PRISMATIC JANE EYRE

Prismatic Jane Eyre

Close-Reading a World Novel Across Languages

Matthew Reynolds

with Andrés Claro, Annmarie Drury, Mary Frank, Paola Gaudio, Rebecca Ruth Gould, Jernej Habjan, Yunte Huang, Abhishek Jain, Eugenia Kelbert, Ulrich Timme Kragh, Ida Klitgård, Madli Kütt, Ana Teresa Marques dos Santos, Cláudia Pazos-Alonso, Eleni Philippou, Yousif M. Qasmiyeh, Léa Rychen, Céline Sabiron, Kayvan Tahmasebian, and Giovanni Pietro Vitali

OpenBook Publishers

https://www.openbookpublishers.com

All external links were active at the time of publication unless otherwise stated and have been archived via the Internet Archive Wayback Machine at https://archive.org/web

Digital material and resources associated with this volume are available at https://doi. org/10.11647/OBP.0319#resources

ISBN Paperback: 978–1-80064–842–5

ISBN Hardback: 978–1-80064–843–2

ISBN Digital (PDF): 978–1-80064–844–9

ISBN Digital ebook (EPUB): 978–1-80064–845–6

ISBN XML: 978–1-80064–847–0

ISBN HTML: 978–1-80064–848–7

DOI: 10.11647/OBP.0319

Cover image: © OpenStreetMap contributors created by Giovanni Pietro Vitali.

Cover design by Katy Saunders

Contents

Acknowledgements

As you can see from the title page, this book is a collaborative publication, the fruit of a populous and intensely conversational project. It was funded from 2016 to 2020 by the AHRC as part of the Open World Research Initiative programme in Creative Multilingualism (led by Katrin Kohl), and hosted by the Oxford Comparative Criticism and Translation Research Centre (OCCT), which is itself sustained by The Oxford Research Centre in the Humanities (TORCH) and St Anne's College, and by a generous benefaction from Jane and Peter Aitken. I am very grateful for all this support.

Sowon S. Park, as co-investigator, helped define the project from its inception, as well as researching material relating to Korean. Alessandro Grilli, Yorimitsu Hashimoto, Adriana X. Jacobs, Magda Szpindler and Kasia Szymanska participated in the workshops, contributing ideas, as well as information on (respectively) Italian, Japanese, Hebrew, Mongolian and Polish. Emrah Serdan provided data on the Turkish translations; Hongtao Wang, and a team of students at Beijing Foreign Studies University, on the Chinese translations; Karolina Gurevich on the vast numbers of re-editions of translations in Russian; Sasha Mile Rudan on translations in Serbian and Croatian; Eunjin Choi on aspects of the reception of *Jane Eyre* in Korea; Vincent Thiery on aspects of the reception in France. The project has also benefited from the intellectual generosity of people not directly connected to it: Patricia González Bermúdez and Marta Ortega Sáez, who shared their expertise in the Spanish translations, Tom Cheesman, who contributed knowledge of the early German translations, Simone Landucci, who brought crucial know-how to the construction of the digital Time Map, and the rare-book expert Jay Dillon, who alerted us to several, otherwise-unknown early editions. I explored the Italian translations with a group of postdocs and postgraduate students in Pisa: Caterina Cappelli, Anna Ferrari, Martina Pastorini, Valeria Ferrà, Benedetta Dini, Chiara Andreoni, Maria Scarmato, Chiara Polimeni, Federica Marsili, Fabio Bassani, Marilena Martucci; I am grateful to them for their enthusiastic participation, and to Alessandro Grilli and the Università di Pisa for hosting me. I am also grateful to my lovely colleagues in the Creative Multilingualism programme for generating a heartening context in which to discuss the progress of the research.

Giovanni Pietro Vitali (the co-author of this volume who created the interactive digital maps) also had a crucial broader role, building the website through which our work was disseminated as it progressed: I am intensely recognizant of his verve and expertise.

The project, and this volume, have benefitted from much able research assistance. Rachel Dryden, postdoctoral research assistant in 2016–17, began the large task of assembling the list of *Jane Eyre* translations; Eleni Philippou (also a co-author of this volume) then stepped into the role and extended the research. Chelsea Haith, Valeria Taddei and Paul Raueiser helped clean publication data and digital texts; Erin Reynolds reconfigured the data for the digital Covers Maps; Michael Reynolds provided some key assistance with coding. Joseph Hankinson did more work on the list of translations, and gave careful editorial attention to the manuscript of this volume. Open Book Publishers called in no less than 19 peer reviewers, and the book has benefitted significantly from their attention, as also from that of Tania Demetriou who read parts of it at a yet later stage. I am enormously grateful to Alessandra Tosi for supporting the idea of this volume from its first glimmer onwards, and to everyone at Open Book for their work on its realisation, especially Jeremy Bowman, who dealt expertly with the many challenges posed by the typesettng.

Some pieces of writing associated with the project have been published elsewhere: Matthew Reynolds, 'Jane Eyre Translated: 57 languages show how different cultures interpret Charlotte Brontë's classic novel', *The Conversation*, 27 September, 2019; Matthew Reynolds, 'Through a Prism', *The Linguist*, 59. 3 (June/July 2020), 18–19; Matthew Reynolds and Giovanni Pietro Vitali, 'Mapping and Reading a World of Translations', *Digital Modern Languages Open*, 1 (2021), http://doi.org/10.3828/mlo.v0i0.375; Eugenia Kelbert, 'Appearances: Character Description as a Network of Signification in Russian Translations of *Jane Eyre*', *Target: International Journal of Translation Studies*, 34.2 (2021), 219–250, https://doi.org/10.1075/target.20079.kel; Kasia Szymanska, 'My Pale Rusalka, a True Heathen: Reading Polish Jane Eyre across Centuries', in *Retracing the History of Literary Translation in Poland: People, Politics, Poetics*, ed. by Magda Heydel and Zofia Ziemann (London: Routledge, 2021), https://doi.org/10.4324/9780429325366. See also the blogposts and other media listed at https://www.creativeml.ox.ac.uk/research/prismatic-translation/.

Above all, I wish to acknowledge the generous and generative energies of collaboration. Authorship is a fuzzy category: all the co-authors of this book have contributed beyond the essays that bear their names, while everyone mentioned above has authored thoughts or information that have helped the volume into being. Of course, these contributions are recorded as far as possible in the text; but there is also a more diffuse shared perceptiveness and energy. I have done my best to honour and channel it in my chapters.

M. R.

Prefatory Note

Our copy-text for quotations from Charlotte Brontë's *Jane Eyre* is the Project Gutenberg e-book which is based on the edition published by Service & Paton in London in 1897, available at: https://www.gutenberg.org/files/1260/1260-h/1260-h.htm. Since this is an electronic text, in which the quotations can easily be located by searching, we do not give page numbers for the quotations; but we do give the chapter to help you locate them in a different edition if you prefer.

The Gutenberg text contains errors of transcription from the 1897 edition, and the 1897 edition itself includes slight variants from any of the editions published during Brontë's lifetime (which also vary slightly among themselves). Quotations have been checked against the authorially sanctioned editions as represented in *Jane Eyre*, ed. by Jane Jack and Margaret Smith (Oxford: Clarendon Press, 2016 [1969]) and any significant divergence has been noted.

Obviously the Gutenberg edition is not a reliable or authoritative text in the terms of traditional scholarship. Why then take it as our copy-text? For two reasons. First, it is readily available to you as a reader: if you wish to plunge in and read around any of the passages we discuss, it is easy for you to do so. And secondly, because the Gutenberg edition is a good representative of the textual condition from which translations arise. In the history of translation — and still today — translators rarely work from what literary scholarship would consider to be an authoritative text. Indeed, as Paola Gaudio shows in her investigation of this issue in Essay 2, the Gutenberg edition is itself increasingly being used as the source text for new translations. A 'source', then, is not a fixed point of origin to which translations orient themselves and from which they diverge. Rather, the source is itself a multiplicitous and shifting entity, which the translational imagination enters and re-makes. All the translations that we have been able to identify, including of course those from which we quote, are given in the List of Translations at the end of the volume. Our general principle for referencing translations has been that it would be repetitious to list them in the Works Cited at the end of each chapter and essay since they are easily locatable in the List of Translations. However, in the case of some essays, which focus on a distinctive subset of translations, it has seemed more helpful to give that subset also in the Works Cited.

Within the volume, the parts written by Matthew Reynolds are referred to as 'chapters' and numbered with Roman numerals. They lay the theoretical foundations, and develop an overarching argument about the close reading of *Jane Eyre* as a world work, articulating the perspective of the project as a whole. The parts written by the other co-authors are referred to as 'essays' and numbered with Arabic numerals. They focus on particular language-contexts and issues, exhibiting a variety of approaches in the arguments they pursue. Unless otherwise noted, English translations of quotations are by the author of the chapter or essay in which they appear.

M. R.

Illustrations

1. A spare chamber. Images of the manuscript (London, British Library, MS 43474–6, vols. I–III), the 1850 edition (London: Smith, Elder & Co.) and the 1897 edition (London: Service & Paton) are courtesy of the © British Library Board. The 1850 edition was digitised by the Google Books project
2. Dusky pictures. Images of the manuscript (London, British Library, MS 43474–6, vols. I–III), the 1850 edition (London: Smith, Elder & Co.) and the 1897 edition (London: Service & Paton) are courtesy of the © British Library Board. The 1850 edition was digitised by the Google Books project
3. A wild man. Images of the manuscript (London, British Library, MS 43474–6, vols. I–III) and the 1850 edition (London: Smith, Elder & Co.) are courtesy of the © British Library Board. The 1850 edition was digitised by the Google Books project
4. Wild and mild. London, British Library, MS 43474–6, vols. I–III, courtesy of the © British Library Board
5. Enchaining stories. London, British Library, MS 43474–6, vols. I–III, courtesy of the © British Library Board
6. Blent, lips and head. London, British Library, MS 43474–6, vols. I–III, courtesy of the © British Library Board
7. The General Map, zoomed out to provide a snapshot of the global distribution of Jane Eyre translations. Created by Giovanni Pietro Vitali; © OpenStreetMap contributors
8. The 'World Map' zoomed in to show the distribution of Jane Eyre translations in Turkey, Greece, Albania, North Macedonia and Bulgaria. Created by Giovanni Pietro Vitali; maps © Thunderforest, data © OpenStreetMap contributors
9. The 'World Map', zoomed in to show the 1992 publication of Stanevich's Russian translation in Krasnoyarsk, Siberia.

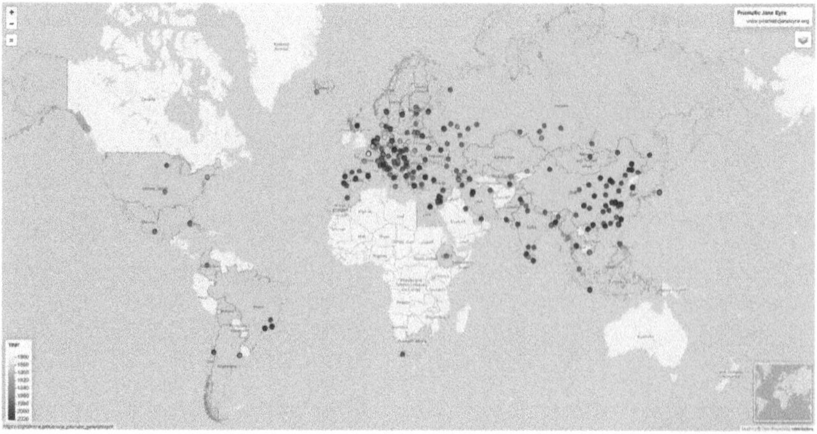

The General Map
https://digitalkoine.github.io/je_prismatic_generalmap/
Created by Giovanni Pietro Vitali; © OpenStreetMap contributors

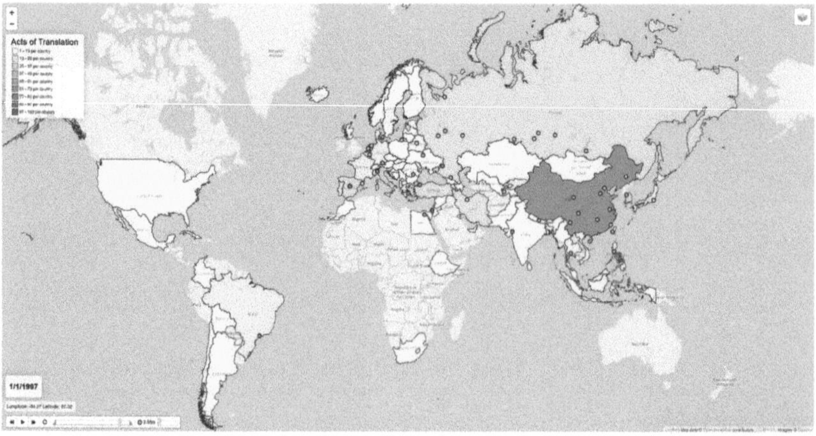

The Time Map
https://digitalkoine.github.io/translations_timemap/
Created by Giovanni Pietro Vitali and Simone Landucci; © OpenStreetMap contributors, © Mapbox

Introduction

Matthew Reynolds

Charlotte Brontë's *Jane Eyre* is not only a novel in English. It is a world work, co-existing in at least 618 translations, by at least as many translators, and spreading over an ever-extending period of years — currently 176 — into at least 68 languages. How can we grasp this vast phenomenon? What questions should we ask of it? With what tactics and tools? What kind of understanding can we hope to achieve? The large and multimodal text that lies before you presents some answers.

In doing so, it aims to contribute to several fields. To world literary studies, by showcasing the complexities inherent in the transnational circulation of a text through language difference, and uncovering the generativity of that process, which involves the imaginative energies of many people, and meshes with their historical moments and political commitments. To English literary studies, by revealing how extremely the reach of a text such as *Jane Eyre*, and therefore the contexts relevant to its interpretation, exceed the boundaries typically drawn around English literature and the English language: both kinds of 'English' are porous, continually tangling and merging with other literature(s) and language(s). To translation studies, by presenting, not only a massively detailed instance, but a corresponding theorisation of translation's inevitably pluralising force, of its role in co-creating the work that is often thought of as simply 'being translated', and of why translation is best seen as happening, not between separate languages, but through a continuum of language difference.

Prismatic Jane Eyre presents some innovations in the methodology of literary history and criticism. It makes use of digital techniques, but braids them into longer-standing practices of literary-critical reading and literary-historical scholarship. Facing the start of this Introduction, you will see links to interactive maps of the kind associated with

 https://doi.org/10.11647/OBP.0319.01

'distant reading', as pioneered by Franco Moretti;[1] and they will recur, in varying configurations, throughout the pages that follow. In the second half of the book, from Chapter IV onwards, you will also find interactive media of an almost opposite character: trans-lingual textual animations inspired by the digital media art of John Cayley.[2] These elements both frame and connect the various literary-critical readings, each anchored in a different location, that are presented by the volume's many co-authors. This intensely co-operative structure is our work's main methodological step forward. The world is made of language difference, and any consideration of a text in world-literary contexts needs to address this fact. Reading collaboratively is a good way to do it, and we hope that the practice we present in this volume may serve as a model for the collaborative close reading of other texts in the world.

So large and varied a book, with so many co-authors, of course builds on many precedents: they are noted and engaged with throughout the chapters and essays that follow. But let me here, as a first orientation, indicate some of our main points of reference. Our overall approach learns from Édouard Glissant in seeing both literature and scholarship as participating in a 'poétique de la relation' [poetics of relatedness]. Our research is therefore not shaped by metaphors of conquest or discovery, but rather by the example of 'l'errant' [the wanderer] who 'cherche à connaître la totalité du monde et sait déjà qu'il ne l'accomplira jamais' [seeks to understand the totality of the world, all the while knowing that he will never manage it].[3] Though we present a large amount of knowledge and discussion of *Jane Eyre* in world-literary contexts, there is a great deal more material that we have not been able to address, and which indeed could never be grasped in full. Selection is basic to our enterprise, and everything we provide here has a metonymic relationship, and therefore a partial one, to the larger phenomenon that is *Jane Eyre* as a world work. No doubt the study of any book, in any context, is always in some sense incomplete; but incompleteness is a pervasive and unignorable feature of the study of literature in world contexts.

---

1 Franco Moretti, *Distant Reading* (London: Verso, 2013).

2 John Cayley, *Programmatology*, https://programmatology.shadoof.net/index.php

3 Edouard Glissant, *Poétique de la relation* (Paris: Gallimard, 1990), p. 33.

The arguments of Francis B. Nyamnjoh have helped us to embrace this condition of our research. He notes that, in Africa, 'popular ideas of what constitutes reality ... are rich with ontologies of incompleteness', and proposes that 'such conceptions of incompleteness could enrich the practice of social science and the humanities in Africa and globally'. He advocates a 'convivial scholarship' which challenges labels that 'oversimplify the social realities of the people, places and spaces it seeks to understand and explain', which recognises 'the importance of interconnections and nuanced complexities', and which 'sees the local in the global and the global in the local by bringing them into informed conversations, conscious of the hierarchies and power relations at play'.[4] In focusing on (only) about 20 of the 68 or more languages spoken by the world *Jane Eyre*, and, for each of them, zooming in on only a few especially interesting or indicative translations, we have made the incompleteness of our project obvious. In this way, we assert the importance of recognising that the world *Jane Eyre* can never be fully known. It is possible to enter into, explore and sample the phenomenon, but not to possess it. It is true that I (Matthew Reynolds) have had what might be called a controlling interest in the project; I initiated and led it; I have edited the essays by my co-authors, and I have written the sequence of chapters that offer a grounding and summation of the research. Some sort of unifying propulsion was necessary for the work to have any coherence. But, at each stage, I have tried to open that propulsion to re-definition and re-direction by my co-authors (hence their being co-authors rather than contributors). I proposed a selection of passages, linguistic features and key words that we might look at together across languages in our practice of collaborative close reading, but that selection changed following input from the group. So also did the structure of this volume. The maps, constructed by Giovanni Pietro Vitali, present data that has been contributed by all the co-authors (and indeed many other participants in and friends of the project, as described in the Acknowledgements). Likewise, the translingual close-readings that I perform in Chapters IV–VII build on observations made by many of the co-authors, and others; as do the arguments about location that I make in Chapter III, and the conceptualization of translation that I offer in Chapters I

4 Francis B. Nyamnjoh, *Drinking from the Cosmic Gourd: How Amos Tutuola can Change our Minds* (Mankon, Bamenda, North West Region, Cameroon: Langaa Research & Publishing CIG, 2017), pp. 2, 5.

and II. In writing these chapters, I have tried to honour and perform this plural authorship, shifting between the 'we' of the project and the 'I' of my own point of view, and opening up a dialogue with my co-authors. That conversation continues on a larger scale across the volume as a whole, in the interplay between the chapters and the essays, and between the written analyses and the visualisations. This dialogic structure embodies our conviction that the heterolingual and multiplicitous phenomenon of the world *Jane Eyre* cannot be addressed by translating it into a monolithic explanatory framework and homolingual critical language. While they meet in the comparative unity of this volume, and the shared medium of academic English, the readings, with their different styles, emphases, rhetorics and points of reference open onto a convivial understanding of differences, interconnections and complexities — they aim to generate Nyamnjoh's 'informed conversations'. Correspondingly, we have very much tried to avoid the imposition of pre-formatted labels onto our material. In the convivial progress of our research, the author of each essay was free to pursue whatever line seemed most interesting to them in their context, while our understanding of all the categories that organise our work, from 'a translation' (see Chapters I and II) to 'an act of translation' (see Chapter III) to 'language(s)' (see Chapter II) developed in response to the texts and situations we encountered.

Our work is also, of course, in dialogue with prominent recent voices in the anglophone and European literary academy. With Pascale Casanova, we rebut 'le préjugé de l'insularité constitutive du texte' [the assumption of the constitutive insularity of a text] and set out to consider the larger, transnational configurations through which it moves[5] — though recognising, more fully than she does, that such configurations can never be known in their entirety, and that circulation can happen in intricate and unpredictable ways. We follow Wai Chee Dimock in realising that, not only '"American" literature', but any literature is 'a crisscrossing set of pathways, open-ended and ever multiplying, weaving in and out of other geographies, other languages and cultures';[6] and we agree with Dipesh Chakrabarty in paying

5 Pascale Casanova, *La République mondiale des lettres*, new edition (Paris: Seuil, 2008), p. 19.

6 Wai Chee Dimock, *Through Other Continents: American Literature across Deep Time* (Princeton, NJ.: Princeton University Press, 2006), p. 3.

'critical and unrelenting attention to the very process of translation'.[7] Our conception of translation builds on research that has been published in *Prismatic Translation* (2019), which in turn is indebted to the work of many translation scholars — debts which are noted both there and here, throughout the pages that lie ahead. *Prismatic Jane Eyre* as a whole enacts in practice an idea of prismatic translation (briefly put, that translation inevitably generates multiple texts which ask to be looked at together), but what that means in theory can be conceived in different ways. Of what is to come, Chapter I develops the prismatic approach in dialogue with the essays in this volume, and with theorists writing in English, Italian and French; Essay 1, by Ulrich Timme Kragh and Abhishek Jain, offers a somewhat different conception, drawing on Indian knowledge traditions and theories of narrative and translation in Sanskrit and Hindi; Essay 8, by Kayvan Tahmasebian and Rebecca Ruth Gould, articulates its argument through Persian conceptions of genre; while Andrés Claro, in Essay 5, takes as his starting point what he calls 'a critical conception of the different possible behaviours of language as a formal condition of possibility of representation and experience'. This plurality of points of view is a crucial element in our practice of convivial criticism. What *Prismatic Jane Eyre* offers is, not a variety of material channelled into a single explanatory structure, but rather a variety of material explored in a range of ways from different theoretical perspectives. It is in this respect that the work we present most differs from that of the figure in the European and North American academy who has most energised this project: Franco Moretti. We have learned from Moretti's ambition to invent techniques for criticism with a wide transnational scope, and in particular from his use of cartography; but we differ decisively from his conviction that world literature can be mapped according to a single explanatory schema, a 'world system' with an inescapable 'centre' and 'periphery'. Most of all, we depart from his view that close reading can have no place in the study of world literature, and that 'literary history will ... become "second-hand": a patchwork of other people's research, *without a single direct textual reading*'.[8] This volume rebuts that assertion. To read closely means to

7 Dipesh Chakrabarty, *Provincializing Europe Postcolonial Thought and Historical Difference*, new edition (Princeton, NJ.: Princeton University Press, 2008), p. 17.

8 Moretti, *Distant Reading*, pp. 48–49.

attend to particularities: of individual style; of linguistic repertoire; of ideological commitments; of historical and geographical location. As I explain further in Chapter IV, and as will be evident throughout this volume, attending to particularities means doing something that is fundamental to world literary study: recognising and responding to difference.

Prismatic Jane Eyre is open to being explored in various ways. This 'Introduction' is really only the first section of a serial discussion which continues through Chapters I–VIII, in which I offer an account of *Jane Eyre* as a world work, addressing successively the theory of translation, conception of language(s) and idea of location that arise from it (Chapters I–III) before presenting a manifesto for multilingual close reading, with examples (Chapters IV–VII), and finally offering some conclusions (Chapter VIII). These chapters are in dialogue with the essays by which they are surrounded, which focus on particular contexts and issues. Each chapter serves as an introduction to the essays that follow it, and the sequence of the essays represents an evolution of theme. Those following Chapters I and II speak most immediately to the conceptualisation of language(s), translation and text. Ulrich Timme Kragh and Abhishek Jain, in 'Jane, Come with Me to India: The Narrative Transformation of Janeeyreness in the Indian Reception of *Jane Eyre*' offer a redefinition of the prismatic approach, drawing on knowledge traditions in Sanskrit and Hindi, before presenting an account of the interplay between translations and adaptations of *Jane Eyre* in many Indian languages. Paola Gaudio, in 'Who Cares What Shape the Red Room is? Or, On the Perfectibility of the Source Text', traces variants between successive English editions of *Jane Eyre*, and discovers how they have played out in Italian translations, showing that 'the source text' in fact consists of texts in the plural. In '*Jane Eyre*'s Prismatic Bodies in Arabic', Yousif M. Qasmiyeh takes an Arabic radio version as the starting point for his argument that *Jane Eyre* is crucially an oral as well as a written work, and that this feature becomes especially charged in Arabic translations; while, in 'Translating the French in the French Translations of *Jane Eyre*', Céline Sabiron shows how French translators have been puzzled by the French that was already present in the language Brontë wrote.

The essays following Chapter III have most to do with location. In 'Representation, Gender, Empire: *Jane Eyre* in Spanish', Andrés Claro finds radical differences between the translations done in Spain and in hispanophone South America; while, in 'Commissioning Political

Sympathies: The British Council's Translation of *Jane Eyre* in Greece', Eleni Philippou showcases one particularly charged translation context from the Cold War. In 'Searching for Swahili Jane', Annmarie Drury investigates why *Jane Eyre* has not been translated into Swahili (and hardly at all into any African language); and, in 'The Translatability of Love: The Romance Genre and the Prismatic Reception of *Jane Eyre* in Twentieth-Century Iran', Kayvan Tahmasebian and Rebecca Ruth Gould demonstrate how a combination of place and political moment impart a distinctive generic identity to translations in late twentieth-century Iran.

The essays following Chapters IV and V, and interspersed by Chapters VI and VII, offer the most tightly focused close readings. After Chapter V's discussion of 'passion' in many languages, you will find Ana Teresa Marques dos Santos and Cláudia Pazos-Alonso's essay on 'A Mind of her Own: Translating the "volcanic vehemence" of *Jane Eyre* into Portuguese', Ida Klitgård's on 'The Movements of Passion in the Danish *Jane Eyre*', and Paola Gaudio's on 'Emotional Fingerprints: Nouns Expressing Emotions in *Jane Eyre* and its Italian Translations'. After Chapter VI's investigation of the many meanings of 'plain' come Yunte Huang's essay on 'Proper Nouns and Not So Proper Nouns: The Poetic Destiny of *Jane Eyre* in Chinese', Mary Frank's on 'Formality of Address and its Representation of Relationships in Three German Translations of *Jane Eyre*', and Léa Rychen's on 'Biblical Intertextuality in the French *Jane Eyre*'. Chapter VII, with its investigation of the distinction between 'walk' and 'wander' and of what becomes of it in different tongues, its presentation of two 'prismatic scenes', and its account of 'littoral reading', then opens onto three essays that attend to grammar and perception: Jernej Habjan's 'Free Indirect *Jane Eyre*: Brontë's Peculiar Use of Free Indirect Speech, and German and Slovenian Attempts to Resolve It', Madli Kütt's '"Beside myself; or rather *out* of myself": First Person Presence in the Estonian Translation of *Jane Eyre*', and Eugenia Kelbert's 'Appearing Jane, in Russian'. After which, you will find some conclusions (Chapter VIII), information about the lives of some of the translators discussed, a list of the corpus of translations that we have worked from, and a link to the code that underlies the interactive maps and JavaScript animations.

Structured as it is by this sequencing of the chapters and essays, the volume has not been formally divided into sections, whether by theme or (for instance) by region, because to do that would be to impose exactly the kind of artificial neatness denounced by Nyamnjoh: close reading can be found in all the essays, as can attention to place and to the conceptualisation of the processes in play. The chapters are, in a sense, written by 'me' (Matthew Reynolds); but in writing them I am endeavouring to speak on behalf of the whole collaborative project, so the narrative voice shifts between more plural and more individual modes. The essays embody more consistently the distinctive styles and approaches of their authors.

Prismatic Jane Eyre is also represented by a website. Depending on when you are reading these words, the website may still be live at https://prismaticjaneeyre.org/, or it may be archived at https://web.archive.org/web/20231026144145/https://prismaticjaneeyre.org/. In either form, the website offers a quick way of sampling the project as a whole. What follows in this volume is obviously very much fuller, and perhaps it may seem a lot to read through from beginning to end. We invite you to follow the sequence of chapters and essays if you wish; but we invite you equally to hop, skip and wander as you will. *Prismatic Jane Eyre* offers, not the encapsulation of a phenomenon, but an opening onto it; and we hope that you, as a reader, may relish entering this incomplete exploration of *Jane Eyre* as a world work, just as we, as readers, and as writers of readings, have done.

Works Cited

Casanova, Pascale, *La République mondiale des lettres*, new edition (Paris: Seuil, 2008).

Cayley, John, *Programmatology*, https://programmatology.shadoof.net/index.php

Chakrabarty, Dipesh, *Provincializing Europe Postcolonial Thought and Historical Difference*, new edition (Princeton, NJ.: Princeton University Press, 2008), https://doi.org/10.1515/9781400828654

Glissant, Edouard, *Poétique de la relation* (Paris: Gallimard, 1990).

Moretti, Franco, *Distant Reading* (London: Verso, 2013).

Nyamnjoh, Francis B., *Drinking from the Cosmic Gourd: How Amos Tutuola can Change our Minds* (Mankon, Bamenda, North West North West Region, Cameroon: Langaa Research & Publishing CIG, 2017), https://doi.org/10.2307/j.ctvh9vw76

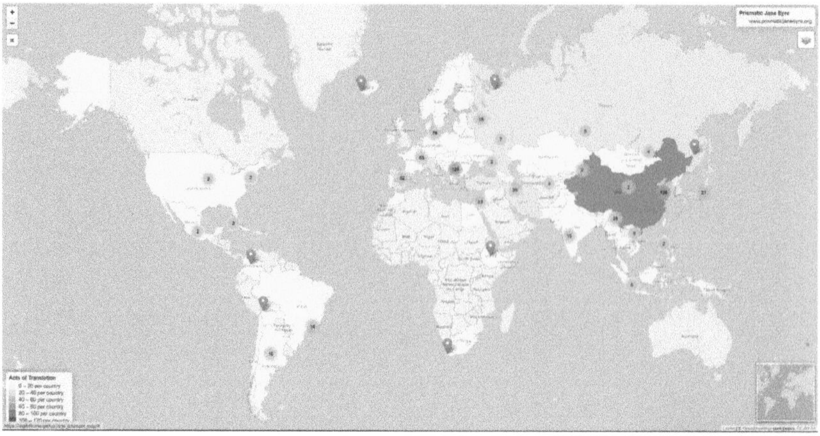

The World Map
https://digitalkoine.github.io/je_prismatic_map
Created by Giovanni Pietro Vitali;
maps © Thunderforest, data © OpenStreetMap contributors

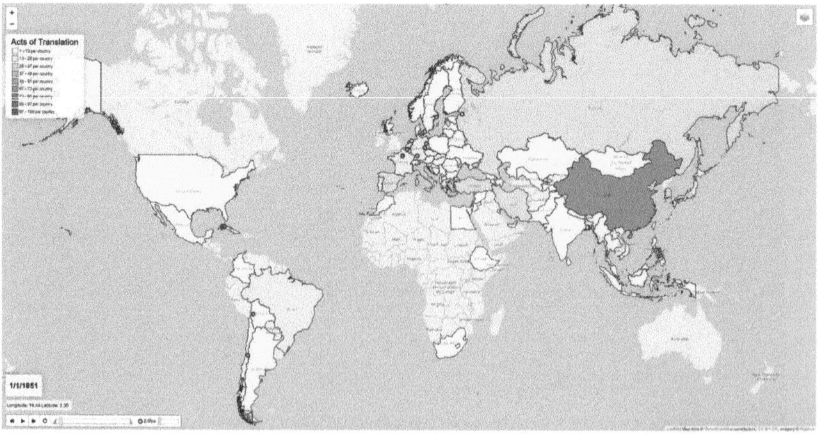

The Time Map
https://digitalkoine.github.io/translations_timemap
Created by Giovanni Pietro Vitali and Simone Landucci;
© OpenStreetMap contributors, © Mapbox

I. Prismatic Translation and *Jane Eyre* as a World Work

Matthew Reynolds

Translations Among Other Texts

The corpus of translations that we have (variably, selectively) explored is vast. Using blunt, quantitative terms which I will qualify in the pages that follow, we can speak of 618 'translations' over 176 'years' into 68 'languages': in short — or rather in long, in very long — a textual multitude of something like 100,000,000 words. Yet this enormous body of material is only a subset of the even larger array of texts — both written and in other media — that have been generated by *Jane Eyre* in one way or another, including adaptations, responses and critical discussion (this publication takes its place among that multitude). There are at least fifty films going back to the earliest days of cinema, most of them in English but with versions also in Arabic, Czech, Dutch, German, Greek, Hindi, Hungarian, Italian, Kannaḍa, Mandarin, Mexican Spanish, Tamil and Telugu.[1] There have been TV series and adaptations for radio, again in many moments, languages and locations.[2] A series of powerful lithographs from the novel has been made by the Portuguese artist Paula Rego. Now there are fan fictions, blogs and at least one vlog, and erotic mash-ups

1 Ulrich Timme Kragh and Abhishek Jain discuss the Hindi, Kannada, Tamil and Telugu films in Essay 1 below. There are lists of adaptations and other *Jane Eyre*-inspired material in *Charlotte Brontë: Legacies and Afterlives*, ed. by Amber K. Regis and Deborah Wynne (Manchester: Manchester University Press, 2017), pp. 280–93; Patsy Stoneman, *Brontë Transformations: The Cultural Dissemination of* Jane Eyre *and* Wuthering Heights, 2nd edn (Brighton: Edward Everett Root, 2018), pp. 254–91; and at *The Enthusiast's Guide to Jane Eyre*, https://sites.google.com/view/eyreguide/adaptations/film?authuser=0

2 Yousif M. Qamiyeh discusses the Arabic radio version by Nūr al-Dimirdāsh in Essay 3 below.

 https://doi.org/10.11647/OBP.0319.02

which interleave Brontë's text with throbbing scenes of passion.[3] Back in the mid-nineteenth century — indeed, almost as soon as it was published — the novel was being re-made for the stage. The most influential dramatization was Charlotte Birch-Pfeiffer's *Die Waise aus Lowood* [*The Orphan of Lowood*] of 1853: it neutered the scandalous heart of the book by changing Bertha from Mr Rochester's own wife to that of his dead brother; she also becomes the mother of Adèle. Over the ensuing decades this play was much performed, in German and other languages, across Europe, the UK and the USA, lending its title also to many translations of the novel.[4] In India, as Ulrich Timme Kragh and Abhishek Jain show in Essay 1 below, *Jane Eyre* was freely re-written first in Bengali and then in Kannada, as *Sarlā* [সরলা] by Nirmmalā Bālā Soma [নির্ম্মালা বালা সোম] and *Bēdi Bandavaḷu* [ಬೇಡಿ ಬಂದವಳು] by Nīla Dēvi [ನೀಳಾ ದೇವಿ] in 1914 and 1959 respectively, well before it was translated.[5] And of course *Jane Eyre* has had a pervasive, energising influence on English-language literary writing, from Elizabeth Barrett Browning's *Aurora Leigh* (1856) to Henry James's *The Turn of the Screw* (1898), from Daphne du Maurier's *Rebecca* (1938) to Jean Rhys's *Wide Sargasso Sea* (1966), together with a scattering of more recent fiction, such as Tsitsi Dangarembga's *Nervous Conditions* (1988), Jamaica Kincaid's *Lucy* (1990), Ali Smith's *Like* (1997), Leila Aboulela's *The*

---

3 Many fan fictions are at *Fan Fiction*, https://www.fanfiction.net/book/Jane-Eyre/; the vlog is *The Autobiography of Jane Eyre*, https://www.youtube.com/channel/UCG1-X6Vhx5Ba84pqBQUDshQ. Examples of blogs are *The Autobiography of Jane Eyre*, https://www.tumblr.com/blog/view/eyrequotes; *Eddie: St John anti*, https://www.tumblr.com/blog/view/mr-rochester-of-thornfield; *Jane Eyre: Everything related with Jane Eyre (Mostly pictures)*, https://www.tumblr.com/blog/view/fyjaneeyre-blog; *My Jane Eyre: Exploring library copies of the seminal nineteenth century novel Jane Eyre by Charlotte Brontë*, https://myjaneeyrelibrary.wordpress.com/. Erotic mash-ups: Charlotte Brontë and Eve Sinclair, *Jane Eyre Laid Bare: The Classic Novel with an Erotic Twist* (London: Pan, 2012); Charlotte Bronte and Karena Rose, *Jane Eyrotica* (London: Piatkus, 2012).

4 See Stoneman, *Brontë Transformations*, pp. 33–34; Patsy Stoneman, *Jane Eyre on Stage 1848–1898: An Illustrated Edition of Eight Plays with Contextual Notes* (Aldershot and Burlington, VT: Ashgate, 2007), pp. 137–98, Lynne Tatlock, *Jane Eyre in German Lands: The Import of Romance, 1848–1918* (New York: Bloomsbury Academic, 2022), pp. 49–82; and the titles of many entries in our List of Translations below.

5 In 'Jane Eyre in Bengal', Olivia Majumdar defines *Sarlā* as a 'free translation', https://www.bl.uk/early-indian-printed-books/articles/jane-eyre-in-bengal-v2. I explain the distinction we draw between translations and other re-writings below in this chapter.

Translator (1999) and Aline Brosh McKenna and Ramón K. Pérez's graphic novel *Jane* (2018).

Alongside these — and many more — proliferating imaginative responses, the novel has always generated vigorous critical discussion, from excited early reviews, through percipient comments by twentieth-century writers such as Virginia Woolf and Adrienne Rich, to the explosion of academic scholarship and criticism which has, since the 1970s, found in *Jane Eyre* a focus for Marxist, feminist and postcolonial literary theories, for research in literature and science and — more recently — for renewed formalist analysis and approaches rooted in environmental and disability studies.[6] Perhaps the most decisive intervention in this critical afterlife was made by Sandra M. Gilbert and Susan Gubar in 1979, with their argument that Mr Rochester's mentally ill and imprisoned first wife, Bertha, who inspired their book's title, *The Madwoman in the Attic*, is Jane's 'double': 'she is the angry aspect of the orphan child, the ferocious secret self Jane has been trying to repress ever since her days at Gateshead'.[7] This interpretation can seem a key to the novel, making sense of its mix of genres as a sign of internal conflict. *Jane Eyre* describes — in a realist vein — the social conditions that make it impossible for Jane fully to act upon or even to articulate her desires and ambitions in her own speaking voice as a character; but it also enables those same unruly energies to emerge through the gothic elements of the text that she is imagined as having written — her *Autobiography* (as the book's subtitle announces it to be).

Another influential line of analysis was launched by Gayatri Chakravorty Spivak, who in 1985 offered a sharp critique of the role that Bertha, a 'native subaltern female', is made to fulfil. For Spivak,

6 In addition to the texts discussed below, see Terry Eagleton, *Myths of Power: A Marxist Study of the Brontës* (London: Macmillan, 1975); Sally Shuttleworth, *Charlotte Brontë and Victorian Psychology* (Cambridge: Cambridge University Press, 1996); Caroline Levine, *Forms: Whole, Rhythm, Hierarchy, Network* (Princeton, NJ: Princeton University Press, 2015), ch. 1; Jennifer D. Fuller, 'Seeking Wild Eyre: Victorian Attitudes Towards Landscape and the Environment in Charlotte Brontë's *Jane Eyre*', *Ecozon@*, 4.2 (2013), 150–65; *The Madwoman and the Blindman: Jane Eyre, Discourse, Disability*, ed. by David Bolt, Julia Miele Rodas and Elizabeth J. Donaldson (Columbus: The Ohio State University Press, 2012).

7 Sandra M. Gilbert and Susan Gubar, *The Madwoman in the Attic: The Woman Writer and the Nineteenth-Century Literary Imagination* (New Haven and London: Yale University Press, 1979), pp. 359–60.

Bertha is 'a figure produced by the axiomatics of imperialism', a manifestation of the 'abject … script' of the colonial discourse that pervaded the linguistic and imaginative materials Brontë had to work with. Across the continuum of imagining between *Jane Eyre* and Rhys's *Wide Sargasso Sea*, this figure (re-named Antoinette in Rhys's novel) serves as 'an allegory of the general epistemic violence of imperialism, the construction of a self-immolating colonial subject for the glorification of the social mission of the colonizer'. Jane's happiness, therefore, comes at the expense of colonial subjects: Spivak takes this to reveal a blindness in readings such as Gilbert and Gubar's, and more generally in the discourses of Anglo-American feminist individualism.[8]

Like *The Madwoman in the Attic*, Spivak's text generated a cascade of quotation and reprinting, as well as of critical contention which pointed to elements of the novel that it downplays. As Susan L. Meyer noted, Bertha, who is identified as a 'Creole' in *Jane Eyre*, is not a straightforwardly representative 'native subaltern' since she comes from a rich, white, slave-owning family.[9] Spivak's response was that her argument still held since 'the mad are subaltern of a special sort'; more interestingly, she suggested that the simplicities of her analysis, as first put forward, had contributed to its popularity among students and readers of the novel: 'a simple invocation of race and gender' was an easier interpretation to adopt than one that would do more justice to the complicated social identities of the participants.[10] This observation indicates how critical analysis, readers' reactions and indeed imaginative re-makings have intertwined in *Jane Eyre*'s afterlife, creating a vivid instance of a general phenomenon that has been described by Roland Barthes:

> Le plaisir du texte s'accomplit … lorsque le texte 'littéraire' (le livre) transmigre dans notre vie, lorsqu'une autre écriture (l'écriture de l'autre) parvient à écrire des fragments de notre propre quotidienneté, bref quand il se produit une coexistence.
>
> [Textual pleasure occurs when the 'literary' text (the book) transmigrates into our life, when another writing (the writing of the other) goes so

8 Gayatri Chakravorty Spivak, *A Critique of Postcolonial Reason: Toward a History of the Vanishing Present* (Cambridge, Mass.: Harvard University Press, 1999), pp. 117, 121, 127.

9 Susan L. Meyer, 'Colonialism and the Figurative Strategy of *Jane Eyre*', *Victorian Studies* 33 (1990), 247–68.

10 Spivak, *Critique*, pp. 117n, 121n.

far as to write fragments of our own everyday lives, in short, when a coexistence comes into being.][11]

Many readers have embraced *Jane Eyre* in this way, and it is evident that the pleasure of such imaginative coexistence comes, not only from agreement, but also from contestation — as for instance when Jean Rhys's passionate involvement with the book led her to re-write it from Bertha's point of view, an imaginative reaction that helped Spivak to frame her critical position. And that critical position has, in turn, both affected readers' views and nourished new creative responses, such as Jamaica Kincaid's novel *Lucy* (1990), in which the governess figure (a modern *au pair*) is herself from the West Indies. There is a similar chain of creativity prompting criticism prompting further creativity in the way Robert Louis Stevenson's *Strange Case of Dr Jekyll and Mr Hyde* (1886), which echoes *Jane Eyre*'s Bertha in its imagining of a monstrous, hidden figure (Hyde), anticipates Gilbert and Gubar's argument when it joins that figure with an apparently irreproachable public one (Jekyll) to form a single conflicted self. And, again, Gilbert and Gubar's critical reading has fed into new creative work, such as Polly Teale's play *Jane Eyre* (1998), where Bertha always accompanies Jane on stage,[12]

A peculiarity of the critico-creative afterlife that I have just sketched is the overwhelming monolingualism of its range of attention. As Lynne Tatlock has noted in her recent study, *Jane Eyre in German Lands*, what has become of the novel in the 'German-speaking realm remains terra incognita for most scholars working in English',[13] and the same is true of translations and responses in all other languages. Together with the (few) studies there have been of them,[14] they tend to be treated

11 Roland Barthes *Œuvres completes*, vol. 3 (1968–1971), new edn, ed. by Éric Marty (Paris: Le Seuil, 1995), p. 704.

12 Jessica Cox, '"The insane Creole": the afterlife of Bertha Mason', Regis and Wynn, *Charlotte Brontë: Legacies and Afterlives*, pp. 221–40 (p. 223).

13 Tatlock, *Jane Eyre in German Lands*, p. 2.

14 Emile Langlois, 'Early Critics and Translators of Jane Eyre in France', *Brontë Society Transactions*, 16 (1971), 11–18; Stefanie Hohn, *Charlotte Brontës* Jane Eyre *in deutscher Übersetzung. Geschichte eines kulturellen Transfers* (Tübingen: Narr, 1998); Inga-Stina Ewbank, 'Reading the Brontës Abroad: A Study in the Transmission of Victorian Novels in Continental Europe', in *Re-Constructing the Book: Literary Texts in Transmission*, edited by Maureen Bell, Shirley Chew, Simon Eliot and James L. W. West (London: Routledge, 2001), pp. 84–99; Emily Eells, 'Charlotte Brontë *en français dans le texte*', *Textes et Genres I: 'A Literature of Their Own'*, ed. by Claire Bazin and Marie-Claude Perrin-Chenour (Nanterre: Publidix, 2003), 69–88; Marta Ortega, 'Traducciones

as something separate from the real business of understanding and re-imagining the novel. It is writing in English (so the assumption goes) that has the power to determine what *Jane Eyre* means, and to give it ongoing life in culture: what happens in other tongues is taken to be necessarily secondary, a pale imitation that can safely be ignored. Yet Tatlock's book is full of illumination, not only of German culture, but also of *Jane Eyre.* I hope the same is true of the pages that follow; that, as they trace the book's metamorphoses through translation, and across time and place, they also offer a refreshed and expanded understanding of *Jane Eyre* — *Jane Eyre* 'in itself', I would say, were it not that, as we have begun to see with the book's afterlife in English, it is impossible to hold a clear line between the book 'in itself', on the one hand, and what has been made of it by readers and interpreters on the other. Interventions like those by Rhys and Spivak change what *Jane Eyre* is; this is no less the case if they happen to be in other languages, and to have been made by translators. After all, translators are especially intimate interpreters and re-writers, who must pay attention to every word.

As we will discover, *Jane Eyre* has been read and responded to at least as often, and just as intensely, in languages other than English; and the way the novel has metamorphosed in translation has sharp relevance to the critical issues I have just sketched (and indeed many others, as we will see). When considering *Jane Eyre*'s feminism, it matters that it was translated by a Portuguese avant-garde feminist for serialization in an alternative Lisbon periodical in the late 1870s, and that it was connected to women's liberation movements in Latin America in the mid-twentieth century (see Essay 9 below, by Ana Teresa Marques dos Santos and Cláudia Pazos-Alonso, and Essay 5 by Andrés Claro). When considering the representation of Bertha, what has been made of that representation by readers in the Global South, and how they have re-made it through translation, is clearly an issue of some pertinence (see again Essay 5, as well as Essay 1 by Ulrich Timme Kragh and Abhishek Jain, and Essay 3 by Yousif M. Qasmiyeh).

del franquismo en el mercado literario español contemporáneo: el caso de *Jane Eyre* de Juan G. de Luaces' (unpublished doctoral thesis, University of Barcelona, 2013); Shouhua Qi, 'No Simple Love: The Literary Fortunes of the Brontë Sisters in Post-Mao, Market-Driven China', in *The Brontë Sisters in Other Worlds*, ed. by Shouhua Qi and Jacqueline Padgett (New York: Palgrave Macmillan, 2014), pp. 19–49; Tatlock, *Jane Eyre in German Lands.*

There are material reasons why these connections have not come into focus until now. It takes a particular conjunction of institutional support and technological development to sustain the degree of collaboration and breadth of reference that are presented in these pages. Yet the material conditions that have hampered work like this in the past have also embodied and sustained a particular ideological stance: a belief in the separateness and self-sufficiency of standard languages, especially English, and a corresponding misunderstanding and under-valuation of the interpretive, imaginative, dialogic power of translation. Some recent work in translation studies and comparative and world literary studies has pushed to reconfigure this regime of 'homolingual address', as Naoki Sakai has defined it, creating alternatives to what Suresh Canagarajah has called 'monolingual orientation' in literary criticism — that is, the assumption (despite all everyday experiential evidence to the contrary) that the default interpretive context, for any work under discussion, possesses 'a common language with shared norms'.[15] *Prismatic Jane Eyre*, in redefining the novel as a multilingual, transtemporal and nomadic work, shares also in the endeavour to open up critical discussion to more diverse voices. I will return to the theory of language that permeates and emerges from this approach in Chapter II.

The proliferation of textuality generated by *Jane Eyre* that I have sketched — the carnival of critique, reading, re-making, reaction, response, and adaptation — matters to the translations of the novel, and they in their turn should be recognised as part of it. As André Lefevere has pointed out, people's idea or 'construct' of a given book comes, not from that book in isolation, but from a plethora of sources:

> That construct is often loosely based on some selected passages of the actual text of the book in question (the passages included in anthologies used in secondary or university education, for instance), supplemented by other texts that rewrite the actual text in one way or another, such as plot summaries in literary histories or reference works, reviews in newspapers, magazines, or journals, some critical articles, performances on stage or screen, and, last but not least, translations.[16]

---

15 Naoki Sakai, *Translation and Subjectivity: On 'Japan' and Cultural Nationalism* (Minneapolis: University of Minnesota Press, 1997), p. 2; Suresh Canagarajah, *Translingual Practice: Global Englishes and Cosmopolitan Relations* (London and New York: Routledge, 2012), p. 1.

16 André Lefevere, *Translation, Rewriting, and the Manipulation of Literary Fame* (London: Routledge, 2016 [1992]), p. 5.

Translations enter into this larger flow of re-writing and re-making, and they are also affected by it, as indeed all the different currents in the ongoing cultural life of the novel may affect one another. Such currents influence the interpretive choices translators make and the way the finished books are marketed and read. They can even bring translations into being: for instance, a successful film version will typically trigger new translations. *Jane Eyre* is therefore a paradigmatic instance of the argument I made in *Prismatic Translation* (2019) that translation should always be seen as happening, not *to* one text, but *among* many texts.[17] The textuality that flows into any given act of translation may include the whole range of other kinds of re-creation; it may also encompass many other sources such as related books in the receiving culture, histories, dictionaries and so on.[18]

In these pages, we follow Lefevere in seeing any translation of *Jane Eyre* as happening among the larger penumbra of versions and responses: they will be referred to and discussed at many points in the chapters and essays that follow. Nevertheless, we draw more of a distinction than he does, albeit a porous and pragmatic one, between all this critical and creative ongoing life and the focus of our investigation, which is the co-existence of the novel in its many translations. For the purposes of our study, we adopt the following rules of thumb for deciding whether to count a given text as a *Jane Eyre* translation. It should be a work intended primarily for reading, whether on page or screen. So we draw a line between the translations that are our focus and the re-makings in other media — such as films, radio versions, and plays — that are less central to our enquiry. It should be a work of prose fiction, so we distinguish between translations on the one hand and reviews and critical discussions on the other. And it should be a work that is offered and/or taken as representing *Jane Eyre* — indeed, as *being Jane Eyre* — for its readers in the receiving culture. So the translations are separated out from responses like *Wide Sargasso Sea*, or versions like *Jane Eyrotica* or Lyndsay Faye's *Jane Steele* (which shadows the plot of *Jane Eyre*, though the heroine is a murderer). Some of these *Eyre*-related books have been translated into other languages — erotic versions have had some success in Russia, for

17 *Prismatic Translation*, ed. by Matthew Reynolds (Cambridge: Legenda, 2019), pp. 7, 31.

18 Essay 6 below, by Kayvan Tahamsebian and Rebecca Ruth Gould, gives a rich account of this phenomenon in Iran.

instance[19] — but such translations are not translations of *Jane Eyre*, any more than the versions and responses themselves are. Readers of such texts know that what they are getting is something different from *Jane Eyre* — indeed, that is why they are reading them.

Another way of describing the (porous, pragmatic) line that we draw is that it distinguishes between translation without an article — the loose, variously fluid and figurative phenomenon — from translation with an article, '*a* translation', that is, a whole work which stands in a particular relationship to another whole work. The entire penumbra of versions and responses can be said to involve translation-without-an-article: for instance, these texts might include translated snippets of dialogue or passages of description, or they might 'translate' (in a loose sense) elements of the source into different genres or locations. To adopt the Indian philosophical terms expounded by Ulrich Timme Kragh and Abhishek Jain in Essay 1 below, 'the *dravya* (substance) *Jane Eyre* can be said to exist in different *paryāy* (modalities) of the source text, adaptations, and translations, which all are *pariṇām* (transformations) sharing a quality of janeeyreness'. But within this larger range, any text that offers itself as 'a translation' is subjected to a tighter discipline. It takes on the task of being the novel *Jane Eyre* for its readers.

Nevertheless, this distinction has to be pragmatic and porous because what it is for a text to 'be the novel *Jane Eyre* for its readers' is not something that can be determined objectively or uncontentiously, especially not when a wide range of different languages and cultures, with varying translational practices, are taken into account. For instance, an immediate and blatant exception to our rules of thumb is the Arabic radio version by Nūr al-Dimirdāsh, first broadcast in 1965. As Yousif M. Qasmiyeh explains in Essay 3 below, this translation reached a 'wide and popular audience across the Arabic speaking region', where access to books 'was restricted by a range of socio-economic and educational barriers'. It also had a significant influence on later print translations. So, in this context, where radio is doing some of the same cultural work as might be done by print elsewhere, it seems best to count al-Dimirdāsh's text as a translation. Even with texts that are indubitably printed, uncertainties of definition arise. Indeed, they flourish. Back in 2004, Umberto Eco proposed what looks

19 As discovered by Eugenia Kelbert and Karolina Gurevich in the course of the Prismatic *Jane Eyre* project.

like it might be an effective — if broad-brush — quantitative measure for distinguishing a text that is a translation from one that is not:

> In terms of common sense I ask you to imagine you have given a translator a printed manuscript in Italian (to be translated, let us say, into English), format A4, font Times Roman 12 point, 200 pages. If the translator brings you back, as an English equivalent of the source text, 400 pages in the same format, you are entitled to smell some form of misdemeanour. I believe one would be entitled to fire the translator before opening his or her product.[20]

Yet, if we applied this principle to our corpus, the number of translations would be radically reduced, not because any of them are twice as long as Brontë's English *Jane Eyre* but because many of them are twice as short, or even shorter. We count such abridged texts as translations by following our rules of thumb: they are intended primarily for reading; they are prose fiction; and they take on the work of being *Jane Eyre* for their readers. In this, we are adopting the classic approach of Descriptive Translation Studies, seeking not to impose on our material an idea of what translation ought to be, but rather to observe and understand what it has been and is: in the words of Gideon Toury, to view translations as 'Facts of a "Target" Culture', and to 'account for actual translational behaviour and its results'.[21]

It follows that a kind of text that counts as a translation in one culture might not if it appeared in another. In France, there is nothing quite like the first Chinese translation, done by Shoujuan Zhou [周瘦鹃] in 1925, with the title 重光记 [*Chong guang ji; Seeing Light Again*]: it is only 9,000 characters in length, and cuts many episodes, as suggested by the titles of its four parts: '(1) Strange Laugh; (2) Budding Love; (3) Mad Woman; (4) Fruit of Love'.[22] Perhaps the nearest French equivalent is that early French review which delighted Charlotte Brontë, written by Eugène Forcade for the *Revue des deux mondes* in 1848: it is 24 pages long, so about 10,000 words, and it includes a full summary of the novel together with close translation of selected passages. Brontë called this review 'one of the most able — the most acceptable to the author of any that has yet appeared', observing that 'the specimens of the translation given are on the whole, good — now

20 Umberto Eco, *Mouse or Rat? Translation as Negotiation* (London: Weidenfeld & Nicolson, 2003), pp. 2–3.

21 Gideon Toury, *Descriptive Translation Studies — and Beyond* (Amsterdam and Philadelphia: John Benjamins, 1995), pp. 23, 3.

22 Qi, 'No Simple Love', p. 21.

and then the meaning of the original has been misapprehended, but generally it is well rendered'.[23] There is no doubt that both texts are involved in translation-without-an-article. And if we were to take them, the Chinese translation and the French review, abstract them as much as possible from their respective cultures and look at them side by side, we might well conclude that the review gives the fuller impression of what Brontë wrote.

But readers of the *Revue des deux mondes* did not think they were being offered a translation. They knew they were reading a review — not only because Forcade frames and permeates the summary and extracts with his own opinions of the novel and indeed of much else, including the 1848 French revolution, but also because, for mid-nineteenth-century French readers, reviews were established as a genre distinct from translations: though a review might well include passages of translation, it was not itself *a* translation. The 1925 Shanghai publication, on the other hand, was part of a ferment of translation of English and European texts in China in the early decades of the twentieth century, during which there was also much debate about different modes of translation and the language appropriate to it. A range of kinds of text were therefore received under the umbrella term *yi* 譯 (translation), with 重光记 [*Chong guang ji; Seeing Light Again*] among them.[24] So, unlike the French review, the Chinese text is a piece of fictional writing that is offered and taken as being a translation, as bodying forth *Jane Eyre* for its readers; and in fact it was the only text in Chinese that did so until the publication of a fuller version ten years later: 孤女飘零记 [*Gunv piaolingji; Record of a Wandering Orphan*] by Wu Guanghua [伍光建]. So it seems to make best sense to count *Chong guang ji* as a translation, while not counting Forcade's review.

Given all this variability and overlap, why seek to distinguish translations from other kinds of re-writing at all? One reason is that

23 *The Letters of Charlotte Brontë*, 2 vols, ed. by Margaret Smith (Oxford and New York: Oxford University Press, 1995–2000), II, p. 140.

24 See Shouhua Qi, *Western Literature in China and the Translation of a Nation* (New York: Palgrave Macmillan, 1912), pp. 32–50 (p. 62); an account of Zhou Shoujuan — though without mention of the translation of *Jane Eyre* — is given in Dechao Li, 'A Study of Zhou Shoujuan's Translation of Western Fiction' (unpublished doctoral dissertation, The Hong Kong Polytechnic University, Department of Chinese and Bilingual Studies, November 2006, UMI Microform no. 3282304); on plural Chinese definitions of translation, see Martha P. Y. Cheung, 'Reconceptualizing Translation — Some Chinese Endeavours', *Meta*, 56 (2011), 1–19.

it enables us to count them, and to locate them in time and space, and therefore to create the interactive maps and other visualisations that I present in Chapter III. Even though the category that we have defined is fuzzy, there is still value in mapping it, and especially so when the synoptic picture provided by the maps is nuanced by the detailed local investigations conducted in the essays. A second reason has to do with the kind of close reading that translations embody and enable. Because translations stick so tightly to the source text, trying to mean the same, or do the same, with different linguistic materials in different times and places, they repay very close comparative attention. As Jean-Michel Adam has observed:

> La traduction présente ... l'immense intérêt d'être une porte d'accès à la boîte noire de la lecture individuelle et secrète qui fait que le même livre est non seulement différent pour chaque lecteur, mais qu'il change même à l'occasion de chaque relecture et retraduction.[25]
>
> [Translation has the enormous interest of giving us an entry into the black box of individual, secret reading which causes the same book, not to be only different for each reader, but to change with every re-reading and re-translation.]

Clive Scott has made a similar point: 'translation is a mode of reading which gives textual substance to reader response'.[26] Because this substantiated reader response, this metamorphic reading and re-reading, translation and re-translation, is done in different moments, cultures and languages, it also gives us a uniquely precise view of the gradations and entanglements of historical, cultural and linguistic difference. This will be amply illustrated in the chapters and essays to come.

The third reason, which follows closely from the second, is that it is only by distinguishing translations from the mass of other *Eyre*-related textuality that we can bring into focus the distinctive, paradoxical challenge that — like translations of any text—they pose to understanding and interpretation. A translation stakes a claim to identity with the source text: to *be Jane Eyre* for the people who read it. And yet that claim is in many respects obviously false, most obviously of all, of course, in the fact that the translated *Jane Eyre* is in a different

25 Jean-Michel Adam, *Souvent textes variant. Génétique, intertextualité, édition et traduction* (Paris: Classiques Garnier, 2018), p. 10.

26 Clive Scott, *Literary Translation and the Rediscovery of Reading* (Cambridge: Cambridge University Press, 2012), p. 10.

language. Pretty much every word, every grammatical construction, and every implied sound in a translation will be different from its counterpart in the source. What is strange is that it is in practice this blatant and unignorable difference which enables the claim to identity to be made. It is the perception of language difference that generates the need to be able to say or write something that counts as *the same* in a different language; and it is the reality of language difference that enables a translation to take the place of its source, since the source will be, for many readers in the receiving culture, difficult or impossible to understand. So, paradoxically, the claim to identity is made possible by the very same factor that announces it to be untrue. To quote again from *Prismatic Translation*, the book that provides much of the theoretical groundwork for *Prismatic Jane Eyre*, this is 'the paradox of all translation'.[27]

From the 1850s onwards, that is, in the early years of *Jane Eyre*'s expanding life in translation, this paradox was confronted by European lawyers, who were trying to establish international copyright agreements that would include translations. As a scholar of the issue, Eva Hemmungs Wirtén, has put it:

> The crux was that the international author-reader partnership also required the multiplication of authorship, and when the need for another author — a translator — was a prerequisite for reaching new readers, the work in question was in danger of alienation from the author. Something happened when a text moved from one language into another, but exactly what was it? Was it reproduction only, or creation of a new work, or rewriting?[28]

The debates culminated in the Berne Convention of 1886, which adopted the view that translations were merely reproductions, no different from a new edition. In consequence, 'authors had the right to translate themselves or authorize a translation of their works within ten years of the first date of publication in a union nation'.[29] Wirtén goes on to explain that national interests played a large part in this decision. States such as France, whose literatures were much translated, sought to expand the rights of the source-text authors who were their citizens. On the other hand, states such as Sweden, which

27 *Prismatic Translation*, ed. by Reynolds, p. 42.

28 Eva Hemmungs Wirtén, 'A Diplomatic Salto Mortale: Translation Trouble in Berne, 1884–1886,' *Book History*, 14 (2011), 88–109, (pp. 92–93).

29 Wirtén, 'A Diplomatic', p. 98.

imported many books through translation, wanted to grant as much liberty as possible to translators, as a document of 1876 asserts:

> För ett folk, hvars språkområde vore så inskränkt, som det svenska, kunde icke ett band på öfversättningsfriheten undgå att verka hämmande på spridning af kunskap och upplysning. Behofvet för ett sådant folk att fullständiga egen litteratur med öfversättningar från utlandets bättre verk vore oändligt mycket större, än det som förefunnes hos folk med vidssträckt språkområde och betydligt rikhaltigare litteratur, än den Svenska.
>
> (For a people whose language is so small and geographically limited as the Swedish, any restriction on freedom of translation could not but have a negative impact on the dissemination of knowledge and education. The need for such a people to complete its own literature by translations of the better works from abroad is infinitely greater than what it is for people with a widespread language and considerably richer literature than the Swedish.)[30]

At Berne, the French view won out over the Swedish; but the debates were not silenced by this triumph of literary power-politics. A revision to the agreement, made in Berlin in 1908, allowed the Swedish view back in, granting translations copyright protection of their own, whether they were authorized or not. This provision was in considerable tension with the protection that continued to be granted to source texts. Wirtén concludes that the Berlin Convention 'implemented a paradox. On the one hand, the rights of the author included translation, but on the other, the translation emerged as a separate work.'[31]

The paradox of translation, as it reared its head in Berlin, reveals the dead end of the terms in which translations and source texts were defined in those debates — terms that persist in much discussion to this day. A source is not a determinate entity that can be either reproduced in translation or not. It consists, not only of its printed words and punctuation, but of all that they mean, and all that they do. As Roland Barthes, Stanley Fish, and other literary theorists have demonstrated in manifold ways since the 1960s, the meaning and affect of a work are not simply given in the text but emerge through the collaborative

30 *Högsta domstolens protokoll*, November 22, 1876, quoted and translated in Wirtén, 'A Diplomatic', p. 92.
31 Wirtén, 'A Diplomatic', p. 101.

involvement of readers.[32] Translators are readers. What is more, as we have seen, their work belongs with those other kinds of re-writing, including literary criticism, that are accepted as characterising and illuminating the book, as subjecting it to continuous rediscovery and reconfiguration. It follows that a translation cannot be judged by how well it 'reproduces' or 'is faithful to' its source, for translation is involved in determining what that source is.

A series of thinkers in Translation Studies have contributed to the view that I am presenting. Focusing on works in classical Greek and Latin, Charles Martindale argued (three decades ago now) that it is misconceived to ask whether a translator has captured what is 'there' in the source, since 'translations determine what counts as being "there" in the first place'. Developing a similar point from his work on nationalist constructions of the Japanese language, Naoki Sakai demonstrated the incoherence of trying to decide whether a translation has or has not successfully transferred the source's meaning, since you cannot define what you think that meaning to be until you have translated it: 'what is translated and transferred can be recognized as such only after translation'. In short, in the crisp, recent formulation by Karen Emmerich, 'each translator creates her own original'.[33] Reading translations in connection with their source, therefore, is not only to engage in transnational literary history and comparative cultural enquiry, though we do a great deal of those two things in the pages that follow. It is also to confront a basic ontological question: what is *Jane Eyre*?

---

32 Key moments in this stream of theory are: Roland Barthes, 'The Death of the Author', *Aspen: The Magazine in a Box*, 5&6 (1967), n.p., https://www.ubu.com/aspen/aspen5and6/threeEssays.html#barthes and its French version 'La mort de l'auteur' *Manteia*, 5 (1968), 12–17; Michel Foucault, 'Qu'est-ce qu'un auteur?', *Bulletin de la Société française de philosophie*, 63 (1969), 73–104; Wolfgang Iser, *Die implicite Leser: Kommunikationsformen des Romans von Bunyan bis Beckett* (Munich: W. Fink, 1972); Stanley Fish, 'Interpreting the "Variorum"', *Critical Inquiry*, 2 (1976), 465–85, and *Is There a Text in This Class? The Authority of Interpretive Communities* (Cambridge, MA: Harvard University Press, 1980); Jerome J. McGann, *The Beauty of Inflections: Literary Investigations in Historical Method and Theory* (Oxford: Clarendon Press, 1985); Eve Kosofsky Sedgwick, 'Jane Austen and the Masturbating Girl', *Critical Inquiry* 17 (1991), 818–37 and *Touching Feeling: Affect, Pedagogy, Performativity* (Durham: Duke University Press, 2003).

33 Charles Martindale, *Redeeming the Text: Latin Poetry and the Hermeneutics of Reception* (Cambridge: Cambridge University Press, 1993), p. 93; Sakai, *Translation and Subjectivity*, p. 5; Karen Emmerich, *Literary Translation and the Making of Originals* (New York and London: Bloomsbury, 2017), p. 13.

What is *Jane Eyre*?

If we focus on the translations as just defined, that is, on the texts that make a claim to be *Jane Eyre*, we discover not only an enormous amount of textuality — several hundreds of translations, several scores of languages, many millions of words — but also a great deal of variety. First, as we have seen, there is variety in size. Many of the translations are roughly the same length as the source (i.e., about 186,000 words, or 919 generously spaced pages in the first edition); none, so far as we have been able to discover, are significantly longer. But many are shorter, sometimes very much so. Zhou Shoujuan's first Chinese translation of 1925, at 9,000 characters, may be an extreme case, but is very far from being the only one. The first translation into an Indian language, Tamil, done by K. Appātturai [கா அப்பாத்துரை] in 1953, with the title [ஜேன் அயர்: உலகப் புகழ் பெற்ற நாவல்] (*Jēn Ayar: Ulakap pukal̲ per̲r̲a naval*; *Jane Eyre: A World-Renowned Novel*), was 150 pages. The first Italian translation, with an anonymous translator and the title *Jane Eyre, o Le memorie d'un'istitutrice* (*Jane Eyre or the Memoirs of a Governess*) was 40,000 words shorter than Brontë's English text. The first version in French, *Jane Eyre ou Mémoires d'une Gouvernante* (*Jane Eyre or Memoirs of a Governess*), published in Paris and Brussels in 1849, written by Paul Émile Daurand Forgues under the pseudonym 'Old Nick', and serialized virtually simultaneously in two newspapers and a literary journal, consisted of 183 pages (I say 'version' here because this text's status as 'a translation' is especially controversial, an issue that I explore further below).

As these instances suggest, abridgement is a common feature of first or early translations, and especially so when they are done into languages and cultures distant from British English. As Kayvan Tahmasebian and Rebecca Ruth Gould observe of the Iranian context in Essay 8, where they build on an idea of Antoine Berman's, it is often the case that successive translations gravitate towards equality of length with the source text. New translations can differentiate themselves from their predecessors by claiming greater accuracy; equally, the passing of time since the mid-nineteenth century has seen enormous growth in the global use of English, as well as in technologies for checking translations against their sources and one another, and in institutions for evaluating them (such as prizes). But other trends push in the opposite direction, and keep abridgements coming. With its childhood beginning, clear narrative line, assertive voice and elements of gothic and romance, *Jane Eyre* is in itself an attractive prospect for re-making as a children's book; and, as it became ever more widely celebrated, market forces must have started to beckon too. In Germany, as Lynne Tatlock has shown, adaptations for children — and especially for girls — date back to as early as 1852 and proliferated through the later nineteenth century, taming the novel by changing it in various ways, including killing Mr Rochester or omitting him entirely.[34] Examples of translations aimed at the same demographic are those done into Russian, anonymously, in 1901; into Turkish in 1946 by Fahrünnisa Seden; into Italian, anonymously, in 1958; into Greek in 1963 by Georgia Deligiannē-Anastasiadē; into Portuguese in 1971 by Miécio Táti (published in Rio de Janeiro); into Hebrew in 1996 by Asi Weistein (published in HaDarom in Israel/Palestine); and into Arabic in 2004 by Ṣabri al-Faḍī (published in Cairo). For similar reasons, abridged translations with parallel text, thesauruses and other learning aids have been made as part of the international industry in English-language tuition: for instance, into Lithuanian by Vytautas Karsevičius (1983); into Hungarian by Gábor Görgey and Mária Ruzitska (1984); and into Chinese by Guangjia Fu [傅光甲] (2005).[35]

Variation in length, then, is not only variation in length. It intersects with differences of audience, use, genre and style. As Yunte Huang explains in Essay 12, Zhou Shoujuan shrank *Jane Eyre* so radically as part of his endeavour to translate it into the conventions of 'the School of Mandarin Duck and Butterfly ... a genre of popular fiction'. The first, abridged Italian translation of 1904 reveals the influence of its target audience too, when it presents itself as meeting a demand from mothers and girls ('e madri e ragazze') to read the celebrated novel, in line with the aim of the imprint in which it appeared, Biblioteca Amena ('Agreeable Library'), to offer 'buone e piacevoli letture accessibili a tutti e a tutte' (virtuous and pleasant reading accessible to all, men and women, girls and boys'). In this pursuit, the 1904 translation does not cut any episodes of dubious virtue: for instance, the story of Mr Rochester's affair with Céline Varens remains intact. Instead, it consistently simplifies the complexities of Brontë's style, and hence of Jane's voice. To give one indicative instance: after the

34 Tatlock, *Jane Eyre in German Lands*, pp. 9, 14–18, 98–99, 105–7.
35 Full details of these editions are given in our List of Translations below.

dramatic episode of the fire in Mr Rochester's bedroom in Chapter 15, the English Jane narrates as follows:

> Till morning dawned I was tossed on a buoyant but unquiet sea, where billows of trouble rolled under surges of joy.

The 1904 Italian Jane, on the other hand, says this:

> Era giorno quando mi pareva di sentirmi portata via da onde torbide mescolate ad onde chiare.
>
> [It was dawn when I seemed to feel myself carried away by turbid waves mixed with clear waves.][36]

Shortening and simplifying go hand in hand, as *Jane Eyre* is translated into a kind of language that can be readily shared by its targeted readers.

The 1849 French version by 'Old Nick', *Jane Eyre ou Mémoires d'une gouvernante* [*Jane Eyre or Memoirs of a Governess*], took a different approach. It was made for serial publication, appearing in 27 instalments in the Paris newspaper *Le National* from 15 April to 11 June, and almost simultaneously in Brussels, in three monthly numbers of a literary magazine *Revue de Paris* (April–June), and in daily segments (though with several interruptions) in the newspaper *L'Indépendance belge* from 29 April to 28 June.[37] It was also published in book form in Brussels the same year, and later in Paris, in 1855.[38] The rare-book expert Jay Dillon, who discovered the serialization in *Le National*, has shown that it must have been the first publication, and argued that the Brussels printings are likely to have been piracies.[39] Certainly, the Brussels-based *Revue de Paris*, which was an imitation of the famous journal of the same name published in Paris, typically plagiarized articles from Paris publications.[40] In this context that was itself strangely, dubiously translated, this *Revue de Paris* published

36 *Jane Eyre, o Le memorie d'un' istitutrice* (Milan: Fratelli Treves, 1904), quoted from the electronic text at Progetto Manuzio, https://www.liberliber.it/online/opere/download/?op=23446798&type=opera_url_pdf, p. 225.

37 Jay Dillon discovered the printing in *Le National* and I am grateful to him to alerting me to it; he described it in '"Reader, I found it": The First *Jane Eyre* in French', *The Book Collector*, 17 (2023), 11–19. I am also grateful to Justine Feyereisen for securing copies of *L'Indépendance belge* for me.

38 *Jane Eyre ou mémoires d'une gouvernante* (Paris: L. Hachette, 1855). In the book version the pseudonym is given with a hyphen, 'Old Nick'.

39 Dillon, '"Reader, I found it"', 14.

40 'Notice Bibliographique', *BnF Catalogue Général*, https://catalogue.bnf.fr/ark:/12148/cb41304908b.public; Langlois, 'Early Critics', p. 13; *Jane Eyre ou*

in Brussels, *Jane Eyre* took its place among other serialisations, short stories, reviews, essays on history, the text of Alfred de Musset's play 'Louison' and an essay on the Louvre by Théophile Gautier. In the two newspapers, meanwhile, it appeared among round-ups of domestic politics and items of economic and international news. *Jane Eyre* was adapted for *Le National* by a man of letters, Paul Émile Daurand Forgues, who was becoming increasingly prominent as a reviewer and translator of British fiction, and whose pseudonym 'Old Nick' (a nickname for Satan) perhaps suggests the devilish liberties he felt entitled to take as he mediated between the two literary worlds.[41]

In shortening *Jane Eyre* for newspaper serialization, perhaps under pressure of time,[42] Old Nick (inevitably) also altered its style and genre. It becomes a letter — apparently one, extremely long letter divided into 27 chapters — addressed to a *'Mistress T……y'*, whom Jane, to begin with, calls her 'digne et sévère amie' ('honoured and austere friend'), but who, in the warmth of narration, becomes 'ma chère Élisabeth' ('my dear Elisabeth') by the start of Chapter 2.[43] The chapters are all of fairly uniform, short length, one for each instalment in *Le National*; this might also be felt to suit the idea of a letter being written sequentially. We could decide that this reconfiguration of the narrative loses the frank challenge of Jane's voice which, in Brontë's English, throws itself equally at all readers. Yet the change also brings *Jane Eyre* into the interpretive frame of the epistolary novel, a form long established in France and employed by writers such as Rousseau and Laclos: this might well seem a welcoming move to make when introducing a text to a new culture. We can, then, view it as part of

mémoires d'une gouvernante (Paris: L. Hachette, 1855). In the book version the pseudonym is given with a hyphen, 'Old Nick'.

41 On Forgues's role as a mediator of English fiction in France, see Marie-Françoise Cachin, 'Victorian Novels in France', *The Oxford Handbook of the Victorian Novel*, ed. by Lisa Rodensky (Oxford: Oxford University Press, 2013). However Cachin mentions only the later publication of Old Nick's version, in book form.

42 Such pressures on C19th French translators are described in the section on 'Prose Narrative', by Anne-Rachel Hermetet and Frédéric Weinman, in *Histoire des traductions en langue française: XIXe Siècle 1815–1914*, ed. by Yvres Chevrel, Lieven D'Hulst and Christine Lombez (Paris: Verdier, 2012), pp. 537–664: see especially pp. 553–55, 600.

43 *Jane Eyre. Mémoires d'une gouvernante* (1re partie), Imité de Currer-Bell, par Old Nick, *Revue de Paris* (Brussels), new series, 4 (1849) 119–79 (pp. 119–20, 129).

the complex process of translation, not only into a language but into a particular genre, medium and set of expectations.

Seeing the shift of narrative form in this way generates a kind of heuristic counter-current. It makes us freshly aware of the distinctiveness of Brontë's choice precisely *not* to organise *Jane Eyre* as an epistolary novel — or indeed as an impersonal, third-person narrative like its closest precedent in English, Charles Dickens's *Oliver Twist* (1837–39) — but instead to create that compelling first-person voice, which makes frequent addresses to an unspecified reader without (puzzlingly, challengingly) having any explicit moment or purpose for the narration. Part of the significance of *Jane Eyre* — or any text — in a transnational and multilingual perspective is created by the forms that it seems to be asking to take on, the shapes that it might itself very well have adopted, but did not. In translation, these shadow forms can step forward and impose themselves on the substance of the text (we will see other examples in the chapters and essays that follow). As they do so, they fulfil what might be described as a potential latent in the source text while, in that very same action, giving salience to the fact that the potential was not realised in the source text itself. This paradoxical dynamic, of what might be called realisation through what might equally be called betrayal, can be found in all translation, and it is one of the engines that power the prismatic proliferation of *Jane Eyre*, or any work. The existence of the Old Nick version must have encouraged Noëmi Lesbazeilles-Souvestre and her publisher D. Giraud to repair Old Nick's realisation/betrayal by producing her more word-for-word translation in 1854, claiming 'l'Autorisation de l'Auteur' ('the Authorisation of the Author') — though no evidence has survived to indicate whether or not any such authorisation was in fact given. And the existence of her translation must in turn have encouraged a rival publisher, Hachette, to re-issue the Old Nick version as a book in 1855 in its 'Bibliothèque des chemins de fer' ('Railway Library'), re-asserting the interest of the different potentials that it fulfils.

Old Nick uses the epistolary voice to summarise some parts of the novel, introducing a more detached tonality of ethical reflection, while at the same time reproducing other sections very closely. Here is an instance of the braiding of the two modes, from the young Jane's conversation with Helen Burns in Chapter 6. Brontë wrote:

> 'But I feel this, Helen; I must dislike those who, whatever I do to please them, persist in disliking me; I must resist those who punish me unjustly.

> It is as natural as that I should love those who show me affection, or submit to punishment when I feel it is deserved.'
>
> 'Heathens and savage tribes hold that doctrine, but Christians and civilised nations disown it.'

Old Nick fuses the first sentence into a summary that represents the immediately preceding exchanges too, before switching to close translation:

> J'essayai de démontrer à Helen que la vengeance était non-seulement un droit, mais un devoir, puisqu'elle sert de leçon à quiconque l'a méritée.
>
> « Il est aussi naturel de résister à l'injustice que de haïr qui nous hait, que d'aimer qui nous aime, que d'accepter le châtiment quand le châtiment est équitable.
>
> —Ainsi pensent les sauvages, et les païens pensaient de même, répondit tranquillement Helen. Mais les chrétiens et les peuples civilisés repoussent et désavouent cette morale.[44]

> [I tried to prove to Helen that revenge was not only a right, but a duty, since it serves as a lesson to whoever has deserved it.
>
> 'It is as natural to resist injustice as to hate those who hate us, to love those who love us, and to accept punishment when punishment is fair.'
>
> 'So think savages, and pagans think the same,' Helen replied calmly; 'but Christians and civilised nations reject and disavow this morality.']

The English Jane's repeated 'I feel' is replaced by impersonal statements of principle and justice, and her tolling 'I's dissolve into infinitive constructions: the novel of feeling is moved towards the novel of philosophy. Inga-Stina Ewbank, in her pioneering and still helpful survey of some of the early European Brontë translations, sees this kind of adjustment as being simply a matter of loss, the imposition of 'a cooling layer between experience and reader', reducing Jane's 'ardour' and weakening her 'force'.[45] Yet Old Nick finds other ways of introducing intensity, adding the phrase about hating those who hate us, and doubling 'disown' into both 'repoussent' ('reject') and 'désavouent' ('disavow'). Other touches too suggest a translator imagining his way into the scene and sensing how best to recreate it, for the context at hand, with the linguistic and stylistic resources at his disposal: for instance, the addition of the speech description 'répondit tranquillement Helen' ('Helen replied calmly'). Brontë is sparing of such tags, having unusual confidence in the power of her dialogue to

44 *Jane Eyre* (1re partie), par Old Nick, 134.
45 Ewbank, 'Reading the Brontës Abroad', p. 88.

make itself heard by her readers, almost like a play script. We could accuse Old Nick — in the Ewbank vein of criticism — of lacking that same daring; but equally, his insertion of the adverb underlines the distinctiveness of Helen's character, accentuating the difference between her view of things and Jane's.

As this brief analysis suggests, Old Nick's version, despite its abridgements, remains a perceptive work of translation. The same holds true on the larger scale of the cuts he makes to the plot. For the most part, what goes are sections that many readers would probably choose to give up if they had to. Jane's visit to Mrs Reed's deathbed is replaced by the receipt of a letter bearing the sad news, and enclosing the note from her uncle John Eyre — which Mrs Reed had suppressed — announcing his intent to make Jane his heir. So we lose the perhaps slightly laboured satire of the grown-up Eliza and Georgiana while the discovery that is needed for the plot is neatly preserved. The long descriptions of the house party with the Ingram and Eshton ladies are reduced to this:

> Je ne vous les décrirai pas; à quoi bon? Avec des nuances plus ou moins prononcées, c'était chez toutes ces fières créatures le même air de calme supériorité, la même nonchalance dédaigneuse, les mêmes gestes appris, la même grâce de convention.
>
> [I won't describe them: what would be the point? With more or less distinctive nuances, all of these proud creatures had the same air of calm superiority, the same disdainful nonchalance, the same studied gestures, the same conventional grace.][46]

The back story of Mr Rochester's affair with Céline Varens is condensed with a similar critical justification:

> Je ne vos répéterai point cette histoire, après tout assez vulgaire, d'un jeune et riche Anglais séduit par une coquette mercenaire appartenant au corps de ballet de l'Opéra. Il s'était cru aimé, il s'était vu trahi.
>
> [I won't rehearse this story, after all a pretty vulgar one, of a young, rich Englishman seduced by a mercenary coquette from the corps de ballet at the Opera. He had believed himself loved; he had seen himself betrayed.][47]

In these self-referential phrases ('I won't describe', 'I won't rehearse'), the narrative decisions of the French Jane about which bits of her

46 *Jane Eyre. Mémoires d'une gouvernante, Suite (1)*, imité de Currer-Bell, par Old Nick, *Revue de Paris* (Brussels), new series, 5 (1849) 51–132 (p. 68).

47 *Jane Eyre, Suite (1)*, par Old Nick, p. 51.

experience to relate to her dear Elizabeth are merged with the translatorial decisions of Old Nick vis-à-vis the English novel. The letter-writer representing her life-story becomes a figure for the translator representing his source. To echo a phrase from Theo Hermans, this shows the translator exhibiting his 'own reading', and marking its difference from other possible interpretations.[48] As the letter-writer chooses to concentrate on what seems most important, so too does the translator; and as she has an eye to the expectations of her readership, so too does he, for the sections cut include those least likely to impress readers familiar with Balzac or Stendhal. The most striking omission is the scene of Bertha's incursion into Jane's bedroom at night, just before her planned wedding — especially as the intimations of Bertha's presence up to that point, as well as the encounter with her after the interrupted wedding, are all fully represented. It is possible to imagine a mix of reasons for this choice: perhaps Old Nick felt the scene to be too melodramatic, and perhaps he also felt it risked spoiling the surprise of the imminent final reveal.

Nevertheless, the main lines of the narrative remain, and many key scenes such as the 'red-room' are attentively translated. Forcade, in his 1848 review, had drawn attention to the way Jane and Mr Rochester become progressively attached 'de causerie en causerie, de confidence en confidence, par l'habitude de cette camaraderie originale' ('from chat to chat, from confidence to confidence, by the habit of this unusual camaraderie'), and Old Nick seems to have felt the same, for the intimate, jousting conversations between the pair are what he most fully translates, and the developing stages of their relationship are what he most closely tracks. Indeed, his tighter focus enables suggestive structural echoes to emerge which may be muffled in the fuller treatment of Brontë's text. For instance, in Chapter 15 of the source (which becomes Chapter 7 in Old Nick's version), Jane saves Mr Rochester from burning in his bed, after which the two of them find it hard to part: '"Good night then, sir," ... "What! ... not without taking leave" ... "Good night again, sir" ... he still retained my hand ... I bethought myself of an expedient ... he relaxed his fingers, and I was gone'.[49] In the next chapter she discovers, after a lonely day of

48 Theo Hermans, *The Conference of the Tongues* (Manchester: St Jerome, 2007), p. 30: 'each rendering exhibits its own reading and, in so doing, marks its difference from other readings, other interpretations'.

49 *JE*, Ch. 15.

puzzled waiting, that Mr Rochester has in his turn departed, leaving Thornfield to stay with a house party some distance away, and is not expected to return at all soon. Reading Brontë's English, it is possible to be struck by and reflect upon this sequence of intimate lingering and departure followed by larger-scale departure and lingering; but Old Nick spotlights the connection with a repeated word. Of leaving Mr Rochester's bedroom, Jane writes 'je le quittai' (I left him); five pages later she learns from Mrs Fairfax that, where Mr Rochester is staying, he will be with the lovely Blanche Ingram, whom he 'ne quitte pas volontiers' ('never leaves willingly').[50] The surge of jealousy which, in Old Nick as in Brontë, takes up the next few pages is heralded by this verbal echo, which hints that Jane may be prey to gnawing thoughts about the consequences of her act of leaving: if she had not left him, perhaps he would not have left the house; or, since she did leave him, perhaps he now will not leave Blanche.

Observing these changes of form and alterations of emphasis which emerge through translation, it is possible to lament, with Ewbank, that this is 'not our Jane Eyre any longer'. Yet Ewbank's phrasing, with its confidently possessive first-person plural, reveals with unusual clarity the nationalist tonality of this mode of translation criticism, in which anything that strikes the critic as significantly different from the source text is marked down as a loss. The assumption underlying this familiar, though unrewarding, line of critique is that success in translation is impossible, because success is taken to mean identity, and translations are by definition different from their sources even as they claim some form of sameness. But once you open yourself to the recognition that the work, *Jane Eyre*, has an existence beyond its first material embodiment in 186,299 particular words (not all of them English words, as we will explore further in Chapter II), the kinds of metamorphosis that occur as the work re-emerges in different linguistic forms can become more interesting. This *Jane Eyre* is not 'our' (English readers') *Jane Eyre* as idealised by Ewbank, but then the actual *Jane Eyre* that is read and lives on in the minds of real English readers is not that either: it encompasses all sorts of varying perceptions, obsessions, expansions and forgettings, as Lefevere pointed out. The idea of there being a consistent, clearly recognisable 'our *Jane Eyre*' is a nationalist and class-based projection, a striking instance of the regime of 'homolingual address' identified by Sakai. It is reinforced by

50 *Jane Eyre, Suite (1)* par Old Nick, 59, 64.

the apparent material sameness of the book as it has been reprinted over the decades in English (even though, as Paola Gaudio outlines in Essay 2, there have also been notable textual variations in successive editions): the apparent solidity of print on paper pushes out of view the varied realisations that the work has in fact had in the imaginings of generations of anglophone readers. As we saw with Jean-Michel Adam, part of the excitement of working with translations is that they provide visible evidence of that interpretive plurality which otherwise remains, to a large extent, hidden in readers' minds.

Nevertheless, one can sympathise with the shock felt by Charlotte Brontë's friend and fellow-novelist Elizabeth Gaskell when sent the book of Old Nick's version in 1855 by the publisher Louis Hachette. She was startled by the 'offensive' pseudonym of the translator, and distressed also by the degree of the abridgement:

> Every author of any note is anxious for a correct and faithful translation of what they do write; and, although from the difference of literary taste between the two nations it may become desirable to abbreviate certain parts, or even to leave them out altogether, yet no author would like to have a whole volume omitted, and to have the translation of the mutilated remainder called an 'Imitation'.[51]

Here we can see, not only Gaskell's loyalty to her friend, together with her emotional investment in the book and her sense of her own professional status, but also the power to provoke that the work of translation, and especially the claim to count as a translation, can possess. Gaskell feels the thrust of this claim even though, as she notes, Old Nick's version was advertised as being 'imité' ('imitated') from Currer Bell, rather than 'translated'; it was also — on its earlier appearances in *Le National* and *Revue de Paris* — described as a 'réduction' ('reduction'), not a translation. As we have been discovering, the borderlines between these terms are in general porous and contested; and they were conspicuously so in French literary culture in the mid-nineteenth century. The prevailing definition of a translation excluded reviews, as we have seen; but on the other hand there was wide acceptance that translations, especially from non-romance languages, needed a fair amount of licence to adapt their sources to the norms of French, and the demands of the publishing market, too, promoted abridgements and adaptations. Four years after his

51 *Further Letters of Mrs Gaskell*, ed. by John Chapple and Alan Shelston (Manchester: Manchester University Press, 2000), p. 130.

version of *Jane Eyre*, Old Nick translated Nathaniel Hawthorne's *The Scarlet Letter*: the text was no less cut and tweaked than his imitation or reduction of Brontë's novel, and the changes were welcomed by a journal, the *Revue britannique*:

> Plus d'un passage nous a paru supérieur à l'original, car il fallait pour le rendre une certaine adresse, lutter avec des phrases un peu redondantes, prêter enfin au romancier américain le goût qui lui fait parfois défaut.[52]
>
> [More than one passage struck us as being superior to the original, because a certain dexterity was required to bring it across, to wrestle with somewhat over-expansive sentences, and to lend the American novelist the taste that he sometimes lacks.]

Yet this book was advertised on the title page as being, not reduced, nor imitated, but 'traduit par Old Nick' [translated by Old Nick].[53]

Looking only at this French context, then, we already get a vivid sense of the instability of the definition of 'a translation'. In consequence, we might choose to discount the markers 'imité' and 'réduction', and view Old Nick's *Jane Eyre* as a translation — as I have been doing — though we might equally choose to accept them, since, after all, they were the terms adopted by him (or his publishers): this is the line taken by Céline Sabiron in Essay 4 below. However, on the larger scale of transnational literary history, those labels, as well as Gaskell's protest, counted for nothing as Old Nick's version was established as a translation by later translators. During 1850–51, Spanish texts titled *Juana Eyre. Memorias de un Aya* [*Jane Eyre: Memoirs of a Governess*] appeared in several locations in South America: Santiago de Chile, Havana and Matanzas in Cuba, and La Paz in Bolivia. The text was initially serialised in newspapers (in *El Progreso*, Santiago; *Diario de la Marina*, Havana; *La Época*, La Paz), though it also appeared in volume form. The conduit for this speedy and distant proliferation of *Jane Eyres* was a Paris-based publishing enterprise connected to the *Correo de Ultramar*, a magazine which conveyed literary and fashion news to Spanish-speaking countries globally.[54] In 1849, 'Administración del Correo de Ultramar' published a Spanish translation of Old Nick's

52 Quoted in *Histoire des traductions*, ed. by Chevrel, D'Hulst and Lombez, p. 609.

53 Nathaniel Hawthorne, *La lettre rouge – A*, trans. by Old Nick (Paris: Gabriel de Gonnet, 1853).

54 See Diana Cooper-Richet, 'La presse hispanophone Parisienne au XIXe siècle: *El Correo de Ultramar* et les autres', *Cedille : revista de estudios franceses* 16 (2019), 81–100 (pp. 81–84); Hernan Pas, 'Eugène Sue en Buenos Aires: Edición,

French version of *Jane Eyre*, crediting Old Nick (spelt 'Oldt Nick' on the title page) as author and making no mention of Brontë.[55] This anonymous translation is the text that was reproduced in Chile, Cuba and Bolivia. Through this process the English source has been erased, and Old Nick's French has become the 'original'; but still, the Spanish text is figuring as the translation of a novel called *Jane Eyre*.

In the Netherlands in 1849, and in Denmark and Saxony (a German kingdom) in 1850, translations were published with subtitles that echoed Old Nick's, though now Currer Bell was credited as author: Dutch, *Jane Eyre, of Het leven eener gouvernante*; Danish, *Jane Eyre, eller en Gouvernantes Memoirer*; German, *Jane Eyre: Memoiren einer Gouvernante*. Of these, the German publication, by Ludwig Fort, turns out to be taken from Old Nick's version; and so too does a Swedish translation from 1850, even though it draws its subtitle from Brontë and not Old Nick: *Jane Eyre: en sjelf-biographie*. So, across Europe and South America in the first few years of the novel's life, you could open a book called *Jane* (or *Juana*) *Eyre* and be as likely to find a translation of Old Nick's text as of Brontë's. This arrogation of Old Nick's text to the status of translation continued in the years that followed: for instance, the 1857 Russian *Dzhenni Ėĭr, ili zapiski guvernantki* [*Jane Eyre, the memoirs of a governess*] was translated by S. I. Koshlakova from Old Nick's text.[56] To Emmerich's observation that 'each translator creates her own original', we can now add that many factors collaborate in the workings of literary history to determine the form of an original and what counts as a translation of it.

These complex strands of what is (so far) only a tiny part of *Jane Eyre*'s translation history show the importance of institutional and material factors such as connections between publishers and the physical movements of texts — what B. Venkat Mani has called 'bibliomigrancy'.[57] Such factors include censorship: as we will see in Essay 17 below, by Eugenia Kelbert, Vera Stanevich's 1950 Russian

circulación y comercialización del folletín durante el rosismo', *Varia história*, 34 (2018), 193–225 (pp. 193–211).

55 My thanks to Jay Dillon who alerted me to the existence of this publication which does not appear in any library catalogues or bibliographies: he discovered the only known copy.

56 Full details of these translations are in our List of Translations below. I am grateful to Eugenia Kelbert for the information about the Russian text.

57 B. Venkat Mani, *Recoding World Literature: Libraries, Print Culture, and Germany's Pact with Books* (New York: Fordham University Press, 2017), passim.

translation was cut by the Soviet censor, with passages relating to Christianity especially being removed; and as Ana Teresa Marques dos Santos and Cláudia Pazos Alonso show in Essay 9, the 1941 Portuguese translation by Mécia and João Gaspar Simões, which came out during the dictatorship of António de Oliveira Salazar, skipped passages that express Jane's desire for greater liberty. Meanwhile — as Andrés Claro reveals in Essay 5 — in Barcelona, Spain, in 1943, the republican Juan G. de Luaces was translating so as to hint at the rebellious energies in the novel that could not be openly expressed under the regime of Francisco Franco. As all three essays suggest, and as other work on translation and censorship has also shown,[58] there is no hard distinction between state coercion on the one hand and individual choices on the other. Marques dos Santos and Alonso discuss an anonymous Portuguese translator writing in 1926, i.e., before Salazar, who took 'a liberdade de cortar desapiedadamente tudo quanto pudesse impedir a carreira dos eventos para o desenlace final' [the liberty to cut ruthlessly everything that could prevent the flow of events towards the final denouement]. This translator was not subject to state censorship, but was still feeling societal pressures from outside as well as interpretive impulses from within. The same is true of Zhou Shoujuan (周瘦鹃), Old Nick and the anonymous 1904 Italian translator, as we have seen in this chapter. Any act of translation involves some negotiation between what a translator might wish to write and what is likely to be acceptable in their publishing context.

Our glimpse of a small part of *Jane Eyre*'s complex life in translation also reveals the productiveness of a prismatic approach; that is, of recognizing that translation generates multiple texts which ask to be analysed together.[59] All the texts that I have mentioned so far, all the texts discussed in the rest of this volume, and indeed all the many translations that we do not have room to discuss — all are manifestations of, and contributions to, the world work that *Jane Eyre* has become and is becoming. As Clive Scott has put it:

> The picture of the translational world that we want to generate is one in which each translation is viewed not as a tinkering with a master-copy, nor as a second order derivation, but as a composition, whose

58 For example, Guido Bonsaver, 'Fascist Censorship on Literature and the Case of Elio Vittorini', *Modern Italy*, 8 (2003), 165–86; Kate Sturge, 'Censorship of Translated Fiction in Nazi Germany', *TTR: traductions, terminologie, rédaction*, 15 (2002), 153–69.

59 *Prismatic Translation*, ed. by Reynolds, pp. 1–18.

> very coming into existence is, as with the ST [source text] before it, conditional upon its being multiplied, on its attracting variations, on its inwardly contesting, or holding in precarious tension, its own apparent finality.[60]

Each new translation establishes a relationship to *Jane-Eyre*-as-it-has-been-hitherto, and especially to the aspects of the world *Jane Eyre* that have been knowable to the translator: the source text they have used (whether it is in English or, in the case of relay translation, another language), and the related texts and ideas that have flowed into the process of translation. At the very same moment, the new translation becomes part of the world *Jane Eyre*, changing it, and also creating a momentum that may help another translation into being, as Old Nick's version helped generate the texts that derived from it, such as the Spanish translation that spread to South America and Lesbazeilles-Souvestre's rival French translation. This is somewhat similar to the dynamic that reigns in English-language contexts (as we saw at the start of this chapter) when the novel is discussed in reviews, academic criticism, debates in book groups or conversations among friends, each new opinion tending to generate another. But what is different about those forms of response is their relationship to the idea of *Jane Eyre*, which is constructed by the organizing power of genre. This relationship is manifest both in their own rhetoric and in the way they are received. They present themselves, and are taken, not as staking a claim to be *Jane Eyre* but merely as saying something about it. They therefore seem not threaten an idea of 'the work itself' as being embodied in the printed words of the English book. In fact, new critical interpretations do alter the words of *Jane Eyre*, but the difference they introduce is invisible. Since Gilbert and Gubar, and since Spivak, the novel has changed, for its words have become part of (we might say) new languages — the languages of feminist and postcolonial critique. Any critical intervention, or any version, has the power to transform the novel in the same way. And such 'new readings', as we tend to call them, even though they are in fact re-writings, are helped into being by pervasive shifts in culture and language that are perpetual and inevitable. As it is reprinted and re-read in English, *Jane Eyre* is in fact being continuously translated. The form of the printed words and punctuation may not alter (or not very much), but the language that

60 Clive Scott, *The Work of Literary Translation* (Cambridge: Cambridge University Press, 2018), pp. 13–14.

surrounds them changes, which is to say, the language that *Jane Eyre* is taken as being 'in'.[61]

Comparison with another kind of continuity through change can help to illuminate the continuing and indeed expanding existence of *Jane Eyre* through translation. In *Reasons and Persons*, the philosopher Derek Parfit dismantles the view that personal identity is 'distinct from physical and psychological continuity', a 'deep further fact' that must be 'all-or-nothing'. Instead, what matters are the links between past, present and future experiences, connections such as 'those involved in experience-memory, or in the carrying out of an earlier intention'. For me to continue being me, it is not necessary for anything to be unchanged between me in the future and me now or as I was at any point in the past: rather, there needs to be a sequence of bodily and experiential links. For instance, no bit of hair on my head may be the same as in my childhood, but it has replaced the hair that replaced the hair (etc.) that I had in that distant period. Likewise, I may not remember what I received for my tenth birthday, but I have a memory of a time when I had a memory of a time when (repeat as often as necessary) I could remember it. What follows is that there is no absolute divide between me and other people, since many experiences are shared. In a beautiful and famous passage, Parfit describes how his sense of himself changed when he had reasoned his way from the first to the second view: 'when I believed that my existence was such a further fact, I seemed imprisoned in myself. My life seemed like a glass tunnel, through which I was moving faster every year, and at the end of which there was darkness. When I changed my view, the walls of my glass tunnel disappeared. I now live in the open air. There is still a difference between my life and the lives of other people. But the difference is less.'[62]

Of course, there are many distinctions to be drawn between a person and a literary work, and also a great many intricacies to Parfit's argument beyond the sound-bite that I have given here. Nevertheless, there are four aspects of his view that are comparable to the argument I am making about texts and translations. The first is that selfhood can consist of a series of linked experiences together with physical

61 This formulation is indebted to George Steiner's somewhat different idea that 'when we read or hear any language-statement from the past ... we translate', *After Babel*, 3rd edn (Oxford: Oxford University Press 1983), p. 28.

62 Derek Parfit, *Reasons and Persons* (Oxford: Clarendon Press, 1984 [1987]), p. 281. I am grateful to Michael Reynolds for advice on this paragraph.

continuity: in our case, *Jane Eyre* inheres in the networked experiences of its readers, including the readers of its texts in translation which, like all English editions, are joined by a sequence of physical links to Brontë's manuscript. Second is the recognition that identity is not 'all-or-nothing': for us, the texts of Old Nick's *Jane Eyre* or Zhou Shoujuan's 重光记 are linked enough to, and generate enough shared experiences with, Brontë's *Jane Eyre* to count as belonging to the same work, as being an instance of it. Third is the overlap between experiences that are mine and experiences that are those of other people: this is like the overlap between *Jane Eyre* and works like Forcade's review or *Wide Sargasso Sea* which, while not being *Jane Eyre*, share some of its features. Finally, there is what happens when you see things in this way. Instead of there being a glass wall around an idealized English *Jane Eyre* ('our Jane Eyre', as Ewbank put it), separating it off from its translations which by definition will never match up to it, nor be as good — instead of that isolationist and dismissive view — we can now see that the translations share in the co-constitution of *Jane Eyre*, enabling what Walter Benjamin, in 'Die Aufgabe des Übersetzers' ('The Task of the Translator'), called its *Fortleben* or 'ongoing life'.[63]

The view of the work and its translations being presented here does not reduce the significance of the text that Brontë wrote, nor scant her genius in writing it. Rather, it offers a better description of the complex mode of existence of a literary work, and of how translations relate to it, than does the still-widespread, 'common-sense' conception, which we saw embodied in the Berne Convention (as well as in Ewbank's essay), where what is in fact just one reading of the source text is reified as 'the original' ('our Jane Eyre') and translations are expected to reproduce it. Academic studies of literary translation nowadays rarely assert this view explicitly, but it still pervades the practice and language of critical discussion: for instance, the introduction to a recent, large study, *Milton in Translation*, presents its chapters as bringing to light 'the keenness on translators' parts to offer as faithful a rendition as they see possible', as aiming at 'feasible degrees of equivalence', as singling out 'aural effects ... that are lost in translation' and as assessing 'translational infelicities'.[64] As Lawrence Venuti has been

63 Walter Benjamin, 'Die Aufgabe des Übersetzers.' *Gesammelte Schriften*, 7 vols (Frankfurt a.M.: Suhrkamp, 1972), IV/i, p. 11.

64 *Milton in Translation*, ed. by Angelica Duran, Islam Issa and Jonathan R. Olson (Oxford: Oxford University Press, 2017), pp. 9, 10, 11, 15.

tireless in pointing out,[65] such attitudes are widespread elsewhere in academia and in literary and media culture. But if you keep hold of the fact that 'there is no "work itself," only a set of signs and a conjunction of reading practices', as the Canadian poet and translator Erín Moure has said,[66] then you can allow yourself to recognize — with Parfit's help — that these signs and practices continue, via a series of links, into the different-though-related signs and practices of the translations, and the reading of them, and the other translations that will arise. When it is seen like this, we can assert, with Antonio Lavieri, that:

> La traduzione acquista una nuova legittimità, mostrando l'inesistenza di un significato transcendentale, resistendo all'ideologia della trasparenza della scrittura, della lingua e del traduttore, diventando oggetto di consocenza che, interrogandosi, interroga e trasforma il senso.[67]
>
> [Translation acquires a new legitimacy, demonstrating the non-existence of a transcendental signified, resisting the ideology of the transparency of writing, of language and of the translator, and becoming an object of knowledge which, questioning itself, questions and transforms the meaning.]

And we can realize, with Henri Meschonnic, that both the work and its translations consist of a perpetual and mutually generating 'mouvement' [movement], so that 'les transformations d'une traduction à l'autre d'un même texte' [the transformations from one translation to another of the same text] are 'à la fois transformations de la traduction et transformations du texte' [at the same time transformations of the translation and transformations of the text].[68] Each translation is an instance of this larger movement by which the work, the world *Jane Eyre*, is constituted.

The translations that I have discussed so far question and transform *Jane Eyre* in various ways. They ask what matters more and matters less in the plot, as shown by the cuts made by Zhou Shoujuan and Old Nick, translating with different generic commitments for the benefit

65 Most recently in Lawrence Venuti, *Contra Instrumentalism: A Translation Polemic* (Lincoln: University of Nebraska Press, 2019).

66 Erín Moure, *My Beloved Wager: Essays from a Writing Practice* (Edmonton: NeWest Press, 2009), p. 174.

67 Antonio Lavieri, *Translatio in fabula : La letteratura come pratica teorica del tradurre* (Roma: Riuniti, 2007), p. 37.

68 Henri Meschonnic, 'Le texte comme mouvement, et sa traduction comme mouvement', *Le texte en mouvement*, ed. by Roger Laufer (Saint-Denis: Presses universitaires de Vincennes, 1987).

of their disparate readerships in different cultures and times. They reveal elements of ideological distinctiveness and challenge, as with the varying excisions made in the Soviet Union and Portugal under Salazar. They give a view of the directness of Jane's style, as it would come through to the 'mothers and girls' targeted by the 'Agreeable Library' in Milan in 1904. And there is the particular emotional and dramatic contour from 'leaving' to 'not leaving' that Old Nick creates with verbal repetition in the aftermath of the fire in Mr Rochester's bedroom. Such transformations show us something about prevailing reading practices in the cultural moments when they occurred, as well as about the individual sensibilities of the translators who created them. And they change *Jane Eyre* itself. Taking inspiration from Parfit, we can talk of both physical (textual) elements and reader experiences that turn out to have either greater or lesser persistence in the ongoing life of the work; and we can see how new elements and experiences can emerge from earlier ones without destroying *Jane Eyre*'s identity. Such changes matter also to the work as it inhabited its first contexts of composition and reception. Those contexts are often assumed to be monocultural and monolingual; but, as we have seen, the novel was being read in Germany, the Netherlands, Belgium, France, Russia, Denmark, Chile, Cuba, Bolivia and Sweden — as well as North America and no doubt elsewhere — in the three years after it came out in London; the review that Brontë most liked was in French; and, as I will explain in Chapter II, Brontë's own linguistic repertoire included French, German and Yorkshire languages (or, as I prefer to say, modes of languaging): it is not quite right to say that *Jane Eyre* was first written 'in English'. Even if we take the most restricted possible conception of interpretive context — what the Brontë family themselves might have made of the novel as they sat at home in the parsonage at Haworth — it is not possible to say with certainty that any transformation through translation makes visible something that was not already in *Jane Eyre* for them, as it was first transformed in their own imaginations as they read it.

The same is true at the level of verbal detail. This will be evident in many of the essays that follow, and will be the focus of my discussion in Chapters IV–VII; but here is a small example. Near the start of the novel, the young Jane has been attacked by her cousin John Reed, and has fought back against him. He has 'bellowed out loud' and Mrs Reed has arrived with the servants Bessie and Abbott. The fighting children are parted, and Jane hears the words:

'Dear! dear! What a fury to fly at Master John!'

'Did ever anybody see such a picture of passion!'

The phrase 'picture of passion' feels as though it might be proverbial; but the *Literature Online* database suggests that it may have appeared only once in English-language literature before this moment.[69] In context, it sounds like a colloquial idiom, more likely to be uttered by Abbott or Bessie than by Mrs Reed. And indeed Mrs Reed chimes in next, in her commanding tones: '"Take her away to the red-room, and lock her in there."' If we focus on 'a picture of passion', as uttered in Bessie's or Abbott's voice, what image do we think it conjures? What do we see and hear? Is the tone sharply disapproving? — or might it include a touch of warmth towards the child? — or even of wonder? How is Jane being viewed? — as understandably emotional? — or incomprehensibly aggressive? We can air such varying possibilities, and different readers might incline to one more than the others; but translations give us a visible spectrum of views. Here are some of them:

He1986 ראיתם פעם תמונה **משולהבת** כזאת [{*ra'item pa'am temuna* ***meshulhevet*** *ka-zot*} Did you ever see such an **ecstatic** picture?]

It1974 Si è mai vista una scena così **pietosa**? [Have you ever seen such a **pitiful** scene?]

F1964 semblable image de la **passion**! [similar image of **passion**!]

Sp1941 ¡Con cuánta **rabia**! [With so much **rage**!]

Por1951 Se já se viu uma coisa destas!... É uma **ferazinha**! [Have you ever seen a thing such as this one?... She's a **little beast**!]

R1950 Этакая **злоба** у девочки! [{*Ėtakaia* ***zloba*** *u devochki*} What **malice** that child has!]

F1946 pareille image de la **colère** [such an image of **anger**]

Por1941 Onde é que já se viu um **monstro** destes?! [Have you ever seen a **monster** such as this one?]

F1919 pareille **forcenée** [such **a mad person / a fury**]

R1901 Видѣлъ-ли кто-нибудь **подобное бѣшенное** созданіе! [{*Vidiel li kto-nibud'* ***podobnoe bieshennoye*** *sozdaníe*} Has anyone seen **such a furious** (lit. driven by rabies) creature!]

69 In James Fenimore Cooper's *Home as Found* (Philadelphia: Lea and Blanchard, 1838). *Proquest (Chadwick-Healey) Literature Online*, https://www.proquest.com/lion

Did ever anybody see such a picture of **passion**!

R1849 Кто бы могъ вообразить такую **страшную** картину! Она готова была растерзать и задушить бѣднаго мальчика! [{*Kto by mog voobrazit' takuiu* ***strashnuiu*** *kartinu! Ona gotova byla rasterzat' i zadushit' biednago ma"chika*} Who could have imagined such a **terrible** sight/picture! She was ready to tear the poor boy apart and strangle him!]

It1904 Avete mai visto una **rabbiosa** come questa? [Have you ever seen a girl as **angry** as this one?]

Por1926 Já viu alguem tal accesso de **loucura**! [Has anyone ever seen such a **madness** fit?]

He1946 הראה אדם מעולם **התפרצות** כגון זו? [{*hera'e adam me-olam* ***hitpartsut*** *kegon zo*} Has anyone ever seen an **outburst** like that one?]

Sp1947 ¿Habráse visto nunca semejante **furia**? [Have you ever seen such **fury**?]

It1951 Non s'è mai vista tanta **prepotenza**! [I've never seen such **impertinence**]

Sl1955 **jeza** [**fury**]

Sl1970 **ihta** [**stubbornness**]

A1985 هل قدر لأي امرئ أن يرى **مثل هذا الانفعال** من قبل؟ [{*hal quddira li ayy imri' an yarā* ***mithla hadha al infi'āl***} Was anyone ever destined to see **such a reaction**][70]

This moment will be discussed in more detail in Chapter IV below, where you will also be able to watch the translations and back-translations unfolding as an animation. Of course, the back-translations do not exactly reproduce the translations they represent, any more than the translations themselves exactly reproduce Brontë's text. But they do serve to give an impression of the imaginative suggestiveness of the phrase (as we will see in Chapters IV–VII, very many phrases in the novel are suggestive in a similar way). We might say that what we are seeing here is a snapshot of the different linguistic and cultural circumstances in which the translations were made — and, certainly, any one of these quotations could be subjected to a discrete critical

70 Details of the translations quoted can be found in the List of Translations. The key in the array indicates the language and the year of publication: for instance, A1985 means the Arabic translation published in 1985, which appears in the List of Translations as جين ايير/*Jane Eyre*, tr. by Munīr al-Baʿalbakī (Beirut, Dār Al-ʿIlm Lil-Malāyīn).

analysis to elucidate its significances in its immediate contexts. But this word cloud also shows us what we might call the potential of the source text — all those meanings which, as Sakai has explained, we cannot know are in the text until after they have been articulated by translation. Word upon word, each translator changes Brontë's text by saying what it is for them.

As we scan the array of translations, we are inevitably struck by the differences between languages. This, after all, is why the translations have had to be made. But we can also notice continuities: 'rabbiosa' in Italian and 'rabia' in Spanish; 'passion' in English and 'passion' in French. Indeed, given the substantial presence of French in *Jane Eyre*, which I will explore in Chapter II, I am not even sure that 'passion', as Brontë wrote it, should be defined as an English word. As we watch the novel being remade across language difference via translation it becomes clear that a view of languages as internally homogeneous and separate from one another, with translation operating between these distinct entities, is inadequate for understanding the phenomenon before us. *Prismatic Jane Eyre* enjoins a refreshed understanding of language difference and of how it relates to translation — an understanding that we will pursue in Chapter II.

Works Cited

For the translations of *Jane Eyre* referred to, please see the List of Translations at the end of this book.

Adam, Jean-Michel, *Souvent textes varient. Génétique, intertextualité, édition et traduction* (Paris: Classiques Garnier, 2018).

The Autobiography of Jane Eyre, https://www.youtube.com/channel/UCG1-X6Vhx5Ba84pqBQUDshQ

The Autobiography of Jane Eyre, https://www.tumblr.com/blog/view/eyrequotes

Barthes, Roland, 'The Death of the Author', Aspen: The Magazine in a Box, 5&6 (1967), n.p., https://www.ubu.com/aspen/aspen5and6/threeEssays.html#barthes

——, 'La mort de l'auteur' Manteia, 5 (1968), 12–17; Michel Foucault, 'Qu'est-ce qu'un auteur?', *Bulletin de la Société française de philosophie*, 63 (1969), 73–104.

——, *Œuvres completes*, vol. 3 (1968–1971), new edn, ed. by Éric Marty (Paris: Le Seuil, 1995).

Benjamin, Walter, 'Die Aufgabe des Übersetzers', *Gesammelte Schriften*, 7 vols (Frankfurt a.M.: Suhrkamp, 1972).

Bolt, David, Julia Miele Rodas and Elizabeth J. Donaldson, *The Madwoman and the Blindman: Jane Eyre, Discourse, Disability* (Columbus: The Ohio State University Press, 2012).

Bonsaver, Guido, 'Fascist Censorship on Literature and the Case of Elio Vittorini', *Modern Italy*, 8 (2003), 165–86, https://doi.org/10.1080/1353294032000131229

Brontë, Charlotte and Eve Sinclair, *Jane Eyre Laid Bare: The Classic Novel with an Erotic Twist* (London: Pan, 2012).

Brontë, Charlotte and Karena Rose, *Jane Eyrotica* (London: Piatkus, 2012).

Cachin, Marie-Françoise, 'Victorian Novels in France' in *The Oxford Handbook of the Victorian Novel*, ed. by Lisa Rodensky (Oxford: Oxford University Press, 2013), pp. 537–664, https://doi.org/10.1093/oxfordhb/9780199533145.013.0010

Canagarajah, Suresh, *Translingual Practice: Global Englishes and Cosmopolitan Relations* (London and New York: Routledge, 2012), https://doi.org/10.4324/9780203073889

Chapple, John and Alan Shelston, eds., *Further Letters of Mrs Gaskell*, ed. by (Manchester: Manchester University Press, 2000).

Cheung, Martha P. Y., 'Reconceptualizing Translation — Some Chinese Endeavours', *Meta*, 56 (2011), 1–19, https://doi.org/10.7202/1003507ar

Cooper, James Fenimore, *Home as Found* (Philadelphia: Lea and Blanchard, 1838). Proquest (Chadwick-Healey) Literature Online, https://www.proquest.com/lion

Cooper-Richet, Diana, 'La presse hispanophone Parisienne au XIXe siècle: El Correo de Ultramar et les autres', *Cedille: revista de estudios franceses* 16 (2019), 81–100, https://www.ull.es/revistas/index.php/cedille/article/view/956

Cox, Jessica, '"The insane Creole": the afterlife of Bertha Mason', Regis and Wynn, *Charlotte Brontë: Legacies and Afterlives*, pp. 221–40.

Dillon, Jay, '"Reader, I found it": The First *Jane Eyre* in French', *The Book Collector*, 17 (2023), 11–19.

Duran, Angelica, Islam Issa and Jonathan R. Olson, *Milton in Translation* (Oxford: Oxford University Press, 2017), https://doi.org/10.1093/oso/9780198754824.001.0001

Eagleton, Terry, *Myths of Power: A Marxist Study of the Brontës* (London: Macmillan, 1975).

Eco, Umberto, *Mouse or Rat? Translation as Negotiation* (London: Weidenfeld & Nicolson, 2003).

Eddie: St John anti, https://www.tumblr.com/blog/view/mr-rochester-of-thornfield

Eells, Emily, 'Charlotte Brontë en français dans le texte', *Textes et Genres I: 'A Literature of Their Own'*, ed. by Claire Bazin and Marie-Claude Perrin-Chenour (Nanterre: Publidix, 2003), pp. 69–88.

Emmerich, Karen, *Literary Translation and the Making of Originals* (New York and London: Bloomsbury, 2017), https://doi.org/10.5040/9781501329944

The Enthusiast's Guide to Jane Eyre, https://sites.google.com/view/eyreguide/adaptations/film?authuser=0

Ewbank, Inga-Stina, 'Reading the Brontës Abroad: A Study in the Transmission of Victorian Novels in Continental Europe', in *Re-Constructing the Book: Literary Texts in Transmission*, ed. by Maureen Bell, Shirley Chew, Simon Eliot and James L. W. West (London: Routledge, 2001), https://doi.org/10.4324/9781315192116-8

Fan Fiction, https://www.fanfiction.net/book/Jane-Eyre/

Fish, Stanley, 'Interpreting the "Variorum"', *Critical Inquiry*, 2 (1976), 465–85.

——, *Is There a Text in This Class? The Authority of Interpretive Communities* (Cambridge, MA: Harvard University Press, 1980).

Fuller, Jennifer D., 'Seeking Wild Eyre: Victorian Attitudes Towards Landscape and the Environment in Charlotte Brontë's Jane Eyre', *Ecozon@*, 4.2 (2013), 150–65, https://doi.org/10.37536/ECOZONA.2013.4.2.534

Gilbert, Sandra M. and Susan Gubar, *The Madwoman in the Attic: The Woman Writer and the Nineteenth-Century Literary Imagination* (New Haven and London: Yale University Press, 1979).

Hawthorne, Nathaniel, *La lettre rouge – A*, trans. by Old Nick (Paris: Gabriel de Gonnet, 1853).

Hermans, Theo, *The Conference of the Tongues* (Manchester: St Jerome, 2007), https://doi.org/10.4324/9781315759784

Hermetet, Anne-Rachel and Frédéric Weinman, 'Prose Narrative', in *Histoire des traductions en langue française: XIXe Siècle 1815–1914*, ed. by Yvres Chevrel, Lieven D'Hulst and Christine Lombez (Paris: Verdier, 2012).

Hohn, Stefanie, *Charlotte Brontës Jane Eyre in deutscher Übersetzung. Geschichte eines kulturellen Transfers* (Tübingen: Narr, 1998).

Iser, Wolfgang, *Die implicite Leser: Kommunikationsformen des Romans von Bunyan bis Beckett* (Munich: W. Fink, 1972).

Jane Eyre: Everything related with Jane Eyre (Mostly pictures), https://www.tumblr.com/blog/view/fyjaneeyre-blog

Langlois, Emile, 'Early Critics and Translators of Jane Eyre in France', *Brontë Society Transactions*, 16 (1971), 11–18.

Lavieri, Antonio, *Translatio in fabula: La letteratura come pratica teorica del tradurre* (Roma: Riuniti, 2007).

Lefevere, André, *Translation, Rewriting, and the Manipulation of Literary Fame* (London: Routledge, 2016 [1992]), https://doi.org/10.4324/9781315458496

Levine, Caroline, *Forms: Whole, Rhythm, Hierarchy, Network* (Princeton, NJ: Princeton University Press, 2015).

Li, Dechao, 'A Study of Zhou Shoujuan's Translation of Western Fiction' (unpublished doctoral dissertation, The Hong Kong Polytechnic University,

Department of Chinese and Bilingual Studies, November 2006, UMI Microform no. 3282304).

Majumdar, Olivia 'Jane Eyre in Bengal', https://www.bl.uk/early-indian-printed-books/articles/jane-eyre-in-bengal-v2

Mani, B. Venkat, *Recoding World Literature: Libraries, Print Culture, and Germany's Pact with Books* (New York: Fordham University Press, 2017), http://doi.org/10.26530/oapen_626400

Martindale, Charles, *Redeeming the Text: Latin Poetry and the Hermeneutics of Reception* (Cambridge: Cambridge University Press, 1993).

McGann, Jerome J., *The Beauty of Inflections: Literary Investigations in Historical Method and Theory* (Oxford: Clarendon Press, 1985).

Meschonnic, Henri, 'Le texte comme mouvement, et sa traduction comme mouvement' in *Le texte en mouvement*, ed. by Roger Laufer (Saint-Denis: Presses universitaires de Vincennes, 1987), n.p., https://doi.org/10.4000/books.puv.1274

Meyer, Susan L., 'Colonialism and the Figurative Strategy of Jane Eyre', *Victorian Studies*, 33 (1990), 247–68.

Moure, Erín, *My Beloved Wager: Essays from a Writing Practice* (Edmonton: NeWest Press, 2009).

My Jane Eyre: Exploring library copies of the seminal nineteenth century novel Jane Eyre by Charlotte Brontë, https://myjaneeyrelibrary.wordpress.com/

'Notice Bibliographique : Revue de Paris ', BnF Catalogue Général, https://catalogue.bnf.fr/ark:/12148/cb41304908b.public

Ortega, Marta, 'Traducciones del franquismo en el mercado literario español contemporáneo: el caso de Jane Eyre de Juan G. de Luaces' (unpublished doctoral thesis, University of Barcelona, 2013), http://hdl.handle.net/2445/46345

Parfit, Derek, *Reasons and Persons* (Oxford: Clarendon Press, 1984 [1987]).

Pas, Hernan, 'Eugène Sue en Buenos Aires: Edición, circulación y comercialización del folletín durante el rosismo', *Varia história*, 34 (2018), 193–225 (pp. 193–211), https://doi.org/10.1590/0104-87752018000100007

Qi, Shouhua, 'No Simple Love: The Literary Fortunes of the Brontë Sisters in Post-Mao, Market-Driven China', in *The Brontë Sisters in Other Wor(l)ds*, ed. by Shouhua Qi and Jacqueline Padgett (New York: Palgrave Macmillan, 2014), pp. 19–49, https://doi.org/10.1057/9781137405159_2

——, *Western Literature in China and the Translation of a Nation* (New York: Palgrave Macmillan, 2012), https://doi.org/10.1057/9781137011947

Regis, Amber K. and Deborah Wynne, eds., *Charlotte Brontë: Legacies and Afterlives*, (Manchester: Manchester University Press, 2017), https://doi.org/10.7228/manchester/9781784992460.001.0001

Reynolds, Matthew, ed., *Prismatic Translation* (Cambridge: Legenda, 2019), https://doi.org/10.2307/j.ctv16km05j

Sakai, Naoki, *Translation and Subjectivity: On 'Japan' and Cultural Nationalism* (Minneapolis: University of Minnesota Press, 1997).

Scott, Clive, *Literary Translation and the Rediscovery of Reading* (Cambridge: Cambridge University Press, 2012).

——, *The Work of Literary Translation* (Cambridge: Cambridge University Press, 2018), https://doi.org/10.1017/9781108678162

Sedgwick, Eve Kosofsky, 'Jane Austen and the Masturbating Girl', *Critical Inquiry*, 17 (1991).

——, *Touching Feeling: Affect, Pedagogy, Performativity* (Durham: Duke University Press, 2003), https://doi.org/10.1215/9780822384786.

Shuttleworth, Sally, *Charlotte Brontë and Victorian Psychology* (Cambridge: Cambridge University Press, 1996).

Smith, Margaret, ed., *The Letters of Charlotte Brontë*, 2 vols (Oxford and New York: Oxford University Press, 1995–2000).

Spivak, Gayatri Chakravorty, *A Critique of Postcolonial Reason: Toward a History of the Vanishing Present* (Cambridge, Mass.: Harvard University Press, 1999).

Steiner, George, *After Babel*, 3rd edn (Oxford: Oxford University Press, 1983).

Stoneman, Patsy, *Brontë Transformations: The Cultural Dissemination of Jane Eyre and Wuthering Heights*, 2nd edn (Brighton: Edward Everett Root, 2018).

——, *Jane Eyre on Stage 1848–1898: An Illustrated Edition of Eight Plays with Contextual Notes* (Aldershot and Burlington, VT: Ashgate, 2007), https://doi.org/10.4324/9781315251639

Sturge, Kate, 'Censorship of Translated Fiction in Nazi Germany', *TTR: traductions, terminologie, rédaction*, 15 (2002), 153–69, https://doi.org/10.7202/007482ar

Tatlock, Lynne, *Jane Eyre in German Lands: The Import of Romance, 1848–1918* (New York: Bloomsbury Academic, 2022), https://doi:10.5040/9781501382383

Toury, Gideon, *Descriptive Translation Studies — and Beyond* (Amsterdam and Philadelphia: John Benjamins, 1995).

Venuti, Lawrence, *Contra Instrumentalism: A Translation Polemic* (Lincoln: University of Nebraska Press, 2019), https://doi.org/10.2307/j.ctvgc62bf

Wirtén, Eva Hemmungs, 'A Diplomatic Salto Mortale: Translation Trouble in Berne, 1884–1886,' *Book History*, 14 (2011), 88–109, https://doi.org/10.1353/bh.2011.0007

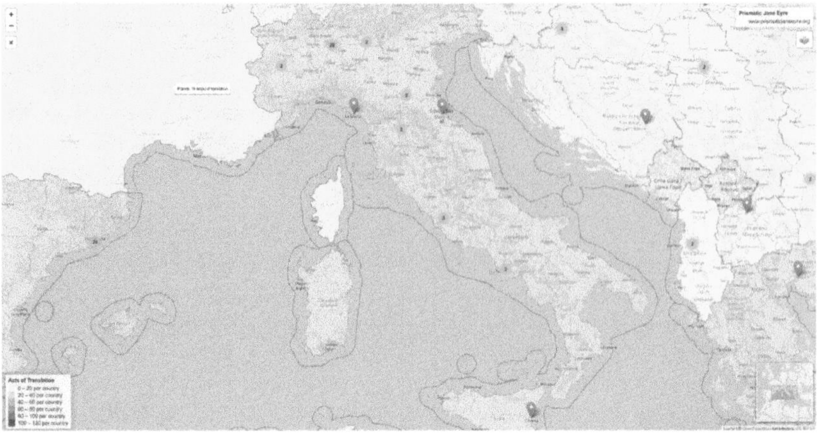

The World Map
https://digitalkoine.github.io/je_prismatic_map
Created by Giovanni Pietro Vitali;
maps © Thunderforest, data © OpenStreetMap contributors

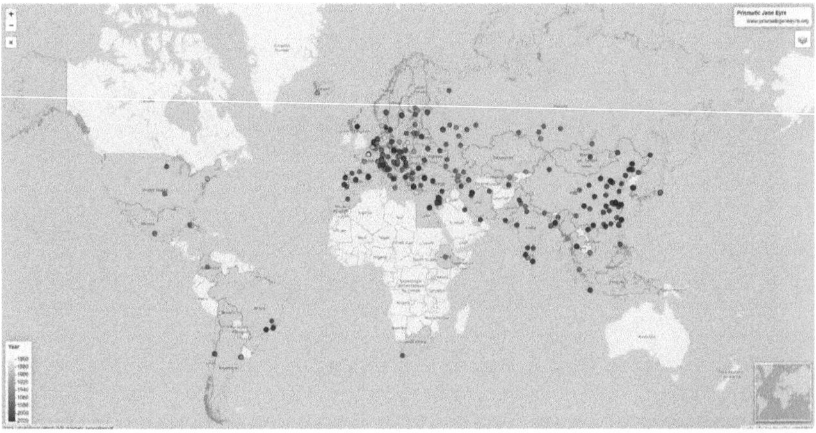

The General Map
https://digitalkoine.github.io/je_prismatic_generalmap/
Created by Giovanni Pietro Vitali; © OpenStreetMap contributors

II. The World Work in Language(s)

Matthew Reynolds

Yu JongHo (유 종호) translated *Jane Eyre* into Korean twice. The first version, published in 1970, 'used ornate and literary Chinese vocabulary' — as Sowon S. Park explains — while the second, which came out in 2004, was in 'more up-to-date modern Korean'.[1] Something similar happened in Croatia, on roughly the same timeline: Giga Gračan and Andrijana Hjuit's 1974 translation (researched by Sasha Mile Rudan) was modernized by Gračan in 2008 to incorporate linguistic forms that had come into being since the country's independence in 1991.[2] As these episodes make clear, the substance that a translation is done into (its 'target language', in the idiom of Translation Studies) is not a fixed entity but a fluid medium. Sometimes it mutates fast — as in Korea and Croatia — but it is always changing to some degree. What is more, the culture that a translation is published into is rarely, if ever monolingual, while — as we began to see in Chapter I — the borders that can be used to distinguish languages from one another, and so differentiate 'monolingual' from 'multilingual', are themselves hazy and porous. How can our thinking about language, and about translation, best grasp this complex, shifting linguistic terrain which world works like *Jane Eyre* inhabit and traverse?

One stark instance of translation in a multilingual context, discovered by Ulrich Timme Kragh, is a 2011 *Jane Eyre* published in Chengdu, Tibet, in which an abridged Chinese version by Daming Li [李大明] and Jing Li [李晶] is reprinted in parallel text with its Tibetan translation by Sonam Lhundrub. Readers with varying degrees of competence in one language, or the other, or both are all catered for by this publication. There is another, though less visible, layering of languages in the anonymous 1904 translation published in Milan,

1 See Sowon S. Park's entry on Yu JongHo in the appendix 'Lives of Some Translators', below.
2 Publication details are in our List of Translations below.

 https://doi.org/10.11647/OBP.0319.03

which one might loosely say is 'in Italian', though it is so closely based on the French of Noëmi Lesbazeilles-Souvestre (1854) as to be more of a linguistic blend. Here is a small example, from the novel's second sentence:

> We had been wandering, indeed, in the leafless shrubbery an hour in the morning

> Le matin, nous avions *erré* pendant une heure *dans le bosquet dépouillé de feuilles*

> La mattina, avevamo *errato* per un'ora *nel boschetto spogliato di foglie*[3]

Observe the closeness, in both structure and vocabulary, of the second translation to the first, and in particular the proximity of 'errato ... nel boschetto spogliato di foglie' to 'erré ... dans le bosquet dépouillé de feuilles' (both of which might be back-translated word for word as 'wandered in the copse stripped of leaves'). Now note the difference in the phrasing from a selection of later Italian translations:

> In verità, nella mattinata, avevamo *girato* un'ora *nel boschetto squallido* (1925)

> A dir vero, la mattina, eravamo state a *gironzare* per un'ora *tra le piante spoglie* (1935)

> La mattina, avevamo *camminato* per un'ora su e giù *per il boschetto spoglio* (1946)

> Veramente alla mattina avevamo *fatto una breve passeggiata* di un ora *nel bosco spoglio* (1950)

> Avevamo, è vero, *camminato* per un'ora *nell'albereta ormai spoglia* (1951)

> La mattina, invece, avevamo *errato* un'ora per *le macchie spoglie* (1956)

> Il mattino, è vero, eravamo *andati vagando* per un'ora *nella brughiera spoglia* (1974)

> La mattina avevamo *vagabondato* per un'ora nel *boschetto spoglio* (1996)

> Avevamo già *vagato tra gli arbusti spogli* per un'ora al mattino (2013)

> In realtà, la mattina avevamo *vagato* per un'ora *tra gli alberi spogli* (2014P)

3 *JE*, Ch. 1; trans by anon. (Milan: Treves, 1904); trans by Noëmi Lesbazeilles-Souvestre (Paris: D. Giraud, 1854).

> Al mattino, in realtà, avevamo *gironzolato* per un'ora *tra gli arbusti spogli* (2014S)[4]

Of course, Standard Italian and Standard French, as closely related romance languages, have a lot of linguistic material in common. Italian syntax and lexis can overlap with French and not sound foreign in the least — as 'mattina' overlaps with 'matin' and 'ora' with 'heure' pretty consistently throughout the translations. Nevertheless, it is clear that the translator and publisher of the 1904 Milan *Jane Eyre* were prepared to print a significantly more Frenchified kind of language than appears in the later translations. The concept of 'linguistic repertoire' can help us describe this phenomenon: it means the range of language actually 'exhibited in the speaking and writing patterns of a speech community', rather than that prescribed by grammar books and dictionaries.[5] So we can say that the linguistic repertoire exhibited in the 1904 translation includes a mix of elements. The same is likely to have been true of the repertoires of many readers, since the translation was published in northern Italy, long open to French culture, only three decades after the formation of the Italian state, when the standardization of the Italian language was not as comprehensive as it has become today.

The history of Italian since the country's unification in 1870 is a textbook instance of the general truth that, as the historian Eric Hobsbawm pointed out, standard national languages are 'almost always semi-artificial constructs'.[6] In the early years of the new state, fewer than 10% of its inhabitants spoke Italian, and a long process of education has been needed to disseminate the official, standardized form of the language, though, even now, very many Italians think of themselves as being bilingual across the standard language and their

---

4 *JE*, Ch. 1; trans by Elivira Rosa (Milan: Sonzogno); trans by C. Marazio (Milan: A. Barion, 1935); trans by Lucilla Kànizsa Jacchia (Rome: Perrella, 1946); trans by Berto Minozzi (Milan: Cavallotti); trans by G. Pozzo Galeazzi (Milan: Rizzoli, 1951); trans by Lia Spaventa Filippi (Rome: R. Casini, 1956); trans by Ugo Dèttore (Milan: Garzanti, 1974); trans by Luisa Reali (Milan: Mondadori, 1996); trans by Berenice Capatti (Milan: Rizzoli, 2013); trans by Monica Pareschi (Vicenza: Neri Pozza, 2014); trans by Stella Sacchini (Milan: Feltrinelli, 2014).

5 Joshua Fishman, *The Sociology of Language* (Rowley, Mass.: Newbury House, 1972), p. 48.

6 E. J. Hobsbawm, *Nations and Nationalism since 1780: Programme, Myth, Reality* (Cambridge: Cambridge University Press, 2012), p. 54.

local dialect.[7] We can see related shifts in usage leaving tiny traces in our *Jane Eyre* translations. Between 1904 and the 1920s and 30s, the form 'avevamo errato' [we had wandered] must have come to seem, though not incorrect, not quite idiomatic in this context, at least to the ears of most of the translators — perhaps too recherché or poetical, or simply too French. The words that seemed best suited both to the imagined scene and to publication in print had become different: 'girato' (which we might back-translate as 'wandered' or 'taken a turn'); 'gironzare' (more like 'wandered around') along with the related 'gironzolato'; 'camminato' (straightforwardly 'walked'); 'fatto una breve passeggiata' [gone for a short stroll]; and finally, becoming established as the go-to translation for 'wandered' over the last 50 years or so, 'vagando'/'vagato', or the semantically very similar but more resounding 'vagabondare'. This group of choices shows phrasing that feels idiomatically Italian branching off from phrasing that overlaps with French (where 'erré' remained a common choice for translators at this point),[8] though the one exception ('errato', 1956) reveals the continuing soft border between the languages. A more consistent difference is that, since 1904, no Italian translator has felt the need to write, in the manner shared with French, 'spogliato di foglie' ('stripped of leaves'): the one word 'spoglio' (or an equivalent) becomes enough. (Another crux in the line, how best to render into either language the very English garden feature that is a 'shrubbery', raises the different issue of realia in translation, which I will not go into here).[9]

These instances give us an idea of the variable linguistic terrain through which translation operates. Languages change, mingle and pull apart, and translation participates in those processes. It can collaborate with the growing standardization of a language, reinforcing, by its choices, the boundary between what is taken to belong to that language

7 Vittorio Coletti, 'Storia della lingua', *Enciclopedia Treccani*, https://www.treccani.it/enciclopedia/storia-della-lingua_%28Enciclopedia-dell%27Italiano%29/

8 For instance, *JE* trans by R. Redon & J. Dulong (Lausanne: J. Marguerat and Éditions du Dauphin, 1946); trans by Charlotte Maurat (Paris: Le Livre de Poche, 1964); trans by Dominique Jean (Paris: Gallimard, 2008).

9 See Javier Franco Aixela, 'Culture-Specific Items in Translation', *Translation, Power, Subversion*, ed. by Roman Alvarez and M. Carmen-Africa Vidal (Clevedon: Multilingual Matters, 1996), pp. 52–78, and Alla Kharina, *Realia in Literary Translation: A Quantitative and Qualitative Study of Russian Realia in Norwegian and English Translations* (Norwegian Open Research Archives, 2019), https://www.duo.uio.no/handle/10852/70895

and what is not. Evidence from corpus-based studies that translations, in general, display less lexical variety than source texts bears witness to this role: translators often prefer words that seem unsurprising so as to demonstrate their obedience to the norms of the language they are translating into.[10] But translation also reveals the work that is continually involved in the maintenance of a standard, and therefore draws attention to the unruly diversity of actual and possible usages with which standardization is always in conflict. It has the power to make unusual choices, even if it does not exercise it often. As Lydia H. Liu has shown in her discussion of interplays between English and Chinese, when languages come into contact, translators venture 'hypothetical equivalences' which may then become solidified through repeated usage and end up in bilingual dictionaries.[11] In our Italian samples, as 'vagato'/'vagando' comes to dominate translation of 'wandered', we can see a tiny instance of the re-adjustment of equivalences between languages that keeps on happening, even centuries after the first Italian-English dictionaries, as the languages continue to interact and change. And translation contributes to such changes — indeed, in the case of Chinese, the encounter with English and other European tongues caused substantial alterations to lexical, grammatical and discursive norms:[12] we will see how this relates to *Jane Eyre* translations in Essay 12 below, by Yunte Huang. Translation, then, cannot be understood as bridging differences between languages that are each internally consistent and separate from one another. Rather, as Mike Baynham and Tong King Lee have suggested, its work is that of 'managing difference' — both the differences that can distinguish one language from what is defined as another, and those within such languages, which are themselves inevitably heterogeneous and changing.[13]

A theory of translation, then, needs to start from a point that is conceptually prior to the organization of linguistic variety into

---

10 Vilma Pápai, 'Explicitation: A Universal of Translated Text?', *Translation Universals: Do they Exist?*, ed. by Anna Mauranen, and Pekka Kujamäki (Amsterdam and Philadelphia: John Benjamins, 2004), pp. 143–64 (pp. 157–59); Sergiy Fokin, 'TTR Changes in Different Directions of Translation', *Translation Journal*, 17 (2013), https://translationjournal.net/journal/63ttr.htm

11 Lydia H. Liu, *Translingual Practice: Literature, National Culture and Translated Modernity — China, 1900–1937* (Stanford, Ca.: Stanford University Press, 1995).

12 Liu, *Translingual*, pp. 153–54.

13 Mike Baynham and Tong King Lee, *Translation and Translanguaging* (London and New York: Routledge, 2019), p. 9.

countable languages conceived as different from one another. It cannot take the separation of languages as a given, and must feel the weight of the argument, made by Robert Young, that 'the idea of a language as a discrete entity was a concept devised by European philologists'. Young gives the telling example of G. A. Grierson, a philologist and civil servant who was tasked with producing a *Linguistic Survey of India* at the end of the nineteenth century. Grierson realised that colonial subjects in India thought of themselves, not as speaking separate languages, but rather as participating in something more like a dialect continuum. As he wrote: 'it thus follows that, while the dialect-names in the following pages have been taken from the indigenous nomenclature, nearly all the language-names have had to be invented by Europeans'.[14] Grierson's predicament is repeated wherever languages, or rather what we are henceforth going to have to call 'language(s)', are studied. The linguist Tore Janson has observed that 'there are few generally accepted rules or criteria for deciding when two ways of speaking should be regarded as being the same language and when they should be seen as two separate ones'.[15] The word 'few' turns out to be an overstatement, for it transpires from his discussion that there are in fact no such generally accepted rules or criteria:

> People who understand each other are usually regarded as speaking the same language, and those who speak the same language are supposed to understand each other. But here, there are many exceptions. For example, Swedes and Norwegians usually understand each other without difficulty, but Swedish and Norwegian are regarded as different languages. On the other hand, many Americans from the Midwest do not understand Londoners, and vice versa, but they are supposed to be using the same English language.[16]

Janson therefore brings in his own preferred test, which is to ask what speakers themselves think. As we have seen with G. A. Grierson, this approach does not necessarily yield the desired answers, and Janson hits an even tougher difficulty in the case of the Khoisan people of Southern Africa:

---

14 Robert J. C. Young, 'That Which is Casually Called a Language', *PMLA*, 131 (2016), 1207–21 (pp. 1208, 1216).

15 Tore Janson, *Speak: A Short History of Languages* (Oxford: Oxford University Press, 2011), pp. 23–24.

16 Janson, *Speak*, p. 24

> When it comes to the Khoisan languages, it is not possible to ask. The speakers in some cases have no names at all for their languages, nor of course for dialects. So, this whole line of reasoning is without meaning for them until the Westernized way of thinking about languages has been taken over into their culture.[17]

It turns out that this 'Westernized way of thinking' did not take shape until a fairly late moment in European history. For instance, the medieval poet Dante, even though he would afterwards be hailed by nineteenth-century nationalists as father of 'the Italian language', did not himself think that he spoke or wrote Italian: 'Dante did not think of Latin as one language and Italian as a completely different one, which is the common view nowadays. In his mind there really existed only one language, which manifested itself either as written Latin or as one of the written popular languages' — those popular languages included what we would now call French and Provençal, as well as all the various dialects that made up what we would now call Italian.[18]

As the idea of there being 'a language' starts to crystallize (in Italy, Janson sees this happening among a small circle of literati in the century after Dante) it becomes codified in writing, with some texts held up as examples, together with the construction of grammars and dictionaries.[19] But this process does not — of course — encompass the great variety of language as it is actually used in a given area, above all in speech. As Alastair Pennycook has put it: 'the codification of languages is not so much a process of writing down what already exists as it is a process of *reducing* languages to writing'. This means that there is — always and everywhere — a yawning, indeed unbridgeable gap between languages as they are recorded and known, and the actual language-use of people to whom the codified languages are attributed. It follows that — in Pennycook's words — 'the notion of [a] "language" does not refer to any real object'.[20] Working from a different range of references, Naoki Sakai reached the same conclusion: 'the unity of [a] language is like a regulative idea. It organizes knowledge, but it

---

17 Ibid.

18 Janson, *Speak*, p. 124.

19 Hayley Davis, 'Typography, Lexicography, and the Development of the Idea of 'Standard English', *Standard English: The Widening Debate*, ed. by Tony Bex and Richard J. Watts (London and New York: Routledge, 1999), pp. 69–88.

20 Alastair Pennycook, 'The Myth of English as an International Language', *Disinventing and Reconstituting Languages*, ed. by Sinfree Makoni and Alastair Pennycook (Bristol, Blue Ridge Summit: Multilingual Matters, 2006), pp. 90–115 (pp. 92, 98).

is not empirically verifiable'.[21] Nevertheless, as Pennycook cautions, 'the effects of repeated construction and reconstruction' of the idea of there being such a thing as a language 'are very real': 'these inventions have a reality for the people who deal with them'.[22] They have reality, for instance, for any anyone told by state powers that their way of speaking does not correspond to 'the language', and that they need to change it. And they have reality for translators.

Translators of novels are typically writing for publication in print, in a state market. Certainly this is the case for all the *Jane Eyre* translators we discuss in the these pages. And so they are subject to the sociopolitical linguistic pressures that bear on that medium, as we saw with the Korean and Croatian translations at the start of this section. Yet what translators are translating *into* is not only the written form of a language, destined for the regulated arena of print publication. They are also translating *Jane Eyre* into a context of reception, a readership; and the readership for a translation — indeed, for any book — is always multilingual, as the Tibetan and Chinese parallel text can serve to remind us. This fact needs emphasizing because, as John C. Mather has pointed out: 'though language diversity is an everyday social fact everywhere, most countries recognize only a small number of "national" languages and "official" languages'.[23] Such limited recognition seems especially to prevail in the study of literary texts, where what Suresh Canagarajah has defined as 'monolingual orientation' is sustained by the generally monolingual and predominantly national structuration of the academic disciplines of literature and languages.[24] But, in fact, printed texts, however regulated their language, always enter into the minds of readers who — however thoroughly schooled they may or may not have been — necessarily bring diverse linguistic repertoires to the collaborative work of reading. And so it is that Juan G. de Luaces, translating into the highly policed, printed language of Franco's Spain, could angle his words so as to enable readers to catch the egalitarian spark of *Jane Eyre* (as Andrés Claro shows in Essay 5 below); and so it

21 Naoki Sakai, 'How Do We Count a Language: Translation and Discontinuity', *Translation Studies*, 2 (2009), 71–88 (p. 73).

22 Pennycook, 'The Myth', 98.

23 John C. Maher, *Multilingualism: A Very Short Introduction* (Oxford: Oxford University Press, 2017), p. 6.

24 Suresh Canagarajah *Translingual Practice: Global Englishes and Cosmopolitan Relations* (London and New York: Routledge, 2012), p. 1; see Mary Louise Pratt, 'Arts of the Contact Zone', *Profession* (1991), 33–40 (p. 38), and the discussion in Chapter I above.

is also that several translators under the Islamic Republic in Iran could signal connections between *Jane Eyre* and a banned genre of romance writing, as Kayvan Tahmasebian and Rebecca Ruth Gould show in Essay 8. When they negotiate the expectations of their publishing markets, translators have the power to make something new happen out of the mix of language(s) that they are working with. As we have begun to see, and will see more fully in the pages that follow, this can happen (or indeed not happen) in a multitude of ways.

The theory of translation that I have been advancing, and the practice of critical scholarship that is presented in this publication, puts translation at the centre of the study of world literature. That is where it should have been at least since David Damrosch launched the latest phase of world-literary theorisation in 2003, with his celebrated announcement that 'I take world literature to encompass all literary works that circulate beyond their culture of origin, either in translation or in their original language'.[25] But this founding utterance did not in fact start an academic vogue for the linguistically informed, textually alert and materially grounded study of the circulation of texts through many languages via translation. Indeed, 'astonishing as it may seem' — as Mary Louise Pratt has said — 'language has not been a category of analysis in the now vast academic literature on globalization'.[26] Instead, there has been an air of shadow-boxing about many of the trend-setting publications that have emerged from the United States academy, with a theoretical commitment to the importance of translation matched by a lack of attention to it in practice. Rebecca Walkowitz's *Born Translated: The Contemporary Novel in an Age of World Literature*, for instance, sets out to approach 'world literature from the perspective of translation', only then to restrict its attention to the thematization of translation in 'anglophone works'.[27] As Damrosch recognises in a 2020 update to his programme, 'we need to develop better ways of working both with original texts and in translation'.[28] The present publication hopes to offer an

25 David Damrosch, *What is World Literature?* (Princeton, NJ: Princeton University Press, 2003), p. 4.

26 Mary Louise Pratt, 'Comparative Literature and the Global Languagescape', *A Companion to Comparative Literature*, ed. by Ali Behdad and Dominic Thomas (Oxford: Wiley-Blackwell, 2011), pp. 273–95 (p. 274).

27 Rebecca Walkowitz, *Born Translated: The Contemporary Novel in an Age of World Literature* (New York: Columbia University Press, 2015), p. 44.

28 David Damrosch, *Comparing the Literatures: Literary Studies in a Global Age* (Princeton, NJ: Princeton University Press, 2020), p. 177.

example of one such 'better way', and so to join the several admirable instances of what Emily Apter has called 'a translational model of comparative literature'[29] which do in fact exist, even if they have perhaps tended to flourish in parts of the world other than the United States. The pioneering *Reception of British and Irish Authors in Europe* series, founded by Elinor Shaffer, dates back to 2002; Barbara Cassin's *Vocabulaire Européen des Philosophies* is from 2004 and Michael O'Neill's *Polyglot Joyce: Fictions of Translation* from 2005. Among more recent work is the expansive research dossier on *Les Mystères urbains au XIXe siècle: Circulations, transferts, appropriations* edited by Dominique Kalifa and Marie-Ève Thérenty (2015), the *Multilingual Locals and Significant Geographies* project led by Francesca Orsini which focuses on North India, the Maghreb and the Horn of Africa (2016–21); as well as the varied research presented in *Migrating Texts: Circulating Translations around the Ottoman Mediterranean* (2019), edited by Marilyn Booth, or *Translation and Literature in East Asia: Between Visibility and Invisibility* by Jieun Kiaer, Jennifer Guest and Xiaofan Amy Li (2019), or *Translation and World Literature,* edited by Susan Bassnett (2018).[30] All this research — and there is much more that could be cited — addresses the complexity of what happens when texts circulate through language(s) and across cultures. The present publication hopes to boost that company, drawing on the resources of multiplicitous cultural and linguistic expertise, digital media and collaborative close reading to give as full an account as we can of what it means for one novel, *Jane Eyre*, to inhabit a world of language(s).

Jane Eyre as a World Work in Language(s)

What it is for *Jane Eyre* to be a world work in language(s) will become more apparent in the chapters and essays to come. It will never be fully evident, however, even when or if every word and every visualisation has been digested. What we offer is — and could only ever be — a partial

29 Emily Apter, *Against World Literature: On the Politics of Untranslatability* (London and New York: Verso, 2013), p. 42.

30 *Les Mystères urbains au XIXe siècle: Circulations, transferts, appropriations* is at https://www.medias19.org/publications/les-mysteres-urbains-au-xixe-siecle-circulations-transferts-appropriations; *Multilingual Locals and Significant Geographies* is at http://mulosige.soas.ac.uk/; *The Reception of British and Irish Authors in Europe* is at https://www.bloomsbury.com/uk/series/the-reception-of-british-and-irish-authors-in-europe/. For full details of the books listed in in this paragraph, see the list of Works Cited at the end of this chapter.

anthology of views. Each discussion grasps only some aspects of the phenomenon it addresses (as is always the case with any critical analysis). And the languages, contexts and translations that we treat are only a sample of those in which *Jane Eyre* exists. It follows that *Jane Eyre* cannot be *known* as a world work in language(s), but only approached with the awareness that that is what it is. Any instance, or group of instances, that we are able to study belongs to the larger network of continuities that embody the world work *Jane Eyre*; but that larger network necessarily exceeds our grasp. Any reader of *Jane Eyre* for pleasure — or any other motive — is in a similar position. Hence, as we saw in the Introduction, the need to accept an ontology of incompleteness, of the kind advocated by Francis B. Nyamnjoh: 'incompleteness as a social reality and form of knowing generative of and dependent on interconnections, relatedness, open-endedness and multiplicities'.[31]

In this, the case of *Jane Eyre* is far from unique. Many texts, having originated in English or another language, have gone on to exist in a similar number and variety of translations. The kind of study that we offer here could be repeated for each of them. Yet, though the broad traits of the phenomenon may recur, the detail in each case is of course different, including the question of how the originary source text — the text in which any work begins its life — relates to and is changed by what the work goes on to become. As we have seen, the idea of 'potential' has a complex temporality. We cannot be sure what potential any text has to generate other texts until after it has done so. By the same token, translations do not just change the world work, whose ongoing life they sustain by their existence as instances of it. They also change the originary source text, because they reveal in it the latent potential that has been realised in them. We have visualised this progressive realisation through space and time in the interactive maps that form part of this publication. I will present them fully in Chapter III, but it may be helpful, in thinking about potential, to open the Time Map. Take a moment to watch the translations unfold through time, then press the pause button at the bottom left of the map, and slide the cursor all the way to the left, to a moment in 1847 before any translations have started to appear. You can feel the shadow of their

31 Francis B. Nyamnjoh, *Drinking from the Cosmic Gourd: How Amos Tutuola Can Change our Minds* (Mankon, Bamenda, Cameroon: Langaa Research & Publishing, 2017), p. 2.

incipience. The potential that they will realise must already be there, as we know because, from our point of view in the present, its realisation has already happened.

How does the originary *Jane Eyre* change in the light of this futurity? Our sense of the structure of the text, and our impression of the power of different moments, is likely to be affected by the re-shapings that we have encountered so far in this volume, as well as those that lie ahead. The figure of Bertha Rochester may take on a somewhat different force as it foreshadows its re-workings in South America, India, Egypt and Lebanon. There is also the question of how the world of language(s) imagined in the novel relates to the world of language(s) through which the novel makes its way. When seen from the perspective of its translational afterlives, the novel's own concern with translation assumes new prominence; above all, the strange scene when, having fled Thornfield, and been reduced to homelessness and hunger at Whitcross, Jane reaches an isolated house where, looking through a window, she sees, in a kitchen, 'two young, graceful women' dressed in mourning: they seem strangely familiar to her, though she has never seen them before. What follows is startling, so I will quote at length:

> A stand between them supported a second candle and two great volumes, to which they frequently referred, comparing them, seemingly, with the smaller books they held in their hands, like people consulting a dictionary to aid them in the task of translation. This scene was as silent as if all the figures had been shadows and the firelit apartment a picture ... When, therefore, a voice broke the strange stillness at last, it was audible enough to me.
>
> 'Listen, Diana,' said one of the absorbed students; 'Franz and old Daniel are together in the night-time, and Franz is telling a dream from which he has awakened in terror — listen!' And in a low voice she read something, of which not one word was intelligible to me; for it was in an unknown tongue — neither French nor Latin. Whether it were Greek or German I could not tell.
>
> 'That is strong,' she said, when she had finished: 'I relish it.' The other girl, who had lifted her head to listen to her sister, repeated, while she gazed at the fire, a line of what had been read. At a later day, I knew the language and the book; therefore, I will here quote the line: though, when I first heard it, it was only like a stroke on sounding brass to me — conveying no meaning:—
>
> '"Da trat hervor Einer, anzusehen wie die Sternen Nacht." Good! good!' she exclaimed, while her dark and deep eye sparkled. 'There you have a dim and mighty archangel fitly set before you! The line is worth a

> hundred pages of fustian. "Ich wage die Gedanken in der Schale meines Zornes und die Werke mit dem Gewichte meines Grimms." I like it!'[32]

Jane is cold, wet through, exhausted and all but starving, and yet her attention is held (and goes on being held long after the extract I have given) by this living picture of two people engaged in translation. Stranger still, the scene is manipulated so that she can hear their words even though they are spoken in a 'low voice' and she is on the other side of a closed, glass window, in the open air, on a 'wild night'. So some authorial magic has been sprinkled over the scene, dislodging it from the constraints of realism. But then, despite this fantastical dissolution of a barrier, a new obstruction appears, for what Jane is able to hear she cannot understand, no more than 'sounding brass' (itself a quotation from a translation, the King James version of the Bible).[33] Yet this obstruction too is overcome, though only partially, by another piece of implausible narrative manipulation: 'at a later day, I knew the language and the book; therefore, I will here quote the line.' Quote it, yes; but translate it? — no, thereby dividing the novel's readership both in 1847 and since. A few will know German and recognise the quoted text; others may be able to read the German words but not know that they are from Friedrich Schiller's lurid, powerful romantic drama *Die Räuber* (*The Robbers*, 1781), and in particular from a vision of the Last Judgement that has come to the villain, Franz, in a dream: 'then one stepped forth who, to look upon, was like a starry night ... [and another figure said:] "I weigh thoughts in the scale of my wrath and deeds with the weight of my fury"'. Perhaps most readers will neither recognise the source nor understand much or any of the language, unless they are using a modern edition that translates these words from a classic English novel into English.

The relevance of *Die Räuber* to *Jane Eyre* is hazy. The play includes a loving couple cruelly pushed apart, and a fractured family, so perhaps Brontë felt it to be a nightmarish pre-echo of her own narrative, haunting it, and making an only semi-comprehensible appearance, like a miniature textual counterpart to the similarly gothic figure of Bertha Rochester. And perhaps this scene of the Last Judgement is a foreshadowing of St John Rivers, who is about to appear, and who,

32 *JE*, Ch. 28.
33 I Corinthians 13. 1.

before long, will be reading out a parallel passage of the Bible.[34] Probably more important than the particular text quoted, however, is the fact that an act of translation should be happening here, and that it should be so foregrounded by the narrative peculiarities that I have noted. The two young women, who are to become Jane's friends, and later turn out to be her cousins, welcome *Die Räuber*, a strange textual visitation from a wild imaginative world, and make the effort to comprehend it; and a moment later they will welcome Jane, a strange human visitation from a wild experiential world, and make the effort to comprehend her. So the framing of the scene suggests a comparison between attending to texts through translation and attending to people through kindness and understanding. In a letter, Brontë had made a similar analogy, describing the minds of others as being like 'hieroglyphical scrolls', a 'hidden language' that needed 'construing',[35] and the same suggestion is brought into our scene by the 'sounding brass' quotation from the Bible. The whole verse from which it is taken is as follows: 'though I speak with the tongues of men and of angels, and have not charity, I am become *as* sounding brass, or a tinkling cymbal'. It is thanks to charity (now often translated 'love') that Jane is taken into the house, and comes in time to learn German, and presumably to discover also from her cousins what it was that they were reading on this fateful night. Her incomprehension at the window points forward to understanding later on, when Jane, currently excluded from the sisterly community of translation, will be translated into it.

This use of translation, and its thwarting, to foreshadow a later translingual and affective community is in tune with the general orientation towards future fluency that is created by the book's narrative structure. As she grows up, Jane encounters many obstacles to understanding and self-expression; but they are all mitigated by our knowledge as readers that she must in the end have achieved both, as they are continually manifested in the narrative that she has written. Attention to the diversity of language(s) is key to this from the beginning. Critical discussion has noted the marked spatial dynamics of the opening pages, the way they articulate a performance of selfhood among constraints as Jane is first excluded from the family group,

34 Revelation 21, in *JE*, Ch. 35. See the discussion by Léa Rychen in Essay 14, below.

35 *The Letters of Charlotte Brontë*, 2 vols, ed. by Margaret Smith (Oxford and New York: Oxford University Press, 1995–2000), i, p. 128.

then secludes herself in the window seat, and later is shut up in the 'red-room' — a succession of positionings that anticipate both her own individualistic disposition and the confinement of Bertha Rochester (to which it is uneasily related).[36] But attention has not been given to the strife of language(s) that is no less marked in this sequence: the haughtily formal tones of Mrs Reed ('she regretted to be under the necessity of keeping me at a distance'); the bullying schoolboy jargon of her son ('Boh! Madame Mope!'); the momentary escape offered by the pictures of remote, northern shores in *Bewick's History of British Birds*, together with the evocative writing that accompanies them, including a quotation from James Thomson's poem *The Seasons*:

> Where the Northern Ocean, in vast whirls
> Boils round the naked, melancholy isles
> Of farthest Thule ....[37]

Then there is the comparatively friendly, colloquial discourse of Mrs Reed's servant Bessie, and the folksy ballads that she sings ('My feet they are sore, and my limbs they are weary'); the attentive professional accents of the apothecary, Mr Lloyd; and the sanctimonious preaching of Mr Brocklehurst: 'all liars will have their portion in the lake burning with fire and brimstone'.[38] And there is French, first this surprising instance as Jane is carried off to the 'red-room':

> The fact is, I was a trifle beside myself; or rather *out* of myself, as the French would say.[39]

And later in Bessie's account of the accomplishments attained by young ladies who went to school:

> She boasted of beautiful paintings of landscapes and flowers by them executed; of songs they could sing and pieces they could play, of purses they could net, of French books they could translate; till my spirit was moved to emulation as I listened.[40]

At the prospect of being able to translate, Jane's spirit is moved. Here too, as in the later scene with German, translation heralds the prospect of joining a community of accomplished self-expression.

---

36 Gayatri Chakravorty Spivak, *A Critique of Postcolonial Reason: Toward a History of the Vanishing Present* (Cambridge, Mass.: Harvard University Press, 1999), p. 119.

37 *JE*, Ch. 1.

38 *JE*, Ch. 3, Ch. 4.

39 *JE*, Ch. 2.

40 *JE*, Ch. 3.

And this provides a solution to the puzzle posed by that odd phrase 'as the French would say' a chapter earlier. Why bring in what the French would say? Because the narrator has become someone whose repertoire includes French and who, as E. C. Gaskell noted of Charlotte Brontë in her celebrated biography:

> would wait patiently searching for the right term, until it presented itself to her. It might be provincial, it might be derived from the Latin; so that it accurately represented her idea, she did not mind whence it came; but this care makes her style present the finish of a piece of mosaic.[41]

The young Jane's powerlessness is salved by the mature Jane's skill with words, skill that draws from a multilingual repertoire.

The warm, almost utopian affect attaching to translation and language-learning continues at Lowood school, for instance when Jane has tea with Helen and Miss Temple:

> ... they seemed so familiar with French names and French authors: but my amazement reached its climax when Miss Temple asked Helen if she sometimes snatched a moment to recall the Latin her father had taught her, and taking a book from a shelf, bade her read and construe a page of Virgil; and Helen obeyed, my organ of veneration expanding at every sounding line.[42]

The unusual adjective 'sounding' there signals a link to the scene of Schiller-translation later in the book with its 'sounding brass'; and there is another link too. In the later scene, Jane describes Schiller's uncomprehended German 'as being in an unknown tongue — neither French nor Latin' — so, though we have heard nothing of Jane's going on to study Latin at Lowood, she must have done. French, on the other hand, we do hear about: it becomes her passport to employment at Thornfield Hall, to conversation with her French pupil Adèle and with Adèle's maid Sophie, and to easy participation in the French world of reference that Mr Rochester has at his disposal. Elaine Showalter and Emily Eells have studied the presence of French in the novel, noting that it is associated with 'sexual response' (Showalter), as well as with 'freedom of speech', being an 'outsider', 'sympathy', 'discipline' and even 'smoking' (Eells).[43] These two perceptive studies are significant

41 E. C. Gaskell, *The Life of Charlotte Bronte*, ed. by Elisabeth Jay (London: Penguin, 1997), p. 234.

42 *JE*, Ch. 8.

43 Elaine Showalter, 'Charlotte Brontë's Use of French', *Research Studies* 42 (1974), 225–34 (p. 228); Emily Eells, 'The French *aire* in *Jane Eyre*', *Cahiers*

in showing that 'bilinguality is an important aspect' of Brontë's style; but the range of associations uncovered by Eells pushes against Showalter's claim (which provides the methodological basis for both essays) that 'French language and allusions to French literature function symbolically'.[44] The assumption here is that *Jane Eyre* presents a language-world of Standard English, to which Standard French is added for strategic signifying purposes. But the novel's linguistic landscape is more complex than that, as we have begun to discover. Roy Harris's word 'languaging' can help us to describe what we are seeing. As Nigel Love explains, 'languaging' is 'a cover term for activities involving language: speaking, hearing (listening), writing, reading, "signing" and interpreting sign language', and it is preferable to phrases like 'using language' or 'language use' because it does not imply 'that what is used exists in advance of its use'.[45] *Jane Eyre* explores a range of language(s), and of the languaging practices which generate it/them, all of which take on distinctive tonalities and connotations in particular circumstances. What can be defined as 'the French language' is prominent among them, but, crucially, it is used in a way that fragments that definition: there is what Eells herself recognises to be the '*franglais*' of little Adèle ('Mademoiselle, I will repeat you some poetry'), and there are also many indeterminate forms that are pieced into the mosaic of Brontë's style — not only 'out of myself' but also 'translate currently' (from 'couramment'), or 'auditress and interlocutrice' (in Mr Rochester's voice — 'interlocutrice' is a French form which it seems likely he pronounces with an English accent), together with very many phrases that, though not alien to English, are a bit unusual, and have perhaps been helped into existence by the presence of French in Brontë's translingual imagination: for example, 'brilliant fire' (less common in English than 'feu brillant' in French), or 'curtains hung rich and ample' ('ample rideau' was an ordinary French collocation).[46]

victoriens et édouardiens, 78 (2013), n.p.

44 Showalter, 'French', p. 225.

45 Roy Harris, *The Language Myth* (London: Duckworth, 1981), p. 36; Nigel Love, 'On Languaging and Languages', *Language Sciences* 61 (2017), 113–47 (p. 115).

46 *JE*, Ch. 8, Ch. 14. Information about the currency of the phrases comes from the databases *Literature Online* and *Gallica*. Céline Sabiron offers a fuller account of what she calls the 'signifying linguistic spectrum' of French and English in Essay 4 below, as well as of the challenges it has posed to translators into French.

This borderless Franco-English languaging coincides with an attention to the fractures that can open up within 'English'. They appear in the narrative voice, as here:

> It was a very grey day; a most opaque sky, 'onding on snaw,' canopied all; thence flakes fell at intervals, which settled on the hard path and on the hoary lea without melting.

The words in inverted commas are not Standard English but northern and Scottish dialect; but it is impossible to know whether they came onto the page from Brontë's everyday conversational soundscape in Haworth, her village in Yorkshire, or as a literary allusion to Sir Walter Scott's novel *The Heart of Midlothian*.[47] Either way, though separated from their surrounding language by the inverted commas (which are also present in Brontë's manuscript),[48] the words are woven into it stylistically through the phonetic harmonies they join ('opaque ... onding ... canopied', 'snaw ... all ...fell ... intervals ... hoary'), as well as by their lexical kinship to 'hoary lea' which, though not markedly dialectal, has a similarly mixed rural and literary pattern of usage.[49] Just as with her writing across the French-English continuum, Brontë shows dialect appearing in the voices of her characters as well as in the narrative she writes through Jane. For instance, immediately after the quotation from Schiller at Moor House, the servant Hannah, who is also in the kitchen, chips in:

> 'Is there ony country where they talk i' that way?' asked the old woman, looking up from her knitting.
>
> 'Yes, Hannah — a far larger country than England, where they talk in no other way.'
>
> 'Well, for sure case, I knawn't how they can understand t' one t' other: and if either o' ye went there, ye could tell what they said, I guess?'
>
> 'We could probably tell something of what they said, but not all ...'[50]

As in the case of 'onding on snaw', difference is created and bridged at the same time: the divergent spelling marks Hannah's speech as something that Diana and Mary, and indeed Jane, would not themselves utter; and yet they are all perfectly able to understand

47 *JE*, Ch. 4. Jane Jack and Margaret Smith note the parallel to Scott in their edition of *Jane Eyre* (Oxford: Oxford University Press, 1969), p. 584.

48 Brontë's fair-copy manuscript of *Jane Eyre* is Add MS 43474, available online at http://www.bl.uk/manuscripts/FullDisplay.aspx?ref=Add_MS_43474

49 Judging from the citations in the *Oxford English Dictionary*.

50 *JE*, Ch. 28.

it, and to recognise it as one of the ways people talk in 'England'. Again, this exploration of disparity within what can be defined as a national language — what Bakhtin called the 'heteroglossia' of 'socio-ideological contradictions' and differing 'points of view on the world'[51] — is opened up by, and compared to, the difference between that language and what can be defined as a different one, German. 'How they can understand t' one t' other' is a question that bears on everyone in the novel, and it is foregrounded by the attention to linguistic diversity in what is shown as being — to adopt Naoki Sakai's terms — a world not of 'homolingual' but of 'heterolingual' address, that is, one where it is recognised that 'heterogeneity is inherent' in any communicative situation.[52]

Brontë's style gives substance to this recognition as it draws from the continuum of French, Standard English and dialects, as well as exhibiting other eclectic features, as critics have recognised ever since the earliest reviews. Margot Peters points to Brontë's 'deliberate and flagrant practice of inverting the normal order of the English language', and Stevie Davis suggests that her knowledge of German may have helped this into being (in the same way as we have seen French influence her phrasing).[53] While the inversions do not typically reproduce German word order exactly, it is plausible that the encounter with German may have opened up Brontë's feeling for how words could be put together. Certainly, the shape of the stand-out inversions transfers more happily into Marie von Borch's 1887 German translation than into Lesbazeilles-Souvestre's French translation of 1854 or the anonymous Italian translation of 1904. For instance, from the very first page:

> Me, she had dispensed from joining the group.
>
> Mich hatte sie davon dispensiert, mich der Gruppe anzuschließen.
> [Me had she from this dispensed ...]

51 M. M. Bakhtin, *The Dialogic Imagination: Four Essays*, ed. by Michael Holquist, tr. by Caryl Emerson and Michael Holquist (Austin, University of Texas Press, 1981), pp. 291–92.

52 Naoki Sakai, *Translation and Subjectivity: On 'Japan' and Cultural Nationalism* (Minneapolis: University of Minnesota Press, 1997), p. 8.

53 Margot Peters, *Charlotte Brontë: Style in the Novel* (Madison: University of Wisconsin Press, 1973), p. 57; *Jane Eyre*, ed. by Stevie Davies (London: Penguin, 2006), p. xxxii. For discussion of Brontë's style in the early reviews, see *Critical Heritage*, ed. by Allott, pp. 79, 116.

> Elle m'avait défendu de me joindre à leur groupe.
> [She me had forbidden ...]
>
> Ella mi aveva proibito di unirmi al loro gruppo.
> [She me had forbidden ...][54]

Then there is Brontë's prolific citation from and reference to other texts, not only the anglophone ones most commonly noticed by scholars in the discipline of English literature, such as Bunyan's *The Pilgrim's Progress*, the King James version of the Bible, and various works by Sir Walter Scott, as well as psychological texts and American slave narratives;[55] but also the German of Schiller (as we have seen) and several works in French, including George Sand's *Indiana* (1832), Bernardin de St Pierre's *Paul et Virginie* (1788) — which had been given to her by her adored French teacher in Brussels, M. Heger — and the Charles Perrault version of the folk tale *Barbe bleue* [*Bluebeard*] (1697). Considered as an aspect of style, *Jane Eyre*'s blending and layering of languages, together with its plurilingual intertextuality, create an expressive medium that presents human languaging as a landscape of heterogeneity.

This heterogeneity involves class and power, so it also becomes a crucial element in the novel's social drama. And from this perspective there turns out to be a striking disparity between Jane's (and Brontë's) eclectic practice as a writer and her more tightly bordered linguistic performances as a character. When Jane has been brought into Moor House and gets into conversation with Hannah, she takes care to entrench the class difference between them, speaking 'with a certain marked firmness' and moving to 'shake hands' only once the disparity of status has been firmly established.[56] A few weeks later, when she takes charge of a nearby village school, her pupils present her with language difference almost as marked as in the encounter with Schiller: 'they speak with the broadest accent of the district. At present,

54 *JE*, Ch. 1; Marie von Borch, *Jane Eyre, die Waise von Lowood, eine Autobiographie* (1887), quoted from TextGrid Repository (2012), n.p. https://hdl.handle.net/11858/00-1734-0000-0002-454D-2; *JE*, trans by Noëmi Lesbazeilles-Souvestre; *JE* (Milan, 1904), p. 10.

55 Sally Shuttleworth, *Charlotte Brontë and Victorian Psychology* (Cambridge: Cambridge University Press, 2004); Julia Sun-Joo Lee, *The American Slave Narrative and the Victorian Novel* (New York and Oxford: Oxford University Press, 2010), pp. 25–52.

56 *JE*, Ch. 29.

they and I have a difficulty in understanding each other's language.'[57] Her response, in line with her duty as a teacher, is to train them in Standard English, along with 'neat and orderly manners'.[58] When she gives up the school, having come into her inheritance, she reveals the nationalist pride, and indeed prejudice, that are associated with this endeavour. She rejoices that her best scholars have become:

> ... as decent, respectable, modest, and well-informed young women as could be found in the ranks of the British peasantry. And that is saying a great deal; for after all, the British peasantry are the best taught, best mannered, most self-respecting of any in Europe: since those days I have seen paysannes and Bauerinnen; and the best of them seemed to me ignorant, coarse, and besotted, compared with my Morton girls.[59]

The same ideology transpires in her attitude to Adèle, of whom we are told that 'as she grew up, a sound English education corrected in a great measure her French defects'.[60] Jane's xenophobia appears most viciously in her response to Bertha Rochester, who is pushed beyond the border between human and animal, described as a 'clothed hyena' standing 'tall on its hind feet', and as possessing a mode of languaging that is past, not only comprehension, but even recognition as language: 'it snatched and growled like some strange wild animal'.[61]

So there is an incongruity between the connotations of the novel's style and the behaviour of its protagonist: that is, between two modes of engaging the aesthetics and politics of language. In the first, a mode of textuality, it is possible for Brontë to welcome the heterolingualism that I have described, because she is producing a work of writing, destined to circulate in the comparatively open interpretive arena of printed literature. But in the second, a mode of individual performance, Jane — as a character — has to be much more guarded in how she behaves with language, because her identity, her status and indeed her ability to survive depend on it. This conflict between the world of language(s) as it can be represented by the narrator, and that same world as it has to be inhabited by the protagonist, provides a powerful instance of what Firdous Azim has called 'the difficulties in being Jane Eyre, that is, the difficulties of a sovereign femininity placed within a system of patriarchy', which — she says — are overlooked when the

57 *JE*, Ch. 31.
58 *JE*, Ch. 32.
59 *JE*, Ch. 34.
60 *JE*, Ch. 38.
61 *JE*, Ch. 26.

novel is simply labelled 'an imperialist text'.[62] In the narrative, Bertha's powerful languaging, her 'mirthless', 'tragic' and 'preternatural' laugh, her 'eccentric murmurs' and her cry, a 'fearful shriek' such as the 'widest-winged condor on the Andes' might have sent out 'from the cloud shrouding his eyrie' can be deployed to suggest feelings that Jane is barred from expressing in her own person, with the connection being hinted at by successive sparks of phonetic play, as here in the word 'eyrie'.[63] But Jane-the-character cannot accept any of this as significant language, even though Bertha is perfectly well able to speak words, as we know from her brother Mr Mason: '"she said she'd drain my heart"'.[64] Mr Mason's own accent is described as 'somewhat unusual, — not precisely foreign, but still not altogether English',[65] but we cannot know whether Bertha's speech is similar or whether she might have used a kind of language that could be defined, like her identity, as 'Creole'.[66] In any case, her languaging asks to be seen together with Schiller's German, Adèle's Franglais, Hannah's Yorkshire, and all the other varieties of speech performance, as a presence — though in her case a significantly occluded one — in the heterolingual landscape of the work.

Susan Meyer, Deirdre David and Carolyn Berman have thoroughly traced the complications of *Jane Eyre*'s involvement with Empire, the way it partially faces and partially evades its wrongs — not least in Jane and Mr Rochester's wounded seclusion at the end, in a society of two, living on funds (both his and hers) whose colonial origins have been made plain, in a house, Ferndean, where Mr Rochester had considered confining Bertha but chose not to because (he said) it was too unhealthy.[67] Meanwhile, St John Rivers pursues his severe

62 Firdous Azim, *The Colonial Rise of the Novel: From Aphra Behn to Charlotte Bronte* (London and New York: Routledge, 1993), p. 196.

63 *JE*, Ch. 11, Ch. 12, Ch.20.

64 *JE*, Ch. 20. Kevin Stevens notes this contradiction in '"Eccentric Murmurs": Noise, Voice and Unreliable Narration in *Jane Eyre*', *Narrative*, 26 (2018), 201–20 (p. 207).

65 *JE*, Ch. 18.

66 Stevens suggests that 'as the daughter of a wealthy merchant from Jamaica, Bertha would likely speak French (and possibly English), perhaps inflected with an accent or an influence of Creolized French or English' ('"Eccentric Murmurs"', p. 207).

67 Carolyn Vallenga Berman, *Creole Crossings: Domestic Fiction and the Reform of Colonial Slavery* (Ithaca, NY: Cornell University Press, 2018), pp. 122–43; Deirdre David, *Rule Britannia: Women, Empire and Victorian Writing* (Ithaca, NY and London: Cornell University Press, 1995), pp. 77–117; Susan L. Meyer,

imperial mission. The language-world of the book is inflected by these complexities and speaks to them, not only in the representation of Bertha's utterances, but also in St John's requirement that Jane give up German and start learning 'Hindostanee' so as — it turns out — to be able to help him in his missionary endeavours. As Ulrich Timme Kragh and Abhishek Jain argue in Essay 1 below, the possibility of going to India can be read as creating an inspiring prospect for Jane; all the same, this is the one experience of language-learning and translation that she does not enjoy.[68] It is another instance, and a stark one, of the politics of language behaviour being negotiated by the protagonist within the heterolingual world created by the work.

Pheng Cheah has argued that literature 'opens a world' by giving shape to its temporality through narrative.[69] It should be added that literature opens a world of language(s). In *Jane Eyre*, that world is one in which multiple linguistic performances are recognised, in all their divergence from one another, as well as in the continuity that joins them. In this textual mode of representing heterolingualism, any utterance, from a shriek to a phrase of Schiller, is welcome as a contribution to the mosaic of Brontë's style. But to move through that world as a character is different: it is to be subjected to the political and social pressures that divide 'correct' from 'incorrect', the standard from the dialectal, and national languages from one another, and which can fix class identity from the pronunciation of a syllable. In this layered language-world of *Jane Eyre*, we can perceive a conflict not unlike that discovered by Édouard Glissant in the 'poétique forcée' ('forced poetics') of Caribbean writing: 'à la fois conscience de la presence contraignante du français comme arrière-fond linguistique et volonté délibérée de renoncer au français' [at the same time an awareness of the constraining presence of French as a linguistic background and the deliberate wish to reject French].[70] The language politics that Jane negotiates are not as violent as those Glissant describes. Nevertheless, as a character, she must take care over the social constraints on behaviour

'Colonialism and the Figurative Strategy of *Jane Eyre*', *Victorian Studies* 33 (1990), 247–68 (the point about the 'atmosphere of Ferndean' is on p. 267).

68 Lesa Scholl points out that St John uses language-learning as a means of control, in *Translation, Authorship and the Victorian Professional Woman: Charlotte Brontë, Harriet Martineau and George Eliot* (Farnham, Surrey & Burlington, VT: Ashgate, 2011), p. 33.

69 Pheng Cheah, *What is a World? On Postcolonial Literature as World Literature* (Durham and London: Duke University Press, 2016), p. 311.

70 Édouard Glissant, *Le discours antillais* (Paris: Gallimard, 1997), p. 409.

in language; while, as a narrator, she has more freedom to channel her — or her author's — eclectic repertoire, one that mixes the local and the transnational like the language-world in which Brontë lived, a world where she had become a writer of novels through intensive exercises in French composition, done in Brussels; where her sister Emily sat in the kitchen at Haworth (like the ladies at Moor House) 'studying German out of an open book, propped up before her, as she kneaded the dough'; and where her friend Mary Taylor's father 'spoke French perfectly ... when need was; but delighted usually in talking in the broadest Yorkshire'.[71] The language of Bertha the Creole is largely excluded from this repertoire, as we have seen, and indeed gains its significance from the vehemence of that exclusion; nevertheless, Glissant's later theorisation of Creole language can also serve as a description of the language-world of *Jane Eyre*: 'la langue créole apparaît comme organiquement liée à l'expérience mondiale de la Relation. Elle est littéralement une conséquence de la mise en rapport de cultures différentes' [the Creole language appears as organically linked to the global experience of inter-relation. It is literally a result of the interplay between different cultures].[72] While showing the constraints on Jane's linguistic performance as a character, *Jane Eyre* also brings into being the more plural linguistic landscape within which she has to define herself. The world of *Jane Eyre*'s writing is broader than the channel of Jane Eyre's speech.

This aspect of the novel grows in prominence when we look back at its originary text from the vantage point of its continuing life through translation. We cannot say, bluntly, that *Jane Eyre*'s heterolingual language-world has helped to cause its prolific re-making through language(s); for other, very different books have been no less frequently translated. But it does affect, and is affected by, the dynamics of that remaking. The novel's continuing life is the continuation of something; and that something is changed by the continuation to which it has given rise. It is safe to say that no individual translation matches the language variety of the text that Brontë wrote. Like Jane the character, the translations are all subject to sociolinguistic constraints that inhibit such a performance. But, looked at together, they of course exceed its

71 Charlotte Brontë and Emily Brontë, *The Belgian Essays: A Critical Edition*, ed. and trans. by Sue Lonoff (New Haven and London: Yale University Press, 1996), p. xxii; Gaskell, *Life*, pp. 105, 116.

72 Glissant, *Le discours*, p. 411.

variety, and massively so. In this sense, the translations extend — and will go on extending — the heterolingualism of the source.

The four essays that follow this chapter focus on several crucial aspects of this dynamic, developing different angles on the practice and theory of translation as they do so. In Essay 1, Ulrich Timme Kragh and Abhishek Jain offer a comprehensive account of *Jane Eyre*'s afterlife in the many languages of India, also presenting a theory of translation built on Indian knowledge traditions which is in some ways in dialogue with the theory I have outlined: this essay is necessarily long, given the large and complex cultural context that needs to be sketched, and the thirteen languages that come into the discussion. Paola Gaudio, in Essay 2, shows how Brontë's eclectic style has given rise to persistent textual variants in English editions which have then expanded through translation; giving examples from Italian, she asks how our understanding of translation might shift when the source text itself is variable. In Essay 3, Yousif M. Qasmiyeh traces the novel's re-materialisations in Arabic, where its linguistic intensities have given rise to a distinctive focus on voice and touch, drawing attention to the importance of sound, not only in a radio version but also in translations for print. And Céline Sabiron, in Essay 4, explores the difficulties that French translators have found in rendering the Franco-English linguistic continuum that I have described in this chapter: what are the possibilities for translation when French has to be translated into French?

Works Cited

For the translations of *Jane Eyre* referred to, please see the List of Translations at the end of this book.

Aixela, Javier Franco, 'Culture-Specific Items in Translation' in *Translation, Power, Subversion*, ed. by Roman Alvarez and M. Carmen-Africa Vidal (Clevedon: Multilingual Matters, 1996), pp. 52–78.

Allott, Miriam, ed., *The Brontës: The Critical Heritage* (Abingdon and New York: Routledge, 2010).

Apter, Emily, *Against World Literature: On the Politics of Untranslatability* (London and New York: Verso, 2013).

Azim, Firdous, *The Colonial Rise of the Novel: From Aphra Behn to Charlotte Brontë* (London and New York: Routledge, 1993).

Bakhtin, M. M., *The Dialogic Imagination: Four Essays*, ed. by Michael Holquist, tr. by Caryl Emerson and Michael Holquist (Austin, University of Texas Press, 1981).

Bassnett, Susan, ed., *Translation and World Literature* (Abingdon, Oxon; New York, NY: Routledge 2018), https://doi.org/10.4324/9781315630298

Baynham, Mike and Tong King Lee, *Translation and Translanguaging* (London and New York: Routledge, 2019). https://doi.org/10.4324/9781315158877

Booth, Marilyn, ed., *Migrating Texts: Circulating Translations around the Ottoman Mediterranean* (Edinburgh: Edinburgh University Press, 2019).

Brontë, Charlotte, *Jane Eyre*, British Library Add MS 43474, http://www.bl.uk/manuscripts/FullDisplay.aspx?ref=Add_MS_43474

——, *Jane Eyre*, ed. by Jane Jack and Margaret Smith (Oxford: Oxford University Press, 1969).

——, *Jane Eyre*, ed. by Stevie Davies (London: Penguin, 2006).

Brontë, Charlotte and Emily Brontë, *The Belgian Essays: A Critical Edition*, ed. and trans. by Sue Lonoff (New Haven and London: Yale University Press, 1996).

Brontë, Charlotte and Eve Sinclair, *Jane Eyre Laid Bare: The Classic Novel with an Erotic Twist* (London: Pan, 2012).

Canagarajah, Suresh, *Translingual Practice: Global Englishes and Cosmopolitan Relations* (London and New York: Routledge, 2012), https://doi.org/10.4324/9780203073889

Cassin, Barbara, ed., *Vocabulaire Européen des Philosophies* (Paris: Dictionnaires Le Robert, Éditions du Seuil, 2004).

Cheah, Pheng, *What is a World? On Postcolonial Literature as World Literature* (Durham and London: Duke University Press, 2016).

Coletti, Vittorio, 'Storia della lingua', *Enciclopedia Treccani* https://www.treccani.it/enciclopedia/storia-della-lingua_(Enciclopedia-del"Italiano)/

Damrosch, David, *Comparing the Literatures: Literary Studies in a Global Age* (Princeton, NJ: Princeton University Press, 2020).

——, *What is World Literature?* (Princeton, NJ: Princeton University Press, 2003).

David, Deirdre, *Rule Britannia: Women, Empire and Victorian Writing* (Ithaca, NY; London: Cornell University Press, 1995).

Davis, Hayley, 'Typography, Lexicography, and the Development of the Idea of 'Standard English' in *Standard English: The Widening Debate*, ed. by Tony Bex and Richard J. Watts (London and New York: Routledge, 1999), pp. 69–88.

Eells, Emily, 'Charlotte Brontë *en français dans le texte*', *Textes et Genres I: 'A Literature of Their Own'*, ed. by Claire Bazin and Marie-Claude Perrin-Chenour (Nanterre: Publidix, 2003), pp. 69–88.

——, 'The French *aire* in *Jane Eyre*', *Cahiers victoriens et édouardiens*, 78 (2013), n.p., https://doi.org/10.4000/cve.839

Fishman, Joshua, *The Sociology of Language* (Rowley, Mass.: Newbury House, 1972).

Fokin, Sergiy, 'TTR Changes in Different Directions of Translation', *Translation Journal*, 17 (2013), https://translationjournal.net/journal/63ttr.htm

Gaskell, E. C., *The Life of Charlotte Brontë*, ed. by Elisabeth Jay (London: Penguin, 1997).

Glissant, Édouard, *Le discours antillais* (Paris: Gallimard, 1997).

Harris, Roy, *The Language Myth* (London: Duckworth, 1981).

Hobsbawm, E. J., *Nations and Nationalism since 1780: Programme, Myth, Reality* (Cambridge: Cambridge University Press, 2012), https://doi.org/10.1017/cbo9781107295582

Janson, Tore, *Speak: A Short History of Languages* (Oxford: Oxford University Press, 2011).

Kharina, Alla, *Realia in Literary Translation: A Quantitative and Qualitative Study of Russian Realia in Norwegian and English Translations* (Norwegian Open Research Archives, 2019), https://www.duo.uio.no/handle/10852/70895

Kiaer, Jieun, Jennifer Guest and Xiaofan Amy Li, *Translation and Literature in East Asia: Between Visibility and Invisibility* (New York, NY: Routledge, 2019), https://doi.org/10.4324/9781351108676

Lee, Julia Sun-Joo, *The American Slave Narrative and the Victorian Novel* (New York and Oxford: Oxford University Press, 2010), https://doi.org/10.1093/acprof:oso/9780195390322.001.0001

Liu, Lydia H., *Translingual Practice: Literature, National Culture and Translated Modernity — China, 1900–1937* (Stanford, Ca.: Stanford University Press, 1995).

Love, Nigel, 'On Languaging and Languages', *Language Sciences* 61 (2017), 113–47, https://doi.org/10.1016/j.langsci.2017.04.001

Maher, John C., *Multilingualism: A Very Short Introduction* (Oxford: Oxford University Press, 2017), https://doi.org/10.1093/actrade/9780198724995.001.0001

Meyer, Susan L. 'Colonialism and the Figurative Strategy of *Jane Eyre*', *Victorian Studies* 33 (1990), 247–68.

Nyamnjoh, Francis B., *Drinking from the Cosmic Gourd: How Amos Tutuola Can Change our Minds* (Mankon, Bamenda, Cameroon: Langaa Research & Publishing, 2017), https://doi.org/10.2307/j.ctvh9vw76

O'Neill, Michael, *Polyglot Joyce: Fictions of Translation* (Toronto, Ontario: University of Toronto Press, 2005), https://doi.org/10.3138/9781442678620

Pápai, Vilma, 'Explicitation: A Universal of Translated Text?', *Translation Universals: Do they Exist?*, ed. by Anna Mauranen, and Pekka Kujamäki (Amsterdam and Philadelphia: John Benjamins, 2004), pp. 143–64, https://doi.org/10.1075/btl.48

Park, Sowon S., 'Yu JongHo 유 종호 (1935–)', https://prismaticjaneeyre.org/yu-jongho-유-종호-1935/

Pennycook, Alastair, 'The Myth of English as an International Language', *Disinventing and Reconstituting Languages*, ed. by Sinfree Makoni and Alastair Pennycook (Bristol, Blue Ridge Summit: Multilingual Matters, 2006), pp. 90–115, https://doi.org/10.21832/9781853599255-006

Peters, Margot, *Charlotte Brontë: Style in the Novel* (Madison: University of Wisconsin Press, 1973).

Pratt, Mary Louise, 'Arts of the Contact Zone', *Profession* (1991), 33–40.

——, 'Comparative Literature and the Global Languagescape' in *A Companion to Comparative Literature*, ed. by Ali Behdad and Dominic Thomas (Oxford: Wiley-Blackwell, 2011), pp. 273–95, https://doi.org/10.1002/9781444342789.ch18

Sakai, Naoki, 'How Do We Count a Language: Translation and Discontinuity', *Translation Studies*, 2 (2009), 71–88, https://doi.org/10.1080/14781700802496266

——, *Translation and Subjectivity: On 'Japan' and Cultural Nationalism* (Minneapolis: University of Minnesota Press, 1997).

Scholl, Lesa, *Translation, Authorship and the Victorian Professional Woman: Charlotte Brontë, Harriet Martineau and George Eliot* (Farnham, Surrey & Burlington, VT: Ashgate, 2011), https://doi.org/10.4324/9781315549927

Showalter, Elaine, 'Charlotte Brontë's Use of French', *Research* Studies 42 (1974), 225–34.

Shuttleworth, Sally, *Charlotte Brontë and Victorian Psychology* (Cambridge: Cambridge University Press, 2004), https://doi.org/10.1017/cbo9780511582226

Smith, Margaret, ed., *The Letters of Charlotte Brontë*, 2 vols (Oxford and New York: Oxford University Press, 1995–2000).

Spivak, Gayatri Chakravorty, *A Critique of Postcolonial Reason: Toward a History of the Vanishing Present* (Cambridge, Mass.: Harvard University Press, 1999).

Stevens, Kevin, '"Eccentric Murmurs": Noise, Voice and Unreliable Narration in *Jane Eyre*', *Narrative*, 26 (2018), 201–20, https://doi.org/10.1353/nar.2018.0010

Tatlock, Lynne, *Jane Eyre in German Lands: The Import of Romance, 1848–1918* (New York: Bloomsbury Academic, 2022), https://doi.org/10.5040/9781501382383

Walkowitz, Rebecca, *Born Translated: The Contemporary Novel in an Age of World Literature* (New York: Columbia University Press, 2015), https://doi.org/10.7312/walk16594

Young, Robert J. C., 'That Which is Casually Called a Language', *PMLA*, 131 (2016), 1207–21, https://doi.org/10.1632/pmla.2016.131.5.1207

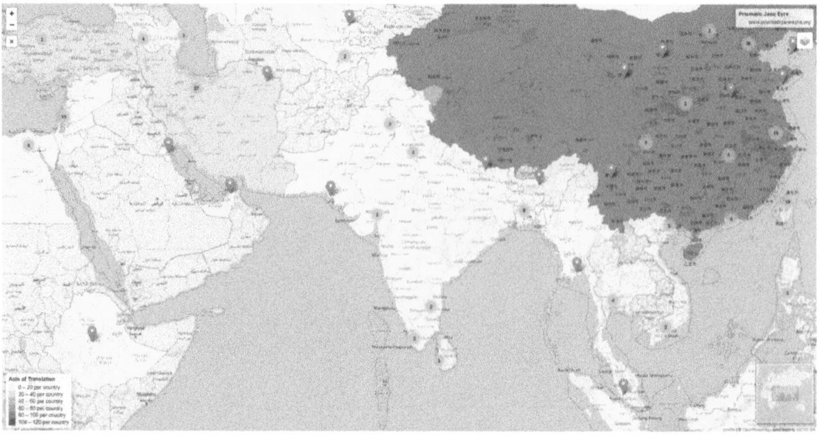

The World Map
https://digitalkoine.github.io/je_prismatic_map
Created by Giovanni Pietro Vitali;
maps © Thunderforest, data © OpenStreetMap contributors

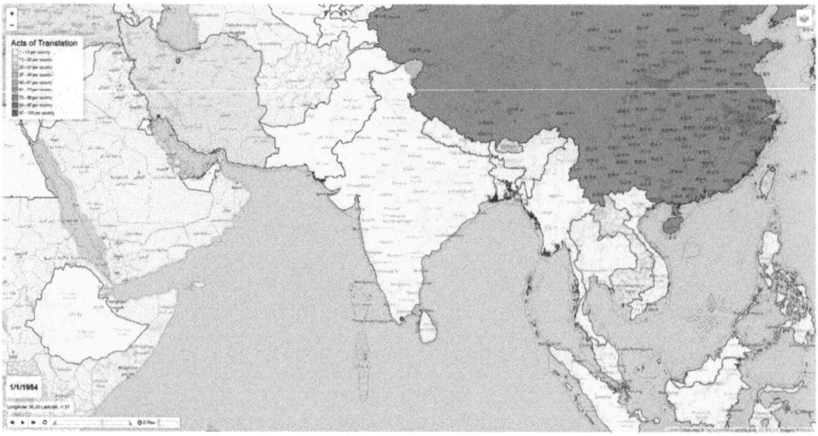

The Time Map
https://digitalkoine.github.io/translations_timemap
Created by Giovanni Pietro Vitali and Simone Landucci;
© OpenStreetMap contributors, © Mapbox

1. Jane, Come with Me to India
The Narrative Transformation of Janeeyreness in the Indian Reception of *Jane Eyre*

Ulrich Timme Kragh and Abhishek Jain[1]

Jane Eyre on India: The Indian Motif as a Suspense Juncture

'I want you to give up German and learn Hindostanee.'[2] These words are spoken by Mr St John Rivers to Jane Eyre as he tries to convince her to become closely involved in his linguistic and theological preparations for leaving England to go on a Christian mission. The quoted passage is one of the several commentaries on India scattered throughout the novel, which, taken together, create a composite of an Indian motif, the full significance of which has hitherto remained unexplored. Its paucity in Brontëan studies detracts not only from understanding the complexities of the literary characters in *Jane Eyre* but more importantly from the exploration at hand of the South Asian reception of the novel across the configurations of the oeuvre of the Indian adaptations and translations. In what follows, an elucidation of

1 The research leading to these results has received funding from the European Research Council under the European Union's Seventh Framework Programme (FP7/2007–2013), ERC Grant Agreement no. 615574, the NAMO Project 'Narrative Modes of Historical Discourse in Asia.' The authors wish to thank Prof. Matthew Reynolds, Prof. Sowon Park, and the other participants of the *Prismatic Jane Eyre* project for the collaboration that led to the writing of this essay. Words of gratitude go to the three anonymous reviewers for their important critiques. Profuse appreciation is extended to Prof. Charles Lock as well as Prof. Peter G. Friedlander for their astute feedback and to Prof. Meera Ashar for her insightful remarks and suggestions.

2 *JE*, Ch. 34.

 https://doi.org/10.11647/OBP.0319.04

the Indian motif will begin by identifying the Indian elements in the novel and be expanded upon by a theoretical appraisal of its narrative function that relies on indigenous Indian narratological theory.

As it turns out, Mr Rivers is hoping to marry Jane so that she may accompany him on his oriental journey as a missionary helpmeet and fellow labourer, a conductress of Indian schools, and a helper amongst Indian women.[3] Dutiful as she is, Jane consents to studying Hindustani, an archaic linguistic term referring to modern Hindi, Urdu, and to some extent Indo-Persian spoken throughout much of northern India.[4] Already fluent in French, the British-born Jane abandons learning German and pursues the study of Hindustani for two months. One passage describes how she sits 'poring over the crabbed characters and flourishing tropes of an Indian scribe'.[5]

Soon thereafter, Mr Rivers purchases a one-way ticket on an East Indiaman ship, bidding farewell to his native England with a foreboding sense of never returning:

> 'And I shall see it again,' he said aloud, 'in dreams when I sleep by the Ganges: and again in a more remote hour — when another slumber overcomes me — on the shore of a darker stream!'[6]

Before leaving for Calcutta,[7] he finally proposes to Jane, saying 'Jane, come with me to India',[8] and although she initially embraces the idea of joining him on this Christian quest, in the end she cannot give her heart to Mr Rivers. The marriage never comes to be and Jane does

---

3 *JE*, Ch. 34.

4 On the term Hindustani as a British colonial linguistic label conceived of by the British Raj as a communal language, see Debarati Goswami, 'Charlotte Bronte's "Imagined" Indianness: Homogenized Othering as a Mimetic Response in *Jane Eyre*', *Rupkatha Journal on Interdisciplinary Studies in Humanities*, 7 (2015), 114–22 (p. 118). In general, the names for Indian languages have throughout the present essay been given in their standard English forms; thus, *Apabhraṃśa, Asamīyā, Bāṅlā, Gujarātī, Hindī, Hindustānī, Kannaḍa, Malayāḷam, Marāṭhī, Nepālī, Oṛiā, Pañjābī, Prākṛta, Saṃskṛta, Tamiḻ*, and *Telugu* have been rendered as Apabhramsha, Assamese, Bangla, Gujarati, Hindi, Hindustani, Kannada, Malayalam, Marathi, Nepali, Odia, Punjabi, Prakrit, Sanskrit, Tamil, and Telugu respectively.

5 *JE*, Ch. 34.

6 *JE*, Ch. 34.

7 The toponym Calcutta can be inferred from a later conversation, when Mr Rivers's sister Diana says to Jane (*JE*, Ch. 34): 'You are much too pretty, as well as too good, to be grilled alive in Calcutta.' Nowadays the city Calcutta has been renamed Kolkata.

8 *JE*, Ch. 34.

not set out to 'toil under eastern suns, in Asian deserts'.[9] Instead, she leaves his home in the English countryside and, in a dramatic turn of events, goes back to her true love, the male protagonist Mr Edward Rochester, whom she finally marries in the book's closing chapter.

Indubitably, the Indian motif is by no means central to the novel in its first twenty-six chapters, which narrate Jane's childhood and her life as a young adult serving as a governess at Mr Rochester's estate, Thornfield Hall. Yet, as the plot unfolds throughout the remaining twelve chapters, India gradually emerges as a place of particular imagination and it is possible to discern its significance at a crucial turn of events, marking a watershed in the narrative. Having, in Chapter 27, discovered the secret life of Mr Rochester and broken off their marriage engagement, Jane wanders away into a new circumstance in her haphazard encounter with the three siblings of the Rivers family throughout Chapters 28 to 33. It is in this new setting of separation from Mr Rochester that India — in Chapter 34 — enters the story with full force.

In the last part of the book, India initially appears in Chapter 32, where the eastern land is brought into focus by Jane in a conversation that she is having with Mr Rivers, as he prepares to set out for the far reaches of the British Empire. Jane has drawn a portrait of Miss Oliver and she offers to make a similar one for Mr Rivers to take on his voyage:

> Would it comfort, or would it wound you to have a similar painting? Tell me that. When you are at Madagascar, or at the Cape, or in India, would it be a consolation to have that memento in your possession?[10]

Here, Jane for the first time mentions India as the ultimate destination of Mr Rivers's voyage, alongside the Cape of South Africa and the island of Madagascar in the Indian Ocean as intermediary ports of call along the traditional shipping route to the Indian subcontinent prior to the opening of the Suez Canal in 1869, twenty-two years after the publication of Brontë's book. Thus, unwitting of its looming momentousness, Jane for the first time broaches the topic of India.

The Indian theme then returns emphatically in Chapter 34, this time raised by Mr Rivers appertaining to Jane. As he, for priestly reasons, beseeches Jane to accompany him on the missionary journey as his wife, India becomes concretised as the fundamental object of

9 *JE*, Ch. 34.
10 *JE*, Ch. 32.

a life-altering decision for Jane. The subcontinent crystallises as a potential destination of escape from the amorous tragedy that she earlier underwent with Mr Rochester. Consequently, Asia becomes a realm in which she might live out a utopian form of religious self-sacrifice unto death. Torn, she reflects on Mr St John Rivers's proposal:

> Of course (as St. John once said) I must seek another interest in life to replace the one lost: is not the occupation he now offers me truly the most glorious man can adopt or God assign? Is it not, by its noble cares and sublime results, the one best calculated to fill the void left by uptorn affections and demolished hopes? I believe I must say, Yes — and yet I shudder. Alas! If I join St. John, I abandon half myself: if I go to India, I go to premature death. And how will the interval between leaving England for India, and India for the grave, be filled? Oh, I know well! That, too, is very clear to my vision. By straining to satisfy St. John till my sinews ache, I shall satisfy him — to the finest central point and farthest outward circle of his expectations. If I do go with him — if I do make the sacrifice he urges, I will make it absolutely: I will throw all on the altar — heart, vitals, the entire victim. He will never love me; but he shall approve me; I will show him energies he has not yet seen, resources he has never suspected. Yes, I can work as hard as he can, and with as little grudging.[11]

India is no longer merely an outer place in the story. By becoming a trope forming a religious-idealist alternative to Jane's former English life of servitude, it is an occasion for the female protagonist gradually to fulfil an inner realisation of a newfound power and independence, which in the end permits the plot's complication to unravel.

Ultimately, in Chapter 35, Jane rejects Mr Rivers's marriage proposal and abandons the prospect of going to India. At this moment of inner strength gushing forth, she intuitively feels that her true love, Mr Rochester, is calling her from afar, and in Chapter 37 she then travels back to Thornfield Hall, while Mr Rivers sets out for India alone. Thereupon, the Indian motif recedes into the background, only to return at the very end of the novel. In the book's closing paragraphs, Jane adopts a changed narrative perspective of reminiscing from the future to recount what later became of Mr Rivers in India, which underscores the Indian theme as a figuration of surrender and personal realisation:

> As to St. John Rivers, he left England: he went to India. He entered on the path he had marked for himself; he pursues it still. A more resolute,

11 *JE*, Ch. 34.

indefatigable pioneer never wrought amidst rocks and dangers. Firm, faithful, and devoted, full of energy, and zeal, and truth, he labours for his race; he clears their painful way to improvement; he hews down like a giant the prejudices of creed and caste that encumber it. He may be stern; he may be exacting; he may be ambitious yet; but his is the sternness of the warrior Greatheart, who guards his pilgrim convoy from the onslaught of Apollyon.[[12]] His is the exaction of the apostle, who speaks but for Christ, when he says — 'Whosoever will come after me, let him deny himself, and take up his cross and follow me.' His is the ambition of the high master-spirit, which aims to fill a place in the first rank of those who are redeemed from the earth — who stand without fault before the throne of God, who share the last mighty victories of the Lamb,[[13]] who are called, and chosen, and faithful.

St. John is unmarried: he never will marry now. Himself has hitherto sufficed to the toil, and the toil draws near its close: his glorious sun hastens to its setting. The last letter I received from him drew from my eyes human tears, and yet filled my heart with divine joy: he anticipated his sure reward, his incorruptible crown. I know that a stranger's hand will write to me next, to say that the good and faithful servant has been called at length into the joy of his Lord. And why weep for this? No fear of death will darken St. John's last hour: his mind will be unclouded, his heart will be undaunted, his hope will be sure, his faith steadfast. His own words are a pledge of this —

'My Master,' he says, 'has forewarned me. Daily He announces more distinctly, — 'Surely I come quickly!' and hourly I more eagerly respond, — 'Amen; even so come, Lord Jesus!'[14]

It is remarkable that such should be the very last words of the novel. Ending the whole book with a Christian pronouncement of devoted service to God by the lone English missionary in India who 'labours for his race, ... clears their painful way to improvement [and] ... hews down like a giant the prejudices of creed and caste that encumber it' is a token of the unexpected prominence of India in the book's narrative.

Literary merits aside, Brontë's construction of India is by no means straightforward and warrants cautious scrutiny. On the one hand, from a contemporary postcolonial perspective, Brontë's India could well be seen as an entirely orientalist *topos* of the heathen presented as being in dire need of moral improvement and social progress.[15] Targeted for

12 The names Greatheart and Apollyon are literary references to John Bunyan's Christian allegorical novel *The Pilgrim's Progress from This World, to That Which Is to Come* (1678).

13 The Lamb, i.e., 'the Lamb of God', is a Christian metaphor for Jesus Christ.

14 *JE*, Ch. 38.

15 For a general introduction to colonial and postcolonial studies, see Ania Loomba, *Colonialism/Postcolonialism* (New York: Routledge, 2015, 3rd edn).

Christian proselytisation, this Indian Other is to be stripped of what is perceived as its baseless religious beliefs and backward social system.[16]

On the other hand, from a literary historicist perspective, Brontë's colonial India could be seen as indispensable to the intercultural poetics at play in the novel's literary portrayal of England in the mid-nineteenth century. The author is evidently familiar with several Indian goods and sporadically employs allusions to Indian mercantile imports, such as rubber, fabric, and ink, embedded in the daily language used by the novel's characters.[17] Brontë's literary allusions to India represent an England saturated by the economic and cultural infusions flowing from its colonial empire. They concord with the historical epoch, when the British colonial trade with India was booming and the Indian languages, religions, and literature had begun to impose a cultural allure on the British mindset, pictured in the story by Jane's foray into her brief study of Hindustani. In fact, the very first English translations from the Indian classical Sanskrit literature had already been published by Sir Charles Wilkins in the 1780s, half a century before Brontë wrote *Jane Eyre*,[18] and the first British chair of Sanskrit Studies had been established at Oxford University in 1833 — a decade and a half prior to Brontë's book — by an endowment from Lt. Colonel Joseph Boden, who had served in colonial India. By the 1840s, when Brontë wrote her novel, contemporaneous English literature was thick with portrayals of India and Indian elements, as encountered in the Indian-born English author Thackeray's novel *Vanity Fair* (1848).

---

16 For a most recent and thorough overview of the broader postcolonial criticism of *Jane Eyre*, see Rachel Willis, '"A Man is Nothing without the Spice of the Devil in him": Jane Eyre and Edward Rochester Navigate an Imperially-Inscribed Masculinity', *Otherness: Essays and Studies*, 6 (2018), 244–59.

17 *JE*, Chs. 14, 17, and 33. The novel's mention of Indian ink (Ch. 33) has been a point of theoretical observation in the postcolonial critiques of *Jane Eyre*; see Susan L. Meyer, 'Colonialism and the Figurative Strategy of *Jane Eyre*', *Victorian Studies*, 33 (1990), 247–68 (p. 267); Susan Meyer, '"Indian Ink": Colonialism and the Figurative Strategy of *Jane Eyre*', in her book *Imperialism at Home: Race and Victorian Women's Fiction* (Ithaca: Cornell University Press, 1996), pp. 60–95; and Partha Sarathi Mandal, Preyona Bhowmik, and Debojyoti Roy, '*Jane Eyre* and its Heteroglossia, Colonialism, Class Struggle, Racial Otherness and the Significance of the British Empire', *International Journal of English, Literature and Social Sciences*, 5 (2020), 190–203 (p. 202).

18 Sir Charles Wilkins, *Bhagvat-geeta, or Dialogues of Kreeshna and Arjoon* (London: Nourse, 1785), and *The Heetopades of Veeshnoo-Sarma, in a Series of Connected Fables, Interspersed with Moral, Prudential and Political Maxims* (London: Nourse, 1787).

It is unknown whether Charlotte Brontë possessed a deeper familiarity with India and its culture. India in her novel is primarily an important place for Christian mission, as reflected in the apparent reason for Jane's study of Hindustani.[19] This Christian depiction of India aligns with some of the early efforts at culturally translating India to the British audience, which were presented as being driven by a religious calling, seen, for instance, in Lt. Colonel Boden's endowment to Oxford University for the Sanskrit chair being explicitly intended to serve 'the conversion of the Natives of India to the Christian Religion, by disseminating a knowledge of the Sacred Scriptures amongst them more effectually than all other means whatsoever'.[20]

While Brontë's portrayal of India certainly is culturally one-sided and religiously hegemonic, there nevertheless is a more profound facet to the Indian motif pertaining to its key function within the novel's plot. The nineteen-year-old Jane's fateful encounter with Mr Rivers, her two-month endeavour to study Hindustani under his tutelage, and finally her expressed yet ultimately unrealised wish to accompany him to India as a fellow missionary cannot be reduced to mere expressions of a fervent Christian calling intrinsic to Jane's character. Rather, these elements in the storyline, along with the reappearance of Mr Rivers and his Indian mission at the very end of the book, suggest that the novel's Indian motif holds a deeper significance aimed at expressing how Jane gradually opens up her young mind to the broader world and the possibilities it holds for her. It offers a way of fulfilling her

19 For an in-depth study of the roles that Victorian women had in Christian mission in India, see Valentine Cunningham, '"God and Nature Intended You for a Missionary's Wife": Mary Hill, Jane Eyre and Other Missionary Women in the 1840s', in *Women and Missions: Past and Present*, ed. by Fiona Bowie, Deborah Kirkwood, and Shirley Ardener (New York: Routledge, 1993), pp. 85–105. For a history of Protestant mission and related colonial governmental policies, see Arthur Mayhew, *Christianity and the Government of India: An Examination of the Christian Forces at Work in the Administration of India and of the Mutual Relations of the British Government and Christian Missions 1600–1920* (London: Faber & Gwyer Limited, 1929).

20 Endowment document for the Oxford University chair in Sanskrit Studies, cited by Richard Gombrich, *On Being Sanskritic: A Plea for Civilized Study and the Study of Civilization* (Oxford: Clarendon Press, 1977), p. 5, and by Gillian Evison, 'The Orientalist, his Institute and the Empire: The Rise and Subsequent Decline of Oxford University's Indian Institute' (bodleian.ox.ac.uk, 2004). Lt. Colonel Boden's proselytising intent was later removed from Oxford University's statutes in 1881, changing the purpose of the Sanskrit chair to simply 'deliver lectures and give instruction on the Sanskrit Language and Literature'; see Gombrich, *On Being Sanskritic*, p. 21.

inner restlessness and deeply felt need for seeing the world that she had already entertained while residing as a governess at Thornfield Hall:

> ... I longed for a power of vision which might overpass that limit; which might reach the busy world, towns, regions full of life I had heard of but never seen.[21]

Consequently, the narrative function of the Indian motif serves as a transformative condition of Jane's character that subsequently triggers in her the telepathic voice of Mr Rochester, which ultimately induces her to return and marry him.

Such plot transitions are commonly interpreted in English literary criticism through the traditional narrative theory of Aristotelian thought. This foundational model espouses plot transitions as driven exclusively by agentive characters and consequently places the action of the plot at its centre. For this reason, it is necessary to consider a theoretical model that would shift the focus from the action to the dramatic purposes of non-agentive motifs. This methodological shift would allow for comprehending Brontë's narrative strategy of letting an outer condition — the possibility of participating in an Indian mission, a non-agentive element — alter Jane's character. By employing a classical Indian model of narratology derived from the dramaturgy of Bharata Muni, a theory of the dramatic purposes of non-agentive motifs may be developed, and applied to *Jane Eyre* and its non-action-based Indian elements.

In the standard Aristotelian model of narrative, a *mythos* (μῦθος plot) is an imitation of a *praxis* (πρᾶξις action) that may be said to consist of five parts: (1) the exposition, (2) the rising action, (3) the climax, (4) the falling action, and (5) the *dénouement* (unravelling) accompanied by revelation.[22] In the final chapters of *Jane Eyre*, the climax of the plot can be identified as Mr Rochester's attempt to marry Jane, which

21 *JE*, Ch. 12.

22 See Gustav Freytag, *Die Technik des Dramas* (Leipzig: S. Hirzel, 1863). In terms of this fivefold Aristotelian division of the plot, it is, moreover, notable that *Jane Eyre* likewise can be divided into five stages as an allegory for the pilgrim's five stations presented in Bunyan's *The Pilgrim's Progress*; see Kalyani Ghosh, 'Charlotte Brontë: A Re-Assessment' (doctoral thesis, University of Burdwan, 1991), pp. 181–90. For an Indian adaptation of *The Pilgrim's Progress*, see Mary Martha Sherwood, *The Indian Pilgrim; or, The Progress of the Pilgrim Nazareenee (Formerly Called Goonah Purist, or the Slave of Sin) from the City of the Wrath of God to the City of Mount Zion. Delivered under the Similitude of a Dream* (Wellington, Salop: F. Houlston and Son, 1818).

fails when it is brought to light that he still is bound by an earlier marriage to the mentally ill Bertha Mason from the West Indies. The falling action follows with Jane's hurried departure from Thornfield Hall and her being taken in by the Rivers family, far away from Mr Rochester. The *dénouement* is then put in motion with the telepathic voice calling Jane back to Mr Rochester, whereby the plot's *agon* (αγων complication) conclusively unravels when she returns and discovers that Thornfield Hall has burned down and Bertha has perished, while the now blind and widowed Mr Rochester has survived, which sets Jane free to marry him.

While these narratological constituents of Aristotelian plot analysis account for the characters' actions, they do not allow a narrative function to be ascribed to the Indian motif, which is not driven by the dramatic action. In Aristotle's model, the motif can be understood only as a minor intensifying context within the falling action, for which there is no Greek term. This limitation originates from the Aristotelian emphasis on the plot being exclusively the dramatic action, which can only be performed by the characters in the drama. Given that the utopian trope of India is not a character, the Aristotelian model cannot ascribe any action to the trope. Consequently, the Indian trope falls outside the explanatory scope of standard narratology. In spite of its evident transformative influence on the main storyline, the Indian motif becomes diminished in a traditional narratological analysis when it is demoted to an entirely passive yet suspenseful outer circumstance in the drama.

The ardent reader of *Jane Eyre*, therefore, might wish to revisit the Indian motif when called by a different classicist voice, that of the dramatologist Bharata Muni resonating from ancient India. For when the storyline of *Jane Eyre* is viewed through the alternative narratological lens of the Bharatic tradition of the *Nāṭyaśāstra* (*A Treatise on Drama*) of Indian dramaturgy, whose theoretical focus lies primarily on the plot's *sandhi* (संधि junctures) rather than on its imitation of a *praxis* (action), it all of a sudden becomes possible to uncover the deeper significance of the Indian ingredients within the plot.[23]

23 For the Bharatic plot theory, see Bharata Muni's classical treatise *Nāṭyaśāstra*, Ch. 19. Sanskrit edition by M. Ramakrishna Kavi, *Nāṭyaśāstra of Bharatamuni with the Commentary Abhinavabhāratī by Abhinavaguptācārya*, 4 vols, 2nd revised edn, ed. by V. M. Kulkarni and Tapasvi Nandi (Vadodara: Oriental Institute, 2003), III, pp. 1–52. English translation by Manomohan Ghosh, *The*

In the Bharatic narratology, the *itivṛtta* (इतिवृत्त plot) is divided into five broad action-oriented *avasthā* (अवस्था stages) that are tied together by five *sandhi* (junctures). The part of the story between Jane's departure from Mr Rochester until her return to him can, in the Bharatic schema, be identified as the penultimate juncture known as *vimarśa* (विमर्श suspense), which is a crisis characterised by deceit, anger, or an obstacle that causes hesitation and doubt in the protagonist.[24] It is within this transitional phase of the plot, the *vimarśasandhi* (विमर्शसंधि suspense juncture), that Brontë introduces the Indian motif.

The suspense juncture generally serves to tie together the plot's middle stage with its final resolution. In the case of *Jane Eyre*, the suspense juncture contains a longer subplot of its own, namely the story of Jane's stay with the Rivers siblings and in particular her platonic relationship with Mr Rivers. In the Bharatic narratology, such a subplot is called a *patākā* (पताका pennant), since it is a story within the story, which tapers out just like the triangular shape of a pennant flag. The pennant type of subplot is defined as an episode that is integral to the main plot, given that it helps to drive the main plot forward. It is marked by having its own distinct *artha* (अर्थ objective), which differs from the overall objective of the main plot.[25]

While the pennant subplot encompasses Jane's encounter and relationship with Mr Rivers, its *artha* (objective) is the Indian motif, i.e., Mr Rivers's proposition for Jane to go with him to India. This *artha* of the subplot represents an alternative to the *artha* of the main plot, which is Jane's marriage to Mr Rochester. In relation to the larger plot structure, the subplot's Indian motif correspondingly signifies an opening up within Jane towards the possibility of a new objective, a different life elsewhere. Although Jane decides not to go to India, it is the maturation of her character brought about by the alternative of the Indian motif that closes the suspense juncture in the plot and propels Jane into the final plot stage, namely the so-called *phalayogāvasthā*

Naṭyaśāstra: A Treatise on Hindu Dramaturgy and Histrionics ascribed to Bharata-Muni, 2 vols (Kolkata: The Royal Asiatic Society of Bengal, 1950–61), I (1950), pp. 380–400. The expression Bharatic is here intended as an adjectival form of Bharata Muni, the ascribed author of the *Nāṭyaśāstra*, parallel to the English expression Aristotelian used for characterising the classical European plot theory.

24 *Nāṭyaśāstra*, verse 19:42.

25 *Nāṭyaśāstra*, verse 19:24.

(फलयोगावस्था stage of reaching the result), which is represented by her return and marriage to Mr Rochester.

In the Bharatic narrative model, the *phalayogāvasthā* ends with another *sandhi* (juncture) of its own, the fifth juncture called *nirvahaṇa* (निर्वहण closure). The *nirvahaṇasandhi* (निर्वहणसंधि closure juncture) is, in the classical Bharatic schema, said to have fourteen possible forms.[26] In the case of *Jane Eyre*, two of these forms of closure can be identified, namely *bhāṣaṇa* (भाषण a closing speech) and *grathana* (ग्रथन a tying together of the action). The *bhāṣaṇa* is the above-cited narration found in the novel's three final paragraphs that recount what later became of Mr Rivers. The *grathana* is the re-emergence of the topos of India in the antepenultimate paragraph of the novel, echoing the Indian motif of the suspense juncture. The fact that Brontë returns to the Indian motif at this concluding point creates a narrative bridge between the living vision of Jane's India and the dying reality of Mr Rivers's India, solidifying the author's overarching resolution to make India a focal point of the plot. Correspondingly, the link between the objective of the *vimarśasandhi* (suspense juncture) and the two narrative expressions of the *nirvahaṇasandhi* (closure juncture) reveals the centrality of the Indian motif for the entire novel.

India on *Jane Eyre*: The Narrative Transformations of the Indian Motif

In the Aristotelian theory of poetics, a turning point defines the moment in a play when the dramatic action begins to unravel, in Greek referred to as *peripeteia* (περιπέτεια reversal). 'Jane, come with me to India' engenders such a *peripeteia* by initiating the gradual return of Jane to Mr Rochester while simultaneously precluding Jane from ever arriving on Indian soil.[27]

In a paradoxical turn of events, Jane nevertheless has been transposed to India, and not by Charlotte Brontë, but by the Indians themselves. Jane first touched Indian soil in 1914 dressed in native *sāṛī* (साड़ी saree) and speaking Bengali as she stepped onto the literary scene in the Indian novel *Sarlā*. In the ensuing popular reception of *Jane Eyre* in India, Jane has ever since lived multifarious lives

26 *Nāṭyaśāstra*, verses 19:65–67.
27 Cf. the *Jane Eyre* sequel novel *A Marble Column* by Cicely Havely (published independently, 2019), wherein Jane, Mr Rochester, and Adele travel to India to meet Mr Rivers.

through numerous adaptations and translations of Brontë's novel into disparate regional Indian languages. Nonetheless, in the Indian academic reception since the 1980s, *Jane Eyre* has forever remained a novel to be read in English, never contemplated with regard to its Indian motif, and invariably confined to the discursive English realm of modern social and literary theory.

As will be argued below, highlighting these different linguistic pathways through a chronological survey of the literary and cinematographic adaptations of the novel, juxtaposed with *Jane Eyre*'s academic reception and circulation in India, uncovers a state of irony in the significance of the Indian motif articulated with a Bharatic narratological awareness. For when the English novel is translocated specifically to India, the Indian motif loses its force and is replaced by other literary devices, signalling a narrative transformation.

In 1914, the Christian schoolteacher Nirmmalā Bālā Soma (নির্ম্মলা বালা সোম) published the Bengali novel *Sarlā* (সরলা *Sarlā*) in 188 pages.[28] It was self-published by the author and printed by N. Mukherjee at Gupta, Mukherjee & Co.'s Press in Calcutta. Soma had been educated at the renowned Bethune women's college in Kolkata and went on to obtain a master's degree in English from the University of Calcutta. The novel, written in Bangla language, i.e., Bengali, is a literary adaptation of *Jane Eyre* which recasts the story into the Bengal region of colonial India. The book consists of thirty chapters, most of which are just four to five pages in length. With a storyline and prose texture closely resembling Brontë's *Jane Eyre*, it tells the story of the Indian female protagonist Ms. Sarlā, a faithful rendering of Jane, from her upbringing as an orphan into her life as a young adult. Sarlā works as a governess for Mr Śacīndrakumār Bandyopādhyāy with whom she gradually becomes romantically involved. Having discovered that he is bound by an existing marriage to the insane wife Unnādinī, Sarlā runs away and is accepted into the Christian family of Mr Śarat Bābu and his two sisters. After Sarlā, with Mr Śarat's help, has obtained a large inheritance from a deceased uncle, Mr Śarat proposes to her, asking her to join him on travels to do Christian work. She rejects the proposal and instead returns to marry Mr Bandyopādhyāy, who, after a fateful fire, is now widowed and blind. Ten years later, Mr Śarat

28 A short introduction by Olivia Majumdar along with a digitised facsimile edition of the original Bengali book is available at the British Library Online, Early Indian Printed Books section.

passes away, having lived an austere, solitary existence devoted to God. Sarlā briefly praises him as a most heroic and devout Christian, whose desires she never fulfilled.

In a short epilogue on the last page of the book, Soma remarks that she does not claim originality for her novel and does not consider it a translation. Without mentioning *Jane Eyre* explicitly, the author notes that the story of *Sarlā* is based on an unnamed English work, deviating from the original in many places. For instance, the novel does not contain the colonial dimension of Englishmen traveling to their Indian colony, but it retains the religious aspect of Christian mission in India. Being quite close to Brontë's novel yet altered in certain ways, Soma's literary work can best be described as an *anurūpaṇ* (अनुरूपण adaptation) of *Jane Eyre*. An adaptation, whether literary or cinematographic, is characterised by the reproduction of a prototypical story in a recognizable fashion while adding certain new elements of its own. Soma's novel never became widespread in India. The writer was not well-known and the book was published independently in just a small number of copies without ever being reprinted. *Sarlā* remains the first Indian adaptation of *Jane Eyre* and also the version that stands the closest to Brontë's original.

Three decades after Soma's literary adaptation, the 1950s mark the period when *Jane Eyre* was introduced to a broader Indian audience. Just a few years after India had gained independence from British colonial rule in 1947, which took place precisely a century after Brontë's publication of *Jane Eyre* in 1847, the first Indian cinematographic adaptation appeared in 1952, followed the next year by the first abridged translation into an Indian language, namely the Tamil translation of 1953. The first cinematographic adaptation was the Hindi-Urdu Bollywood film *Saṅgdil* (संगदिल سنگدل *Stone-Hearted*),[29] bearing the English subtitle *An Emotion Play of Classic Dimensions*. Produced and directed by Ār. Sī. Talvār (b. 1910), it was shot at the Eastern Studios and Prakash Studios in Mumbai.[30] The film stars the actress Mumtāz Jahāṃ Begham Dehlavī (1933–1969, stage name

29 Some Hindi speakers though understand the title *Saṅgdil* to mean true-hearted, which reflects another, more common meaning of the adjective *saṅg* as 'true' in Hindi.

30 Ār. Sī. Talvār, *Saṅgdil*, released by Talvār Films in 1952, screenplay by Rāmānand Sāgar, photography by Prakāś Malhotrā, music by Sajjād Hussain, and lyrics by Rājindar Kṛṣṇa.

Madhubālā) in the female lead role of Kamlā and Muhammad Yūsuf Khān (b. 1922, stage name Dilīp Kumār) in the male lead role of Śaṅkar.

Although *Saṅgdil* displays many elements detectable from the original novel, in his screenplay Rāmānand Sāgar (1917–2005)[31] takes many liberties in constructing the female and male protagonists. The major difference is that while Jane and Mr Rochester first become acquainted as adults in Brontë's narrative, the film portrays Kamlā and Śaṅkar as living in the same household since early childhood. Śaṅkar's father adopts Kamlā after the death of her father, a close friend of his, and secretly usurps Kamlā's inheritance, leaving her to the cruelty of his wife, who treats her like a servant. After the death of Śaṅkar's father, the stepmother sends Kamlā to an orphanage. On the way to the orphanage, Kamlā manages to escape and is adopted by a group of Hindu *pujārīn* (पुजारीन priestesses) living in a local Śiva temple, where she grows up. Later in the film, the childhood friends Kamlā and Śaṅkar are gradually reunited as adults, when Kamlā visits Śaṅkar's new estate in order to carry out religious worship as a *devadāsī* (देवदासी) performer of Hindu sacred dance.[32]

A series of events then unfolds, which is highly reminiscent of the second half of Brontë's novel with certain alterations. When Kamlā leaves Śaṅkar on their wedding day as she discovers that he already is married to the insane woman Śīlā, she returns to the temple where she grew up in order to pursue a wholly celibate life as a Hindu priestess. There is, accordingly, no character in the film matching Mr Rivers and consequently Kamlā is never exposed to the element of having to learn a foreign language nor of having to go abroad as a missionary. Instead, while Kamlā places her personal belongings one by one into a sacrificial fire during a purification ritual aimed at fully devoting herself to the new religious life of a renunciate, Śaṅkar's estate is set ablaze by Śīlā and burns to the ground, with Śīlā being consumed by the fire. When, during the ritual, Kamlā is asked by the high priestess

---

31 Rāmānand Sāgar went on to become an acclaimed Indian director famous for creating a TV serial adaptation of the classical Indian epic *Rāmāyaṇa* (1987) in 78 episodes, which has been rated as the most-watched television series in the world, setting another world record when it re-aired in 2020.

32 On the tradition of female *devadāsī* performers, see Anne-Marie Gaston, 'Dance and the Hindu Woman: Bharatanāṭyam Re-Ritualized', as well as, Saskia C. Kersenboom, 'The Traditional Repertoire of the Tiruttaṇi Temple Dancers', both in *Roles and Rituals for Hindu Women*, ed. by Julia Leslie (Rutherford: Fairleigh Dickinson University Press, 1991), pp. 149–71 and pp. 131–47 respectively.

whether she still has an attachment to anyone in the world, she internally hears Śaṅkar's voice calling her name and realises her strong bond to him. Kamlā interrupts the ritual and returns to her beloved Śaṅkar, who has by then become blind and widowed.

Saṅgdil, which was an Indian box office hit, can certainly be considered an adaptation of *Jane Eyre*, in that it thoroughly rewrites the prototypical story of the English novel while retaining some familiar elements. The film is, though, not much further removed from the original than, for instance, the 1934 Hollywood movie adaptation of *Jane Eyre* directed by Christy Cabanne, starring Virginia Bruce and Colin Clive, which likewise makes many omissions and changes of its own to the story.[33] *Saṅgdil* may thus be said to belong to a film genre similar to that of its literary ancestor, with the proviso that the change of medium from text to screen naturally involves transformations that transcend the strictly narrative aspect of the literary genre.[34] This is particularly evident in the film's inclusion of several song and dance segments, as is characteristic of most Bollywood films, such as the celebrated song *Dhartī se dūr gore bādloṃ ke pār* (धरती से दूर गोरे बादलों के पार *Far from the Earth, Across the White Clouds*).

Some of the creative modifications of narrative found in *Saṅgdil* were perhaps culturally necessitated when placing the story in an Indian setting inhabited by Indian characters. One such requisite is Kamlā's upbringing as a temple priestess, because this is a profession that allows her as an adult to enter Śaṅkar's estate. It would have been improbable for Kamlā to come to the estate as a governess, since Indian unmarried women normally did not hold such positions in the nineteenth century.

Other changes in the storyline may have been motivated by literary concerns aimed at opening up the story to the Indian audience, which may have served to draw the film into intertextual connections with

33 Christy Cabanne, *Jane Eyre*, released in the United States by Monogram Pictures in 1934, produced by Ben Verschleiser, and screenplay by Adele Comandini.

34 For a general discussion of cinematographic adaptation practices, including *Jane Eyre* filmizations with reference to further theoretical literature, see Erik Svendsen, 'Genre and Adaptation in Motion', in *Genre And ...*, ed. by Sune Auken, Palle Schantz Lauridsen, and Anders Juhl Rasmussen, *Copenhagen Studies in Genre* vol. 2 (Copenhagen: Ekbátana, 2015), pp. 221–50, and Papiya Nabi, 'From Texts to Films: Adaptations of Pride and Prejudice, Jane Eyre and Great Gatsby across the 20th and the 21st Centuries' (master's thesis, BRAC University, Bangladesh, 2016), pp. 9–18.

distinctively Indian literary genres. In particular, the reunion of Kamlā and Śaṅkar in the middle of the film made possible by their childhood friendship echoes a beloved Indian literary device of *abhijñāna* (अभिज्ञान recognition). Famous across India from the Sanskrit poet Kālidāsa's (4th-5th centuries) classic drama *Abhijñānaśākuntala* (*The Recognition of Śakuntalā*), this literary theme is a transformation of the lovers' estrangement into their mutual recall and subsequent conjugal union. The film innovatively draws on Kālidāsa's story to infuse *Jane Eyre* with a new potent reason for the love to unfold.

Saṅgdil is the Indian adaptation that portrays its female protagonist in the most powerful way, because it entirely leaves out any Mr Rivers character and instead has Kamlā seek an independent religious life as a Hindu renunciate priestess. Kamlā's decision to return to Śaṅkar is not based on having been offered an alternative marriage to another man. It instead flows from her inner awakening that she still has an emotional connection to Śaṅkar, which she wishes to confront and eventually pursue. In this version, there is no manifest colonial aspect and the story's religious dimension has been transformed from Christian to Hindu, and transposed onto Kamlā.

In 1959, Jane emerged in yet another Indian adaptive guise. The lauded South Indian writer Nīḷā Dēvi (ನೀಳಾ ದೇವಿ, b. 1932) from Bengaluru, Karnataka, published the Kannada novel *Bēḍi Bandavaḷu* (ಬೇಡಿ ಬಂದವಳು *The Woman Who Came out of Need*) in 240 pages. This was the second Indian book adaptation of *Jane Eyre*. The book was published by Mōhana Prakāśana in Mysuru.[35] Analogous to the earlier Bengali novel by Soma, Dēvi recasts Brontë's story into an Indian setting, keeping the plot close to the storyline of the English novel. The female protagonist Indu takes up a position as a private teacher for a young girl at the estate of Mr Prahlāda. The story then unfolds along the lines of the English novel, although all of the dialogue has been rewritten and Indu is a softer, less individualistic character than her British counterpart. Having left Mr Prahlāda's estate upon the discovery of a mad wife in the attic, Indu is taken in to the home of Mr Nārāyaṇa and his two sisters. He is a young Brahmin, who works at a Hindu temple and is involved in distributing herbal medicine to the local rural community. When offered a job at a textile mill in

35 The authors wish to thank Professor Emeritus B. A. Viveka Rai, Mangalore University, for drawing our attention to Dēvi's novel and for his help in discussing the book and its filmization.

faraway Ahmedabad in the Indian state of Gujarat, he proposes to Indu and asks her to accompany him. She rejects his proposal. At this moment, she remembers Mr Prahlāda and is overcome with longing. Soon thereafter, she telepathically hears Prahlāda crying out her name as he is blinded in a fire that burns down his estate, whereupon she returns and marries him. Mr Nārāyaṇa does not reappear in the story.

While the Kannada novel resembles Soma's earlier Bengali work in the manner in which it adapts the English novel into an Indian setting, the Kannada version entirely lacks the Christian dimension, which remains prominent in the Bengali adaptation. The novel is the first Indian adaptation to replace, or at least substantially downplay, the religious mood of *Jane Eyre* in favour of a secular choice. Mr Nārāyaṇa proposes marriage to Indu, not for the sake of religious mission, which traditionally is a relatively unimportant aspect of Hinduism, but instead with the secular prospect of moving for his new job at a textile mill. The novel presents Indu as finding independence through her new position as a schoolteacher, and by the financial security that she obtains from getting an inheritance, without suggesting any inner transformation taking place within Indu that could explain her decision to return to Mr Prahlāda. In this sense, Indu's character is slightly weakened in the Kannada novel.

In 1968, a decade after the publication of Dēvi's *Bēḍi Bandavaḷu*, the novel was picked up and filmed under the same title *Bēḍi Bandavaḷu* (ಬೇಡಿ ಬಂದವಳು *The Woman Who Came out of Need*) by the South Indian director Si. Śrīnivāsan.[36] The Kannada language film features the actress Candrakalā (1950–1999) as Indu and the actor Kalyāṇ Kumār (1928–1999) as Prahlāda. The filmization entails several minor changes to the story of the Kannada novel. A new element is the interspersed comic relief provided in the film by the supporting character Kṛṣṇa, a male servant at the estate, played by the South Indian comedian Baṅgle Śāma Rāv Dvārakānāth (stage name Dvārakīś, b. 1942). Another narrative difference from the Kannada novel is that Indu in the film serves as the governess not for one but for four girls at the estate. The film deals only briefly with Indu's stay at the Nārāyaṇa family and Mr Nārāyaṇa does not propose marriage to Indu. Instead, he asks her about her general intentions to marry, which causes her to remember

36 Si. Śrīnivāsan, *Bēḍi Bandavaḷu*, released by Śrīnivāsa Ārṭs Proḍakṣans in 1968, produced by Ṭi. En. Śrīnivāsan, photography by Vijaya Nañjappa, and music by Ār. Sudarśanaṃ.

Prahlāda. Finally, the ending of the film differs slightly from the novel. When Indu discovers that Prahlāda has turned blind, she wishes to destroy her own eyesight with a lit candle. She is prevented from doing so by a doctor who enters the scene just in time to assure her that Prahlāda's sight can be restored with surgery at a hospital in Bengaluru. The film ends with Prahlāda and Indu driving away for Bengaluru in the back of a jeep. In terms of filmic adaptative transformations, like *Saṅgdil*, the Kannada film includes several genre-altering song and dance routines not found in the Kannada novel, thereby imbuing the film with an added feature of the musical genre. Some of these are the song *Ēḷu svaravu sēri* (ಏಳು ಸ್ವರವು ಸೇರಿ *Uniting the Seven Musical Notes*) performed by the playback singer Pi. Suśīla (b. 1935) and the amorous tune *Nīrinalli aleya uṅgura* (ನೀರಿನಲ್ಲಿ ಅಲೆಯ ಉಂಗುರ *Rings of Waves in the Water*) performed by Suśīla and Pi. Bi. Śrīnivās (1930–2013).

Character-wise, the filmization of *Bēḍi Bandavaḷu* weakens Indu's role even further. It omits both Indu's employment as a schoolteacher and Mr Nārāyaṇa's marriage proposal, and as a result it does not give Indu any concrete choice of another way to fulfilment. Indu finds financial independence through an inheritance, but is uncertain about what to do with her life. Her hesitancy builds up in the scene when Mr Nārāyaṇa inquires about her general plans to marry, which causes her to remember and long for Mr Prahlāda. Indu undergoes no emotional transformation at all and returns to Mr Prahlāda when, in her solitude, she realises that her heart belongs to him.

In the following year, 1969, after the commercial success of *Bēḍi Bandavaḷu*, a remake of the film was produced in the Tamil language entitled *Cānti Nilaiyam* (சாந்தி நிலையம் *A Peaceful Home*) directed by Ji. Es. Maṇi.[37] Remarkably, it is the only production of the five Indian cinematographic adaptations made in colour. The film script was rewritten for the Tamil version by the screenwriter Citrālayā Kōpu (pen name Caṭakōpaṉ, 1959–1990) in a decidedly more melodramatic form, leading the plot even further away from the storyline of Brontë's *Jane Eyre*. The film features Vacuntarā Tēvi (stage name Kāñcaṉā, b. 1939) in the female lead as Mālati and Kaṇapati Cuppiramaṇiyaṉ Carmā (stage name Jemiṉi Kaṇēcaṉ, 1920–2005) in the male lead as Pācukar. Mālati is hired as a governess at Pācukar's

37 Ji. Es. Maṇi, *Cānti Nilaiyam*, released by Jēm Mūvīs in 1969, produced by Ji. Es. Maṇi and Es. Es. Vācaṉ, written by Citrālayā Kōpu, cinematography by Marcus Bartley, and music by Em. Es. Visvanātaṉ.

estate to look after four girls and one boy, all of whom are very rowdy and naughty. The developing romance between Pācukar and Mālati is haunted by Pācukar's mad wife, Janakī, who lives hidden in the attic. Janakī's role is, though, relatively minor, since the plot's main conflict has been shifted to Pācukar and Janakī's brother Pālu, correlative to Brontë's character Richard Mason, the brother of Bertha Mason. Pālu aggressively pressures Pācukar to pay him money in order to settle an old family feud. Long ago, Pācukar's father was wrongfully accused of murder and the legal settlement forced Pācukar to marry the insane Janakī. Pācukar's family was required to pay compensation, part of which Pācukar still owes Pālu. When Pālu interrupts the wedding of Mālati and Pācukar, Mālati runs away on foot. Pācukar and Pālu have a dramatic fist fight, during which Janakī sets the house on fire. Mālati does not manage to get far, since one of the children runs after her and is hit by a car, whereupon Mālati rushes back to bring the child to a hospital. Janakī and her atrocious brother both perish in the fire, while Pācukar survives with his sight intact. The film ends happily with Pācukar, Mālati, and the children reunited at the family table in the still-standing and now peaceful house, which has survived the fire. The Tamil version tends to reduce the female protagonist Mālati's emotional independence to the extent that she only briefly escapes on foot, whereupon she immediately has to return to help the injured child, leaving Mālati no time or possibility to reflect on seeking a new life of her own.

In the same year, 1969, that Ji. Es. Maṇi released the Tamil film *Cānti Nilaiyam*, the director Pi. Sāmbaśivarāvu created his debut film, the Telugu thriller *Ardharātri* (అర్ధరాత్రి *Midnight*).[38] While not exactly an adaptation but rather an appropriation of *Jane Eyre* that is here recast in a completely different filmic genre of suspense, this cloak-and-dagger Telugu film contains the *Jane-Eyre*-inspired themes of an orphan woman and a mad wife, two characters already well-known to Indian cinemagoers from the earlier *Jane Eyre* adaptations.[39] The film starts with a murder and a prison escape. It then tells the story of a young orphan woman, Saraḷa, a name reminiscent of the Bengali Sarlā character from the 1914 novel by Soma. The female lead is played by

---

38 Pi. Sāmbaśivarāvu, *Ardharātri*, released by Haidarābād Mūvīs in 1969, produced by Pi. Gaṅgādhararāvu, script by Ārudra, and music by Māsṭar Vēṇu.

39 In Telugu, the novel *Jane Eyre* is known as *Jēn Air* (జేన్ ఐర్).

the actress Bhāratī Viṣṇuvardhan (b. 1948). After being expelled from her childhood home by a mean stepmother, Saraḷa is hit by a car and is taken into the household of the driver, a childless rich man named Śrīdhar, played by the actor Koṅgara Jaggayya (1926–2004). Saraḷa looks after Śrīdhar and a romance develops between them. Every midnight the house is haunted by a strange female presence emerging from a cottage in the garden, which terrifies the household's male servants. Intrigued by the mysterious phenomenon, Saraḷa unsuccessfully tries to find out what lies behind the apparition. When Śrīdhar and Saraḷa are to be married, their wedding is interrupted by the antagonist Kēśav. He reveals that Śrīdhar already is married to the mad woman Rāṇi, Kēśav's sister, who lives in the mysterious cottage in the garden. Onto the scene steps Śrīdhar's long-lost father, who escaped from prison at the beginning of the film. The father discloses that Kēśav long ago murdered Rāṇi's boyfriend, referring back to the murder shown at the beginning of the film. The fatal event drove Rāṇi insane. Kēśav managed to pin the murder on Śrīdhar's father, which in turn forced his son, Śrīdhar, to marry the traumatised Rāṇi. In a dramatic twist of events, Kēśav sets the garden cottage on fire, in which he and Śrīdhar get into a fight to the death. Rāṇi saves Śrīdhar from being killed by Kēśav. Badly hurt in the fire, she dies from her wounds while lying on the ground calling out the name of her beloved murdered boyfriend. The police arrive and arrest Kēśav and his thuggish servant. The last scene shows Śrīdhar and Saraḷa as a married couple.

In 1972, a Telugu cinematographic remake of the 1969 Tamil film *Cānti Nilaiyam* was released under the similar title *Śānti Nilayaṃ* (శాంతి నిలయం, *A Peaceful Home*) directed by Si. Vaikuṇṭha Rāma Śarma.[40] It features the actress Añjalīdēvi (1927–2014) in the role of Mālati.

The two Indian novels and five cinematographic renditions, starting with the Bengali novel *Sarlā* in 1914 up to the Telugu film *Śānti Nilayam* in 1972, can all be characterised as widely differing from the English *Jane Eyre* in terms of their outer setting, culture, religion, and language, while sharing certain elements with Brontë's storyline and the typological features of its characters. None of these works explicitly acknowledges its indebtedness to *Jane Eyre* and yet,

40 Si. Vaikuṇṭha Rāma Śarma, *Śānti Nilayaṃ*, released by Annapūrṇa Sinī Eṇṭarpraijes in 1972, screenplay by Si. Vaikuṇṭha Rāma Śarma, and music by Es. Pi. Kōdaṇḍapāṇi. Only the songs excerpted from the film are currently available online for viewing.

in spite of all the narrative transformations introduced in the Indian books and films, a reader or viewer familiar with Brontë's novel would undoubtedly be able to pinpoint the resemblances. In particular, the motifs of the orphan girl, the romantic relationship with the estate owner, his hidden mad wife, and the portentous fire are repeated points of similitude.

Their common denominator of relocating the story to an India inhabited by Indian characters creates a quaint sense of fictionalised displacement. The new native soil, however, is extrapolated not through cultural comparison but by a hybridised substitution of English manner and tongue with Indian demeanour and vernacular in a Western-inspired *mise en scène*. Through this narrative process of metonymic transposition, the *sāṛī*-clad acculturated Janes amplify the subsidiary Indian features of Brontë's novel into their preponderant trait, nonetheless with one inadvertent consequence for the anticipated metamorphosis of Jane's character. The full transference of the story to India causes the Indian motif in Brontë's novel, with its specific function as a transformative transition of *peripeteia* in the plot's *dénouement*, to be rendered mute. Depriving the Indian Janes — Sarlā, Kamlā, Indu, Mālati, and Saraḷa — of the opportunity to go on a Christian mission to India with the Mr Rivers characters circumscribes the story's *vimarśasandhi* (suspense juncture) that in Brontë's novel enabled Jane to realise her sovereign self. Facing this inherent dilemma, the authors of the Indian adaptations are forced to provide their Jane characters with alternatives for finding closure after the betrayal they suffer from the Mr Rochester personas — Bandyopādhyāy, Śaṅkar, Prahlāda, Pācukar, and Śrīdhar — which inevitably leads to the progressive weakening of Jane's internal character.

Diminishing the Indian Janes inexorably brings the otherwise obscure figure of Bertha Mason to the fore as a catalyst for unravelling the plot. The desperation and madness of the wife in the attic becomes a prominent feature, especially in the 1969 Telugu thriller *Ardharātri*, wherein the female protagonist Saraḷa is portrayed as an extraordinarily passive individual unable to react even when learning that her suitor is already married. To resolve the plot's consequent *impasse*, the mad Rāṇi is made to stop the villain brother from killing Śrīdhar by sacrificing herself in the flames. In this sense, *Ardharātri* could be regarded as the ultimate adaptation of *Jane Eyre*, since it is here that the mad Rāṇi's suppressed rage and not Saraḷa's dullness and indecisiveness becomes the actual dramatic device for the *dénouement*.

The character of the mad wife Bertha Mason with its gothic determinism has been a topic of enduring fascination for academic Brontë studies in South Asia. Remarkably, the discourse on madness in Indian scholarship focusses on *Jane Eyre* solely as a Victorian novel to be scrutinized in English, never beheld through the prism of the Indian adaptations and translations. In their discussion, South Asian scholars have relied primarily on the Western classics of feminist theory and postcolonial critique while entirely leaving out literary and cinematographic adaptations in Indian languages.[41] Therefore, when India's leading scholar on the Brontë sisters, Kalyani Ghosh,[42] examines the figure of Bertha, she does so in terms of an argument largely drawn from the feminist analysis put forth earlier by the American literati Sandra Gilbert and Susan Gubar.[43] Ghosh argues that Bertha is an archetypal figure of hunger, rebellion, and rage, who has been victimised and repressed under a patriarchal social order, highlighting a degree of affinity between Bertha and Jane as to their entrapment in their inner and outer imprisonments.[44] In a similar vein, Ratna Nandi maintains that Bertha's volcanic rage is a projection of Jane's fiery nature, representing a forbidden female expression, the explosiveness of which symbolises a destructive end to the despotic rule of man.[45]

---

41 One minor exception is a mention in passing of the 1952 Bollywood film *Saṅgdil* in Nabi, 'From Texts to Films', p. 52.

42 Ghosh's scholarship on Brontëan literature includes her doctoral thesis 'Charlotte Brontë: A Re-Assessment', published under the title *The Novels of Charlotte Brontë: A Reassessment* (Kolkata: Papyrus Publishers, 2003), and the following articles: 'Satire in Charlotte Bronte's *Shirley*', *Punjab Journal of English Studies* (Amritsar, 1995); 'The Last Fragments of Charlotte Bronte: Some Inconclusive Conclusions', *Dibrugarh University Journal of English Studies*, 12 (1996–1997), 77–84; 'The Poetry of Anne Bronte', *Pegassus* (Kolkata, 2010); and 'Romanticism with a Difference: Anne Bronte's *The Tenant of Wildfell Hall*', *Heteroglossia* (2014).

43 Sandra Gilbert and Susan Gubar, *The Mad Woman in the Attic: The Woman Writer and Nineteenth-Century Literary Imagination* (New Haven: Yale University Press, 1979).

44 Ghosh, 'Charlotte Brontë: A Re-Assessment', p. 211.

45 Ratna Nandi (Guha Mustaphi), 'Narrativizing Female Consciousness: Re-Reading the Fictional Texts of the Brontë Sisters' (doctoral thesis, University of Calcutta, 2008), pp. 100 and 107. For further references to gender studies in *Jane Eyre* by Indian scholars, see Jitendra Singh, 'The Novels of Bronte Sisters: A Study in the Theme of Feminism' (doctoral thesis, Chhatrapati Shahu Ji Maharaj University, 2002); Deetimali Barua, 'The Victorian Family: An Analysis of the Role of the Family in the Victorian Novel with Special Reference to the Brontë Sisters' (doctoral thesis, Gauhati

Already in 1957, the Indian-Canadian scholar Devendra P. Varma observed that Brontë's idea of the hidden mad wife seems to have been borrowed from a comparable motif in Ann Radcliffe's gothic novel *A Sicilian Romance* (1790).[46] It needs to be remarked that the ubiquitous character of the mad wife in all seven adaptations speaks to the power of the ancient Indian trope of female madness present throughout centuries of classical Indian literature, with its prototype in Princess Ambā from the ancient Hindu epic *Mahābhārata*.[47] This most famous scorned mad woman in the Indian literary tradition is the quintessential figure of female resistance to male repression and ultimate self-sacrifice on the altar of revenge. When the love and life of Princess Ambā have been ruined after a violent intervention by the male anti-hero Bhīṣma, Ambā wanders the earth in a state of madness and pursues extreme religious renunciation in search of vengeance. By committing religious suicide, she returns in a reincarnation as Śikhaṇḍin, becoming an instrument for the hero Arjuna to slay Bhīṣma on the epic battlefield of Kurukṣetra. In contrast, in the context of Indian Buddhist narratives, the thread of madness is a common literary device allowing female protagonists to escape from the clutches of unwanted arranged marriages and pursue alternative lifestyles as religious mendicants for the sake of enlightenment, exemplified by the female Buddhist saint Lakṣmī in the twelfth-century biography by Abhayadattaśrī. Feigning insanity, Princess Lakṣmī deters her suitor from marrying her and thereby avoids a marriage with an unvirtuous

University, 2006); Shukla Banerjee, 'Portrait of Women in the Novels of Charlotte Brontë' (doctoral thesis, Pt. Ravishankar Shukla University, 2014); Deepika Elizabeth, 'Re-Visioning Women's Writing: A Study of George Eliot's The Mill on the Floss and Charlotte Brontë's Jane Eyre' (doctoral thesis, University of Madras, 2015); Ahmed Taher Abdu Nagi, 'Victorian Gentlemen and the Concept of Masculinity in the Novels of Charlotte Bronte and Jane Austen' (doctoral thesis, Swami Ramanand Teerth Marathwada University, 2016); and Abhinav Bhardwaj, 'Echoes of *Jane Eyre* in the Novels of Margaret Atwood', *Contemporary Literary Review India*, 7.2 (2020), 1–11. For a broad treatment of *Jane Eyre* by an Indian scholar, see S. N. Singh, *Charlotte Bronte: A Thematic Study of Her Novels* (Delhi: Mittal Publications, 1987).

46 See Devendra P. Varma, *The Gothic Flame, being a History of the Gothic Novel in England: Its Origins, Efflorescence, Disintegration, and Residuary Influences* (London: Arthur Barker, 1957), p. 200.

47 On the figure of Ambā, see Lavanya Vemsani, *Feminine Journeys of the Mahabharata: Hindu Women in History, Text, and Practice* (Cham, Switzerland: Palgrave Macmillan, 2021), pp. 175–92.

prince, who through his indulgence in hunting breaks the fundamental Buddhist ethic of non-violence.[48]

While the relocation of *Jane Eyre* to India in the literary and cinematographic adaptations may evoke such classic Indian literary portrayals of insanity, it at the same time eradicates the overt colonial implications of madness first pointed out by the Indian-American Gayatri Chakravorty Spivak in her highly influential postcolonial critique of the English novel.[49] Spivak views Brontë's Bertha as involving the construction of a self-immolating colonial subject who had to kill herself for the glorification of the coloniser's social mission, thereby allowing Jane to realise her role as 'the feminist individualist heroine of British fiction'.[50] She notes that the underlying imperialistic staging of Bertha's role remains obscure unless the reader is familiar with the British colonialist history of legal manipulation surrounding the former Hindu practice of widow self-immolation.[51] In 1829, eighteen years prior to the publication of Brontë's *Jane Eyre*, following a long political campaign in both Britain and India, the British government in India banned widow self-immolation, which Spivak maintains was a law imposed primarily for the sake of the colonial government to mandate itself as the protector of the Indian people against themselves.[52]

Spivak's postcolonial critique has been bolstered by the Bangladeshi feminist scholar Firdous Azim.[53] Azim extends Spivak's earlier appraisal by asserting that the rise of the entire Western genre of the novel served an outright imperialistic purpose aimed at silencing and excluding women as well as persons of colour. Her analysis of *Jane Eyre* is — like Spivak's — centred on the figure of Bertha Mason as

48 On Lakṣmī's feigned insanity, see Ulrich Timme Kragh, 'Appropriation and Assertion of the Female Self: Materials for the Study of the Female Tantric Master Lakṣmī of Uḍḍiyāna', *Journal of Feminist Studies in Religion*, 27 (2011), 85–108 (pp. 92–94).

49 Gayatri Chakravorty Spivak, 'Three Women's Texts and a Critique of Imperialism', *Critical Inquiry*, 12 (1985), 243–61.

50 Spivak, 'Three Women's Texts', p. 251.

51 For the Indian practice of *satī* (widow self-immolation), see Julia Leslie, 'Suttee or *Satī*: Victim or Victor', in *Roles and Rituals for Hindu Women*, ed. by Julia Leslie (Rutherford: Fairleigh Dickinson University Press, 1991), pp. 175–91.

52 Spivak, 'Three Women's Texts', p. 259.

53 Firdous Azim, *The Colonial Rise of the Novel: From Aphra Behn to Charlotte Bronte* (London: Routledge, 1993).

Jane's antithesis, her binary Other, who in a colonialist sense embodies attributes of savagery, madness, and sexuality.[54]

In the adaptations, strikingly the Indian Bertha characters do not hail from the West Indies and their stories do not entail the same imperialist subtext as found in Brontë's work. Hence, the postcolonial critiques of the English novel raised by Spivak and Azim cannot be transferred outright to these adaptations. Nevertheless, the psychological antithesis between Bertha and Jane remains present throughout all the adaptations, magnifying the image of the mad wives' rage proportionately as the Jane characters diminish in independence and strength in the later Indian film adaptations.

An issue closely related to the theme of madness is Brontë's use of literary imagery. In a sophisticated feminist deconstruction of *Jane Eyre*, the Indian scholar Sonia Sarvipour,[55] relying on Elaine Showalter's feminist poetics,[56] argues that the abundant images of dark corridors, locked rooms, and barely contained fires are significant examples of a unique female literary style characterised by recurrent themes of imprisonment, hidden rooms, and fantasies of mobility.[57] She contends that such tropes are suggestive of a thick mist of female repression, which enveloped the lives of Victorian women, and that Brontë's language fundamentally is a masculine form of prose in spite of its frequent use of feminine figuration and imagery. Ultimately, Sarvipour defines this multivalence as a literary mode of unreadability or undecidability, which she argues lies at the very heart of feminist writing.

---

54 Azim, *The Colonial Rise*, pp. 175–83. For further feminist studies on *Jane Eyre* by Indian scholars, see Seema Jauhari, 'Female Self Assertiveness: A Study in the Novels of Charlotte Brontë, Emily Brontë, and George Eliot' (doctoral thesis, Chhatrapati Shahu Ji Maharaj University, 1992); B. Janaki, 'The Variegated Voices: Feminine Consciousness in Selected Novels of Jane Austen, Charlotte Brontë and Anita Brookner' (doctoral thesis, Dayalbagh Educational Institute, 2008); and Sharmita Lahiri, 'Jane Eyre: A Unique Vision of Feminism', *The Atlantic Literary Review* (New Delhi), 12 (2014), 15–26.

55 Sonia Sarvipour, 'Aspects of Feminism in the Bronte Sisters' Novels' (doctoral thesis, Savitribai Phule Pune University, 2011).

56 See Elaine Showalter, *A Literature of Their Own: British Women Novelists from Brontë to Lessing* (Princeton: Princeton University Press, 1977).

57 On the related gothic interpretations of such elements, see Varma, *The Gothic Flame*, p. 200; Brian M. Mendonca, 'Irrationality in the Novels of Ann Radcliffe and Charlotte Brontë' (doctoral thesis, Central Institute of English and Foreign Languages, 1997); and Aparajita Hazra, 'Elements of the Gothic in the Brontes' (doctoral thesis, University of Burdwan, 2004).

The diverse ways in which the Bertha character has been portrayed in the popular adaptations versus how she has been conceived of in the scholarly reception in India illustrates that there exists a dialectic tension between the adaptations within the popular reception and the scholarly critiques within the academic debate. The popular adaptations voice the narratives in Indian vernaculars and Indianize the characters, whereas every academic study limits the story to its English source text, discussing it primarily in the framework of Western discourse.[58] The opposition between the popular and academic forms of reception is embedded in a particular politics of language and audience, whereby Indian scholars, writing for an educated English readership, are primarily in dialogue with research by non-Indian scholars, giving minimal cross-reference to the work by their Indian academic peers. They deliberate, acquiesce, or expostulate without heeding the prevailing adaptations and translations of *Jane Eyre* in the Indian regional languages.

The politics of language and audience can only be understood against the backdrop of the nature of the broader status of the English language, the circulation of English classics, and their presence in higher education in India. For to read a literary classic directly in English signals on the subcontinent a cosmopolitan standing, and accordingly every Indian city has a number of well-stocked bookstores specialising in English literature, such as the store chains *Crossword Bookstore* or *Sapna Book House*, each of which is sure to have a copy of *Jane Eyre* in its section of English classics. The considerable acclaim received today by the major works of nineteenth-century English literature imported to India is closely linked with the high social status and widespread use of the English language throughout South Asia in spite of, as well as because of, the language's colonial history on the subcontinent. In short, English 'is the "master language" of the urban *nouveaux riches*'.[59] The English language functions governmentally and often practically as an unofficial *lingua franca* between the different speakers of the twenty-two Indian languages officially endorsed in the Indian Constitution, for which reason learning English

58 For a critical analysis of Brontë's *Jane Eyre* read from the perspective of an Indian-American heritage student, see Sangeeta Parashar, '"Not Fit to Associate with Me": Contradictions of Race, Class, and Gender in Charlotte Brontë's Jane Eyre' (master's thesis, Iowa State University, 1999).

59 Robert J. Zydenbos, *A Manual of Modern Kannada* (Heidelberg: Cross-Asia Ebooks, 2020), p. xv.

and achieving cultivation in English literature are of economic and cultural importance both to the state and the individual.

As evidenced in the Indian system of education, an extraordinary seventeen percent of Indian children attend schools where English is the main medium of instruction, while the remaining pupils receive five to ten English language classes per week within the frame of a primary school education in Hindi (49%) or other Indian regional language (33%).[60] English literature and its classics are indisputably valuable to Indians, although this statement must be read with the caveat in mind that India has a highly prolific production of Indian English literature involving its own English classics, to mention but a few, the writings by the Indian poets and novelists Mulk Raj Anand (1905–2004), R. K. Narayan (1906–2001), Raja Rao (1908–2006), A. Salman Rushdie (b. 1947), Vikram Seth (b. 1952), Amitav Ghosh (b. 1956), S. Arundhati Roy (b. 1961), and Kiran Desai (b. 1971). The British Victorian literature, to which *Jane Eyre* belongs, is without doubt just one among several forms of English literary classics in India.

The popularity of *Jane Eyre* as an English classic throughout India is demonstrated by its wide distribution and presence in school curricula. Aside from the many print and e-book English editions available on the continent from large multinational publishers, such as Penguin, HarperCollins, and Macmillan India, the novel has frequently been reprinted in English by a number of smaller domestic Indian publishers, including Atlantic Publishers and Distributors (New Delhi), Om Books (Hyderabad), Maple Press (Noida), Rupa Publications (New Delhi), Rama Brothers India (New Delhi), and Gyan Publishing House (New Delhi). Indian publishers have likewise brought out several abridged English versions of the novel, some of them illustrated, mainly intended for the children and student book market, e.g., those published by S. Chand Publishing (New Delhi) as part of their 'Great Stories in Easy English' series, Har-Anand Publications (New Delhi), and Om Kidz Books (Hyderabad) in their 'Om Illustrated Classics' series.

---

60 Human Resource Development Ministry, answer to parliament, 2016. The percentage of English-medium schools differs widely from state to state within the Indian federation. The states with the highest proportion of English-medium schools are Jammu-Kashmir (99.9%), Kerala (49.2%), Delhi (48.6%), Andhra Pradesh (44.1%), and Tamil Nadu (40.6%); see *The Times of India*, September 28, 2015, 'Children Attending English-Medium Schools: 2008–14'.

In the system of higher education, *Jane Eyre* appears frequently on the curricula of English departments at many Indian universities. The book is a standard component of the undergraduate course 'Analysis of English Literature', where it is read alongside Charles Dickens' *Great Expectations* (1861), D. H. Lawrence's *Sons and Lovers* (1913), and William Golding's *The Lord of the Flies* (1954), albeit not always in its entirety and typically in the form of excerpts.[61]

In spite of the omnipresence of the novel in English throughout India and its primary importance to Indian academic discourse, it could be argued that the cinematographic adaptations in Indian vernaculars supersede the permeability of *Jane Eyre* across social strata, because an English-clad Jane stays perpetually aloof and exotic. While the English *Jane Eyre* is widespread, it is no match for the familiarity with the story effected by the box-office hits of the Indian film adaptations delivered in several major regional languages. Adaptation is thus the literary form that most eminently captures acculturation. *Jane Eyre* in India is accordingly not exclusively a literary classic in English or an Indian translation, but through its literary and cinematographic adaptations the Jane character has metamorphosed from a British governess to a polyglot South Asian maiden. The creative license exercised by the novelists and filmmakers to adjust and transform the story whilst retaining the recognizability of the original comprises the hallmark of these adaptations.

Jane Eyre in *Anuvād*: The Substance of Janeeyreness

Translation is, in a sense, the opposite of adaptation. While adaptation stands out through a difference to the original due to its distinctive feature of modifying the plot, the setting, or the medium, translation has conventionally been qualified by an expectation to reproduce the source text so adequately that the text itself becomes fully meaningful in the target language, whether it be an interlingual or intralingual

61 Salma Ahad, 'English Studies in Kashmir: An Examination of the Relationship between Undergraduate English Courses and Literary Studies in English at the M. A. Level' (doctoral thesis, University of Kashmir, 2002), pp. 86 and 90. For a broader postcolonial critique of English literary education in India, see Vishwanathan Guari, *Masks of Conquest: Literary Study and British Rule in India* (Oxford: Oxford University Press, 1989).

rendering.[62] This understanding of translation, which has been termed semantic equivalence, remains common to contemporary academic traditions across the West and India, despite the critique levelled against the idea in more recent Translation Studies.[63]

As will be argued, defining translation by equivalence, as opposed to the modification that is characteristic of adaptation, accidentally hides and suppresses many thriving forms of South Asian translational performativity. In light of this, to be able to discern the distinct qualities of the multifarious Indian translations of *Jane Eyre* presented below, it is first necessary to digress into the historical forms of Indian translational practices. Using these as a frame, it will be possible to arrive at a suitable definition of translation that may uncover a unique episteme of literary criticism for Indian translation theory.

At its very foundation, Indian civilisation is not culturally anchored in interlingual translation, unlike its European counterpart. In Europe, intellectual cultivation has been built on the edifice of translation, at first through Latin translations of the ancient Greek texts during the Roman Empire and subsequently through the Latin and later vernacular translations of the Bible.[64] Europe — with its borrowed cultural roots transplanted through careful translation from Greek, Hebrew, Aramaic, Syriac, and Arabic — turned translation into such an art of significance and exactitude that it could unequivocally be

---

62 The term source text refers to the original work that the translation is intended to represent, whereas the term target language denotes the language into which the translation renders the text. For the contrasting terms interlingual and intralingual, see Roman Jakobson's seminal article 'On Linguistic Aspects of Translation', in *On Translation*, ed. by Reuben A. Brower *et al.* (Cambridge, MA: Harvard University Press, 1959), pp. 232–39 (p. 233).

63 The term semantic equivalence derives from Jakobson, 'On Linguistic Aspects', pp. 233ff. For critiques of translation interpreted as equivalence, see, for instance, the notion of 'translingual practice' in the broader phenomenon of cross-cultural translation discussed by Lydia H. Liu in *Translingual Practice: Literature, National Culture, and Translated Modernity: China, 1900–1937* (Stanford: Stanford University Press, 1995); the issue of incommensurability and the notion of 'the schema of co-figuration' in Naoki Sakai, 'Translation', in *Theory, Culture & Society*, 23 (2006), 71–86; the critique of the terms 'original' and 'source text', along with the view of translation as interpretive iteration in Karen Emmerich, *Literary Translation and the Making of Originals* (New York: Bloombury, 2017); and the prismatic approach to translation studies with its view of translation as involving change and difference presented in Matthew Reynolds (ed.), *Prismatic Translation* (Cambridge: Legenda, 2019).

64 For the formative role of translation in the Roman Empire, see Denis Feeney, *Beyond Greek: The Beginnings of Latin Literature* (Cambridge, MA: Harvard University Press, 2016).

considered a keystone in the historical formation of Europe's many vernacular political and cultural identities, in the building of the modern European nation states, and in the wider European colonialism across the globe.[65] The Christian Protestant Reformation of the early sixteenth century, for instance, coincided with the Latin and German Bible translations by Erasmus of Rotterdam and Martin Luther,[66] while the Early Modern English language itself often is defined as commencing in 1611 with the printing of the *King James Bible*, a new English translation of the Christian scripture. Even the most recent global technological advances in digital machine translation in the twenty-first century have had their quantitative linguistic basis in the exactitude of the digital data corpus of the documents translated by the administrations of the European Union and the United Nations.

There is absolutely no comparable instance prior to modernity of any major text translated interlingually into an Indian language having a similar cultural impact on India, at least not if translation is understood narrowly as involving 'equivalence' in the sense in which translation was defined in 1959 by the influential Russian-American linguist Roman Jakobson, namely as a process of substituting linguistic codes entailing 'two equivalent messages in two different codes'.[67]

There are, however, a few minor texts that were imported from outside of India in premodernity that continue to be influential. These include Persian and Arabic texts that were translated into Sanskrit and Indian vernaculars from the sixteenth century onwards, mostly into the South Indian Dakanī and Tamil languages as well as the Northeast Indian Middle Bengali language, as represented by the Bengali poets Ālāol ('Alāwal, 1607–1673) and Abdul Hakim ('Abd al-Ḥakīm, c.1600-c.1670).[68] The translations are literal in nature and, anachronistically,

65 On the intricate relations between language, nation, colony, and translation, see Antoine Berman, *L'épreuve de l'étranger: Culture et traduction dans l'Allemande romantique* (Paris: Gallimard, 1984), pp. 250–78; Naoki Sakai, *Translation and Subjectivity: On Japan and Cultural Nationalism* (Minneapolis: University of Minnesota Press, 1997); Susan Bassnett and Harish Trivedi (eds.), *Post-Colonial Translation: Theory and Practice* (London: Routledge, 1999); and Matthew Reynolds, *Translation: A Very Short Introduction* (Oxford: Oxford University Press, 2016), pp. 21–23.

66 See Peter Mack, *A History of Renaissance Rhetoric 1380–1620* (Oxford: Oxford University Press, 2011), p. 76.

67 Jakobson, 'On Linguistic Aspects', p. 233.

68 For an example of a Persian text translated into Sanskrit, see the Kashmiri court-poet Śrīvara's (fifteenth to sixteenth centuries) Sanskrit translation *Kathākautuka* of the Persian narrative poem *Yūsuf u Zulaykhā* composed

this trait of semantic equivalence qualifies them as falling within the ambit of the modern Indian term *anuvād* (अनुवाद translation), which was introduced into Hindi in the late nineteenth century as a response to the English concept of translation.[69] This is significant, because these seventeenth-century translations predate the introduction of the modern translational practices promulgated by Christian missionaries and European colonialists from the eighteenth century onwards.

It is worth mentioning that, parallel to these developments, in India itself other translations marked by semantic equivalence sprang up in the non-Islamic Jain communities in Western India, represented by poets such as Banārsidās of Agra (1587-c.1643) and the contemporary Hemrāj Paṇḍe, who translated entire texts from Sanskrit into Brajbhāṣā, an early form of the Hindi language that evolved from

---

by ʻAbd al-Raḥmān Jāmī (1414–1492 CE) in Luther Obrock, ʻŚrīvara's *Kathākautuka*: Cosmology, Translation, and the Life of a Text in Sultanate Kashmir', in *Jāmī in Regional Contexts: The Reception of ʻAbd al-Raḥmān Jāmī's Works in the Islamicate World, ca. 9th/15th-14th/20th Century*, ed. by Thibaut d'Hubert and Alexandre Papas (Leiden: Brill, 2019), pp. 752–76. On Dakanī literature, adaptation, and translation, see David John Matthews, ʻDakanī Language and Literature: 1500–1700 A. D.' (doctoral thesis, School of Oriental and African Studies, University of London, 1976), pp. 99–101, 125, 137–39, 157–58, 257, and 277. On a sixteenth-century translation from Persian into Tamil of the *Book of One Thousand Questions of Abdullah ibn Salam* (*Kitāb Masā'il Sayyidī ʻAbdallāh Bin Salām*), see Ronit Ricci, *Islam Translated: Literature, Conversion, and the Arab Cosmopolis of South and Southeast Asia* (Chicago: The University of Chicago Press, 2011), pp. 98–128. For the Middle Bengali translations by Ālāol and ʻAbd al-Ḥakīm, see the two *lemmata* by Thibaut d'Hubert in the *Encyclopedia of Islam*, 3rd edn, ed. by K. Fleet, G. Krämer, D. Matringe, J. Nawas, and E. Robson, III (Leiden: Brill, 2013). For Hindi translations of Persian medical works during the late seventeenth to early eighteenth centuries, see Peter G. Friedlander, ʻBefore Translation?', in *Translation in Asia: Theories, Practices, Histories*, ed. by Ronit Ricci and Jan van der Putten (Manchester: St Jerome Publishing, 2011), pp. 45–56 (pp. 52–54). For a brief mention of the known cases of translations from Arabic into Persian produced on the Indian subcontinent, see Ricci, *Islam Translated*, p. 39. The authors wish to thank Prof. Thibaut d'Hubert at the University of Chicago and Prof. Sunil Sharma at Boston University for their advice on the cases of Persian and Arabic translations into Indian languages.

69 For the nineteenth-century history of *anuvād*, see Friedlander, ʻBefore Translation?', pp. 54–55. Friedlander demonstrates that the Hindi word *anuvād* is attested in the sense of ʻtranslation' in the writings of the author and Hindi language reformer Bharatendu Hariścandra (1850–1885) during the early 1870s. However, as also confirmed by Friedlander (p. 55), an exhaustive and precise determination of when the Sanskrit term *anuvāda* first became appropriated as the modern Indian term for English ʻtranslation' is still wanting.

Prakrit and Apabhramsha.[70] As for foreign major works of high cultural impact, it was first in modernity that they were transmitted into Indian languages. In this regard, the Bible translated into Tamil in 1706 and the Qur'an translated into Bengali in 1886 and then into Urdu in 1902 stand out.

While, in premodern times, there was no import of foreign cultures into Indian educational and intellectual institutions through interlingual translation, there nevertheless was a historic opposite movement of translation flowing out of India having far-reaching impact. From the second to the fifteenth centuries, interlingual translation of texts for the export of Indian religions and literature was prevalent, with numerous works written in Sanskrit and other Indian languages being translated into foreign languages. Thousands of Indian Buddhist scriptures and commentaries were translated into East and Inner Asian languages, in particular Chinese and Tibetan.[71] Moreover, from the sixth century onwards, a number of literary and religious works were translated into Persian and Arabic, including story collections, poems, epics, and Hindu mystical works.[72]

70 See John E. Cort, 'Making It Vernacular in Agra: The Practice of Translation by Seventeenth-Century Jains', in *Tellings and Texts: Music, Literature and Performance in North India*, ed. by Francesca Orsini and Katherine Butler Schofield (Cambridge: Open Book Publishers, 2015), pp. 61–105 (pp. 77–88).

71 On the nature and history of translation of Indian Buddhist texts into Chinese, see Jan Nattier, *A Guide to the Earliest Buddhist Translations: Texts from Eastern Han 東漢 and Three Kingdoms 三國 Periods* (Tokyo: The International Research Institute for Advanced Buddhology, Soka University, 2008). On some of the complexities of the translation concept in relation to the Chinese Buddhist canonical texts, see Tōru Funayama, 'Masquerading as Translation: Examples of Chinese Lectures by Indian Scholar-Monks in the Six Dynasties Period', *Asia Major*, 19 (2006), 39–55. On the translation of Indian texts into Tibetan, see Cristina Scherrer-Schaub, 'Translation, Transmission, Tradition: Suggestions from Ninth-Century Tibet', *Journal of Indian Philosophy*, 27 (1999), 67–77.

72 On the sixth-century Persian translation of the Sanskrit *Pañcatantra* collection of edifying fables and its subsequent Arabic and Syriac versions, see McComas Taylor, *The Fall of the Indigo Jackal: The Discourse of Division and Pūrṇabhadra's Pañcatantra* (Albany: State University of New York Press, 2007), pp. 3–6. On al-Bīrūnī's (973-c.1050 CE) Arabic translation of Patañjali's mystic Hindu text *Yogasūtra*, see Shlomo Pines and Tuvia Gelblum, 'Al-Bīrūnī's Arabic Version of Patañjali's *Yogasūtra*: A Translation of his First Chapter and a Comparison with Related Sanskrit Texts', *Bulletin of the School of Oriental and African Studies*, 29 (1966), 302–25, with follow-up articles covering chs 2–4 in vols 40 (1977), 46 (1983), and 52 (1989) of the same journal.

Although Indian scholars often supervised the translation endeavours from Indian into foreign languages as presiding experts, these specialists never felt compelled to translate non-Indian works into the classical languages of South Asia. In fact, the dominant literary form of translation from the very inception of Indian literature has always been intralingual. Its embodiment is exegesis entailing interpretation and commentarial reiteration, as represented by the exegetic device of *anuvāda* (अनुवाद repetition, paraphrase). Etymologically, Sanskrit *anuvāda* consists of two distinct morphemes *anu* (अनु after) and *vāda* (वाद speech), and has a specific technical application in the context of a Sanskrit commentarial literary method of intralingual rewriting and supplementing of an earlier stated *vidhi* (विधि rule) or *pakṣa* (पक्ष assertion) within the one language of Sanskrit.[73] For instance, a seventh-century commentator makes use of *anuvāda* in the sense of reiterating an opponent's position, in Sanskrit *parapakṣānuvāda* (परपक्षानुवाद reiteration of others' position), in a scholastic debate.[74]

Given that the hallmark of intralingual hermeneutics is a non-equivalence between the source and target texts, the early history of Indian translation is marked by a flexible intertextuality that has influenced both the interlingual exchange between the Indian indigenous languages and the degree of semantic equivalence in their literary representations.[75] These translational forms range within the classical spectrum from the non-literal Kannada *varṇaka* (ವರ್ಣಕ retelling) to the word-for-word Sanskrit *chāyā* (छाया shadow), often transferring a text into multiple Indian languages as well as displaying non-linear multitextuality across traditions.

A typical exemplification of an ancient source transmitted interlingually and intertextually is the Prakrit epic *Paümacarẏa* (*The Passage of Padma*). Belonging to a genre of *mahākāvya* (महाकाव्य grand

73 For a brief discussion of the historical Sanskrit background of the term *anuvāda*, see the *lemma* in Theodor Goldstücker, *A Dictionary, Sanskrit and English, Extended and Improved from the Second Edition of the Dictionary of Professor H. H. Wilson with His Sanction and Concurrence* (Berlin: A. Asher & Co., 1856), pp. 102–3.

74 See Anne MacDonald, *In Clear Words: The Prasannapadā, Chapter One*, 2 vols. (Vienna: Verlag der Österreichischen Akademie der Wissenshaften, Philosophisch-Historische Klasse Sitzungsberichte, 863. Band, 2015), I, p. 126 and II, pp. 26–27 (§8).

75 Moreover, Peter G. Friedlander has brought up the closely related problems of defining the terms 'language' and 'literary work' in premodern Indian traditions; see Friedlander, 'Before Translation?', pp. 47–50.

poem, epic), this Jain work has many commonalities with the Hindu epic *Rāmāyaṇa* (*The Course of Rāma*). The first version of the text was composed in an ancient Prakrit vernacular by the Jain monk Vimalasūri around the fifth century CE, entitled *Paümacarẏa* (*The Passage of Padma*). It was then adapted into a Sanskrit version, the *Padmacarita* (*The Passage of Padma*), in the seventh century by Raviṣeṇa. Finally, during the ninth century, the South Indian poet Svayambhūdeva adapted the story under the title *Paümacariu* (*The Passage of Padma*) into the medieval Apabhramsha vernacular, which linguistically was a precursor for Old Hindi. Although the three linguistic versions of the *Paümacarẏa* share the same narrative structure, they are by no means word-for-word translations of semantic equivalence and therefore could be said to belong under the notion of *varṇaka* (retelling).[76]

Another form of *varṇaka* (retelling) is represented in the genre of the scholarly writing of *śāstra* (शास्त्र treatise). Its classic example is the ninth-century text on poetics written in Old Kannada entitled *Kavirājamārga* (*The Royal Road of Poets*) by Śrīvijaya. Being an interlingual and intertextual translation of the major Sanskrit treatise on literary theory *Kāvyādarśa* (*The Mirror of Poetry*), it parallels 230 verses from this late-seventh-century classic by the poetician Daṇḍin while innovating the remaining 302 verses of the text.[77]

Neither of the two texts proclaim themselves as *varṇaka* (retelling), however, there is a medieval epic that specifically identifies itself as such, directly acknowledging its reliance on an earlier work. The case in point is the Old Kannada *Vikramārjunavijaya* written by Pampa

76 For a short comparison of the three texts, see Eva De Clercq, '*Paümacariẏa — Padmacarita — Paümacariu*: The Jain Rāmāyaṇa-Purāṇa', in *Epics, Khilas, and Purāṇas: Continuities and Ruptures*, ed. by Petteri Koskikallio under the general editorship of Mislav Ježić (Zagreb: Croatian Academy of Sciences and Arts, 2005), pp. 597–608, especially the synoptic comparison given in Table 1 of her article.

77 For the *Kavirājamārga* and its dependence on the *Kāvyādarśa*, see the annotated Kannada edition of the *Kavirājamārgam* by M. V. Seetharamaiah, *Śrīnṛpatuṅgadēvānumatamappa Śrīvijayakṛta Kavirājamārgaṃ* (Bengaluru: Kannaḍa Sāhitya Pariṣattu, 2015). For an English translation of the text, see R. V. S. Sundaram and Deven M. Patel, *Kavirājamārgaṃ: The Way of the King of Poets* (New Delhi: Manohar, 2017). For a short outline of other medieval adaptations of Daṇḍin's *Kāvyādarśa* into various Indian languages, see Sheldon Pollock, *The Language of the Gods in the World of Men: Sanskrit, Culture, and Power in Premodern India* (Berkeley: University of California Press, 2006), p. 163.

(902–75 CE), which is a rendering of the Sanskrit epic *Mahābhārata* by Vyāsa. Already at the outset of the poem, Pampa declares:

> No past poet has given a *varṇaka* (retelling) in Kannada of the long story of the *Mahābhārata* in its entirety and without any loss to its structure. In doing so, to fuse poetic description with the story elements, only Pampa is competent.[78]

The author describes his style of writing as a *varṇaka* (retelling) of the *Mahābhārata* as its source text. Pampa's perception of the question of equivalence is encapsulated in one of the poem's verses, wherein he describes himself as 'swimming across the vast and divine ocean of the sage Vyāsa.'[79] It is notable that in spite of telling the story of the Sanskrit *Mahābhārata* in its entirety and maintaining the internal structure of the epic, Pampa shortened the epic down to a mere 1609 verses as compared to the more than 89000 verses of the Sanskrit text. If swimming were to be seen as a trope for fluid translation of non-semantic equivalence, it could be deemed that Pampa's poem is not only a translational adaptation but also a paradigmatic medieval example of an abridgement and, as shall be argued further on, abridgement is a defining characteristic of many of the modern Indian translations of *Jane Eyre*.

Parallel to *varṇaka* (retelling), *chāyā* (shadow) proliferated over the course of the first millennium CE, bringing to the fore word-for-word interlingual translation of smaller textual passages consisting of individual verses or prose sentences from the Prakrit vernaculars into Sanskrit. It was practised especially by Jain exegetes, who were masters of transposing Jain Prakrit scriptures into Sanskrit commentarial writing. *Chāyā* (shadow) could be considered the earliest Indian term for translation.[80] Its usage is limited to commentaries and dramatic

78 Pampa, *Vikramārjunavijaya* (*The Victory of Vikrama Arjuna*), verse 1.11, ed. by T. V. Venkatachala Sastry, *Pampa Sampuṭa: Ādipurāṇa, Vikramārjuna Vijaya* (Hampi: Prasaranga Kannada University, 2006), p. 357. The above English translation of the verse has been adapted from the translation given in C. N. Ramachandran and B. A. Viveka Rai, *Classical Kannada Poetry and Prose: A Reader* (Hampi: Prasaranga Kannada University, 2015), p. 115.

79 Pampa, *Vikramārjunavijaya*, verse 1.13.

80 For some short remarks on Sanskrit *chāyā* translation of Prakrit and Apabhramsha verses, see Pollock, *The Language of the Gods*, pp. 104–5. For general discussion of ancient Indian translation practices, see G. Gopinathan, 'Ancient Indian Theories of Translation: A Reconstruction', in *Beyond the Western Tradition: Essays on Translation outside Standard European Languages*, ed. by Marilyn Gaddis Rose (Binghamton: State University of New

stage writing in Sanskrit, wherein it features as interpolated translation of Prakrit linguistic elements that are of non-Sanskritic provenance.

In the case of a commentary, a Prakrit pericope is first cited in its original form, then furnished with a literal Sanskrit *chāyā* translation, and thereupon expounded in Sanskrit prose. In the case of stage writing, a Prakrit dialogue spoken by either a woman or lower-caste man is first cited in its original form and then furnished with a literal Sanskrit *chāyā* translation. The use of *chāyā* translation, a tradition that has continued to the present day, is necessitated by the fact that the older Prakrit vernacular forms had become linguistically archaic by the middle of the first millennium.[81]

The indicative feature of *chāyā* is its precise equivalence between the Prakrit source text and the Sanskrit translation, obtained through the application of systematic principles of phonetic correspondence and through the faithful reproduction of grammatical and syntactical structures. *Chāyā* positively fulfils the trademarks of the modern definition of translation as 'two equivalent messages in two different codes' with a characteristic leeway for some level of interpretation common to all forms of literal translation.

Dictated by the rather undifferentiated nature of the Prakrit phonetic forms, subtle yet at times considerable interpretative compromises are required because the Sanskrit language is phonetically more elaborate. A conspicuous instance of such a translational interpretation from Prakrit to Sanskrit is the rendering of the Buddhist scriptural term *sutta* (सुत्त sermon) into the Brahmanical literary term *sūtra* (सूत्र् thread, mnemonic formula). Instead of translating the Prakrit

York, 2000), pp. 165–73, and G. Gopinathan, 'Translation, Transcreation and Culture: Theories of Translation in Indian Languages', in *Translating Others*, ed. by Theo Hermans, 2 vols (New York: Routledge, 2014), I, pp. 236–46. A detailed study and history of *chāyā* and other old Indian forms of translation remains a desideratum.

81 While Sanskrit *chāyā* translations appear in the modern printed text editions, it remains an open question to which extent such *chāyā* are attested in medieval manuscript copies. Esposito remarks in her study of several South Indian drama manuscripts in Malayalam script dating from between the fifteenth to twentieth centuries that none of the examined manuscripts contains any *chāyā* of the Prakrit passages, where such would be expected, as they are given in the modern printed editions of the text; see Anna Aurelia Esposito, 'The South Indian Drama Manuscripts', in *Aspects of Manuscript Culture in South India*, ed. by Saraju Rath (Leiden: Brill, 2012), pp. 81–97 (p. 87). A detailed study investigating the attestation of *chāyā* in the older manuscript tradition is a desideratum.

sutta into Sanskrit *sūkta* (सूक्त well-spoken, aphorism), which would likely have been the linguistically correct equivalent, the Buddhist translators selected the Brahmanical Sanskrit term *sūtra* in order to appropriate the prestige of this well-established Brahmanical term. Under the circumstances, a translational decision was made to avoid a rhetorically less compelling Sanskrit word *sūkta*, even though it was phonetically and semantically equal to the Prakrit *sutta*.[82]

It would be remiss to omit mention of the precursors to *chāyā* in the older Indic literature. Verily, the history of writing in India begins with a translation in the year 260 BCE, when the Indian Emperor Aśoka issued an edict incised on a rock in the frontier region of Kandahar, Afghanistan. The edict features a bilingual proclamation in Greek and Aramaic believed to have been a literal translation from a now lost common source text in a Prakrit vernacular.[83]

Later precursors to *chāyā* dating to the first century BCE involve literal translations of Prakrit portions of texts into another Prakrit vernacular or Sanskrit. These include the early Buddhist aphoristic treatise *Dhammapada* (*Words of Dharma*) rendered from the Prakrit Pāli language into the Prakrit Gāndhārī language under the same title and into an enlarged Sanskrit recension entitled *Udānavarga* (*Chapters of Utterances*). The translations share with their source an underlying textual structure and some of the chapter headings and verses.[84]

The above short exposition of the history of translation in premodern India demonstrates a varying degree of equivalence in the classical textual practices of literary transmission within one language or across languages through *anuvāda* (paraphrase), *varṇaka* (retelling), and *chāyā* (shadow). Accordingly, Jakobson's definition for translation would, if applied to the Indian literary heritage, eclipse and consequently reject the premodern translational practices. Although the theory of equivalence has been dislodged in recent scholarship, it reverberates in the proclamations made by some contemporary literary critics, who argue that speaking of translation in premodern

82 See K. R. Norman, *A Philological Approach to Buddhism: The Bukkyō Dendō Kyōkai Lectures 1994* (London: School of Oriental and African Studies, University of London, 1997), pp. 87–88 with further references.

83 See D. D. Kosambi, 'Notes on the Kandahar Edict of Asoka', *Journal of the Economic and Social History of the Orient*, 2 (1959), 204–6.

84 See John Brough, *The Gandhari Dhammapada* (Delhi: Motilal Banarsidass Publishers, 2001).

India 'makes no cultural sense in this world',[85] amounts to 'a non-history' prior to the colonial impact in the nineteenth century,[86] or requires demoting premodern Indian translation to transcreation.[87] In contrast, it could be argued that the classical Indian intertextual processes fall well within the bounds of the etymological configuration of the classical Latin notions of *translatio* (carrying across), *transferre* (transfer), and *vertere* (turning) of a text,[88] whereby the European metaphor of semantic movement is echoed in the Indian images of verbal repetition. Among contemporary Indian academics, there are therefore some who have consistently employed the term translation for the premodern period also.[89]

Counterintuitively, the classical translational practices of *anuvāda* (paraphrase), *varṇaka* (retelling), and *chāyā* (shadow) have not abated in modern India and exist side by side with the new forms of interlingual translation that became commonplace in British colonial India. By the nineteenth century, numerous translations of European and non-European works were produced in all Indian languages and

85 Pollock, *The Language of the Gods*, pp. 344–45.

86 Harish Trivedi, 'In Our Own Time, on Our Own Terms: "Translation" in India', in *Translating Others*, ed. by Theo Hermans, 2 vols (New York: Routledge, 2014), I, pp. 102–19 (p. 103), and 'Translation in India: A Curious History', in *The Book Review* (New Delhi), 42.2 (2018). For Trivedi's earlier notion of an 'older pre-colonial translational practice in India', cf. Susan Bassnett and Harish Trivedi, 'Introduction: Of Colonies, cannibals and vernaculars', in *Post-Colonial Translation: Theory and Practice*, ed. by Susan Bassnett and Harish Trivedi (London: Routledge, 1999), pp. 1–18 (p. 10). For an extended critique of Trivedi's view, see Francesca Orsini, 'Poetic Traffic in a Multilingual Literary Culture: Equivalence, Parallel Aesthetics, and Language-Stretching in North India', in *Prismatic Translation*, ed. by Matthew Reynolds (Oxford: Legenda, 2019), pp. 51–71.

87 For the proposition of the theoretical term 'transcreation', see P. Lal, *Transcreation: Two Essays* (Kolkata: Writers Workshop, 1972).

88 On the common senses of the English word translation and the term's etymological Latin metaphors, see Matthew Reynolds, *The Poetry of Translation: From Chaucer & Petrarch to Homer & Logue* (Oxford: Oxford University Press, 2011), pp. 3–11. Also, see Samuel Johnson's traditional definition of translation as 'the act of turning into another language', in *A Dictionary of the English Language*, 2 vols (London: Knapton, Longman, Hitch, Hawes, Millar, & Dodsley, 1755), II, p. 2086.

89 For instance, Ganesh N. Devy, *In Another Tongue: Essays on Indian English Literature* (Frankfurt am Main: Peter Lang, 1993), pp. 117–18, and T. Vijay Kumar, 'Translation as Negotiation: The Making of Telugu Language and Literature', in *History of Translation in India*, ed. by Tariq Khan *et al.* (Mysuru: National Translation Mission, Central Institute of Indian Languages, 2017), pp. 13–32 (p. 19).

copious translations between the different Indian regional languages themselves began to flourish across the continent initiating the era of modern translational practices alongside scholarly methods of philology.[90]

Post-independence India has become home to new sophisticated paradigms of semantic equivalence, fusing traditional forms of linguistic sciences with modern forms of vernacular textualities. Innovative efforts to produce modern literal translations of classical Indian works have drawn on indigenous reading practices to balance the subjectivity of translation with the objectivity of grammatical scrutiny. It suffices to mention the large body of work by the contemporary Rajasthani scholar Kamal Chand Sogani employing what is known as the *samjhane kī Sogāṇī paddhati* (समझने की सोगाणी पद्धति Sogāṇī Comprehension Method) of *vyākarṇātmak anuvād* (व्याकरणात्मक अनुवाद grammatical translation).[91]

It is in this ambience that the modern Hindi concept of *anuvād* (translation) was coined and persists as a household term into the twentieth and twenty-first centuries in the complex literary landscape of India, and it is in this sense that the Indian translations of *Jane Eyre* are referred to as *anuvād* (translations).[92]

---

90 For the emergence of modern translation practices in colonial India, see, e.g., the study of Odia translation in nineteenth-century Orissa by Ramesh C. Malik and Panchanan Mohanty, 'History of Odia Translations (1803–1936): A Bottom-up Approach', in *History of Translation in India*, ed. by Tariq Khan *et al.* (Mysuru: National Translation Mission, Central Institute of Indian Languages, 2017), pp. 33–100, and the study of Marathi translation in nineteenth-century Maharashtra by Maya Pandit, 'History of Translation Culture in Nineteenth Century Maharashtra: An Exercise in Colonial Cultural Politics', in *History of Translation in India*, ed. by Tariq Khan *et al.* (Mysuru: National Translation Mission, Central Institute of Indian Languages, 2017), pp. 135–59. For a theoretical discussion of translation in India with a focus on Bengali literature, see Sukanta Chaudhuri, *Translation and Understanding* (New Delhi: Oxford University Press, 1999).

91 See, for example, Kamal Cand Sogāṇī and Śakuntalā Jain, *Ācārya Kundkund-racit Samayasār*, 5 vols. (Jaipur: Apabhraṃśa Sāhitya Akādamī, 2015–2016). This translation into Hindi of Kundakunda's Prakrit work *Samayasāra*, dated to the early first millennium, parses with precision the entire work through a *vyākarṇik viśleṣaṇ* (व्याकरणिक विश्लेषण grammatical analysis), transforms the meter into prose through the method of *anvay* (अन्वय reiteration), and creates an exact translation relying on an approach of *vyākarṇātmak anuvād* (व्याकरणात्मक अनुवाद grammatical translation).

92 *Anuvād* is the most common word for translation in the many different Indian regional languages. The writing of the Hindi word is identical to its Sanskrit ancestor in the Devanāgarī script. Other Indian words for translation include,

The below examination of the numerous *anuvād* (translations) of *Jane Eyre* into Indian *bhāṣā* (भाषा vernaculars) accordingly reveals a plethora of underground renditions of the literary work that stubbornly resist the superimposition of academic universalising definitions onto their proliferating *praxis*. The publications will be reviewed in chronological order in terms of their geographical, linguistic, and bibliographical distinctions. Through considering their varying length and degree of abridgement, through identifying their paratextual self-proclamations as translations or other textual forms, and through unpacking their modes of acknowledgement of the original novel and its author, it is hoped to reach a conclusion as to their translational status.

Following the period of the six decades of Indian *Jane Eyre* adaptations bracketed by the appearance of the Bengali novel *Sarlā* in 1914 and the release of the Telugu film *Śānti Nilayam* in 1972, the late 1970s witnessed the dawn of the era of Indian *Jane Eyre* translations. Only a single translation into Tamil had been produced earlier in the 1950s. To date, at least nineteen translations of *Jane Eyre* into nine South Asian languages have been published throughout India, Bangladesh, and Nepal: Tamil (1953), Bengali (1977, 1990, 1991, 2006, 2010, 2011, 2018, 2019), Punjabi (1981), Malayalam (1983, 2020), Gujarati (1993, 2009), Nepali (1997), Assamese (1999, 2014), Hindi (2002), and Kannada (2014).

The very first translation of *Jane Eyre* into an Indian language was published in 1953 by the Tirunelvēlit Te<u>n</u><u>n</u>intiya Caiva-cittānta Nū<u>r</u>patippuk Ka<u>l</u>akam (திருநெல்வேலித் தென்னிந்திய சைவசித்தாந்த நூற்பதிப்புக் கழகம் The South India Saiva Siddhanta Publishing Society of Tirunelveli) in the South Indian city of Tirunelveli, Tamil Nadu. It is a translation into Tamil language bearing the title *Jē<u>n</u> Ayar* (ஜேன் அயர் *Jane Eyre*). The translator is given as Kācināta Piḷḷai Appātturai (காசிநாத பிள்ளை அப்பாத்துரை, 1907–1989). The book consists of 110 pages. A slightly enlarged reprint in 143 pages was brought out under the title *Jē<u>n</u> Ayar: Ulakap puka<u>l</u> pe<u>r</u><u>r</u>a nāval* (ஜேன் அயர்: உலகப் புகழ் பெற்ற நாவல் *Jane Eyre: A World-Renowned Novel*) in 2003 by the publishing house Cāratā Māṇikkam Patippakam (சாரதா மாணிக்கம் பதிப்பகம்) in

inter alia, Hindi *rūpāntar* (रूपांतर), *bhāṣāntar* (भाषांतर), *svakaraṇ* (स्वकरण), Urdu *tarjuma* (ترجمہ), Tamil *mo<u>l</u>ipeyarppu* (மொழிபெயர்ப்பு), and Malayalam *vivarttanaṃ* (വിവർത്തനം).

Chennai, Tamil Nadu. The translator's name is given in the reprint as Kā Appātturaiyār (கா அப்பாத்துரையார்).

The second translation was issued in 1977 in Dhaka, Bangladesh, by the publishing house Muktadhārā (মুক্তধারা). Entitled *Jen Āẏār* (জেন আয়ার *Jane Eyre*), it was translated into Bengali by Surāiyā Ākhtār Begam (সুরাইয়া আখতার বেগম) in merely 43 pages.[93]

The third translation appeared four years later in 1981. It was rendered into the Punjabi language in the North-Western Indian state of Punjab under the title *Sarvetam viśva mārit Jen Āir* (ਸਰਵੇਤਮ ਵਿਸ਼ਵ ਮਾਰਿਤ ਜੇਨ ਆਇਰ *The World-Renowned Jane Eyre*) and was printed in 2000 copies by the Bhāṣā Vibhāg (ਭਾਸ਼ਾ ਵਿਭਾਗ Language Department) in the city of Patiala, Punjab. The book's front matter lists Charlotte Brontë as the *mūl lekhak* (ਮੂਲ ਲੇਖਕ original author) and the *anuvādak* (ਅਨੁਵਾਦਕ translator) as Kesar Siṅgh Ūberāi (ਕੇਸਰ ਸਿੰਘ ਊਬੇਰਾਇ, 1911–1994), who was a university professor. The precise number of pages of the slim volume is not known.[94]

In 1983, a translation into Malayalam was published in the South Indian state of Kerala under the title *Ṣārlaṟṟ Brōṇṭi: Jeyn Eyar* (ഷാർലറ്റ് ബ്രോൺടി ജെയ്ൻ എയർ *Charlotte Brontë: Jane Eyre*). The volume was published by Ḍi Si Buks (ഡി സി ബുക്സ് D. C. Books) in the city of Kottayam. The front matter characterises it as a *punarākhyānaṃ* (പുനരാഖ്യാനം retelling) that was made by Yōgācārya En Gōvindan Nāyar (യോഗാചാര്യ എൻ ഗോവിന്ദൻ നായർ). The book consists of 151 pages. The latest fourth reprint was published in 2015 by the same press.

Another translation into Bengali language was published in 1990, again released by Muktadhārā in Dhaka, Bangladesh. It is entitled *Jen Āẏār* (জেন আয়ার *Jane Eyre*). The book cover states that the version is *saṃkṣepit o rūpāntarit* (সংক্ষেপিত ও রূপান্তরিত abridged and transformed). The descriptive term *saṃkṣepit* (abridged) can etymologically be broken down into *saṃ* (সং altogether) and *kṣepit* (ক্ষেপিত contracted).

93 The Bengali language is used in Bangladesh as well as in the Indian state of Western Bengal, the capital of which is Kolkata, formerly known as Calcutta. It is remarkable that the majority of *Jane Eyre* translations have appeared in the Bengal region, which coincides with the fact that the very first literary adaptation of *Jane Eyre* from 1914 likewise appeared in Calcutta, Bengal. During colonial times, Calcutta was the cultural and maritime epicentre for British rule.

94 The authors wish to thank Prof. Ronki Ram, the University of Panjab, and Prof. Kuldip Singh, Punjabi University Patiala, for their assistance with obtaining the bibliographical information of the Punjabi translation.

The word *rūpāntarit* is an adjectival form of the noun *rūpāntar* (রূপান্তর rendition). Moreover, the cover states that the book was created by Kabīr Caudhurī (কবীর চৌধুরী, 1923–2011), an award-winning Bangladeshi writer and translator. The volume consists of 50 pages.

A different translation into Bengali was published in Kolkata, India, in 1991 by the publishing house Dev Sāhitya Kuṭīr Prāibheṭ Limiṭeḍ (দেব সাহিত্য কুটীর প্রাইভেট লিমিটেড). It is entitled *Jen Āẏār* (জেন আয়ার *Jane Eyre*) and was translated by Sudhīndranāth Rāhā (সুধীন্দ্রনাথ রাহা, 1897–1986). It has 88 pages.

The first translation into Gujarati was issued in the West Indian state of Gujarat in 1993 by the publishing house Navbhārat Sāhitya Mandir (નવભારત સાહિત્ય મંદિર) in the city of Ahmedabad. The book is entitled *Śārloṭ Bronṭe kṛt Jen Eyar* (શાર્લોટ બ્રોન્ટે કૃત જેન એયર *Jane Eyre written by Charlotte Brontë*), while the front matter adds the English title *Jane Eyre (Novel) by: Charlotte Bronte*. It was translated by Hansā Sī. Paṭel (હંસા સી. પટેલ). It is notable that the book cover names Paṭel as the *anu.*, which stands for *anuvādak* (અનુવાદક translator), while the front matter mentions her as the *bhāvānuvādak* (ભાવાનુવાદક gist translator). Additionally, the front matter informs in English that the book was translated by Paṭel and that the *mūḷ lekhikā* (મૂળ લેખિકા original authoress) is Śārloṭ Bronṭe (શાર્લોટ બ્રોન્ટે Charlotte Brontë). The volume consists of 210 pages. This highly abbreviated Gujarati translation in conjunction with the complete Hindi (2002) and Kannada (2014) translations will be critical to the subsequent synoptic assessment of literalness and abridgement in the Indian reception of *Jane Eyre*.

A translation into Nepali was made by Sairu Rai in 1997, as can be determined from its citation in an article by the Indian literary historian Sudesh Manger.[95]

In 1999, a translation into Assamese was published in the city of Guwahati, Assam, in North-Eastern India by the publishing house Pūrbāñcal Prakāś (পূৰ্বাঞ্চল প্ৰকাশ). The volume is entitled *Jen Āẏār* (জেন আয়াৰ *Jane Eyre*) and was translated by Subhadrā Baruwā (সুভদ্ৰা বৰুৱা). It has 151 pages.

In the year 2002, the first-ever translation into Hindi appeared. It was published by Rājkamal Prakāśan Prāiveṭ Limiṭeḍ (राजकमल प्रकाशन

95 See Sudesh Manger, 'History of English Translations and Its Influence on Nepali Literature', in *History of Translation in India*, ed. by Tariq Khan *et al.* (Mysuru: National Translation Mission, Central Institute of Indian Languages, 2017), pp. 371–412 (p. 391). For further bibliographical detail of the Nepali translation, see the List of Translations at the end of this book.

प्राइवेट लिमिटेड) in New Delhi and is entitled *Jen Āyar* (जेन आयर *Jane Eyre*) with added mention of the author *Śārloṭ Bronṭe* (शार्लोट ब्रॉन्टे Charlotte Brontë). The front matter repeats the title and adds in parenthesis the word *upanyās* (उपन्यास novel). Translated by Vidyā Sinhā (विद्या सिन्हा),[96] who is characterised in the front matter as the *anuvādikā* (अनुवादिका female translator), it consists of 472 pages and was printed in 450 copies. Remarkably, this publication constitutes a fully unabridged and literal translation of the English novel. Only two other Indian publications can claim such status.

Another translation into Bengali was published in 2006 by the publishing house Sebā Prakāśanī (সেবা প্রকাশনী) in Dhaka, Bangladesh. The book is entitled *Kiśor klāsik: Jen Āẏār, Liṭl Uimen, Bhyāniṭi Pheẏār* (কিশোর ক্লাসিক জেন আয়ার লিটল উইমেন ভ্যানিটি ফেয়ার *Teenager Classics: Jane Eyre, Little Women, Vanity Fair*). The book cover states that it is a *rūpāntar* (রূপান্তর rendition) and that it was translated by Kājī Śāhnūr Hosen (কাজী শাহনূর হোসেন). On page five of the book, *Śārlaṭ Branṭi* (শার্লট ব্রনটি Charlotte Brontë) features as the author. The *Jane Eyre* portion of the book is found on pages 5–83. The literary term *rūpāntar* generally means translation and is likely to be taken as such by the Bengali reader. However, here it could have a narrower etymological sense of remaking a text into *antar* (অন্তর another) *rūp* (রূপ form), hinting at a textual practice other than literal translation.

In 2009, a second translation into Gujarati was brought out by Bālvinod Prakāśan (બાલવિનોદ પ્રકાશન), a publishing house for children's books in Ahmedabad, Gujarat. The book is a compilation of Oliver Goldsmith's eighteenth-century novel *The Vicar of Wakefield* and Charlotte Brontë's *Jane Eyre*. Entitled *Veīkphīlḍano bhalo pādrī, Bicārī Anāth Chokarī* (વેઈકફીલ્ડનો ભલો પાદરી, બિચારી અનાથ છોકરી *The Vicar of Wakefield, The Poor Orphan Girl*), it preserves the original title of Goldsmith's novel in translation, while it modifies the title *Jane Eyre* into *The Poor Orphan Girl*. The book cover adds the English subtitle *Jane Eyre: By Charlotte Bronte*, announces that it is a *saṃkṣipt bhāvānuvād* (સંક્ષિપ્ત ભાવાનુવાદ abridged gist translation), and informs the reader that

96 Sinhā (b. 1935) grew up in Motihari, Bihar, and obtained her Ph.D. degree in English literature from Lalit Nārāyaṇ Mithilā University in Darbhanga, Bihar, in 1962. She has been involved in social service for women and children and has worked professionally at various educational institutions. In 1995, she was bestowed the National Teacher Award by the Government of India for her dedicated service in the field of women's education. She is the author of several short stories and poems published in a number of magazines.

it was translated by Manasukh Kākaḍiyā (મનસુખ કાકડિયા). The combined volume consists of 248 pages.

In 2010, a fifth translation into Bengali was released by Pāñjerī Pāblikeśans (পাঞ্জেরী পাবলিকেশন্স Panjeri Publications) in Dhaka, Bangladesh. The book is entitled *Śārlaṭ Branṭi: Jen Āẏār* (শার্লট ব্রন্ট জেন আয়ার *Charlotte Brontë: Jane Eyre*) and was published in the series Pāñjerī Sacitra Kiśor Klāsik Sirij (পাঞ্জেরী সচিত্র কিশোর ক্লাসিক সিরিজ Panjeri Illustrated Teenage Classics Series). The book cover defines the book as a *rūpāntar* (রূপান্তর rendition) made by Dhrub Nīl (ধ্রুব নীল), a writer of numerous children's books. It consists of 168 pages and contains hand-drawn illustrations.

A sixth translation into Bengali was made in 2011 by the publishing house Phrenḍs Buk Karṇār (ফ্রেন্ডস্ বুক কর্ণার Friends Book Corner) in Dhaka, Bangladesh, under the title *Śārlaṭ Branṭi: Jen Āẏār* (শার্লট ব্রন্টি জেন আয়ার *Charlotte Brontë: Jane Eyre*). The cover states that the *anubād* (অনুবাদ translation)[97] was made by Khurram Hosāhin (খুররম হোসাইন). The volume amounts to 138 pages.

The year 2014 saw the release of the sole translation of *Jane Eyre* into Kannada to date. It was published by Tēju Pablikēṣans (ತೇಜು ಪಬ್ಲಿಕೇಷನ್ಸ್ Tēju Publications) in Bengaluru, Karnataka, and is entitled *Jēn Air* (ಜೇನ್ ಏರ್ *Jane Eyre*). The book cover states that the *mūla* (ಮೂಲ original) was composed by Śāleṭ Brāṇṭi (ಶಾಲೆಟ್ ಬ್ರಾಂಟಿ Charlotte Brontë) and that it is a *Kannaḍakke anuvāda* (ಕನ್ನಡಕ್ಕೆ ಅನುವಾದ Kannada translation) made by Śyāmalā Mādhava (ಶ್ಯಾಮಲಾ ಮಾಧವ).[98] The front matter gives the English title *Jane Eyre* (*Charlotte Bronte's English Novel*) and specifies in Kannada *Iṅgliṣ mūla: Śālaṭ Brāṇṭi* (ಇಂಗ್ಲಿಷ್ ಮೂಲ ಶಾಲಟ್ ಬ್ರಾಂಟಿ *English Original: Charlotte Brontë*). It consists of 488 pages and was printed in 1000 copies. This literal translation of *Jane Eyre* is fully unabridged and is the second Indian publication of such status.

97 The Bengali word *anubād* is phonetically equivalent to Hindi *anuvād*.

98 The Mumbai-based Mādhava (b. 1949) grew up in Mangalore, Karnataka, where she graduated from St Agnes College. She published her first poem at the age of eleven and went on to produce numerous stories, memoirs, translations, poems, travelogues, and articles in different magazines and journals. This award-winning translator served as the president of *Śrījan* (Excellent Persons), a forum for women writers in Mumbai. She has distinguished herself through translations into Kannada of Rafia Manzurul Amin's Urdu novel *Ālampanāh* (1994), Margaret Mitchell's English novel *Gone with the Wind* (2004), Mary Shelley's English novel *Frankenstein* (2007), and S. V. Raju's English biography *M. R. Pai: The Story of an Uncommon Man* (2013).

In 2014, a second translation into Assamese appeared. The book is published by Śarāighāṭ Prakāśan (শৰাইঘাট প্ৰকাশন) in Guwahati, Assam, and bears the title *Jen Eẏār* (জেন এয়াৰ *Jane Eyre*) and the subtitle *Śbārlaṭ Branṭir 'Jen Eẏār'ra anubād* (শ্বাৰলট ব্ৰণ্টিৰ 'জেন এয়াৰ'ৰ অনুবাদ Translation of Charlotte Brontë's *Jane Eyre*). The book, which is the second edition, was published in the series *Kāljaẏī Sāhitya* (কালজয়ী সাহিত্য Timeless Literature). It was translated by Junu Mahanta (জুনু মহন্ত) and has 147 pages.

The seventh translation into Bengali was brought out in 2018 by the publishing house Biśbasāhitya Bhaban (বিশ্বসাহিত্য ভবন) in Dhaka, Bangladesh. It is entitled *Śārlaṭ Branṭir pāṭhaknandit o śilpottīrṇa upanyās: Jen Āẏār* (শার্লট ব্রন্টির পাঠকনন্দিত ও শিল্পোত্তীর্ণ উপন্যাস জেন আয়ার *Charlotte Brontë's Delightful and Artistic Novel: Jane Eyre*). The book cover states that it is an *anubād o sampādanāy* (অনুবাদ ও সম্পাদনায় translation and edition) and a *kiśor saṃskaraṇ* (কিশোর সংস্করণ version for teenagers) created by Muhaḥ Jākir Hosen (মুহঃ জাকির হোসেন). It consists of 144 pages.

An eighth translation into Bengali appeared the following year in 2019, published by Uttaraṇ (উত্তরণ) in Dhaka, Bangladesh. The title is *Jen Āẏār* (জেন আয়ার *Jane Eyre*). The cover states that it is a *bhāṣāntar* (ভাষান্তর translation) made by Sālehā Caudhurī (সালেহা চৌধুরী) and that the *mūl* (মূল original) is by *Śārlaṭ Branṭi* (শার্লট ব্রন্টি *Charlotte Brontë*). It has 128 pages.

Finally, in 2020 there appeared a second translation into Malayalam language by Saikataṃ Buks (സൈകതം ബുക്സ് Saikatham Books) in the South Indian city of Kothamangalam, Kerala. The Malayalam title of the translation is *Jeyn Eyr* (ജെയ്ൻ എയ്ർ *Jane Eyre*) with the added English subtitle *Jane Eyre: Charlotte Brontë*. The back cover states that it is a *vivarttanaṃ* (വിവർത്തനം translation) created by Sāṟa Dīpa Ceṟiyān (സാറ ദീപ ചെറിയാൻ). It consists of 304 pages. Its voluminous size suggests that the translation might be unabridged and literal, perhaps constituting the third publication of that nature. The Malayalam term *vivarttanaṃ* is etymologically derived from Sanskrit *vivartana* (विवर्तन turning) and is cognate with the Latin *vertere* (turning), which when speaking of translation evokes an image of turning a text from one language into another.

From the above treatment of the nineteen South Asian *Jane Eyre* renderings, it transpires that modern Indian languages employ a wide array of literary terms to denote the creators of textual transference and their activities. Whereas the literary and cinematographic adaptations of *Jane Eyre* do not in any way acknowledge their debt to Charlotte Brontë and accordingly leave out any technical term to identify themselves as reworkings of the novel, the translations invoke the name of the English writer, provide the original title of the novel, and explicitly characterise themselves using labels that describe translational forms that signify their makers as translators and their literary products as translations. These important classificatory markers allow for a theoretical reflection on translation as fundamentally characterised by exhibiting semiotic signs of textual transference, which sets it apart from adaptation, and will open onto the ensuing discussion of what distinguishes translation from adaptation and abridgement.

The designation used most frequently for the makers of the *Jane Eyre* translations is the term *anuvādak* (translator) employed in the abridged translations into Punjabi (1981) and Gujarati (1993). The gender-specific *anuvādikā* (female translator) appears but once in the unabridged and literal translation into Hindi (2002), even though many of the nineteen *Jane Eyre* translators are women. Finally, a unique Indian appellative *bhāvānuvādak* (gist translator) surfaces in the context of the abridged Gujarati translation (1993) and notably it appears in an abstract form as *bhāvānuvād* (gist translation) in the other abridged Gujarati translation (2009). The two Gujarati translations are the only cases where the notion of *bhāv* (ભાવ gist) is stressed. Literally, the word *bhāv* carries the sense of gist, or main idea, i.e., it denotes the quintessence or general meaning of a work. Additionally, the word *bhāv* may in some contexts carry the sense of emotion, particularly a poetic sentiment, which could be taken as expressing the general spirit of a work. To capture this semantic range, the term *bhāv* shall here be rendered into English as 'gist' understood in the sense of general contents. The compound form *bhāvānuvād* (gist translation) can then be broken down into the two constituent parts *bhāv* (gist) and *anuvād* (translation). At times, it has been rendered into English as free translation although more precisely it denotes a gist translation in the sense that the translation attempts to convey only the main drift, including the overall emotional sentiment, of the source text. In this sense, it is in opposition to the Hindi term *śābdik anuvād* (शाब्दिक अनुवाद literal translation) connoting an unabridged *anuvād* (translation) of each *śabd* (शब्द word).

More broadly, the term *bhāvānuvād* (gist translation) has especially been used by contemporary Gujarati Jain scholars for their free translations of classical Prakrit and Sanskrit texts into modern Gujarati,

Hindi, or English languages.[99] Appropriately, the objective of the *bhāvānuvādak* (gist translator) is not to create an exhaustive semantic *anuvād* (translation) of the individual *śabd* (words) but to encapsulate the *bhāv* (gist, sentiment) behind the textual passages without changing the storyline, as it is done in an *anurūpaṇ* (adaptation). In this sense, *bhāvānuvād* could be taken as an overall Indian term for abridged translation.

Nevertheless, perhaps the most intriguing aspect of the Indian translational nomenclature is the insistence on assigning the Hindi, Bengali, Assamese, Kannada, and Malayalam translations with the respective standard terms *anuvād* (translation), *anubād* (translation) or bhāṣāntar (translation), *anuvāda* (translation), and *vivarttanaṃ* (translation), applied to both unabridged as well as abridged publications. At the same time, not all the abridged *Jane Eyre* translations label themselves in such definite terms. The 1983 abridged Malayalam translation of *Jane Eyre* characterises itself as a *punarākhyānaṃ* (retelling), whose morphemes *punar* (പുനർ again) and *ākhyānaṃ* (ആഖ്യാനം telling) echo the medieval South Indian poet Pampa's description of his own abridged *Mahābhārata* poem in the Old Kannada language as a *varṇaka* (retelling) of the larger Sanskrit source text. By the same token, some of the Bengali abridged translations label themselves as *rūpāntar* (rendition) and not as *anubād* (translation), as it is the case with the Bengali publications implicitly intended for teenage readers (1990, 2010, 2019) or specified as such with the phrases *kiśōr klāsik* (teenager classic) and *kaiśōr saṃskaraṇ* (version for teenagers) in three other Bengali editions (2006, 2010, 2018).

Overall, when considering the nineteen Indian *Jane Eyre* translations, the basic distinction underlying the principle of equivalence is between *saṅkṣipt* (संक्षिप्त abridged) and *asaṅkṣipt* (असंक्षिप्त unabridged). Although only two publications (Bengali 1990, Gujarati 2009) make explicit use of the technical term *saṅkṣipt* or *saṃkṣepit* (abridged), the textual analysis as well as the condensed volume size of fourteen other publications (Tamil 1953, Bengali 1977, 1991, 2006, 2010, 2011, 2018, 2019, Punjabi 1981, Malayalam 1983, Gujarati 1993, Nepali 1997, Assamese 1999, 2014) corroborate that

---

99 See, for instance, the Prakrit canonical work with *bhāvānuvād* translations into Hindi and English by Amarmuni, Śrīcand Surānā, and Rājkumār Jain, *Sacitra Antakṛddaśā sūtra: mūl pāṭh, Hindī-Aṅgrejī bhāvānuvād tathā vivecan sahit (viśoṣ pariśiṣṭa, Antakṛddaśā mahimā)* (Delhi: Padma Prakāśan, 1999).

they too must be considered *saṅkṣipt* (abridged) in contrast to the 918 pages found in the first edition of Brontë's English novel from 1847, or the 400 to 600 pages typical of modern English editions. The remaining three literal translations (Hindi 2002, Kannada 2014, Malayalam 2020) must conversely be defined as *asaṅkṣipt* (unabridged), a term whose individual morphemes mean *a* (अ not), *saṃ* (सं altogether), and *kṣipt* (क्षिप्त contracted).

On the whole, in view of the fact that the Indian *Jane Eyre* translations consistently acknowledge their reliance on Charlotte Brontë's novel and that nine of the nineteen publications, including both abridged and unabridged versions, explicitly declare themselves as *anuvād* (translation) through some form of translational nomenclature, such as *rūpāntar* (rendition), it must be concluded that the totality of the nineteen *Jane Eyre* publications in Indian *bhāṣā* (vernaculars), in spite of their varying forms and degrees of equivalence, uniformly are to be considered translations in the broad sense of the English term denoting textual transference. Ergo, they are all translations.

At the same time, the limitation dictated by the provision of Jakobsonian semantic equivalence makes it impossible to include the full range of these Indian adaptational and translational forms under the English notion of translation and to appreciate these renderings on their own terms. To encompass and study the full range of Indian *Jane Eyre* renditions, it is necessary to put forth a new and more inclusive theoretical elucidation of the term translation. Such broadened principles shall here be rooted in India's own literary terminology, formal analysis, conceptual history, and philosophy. The proposed theory has to step away from the pitfalls of semantic equivalence and be sufficiently non-hierarchical to acknowledge the actual *praxis* of adaptation and translation on the subcontinent. It must stretch the Jakobsonian notion to encompass both premodern and modern, classical and non-classical, as well as theoretical and practical manifestations of Indian literary practices. Furthermore, the ramifications of the definition must make it possible to apply the term in the interpretation of actual literary texts. The proposed definition is thus:

> An *anurūpaṇ* (अनुरूपण adaptation) or *anuvād* (अनुवाद translation) is a *pariṇāmī paryāy* (परिणामी पर्याय transformed modality) derived from the *dravya* (द्रव्य substance) of a *srot pāṭh* (स्रोत पाठ source text) through *dravyārthik samtulyatā* (द्रव्यार्थिक समतुल्यता substantive equivalence) in a *kathātmik vyākhyā* (कथात्मिक

> व्याख्या narrative interpretation) instantiating a *sāhityik prakār* (साहित्यिक प्रकार literary type).

Without the use of the technical literary terms in Hindi, the proposed definition is:

> An adaptation or translation is a transformed modality derived from the substance of a source text through substantive equivalence in a narrative interpretation instantiating a literary type.

The proffered definition juxtaposes and puts on equal footing what are normally regarded as two distinct literary forms, *anurūpaṇ* (adaptation) and *anuvād* (translation). The postulated correspondence between the two is a consequence of broadening *anuvād* (translation) to include forms of non-semantic equivalence. Nevertheless, the differentiation between the two terms is maintained in order to uphold a narrative criterion, whereby *anurūpaṇ* (adaptation) is understood as involving changes to the overall storyline and setting whereas *anuvād* (translation) does not.

Both *anurūpaṇ* (adaptation) and *anuvād* (translation) are in the proposed definition philosophically characterised as *pariṇāmī paryāy* (transformed modality) entailing an evolution of a *dravya* (substance). In Indian philosophy, the ancient Sanskrit concept of *pariṇāma* (परिणाम transformation), in Hindi romanized as *pariṇām*, is an ontological position linked with a processual view of causation, according to which causes evolve into effects that inhere in their causes. The causes and effects are all *paryāy* (पर्याय modalities) existing as individual states within the single continuum of a given entity. The continuum is a *dravya* (substance) being an abstract form that permeates all its *paryāy* (modalities) from the first cause to any subsequent effect.

The traditional exemplifications for this ontological principle presented in the classical Indian sources are the element of *jal* (जल water) and *kanak* (कनक gold). The *dravya* (substance) *jal* (water) is said to exist in different *paryāy* (modalities) of liquid, ice, and vapour, which are *pariṇām* (transformations) of the same *dravya* (substance) sharing a quality of *jaltva* (जलत्व waterness). Similarly, the *dravya* (substance) *kanak* (gold) exists in different *paryāy* (modalities) of gold ore, unwrought purified gold, and gold jewellery, which are *pariṇām* (transformations) sharing a characteristic of *kanaktva* (कनकत्व goldness). Significantly, none of these *paryāy* (modalities) is more important or original than the other, each being just a mere instantiation of the same underlying *dravya* (substance).

When applied to translation theory, the ontological principles of (1) *pariṇām* (transformation), (2) *paryāy* (modalities), and (3) *dravya* (substance) respectively correspond to (1) the creative process, (2) the limitless versions of source texts, adaptations, and translations, and (3) the shared literary type. In the case at hand, the *dravya* (substance) *Jane Eyre* can be said to exist in different *paryāy* (modalities) of the source text, adaptations, and translations, which all are *pariṇām* (transformations) sharing a quality of janeeyreness. None of these *paryāy* (modalities) is more important or original than the other, each being a mere instantiation.

The *dravya* (substance) *Jane Eyre* then signifies an abstraction of the literary text as a prototype or archetype. The prototype is a *sāhityik prakār* (literary type), which incorporates within it all the concrete instances of the novel. Notably, the substance is not limited to the source text, which means that the prototype or hypotext for a given translation is not necessarily confined to the work in the original language. Rather, the abstract substance is augmented by each new instance. This may be seen in the way in which the Indian cinematographic adaptations of *Jane Eyre* display a clear progressive development of certain elements of the story over the course of the individual adaptations. The later adaptations simulate not only Brontë's original work but also the earlier Indian film adaptations. For instance, the 1969 Telugu thriller *Ardharātri* bears more resemblance to the preceding Indian film adaptations than it does to Brontë's novel. The process of augmentation of the substance may be seen in the way in which a given translation may bear close resemblance to the style of earlier translations of the work and, in such a case, exhibits equivalence with its source text in the original English language as well as with certain earlier translations in the target language.

Janeeyreness is the quality that identifies a given text as belonging to a prototype, consisting in the elements of the text that exhibit comparative equivalence to that type. In the case of the Indian *Jane Eyre* adaptations, these elements are primarily the repeated motifs of the orphan girl, the romantic relationship with the estate owner, his hidden mad wife, and the portentous fire, which, as points of typological similitude, provide the reader or viewer with a recognition of the literary type in the given textual or filmic instance.

The concept of *samtulyatā* (equivalence) can consequently be broadened to include the new notion of *dravyārthik samtulyatā* (substantive equivalence) encompassing but not limited to *śābdārthik samtulyatā* (शाब्दार्थिक समतुल्यता semantic equivalence), since the different *paryāy* (modalities) are considered equal in the common *dravya* (substance) as a shared *sāhityik prakār* (literary type). Each *paryāy* (modality) is different through its *pariṇāmī* (transformed) *kathātmik vyākhyā* (narrative interpretation) into, for example, an adapted screenplay or a rendition for teenagers. Each *paryāy* remains a unique instantiation of the *dravya* (substance) *Jane Eyre* as the *sāhityik prakār* (literary type) of janeeyreness. In modern literary discourse, the polarity between *dravya* (substance) and *paryāy* (modality) is reminiscent of the differentiation between the singular work (French *oeuvre*) and the pluralised texts (French *texte*) introduced by the literary critic Roland Barthes.[100]

In the classical Indian context, this polarity harks back to the Indian notion of *naya* (नय perspective), which opens the door to a new literary dialectical hermeneutic, which could be termed *anuvādik nayavād* (अनुवादिक नयवाद translational perspectivism).[101] The hermeneutic of translational perspectivism entails bifurcated aspects of a *dravyārthik naya* (द्रव्यार्थिक नय substantive perspective) and a *paryāyārthik naya* (पर्यायार्थिक नय modal perspective).[102] From a *dravyārthik naya* (substantive perspective) there is an emphasis on sameness and belonging to an abstract literary type. Oppositely, from a *paryāyārthik naya* (modal perspective) there is emphasis on difference and being unique, resulting in a dialectic between the various instances of the *dravya* (substance).

In the former case of adopting a substantive perspective, there is a sense of continuity, as when viewing *Jane Eyre* as a singular literary work across all its many different textual instantiations in both the source and target languages. This would include the various editions and reprints of the English text, the literal translations into other languages,

100 Roland Barthes, 'From Work to Text', in *The Rustle of Language*, trans. by Richard Howard (New York: Hill and Wang, 1986), pp. 56–64.

101 The proposed theoretical term perspectivism creates an intercultural parallel to the philosophy of perspectivism in the European continental tradition associated especially with the thought of the German mathematician Gottfried Wilhelm Leibniz (1646–1716).

102 On the Indian distinction between substantive and modal perspectives, see the eleventh-century Indian philosophical treatise *Ālāpapaddhati* by the Jain author Devasena, *sūtra* no. 40, Sanskrit edition by Mukhtār Ratancand Jain, *Śrīmaddevasenācāryaviracitā Ālāpapaddhati aparanāma dravyānuyogapraveśikā* (Saharanpur, Uttar Pradesh: Prācīn Ārṣ Granthāyatan, 1940; reprint 2003, pp. 8–10.

as well as other forms of reworking the text that are semantically more divergent, as seen with the abridged versions and gist translations. It would also include the more creative adaptations of *Jane Eyre* in literature, film, or other media, such as illustrated comic books. All these versions can then be considered multifarious instances of the same underlying literary work in the abstract sense of a substance, given that they all share certain defining characteristics of janeeyreness, i.e., they are recognizable as individual forms of that literary type.

In the latter case of adopting a modal perspective, the accentuation shifts from viewing sameness to perceiving the individual differences between one instantiation and the next in a non-hierarchical sense, even when a given instance exhibits little or no semantic equivalence to its source text.

The hermeneutic of translational perspectivism has the advantage that it allows for the continued use of the common terms adaptation, abridgement, and translation while dispensing with any textual hierarchy between them. All modalities of the novel in any form may be regarded as pluralised texts that are instantiations of the same singular literary work and each modality augments the substance of the literary work with a new reiteration. In this view, an abridged translation of *Jane Eyre*, in spite of its brevity, can rightfully be regarded as a translation *tout court*, because each rendering exhibits a unique modality of shared janeeyreness.

Bhāṣā in *Jane Eyre*: The Epiphany of Substantive Equivalence

Although itself a classic, *Jane Eyre* was not written in a European classical language such as Latin. Rather, like many other authors of the Victorian era, Charlotte Brontë made use of a colloquial English language in a written literary form, which is far removed from the European classical notion of prose.[103] Aptly, the Indian translations of *Jane Eyre* display a comparable vernacularity that is embedded in the myriad of Indian *bhāṣā*, a term literally meaning speech, which since the early nineteenth century onwards has generally come to denote language in a vernacular

103 For the argument that *Jane Eyre* is not written in prose, see Charles Lock, 'Why Novels Are Not Written in Prose', *Ink*, 2 (Copenhagen: University of Copenhagen, Department of English, Germanic and Romance Studies, 2010), 14–16.

non-classical sense.[104] The Indian *bhāṣā* (vernacular) of Hindustani was, in point of fact, what Jane herself engaged in learning when presented with the prospect of going to India in the early nineteenth century. Globally, the nineteenth century witnessed a swell of the vernaculars and as the tremendous wave of translational activities swept the world, universities were propelled to establish numerous language departments, a development also seen in India.

Correspondingly, *Jane Eyre* was never translated into any classical language of India and the colloquial character of Brontë's English is closely reflected in the Indian translations of *Jane Eyre* of the twentieth and twenty-first centuries. Brontë's Victorian English is not readily understandable to most Indian readers and the fact that the Indian book market is dominated by abridged Indian versions of *Jane Eyre* aimed especially at an adolescent audience confirms the complexities that Indian school pupils face when studying the English classics of the nineteenth century.

Fittingly, the Indian translators of *Jane Eyre* are mostly from an educational background and the majority of them are women. The translations are typically produced by retired Indian schoolteachers and small Indian publishing houses warmly welcome new abridged translations of any well-known English classic.[105] An abridged translation offers an easier read free from the many difficulties that exist in accessing and comprehending all the literary, cultural, and historical intricacies of nineteenth-century English writing, which undoubtedly persist for the average Indian reader even when served in a good literal translation. The abridged translations likewise have the purpose of providing school pupils with book summaries of the major classics. Reading *Jane Eyre* in a local *bhāṣā* (vernacular) makes the novel intelligible but in a cultural frame that differs from that of the English language.

---

104 For a historical overview of the term *bhāṣā* and other Indian linguistic forms and registers of speech, see Friedlander, 'Before Translation?', pp. 47–49.

105 Oral information (November, 2018) obtained from the owners of the publishing house Navbhārat Sāhitya Mandir in Ahmedabad, Gujarat, the publisher of the first Gujarati abridged translation of *Jane Eyre* in 1993. The same publishing house has also brought out Gujarati abridged translations of many other English and French classics, such as Jane Austen's *Pride and Prejudice*, Mary Ann Evans's (pen name George Eliot) *Silas Marner*, Victor Hugo's *Les Miserables*, Thomas Hardy's *The Mayor of Casterbridge*, Charles Dickens's *Great Expectations*, Jules Verne's *Around the World in Eighty Days*, and Jonathan Swift's *Gulliver's Travels*.

Whether abridged or literal, a translation into an Indian *bhāṣā* (vernacular) transforms the source text in a way that empowers the reader to create a new *kathātmik vyākhyā* (narrative interpretation) of the story within the *bhāṣā* itself. Reading a foreign classic in a native *bhāṣā* transports the story into the richness of the *bhāṣā*'s own language, culture, and aesthetic sense. Poetically, such transformation can be compared to a scene early in Ār. Sī. Talvār's *Jane Eyre* film adaptation *Saṅgdil*. In the act, the orphan girl Kamlā and her childhood friend Śaṅkar go to the household nursemaid to hear a fairy tale.[106] As Kamlā listens attentively to the story about a princess and a prince, the stage instantly transforms from the outer setting of the nursemaid's quarters into Kamlā's inner imagination, where she places herself into the narrative as its central female character, the princess. At this point, the princess is attacked in her palace by an evil witch in the form of Kamlā's strict stepmother. When she escapes up a flight of stairs leading to the top of a tower, she calls out to her friend, the prince in the form of Śaṅkar, who swiftly comes to her rescue. Abandoning the confines of the palace, the prince and princess then ride together on his white stallion through the sky among white clouds while singing a duet about their love far away from this stern world.[107] The refrain of the song goes *ājā basā leṃ nayā saṅsār* (आजा बसा लें नया संसार 'Come, let's inhabit a new world!').[108] This transfiguration from outer realism to inner self-imagination is an apt allegory for the transformative nature of translation, which changes the literal strictures of the source text into a new imaginative world in the target language, augmenting the substance of the literary work. In this vein, the transformative aspect of the *bhāṣā* is closely linked with how the equivalence of translation is to be understood. Jakobson's principle of equivalence, which could be compared to an equals sign placed between the source and target languages in the translational equation, is semantic in nature.

---

106 The scene starts at minute 04:57.

107 The clouds and the landscape below could be taken as a literary allusion to the famous lyric poem *Meghadūta* (*The Cloud Messenger*) by the classical Sanskrit poet Kālidāsa, wherein a newly-wed young god exiled to a mountain top in central India implores a monsoon cloud drifting by to carry a deep-felt love message to his beloved wife living in the divine city on Mt. Kailash in northern India, describing in florid detail the varied landscapes that the cloud must traverse on its path going north.

108 The song is entitled *Dhartī se dūr gore bādloṃ ke pār* (धरती से दूर गोरे बादलों के पार *Far from the Earth, Across the White Clouds*). It was performed in the film as vocal playback by the singers Āśā Bhosle (b. 1933) and Gītā Datt (1930–1972).

However, close examination of the Indian literal translations of *Jane Eyre* reveals that sameness in meaning not only tends to be transferred interlingually from English to Indian *bhāṣā* (vernacular) but intermittently emerges intralingually from within the linguistic structure of the *bhāṣā* itself, because the very nature of language is the intralingual and not interlingual generation of meaning 'through differences without positive terms'.[109] Accordingly, words take on their own meaning in the *bhāṣā* (vernacular) through internal semantic contrasts rather than through semantic equivalence between the English word and its Indian *bhāṣā* correlate. The translational equation has *dravyārthik samtulyatā* (substantive equivalence), encountered oftentimes in abridged translation and adaptation. The greater freedom of creative license afforded by abridged translation and adaptation in recreating the original work in the *bhāṣā* (vernacular) at times endows both with a stronger transformative power than is usually met with in a translation that is strictly literal and espouses semantic equivalence. On that account, the equals sign becomes the shared *dravya* (substance) of the abstract literary work rather than a reciprocal word-for-word signification.

To illustrate the unstable nature of equivalence, two sets of synoptic parallels presented below will serve as a basis for discussing its ramifications. To begin with, two literal *bhāṣā* translations will be juxtaposed against the English original exemplified by three selected passages. Thereafter, an abridged *bhāṣā* translation will be contrasted with the same two literal *bhāṣā* translations and the English original exemplified by two selected passages.

In the first synoptic survey, the two *bhāṣā* translations into Hindi (2002) and Kannada (2014) will be considered, representing a North Indian Indo-European language and a South Indian Dravidian language respectively. Overall, the translational equation between the English original *Jane Eyre* and the Hindi and Kannada literal translations can be said to be predominantly of a semantic character reflected both in the Indian *bhāṣā* (vernacular) and in the back-translations.[110] A typical example would be the faithful rendering of the following:

---

109 Ferdinand de Saussure, *Course in General Linguistics*, trans. by Wade Baskin, 3rd edn (New York: McGraw-Hill Book Company, 1959), p. 12.

110 The term back-translation means a literal re-translation of a translated sentence back into its original language, which in the present case is the literal re-renderings of the Hindi and Kannada translations back into English found beneath the romanizations.

English[111]	Hindi[112]	Kannada[113]
'I want you to give up German and learn Hindostanee'	मैं चाहता हूँ कि तुम जर्मन सीखना छोड़ दो और हिन्दुस्तानी भाषा सीखो। *maiṃ cāhtā hūṁ ki tum jarman sīkhnā choṛ do aur Hindustānī bhāṣā sīkho.* I want that you give up learning German and [instead] learn Hindustani language.	ನೀನು ಜರ್ಮನ್ ಬಿಟ್ಟುಬಿಟ್ಟು ಹಿಂದುಸ್ತಾನೀ ಕಲಿಯಬೇಕೆಂದು ಬಯಸುತ್ತೇನೆ. *nīnu jarman biṭṭubiṭṭu hindustānī kaliyabēkendu bayasuttēne.* I want you to give up German [and] learn Hindustani.

The Hindi and Kannada translations here transfer the source text into the target languages with complete and equivalent meaning.

Among the sentences that closely reproduce the original text, a fraction exhibits minor semantic variance, especially when the English text uses culturally specific elements:

111 *JE*, Ch. 34.
112 Sinhā, *Jen Āyar*, p. 413.
113 Mādhava, *Jēn Air*, p. 421.

English[114]	Hindi[115]	Kannada[116]
‘And I shall see it again,’ he said aloud, ‘in dreams when I sleep by the Ganges: and again in a more remote hour — when another slumber overcomes me — on the shore of a darker stream!’	फिर जोर से बोले, ‘मैं इन्हें फिर देखूँगा, स्वप्न में, जब मैं गंगा के पास सो रहा हूँगा, और फिर किसी सुदूर घड़ी में जब चिर-निद्रा मुझे किसी अँधेरी नदी के पास गोद में ले लेगी ।’ *phir jor se bole, ‘maiṃ inheṃ phir dekhūṅgā, svapna meṃ, jab maiṃ gaṅgā ke pās so rahā hūṅgā, aur phir kisī sudūr ghaṛī meṃ jab cir-nidrā mujhe kisī andherī nadī ke pās god meṃ le legī.’* Then he said loudly, ‘I will see them again, in dreams, when I will be sleeping near the Gaṅgā [river], and then again in a remote moment, when a deep sleep will take me into [its] lap near some dark river.’	‘ನಾನದನ್ನು ಪುನಃ ಕಾಣುವೆ’ ಅವರು ಗಟ್ಟಿಯಾಗಿ ಅಂದರು, ‘ಗಂಗಾತೀರದಲ್ಲಿ ಮಲಗಿರುವಾಗ, ಮತ್ತೆ ಇನ್ಯಾವುದೋ ನದೀದಡದಲ್ಲಿ, ಮಲಗಿರುತ್ತಾ, ಕನಸಿನಲ್ಲಿ ಮತ್ತೆ ಕಾಣುವೆ.’ *‘nānadannu punaḥ kāṇuve’ avaru gaṭṭiyāgi andaru, ‘gaṅgātīradalli malagiruvāga, matte inyāvudō nadīdaḍadalli, malagiruttā, kanasinalli matte kāṇuve.’* ‘I will see it again,’ he said loudly, ‘while sleeping on the bank of the Gaṅgā [river], [and] then again while sleeping on the shore of another river, I will see it again in [my] dreams.’

The Hindi translation displays minor semantic variance to the source text in its slightly nondescript rendering of the English ‘on the shore of a darker stream’ into *kisī andherī nadī ke pās* ‘near some dark river’, while the Kannada translation employs a less distinguished expression *inyāvudō nadīdaḍadalli* ‘on the shore of another river’. Both translations in varying degree lack the deeper connotation of the English phrase ‘a darker stream’, which in the passage symbolises death by implying the ancient Greek notion of the mythological river Styx in the afterlife or the Christian trope of mythological rivers in the underworld appearing in Dante’s *Divine Comedy*. The Hindi translation manages to convey the sense of dying with its images of deep sleep and a dark river, but does not evoke any allegorical reference to Greek or Christian mythology. The Kannada translation, in contrast,

114 *JE*, Ch. 34.
115 Sinhā, *Jen Āyar*, p. 417.
116 Mādhava, *Jēn Air*, p. 425.

completely misses the point with its overtly general phrase 'another river' and altogether fails to convey the implication of the scene where Mr Rivers in a moment of prescience sees himself remembering the English countryside at the future time of his death. The Kannada rendering of the phrase is a typical example of a translation that falls short in terms of the full semantic range of the source text due to the fact that the indefinite expression 'another river' does not in any way evoke the corresponding Indian notion of the mythic Vaitaraṇī river, which a deceased person in the afterlife has to cross to enter the realm of the dead, and Indian readers unfamiliar with Greek or Christian mythologies will therefore not perceive the allegory. Thence, although being literal, translations of semantic equivalence regularly leave out some of the deeper semantic connotations of the source text, as discussed theoretically by Jakobson.[117]

In contradistinction to an aim for semantic equivalence, literal translations on occasion consciously curtail the semantic equivalence by circumnavigating uncomfortable or controversial aspects of the original:

117 See fn. 121.

English[118]	Hindi[119]	Kannada[120]
'Firm, faithful, and devoted, full of energy, and zeal, and truth, he labours for his race; he clears their painful way to improvement; he hews down like a giant the prejudices of creed and caste that encumber it.'	पक्का, आस्थावान और विश्वासी, शक्ति, उत्साह और सच्चाई से भरे, वह व्यक्ति अपनी जाति के लिए परिश्रम कर रहा है, उसकी कष्ट-भरी राहों को साफ करके उसे प्रगति की ओर ले जा रहा है। रास्ते में आनेवाले, धर्म और जाति के व्यवधानों को वह राक्षस की भाँति चूर-चूर कर रहा है। *pakkā, āsthāvān aur viśvāsī, śakti, utsāh aur saccāī se bhare, vah vyakti apnī jāti ke lie pariśram kar rahā hai, uskī kaṣṭ-bharī rāhoṃ ko sāph karke use pragti kī or le jā rahā hai. rāste meṃ ānevāle, dharm aur jāti ke vyavdhānoṃ ko vah rākṣas kī bhānti cūr-cūr kar rahā hai.* Determined, faithful and devoted, powerful, full of zeal and truth, that man is doing efforts for his caste, having cleared his ways full of hardship, taking him towards improvement. Like a demon, he is shattering whatever comes in the way as obstacles to religion and caste.	ದೃಢ, ನಿಷ್ಠಾವಂತ ಸಮರ್ಪಣಾ ಭಾವದ, ಶಕ್ತ್ಯುತ್ಸಾಹಗಳ ಆತ ತನ್ನ ಜನರಿಗಾಗಿ ಶ್ರಮಿಸುತ್ತಿದ್ದಾರೆ. ಅವರನ್ನು ಸುಧಾರಿಸಲು ಯತ್ನಿಸುತ್ತಿದ್ದಾರೆ; ಜಾತಿ, ಪಂಥದ ಭೇದ ಭಾವವನ್ನು ತೊಡೆದುಹಾಕಲು ಯತ್ನಿಸುತ್ತಿದ್ದಾರೆ. *dṛḍha, niṣṭhāvanta samarpaṇā bhāvada, śaktyutsāhagaḷa āta tanna janarigāgi śramisuttiddāre. avarannu sudhārisalu yatnisuttiddāre; jāti, panthada bhēda bhāvavannu toḍeduhākalu yatnisuttiddāre.* Firm, faithful, devoted, with energy and enthusiasm, he labours for his people. He strives to improve them. He strives to expunge the discriminatory attitude of caste and creed.

Both the Hindi and Kannada translators clearly struggle with this passage so imbued with polemical undertones for the modern postcolonial reader. Words ripe with controversial meanings are either omitted or altered in the Indian *bhāṣā* (vernacular). A particular

118 *JE*, Ch. 38.
119 Sinhā, *Jen Āyar*, p. 471.
120 Mādhava, *Jēn Air*, p. 480.

exemplification is the English word 'race' in the expression 'he labours for his race' and the word 'caste' in the clause 'he hews down like a giant the prejudices of creed and caste that encumber it.'

In the context of England in the mid-nineteenth century, by 'race' Brontë must surely have intended 'mankind' in a Christian universalist sense, as is evident from the remainder of the sentence that qualifies the antecedent noun 'race' with the clause 'he clears their painful way to improvement' as well as with the agreement of the pronoun 'it'. In this way, when Mr Rivers as a Christian missionary is portrayed to be working towards the moral-religious improvement of his Indian converts, these Indian persons must be understood as included in the labours that Mr Rivers undertakes for the sake of 'his race', i.e., for the sake of mankind. It must be added that in the twenty-first century, the English word 'race' no longer implies humankind in general and primarily carries association with the issue of race theories. This latter connotation has found its way into the modern Hindi and Kannada languages through the English homophonous loanwords *res* (रेस) and *rēs* (ರೇಸ್) respectively, which correctly are not employed in either translation of the passage. Still, the Hindi translator misinterprets 'race' by rendering it with the unfitting word *jāti* (caste) and the Kannada translator chooses the word *jana* (people), which is closer in meaning yet nevertheless imperfect. Neither of the two Indian words conveys the intended English universalist sense 'mankind', which in Hindi and Kannada would be *manuṣyajāti* (मनुष्यजाति, ಮನುಷ್ಯಜಾತಿ) or similar. Devoid of universality, the Hindi *apnī jāti ke lie* (for his caste) and the Kannada *tanna janarigāgi* (for his people) diminish the stature of Mr Rivers and his mission by insinuating that he labours exclusively for his own ethnic group.

By the word 'caste' Brontë seems to be referring primarily to the Indian 'caste system' in a Hindu socio-religious sense. The word has retained its European nineteenth-century meaning and has today become common parlance in Indian English. The English concept originates from the sixteenth-century Portuguese and Spanish *casta* (racial lineage, ethnic descendance). There are two primary words for the indigenous caste system in India, namely *varṇa* (caste, literally 'colour') and *jāti* (birth group), dating back to ancient times and having their own connotations different from that of the Portuguese-Spanish word. Both the Hindi and Kannada translators accurately choose the word *jāti*, which is the closest to represent the English word 'caste'.

Remarkably, when the Hindi translator first employs the word *jāti* to render 'race' and again uses the same word *jāti* to signify the word 'caste', the circumscribed meaning of the first occurrence in *apnī jāti* 'his caste' foreshadows and thereby alters the meaning of the second occurrence of *jāti*, changing 'caste' in the general sense of the Indian caste system to 'his caste'. The implication of the Hindi passage becomes that the missionary Mr Rivers is not at all concerned with removing the social prejudices of the Hindu caste system but rather that he like a demon shatters any obstacle to his own ethnic kind. Though the second *jāti* is technically equivalent to the semantic sense of the English word 'caste', this intentional yet subtle shift in meaning on the part of the Hindi translator removes the English novel's implied critique of the Indian caste system and shifts it onto the British missionary, thereby circumventing a passage in the English source text which might otherwise have seemed accusatory to the Indian reader.

The three synoptic instances of literal *bhāṣā* translation provided above all involve a certain dialectical oscillation between equivalence and variance in relation to the source text. Jakobson called this phenomenon 'equivalence in difference', which he exemplified with circumlocutions in neologisms and subtle interlingual variations in grammatical patterns.[121] The case in point is that the English word 'race' and its decisively unequal translations into Hindi and Kannada exceed Jakobson's notion of semantic equivalence in difference. *Per contra*, when translation instead is defined as a *pariṇāmī paryāy* (transformed modality), the transformative character of the translation comes to the fore, acknowledging the many ways in which a translation can create new meaning.

In the second synoptic survey, the West Indian Gujarati *bhāṣā* abridged translation (1993) will be contrasted against the original *Jane Eyre* in English and the same two literal *bhāṣā* translations in Hindi and Kannada. Overall, the Gujarati abridged translation is transformative in its substantive equivalence by radically condensing the source text, which is a translational equation quite unlike any form of semantic equivalence. An illustrative example is the diffused Gujarati rendering of an English passage describing the ten-year-old Jane being sent off to a boarding school by her heartless stepmother Mrs Reed, at which point Jane is subjected to an interview by the intimidating school principal,

121 Jakobson, 'On Linguistic Aspects', p. 233.

Mr Brocklehurst. First the full passage is given in English, Hindi, and Kannada, whereupon the highly truncated Gujarati rendering follows:

English[122]	Hindi[123]	Kannada[124]
'No sight so sad as that of a naughty child,' he began, 'especially a naughty little girl. Do you know where the wicked go after death?'	उन्होंने बोलना आरम्भ किया, 'एक दुष्ट बच्चे को देखने से बुरा कोई और दृश्य नहीं होता, विशेषकर जब वह दुष्ट एक छोटी लड़की हो। तुम्हें पता है कि मरने के बाद दुष्ट कहाँ जाते हैं?' *unhonne bolnā ārambh kiyā, 'ek duṣṭ bacce ko dekhne se burā koī aur dṛśya nahīṃ hotā, viśeṣkar jab vah duṣṭ ek choṭī laṛkī ho. tumheṃ patā hai ki marne ke bād duṣṭ kahām̐ jāte haiṃ?'* He started speaking, 'There is no worse sight than seeing a wicked child, especially when that wicked one is a little girl. Do you know where the wicked go after death?'	[*sentence omitted in the Kannada translation*]
'They go to hell,' was my ready and orthodox answer.	मैंने तुरन्त परम्परागत उत्तर दिया, 'नरक में जाते हैं।' *maiṃne turant paramparāgat uttar diyā, 'narak meṃ jāte haiṃ.'* I immediately replied traditionally, 'They go to hell.'	'ಅವರು ನರಕಕ್ಕೆ ಹೋಗುವರು.' ಶಾಸ್ತ್ರಬದ್ಧವಾದ ಸಿದ್ಧ ಉತ್ತರ ನನ್ನಿಂದ ಹೊರಬಿತ್ತು. *'avaru narakakke hōguvaru.' śāstrabaddhavāda siddha uttara nanninda horabittu.* 'They go to hell.' I had a readymade orthodox answer.

122 *JE*, Ch. 4.
123 Sinhā, *Jen Āyar*, pp. 32–33.
124 Mādhava, *Jēn Air*, pp. 34–35.

English	Hindi	Kannada
'And what is hell? Can you tell me that?'	'नरक क्या होता है? बता सकती हो?' *'narak kyā hotā hai? batā saktī ho?'* 'What is hell? Can you tell?'	'ಈ ನರಕವೆಂದರೇನು, ಹೇಳಬಲ್ಲೆಯಾ?' *'ī narakavendarēnu, hēḷaballeyā?'* 'Can you tell what this hell is?'
'A pit full of fire.'	'अग्नि से भरी एक खाई।' *'agni se bharī ek khāī.'* 'A chasm full of fire.'	'ಅದೊಂದು ಅಗ್ನಿಕುಂಡ.' *'adondu agnikuṇḍa.'* 'It is a fire pit.'
'And should you like to fall into that pit and to be burning there for ever?'	'क्या तुम उस खाई में गिरना और जलते रहना चाहोगी?' *'kyā tum us khāī meṃ girnā aur jalte rahnā cāhogī?'* 'Would you like to fall into that chasm and keep burning?'	'ಆ ಅಗ್ನಿಕುಂಡಕ್ಕೆ ಬಿದ್ದು ನಿರಂತರ ಉರಿಯುತ್ತಿರಬೇಕೇ, ನಿನಗೆ?' *'ā agnikuṇḍakke biddu nirantara uriyuttirabēkē, ninage?'* 'Do you want to fall into that fire pit and be burning there forever?'
'No, sir.'	'नहीं, श्रीमान!' *'nahīṃ, śrīmān!'* 'No, sir!'	'ಇಲ್ಲ, ಸರ್.' *'illa, sar.'* 'No, sir.'
'What must you do to avoid it?'	'तो इससे बचने के लिए तुम्हें क्या करना चाहिए?' *'to isse bacne ke lie tumheṃ kyā karnā cāhie?'* 'So what should you do to avoid it?'	'ಅದನ್ನು ತಪ್ಪಿಸಿಕೊಳ್ಳಲು ಏನು ಮಾಡಬೇಕು?' *'adannu tappisikoḷḷalu ēnu māḍabēku?'* 'To avoid it, what should be done?'

English	Hindi	Kannada
I deliberated a moment; my answer, when it did come, was objectionable: 'I must keep in good health, and not die.'	मैं एक क्षण सोचती रही और फिर जो उत्तर मैंने दिया वह आपत्तिजनक था, 'मुझे अपना स्वास्थ्य अच्छा रखना चाहिए, ताकि मरूँ नहीं।' *maiṃ ek kṣaṇ soctī rahī aur phir jo uttar maiṃne diyā vah āpattijanak thā, 'mujhe apnā svāsthya acchā rakhnā cāhie, tāki marūm̐ nahīṃ.'* I kept thinking for a moment and then the answer I gave was objectionable, 'I must keep my health good, so that I do not die.'	ಕ್ಷಣ ತಡೆದು ನಾನು ಉತ್ತರಿಸಿದೆ, 'ಸಾಯದಂತೆ ಒಳ್ಳೆಯ ಆರೋಗ್ಯದಿಂದಿರಬೇಕು.' *kṣaṇa taḍedu nānu uttariside, 'sāyadante oḷḷeya ārōgyadindirabēku.'* Waiting for a moment, I replied: 'One should keep in good health in order not to die.'

English	Hindi	Kannada
'How can you keep in good health? Children younger than you die daily. I buried a little child of five years old only a day or two since, — a good little child, whose soul is now in heaven. It is to be feared the same could not be said of you, were you to be called hence.'	'तुम स्वास्थ्य अच्छा बनाकर कैसे रख सकती हो? तुमसे भी छोटे बच्चे प्रतिदिन मरते हैं। एक-दो ही दिन पहले मैंने एक पाँच वर्ष के बच्चे को दफनाया था — एक भला बच्चा जिसकी आत्मा स्वर्ग में चली गई। यदि तुम्हें वहाँ से बुलावा आ जाए, तो तुम्हारे विषय में तो भला नहीं कहा जा सकता।' *'tum svāsthya acchā banākar kaise rakh saktī ho? tumse bhī choṭe bacce pratidin marte haiṃ. ek-do hī din pahle maiṃne ek pāñc varṣ ke bacce ko daphnāyā thā — ek bhalā baccā jiskī ātmā svarg meṃ calī gaī. yadi tumheṃ vahāṁ se bulāvā ā jāe, to tumhāre viṣay meṃ to bhalā nahīṃ kahā jā saktā.'* 'How can you maintain good health? Children even younger than you die every day. One or two days ago, I buried a five-year-old child — a virtuous child whose soul has gone to heaven. If a call for you comes from there, then such good words could not be said about you.'	'ಒಳ್ಳೆಯ ಆರೋಗ್ಯದಿಂದಿರುವುದೆಂತು? ದಿನವೂ ನಿನಗಿಂತಲೂ ಎಳೆಯ ಮಕ್ಕಳು ಸಾಯುತ್ತಿರುತ್ತಾರೆ. ಐದು ವರ್ಷದ ಪುಟ್ಟ ಬಾಲೆಯೊಬ್ಬಳನ್ನು ಇದೀಗ ಒಂದೆರಡು ದಿನಗಳ ಹಿಂದಷ್ಟೇ ಮಣ್ಣುಮಾಡಿ ಬಂದೆ. ಒಳ್ಳೆಯವಳಾದ ಪುಟ್ಟ ಹುಡುಗಿ; ಅವಳ ಆತ್ಮವೀಗ ಸ್ವರ್ಗದಲ್ಲಿದೆ. ನಿನಗೆ ಕರೆ ಬಂದುದೇ ಆದರೆ, ನಿನ್ನ ಬಗ್ಗೆ ಈ ಮಾತನ್ನು ಹೇಳಲಾಗದು.' *'oḷḷeya ārōgyadindiruvudentu? dinavū ninagintalū eḷeya makkaḷu sāyuttiruttāre. aidu varṣada puṭṭa bāleyobbaḷannu idīga onderaḍu dinagaḷa hindaṣṭē maṇṇumāḍi bande. oḷḷeyavaḷāda puṭṭa huḍugi; avaḷa ātmavīga svargadallide. Ninage kare bandudē ādare, ninna bagge ī mātannu hēḷalāgadu.'* 'What is it to be in good health? Children younger than you die daily. I buried a five-year-old girl just one or two days back. A good little girl. Her soul is now in heaven. If you get [such] a call, one could not say such a word about you.'

English	Hindi	Kannada
Not being in a condition to remove his doubt, I only cast my eyes down on the two large feet planted on the rug, and sighed; wishing myself far enough away.	उसकी शंकाओं को दूर करने की स्थिति में नहीं होने के कारण मैंने अपनी आँखें नीचे गड़ा दीं और कालीन पर रखे उसके दो चौड़े-चौड़े पैरों को देखने लगी। उससे दूर भागने की इच्छा करते हुए मैंने आह भरी। *uskī śaṅkāoṃ ko dūr karne kī sthiti meṃ nahīṃ hone ke kāraṇ maiṃne apnī āṅkheṃ nīce gaṛā dīṃ aur kālīn par rakhe uske do cauṛe-cauṛe pairoṃ ko dekhne lagī. usse dūr bhāgne kī icchā karte hue maiṃne āh bharī.* Not being in a position to dispel his doubts, I put my eyes down and kept watching his two wide feet on the carpet. Wishing to run away from him, I sighed.	ಆತನ ಸಂಶಯವನ್ನು ನಿವಾರಿಸುವುದು ಸಾಧ್ಯವಿಲ್ಲವಾಗಿ, ನನ್ನೆದುರಿಗೆ ನೆಲದಲ್ಲಿ ಊರಲಾಗಿದ್ದ ಆ ದೊಡ್ಡ ಪಾದಗಳನ್ನೇ ದಿಟ್ಟಿಸುತ್ತಾ, ದೂರವೆಲ್ಲಾದರೂ ಹೋಗುವುದು ಸಾಧ್ಯವಾದರೆ, ಎಂದಾಶಿಸುತ್ತಾ ನಾನು ನಿಡುಸುಯ್ದೆ. *ātana sañśayavannu nivārisuvudu sādhyavillavāgi, nannedurige neladalli ūralāgidda ā doḍḍa pādagaḷannē diṭṭisuttā, dūravellādarū hōguvudu sādhyavādare, endāśisuttā nānu niḍusuyde.* Since it was not possible to remove his doubt, looking at his large feet resting on the ground in front of me, wishing to go somewhere far away, I sighed.

English	Hindi	Kannada
'I hope that sigh is from the heart, and that you repent ever having been the occasion of discomfort to your excellent benefactress.'	'मुझे आशा है कि यह आह तुम्हारे हृदय से निकली है और अपनी परम् उपकारिन को कभी दुख पहुँचाने के लिए तुम्हें पश्चात्ताप हो रहा है।' *'mujhe āśā hai ki yah āh tumhāre hṛday se niklī hai aur apnī param upkārin ko kabhī dukh pahuñcāne ke lie tumheṃ paścāttāp ho rahā hai.'* 'I hope that this sigh comes from your heart and that you are repenting ever causing suffering for your excellent benefactor.'	'ಇದೀಗ ಈ ನಿಟ್ಟುಸಿರು ನಿನ್ನ ಹೃದಯದಾಳದಿಂದಲೇ ಬಂದಿರುವುದು ಎಂದುಕೊಳ್ಳುತ್ತೇನೆ. ಶ್ರೇಷ್ಠಳಾದ ನಿನ್ನ ಪೋಷಕಿಗೆ ಅಹಿತವೆನಿಸುವಂತೆ ನಡಕೊಂಡ ಬಗ್ಗೆಯೂ ನೀನು ಪರಿತಪಿಸುವೆ, ಎಂದಂದುಕೊಂಡಿದ್ದೇನೆ.' *'idīga ī niṭṭusiru ninna hṛdayadāḷadindalē bandiruvudu endukoḷḷuttēne. śrēṣṭaḷāda ninna pōṣakige ahitavenisuvante naḍakoṇḍa baggeyū nīnu paritapisuve, endandukoṇḍiddēne.'* 'Now, I think this sigh has come out from the depth of your heart. I think you are repenting for the misbehaviour to your benefactress.'
'Benefactress! benefactress!' said I inwardly: 'they all call Mrs. Reed my benefactress; if so, a benefactress is a disagreeable thing.'	'उपकारिन! उपकारिन! सभी श्रीमती रीड को मेरी उपकारिन कहते हैं। यही यदि उपकार है तो उपकारिन निश्चय ही एक अप्रिय वस्तु है,' मैंने मन-ही-मन कहा था। *'upkārin! upkārin! sabhī śrīmatī rīḍ ko merī upkārin kahte haiṃ. yahī yadi upkār hai to upkārin niścay hī ek apriy vastu hai,' maiṃne man-hī-man kahā thā.* 'Benefactor! Benefactor! Everyone calls Mrs. Reed my benefactor. If this is a benefit, then a benefactor is certainly an unpleasant thing,' I said inwardly in my mind.	ಪೋಷಕಿ! ಎಲ್ಲರೂ ಮಿಸೆಸ್ ರೀಡ್ ರನ್ನು ನನ್ನ ಪೋಷಕಿಯೆನ್ನುತ್ತಾರೆ. ಇಂಥ ಪೋಷಕಿ ಬೇಡವೇ ಬೇಡ, ಎಂದಂದುಕೊಂಡೆ. *pōṣaki! ellarū mises rīḍ rannu nanna pōṣakiyennuttāre. intha pōṣaki bēḍavē bēḍa, endandukoṇḍe.* Benefactress! Everyone calls Mrs. Reed my benefactress. I do not need such a benefactress. So I thought.

English	Hindi	Kannada
'Do you say your prayers night and morning?' continued my interrogator.	प्रश्नकर्ता ने पूछना जारी रखा, 'क्या तुम सुबह-शाम प्रार्थना करती हो?' *praśnakartā ne pūchnā jārī rakhā, 'kyā tum subah-śām prārthnā kartī ho?'* The questioner continued to ask questions: 'Do you pray in the morning and evening?'	'ಬೆಳಗೂ ರಾತ್ರಿಯೂ ನೀನು ಪ್ರಾರ್ಥನೆ ಪಠಿಸುತ್ತೀಯಾ?' – ನನ್ನಾ ಪರೀಕ್ಷಕ ಮುಂದುವರಿಸಿದರು. *'beḷagū rātriyū nīnu prārthane paṭhisuttīyā?' – nannā parīkṣaka munduvarisidaru.* 'Do you recite your prayers in the morning and at night?' – my interrogator continued.
'Yes, sir.'	'हाँ, श्रीमान।' *'hām̐, śrīmān.'* 'Yes, sir.'	'ಹೌದು, ಸರ್.' *'haudu, sar.'* 'Yes, sir.'
'Do you read your bible?'	'क्या तुम बाइबिल पढ़ती हो?' *'kyā tum bāibil paṛhtī ho?'* 'Do you read the Bible?'	'ಬೈಬಲ್ ಓದುತ್ತೀಯಾ?' 'baibal ōduttīyā?' 'Do you read the Bible?'
'Sometimes.'	'कभी-कभी।' *'kabhī-kabhī.'* 'Sometimes.'	'ಕೆಲವೊಮ್ಮೆ.' *'kelavomme.'* 'Sometimes.'
'With pleasure? Are you fond of it?'	'प्रसन्नता से? क्या तुम्हें बाइबिल अच्छा लगता है?' *'prasanntā se? kyā tumheṃ bāibil acchā lagtā hai?'* 'With pleasure? Do you like the Bible?'	'ಸಂತೋಷದಿಂದಲೇ? ಬೈಬಲ್ ನಿನಗಿಷ್ಟವೇ?' *'santōṣadindalē? baibal ninagiṣṭavē?'* 'With pleasure? Do you like the Bible?'

English	Hindi	Kannada
‘I like Revelations and the Book of Daniel, and Genesis and Samuel, and a little bit of Exodus, and some parts of Kings and Chronicles, and Job and Jonah.’	‘मुझे रिवीलेशन, डेनियल की किताब, जेनेसिस और सैमुएल थोड़ा एक्जोडस, किंग और क्रोनिकिल का कुछ भाग तथा जॉब और जोना अच्छे लगते हैं।’ *‘mujhe rivīleśan, ḍeniyal kī kitāb, jenesis aur saimuel thoṛā ekjoḍas, kiṅg aur kronikil kā kuch bhāg tathā job aur jonā acche lagte haiṃ.’* ‘I like Revelations, the Book of Daniel, Genesis and Samuel, a little bit of Exodus, some parts from Kings and Chronicles, as well as Job and Jonah.’	‘ರಿವಿಲೇಶನ್ಸ್, ಡ್ಯಾನಿಯೆಲ್, ಜೆನೆಸಿಸ್, ಸ್ಯಾಮ್ಯುಯೆಲ್, ಜಾಬ್, ಜೋನಾ, ರಾಜರ ವೃತ್ತಾಂತಗಳು, ಇವೆಲ್ಲ ನನಗಿಷ್ಟ.’ *‘rivilēśans, ḍyāniyel, jenesis, syāmyuyel, jāb, jōnā, rājara vṛttāntagaḷu, ivella nanagiṣṭa.’* ‘I like Revelations, Daniel, Genesis, Samuel, Job, Jonah, [and some] episodes of Kings and Chronicles.’
‘And the Psalms? I hope you like them.’	‘और साम (Psalms)? आशा है, उन्हें भी तुम पसन्द करती हो?’ *‘aur sām (Psalms)? āśā hai, unheṃ bhī tum pasand kartī ho?’* ‘And the Psalms? I hope you like them too?’	‘ಮತ್ತು ಕೀರ್ತನೆಗಳು? ಅವು ನಿನಗೆ ಇಷ್ಟವಷ್ಟೇ?’ *‘mattu kīrtanegaḷu? avu ninage iṣṭavaṣṭē?’* ‘And the Psalms? Do you like them too?’
‘No, Sir.’	‘नहीं, श्रीमान!’ *‘nahīṃ, śrīmān!’* ‘No, sir!’	‘ಇಲ್ಲ, ಸರ್.’ *‘illa, sar.’* ‘No, sir.’

English	Hindi	Kannada
'No? Oh, shocking! I have a little boy, younger than you, who knows six Psalms by heart; and when you ask him which he would rather have, a gingerbread-nut to eat, or a verse of a Psalm to learn, he says: 'Oh! The verse of a Psalm! Angels sing Psalms;' says he, 'I wish to be a little angel here below;' he then gets two nuts in recompense for his infant piety.'	'नहीं! बड़े दुख की बात है। अरे, मेरा एक छोटा लड़का है, तुमसे भी छोटा। वह छह साम रटे हुए है। यदि तुम उससे पूछोगी कि चॉकलेट लोगे या साम की एक कविता सीखोगे, तो वह कहेगा कि 'साम की कविता। देवदूत भी साम गाते है! मैं इसी संसार में एक छोटा-सा देवदूत बनना चाहता हूँ।' अपनी शैशव-भक्ति के बदले तब उसे दो चॉकलेट मिल जाते हैं।' *'nahīṃ! baṛe dukh kī bāt hai. are, merā ek choṭā laṛkā hai, tumse bhī choṭā. vah chah sām raṭe hue hai. yadi tum usse pūchogī ki cokleṭ loge yā sām kī ek kavitā sīkhoge, to vah kahegā ki 'sām kī kavitā. devdūt bhī sām gāte hai! maiṃ isī sāṅsār meṃ ek choṭā-sā devdūt bananā cāhtā hūṁ.' apnī śaiśav-bhakti ke badle tab use do cokleṭ mil jāte haiṃ.*	'ಇಲ್ಲವೇ? ಆಶ್ಚರ್ಯ! ನಿನಗಿಂತ ಕಿರಿಯನಾದ ಚಿಕ್ಕ ಹುಡುಗನಿದ್ದಾನೆ; ಅವನಿಗೆ ಆರು ಕೀರ್ತನೆಗಳು ಕಂಠಪಾಠ ಆಗಿವೆ. ತಿನ್ನಲು ಒಂದು ಜಿಂಜರ್ ಬ್ರೆಡ್ ನಟ್ ಬೇಕೇ, ಇಲ್ಲಾ, ಕಲಿಯಲು ಕೀರ್ತನೆಯ ಚರಣ ಒಂದಿರಲೇ, ಎಂದು ಕೇಳಿದರೆ, 'ಓ! ಕೀರ್ತನೆಯ ಚರಣ! ದೇವ ಕಿನ್ನರರು ಕೀರ್ತನೆಗಳನ್ನು ಹಾಡುತ್ತಾರೆ. ನಾನು ಭೂಮಿಯ ಮೇಲಿನ ಪುಟ್ಟ ಕಿನ್ನರನಾಗಬಯಸುತ್ತೇನೆ.' ಎಂದು ಅವನನ್ನುತ್ತಾನೆ. ಅವನ ಈ ಮುಗ್ಧ ಮಗುತನವೇ ಅವನಿಗೆ ಇಮ್ಮಡಿ ನಟ್ಸ್ ಸಿಗುವಂತೆ ಮಾಡುತ್ತದೆ.' *'illavē? āścarya! ninaginta kiriyanāda cikka huḍuganiddāne; avanige āru kīrtanegaḷu kaṇṭhapāṭha āgive. tinnalu ondu jiñjar breḍ naṭ bēkē, illā, kaliyalu kīrtaneya caraṇa ondiralē, endu kēḷidare, 'ō! kīrtaneya caraṇa! dēva kinnararu kīrtanegaḷannu hāḍuttāre. nānu bhūmiya mēlina puṭṭa kinnaranāgabayasuttēne.' endu avanannuttāne. avana ī mugdha magutanavē avanige immaḍi naṭs siguvante māḍuttade.'*

	'No! That is very sad. Well, I have a little boy, even younger than you. He memorised six Psalms. If you ask him whether he would rather have a chocolate or learn a poem from the Psalms, then he replies, 'A poem from the Psalms. Angels too sing the Psalms! I want to be a little angel in this world.' In exchange for his infant devotion, he then gets two chocolates.'	'No? Surprising! There is a little boy younger than you. He has six psalms memorised. If asked, do you want a gingerbread nut to eat or a verse of a psalm to learn, he says 'Oh, a verse of the Psalms. Divine *kinnaras* [celestial musicians, angels] sing psalms. I want to be a little *kinnara* on earth.' This kind of innocent infancy gets him two nuts.'
'Psalms are not interesting,' I remarked.	'साम पढ़ने में मन नहीं लगता,' मैंने विचार प्रकट किया। *'sām paṛhne meṃ man nahīṃ lagtā,' maiṃne vicār prakaṭ kiyā.* I expressed the opinion, 'I do not have a mind for reading the Psalms.'	'ಕೀರ್ತನೆಗಳು ಆಸಕ್ತಿಕರವಾಗಿಲ್ಲ' ನಾನಂದೆ. *'kīrtanegaḷu āsaktikaravāgilla' nānande.* 'The Psalms are not interesting,' I said.

English	Hindi	Kannada
'That proves you have a wicked heart; and you must pray to God to change it: to give you a new and a clean one: to take away your heart of stone and give you a heart of flesh.'	'इससे प्रमाणित हुआ की तुम दुष्ट हृदय की हो। ईश्वर से प्रार्थना करो कि वे इसे बदल दें, तुम्हें नया और स्वच्छ हृदय दें, तुम्हारे पत्थर का हृदय हटाकर हाड़-मांस का हृदय दें।' *'isse pramāṇit huā kī tum duṣṭ hr̥day kī ho. īśvar se prārthnā karo ki ve ise badal deṃ, tumheṃ nayā aur svacch hr̥day deṃ, tumhāre patthar kā hr̥day haṭākar hāṛ-māṃs kā hr̥day deṃ.'* 'This proves that you have a wicked heart. Pray to God that He will change it, that He will give you a new and clean heart, that He will remove your heart of stone and instead give you a heart of flesh.'	'ನಿನ್ನದು ಕೆಡುಕು ಹೃದಯವೆಂದು ಇದರಿಂದಲೇ ತಿಳಿಯುತ್ತದೆ. ಅದನ್ನು ಬದಲಿಸಿ ಹೊಸತೊಂದು ಪರಿಶುದ್ಧ ಹೃದಯವನ್ನೀಯುವಂತೆ, ಈ ಕಲ್ಲು ಹೃದಯದ ಬದಲಿಗೆ ರಕ್ತ ಮಾಂಸದ ಹೃದಯವನ್ನೀಯುವಂತೆ ನೀನು ದೇವರಲ್ಲಿ ಪ್ರಾರ್ಥಿಸಬೇಕು.' *'ninnadu keḍuku hr̥dayavendu idarindalē tiḷiyuttade. adannu badalisi hosatondu pariśuddha hr̥dayavannīyuvante, ī kallu hr̥dayada badalige rakta mānsada hr̥dayavannīyuvante nīnu dēvaralli prārthisabēku.'* 'This shows that your heart is wicked. You should pray to God to change your heart to a pure heart, to give [you] a heart of blood and flesh in place of your heart of stone.'

	Gujarati[125]
	બ્રોકલહર્સ્ટે મને સ્કૂલે જવાનું ગમશે કે કેમ અને પ્રાર્થના કરું છું કે નહીં, એમ પ્રશ્નો પૂછ્યા. અને હું તે બધું કરું છું. એમ મેં કહ્યું ત્યારે તેમણે મને ભક્તિગીતો આવડે છે કે નહીં, પૂછ્યું. તેના જવાબમાં મેં જ્યારે ના પાડી ત્યારે તેઓ બોલી ઊઠ્યા કે ભક્તિગીતો આવડે નહીં તે નર્કમાં જાય છે. તે પછી તેમણે નર્કમાં ભયંકર તેજ અગ્નિમાં તેવા માણસોને બાળવામાં આવે છે. એમ કહી મને સારી છોકરી બનવા કહ્યું. *brokalharsṭe mane skūle javānuṃ gamśe ke kem ane prārthnā karuṃ chuṃ ke nahīṃ, em praśno pūchyā. ane huṃ te badhuṃ karuṃ chuṃ. em meṃ kahyuṃ tyāre temṇe mane bhaktigīto āvḍe che ke nahīṃ, pūchyuṃ. tenā javābmāṃ meṃ jyāre nā pāḍī tyāre teo bolī ūṭhyā ke bhaktigīto āvḍe nahīṃ te narkmāṃ jāy che. te pachī temṇe narkmāṃ bhayaṃkar tej agnimāṃ tevā māṇsone bāḷvāmāṃ āve che. em kahī mane sārī chokrī banvā kahyuṃ.* Brocklehurst asked me questions, such as whether I like to go to school and whether I pray, and [I said that] I do all of that. When I had said so, he asked whether I know [how to sing] devotional songs. When I replied in the negative, he declared at once that those who do not know devotional songs go to hell. He then said that such humans are burnt in a terrifying blazing fire in hell. Having said so, he asked me to be a good girl.

The Gujarati abridged translation condenses the long original passage into a brief paraphrase in the form of a short third-person diegetic narrative without any dialogue in direct speech. It does so by fully removing any culture-specific elements, in this case the theological references to the Bible. It preserves only one technical term, but alters its meaning from Psalms in English to *bhaktigīto* (devotional songs) in Gujarati *bhāṣā* (vernacular). By using a term that is associated with daily Hindu religious rituals in Indian society, it manages to align a familiar Gujarati notion with a corresponding Christian concept. The unabridged Hindi and Kannada translations, on the other hand, effortlessly manage to express the rather specialised wording of the English passage with near semantic equivalence.

125 Paṭel, *Śārloṭ Bronṭe*, p. 5. It is notable that the Gujarati passage occurs in Ch. 1 of the translation, unlike in the original English version where it is found in Ch. 4.

The stark difference between the Gujarati abridged translation and the source text provokes the question whether such a form of textual reproduction ought to be called a translation at all. It is probably not possible to subsume this type of rendering under Jakobson's 'equivalence in difference', but it could be understood as a *pariṇāmī paryāy* (transformed modality). The abridged paraphrase of the source text retains the janeeyreness as a *sāhityik prakār* (literary type) in a sufficient degree to perceive the Gujarati text as an instantiation of the work, even if condensed. Hence, it is here only possible to speak of a *dravyārthik samtulyatā* (substantive equivalence).

Yet, abridged translation is not only paraphrase, for it may also contain more elaborate passages that are closer to word-for-word translation. In such portions, even an abridged translation may introduce transformed meanings in the *bhāṣā* (vernacular) that augment the substance of the source text markedly. In the case of *Jane Eyre*, a very suitable example is the scene where Jane and Mr Rochester have their first formal conversation at Thornfield Hall. The topic of the exchange is their chance encounter during the preceding evening when Mr Rochester fell off his horse. The full passage is first given in English, Hindi, and Kannada, whereupon the rather surprisingly literal rendering of the same passage in the otherwise abridged Gujarati translation follows:

English[126]	Hindi[127]	Kannada[128]
'I thought not. And so you were waiting for your people when you sat on that stile?'	'मैं भी यही समझता था। तो तुम उस घुमावदार पुलिया पर बैठकर अपने मित्रों की पूतीक्षा कर रही थी?' *'maiṃ bhī yahī samajhtā thā. to tum us ghumāvdār puliyā par baiṭhkar apne mitroṃ kī pratīkṣā kar rahī thī?'* 'I also thought so. And so you were sitting on that round culvert waiting for your friends?'	'ಇಲ್ಲವೆಂದೇ ನಾನೂ ಎಣಿಸಿದೆ. ಹಾಗಾದರೆ ನೀನಲ್ಲಿ ಆ ಶಿಲಾಹಾಸಿನಲ್ಲಿ ಕುಳಿತು ನಿನ್ನ ಜನರಿಗಾಗಿ ಕಾಯುತ್ತಿದ್ದೆಯಾ?' *'illavendē nānū eṇiside. hāgādare nīnalli ā śilāhāsinalli kuḷitu ninna janarigāgi kāyuttiddeyā?'* 'I thought not. If so, were you sitting on that stone waiting for your people?'
'For whom, sir?'	'किसकी महाशय?' *'kiskī mahāśay?'* 'For whom, sir?'	'ಯಾರಿಗಾಗಿ ಸರ್?' *'yārigāgi sar?'* 'For whom, sir?'
'For the men in green: it was a proper moonlight evening for them. Did I break through one of your rings, that you spread that damned ice on the causeway?'	'जंगल में रहनेवाली परियों की। कल की चाँदनी पूर्णतः उनके अनुकूल थी। क्या मैंने तुम लोगों का कोई गोल तोड़ दिया था जिससे कुद्ध होकर तुमने रास्ते पर वह दुखदायी बर्फ बिछा दिया?' *'jaṅgal meṃ rahnevālī pariyoṃ kī. kal kī cāndnī pūrṇtaḥ unke anukūl thī. kyā maiṃne tum logoṃ kā koī gol toṛ diyā thā jisse kruddh hokar tumne rāste par vah dukhdāyī barph bichā diyā?'* 'For those beings living in the jungle. Yesterday's moonlight was perfectly suited for them. Did I break some sphere of yours, due to which you got angry and spread that painful ice on the road?'	'ಹಸಿರುಡುಗೆಯವರಿಗಾಗಿ; ಅದು ಅದಕ್ಕೆ ತಕ್ಕ ಬೆಳದಿಂಗಳ ರಾತ್ರಿಯಾಗಿತ್ತು. ನಾನೇನು ನಿನ್ನ ಪರಿಧಿಯನ್ನು ಅತಿಕ್ರಮಿಸಿದೆನೇ, ನೀನು ಹಾಗೆ ನನ್ನ ದಾರಿಯಲ್ಲಿ ಹಿಮ ಚೆಲ್ಲಲು?' *'hasiruḍugeyavarigāgi; adu adakke takka beḷadiṅgaḷa rātriyāgittu. nānēnu ninna paridhiyannu atikramisidenē, nīnu hāge nanna dāriyalli hima cellalu?'* 'For the people dressed in green. It was a proper moonlight night. Did I cross your circle that you spread snow on my path?'

126 *JE*, Ch. 13.
127 Sinhā, *Jen Āyar*, p. 126.
128 Mādhava, *Jēn Air*, p. 130.

	Gujarati[129]
	‘મને ખબર જ હતી કે નહીં જ હોય. તો તમે પથ્થર ઉપર બેસીને તમારા સાગરીતોની રાહ જોતાં હતાં?’ ‘શું કહ્યું સાહેબ?’ ‘કેમ, પેલા લીલા રંગના માણસો … ચાંદની રાત પણ હતી. તે જ તમને ગમે છે ને? મેં તે લક્ષ્મણરેખા ઓળંગી? તમે જે બરફ ઉપર દોરી હતી તે?’ *‘mane khabar ja hatī ke nahīṁ ja hoya. to tame paththar upar besīne tamārā sāgarītonī rāh jotāṃ hatāṃ?’ ‘śuṃ kahyuṃ sāheb?’ ‘kem, pelā līlā raṅgnā māṇso … cāndnī rāt paṇ hatī. te ja tamne game che ne? meṃ te lakṣmaṇrekhā oḷaṅgī? tame je baraph upar dorī hatī te?’* ‘I knew for sure that would not be the case. So were you sitting on that stone waiting for your accomplices[?]’ ‘What did you say, sir?’ ‘Well, those green-coloured men … It was a moonlit night too. That is exactly what you like, isn’t it? Did I cross the line of Lakṣmaṇ, which you had drawn on the ice?’

In the original English text, attention must here be drawn to the sentence ‘Did I break through one of your rings, that you spread that damned ice on the causeway?’, where the purport of the word ‘rings’ needs to be considered. The allegorical source of the rings stems from a folkloristic belief in fairies found in the pre-Christian culture of Europe. The idea of a fairy ring or fairy circle originates with an actual physical indentation of varying size caused by a certain kind of subterranean fungi that naturally occurs on the ground or in the grass.[130] In European folklore, these rings are associated with magical beings such as fairies, elves, or witches, who are believed to dance within their boundaries on moonlit nights. Thus, when in the same passage Mr Rochester speaks of ‘the men in green’, he is referring to supernatural beings of the forest, who typically are portrayed in green clothes. He thereby implies that Jane conspired with those beings and caused him to fall from his horse as a punishment for having transgressed the sacred boundary of the circle. In folkloric beliefs,

129 Paṭel, *Śārloṭ Bronṭe*, p. 54.

130 For details of the belief and the physical phenomenon, see Gordon Rutter, ‘Fairy Rings’, *Field Mycology*, 3.2 (2002), 56–60. On European beliefs in fairies, see Carole G. Silver, ‘Fairies and Elves: Motifs F200–F399’, in *Archetypes and Motifs in Folklore and Literature*, ed. by Jane Garry and Hasan El-Shamy (Armonk, New York: M. E. Sharpe, 2005), pp. 203–9.

trespassing a fairy ring is considered a violation and dangerous for humans.

When reproducing the English 'Did I break through one of your rings', the Hindi translation in its literal attempt to formulate the clause betrays the allegorical aspect of the idiom. The result is a somewhat dull and overly literal reading *kyā maiṃne tum logoṃ kā koī gol toṛ diyā* (Did I break some sphere of yours). The chosen word for ring, in Hindi *gol* (गोल) meaning sphere or circle, does not evoke the full connotation of the English word in its mythical sense. Although the Kannada translation for ring, *paridhi* (ಪರಿಧಿ), approximates the meaning of the English word as it signifies an enclosure or boundary and from a purely semantic point of view is a correct choice, it too lacks the folkloristic force of the image.

Astoundingly, the Gujarati translation, which otherwise tends to discard cultural complexities from the source text, approaches the clause at hand through a highly effective translational strategy. Instead of resorting to a literal translation, it captures the imagination of the audience by employing a corresponding Indian allegory. Drawing on an Indian folkloric belief, Paṭel translates the English word 'rings' with *lakṣmaṇrekhā* (લક્ષ્મણરેખા the line of Lakṣmaṇ).[131] This Indian adage, referring to a strict boundary or rule that may never be broken or crossed, has its origin in the folk theatre tradition of *rāmlīlā* (रामलीला plays of Rām).[132] Just as in the case of the fairy ring, crossing the *lakṣmaṇrekhā* (the line of Lakṣmaṇ) brings bad luck and danger. The central scene common to all the *rāmlīlā* plays is the abduction of Sītā. While staying in a forest exile, the hero Rām goes out to catch a golden deer for his wife Sītā. When he does not return, Sītā requests Rām's younger brother Lakṣmaṇ to go and look for him. Concerned for her safety, Lakṣmaṇ draws a *rekhā* (line) on the ground encircling Sītā to form a protective boundary that she is told not to cross. During his absence, however, the evil Rāvaṇ, disguised as a noble ascetic, tricks

131 On the *lakṣmaṇrekhā*, its origin, and use, see Danuta Stasik, 'A (Thin) Boundary Not to Be Crossed, or *Lakṣman-rekhā*', *Cracow Indological Studies*, 21 (2019), 207–24, and Uma Chakravarti, 'The Development of the Sita Myth: A Case Study of Women in Myth and Literature', *Samaya Shakti: A Journal of Women's Studies*, 1 (1983), 68–75.

132 The dramatic tradition of *rāmlīlā* is related to the vernacular versions of the *Rāmāyaṇa* epic, for which see Paula Richman (ed.), *Many Rāmāyaṇas: The Diversity of a Narrative Tradition in South Asia* (Berkeley: University of California Press, 1991) and Danuta Stasik, *The Infinite Story: Past and Present of the Rāmāyaṇas in Hindi* (New Delhi: Manohar, 2009).

Sītā to step out of the circle, at which point he snatches her and carries her away. This turn of events constitutes the primary complication in the plot, leading to Rām's epic struggle to rescue Sītā. Over the centuries, the dictum *lakṣmaṇrekhā* (the line of Lakṣmaṇ) became so widespread that it has become an Indian household turn of phrase for any limit or boundary not to be transgressed.[133]

The clever narrative device of the *lakṣmaṇrekhā* (the line of Lakṣmaṇ) may serve as a fitting example of the intertwined relationship between *anuvād* (translation), *bhāṣā* (vernacular), and *kathātmik pariṇām* (कथात्मिक परिणाम narrative transformation). The translational dependency is a transformative escape from the confines of literalness that allows immersion into the story within the innovative narrative setting of the *bhāṣā* (vernacular), quite like Kamlā's imaginative flight from the evil witch in *Saṅgdil*. In this manner, the Gujarati abridged translation opens up the substance of janeeyreness to the literary world of the *rāmlīlā*, adding another modality to what the janeeyreness may mean by creating a *sandhi* (juncture) of substantive equivalence between Jane and Sītā.

Kathātmik pariṇām (narrative transformation) is intrinsic to *anuvād* (translation) into a *bhāṣā* (vernacular), as has been instantiated through the selected synoptic readings of *Jane Eyre* in Hindi, Kannada, and Gujarati. Whether in the exemplification of the literal Hindi translation's subtle rendering of the English word race into *jāti* (caste) or the overt occurrence of the Gujarati abridged translation's substitution of the English fairy ring with the allegory of *lakṣmaṇrekhā* (the line of Lakṣmaṇ), translation transforms the narrative of a novel into the literary realm of the *bhāṣā* (vernacular). In such cases, the equivalences between the source text and the translation are more substantive than semantic, inasmuch as the formation of meaning in the *bhāṣā* (vernacular) occurs primarily within the intralingual linguistic, poetic, and literary formations of the *bhāṣā* itself, whereas the interlingual transference between the source and target languages is secondary.

Dravyārthik samtulyatā (substantive equivalence), being a broader term than *śabdārthik samtulyatā* (semantic equivalence), therefore

133 It may be added that the Hindi translation also employs the expression 'the line of Lakṣmaṇ' (*lakṣmaṇrekhā*) in a passage elsewhere when translating the English clause 'the Rubicon was passed'; see *JE*, Ch. 7, and Sinhā, *Jen Āyar*, p. 66. The Rubicon sentence is omitted in Paṭel's Gujarati abridged translation (Ch. 3, p. 16) and therefore has no correspondence.

comes to include not only literal translation but also abridged translation and even adaptation. The breadth of the concept tallies with the great variety of translational practices that are observable in the long history of translation in classical and modern Indian sources. An adaptation, such as the film *Saṅgdil*, or an abridged translation, such as Paṭel's Gujarati version, is no less substantively equivalent to *Jane Eyre* than is the Hindi or Kannada literal translation, given that they similarly coalesce in the *dravya* (substance) *Jane Eyre*, having qualities of janeeyreness.

The notion of *dravyārthik samtulyatā* (substantive equivalence) has the potential to create a sense of continuity and consolidation between the classical and modern Indian practices of intertextuality and translation, without any need to dismiss certain forms of textual transformation, such as abridgement or gist translation, as being inferior or outright inadmissible. The very widespread Indian use of abridgement, which is so evident in the case of the modern Indian *Jane Eyre* renditions, is unsurprising when this contemporary translational practice is viewed historically in comparison to the common literary practices of textual adaptation and retelling within the classical Indian traditions. Summary, paraphrase, and reworking were more widespread writing styles in the classical traditions than literal word-for-word translation. Hence, the textual expectations raised by the modern Indian term *anuvād* (translation) may differ somewhat from the assumptions invoked by the English term translation.

The generic quality of substantive equivalence prompts the critical question of what the cognitive principle for distinguishing between the Indian phenomena of literal translation, abridged translation, and adaptation might be. Unpacking a universal notion of translation for the purpose of discerning its particulars necessitates recourse to a new theoretical criterion that would allow for setting these three distinct literary practices apart, without the drawback of misconstruing them as mutually exclusive counterparts. Avoiding the proclivity in the European tradition to treat adaptation, abridgement, and translation as diametrical opposites must be at the core of such a *modus operandi*, which in turn has to take advantage of a theoretical discourse outside the boundaries of occidental parameters.

In the Indian context of poetics, such a criterion may be derived from the classical Indian theory of *alaṃkāra* (अलंकार tropes), wherein the cognitive term *dīpaka* (दीपक illumination, epiphany) could serve as a basis for proposing a contiguity between the three practices without asserting an opposition.

The *dīpaka* (epiphany) is a poetic element that triggers an understanding in the reader of the overall character and meaning of a text. According to the late seventh-century poetician Daṇḍin, the *dīpaka* takes the form of a hint or sign provided either at the outset, in the middle, or at the end of a work that causes the reader to understand what the given poem is about, for instance the topic of springtime.[134] Using such a cognitive principle, it will be argued that engaging the literary notion of *dīpaka* in translation theory makes it possible to distinguish between literal translation, abridged translation, and adaptation.

A literal translation tends to signal its translational character from the very outset of the publication, for instance, by the fact that the title of the translation corresponds to that of a known work or that concrete paratextual statements are provided on the book cover or in the front matter naming the original author and the translator. These elements given already at the outset of the book can be understood as signs that trigger a *dīpaka* (epiphany) enabling the reader to identify the text at hand as a literal translation.

Disregarding such hints at the start of the publication, the true character of an abridgement first becomes fully assessable towards the middle of the reading, when the reader is in a position to realise the full extent of the omissions and paraphrases in the rendering. Therefore, in the case of an abridged translation, the *dīpaka* (epiphany) arises only in the middle of the reading.

Whether a work is an adaptation can be determined solely at the very completion of the reading or viewing, at which point the congruence of the parallels in the storylines between the adaptation and its source text as a whole becomes evident. On this assumption, with adaptations, the *dīpaka* (epiphany) arises at the end.

These three types of observable signs of transformational configuration are tropes of *dīpaka* (epiphany) enabling the audience to realise a particular modality as being either literal translation, abridged translation, or adaptation. From a *dravyārthik naya*

134 On the rhetorical figure *dīpaka*, see Daṇḍin, *Kāvyādarśa*, verses II.97–115; Sanskrit edition and English translation in John F. Eppling, 'A Calculus of Creative Expression: The Central Chapter of Daṇḍin's *Kāvyādarśa*' (doctoral thesis, The University of Wisconsin, 1989), pp. 671–726.

(substantive perspective), the three literary practices are similar with regard to being equal instantiations of a given literary work sharing substantive equivalence. From a *paryāyārthik naya* (modal perspective), they differ in terms of their internal tropological figuration of when and how the *dīpaka* (epiphany) arises and it is this difference that distinguishes the three translational practices. By regarding the three literary practices analogously as *pariṇām* (transformations), any irreconcilable dichotomy between equivalence and difference falls away and there need not be an opposition between translation, abridgement, and adaptation.

Dīpaka (epiphany), being a cognition, is a state of consciousness. The tropological cognition of the *dīpaka* is what induces the consciousness of the reader to conceive of a relation between the source text and the translation in a moment of revelation or illumination. This translational consciousness[135] is at once etic and emic.[136] It is etic owing to the interlingual nature of that relation induced by perceiving a form of equivalence across cultures, while it is emic in as much as the consciousness is mythically enmeshed in an intralingual deep structure of the reader's personal set of languages, which erects borders of heterolinguistic difference.[137]

Through the synchronicity of these etic and emic aspects, the consciousness transcends the dichotomy of equivalence and difference. The outcome is a metonymic interplay of the source text and the translation, meeting at the *sandhi* (juncture), as it were, formed by the *dīpaka* cognition. Accordingly, the nature of a *dīpaka* cognition is to create a *sandhi* (juncture) that transforms the initially separate poetic elements into a perception of a then-unified literary substance. Seeing

135 For a different use of the term 'translational consciousness', cf. Ganesh N. Devy, "Translation and Literary History: An Indian View", in *Post-Colonial Translation: Theory and Practice*, ed. by Susan Bassnett and Harish Trivedi (London: Routledge, 1999), pp. 182–88 (184–85).

136 For the anthropological distinction between etic and emic in literary theory, see Gunilla Lindberg-Wada, *Literary History: Towards a Global Perspective* (Berlin: de Gruyter, 2006), II, pp. 2–3.

137 The word mythic is here to be understood in the tropological sense as propounded by Hayden White in a different context of historical writing being prefigured by a culturally-determined mythic consciousness; see Hayden White, "Interpretation in History", in *New Literary History*, 4.2 (1973), 281–314 (pp. 292–94); reprint in Hayden White, *Tropics of Discourse: Essays in Cultural Criticism* (Baltimore: Johns Hopkins University Press, 1978), pp. 51–80. On the notion of the heterolingual as a critical response to Jakobson's concepts of interlingual and intralingual, see Sakai, *Translation and Subjectivity*, pp. 1–17.

the narrative transformation of janeeyreness in the given instance of *Jane Eyre*, whether it be translation, abridgement, or adaptation, thereby offers a pathway to a consolidated theory of translation.

Works Cited

For the translations of *Jane Eyre* referred to, please see the List of Translations at the end of this book.

Ahad, Salma, 'English Studies in Kashmir: An Examination of the Relationship between Undergraduate English Courses and Literary Studies in English at the M. A. Level' (doctoral thesis, University of Kashmir, 2002).

Amarmuni, Śrīcand Surānā, and Rājkumār Jain, *Sacitra Antakr̥ddaśā sūtra: mūl pāṭh, Hindī-Aṅgrejī bhāvānuvād tathā vivecan sahit (viśoṣ pariśiṣṭa, Antakr̥ddaśā mahimā)* (Delhi: Padma Prakāśan, 1999).

Appātturai, K., *Jēn Ayar: Ulakap pukaḻ peṟṟa nāval* (Tirunelvēli: Tirunelvēlit Teṉṉintiya Cavacittānta Nūṟpatippuk Kaḻakam, 1953; Chennai: Cāratā Māṇikkam Patippakam, reprint 2003).

Azim, Firdous, *The Colonial Rise of the Novel: From Aphra Behn to Charlotte Bronte* (London: Routledge, 1993).

Banerjee, Shukla, 'Portrait of Women in the Novels of Charlotte Brontë' (doctoral thesis, Pt. Ravishankar Shukla University, 2014).

Barthes, Roland, 'From Work to Text', in *The Rustle of Language*, trans. by Richard Howard (New York: Hill and Wang, 1986), pp. 56–64.

Barua, Deetimali, 'The Victorian Family: An Analysis of the Role of the Family in the Victorian Novel with Special Reference to the Brontë Sisters' (doctoral thesis, Gauhati University, 2006).

Baruwā, Subhadrā, *Jen Āẏār* (Guwahati: Pūrbāñcal Prakāś, 1999).

Bassnett, Susan and Harish Trivedi (eds.), *Post-Colonial Translation: Theory and Practice* (London: Routledge, 1999).

Begam, Surāiyā Ākhtār, *Jen Āẏār* (Dhaka: Muktadhārā, 1977).

Berman, Antoine, *L'épreuve de l'étranger: Culture et traduction dans l'Allemande romantique* (Paris: Gallimard, 1984).

Bhardwaj, Abhinav, 'Echoes of *Jane Eyre* in the Novels of Margaret Atwood', *Contemporary Literary Review India*, 7.2 (2020), 1–11.

Brontë, Charlotte (penname Currer Bell), *Jane Eyre: An Autobiography*, first edition 1847, 3 vols (London: Smith, Elder, and Co., 1847; London: Service & Paton, reprint 1897). The citations given in the article are to the 1897 reprint, with its standard chapter numbers common to the single-volume editions of the novel.

Brough, John, *The Gandhari Dhammapada* (Delhi: Motilal Banarsidass Publishers, 2001).

Bunyan, John, *The Pilgrim's Progress from This World, to That Which Is to Come*, edn by Roger Sharrock and J. B. Wharey (Oxford: Oxford University Press, 1975 (1678)).

Caudhurī, Kabīr, *Jen Āẏār: Saṃkṣepit o rūpāntarit* (Dhaka: Muktadhārā, 1990).

Caudhurī, Sālēhā, *Śārlaṭ Branṭi: Jen Āẏār* (Dhaka: Uttaraṇ, 2019).

Ceṟiyān, Sāṟa Dīpa, *Jeyn Eyar: Jane Eyre: Charlotte Brontë* (Kothamangalam: Saikataṃ Buks, 2020).

Chakravarti, Uma, 'The Development of the Sita Myth: A Case Study of Women in Myth and Literature', *Samaya Shakti: A Journal of Women's Studies*, 1 (1983), 68–75.

Chaudhuri, Sukanta, *Translation and Understanding* (New Delhi: Oxford University Press, 1999).

De Clercq, Eva, '*Paümacariẏa—Padmacarita—Paümacariu*: The Jain Rāmāyaṇa-Purāṇa', in *Epics, Khilas, and Purāṇas: Continuities and Ruptures*, ed. by Petteri Koskikallio under the general editorship of Mislav Ježić (Zagreb: Croatian Academy of Sciences and Arts, 2005), pp. 597–608.

Cort, John E., 'Making It Vernacular in Agra: The Practice of Translation by Seventeenth-Century Jains', in *Tellings and Texts: Music, Literature and Performance in North India*, ed. by Francesca Orsini and Katherine Butler Schofield (Cambridge: Open Book Publishers, 2015), pp. 61–105, https://doi.org/10.11647/obp.0062.12

Cunningham, Valentine, '"God and Nature Intended You for a Missionary's Wife": Mary Hill, Jane Eyre and Other Missionary Women in the 1840s,' in *Women and Missions: Past and Present*, ed. by Fiona Bowie, Deborah Kirkwood, and Shirley Ardener (New York: Routledge, 1993), pp. 85–105.

Dēvi, Nīḷā, *Bēḍi Bandavaḷu* (Mysuru: Mōhana Prakāśana, 1959).

Devy, Ganesh N., *In Another Tongue: Essays on Indian English Literature* (Frankfurt am Main: Peter Lang, 1993), pp. 117–18.

——, 'Translation and Literary History: An Indian View,' in *Post-Colonial Translation: Theory and Practice*, ed. by Susan Bassnett and Harish Trivedi (London: Routledge, 1999), pp. 182–88.

Elizabeth, Deepika, 'Re-Visioning Women's Writing: A Study of George Eliot's The Mill on the Floss and Charlotte Brontë's Jane Eyre' (doctoral thesis, University of Madras, 2015).

Emmerich, Karen, *Literary Translation and the Making of Originals* (New York: Bloomsbury, 2017), https://doi.org/10.1093/fmls/cqy033

Eppling, John F., 'A Calculus of Creative Expression: The Central Chapter of Daṇḍin's *Kāvyādarśa*' (doctoral thesis, The University of Wisconsin, 1989).

Esposito, Anna Aurelia, 'The South Indian Drama Manuscripts', in *Aspects of Manuscript Culture in South India*, ed. by Saraju Rath (Leiden: Brill, 2012), pp. 81–97, https://doi.org/10.1163/9789004223479

Evison, Gillian, 'The Orientalist, his Institute and the Empire: The Rise and Subsequent Decline of Oxford University's Indian Institute' (Oxford

University, 2004), https://www.bodleian.ox.ac.uk/__data/assets/pdf_file/0009/27774/indianinstitutehistory.pdf

Feeney, Denis, *Beyond Greek: The Beginnings of Latin Literature* (Cambridge, MA: Harvard University Press, 2016), https://doi.org/10.4159/9780674496026

Freytag, Gustav, *Die Technik des Dramas* (Leipzig: S. Hirzel, 1863).

Friedlander, Peter G., 'Before Translation?', in *Translation in Asia: Theories, Practices, Histories*, ed. by Ronit Ricci and Jan van der Putten (Manchester: St Jerome Publishing, 2011), pp. 45–56, https://doi.org/10.4324/9781315760117

Funayama, Tōru (船山 徹), 'Masquerading as Translation: Examples of Chinese Lectures by Indian Scholar-Monks in the Six Dynasties Period', *Asia Major*, 19 (2006), 39–55.

Gaston, Anne-Marie, 'Dance and the Hindu Woman: Bharatanāṭyam Re-Ritualized', in *Roles and Rituals for Hindu Women*, ed. by Julia Leslie (Rutherford: Fairleigh Dickinson University Press, 1991), pp. 149–71.

Ghosh, Kalyani, 'Charlotte Brontë: A Re-Assessment' (doctoral thesis, University of Burdwan, 1991). Revised edition: Kalyani Ghosh, *The Novels of Charlotte Brontë: A Reassessment* (Kolkata: Papyrus Publishers, 2003).

——, 'Satire in Charlotte Bronte's *Shirley*', *Punjab Journal of English Studies* (1995).

——, 'The Last Fragments of Charlotte Bronte: Some Inconclusive Conclusions', *Dibrugarh University Journal of English Studies*, 12 (1996–1997), 77–84.

——, 'The Poetry of Anne Bronte', *Pegassus* (Kolkata, 2010).

——, 'Romanticism with a Difference: Anne Bronte's *The Tenant of Wildfell Hall*', *Heteroglossia* (2014).

Ghosh, Manomohan, *The Naṭyaśāstra: A Treatise on Hindu Dramaturgy and Histrionics ascribed to Bharata-Muni*, 2 vols (Kolkata: The Royal Asiatic Society of Bengal, 1950–1961).

Gilbert, Sandra and Susan Gubar, *The Mad Woman in the Attic: The Woman Writer and Nineteenth-Century Literary Imagination* (New Haven: Yale University Press, 1979).

Goldstücker, Theodor, *A Dictionary, Sanskrit and English, Extended and Improved from the Second Edition of the Dictionary of Professor H. H. Wilson with His Sanction and Concurrence* (Berlin: A. Asher & Co., 1856).

Gombrich, Richard, *On Being Sanskritic: A Plea for Civilized Study and the Study of Civilization* (Oxford: Clarendon Press, 1977).

Gopinathan, G., 'Ancient Indian Theories of Translation: A Reconstruction', in *Beyond the Western Tradition: Essays on Translation outside Standard European Languages*, ed. by Marilyn Gaddis Rose (Binghamton: State University of New York, 2000), pp. 165–73.

——, 'Translation, Transcreation and Culture: Theories of Translation in Indian Languages', in *Translating Others*, ed. by Theo Hermans, 2 vols (New York: Routledge, 2014), I, pp. 236–46, https://doi.org/10.4324/9781315759869

Goswami, Debarati, 'Charlotte Bronte's "Imagined" Indianness: Homogenized Othering as a Mimetic Response in *Jane Eyre*', *Rupkatha Journal on Interdisciplinary Studies in Humanities*, 7 (2015), 114–22.

Guari, Vishwanathan, *Masks of Conquest: Literary Study and British Rule in India* (Oxford: Oxford University Press, 1989).

Havely, Cicely, *A Marble Column*, published independently, 2019.

Hazra, Aparajita, 'Elements of the Gothic in the Brontes' (doctoral thesis, University of Burdwan, 2004).

Hosāhin, Khurram, *Śārlaṭ Branṭi: Jen Āẏār* (Dhaka: Phrēnḍs Buk Karṇār, 2011).

Hosen, Kājī Śāhnūr, *Kiśor klāsik: Jen Āẏār, Liṭl Uimen, Bhyāniṭi Pheẏār* (Dhaka: Sebā Prakāśanī, 2006).

Hosen, Muhaḥ Jākir, *Śārlaṭ Branṭi pāṭhaknandit ō śilpottīrṇa upanyās: Jen Āẏār* (Dhaka: Biśbasāhitya Bhaban, 2018).

d'Hubert, Thibaut, 'Ālāol' and "Abd al-Ḥakīm', in the *Encyclopedia of Islam*, 3rd edn, ed. by K. Fleet, G. Krämer, D. Matringe, J. Nawas, and E. Robson (Leiden: Brill, 2013), III.

Jain, Mukhtār Ratancand, *Śrīmaddevasenācāryaviracitā Ālāpapaddhati aparanāma dravyānuyogapraveśikā* (Saharanpur, U. P.: Prācīn Ārṣ Granthāyatan, 1940; reprint 2003).

Jakobson, Roman, 'On Linguistic Aspects of Translation', in *On Translation*, ed. by Reuben A. Brower *et al.* (Cambridge, MA: Harvard University Press, 1959), pp. 232–39.

Janaki, B., 'The Variegated Voices: Feminine Consciousness in Selected Novels of Jane Austen, Charlotte Brontë and Anita Brookner' (doctoral thesis, Dayalbagh Educational Institute, 2008).

Jauhari, Seema, 'Female Self Assertiveness: A Study in the Novels of Charlotte Brontë, Emily Brontë, and George Eliot' (doctoral thesis, Chhatrapati Shahu Ji Maharaj University, 1992).

JE: see Brontë, Charlotte, *Jane Eyre*.

Johnson, Samuel, *A Dictionary of the English Language*, 2 vols (London: Knapton, Longman, Hitch, Hawes, Millar, & Dodsley, 1755).

Kākaḍiyā, Manasukh, *Veīkphīlḍano bhalo pādrī, Bicārī Anāth Chokarī* (Ahmedabad: Bālvinod Prakāśan, 2009).

Kavi, M. Ramakrishna, *Nāṭyaśāstra of Bharatamuni with the Commentary Abhinavabhāratī by Abhinavaguptācārya*, 4 vols, 2nd revised edn, ed. by V. M. Kulkarni and Tapasvi Nandi (Vadodara: Oriental Institute, 2003).

Kersenboom, Saskia C., 'The Traditional Repertoire of the Tiruttaṇi Temple Dancers', in *Roles and Rituals for Hindu Women*, ed. by Julia Leslie (Rutherford: Fairleigh Dickinson University Press, 1991), pp. 131–47.

Kosambi, D. D., 'Notes on the Kandahar Edict of Asoka', *Journal of the Economic and Social History of the Orient*, 2 (1959), 204–6.

Kragh, Ulrich Timme, 'Appropriation and Assertion of the Female Self: Materials for the Study of the Female Tantric Master Lakṣmī of Uḍḍiyāna', *Journal of Feminist Studies in Religion*, 27 (2011), 85–108.

Kumar, T. Vijay, 'Translation as Negotiation: The Making of Telugu Language and Literature', in *History of Translation in India*, ed. by Tariq Khan *et al.* (Mysuru: National Translation Mission, Central Institute of Indian Languages, 2017), pp. 13–32, https://doi.org/10.46623/tt/2019.si1

Lahiri, Sharmita, 'Jane Eyre: A Unique Vision of Feminism', *The Atlantic Literary Review*, 12 (2014), 15–26.

Lal, P., *Transcreation: Two Essays* (Kolkata: Writers Workshop, 1972).

Leslie, Julia, 'Suttee or *Satī*: Victim or Victor', in *Roles and Rituals for Hindu Women*, ed. by Julia Leslie (Rutherford: Fairleigh Dickinson University Press, 1991), pp. 175–91.

Lindberg-Wada, Gunilla, *Literary History: Towards a Global Perspective* (Berlin: de Gruyter, 2006), II, "Literary Genres: An Intercultural Approach," https://doi.org/10.1515/9783110894110

Liu, Lydia H., *Translingual Practice: Literature, National Culture, and Translated Modernity: China, 1900–1937* (Stanford: Stanford University Press, 1995).

Lock, Charles, 'Why Novels Are Not Written in Prose', *Ink*, 2 (Copenhagen: University of Copenhagen, Department of English, Germanic and Romance Studies, 2010), 14–16.

Loomba, Ania, (2015): *Colonialism/Postcolonialism*, (New York: Routledge, 3rd edn, 2015), https://doi.org/10.4324/9781315751245

MacDonald, Anne, *In Clear Words: The Prasannapadā, Chapter One*, 2 vols., (Vienna: Verlag der Österreichischen Akademie der Wissenshaften, Philosophisch-Historische Klasse Sitzungsberichte, 2015), 863. Band, https://doi.org/10.2307/j.ctt1zctspn

Mack, Peter, *A History of Renaissance Rhetoric 1380–1620* (Oxford: Oxford University Press, 2011), https://doi.org/10.1093/acprof:osobl/9780199597284.001.0001

Mādhava, Śyāmalā, *Jēn Air* (Bengaluru: Tēju Pablikēṣans, 2014).

Malik, Ramesh C. and Panchanan Mohanty, 'History of Odia Translations (1803–1936): A Bottom-up Approach', in *History of Translation in India*, ed. by Tariq Khan *et al.* (Mysuru: National Translation Mission, Central Institute of Indian Languages, 2017), pp. 33–100, https://doi.org/10.46623/tt/2019.si1

Mandal, Partha Sarathi, Preyona Bhowmik, and Debojyoti Roy, '*Jane Eyre* and its Heteroglossia, Colonialism, Class Struggle, Racial Otherness and the Significance of the British Empire', *International Journal of English, Literature and Social Sciences*, 5 (2020), 190–203.

Manger, Sudesh, 'History of English Translations and Its Influence on Nepali Literature', in *History of Translation in India*, ed. by Tariq Khan *et al.* (Mysuru: National Translation Mission, Central Institute of Indian Languages, 2017), pp. 371–412, https://doi.org/10.46623/tt/2019.si1

Matthews, David John, 'Dakanī Language and Literature: 1500–1700 A. D.' (doctoral thesis, School of Oriental and African Studies, University of London, 1976).

Mayhew, Arthur, *Christianity and the Government of India: An Examination of the Christian Forces at Work in the Administration of India and of the Mutual Relations of the British Government and Christian Missions 1600–1920* (London: Faber & Gwyer Limited, 1929).

Mendonca, Brian M., 'Irrationality in the Novels of Ann Radcliffe and Charlotte Brontë' (doctoral thesis, Central Institute of English and Foreign Languages, 1997).

Meyer, Susan L., 'Colonialism and the Figurative Strategy of *Jane Eyre*', *Victorian Studies*, 33 (1990), 247–68.

——, '"Indian Ink": Colonialism and the Figurative Strategy of *Jane Eyre*', in Susan L. Meyer, *Imperialism at Home: Race and Victorian Women's Fiction* (Ithaca: Cornell University Press, 1996), pp. 60–95; reprint in Harold Bloom, *Charlotte Brontë's Jane Eyre* (New York: Chelsea House, 2007), pp. 43–74.

Nabi, Papiya, 'From Texts to Films: Adaptations of Pride and Prejudice, Jane Eyre and Great Gatsby across the 20th and the 21st Centuries' (master's thesis, BRAC University, Bangladesh, 2016).

Nagi, Ahmed Taher Abdu, 'Victorian Gentlemen and the Concept of Masculinity in the Novels of Charlotte Bronte and Jane Austen' (doctoral thesis, Swami Ramanand Teerth Marathwada University, 2016).

Nandi, Ratna (Guha Mustaphi), 'Narrativizing Female Consciousness: Re-Reading the Fictional Texts of the Brontë Sisters' (doctoral thesis, University of Calcutta, 2008).

Nattier, Jan, *A Guide to the Earliest Buddhist Translations: Texts from Eastern Han* 東漢 *and Three Kingdoms* 三國 *Periods* (Tokyo: The International Research Institute for Advanced Buddhology, Soka University, 2008).

Nāyar, Yōgācārya En Gōvindan, *Ṣārlaṟṟ Brōṇṭi: Jeyn Eyar* (Kottayam: Ḍi Si Buks, 1983; 4th reprint, 2015).

Nīl, Dhrub, *Śārlaṭ Branṭi: Jen Āẏār* (Dhaka: Pāñjērī Pāblikēśans, 2010).

Norman, K. R., *A Philological Approach to Buddhism: The Bukkyō Dendō Kyōkai Lectures 1994* (London: School of Oriental and African Studies, University of London, 1997).

Obrock, Luther, 'Śrīvara's *Kathākautuka*: Cosmology, Translation, and the Life of a Text in Sultanate Kashmir', in *Jāmī in Regional Contexts: The Reception of 'Abd al-Raḥmān Jāmī's Works in the Islamicate World, ca. 9th/15th-14th/20th Century*, ed. by Thibaut d'Hubert and Alexandre Papas (Leiden: Brill, 2019), pp. 752–76, https://doi.org/10.1163/9789004386600

Orsini, Francesca, 'Poetic Traffic in a Multilingual Literary Culture: Equivalence, Parallel Aesthetics, and Language-Stretching in North India', in *Prismatic Translation*, ed. by Matthew Reynolds (Oxford: Legenda, 2019), pp. 51–71, https://doi.org/10.2307/j.ctv16km05j

Pandit, Maya, 'History of Translation Culture in Nineteenth Century Maharashtra: An Exercise in Colonial Cultural Politics', in *History of Translation in India*, ed. by Tariq Khan *et al.* (Mysuru: National Translation Mission, Central Institute of Indian Languages, 2017), pp. 135–59, https://doi.org/10.46623/tt/2019.si1

Parashar, Sangeeta, '"Not Fit to Associate with Me": Contradictions of Race, Class, and Gender in Charlotte Brontë's Jane Eyre' (master's thesis, Iowa State University, 1999).

Paṭel, Hansā C., *Śārloṭ Bronṭe kṛt Jen Eyar* (Ahmedabad: Navbhārat Sāhitya Mandir, 1993).

Pines, Shlomo and Tuvia Gelblum, 'Al-Bīrūnī's Arabic Version of Patañjali's *Yogasūtra*: A Translation of his First Chapter and a Comparison with Related Sanskrit Texts', *Bulletin of the School of Oriental and African Studies*, 29 (1966), 302–25.

——, 'Al-Bīrūni's Arabic Version of Patañjali's *Yogasūtra*: A Translation of the Second Chapter and a Comparison with Related Texts', *Bulletin of the School of Oriental and African Studies*, 40 (1977), 522–49.

——, 'Al-Bīrūni's Arabic Version of Patañjali's *Yogasūtra*: A Translation of the Third Chapter and a Comparison with Related Texts', *Bulletin of the School of Oriental and African Studies*, 46 (1983), 258–304.

——, 'Al-Bīrūni's Arabic Version of Patañjali's *Yogasūtra*: A Translation of the Fourth Chapter and a Comparison with Related Texts', *Bulletin of the School of Oriental and African Studies*, 52 (1989), 265–305.

Pollock, Sheldon, *The Language of the Gods in the World of Men: Sanskrit, Culture, and Power in Premodern India* (Berkeley: University of California Press, 2006), https://doi.org/10.1525/9780520932029

Rāhā, Sudhīndranāth, *Jen Āẏār* (Kolkata: Dev Sāhitya Kuṭīr Prāibheṭ Limiṭeḍ, 1991).

Ramachandran, C. N. and B. A. Viveka Rai, *Classical Kannada Poetry and Prose: A Reader* (Hampi: Prasaranga Kannada University, 2015).

Reynolds, Matthew, *The Poetry of Translation: From Chaucer & Petrarch to Homer & Logue* (Oxford: Oxford University Press, 2011).

——, *Translation: A Very Short Introduction* (Oxford: Oxford University Press, 2016), https://doi.org/10.1093/actrade/9780198712114.001.0001

——, (ed.), *Prismatic Translation* (Cambridge: Legenda, 2019), https://doi.org/10.2307/j.ctv16km05j

Ricci, Ronit, *Islam Translated: Literature, Conversion, and the Arab Cosmopolis of South and Southeast Asia* (Chicago: The University of Chicago Press, 2011), https://doi.org/10.7208/chicago/9780226710907.001.0001

Richman, Paula (ed.), *Many Rāmāyaṇas: The Diversity of a Narrative Tradition in South Asia* (Berkeley: University of California Press, 1991).

Rutter, Gordon, 'Fairy Rings', *Field Mycology*, 3.2 (2002), 56–60.

Sakai, Naoki, *Translation and Subjectivity: On Japan and Cultural Nationalism* (Minneapolis: University of Minnesota Press, 1997).

——, 'Translation', in *Theory, Culture & Society*, 23 (2006), 71–86.

Sarvipour, Sonia, 'Aspects of Feminism in the Bronte Sisters' Novels' (doctoral thesis, Savitribai Phule Pune University, 2011).

de Saussure, Ferdinand, *Course in General Linguistics*, trans. by Wade Baskin, 3rd edn (New York: McGraw-Hill Book Company, 1959).

Scherrer-Schaub, Cristina, 'Translation, Transmission, Tradition: Suggestions from Ninth-Century Tibet', *Journal of Indian Philosophy*, 27 (1999), 67–77.

Seetharamaiah, M. V. (ed.), *Śrīnṛpatuṅgadēvānumatamappa Śrīvijayakṛta Kavirājamārgam* (Bengaluru: Kannaḍa Sāhitya Pariṣattu, 2015).

Sherwood, Mary Martha, *The Indian Pilgrim; or, The Progress of the Pilgrim Nazareenee (Formerly Called Goonah Purist, or the Slave of Sin,) from the City of the Wrath of God to the City of Mount Zion. Delivered under the Similitude of a Dream* (Wellington, Salop: F. Houlston and Son, 1818).

Showalter, Elaine, *A Literature of Their Own: British Women Novelists from Brontë to Lessing* (Princeton: Princeton University Press, 1977).

Silver, Carole G., 'Fairies and Elves: Motifs F200–F399', in *Archetypes and Motifs in Folklore and Literature*, ed. by Jane Garry & Hasan El-Shamy (Armonk, New York: M. E. Sharpe, 2005), pp. 203–9, https://doi.org/10.4324/9781315097121

Singh, Jitendra, 'The Novels of Bronte Sisters: A Study in the Theme of Feminism' (doctoral thesis, Chhatrapati Shahu Ji Maharaj University, 2002).

Singh, S. N., *Charlotte Bronte: A Thematic Study of Her Novels* (Delhi: Mittal Publications, 1987).

Sinhā, Vidyā, *Jen Āyar* (New Delhi: Rājkamal Prakāśan Pvt. Ltd, 2002).

Sogāṇī, Kamal Cand and Śakuntalā Jain, *Ācārya Kundkund-racit Samayasār*, 5 vols. (Jaipur: Apabhraṃśa Sāhitya Akādamī, 2015–2016).

Soma, Nirmmalā Bālā, *Sarlā* (Calcutta: Gupta, Mukherjee & Company's Press, 1914).

Spivak, Gayatri Chakravorty, 'Three Women's Texts and a Critique of Imperialism', *Critical Inquiry*, 12 (1985), 243–61; reprint in *Feminisms: An Anthology of Literary Theory and Criticism*, ed. by Robyn R. Warhal and Diane Price Hernal (Hampshire: Macmillan Press, 1997), pp. 896–912.

Stasik, Danuta, *The Infinite Story: Past and Present of the Rāmāyaṇas in Hindi* (New Delhi: Manohar, 2009).

——, 'A (Thin) Boundary Not to Be Crossed, or *Lakṣmaṇ-rekhā*', *Cracow Indological Studies*, 21 (2019), 207–24.

Sundaram, R. V. S. and Deven M. Patel, *Kāvirājamārgaṃ: The Way of the King of Poets* (New Delhi: Manohar, 2017).

Svendsen, Erik, 'Genre and Adaptation in Motion', in *Genre And …*, ed. by Sune Auken, Palle Schantz Lauridsen, & Anders Juhl Rasmussen, Copenhagen Studies in Genre (Copenhagen: Ekbátana, 2015), II, pp. 221–50.

Taylor, McComas, *The Fall of the Indigo Jackal: The Discourse of Division and Pūrṇabhadra's Pañcatantra* (Albany: State University of New York Press, 2007).

Trivedi, Harish, 'In Our Own Time, on Our Own Terms: "Translation" in India', in *Translating Others*, ed. by Theo Hermans, 2 vols (New York: Routledge, 2014), I, pp. 102–19, https://doi.org/10.4324/9781315759869

——, 'Translation in India: A Curious History', in *The Book Review*, 42.2 (2018).

Ūberāi, Kesar Siṅgh, *Sarvetam viśva mārit Jen Āir* (Patiala: Bhāṣā Vibhāg, 1981).

Varma, Devendra P., *The Gothic Flame, being a History of the Gothic Novel in England: Its Origins, Efflorescence, Disintegration, and Residuary Influences* (London: Arthur Barker, 1957).

Vemsani, Lavanya, *Feminine Journeys of the Mahabharata: Hindu Women in History, Text, and Practice* (Cham, Switzerland: Palgrave Macmillan, 2021), https://doi.org/10.1007/978-3-030-73165-6

Venkatachala Sastry, T. V., *Pampa Sampuṭa Ādipurāṇa, Vikramārjuna Vijaya* (Hampi: Prasaranga Kannada University, 2006).

White, Hayden, "Interpretation in History," in *New Literary History*, 4.2 (1973), 281–314; reprint in Hayden White, *Tropics of Discourse: Essays in Cultural Criticism* (Baltimore: Johns Hopkins University Press, 1978), pp. 51–80.

Wilkins, Charles, *Bhagvat-geeta, or Dialogues of Kreeshna and Arjoon* (London: Nourse, 1785).

——, *The Heetopades of Veeshnoo-Sarma, in a Series of Connected Fables, Interspersed with Moral, Prudential and Political Maxims* (London: Nourse, 1787).

Willis, Rachel, '"A Man is Nothing without the Spice of the Devil in him": Jane Eyre and Edward Rochester Navigate an Imperially-Inscribed Masculinity', *Otherness: Essays and Studies*, 6 (2018), 244–59.

Zydenbos, Robert J., *A Manual of Modern Kannada* (Heidelberg: Cross-Asia Ebooks, 2020).

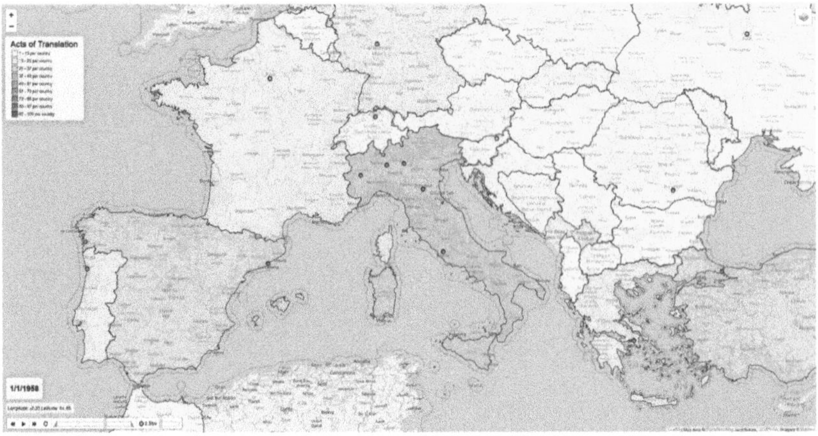

The Time Map
https://digitalkoine.github.io/translations_timemap
Created by Giovanni Pietro Vitali and Simone Landucci;
© OpenStreetMap contributors, © Mapbox

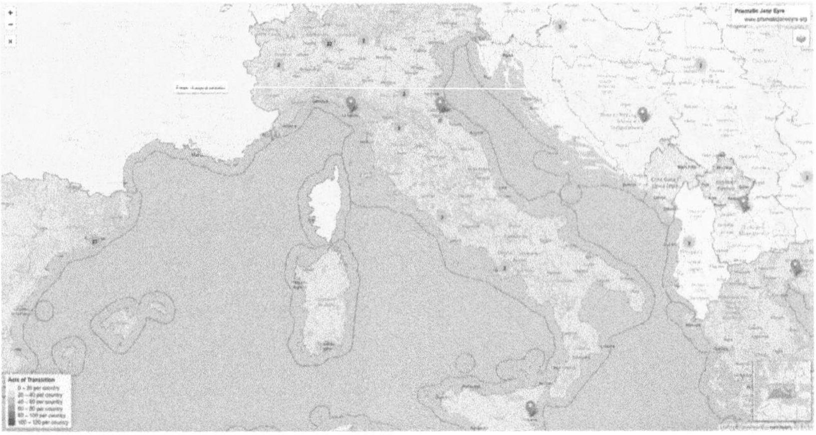

The World Map
https://digitalkoine.github.io/je_prismatic_map
Created by Giovanni Pietro Vitali; maps © Thunderforest,
data © OpenStreetMap contributors

2. Who Cares What Shape the Red Room is?

Or, On the Perfectibility of the Source Text

Paola Gaudio

Marks

In 2003, when I was studying for my Master's degree in Literary Translation at the University of East Anglia, I wrote a paper for my Case Studies class. It revolved around the translation of the red room episode in Charlotte Brontë's *Jane Eyre* and, among other things, it pointed out a discrepancy between the description of the room in the original version as a 'spare chamber', and its Italian translation as a *square* one by Giuliana Pozzo Galeazzi (1951) and Ugo Dèttore (1974). I was quite confident the professor would appreciate my discovery and reward my effort with high marks, so I was appalled when I found out my essay only got a score of 65% — the lowest in my career as a postgraduate student — possibly my lowest ever. I was even more appalled by the reason for such a low score: the professor claimed it was indeed a *square* chamber, not a *spare* one — therefore the translations were perfectly in line with the source text and my essay was inaccurate, based as it was on my assumed negligence.

I could not believe my eyes as I was reading the professor's comments on my paper, so I went over my English edition again, and I was elated to find out that it did read *spare* — the mistake was not mine, it was in the translations — and the professor was wrong. I reckoned I had grounds for appeal, and that is exactly what I did, this time attaching a photocopy from my 1966 Penguin edition in order to prove beyond any reasonable doubt that there was nothing wrong with my thesis, and that the red room was actually spare, not square. To cut a long story short, although (or maybe precisely because) I became quite insistent about it, my score was lowered even more. Luckily, this did not prevent

 https://doi.org/10.11647/OBP.0319.05

me from graduating with distinction, given the high scores I was awarded in all the other classes, but still it left a sour taste. When, more recently, I happened to analyse some of the new translations (Lamberti 2008, Capatti 2013, Sacchini 2014) which, in the meantime, had been published in Italian, it was with great surprise that I noticed the red room was square — yet again.

I know now that not only the score I received twenty-ish years ago was indeed unfair, but what I had stumbled upon was not a simple mistake on the part of a couple of translators: it was a pattern — a pattern which has been perpetuating itself over many decades — at least from the 1951 translation by Pozzo Galeazzi, up until the 2014 one by Sacchini. At this point, it seemed important to trace the origin of these variations, so I investigated them further, and here are my findings.

'The red room was a spare chamber': this is what Charlotte Brontë actually hand-wrote in 1847, i.e., in the manuscript currently held at the British Library, and on which the first editions are based. The first four editions all faithfully read *spare* as well. In the 1897 Service & Paton edition, however, *spare* becomes *square*. That this mutation in the source text may also have occurred in other print editions cannot be ruled out,[1] but what makes the 1897 edition so special is that it was used as a basis for the digitized edition that can most easily be found online, published by Project Gutenberg back in 1998 — at the dawn of the digital revolution.

Because of the vast popularity of Project Gutenberg, it is no surprise that this edition has spread exponentially,[2] not only among the reading public but also among publishers who, in the digitized version, can find a handy source for new e-book editions. It is not far-fetched to assume that translators, who by now work exclusively at computers, might have been using the digitized 1897 edition. This would explain why the error is being perpetuated more and more, both in the original English electronic versions (for example the Amazon Classics e-book,

1 The vast majority of early anglophone editions do read *spare*, both in the UK (an exception is the 1933 Oxford edition, later amended) and in the USA. In this regard, it is interesting to notice that the 1848 Harper & Brothers edition, published in New York, is correct with regard to the spare room, but the *red* room is turned into a *bed*room ('the bed room was a spare chamber'). *Square* tends to become more common only in later American editions, such as the 2002 Dover Classics and the 2006 Borders Classics.

2 The Victorian Web also contributed to the increased exposure of the Gutenberg file, using it as its reference text (http://www.victorianweb.org/authors/bronte/cbronte/janeeyre/1.html).

which is clearly based on the Project Gutenberg file) and in their translations. The same error would be found in any English printed book based either on the 1897 edition or its digitized version. The truth is that, in the now long-gone era of mechanical reproduction, this mutation would have concerned only prints and reprints of that edition or of those based on it: it would certainly have spread, but its scope would still have been limited. Not so in the digital world, where the power of a digital item — a file freely distributed on the Internet — becomes stronger than any book-as-object, defined as the latter is by its insurmountable yet finite physicality.

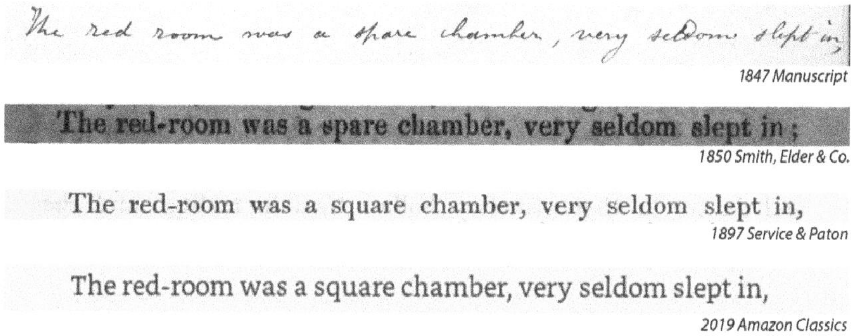
The red room was a spare chamber, very seldom slept in;
1847 Manuscript
The red-room was a spare chamber, very seldom slept in;
1850 Smith, Elder & Co.
The red-room was a square chamber, very seldom slept in,
1897 Service & Paton
The red-room was a square chamber, very seldom slept in,
2019 Amazon Classics

Fig. 1 A spare chamber. Images of the manuscript (London, British Library, MS 43474, vol. I, fol. 12r), the 1850 edition (London: Smith, Elder & Co., p. 7) and the 1897 edition (London: Service & Paton, p. 7) are courtesy of the © British Library Board. The 1850 edition was digitised by the Google Books project.

Square replaces *spare* in many translations, and not only Italian ones, since it is likely that the same mistake can and will be found in other languages as well, as is the case with Luise Hemmer Pihl's 2016 Danish translation.[3] If this is so, it is only because *square* is what both digitizers and translators have found in their source text: the optical character recognition process is not to blame in this case, but the source text of choice is not the one which best reproduces Charlotte Brontë's masterly depiction of this uncanny red room. In an era when the distinction between original and reproduction seems to be dead and buried, the digitized version appears to (yet should not) be more authoritative than the original because of its greater availability, and because sometimes virtual reality tends to be more real than reality

3 *'Det røde værelse var et kvadratisk rum'* (the red room was a square chamber).

itself. In this case, the digitized version has become the original text for quite a few readers and translators. Be that as it may, in this widely available digitized file based on the 1897 edition, crucial information about the function of the room (it was spare, therefore seldom used, therefore haunted — as little Jane would soon find out) is replaced by an uninformative, even obvious, detail about its shape: after all, most rooms are quadrangles, either square or rectangular, with fewer cases of oval or circular rooms, and even fewer other shapes — but who would really care?

Because the squareness of the room has become so prominent over the years — not only to me but in the translations as well — I could not help inquiring even further into the matter. I asked the following questions: is the occurrence of the words *spare* and *square* of any significance in the rest of the novel? Are there other imprecisions in the 1897 edition? Are there variations in other authoritative English editions, such as the Penguin one? If the optical character recognition (OCR) process did not cause the mutation from *spare* to *square*, did it create others? Is it possible to identify errors that are common to most editions? Can patterns of textual variation provide insights into the translations? The quick answer to all these questions is 'yes'. In what follows, I show why.

Spare and Square

First, it should be made clear that the red-room instance is the only substitution of *spare* by *square* that I have discovered: the error is therefore not systematic within any edition of the novel itself. As an adjective, *spare* is used only three times in *Jane Eyre*: once it refers to cash ('some of that *spare* cash', Chapter 24), which is a common collocation; the other two concern the description of rooms, such a collocation being similarly very common. The first room, of course, is the red chamber at Gateshead, whereas the other is 'a spare parlour and bedroom' at Moor House (Chapter 34), which Jane refurbished as she was expecting her cousins' return for the Christmas season. However, if the use of *spare* is straightforward and unproblematic in both frequency and collocation throughout the original novel, not so are its translations.

One issue follows from the ambiguity of the coordinating conjunction 'and' in the occurrence 'a spare parlour and bedroom', which does not make it possible to determine whether *spare* refers to the parlour only or to both the parlour and the bedroom. This is complicated even further by the fact that, no matter how it is translated, the English pre-modifier *spare* necessarily becomes a post-modifier in Italian. The translations considered here[4] range from '*di riguardo*' (for special occasions), and '*di riserva*' (extra) to '*per gli ospiti*' (for guests). The translation of *spare* with '*riservato*' (reserved) would also be a feasible option, just as '*spoglio*' (bare) or '*spartano*' (spartan, basic) would be conceivable in this context. However, none of the translators chooses these latter options, and some prefer to simplify things by omitting *spare* altogether, whereas others modify the ambiguity implicit in the conjunction 'and' by inverting the order of constituents:

Spare omission:

> *un salottino e una camera da letto* (Pozzo Galeazzi, 1951; D'Ezio, 2011)
>
> [a small parlour and a bedroom]
>
> *il salotto e una camera da letto* (Spaventa Filippi, 1956; Lamberti, 2008)
>
> [the parlour and a bedroom]

Ambiguity inversion:

> *un salotto e una stanza da letto di riguardo* (Dettore, 1974)
>
> [a parlour and a guest room]
>
> *un salottino e una camera da letto di riserva* (Gallenzi, 1997)
>
> [a small parlour and a spare bedroom]
>
> *un salottino e una camera di riserva* (Sacchini, 2014)
>
> [a small parlour and a spare room]
>
> *il salottino e una stanza per gli ospiti* (Capatti, 2013)
>
> [the small parlour and a guest room]
>
> *un salottino e una camera per gli ospiti* (Pareschi, 2014; Manini, 2019)
>
> [a small parlour and a guest room]

---

4 For the purposes of the present research, eleven unabridged translations have been selected, all currently available on the market. Of these, Alessandro Gallenzi's 1997 translation, which is based on the 1980 Oxford University Press edition (as stated in the copyright page of his *Jane Eyre*, published by Frassinelli), follows the three-volume division — therefore chapter references used for the others do not apply to either Gallenzi's translation or the Oxford editions (including the Clarendon one, but excluding the 1933 OUP edition) — unless the reference is to the chapters in the first volume (Ch. 1–15).

Explicitation:

> *un salotto che non veniva mai usato e una camera per gli ospiti* (Reali, 1996)
>
> [a parlour that was seldom used and a room for guests]

In the inversions, the postmodifying prepositional groups '*di riguardo*', '*di riserva*', and '*per gli ospiti*' certainly refer to the bedroom but, because of the inherent ambiguity of the conjunction *and* ('*e*' in Italian), they might also refer to the parlour. In English it is the other way round (i.e., the parlour is certainly spare, the bedroom might or might not be spare as well, depending on the reader's interpretation). Reali is the only one to eliminate the ambiguity by making the postmodification explicit: therefore — and not without reason — she interprets *spare* as referring to both the parlour and the bedroom. To sum up, whether because it was misprinted in the source text, or because of the asymmetries between English premodification and Italian postmodification, in Charlotte Brontë's masterpiece the adjective *spare* has a tendency to get either lost or misrepresented in translation.

Square presents completely different characteristics. It occurs fifteen times (sixteen if you include the red room), of which one is the comparative *squarer*, and another is the abstract noun *squareness*. It is never used to describe the shape of rooms — with only one exception. Much more poignantly, it serves the purpose of metaphorically (and skilfully) pointing to the hard-edged nature of some characters in the novel. Mrs Reed is the first one to be described in such terms:

> she was a woman of robust frame, *square*-shouldered and strong-limbed, not tall, and, though stout, not obese [...].[5]

Then there is Mr Brocklehurst, whose squareness is to be found not so much in his appearance — when little Jane is convened to meet him, all she sees is a 'black pillar' — as in what he does when he faces her at Gateshead. Such action suits him perfectly:

> he placed me *square* and straight before him. What a face he had, now that it was almost on a level with mine! what a great nose! and what a mouth! and what large prominent teeth![6]

St John Rivers is another character associated with the word *square*. Given his austere nature, it is not surprising that, while suppressing

5 *JE*, Ch. 4.
6 Ibid.

what appears to be full-fledged jealousy for his beloved Rosamond Oliver, his face should take on some squareness as well:

> Mr St John's under lip protruded, and his upper lip curled a moment. His mouth certainly looked a good deal compressed, and the lower part of his face unusually stern and *square* [...].[7]

It is at Thornfield, though, that the word *square* occurs most often. The reference is to Rochester's forehead and his masculine jaw, of course, but also to Thornfield itself, its inhabitants — Grace Poole — and its objects, tokens of Rochester's failed wedding attempt. It is also here — as Jane enters the property for the first time — that the only use of *square* to describe a room occurs, justified by the need to emphasize the magnificence of the hall:

> I followed her across a *square* hall with high doors all round [...].[8]

However, it is Rochester who is primarily described in terms of squareness:

> The fire shone full on his face. I knew my traveller with his broad and jetty eyebrows; his *square* forehead, made *squarer* by the horizontal sweep of his black hair. I recognised his decisive nose, more remarkable for character than beauty; his full nostrils, denoting, I thought, choler; his grim mouth, chin, and jaw — yes, all three were very grim, and no mistake. His shape, now divested of cloak, I perceived harmonised in *squareness* with his physiognomy: I suppose it was a good figure in the athletic sense of the term — broad-chested and thin-flanked, though neither tall nor graceful.[9]

Again:

> My master's colourless, olive face, *square*, massive brow, broad and jetty eyebrows, deep eyes, strong features, firm, grim mouth — all energy, decision, will — were not beautiful, according to rule; but they were more than beautiful to me.[10]

Even at Gateshead, when Jane visits Mrs Reed on her deathbed, Rochester's image looms with the squareness of his lineaments:

> One morning I fell to sketching a face: what sort of a face it was to be, I did not care or know. I took a soft black pencil, gave it a broad point, and worked away. Soon I had traced on the paper a broad and prominent forehead and a *square* lower outline of visage: that contour

7 *JE*, Ch. 34.
8 *JE*, Ch. 11.
9 *JE*, Ch. 13.
10 *JE*, Ch. 17.

> gave me pleasure; my fingers proceeded actively to fill it with features [...]. I looked at it; I smiled at the speaking likeness: I was absorbed and content.
>
> 'Is that a portrait of some one you know' asked Eliza, who had approached me unnoticed. I responded that it was merely a fancy head, and hurried it beneath the other sheets. Of course, I lied: it was, in fact, a very faithful representation of Mr Rochester.[11]

Grace Poole too, a Thornfield inhabitant herself, has a square figure, as Jane points out not once but twice in her narrative:

> The door nearest me opened, and a servant came out — a woman of between thirty and forty; a set, *square*-made figure, red-haired, and with a hard, plain face: any apparition less romantic or less ghostly could scarcely be conceived.[12]

> Mrs Poole's *square*, flat figure, and uncomely, dry, even coarse face.[13]

The remaining squares are tokens of the failed wedding attempt: the square of blond that Jane had prepared as a head-covering for the ceremony (in contrast to the rich veil supplied by Mr Rochester and torn by Bertha), and the 'cards of address' where the newly-weds' luggage was supposed to be sent:

> The cards of address alone remained to nail on: they lay, four little *squares*, in the drawer.[14]

> I thought how I would carry down to you the *square* of unembroidered blond [...].[15]

> She was just fastening my veil (the plain *square* of blond after all) [...].[16]

Finally, in light of these occurrences, the fact that the word *square* should be used in connection with another rigid and hard-edged character like Eliza Reed acquires a deeper meaning. She is not described as square herself but, as her mother is lying on her deathbed upstairs,

> three hours she gave to stitching, with gold thread, the border of a *square* crimson cloth, almost large enough for a carpet.[17]

---

11 *JE*, Ch. 23.
12 *JE*, Ch. 11.
13 *JE*, Ch. 14.
14 *JE*, Ch. 25.
15 Ibid.
16 *JE*, Ch. 26.
17 *JE*, Ch. 21.

Such unwieldy square crimson cloth may well be the objective correlative to her personality, and its colour a subtle reminder of the spare room in the house.

From the point of view of translation, the word *square* finds a straightforward enough equivalent in the Italian '*quadrato*' (noun, adjective) and '*squadrato*' (adjective). Notwithstanding, their occurrence is not always consistent and, unfortunately, the word disappears altogether in the translation of the expression *square and straight* ('he placed [Jane] square and straight before him', Chapter 4) into Italian, variously rendered as just '*dritta*' (straight) in Dèttore, Gallenzi, Capatti, and Pareschi; '*dritta impalata*' (straight and stock-still) in Sacchini; '*proprio*' (right) in Pozzo Galeazzi, Reali, Lamberti, D'Ezio and Manini; and altogether omitted in Spaventa Filippi '*egli mi pose dinanzi a lui*' (he placed me before him).

Nonetheless, on the whole, these significant instances of squareness come through strongly in Italian *Jane Eyre*s: 'square' not only edges out 'spare' from the red room, but makes itself squarely felt throughout the translations.

The 1897 Service & Paton Edition

By comparing the 1897 edition with the manuscript and early editions, several divergences emerge. These mostly concern spelling variations and do not generally involve any substantial difference or malapropism. However, in addition to the replacement of *spare* by *square* in Chapter 2, there are three more cases that appear noteworthy.

The first occurs towards the end of Chapter 6, in Helen's outline of her doctrine of acceptance and hope, according to which there is no point in letting oneself being burdened by the faults of this world if, some day, what will remain of our mortal flesh is only 'the impalpable principle of life and thought' (MS 43474, vol. I, fol. 93r and the first four editions). In the 1897 Service & Paton edition, *life* becomes *light*. The reverberations of this substitution, which can also be found in the 1933 Oxford edition, are far-reaching in terms of translation, with half the translators replacing '*vita*' (life) with '*luce*' (light): Pozzo Galeazzi, Dettore, Capatti, Sacchini and Manini.

In Chapter 12, just before Rochester and Jane meet for the very first time, Jane sees from afar Rochester's horse approaching on the solitary road, then perceives his big dog: 'it was exactly one *mask* of Bessie's Gytrash — a lion-like creature with long hair and a huge head'. The discrepancy concerns the replacement of the original *mask* (to be found in the manuscript and first four editions) with *form* in the 1897 edition. Indeed, Charlotte Brontë had just mentioned — in the preceding paragraph — that the Gytrash 'comes upon belated travellers in the *form* of a horse, mule, or large dog'. *Form*, in this particular context, can be considered the generic hypernym of the more specific hyponym *mask*, with the former referring to the form of the body and the latter to the mask one wears on the face.[18] Brontë's unusual use of 'mask' here, which is not attested in the *OED*, must mean something like 'avatar' or 'manifestation', but still suggests, in Jane's perception, an actual Gytrash wearing a mask — which is a lot more frightening than the mere resemblance of a form. With the shift from *mask* to *form*, the 1897 edition thus loses some intensity in the suspense of the scene.

In the translations, however, this difference becomes blurred, since the translators tend to use more indefinite expressions such as '*copia*' (copy) or '*immagine*' (image), for example in Dèttore and Manini:

> Era la copia esatta di una delle personificazioni del Gytrash di Bessie (Dèttore, 1974)
>
> [it was the exact copy of one of the personifications of Bessie's Gytrash]
>
> Era un'immagine esatta del Gytrash di Bessie (Manini, 2019)
>
> [it was an exact image of Bessie's Gytrash]

Only D'Ezio (albeit with an omission), Pareschi, and Sacchini express how it was not merely 'an exact image' or 'a copy', but rather the actual Gytrash:

> Era esattamente il Gytrash di Bessie (D'Ezio, 2011)
>
> [It was exactly Bessie's Gytrash]

18 Of the three occurrences of *mask* in *Jane Eyre*, two are associated with *form* and, in both cases, there is a hyponymy-hypernymy relation between the two. Besides the Gytrash's mask, the other occurrence is used to describe Bertha Mason's features. Here as well, *mask* refers to the face (hyponym) and *form* to the body (hypernym): 'compare [...] this face with that mask — this form with that bulk' (in Ch. 26, soon after the failed wedding, when Rochester takes his guests to see for themselves who or what his wife was). In this case, though, the translations of *mask* and *form* are unanimously consistent and literal: '*maschera*' and '*forma*' (form) in Reali, Gallenzi, D'Ezio, Capatti; '*maschera*' and '*forme*' (forms) in Spaventa Filippi and Lamberti; '*maschera*' and '*figura*'(figure) in Dèttore, Sacchini, Pareschi, Manini; and '*maschera*' and '*corpo*' (body) in Pozzo Galeazzi.

Era esattamente una delle personificazioni del Gytrash (Pareschi, 2014)

[It was exactly one of the Gytrash's personifications]

Era proprio uno dei travestimenti del Gytrash di Bessie (Sacchini, 2014)

[It was indeed one of the costumes of Bessie's Gytrash]

The other noteworthy difference between the 1897 edition and the manuscript and first four editions is interesting because it also affects all Penguin editions (1966, 2006 and 2015). In Chapter 29, when Jane speaks to St John for the first time after recovering from her four-day wanderings, he is depicted as 'sitting as still as the *study* pictures on the walls'. *Study* here is inappropriate: for one, Jane and St John are in the parlour, not in the study, and even if its reference were not to a room, the meaning of study would remain unclear. It simply is not the word used by Charlotte Brontë, and this also explains why so many translators prefer to omit it altogether.

The 1897 edition makes more sense: St John is here 'sitting as still as one of the *dusty* pictures on the walls'. It does seem quite likely that St John should appear *dusty* — at least in countenance. However, the 1847 manuscript, and the four first editions all read neither *study* nor its anagram *dusty*, but *dusky*. This matters because it shifts the description to the realm of colours, rather than that of location or of sloppiness in house cleaning.

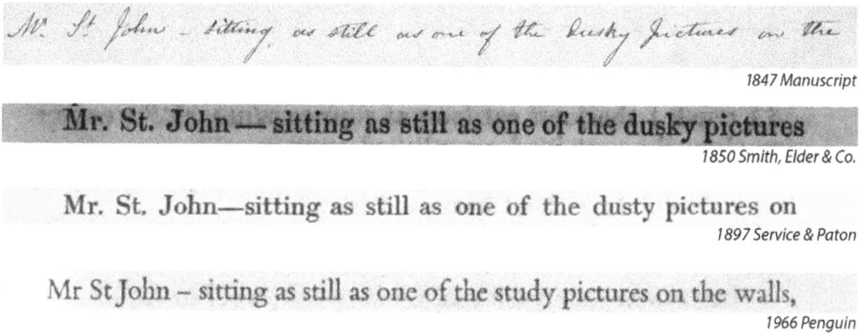
Mr St John – sitting as still as one of the dusky pictures on the

1847 Manuscript

Mr. St. John — sitting as still as one of the dusky pictures

1850 Smith, Elder & Co.

Mr. St. John—sitting as still as one of the dusty pictures on

1897 Service & Paton

Mr St John – sitting as still as one of the study pictures on the walls,

1966 Penguin

Fig. 2 Dusky pictures. Images of the manuscript (London, British Library, MS 43476, vol. III, fol. 84r), the 1850 edition (London: Smith, Elder & Co., p. 353) and the 1897 edition (London: Service & Paton, p. 331) are courtesy of the © British Library Board. The 1850 edition was digitised by the Google Books project.

As in a piece of classical music, there are here three variations on the theme — the theme being St John sitting still, the variations being the similes. In Italian, '*polveroso*' (dusty) can be found in Capatti, Pareschi and Sacchini. A few, like Lamberti, D'Ezio and Manini, omit the word altogether. *Dusky* is aptly translated as '*scuri*' (dark), by Pozzo Galeazzi and Dettore; as '*anneriti*' (blackened), by Reali; and as '*cupi*' (sombre), by Gallenzi.

The Penguin Editions (1966, 2006 and 2015)

As already shown, the Service & Paton 1897 edition is not the only one to contain imprecisions. The Penguin editions have their share too. In addition to the replacement of *dusky* with *study* in Chapter 29, and the replacement of *enchaining* with *enchanting* in Chapter 4, which we will explore in the next section, there are a few more striking malapropisms.

In Chapter 36 of all Penguin editions, when Jane is being told by the inn's host about the misfortunes that befell Thornfield and its inhabitants, and specifically about Rochester's reaction when he lost Jane, 'the most precious thing he had in the world', the host adds that 'he never was a *mild* man'. Penguin was not the only one to prefer *mild* over *wild*: the authoritative 1969 Clarendon edition does the same.[19]

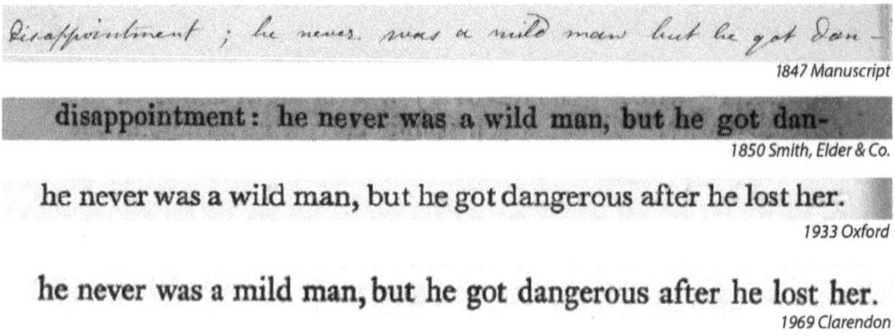
1847 Manuscript
disappointment: he never was a wild man, but he got dan-
1850 Smith, Elder & Co.
he never was a wild man, but he got dangerous after he lost her.
1933 Oxford
he never was a mild man, but he got dangerous after he lost her.
1969 Clarendon

Fig. 3 A wild man. Images of the manuscript (London, British Library, MS 43476, vol. III, fol 225r) and the 1850 edition (London: Smith, Elder & Co., p. 440) are courtesy of the © British Library Board. The 1850 edition was digitised by the Google Books project.

19 The Oxford Clarendon Press edition may have been the most authoritative, but it was not the first one, as the earliest occurrence of *mild* can be traced back at least to 1906, with the American edition The Century & Co., New York, p. 459. The 1966 Penguin edition also anticipates Jane Jack and Margaret Smith's 1969 emendation.

That Rochester was never mild in nature is well understood by the readers as well as by the characters in Jane's story. But he was not altogether wild either, at least not until Jane's departure — and that is what the host is pointing out. After losing her, Rochester did become wild — and utterly so — to the point of being dangerous, as 'he grew savage, quite savage on his disappointment'.

The first four editions, just like the manuscript and several others,[20] up to the recent 2019 Collins Classics edition, all read: 'he never was a *wild* man, but he got dangerous after he lost her'. Yet, in the Penguin editions, the original adjective *wild* is replaced by its antonym. This may be a slip, but it might also be a deliberate choice, like that made by the Clarendon editors Jane Jack and Margaret Smith. These mutations in the English source text do bear consequences in the translations: '*un uomo mite*' (a mild man) can be found in Spaventa Filippi, Reali, Gallenzi, Lamberti, D'Ezio and in the most recent 2019 translation by Luca Manini. Pozzo Galeazzi emphasizes Rochester's mildness even more: '*egli era sempre stato un uomo tranquillo*' (he had always been a tranquil man). From never wild to always mild — that is quite a leap.

For the sake of complete disclosure, it should be pointed out that the manuscript's handwriting of *wild* (MS 43476, vol. III, fol. 225r) might easily be confused with *mild* — which was at the basis of the Clarendon editors' choice to replace it with *mild*.[21] However, by comparing *wild* in 'a wild man' with random occurrences of both *mild* and *wild* in the same manuscript, the difference — however subtle — does appear.[22]

---

20 1848 Harper & Brothers, 1908 Dents & Sons, 1911 G. Bells & Sons, 1933 Oxford University Press, all Norton Critical Editions, among others.

21 'The MS states that Mr Rochester "never was a mild man", whereas the printed editions tell us that he "never was a wild man"', in Charlotte Brontë, *Jane Eyre*, ed. by Jane Jack and Margaret Smith (Oxford: Clarendon Press, 1969), p. xxi. In the note on p. 547, the editors again specify that *mild* is their reading of the manuscript. It goes without saying that, because of the authoritative standing of the Clarendon edition, it influenced not only the OUP editions to follow but also editors of other publishing houses, like Penguin itself, whose 1966 reading as *mild* was tacitly validated by Jack and Smith.

22 Figure 4 highlights the stroke that distinguishes the 'w' from the 'm', but — as Joseph Hankinson aptly pointed out when he read the first draft of this Essay — there is another interesting difference to be appreciated here: in Charlotte Brontë's calligraphy, the letter 'd', especially but not exclusively at the end of a word, appears sometimes to be curved (as in *wild man*), sometimes straight (as in *wild rain*). Even though in *mild* the 'd' tends to be straight, this has no bearing on the wild/mild difference, as the alternative calligraphies happen for no obvious reason other than — probably — fluctuations in writing speed.

That Charlotte Brontë never meant to write *mild* is also supported by her never amending any of the first three editions (all of which read *wild*).

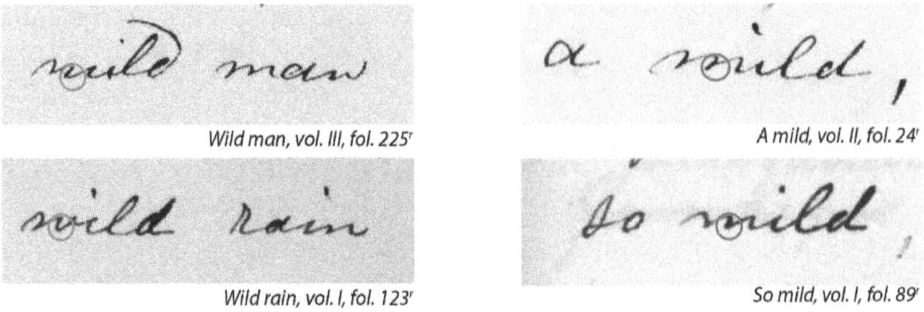

Fig. 4 Wild and mild. London, British Library, MS 43474, vol. I, fol. 89^{r} and 123^{r}; MS 43475, vol. II, fol. 24^{r}; MS 43476, vol. III, fol. 225^{r}, courtesy of the © British Library Board.

Another Penguin variation occurs in Chapter 30, when St John offers to help Jane by appointing her as the mistress of the new girls' school, and asks her to recall his 'notice, *early* given, that if I helped you, it must be as the blind man would help the lame'. All the other editions I have consulted, as well as the manuscript, read *clearly*, not *early*. This bears consequences for a substantial number of translations, as Pozzo Galeazzi replaces *clearly* with '*già*' (already), Speranza Filippi with '*subito*' (right away), Lamberti, D'Ezio and Sacchini go with '*dall'inizio*' (since the beginning) and similarly Manini provides a temporal specification with his '*un giorno*' (some day). Although less conspicuous, worth mentioning are also the replacements of 'no *signal* deformity' with 'no *single* deformity' in Chapter 7, of '*threading* the flower and fruit parterres' with '*trading* the flower and fruit parterres' in Chapter 23 and of 'hazarding *confidences*' with 'hazarding *conferences*' in Chapter 27.

The Project Gutenberg File

Once so many differences have come to the surface in the print editions, it seems natural to wonder whether anything of the sort can also be observed in the Project Gutenberg file — i.e., in the digitized version of the 1897 Service & Paton edition — which, as already mentioned, was first released in 1998, the current release dating to 2007. As with the other editions considered, variations in spelling and obvious typos (e.g., quiet → quite) have but little relevance. What is of greater interest are meaning-bearing changes, especially malapropisms. In the Gutenberg file, there are a few such cases, listed here in order of occurrence.

The first one is in Chapter 4 and has a rather hilarious effect: John Reed, scared of Jane's aggressive reaction, runs away from her — not '*uttering* execrations', as in the manuscript, but '*tittering* execrations'.

Then, the words *enchanting* (in 'enchanting stories', Chapter 4) and *enchanted* (in 'enchanted my attention', Chapter 7) — which at first sight do not attract any attention because of the common collocation of both enchanting + stories and enchanted + attention — are in fact a substitution for the '*enchaining* stories' and '*enchained* my attention' of the original manuscript. This is interesting, because there are also some print editions, such as the 2019 Collins Classics, which mistakenly replace the verb *to enchain* with *to enchant* in 'enchaining stories'. The 1966 Penguin edition had 'enchanting stories' but it was afterwards replaced with the correct 'enchaining stories' in 2006. Unfortunately, Penguin went back to 'enchanting stories' in 2015. Likewise, the translations tend to maintain the *enchanting* version, as for example that by Manini, which reads '*storie incantevoli*' (enchanting stories). Though the change in meaning is not dramatic, still such substitutions reveal the tenuous yet salient difference between narrative commonplace and stylistic mastery.

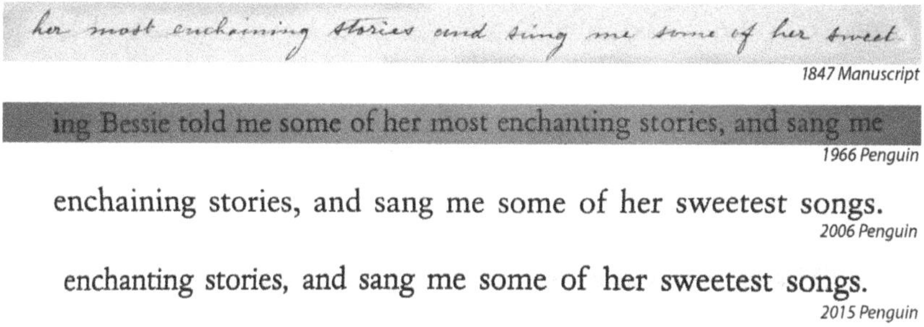
her most enchaining stories and sing me some of her sweet
1847 Manuscript

ing Bessie told me some of her most enchanting stories, and sang me
1966 Penguin

enchaining stories, and sang me some of her sweetest songs.
2006 Penguin

enchanting stories, and sang me some of her sweetest songs.
2015 Penguin

Fig. 5 Enchaining stories. The image of the manuscript (London, British Library, MS 43474, vol. I, fol. 61r) is courtesy of the © British Library Board.

The next variation occurs in Chapter 21, when Jane goes back to Gateshead to visit her dying aunt. There, Jane finds her cousins Georgiana and Eliza, who have by now developed incompatible personalities. As Eliza speaks harshly to her sister, she advises her to 'suffer the results of [her] idiocy, however bad and *insuperable* they may be'. Those results are indeed not *insuperable* — as in the Gutenberg file — but *insufferable*, as in the 1897 Service & Paton edition and in the 1847 manuscript.

In Chapter 27, Rochester tells Jane about his unsuccessful chase after true love, and, in the Gutenberg edition, he says 'I was presently undeserved' — as if he were himself a prize not deserved by the women he fell for. The effect is totally different from the original *undeceived*, meaning that Rochester's expectations to find a soulmate were repeatedly disappointed.

An even more substantial case can be observed in Chapter 34. The context is St John's marriage proposal to Jane. As she contemplates his words, Jane finally comprehends him and understands his limits: 'I sat at the feet of a man, *erring* as I'. St John's arduous crusade to save humanity — possibly with Jane as wife — is based exactly on this, on the fallibility of the human race and his wish to make amends, to atone for original sin. If, at this very moment, Jane realizes the true nature of St John by perceiving him as a flawed human being, in the Gutenberg file such human fallibility is transformed into affection: in an ironic twist, '*erring* as I' becomes '*caring* as I'.

Further cases worth mentioning are: the replacement of 'flakes fell at intervals' with 'flakes *felt it* intervals' in Chapter 4; 'by dint of' becomes 'by drift of' in Chapter 11; the transformation into *muffed* to be found in Chapter 15, when Rochester does not hesitate to recognize his unfaithful Céline '*muffled* in a cloak'; the 'sweetest *hues*' to be used by Jane for Blanche Ingram's portrait become 'sweetest *lines*' in Chapter 16; the change from *shake* to *shade* in St John's confession to Jane about his feelings for Rosamond ('when I *shake* before Miss Oliver, I do not pity myself', Chapter 32); in Chapter 35, *malice* is replaced by *force* in the expression 'by malice'; and *blent* becomes *blest* in Chapter 37.

Finally, there are a few omissions: of the word *small* in a 'small breakfast room' in Chapter 1; of 'ear, eye and mind were alike' in Chapter 3; of *necessary* in 'thoughts I did not think it necessary to check' in Chapter 17; of Jane's words to Rochester 'quite rich, sir!' in Chapter 37.[23]

Even though some of these variations occur in other editions as well, they are relevant here because they diverge from the 1897 edition, on

23 There are a couple more variants in this chapter, which are not specific to the Gutenberg file, and concern most editions: these are dealt with in the following section.

which the Gutenberg file is based, and are therefore to be considered consequences of a faulty passage from paper to digital format.

Errors Common to Most Editions

The red room is a mysterious place indeed. Strange things happen there, not only in the context of the development of the story, but also in its textual *detours*. The one which spurred this research has been extensively discussed, with the square room error inevitably projected into the translations — in a reflection game not dissimilar from what Jane experiences by looking into the mirror when she is locked up in there. Towards the end of Chapter 2, there is another anomaly, and this time it affects most editions, anglophone or otherwise. It is an omission fraught with meaning because it makes the red-room scene even more surreal than it actually is. This is the excerpt from the manuscript: 'I was oppressed, suffocated: endurance broke down — I uttered a wild, involuntary cry' (MS 43474, vol. I, fol. 20r). This last clause, 'I uttered a wild, involuntary cry', is omitted in the first edition and is not amended in the following ones. The consequence is that what happens next in the scene loses coherence, because it is supposed to be Jane's screaming that attracts Bessie and Abbot's attention and makes them run to check in on her. Without this clause, Abbot's words 'What a dreadful noise!' would not make sense, unless such noise were caused by a ghost or some other supernatural creature (this could easily be expected in a haunted place like the red room, but it is not in fact the case). This clause remained omitted both in Great Britain (first four editions, 1897 Service & Paton, 1908 J.M. Dent & Sons, 1933 Oxford edition, 1966 Penguin edition) and in the United States (1848 Harper & Sons, 1943 Random House, 1969 Cambridge Book Company, 2003 Barnes & Noble, the first three Norton Critical editions — the list is not exhaustive). The error was clearly pointed out in the Clarendon edition, but not all publishers followed suit. It still remains omitted, for example, in the Collins Classics editions as well as in most translations — with the exceptions of Gallenzi, Sacchini and Manini.

At the beginning of the penultimate chapter (37), Jane is about to be reunited with Rochester and observes him from a distance. She addresses the reader by asking whether we believe Rochester's blind ferocity scared her at all. It does not:

> A soft hope *blent* with my sorrow that soon I should dare to drop a kiss on that very brow of rock, and on those *lips* so sternly sealed beneath it [...]. He lifted his *hand* and opened his eyelids.

This passage is peculiar: it contains three variations within just a few lines, and two of them concern most anglophone editions, hence most translations. The first one has already been mentioned and pertains to the Gutenberg file ('a soft hope *blest* with my sorrow'): it resurfaces again in the Italian translation by Sacchini, in which Jane's hope is '*sacra*' (blessed). The second one follows immediately and is reproduced in most English editions. It has to do with where Jane wants to kiss Rochester after kissing his brow. Beneath the brow, there are Rochester's eyes and *lids*, not his *lips*, and it is his lids that are so sternly sealed because of the injuries he suffered: his lips can open all right. The Clarendon edition specifies how the error arose in the second edition and was repeated in the third. The fourth perpetuated the error, which inevitably spread in time and space. *Lips* is to be found, among others, in: 1897 Service & Paton, 1906 The Century & Co., 1908 J. M. Dent & Sons, 1911 G. Bells & Sons, 1933 Oxford University Press, all Penguin editions, all Collins Classics, all Norton Critical Editions.[24] It is no surprise that '*labbra*' (lips) is in all the translations, the only exception being Reali, who writes '*palpebre*' (lids).

The third variation also refers to Rochester's maimed physicality and, like the previous one, is a direct consequence of a misprint which can be traced back to the first edition — as pointed out in the notes to the 1969 Clarendon edition. The result is a slightly graphic scene where Rochester rises his *hand* to pry his eyelids open. The truth is that he simply lifts his *head* and then opens his eyes, without any help from his hand — as in the manuscript: 'he lifted his *head* and opened his eyelids'. Just like the previous case, this same error shows up in most anglophone editions and Italian translations, with only Reali and Gallenzi getting it right.

24 Not all editions perpetuate the error: the 1948 Harper & Brothers, New York, is correct, and so are the Oxford editions following the Clarendon amendment.

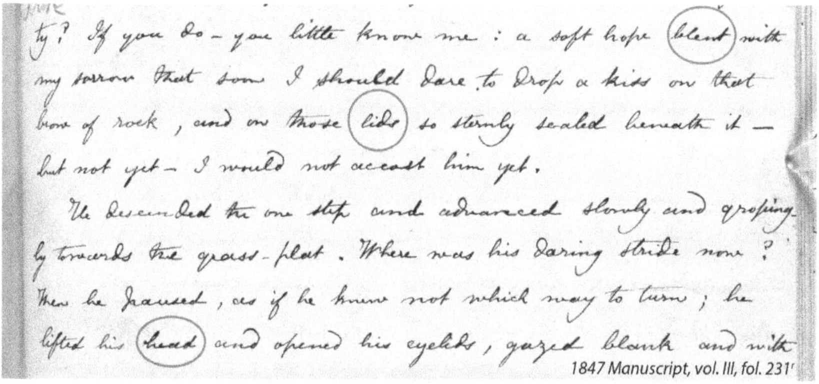
ty? If you do – you little know me: a soft hope blent with
my sorrow that soon I should dare to drop a kiss on that
brow of rock, and on those lids so sternly sealed beneath it –
but not yet – I would not accost him yet.
He descended the one step and advanced slowly and groping-
ly towards the grass-plat. Where was his daring stride now?
Then he paused, as if he knew not which way to turn; he
lifted his head and opened his eyelids, gazed blank and with
1847 Manuscript, vol. III, fol. 231r

Fig. 6 Blent, lids and head. London, British Library, MS 43476, vol. III, fol. 231r, courtesy of the © British Library Board.

Insights into Translations Based on Non-Negligible Patterns

In general, it can be hard to be certain whether a variance in a translation derives from a similar variance in the source text or has been introduced by the translator: such is the fluidity that is always available in translation. However, when patterns emerge, claims can be ventured. The claims put forward in this section are that Stella Sacchini and Monica Pareschi both used the Gutenberg file as their main source text, and that the translation by Luca Lamberti is strongly based on Spaventa Filippi's. Debatable as they may be, these claims result from the observation of a pattern arising from a non-negligible consistency in the anomalies of the texts at stake. In spite of the plethora of alternative translations of the same text (after all, translation is a never-ending task), there are some crucial words and expressions that either give away the influence from previous translations or reveal what source texts were used.

In Stella Sacchini's prize-winning translation (2014), the following signs suggest that her work may have been directly affected by the Project Gutenberg file:

> Ch. 1: omission of *small* in 'a small breakfast room' (Sacchini's is the only translation to omit the adjective, as the Gutenberg file does);
>
> Ch. 2: replacement of *spare* with *square* ('*quadrata*') in the red-room episode;
>
> Ch. 6: replacement of *life* with *light* ('*luce*');

> Ch. 16: replacement of *hues* with *lines* (‘*linee*’ — hers is the only translation to be faithful to the Gutenberg file);
>
> Ch. 21: *insufferable* becomes *insuperable* (‘*insormontabili*’ — the only instance among the translations);
>
> Ch. 29: *dusky* is replaced by *dusty* (‘*polverosi*’);
>
> Ch. 37: replacement of *blent* with *blest* (‘*sacra*’ — again, the only instance among the translations to be faithful to the Gutenberg file); replacement of *head* with *hand* (common to most translations); replacement of *lids* with *lips* (common to most translations).

In the cases above, Sacchini’s are all faithful translations of the variations as they appear in the Gutenberg text: some pertain exclusively to it, while some are common to other editions as well. However, the influence exerted by the Gutenberg version on her text is limited to these instances, which suggests that she did also refer to other source texts or translations.

Another translation that appears to have suffered from the same influence is that by Monica Pareschi: according to her unique interpretation — and perfectly in line with the Gutenberg transcription — St John is *caring* (‘*capace di affetti*’) rather than *erring*; he does not *shake* before Miss Olivier, but *shades* before her (‘*mi faccio scuro*’); the stories are ‘*più belle*’ (more beautiful, which is a loose translation of *enchanting*) rather than *enchaining*; and — here again — St John sits still like ‘*polverosi*’ (dusty) pictures, not *dusky* ones. Like most translators, she omits “I uttered a wild, involuntary cry” in Chapter 2, and replaces *lids* with *lips* and *head* with *hand* in Chapter 37, all of which are consistent with, although not exclusive to, the Gutenberg file.

Then there is the case of the one-of-a-kind translator ‘Luca Lamberti’: this is not a real person but rather the *nom de plume* of a variety of translators working anonymously for the publishing house Einaudi, one of the most prestigious in Italy.[25] What is peculiar about him — besides the undetermined authorship — is that he repeats some of the idiosyncratic phrasings used by Lia Spaventa Filippi. The anomaly emerges with suggestive precision in those strings of text where Spaventa Filippi tends to creatively paraphrase the source text

25 See Ernesto Ferrero, ‘Il più longevo, prolifico e poliedrico traduttore dell’Einaudi’, in *Tradurre. Pratiche, teorie, strumenti*, 11 (2016), https://rivistatradurre.it/2016/11/il-piu-longevo-prolifico-e-poliedrico-traduttore-delleinaudi/

rather than provide a word-for-word translation. In Chapter 3, the source text reads 'ear, eye and mind were alike strained by dread': she does not mention the ear, the eye nor the mind (which all other translators do), but summarizes the expression with a concise '*i miei sensi*' (my senses). Lamberti uses the same wording.

Spaventa Filippi translates 'his gripe was painful' (Chapter 27), with an unusual '*sotto la sua stretta*' (under his grip), thus transforming the subject into a prepositional phrase and omitting the adjective *painful*. Lamberti does the same. In Chapter 31, 'perfect beauty is a strong expression; but I do not retract or qualify it' is uniquely interpreted by Spaventa Filippi as '*perfetta, per quanto forte possa sembrare questa espressione*' (perfect, no matter how strong this expression may seem), where the first part of the sentence is transformed by the addition of *no matter how* and of the verb *to seem*, while the second part is omitted. Such elaborate rewriting is echoed — again — by Lamberti. One last suggestive example is 'a soft hope blent with my sorrow' (Chapter 37), which Spaventa Filippi transforms into '*la mia pena mi ispirava*' (my sorrow inspired me) — clearly a loose translation of the original, repeated verbatim by Lamberti.

Conclusion

If we merge all the source text variations, the spare room appears squarer and squarer; in that same room little Jane remains dumbstruck even as she is heard screaming out; Rochester is not that wild after all; and St John looks like a dusty and caring mortal soul, rather than a tragically dusky, erring one. Charlotte Brontë's mid-nineteenth-century masterpiece has gained new features as a consequence of the inevitable imprecisions stemming from reproduction techniques such as printing, transcription, optical character recognition processes and indeed translations into whatever language. These are not necessarily mistakes or degradations though, since involuntary imprecisions or intentional translatorial choices can actually be ameliorative of the original — at least in theory, and assuming universally acknowledged quality standards can be set.[26] Besides, it was because, at some point in

26 In this regard, Umberto Eco devotes a section of his *Dire quasi la stessa cosa: Esperienze di traduzione* (Milano: Bompiani, 2003, pp. 114–25) to the possible improvements of a source text following misreadings that are sometimes intentional, sometimes not, but which can, in both cases, still be very poetic, and actually improve the source text. He does, however, warn

time, *spare* was replaced by *square*, that the scattered yet meaningful occurrences of the word *square* have come to the forefront, lending the novel as a whole an extra shade of squareness, and not only the red room.

Textual variations simply mean that novels can and do develop well beyond the borders of the author's manuscript. The claim that texts have a life of their own was never truer than in the cases analysed here. And each translation is indeed different from the others, no matter the degree to which it may have been influenced by the previous ones: they do change incessantly, but the most basic reason for such variety is that the source text itself varies, as it appears to be slowly evolving or devolving. Not all errors are horrors, though, and perhaps it cannot even be asserted that one edition or translation is ultimately better than the others, or that the digital revolution is to be blamed for perpetuating the horror of the square chamber (malapropism intended). If anything, the digital turn in the humanities, whose full potentialities are still being uncovered, represents a breakthrough in the study of the novel.

Texts are always characterized by their own idiosyncrasies and tend to be susceptible to improvement. Any novel and any translation, not unlike all things human, is subject to amelioration. In fact, because of their very nature, complex human endeavours — like human beings themselves — are defined much less by perfection and a lot more by perfectibility, and that striving is precisely what history — and scholarship — are made of.

Works Cited

For the translations of *Jane Eyre* referred to, please see the List of Translations at the end of this book.

Eco, Umberto, *Dire quasi la stessa cosa: Esperienze di traduzione* (Milano: Bompiani, 2003).

Ferrero, Ernesto, 'Il più longevo, prolifico e poliedrico traduttore dell'Einaudi', in *Tradurre. Pratiche, teorie, strumenti,* 11 (2016), https://rivistatradurre.it/2016/11/il-piu-longevo-prolifico-e-poliedrico-traduttore-delleinaudi

The Victorian Web, http://www.victorianweb.org

against the dangers of misreading the original and advises against this sort of manipulation.

English-Language Editions of *Jane Eyre*

Brontë, Charlotte, *Jane Eyre*, manuscript, MS 43474–6, vol. I–III, (London: British Library, 1847).

——, (New York: Harper & Brothers, 1848).

——, (London: Smith, Elder & Co., 1850).

——, (London: W. Nicholson & Sons, 1890).

——, (New York: Thomas Y. Crowell & Company, 1890).

——, (London: Service & Paton, 1897).

——, (New York and London: Harper & Brothers Publishers, 1899).

——, (New York: The Century Co., 1906).

——, (London and Toronto: J.M. Dent & Sons; New York: E.P. Dutton & Co.,1908).

——, (London: G. Bell & Sons, 1911).

——, (Oxford: Oxford University Press, 1933).

——, (New York: Random House, 1943).

——, (London: Penguin, 1966).

——, (New York: Cambridge Book Company, 1969).

——, (Oxford: Clarendon Press, 1969).

——, *A Norton Critical Edition* (New York and London: W. W. Norton Company, 1971).

——, *2nd Norton Critical Edition* (New York and London: W. W. Norton Company, 1987).

——, (Oxford: Oxford University Press, 2000, 2008).

——, *3rd Norton Critical Edition* (New York and London: W. W. Norton Company, 2001).

——, (London: Penguin, 2006).

——, (Gutenberg Project, 1998, 2007), https://www.gutenberg.org/files/1260/1260-h/1260-h.htm.

——, (London: Collins Classics, 2010).

——, (London: Penguin, 2015).

——, *4th Norton Critical Edition* (New York and London: W. W. Norton Company, 2016).

——, (London: Collins 2019).

——, (Seattle: Amazon Classics, 2019).

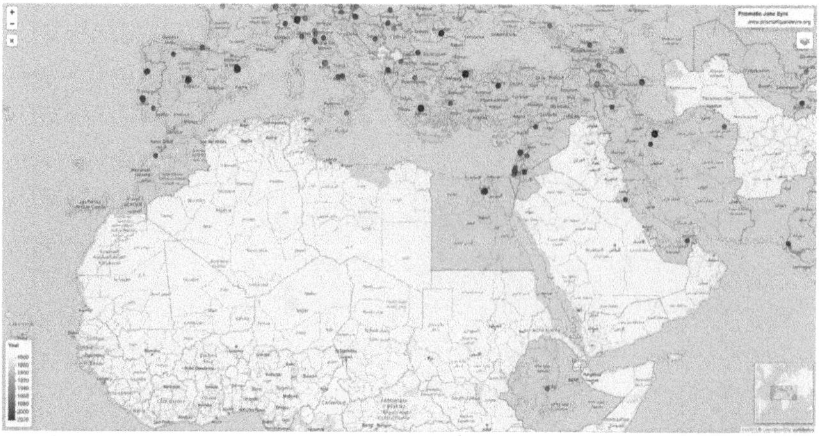

The General Map
https://digitalkoine.github.io/je_prismatic_generalmap/
Created by Giovanni Pietro Vitali; © OpenStreetMap contributors

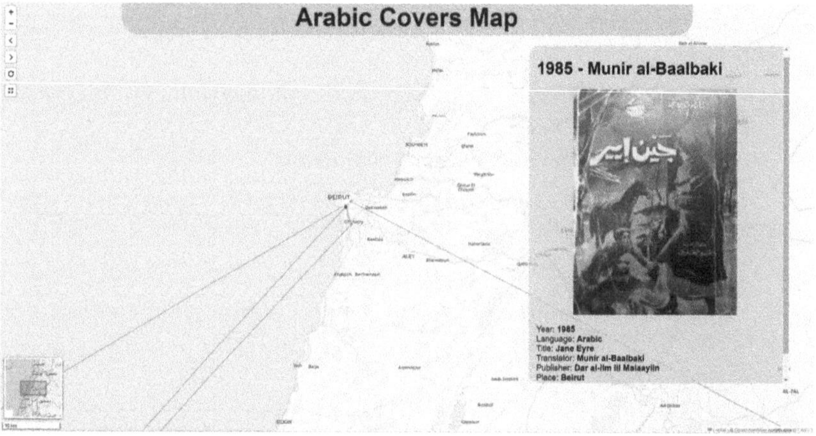

The Arabic Covers Map
https://digitalkoine.github.io/arabic_storymap/
Researched by Yousif M. Qasmiyeh; created by Giovanni Pietro Vitali and Simone Landucci

3. *Jane Eyre*'s Prismatic Bodies in Arabic

Yousif M. Qasmiyeh

This chapter explores the *body* in translation in Arabic versions of Charlotte Brontë's *Jane Eyre*.[1] In doing so, I focus on three interpretations of the body: firstly, viewing *Jane Eyre* itself as a *corpus* which engenders more corpuses through translation across languages and genres; secondly, tracing the multiple Arabic renderings of the body's *name*, Jane Eyre, in the context of naming and titling; and finally, through a focus on one material aspect of the body in the novel: touching. Throughout the chapter I am guided by Matthew Reynolds's proposition that '[t]ranslation is inherently prismatic', a view which 'is alert to translation's proliferative energies' but also one that re-centres 'the particularity of the language of the translation'.[2] Moreover, in exploring the relationship between translation and the body, in particular through my discussions of naming and touching, I build on the work of Jacques Derrida and his specific attention to the body in his pivotal article 'What Is a "Relevant" Translation?'.[3] In this article, originally titled 'Qu'est-ce qu'une traduction "relevante"?',[4] Derrida attempts to locate a 'relevant translation' by astutely attributing the act of religious conversion — in Shylock's case from Judaism to Christianity — to the transformation of the body proper. Derrida's essay has long been viewed as canonical in translation studies, and yet

1 I am hugely indebted to Prof. Matthew Reynolds for his invaluable feedback and suggestions on different iterations of this chapter. I am also grateful to the two anonymous reviewers for their helpful comments and recommendations.

2 Matthew Reynolds, 'Introduction', in *Prismatic Translation*, ed. by Matthew Reynolds (Oxford: Legenda, 2019), pp. 1–18 (pp. 6, 9).

3 Jacques Derrida, 'What Is a "Relevant" Translation?', trans. by Lawrence Venuti, *Critical Inquiry*, 27.2 (2001), 174–200.

4 Jacques Derrida, 'Qu'est-ce qu'une traduction "relevante"?' in *Quinzièmes assises de la traduction littéraire* (Arles: Actes Sud, 1998), pp. 21–48.

 https://doi.org/10.11647/OBP.0319.06

more recently its precise 'relevance' (as in pertinence) to translation studies has been queried. In particular, Kathryn Batchelor argues that the particular power of Derrida's essay stems from his attention to the 'multiplication of touches, caresses, or blows' throughout translation, noting that it is the duty of undertaking 'the movement between languages to open up multiple readings of the original text' that should be of 'far greater interest to today's translation studies scholars than Derrida's discussions of the traditional paradigm of translation'.[5] What is of particular interest in this chapter is precisely the prismatic multiplication that arises through the movement between English and Arabic, and more concretely as it pertains to the body, in the case of *Jane Eyre*.

While Derrida notes that 'any translation' can be considered to 'stand between... absolute relevance, the most appropriate, adequate, univocal transparency, and the most aberrant and opaque irrelevance',[6] throughout his essay, Derrida 'prowl[s]'[7] around the 'inter- and multilingual' term *relevant*,[8] in particular through its French roots and connotations. In so doing, he ties relevance, translation and the body closely together by 'describing [relevance] not simply as a "corps" [body] but as a "corps de traduction" [translative body]':[9]

> this word, 'relevant' carries in its body an on-going process of translation...; as a translative body, it endures or exhibits translation as the memory or stigmata of suffering [passion] or, hovering above it, as an aura or halo.[10]

In his essay, Derrida thus mainly talks about translation as a lifting away from the body (from the French *relever*),[11] a movement from body to word. In turn, my chapter takes a step forward from Derrida by exploring translation in relation to new kinds of embodiment.

On the one hand, I build upon existing elements of Derrida's oeuvre; for instance, as Derrida attributes to the title of his own essay,[12] I would argue that the title of *Jane Eyre*, or even the entire corpus

5 Kathryn Batchelor, 'Re-reading Jacques Derrida's 'Qu'est-ce qu'une traduction "relevante"?' (What is a 'relevant' translation?)', *The Translator*, (2021), 1–16 (p. 4).
6 Derrida, 'What Is a "Relevant" Translation?', p. 179.
7 Derrida, 'What Is a "Relevant" Translation?', p. 178.
8 Batchelor, 'Re-reading', p. 8.
9 Batchelor, 'Re-reading', p. 8.
10 Derrida, 'What Is a "Relevant" Translation?', p. 177.
11 Derrida, 'What Is a "Relevant" Translation?', p. 199.
12 Derrida, 'What Is a "Relevant" Translation?', p. 178.

of *Jane Eyre*, has an 'apparent untranslatability' into Arabic, due to factors related to voice and materiality. On the other hand, I expand the remit of other elements underpinning Derrida's essay. Most notably, perhaps, where Derrida concentrates on the 'Abrahamic and post-Lutheran Europe[an]'[13] traditions, and 'insist[s] on the Christian dimension'[14] of conceiving the body and translation, I focus on the distinctiveness of translation into Arabic and its related traditions. Like Derrida, my interest thus lies in the body, and yet working through the Arabic translations emphasises not only how the body in translation can emerge differently, but also how such translations are rendered accessible to audiences who may not have so 'thoroughly assimilated the ideas and images of Christianity' as Charlotte Brontë herself.[15] Indeed, *Jane Eyre* has often been read through a specifically Christian frame of reference — as Brown Tkacz notes, there are 176 scriptural allusions, circa 81 and 95 quotations and paraphrases from the Old Testament and the New Testament respectively[16] — and yet I suggest that a critical reading of Arabic translations must also acknowledge traditions that go beyond 'the Christian dimension'.[17] In essence, where Derrida posits the relevance of the *Merchant of Venice* to the concerns of translation, in my analysis of Arabic translations of *Jane Eyre* I make reference to the Qur'an and *The Arabian Nights* alike, thereby echoing the very duality in *Jane Eyre*, as a novel that refers repeatedly to the Bible (see also Essay 14 by Léa Rychen, below) and to the *Arabian Nights* themselves (representing transformative storytelling and self-fashioning).[18] In drawing on these references, I seek to develop a view of the body in translation rooted in Arabic, in contrast to Derrida's theory with its Judeo-Christian roots.

13 Derrida, 'What Is a "Relevant" Translation?', p. 179.
14 Derrida, 'What Is a "Relevant" Translation?', p 199.
15 Catherine Brown Tkacz, 'The Bible in *Jane Eyre*', *Christianity and Literature*, 44 (1994), 3–27 (p. 3).
16 Brown Tkacz, 'The Bible in *Jane Eyre*', p. 3.
17 Derrida, 'What Is a "Relevant" Translation?', p. 199.
18 On the position of *The Arabian Nights* in relation to storytelling in both Arabic and European literatures, see Wen-Chin Ouyang 'Genres, ideologies, genre ideologies and narrative transformation', *Middle Eastern Literatures*, 7.2 (2004), 125–31; Abdelfattah Kilito, *Arabs and the Art of Storytelling*, trans. by Mbarek Sryfi and Eric Sellin (Syracuse, N. Y.: Syracuse University Press, 2014), pp. 116–25; and Muhsin Jassim Al-Musawi, *The Postcolonial Arabic Novel: Debating Ambivalence* (Leiden and Boston: Brill, 2003).

Another way in which I expand Derrida's analysis is that where he views translation as 'preserving the debt-laden memory of the singular body',[19] I develop a different line of argumentation by challenging the equation of translation with 'preservation' and, indeed, by highlighting the prismatic and pluralistic nature of bodies in translation.[20] To do so, and echoing Batchelor's recognition that it is precisely the 'multiplication of touches, caresses, or blows' that is of particular significance to translation,[21] I divide my discussion as follows. Taking the *corpus* of *Jane Eyre* as my starting point, I begin by introducing the first radio adaptation (and, indeed, the first *popular* translation) of *Jane Eyre* in Arabic, examining how orality and narration in Arabic, and their employment in Arabic translations of Brontë's text, usher in the birth of new versions which are themselves not direct equivalences, but 'prismatic' bodies in translation. Nūr al-Dimirdāsh's 1965 radio adaption evidences the significance of voice and localisation, and in the second part of the chapter I examine how the importance of voice continues to figure in the print translations of Jane Eyre in Arabic, especially in the 1985 translation by Munīr al-Baʿalbakī. In particular, I focus on how translators have, in fluid ways, engaged with *Jane Eyre*'s genres, and on different written and voiced iterations of the name Jane Eyre in Arabic. Through my discussions of both the radio and printed translations, I thus complicate the distinction between speech and writing, or the binary of the oral and the written, instead noting that there can be elements of orality in writing, and, equally, 'writtenness' in oral performances. Finally, through an analysis of the different forms of touching and caressing the body, as written/voiced in the Arabic verbs employed in the various translations of the text, I emphasise the materiality of the body in translation, thereby complicating the positionality of the body proper in translation.

Orality as a Vehicle for Multiplicity

In the first section of this chapter, I examine Nūr al-Dimirdāsh's 1965 serialised adaptation of *Jane Eyre* for the Egyptian national radio,[22]

---

19 Derrida, 'What Is a "Relevant" Translation?', p 199.

20 In this way, I adopt the definition of translation advocated throughout this volume (see Chapter I, by Matthew Reynolds).

21 Batchelor, 'Re-reading', p. 4.

22 Nūr al-Dimirdāsh, *Jane Eyre* (Cairo: Egyptian Radio Station, 1965). The radio adaptation is available at https://youtu.be/GF2sj8QiPfQ

inter alia highlighting the significance of the aural transmission of *Jane Eyre* on subsequent textual Arabic translations. Although the radio adaption was not the first translation per se into Arabic,[23] in this chapter I focus on the first serialised radio adaption, given its broader significance as it reached a particularly wide and popular audience across the Arabic-speaking region. This is highly relevant given that access to the cinema and books alike was restricted by a range of socio-economic and educational barriers.[24] In particular, I argue that al-Dimirdāsh's version not only bridges the gap between Arabic and English, but, equally, is a medium through which the formal Arabic (*Fuṣḥā*) and the Egyptian vernacular have been reconciled, thereby demonstrating the complex relationship between writing and speech. At this stage, it is worth noting that, while its aim is not to offer a purely formal rendition of *Jane Eyre*, al-Dimirdāsh's version nonetheless sheds light on diglossia within the Arab-speaking region and the rupture between the formal Arabic register (*Fuṣḥā*) and the many national dialects (*lahajāt*, sing. *lahja*) that are spoken across the region.[25] Such a distinction is essential to our discussion, since *Fuṣḥā* has long been assigned to the written in Arabic, whereas *lahja* primarily refers to the spoken.[26] In al-Dimirdāsh's case, one might say

---

23 Ismāʿīl Kāmil's translation, published in Cairo as part of the Kitābī Series in 1956, is seen as the first translation of the novel into Arabic, and the first adaptation itself was a cinematographic one, with the first film directed by ḥusayn ḥilmī in 1961, under the title *This Man, I Love*. In this film, Jane Eyre's name is transformed into 'Ṣabrīn', a term from the word *ṣabr*, meaning patience in Arabic (Maḥmūd Qāsim, *Al-Iqtibās: 'Al-Maṣādir al-Ajnabiyya fī al-Sinamā al-Misriyya'* (Adaptation: Foreign Sources in Egyptian Cinema) (Cairo: Wikālat al-Ṣiḥāfa al-ʿArabiyya, 2018), p. 1911.

24 On the popular reach of Egyptian radio during the 1960s, see Salwa El-Shawan Castelo-Branco, 'Radio and Musical Life in Egypt', *Revista de Musicologia*, 16 (1993), 1229–1239.

25 While beyond the scope of this chapter, it is worth noting the significance and particular challenges of diglossia in Arabic for translation, where the formal register and the local dialects coexist but also clash — for instance, see Muhammad Raji Zughoul and Mohammed El-Badarien, 'Diglossia in Literary Translation: Accommodation into Translation Theory', *Meta*, 49.2 (2004), 447–56.

26 Building on the present discussion of voice in the radio adaptation, in subsequent sections of this chapter I continue to dwell on the significance of voice in the written translations, in particular in relation to the multiple renderings of the name Jane Eyre. On the question of the *Fuṣḥā*'s purity versus the contamination of dialects see Tetsuo Nishio, 'Language nationalism and consciousness in the Arab world', *Senri Ethnological Studies*, 55 (2001), 137–46. Also see Salameh on how certain dialects are purported (by their speakers

that the *Fuṣḥā-lahja* dynamic is inverted: instead of employing the Egyptian vernacular in the transmission of the radio adaptation of *Jane Eyre*, he opts for *Fuṣḥā* with vernacular traces (as I discuss below) which can be easily detected by the listener and, as such, nationally located in the radio broadcast.[27]

It is not insignificant that, when *Jane Eyre* was transmitted to the Arab reader/listener regionally, it was transmitted through a serialised form completed not by a professional translator but by the Egyptian actor and director Nūr al-Dimirdāsh's himself, who understood and spoke English, and enjoyed adapting and abridging world literature,[28] to subsequently be voiced by first-class Egyptian actors and actresses, including Ḥamdī Ghayth and Karīma Mukhtār, and broadcast on the Egyptian national radio to acclaim.[29] Radio, as a medium, was particularly significant during this period (part of Egypt's 'Radio Era'),[30] since it provided access to people who would otherwise be unable (due to socio-economic and educational barriers, amongst other things) to read a translation.

Guided and inspired by Jerome's *Jane Eyre: A Drama in Three Acts* (1938), and the novel itself, as announced by al-Dimirdāsh at the start of the broadcast, the adaptation was almost entirely performed in *Fuṣḥā* Arabic, notwithstanding some inflections that belong solely to the Egyptian vernacular, in particular those pertaining to the pronunciation of the letter/sound *j* (a highly significant sound, given the title and eponymous protagonist), which in the Egyptian vernacular

---

and external analysts alike) to be closer to *Fuṣḥā*, leading to hierarchical frames of stronger or weaker understandings of the Arabic language (Franck Salameh, 'Does anyone speak Arabic?', *Middle East Quarterly*, 18 (2011), 47–60).

27 As a brief note, I consider this adaptation to embody an attempt at conveying hybridity: first, in its reliance on both Brontë's *Jane Eyre* and Helen Jerome's *Jane Eyre: A Drama in Three Acts* (first performed and published in 1936) and secondly, and more importantly, in presenting this version as an attempt to introduce *Jane Eyre* to Arabic-speaking audiences and in so doing honouring the incompleteness that surrounds any translation.

28 For instance, he translated, adapted, and/or directed *Widowers' Houses*, by George Bernard Shaw, and Richard Sheridan's *The School of Scandal* for radio, the latter of which can be accessed at https://archive/org/details/P2-Dra-SchoolForScandal

29 See Said Yassin, '*Nūr al-Dimirdāsh.. Madrasa ikhrajiyya farīda*' (Nūr al-Dimirdāsh: A unique "school" in directing'), *Al-Ittihād*, May 2020, https://www.alittihad.ae/news/دنيا/٧٦٠١٩٩٣/نور-الدمرداش----مدرسة--إخراجية-فريدة

30 See El-Shawan Castelo-Branco, 'Radio and Musical Life in Egypt'.

is pronounced as a hard *g*.[31] To provide two minor examples (the radio adaption is replete with such instances throughout), in the midst of an otherwise 'formal' sentence, the words *'yagib'* and *'igāba'* (the auxiliary, 'must' and the noun 'answer', respectively) are enunciated with the hard 'g' that does not exist in *Fuṣḥā*, instead of the formal *'yajib'* and *'ijāba'* (with the soft *j* of 'journal').[32] Subsequently, in the final scene, words related to the body (and as such of particular bearing to this chapter) including *'jiwār'* (side, as in by your side), *'jasad'* (body) and *'jamīl'* (handsome) are converted to *'giwār'*, *'gasad'* and *'gamīl'*.[33]

What is of interest to us here is how such a translation, completed from and in conjunction with different sources (i.e., the original novel and a theatrical adaptation of it), has brought to life a new body which sits between the original and the literally translated. In other words, al-Dimirdāsh's creation, which runs for a total of two hours and just under sixteen minutes and maintains the plot and spirit of *Jane Eyre*, even though it is incomplete in so far as it is not a verbatim translation of the novel, carries within its folds a high degree of *relevance*, which, in turn, following Derrida, 'carries in its body an ongoing process of translation [...] as a translative body'.[34] This 'translative body' is also what '[leaves] the other body intact but not without causing the other to appear', meaning that it is progressively moving and is always viewed *apropos* the originals and other translations at the same time.[35] Expanding the remit of Derrida's analysis, I posit that this somatic outlook of a 'relevant translation' places the original and the translation in close (physical) proximity to each other, as two or more corpora whose materialities are continually shared.[36] Indeed, it is notable that al-Dimirdāsh's script for radio itself became

31 Building on Zughoul and Al-Badarien, who emphasise the challenges that exist vis-a-vis diglossia and translation in Arabic and who identify the 'phonemic substitution' of the 'Classical Arabic voiced palatal affricate /j/ or /dg/' with the 'colloquial Egyptian Arabic' 'voiced velar stop /g/' as a key characteristic that enables the audience to 'directly recognise' the vernacularisation therein, I maintain that the radio adaption of *Jane Eyre* is immediately recognisable as 'naturally dialectal' precisely due to this vernacular substitution and inflection (see Zughoul and El-Badarien, 'Diglossia in Literary Translation', p. 452).

32 Al-Dimirdāsh, *Jane Eyre*, 17' 20".

33 Al-Dimirdāsh, *Jane Eyre*, 2' 11".

34 Derrida, 'What is a "Relevant" Translation?', p. 177.

35 Derrida, 'What is a "Relevant" Translation?', p. 175.

36 On translation and the body, see Derrida 'What is a "Relevant" Translation?', and also Waïl S. Hassan, 'Translator's Note', in Abdelfattah Kilito, *Thou*

the foundation for multiple theatre productions, each one a minor adaptation of the 'relevant' text.

While the general aim of the serialised radio broadcast (as announced orally by the narrator at the beginning of the broadcast and subsequently in writing when it was adapted in turn to the stage) was 'to transmit some of the wonders of world literature in Arabic',[37] other aims may come to the fore when the medium itself is scrutinized. For example, radio broadcasting in Egypt during that particular time was on a par with the unmatched role of Egyptian cinema both worldwide and in the Arab region. That said, translating this quintessentially English text, not only into Arabic but into Arabic voices and sounds,[38] simultaneously built an ever-expanding audience but equally centralised orality in Arabic as a vital medium for such translations, narrating a story whose ethical and social specifics are distinct from the language to which it is translated.[39] This, as highlighted by the adaptation's reception, has offered an engagement and a subsequent debate that are triggered, strictly speaking, by the fluid nature of the broadcast and its translation, inviting people to listen to *an* Arabic (or a version of Arabic) that is set against or in conjunction with other Egyptian dramatisations in the Arabic language.

What appeared to be at stake in translating and broadcasting *Jane Eyre* on the national Egyptian radio is how, in privileging *listening* to a story, the narrative itself is consumed by the voices enacting the novel and their traces of Egyptian vernacular. Notably, in a medium that requires listening, rather than *reading* a novel whose narrative includes key speech-like elements, the line for which this novel is

---

Shalt Not Speak My Language, trans. by Waïl S. Hassan (Syracuse: Syracuse University Press, 2008), pp. vii–xxvi (p. x).

37 Many other plays and novels were serialised in this way, including *The Lady from the Sea* and *A Doll's House*, both by Henrik Ibsen, and available at https://youtu.be/Qbe_W8gs7Sk and https://youtu.be/-ruLNVygRyw; *Doctor Faustus*, by Christopher Marlowe, available at https://youtu.be/ben5H0dfhgw; and *The Cherry Orchard*, by Anton Chekov, available at https://youtu.be/UOVdlkoGZm0

38 Here I do not refer to sound effects (noting that the music playing in the background of the broadcast is associated with organ music for instance), but rather the specific sounds of the letters and words pronounced by the actors, who, as noted above, spoke in *Fuṣḥā* with vernacular (specifically Egyptian) inflections.

39 See Abdelfattah Kilito, *Thou Shalt Not Speak My Language*, trans. by Waïl S. Hassan (Syracuse: Syracuse University Press, 2008); Joanna Druggan and Rebecca Tipton, 'Translation, ethics and social responsibility', *The Translator*, 23 (2017), 119–25.

widely known in English — 'Reader, I married him' — is poignantly missing. Instead, the radio broadcast concludes with Jane answering Mr Rochester's question 'Will you marry me?' through the passionately enunciated responses '*bi kulli surūr*' (with pleasure) and '*bi muntahā ar-riḍā*' (with full acceptance) (circa min. 2h13). In a closing scene consumed with heavy breathing and eroticism, the broadcast ends with Mr Rochester asking Jane to kiss him, followed by dramatic music reaching a crescendo.

While the line is absent in al-Dimirdāsh's adaptation, Munīr al-Baʿalbakī's Arabic 1985 translation of the novel (discussed in more detail below) beautifully captures the agency which belongs to 'I married…', by omitting the first person subject pronoun *anā* in order to rely only on the implied subject in the verb conjugation, thereby maintaining the emphasis on the verb/verbal sentence and, importantly, centralising Jane as the woman who 'actively married him':[40] *wa tazawajtu minhu, ayyuhā al-qārī*',[41] which, back translated into English would be: 'And I married (from) him, O Reader.'

In spite of sacrificing one of the novel's defining lines ('Reader, I married him') by privileging listening, rather than reading, the radio adaptation inadvertently introduces the audience to a translation that is only recognisable as a translation through its inclusion of English names and sites, and more importantly through the foreignness of such names contra what is considered local and non-foreign by the listener. As the broadcast itself focuses on the audible and not the written, as explained by al-Dimirdāsh in his introduction to the adaption, the written only appears schematically in adverts for the programme in the form of an introductory list comprising: the title of the original work and its author in English, the sources, the radio station, the translator/director's name and the main cast. As this is still a translation, albeit incomplete, of *Jane Eyre* — one that has ushered in further and more textually complete versions — in this sense, this translation can be regarded as 'prismatic': 'one which is alert to translation's proliferative energies', contra the solely reproductive modes that engender sameness in translation, as theorised by

40 In the Arabic translations more broadly, two scenarios have been offered: 1) I married him and 2) We married. As noted above, the former was captured in the 1985 translation.

41 Munīr al-Baʿalbakī, *Jane Eyre* (Casablanca: Al-Markaz al-Thaqāfī Al-ʿArabī/ Beirut, Dār Al-ʿIlm Lil-Malāyīn, 2006), p. 727.

Reynolds.[42] If they were to be pinpointed, these 'proliferative energies' in al-Dimirdāsh's version would be the afterlives of his translation; its role was to propel the texts involved to new lives of their own, not only in connection to one another but also independent of one another. When al-Dimirdāsh offered the listener the opportunity to listen to and learn from this version, he did so by creating an enacted narrative performed by Egyptians to be received through radio broadcast across Egypt and beyond.

In all, it is not an exaggeration to maintain that al-Dimirdāsh's 1965 version has contributed immeasurably to *Jane Eyre*'s reception in Arabic; first, by recentring orality in the Arabic tradition as a medium whereby new knowledge is transmitted and contested,[43] this time in translation, and secondly, in crafting a scripted version in which difference is inherent to every subsequent performance of the script, which travelled across media from the radio to theatre, in a process of intersemiotic translation. In brief, this version is in itself multiple versions of *Jane Eyre*, both in translation and in reception.

Jane Eyre's Corpora: *ḥikāya* or *qiṣṣa?*

Following this introduction to al-Dimirdāsh's adaptation and serialisation of this prismatic body, focusing on orality and translational fluidity in radio, in this section I explore how these issues continue into printed translations of the novel into Arabic. In particular, my discussion of al-Dimirdāsh paves the way for an interrogation, firstly, of how translators have engaged with *Jane Eyre*'s genres, and subsequently how the name Jane Eyre is inscribed and pronounced in its Arabic translations.

With reference to the genres invoked by the novel's translators, as I set out below, in Arabic the question of storytelling falls under two complementary, albeit technically different, spheres: the *ḥikāya* and the *qiṣṣa*, which, in turn, convey varied hierarchical schemata with regards to the orality and the indefiniteness of the former (as also explained in relation to al-Dimirdāsh's 1965 adaptation) and

42 Reynolds, 'Introduction', pp. 2, 9.

43 See Kilito, *Thou Shalt Not Speak My Language*, p. 54, on the relationship between speech, transcription and rewriting; while discussing Ibn Battuta, I would posit that the broader process discussed by Kilito demonstrates the centrality of the oral as a prerequisite for writing and rewriting.

the solidity and the testimonial nature of the latter.[44] In this section, I shed light on the translators' labelling of *Jane Eyre* variously as a *ḥikāya* (a tale transmitted orally, and attributed to orality and fluidity in the Arabic tradition), *qiṣṣa* (a story, intimately related to the fixed/written and the Qur'an[45]) and/or *riwāya* (the contemporary novel).[46] In particular, I focus on al-Baʿalbakī's 1985 translation, given the particular pertinence of this text on multiple levels. Indeed, contra Derrida's assertion that translations carry and maintain 'a debt-laden memory of the singular body',[47] in Arabic, al-Baʿalbakī's translation has in a sense taken over from the English text and as such, the most recent translations still rely heavily and at times 'adopt' and 'adapt' sections from al-Baʿalbakī's.[48] It is very likely that the legacy of this translator's family — the owners and founders of the authoritative Al-Mawrid English-Arabic Dictionary series and the publishing house Dār Al- ʿIlm Lil-Malāyīn — significantly contributed to the centrality and popularity of this translation.[49]

---

44 On genres in Arabic literature, including the very question of locating a text's genre, see Ouyang, 'Genres, ideologies, genre ideologies and narrative transformation'; Wen-chin Ouyang (2003) 'The Dialectic of Past and Present in Riḥlat Ibn Faṭṭūma by Najīb Maḥfūẓ', *Edebiyat: Journal of Middle Eastern Literatures*, 14.1 (2003) 81–107; Edward Said's chapter, 'Arabic Prose and Prose Fiction After 1948', in *Reflections On Exile and Other Essays* (Cambridge: Harvard University Press, 2000); Al-Musawi, *The Postcolonial Arabic Novel;* Abdelfattah Kilito, 'Qiṣṣa', in Franco Moretti (ed.) *The Novel, Volume 1: History, Geography and Culture*, (Princeton and Oxford: Princeton University Press, 2006), pp. 262–68.

45 Noting its inherent plurality in this tradition, it is the plural term '*qaṣas*' that appears in the Qur'an, and never the singular noun '*qiṣṣa*'.

46 What is of particular 'relevance' in this regard, is not whether the text 'actually' belongs to one genre or another, but rather precisely the *translators*' choice — which once again relays the fluidity of the process — to label the text variously as *ḥikāya, qiṣṣa,* and/or *riwāya.*

47 Derrida, 'What is a "Relevant" Translation?', p. 199.

48 See Nabīl Rāghib, *Jane Eyre* (Cairo: Gharīb Publishing House, 2007); and Amal al-Rifāʿī, *Qiṣṣat Jane Eyre (Story of Jane Eyre)* (Kuwait: Dār Nāshirī Lil Nashr al-Ilikitrūni, 2014).

49 Al-Baʿalbakī is considered a giant of the field, having been nicknamed the 'sheikh of translators in the modern era' by fellow translators, literary critics and philologists alike. The vast majority of the translations of *Jane Eyre* that I reviewed for the Prismatic Jane Eyre project relied extensively on al-Baʿalbakī's 1985 translation. It is as if al-Baʿalbakī's translation had become 'the original of the original' by virtue of constituting itself as a new canon within translation studies in Arabic. Eventually run by his family, al-Baʿalbakī founded, with his friend Bahīj ʿUthmān, the publishing house Dār Al- ʿIlm Lil-Malāyīn (House of Education for the Millions) which has continued to publish

What is particularly notable in the original introduction to his 1985 translation is that, rather than characterising his translation as embodying one specific genre, al-Baʿalbakī refers to *Jane Eyre* interchangeably as a *ḥikāya, qiṣṣa,* and/or *riwāya.*[50] Importantly, the use of such overlapping labels is not specific to translations alone, as we can also see in the classical case of the *Arabian Nights* (also *One Thousand and One Nights, Alf Layla wa-Layla*)[51] — a text that was itself read by the eponymous heroine as a child and through which *Jane Eyre* has often been analysed[52] — which has been referred to in Arabic simultaneously as *ḥikāya* (pl. *ḥikāyāt*) and *qiṣṣa* (pl. *qaṣaṣ*). In defining the *Arabian Nights* as *ḥikāyāt,* the stories are situated within traditions of orality and oral story-telling (whereby each retelling leads to new versions of the story itself), while the term *qiṣṣa* invokes the salience of the written, recognising the *Arabian Nights* as semi-complete, semi-textual tales.[53]

In Arabic, *qiṣṣa* (*Q–Ṣ–Ṣ*) (pl. *qaṣaṣ*) refers to 'that which is written'[54] and as such that which is demarcated by a fixity that prevents the reader (hence the interpreter) from tampering with it, thus accepting

---

his English-Arabic dictionary *Al-Mawrid* (now in different formats: complete, concise, pocket, bilingual, middle-sized, etc.) which has exceeded its 40th edition. He translated more than a hundred books from English, including *The Story of My Experiments with Truth* by Mahatma Ghandi, *A Tale of Two Cities* by Charles Dickens, *Farewell to Arms, The Old Man and the Sea* and *The Snows of Kilimanjaro* by Ernest Hemingway, *A History of Socialist Thought* by G. D. Cole, *The Iron Heel* by Jack London, and *History of the Arabs* by Philip Hitti.

50 The multiple invocations of these three labels are indicative of how the Arabic translations of the text have been viewed by the translators themselves. In making this point, I do not seek to delimit the genre of the novel, but more importantly I refer to the multiple invocations of *ḥikāya* and *qiṣṣa* as a way of further developing a theory of translation.

51 Muḥammad Qiṭṭa al- ʿAdawī, ed., *Alf Layla wa-Layla* (One Thousand and One Nights) (Beirut: Dār Ṣādir Lil Ṭibāʿa wa al-Nashr, 1999).

52 See Melissa Dickson, 'Jane Eyre's 'Arabian Tales': Reading and Remembering the Arabian Nights', *Journal of Victorian Culture,* 18.2 (2013), 198–212; on the 'influence' of the Arabian Nights on Charlotte Brontë and on *Jane Eyre,* see Muhsin J. Al-Musawi, 'The Taming of the Sultan: A Study of Scheherazade Motif in *Jane Eyre*', *Adab al-Rafidayn* 17 (1988), 59–81, p. 60, and Melissa Dickson, *Cultural Encounters with the Arabian Nights in Nineteenth-Century Britain* (Edinburgh: Edinburgh University Press, 2019).

53 See Richard van Leeuwen, *The Thousand and One Nights and Twentieth-Century Fiction* (Leiden: Brill, 2018).

54 Muḥammad ibn Mukarram Ibn Manẓūr, *Lisān al-ʿArab* (The Language of the Arab People) (Cairo: Dār Ibn al-Jawzī, [1970] 2015], IV, pp. 53–57.

it as a complete version which is in no need of any addition or subtraction. Given its intimate linkage with the stories narrated in the Qur'an — such stories are called *qaṣaṣ* in the Qur'an, always in the plural — the *qiṣṣa* carries connotations of holiness and definiteness such that its borders are rarely violated. For instance, *Sūrat Joseph* (Chapter Yousif) reads: 'We tell you [Prophet] the best of stories [*aḥsan al-qaṣaṣ*] in revealing this Qur'an to you' (11:118–12:4).[55] In these Qur'anic chapters, stories of past prophets and messengers; their wives and other significant women; elders; animals and insects are recounted for the listener (before the reader, given that the Qur'an was transmitted orally before being transcribed) so that lessons can be gleaned from these parables.

As stories reported in the Qur'an are considered to be undeviating texts, their fixity is not only attributed to the divine; that is, the narrative that is owned by and referred to God in all its predetermined facets and specifics, but it is also attributed to the authority that dominates (in) as well as guards the parameters of the storyline, in this case the author and the original language of the text under study. When the narratorial fixity of the *qiṣṣa* becomes a literary itinerary towards all things in the text, be they real, imagined, sacred, truthful (to an extent) and/or allegorical, its status becomes that of a witness statement insofar as the act of reporting or bearing witness takes place through the eyes of an authority figure who is supposed to be all-knowing, or at least who knows better.[56]

Such an attribute, still within the Arabic canon, can be easily contradicted, on the other hand, by the ability of the *ḥikāya* — (Ḥ–K–Y), 'a speech like a story'[57] — to transcend its text and in turn refuse to adhere to a discursive linearity which is simply that of a tale. Since it is the narrative or the storyline that the *ḥikāya* is transmitting in multiple forms, this transmission becomes less of a text and more of an ongoing narrative, which is based on a direct relationship between an author or a narrator and an audience (notably echoing *Jane Eyre*'s narrative style in English). In this sense, the *ḥikāya* represents the

55 M. A. S. Abdel Haleem, *The Qur'an: Parallel Arabic Text*, trans. by M. A. S. Abdel Haleem (Oxford: Oxford University Press, 2000), p. 236.

56 On the relationship between writing and fixity in the case of the Qur'an, see Tim Winter, 'God the Speaker: The Many-Named One' in *The Routledge Companion to the Qur'an*, ed. by George Archer, Maria M. Dakake and Daniel A. Madigan (New York: Routledge, 2021), pp. 45–57 (p. 49).

57 Ibn Manẓūr, *Lisān Al-'Arab*, VII, pp. 563–4.

collective, which is normally maintained as multiple versions of itself through a continual series of narrations, in direct contrast to the *qiṣṣa* whose own survival is solely contingent on the specificity within the text, which is supposed to be passed on as it is.[58] Such a direct variance between the *qiṣṣa*, on the one hand, and the *ḥikāya*, on the other, takes us to the question of orality and its centrality in the latter, as explained earlier with reference to al-Dimirdāsh's adaptation of *Jane Eyre*. This orality, which can be likened to a nerve that goes through the *ḥikāya*'s entire body, counters the *qiṣṣa*, whose wholeness is guarded across time and space in the form of a text (even if it originated in the oral transmission that was subsequently written down). As the integrity of the *ḥikāya* is not contingent on the specific but on the collective instead, the multiple, the progressive and the tendency to evolve in terms of length and popularity are more palpable.

Such a distinction becomes increasingly critical when 'stories' such as *Jane Eyre* are translated into Arabic, and when the corpus of *Jane Eyre* is itself labelled by the translators variously as not only a *riwāya* (novel) but also simultaneously as a *qiṣṣa* or *ḥikāya*, as is the case with al-Baʿalbakī's translation. While acknowledging that *Jane Eyre* is indeed technically both a *riwāya* (novel) and a *qiṣṣa* (story), and noting that these are at times used to refer to the genre that the text belongs to rather than to name the tale itself, the term *ḥikāya* is also used — as a descriptor of the story — throughout the prefaces and introductions of selected translations of *Jane Eyre*, including those by al-Dimirdāsh, al-Baʿalbakī, Rāghib and Ṣabrī Al-Faḍl.[59] Such invocations, I would posit, are not circumstantial, but a clear indication of the way in which translation has been conceived of — in other words, the fluidity that is attributed to *ḥikāya* (a story that changes in its retelling) contra the fixity of the text-based *qiṣṣa*, which in turn resonates with Derrida's abovementioned reflections on the tension between translation-as-staying-the-same and translation-as-change. The latter is of particular relevance given the employment of *qiṣṣa* in the Qur'an and the particular approach to translation that has historically been applied in translations of the holy text: far from ascertaining that the Qur'an is

58 Also see Abdelfattah Kilito, *Arabs and the Art of Storytelling*, trans. by Mbarek Sryfi and Eric Sellin (Syracuse, N. Y.: Syracuse University Press, 2014), pp. 116–25.

59 See al-Dimirdāsh, *Jane Eyre*; Munīr al-Baʿalbakī, *Jane Eyre* (Beirut: Dār Al- ʿIlm Lil-Malāyīn, 1985); al-Baʿalbakī, *Jane Eyre* (2006); Rāghib, *Jane Eyre*; and Ṣabrī Al-Faḍl, *Jane Eyre* (Cairo: Al-Usra Press, 2004).

untranslatable per se, its translations are generally viewed as a means of capturing the *meaning* (*maʿnā*) of the text, rather than translating the text itself.[60]

I would thus argue that the abovementioned translators' references to *Jane Eyre* as a *ḥikāya* — a choice that I would argue may have been facilitated by the first-person narrative with its speech-like elements in the novel — can be interpreted as a desire not to depict translation as a production of one equivalent of *the* origin, but rather as a creation of a version that is susceptible to other versions and interpretations. For instance, in line with the fluidity of story-telling, al-Baʿalbakī's willingness (among other translators) to shift at times from the static to the fluid is worth noting. Tying back to the question of translating religious texts, al-Baʿalbakī handled the numerous references to the Bible and the Old Testament in *Jane Eyre* not only by including verbatim extracts from existing Arabic versions of the Bible, but also — given that many of the translation's readers would be Muslim — by adding explanatory footnotes throughout to explain the significance of key Christian personae. In turn, al-Baʿalbakī adopted fluid means when facing the challenge of translating a text replete with references to the soul and the spirit, as these relate to Christian doctrine. On the one hand, he adopts the term *rūḥ* (pl. *arwāḥ*) throughout the text to refer to both 'soul' and 'spirit', as noted in Table 1; in spite of theologically-charged debates pertaining to Arabic and Islamic approaches to the meanings and translation of the terms 'soul' and 'spirit',[61] this

---

60 Starting from the premise that 'translation is both necessary and impossible', Derrida offers the following reflection on Benjamin's *The Task of the Translator*: 'A sacred text is untranslatable, says Benjamin, precisely because the meaning and the letter cannot be dissociated'. See Jacques Derrida, *The Ear of the Other: Texts and Discussions with Jacques Derrida: Otobiography, Transference, Translation*, English edition ed. by C. McDonald. (Lincoln: University of Nebraska Press, 1988), p. 103.

61 On the widespread usage of the term '*rūḥ*' and related constructs to refer both to the soul and to the spirit in Arabic, see Mustafa Ali Harb, 'Contra stive Lexical Semantics of Biblical Soul and Qur'anic Ruh: An Application of Intertextuality', *International journal of Linguistics*, 6.5 (2014), 64–88. It is beyond the scope of this chapter to discuss the theologically-charged debates pertaining to Arabic and Islamic approaches to the concepts of the soul and spirit, but it is worth noting that *rūḥ* is widely identified as referring to both 'soul' and 'spirit', with *nafs* also being used at times to translate 'soul' (see Hard, 'Contrastive Lexical'; cf. M. S. Zahir al-Din, 'Man in Search of His Identity: A Discussion on the Mystical Soul (Nafs) and Spirit (Ruh)', *Islamic Quarterly*, 24.3 (1980), 96; Abdulaziz Daftari, 'The Dichotomy of the Soul and Spirit in Shi'a Hadith', *Journal of Shi'a Islamic Studies*, 5. 2 (2012), 117–29.

approach could be viewed as reflecting what Abdulaziz Daftari refers to as the 'common perception in the Islamic tradition that there is no distinction between the soul and the spirit'.[62]

Original	Arabic Translation
'a good little child, whose soul is in heaven' (Ch. 4)	طفلا صغيرا صالحا تقيم روحه الآن في السماء Back translation: 'a good little child, his soul [*rūḥ*] now lives in heaven
'punish her body to save her soul' (Ch. 7)	وعاقبن جسدها لكي تنقذن روحها... Back translation: 'punish [you pl, f.] her body in order for you [pl, f] to save her soul [*rūḥ*]...'
'your soul sleeps' (Ch. 15)	إنّ روحك هاجعة الآن Back translation: 'indeed your soul [*rūḥ*] is [a] sleep[ing] now'
'and only the spark of the spirit will remain' (Ch. 6)	فلا يبقى غير شرارة الروح – أصل الحياة والفكر وجوهرهما اللطيف... Back translation: 'and nothing remains except the spark of the spirit [*rūḥ*]'
'Besides this earth, and besides the race of men, there is an invisible world and a kingdom of spirits' (Ch. 8)	وبالاضافة الى الجنس البشري هناك عالم غير منظور ومملكة أرواح... Back translation: 'And in addition to the human race, there is an invisible world and a kingdom of spirits [*arwāḥ*]'

Table 1 Examples of 'soul' and 'spirit' being translated as '*rūḥ*'; with back translations by Y. M. Qasmiyeh.[63]

On the other hand, while consistently translating the term 'spirit' as '*rūḥ*' throughout the novel, in a series of notable examples, al-Baʿalbakī astutely converts 'the soul' into individual parts of the body, through what I refer to as 'bodily inflections', and in so doing he renders the soul concrete in some instances:

62 Daftari, 'The Dichotomy of the Soul and Spirit in Shi'a Hadith', p. 117.
63 Other similar examples of the translation of 'spirit' are found in Chs. 10, 12, and 19.

Original	Arabic Translation followed by back translations
'Then her soul sat on her lips, and language flowed, from what source I cannot tell' (Ch 8)	ثم جرى لسانها بما تكنُّه نفسها، وتدفقت لغتها من معين لست أدري حقيقته. Back translation: 'Then her tongue moved in synchrony with what her [inner] self [*nafs*] was concealing'
'The fury of which she was incapable had been burning in my soul all day' (Ch. 8)	إنّ صورة الغضب التي امتنعت هيلين عليها كانت تضطرم في جوانحي طوال النهار... Back translation: 'was burning in all my limbs [*jawaaniḥ sing. janaaḥ*] all day'
'the reader knows I had wrought hard to extirpate from my soul the germs of love there detected' (Ch. 17)	والقارئ يعرف أني بذلت جهدا كبيرا لكي أستأصل من قلبي بذور الحب التي اكتشفتها هناك Back translation: '... in order [for me] to extirpate from my heart [*qalb*] the seeds of love...'

Table 2 Examples of 'soul' being translated through what I refer to as 'bodily inflections'; with back translations by Y. M. Qasmiyeh.

Finally, and most powerfully perhaps, al-Baʿalbakī reclaims in translation the position of Palestine in rendering the second part of the English line 'I saw beyond its wild waters a shore, sweet as the hills of Beulah' (Chapter 15) as '*jamīlan ka hiḍāb Filastīn*' ('as beautiful as the hills of Palestine').[64] Such a retelling is poignant since it enables the novel to be situated not only in the Arabic language but also within Arab readers' cultural and historical frameworks, and both geographical and imaginary landscapes.

In these ways, al-Baʿalbakī's multiple categorisations of *Jane Eyre* as not only a *riwāya* (novel) and *qiṣṣa* (story) but also a *ḥikāya* demonstrate the fluidity that characterises the retelling of *Jane Eyre* in translation, a fluidity inherent within the materiality of story-telling and its capacity to articulate (or perhaps 'domesticate') a foreign text in a popular way and to a wider audience. Indeed, this approach to the textual (corpus) as materiality can be viewed as being closely linked to 'conversion', in line with Derrida's conceptualisation. In this vein, the materiality of the text is connected to the materiality of the translator's voice and location, with the translation of Beulah as Palestine being

64 Al-Baʿalbakī, *Jane Eyre* (2006), p. 245.

an instance of how, far from being fixed, the source's signifieds can undergo transformation as they pass into another body and location.

As I argue in the remainder of this chapter, to translate a story into another story, it is important to examine the body of the story in the target language in order to see whether all of the elements — including, in particular, literality, sounds and names — are consciously preserved as they are (however impossible this might ultimately be) or whether, in particular, the narratives are privileged at the expense of other features. It is to this question that I now turn, firstly with reference to the different written and voiced iterations of the name Jane Eyre, and, subsequently, to touching as a means of calling out the mutable nature of the body in translation.

Naming and Titling in *Jane Eyre*

In 'Des tours de Babel', Derrida poses the question: '"Babel": first a proper name, granted. But when we say "Babel" today, do we know what we are naming? Do we know whom?'[65] Echoing this question, how can proper nouns that belong to one language[66] — to spaces demarcated by the particularities of sounds, inflections and enunciations — be translated into another language? In this section on translating the name, I begin with the notion of the proper noun and the title in the Arabic tradition while assembling some of the many 'Jane Eyres' that have appeared in Arabic thus far. In so doing, I seek to trace the ways that the name itself engenders new names, identifying the writing and pronunciation of the proper name as a particular instance of the materiality and fluidity of the text.

Building on the extent to which the word 'title' in Arabic — according to the encyclopaedic *Lisān Al-'Arab*, for instance — is understood as the 'container' of the text (from the first to the final word), I would argue that such a conceptualisation makes the title the protector of the beginning and the end of a given text, and everything in between. In other words, the title, alongside its different interpretations, is the

65 Jacques Derrida, 'Des Tours de Babal', trans. by Joseph F. Graham, in *Difference in Translation* ed. by Joseph F. Graham (Ithaca and London: Cornell University Press, 1985), pp. 165–205 (p. 165).

66 As Bennington notes, however, 'we shall have to say that the proper name belongs without belonging to the language system.' See George Bennington and Jacques Derrida, *Jacques Derrida* (Chicago: Chicago University Press, 1999), p. 170.

only element within a text that is capable of delimiting the text itself.[67] In Arabic, the verb *ʿanan* — that is, 'to bestow a title on something' — is also understood as follows: 'to be or to appear in front of something or somebody' and/or 'to block the line of vision'. In turn, the noun *ʿunwān* (title)[68] is the trait of the book and also the sign or the trace that appears (gradually) on a person's forehead as a result of excessive prostration;[69] this trace, in turn, is perceived to be a sign of total submission to God and a reiteration of piety. As such, through the title *Jane Eyre* (whose full original title in English is *Jane Eyre: An Autobiography*) or its translations alone we can identify a direct correspondence between two corpuses, or more than two: the English, the Arabic and the multiple transliteration(s) of specific sounds from English into Arabic. With reference to the latter, although transliteration belongs to and is managed by Arabic on the basis of the Arabic alphabet, the sounds themselves and their combinations therein are *quasi-shared* between English and Arabic, a dynamic I explore in more detail below.

In two of the Arabic translations consulted for the purposes of this chapter,[70] the name 'Jane Eyre' in the title of the book has been either

67 Also see Gérard Genette, 'Introduction to the Paratext', *New Literary History*, 22.2 (1991), 261–72.

68 In contemporary Arabic, the term also refers to 'the address', hence a marker of emplacement. It refers to the 'structure on or in which something is firmly placed', and 'the process through which something is set in place', 'the location'.

69 One of the five pillars of Islam is to pray five times a day, a process which involves physically kneeling and prostrating, touching the ground with one's forehead. In some instances, some believers undertake such regular and vigorous prostration that this can leave a visible mark or sign on their foreheads.

70 For the purposes of this section of the chapter, the translations of *Jane Eyre* that I have consulted are as follows: Ismāʿīl Kāmil, *Jane Eyre* (Cairo: Kitābī Series, 1956); al-Dimirdāsh, *Jane Eyre*; Unnamed group of translators, *Jane Eyre aw Qiṣṣat Yatīma* (*Jane Eyre, or Story of an Orphan*) (Beirut: Al-Mʿārif Press, 1984); al-Baʿalbakī, *Jane Eyre* (1985 and 2006); Unnamed translator, *Jane Eyre*, ed. by Nabīl Rāghib (Bilingual edition, Cairo: Dār al-Hilāl, 1993); Unnamed translator, *Jane Eyre* (Damascus: Dār al-Biḥār/Cairo: Dār Wa Maktabat Al-Hilāl, 1999); al-Faḍl, *Jane Eyre*; Samīr Izzat Naṣṣār, *Jane Eyre* (Amman: Al-Ahliyya Press, 2005); Rāghib, *Jane Eyre*; Unnamed group of translators, *Jane Eyre* (Beirut: Dār Maktabat Al Maʿārif, 2008); Riḥāb ʿAkāwī, *Jane Eyre* (Beirut: Dār Al-Ḥarf al-ʿArabī, 2010); Ḥilmī Murād, *Jane Eyre* (Cairo: Modern Arab Foundation, 2012); al-Rifāʿī, *Qiṣṣat Jane Eyre (Story of Jane Eyre)*; Unnamed translator, *Jane Eyre* (Dubai: Dār Al Hudhud For Publishing and Distribution, 2016); Unnamed translator, *Jane Eyre* (Giza: Bayt al-Lughāt al-Duwaliyya, 2016); Yūsif ʿAṭā al-Ṭarīfī, *Jane Eyre* (Amman: Al-Ahliyya Press, 2017); Aḥmad Nabīl al-Anṣārī, *Jane Eyre* (Aleppo: Dār al-Nahj/Dār al-Firdaws:

preceded or followed by 'Story of' or 'Story of An Orphan', making the Arabic title 'Story of Jane Eyre' (*Qiṣṣat Jane Eyre*) or 'Jane Eyre or Story of an Orphan' (*Jane Eyre aw Qiṣṣat Yatīma*) respectively.[71] While the addition of 'an orphan' within the title marks out these Arabic titles from other languages, given that 'orphan' has been incorporated *into* the formal title rather than being presented as a *subtitle*,[72] in some sense this retitling process echoes translations into other languages, whereby the original English subtitle ('An Autobiography') was replaced by references to 'the orphan' or 'a governess' (following the 1849 publication of *Jane Eyre ou Mémoires d'une gouvernante/Jane Eyre or Memoirs of a Governess*, and Charlotte Birch-Pfeiffer's 1853 stage version *Die Waise von Lowood*, the Orphan of Lowood). The inclusion of the term 'orphan' within the title is paralleled by the exclusion of the original subtitle: even though some of the reviews of the Arabic translations, as well as some of the bilingual (normally abridged) translations published by Dar Al-Bihar in Syria (with no named individual translators), have used words such as 'autobiography' and/or 'autobiographical' to describe the novel and therefore situate it in a wider genre, the translators themselves have never done so in any of the texts consulted. Of particular relevance in light of my discussion of the multiple labels used by translators themselves to describe the genre (variously as *qiṣṣa*, *ḥikāya* or *riwāya*), is that the Arabic retitling in these two instances is relatively unique, writ large, precisely due to the insertion of 'story' into the title itself (with notable exceptions being two recent translations in the Thai language[73]). Importantly, the prominence of *qiṣṣa* on the covers of these translations is nonetheless often complemented, as discussed above, by the translators situating the text within the framework of the *ḥikāya*.

Whether with or without subtitles, and the above-mentioned additions and exclusions, we can argue that we bestow a proper noun/ name on the text mainly to view everything through the eyes of the

---

2017); Unnamed translator, *Jane Eyre* (Cairo, Dār al-Alif for Printing and Distribution, 2017); Munīr al-Baʿalbakī, *Jane Eyre* (Morroco: Maktabat al-Yusr, n.d. print on demand).

71 Given the lack of a direct equivalent or the name 'Jane Eyre', as I discuss below, here I have opted to maintain the English spelling of the name as it is.

72 It is worth noting that the way that subtitles are appended to titles in the English language does not correspond to the Arabic tradition. Of late, subtitles have started to be used in Arabic texts.

73 With thanks to Matthew Reynolds for drawing my attention to these translations. See, for instance, *Khwām rak khọ̄ng yēn 'œ/Jane Eyre: Love Story*, trans. by Sotsai Khatiwọ̄raphong (Bangkok: Phrǣ, 2007).

named. In this context, for example, the name is itself the title, and vice versa. To take it (back) to Arabic and to find an equivalence, we resort to multiple transliterations of the name or names (Jane Eyre) to substitute another name or names. But should names always be perceived as transferable, interpretable and translatable as names? What if, for example, this vocal directness — that is, the preservation of the name as it is, with its unique pronunciation which only belongs to itself — cannot be sustained in other languages, as is the case in Arabic? Would such a transfer convey the same name, or could we simply assume that all names are pseudonyms in translation? Such questions push against Derrida's argument in 'Des tours de Babel' and expand the focus developed in 'What is a relevant translation?' in so far as Derrida, in those essays, does not acknowledge the importance of the traces of vocality — the implied pronunciations — that are inscribed in writing; it is by emphasizing their significance that I therefore seek to move on from Derrida's work.

To ponder the untranslatability of the proper noun, Jane Eyre, from English into Arabic, it is worth examining the title's two constituent parts: Jane and Eyre. As demonstrated in Table 3, which lists the transliterations of the title alongside the translators' names and years of publication, in the Arabic translation, Ja (in Jane) = J+a and Ey (in Eyre) = E+y have been matched with either J جا or Jī جي or Ā آ or Ī إي respectively, as a result of the absence in Arabic of direct equivalents of the elongated and wide sound combinations that exist in English. Such appropriations and/or distortions, in the form of alternative Arabic pronunciations to the original, open the title up to different readings that, in turn, engender new titles/translations, which act independently of the original title itself.[74] Notably, Derrida does not discuss pronunciation in 'Des tours de Babel' and as such in this discussion I build and expand upon his approach, with my analysis aligned to this volume's emphasis on the prismatic nature of translation, as I argue that the very reiteration of a proper name through language difference has a prismatic effect.

The way that *Jane* has been transliterated is closely aligned with the word *jinn* (spirit or genie), in particular when the diacritics (signs written above and below the letter to mark its corresponding short

74 Miss, Mr and Mrs are also transliterated in Arabic letters in the 1985, 2006 and 2012 translations by al-Baʿalbakī. The word Master was translated as Sayyid (the head of...).

vowel sound) on the word *jinn* are not visible.[75] Of particular relevance to the focus of this chapter on the body, the word *jinn* is itself derived from the root *J–N–N* which refers to concealment and the lack of physical presence. In turn, the equivalent of Eyre, when commonly transliterated into Arabic, ties to another aspect of the body: that is, *ʾayr*, which is the penis.[76] This may be one reason why the titles of the book rarely bear diacritics — even though such signs would make the transliteration more accurate sound-wise — as these signs would more concretely pin down the pronunciation of the name and tie it to such connotations. At the same time, we can assume that the general absenting of the glottal stop in the transliteration of Eyre (*ʾayr*) may have purposely been applied in order to move the transliteration away from its close Arabic homophone.

Standing out from the other transliterations is al-Baʿalbakī's rendition of the title, both in its usage of diacritics in the 1985 version, and its unique approach to transliterating the surname: إيير (al-Baʿalbakī's choice) and آيير (used posthumously, and we can assume amended by the publishing house). As per Table 4 below, the sound choices here are difficult to recapture closely in English — the first broadly corresponds to an elongated 'ee' ('eeer') and the second to 'aayir'. Importantly, each and every reader, especially those unfamiliar with the pronunciation of the English title, would imagine and enunciate these nominal alternatives differently.

75 Ibn Manẓūr, *Lisān al-ʿArab*, VII, p. 71.
76 Ibn Manẓūr, *Lisān al-ʿArab*, II, p. 422.

Translations bearing the specified title	Title as written in Arabic (*Jane Eyre* unless specified otherwise)
Nūr al-Dimirdāsh, 1965 Unknown Translator, 1993 Unnamed Translator, 1999 Ṣabrī al-Faḍl, 2004 Samīr Izzat Naṣṣār, 2005 Nabīl Rāghib, 2007 Unknown, 2007 Riḥāb ʿAkāwī, 2010 Ḥilmī Murād, 2012 Unknown translator, 2016 Yūsif ʿAṭā al-ṭarīfī, 2017 Unknown translator, 2017	جين اير
Munīr al-Baʿalbakī, 1985	جَيْن إيير
Munīr al-Baʿalbakī, 2006	جين آيير
Aḥmad Nabīl al-Anṣārī, 2017	جين آير
Unnamed group of translators, 2008	جاين إير
Unnamed group of translators, 1984 *Jane Eyre, or Story of an Orphan*	جين إير أو قصّة يتيمة
Amal al-Rifāʿī, 2014 *Story of Jane Eyre*	قصّة جين إير

Table 3 Some of the Arabic 'Jane Eyres' compiled from different translations completed between 1965 and 2017.

Guiding Sounds and Letters	Transliteration
ج	'j'
جْ	'muted j'
جَ جا	'ja jā'
جُ جو	'ju jū'
جِ جي	'ji jī'
ا	'elidable hamza'
أْ	'muted a'
أَ آ	'short and long a'
أُ أو	'short and long u'
إ إي	'short and long i'
ن	'n'
ي	'the consonant y or as a long vowel ī'

Table 4 Guiding sounds and letters with their transliterations in the Arabic transliterations of the name 'Jane Eyre'.

As it is the name that we are carrying from one language to another, not as the same name, but as a metaphor of a name, it becomes clear in Arabic that the 'foreign' (*aʿjamī*) (that which has no equivalence in Arabic) becomes 'more foreign' in translation by being moved away from its autochthonous sounds. To draw the name-metaphor apposition closer, the words *kunya* and *kinya* (كُنية or كِنية) in Arabic (epithet, title, name, surname, nickname) are etymologically related to the word *kināya* (كِناية) (metonymy, metaphor, sign, symbol). Such an affinity is relevant in this context in the interpretation of the translation of names as a production of 'new' metaphors and/or signs that will eventually take over from the name, as is the case in the Arabic titles. Indeed, such processes arise throughout Arabic translations of novels bearing 'foreign' proper nouns, and yet perhaps have especial salience in the case of *Jane Eyre* because of the challenge of the repeated vowel sounds and also because of the suggestiveness of the name in the novel.

Despite the fact that these Arabic transliterations belong to or are derived from the English *Jane Eyre*, I would argue that they equally sit outside the text as written and, as such, they become extra-textual within the origin. This extra-textuality being established in the Arabic text may be seen as a third text:[77] it is neither English (entirely) nor Arabic (entirely) but a combination of both, whose main aim is to produce an equivalent that resembles the English *Jane Eyre* as best as Arabic sounds can do. Importantly, since it is the female name that is engendering all these names, it becomes apparent how some Arabic translators, when transliterating the name Brontë, at times opted to use the feminine marker (*al-tā' al-marbūṭa*) (*Bruntah*) and not an elongated ee (*Bruntee*) (which is more common) in order to make the feminine more physically present through the suffix.

In the absence of capital letters in Arabic to mark the proper nouns, most Arabic translations have relied on brackets to declare and concretise the names of people, places, titles and languages throughout the novel. In so doing, they have reinforced physical borders (to borrow Reynolds's words[78] in another context) around the proper nouns for the sake of foreclosing any other assumptions beyond the proper noun and the title. Such an approach in the Arabic translations has transformed the name itself into a border, firstly, in its potentiality to (re)assert as well as delineate the linguistic 'difference' between Arabic and English, and secondly, in positing the name's life as that which transcends the life of the translation itself.

'Touching' *Jane Eyre*

Rather than seeing translating as lifting above materiality and then mourning it (as argued by Derrida), I have shown that translation does not rise *above*, but moves *through* materiality, thereby not only generating change but also, in so doing, producing a questioning textuality in which translation is more like touching than like transfer, with the concomitant question arising: how much can a touch accurately apprehend? Building on the preceding analyses, in this final section, I discuss touch in more detail, arguing that the Arabic is not only different from the English, but is also arguably more nuanced: in a sense, it apprehends more than the English knows. I thus examine

77 Homi K. Bhabha, 'Cultural Diversity and Cultural Differences' in *The Post-Colonial Studies Reader*, ed. by Bill Ashcroft, Gareth Griffiths and Helen Tiffin, 2nd edition (London: Routledge, 2006), pp. 155–57 (p. 156).

78 Here I am referring to Reynolds where he writes: 'translationese (with its many sub-varieties) is a different kind of translation, or "translation", than the reiteration of a proper name: it creates boundaries between languages by the very act of bridging them.' Matthew Reynolds, *Likenesses: Translation, Illustration, Interpretation* (London: Routledge, 2013), p. 104.

the multiplicity (and inherently metaphoric nature) of the Arabic translations of the verb 'to touch' in *Jane Eyre*, thereby elucidating how 'touching' is rendered in Arabic and in what ways its translation goes beyond the English, not with the aim of identifying similarities across the languages, but to engender *prismatic* readings in both the English *and* its Arabic equivalent. To develop this text-based reading of the translation of 'touching' in *Jane Eyre*, I continue referring to Munīr al-Baʿalbakī's 1985 Arabic translation of the novel, which, as noted above, is still considered to be the most reliable of the Arabic literary translations, to the extent of being elevated to the status of a quasi-source text. In this translation, three key Arabic verbs are used to refer to 'touching': *massa, lamasa* and *lāmasa.*

In *Sūrat Maryam* (Chapter Mary) in the Qur'an, Maryam asks: 'How can I have a son while no man has *touched* me and I have not been unchaste?'[79] The Arabic verb used in this verse to convey 'touching' is *massa* (from the Classical Arabic root M-S-S) which connotes the most delicate of touches, which can only be captured or sensed if the touched person is fully in tune with an emanating touch. Since the overriding aim of this Qur'anic verse is to dispel the possibility of conceiving through touching (Maryam is supposed to be a virgin), the verb *massa* is employed as an alibi for no perceptible touch. The other verb that is used in Arabic to convey touching is *lamasa* (L–M–S), which is attributed to the hand touching another part of the body, thereby highlighting precisely the corporeal aspect of, and in, touching. The third verb, which is in fact a variant of the second, is *lāmasa* (L–M–S); unlike *lamasa, lāmasa* (with an elongated first *ā* sound) is interactive and connotes interchangeable movements. This thereby makes both parties (the touch*er* and the touch*ed*) equally involved in the process of touching.

In the following examples — quoted from the original (English) version of the text — I start from the premise that al-Baʿalbakī's treatment of the act of touching in his translation of *Jane Eyre* embodies interpretations (and/or versions of translations) that occur first within Arabic, before being perceived as equivalences, alternatives and/or substitutes for the English.

With the word 'touch' absent from the first phase of the novel at Gateshead, where physical contact is primarily aggressive, it is only when the as yet unnamed Miss Temple encounters 'Jane Eyre' that

79 Abdel Haleem, *The Qur'an*, 19:20.

touch becomes an important motif in the novel, bringing the name, the body and touch together: '"Is there a little girl called Jane Eyre, here?" she asked. I answered "Yes," and was then lifted out.'[80] The initial bodily encounter — being 'lifted out' or, returning to Derrida, perhaps '*relevée*' — not only arises a few short paragraphs after a noteworthy instance of the whole name 'Jane Eyre' (rather than solely the first name, Jane) being enunciated, but is followed by an unusually gentle touch for Jane to experience:

> She inquired how long they had been dead; then how old I was, what was my name, whether I could read, write, and sew a little: then she *touched* my cheek gently with her forefinger...

In his translation of this sentence (p. 68), al-Baʿalbakī acknowledges the gentleness of the touch as reiterated in the original by opting to use the verb *massa* (transliterated as '*thumma massat wajnatayy bi subbabatihā massan rafīqan*', literally, 'then she touched my cheek with her forefinger a delicate touching').[81] In doing so, the touch(ing) becomes a marker of a beginning, in other words, a gentle initiation — as interpreted in Arabic — that is performed in/on/through body parts that are considered less intrusive and therefore less physical than others.

In the second instance of physical touching in the novel, which comes immediately after the first, when Jane is new at Lowood and is determining how to connect to the place and the people there, *massa* again (and not *lamasa*) is used in the Arabic version:

> When it came to my turn, I drank, for I was thirsty, but did not *touch* the food.[82]

It would not be entirely unusual to use the verb *lamasa* in this context, precisely because this verb is used to convey the process of palpably touching food. However, al-Baʿalbakī invokes the verb *massa* to reflect the nature of the rejection of the food: it is an outright rejection, a rejection even of the *intention* of touching. In this way, the Arabic verbs — *massa* versus *lamasa* — are placed in a hierarchy according to subtle proximities and, through these nuances, the involved subjects are separated or united. In other words, translating touching in Arabic

80 *JE*, Ch. 5.
81 Al-Baʿalbakī, *Jane Eyre* (2006), p. 68.
82 *JE*, Ch. 5; al-Baʿalbakī, *Jane Eyre* (2006), p. 70.

seems to touch first and foremost on multiple degrees of touching inherent in the language itself.

In turn, the third (and last) example of touching in Lowood pertains to Helen — 'but I think her occupation touched a chord of sympathy somewhere; for I too liked reading' — and once again the verb *massa* is used by the translator, indicating the subtlety and profundity of such touching.[83]

Contra the consistent usage of *massa* in Lowood, the first touches that occur after Lowood arise from the earlier encounter with Rochester and his horse, and move us away from this first 'touching' verb. The original version in English reads 'I should have been afraid to touch a horse when alone, but when told to do it, I was disposed to obey', followed by 'A touch of a spurred heel made his horse first start and rear, and then bound away.'[84] In both of these instances, the translation of 'touch' through the verbal noun *lams* and then *lamasa,* embodies the greater physicality that is taking place, and the active and direct process of touching by the subjects (pages 187 and 188): the latter is demonstrated clearly in the back-translation of the second line: 'and *he touched his horse* with his heel (the one) which has spurs…'.[85]

In contrast, al-Baʿalbakī chooses to use the verb *lāmasa* (with an elongated *ā*) to exemplify the outward and interactive nature of the process, as clearly illustrated in the following quotation from the English, which once again brings together touch and an enquiry about a name:

> Just then it seemed my chamber-door was *touched*; as if fingers had *swept* the panels in groping a way along the dark gallery outside. I said, 'Who is there?'[86]

In the Arabic translation, the first touch is converted into the active voice ('And at that moment it seemed to me as though a thing had touched the door of my room'), using the verb *massa* to allude to the fact that this touch has originated from an unidentifiable source, whereas the verb 'swept' is translated with *lāmasa,* as if the fingers and the panels are rubbing against one another.[87] Amongst other

83 *JE*, Ch. 5; al-Baʿalbakī, *Jane Eyre* (2006), p. 78.
84 *JE*, Ch 12.
85 Al-Baʿalbakī, *Jane Eyre* (2006), pp. 187, 188.
86 *JE*, Ch 15.
87 Al-Baʿalbakī, *Jane Eyre* (2006), p. 239.

things, opting to use *lāmasa* for 'swept' highlights the multiple levels of touching taking place within the same context.

As a final cluster of examples,[88] included here in the English, touch re-emerges powerfully in the penultimate chapter, when Jane goes to Mr Rochester at Ferndean.

> He put out his hand with a quick gesture, but not seeing where I stood, he did not *touch* me.
>
> "And where is the speaker? Is it only a voice? Oh! I cannot see, but I must *feel*, or my heart will stop and my brain burst. Whatever — whoever you are — be perceptible to the touch or I cannot live!"
>
> "You touch me, sir — you hold me, and fast enough: I am not cold like a corpse, nor vacant like air, am I?"

In these examples from Chapter 37, the verbs *massa* and *lamasa* are both used in various forms. The first verb 'touch' is rendered *massa*. '[H]e did not touch me' is translated as '*lamm yasammanī*' (sic) — '*lamm yamassanī*' which invokes a touching that did not actually happen, hence the use of a form of touching that is too discreet in *massa* instead of the physicality inherent in *lamasa*.[89] As a brief aside, and prompted by the typographical error included on page 701, where *yamassanī* is incorrectly written as *yasammanī* by inverting the order of the s and the m, the verbs *massa* (to touch) and *sammā* (to name) that are conflated here draw powerful attention to the very connection that is

88 Other examples of 'touch' in the translation include the following: in Chapter 18, the text reads 'I see Mr. Rochester turn to Miss Ingram, and Miss Ingram to him; I see her incline her head towards him, till the jetty curls almost touch his shoulder and wave against his cheek; I hear their mutual whisperings; I recall their interchanged glances; and something even of the feeling roused by the spectacle returns in memory at this moment.' Here, the relevant part of the Arabic translation (p. 298) can be back-translated as 'I can see her inclining/tilting her head towards him to the extent that/until her tresses were about to touch his shoulder...' Subsequently, 'I have told you, reader, that I had learnt to love Mr. Rochester: I could not unlove him now, merely because I found that he had ceased to notice me — because I might pass hours in his presence and he would never once turn his eyes in my direction — because I saw all his attentions appropriated by a great lady, who scorned to touch me with the hem of her robes as she passed...' becomes (through the back translation from Arabic, p. 298) 'to touch me with the hems [idiomatically, in Arabic we use the plural of 'hem'] of her dress as she walks past me...' In both of these instances, the verb *massa* is used, in line with the touching of objects of a delicate nature — the hair and the hem.

89 Al-Baʿalbakī, *Jane Eyre* (2006), p. 701.

at the heart of this chapter on the relationship between the body and the name.

In the following two lines included above, 'I feel' is rendered 'I touch' (*almis*, from *lamasa*) in line with the English 'to palpate', which in this case mainly refers to the movement of the body towards another body, with the intention of physically reaching out; in turn, 'perceptible to touching' is translated through the verbal noun of *lamasa*, *lams*, thereby once again highlighting the physical attribute of this type of touching.[90] Finally, exemplifying the actual act of touching taking place, 'You touch me, sir' is translated by al-Baʿalbakī as *'anta talmisunī ya sayyidī'*: 'You are touching me, sir'.[91] With no doubt, the urgency and definiteness of this touching rebuts any suggestion that Jane Eyre could be 'cold like a corpse' or 'vacant like air'.

Since touching does not solely involve one specific body part, as Derrida contends,[92] or more precisely as it escapes the local or localised in other senses, one might argue that this multidirectional touching retains the inherent prisms in language. In this sense, these multiple and yet particular readings of touching in *Jane Eyre* and al-Baʿalbakī's Arabic translation of this important novel cannot but usher in a constant return to both languages, not to limit meaning in any way, but rather to open more possibilities within and beyond both texts.

Conclusion

In this chapter I have sought to build upon, and in so doing move on from, Derrida's pivotal article, 'What Is a "Relevant" Translation?', advocating for the development of a more nuanced, and indeed prismatic, approach to translation and embodiment, one that conceives of translation as a touching of bodies rather than a (guilt-ridden) rising above them. Throughout, I have complicated the distinction between speech and writing, and highlighted the pluralistic relationships between the body and translation, arguing that the Arabic translation is not merely 'different' but at times apprehends more than the English knows. In the scene that draws both this chapter, and *Jane Eyre* itself, to a close, the relationship between speech and touch is (to return to Derrida) particularly 'relevant'. As Mr Rochester has become

90 Al-Baʿalbakī, *Jane Eyre* (2006), p. 702.
91 Al-Baʿalbakī, *Jane Eyre* (2006), p. 703.
92 Jacques Derrida, *On Touching – Jean Luc Nancy*, trans. by Christine Irizarry (Stanford C. A.: Stanford University Press, 2005).

blind and can no longer read, Jane instead reads to him out loud, thereby undertaking a particular form of translation — from the text to the oral and the aural — which resonates with al-Dimirdāsh's 1965 adaptation of the novel: from the text, to the script that is performed by the actors on radio and subsequently consumed by the listener. While al-Dimirdāsh's adaptation is subsequently reborn as a play, to be observed as well as heard, Jane Eyre's reading out loud (or storytelling) to Mr Rochester takes precedence over sight, pushing sound to the forefront while relegating sight to the background: 'never did I weary of ... impressing by sound on his ear what light could no longer stamp on his eye.' At the same time as sound becomes a form of touch, and as emotional and physical sensing and feeling come together as one, so too does touch itself appear as a dynamic that is not only *felt* but is also a new language (literally) that gathers two corpuses afresh within its folds: Jane's and Mr Rochester's.[93]

The relationship between translation and the body is further concretised in al-Baʿalbakī's retelling of this scene, since, in the Arabic translation, both 'impressing' and 'stamp' are rendered with the same verb, *ṭabaʿa*, which, importantly, mean 'to print' and 'to inscribe', as though to remind the reader that senses are always in translation — so to speak — and can therefore be expressed differently.[94] While *ṭabaʿa* refers, inter alia, to the written, this closing account demonstrates the interconnectedness between the multiple senses of translation, and the processes of conversion, both bodily and textual, that take place throughout. The retelling of *Jane Eyre* that takes places through translation highlights the ways that languages and genres alike are converted, including through the labelling of *Jane Eyre* as both *ḥikāya* and *qiṣṣa*, and the fluidity that exists between and through the oral and the written. Creating versions that are susceptible to other versions in this case is also intimately linked to the complexity of translating the name, including in the very title of the novel under analysis. In light of the variable, and suggestive, sounds of the name in Arabic, the not-one Jane Eyre captured in transliterations of the proper noun engenders different versions of the novel, as the Arabic *Jane Eyre*s will always

93 I am grateful to Matthew Reynolds for encouraging me to develop this line of analysis further.

94 Al-Baʿalbakī, *Jane Eyre* (2006), p. 731. Interestingly, its cognates, *ṭabʿ* and *ṭibāʿ*, also mean 'mannerism' and 'character' respectively.

be subject to readers' differing interpretations and voicings; readings and translations that are, at their very core, inherently prismatic.

Works Cited

For the translations of *Jane Eyre* referred to, please see the List of Translations at the end of this book.

Abdel Haleem, M. A. S., *The Qur'an: Parallel Arabic Text*, trans. By M. A. S. Abdel Haleem (Oxford: Oxford University Press, 2000).

Al-ʿAdawī, Muḥammad Qiṭṭa, ed., *Alf Layla wa-Layla* (One Thousand and One Nights) (Beirut: Dār ṣādir Lil ṭibāʿa wa al-Nashr, 1999).

Batchelor, Kathryn, 'Re-reading Jacques Derrida's 'Qu'est-ce qu'une traduction "relevante"?' (What is a 'relevant' translation?), *The Translator*, (2021), 1–16.

Bennington, George and Derrida, Jacques, *Jacques Derrida* (Chicago: Chicago University Press, 1999).

Bhabha, Homi K., 'Cultural Diversity and Cultural Differences' in *The Post-Colonial Studies Reader*, ed. by Bill Ashcroft, Gareth Griffiths and Helen Tiffin, 2nd edition (London: Routledge, 2006), pp. 155–57.

Brown Tkacz, Catherine, 'The Bible in *Jane Eyre*', *Christianity and Literature*, 44.1 (1994), 3–27.

Daftari, Abdulaziz, 'The Dichotomy of the Soul and Spirit in Shi'a Hadith', *Journal of Shi'a Islamic Studies*, 5.2 (2012), 117–29.

Derrida, Jacques, 'Des Tours de Babel', trans. by Joseph F. Graham, in *Difference in Translation*, ed. by Joseph F. Graham (Ithaca and London: Cornell University Press, 1985), pp. 165–205.

——, *The Ear of the Other: Texts and Discussions with Jacques Derrida: Otobiography, Transference, Translation*, English edition ed. by C. McDonald (Lincoln: University of Nebraska Press, 1988).

——, *On the Name* (Stanford: Stanford University Press, 1995).

——, *On Touching – Jean Luc Nancy*, trans. by Christine Irizarry (Stanford C.A: Stanford University Press, 2005).

——, 'Qu'est-ce qu'une traduction "relevante"?' in *Quinzièmes assises de la traduction littéraire* (Arles: Actes Sud, 1998), pp. 21–48.

——, 'What Is a "Relevant" Translation?', trans. by Lawrence Venuti, *Critical Inquiry*, 27.2 (2001), 174–200.

Dickson, Melissa, *Cultural Encounters with the Arabian Nights in Nineteenth-Century Britain* (Edinburgh: Edinburgh University Press, 2019).

——, 'Jane Eyre's 'Arabian Tales': Reading and Remembering the Arabian Nights', *Journal of Victorian Culture*, 18.2 (2013), 198–212.

Druggan, Joanna and Tipton, Rebecca, 'Translation, ethics and social responsibility', *The Translator*, 23.2 (2017), 119–25.

El-Shawan Castelo-Branco, Salwa, 'Radio and Musical Life in Egypt', *Revista de Musicología*, 16. 3 (1993), 1229–1239.

Genette, Gérard, 'Introduction to the Paratext', *New Literary History*, 22.2 (1991), 261–72.

Harb, Mustafa Ali, 'Contrastive Lexical Semantics of Biblical Soul and Qur'anic Ruħ: An Application of Intertextuality', *International Journal of Linguistics*, 6.5 (2014), 64–88.

Hassan, Waïl, 'Translator's Note', in Abdelfattah Kilito, *Thou Shalt Not Speak My Language*, trans. by Waïl S. Hassan. (Syracuse: Syracuse University Press, 2008), pp. vii–xxvi.

Ibn Manẓūr, Muḥammad ibn Mukarram, *Lisān al-ʿArab* (The Language of the Arab People) (Cairo: Dār Ibn al-Jawzī, [1970] 2015).

Kilito, Abdelfattah, *Arabs and the Art of Storytelling*, trans. Mbarek Sryfi and Eric Sellin (Syracuse: Syracuse University Press, 2014).

——, 'Qiṣṣa', in Franco Moretti (ed.) *The Novel, Volume 1: History, Geography and Culture*, (Princeton and Oxford: Princeton University Press, 2006), pp. 262–68.

——, *Thou Shalt Not Speak My Language*, trans. by Waïl S. Hassan. (Syracuse: Syracuse University Press, 2008).

Leeuwen, Richard van, The Thousand and One Nights *and Twentieth-Century Fiction* (Leiden: Brill, 2018).

Al-Musawi, Muhsin Jassim, *The Postcolonial Arabic Novel: Debating Ambivalence* (Leiden and Boston: Brill, 2003).

——, 'The Taming of the Sultan: A Study of Scheherazade Motif in *Jane Eyre*', *Adab al-Rafidayn*, 17 (1988), 59–81.

Nishio, Tetsuo, 'Language nationalism and consciousness in the Arab world', *Senri Ethnological Studies*, 55 (2001), 137–46.

Ouyang, Wen-Chin, 'The Dialectic of Past and Present in *Riḥlat Ibn Faṭṭūma* by Najīb Maḥfūẓ', *Edebiyat: Journal of Middle Eastern Literatures*, 14.1 (2003), 81–107.

——, 'Genres, Ideologies, Genre Ideologies and Narrative Transformation', *Middle Eastern Literatures*, 7.2 (2004), 125–31.

Qāsim, Maḥmūd, *Al-Iqtibās: 'Al-Maṣādir al-Ajnabiyya fī al-Sinamā al-Misriyya'* (Adaptation: Foreign Sources in Egyptian Cinema), (Cairo: Wikālat al-ṣiḥāfa al-ʿArabiyya, 2018).

Reynolds, Matthew, 'Introduction' in *Prismatic Translation*, ed. by Matthew Reynolds (Oxford: Legenda, 2019), pp. 1–19.

——, *Likenesses: Translation, Illustration, Interpretation* (London: Routledge, 2013).

Said, Edward, *Reflections On Exile and Other Essays* (Cambridge: Harvard University Press, 2000).

Salameh, Franck, 'Does anyone speak Arabic?', *Middle East Quarterly*, 18 (2011), 47–60.

Winter, Tim, 'God the Speaker: The Many-Named One', in *The Routledge Companion to the Qur'an*, ed. by George Archer, Maria M. Dakake, Daniel A. Madigan (New York: Routledge, 2021), pp. 45–57.

Yāsīn, Saʿīd, *'Nūr al-Dimirdāsh.. Madrasa ikhrajiyya farīda'* (Nūr al-Dimirdāsh: A unique "school" in directing'), *Al-Ittiḥād*, May 2020, https://www.alittihad.ae/news/دنيا/٧٦٠١٩٩٣/نور-الدمرداش---مدرسة--إخراجية-فريدة

Zahir al-Din, M S., 'Man in Search of His Identity: A Discussion on the Mystical Soul (Nafs) and Spirit (Ruh)', *Islamic Quarterly*, 24.3(1980), 96.

Zughoul, Muhammad Raji and El-Badarien, Mohammed, 'Diglossia in Literary Translation: Accommodation into Translation Theory', *Meta*, 49.2 (2004), 447–56.

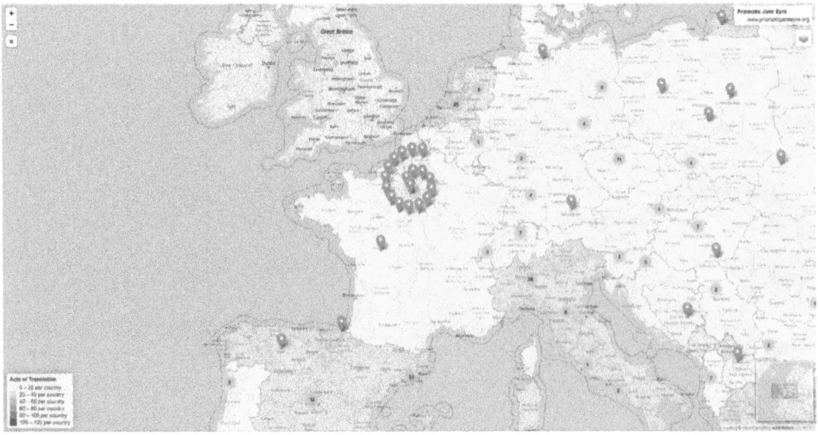

The World Map
https://digitalkoine.github.io/je_prismatic_map
Created by Giovanni Pietro Vitali;
maps © Thunderforest, data © OpenStreetMap contributors

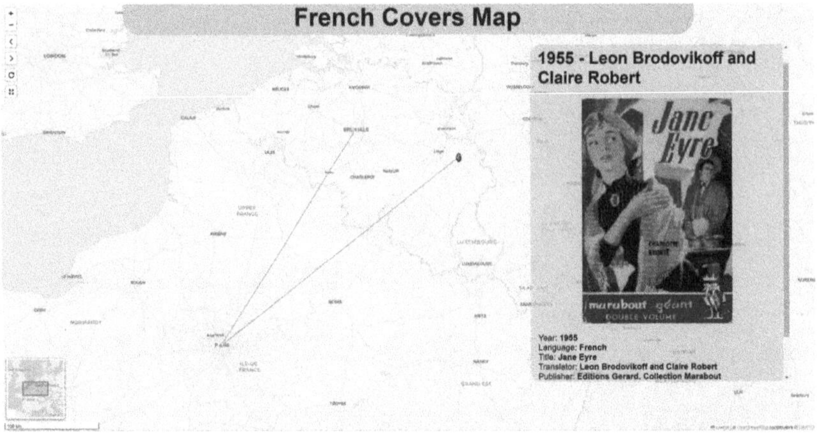

The French Covers Map
https://digitalkoine.github.io/french_storymap/
Researched by Céline Sabiron, Léa Rychen and Vincent Thierry;
created by Giovanni Pietro Vitali and Simone Landucci

4. Translating the French in the French Translations of *Jane Eyre*

Céline Sabiron

Introduction: 'it loses sadly by being translated'

'(I wish I might write all she said to me in French — it loses sadly by being translated into English)', Charlotte Brontë's narrator regrets in an aside, in her posthumously published novel *The Professor* (1857).[1] Nevertheless, she does sometimes boldly grant herself the freedom to write in French, as in her more bestselling *Jane Eyre* (1847), which was written after *The Professor* but published ten years before it, since her first novel had been repeatedly turned down by publishing houses. Impulsive young Adèle babbles in French to discuss the 'cadeau'[2] that Mr Rochester has bought her and that consists of a 'robe': '"Il faut que je l'essaie!" cried she; "et à l'instant même!"'.[3] However, Charlotte Brontë does not overuse this linguistic license and often reverts to English, as in *Shirley* (1849) where she translates the French conversation between Hortense Moore and Caroline Helstone: '[t]he answer and the rest of the conversation was in French, but as this is an English book, I shall translate it into English', she explains through the voice of her narrator.[4] Translation is therefore presented as both a loss ('it loses sadly by being translated') and an injunction ('shall') imposed by the dictates of the publishing industry in an English context and that she has to subject herself to. This goes against her spontaneous inner wish

1 Charlotte Brontë, *Shirley and The Professor* (New York: Everyman's Library, 2008), p. 810.
2 *JE*, Ch. 13.
3 *JE*, Ch. 14.
4 Brontë, *Shirley and The Professor*, p. 64.

 https://doi.org/10.11647/OBP.0319.07

to write a multilingual text in which her language of expression would vary within the very same text depending on the object of her writing.

Nevertheless, this caution about language did not prevent her from receiving harsh and somewhat exaggerated criticisms from a few English reviewers mocking her 'peculiar'[5] style and her 'unintelligible'[6] language linked to her extensive use of French. Her English-speaking audience was not the only one tearing their hair out over her text, however popular it was in the United Kingdom. The novel was also extremely testing for the translators who endeavoured to translate it for a French readership, eager in the context of utmost social discontent and political upheavals to emulate the stable Victorian values conveyed in the novel. Published in 1847, *Jane Eyre* was not officially translated into French until 1854, even if French newspaper publisher and reviewer Eugène Forcade alludes to the novel as early as 1849 in his review of *Shirley* for *Revue des Deux Mondes*.[7] While well-off French readers could afford to buy the English 1847 Smith, Elder edition circulating from the start on the Continent in selected bookshops in large French cities like Paris, the majority of copies available in France came from the Leipzig firm of Tauchnitz that had been allowed to distribute cheap and portable original novels since the 1844 International Copyright Act.[8] Within four months of the English publication of *Jane Eyre* in 1847, the French could thus access the English text that might then be read out and translated on the spot

5 'The style of *Jane Eyre* is peculiar; but, except that she admits too many Scotch or North-country phrases, we have no objection to make to it, and for this reason: although by no means a fine style, it has the capital point of all great styles in being personal, — the written speech of an individual, not the artificial language made up from all sorts of books', George Henry Lewes, 'Recent Novels: French and English', *Fraser's Magazine for Town and Country, 1830–1869*, 36.216 (Dec. 1847), 686–95 (p. 693).

6 'The first volume will be unintelligible to most people, for it is half in French and half in broad Yorkshire. There are many who know "Yorkshire", and don't know French; and others, we fear, who know French and don't know Yorkshire', from an unsigned review, in *Fraser's Magazine for Town and Country, 1830–1869*, 40.240 (Dec. 1849), 691–702 (p. 693), cited in *The Brontes: The Critical Heritage*, ed. by Miriam Allott (London: Routledge, 1974), pp. 153–54.

7 Eugène Fourcade, 'Le roman anglais contemporain en Angleterre: *Shirley*, de Currer Bell', *Revue des Deux Mondes*, 1.4 (Nov. 1849), 714–35 (p. 714).

8 Inga-Stina Ewbank, 'Reading the Brontës Abroad: A Study in the Transmission of Victorian Novels in Continental Europe', in *Re-Constructing the Book: Literary Texts in Transmission*, ed. by Maureen Bell, Shirley Chew, Simon Eliot and James L. W. West (London: Routledge, 2001), pp. 84–99.

during family gatherings. They could also read an abridged version, adapted in French by Paul Émile Daurand Forgues, nicknamed 'Old Nick', that ran as a feuilleton from April to June 1849 in *Le National* (Paris) as well as the Belgian *Revue de Paris* and *L'Indépendance belge*,[9] before being published as a single volume in 1855 by the Paris-based firm Hachette. When the first adaptation by 'Old Nick' (1849) and the first translation by Madame Lesbazeilles-Souvestre (1854) came out in France, no review mentioned the use of French in the original text. In *Journal des débats politiques et littéraires*, Louis Ratisbonne praised the former's skill at shortening the text and the latter's elegance and fidelity to the original.[10] These remarks, and especially the unspoken topic of the language choice, raises the question of the way the French used by Charlotte Brontë in her text was translated in the French versions of her novel. 'How do you translate French into French?' Véronique Béghain aptly wondered in her 2006 study of Charlotte Brontë's *Villette*.[11]

Seventeen different translators have gritted their teeth and worked on *Jane Eyre*, but the present study will mostly focus on seven of them, leaving aside Old Nick's adaptation, and dedicating rather little time to the 1919 French version (Flammarion) by two feminist activists, the sisters Marion Gilbert and Madeleine Duvivier, and the 1946 Redon and Dulong's translation, published simultaneously in Lausanne (J. Marguerat), Switzerland, and in Paris (Édition du Dauphin) because of their almost systematic tendency to simplify the original text by omitting large parts. This analysis will therefore concentrate on Noëmi Lesbazeilles-Souvestre's first ever translation in 1854 (first published by D. Giraud and now accessible electronically), Léon Brodovikoff and Claire Robert's 1946 translation, as well as the more recent 1964 (Charlotte Maurat, with Hachette, Paris), 1966 (Sylvère Monod, with Garnier-Frères, Paris), and 2008 (Dominique Jean, with Gallimard, Paris) French versions. It will deliberately not discuss the translators' biography or the identity and history of the publishing houses through

9 Jay Dillon, '"Reader, I found it"': The First *Jane Eyre* in French', *The Book Collector*, 17 (2023), 11–19. See Chapter I in this volume for discussion.

10 'l'une, élégante et fidèle due à la plume de Mme de Lesbazeilles; l'autre a été habilement abrégée pour la Bibliothèque des Chemins de Fer par Old Nick (M. Forgues)', Louis Ratisbonne in *Journal des débats politiques et littéraires* (4 Jan. 1856), https://gallica.bnf.fr/ark:/12148/bpt6k4507688.item

11 Véronique Béghain, 'How do you translate French into French? Charlotte Brontë's *Villette* as a borderline case in Translatability', *Interculturality & Translation, 2* (2006), 41–62.

which their works came out, even though they do play a major part in the text production.[12] Neither is our aim to compare and contrast individual translation choices. Rather, following the concepts and theories developed by translation and reception specialists, this article proposes to combine literary, linguistic, and translatological approaches and study the French translators' responses to Charlotte Brontë's interplay between familiarity and otherness, proximity and distance, feelings of closeness and estrangement when she both 'imposes and forbids translation', thus making the latter altogether both necessary and impossible in *Jane Eyre*.[13] In order to do that, it will rely on the three different levels of significance of the French language in the original text ('effet de réel', cultural and ideological, or ontological differences) as highlighted by three ground-breaking articles on the subject: Véronique Béghain's 2006 theoretically-based essay on the translation of the French language in *Villette*, and two literary studies published in 2013: Emily Eells's examination of the signification of the French in *Jane Eyre*, and Hélène Collins's focus on plurilingualism in *The Professor* and the various strategies used by the author to allow coherence between the foreign words and their co-texts, or their translations within the novel.[14] The chain of signification from the author to the French reader will be examined through a detailed analysis of the translators' practices and illustrated with a comparative study of examples taken from the original text and its various French translations.

---

12 'the text may pass through many hands on its way from author to printed form: those of scribe or copyist, amanuensis, secretary, typist, editor, translator, compositor, printer, proofreader and publisher. The work of all these agents alters the text (directly or indirectly, intentionally or not) and — by the addition or deletion of material, by errors and accidents in copying or typesetting, by supplying new contexts (prefaces, dedications, postscripts, indexes) or by repackaging the text among other texts (in compilations and anthologies) — substantially conditions what and how the text *means*', Maureen Bell, 'Introduction: The Material Text', in *Re-Constructing the Book: Literary Texts in Transmission*, ed. by Maureen Bell, Shirley Chew, Simon Eliot, Lynette Hunter and James L. W. West (Burlington: Ashgate, 2001), p. 3.

13 'Il impose et interdit à la fois la traduction', Jacques Derrida, 'Des tours de Babel', in *Psyche: Inventions de l'autre*, 2 vols (Paris: Galilée, [1985] 1998), I, 203–35 (p. 207).

14 Véronique Béghain, 'How do you translate French into French', 41–62; Emily Eells, 'The French *aire* in *Jane Eyre*', *Cahiers victoriens et édouardiens*, 78 (2013); Hélène Collins, 'Le plurilinguisme dans *The Professor* de Charlotte Brontë: entre fascination et neutralisation de l'altérité', *Cahiers victoriens et édouardiens*, 78 (2013).

Speaking French: A Signifying Linguistic Spectrum in *Jane Eyre*

Even though other foreign languages, like German and 'Hindostanee', appear in Charlotte Brontë's hetero-glossic work, French dominates so much that it constantly invades and interferes with the English script revolving, as is often the case in Brontë's novels, around the teaching of French. In *Jane Eyre*, she weaves a French linguistic thread throughout her text by recreating a French domestic bubble at Thornfield Hall. Jane thus joins Mr Rochester's home as a governess to teach his ward Adèle, the daughter of French opera dancer Céline Varens whom he had an affair with in Paris.[15] The little French girl came to Thornfield with her French nurse, Sophie, six months before Jane's arrival. *Jane Eyre* is thus strewn with vocabulary, phrases, and idiomatic expressions borrowed from French, which even contaminates the English text through clumsy constructions based on French grammatical structures. The text exemplifies a whole range of language proficiency from Adèle's native French, which she speaks in full phrases, to Jane's fluency as the result of her dutiful language learning and mimicry of French native speakers ('Fortunately I had had the advantage of being taught French by a French lady [...] applying myself to take pains with my accent, and imitating as closely as possible the pronunciation of my teacher'[16]). Mr Rochester's approximate mastery of French features in the middle of the linguistic spectrum provided. He is conversant in several foreign languages, including Italian and German through the liaisons he has had, and he thus mostly sprinkles French words throughout his conversations with his ward.[17] As brilliantly demonstrated by Emily Eells in her article dedicated to the significance of Brontë's use of French, the latter is 'not merely ornamental and circumstantial'. It serves to 'encod[e] issues of gender and education, and [to voice] the conflict of individualism and conformity in a Victorian context. True to cliché, it is [also] the language of romance'[18] and it embodies passion, fantasy and everything that is associated with French values,

15 *JE*, Ch. 11.
16 *JE*, Ch. 11.
17 Anne O'Neil-Henry, 'Domestic Fiction Abroad: Jane Eyre's Reception in Post-1848 France', in *Aller(s)-Retour(s): Nineteenth-Century France in Motion*, ed. by Loic Guyon and Andrew Watts (Cambridge: Cambridge Scholars Publishing, 2013), pp. 111–24.
18 Eells, 'The French *aire* in *Jane Eyre*'.

mores, and customs at the time as opposed to reason, morality, and reality represented by the English language. As a result, French is not just thoughtlessly sprinkled throughout her text to create a Barthesian 'effet de réel'. It is rooted in Brontë's deep interest in languages, and French in particular, which she had learnt at Professor Constantin Héger's boarding school in Brussels in 1842 and 1843.[19] It also comes from her real fascination for foreign words, their musical signification, as well as their textual, almost physical, presence on the material page.

Visualising the 'effet de réel étranger' (Collins): The Translator's vs. the Editor's Roles

In *Jane Eyre*, a French signifier is often preferred to its English equivalent owing to its additional aesthetic value, as demonstrated by Hélène Collins in her analysis of plurilingualism in Charlotte Brontë's *The Professor*.[20] The English text is thus interspersed with French words because of the exotic sensation and the feeling of otherness they convey to readers. The experience of reading foreign written characters is meant to mimic the experience of hearing the syllable-timed language that is French. This 'effet de réel étranger', as coined by Collins, is used when 'Adèle [...] asked if she was to go to school "sans mademoiselle?"'.[21] Direct speech — as symbolized by the inverted commas — enables Adèle's voice and language to be heard. What is interesting to mention at this point is that, contrary to the first edition, or the more scholarly Clarendon Edition, the widely available, affordable, and therefore very popular, World's Classics edition of *Jane Eyre* (published in paperback by Oxford University Press since 1980, and constantly reissued with the latest edition dating from September 2019) translates Brontë's plurilingual text. While 'mademoiselle' is a lexical borrowing that is transparent in English, the more recent English editions have followed the preposition by an asterisk (*) and an explanatory endnote saying '*sans*: without'. Even though 'sans' has been found in English since the early fourteenth-century, it is extremely rarely used and is mostly part of the cultural, and in particular literary, baggage that a *Jane Eyre* reader is expected to have, with the anaphorical repetition of the preposition '*sans*' emphatically closing

19 Eells, 'The French *aire* in *Jane Eyre*'.
20 Collins, 'Le plurilinguisme'.
21 *JE*, Ch. 24.

the last line of Jaques's 'All the world's a stage' speech in Shakespeare's *As You Like It* ('Sans teeth, sans eyes, sans taste, sans everything', II.7). The implied modern readership is thus felt to be more monolingual and less well versed in classic literature, hence the necessary note added in more recent editions. When the phrase is taken up by Mr Rochester immediately afterwards 'sans' no longer needs a note: the otherness has been recognized and got over. The feeling of otherness is greatly toned down in the French translations: all of them, except Gilbert and Duvivier's version, simply resort to italics to indicate that the words were written in French in the original. Most translators have then chosen to add a second mark and used either a footnote saying 'En français dans le texte'[22] or a superscript black star.[23] Only Sylvère Monod's translation does not show any other mark, but this was an editor's choice rather than the translator's. His work came out with 'Pocket', a French generalist publisher of literature in pocket format that targets a broad range of readers by producing cheap fiction and non-fiction books composed of uncluttered, almost bare, texts with very few endnotes, and no introduction or critical apparatus. In the French translations, then, exoticism is visually conveyed, through written marks (italics, stars, and notes), whereas in the original English it is phonetically conveyed, through the bare use of French words, i.e., through French rhythm and sound. The translation work affects the reader's sensory experience as it shifts from the ear to the eye, from a sonorous to an ocular effect. In the French translation, otherness is the fruit of decisions that involve both translators and editors; it is moved out of the author's text to feature as part of what Genette calls 'paratext' since it is imprinted into the text, materially inscribed as part of the printed page.

Translating Otherness: A Shift to the Paratext, or even Off the Text

In the English *Jane Eyre*, French words are not only used for their aesthetic value, their exoticism, and musicality. They are often strategically employed by the author who, as Collins says, 'relegates the signified of the foreign word to an irreducible otherness' (my

22 Charlotte Brontë, *Jane Eyre*, trans. by Charlotte Maurat (Paris: Le Livre de Poche, [1984] 2012), p. 309.

23 Charlotte Brontë, *Jane Eyre*, trans. by Dominique Jean (Paris: Gallimard, [2008] 2012), p. 441.

translation; *'reléguer le signifié du mot étranger dans une irréductible altérité'*).[24] The phrase '"*Jeune encore*," as the French say', thus sounds very derogatory, not to say condescending, in Mr Rochester's mouth, since it is loaded with illocutionary force by being put aside (through the lack of translation) and labelled as belonging to a different people.[25] The meaning of the French expression — used out of politeness and respect to mean 'not old yet' — is thus perverted and even inverted in this very case owing to Mr Rochester feeling jealous towards St John Rivers. The French translators have mostly chosen to displace the issue from lexico-modal terms to grammatical terms by using the indefinite personal pronoun '*on*' (Monod's '*Jeune encore*, comme on dit en français';[26] or Maurat's '*Jeune encore*[1], comme on dit en français', with the note 'En français dans le texte'[27]). The latter serves to exclude the speakers, to move away the referent and eventually disembody the French who are reduced to an empty signifier. Dominique Jean used a similar kind of grammatical distanciation through the personal pronoun '*le*' that substitutes the French phrase, thus belittling it by reducing it to a two-letter word: '"*Jeune encore**", comme le disent les Français'.[28]

If the translations usually try to bring forward the negative connotation often associated with the use of French in the English text, in particular through grammatical means, they often fail to convey the moral or cultural clichés that the British, and Charlotte Brontë in particular, tend to attach to the French and that are reflected in the author's use of the French language. 'The production of translations involves the cognitive representation of perceived potential reception (in other words, the translator's mental construction of "the reader" and their horizon of expectations), which affects decision making during translation and is inscribed in the translation in the form of an "implied reader"'.[29] *Jane Eyre*'s French translators thus tend to privilege a linguistic take over socio-cultural and ideological approaches to

24 Collins, 'Le plurilinguisme'.

25 *JE*, Ch. 37.

26 Charlotte Brontë, *Jane Eyre*, trans. by Sylvère Monod (Paris: Pocket, [1984] 2012), p. 742.

27 Brontë, *Jane Eyre*, trans. by Charlotte Maurat, p. 507.

28 Brontë, *Jane Eyre*, trans. by Dominique Jean, p. 715.

29 Haidee Kruger and Jan-Louis Kruger, 'Cognition and Reception', in *The Handbook of Translation and Cognition*, ed. by John W. Schwieter and Aline Ferreira (Oxford: Wiley Blackwell, 2017), 71–89 (pp. 72–73).

translation. There cannot be any 'dynamic equivalence'[30] between the messages conveyed in the source text and the translated text because the ideology and culture targeted in Brontë's novel are those inherently carried by the translators and readers of the translated text. As defined by Eugène A. Nida, 'dynamic equivalence' is the process by which 'the relationship between receptor and message should be substantially the same as that which existed between the original receptors and the message'.[31] Besides, as Iser argued of all texts (1972 and 1978), a translation is not complete once the translator has finished his task: it is the result of two cognitive processes, consisting of both production and reception. A translation is thus 'reconstituted every time it is read, viewed, or heard by a receiver, in an active and creative process of meaning making'.[32] The meaning of a translation is not inherent in the text; it is conjured up by the interaction between the text and the reader coming with their own linguistic and cultural backgrounds. These necessarily affect their reading and construction of meanings, as illustrated in the following example that points at the ineluctably partial 'dynamic equivalence' between the messages conveyed in the source and target texts because of a difference in mental representations.[33] 'I wished the result of my endeavours to be respectable, proper, *en règle*', the narrator, Jane Eyre, says as she contemplates Mrs Fairfax's response to her advertisement.[34] Her use of the French expression '*en règle*' is fraught with meaning as it comes at the end of her sentence, just before the full stop. It adds extra weight and features as a final point to her rather strong declaration which is structured around a ternary rhythm with a double decrescendo-crescendo effect: first grammatically from the two quadrisyllabic ('respectable') and disyllabic ('proper') mono-phrastic adjectives to the two-word phrase ('*en règle*'), and then linguistically from two English words subtly blending into French lexis ('*respectable*' and '*propre*') to the borrowed French expression meaning in order, in accordance with the rules. There is a clear gradation from what is considered socially and morally acceptable (British values associated

30 Eugène A. Nida and Charles R. Taber, *The Theory and Practice of Translation* (Leiden: Brill, 2003).
31 Eugène A. Nida, *Toward a Science of Translating* (Leiden: Brill, 1964), p. 159.
32 Kruger and Kruger, 'Cognition and Reception', p. 72.
33 Hans Robert Jauss, *Toward an Aesthetic of Reception* (Minneapolis, MN: University of Minnesota Press, 1982).
34 *JE*, Ch. 10.

with the English language) to what is legally acceptable (Law French). The two adjectives also serve to throw some light on the meaning of the French expression through a paraphrastic technique (using more or less close levels of equivalence), should the latter remain inaccessible to an English reader. Some French translators have chosen to compress the sentence by using one encompassing adjective ('honorable' Lesbazeilles-Souvestre). In that case, they have considered that the main function of the surrounding words was that of a co-text paraphrasing — through the use of more or less close equivalences — the French phrase. Others have kept '*en règle*' with italics and an endnote, thereby only pointing at the change of language.[35] However, Dominique Jean has chosen a different strategy; he has used a synonymous expression '*dans les formes*' meaning 'done according to custom' ('honorable, convenable, dans les formes'), thus displacing the topic from the legal field to that of tradition.[36] Besides, he has actually replaced the clichéd cultural reference by an intertextual reference to a literary classic. In the French text, the endnote specifies that Brontë here alludes to Samuel Richardson's *Pamela* in her portrayal of a young woman, with no protection, in the service of an unscrupulous master.[37] Jean has thus mimicked Brontë's process of associating the expression with France, through her use of French and reference to legality (as a typically French concern), by linking his chosen phrase to a canonical English text and to tradition. It is interesting to note that because of his academic background, the relatively recent discoveries (dating to the 1990s)[38] in the fields of translation and cognition, and his own take on the cognitive processing at stake in the reception of translation, Jean is

35 Brontë, *Jane Eyre*, trans. by Charlotte Maurat, p. 109.

36 Brontë, *Jane Eyre*, trans. by Dominique Jean, p. 163.

37 The endnote says 'Allusion à la situation critique de la jeune femme sans protection au service d'un maitre peu scrupuleux, dont le modèle littéraire remontait au roman épistolaire de Samuel Richardson Pamela (voir n.1, p. 38). Charlotte Brontë admirait l'œuvre de Richardson' [An allusion to the plight of the unprotected young woman in the employment of an unscrupulous master, whose literary model was Samuel Richardson's epistolary novel Pamela (see n.1, p. 38). Charlotte Brontë admired Richardson's work], my translation), Brontë, *Jane Eyre*, trans. by Dominique Jean, p. 807.

38 See Newmark's concept of pragmatic translation, requiring that 'the translator must take into account all aspects involving readership sensitivity in order to stimulate the appropriate frame of mind in the reader', Peter Newmark, 'Pragmatic Translation and Literalism', *TTR: Traduction, Terminologie, Rédaction*, 1 (1988), 133–45 (pp. 133–34).

the only translator who reproduces the distanciation effect through a parallel reversed strategy.

The French translations of *Jane Eyre* under study thus tend to move any signs of exoticism to the paratext, leaving the editor, as well as the translator, in charge of expressing foreignness through visual tokens, while they ignore any cultural and moral connotations — which are part of the readers' mental representations, of their cognitive baggage — by removing any subjective evocations linked to the readers' nationality. Hence the potential pitfall which Véronique Béghain calls 'the greying risk' ('*risque de grisonnement*') that covers up nuances and standardizes differences.[39] This overall tendency must yet be qualified with the 2008 translation which does resort to 'transfer' strategies, taking into account the cognitive dimension of producing and receiving translated materials, with Jean displaying what Wolfram Wilss calls 'a super-competence',[40] that is, the ability to transfer messages between the linguistic and textual systems of the source culture and the linguistic and textual systems of the target culture.

Translating 'Frenglish': Continuum (ST) vs. Continuity (TT)

In Brontë's English text, French words are not only scattered throughout, they are gradually woven into the fabric of the English text, so that the language-origin is smoothed out to create a form of continuum between French and English, a sort of 'Frenglish'. The author thus tends to privilege English words from Latin and/ or French origin ('mediatrix';[41] 'auditress and interlocutrice'[42]) in order

39 Véronique Béghain, '"A Dress of French gray": Retraduire *Villette* de Charlotte Brontë au risque du grisonnement', in *Autour de la traduction: Perspectives littéraires européennes*, ed. by Enrico Monti and Peter Schnyder (Paris: Orizons, 2011), p. 99.

40 For Wolfram Wilss three complementary competences are needed in translation: receptive competence in the source language (the ability to understand the source text), productive competence in the target language (the ability to use the linguistic and textual resources of the target language), and super-competence as defined above. See Wolfram Wilss, 'Perspectives and Limitations of a Didactic Framework for the Teaching of Translation', in *Translation*, ed. by Robert W. Brislin (New York: Gardner, 1976), pp. 117–37 (p. 120).

41 *JE*, Ch. 10.

42 *JE*, Ch. 14.

to erase the language boundary as if she dreamt of creating a form of universal language. She therefore often resorts to words that, through various past cultural contacts and transfers, have been borrowed from the French language. They usually pertain to the fields of clothing ('pelisse'; 'a surtout'; 'calico chemises'[43]), hairstyle ('a false front of French curls'[44]), food and gastronomy ('forage'; 'repast'[45]), love ('"grande passion"'[46]); architecture ('a boudoir';[47] 'consoles and chiffonières';[48] 'lustre';[49] 'balustrade'[50]), and character traits ('minois chiffoné'[51]), to name but a few.

French gradually contaminates the text as the narrator imports French words and even full expressions verbatim into her sentences ('This, par parenthèse, will be thought cool language'[52]), so much so that the italics indicating foreign borrowings progressively disappear, French words being even anglicized and spelt with a mix of English and French letters: Adèle is said to sing with 'naiveté',[53] instead of naïveté in French, through an act of transliteration, i.e., the conversion from one script to another involving swapping letters ([i] instead of [ï] and [é] instead of [e]). The Englished form 'naivety', attested in English from 1708, has been avoided, as well as the English spelling ('naivete') of the French word. Brontë has deliberately chosen the Old French spelling ('naiveté'), literally meaning 'native disposition', thus indirectly raising the issue of the origin and subtly pointing at Adèle's French descent. The foreign character of the letter [é] has also been preferred for its French musicality. The diacritical mark — mostly found in the Latin, Greek, and Cyrillic alphabets and their derivatives — allows the distinction between the phoneme with the closed tone /e/ which is that of naiveté and the /ə/ sound ('naivete'). It serves to convey the French imprint on the musical rhythm of the language. In the translations, however, this continuum between languages becomes a continuous flow within the same language since they tend to erase all traces

43 *JE*, Ch. 5, and Ch. 7.
44 *JE*, Ch. 7.
45 *JE*, Ch. 17.
46 *JE*, Ch. 15.
47 *JE*, Ch. 11.
48 *JE*, Ch. 13.
49 *JE*, Ch. 14.
50 *JE*, Ch. 17.
51 *JE*, Ch. 17.
52 *JE*, Ch. 12.
53 *JE*, Ch. 11.

of foreignness by choosing existing French equivalents. The noun 'naiveté' is thus systematically translated into 'naïveté'.[54] Similarly, the adjective 'piquant' from Middle French is often translated as such, with French grammar applied ('piquante' in Maurat's and Monod's translations), or with a synonym ('bizarre' in Gilbert and Duvivier's).[55] Jean has opted for a different expression ('avait du piment') that ignores the etymology, and therefore the French history, of the term in order to privilege an equivalent semantic effect for the modern French reader.[56] The adjective 'piquant' was carefully chosen by the author: even if the narrator Jane uses it to mean 'stimulating', as in piquing her interest, the word can also mean 'pricking', thus programmatically alluding to future episodes in the plot and the eponymous character's pain to come.

Jane Eyre's English is so contaminated by French that it is affected by it in strange and subtle ways, as when the young protagonist mentions her dream of being able to 'translate currently a certain little French story-book which Madam Pierrot had that day shewn [her]'.[57] The lexical mistake — caused by the fact that 'currently' and '*couramment*' are cognates, i.e., false friends with '*couramment*' actually meaning 'fluently' in French — is identified as such by an asterisk (and an endnote in the Oxford World's Classics edition even though there was none in the editions approved by Charlotte Brontë). Yet, it has been fully ignored by all the French translators who have chosen to translate the expression as '*traduire couramment*' with no reference to the confusion between the bilingual homophones. Only Jean shifts the lexical confusion by playing on the metaphor of the book through the figurative expression 'traduire à livre ouvert', meaning 'translate easily and perceptively'.[58] Semantic continuity thus prevails in the French translations that do not bring out the blending of meanings within the same language.

54 Brontë, *Jane Eyre*, trans. by Dominique Jean, p. 185; Brontë, *Jane Eyre*, trans. by Charlotte Maurat, p. 125; Brontë, *Jane Eyre*, trans. by Sylvère Monod, p. 177; Brontë, *Jane Eyre*, trans. by Marion Gilbert and Madeleine Duvivier (Paris: GF Flammarion, 1990), p. 117.

55 *JE*, Ch. 13; Brontë, *Jane Eyre*, trans. by Charlotte Maurat, p. 146; Brontë, *Jane Eyre*, trans. by Sylvère Monod, p. 208; Brontë, *Jane Eyre*, trans. by Marion Gilbert and Madeleine Duvivier, p. 134.

56 Brontë, *Jane Eyre*, trans. by Dominique Jean, p. 213.

57 *JE*, Ch. 8.

58 Brontë, *Jane Eyre*, trans. by Dominique Jean, p. 141.

Charlotte Brontë's text relies on semantic but also grammatical continuum since it is fraught with 'barbarisms', i.e., words and even phrases that are 'badly' formed according to traditional philological rules as they are coined with a mixture of French and English elements. The sentence 'The old crone "nichered" a laugh' points at both the gap and the proximity between languages: the French verb '*nicher*' (to hide in), conjugated in the preterite tense with its English-ed ending, is phonetically (and lexically) very close to Old English 'snicker', meaning 'to laugh in a half-suppressed way'.[59] However, this overlapping of languages automatically disappears in the French translations, which, at best, focus on conveying the concealed nature of the character's laughter, when they do not bypass the issue (Redon and Dulong, Monod), or displace it altogether. For instance, Jean has chosen to change the characteristics of the woman's laughter described as neighing or whinnying, following his process-oriented method.

Translators	French Translations
Noëmi Lesbazeilles-Souvestre	'La vieille femme cacha un sourire' (etext)
Marion Gilbert and Madeleine Duvivier	'La vieille sorcière eut un rire étouffée' (p. 208)
R. Redon and J. Dulong	'La vieille fit entendre un rire sarcastique' (p. 181)
Sylvère Monod	'La vieille commère fit entendre un ricanement' (p. 334)
Léon Brodovikoff and Claire Robert	'La vieille riait' (p. 234)
Charlotte Maurat	'La vieille sorcière ricana' (p. 230)
Dominique Jean	'La vieille commère lança [...] un rire comme une sorte de hennissement' (p. 331)

Lexical and grammatical barbarisms can occur when the narrator expresses a feeling of rebellion and yearns for freedom, her expression mimicking the content of her thoughts and flouting any language rule, as in 'I was a trifle beside myself; or rather *out* of myself, as the French would say' or 'I was debarrassed of interruption'.[60] The past participle 'debarrassed', here used to mean 'relieved' or 'free'

59 *JE*, Ch. 19.
60 *JE*, Ch. 2, and Ch. 10.

is a mix of French 'débarrassé', and the more usual English form 'disembarrassed', employed by Jane later on ('I sat down quite disembarrassed') in the sense of 'freed from embarrassment'.[61] The two notions of freedom and self-respect, thus blended together in the newly coined word, organically grow from the surrounding English text made up of words shared with French such as 'with satisfaction', 'revived', and the opposites 'Liberty'/'Servitude'.[62] None of the French translations hint at the barbarism created by the merging of the two languages. While Monod has ignored the sentence altogether, Brodovikoff and Robert have simplified and thereby neutralized it ('je n'allais plus être interrompue').[63] The other translators have opted for one interpretation or the other, privileging either the idea of shelter and protection ('j'étais désormais à l'abri de toute interruption' in Lesbazeilles-Souvestre; 'Je n'étais plus en butte aux interruptions' in Jean) or that of freedom ('ainsi délivrée de toute interruption' in Maurat).[64] Brontë's patchwork approach to languages gives way to a seamless fabric of French words in the translations.

This sense of a language continuum between French and English fails to be translated in the French versions. What is often translated, though, is imagery; that is to say the language that produces pictures in the minds of people reading or listening to the text, as demonstrated through the verb 'disembowel' used by Mr Rochester to summon Adèle to unwrap her 'boîte'.[65] Even if the word has been attested in English since the 1600s to mean 'eviscerate, wound so as to permit the bowels to protrude', it is deliberately employed by Brontë because it sounds like a portmanteau word in the master's mouth.[66] Mr Rochester wishes to play on French images (through the phonetic pun, the near-homophony between 'disembowelling' and the French verb 'désemballer', 'to unwrap') mixed with references to guts and interior parts as an ironic allusion to Adèle's illegitimate origin. About half of the translations under study have simply focused on the idea of unwrapping ('déballer' in Lesbazeilles-Souvestre), of opening

61 *JE*, Ch. 13.
62 *JE*, Ch. 10.
63 Brontë, *Jane Eyre*, trans. by Sylvère Monod, p. 148; Brontë, *Jane Eyre*, trans. by Léon Brodovikoff and Claire Robert (Verviers, Belgique: Gérard & Co., 1950), p. 106.
64 Brontë, *Jane Eyre*, trans. by Dominique Jean, p. 158; Brontë, *Jane Eyre*, trans. by Charlotte Maurat, p. 106.
65 *JE*, Ch. 14.
66 See 'disembowel, *v.*', https://oed.com/view/Entry/54194

up ('ouvrir' in Redon and Dulon) a present, with only Brodovikoff and Robert twisting its meaning a bit through the use of the verb 'inventorier', that is 'to list', thus pointing at the formal staging of Adèle's gesture.[67] The other translators have rather cleverly played on the imagery of the bowels by picking up the analogy and stretching it further into their translations, from the rather descriptive phrase 'vider les entrailles' (in Maurat) to the slightly more brutal and gory-sounding phrases 'éventrer' (in Monod) — literally meaning 'to gut', 'cut open' or 'to rip open' when used figuratively — or 'éviscérer' (in Jean), i.e., 'to eviscerate'.[68] If there is no language continuum but rather a language continuity through the single use of French in the translations and the absence of any reference to the subtle blending of languages in the source text, the translations mostly focus on the language of mental images.

Conclusion: Foreign Language Instruction and the Reader's Role in *Jane Eyre*

The question of which language to favour and Charlotte Brontë's refusal to resort to translation systematically is recurrently raised throughout her work in a metafictional discourse that betrays the author's inner turmoil between her wish to keep foreign words for linguistic authenticity, to be coherent with her co-text, and the risk she runs of making her text inaccessible to those of her readers who knew only English due to an irreducible sense of unfamiliarity, and even otherness. This hesitation reveals the author's deep reflection around the use of untranslated French words. She constantly reconsiders her choice of language, which is never only artificial but serves a purpose, as demonstrated by Emily Eells. Through her 'superimposition of languages', her choice not to use equivalences and to keep a feeling of otherness in her text,[69] she privileges cultural decentering and asks for the reader's cooperation as analysed by Umberto Eco.[70]

67 Brontë, *Jane Eyre*, trans. by R. Redon and J. Dulong (Paris: Éditions du Dauphin, 1946), p. 123; Brontë, *Jane Eyre*, trans. by Léon Brodovikoff and Claire Robert, p. 160.

68 Brontë, *Jane Eyre*, trans. by Charlotte Maurat, p. 155; Brontë, *Jane Eyre*, trans. by Sylvère Monod, p. 223; Brontë, *Jane Eyre*, trans. by Dominique Jean, p. 227.

69 Antoine Berman, *La traduction et la lettre ou l'Auberge du lointain* (Paris: Seuil, 1991); Henri Meschonnic, *Poétique du traduire* (Paris: Verdier, 1999).

70 Umberto Eco, *Lector in Fabula*, trans. by Myriam Bouzaher (Paris: Grasset, 1979).

Brontë dreams of freeing languages viewed as tools that must serve a subject matter, an idea, or an emotion. For the latter to bloom and take on their full meanings, the author feels she cannot be constricted to one language system, but conversely wished she could dig into multiple language systems, ideally viewed as a continuum. She thus relies on her readers to produce textual meaning, and when there are no editorial signs to guide them, they must look for interpretative clues — be they etymological, phonetic (through near-homophonies), or contextual — to unlock the meaning of the passage. In her book *The Foreign Vision of Charlotte Brontë* (1975), Enid Duthie points at the author's great skill at introducing foreign words since she almost systematically places interpretative keys to domesticate the foreign text and thus make the signified more accessible to English-speaking readers. The latter must then trust that the author has done everything in her power to facilitate their entry into the text (Collins), and rely on their expertise in the domain of reading and their own comprehension abilities. 'She [Adèle] would have Sophie to look over her 'toilettes' as she called her frocks; to furbish up any that were 'passées', and to air and arrange the new', can be read in Chapter 17. After first giving the readers a leg-up and guiding them within the text through an act of self-translation — 'toilettes' being immediately given its English equivalent 'frocks' — Brontë gradually leads the readers to autonomy. 'Reading is a pact of generosity between author and readers; each one trusts the other, each one counts on the other', wrote Jean-Paul Sartre in *Qu'est-ce que la littérature?* (1948).[71] The past participle 'passées' therefore no longer needs to be translated, but its meaning can be inferred from the context and the structure of the sentence, i.e., the opposition between 'passées' and 'new' which echoes through a grammatical parallelism, referring to Adèle's clothes. French and English signifiers work together to produce meaning; hence their complementarity, and the creation of a Franco-English union within the source text. This whole framework set up by the author for reader autonomy is absent from the French translations. The French reader is effortlessly given the meaning of the word, as in Lesbazeilles-Souvestre's translation ('ses toilettes, ainsi qu'elle appelait ses robes, afin de rafraîchir celles qui étaient passées et d'arranger les autres').

---

71 My translation; '*la lecture est un pacte de générosité entre l'auteur et le lecteur; chacun fait confiance à l'autre, chacun compte sur l'autre*', Jean-Paul Sartre. *Qu'est-ce que la littérature?* (Paris: Gallimard, 1948), p. 62.

While Léon Brodovikoff and Claire Robert have opted for a lexical translation that goes unnoticed for the reader through the use of the synonym 'défraîchies', that is to say 'faded' ('ses toilettes, comme elle appelait ses robes, pour renouveler celles qui étaient défraîchies et arranger les neuves' Brodovikoff and Robert), other translators have chosen to keep the French word, but to use a visual sign to point at its foreign origin, such as italics, and, as aforementioned either a footnote 'en français dans le texte' (Redon and Dulong, and Maurat) or a superscript black star (Jean).[72]

In their take on the target culture, translators have mostly switched from the 'domesticating (19th and early 20th centuries)/ foreignizing' (1960s) strategies, as developed by Lawrence Venuti,[73] to the archaizing (1960s)/modernizing (1990s–2000s) approaches in the latest French versions. While the translators' former stress was on culture — 'domesticating' the text to make it closely conform to the target culture, or conversely 'foreignizing' the text to respect the source culture as advocated by Friedrich Schleiermacher and other German Romantics before being theorized by Antoine Berman as an ethics of translation in the 1980s[74] — their current emphasis seems to be more on lexis, opposing outdated to modern day vocabulary and lexical uses. Charlotte Brontë's pedagogical approach into textual deciphering is not translated into the French versions of her work, so that readers are not educated to reading. They are spoon-fed by the translators who have worked around the problem and also 'défraîchi' the text by fading out the latter's sense of otherness. They remain passive and external to the foreign character of the text before them. Meaning is not gradually allowed to emerge through the harmonious blending of the two languages since it is already *a priori* given. The Franco-English linguistic union is definitely broken in the translation which privileges one language viewed as independent from the

72 Brontë, *Jane Eyre*, trans. by Léon Brodovikoff and Claire Robert, p. 201.

73 'Admitting (with qualifications like "as much as possible") that translation can never be completely adequate to the foreign text, Schleiermacher allowed the translator to choose between a domesticating method, an ethnocentric reduction of the foreign text to target-language cultural values, bringing the author back home, and a foreignizing method, an ethno-deviant pressure on those values to register the linguistic and cultural difference of the foreign text, sending the reader abroad'. Lawrence Venuti, *The Translator's Invisibility: A History of Translation* (London: Routledge, 1995), p. 20.

74 Antoine Berman, *L'épreuve de l'étranger: Culture et traduction dans l'Allemagne romantique* (Paris: Gallimard, 1984).

other. 'Perhaps, therefore, it is more useful to understand the role of foreign language instruction and not simply the role of language in the original version and in the translation of *Jane Eyre* when trying to comprehend its transnational reception', Anne O'Neil-Henry writes.[75] As the teaching-learning process fails to be reproduced in the French translations and despite the recent tendency to take the audience's response into account, it seems that there is an urgent need for the translators to implement a full 'dynamic equivalence' between the source text and the target text, and acknowledge the cognitive processing in the production and the reception of translation.

Works Cited

Translations of *Jane Eyre*

Brontë, Charlotte, *Jane Eyre*, trans. By Noëmi Lesbazeilles-Souvestre (Paris: D. Giraud, 1854). The version used here is the electronic 1883 version published by Hachette.

——, *Jane Eyre*, trans. By R. Redon and J. Dulong (Paris: Éditions du Dauphin, 1946).

——, *Jane Eyre*, trans. By Marion Gilbert and Madeleine Duvivier (Paris: GF Flammarion, [1919] 1990).

——, *Jane Eyre*, trans. By Léon Brodovikoff and Claire Robert (Verviers, Belgique: Gérard & Co., [1946] 1950).

——, *Jane Eyre*, trans. By Charlotte Maurat (Paris: Le Livre de Poche, [1964] 2016).

——, *Jane Eyre*, trans. By Dominique Jean (Paris: Gallimard, [2008] 2012).

Other Sources

Allott, Miriam, ed., *The Brontës: The Critical Heritage* (London: Routledge, 1974). https://doi.org/10.4324/9781315004570

Armstrong, Nancy, *Desire and Domestic Fiction: A Political History of the Novel* (Oxford: Oxford University Press, 1989).

Barthes, Roland, 'L'effet de réel', *Communications*, 11 (1968), 84–89. https://doi.org/10.3406/comm.1968.1158

Béghain, Véronique, 'How do you translate French into French? Charlotte Brontë's Villette as a borderline case in Translatability', *Interculturality & Translation*, 2 (2006), 41–62.

——, '"To retain the slight veil of the original tongue": traduction et esthétique du voile dans Villette de Charlotte Brontë', in *Cahiers Charles V*, 'La

75 O'Neil-Henry, 'Domestic Fiction Abroad', p. 121.

traduction littéraire ou la remise en jeu du sens', ed. by Jean-Pierre Richard, 44 (2008), 125–42. https://doi.org/10.3406/cchav.2008.1518

——, '"A Dress of French gray": Retraduire Villette de Charlotte Brontë au risque du grisonnement', in *Autour de la traduction: Perspectives littéraires européennes*, ed. by Enrico Monti and Peter Schnyder (Paris: Orizons, 2011), pp. 85–104.

Bell, Maureen, Shirley Chew, Simon Eliot, Lynette Hunter and James L. W. West, eds., *Re-Constructing the Book: Literary Texts in Transmission* (Burlington: Ashgate, 2001). https://doi.org/10.4324/9781315192116

Berman, Antoine, *La traduction et la lettre ou l'Auberge du lointain* (Paris: Seuil, 1991).

——, *L'épreuve de l'étranger: Culture et traduction dans l'Allemagne romantique* (Paris: Gallimard, 1984).

Brontë, Charlotte, *Shirley and The Professor* (New York: Everyman's Library, [1849, 1857] 2008).

Buzard, James, *Disorienting Fictions: The Autoethnographic Work of Nineteenth-Century Novels* (Princeton: Princeton University Press, 2005).

Collins, Hélène, 'Le plurilinguisme dans The Professor de Charlotte Brontë: entre fascination et neutralisation de l'altérité', *Cahiers victoriens et édouardiens*, 78 (2013), https://doi.org/10.4000/cve.818

Derrida, Jacques, 'Des tours de Babel', in *Psyche: Inventions de l'autre*, 2 vols (Paris: Galilée, [1985] 1998), I, pp. 203–35.

Devonshire, Marian Gladys, *The English Novel in France: 1830–1870* (New York: Octagon Books, 1967).

Dillon, Jay, '"Reader, I found it": The First *Jane Eyre* in French', *The Book Collector*, 17 (2023), 11–19.

Duthie, Enid L., *The Foreign Vision of Charlotte Brontë* (London: Macmillan, 1975). https://doi.org/10.1177/004724417600602107

Eco, Umberto, *Lector in Fabula*, trans. By Myriam Bouzaher (Paris: Grasset, 1979).

Eells, Emily, 'The French aire in Jane Eyre', *Cahiers victoriens et édouardiens*, 78 (2013), https://doi.org/10.4000/cve.839

——, 'Charlotte Brontë en français dans le texte', in *Textes et Genres I: 'A Literature of Their Own'*, ed. by Claire Bazin and Marie-Claude Perrin-Chenour (Nanterre: Publidix, 2003), pp. 69–88.

Ewbank, Inga-Stina, 'Reading the Brontës Abroad: A Study in the Transmission of Victorian Novels in Continental Europe', in *Re-Constructing the Book: Literary Texts in Transmission*, ed. by Maureen Bell, Shirley Chew, Simon Eliot and James L. W. West (London: Routledge, 2001), pp. 84–99. https://doi.org/10.4324/9781315192116

Forcade, Eugène, 'Le roman anglais contemporain en Angleterre: *Shirley*, de Currer Bell', *Revue des Deux Mondes*, 1.4 (Nov. 1849), 714–35.

Fraser's Magazine for Town and Country, 1830–1869, 40.240 (Dec. 1849), 691–702.

Genette, Gérard, *Palimpsestes: La littérature au second degré* (Paris: Seuil, 1982).

Gilbert, Sandra M. and Susan Gubar, *The Madwoman in the Attic: The Woman Writer and the Nineteenth-Century Literary Imagination* (New Haven: Yale University Press, 1979).

Guyon, Loïc and Andrew Watts, eds., *Aller(s)-Retour(s): Nineteenth-Century France in Motion* (Cambridge: Cambridge Scholars Publisher, 2013).

Iser, Wolfgang, 'The Reading Process: A Phenomenological Approach', *New Literary History*, 3 (1972), 279–99. https://doi.org/10.2307/468316

——, *The Act of Reading: A Theory of Aesthetic Response* (Baltimore, MD: Johns Hopkins University Press, 1978).

Jauss, Hans Robert, *Toward an Aesthetic of Reception* (Minneapolis, MN: University of Minnesota Press, 1982).

Kruger, Haidee and Jan-Louis Kruger, 'Cognition and Reception', in *The Handbook of Translation and Cognition*, ed. by John W. Schwieter and Aline Ferreira (Oxford: Wiley Blackwell, 2017), pp. 71–89.

Lawrence, Karen, 'The Cypher: Disclosure and Reticence in Villette', *Nineteenth-Century Literature*, 42 (1988), 448–66. https://doi.org/10.2307/3045249

Lewes, George Henry, 'Recent Novels: French and English', *Fraser's Magazine for Town and Country*, 1830–1869, 36.216 (Dec. 1847), 686–95.

Longmuir, Anne. '"Reader, perhaps you were never in Belgium?": Negotiating British Identity in Charlotte Brontë's The Professor and Villette', *Nineteenth-Century Literature*, 64 (2009), 163–88. https://doi.org/10.1525/ncl.2009.64.2.163

Lonoff, Sue, 'Charlotte Brontë's Belgian Essays: The Discourse of Empowerment', *Victorian Studies*, 32 (1989), 387–409.

Meschonnic, Henri, *Poétique du traduire* (Paris: Verdier, 1999).

Newmark, Peter, 'Pragmatic Translation and Literalism', *TTR: Traduction, Terminologie, Rédaction*, 1 (1988), 133–45. https://doi.org/10.7202/037027ar

Nida, Eugène A., *Toward a Science of Translating* (Leiden: Brill, 1964).

Nida, Eugène A. and Charles R. Taber, *The Theory and Practice of Translation* (Leiden: Brill, 2003). https://doi.org/10.1163/9789004496330

O'Neil-Henry, Anne, 'Domestic Fiction Abroad: Jane Eyre's Reception in Post-1848 France', in *Aller(s)-Retour(s): Nineteenth-Century France in Motion*, ed. by Loïc Guyon and Andrew Watts (Cambridge: Cambridge Scholars Publishing, 2013), pp. 111–24.

Ratisbonne, Louis, in *Journal des débats politiques et littéraires* (4 Jan. 1856),

Sartre, Jean-Paul, *Qu'est-ce que la littérature?* (Paris: Gallimard, 1948).

Schwieter, John W. and Aline Ferreira, eds., *The Handbook of Translation and Cognition* (Oxford: Wiley Blackwell, 2017).

Showalter, Elaine, 'Charlotte Brontë's Use of French', *Research Studies*, 42 (1974), 225–34.

Venuti, Lawrence, *The Translator's Invisibility: A History of Translation* (London: Routledge, 1995). https://doi.org/10.4324/9781315098746

Wilss, Wolfram, 'Perspectives and Limitations of a Didactic Framework for the Teaching of Translation', in *Translation*, ed. by Robert W. Brislin (New York: Gardner, 1976), pp. 117–37.

Yaeger, Patricia, *Honey-Mad Women: Emancipatory Strategies in Women's Writing* (New York: Columbia University Press, 1988). https://doi.org/10.7312/yaeg91456

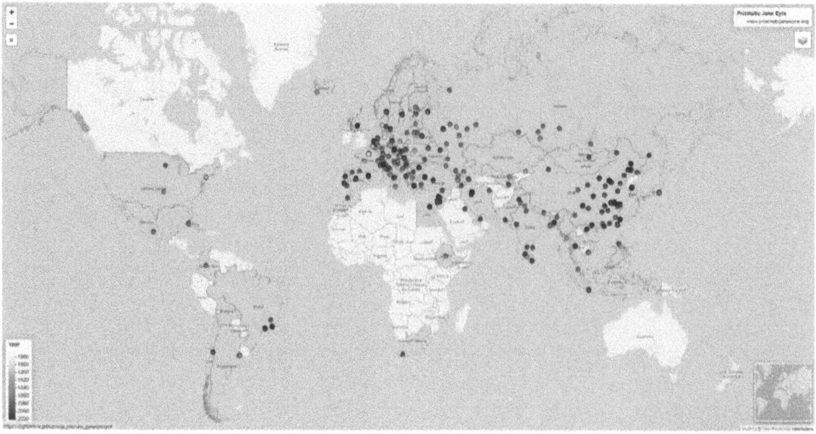

The General Map
https://digitalkoine.github.io/je_prismatic_generalmap/
Created by Giovanni Pietro Vitali; © OpenStreetMap contributors

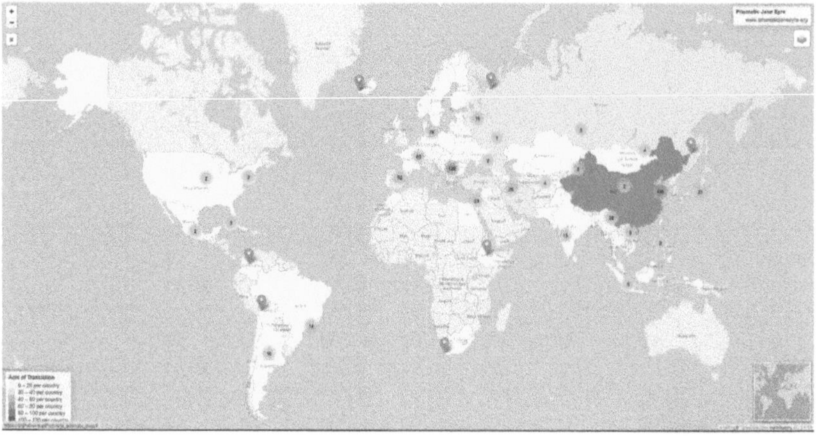

The World Map
https://digitalkoine.github.io/je_prismatic_map
Created by Giovanni Pietro Vitali;
maps © Thunderforest, data © OpenStreetMap contributors

III. Locating the Translations

Matthew Reynolds

'Locating', here, has layered and intermingled senses.[1] There is tracking down any given translation now, in a database, library catalogue or bookshop. There is situating its first appearance and its circulation geographically, as on a map. There is placing it in time. And then there is the whole intricate and finally unanswerable question of how to locate a translation vis à vis everything it is 'into': not just 'a language', but a particular linguistic idiom and style, in a cultural context (or better, as we will see, a complex of contexts), with some kind of purpose, among expectations, in conversation with other texts, in, or in connection to, a genre. The pages that you have read so far have already raised these issues in abundance, and the essays that immediately follow this chapter focus on them with special intensity. So this chapter serves as a hinge, aiming to open general issues of location, and explore them across several languages and contexts before the essays to come zoom in on more particular places.

In this endeavour, I will ask you, from time to time, to open one or other of the interactive maps, built by Giovanni Pietro Vitali, to which these pages are linked. Our use of maps has drawn inspiration from the work of Franco Moretti, and we agree with him that it is important to 'make the connection between geography and literature explicit'.[2] However, learning from Karima Laachir, Sara Marzagora and Francesca Orsini, we have also been wary of the process of abstraction that is inevitably involved in cartography, and of the detached, synoptic and thin kind of knowledge that a map therefore tends to provide. In harmony with those scholars, we hope that our discussion

1 An earlier treatment of some of the material in this chapter was published as Matthew Reynolds and Giovanni Pietro Vitali, 'Mapping and Reading a World of Translations', *Digital Modern Languages Open*, 1 (2021).

2 Franco Moretti, *Atlas of the European Novel, 1800–1900* (London and New York: Verso, 1998), p. 3.

 https://doi.org/10.11647/OBP.0319.08

shows 'sensitivity to the richness and plurality of spatial imaginings that animate texts, authors, and publics in the world'.[3] As we have already begun to see, the 'world' that is inhabited by the world work *Jane Eyre* is not some featureless international zone — not a world of airports — but a network of particular locations, each thickly striated and complicatedly entangled, with variable degrees of connection between them. It is a world unevenly patched together from a collection of 'significant geographies', to adopt Laachir, Marzagora and Orsini's term. Places that are distant in space may be closely linked in the history of *Jane Eyre* translation, as with the connection from Brussels and Paris to Havana, Santiago de Chile and La Paz which we discovered in Chapter I. Or the same city may, both in relation to *Jane Eyre* and in other ways, be split from itself by a historical event, like Tehran before and after the Islamic Revolution, as we will see in Essay 8 by Kayvan Tahmasebian and Rebecca Ruth Gould. We have tried to bring something of this awareness of complexity into the maps themselves, in two ways. First, by making them interactive, so that you can zoom in on any given point and click for more information about it; and second, by providing several different kinds of map, each offering a distinct view, so that the ensemble enables varied kinds of perception to emerge. We hope to generate an understanding of the significant geographies of *Jane Eyre* translation from the interplay between the varied modes of representation, and different critical voices, that are brought together in these pages. The mobile visuals of the maps are in dialogue with the broad interpretive arguments in the chapters, such as this one; and also with the more tightly focused analyses in the essays.

3 Karima Laachir, Sara Marzagora and Francesca Orsini, 'Significant Geographies: In Lieu of World Literature', *Journal of World Literature*, 3, 3 (2018), 290–310, p. 293.

The Point of a Point on a Map

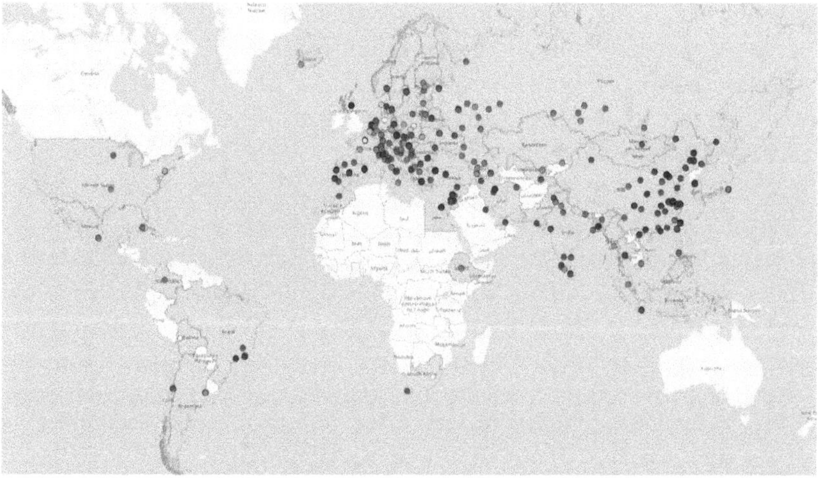

Fig. 7 The General Map, zoomed out to provide a snapshot of the global distribution of *Jane Eyre* translations. Created by Giovanni Pietro Vitali; © OpenStreetMap contributors

Each little circle represents what we call an 'act of translation' — that is, either the first appearance of a new translation, or the re-publication of that translation in a new place (I will expand on this definition below).[4] The darker the circle, the more recent the act of translation. The impression we get is very imperfect, for many earlier acts of translation are hidden by later ones; but still, looking at the map, we can immediately see the very broad spread of *Jane Eyre* translations. No longer is this a novel that was begun in Manchester and written mainly in Haworth, Yorkshire, in Charlotte Brontë's distinctive language(s). Rather, it has been — and is still being — written in many hundreds of locations, with as many different linguistic repertoires.[5] We can also register the uneven distribution of the translations, the thick crowds in Europe, China, Japan, Korea and Iran, for instance; and the patchier scattering in the Americas. Here is a first visual indication of the world of *Jane Eyre* translation as a mesh of significant geographies. Finally, there are the large tracts of the world where no

4 I am grateful to Eugenia Kelbert for suggesting the phrase 'an act of translation'.

5 See Chapter I above for an account of Brontë's language(s) and an explanation of 'repertoire'.

translations have appeared. These include places where one would not expect them to, such as Greenland, together with countries where they perhaps might have done, such as Côte d'Ivoire, Venezuela or Peru. They also include, of course, countries where English is a — or the — dominant language, such as Australia, Ghana, Nigeria, Canada, and England itself (the United States does not figure in this group because translations have appeared there, into Russian, Vietnamese and Spanish, and neither does Scotland, because of recent translations into North-East Scots, Cornish and West Frisian published there by Evertype). In Essay 1 we discovered, with Ulrich Timme Kragh and Abhishek Jain, the effect on *Jane Eyre* translations in India of the widespread use of English in that country, as well as of colonial and post-colonial education structures; and in Essay 7, below, Annmarie Drury explores related reasons that explain, and give significance to, the paucity of *Jane Eyre* translations in sub-Saharan Africa: different significant geographies are revealed by these detailed examinations. Nevertheless, reflecting on this aspect of the map as a whole, what is striking is the negative it gives to what one might naively think to be the global distribution of English literature, as happening primarily in 'English-speaking countries'. Though we have not attempted the impossible task of tracking the circulation of English-language copies of *Jane Eyre*, it is the case that they might be found anywhere: from the first year of the novel's existence, when a cheap English edition was published in Leipzig by Tauchnitz, the book has travelled widely, and many people with English as an additional language have read the text that Brontë wrote.[6] Even more important is the obvious, though neglected, fact that is made starkly visible by our map: it is in countries where English is not a primary language that *Jane Eyre* has been most translated — that is, where it has generated the particular, intense imaginative life that goes into making a translation, and attracted the distinctive sorts of attention that go into reading one (though of course these vary in different cultures and times). There is a kind of energy in an ongoing life through translations that a continuing existence in a source language does not have.

---

6 For French readers of the early English-language Tauchnitz editions, see Essay 4 above, by Céline Sabiron.

If you now open the General Map and zoom in wherever you like, you will see that the little circles representing each act of translation are located in cities and towns (and the occasional village). We have not attempted to show the spread of each translation's readership, because that cannot be known. Equally we have not tried to visualise the geographical reach of the language that each translation might be thought to be 'into'. There are two, interrelated reasons for this, which I have already touched upon in Chapter I. Languages, conceived as entities that are internally consistent and separate from one another, are brisk abstractions from actual linguistic usage which is always complex and changeable, with boundaries — if they exist at all — that are fuzzy and shifting.[7] The account of *Jane Eyre* in Arabic, or Arabics, given by Yousif M. Qasmiyeh in Essay 3 above is a case in point. And translations are never merely into 'a language', but are made with a particular linguistic repertoire, in a given context and moment, with aims in view and stylistic preferences in play. Neither a translation's mode of relating to language(s), nor the mode of existence of language(s) in the world, can adequately be represented on a map.

Another entity a translation might be thought to be 'into' is the ongoing literary culture of a nation-state. Here again the picture is complicated, for nation-states are of course political constructions, and their borders, though more distinct than those of languages, can also change, and radically so. Indeed, the State in which a translation was done may now no longer exist: the former Yugoslavia and former USSR are obvious examples. Nevertheless, the hope of contributing to the growth of a national culture can be an important driver of translation, as Andrés Claro will outline for the Latin American context in Essay 5 below; and successive translations in the same publishing market can be in dialogue or competition with one another, as we have begun to see in the case of France in Essay 4 by Céline Sabiron, and as many of the essays to come will also reveal. So our maps do show the borders of States, together with the number of acts of translation that have happened within them, though with the proviso

7 At first sight, the expensively commercialized language maps produced by *Ethnologue* appear to give an impressive rendition of the intricacy of language borders and borderlands. But the approximation inherent in these visualisations is evident from the description of their data sources and processes given here: https://www.ethnologue.com/methodology

that the borders indicated are those that hold at present (or rather, that held at a moment in the twenty-teens when the ground-maps that we have employed were created) — so the State in which a translation was published may not be the same as the State within whose boundaries it now appears. The maps, then, need to be read with an awareness of the historical shifts which their presentist representation of borders conceals. In the General Map, as you can see, the different States where acts of translation have occurred are all indiscriminately coloured green, giving the impression of a continuity of activity across them. However, in another map, the World Map , we have taken a different approach, and coloured them differently according to the number of acts of translation that each has hosted. This makes the difference between the States look more substantial, and provides a rough contour diagram of the intensity of translation activity in different places.

So one thing that mapping helps us to understand is, paradoxically, how much about the spatial distribution of translations we cannot represent, or indeed know; as well as how much we can know and represent only very imperfectly. But what the maps do show clearly, as Giovanni Pietro Vitali pointed out while we were making them, is the importance of cities as centres for the publication of translations (as they are for the publication of books in general). The World Map, though it gives a less immediate impression of the world-wide spread of *Jane Eyre* than the General Map, is a better tool for exploring the phenomenon of the city because it groups the translations numerically. For instance, Figure 8 presents the World Map zoomed in to show the distribution of *Jane Eyre* translations in Turkey, Greece, Albania, North Macedonia and Bulgaria: you can see that Istanbul and Athens are very prominent sources, with lesser contributions emerging from Ankara, Izmir, Thessaloniki, Sofia, Tirana and Skopje.

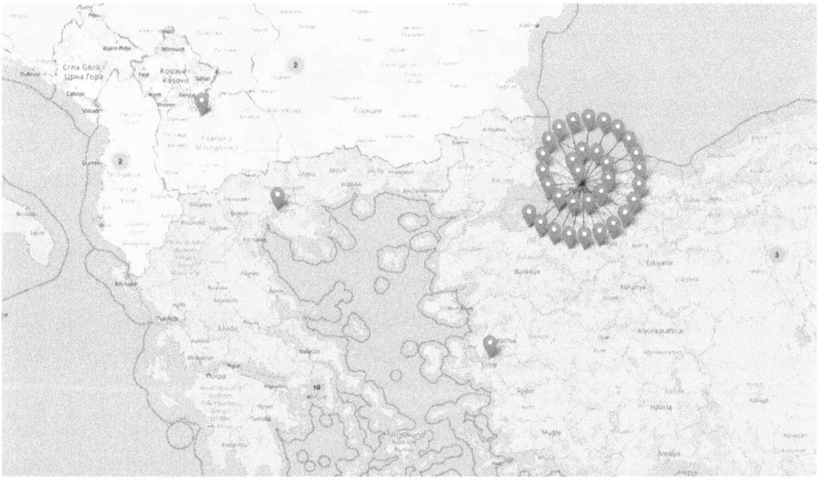

Fig. 8 The World Map zoomed in to show the distribution of *Jane Eyre* translations in Turkey, Greece, Albania, North Macedonia and Bulgaria. Created by Giovanni Pietro Vitali; maps © Thunderforest, data © OpenStreetMap contributors

If you move around in the World Map you will find that this pattern, with acts of translation being concentrated in a capital city, is fairly common. In South Korea, all 27 acts of translation into Korean occurred in Seoul; in Japan, all 22 took place in Tokyo except for one (Kyoto, 2002); in Iran, 26 translations into Persian have been published in Tehran, and 1 each in Mashad, Qom and Tabriz. In Europe, you sometimes find a similar distribution: Greece, 19 acts of translation in Athens and 1 in Thessaloniki (1979), as we can see in Figure 2; France, 18 in Paris and 1 in Poitiers (1948). But there are also more dispersed environments. Of Italy's 39 acts of translation, 19 occurred in Milan, but the rest are shared out among 12 other places. German has a yet flatter configuration which spreads across Germany and beyond: 7 in Berlin; 3 for Stuttgart; 2 each for Leipzig and Frankfurt; 1 each for six other German locations; and then 6 in Zurich, 2 in Vienna and 1 each in Klagenfurt and Budapest.[8] The markets, the distribution networks, and the socio-political dynamics are different in each case; and so therefore are the reach and significance of each act of translation.

8 These translations listed in this paragraph were researched by Emrah Serdan, Sowon S. Park, Kayvan Tahmasebian, Yorimitsu Hashimoto, Eleni Philippou, Céline Sabiron, Léa Rychen, Vincent Thierry, Alessandro Grilli, Caterina Cappelli, Anna Ferrari, Paola Gaudio, and Mary Frank.

Seeing translations emerge physically into the world in this way brings the work of translation and the business of publication close together. Both are needed for *Jane Eyre*, or any text, to find readers in new language(s) in another place. This is why, for the purposes of our maps, we chose to define an 'act of translation' in the way I have described — as either the first appearance of a new translation, or the re-publication of that translation in a new place — and to create a separate entry for each such act (we have identified 683 of them in total). The result is that, when you look at our maps, translation's activity of making *Jane Eyre* available in a spread of new locations comes to the fore. In particular, two striking instances of such migratory re-publication are made visible.

The first, researched by Eugenia Kelbert and Karolina Gurevich, is the case of a classic translation of *Jane Eyre* into Russian by V. O. Stanevich. This text was first published simultaneously in Moscow and Leningrad in 1950. It was much reprinted in both those cities; but its geographical publication-life also extended a great deal further. On our maps, you can watch it appearing in Alma-Ata, in what is now Kazakhstan, and Kiev, in Ukraine (1956), Minsk, in modern Belarus, Barnaul, in Altai Krai, and Gorkji, now Nizhny Novgorod (1958), Tashkent, in what is now Uzbekhistan (1959); and then Krasnodar, on the Eastern edge of the Black Sea (1985), Makhachkala on the Caspian Sea (1986), Saransk, in Mordovia (1989), Baku, in Azerbaijan (1989), Voronezh (1990), Izhevsk, in the Urals (1991), Krasnoyarsk, in Siberia (1992 — see Figure 12), Omsk, again in Siberia (1992), Kalinigrad on the Baltic (1993), Kazan, on the Volga (1993), Tomsk (1993), Ulan-Ude, in the Russian Far East (1994), and Nal'chik, in the Caucasus Mountains (1997).

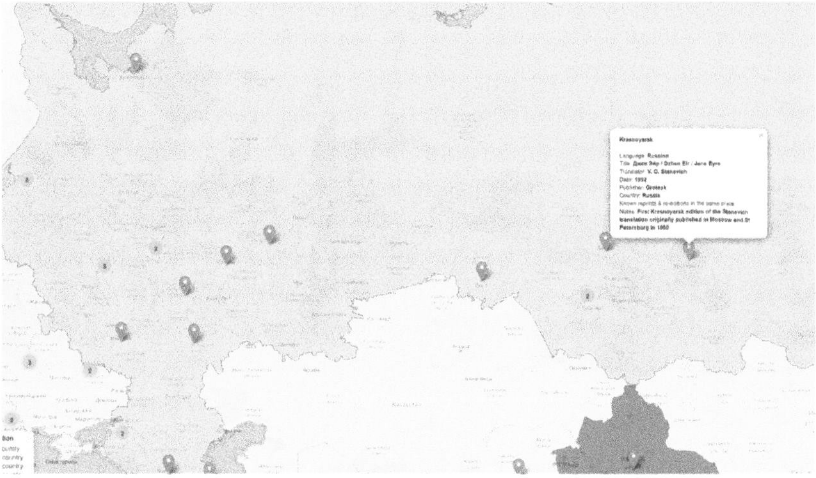

Fig. 9 The World Map, zoomed in to show the 1992 publication of Stanevich's Russian translation in Krasnoyarsk, Siberia. Created by Giovanni Pietro Vitali; maps © Thunderforest, data © OpenStreetMap contributors

This distribution gives us a window onto the conditions of publication, first of all during the 1950s and then during the period of Glasnost and the dissolution of the USSR. The very fact that these successive publications in different locations were necessary shows that the first acts of translation in Moscow and Leningrad did not translate the novel 'into Russian', in the sense of making it available to all Russian speakers, nor 'into the USSR' or 'into Soviet culture', in the sense of conveying it to all inhabitants of that state or participants in that culture. The first acts of translation brought the novel to smaller linguistic, topographical and cultural areas (that is, significant geographies); and more acts of translation were needed to carry it further.

The second instance is the vivid and absorbing translation of *Jane Eyre* into Spanish by Juan González-Blanco de Luaces, first published in Barcelona in 1943. As Andrés Claro will describe in Essay 5, Luaces, a republican, had had a career as a novelist before the establishment of Franco's regime, and turned to translation both to make a living and as a way of continuing the imaginative life that was no longer available to him as an author. His version of *Jane Eyre* was much reprinted in Barcelona; it then crossed the Atlantic to Argentina where it appeared in Buenos Aires in 1954, joining four other *Jane Eyre* translations that had been published there during the 1940s. Claro explains how the significance of the act of translation changed in the new context: the same text that, in Barcelona, had enabled Luaces to 'write between the lines' in resistance to Franco became, when transplanted to Buenos Aires, 'part of an explicit programme of opening up to and interacting with foreign languages and literatures as a way of creating a local ethos and literature emancipated from Spanish colonialism', taking on particular significance because 'the novel became widely known at the very time the female vote and other civil rights for women were being secured'. It was only after this that Luaces's translation came out in Madrid, where Claro notes that the literary scene was more Francoist than in Barcelona: it was first published there in 1967, by the same transnational firm, Espasa-Calpe, that had brought it to Buenos Aires. Reprints continued (and still do) in all these cities; and in 1985 Luaces's translation appeared in a second South American location, Bogotá, from a different publisher, Oveja Negra. Tracking this text shows us an instance of the transnational dynamics of Spanish-language publishing, and the varying pressures that have encouraged translation in different locations and times.

All these cases reveal the productive interplay between, on the one hand, the pressure to visualise which comes from trying to make a map and, on the other, the resistance to being visualised which comes from the complex nature of the linguistic and cultural locations that translations are actually in. Maps make blatantly obvious what we cannot know: we cannot put boundaries around a language, and we cannot trace where translations travelled or were read. But we can see where they were published, and reflecting on that single parameter can — in dialogue with more detailed knowledge — open onto an understanding of the significant geographies that they inhabited. To move through such geographies is also to advance through time; and we have tried to capture something of this phenomenon in our Time Map .

Translation in Time

The Time Map , created by Giovanni Pietro Vitali and Simone Landucci, should be tranquilly running through history when you open it (if it isn't, click the 'play' button at the bottom left). Note that each dot representing an act of translation lasts for six years, before disappearing: this is to help the map be legible, but it also hints at the temporal life of a translation which, though it may be reprinted, become a classic, or indeed simply be stumbled across, picked up and read at any time, nevertheless tends on the whole to have a brief moment of higher visibility in culture, followed by a long stretch of comparative obscurity. If you wish to freeze time in a particular year, you will see that there is a 'pause' button at the bottom left that enables you to do so.

When we watch the ongoing, proliferative pulse of the world-novel *Jane Eyre* in this map, what do we see? In *Atlas of the European Novel* (1998), Franco Moretti offered a pattern that we too might discover. Focusing on Europe, and generalising initially from the case of *Don Quixote*, he suggests that the diffusion of translations tends to happen in three 'waves': first, nearby literary cultures (which he calls 'core'), then a pause; then somewhat further afield ('semi-periphery'); and after that more distant cultures — the 'periphery'.[9] The approach builds on Itamar Even Zohar's polysystem theory, and adopts its tripartite structure from Immanuel Wallerstein's theorization of 'The Modern World-System', in which 'core' economies accomplish tasks that require 'a high level of skill', the periphery provides '"raw" labour power', and the semi-periphery contributes 'vital skills that are often politically unpopular'.[10] It is not immediately obvious why this particular economic model should apply to literary writing: as Johan Heilbron has pointed out, 'the world-system of translation ... does not quite correspond to the predominant view in world-systems theory ... Cultural exchanges have a dynamic of their own'.[11] We might also demur at the implicitly low valuation that this picture of waves emanating from a centre gives to the skill and creativity inherent in translation, and to the imaginative energies of the translating cultures — factors that are abundantly evident throughout the essays and chapters that you are reading. Still, there is also something attractive about the metaphor of translation as a wave spreading through many locations, in that it seems as though it might, to some extent, register the proliferative dynamics that we began to explore in Chapter I, with Old Nick's version prompting others which then prompted others again. So how far does the translation history of *Jane Eyre* conform to this possible blueprint of three waves?

9 Moretti, *Atlas*, p. 171.

10 Wallerstein, Immanuel Maurice, *The Modern World System*, 4 vols (Berkeley, University of California Press, 2011), vol. 1, p. 350.

11 Johan Heilbron, 'Towards a Sociology of Translation: Book Translations as a Cultural World-System', *European Journal of Social Theory*, 2, 4 (1999), 429–44.

Well, the novel was translated into cultures well-connected to English in the three years after its first publication in 1847: Germany, France, Belgium, Russia, the Netherlands, Denmark and Sweden. It is plausible to see this group of countries as closely linked both culturally and economically — as forming a multilingual and transnational significant geography — a 'core' in Moretti's terms. But, as we discovered in Chapter I, these are not the only places where *Jane Eyre* was translated in those early years. During 1850–51 it appeared in South America and the Caribbean, first in Santiago de Chile, where it was serialized in the newspaper *El Progreso*, then Havana, in another newspaper, *Diario de la Marina*, then elsewhere in Cuba (Matanzas) and Bolivia (La Paz). As we saw, the mediate source for these texts was Old Nick's French version, first published in the French newspaper *Le National* and the Brussels-based *Revue de Paris* and *L'Indépendance belge*, which had been put into Spanish for the *Correo de Ultramar* in Paris, an act of translation that was designed to travel to Spanish-speaking locations overseas. The detour via French helped *Jane Eyre* to be catapulted across the Atlantic, for the Caribbean and South American publications drew their cultural material primarily from France as well as Spain, with only the very occasional bit of English. In *El Progresso*, the novel serialised immediately after *Juana Eyre* was Edward Bulwer-Lytton's *Leila; or, The Siege of Granada* (1838), but that — as its title suggests — is an English novel with a strong Spanish connection; the other texts appearing in the preceding and following months were translations of two novels by Alexandre Dumas, and an account of the 1847 murder of Fanny, duchesse de Praslin 'traducida del francés' ['translated from French'].[12] Likewise, in *Diario de la Marina*, books serialized in the years before and after *Jane Eyre* included Fédéric Soulié's *Les Drames inconnus*, Alexandre de Lavergne's *La Circassienne*, José María de Goizueta's *Leyendas vascongadas*, Antonio Flores's *Fé, esperanza y caridad*, and multiple novels by Dumas: *Le Comte de Monte-Cristo, Les Quarante-cinq* and *Le Vicomte de Bragelonne*.[13] The international news coverage in both papers tended to have a similar geographical orientation. So in this leap of *Jane Eyre* across the Atlantic we can see a particular set of connections enabling an act of translation that does not fit the model of a generalized wave.

12 *El Progreso*, 1 November 1849 – 18 June 1851.
13 *Diario de la Marina*, 18 January 1848 – 12 December 1851.

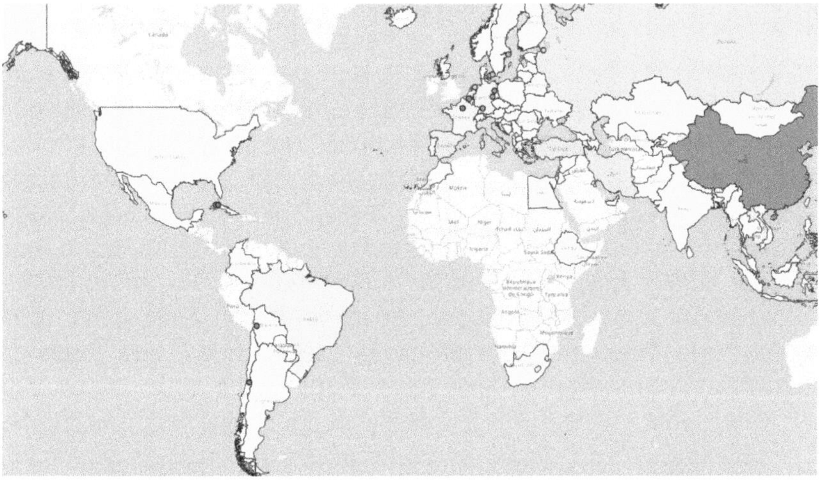

Fig. 10 Time Map: translations 1848–53. Created by Giovanni Pietro Vitali and Simone Landucci. © OpenStreetMap contributors, © Mapbox

After this early rush, there was something of a slowdown. If we confine our attention to Europe, we might take this to show that a group of cultures more immediately connected to English should be distinguished from a spread of those that were somewhat more detached — or, on Moretti's schema, first from second 'waves'. Despite the substantial exception presented by the Chilean, Cuban and Bolivian *Juana Eyre*s, the model does retain some explanatory power. After 1850 there was a second translation into French, in 1854 (this time published in Paris) as we saw in Chapter I, and re-translations also in German, Swedish and Russian between 1855 and 1857. The first translation into a new language, however, was not until 1865, into Polish, serialized in the Warsaw magazine *Tygodnik Mód* (*Fashion Weekly*).[14] It was followed by the first Hungarian translation in 1873, then Czech in 1875 and Portuguese in 1877 (an incomplete version serialised in a Lisbon magazine). Perhaps here we can discern another pause, before first translations then happen in Japan (1896 — albeit an incomplete version), Norway (1902), Italy (1904), Armenia (1908), Finland (1915), Brazil (c. 1916), China (1925), Romania (1930), into Esperanto in 1931 (in the Netherlands), Ukraine (1939), Argentina (1941), Brazil and Turkey (1945), Mandatory Palestine, into Hebrew

14 We are grateful to the book collector Jay Dillon for alerting us to this 1865 translation.

(1946), Iceland (1948), Greece (1949), Iran (1950), India, into Tamil (1953), Burma (1953), Slovenia and Bulgaria (1955), Sri Lanka, into Sinhalese (1955), Lithuania (1957), Estonia (1959), Korea and Vietnam (1963), Serbia (1965), Croatia (1974), Latvia (1976), Bangladesh, into Bengali (1977), Malaysia (1979), Ethiopia, into Amharic (1981); India, into Punjabi (1981); India, into Malayalam (1983), North Macedonia (1984), the Philippines, into Tagalog (1985), Spain, into Catalan (1992); India, into Gujarati (1993), Nepal (1993), Thailand (1993), Spain, into Basque (1998), India, into Assamese (1999), India, into Hindi (2002), Albania (2003), South Africa, into Afrikaans (2005), Tajikistan (2010), China, into Tibetan (2011), Mongolia (2014), India, into Kannada (2014), and Scotland, into Doric Scots (2018).

As we look at this broad, complicated scattering of first translations, the idea that it can be organised into three waves that correspond to 'core', 'semi-peripheral' and 'peripheral' cultural and economic status, comes to pieces, and with it the assumption that the agency involved is predominantly an emanation from a cultural centre, with *Jane Eyre* being passively received in all these locations like a delivery of international aid. Is Bolivia 'core' while Hungary is 'semi-peripheral'? Is Italy 'peripheral' while Sweden is 'core'? Clearly more varied and particular forces are at work — and several of them are detailed in the essays that follow this chapter. In at least one case, an endeavour conducted from England, to disseminate English culture, is indeed a decisive element. As Eleni Philippou will explain in Essay 6, the first Greek translation came about in 1949 as part of a programme of soft power in the context of the Cold War. But, in many other instances, the energies that most drive acts of translation originate in the locations which we should no longer think of, in the habitual terms of Translation Studies, as 'target' or 'receiving' cultures, but rather as ingurgitating cultures, along the lines of the Latin American anthropophagous manifestoes penned by Haroldo de Campos and Osvaldo de Andrade, and mentioned by Andrés Claro in Essay 5. As Claro shows, translations such as M. E. Antonini's, published in Buenos Aires by Acme Agency in 1941, should be seen, not as being subjected to 'the foreign' but rather as choosing to 'journey through' it. Likewise, in Iran after the Islamic Revolution — as Kayvan Tahmasebian and Rebecca Ruth Gould will explain in Essay 8 — translators turned to *Jane Eyre* to answer specific imaginative needs. In this vein of interpretation, an absence of *Jane Eyre* translations, as in many sub-Saharan African countries, need not be configured as a lack, since it can also be a sign of resistance or sufficiency: of there being no desire to translate *Jane Eyre* because interests are directed elsewhere. As soon as you begin to register the complexity of each situation in which translation is (or is not) happening, and of the dynamics that drive it, the broad-brush geometry of a single core and generalised periphery comes to seem more a matter of imperialistic assumption than of observation or reading. A better description would recognise that there are many cores, with energies sparking in multiple directions.[15]

Seeing this can help us to understand why the proliferative life of the world work *Jane Eyre* does not only happen via the first translation into any given language. It is not that, once translated, *Jane Eyre* has simply arrived. Rather, a first translation can open onto a phase of intense imaginative engagement conducted through re-translations which are in dialogue with one another as well as with Brontë's text. Tahmasebian and Gould illuminate one such phenomenon, the 28 new translations into Persian since 1982. Another, startling instance consists of the 108 new translations into Chinese since 1990 (see Figure 11).

15 Somewhat similarly, the *Mystères urbains au XIXe siècle* project identifies three centres 'qui vont chacun autonomiser leur série de mystères urbains: les Etats-Unis, la Grande Bretagne et la France' ['each of which establishes its own series of urban mysteries: the United States, Great Britain and France'], Dominique Kalifa and Marie-Ève Thérenty, 'Introduction', https://www.medias19.org/publications/les-mysteres-urbains-au-xixe-siecle-circulations-transferts-appropriations/introduction

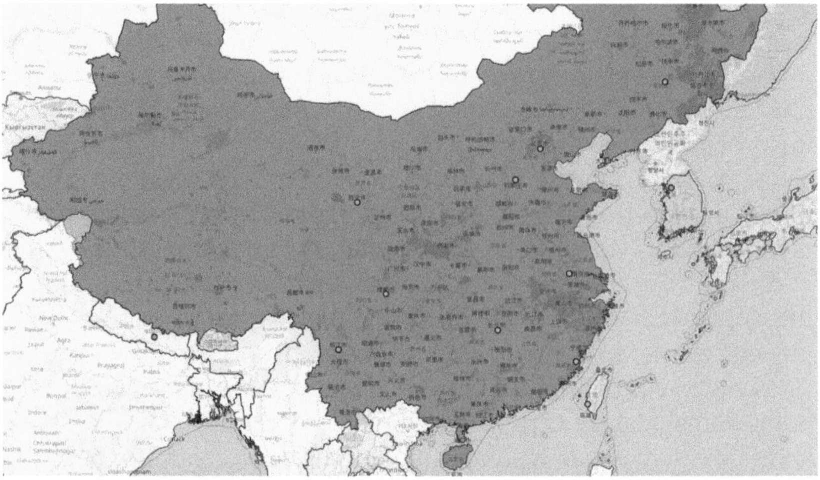

Fig. 11 The Time Map, zoomed in to show intense *Jane Eyre* translation activity in China, South Korea, Taiwan and Nepal, 1992–97. Created by Giovanni Pietro Vitali and Simone Landucci. © OpenStreetMap contributors, © Mapbox

No doubt there is some reiteration of material between these multitudinous publications, though we have not been able to establish how much. Nevertheless, it remains the case that, during the last three decades, *Jane Eyre* has been more voluminously re-written and reprinted in China than anywhere else. Once you start paying attention to re-translations there are other distributions of energy that emerge. During the 1980s there were 8 new translations into Korean but none into French or German. Where shall we say the 'core' of *Jane Eyre* translation is located at such times? Similar phases of intensity can spread across national boundaries. For instance, there was a surge of *Jane Eyre* translation, concentrated in Europe, at the end of the Second World War (see Figure 12), with 25 new translations being published between 1945 and 1948: 8 each into French and Spanish, 3 into German, 2 into Turkish, and 1 each into Dutch, Italian, Norwegian and Hebrew (written by the Paris-based modernist artist Hana Ben Dov, and published in Jerusalem in 1945). The post-war prestige of English can be seen here, abetted by the glamour of the widely distributed 1943 American film, directed by Robert Stevenson and starring Orson Welles and Joan Fontaine. Significance can be found also in a longer, narrower dispersion, such as the 39 translations into Italian since 1904: they have followed one another at intervals which, though decreasing recently, have remained comparatively regular across the twelve decades. *Jane Eyre* in Italy has been a continuing presence that publishers and translators have found reason to turn to, to re-angle or re-juvenate, from time to time.

Fig. 12 Time Map: translations 1945–50. Created by Giovanni Pietro Vitali and Simone Landucci. © OpenStreetMap contributors, © Mapbox

Looking at the Time Map, and indeed the World and General maps, in dialogue with the detailed analyses conducted in the essays, helps us to see that each translation of *Jane Eyre* involves a mix of sources of agency. Translation is not a passive reception but an active engagement. To be sure, elements of cultural domination or encroachment are in play: the power of English, growing globally throughout the period of *Jane Eyre* translations so far, is a crucial factor in the way they have spread. But also in play is the agency of translators, publishers, readers, and other elements in the ingurgitating culture. There is the choice to translate, the recognition of why the book might be needed or liked, the power to cut large stretches of it (as we saw in Chapter I), the labour of re-making the work with different linguistic materials, re-orienting it with an eye to the new market and in collaboration with the translator's imaginative disposition and style. Each culture where this happens is not merely peripheral to a centre that lies elsewhere: it is in many respects a centre to itself. Seeing this brings us back to the idea of the world as a network or patchwork of significant geographies. But what kind of significance are we talking about?

Locational Textures

By significant geographies, Laachir, Marzagora and Orsini mean 'the *conceptual, imaginative*, and *real* geographies that texts, authors, and language communities inhabit, produce, and reach, which typically extend outwards without (ever?) having a truly global reach'.[16] In the case of translation, all three of these geographies are doubled — or more than doubled — because there are always at least two points of view from which each of them can be projected. On the one hand, there are the material ('*real*') factors that have enabled the novel to travel from its first publication in London, perhaps through the medium of other languages and re-imaginings, to the place where it is being translated. On the other, from the point of view of the ingurgitating culture, there are the material factors that have enabled it to be sourced, brought in, translated and distributed. On the one hand, the '*conceptual*' frame that starts from London and that tends to see the world work *Jane Eyre* in terms of spread; on the other, the conceptual frame that starts from the place of translation, and which is likely to be built from other elements, including perhaps emulation, but also interest, choice or a perception of need. And then there is the '*imaginative*' geography that has been generated in collaboration with the text — a shifting landscape that has been variously inhabited by Charlotte Brontë, many millions of readers in English(es) and other language(s), and many hundreds of translators. This imaginative geography is affected by the other two kinds: what you see in the novel will be influenced by where you are standing, and the frame through which you are looking. But it can also permeate them in its turn, altering their significance and shape. The world that is in *Jane Eyre* is changed by and also changes the world that it is in.

The *Jane Eyre* that Brontë wrote is a novel full of significant migrations. From her unhappy childhood home, Gateshead Hall, Jane is sent fifty miles away to Lowood School, a whole day's journeying which seems, to the ten-year-old girl who is travelling alone, much longer: 'I only know that the day seemed to me of a preternatural length, and that we appeared to travel over hundreds of miles of road'.[17] Eight years later Jane moves again, to Thornfield Hall: this means another long spell of coach-travel as Thornfield is situated in a

16 Laachir, Marzagor and Orsini, 'Significant Geographies', p. 294.
17 *JE*, Ch. 5.

'shire' that was 'seventy miles nearer London than the remote county where I now resided' — though the older Jane is now better able to cope with the journey.[18] After many months at Thornfield she makes a visit back to Gateshead to see Mrs Reed on her deathbed: this is 'a hundred miles' each way.[19] Then, six weeks or so later, after the failed wedding, she flees Thornfield, getting on a coach that is travelling to 'a place a long way off', though she only has twenty shillings instead of the thirty-shilling fare; she is therefore set down before the coach reaches its destination, at a place called 'Whitcross', in a 'north-midland shire', 'dusk with moorland, ridged with mountain': it is 'two days' since she left Thornfield.[20] She wanders the landscape, spends two nights in the open, walks 'a long time', and ends up at Moor House, also known as Marsh End. From there, after some weeks, she moves a little way to the village of Morton when she becomes a schoolteacher. After some months, just before Christmas, and after she has come into her surprise inheritance, she moves back to Moor House; from there, on the 'first of June' she returns to Thornfield, a journey of 'six-and-thirty hours', followed, when she has found Thornfield in ruins, by another 'thirty miles' to Ferndean.

If we try to plot these distances against some of the real places thought to have inspired *Jane Eyre*'s five key locations (as gathered by Christine Alexander in *The Oxford Companion to the Brontës*), we can find a shadow of resemblance, albeit a somewhat truncated one. If we located Gateshead not far from Stonegappe, the house in Lothersdale, near Skipton, where Brontë was unhappy as a governess, then it would be a bit more than forty miles north-west from there to the site of the Clergy Daughters' School at Cowan Bridge, the inspiration for Lowood. If we sited Thornfield near Rydings, the battlemented home of Charlotte's friend Ellen Nussey, in Birstall Smithies, just outside Leeds, then that would be about fifty-five miles back to the south-east. If we followed Ernest Raymond and equated Whitcross with Lascar Cross on the Hallam Moors, in the Peak District outside Sheffield, then that would be about forty miles south of our site for Thornfield. Finally, from Thornfield it is thirty miles to Ferndean; and so it is also from Rydings to Wycoller Hall, the ruined house that may have helped Ferndean to be imagined. Wycoller is also only ten miles

18 *JE*, Ch. 10.
19 *JE*, Ch. 21.
20 *JE*., Chs 27 and 28.

from the Brontës' home at Haworth: perhaps Brontë liked to think of Jane ending up nearby.

Obviously these equations are very approximate. The imagined places are not the real ones, and even their names dislodge them from any actual geography, locating them in a gently symbolic landscape of gates, woods, thorns, a marsh, a moor and a cross. Nevertheless, looking at a map of England does give us a sense of the kind of span that is crossed in the novel. It makes sense to pin Lowood to Cowan Bridge, in the North-West, near the Lancashire coast, since that episode is so tightly rooted in the harrowing facts that Brontë lived through at the Clergy Daughters' School. And Whitcross and Moor House must be somewhere in the Peak District, in the North Midlands, given the topography as well as the likely equation of 'S—' (mentioned in Chapter 31) with Sheffield. Between these two extremities, which are in fact only a hundred miles apart, we could amuse ourselves by sliding the other locations around on the map, to try to make the distances between them match up. Or, better, we could realise that the journeyings in the novel are simply longer, more expansive, than those that Brontë herself took between the loosely equivalent actual English places. *Jane Eyre* does not inhabit a realist geography, but a more malleable kind of imaginative landscape. The novel's major locations, encountered in sequence, are also stages of life: early childhood; school; adulthood and romance; despair and an alternative future; back to the ruins of romance and a more secure, because damaged, living-on of the relationship. Various textualities flow into these locations, shaping them and giving them significance. There is the textuality of Brontë's life, as we have begun to see. Part of the reason why Thornfield is so far from everywhere is that the emotional experience Brontë is most channelling in these pages took place further away still, in Brussels: her exhilarating, heartbreaking attachment to her married French teacher M. Heger. This is also why there is so much French spoken at Thornfield. There are also literary models, of course. Most prominent among them are John Bunyan's *The Pilgrim's Progress*, with its Christian journey through a series of allegorical locations (including a gate, a 'slough' — or marsh — and several houses); Jonathan Swift's *Gulliver's Travels* (which the young Jane likes to read), in which the protagonist journeys from one anthropologically instructive fantasy location to another, each imagined as a different country; the *Arabian Nights* (also read by the young Jane), with its succession of different stories and settings, all linked in the person of the spellbinding woman narrator; and Dickens's *Oliver Twist*, in which the protagonist (a young boy) makes a long journey to London where he encounters two possible homes and associated family-style attachments — one disreputable, the other genteel — and moves back and forth between them.

So far, we have seen the significant geography imagined in the novel blending elements from realistic topography, biographical experience and literary analogues. These factors all contribute to *Jane Eyre*'s distinctive, and unusually complex, generic makeup, with its blend of precise observation, fierce personal feeling and occasionally fantastical narrative developments. But there is also another dimension to the world within the book, one which it shares with other nineteenth-century British novels such as Austen's *Mansfield Park*, Thackeray's *Vanity Fair* or Dickens's *Great Expectations*. This is created by the connections drawn between locations that are book's focal points and places elsewhere — in Europe and especially in the British Empire — which are all, in various ways, brought home to the English setting. The presence of Adèle at Thornfield Hall is the first prominent instance of this dynamic. Whatever her biological relationship to Mr Rochester, she is there as witness to his dissolute time in Paris, itself (as we later learn) only part of a decade-long, Don Juan-esque romp around Europe.[21] As a figure, Adèle is a kind of prelude to the revelation of Bertha Rochester's presence in the house: both the girl and the woman have been brought there from elsewhere, and are — as Rochester sees it — left-overs from rejected phases of his life. But Bertha is, of course, from further away — from Spanish Town, Jamaica — and is much more fiercely rejected than Adèle, both by Mr Rochester and by the narrator. If the girl is a channel for Francophobia, Bertha is charged with the racist attitudes, and fear and guilt about Empire, which I discussed in Chapter I. St John Rivers, with his evangelizing mission somewhere in India, is another kind of embodiment of those attitudes, and another textual manifestation of fear and guilt. Where Bertha is said to be 'incapable of being led to anything higher', St John is presented as labouring on behalf of people subject to the 'informal' Indian empire of that period, clearing 'their painful way to improvement'.[22] The novel does not wholly support his endeavour (after all, Jane chooses a different path), but it does not wholly condemn it either (St John writes the book's last words).

21 *JE*, Ch. 27.
22 *JE*, Chs 27 and 38.

These two conflicting figures, Bertha and St John, who take contrasting journeys to and from virtually opposite points on the globe — Jamaica and India — show the strange, profoundly uneasy and yet also merely gestural way in which *Jane Eyre* sees locations in England as being intimately joined to places elsewhere in the world. As Susan Meyer has pointed out, the fact that Jane's inheritance comes from an uncle who is a wine-merchant in Madeira, that is, someone who is embedded in imperial structures of trade, leaves her with wealth from a troubled source, just like the money that came to Mr Rochester from Bertha's family, the Masons. In fact, this uncle, John Eyre, is the first of all the emissaries of Empire in the book, turning up, as Mrs Reed's maid Bessie tells the story in Chapter 10, to look for Jane at Gateshead just a year or so after she had moved to Lowood. The account is brief, and seems inconsequential, so the connection may not strike a reader as significant until its consequences play out much later in the novel. But its uncanny intimacy with Jane, and indeed eery joining of Jane and Bertha, is suggested right from the start by the phonetic play around the location of John Eyre's business: Mad-eira. Of course many other flickers of suggestiveness have been noticed in Jane's surname: 'air', 'ire', even 'Eire' in the sense of Ireland. Nevertheless, it is striking that the other dominant surnames in the novel attach characters physically to a landscape, in the same vein as the names of the houses: Rivers, Reed, Roch(rock)ester, Burns, even Temple. But Eyre floats weirdly free, and can attach itself, not only to Madeira but to that 'eyrie' in the 'Andes' which — as we saw in Chapter I — is called to mind, much later on in the novel, by Bertha's cry. So this fourth, world-spanning dimension of the significant geography imagined in the book cuts across the others, opening yawning spatial voids and throwing sudden bridges across them.

How does this complicated envisaging of location within the novel matter to the translations? In several ways, one of which occurs when there is a conjunction between a translator's geographical situation and a place imagined in the novel. Ulrich Timme Kragh and Abhishek Jain, in Essay 1, have already explored how writers, film-makes and translators in India have responded, in their re-makings of the novel, to the role of India within it. Another example will appear in Essay 5, by Andrés Claro, with its analysis of the reactions of Spanish-speaking translators in South America to the representations of Bertha Rochester and of Spanish Town, Jamaica. A further consideration is how the English place-names are, or are not, translated. Studying European

Portuguese translations, Ana Teresa Marques dos Santos has noted a consistent practice of reproducing the English names, rather than attempting to render their significance. This means that their gentle symbolism is pushed into the background (though of course some readers of Portuguese translations will also have sufficient knowledge of English and be able to register it); and instead 'Thornfield', 'Rivers' and the rest become insistent reminders of the book's primary location in England.[23] This kind of change alters location and genre together, shifting the book a bit more in the direction of documentary realism.

Genre is the clearest bridge between location in the book and the location of the book. How places are imagined is a key part of the novel's generic identity; and the novel's identity affects where it sits in the culture it is published into, and how readers relate to it. Book covers signal genre and often they do so by choosing to represent particular scenes and locations from the novel. Our last set of maps, the Covers Maps, enables you to explore this phenomenon in conjunction with the locations where the books were published.

Arabic Danish Dutch Estonian

Finnish French German Greek

23 Marques dos Santos presented these findings as part of her collaboration in the Prismatic *Jane Eyre* project.

Hebrew

Hungarian

Japanese

Persian

Polish

Brazilian Portuguese

Romanian

Slovenian

Spanish

Swedish

Turkish

These maps are necessarily partial: often we were not able to source cover images; and the covers of most of the earlier translations were of course unrevealingly plain. Nevertheless, working with these maps, we can discern international trends: favourite images for *Jane Eyre* covers are a solitary woman (often the 1850 George Richmond pencil portrait of Brontë); a solitary woman reading or writing; a romantic couple; a young woman with a big house in the distance; the house burning; and many variants of Jane's first encounter with Rochester when he falls from his horse. Both the house and the landscape are sometimes plausibly English and sometimes not. We can observe the global influence of film versions and BBC adaptations, which bring with them their own visualisations: a cover inspired by the 1943 Robert Stevenson film with Orson Welles appears in Buenos Aires in 1944; the 1996 Zeffirelli version prompts covers in Paris (1996), Sâo Paolo (1996) and Istanbul (2007); and the 2006 BBC series with Ruth Wilson and Toby Stephens leaves its mark again in Istanbul (2009), as well as in Colombo (2015) and Giza (2016). And we can also discern national trends: Germany has a long-standing preference for the solitary woman, while the romance scenes prominent on the covers of Persian translations announce a significant shifting of the book into the genre of romance, as part of its re-location in Persian literary culture: Kayvan Tahmasebian and Rebecca Ruth Gould explore this development in Essay 8.

Partial as they are, the Covers Maps help one to shift perspective from the global view of our other maps, and register the look of the individual books, and thereby sense something of the market conditions in which they were produced and the presence of the people involved in the design and production process. Of the translators themselves, generally very little is known. About eighty of them are anonymous and, of the others, it is only in rare cases such as Marion Gilbert (French), Juan González-Blanco de Luaces (Spanish), Munīr' al-Baʿalbakī (Arabic) and Yu JongHo [유 종호] (Korean) that more than the barest details are recoverable — as you can discover from the selected brief biographies provided in the appendix, Lives of Some Translators, below.

Likewise, much detail about the cultural location of translations — where they are being read, and the uses to which they are being put — is necessarily unknowable. For instance, it is only by chance, and thanks to the mediating work of Sowon S. Park, that I came to know of Seo SangHoon, who works at Reigate Grammar School Vietnam in Hanoi, and who uses *Jane Eyre*, in the Korean translations by Ju JongHo and Park JungSook, to teach students about narrative voice and, as he says, 'why we should accept information around us critically'.[24] There are innumerable other instances of the enterprise of *Jane Eyre* translation finding distinct significance in particular locations. Some of the most striking are gathered in the sequence of essays that follows this chapter. Andrés Claro traces differences between the Spanish translations published in Spain and in Latin America, focusing especially on issues of gender, race and empire (like Essay 1, this essay is necessarily long, given the wide range of material considered). Eleni Philippou shows how the British Council supported the translation of *Jane Eyre* in Greece as part of an exertion of soft power during the Cold War. Annmarie Drury explores the complex

24 Seo SangHoon, email to the author, 09.13, 20 March 2020. Quoted with permission.

of reasons behind the lack of *Jane Eyre* translations into Swahili and most other African languages both during the period of the British Empire and after. And Kayvan Tahmasebian and Rebecca Ruth Gould uncover the intricate relationship between *Jane Eyre* and ideas of romance in twentieth-century Iran, which accounts for the surprising surge in translations that followed the 1979 revolution.

Works Cited

For the translations of *Jane Eyre* referred to, please see the List of Translations at the end of this book.

Diario de la Marina (Habana: s.n., 1850–51).

Ethnologue, https://www.ethnologue.com/about/language-maps

Heilbron, Johan, 'Towards a Sociology of Translation: Book Translations as a Cultural World-System', *European Journal of Social Theory*, 2, 4 (1999) 429–44.

Kalifa, Dominique and Marie-Ève Thérenty, 'Introduction', https://www.medias19.org/publications/les-mysteres-urbains-au-xixe-siecle-circulations-transferts-appropriations/introduction

Laachir, Karima, Sara Marzagora and Francesca Orsini, 'Significant Geographies: In Lieu of World Literature', *Journal of World Literature*, 3.3 (2018), 290–310, https://doi.org/10.1163/24056480-00303005

Franco Moretti, *Atlas of the European Novel, 1800–1900* (London and New York: Verso, 1998).

El Progreso (Santiago de Chile: Imprenta del Progreso, 7th February – 4th April, 1850).

Reynolds, Matthew and Giovanni Pietro Vitali, 'Mapping and Reading a World of Translations', *Digital Modern Languages Open*, 1 (2021), http://doi.org/10.3828/mlo.v0i0.375

Wallerstein, Immanuel Maurice, *The Modern World System*, 4 vols (Berkeley, University of California Press, 2011).

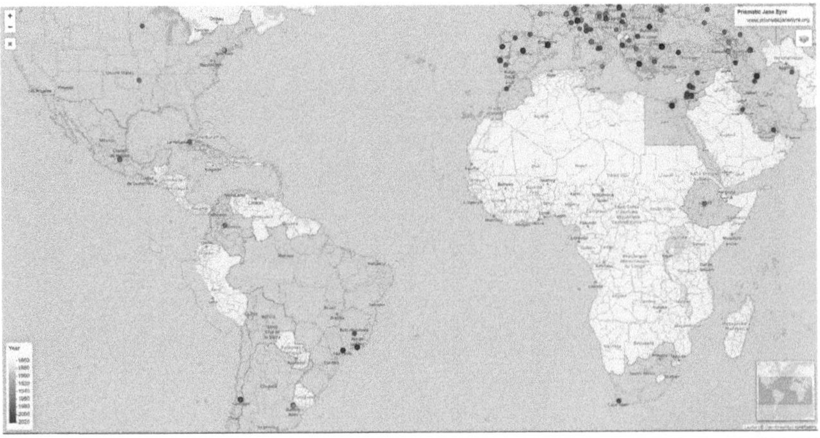

The General Map
https://digitalkoine.github.io/je_prismatic_generalmap/
Created by Giovanni Pietro Vitali; © OpenStreetMap contributors

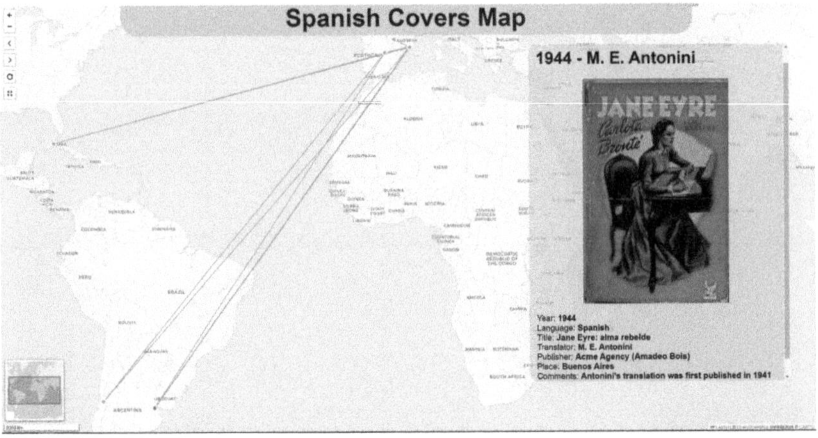

The Spanish Covers Map
https://digitalkoine.github.io/spanish_storymap/
Researched by Andrés Claro; created by Giovanni Pietro Vitali and Simone Landucci

5. Representation, Gender, Empire
Jane Eyre in Spanish

Andrés Claro

I cannot call them handsome — they were too pale and grave for the word [...], like people consulting a dictionary to aid them in the task of translation. This scene was as silent as if all the figures had been shadows [...], not one word was intelligible to me; for it was in an unknown tongue [...]; it was only like a stroke of sounding brass to me — conveying no meaning [...].

'Is there ony country where they talk i' that way?' [...]

'Yes [...] — a far larger country than England; where they talk in no other way.'

'Well, for sure case, I knawn't how they can understand t' one t' other: and if either o' ye went there, ye could tell what they said, I guess?'

'We could probably tell something of what they said, but not all'

C. Brontë, *Jane Eyre*[1]

Where meaning is many-faceted, language can become prismatic as easily as it can become crystal-clear — the meanings projected by one and the same form of words can splay into a spectrum of colour without loss of definition [...]. The first question, then, would seem to be, not whether the poet can bring a prismatic splay of distinct meanings, but why he does it and why we like it.

W. Nowottny, *The Language Poets Use*[2]

1 *JE*, Ch. 28.

2 Winifred Nowottny, *The Language Poets Use* (London: Athlone Press, 1996), p. 147.

https://doi.org/10.11647/OBP.0319.09

Translations of *Jane Eyre* in Latin America and Spain: The Context of their First Widespread Impact in the 1940s

'As far as I can see, it would be wiser and more judicious if you were to take to yourself the original at once'.[3] Jane Eyre's recommendation to St John could never have become the motto of Spanish and Latin American readers of British novels since the mid-nineteenth century. For them, for reasons that range from a constitutive relationship with the linguistic and cultural fabric making up the multiform literature and mestizo ethos of Latin America to what has been called modern Spain's relative cultural dependency on its northern neighbours, translation has played and continues to play a decisive and inescapable role. Thus, it is not altogether surprising to find that an indirect Spanish version of *Jane Eyre* appeared in Santiago, Chile and Havana, Cuba, as early as 1850, i.e., only three years after the first edition of the English original, but also four decades before a first direct Spanish rendering appeared in New York (1889), and almost a century before several complete Spanish translations done directly from the English text began to have a widespread impact on both sides of the Atlantic from the 1940s onwards.[4]

Indeed, whereas translations of the novel up to the start of the Second World War can be counted on the fingers of one hand, from the early 1940s onwards there was a veritable burgeoning of versions

3 *JE*, Ch. 32.

4 The first translation of *Jane Eyre* in Spanish, published without naming the translator as *Juana Eyre. Memorias de una aya* [*Jane Eyre: Memoirs of a governess*], was initially printed in Paris and then serialised in newspapers in Santiago and Havana. It was an indirect version based on the French adaptation produced a year earlier by Old Nick (P. É. Daurand Forgues): see Chapter I above for discussion, and the List of Translations below for publication details. Two decades later, an even freer version was published in Spain in the form of a play by F. Morena y Vals, *Juana Eyre. Drama en cuatro actos y un prólogo* [*Jane Eyre: A drama in four acts and a prologue*] (Barcelona: Manero, 1869). Another two decades would pass before the first direct and fairly complete version of the novel was brought out in Spanish, published in the United States as *Juana Eyre* (New York: Appleton & Co., 1889). Since then, at least twenty versions have been published in Latin America and as many in Spain, starting with *Juana Eyre* (Barcelona: Mentora, 1928) and *Juana Eyre* (Barcelona: Juventud, 1928). Most of these versions have been reprinted numerous times by different publishers as the rights have been transferred or lapsed, so that there have been more than a hundred editions to date.

and editions, both in Latin America, with particularly active centres in Buenos Aires (e.g., M. E. Antonini's popular version for Acme Agency in 1941, marketed suggestively from 1944 onwards under a title that translates as *Jane Eyre, Rebel Soul*) and in Spain, with Barcelona clearly predominating over Madrid (e.g., J. G. de Luaces' popular version for Iberia first published in 1943). Certainly, this proliferation of *Jane Eyre* translations can be explained in part by the renewed prestige acquired by English language and culture after the Second World War. But it started somewhat earlier, and can be put down as well, and especially, to differentiated local processes in the Latin American and Spanish contexts that led to the promotion of foreign literature generally and this English novel in particular. For whereas the translation boom that began in Spain in the early 1940s, in the face of censorship and abrupt stifling of local creative expression by the Franco dictatorship (1939–1975), can be understood as a literary compensation and even an implicit alibi serving to avoid oppression and write between the lines, not least in relation to the Francoist National-Catholic programme and the domestic role for women that it promoted, the *Jane Eyre* translation boom in Latin America was part of an explicit programme of opening up to and interacting with foreign languages and literatures as a way of creating a local ethos and literature emancipated from Spanish colonialism, especially in the young republics of the Southern Cone, where the novel became widely known at the very time the female vote and other civil rights for women were being secured.

As regards the context of reception in Spain, then, it should be recalled that Franco's dictatorship not only began by abolishing a number of progressive reforms implemented by the previous Republican constitution, such as freedom of worship, equal rights between the sexes, and thence universal suffrage, but also set up a powerful and energetic system of censorship that directly impacted literary work and books, with side effects for translation. First of all, in what can be seen as a kind of *sui generis* reissuing of the *Index librorum prohibitorum et derogatorum* of the old Spanish Inquisition, Francoist censorship banned all kinds of works and authors seen as criticising the National-Catholic movement or threatening its orthodox imaginary, including not only pacifist, anti-fascist, Marxist, and separatist writings, but also theosophical and Masonic works, together with any dealing openly with sexual matters (whether scientific or otherwise) or including explicitly sexual scenes; in short, a whole array of works that, if encountered, were to be destroyed. Then, unpublished works had to undergo prior censorship before they could be published and distributed, to evaluate them in terms of respect for and compatibility with the ideology of the regime and dogmas of the Church, with verdicts that could range from the removal of certain passages to prohibition of the entire work. Thus, in a country where many of the leading women and men of literature, the arts, and the sciences had disappeared, either killed during the Civil War or forced into exile, among those who remained in Spain translation became not just a means of economic survival in extremely hard times, but also a possible way of exercising literary activity despite censorship, and even of establishing an alibi of anonymity that made it possible to write between the lines, dividing readerships into accomplices and dupes, creating complicity in resistance, a negative freedom by way of subtle gestures that made it impossible for the censors and other guardians of the law to arrive at forthright rulings. This partly explains the seeming paradox of a proliferation of translations amid the acute crisis of Spanish post-war economy, culture and literary production, with most of them being made from the European languages that the literati of the time were familiar with, and most particularly English (to the relative detriment of French and German, which had been dominant before the War), a proliferation that unsettled the guardians of orthodoxy on more than one occasion.[5]

As regards Latin America, the political and literary context in which translations and editions of *Jane Eyre* began to be multiplied and widely circulated was quite different. Certainly, the new relative predominance of English can be seen here as well, being further associated with the growing political power, influence, and intervention of the United States. But from the late 1930s to the late 1960s (i.e., before the era of North American-backed military dictatorships), the young republics of Latin America, independent of Spain for just over a century, embarked upon a period of relative industrial progress and new political, cultural, and literary awareness, where translation was

5 For the context of translation in Spain during Franco's dictatorship, see *Traducción y censura inglés-español: 1939–1985*, ed. by Rosa Rabadán (León: Universidad de León, 2000). A broader context is provided by Ángel Llorente, *Arte e ideología en el franquismo, 1936–1951* (Madrid: Visor, 1995). For a particular emphasis on the Spanish translation of *Jane Eyre* by J. G. de Luaces (1943) in this context, see Marta Ortega Sáez's 'Traducciones del franquismo en el mercado literario español contemporáneo: el caso de *Jane Eyre* de Juan G. de Luaces' (unpublished doctoral thesis, University of Barcelona, 2013).

often encouraged and understood explicitly as a necessary process in view of what Latin America's literature and culture had been and ought to be, including as regards its emancipation and differentiation from Spain itself. This explicit awareness of translation as constitutive to the Latin American ethos can be traced from period to period and from north to south: at least as early as the reflections on the mestizo constitution which appear in the ambiguity of malinchism in Mexico (where a symbol of foundational linguistic and political betrayal of the native metamorphoses into a symbol of formative heterogeneity and female liberation from oppression),[6] through the romantic republican project of the mid-nineteenth century (which sought to break away from the Spanish substratum and transform the language and culture of the southern countries by grafting other languages and cultures onto them),[7] to the more recent conceptions of an anthropophagic relationship inspired by Amazonian culture (where what is posited is a relationship of capture, digestion, and assimilation of European,

6 Regarding malinchism, see for example Octavio Paz's well-known interpretation, 'Los hijos de la Malinche', in *El laberinto de la soledad* (Mexico City: Fondo de Cultura Económica, 1989), pp. 59–80. For its repercussions and interpretations, see *La Malinche, sus padres y sus hijos*, ed. by Margo Glantz (Mexico City: Taurus, 2001). For a historical overview, see also Juan Francisco Maura, *Women in the Conquest of the Americas* (New York: Peter Lang, 1997), and Sandra Messinger Cypress, *La Malinche in Mexican Literature: From History to Myth* (Austin: University of Texas Press, 1991).

7 See Juan María Gutiérrez, 'Discurso Inaugural del Salón Literario' (1837), in Marieta Gargatagli and Nora Catelli (eds.), *El tabaco que fumaba Plinio. Escenas de la traducción en España y América: relatos, leyes y reflexiones sobre los otros* (Barcelona: Serbal, 1998), pp. 360–86. Thus, Gutiérrez summarizes: 'Spanish science and literature being negligible, then, we need to divorce ourselves from them completely and emancipate ourselves in this respect from peninsular traditions, as we succeeded in doing in politics, when we proclaimed our freedom. We are still joined by the close, strong tie of the language; but this should loosen day by day as we enter into the intellectual movement of the advanced peoples of Europe. For this it is necessary for us to familiarize ourselves with foreign languages and make it our constant study to acclimatize ours to anything good, intelligent and beautiful that might arise in these'. Juan Bautista Alberdi would likewise write: 'Have no fear of mingling races and languages. Out of Babel, out of chaos, the South American nationality will arise some clear, bright day' (*Las bases*, Buenos Aires: La Facultad, 1915, p. 94). For an evaluation of this stance on emancipation from Spain by way of other European languages and cultures, including its violence towards the indigenous substratum, see Beatriz Sarlo, 'Oralidad y lenguas extranjeras: el conflicto en la literatura argentina durante el primer tercio del siglo XX', in Beatriz Sarlo and Carlos Altamirano, *Ensayos argentinos: de Sarmiento a la vanguardia* (Buenos Aires: Siglo XXI, 2006), pp. 253–69.

Oriental, and more broadly universal cultural strength in pursuit of local prowess).[8] Amid this multiplicity of scenes — all very different, of course, and all complex in themselves and not without violence, but also evincing this common denominator of a constitutive translation experience — if the focus is narrowed to the River Plate context whence *Jane Eyre* was disseminated in the 1940s, it is worth considering Borges' well-known admonitions in 'The Argentine Writer and Tradition' (1951), a good synecdoche for the simultaneously constitutive and emancipatory role explicitly assigned in the Southern Cone to the process of passing through the foreign. Activating his own sense of paradox, Borges reviews and rebuts three common claims about what literature and culture ought to be in Argentina and South America generally:

> [1] *The idea that Argentine poetry should abound in distinctive Argentine features and Argentine local colour seems to me a mistake* [...]. The Argentine cult of local colour is a recent European cult that nationalists should reject as foreign.
>
> [2] *It is said that there is a tradition to which we Argentine writers must adhere, and that tradition is Spanish literature* [.... But] Argentine history can be defined without inaccuracy as a desire for separation from Spain, as a voluntary distancing from Spain.
>
> [3] *This opinion is that we, the Argentines, are detached from the past* [...]. However [...,] I believe that our tradition is the whole of Western culture, and I also believe that we have a right to this tradition, a greater right than the inhabitants of one or another Western nation may have [...]. I believe that Argentines, South Americans in general, [...] can deal with all European themes, deal with them without superstition, with an irreverence that may have, and is already having, happy consequences

8 Among the anthropophagous manifestos, see especially Haroldo De Campos, *De la razón antropofágica y otros ensayos* (Madrid: Siglo XXI, 2000), esp. 'De la razón antropofágica: diálogo y diferencia en la cultura brasilera', pp. 1–23; and 'De la traducción como creación y como crítica', pp. 185–203. The background to this position on translation can be found in Osvaldo de Andrade, 'Manifiesto Antropofágico', in Jorge Schwartz (ed.), *Las vanguardias latinoamericanas: textos programáticos y críticos* (Mexico City: Fondo de Cultura Económica, 2002), pp. 173–80. More broadly, see Osvaldo De Andrade, *Escritos antropofágicos* (Buenos Aires: Corregidor, 2001). Lastly, for a wide-ranging study of this complex opening via translation in Brazilian and Spanish American literature, see Horácio Costa, *Mar abierto: ensayos sobre literatura brasileña, portuguesa e hispanoamericana* (Mexico City: Fondo de Cultura Económica, 1998), esp. 'El centro está en todas partes', pp. 437–46.

> [...]. And so I say again that we must be fearless and take the whole universe as our inheritance.[9]

Certainly, setting out from the paradoxical aesthetics of 'originality as rewriting' and '*finis terrae* cosmopolitanism' that his particular vantage point on the River Plate allows him, Borges omits the dimension of conflict that has often been part of the translation experience in Latin America, ignoring the violence perpetrated on that which resists assimilation, as has often been the case with indigenous languages and cultures, while unilaterally emphasising the outlook of sceptical tolerance that a large-scale translation movement encourages. But Borges' awareness of the extent to which South American literature and culture should be thought of as a journey through the foreign transcending any boundary between traditions and continents is characteristic of the women and men of letters of the Southern Cone, and particularly those of Buenos Aires (a city shaped by a succession of rapid and large-scale immigrations of Italians, Russians, Jews, Central Europeans, Asians, and others superadded to substrates of Spanish and indigenous descent), further resonating in this particular case on the cultural scene of the 'translation machine' that was *Sur* magazine, where Borges' text was published.[10] Since from the late 1930s onwards, everyone in South America who could translate did so; and everyone, whether they translated literature or not, understood each other through access to the foreign in translation, whether this meant intelligibility across the different languages that tend to be hastily grouped under the label of Latin American Spanish (themselves the product of different genealogies and translational emphases over the course of the particular history of each of their regions), or literary versions such as the ones from *Jane Eyre* that concern us here, which became accessible to a wide and varied readership extending far

9 Jorge Luis Borges, *Obras completas*, 4 vols (Buenos Aires: Emecé, 1974–96), I (1989), pp. 267–74. My emphases.

10 'El escritor argentino y la tradición', a lecture originally given by Borges at the Colegio Libre de Estudios Superiores in 1951, following an earlier version in *Cursos y conferencias* (1953), was published in *Sur* magazine in 1955, after which Borges incorporated it into his work *Discusión* (originally published in 1932 and reissued in 1957), where the essay would find its final place. For this immediate context of *Sur* as a 'translation machine', see especially Beatriz Sarlo, *La máquina cultural. Maestras, traductores y vanguardistas* (Buenos Aires: Seix Barral, 1998). Additionally see Beatriz Sarlo, *Borges, un escritor en las orillas* (Buenos Aires: Seix Barral, 2007).

beyond the narrow circle of the polyglot elite to which someone like Borges himself belonged.

In this sense, as one moves from the general and differentiated outline of the contexts of reception in Spain and Latin America to the characteristics of the translations of *Jane Eyre* themselves in relation to their readerships, one can add that the more than thirty Spanish versions and hundreds of editions of the novel brought out since the 1940s on the two sides of the Atlantic reveal at least three different general approaches, manifested in decisions pertaining to both content and style, and driven by literary, commercial, and ideological constraints. That is, in what already constitutes a first, very general instance of literary and cultural prismatisation, one can distinguish between: (i) 'relatively unabridged translations', which preserve most of the literal surface of the novel, permitting a line-by-line comparison with the original; (ii) 'edited compressed versions', which often drop or merge sentences, cut passages and sometimes redistribute chapters, reducing the novel by up to half its length; and (iii) 'highly condensed paraphrases', which rewrite the novel as didactic material, reducing it to less than a third of its original length. While in each particular case it is possible to observe the extent to which excisions, as well as changes of style and content, are driven by considerations ranging from the ideological to the commercial, these three different, recurring approaches testify to a settled belief on the part of publishers that the novel could have just as much success as (i) a classic of world literature in the form of a female *Bildungsroman*, (ii) a romantic best-seller for the general public, or (iii) an edifying tale for the young.[11]

11 This general prismatisation is also made clear by an examination of some of the paratextual elements, starting with the changes to the title in the post-war years, which range from *Juana Eyre: alma rebelde* [*Jane Eyre: Rebel Soul*] (Buenos Aires: Acme Agency, 1944) in Latin America to *Juana Eyre. Una obra maestra rebosante de ternura y bondad, cuya emoción sabe llegar al alma. Creación que labró la reputación de su autora, popularizándola en todos los países* [*Jane Eyre. A masterpiece overflowing with tenderness and goodness that can move the very soul. A creation that established the author's reputation, making her popular in all countries*] (Madrid: Revista Literaria, 1945) in Spain. No less significant are the cover designs, which run the gamut from classical Victorian portraits of an educated lady to portrayals of female determination in situations of adversity and romance, right up to the gothic imaginary associated with adventure. In fact, while the same main emphases and broad changes recur in cover styles time and again, it can be seen that the covers of the post-war editions (1940s and 1950s) tend to stress gothic mystery/aesthetics, a Victorian female ethos and values, determination in adversity,

Finally, moving on from the foregoing introductory and contextual observations to the transcendental perspective on language that will determine many of the analyses to follow — i.e., to a point of view that interrogates linguistic and literary behaviour as the formal condition of possibility for the representation of reality and experience — it is worth clarifying that the aim in what follows is not to denounce the translative limits that the various modes of passage of *Jane Eyre* into Spanish reveal, but to evaluate the levels of refraction between the English and Spanish languages, literatures, and cultures arising in the process: the possibilities opened up or not by the formal insemination and the semantic afterlife involved in these different forms of translation, which, when strong and achieved, are capable both of changing modes of representation in the receiving language and of generating a backward effect on the original, unfolding its signification over time.

These formal inseminations and prismatisations can already be noticed to a certain degree at a stylistic micro-level, as can be seen in the next section ("The literary synthesis and representation of reality: evaluating the recreation of lexical, syntactic, musical, imagistic, and contextual forms of meaning"), while examining the variety of significant behaviours that the Spanish language takes on as it either echoes or, very often, departs from the English original lexicon, syntax, verbal music, verbal images or contextual forms of meaning, with the corresponding forms of experience and representation that they give rise to.

---

and some romance. Those of the 1960s and 1970s add pre-Raphaelite aesthetics and a clear emphasis on adventure and romance in contemporary terms, with the iconography for Jane shifting from virtue to eros. Those of the 1980s and 1990s add at least three new iconographies, tailored to the readership targeted: (1) classical portrayal (making it clear that this is a classic of world literature, serious writing), (2) film imagery (especially scenes from Zeffirelli's adaptation, promoting the idea of an entertainment classic), and (3) a didactic approach, when children are the intended readership (abridged versions). Those from the 2000s and 2010s show a new relative emphasis on solitude and suffering (Jane portrayed alone, meditative). As a final contrast, it is worth noticing that in the last half century the novel has not only been frequently published in the 'classic' collections of the large publishing houses — including Colección Obras Maestras (Iberia), Clásicos Universales (Planeta), Letras Universales (Cátedra), Colección Centenario (Espasa), Grandes Clásicos (Mondadori) and Clásicos (Ediciones B) — but has also been adapted as English-language teaching material, in 'English Graded Readers. Simplified Fiction Series, Grade 4' (Pearson Educación) and 'Richmond Readers' (Santillana).

But it is above all while looking from a broader, contextual and cultural point of view on the impact of *Jane Eyre* in Latin America as compared to Spain (as we do in the subsequent two sections under the rubrics "Gender refractions: human individuality as feminist emancipation" and "Empire refractions: from savage slave to gothic ghost"), that one can see how the afterlife and refraction of the novel, starting with those of its crucial gender and colonial motifs, become particularly significant. Especially bearing in mind that Spanish-language versions of *Jane Eyre* became popular at a time when the women's vote was being fought for and achieved in the newly independent Latin American republics, which had succeeded only a century earlier in shaking off the imperial yoke of Spain, where Franco's National-Catholic programme was, during this same period, pursuing the restoration of so-called 'traditional family values'.

The Literary Synthesis and Representation of Reality: Evaluating the Recreation of Lexical, Syntactic, Musical, Imagistic and Contextual Forms of Meaning

As one focuses on a comparative analysis of the ways the characteristic signifying behaviours of Charlotte Brontë's English are rendered in the different Spanish translations — taking sample passages from the original that present distinctive organic textures to evaluate the difficulties encountered and the re-creations devised in the unabridged, compressed, and highly condensed versions — the aim is not to arrive at a value judgement of the quality of the translations or the translators, much the less to list blunders or significant losses relative to the original, but to evaluate prismatisation from a transcendental point of view, shedding light on the refractions arising out of these encounters between the English and Spanish languages, literatures, and cultures, and pointing to the possibilities of experience or literary representation they do or do not give rise to.

As a basis for the analyses that follow, we have selected seven of the most published and read translations of the last eighty years, produced for different readerships and purposes by translators situated differently in place, ideological stance, and time. To begin with, three unabridged translations (marked as 'A' alongside the translator's name and date of publication in references below): (1) María Fernanda de Pereda's 1947 *Jane Eyre* (Madrid: Aguilar, 780 pages, with at least fifteen editions since); (2) Carmen Martín Gaite's 1999 *Jane Eyre* (Barcelona: Alba, 656 pages, with at least six editions since); and (3) Toni Hill's 2009 *Jane Eyre* (Barcelona: Mondadori, 608 pages, with at least six editions since). Then, there are the two pioneering and most widely read compressed versions, published in Latin America and Spain just two years apart in the early forties (marked as 'B' alongside the translator's name and date of publication in references below): (4) M. E. Antonini's 1941 *Jane Eyre* (Buenos Aires: Acme Agency, 287 pages, with at least five editions in the next ten years as *Jane Eyre, Alma Rebelde*, and many more official editions and pirate versions since); and (5) Juan de Luaces' 1943 *Jane Eyre* (Barcelona: Iberia-J. Gil, 518 pages, with at least thirty-five editions since). Lastly, the selection is completed by two highly condensed paraphrases for children, both of which rely heavily on Antonini's earlier compressed version and have been published on both sides of the Atlantic over the years (marked as 'C' alongside the translator's name and date of publication in references below): (6) Jesús Sánchez Díaz's 1974 *Jane Eyre* (Santiago de Chile: Paulinas, 191 pages) and (7) Silvia Robles' 1989 further condensed adaptation (*Jane Eyre*, Santiago de Chile: Zig Zag, 123 pages). Thus, while the selection concentrates on examples of the three different forms of passage into Spanish identified that have been repeatedly published and had large readerships, it also offers a broad spectrum as regards the individuality and positioning of the translators in the Spanish and Latin American contexts: from the Catalan Republican Juan de Luaces (tr. 1943), a promising writer and literary critic before the Civil War who, after a number of vicissitudes, including censorship and prison, became the most prolific of the post-war Spanish translators, to María Fernanda de Pereda (tr. 1947), who worked in close contact with the orthodox Madrid establishment; from M. E. Antonini (tr. 1941), who essentially translated adventure books for the young (*Buffalo Bill*, *Robin Hood*) for a popular collection issued by Acme Agency in Buenos Aires, to Jesús Sánchez Díaz (tr. 1974) in Spain, who translated mainly educational religious literature for the young for the Catholic publisher Ediciones Paulinas; from the very well-known prize-winning Spanish novelist Carmen Martín Gaite (tr. 1999), born in 1925 and associated with the Madrid literary world, to the psychologist and successful author of police novels Toni Hill (tr. 2009), born in Barcelona in 1966.[12]

In what concerns the sample passages highlighted below, the focus has been guided first and foremost by the characteristic elements of Brontë's style in the English original, involving an examination of units of meaning from lexical networks and syntactic forms to the more sophisticated forms of verbal music, verbal imagery, and contextual effects (it being understood that many of these forms of representation overlap and work together), to analyse the way these have been re-created, dropped, or transformed in the different types of Spanish-language versions, with the corresponding impact on literary representation and experience.

Lexical Networks

To start with the most basic aspects, such as the taxonomy of reality produced by lexical networks, there are no drastic difficulties or prismatisations here, insofar as translation is facilitated by the partial overlap between the genealogies of the Spanish and English languages. Thus, most of the keywords that organise the world of the novel (passion, conscience, reason, feelings, resolve, nature, etc.) are translated in the unabridged editions by their usual Spanish synonyms or calques (*pasión*, *consciencia*, *razón*, *sentimientos*, *resolución*, *naturaleza*, etc.), with only some slight allusive refraction, mainly because of the differentiated impact of key concepts in Protestantism such as 'conscience', 'reason', and 'resolve' when it comes to describing female determination in the Latin American and Spanish contexts respectively.

Among the notable exceptions to this lexical straightforwardness are the twofold denotation and symbolism attached to the names that Brontë chooses for many of the characters and places in the novel: Burns, Reed, Temple, Rivers, Lowood, Thornfield. For, notwithstanding that the compressed versions and reduced paraphrases often adopt what was a common practice until the mid-twentieth century of Hispanicising names (as in Juana Eyre by Carlota Brontë), none of the Spanish versions sets out to account for this way in which Brontë charges the place-names with meaning. A partial exception in

12 For more details on these translators, see the appendix 'Lives of Some Translators' below.

respect of Thornfield can be found in Luaces and Gaite, who resort to annotation. Thus, the latter, whose unabridged translation is the only one to provide systematic notes (more than a hundred in all), explains: 'Thornfield significa "campo de espinos". Con esta metáfora volverá a jugar más tarde' ['The name means 'field of thorns'. The author will play on this metaphor again later'] (Gaite 1999A). Luaces, whose compressed edition provides only four footnotes, explains in the third of them: 'Thornfield significa, literalmente, campo de espinos' ['The name literally means field of thorns'] (Luaces 1943B). Luaces will have nothing to say about the 'fiery' allusions of Burns or the 'religious' ones of Temple, however, which is perhaps already revealing of the kind of more-or-less automatic self-censorship that he applied under Franco's dictatorship. For, as he tactically puts it in the prologue to his 1946 Spanish edition of *The Canterbury Tales*, dividing readerships into accomplices, innocents, and dupes: 'I have resisted the itch to multiply footnotes. My contention is that the well-informed rarely need them and that they are of very limited value to the unlearned [...]. In attempting to interpret and unpick all allusions and overtones, the annotator will often err and provide the reader in turn with a misleading picture.'[13]

Syntactic Forms

More dramatic are the transformations at a syntactic level, where forms characteristic of the novel, such as the direct presentation and detailed descriptions that reinforce testimonial and autobiographical experience, the syntactic repetitions and inversions that help to express altered states of mind and perception, and verbal time shifts used to convey emotion, are often simplified, creating a more straightforward texture and a more homogeneous, linear, logical, and distant representation of events.

In the first place, whereas the general style of the novel, although highly elaborate and reflexive, gives the impression of spontaneity — more precisely, whereas this fiction written as first

13 'He huido del prurito de prodigar notas. Sostengo que el informado pocas veces las necesita, y que al indocto le son de muy parco valor [...]. Interpretar y desmenuzar todas las alusiones y sobrentendidos, llevan al anotador a errar con frecuencia, y subsiguientemente a dar al lector una visión falaz de las cosas', Ortega Sáez, 'Traducciones del franquismo en el mercado literario español contemporáneo', p. 123.

person autobiography has a direct, almost epistolary style, often highly detailed in its descriptions, which allows things to be touched and felt — this is an aspect that is not only predictably curtailed in the compressed versions, and simply omitted in the condensed paraphrases, but also modified in the unabridged Spanish translations. Thus, a brief negative description such as 'I know not what dress she had on: it was white and straight; but whether gown, sheet, or shroud, I cannot tell',[14] can become anything from a relatively literal 'No sé cómo era su traje: si vestido, o manto, o mortaja; sólo distinguí que era blanco' (Pereda 1947A),[15] to a condensed version like 'No me fijé cómo iba vestida; sólo sé que llevaba un traje blanco' (Luaces, 1943B: 'I did not pay attention to how she was dressed; I only know she had a white garment on'), to complete omission in Sánchez's and Robles' condensed paraphrases.

Secondly, while the novel's syntax tends to be direct and relatively straightforward, something that heightens the naturalness and spontaneity of the tale and its emotions, confusion and excitement are often staged through parataxis, repetitions, and inversions. These ways of disrupting linear movement are often softened or transformed even in the unabridged Spanish-language versions, which tend to clarify and simplify, transforming such passages of fragmented, heightened, or confused perception into a more straightforward presentation. Take for instance the dramatic tension achieved in a passage describing Bertha's night visit to Jane, who is still unaware of her existence:

> I had risen up in bed, I bent forward: first surprise, then bewilderment, came over me; and then my blood crept cold through my veins. Mr. Rochester, this was not Sophie, it was not Leah, it was not Mrs. Fairfax: it was not — no, I was sure of it, and am still — it was not even that strange woman, Grace Poole.[16]

---

14 JE, Ch. 25.

15 In the other unabridged translations, the passage reads: 'No sé qué clase de vestimenta llevaba, aunque sí que le caía en pliegues rectos y blancos, pero no puedo decirle si era un camisón, una sábana o una mortaja' (Gaite 1999A); 'Ignoro que vestido llevaba: era blanco y recto, pero no puedo decir si era un camisón, una sábana o una mortaja' (Hill 2009A). Antonini's condensed version does not cut much here, although it generalises at the end of the passage: 'No puedo decir cómo iba vestida, sólo sé que llevaba una túnica blanca y estrecha; pero no sé si era un batón u otra forma de vestido' (Antonini 1941B).

16 *JE*, Ch. 25.

Confronted with these syntactic parataxes, inversions, and repetitions, even the unabridged versions, from Pereda (1947) to Gaite (1999), clarify the text, using resources such as logical connectives and explanation. Pereda gives:

> Me incorporé en la cama **y** me incliné hacia adelante, **sintiendo** primero sorpresa, luego duda, **y al darme cuenta de la realidad**, la sangre se me heló en las venas. Señor Rochester, **aquella mujer** no era Sophie, ni Leah, ni la señora Fairfax, ni era, ... **de ello estoy absolutamente segura**..., ni era siquiera esa mujer espeluznante **que se llama** Grace Poole.
>
> (Pereda 1947A: 'I sat up in the bed **and** [adds connective that avoids parataxis] leant forward, **feeling** [adds clarification and link that avoids parataxis] first surprise, then doubt, **and as I became aware of the reality** [interpolates a phrase to explain the confusion which in the original is staged by the behaviour of language], the blood froze in my veins. Mr. Rochester, **that woman** [introduces clarification] was not Sophie, nor Leah, nor Mrs. Fairfax, nor was it, ... **of this I am absolutely sure**... [omits the time juxtaposition between past and present], it was not even that terrifying woman **whose name is** [introduces clarification] Grace Poole'.)[17]

The compressed versions provide similarly logic-oriented clarification; Antonini, for instance, while reducing the passage, explains: 'y la sangre se heló en mis venas, **porque** la persona que estaba allí no era Sophia, ni la señora Fairfax, ni Lía, ni aun esa extraña Gracia Poole' (Antonini 1941B: 'and the blood froze in my veins, **because** the person who was there was not Sophie, nor Mrs Fairfax, nor Leah, nor even that strange Grace Poole').[18]

Finally amid these syntactic characteristics, while *Jane Eyre* is narrated *ex post facto* by the protagonist, using the past tense to recount experiences which are over and done with and of which she knows the outcome, it often shifts to the present to express emotional tension, fading across from the point of view of Jane the narrator to the point of view of Jane the character to make us feel her emotions as

---

17 In a similar vein, Gaite gives: 'Me había incorporado en la cama **y** me incliné **a mirar en aquella dirección**. Primero **me quedé** estupefacta, **pero** enseguida **el pasmo se convirtió** en una perturbación que hizo presa en mí y me heló la sangre. No era Sophie, señor Rochester, ni tampoco Leah, ni la señora Fairfax, no, no lo eran, **estoy segura,** y ni siquiera esa misteriosa Grace Poole, tampoco ella' (Gaite 1999A).

18 Sánchez uses Antonini's solution with *very minor adaptations*: 'y la sangre se heló en mis venas, **porque** la persona que estaba allí no era *Sofía*, ni la señora Fairfax, ni Lía, ni aun *la* extraña Gracia Poole' (Sánchez, 1974C).

they arise. Take for instance a passage that stages Jane's tension when she sees Rochester flirting with Miss Ingram:

> Miss Ingram **placed** herself at her leader's right hand; the other diviners **filled** the chairs on each side of him and her. I **did** not now watch the actors; I no longer **waited** with interest for the curtain to rise; my attention **was absorbed** by the spectators; my eyes, erewhile fixed on the arch, **were** now irresistibly **attracted** to the semicircle of chairs… *I **see** Mr. Rochester turn to Miss Ingram, and Miss Ingram to him; I **see** her incline her head towards him, till the jetty curls almost touch his shoulder and wave against his cheek; I **hear** their mutual whisperings; I **recall** their interchanged glances* (my italics).[19]

These shifts of verbal tense into the present to express emotional tension in the current scene, as in the second half of the excerpt, are re-created by Pereda's unabridged Spanish translation and especially by those of Gaite and Hill.[20] Luaces' condensed version, however, unifies the point of view by keeping all verbs in the past (Antonini and Sánchez cut the whole scene). Luaces renders it:

> Miss Ingram se **colocó** al lado de Rochester. Los demás, en sillas inmediatas, a ambos lados de ellos. Yo **dejé** de mirar a los actores; **había** perdido todo interés por los acertijos y, en cambio, mis ojos se **sentían** irresistiblemente atraídos por el círculo de espectadores… **Ví** a Mr. Rochester inclinarse hacia Blanche para consultarla y a ella acercarse a él hasta que los rizos de la joven casi tocaban los hombros y las mejillas de sus compañeros. Yo **escu*ch*aba** sus cu*ch*i*ch*eos y **notaba** las miradas *q*ue *c*ambiaban entre sí (Luaces 1943B; my italics).[21]

---

19 *JE*, Ch. 18. Emphases my own.

20 The second part of the excerpt becomes: '**Veo** al señor Rochester inclinado hacia su compañera, y a ella inclinada hacia él. **Veo** los rizos de azabache rozar su espalda y sus mejillas, y sigo escuchando los murmullos de su conversación y recordando sus miradas' (Pereda 1947A). '**Veo** al señor Rochester volviéndose hacia la señorita Ingram, y ella lo mismo; la **veo** inclinar la cabeza hacia él hasta que sus rizos negros casi le rozan el hombre y acarician su mejilla, **oigo** sus cuchicheos, **recuerdo** las miradas que se intercambiaron' (Gaite 1999A); '**Veo** al señor Rochester volviéndose hacia la señorita Ingram, y a esta mirándolo; la **veo** inclinar la cabeza hacia él hasta rozar su hombro con los rizos o acariciar con ellos su mejilla; **oigo** sus murmullos de complicidad y **recuerdo** las miradas' (Hill 2009A).

21 Retranslated into English: 'Miss Ingram **placed** herself at Rochester's side. The others, in adjoining chairs, on either side of them. I **ceased** to watch the actors; I **had** lost all interest in the riddles, and instead my eyes **felt** irresistibly attracted to the circle of spectators […]. I **saw** Mr. Rochester lean towards Blanche to consult her, and her draw nearer to him until the young woman's curls almost touched her companion's shoulders and cheeks […]. I **heard** their whisperings and **observed** their interchanged glances.'

The original fade-out from the narration in the present to the intensity of the past emotion, produced by the change in verbal tense, is thus unified in a single viewpoint, a texture without time inflections, where what does stand out though is the vividness of Luaces' onomatopoeias ('es*cuch*aba sus *cuchich*eos'), conveying a musicality which he is often more alert to and re-creates more effectively than the other Spanish translators being considered.

Verbal Music

Even as the Spanish renderings of *Jane Eyre* tend to simplify the syntax, they also, more often than not, do not recreate the verbal music, at least locally. There are some variously prominent exceptions in Pereda, Gaite, and Hill when the musicality of the original passages themselves is particularly significant; thus, 'the **w**est **w**ind **w**hispered in the ivy'[22] becomes 'El viento **s**u**s**u**rr**aba en**tr**e las hojas de hie**dr**a' (Pereda 1947A); similarly, and more sustainedly, 'A waft of **win*d*** came s**wee**ping ***d***own the laurel-**w**alk [...]: it **w**an***d***ere***d*** away — a**w**ay to an in***d***efini**t**e ***d***i**st**ance — it ***d***ie***d***'[23] is rendered in a way that re-creates the harder consonance: 'El vien**t**o **p**a**s**ó de**p**ri**s**a **p**or nues**t**ro sen**d**ero [...], y fue a extinguirse lejos, muy lejos [...] a infini**t**a **d**i**st**ancia **d**e **d**on**d**e estábamos' (Pereda 1947A); or 'Una ra**ch**a impre**v**ista de **v**iento **v**ino a barrer el camino de los laureles [...]. Luego se ale**j**ó hasta morir le**j**os' (Gaite 1999A); lastly, lines from songs such as '**Li**ke heather **th**at, in **th**e **wil**derness, / **Th**e **wil**d **w**ind **wh**irls away'[24] are rendered in a way that retains the consonance (but not the clear vowel sounds): '**C**omo el **b**rezo, arran**c**ado del **b**os**q**ue / por una ráfaga de **v**iento sal**v**aje' (Hill 2009A).[25] But the sound iconicity of the original is usually disregarded, even in very noticeable instances similar to those quoted above, especially when it comes to the hard alliteration

22 *JE*, Ch. 20.
23 *JE*, Ch. 23.
24 *JE*, Ch. 12.
25 See also the versions by Luaces and Hill of Rochester's song 'The truest love that ever heart [...]' in Chapter 24, for instance, where, while they are able to shape a rhymed version, they fall short of the abundant alliteration of the original. Thus, 'I **d**angers **d**ared; I hin**d**'rance scorne**d**; I omens **did** **d**efy' becomes, in the mainly octo- and heptasyllabic reduction in Luaces: 'obstáculos venceré/ desafiaré peligros' (Luaces, 1943B), while Hill's version in alternate rhymes gives: 'Desafié peligros, desoí advertencias / todo lo ignoraba por tenerla cerca, / ni las amenazas de los peores llantos / pudieron quebrar mi decisión terca' (Hill 2009A).

and the *staccato* effect that the predominance of monosyllables in the English language is able to create, and that can be very effective at staging extreme emotions, as in: 'Up the blood rushed to his **f**ace; **f**orth **fl**ashed the **fi**re **f**rom his eyes [...]. "**F**arewell, **f**or e**v**er!"',[26] a musicality that is hard to re-create given the general sonority of Spanish, with its predominance of polysyllables, its more spaced-out accentuation and its *legato* sounds.

In this sense, even concerning a unique sound effect of Brontë's in *Jane Eyre*, namely her play on the 'eir' sound in words such as 'dare', 'rare', 'err', and many others to make the name of the protagonist resonate by homophony, the Spanish translators devise no way of re-creating it, with the partial exception of Luaces. Take a particularly emphatic use of the resource in Chapter 35: the dreamlike state in which Jane hears Rochester's voice calling her, where the sound-play makes her name echo time and again from beyond the immediacy of the scene and the linearity of the prose:

> I might have said, 'Wh**ere** is it?' for it did not seem in the room — n**or** in the house — n**or** in the g**ar**den; it did not come out of the **air** — n**or** from under the **ear**th — n**or** from overh**ead**. I had **heard** it — wh**ere**, or whence, for**ever** impossible to know! And it was the voice of a human being — a known, loved, well-rem**embere**d voice — that of **Edward** F**air**fax Roch**ester**; and it spoke in pain and woe, wildly, **eer**ily, **ur**gently.[27]

The ghostly sounds of the homophonies and half-homophonies contributing to the sensuous feeling of the scene, with 'where', 'air', 'earth', 'heard', 'eerily', 'urgently', and other words making us hear how Jane 'Eyre' is being called by name even before the language of the novel literally tells us so, are not easy to re-create in Spanish. Thus, none of the translators even of the unabridged versions attempted to stage the effect locally, and it is possible that they were unaware of it. Luaces, though, who was certainly aware of the sound pattern, devised a partial and indirect way of conveying its import to the reader in his condensed version, writing:

> En vez de *qué*, debía haber preguntado *dónde*, porque ciertamente no sonaba ni en el cuarto, ni encima de mí. Y sin embargo era una **voz**, una **voz** inconfundible, una **voz** adorada, la **voz** de Edward Fairfax

26 *JE*, Ch. 27.
27 *JE*, Ch. 35.

> Rochester, hablando con una expresión de agonía y dolor infinitos, penetrantes, urgentes.
>
> (Luaces 1943B: 'Instead of *what*, I should have asked *where*, for certainly it came neither from the bedroom, nor from above me. And yet it was a **voice**, an unmistakable **voice**, a beloved **voice**, Edward Fairfax Rochester's **voice**, speaking with an expression of infinite, penetrating and urgent agony and pain'.)

By repeating the word 'voice' several times, Luaces takes what the homophonies of the original do between the lines and repeatedly and explicitly says it in the Spanish-language version, laying out in literal terms the fact that Jane is being called insistently.

Verbal Images

It is as one moves on to the translation of verbal images, which are usually easier to reproduce in another language than syntax, music, or contextual effects, that one finds a more sustained and massive re-creation in Spanish of Brontë's idiosyncratic forms of representation and experience. This can be observed not only in the networks of metaphors and the corresponding analogical presentation of feelings, entities, and events, but also in the biblically inspired parallelistic forms promoting correlative presentation and, less frequently, in the perspectivism on reality activated by the paratactic superposition of points of view, all of which have a decisive impact on the way the representation of reality is topologically organized.

In general, as might be expected, metaphorical patterns and other classical tropes reappear in Spanish even when the translator is not being particularly re-creative, as does their effect of dualistic representation of the real, which analogically relates the dispersion of the sensible comparison to the ideal meaning that unifies it. Thus, for instance, the whole panoply of well-worn metaphors drawing on an imaginary of war or slavery to represent the 'conquests' and 'submissions' of love — 'Jane: you please me, and you **master** me — you seem to **submit**, and I like the **sense of pliancy** you impart; and while I am twining the soft, silken skein round my finger, it sends a thrill up my arm to my heart. I am **influenced** — **conquered**; and the **influence** is sweeter than I can express; and the **conquest** I undergo has a **witchery** beyond any **triumph *I* can win**'[28] — are re-created

28 *JE*, Ch. 24.

relatively automatically, with few omissions or transformations in the unabridged Spanish translations, omnipresent as these metaphors are in the so-called Western tradition and European languages.[29] Because of this largely shared background, even the symbols of the novel tend to remain quite stable (less so the personifications of faculties such as Reason, Memory, etc., which describe Jane's inner conflict and growing spirituality in a Protestant ethos).

Among the composite figurations characteristic of the novel that are actively re-created by Spanish-language translators, mention must be made of biblically inspired semantic parallelism, a form of representation by repetition or correlation of complementary entities that Charlotte Brontë will have imbibed naturally from the Scriptures and from the sermons she heard from her minister father, projecting a correlative topology of the real.[30] Such parallelisms often appear

29 The unabridged Spanish versions give: 'Jane; tú me atraes, me **dominas**, pareces **someterte** y me gusta esa impresión que sabes dar de **sumisa y dócil**; y mientras devano la madeja fina y sedosa, ella misma se enrolla en mis dedos; y a través de mi cuerpo, hasta llegar al corazón, me sacude un estremecimiento que me **domina** y que me envuelve. Me **sometes** tú y me **influyes** tú, y esta sensación que experimento tiene para mí el encanto del **hechizo** y de la **brujería** que hay en tu persona' (Pereda 1947A). 'Nunca he conocido a nadie como tú, Jane, a nadie. Me gustas y me **dominas**. Da la impresión de que te **doblegas** y me complace esa aparente **sumisión**, pero de repente, cuando estoy enroscando en mis dedos un suave y sedoso mechón de tu pelo, éste despide una corriente eléctrica que me recorre el brazo y me llega al corazón. Me has **conquistado**, estoy **entregado** a tu **influjo**, tan dulce que no puede expresarse con palabras. Me **rindo** porque tu **conquista** entraña un **hechizo** muy superior a cualquier **hazaña** en la que yo saliera **victorioso**' (Gaite 1999A). 'Jane: me complaces y a la vez me **dominas**; pareces **someterte** y me gusta la sensación de **docilidad** que emana de ti, pero cuando acaricio un mechón sedoso de tus cabellos, siento un escalofrío que me sube por el brazo directamente hasta el corazón. Me has **conquistado**, me has **dominado**, y ejerces sobre mí un **poder** más dulce del que soy capaz de expresar. Me dejo llevar por tu **hechizo**, la muestra de **una** brujería a la que no sé **resistirme**' (Hill 2009A). Luaces' condensed version, however, replaces part of the metaphorical hyperbolic imaginary by literally asserting the implicit significance of this tropological multiplication, namely, that the feelings are 'inexpressible' ('Nadie me ha **sometido**, nadie ha **influido** tan dulcemente como tú los has hecho. Esta influencia que ejerces sobre mí es **mucho más encantadora de cuanto se pueda expresar**' (Luaces 1943B)), a decision due most probably to self-censorship, since he usually plays down the erotic intensity of the imaginary. Antonini reduces more, cutting out the sustained metaphorics of the passage in their entirety, as also happens, more predictably, in the condensed paraphrases.

30 Charlotte Brontë quotes profusely from the Bible in her writings, often using for her own purposes passages from Genesis, Samuel, Job, the Psalms, Isaiah,

when biblical passages are quoted verbatim in the novel: 'Better is a dinner of herbs where love is, **[/]** than a stalled ox and hatred therewith'.[31] But Brontë also uses parallelism as a literary device when she wants to express extreme emotion, changes of fortune suffered by the protagonist, and other tensions suited to a correlative or contrasted representation of reality. Thus, at the beginning of the novel, parallelism is activated in Jane's emotional description of her confinement in the red room: 'This room was chill, because it seldom had a fire; **[/]** it was silent, because remote from the nursery and kitchens'.[32] Again, later in the novel, it determines the way she describes the lonely pathway on which she first meets Rochester: 'The ground was hard, **[/]** the air was still [...]. **[//]** I walked fast till I got warm, **[/]** and then I walked slowly to enjoy [...] **[//]** the charm of the hour lay in its approaching dimness, **[/]** in the low-gliding and pale-beaming sun'.[33] An even more emphatic example can be found towards the end of the novel, as she describes her definitive change of destiny after meeting Rochester again: 'Sacrifice! **[/]** What do I sacrifice? **[//]** Famine for food, **[/]** expectation for content. **[//]** To be privileged to put my arms round what I value — **[/]** to press my lips to what I love'.[34]

Unquestionably, the passage most continuously shaped by these forms of biblically inspired parallelism, oscillating between the repetition and the complementation of an idea through its correlative,

---

Matthew, and Revelation (to the point where orthodox Anglican reviewers complained of her profanity in quoting texts of Scripture disagreeably): see essay 14 below, by Léa Rychen, for discussion of the translation of these quotations into French. But it is above all the metrical psalter in the *Book of Common Prayer* (1662 version), with its solemn cadenced language, which may have been critical in influencing this parallelistic form of representation of entities and events.

31 *JE*, Ch. 8. All the unabridged and compressed Spanish renderings keep the parallelism well here, with different emphases over time. Thus, Antonini emphasises the proverbial aspect of the parallelism rather than the biblical language: 'Mejor es comer hierbas donde hay amor, **[/]** que buenas tortas con nuestros enemigos' (Antonini 1941B); Luaces is more literal: 'Más vale comer hierbas en compañía de quienes os aman, **[/]** que buena carne de buey con quien os odia' (Luaces 1943B); and then we have: 'Mejor es comer hierba con quienes nos aman, **[/]** que un buey con quienes nos odian' (Pereda 1947A); 'Más vale comer hierbas donde reina el amor, **[/]** que un buey bien cebado en el seno del odio' (Gaite 1999A); finally, Hill generalises in more secular terms: 'Sabe mejor una comida sencilla hecha con amor **[/]** que un festín suculento aderezado con odio' (Hill 2009A).

32 *JE*, Ch. 2.

33 *JE*, Ch. 12.

34 *JE*, Ch. 37.

is found in the last pages of Chapter 26, where the stylistic device serves to express the contrasts in Jane's change of fortune and the extreme emotion with which she contemplates the cancellation of her marriage with Rochester. This very long passage, written in parallel prose throughout, opens:

> Jane Eyre, who had been an ardent, expectant woman — almost a bride —, [/] was a cold, solitary girl again: [//] her life was pale; [/] her prospects were desolate. [//] A Christmas frost had come at midsummer; [/] a white December storm had whirled over June; [//] ice glazed the ripe apples, [/] drifts crushed the blowing roses; [//] on hayfield and cornfield lay a frozen shroud: [/] lanes which *last night* blushed full of flowers, *to-day* were pathless with untrodden snow.

After some thirty more lines in a similar vein, this extended passage in parallel prose ends by flowing into the actual words of Psalm 69:

> The whole consciousness of my life lorn, my love lost, [/] my hope quenched, my faith death-struck, [/] swayed full and mighty above me in one sullen mass. [/] That bitter hour cannot be described: [/] in truth, 'the waters came into my soul; I sank in deep mire: [/] I felt no standing; I came into deep waters; the floods overflowed me'.[35]

Of the unabridged Spanish translations, both Gaite's and Hill's re-create most of the parallelistic form of presentation, with the corresponding representation of reality as contrast and correlation of entities, events, and experiences.[36] Pereda, for her part, somewhat relaxes the effect by

35 See Essay 13, below, for further discussion of this quotation.

36 Gaite begins: 'Aquella Jane Eyre ardiente y esperanzada, disfrazada de novia, [/] volvía a ser una muchacha solitaria y encogida, [/] su vida era desvaída, [/] su porvenir desolador. [/] Una helada navideña había sobrevenido en la plenitud del verano, [/] sobre el mes de junio cayeron las ventiscas de nieve de diciembre; [/] el hielo congeló las manzanas en sazón [/] y aplastó los rosales'; and ends without marking the internal quotation from the Bible: 'Toda la consciencia de mi vida solitaria, [/] de mi amor perdido, [/] del naufragio, de mi esperanza, [/] de mi fe agonizante se abatió sobre mí de lleno, como un macizo de sombras. No es posible describir la amargura de aquella hora; las aguas anegaron mi alma, [/] me hundí en un cenagal sin fondo, [/] donde no se hacía pie, [/] hasta lo más profundo de las aguas' (Gaite 1999A). Hill begins: 'La Jane Eyre ilusionada, ardiente, casi una novia, [/] había dejado paso de nuevo a una chica fría y solitaria, [/] que se enfrentaba a una vida desvaída y a un futuro desolador. [/] Una helada navideña había invadido el verano. [/] Una tormenta de nieve había secuestrado el mes de junio: [/] el hielo había petrificado los frutos del manzano, [/] el viento había deshojado las rosas que despuntaban', and ends: 'La absoluta conciencia de una vida sin valor, de un amor perdido, [/] de las esperanzas mutiladas y de una fe derribada a golpes, [/] cayó sobre mí con la intensidad de un alud. No soy capaz de describir

using, as she tends to do, illative words and other particles that soften the predominantly binary parataxis, while preserving something of the parallel style of representation in the passage as a whole; she further ends with a dissolve, omitting the quotation marks around the biblical passage.[37] As for the condensed literary versions, Antonini reduces the passage to little more than a quarter of its original length, dissolving most of the biblically-inspired parallelism, including the quotation at the end. Luaces, though, while condensing, maintains the parallelistic figuration of entities and feelings throughout the passage — 'Mis esperanzas habían muerto de repente; **[/]** mis deseos, el día anterior rebosantes de vida, estaban convertidos en lívidos cadáveres... **[//]** Cerré los ojos. **[/]** La oscuridad me rodeó' (Luaces 1943B) — highlighting the verbatim intrusion of the Psalms at the end by using quotation marks, just as the English original does: 'La conciencia de mi vida rota, de mi amor perdido, de mi esperanza deshecha, me abrumó como una inmensa masa. Imposible describir la amargura de aquel momento. Bien puede decirse que "las olas inundaron mi alma, me sentí hundir en el légamo, **[/]** en el seno de las aguas profundas, y las ondas pasaron sobre mi cabeza"' (Luaces 1943B).

Less re-creation and more simplification are to be found in the renderings of complex images formed by the paratactic juxtaposition of points of view, a perspectivism capable of providing a kaleidoscopic experience. Indeed, other than in quite limited instances, moments of kaleidoscopic perspectivism are dissolved into a more homogenous texture in the Spanish, even into a single point of view, with the resultant simplification of space-time representation.

A limited form of perspectivism is often constructed by the narrator's voice addressing the reader of the novel — 'oh, **romantic reader, forgive me** for telling the plain truth!'[38] — juxtaposing the space-time of the fictitious Jane as a very self-conscious narrator, the space-time

esa hora tan amarga: la única verdad es que "aquel mar siniestro invadió mi alma y me hundí en una ciénaga; **[/]** rodeada de agua, sin encontrar un solo punto de apoyo, **[/]** la corriente me arrastró hasta el fondo"' (Hill 2009A).

37 'La evidencia de mi soledad, de mi amor perdido para siempre, [/] de mis esperanzas destrozadas y lejanas, la idea de mi fe muerta..., [/] todo ello me abrumó con infinito desconsuelo. [/] No podría expresar la amargura y el desaliento de aquellas horas interminables. [/] Bien puedo decir que las olas inundaron mi espíritu, que me sentí sumergida en el espeso fango, [/] que caí en las aguas profundas y que sus oleajes me cubrieron' (Pereda 1947A).

38 *JE*, Ch. 12.

of the story itself with Jane as a character, and the space-time of the empirical reader, which is multiple and changeable over time. These forms of superposition, which can be used to create complicity and allow the narrator to impose her preferences and better control the reader's reactions, offer no difficulty and are for the most part re-created in the unabridged Spanish-language translations — '**perdona, lector romántico**, que te diga la verdad escueta' (Pereda 1947A), 'oh, **lector romántico, perdóname** por contarte la verdad sin adornos' (Hill, 2009A), less literally in '**perdona, lector,** si te parece poco **romántico**, pero la verdad es que...' (Gaite 1999A) — as they are about two thirds of the time in Luaces' condensed version, including as it happens in this particular instance: 'perdona, **lector romántico**, que te diga la verdad desnuda' (Luaces 1943B).[39]

The same can be said of the limited perspectivism obtained by the juxtaposition of linguistic planes, interrupting the unity of the English language. This can be seen very obviously in the intrusion of foreign tongues, such as Miss Temple's Latin, Diana and Mary River's German and Blanche Ingram's Italian, with the most sustained instance being Adèle's French — 'having replied to her "***Revenez bientôt, ma bonne amie, ma chère Mdlle. Jeannette***," with a kiss, I set out'[40] — which serves to outline the girl's character, but also to create complicity with the reader through the traditional nineteenth-century education shared by the 'highly educated' (thus, French is also used occasionally by Jane the character, who learned it at Lowood, as well as by Rochester and the friends he receives at Thornfield).[41] Pereda and Hill's un-abridged translations almost always re-create these juxtapositions of linguistic planes — 'y contestando con un beso a sus frases cariñosas de ***Revenez bientôt, ma bonne amie, ma chère mademoiselle Jeannette***, salí de casa y me puse en camino' (Pereda 1947A), 'respondí con un beso a su despedida, "***Revenez bientôt ma bonne amie, ma chère mlle. Jeannette***", y salí de la casa' (Hill 2009A) — while Gaite also adds notes giving the Spanish translation of the French in the text: '***Revenez bientôt, ma bonne amie, ma chère mademoiselle Jeannette*** **[Note: Vuelva pronto, mi buena**

39 These addresses to the reader are not kept in the condensed version of Antonini 1941B, nor in, predictably, the abridged ones of Sánchez 1974C or Robles 1989C.

40 *JE*, Ch. 12.

41 See the discussion of the novel's multilingualism in Chapter II above by Matthew Reynolds.

amiga, mi querida señorita Jeannette].' Le contesté con un beso, y salí' (Gaite 1999A). Not so the condensed versions, however, where even Luaces, at least when it comes to Adèle's French, homogenizes to a single Spanish perspective in all but a couple of cases, giving in this instance: 'respondí con un beso a su "**Vuelva pronto, mi buena amiga Miss Jane**", y emprendí la marcha' (Luaces 1943B). They are likewise omitted from Antonini's version and predictably in the reduced paraphrases, produced as they were with young readers in mind. This same unification of linguistic planes is also found in all the different kinds of Spanish versions when they come to deal with the linguistic perspectivisms produced by the juxtaposition of different English registers, such as John's local form of speech — 'You're noan so far fro' Thornfield now'[42] — or Hannah's — 'Some does one thing, and some another. Poor folk mun get on as they can'[43] — which are dissolved into the general texture in all the different kinds of Spanish versions.

Leaving aside these simple and limited cases of addresses to the reader and inclusion of foreign languages or local registers, a more frequent and complex form of perspectivism in the novel is created by the juxtaposition without transition of points of view such as direct and indirect address, present and past tense, narration, and dialogue, etc., creating an almost kaleidoscopic presentation of reality with great dramatic potential. Take Jane's account of Bertha's nocturnal visit before the cancelled wedding (in which Jane-the-character in the past is already taking the place of Jane-the-narrator in the present). It begins:

> All the preface, sir; the tale is yet to come [a literary register — preface, tale — in the present which announces the future to narrate the past]. On waking, a gleam dazzled my eyes; I thought — Oh, it is daylight! [direct account of her thoughts in the past, staged in the present tense; but then back to the narration:] But I was mistaken; it was only candlelight. Sophie, I supposed, had come in. There was a light on the dressing-table, and the door of the closet, where, before going to bed, I had hung my wedding-dress and veil, stood open [introduction of pluperfect time, and then back to past:]; I heard a rustling there. I asked, 'Sophie, what are you doing?' [new change to her voice in the

42 *JE*, Ch. 11.
43 *JE*, Ch. 28.

past staged in the present tense, and then back to the narration:] No one answered; but a form emerged from the closet.[44]

Even among the unabridged translations, only Gaite keeps the general juxtaposition of points of view,[45] while Pereda and Hill reduce the perspectivism, dissolving some of the dramatic intensity by cutting out references in the future and pluperfect tense as well as some direct accounts of Jane's thoughts in the past.[46] Something similar

---

44 *JE*, ch. 25. For further discussion of this passage, with an animation, see Chapter VII below.

45 Gaite gives: 'Pasó el prólogo, señor; aún le queda por oír la historia. Al despertar, un resplandor deslumbró mis ojos. 'Ya es de día', pensé en un primer momento. Pero estaba equivocada: se trataba simplemente de la luz de una vela. Supuse que sería Sophie, que había entrado a buscar algo. Había una vela encendida sobre el tocador, y la puerta del armario donde había colgado mis atavíos de boda y que cerré antes de acostarme estaba abierta. Escuché un crujido procedente de allí. "¿Qué estás haciendo, Sophie?", pregunté. No obtuve respuesta, pero sí vi que una silueta surgía del armario' (Gaite 1999A).

46 Pereda gives: 'He terminado el prólogo señor; la historia es más larga [no reference to future to narrate past]. Al despertarme noté que una luz cargaba mis ojos, y pensé que sería el día [no direct account of thoughts]; pero me equivocaba; en efecto: era una luz; creí que Sophie habría entrado, pues la luz brillaba sobre el tocador, frente al armario de mis vestidos, donde, antes de acostarme, colgué [no pluperfect] mi velo y mi traje de boda, y cuya puerta se hallaba abierta. Al oír el ruido, pregunté: "Sophie, ¿qué está usted haciendo?" Nadie me contestó; pero una persona se separó del armario' (Pereda 1947A; 'I have finished the prologue sir; the story is longer. When I woke up I realised that a light shone on my eyes, and I thought that it must be day; but I was mistaken; indeed: there was a light; I thought Sophie had come in, since the light was shining on the dressing table, in front of the closet where, before going to bed, I hung my veil and wedding dress, and the door of which was open. When I heard the noise, I asked: "Sophie, what are you doing?" Nobody answered me; but a person moved away from the closet.')

Hill gives: 'Esto fue solo el principio, señor. La historia acaba de empezar [no reference to future to narrate past]. Cuando desperté, distinguí un resplandor. Pensé que ya era de día [no direct account of thoughts], pero me equivoqué: era sólo la luz de una vela. Supuse que se trataba de Sophie. Había luz en el tocador, y la puerta del armario donde había colgado el vestido de novia antes de acostarme estaba abierta. Oí un crujido procedente de allí y grité: "*¿Eres tú, Sophie? ¿Qué haces allí?*" Nadie respondió, pero una silueta emergió del armario' (Hill 2009A: 'This was only the beginning, sir. The story has just begun. When I awoke, I was aware of a glow. I thought that it was already daytime, but I was mistaken: it was only the light of a candle. I assumed it was Sophie. There was light on the dressing table, and the door of the closet where I had hung the wedding dress before going to bed was open. I heard a creak from there and shouted: "*Is that you, Sophie? What are you doing there?*" Nobody replied, but a silhouette emerged from the wardrobe.')

can be observed in Luaces' condensed version,[47] while in Antonini and the two reduced paraphrases the passage is fused with Jane's earlier dream as a continuation of it, omitting all reference to the prologue and unifying them into a single perspective.[48] Most of the English perspectivism is thus transformed into a single point of view, a kind of counter-prismatisation that unifies the juxtaposition of time and narrative forms of indirect and direct presentation into a sort of omniscient narrative voice, no longer confronting us with the drama inside the protagonist as a kaleidoscopic consciousness.

Contextual Effects

Turning finally to contextual effects, to those forms of language that generate meaning and project representation by appealing to and playing with the reader's expectations within a certain historical and literary context (such as allusion, connotation, irony, intertextuality, etc.), the enormous difficulties they impose on the re-creative task of a literary translator who wants to keep meaning under control are increased when the new text is to be read in more than one context, as was often the case with the Spanish versions of *Jane Eyre* in the second half of the twentieth century. In principle, confronted with the variously noticeable change of linguistic, literary, cultural, and epochal contexts between Victorian England and twentieth-century Spanish-speaking

47 Luaces gives: 'Todo el prólogo. Ahora falta el relato. Al despertarme, una luz hirió mis ojos. Pensé que ya era de día [no direct account of thoughts]. Pero no era más que el resplandor de una vela. Supuse que Sofía estaba en la alcoba. Alguien había dejado una bujía en la mesa, y el cuartito guardarropa, donde yo colocara mi velo y mi vestido de boda, se hallaba abierto. "*Qué hace usted, Sofía*", pregunté. Nadie contestó, pero una figura surgió del ropero' (Luaces 1943B: 'All the prologue. The story is still to come. When I awoke, a light hurt my eyes. I thought that it was already daytime. But it was only the glow of a candle. I assumed that Sophie was in the bedchamber. Someone had left a candle on the table, and the closet where I had put my veil and my wedding dress was open. "*What are you doing there, Sophie?*" I asked. No one answered, but a figure emerged from the closet.')

48 Antonini gives: 'Vi luz y creía que era el alba; pero no: era una bujía que estaba en mi tocador. Al mismo tiempo sentí que alguien revisaba mi armario y creyendo que era Sofía, le pregunté qué estaba haciendo. Nadie me respondió, pero un bulto se desprendió de la sombra' (Antonini 1941B: 'I saw light and thought it was the dawn; but no: it was a candle on my dresser. At the same time I noticed that somebody was looking in my wardrobe, and, thinking that it was Sophie, I asked her what she was doing. Nobody replied, but a shape came out of the shadows.') Sánchez 1974C and Robles 1989C use this earlier translation by Antonini, with only minor changes of vocabulary.

countries, preserving the effect of allusions, intertextuality, or other contextual forms of meaning (such as political preferences conveyed through literary allusion to the traditional canon or defiance of religious authority conveyed by intertextuality), would often involve creating new equivalent events capable of activating these effects by reference to the new context, including new representatives of the approved literary, political or religious law — an effort at re-creation that is not found in a sustained way in the Spanish-language versions of *Jane Eyre* (or in commercial literary translation of novels into Spanish generally in contemporary times). Moreover, one must be aware that, owing to the significant differences between the literary and political contexts of reception during most of the twentieth century in Latin America as compared to Spain, the same factual translation of *Jane Eyre* could generate different overtones on either side of the Atlantic, an added difficulty which resulted, not in strong re-creation, but in calculations and self-censorship of various kinds, especially among the translators working within the context of Franco's dictatorship, and, in any case and often, in strong forms of refraction.

Certainly, most Spanish versions manage, more or less automatically, to activate some of the original meanings that depend on a relatively shared context, which existed for most of the twentieth century. This is the case with a significant number of the biblical allusions in the novel, for instance, which tend to preserve their effect when the translators maintain them as such. The same is true of the many proverbial expressions — 'Beauty is in the eye of the beholder', 'All is not gold that glitters', 'To each villain his own vice'[49] — often activated by naturally arising Spanish-language proverbial equivalents: 'La belleza está en los ojos del que mira' (Luaces 1943B); 'La belleza está en los ojos de aquel que mira' (Gaite 1999A); 'No es oro todo lo que reluce' (Luaces 1943B, Pereda 1947A, Gaite 1999A, Hill 2009A); 'A cada vicioso con su vicio' (Pereda 1947A), 'Cada villano tiene su vicio' (Gaite 1999A). Even some of the religious-political allusions in the context of the relationship and tension between the Anglican and Catholic churches can reappear more or less spontaneously, or when annotated and literalised; thus, a reference such as the one in Chapter 3 to Guy Fawkes — 'Abbot, I think, gave me credit for being a sort of infantile Guy Fawkes' — who was known as Guido Fawkes when he fought with the Spanish army, can be maintained and work as such, both in Luaces'

49 *JE*, Ch. 17, Ch. 24, and Ch. 27.

condensed version (1943) and Hill's unabridged version (2009) (Gaite also keeps it, telling the reader in a note that he was a 'conspirator in the time of James I in England, in the early seventeenth century' (Gaite 1999A)). Pereda literalises the meaning of the reference by using the word 'conspiradora' ('conspirator') instead of the proper name, while Antonini is more creative, refracting the reference as: 'Creo que para la Abbot era yo una especie de **bruja infantil**' (Antonini 1941B: 'I think that for Abbot I was a kind of **child witch**')). The same re-creation can be found in the case of meaningful contrasts such as the one between 'stylish' and 'puritanical' in Chapter 20, with both erotic and religious harmonics — 'The hue of her dress was black too; but its fashion was so different from her sister's — so much more flowing and becoming — it looked as **stylish** as the other's looked **puritanical**' — which quite naturally maintains its effectiveness in the Spanish tradition, where these connotations of puritanism, including the use of the adjectival form of the word as a well-worn image in opposition to the sensual, are well established. Thus, Antonini's condensed version published in Argentina gives: 'Vestía también de negro como su hermana, pero no en estilo **puritano** sino **elegante**' (Antonini 1941B); while an orthodox establishment figure such as Pereda can allow herself to render it: 'Vestía también de negro, pero con un traje tan **estilizado y tan a la moda** como lo era el de su hermana **sencillo y puritano**' (Pereda 1947A). But someone like Luaces, a Republican translating in the immediate aftermath of the Spanish Civil War, avoids murky religious waters and omits all reference to puritanism, especially its contrast to the sensual, rendering the sentence: 'Su vestido era negro también, pero absolutamente distinto al de su hermana. Una especie de luto estilizado' (Luaces 1943B: 'Her dress was black too, but completely different to her sister's. A kind of stylised mourning.') Gaite, lastly, translating half a century later, in post-Franco times, allows herself to unpack and strongly emphasise the implications of the strict parallelism in the original: 'También iba de luto, pero su vestido, **ceñido y a la moda**, no llamaba la atención precisamente por su **puritanismo** como el de la hermana' (Gaite 1999A: 'She wore mourning too, but her dress, **close-fitting and fashionable**, was not exactly remarkable for its **puritanism** like her sister's.').[50]

50 Hill renders it: 'También llevaba un vestido de color negro, pero su corte era muy distinto del de su hermana: mucho **más favorecedor y vaporoso, menos puritano y más elegante**' (Hill, 2009A).

Aside from these instances of more or less automatic reactivation when the references are not cut out, most of the contextual forms of meaning either dissolve or refract in more unpredictable directions in the Spanish-language versions, which do not establish new references to activate the same effects in the context of the new culture. Nor do they use sustained annotation, with the notable exception of Gaite's translation, which has more than a hundred notes clarifying historical and geographical references, mythological, biblical, and literary allusions, and even some possible ironies; in sum, informing the modern Spanish reader of what the contextual literary forms of meaning of the original would make complicit English readers experience directly.[51]

Thus, where the linguistic-literary context is concerned, these forms of meaning can be seen predictably to disappear when they depend on intertextuality with earlier works of English literature, or with books fashionable at the time, since the prodigious web of textual allusion in the original, whether retained or not, does not activate easily in the Spanish context of reception (and the same probably holds true for most contemporary English readers, as the increasing annotation in current commercial editions suggests). These instances range from references to classics such as Bunyan, Shakespeare, Milton, Johnson, Swift, Burns, Richardson, Byron, Scott, Keats, and others, up to the works that Jane reads during her formative years: the childhood vision of exotic faraway sea coasts obtained from Bewick's *History of British Birds* (Chapter 1), or even the exotic stories of the 'Arabian Tales' (Chapter 2) (which some of the translators do not seem to realise are *The Arabian Nights*, known in Spanish as *Las mil y una noches — The Thousand and One Nights)*. Even when very obvious references crop up in the original English, such as an interpolation taken from one of Shakespeare's best-known works in the conversation between Mrs Fairfax and Jane after her arrival at Thornfield, while they are touching with ominous humour the possible presence of ghosts in the house — 'Yes — "**after life's fitful fever they sleep well** [*Macbeth* 3.2.23]," I muttered' — the effect is mostly lost.[52] A partial exception is Gaite, who translates in high tone: '"Sí — murmuré yo — tras la fiebre

51 More generally, Gaite states in these same notes: 'Many of the learned allusions in this novel reveal the Brontë sisters' fondness for Bible reading and their belief that their readers will have had exactly the same education' (Gaite 1999A; note 6).

52 *JE*, Ch. 11.

caprichosa de la vida, duerme plácidamente"' ('"Yes, — I muttered —, after life's fitful fever, he sleeps peacefully"'), and who adds a footnote explaining the reference, as she does for other contextual aspects: 'Charlotte Brontë liked to display her knowledge of literature. This is a phrase from act III of Shakespeare's *Macbeth* and refers to the King of Scotland, Duncan, whom he has recently murdered' (Gaite 1999A).[53] But in the other editions, whether the inverted commas and attendant superposition of planes are preserved as they stand, as in Hill's unabridged version — 'Sí. "**Tras la intensa fiebre de la vida llega el reposo más plácido**" — murmuré' (Hill 2009A) — or are done away with, so that these appear to be Jane's own words — 'Sí, **después de una vida borrascosa bueno es dormir** — murmuré' (Antonini 1941B), '**Hartos de turbulencia, reposan tranquilos,** ¿no? — comenté' (Luaces 1943B), 'Claro; **duermen en paz después de una vida de emociones y de agitación** — murmuré' (Pereda 1947A) — the effect of intertextuality is diluted and the ominous parallelisms with Duncan's death, or more broadly with the ghosts and events of *Macbeth* as a whole, are not activated.

Generally speaking, whether or not all the individual translators were familiar with these and other less well-known passages of English literature, they tended to submit to the current imperative in commercial editions of prioritising the plot of the story without 'distractions' for the Spanish-speaking reader, removing — or at least not re-creating via new references — the allusions and other effects of intertextual forms. Thus, whereas in the original context this whole web of literary allusion was able to divide readers between those who noticed it and extract its meaning and those who did not (starting with the significant fact that literary allusion is as important in *Jane Eyre* as biblical allusion, with both being placed at the same level of importance in the protagonist's development and generating a potential complicity with the novel's readership in this respect), in the Spanish translations, where they are not simply done away with — as they often are in the compressed versions and almost always are in the condensed paraphrases — their literal preservation, without any re-creative effort to reflect the difference in context and literary expectations, means they are left adrift like messages in a bottle.

53 'A Charlotte Brontë le gustaba exhibir sus conocimientos de literatura. Es una frase del acto III de *Macbeth* de Shakespeare, y alude al rey de Escocia, Duncan, recién asesinado por él' (Gaite 1999A).

Where the historical context is concerned, however, there is a much greater tendency towards refraction in the transition from Victorian England to post-Second World War Spain and Latin America. This can already be seen in the case of religious references and their moral and political overtones, which are capable of generating a renewed meaning when transposed from Protestant England to Catholic Spain, leading some translators to variously emphatic self-censure and writing between the lines, especially if they were working under Franco's censorship and programme to restore traditional National-Catholic values (Spain remained a confessional state until 1978).

In general terms, Charlotte Brontë had no particular liking for the Roman Catholic form of Christianity, dominant in Spain and Latin America, or for rigid Pharisaic forms of Protestantism and Anglicanism. 'I consider Methodism, Quakerism, and the extremes of High and Low Churchism foolish, but Roman Catholicism beats them all',[54] she wrote some time after publishing *Jane Eyre*, a statement that helps to unfold her true intentions behind some of the religious references and overtones in her novel. For the effect even of the English original in the context of the religious conventions of Victorian England was felt to be discordant and was attacked as anti-Christian, prompting Brontë to mount a tactical defence; as she summarises it in a well-known passage of her Prologue to the Second Edition (1848): 'Having thus acknowledged what I owe those who have aided and approved me, I turn to another class [...] I mean the timorous or carping few who doubt the tendency of such books as 'Jane Eyre:' in whose eyes whatever is unusual is wrong; whose ears detect in each protest against bigotry — that parent of crime — an insult to piety, that regent of God on earth. I would suggest to such doubters certain obvious distinctions [...]. Conventionality is not morality. Self-righteousness is not religion. To attack the first is not to assail the last. To pluck the mask from the face of the Pharisee, is not to lift an impious hand to the Crown of Thorns.'

Symptomatically, of the seven versions being considered here, only Gaite's translation, done in 1999 from the second English edition, reproduces Brontë's Preface. More broadly, when confronted with religious references, especially with dissident overtones, one often finds either transformation or self-censorship according to the

54 Elizabeth Gaskell, *The Life of Charlotte Brontë* (London: J. M. Dent, 1971 [1857]), p. 160.

religious orthodoxy or the position of the translator relative to the political regime and apparatus of censorship in the new Spanish context.

Take the different ways of translating a passage such as Jane's 'innocent' and 'spontaneous' words when she is faced with Helen's imminent death: 'How sad to be lying now on a sick bed, and to be in danger of dying! This world is pleasant — it would be dreary to be called from it, and to have to **go who knows where**?'.[55] Pereda, as one would expect, reconciles the anxiety about death with orthodox Catholic dogma, making Jane doubt the exact location but not the existence of the realm of the dead: '¡Qué triste debe de ser verse tendido en una cama y en peligro de muerte, con lo hermoso que es el mundo! ¡Será espantoso dejarlo para **ir a un lugar desconocido que no se sabe en dónde está [go to a place whose whereabouts are unknown]**!' (Pereda, 1947A). Luaces, a Republican, accentuates between the lines, using a religious expression (*God knows where*) to subvert religion; stressing the subversion of consolation vis-à-vis death, he renders it: '¡Qué triste estar enfermo, en peligro de muerte! El mundo es hermoso. ¡Qué terrible debe ser que le arrebaten a uno de él **para ir a parar Dios sabe dónde [to end up God knows where]**!', a passage whose rendering acquires further political overtones from the fact that it was published just a few years after the massacres of the Spanish Civil War.

Conversely, a revealing example of the removal of allusive references can be found in the treatment of the interpolation of Esther 5.3 in Chapter 24 — 'Now, King Ahasuerus! What do I want with half your estate? Do you think I am a Jew-usurer, seeking good investment in land?' — which takes on a particularly ominous meaning in the years after the Spanish Civil War and the Second World War. Once again, the positions of these two Spanish translators working in the forties are symptomatic. Thus, whereas Pereda keeps this intact in her translation, just as she does other biblical allusions — 'Bueno, rey Asuero. ¿Para qué necesito yo la mitad de su hacienda? ¿Es que se figura que soy un judío usurero que voy buscando la manera de sacar partido de unos caudales?' (Pereda 1947A) — Luaces cuts out the

55 *JE*, Ch. 9.

entire reference (as does Antonini in Argentina at the same time, by contrast with the more recent versions, which are more literal here).[56]

Finally, in less conscious but no less revealing modes, one can consider the way the turn of phrase '*my* master' is avoided by Luaces and the rest of the early Spanish translators when used by Jane for Rochester (while this same word 'master' is kept as 'maestro' when confined to its social and educational uses). That is, confronted with expressions such as '"It must have been one of them," interrupted **my master**',[57] whereas Antonini in Argentina (1941) or Hill much later in Spain (2009) would often render the expression as 'mi señor', with clear erotic overtones, none of the early versions published in Spain offer this turn of phrase 'mi señor', using rather expressions such as 'Rochester' (Luaces 1943) or 'el señor Rochester' ('mister Rochester': Pereda 1947, as well as later in Sánchez 1974). For despite a possible literal reading (Jane was in fact employed by Rochester), the immediate literal equivalent of 'my master' as 'mi señor' would have had disruptive religious overtones in mid-century Spain, being normally reserved in the Spanish language and Catholic tradition for Christ who, according to his biographers in the Gospels, was already thus called by his disciples: master. In synthesis, it would be giving to a man what belongs to God.

One can realize how in two of the three instances just examined, as in other examples commented on before, Luaces takes advantage of the cover of anonymity provided by his position as translator to write episodically between the lines, shielded as he is by the canonical authority of Charlotte Brontë, whom he recalls in the brief introductory note to his Spanish edition is one of the greatest women writers of all time, concluding, no less surreptitiously in the context of the immediate situation in Spain, that 'Jane Eyre is, in summary, a bright picture on a dark background' (Luaces 1943B). But this is a way of dividing readerships between accomplices and dupes that Luaces only activates occasionally, when opportunity allows or the passage

56 Indeed, Gaite and Hill, translating more than half a century later (1999 and 2009), reinstate the words of the original: '¿Y para qué quiero yo la mitad de su patrimonio, rey Asuero [nota: 'Rey persa inmensamente rico que prometió a su mujer entregarle cuanto pidiera]? ¿Me toma por un judío usurero en busca de una provechosa inversión? (Gaite 1999A); '¿Y para qué quiero yo la mitad de su herencia, rey Asuero? ¿Acaso cree que soy un usurero judío que desea hacer una buena inversión?' (Hill 2009A).

57 *JE*, Ch. 25.

merits it, while he acts cautiously and censors himself in many other instances when it comes to translating religious or social references with local harmonics, since out of political considerations and the need to earn a living he could not risk his manuscripts being rejected by the censor (something he was familiar with, since his text *Fuera de su sitio* was banned in 1939, probably because of its open treatment of sexual matters).[58] Luaces' duplicity was effective, in any event, and the guardians of the law took the bait; in its prior censorship ruling, the Department of Propaganda decreed (13 October 1942) that *Jane Eyre* was 'A good novel that tells the life story of an orphan girl, her sufferings and her struggle to attain to a decent living. It is completely moral, but because it is an English work, all its action takes place within

---

58 It is enough to look again in more detail at the childlike innocence of these scenes of friendship between Jane and Helen (where the former, albeit admiringly, shows doubts about religious beliefs and rebels against the latter's submissiveness) to find several instances of moderation and self-censorship in Luaces; thus, when confronted with a kind of programmatic summary like 'I could not comprehend **this doctrine of endurance; and still less could I understand or sympathise with the forbearance she expressed for her chastiser**' (*JE*, Ch. 6), a defiance with religious and political overtones in Franco's Spain, Luaces cuts out almost everything, leaving just: 'No podía estar de acuerdo con **aquella opinión**' (Luaces 1943B; 'I could not agree with **this opinion**').

More broadly, and on a strictly religious issue, one may take the most sustained instance of doubt on Jane's part about existence in the other world that follows. The original reads:

'I believe; I have faith: I am going to God.'

'Where is God? What is God?'

'My Maker and yours, who will never destroy what He created. I rely implicitly on His power, and confide wholly in His goodness: I count the hours till that eventful one arrives which shall restore me to Him, reveal Him to me.'

'You are sure, then, Helen, that there is such a place as heaven, and that our souls can get to it when we die?'

'I am sure there is a future state; I believe God is good; I can resign my immortal part to Him without any misgiving. God is my father; God is my friend: I love Him; I believe He loves me.' (*JE*, Ch. 9)

Luaces avoids any dissonance with dogma and doubt vis-à-vis religious authority by condensing this whole anguished dialogue into a single speech uttered by Helen: 'Sí, lo sé, porque tengo fe. Voy a reunirme con Dios, nuestro creador. Me entrego en sus manos y confío en su bondad. Cuento con impaciencia las horas que faltan para ese venturoso momento. Dios es mi padre y mi amigo: le amo y creo que Él me ama a mí' (Luaces 1943B: 'Yes, I know, because I have faith. I shall be reunited with God, our creator. I resign myself into his hands and trust in his goodness. I impatiently count the hours until that happy moment. God is my father and my friend: I love Him and believe that he loves me.)

the Protestant religion,'[59] in view of which nothing was required to be removed or altered, it being considered that these dissonances characteristic of the Protestant religion had been duly toned down and transformed (which is indeed the case with other additional aspects, such as the harsh and punitive Calvinist God, or the evangelism of St John Rivers, which are played down, not to mention occasional allusions to non-Christian religions, which Luaces simply removes).

Nonetheless, despite Luaces' self-censorship and transformations by other translators, dissident or otherwise, to avoid problems with the guardians of the law, the difference in cultural and historical horizon between Victorian England and post-war Spain and Latin America could not but produce a sharp refraction of the contextual effects in *Jane Eyre*. Leaving aside all explicit self-conscious censorship to dupe the guardians of the law, and to a more acute degree than with the recreations and refractions in lexical, grammatical, musical, and imagistic aspects reviewed earlier, it is mainly when these contextual effects come to be evaluated that one finds a sharp prismatisation of the work in the Spanish language. And of these refractions between the different cultural contexts, it is above all the prismatisations concerning gender and colonial motifs in the new differentiated contexts of the Latin American republics as compared to Spain under Franco's dictatorship which become particularly significant, as will be examined in the two sections that follow.

Gender Refractions: Human Individuality as Feminist Emancipation

Among the cultural instances that refract most decisively in the passage of *Jane Eyre* from its original context of inscription in mid-nineteenth century Victorian England to the mid-twentieth century contexts in which its Spanish translations were popularized in Latin America and Spain, one finds first and foremost its potential as a feminist emancipation manifesto. For, even beyond the different levels of emphasis or self-censorship that can be found in the translations, whether emphasizing or downplaying the protagonist's passion and sense of independence, the very sense of individuality congenial to Protestant English culture, key to the pathos and plot of this kind of

59 Ortega Sáez, 'Traducciones del franquismo en el mercado literario español contemporáneo', p. 183.

Bildungsroman presentation of a female character's development against adversity, is refracted in decisive and differentiated ways in the young republics of South America, on the one hand, where struggles for the women's vote and other civil rights were in their critical stages, and in the Iberian Peninsula, on the other, where Franco's National-Catholic programme sought to re-establish traditional family values that assigned women a domestic role.

Certainly, the force of the novel as a provocative statement about women's emancipation can easily be lost on contemporary Spanish readers (or indeed English ones) — they might be confused, for instance, by the way Jane, despite her disdain for John Reed or for St John Rivers' ambitions, seems to aspire to marriage as a woman's ultimate fulfilment — so that contextual adjustments are required to take the full measure of its original impact and likewise its potential for refraction in mid-twentieth century translations in Latin America and Spain. Regarding the English text in its original context of inscription, the reader must be reminded that this mid-nineteenth century portrait of the desires and frustrations of an educated woman not enjoying all the privileges of class, written at a time when women had few civil rights, was experienced by its Victorian readership as depicting an impetuous, rebellious figure who broke the traditional moulds and was described as 'unfeminine' by her detractors (within and outside the novel itself),[60] being seen as a direct assertion of women's rights by complicit readers. As for the Spanish language versions done during the first large wave of translation of the novel in the 1940s, of which there were at least six issued in dozens of editions between 1941 and 1950, including the most re-printed ones by Antonini (1941), Luaces (1943), and Pereda (1947), the contemporary reader would have to be reminded of the differentiated social and cultural contexts in which the emancipatory potential of the novel was refracted during this first widespread reception in Latin America and Spain respectively.

For in the South American republics, on the one hand, this popularity of *Jane Eyre* was exactly contemporary with the explicit political and social struggle for women's civil rights and achievement of suffrage (attained in 1946 in Venezuela, 1947 in Argentina, 1949 in Chile, 1955 in Peru, and 1957 in Colombia, and earlier in some countries: 1924 in Ecuador, 1932 in Uruguay, and 1938 in Bolivia), an event regarded as a fundamental advance in the long and as-yet

60 For instance *JE*, Ch. 35.

unfinished movement towards equal rights. Thus, whereas the Seneca Falls Declaration of Sentiments (1848), usually identified as the founding moment of suffragism, is strictly contemporary with the publication of the original English version of *Jane Eyre* (1847), it was around the time of what is viewed as its final international recognition a hundred years later with the Universal Declaration of Human Rights (1948) that the novel had its translation boom in Latin America, just as women were attaining equal civil rights in many of the young South American republics following a struggle that had begun in the early twentieth century. In Argentina itself, where this *Jane Eyre* translation boom began with Antonini's pioneering 1941 version, Eva Duarte (Evita, 1919–1952) — whose own life story, from humble beginnings and a career as an actress to her work as a trade unionist, political leader and final explicit proclamation as 'Spiritual Head of the Nation' (Jefa espiritual de la nación) before she died at the age of thirty-three, offers a no-less sui generis formation narrative in this respect — spoke as follows on national radio about the enactment of the law on women's suffrage, in which she had been actively involved: 'My fellow countrywomen, I am even now being presented by the national government with the law that enshrines our civil rights. And I am being presented with it in your company, in the assurance that I do so on behalf and as the representative of all Argentine women, jubilantly feeling how my hands tremble as they touch the laurels that proclaim our victory. Here it is, my sisters, summed up in the cramped print of a few paragraphs — a long history of struggles, setbacks and hopes. And so it contains flares of indignation, the shadows of threatening eclipses, but also the joyous awakening of triumphant dawns, heralding the victory of women over the incomprehension, denials and vested interests of the castes repudiated by our national awakening.'[61]

61 'Mujeres de mi Patria, recibo en este instante, de manos del Gobierno de la Nación, la ley que consagra nuestros derechos cívicos. Y la recibo ante vosotras, con la certeza de que lo hago en nombre y representación de todas las mujeres argentinas, sintiendo jubilosamente que me tiemblan las manos al contacto del laurel que proclama la victoria. Aquí está, hermanas mías, resumida en la letra apretada de pocos artículos, una historia larga de luchas, tropiezos y esperanzas. Por eso hay en ella crispaciones de indignación, sombras de ocasos amenazadores, pero también alegre despertar de auroras triunfales. Y esto último que traduce la victoria de la mujer sobre las incomprensiones, las negaciones y los intereses creados de las castas

Franco's dictatorship in Spain, on the other hand, did not just abolish the female suffrage sanctioned by the 1931 constitution enacted under the Second Republic and repeal other civil rights won during the previous period, such as the equality of the sexes before the law and the ability to dissolve a marriage. More radically, as part of what was conceived as a struggle of Good against Evil projected on to the two sides that had confronted each other in the Civil War, Francoism applied an explicit National-Catholic programme to restore traditional family values, making canonical marriage the only valid kind and encouraging women to leave the workforce and devote themselves to domestic tasks (so that from 1944 Spain's labour laws required married women to have their husband's permission to work). The result was the establishment of a nationalist and religious traditionalism unequalled in the Europe of the day.

It is this contextual difference and relative separation of the cultural destinies of South America and Spain between the 1940s and 1970s, then, that substantially accounts for the different forms of emphasis or self-censorship regarding the potential for female emancipation that are observed in the various translations of *Jane Eyre* that came out at the time, starting with those of Antonini (1941) and Luaces (1943), two compressed versions that are to some extent equivalent, and that would enjoy great commercial success in their respective regions.

Thus, in South America, it is symptomatic that Antonini's pioneering Argentine translation was sold, beginning in 1944 and for the three decades to come, in the series of editions published by Acme Agency in Buenos Aires, under the composite title of *Jane Eyre: Rebel Soul* (*Juana Eyre: alma rebelde*), with the iconography of its cover design emphasising the idea of the independent and educated woman (you can see the cover, together with the book's place of publication, on the third screen of the Spanish Covers Map). While this addition to the title, 'Rebel Soul', matches that of the Spanish-language version of the 1943 film adaptation of *Jane Eyre* by Robert Stevenson, with Joan Fontaine and Orson Welles in the roles of Jane and Rochester, it summarizes well the emphasis Antonini would give both to proclamations of gender equality and to the heroine's erotic intensity.

In the way *Jane Eyre* translation was approached in Spain in those same years, conversely, starting with Luaces' version, it is possible

---

repudiadas por nuestro despertar nacional'. Eva Perón, *Dicursos* (Buenos Aires: Biblioteca del Congreso Nacional, 2012), p. 46.

to see how the conditioning of the Francoist National-Catholic programme in relation to the social role of women led to varying degrees of self-censorship when it came to the novel's potential for female emancipation, including its variously explicit eroticism. Insofar as Franco's dictatorship prescribed the re-establishment of traditional patriarchal culture against the conquests made in the previous Republican period, promoting values and a role for women that did not actually differ greatly from those of the Victorian context in which *Jane Eyre* originally appeared, it was precisely those moments of the novel that created dissonance in its original context of inscription by deviating from expectations about the social role of women, starting with its claim to equality and its erotic passion, that activated the Spanish translator's self-censorship in the new context a century later. In fact, Luaces also acted here in a very deliberate and often astute manner, decisively moderating the energy with which Jane asserts her emancipatory positions and experiences her passions, especially the erotic impetus, but also allowing a hidden agenda to show through for those prepared to understand, so that his translation divides readers into accomplices and dupes in more or less subtle and probably automatic ways within this context of censorship in which he was operating.

For this ability to divide readers into accomplices and dupes was something that Luaces exercised from early on, even before he was imprisoned or censored, as can be seen in his work as a writer under the previous dictatorship of Miguel Primo de Rivera (1923–1930), and not least in relation to the civil oppression and erotic repression of women. Take his journalistic text 'Feminismo y desvergüenza' ('Feminism and Shamelessness'), written when he was just 19 and published in the *Heraldo Alavés* (25 February 1925), not only because it can effectively divide readerships even now, but also because the picture it provides of the female oppression and tension in which his compressed version of *Jane Eyre* was to appear somewhat later could hardly be bettered. Luaces, the young Republican poet, thunders:

> Not in fancy dress but in undress, their pink flesh covered only by the flimsiest of shifts, two graceful women, identity unknown, shielded behind never-raised masks, had the absurd — or shamelessly insolent — fancy of mingling with the colourful crowd of masked figures at the Press ball in the Theatre Royal. This public display of brazenness and unseemliness is yet another treacherous blow dealt us severe Spaniards of the old stock, enamoured of Christian modesty and southern mystery, by the foul, misshapen monster of feminism without

> femininity. Women voting, women writing, women in government and at the bar, women naked in public, open prostitution proliferating, sterility rampant, bestiality triumphant, spirituality groaning: ambiguity, destitution, decadence... This is the work of feminism. Where is this path leading us? Is there in Spain no morality, no conscience, no masculinity even? Must we forever indulge the repellent spectacle of pseudo-women alienated from the home, from motherhood and from Religion, the artist's or lawyer's cloak draped over the garb of harlotry? I know that these and worse outrages are common currency abroad, but are we to measure Spain, severe, virile, noble, conquering Spain, by the same yardstick as the frivolous French or the Yankee bacon mongers? [...] Against the barefaced shamelessness of women unworthy to be called Spanish, against the increasing womanishness of men, against indifference, scepticism and denial of all that is good, beautiful and grand, we must raise a wall of sound tradition, of sincere austerity, of triumphant manhood. We must preach an ethical and aesthetic Crusade to restore all the old foundations of the true Spanish ways.[62]

By taking the attire of two women supposed to have attended a ball at the Theatre Royal as a pretext for a hyperbolic condemnation of both

62 See Marta Ortega Sáez, 'Traducciones del franquismo en el mercado literario español contemporáneo: el caso de *Jane Eyre* de Juan G. de Luaces', (unpublished doctoral thesis, University of Barcelona, 2013), p. 103. ('No disfrazadas sino desvestidas, cubiertas solo sus carnes rosadas por una camisilla muy sutil, dos gentiles mujeres desconocidas, parapetadas en el no levantado antifaz, tuvieron el absurdo capricho o la insolente desvergüenza de mezclarse a la multicolor algarabía de las máscaras del baile de la Prensa en el Teatro Real. Nosotros, los recios españoles de añeja casta, enamorados del cristiano recato y del misterio meridional, hemos, con esta pública demostración de impudicia y antiestética, sufrido un nuevo traidor zarpazo del deforme y hediondo monstruo del feminismo sin feminidad. Mujeres electoras, mujeres regidoras, mujeres escritoras y togadas, mujeres públicamente desnudas, libre prostitución multiplicada, esterilidad que aumenta, bestialidad triunfante, espiritualidad mugiente: ambigüedad, miseria, decadencia... He aquí la labor del feminismo. ¿A dónde vamos por este camino? ¿Es que no hay en España moralidad, conciencia, ni siquiera masculinidad? ¿Es que hemos de tolerar indefinidamente el repelente espectáculo de las pseudo-mujeres alejadas del hogar, de la maternidad y de la Religión, que, bajo un manto de artistas o letradas ocultan la deshonesta falda de picos pardos? Ya sé que estas, y aún mayores atrocidades son en el extranjero moneda corriente, pero ¿mediremos a la España severa, viril, noble y conquistadora con el mismo metro que a la Francia frívola o la Yanquilandia tocinera? [...] Ante la descarada desvergüenza de esas mujeres indignas de ser dichas españolas, ante el afeminamiento de los varones, ante la indiferencia, la negación y el escepticismo, de todo lo bueno, lo bello y lo grande, hemos de alzar un muro de sanas tradiciones, de sincera austeridad, de virilidad triunfante. Hemos de predicar una Cruzada ética, estética, y restauradora de todos los antiguos sustentáculos del verdadero españolismo').

literary feminism (of which Charlotte Brontë was a pioneering and archetypal figure) and foreign influence on Spain (which he would devote the whole of his subsequent literary labour to furthering), Luaces not only subverts by *reductio ad absurdum* the traditionalist and nationalist programme pursued by the dictatorship of Miguel Primo de Rivera, but also illustrates his ability to write between the lines and separate readerships, deployed here with a youthful assurance and effrontery less subtle than the approach he would take during the Francoist oppression two decades later. In all cases, while separating accomplices from dupes, he could not be accused by the duty censor of saying anything but what 'his words in the text literally say', making the guardians of the law take the bait (as they still do).[63] But whatever attitude the reader of the day might have taken to Luaces' text, and whatever today's reader might choose to think his real intentions were, what it leaves in no doubt is the cultural outlook and traditional view of women officially promoted by the authorities in the 1920s, before the Second Republic (1931–1936) — the same traditional view that the National-Catholic programme implemented by Franco's dictatorship after the Civil War would be seeking to restore at the time Luaces was undertaking and publishing his successful version of *Jane Eyre*.

As one thus returns from the Spanish and Latin American contexts to the text of the novel itself and its translations into Spanish, if Jane's development in the face of adversity includes her repeated rebellions against oppression (not least oppression by a number of male characters, from her cousin John Reed's physical abuse and Mr Brocklehurst's psychological abuse to St John Rivers's attempts at control), alternating with a series of explicit reflections about the need for women to be independent of and equal to men, and an explicit staging of her erotic passion for Rochester, a married man, one can

63 For the unstable and undecidable nature of meaning when an author writes effectively between the lines, which constitutes an '*art* of writing' very different from 'logical encoding', not allowing censors (including scholarship) to 'prove' their point by methods of *inquisitio* or factual research, see Leo Strauss, *Persecution and the Art of Writing* (London: Chicago University Press, 1988, esp. "Introduction" and "Persecution and the Art of Writing"), pp. 1–37. For Juan de Luaces' political stance, his problems with censorship, imprisonment, as well as his attempt to escape to Latin America during the Spanish Civil War, see the appendix 'Lives of Some Translators' below. More broadly, see Marta Ortega Sáez's 'Traducciones del franquismo en el mercado literario español contemporáneo: el caso de *Jane Eyre* de Juan G. de Luaces' (unpublished doctoral thesis, University of Barcelona, 2013).

notice how the versions produced by Antonini in Argentina and Luaces in Spain proceed quite differently in relation to this series of aspects with a common potential for female liberation, notwithstanding that both appear to be extremely alert to such a potential in their respective contexts.

Thus, bearing in mind that Antonini's version is far more compressed than Luaces' (having 287 pages as compared to 518, in a similar format), whereas the Argentine translator cuts substantially more than the Spaniard at all other times, when it comes to declarations about female liberation or Jane's erotic passion he translates emphatically, stressing the novel's impact as a romantic bestseller at a time of female emancipation. Luaces, on the other hand, acting just as consciously, cuts much more in those passages than he does elsewhere, obscuring Jane's demand for emancipation and particularly her erotic passion, portraying her as a more resigned and restrained woman; as one who is less passionate and more demure and chaste. This is so, at least, in the literal façade his Spanish version presents to the censor; since some of what he does, often no doubt spontaneously, gives grounds for suspecting second intentions here as well.

To recommence the analyses, let us take a passage of the novel where a proclamation of equality is made in a context of eroticism, like the one Jane makes during her conversation with Rochester in the garden at Thornfield, when she confesses her love to him although believing him to be engaged to another woman. The original reads:

> 'I am not talking to you now through the medium of custom, conventionalities, nor even of mortal flesh; — it is my spirit that addresses your spirit; just as if both had passed through the grave, and we stood at God's feet, **equal, — as we are**!'
>
> **'As we are!'** repeated Mr. Rochester — **'so,'** he added, enclosing me in his arms. Gathering me to his breast, **pressing** his lips on my lips: **'so, Jane!'**[64]

Amid this explicit opposition to 'conventionalities and custom', apparently diminished by the contraposition between body and spirit, life and death, which in fact ultimately makes it even more suggestive (i.e., 'men and women may be physically different, but our minds are alike and have the same rights'), an initial moment of emphasis comes at the end of the first paragraph of the excerpt, where it is proclaimed in the present tense and with a final exclamation mark: '"equal, — as

64 *JE*, Ch. 23. Emphases my own.

we are!"' This is what Rochester apparently assents to ('"As we are!" repeated Mr Rochester'), even if the conclusions he draws from this primarily concern sexual freedom (centring on the body, not the spirit): '"so," he added, enclosing me in his arms. Gathering me to his breast, pressing his lips on my lips: "so, Jane!"'

Antonini, whose quite compressed version translates less than half the original overall, departs from his usual procedure on this occasion and, instead of condensing, emphasises throughout:

> No le estoy hablando como se acostumbra, ni aun habla mi cuerpo; es mi espíritu que se dirige a su espíritu..., como si ya estuvieran más allá de la tumba, y estuviésemos a los pies de Dios, **iguales, como somos.**
>
> –¡**Cómo somos**! repitió el señor Rochester –. ¡**Así**! –y me estrechó entre sus brazos, apartándome contra su pecho y **oprimiendo** mis labios con los suyos–. '¡**Así, así**!' (Antonini 1941B).

Besides the suggestive ellipsis that Antonini adds after the idea of the two minds being on equal terms — 'es mi espíritu que se dirige a su espíritu...,' — his use of the present tense in the Spanish — 'iguales, como somos' — as in the English makes it clear that the spiritual equality proclaimed by Jane exists in the present. His translation of 'So' as 'Así' ('Like this'), privileging the physical over the logical aspect of the expression, and likewise the literalness of the passionate kiss — 'oprimiendo mis labios con los suyos' — serve to emphasise the physical eroticism of the scene.

But see now what happens in Luaces' version, which, far less compressed overall, on this occasion not only cuts out much more than usual but includes additional precautions so that this proclamation of gender equality in an eroticised context does not draw the attention of the guardians of the law. He renders it:

> Le hablo prescindiendo de convencionalismos, como si estuviésemos más allá de la tumba, ante Dios, y **nos hallásemos en un plano de igualdad, ya que en espíritu lo somos.**
>
> ¡**Lo somos!** — repitió Rochester. Y tomándome en sus brazos me oprimió contra su pecho y **unió** sus labios a los míos —. ¡Sí, Jane! (Luaces 1943B).

Luaces' self-censorship is not unskilful, for he is able to allow different meanings to activate depending on how complicit and suspicious the reader is. On the face of it, his translation does not explicitly stage Jane's manifesto of equality in the present, saying literally: 'as though... we were on a footing of equality, since in spirit we are' ('como si... nos hallásemos en un plano de igualdad, ya que en espíritu lo somos'); in other words, although men and women cannot be regarded as equal on earth, we are equal as sinners before God on the Day of Judgement. This is all beautifully orthodox. And the same can be said of the way the lovers' lips barely touch — '**unió** sus labios a los míos' ('he **joined** his lips to mine') — without the passion entailed by the 'pressing' of the English original. Implicitly, though, what Brontë is really saying can also be understood: that while men and women are not equal in their bodies, they are as minds, which gives them equal rights, breaking with social 'conventionalities', including sexual oppression. However Luaces' version is read, though, his self-censorship is as apparent as it is revealing.

These levels of emphasis and self-censorship tend to be even more obvious at times when Antonini and Luaces translate scenes where the protagonists' amorous passion is manifested, especially when there are erotic overtones present in the original or liable to appear when it is translated into Spanish. We may take what is on the face of it a fairly innocent scene in Chapter 16, where Jane becomes aware that she 'desires' to meet Rochester while she is looking after Adèle:

> 'Qu'avez-vous, mademoiselle?' said she. 'Vos doigts tremblent comme la feuille, et vos joues sont rouges: mais, rouges comme des cerises!'
>
> **'I am hot, Adèle, with stooping!' She went on sketching; I went on thinking.**
>
> I hastened to drive from my mind the hateful notion I had been conceiving respecting Grace Poole; it disgusted me. I compared myself with her, and found we were different. **Bessie Leaven had said I was quite a lady; and she spoke truth — I was a lady.** And now I looked much better than I did when Bessie saw me; I had more colour and more flesh, more life, more vivacity, because I had brighter hopes and keener enjoyments.
>
> 'Evening approaches,' said I, as I looked towards the window. 'I have never heard Mr. Rochester's voice or step in the house to-day; but surely I shall see him before night: I feared the meeting in the morning; **now I desire it, because expectation has been so long baffled that it is grown impatient.**'

Brontë operates subtly here. Besides veiling the question about what is really happening to Jane in Adèle's French — 'Qu'avez-vous, mademoiselle? ...' — she establishes a parallel between the explicit reality that is briefly outlined and the implicit thought — 'I am hot, Adèle, with stooping!' **[:]** She went on sketching; **[/]** I went on thinking' — something that gives rise to a new contrast between

Jane's wishful thinking in the third paragraph of the excerpt — 'Bessie Leaven had said I was quite a lady; and she spoke truth — I was a lady' — and what is implied in the final paragraph: 'now I desire it, because expectation has been so long baffled that it is grown impatient'.

Antonini, who does cut this time, following his normal practice in his compressed version, does so only to construct a suggestive montage that emphasises what is only implicit in the original passage, enhancing the eroticism of the scene; he reduces the whole to:

> — ¿Qué tiene, señorita? Sus dedos tiemblan como las hojas y sus mejillas están rojas como cerezas...
>
> — **Tengo calor, Adela.**
>
> Yo esperaba, con desconocida impaciencia, la hora de ver al señor Rochester. Pensaba interrogarlo sobre Grace Poole, y aun hacerle rabiar un poco, **para después contentarlo**... (Antonini 1941B)

Retranslated into English it gives:

> 'What is the matter, Miss? Your fingers are trembling like leaves and your cheeks are as red as cherries...'
>
> **'I am hot, Adèle.'**
>
> I was waiting, with unwonted impatience, until I could see Mr. Rochester. I planned to question him about Grace Poole, and even anger him a little, **and then make him content**...

Antonini's swingeing cuts are placed at the service of an emphatic refraction. First of all, Adèle's words are in Spanish (not veiled by the French), and he adds a final ellipsis (...) which indicates to the reader that there is 'something else', something unsaid about Jane's appearance. Thus, Antonini replaces the original's parallelism between the explicit physical description and the implied thoughts — '"I am **hot**, Adèle, with **stooping**!" She went on **sketching**; I went on **thinking**' — with a unilateral emphasis in '**I am hot, Adela**', an isolated expression that, cutting out the whole of the reflection about being 'quite a lady' which follows in the next paragraph of the original, he juxtaposes directly with the desire to 'see Mr. Rochester', her aim being, we are suggestively told, to 'anger him a little, and then make him content...', with the new ellipsis added by Antonini at the end suggesting to the complicit reader something considerably more physical than spiritual, and in any event something unsaid implicit in this desire to 'make him content...'.

As might be expected by now, Luaces operates quite differently, taking the opposite direction at each of the crossroads that occur in the original. Thus, while he cuts much less than Antonini, he presents, at least for the literal reader, a Jane who is far more demure, with the implied eroticism concealed. His rendering is:

> — ¿Qué tiene usted, señorita? — dijo —. Sus dedos tiemblan y sus mejillas están encarnadas como las cerezas...
>
> — **Es que al inclinarme estoy en una posición incómoda,** Adèle.
>
> Ella continuó dibujando y yo me sumí otra vez en mis pensamientos.
>
> Me apresuré a eliminar de mi mente la desagradable idea que había formado a propósito de Grace Poole. Comparándome con ella, concluí que éramos muy diferentes. **Bessie Leaven decía que yo era una señora, y tenía razón: lo era.** Y ahora yo estaba mucho mejor que cuando me viera Bessie: más gruesa, con mejor color, más viva, más animada, porque tenía más esperanzas y más satisfacciones.
>
> «Ya está oscureciendo -medité, acercándome a la ventana —, y en todo el día no he visto ni oído a Mr. Rochester. Seguramente le veré antes de la noche. Por la mañana lo temía, pero **ahora estoy impaciente por reunirme con él.»** (Luaces 1943B)

Luaces' translation conceals all the overtones that reveal erotic passion in the original or could be understood as having a double meaning in the Spanish context. To start with the most obvious, his rendering of 'I am hot, Adèle, with stooping!', cuts out the reference to the temperature and unilaterally emphasizes Jane's position, to give 'Es que al inclinarme estoy en una posición incómoda' ('I am uncomfortable from stooping'), a phrase that turns away from the implications created by Brontë (it is also a phrase that describes Luaces' position as a translator under the Francoist regime quite well!) Similarly, Jane is made into a mature 'señora' not a young 'señorita', and her impatient *desire* to see Rochester is unilaterally turned into 'impatience', removing any erotic implication. The result is a passage in which there is nothing to alarm the guardians of orthodoxy in the Spanish context, with both the expression of female desire and the very intensity of Jane's emotions being attenuated.

Similar decisions about emphasis and self-censorship are observed when Antonini and Luaces deal with other erotic situations, such as the possibility of becoming the lover of a married man. This happens, for example, when Jane, after discovering Rochester's deception, struggles with her conflicting feelings. Rochester notices and says to her:

> 'You intend to make yourself a complete stranger to me: to live under this roof only as Adèle's governess; if ever I say a friendly word to you, if ever a friendly feeling inclines you again to me, you will say, — 'That

> man had **nearly made me his mistress**: **I must be ice and rock to him**;' and ice and rock you will accordingly become.'[65]

Confronted with this passage, Antonini decides to preserve more than usual; consistently with his version, which makes *Jane Eyre* a romantic bestseller and female emancipation novel (paradoxical as these two aspects might seem now), he gives:

> — Piensa en el medio de volver a ser para mí una extraña: vivir aquí como la institutriz de Adela solamente; y si le digo alguna vez una palabra amistosa, se dirá: 'Este hombre **piensa hacerme su amante**; **¿necesito ser roca y hielo para él?**'; hielo y roca llegaría usted a ser (Antonini 1941B).

It will be noted that Antonini not only makes the possibility of her becoming Rochester's *mistress* a firm decision — 'piensa hacerme su amante' ('intends to make me his lover') — but also adds a question mark of his own to Jane's thought — '¿necesito ser roca y hielo para él?' ('must I be rock and ice to him?') — thus emphatically spelling out the doubts she actually has about whether or not to give herself to him, whether or not to become his lover. Luaces, on the other hand, who once again cuts more than usual here, and removes all double meanings, gives:

> 'Te propones convertirte para mí en una extraña, vivir bajo mi mismo techo exclusivamente como institutriz de Adèle, rechazando mis palabras y mis aproximaciones **como si fueras de piedra y de hielo**' (Luaces 1943B).

The Spanish translator not only cuts out the word 'mistress' but, by removing the perspectivism of the protagonist's inner thoughts, makes the state of 'rock and ice' a simile of Rochester's for the distance Jane may take from him, not a staging of the inner doubt in Jane's own passionate consciousness, as she struggles in the double bind between her amorous passion and social convention.

In fact, even when the erotic passion is attributed to Rochester himself, with the description of his physical movements often providing the necessary suggestion, there is a radical difference in the ways Antonini and Luaces translate for their respective Latin American and Spanish contexts. Take one last scene, from Chapter 23: Rochester has now proposed to Jane and for the first time we are given

---

65 *JE*, Ch. 27.

a description of physical contact between the lovers, in which she by no means rejects his advances. The original reads:

> 'Come to me — **come to me entirely now,'** said he; and added, in his deepest tone, speaking in my ear as his cheek was laid on mine, **'Make my happiness — I will make yours.'**
>
> **'God pardon me!'** he subjoined ere long; 'and man meddle not with me: **I have her, and will hold her.'**
>
> 'There is no one to meddle, sir. I have no kindred to interfere.'
>
> **'No — that is the best of it,' he said.**

Several of the highlighted expressions of Rochester's are racy for the period, revealing literally the intensity of his amorous passion and implicitly the desire for sexual intercourse. His 'God pardon me!' thus refracts in other directions apart from the secret he still keeps. Likewise with what follows, the suggestion that for this passion to be realised it is desirable to be free of the pressures brought by traditional family ties, something that is expressed with seeming innocence by Jane, for whom this absence is consubstantial with her development as an independent woman against adversity — 'There is no one to meddle, sir. I have no kindred to interfere' — but which Rochester reformulates into a kind of aside with various underlying implications: 'No — that is the best of it.'

Antonini not only preserves the whole passage but, as we would now expect, employs his usual resources to emphasise the passion and some of the double meanings:

> — **Ven a mis brazos, ven ahora**... dijo, y estrechándome la cabeza mururó a mi oído: — **Haz mi felicidad que yo haré la tuya. ¡Dios me perdone!** — añadió — ; y que los hombres no se me traviesen. **Te poseo y te poseeré.**
>
> — **No hay nadie que se resista** — dije — ; yo no tengo parientes que puedan pretenderlo.
>
> — **Sí, y eso es lo mejor** — dijo. (Antonini 1941B).

Although Antonini leaves out 'entirely' at the beginning of the passage as a whole — 'Come to me — come to me *entirely* now' — he adds one of his usual ellipses — 'Ven a mis brazos, ven ahora...' ('Come to my arms, come now...') — highlighting what is left unsaid, what the surrender implies. This is reinforced by his emphatic translation of Rochester's 'I have her, and will hold her' as **'Te poseo y te poseeré'** (**'I possess you and will possess you'**), just as Jane's 'There is no one to meddle, sir' becomes **'No hay nadie que se resista'** (**'There is no-one to resist'**), giving it a bolder tone than the original.

Luaces, whose version, it should be recalled, is at least fifty percent longer than Antonini's, cuts out most of the scene here, removing the idea of total surrender and the other sexual overtones. He leaves just:

> —Ven, ven conmigo—y rozando mis mejillas con las suyas y hablándome al oído, murmuró—: Hazme feliz y yo te haré feliz a ti. (Luaces 1943B).

Besides playing down the initial request for total surrender with his rendering 'Ven, ven conmigo' ('Come, come with me'), Luaces symptomatically excises both the idea of divine forgiveness associated with the extramarital relation with Jane and the idea that the absence of traditional family ties creates the opportunity for amorous union, aspects that would undoubtedly have been subject to censorship by the guardians of the family values and female chastity promoted in Franco's National-Catholic programme. (One can see in fact how Luaces cuts throughout the novel the references to or justification of Jane's development away from family and social ties; expressions such as 'I am absolutely destitute' and 'Not a tie holds me to human society at this moment', or, more emphatically, 'Some of the best people that ever lived have been as destitute as I am',[66] are all symptomatically cut by Luaces—who does translate the passages where these sentences appear, though—an omission that can also be explained in terms of their allusive refraction as a more general description of the situation of opposers to Franco's regime).

In the light of this, the obvious differences between Antonini's and Luaces' pioneering versions when it comes to refracting the potential of *Jane Eyre* for female emancipation, both in the book's proclamations of women's rights and in the scenes where Jane's amorous passion and the sexual freedom it can potentially give rise to are manifested, show the extent to which they were aware of the role the novel could play in this respect for a contemporary readership, on both sides of the Atlantic. On the one hand, certainly, in no area so much as that of female emancipation do we find such radical, systematic differences between the versions produced by Antonini (1941) and Luaces (1943), for while the South American version betrays obvious efforts to emphasise the novel's emancipatory and erotic potential, consistently with the way it was marketed as a romantic bestseller (*Jane Eyre*) and a *Bildungsroman* depicting a woman struggling against social convention

66 See *JE*, Ch. 28, and Ch. 19.

(*Rebel Soul*), it is in this very area that the Peninsular Spanish version evinces the greatest self-censorship, with Luaces moving carefully so as not to attract the attention of the guardians of Francoist orthodoxy. On the other hand, however, whether the erotic passion and potential for female emancipation in *Jane Eyre* were played up or concealed in the Spanish translations, its liberating effect would be strongly felt by readers who were able to understand, on both sides of the Atlantic. For them, it would be enough to consider the work's authorship and engage with its plot as a novel of a woman's development in the face of social adversity to extract its transformative potential.

For, ultimately, it is not only the protagonist's more explicitly rebellious attitudes towards female submission, which the translators could transform at will as has been seen, but also the female individualism characteristic of the Protestant tradition, which defines its authorship, pathos, and plot in ways that could not be changed by the translators, that would refract *Jane Eyre* as a manifesto of female liberation in the new Hispano-American context. Before even opening the translated volume, it was enough to be presented with a work by one of the 'Brontë sisters', who by the mid-twentieth century had acquired a symbolic aura directly associated with their status as 'women writers', to feel an emancipatory potential (redoubled among informed readers by the awareness that, from Jane Austen to the Brontë sisters and George Eliot, women writers had made the decisive contribution to the English novel in the Victorian era). Then, focusing on *Jane Eyre* in particular, the emancipatory refraction intensifies when one considers its plot as a kind of *Bildungsroman* of female liberation, its presentation of woman's individual triumph over social adversity, which would have produced its own differentiated harmonics for those living in Francoist Spain, with its regressive female policies, and those living through the earliest conquests of civil rights in Latin America.

Indeed, the very Protestant idea of an individual directly responsible for her acts, embodied in this case in an emphasis on a woman's will as a path to gradual spiritual growth — 'seized against your will', Rochester recognises, 'you will elude the grasp like an essence'[67] — will have been regarded in the mainly Catholic contexts of South America and Spain as a model for female emancipation. In other words, the way a female orphan becomes a mature and responsible woman through

67 *JE*, Ch. 27.

a combination of rebellion and learning experiences comes through in the Spanish translations as a model of individual behaviour and responsibility that not only subverts traditional male domination and traditional ideas about the family space as the exclusive realm for female growth and fulfilment, but also the Catholic emphasis on hierarchy, whereby priests impose control, penance, and absolution. If one of Brontë's *bêtes noires* was the priestly control of women's education — 'given up independence of thought and action into the hands of some despotic confessor', 'conjured by Romish wizard-craft' (*The Professor*, Chapter 12) — it was precisely this liberation of women from the Catholic hierarchy, Catholic tutelage, and Catholic education that was explicitly and repeatedly identified in twentieth-century Hispano-America as a prerequisite for obtaining and sanctioning full civic rights for women.[68]

It is this significant change of context, then, in which the Protestant individualism staged by the novel is refracted as a relative emancipation

68 This issue of the power of Catholic priests over women created paradoxical situations in both Spain and Latin America, where female suffrage was supported right across the political spectrum, whether out of principle or pragmatism. Thus, in Chile, where intellectuals had upheld women's right to vote since the beginning of the twentieth century as part of their civic, cultural, and educational emancipation, that same right was also upheld by sections of the Conservative Party allied to the Church in the hope that it would work in their favour, given that women received a Catholic education (in fact, the Conservative Party was the first to present a bill to bring in female suffrage, in 1917, and this was rejected by the centre-left, which feared that the generally Catholic education of women would favour right-wing parties in elections). A similar argument against female suffrage was put forward by some Spanish Republicans: giving the vote to women would lead to a conservative and theocratic state, they thought, because of the influence of the Catholic Church on women's education. Even Victoria Kent, the Spanish lawyer and Republican politician — and the first woman to be admitted to the College of Lawyers in Madrid — argued in 1931, against what she acknowledged were her own principles, for the female vote to be postponed because women's generally limited political knowledge as a result of Church influence would ensure that they inclined towards the conservatives. As she summarised it: 'I don't think it's the right time to give Spanish women the vote. I say that as a woman who at the critical juncture of having to come down on one side or the other finds herself forsaking an ideal'. (The law was passed with support from the right, the Spanish Socialist Workers' Party and small Republican groups, but the great majority of Republican Action, the Radical Republican Party and the Radical Socialist Republican Party voted against it. As was observed earlier, this law conferring suffrage was repealed by Franco, who would ultimately proscribe all voting rights, for both men and women).

from religious male authority and education as such, associated with the influence of Castilian-style Catholicism, that explains how a novel written a hundred years earlier (and in which a clear sexual hierarchy and sexist prejudices doubtless persist) could become a manifesto for women's liberation, the *Bildungsroman* of the 'rebel soul' fighting against the prejudices of tradition and the oppressiveness of society. If the traditional religious menace was most clearly recognisable in the formalism of St John — who, in the face of Jane's resistance, exclaims 'Your words are such as ought not to be used: violent, unfeminine, and untrue. They betray an unfortunate state of mind: they merit severe reproof: they would seem inexcusable' — Jane's imaginary of individual liberation when faced with the pressures of her context could only be read as an explicit manifesto for women's emancipation: 'I am no bird; and no net ensnares me; I am a free human being with an independent will'.[69] It is symptomatic that Luaces' compressed version leaves only the first metaphor here — 'No soy un **ave**' ('I am not a bird') — which is somewhat obscure by itself, whereas the other translation done in Spain in the period, the unabridged one by the orthodox Pereda, reads 'nest' instead of 'net' — 'No soy ningún **pájaro** y no hay **nido** que me retenga' (Pereda 1947A: 'I am no **bird** and no **nest** holds me back') — replacing the image of oppression with a metaphor of family belonging.

For there is perhaps no aspect of the novel that produces a stronger refraction in Spanish than these liberation metaphors presented by the protagonist throughout, which rise to something of a climax in the imaginary of rebellion against slavery, the passages comparing the situation of women to that of slaves in need of freedom. Not least because, as might be expected, this comparison was omnipresent from the outset of the struggle for equal rights in Hispano-America; as Gabriela Mistral would put it in the early twentieth century: 'As minds are illuminated, her mission and value are beginning to be understood and she is becoming a companion, an equal, instead of the slave of yesterday. Compared with her old humiliation, she has already won significant ground, but there is still much to explore before she can declare victory.'[70] Thus, the refraction of new meaning can be

69 *JE*, Ch. 35, Ch. 23.

70 Gabriela Mistral, 'La instrucción de la mujer [1906]', in *Mujeres Chilenas. Fragmentos de una historia*, ed. by Sonia Montecino (Santiago: Catalonia, 2008), p. 97.

envisioned even in passages such as the following from Chapter 24, where Jane compares the situation of a woman regaled with all kinds of unwanted luxuries to that of prisoners in an oriental harem who should be liberated:

> The Eastern allusion bit me again. 'I'll not stand you an inch in the stead of a seraglio,' I said; 'so don't consider me an equivalent for one. If you have a fancy for anything in that line, away with you, sir, to the bazaars of Stamboul without delay, and lay out in extensive slave-purchases some of that spare cash you seem at a loss to spend satisfactorily here.'
>
> 'And what will you do, Janet, while I am bargaining for so many tons of flesh and such an assortment of black eyes?'
>
> 'I'll be preparing myself to go out as a missionary to preach liberty to them that are enslaved — your harem inmates amongst the rest. I'll get admitted there, and I'll stir up mutiny; and you, three-tailed bashaw as you are, sir, shall in a trice find yourself fettered amongst our hands: nor will I, for one, consent to cut your bonds till you have signed a charter, the most liberal that despot ever yet conferred.'
>
> 'I would consent to be at your mercy, Jane.'
>
> 'I would have no mercy, Mr. Rochester, if you supplicated for it with an eye like that. While you looked so, I should be certain that whatever charter you might grant under coercion, your first act, when released, would be to violate its conditions.'

Jane's refusal to accept the presents Rochester wants to give her, which for many of Brontë's English contemporaries would have constituted a scene not devoid of flirtation, could be (and increasingly was) construed in the new twentieth-century Spanish-speaking contexts as a scene of resistance to the traditional image of the woman dependent on the will, praise, and respect of a man, valued for her beauty as an adornment to him. In fact, several of the motifs making up this quasi-allegory of the slave in need of liberation take on clear and immediate cultural and political overtones, including the mention of a 'liberal charter', which Luaces capitalises as 'Constitución' in a suggestive rendering of the phrase — 'una Constitución tan liberal como jamás déspota alguno haya concedido' (Luaces 1943B: 'a Constitution more liberal than any despot has yet granted') — writing once more between the lines for his local readership, while there are further echoes with the struggle for equal civil rights in the South American republics, liberated barely a century earlier from European imperialism.

Empire Refractions: From Savage Slave to Gothic Ghost

The imaginary of slavery staged in *Jane Eyre* had a strong refraction not only due to its significance for female emancipation, but also in terms of the criticism it activated of European colonialism and the racial prejudices that fed it, towards which there was a particularly acute sensibility in Latin America, leading the translators into Spanish to make variously drastic and deliberate transformations. Certainly, as one focuses on the original Victorian British context, when there were colonies from the Americas to India, all further applications of this slave imaginary to Chartism and industrial capitalism would have been lost on the twentieth-century Spanish-speaking reader, including the echoes and condemnation of 'white slavery', which would have given the original English novel, appearing only a year before the 1848 Revolution, certain subversive overtones, however far its author was from seeming to be a revolutionary in this respect. But Jane's episodic denunciation of slavery throughout the novel takes on a new meaning when read either from the perspective of the former colonial territories of Latin America, now emancipated republics, or from the perspective of the old colonial power, Spain, where Franco's National-Catholic programme had renewed its universalist imaginary of imperial evangelisation. (As Luaces parodically summed it up in the article 'Feminism and Shamelessness' quoted earlier, when confronted in his youth with a similar renewal of imperial evangelism during the dictatorship of Primo de Rivera: 'Spain is a nation upon which God has conferred the highest governing and civilising mission that a people ever received. But if we Spaniards are to be worthy once again to wear the crown of dominion on our brows, it is indispensably necessary for us to extirpate from the fertile garden of our land the weeds of foreign influences, feminisms, and all other pernicious isms').[71]

Already a scene such as the childhood episode in which John Reed's cruelty and violence are likened to those of slave drivers and Roman emperors — '"Wicked and cruel boy!" I said. "You are like a murderer — you are like a slave-driver — you are like the Roman emperors!"'[72] — refracts in a symptomatic manner, superimposing as

71 Ortega Sáez, 'Traducciones del franquismo en el mercado literario español contemporáneo', p. 103.

72 *JE*, Ch. 1.

it does slavery on to the quintessential model of imperialism, while the historical parallels with the contemporary situation are explicitly brought forward by the introspective commentary that Brontë adds immediately afterwards, with Jane as her mouthpiece: 'I had drawn parallels in silence, which I never thought thus to have declared aloud'. Suggestive parallels of precisely this kind were activated in the early translations published in Spain through the rendering of 'slave-drivers' as 'negreros' — '¡Malvado! — le dije —. Eres peor que un asesino, que un **negrero**, que un emperador romano' (Luaces 1943B); '¡Empecatado, cruel! — dije —. ¡Eres como los asesinos, como los **negreros**, como los emperadores romanos!' (Pereda 1947A) — which not only anchors the image unequivocally in the context of modern authoritarian rule and imperialism, modelled on Rome, but also in the trade in humans from Africa, and which finally resonates critically with the situation of the working class, since the word 'negrero' is a well-worn Spanish metaphor commonly used to denote somebody who is exploitative in his treatment of those working under him.[73]

This same type of refraction, where imperial exploitation overlaps with the exploitation of workers, is activated when Brontë next returns to the analogy between childhood violence and slavery at the start of the second chapter, where we find Jane confined to the red room:

> I was conscious that a moment's **mutiny** had already rendered me liable to strange penalties, and, like any other **rebel slave**, I felt resolved, in my desperation, to go all lengths.
>
> 'Hold her arms, Miss Abbot: she's like a mad cat.'
>
> 'For shame! for shame!' cried the lady's-maid. 'What shocking conduct, Miss Eyre, to strike a young gentleman, your benefactress's son! **Your young master**.'
>
> **'Master! How is he my master? Am I a servant?'**[74]

Of the early versions in Spanish, Antonini's in Argentina, which symptomatically cuts nothing here, is the most emphatic, strongly

73 Antonini misreads the original here, rendering 'slave-driver' as 'cochero eslavo', i.e., a 'Slav coachman': '¡Malvado y cruel muchacho — exclamé —, eres un asesino, más bruto que un **cochero eslavo** y semejante a los emperadores romanos!' (Antonini 1941B). Gaite's later translation removes the reference to African slaves and the work connotations: ' — ¡Maldito canalla! — le increpé —. Eres un asesino, un déspota, como los emperadores romanos' (Gaite 1999A). Hill is more literal, but has a less effective and natural rhythm: '¡Chico malvado y cruel! — grité —. Eres igual que un asesino, te comportas como un **tratante de esclavos**, como un emperador romano' (Hill 2009A).

74 *JE*, Ch. 2.

refracting this overlap between the imperial imaginary and that of social subjection:

> Tenía el convencimiento de que un momento de **rebeldía** me haría merecedora de severos castigos y, como una verdadera **esclava rebelde**, resolví, en mi desesperación, arrostrar hasta el fin las consecuencias.
>
> — ¡Agárrela por los brazos, señorita Abbot; mire, parece un gato montés!
>
> — ¡Qué vergüenza!, ¡qué vergüenza! — exclamaba la doncella —. ¡Qué conducta tan escandalosa la suya, señorita Eyre! Golpear a un joven caballero, hijo de su benefactora! ¡**Su joven amo!**
>
> — **¡Amo! ¿Quién es mi amo? ¿Soy acaso una sirvienta?** (Antonini 1941B).

Besides the retention of the reference to the rebellious slave, Antonini's decision to translate 'master' by 'amo' (which brings in the senses of 'owner' and 'boss') reactivates the parallelism between the childhood scene and social exploitation. This is not done in the two translations produced in Spain at about this time, however, which render 'master' as 'señorito' ('young master' in the sense of 'young gentleman'), limiting the reference to the childhood scene in a domestic context. Thus, Luaces gives:

> Comprendía, además, las consecuencias que iba a aparejar mi **rebeldía** y, como un **esclavo insurrecto**, estaba firmemente decidida, en mi desesperación, a llegar a todos los extremos.
>
> — Cuidado con los brazos, Miss Abbot: la pequeña araña como una gata.
>
> — ¡Qué vergüenza! — decía la criada —. ¡Qué vergüenza, señorita Eyre! ¡Pegar al hijo de su bienhechora, a su **señorito**!
>
> — **¿Mi señorito? ¿Acaso soy una criada?** (Luaces 1943B).

While Luaces preserves the imaginary of a slave in rebellion at the beginning, his rendering of 'amo' by 'señorito' at the end dissipates somewhat the strength of the parallel between the domestic childhood realm and the social and employment realm. As for the other version published in Spain during the period, Pereda cuts out some expressions: this is rather surprising, on the face of it, given that hers is an unabridged translation, though less so when her relative orthodoxy is considered. She gives:

> Comprendía que aquellos instantes de rebeldía me traerían consecuencias funestas, y en mi desesperación, estaba decida a llegar al final.
>
> — ¡Sujétale los brazos, Abbot! ¡Parece un gato rabioso!

> — ¡Señorita, qué vergüenza, qué vergüenza haberse atrevido a pegar al hijo de su bienhechora, que es todo un caballero, **a su señorito**!
> — ¿Por qué va a ser **mi señorito**? **¿Es que soy una criada**? (Pereda 1947).

Repressing any imperial and social refraction that might take us away from the childhood scene as such, Pereda not only translates 'master' as 'señorito', but excises the imaginary of the rebel slave. In Spain, only the post-Franco translations by Gaite and Hill convey the passage with a completeness equivalent to that provided by Antonini in Argentina in 1941, in circumstances where the refraction would connect more to the situation of 'maidservants' than to liberation in a colonial context.[75]

More broadly, although *Jane Eyre* betrays many of the middle-class social and racial prejudices which lay at the heart of both the exploitation of the working class and the slavery that upheld nineteenth-century British imperialism (and European colonialism more generally), these refract in a quite different manner and direction through the transformations wrought in the Spanish versions over time, a refraction that becomes once again particularly significant when the decisions taken in Latin America and Spain, respectively, are compared.

Thus, the early translations published in Spain, unlike Antonini's in Argentina, make no difficulty about reproducing clichés concerning the relations between European nations, as when Jane chauvinistically contrasts the supposed constancy of the English to

75 These unabridged translations published much later in Spain give:
Me daba cuenta de que algunos instantes de rebelión ya me había hecho acreedora de extrañas penitencias y, como cualquier **esclavo rebelde** en mi caso, decidí, llevada por la desesperación, llegar todo lo lejos que hiciera falta.
— Sujétele bien los brazos, señorita Abbot; está igual que un gato furioso.
— ¡Qué bochorno! — gritaba la doncella — ¿no le parece una conducta bochornosa señorita Eyre, atacar a un muchacho que además es hijo de su bienhechora? ¡A su **joven amo**!
— ¿**Amo**? ¿Por qué va a ser él mi **amo**? **Yo no soy ninguna criada**. (Gaite 1999A).
Era consciente de que un sólo momento de desobediencia me había reportado un injusto castigo y, como cualquier otro **esclavo rebelde**, estaba tan desesperada que habría hecho lo que fuera para escapar.
— ¡Tómela por los brazos, señorita Abbot! ¡Parece un gato salvaje!
— ¡Qué vergüenza! ¡Qué vergüenza! — exclamaba la doncella de la señora —. ¿Cómo se ha atrevido a golpear al joven **señorito**? ¡Al hijo de su benefactora! ¡A su **señor**!
— ¡Mi **señor**! ¿Cómo va a ser mi **señor**? **¿Acaso soy una criada?** (Hill 2009A).

the supposed fickleness of the French. Prejudices such as 'a **sound English education** corrected in a great measure her **French defects**',[76] summarising at the end of the novel the way in which Adèle has apparently been transformed from a frivolous and capricious young girl into a docile, good-tempered and well-principled woman, are fully reproduced in the mid-twentieth-century versions published in Spain by both Luaces — 'una **sana educación inglesa** corrigió en gran parte sus **defectos franceses**' (Luaces 1943B) — and Pereda — 'una **sólida educación inglesa**, que corrigió, en todo lo posible, los **defectos propios de la educación francesa**' (Pereda 1947) — a passage that would certainly have chimed with the animosity towards France of Francoism (onomastic paradoxes aside): 'Are we to measure Spain, severe, virile, noble, conquering Spain, by the same yardstick as the frivolous French?', as we read in Luaces' own parody. In Argentina, conversely, where the journey through the French language and French culture (and, more broadly, through the languages and cultures of a number of other European nations) had since the Romantic period been part of an explicit programme of liberation from Spanish literary and cultural colonialism, Antonini completely omitted this contemptuous prejudice against the French, vaguely attributing Adèle's faults to her personal 'inheritance' (i.e., it is hinted, to the habits of her dancer mother): 'la **perfecta educación inglesa** que había recibido le corrigió los **defectos heredados**' (Antonini 1941B: 'the **perfect English education** she had received corrected her **inherited defects**'). This kind of transformation is also found in the translations published in Spain much later, in the post-Franco period, with both Gaite and Hill watering down the anti-French prejudice by attributing the defects once again to Adèle's personal constitution: 'La sólida educación inglesa corrigió en gran medida sus **defectos de origen [her defects of origin]**' (Gaite 1999A); 'los sólidos principios de la educación inglesa fueron corrigiendo **los defectos de su naturaleza [the defects of her nature]**' (Hill 2009A).

Where racial prejudices towards non-European peoples are concerned, meanwhile, all the early Spanish-language translations curtail or omit them, even when the word 'race' was used to mean (as the Spanish word 'raza' also commonly was during the first half of the twentieth century) 'feature', 'family', 'nation', or 'humanity'. Thus, an expression of Rochester's such as 'Her family wished to secure me

76 *JE*, Ch. 18.

because I was of a **good race'**, used to explain why the Mason family wished him to marry Bertha, is stripped of all its racial overtones when translated into Spanish.[77] The most extreme suppression, as we have learned to expect, comes from Antonini in Argentina, who does translate this whole passage containing Rochester's explanation to Jane, but cuts out precisely this sentence about Bertha's Jamaican family being pleased by his 'English race'. The early Spanish translators, for their part, although they did not cut out the sentence, restricted the implications of 'race' to social genealogy: 'Su familia deseaba asegurarme, porque yo pertenecía a una **casta ilustre** [illustrious caste, heritage]' (Luaces 1943B); 'Su familia quería engatusarme, ya que pertenecía a una **ilustre casa** [illustrious household, heritage]' (Pereda 1947A). Even when used as a synonym for humanity, in a way that 'race' often was by extension in both English and Spanish until the 1940s, the word tended to be avoided in the translations published in Spain; thus, a phrase such as 'he labours **for his race**',[78] summarising St John's missionary task at the very end of the novel, becomes in the translations 'labora por **sus semejantes** [his kind]' (Luaces, 1943B), 'trabajar a favor de **sus prójimos** [his fellow men]' (Pereda, 1947A), unequivocally emphasising the Christian universalist imaginary (the same holds for Gaite's 'se desvive por **sus semejantes**' (1999) and for Hill's 'mejorar la **raza humana**' (2009)). Antonini, however, in what is a less favourable presentation of the Christian missionary destiny associated with British imperialism, translates literally this time — 'él trabaja para **su raza**' (Antonini 1941B ['he works for **his race**']) — which refracts differently, also suggesting that St John works in the interests of his own colonizing nation.

These imperial refractions and associated transformations in the Spanish translations of Jane Eyre reach something of a climax when it comes to the colonial conception of the 'savage', that European anthropological invention of the nineteenth century used to describe a sort of proto-man, characterised by both his cultural backwardness and his position in a teleology leading towards the civilised European man, which finds its paradigmatic embodiment in the figure of Bertha. For when 'the madwoman in the attic' is presented as a dangerous being, a monstrous savage endowed with an enormous sexual passion, her aura of mystery and characterisation as an absolute

77 *JE*, Ch. 27.
78 *JE*, Ch. 38.

alterity, likened at times to either the animal imaginary or the ghostlike, vampiric gothic imaginary, are defined first and foremost by her mestizo genealogy (she is the daughter of an English merchant, Jonas Mason, and a Jamaican Creole, Antoinetta). In other words, she is defined by the absence of a pure identity, culturally and historically speaking, by a sort of degeneracy — 'she came of a mad family; idiots and maniacs through three generations!' — that contrasts with Jane's stable identity and healthy constitution as an unquestionably white European woman (at least literally speaking, leaving aside for the moment psychoanalytical interpretations of Bertha as an alter ego of the protagonist).[79] Thus, it is not fortuitous, and it becomes significant in the translations, that Rochester should have married Bertha in 'Spanish Town, Jamaica', just as it is significant that, bringing together a number of these imaginaries, Bertha's 'savage' cry should be determined by comparison with that of the largest bird which flies over the highest South American peaks: 'Good God! What a cry!... not the widest-winged condor on the Andes could, twice in succession, send out such a yell from the cloud shrouding his eyrie'.[80]

Faced with this particular conception of the 'savage', which had been applied across the board to the indigenous peoples of America — and which, more broadly, Europeans had used in their discourse to characterise the exotic cultures they came into contact with on their colonial campaigns, incorporating them into a supposedly inevitable evolution running from primitive savagery through gothic-medieval barbarism to modern civilisation — it is once again symptomatic that, while the orthodox editions published in Spain tended to stage at least some of these imperial and racial prejudices, likening Bertha to an animal, the more dissident ones, as well as those translated in Latin America, tend to emphasise a more gothic imaginary, the well-known ghost motifs of British culture that are also present in Brontë's novel, likening Bertha to a night spectre.

Take one of the standout moments of the novel in this respect, the scene where Bertha's nocturnal visit is described by Jane to Rochester. Amid the long portrayal in the original, one reads:

79 *JE*, Ch. 26. For a discussion of the idea of Bertha as an alter ego, see Chapters I & II above.

80 *JE*, Ch. 20.

> 'Fearful and ghastly to me — oh, sir, I never saw a face like it! It was a discoloured face — it was a **savage face**. I wish I could forget the roll of the red eyes and the fearful blackened inflation of the lineaments!'
>
> 'Ghosts are usually pale, Jane.'
>
> 'This, sir, was purple: the lips were swelled and dark; the brow furrowed: the black eyebrows widely raised over the bloodshot eyes. Shall I tell you of what it reminded me?'
>
> 'You may.'
>
> 'Of the foul German spectre — the Vampyre.'[81]

Confronted with this amalgam of racial prejudice and gothic imaginary, which the reader of the original would divide automatically between the actual facts — Bertha's 'savage' face (red eyes, blackened lineaments, broad dark lips), suggesting a mulatto constitution — and Jane's fanciful comparison of her to a spectre, the different Spanish versions react not only by omitting details, but also by modifying the words of the description that present Bertha in the light of a primitive savage, promoting the animal and the gothic rather than the colonial imaginary. Even Pereda, while generally remaining literal and orthodox, so that most of the implications of the original come out, does not allow herself to reproduce the reference to the 'savage' as such, but gives:

> —¡Espantosa y como un fantasma, señor! No puede concebirse nada parecido: **la cara, sin color humano; la expresión, de fiera [her expression that of a wild beast]**. ¡Qué daría por olvidar la mirada de aquellos ojos sanguinolentos y aquellas facciones ennegrecidas y abultadas!
>
> —Los fantasmas suelen ser muy pálidos, Jane.
>
> —Pues este no lo era; tenía un color amoratado, los labios cárdenos y como hinchados, el ceño de furia y una espesas y negras cejas. ¿Sabe lo que me recordaba señor?
>
> —¿A qué?
>
> —Al inmundo espectro de las leyendas alemanas, al vampiro. (Peredá 1947A)[82]

---

81 *JE*, Ch. 25.

82 Retranslated into English:

> 'Horrifying and ghostlike, sir! It is impossible to conceive of anything like it: the face, without human colour; the expression, that of a wild beast. What would I give to forget the look in those bloodshot eyes and those blackened and swollen features.'
>
> 'Ghosts are usually very pale, Jane.'
>
> 'Yet this one was not; it had a purple colour, the lips violet and as though swollen, a furious brow and thick black eyebrows. Do you know what it reminded me of, sir?'

Pereda's unabridged translation reproduces the whole portrait of Bertha's features (black face, red eyes, broad purple lips, etc.), adding explicitly that its colour was 'not human' ('la cara, sin color humano'). But instead of summarising the whole as a 'savage face' (which would be *cara salvaje* or *cara de salvaje* in Spanish), she speaks about the expression of a wild beast (*expresión de fiera*), pushing the translation of the word savage towards its original meaning of an undomesticated animal or plant before it became a conventional anthropological metaphor to designate 'uncultivated' human beings. Thus, instead of emphasising the image of the lustful, promiscuous and supposedly inferior inhabitant of the colonized regions — 'her vices sprang up fast and rank [...] What a pigmy intellect she had, and what giant propensities!',[83] in Rochester's words this time — Pereda emphasises the bestial side, matching the frequent animalisation of Bertha in other passages of the novel — 'whether beast or human being, one could not, at first sight, tell',[84] as Brontë puts it when Jane confronts Bertha in the knowledge of who she is. Luaces, meanwhile, is more emphatic in his transformations, giving:

> — Me pareció horrible. Nunca he visto cara como aquella: una cara descolorida, espantosa. Quisiera poder olvidar aquel desorbitado movimiento de sus ojos inyectados en sangre, y sus facciones hinchadas como si fuesen a estallar.
>
> — Los fantasmas son pálidos, por regla general.
>
> — Pues éste no lo era. Tenía los labios protuberantes y amoratados, arrugado el entrecejo, los párpados muy abiertos sobre sus ojos enrojecidos. ¿Sabe lo que me recordaba?
>
> — ¿El qué?
>
> — La aparición de las leyendas germanas: el vampiro... (Luaces 1943B)[85]

'What?'

'Of the foul spectre of German legend, the vampire.'

83 *JE*, Ch. 27.

84 *JE*, Ch. 26.

85 Retranslated into English:

'It looked horrible to me. I have never seen a face like that: a face discoloured, horrifying. I would like to forget that bulging movement of its bloodshot eyes, its features swollen as though about to burst.'

'Ghosts are pale, as a general rule.'

'This one was not, though. It had protuberant, purplish lips, the brow was wrinkled, the eyelids wide open over its reddened eyes. Do you know what it reminded me of?'

'What?'

'The apparition of the Germanic legends: the vampire...'

Luaces, who tried to escape to South America during the Spanish Civil War, cut out most of the key details that would make the reader construe the figure as a native of Africa or some other southern or colonized region, starting with the words 'savage' and 'black'. For, as regards the way the scene had been received and translated in South America itself a couple of years earlier, Antonini's version not only omits the 'savage' reference but cuts even more emphatically to tilt the scales towards the gothic imaginary and away from the colonial, giving:

> — Me pareció espantoso: nunca he visto una cara como aquélla. ¡No puedo olvidar esos sanguinolentos ojos y esas inflamadas facciones!
> — Los espíritus ordinariamente son pálidos.
> — El color de éste era púrpura, los labios renegridos y las cejas espesas y levantadas. Me pareció un espectro, un vampiro. (Antonini 1941B)[86]

As one goes back to Antonini's pioneering version in Buenos Aires, then, Bertha's apparition is no longer simply likened by Jane to a vampire — 'Shall I tell you of what it reminded me? [...] Of the foul German spectre — the Vampyre' — but actually seems to her to be one — 'It seemed to me a spectre, a vampire' — more unilaterally emphasising the English imaginary of ghosts and spectres that is deployed at other points in the novel to present the threat of Bertha at Thornfield: 'This accursed place, [...] this insolent vault, offering the ghastliness of living death to the light of the open sky — this narrow stone hell, with its one real fiend, worse than a legion of such as we imagine. [...] I was wrong ever to bring you to Thornfield Hall, knowing as I did how it was haunted'.[87] In the refraction of Antonini's South American version, then, the threat enclosed in the attic is no longer that of an anthropological creation, the savage emerging from the southern seas, but rather that of a mythological creation, the vampire or spectre inhabiting the misty northern climes.[88]

---

86 Retranslated into English:
'I found it frightful: I have never seen a face like that one. I cannot forget those bloodshot eyes and inflamed features!'
'Spirits are usually pale.'
'This one was purple in colour, with blackened lips and thick raised eyebrows. It seemed to me a spectre, a vampire.'

87 *JE*, Ch. 27.

88 The much later unabridged translations by Gaite (1999) and Hill (2009) restore the '*savage*' face, but using 'savage' unambiguously as an adjective ('the face was savage' in Gaite, 'the face had something savage' in Hill), thus no longer

Some Final Remarks on Literary Simplification and Cultural Refraction

The refraction of *Jane Eyre* in the Spanish language was as limited at a literary micro level, in stylistic terms, as it was strong at a contextual level, in cultural terms. On the one hand, if editorial policies influencing the translation of novels into Spanish often promote various forms of literary simplification and domestication — especially when a book is recognised as having potential not only as a literary classic for an instructed audience, but also as a bestseller and youth story, as has been the case with *Jane Eyre* — the resulting only partial re-creation of the characteristic forms of meaning of the English original, eschewing any stronger poetic insemination of language and corresponding ways of representing reality, does not preclude an important prismatisation in Spanish at such an intratextual level. On the other hand, though, one observes a quite strong refraction resulting from the contextual differences between the English culture of the mid-nineteenth century and the respective Spanish and Latin American cultures of the twentieth, unfolding the potential signification of gender and colonial motifs in Brontë's novel in an effective and often differentiated afterlife in both sides of the Atlantic.

On the face of it, the interrogation of linguistic behaviours as formal conditions of possibility of representation in the various kinds of Spanish-language renderings (the relatively unabridged translations, the edited compressed versions, and the highly condensed paraphrases), paying attention to the wide spectrum of forms that the Spanish language enacts or not in response to the lexical, syntactic, imagistic and musical behaviours of the English novel, reveals at least three interrelated simplifying tendencies that are relatively common in mainstream translation, namely (i) a realistic and intentional semantics, (ii) a literary hypertextualism, and (iii), to a lesser extent, a relative ideological domestication.

From a semantic point of view, the Spanish translations operate with an inherited horizon of realism and intentionality. In objective terms, the meaning is more often than not understood as an ideality that transcends the linguistic and formal behaviour of the text. In

---

referring explicitly to the supposedly uncultivated native inhabitants of the colonies, but evoking someone with a fiery look, an expression like a wild beast's, like Pereda before them.

subjective terms, it is assumed that the apprehension and translation of this meaning does not depend on a poetic receptiveness towards the unpredictable effects of grafting the foreign literary forms onto the Spanish language, but rather on an intentional act that involves grasping this ideality and then presenting it once again with all the resources of the new language. This procedure works relatively well at the basic level of the taxonomy of experience produced by the lexical networks of Spanish and English (given the partial overlap between the genealogies of these languages), and likewise in the transmission of metaphorical imaginaries, parallelisms, and other forms of verbal imagery that translate more or less effortlessly when it is ideas that are privileged; but it becomes more problematic when it comes to syntactic and musical forms, for instance, with the array of stylistic peculiarities that Charlotte Brontë deploys in the context of the English language (parataxis, time perspectivism, sound iconisms, etc.) being disregarded by translators, with some exceptions in Luaces and Gaite.

This is why the general approach can be summarized as 'hypertextual'. Far from privileging the materiality and behaviour of Brontë's idiosyncratic forms of representation, most translators deploy either a general *imitatio*, prevalent in the longer unabridged translations, or an adaptive *inventio*, prevalent in the more compressed versions. Whereas the former already involve all kinds of rationalisations, clarifications and simplifications — very obviously so in the case of Pereda (1947) and still in evidence with Hill (2009) — that generate a more straightforward, logical texture and a more distant representation of the facts, the latter clearly drop the signifying system of the original. In fact, the only common form of hypertextualism not observed in a systematic way in the Spanish-language versions examined here is 'embellishment', an absence which tells us something about the power relations, in literary and cultural terms, between the Spanish-speaking and English-speaking countries in the second half of the twentieth century, when British and Anglo-American traditions had acquired enormous influence and prestige.

For the same reason, within the typically interrelated domesticating tendencies, one can observe a certain degree of cultural-ideological adaptation, a process that may include anything from acts of omission to stronger transformation of aspects that are dissonant or difficult to understand for the new readership. As might be expected, the largest cuts are to be found in the highly condensed paraphrases aimed at a young readership, whose translators or editors seek to turn the novel into an edifying story, transforming any content that might be potentially dissonant and any phrases that could break the spell of fiction, even Hispanicising some of the names to make them more familiar and immediate to the reader. But a slightly different process of adaptation is also evident in the unabridged translations and compressed versions, with the difference in ideological-cultural context between the first inscription of the English original and the later inscriptions of the Spanish-language versions leading translators to remove aspects that could offend Spanish or Latin American sensibilities, such as the characterisation of Bertha as a savage from colonised regions, while exploiting the novel's potential for the new place and time, including its important impact as a manifesto for female emancipation.

In this sense, having recognised the semantic realism and intentionality, the literary hyper-textualism and the relative cultural adaptation in the Spanish renderings of *Jane Eyre*, one can end by insisting that the change of the ideological-cultural context activated a decisive refracting of the work, a Spanish-language after-life to the English novel that detonated new signification, as has been seen especially concerning the motifs of empire and gender in their differentiated reception in Latin America and Spain. It is above all the effect produced by these gender and imperial motifs that differentiates the refraction of meaning between the first large-scale reception of *Jane Eyre* in Spain and in Latin America in the aftermath of the Second World War. That is, the differences are to be found not only in the divergent choices made in the Spanish-language texts, but also in the significations these texts activate in the different contexts.

Thus, firstly, one can witness the different significance of the motifs of female liberation. In the context of the struggle for women's civil rights in the Latin American republics — where there existed a separation between Church and State, and where the vote for women was fought for and obtained in one country after another from the late 1930s to the late 1950s — one finds that not only the explicitly emancipatory aspects of the novel, but also a large part of the individualism characteristic of the English Protestant tradition, are refracted spontaneously as a manifesto of female liberation. On the other hand, in the Francoist context of promotion of traditional Catholic values in a confessional state, translators had to censor themselves or write between the lines to varying degrees.

Then, there is the refracted meaning of the imperial motifs — with symptomatic cases in the treatment of the imaginary of 'slavery' and the racial representations of the 'savage', instances where European power and knowledge had come together to justify the hierarchy between human beings and territories that are at the root of colonial conquest — with a certain contrast between the versions produced in the Latin American countries, liberated from colonialism a century earlier, and those coming out of Spain, which was redefining itself at the time as a somewhat backward post-colonial nation among the European countries, although in both cases effecting significant transformations when they come to deal with racial prejudices.

Lastly, within Spain itself, there are noticeable differences in the translations and promotion of the text between Castile and Catalonia. For among the reasons that the publishing of *Jane Eyre* in Madrid during Franco's dictatorship was quite backward relative to publishing in Barcelona were not only the death, imprisonment, and exile of many literary figures during the Civil War, but also the fact that translating and commenting on foreign works, including one with the kind of potential for female and colonial liberation offered by *Jane Eyre*, can be a very effective way of writing between the lines in dissident regions under pressure, of projecting one's own voice onto others' at times of political persecution or intellectual repression, as was the case for literary resistance through translation in Barcelona.

Works Cited

Translations of *Jane Eyre*

Brontë, Charlotte, *Jane Eyre ou mémoires d'une gouvernante*, trans. By Old Nick (P. É Daurand Forgues (Paris: *Le National*, 1849).

——, *Juana Eyre. Memorias de un aya* (Santiago de Chile: Imprenta del Progreso, 1850).

——, *Juana Eyre: Memorias de una aya*, 2 vols (Havana: Diario de la Marina, 1850–1851).

——, *Juana Eyre* (New York: Appleton & Co., 1889).

——, *Juana Eyre*, trans. By José Fernández Z (Barcelona: Juventud, 1928).

Brontë, Carlota, *Juana Eyre* (Barcelona: Mentora, 1928).

Brontë, Charlotte, *Jane Eyre*, trans. By M. E. Antonini (Buenos Aires: Acme Agency, 1941).

——, *Jane Eyre*, trans. By J. de Luaces (Barcelona: Iberia-J. Gil, 1943).

Brontë, Carlota, *Juana Eyre. Una obra maestra rebosante de ternura y bondad, cuya emoción sabe llegar al alma. Creación que labró la reputación de su autora, popularizándola en todos los países* (Madrid: Revista Literaria, 1945).

Brontë, Charlotte, *Jane Eyre*, trans. by M. F. Pereda (Madrid: Aguilar, 1947).

——, *Jane Eyre*, trans. by J. Sánchez Díaz (Santiago de Chile: Paulinas, 1974).

——, *Jane Eyre*, trans. by S. Robles (Santiago de Chile: Zig Zag, 1989).

——, *Jane Eyre*, trans. By C. M. Gaite (Barcelona: Alba, 1999).

——, *Jane Eyre*, trans. By Toni Hill (Barcelona: Mondadori, 2009).

Other Sources

Alberdi, Juan Bautista, *Las bases* (Buenos Aires: La Facultad, 1915).

Borges, Jorge Luis, 'El escritor argentino y la tradición', in *Obras completas*, 4 vols (Buenos Aires: Emecé, 1974–96), I (1989), pp. 267–74.

Costa, Horácio, *Mar abierto: ensayos sobre literatura brasileña, portuguesa e hispanoamericana* (Mexico City: Fondo de Cultura Económica, 1998).

De Andrade, Osvaldo, 'Manifiesto Antropofágico', in *Las vanguardias latinoamericanas: textos programáticos y críticos*, ed. by Jorge Schwartz (Mexico City: Fondo de Cultura Económica, 2002), pp. 173–80.

——, *Escritos antropofágicos* (Buenos Aires: Corregidor, 2001)

De Campos, Haroldo, *De la razón antropofágica y otros ensayos* (Madrid: Siglo XXI, 2000).

Glantz, Margo, ed., *La Malinche, sus padres y sus hijos* (Mexico City: Taurus, 2001).

Gutiérrez, Juan María, 'Discurso Inaugural del Salón Literario' (1837), in *El tabaco que fumaba Plinio. Escenas de la traducción en España y América: relatos, leyes y reflexiones sobre los otros*, ed. by Marieta Gargatagli and Nora Catelli (Barcelona: Serbal, 1998), pp. 360–86.

Llorente, Ángel, *Arte e ideología en el franquismo, 1936–1951* (Madrid: Visor, 1995).

Maura, Juan Francisco, *Women in the Conquest of the Americas* (New York: Peter Lang, 1997).

Messinger Cypress, Sandra, *La Malinche in Mexican Literature: From History to Myth* (Austin: University of Texas Press, 1991).

Mistral, Gabriela, 'La instrucción de la mujer', in *Mujeres Chilenas: Fragmentos de una historia*, ed. by Sonia Montecinos (Santiago: Catalonia, 2008).

Morena y Vals, F., *Juana Eyre: Drama en cuatro actos y un prólogo* (Barcelona: Manero, 1869).

Nowottny, Winifred, *The Language Poets Use* (London: Athlone Press, 1996).

Ortega Sáez, Marta, 'Traducciones del franquismo en el mercado literario español contemporáneo: el caso de *Jane Eyre* de Juan G. de Luaces' (unpublished doctoral thesis, University of Barcelona, 2013).

Paz, Octavio, *El laberinto de la soledad* (Mexico City: Fondo de Cultura Económica, 1989).

Perón, Eva, *Dicursos* (Buenos Aires: Biblioteca del Congreso Nacional, 2012).

Rabadán, Rosa, ed., *Traducción y censura inglés-español: 1939–1985* (León: Universidad de León, 2000).

Sarlo, Beatriz, 'Oralidad y lenguas extranjeras: el conflicto en la literatura argentina durante el primer tercio del siglo XX', in Beatriz Sarlo and Carlos Altamirano, *Ensayos argentinos: de Sarmiento a la vanguardia* (Buenos Aires: Siglo XXI, 2006), pp. 253–69.

——, *Borges, un escritor en las orillas* (Buenos Aires: Seix Barral, 2007).

——, *La máquina cultural: Maestras, traductores y vanguardistas* (Buenos Aires: Seix Barral, 1998).

Strauss, Leo, *Persecution and the Art of Writing* (London: Chicago University Press, 1998).

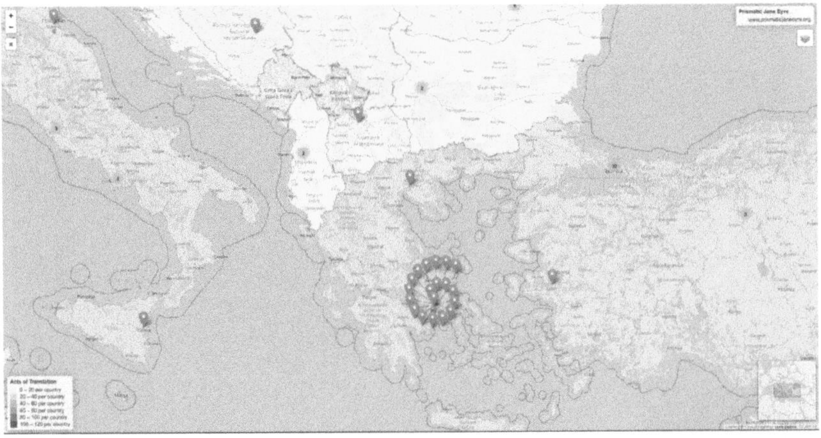

The World Map
https://digitalkoine.github.io/je_prismatic_map
Created by Giovanni Pietro Vitali;
maps © Thunderforest, data © OpenStreetMap contributors

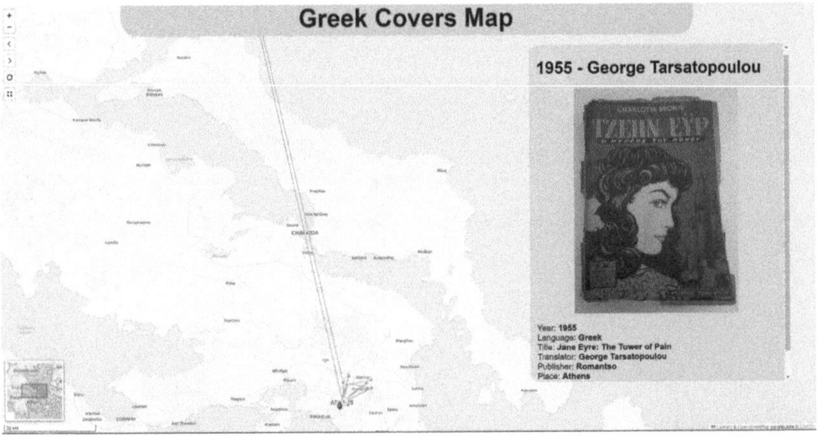

The Greek Covers Map
https://digitalkoine.github.io/greek_storymap/
Researched by Eleni Philippou; created by Giovanni Pietro Vitali and Simone Landucci

6. Commissioning Political Sympathies

The British Council's Translation of *Jane Eyre* in Greece

Eleni Philippou

Jane Eyre's First Translation: A Prelude

The first full translation of *Jane Eyre* into Modern Greek was translated by Ninila Papagiannē, and published in 1949 by Ikaros publishers under the aegis of the British Council in Greece. It was reprinted by Ikaros in 1954/1955, and the same translation was later reprinted in 1993 by S. I. Zacharopoulos Press. Since this initial translation, abridged, juvenile, and scholarly editions of *Jane Eyre* have been published in Greece, not to mention more low-brow popular adaptations of the book, such as a Classics Illustrated comic. It may seem surprising that it took over a hundred years for *Jane Eyre* to be translated into Greek, but up until the 1940s translations from French were pervasive across the Greek literary market. In fact, in the 1800s French and Italian largely dominated the translation scene, with French gaining ascendency with the decline of the Venetian Democracy of 1797.[1] French texts constituted over 60 percent of the translations during this period, with English translations only starting to appear in Greece in 1817 when the British took over the Ionian islands.[2] Although Shakespeare and Lord Byron feature on the list of the most translated authors of the period

1 K. G. Kasinēs, *Bibliography of Foreign Literature into Greek, 19th–20th Centuries Volume I 1801–1900* [*Vivliographia Tōn Hellēnikōn Metaphraseōn Tēs Xenēs Logotechnias 19.-20. Ai. Prōtos Tomos 1801–1900*] Autoteleis ekdoseis (Athēnai: Syllogos Pros Diadosin Ōphelimōn Vivliōn, 2006), p. χα′–χβ′.

2 Kasinēs, *Bibliography (Volume 1) 1801–1900*, p. χδ′.

https://doi.org/10.11647/OBP.0319.10

(Shakespeare at number nine and Byron at number seventeen), the list is overwhelmingly French.[3]

Interestingly, Sophia Denisi points out that in the second half of the nineteenth century, household literary magazines contributed decisively to the dissemination of translated novels, which initially had been treated with distrust when first arriving in Greece, and only were accepted as a serious literary form after decades.[4] However, it is difficult to collect accurate information on the translation scene in Greece in the period between 1900–1950, owing to both local and global events. Statistical information was affected by Greece's chequered twentieth-century history. Greece experienced a series of massive political upheavals: the Balkans Wars (1912–1913), World Wars (1914–1918; 1939–1945), and the Civil War (1946–1949), and the Asia Minor Catastrophe (1922), preceded by the Greco-Turkish War. These events not only affected the production of books and their current existence (bad quality paper was used), but contributed to the lack of care for and cataloguing of books in public libraries.[5] Despite these significant problems, K. G. Kasinēs has been able to determine that between 1901–1950, French texts were most translated, then English (out of 537 titles, 110 were American and one Australian), followed by Russian, German, and Scandinavian languages.[6] In contrast to the nineteenth

3 Kasinēs, *Bibliography (Volume 1) 1801–1900*, p. χθ′. Other Anglophone authors circulating at the time included Jonathan Swift and Walter Scott. Alexandre Dumas was reprinted multiple times, perhaps as many as 250.000 times over the period 1801–1900 (Kasinēs, *Bibliography (Volume 1) 1801–1900*, p. λ′).

4 Sophia Denisi, *The Translation of Novels and Novellas 1830–1880: An Introductory Study and Record* [*Metafrasis Mithistorimatōn kai Diēgēmatōn 1830–1880: Eisagōgiki Meletē kai Katagrafē*] (Athens: Periplus, 1995), pp. 13–14.

5 K. G. Kasinēs, *Bibliography of Greek Translations of Foreign Literature, 19th–20th Centuries Volume II 1901–1950* [*Vivliographia Tōn Hellēnikōn Metaphraseōn Tēs Xenēs Logotechnias 19.-20. Ai. Deyphteros Tomos 1901–1950*] Autoteleis ekdoseis (Athēnai: Syllogos Pros Diadosin Ōphelimōn Vivliōn, 2013), p. ι′. Kasinēs notes that there is often evidence for a text existing in the national catalogues but it was impossible to secure a hard copy of the book when researching it. He comments that bad spinoffs or imitations of the original texts were sometimes the only versions available, and about 30 percent of books of the 1901–1950 period were without a publication date (Kasinēs, *Bibliography (Volume II) 1901–1950*, pp. ι′–ιγ′).

6 Kasinēs, *Bibliography (Volume II) 1901–1950*, p. ιη′. Between 1901–1950, novels were the most commonly translated literary form, with more than 50 percent of translations, followed by theatre and then poetry. Oscar Wilde was translated multiple times by different translators, as was Eugene O'Neil (Kasinēs, *Bibliography (Volume II) 1901–1950*, pp. κα′, κη′).

century, the twenty most translated authors were a more balanced mix of English and French writers, with Shakespeare holding first place.[7]

The proliferation of French translations in the nineteenth century was primarily a manifestation of Greece's political and cultural sympathy towards France. The Greek War of Independence (1821–1830) was inspired by the French Revolution, and up until the 1940s, French was the only foreign language taught in state schools. English began to gain ascendancy in twentieth-century Greece. During the 1930s, Greek intellectuals became more interested in English, partly owing to their interest in the modernist movement. Key Greek literary figures, such as George Seferis, spent time in Britain before the Second World War which allowed for greater receptivity towards British culture. Furthermore, English was introduced into state schools in 1945. The most important feature of the increasing engagement with English was the presence of the British Council in Greece from the late 1930s onwards, with the explicit aim of promoting cultural dialogue between the two nations. In the March 1946 issue of the *Anglo-Greek Review* (a publication of the British Council that we will discuss in due course) the role of the British Council was outlined thus:

> The main purpose of the British Council is to give the inhabitants of the other countries of the world the opportunity to understand British culture and the British way of life, and to give the British the opportunity to understand the culture of other countries [...]. What needs to be remembered above all the details is the ultimate aim of the Council's activities: that is, the spreading of mutual understanding, respect and love between the peoples of the world. And that, above all, is the Propaganda of Peace.[8]

7 Kasinēs, *Bibliography (Volume II) 1901–1950*, p. κε′. The shift in publishing locations between the nineteenth and twentieth century may have affected which texts were translated into Greek. Between 1901–1950, the majority of translated texts were published in Athens, or mostly Greek cities, whereas in the nineteenth century, places where Greek books were printed included a number of cities or towns outside of the geographical confines of modern-day Greece, which became independent of Ottoman rule in the years 1821–1829 and was established as an independent kingdom in 1832. Before 1835, the biggest number of translations were published in Venice, whereas after 1835, publishing took place in Greece (e.g., Athens, Ermoupoli on the island of Syros) as well as in places with Greek inhabitants (e.g., Alexandra in Egypt) (Kasinēs, *Bibliography (Volume II) 1901–1950*, pp. κγ′, χδ′).

8 Cited in Dimitris Tziovas, 'Between Propaganda and Modernism: The *Anglo-Greek Review* and the Discovery of Greece', in *The British Council and Anglo-Greek Literary Interactions, 1945–1955*, ed. by Peter Mackridge and David Ricks (London: Routledge, 2018), pp. 123–54 (p. 146).

Although this passage expresses admirable sentiments, proclaiming that the British Council is an open and inclusive space set up with an emphasis on cultural exchange, in fact the British Council as an institution was not entirely innocuous, especially considering that the Council was founded before the Second World War by Sir Reginald Leeper, a British civil servant and diplomat.[9] Leeper's founding of the British Council was inspired by his recognition of the importance of 'cultural propaganda' in promoting British political interests both during peacetime and in war, a view no doubt informed by his time in the Department of Information's Intelligence Bureau (1916–1918), and as Director of the Political Intelligence Department (1938–1943).[10] Leeper saw the establishment of the British Council as a means of asserting 'soft power'.[11] For Leeper, cultural diplomacy was an effective manner of securing political power, especially if such diplomacy projected forth an image of cultural reciprocity and exchange between different countries.[12] Leeper supported 'qualitative rather than quantitative propaganda' and an avoidance of 'one-sided methods of cultural infiltration'.[13]

Although the British Council first opened in Athens in 1937, its presence was relatively short-lived as in 1941 it was forced to close owing to the Second World War.[14] Greece was occupied by German forces in April of 1941. Within a few months, as Greece's national

---

9 Leeper had a vested interest in Greece. In the interests of recouping British influence on Greece, he was tasked with the responsibility of restoring the exiled Greek monarchy, and quashing 'any threats to national stability, principally that posed by the communists' after the end of the German occupation (see Derek Drinkwater, 'Leeper, Sir Reginald Wildig Allen [Rex] '1888–1969', *Oxford Dictionary of National Biography* (2011). It is unclear how these mandates locked into the activities of the British Council in Greece after the German forces left the country (see Peter Mackridge, 'Introduction', in *The British Council and Anglo-Greek Literary Interactions*, pp. 1–20 (p. 3)).

10 Tziovas, 'Between Propaganda and Modernism', p. 125; Drinkwater, 'Leeper'.

11 The *Oxford English Dictionary* defines soft power as a power 'deriving from economic and cultural influence, rather than coercion or military strength'. See 'soft power', in 'soft, *adj.*', *Oxford English Dictionary*, https://oed.com/view/Entry/183898

12 Tziovas, 'Between Propaganda and Modernism', p. 125.

13 Ibid. In a memorandum written in April 1934, Leeper states, 'It is just as good propaganda for this country to bring distinguished foreigners to lecture and meet people here as it is to send our own speakers abroad. We shall obtain better publicity for our own culture in other countries if we take an equal interest in their culture.'

14 This opening coincided with the British Council funding the Byron Chair at the Athens University for the teaching of English language and literature. In

economy collapsed and the official state lost its authority, inflation, black-marketeering, food shortages (eventually escalating into famine) became rampant.[15] Arising from this bleak reality, Greece developed a robust resistance against the Axis powers which was riven along two political lines: EAM/ELAS and EDES. The former was roughly composed of two bodies — the National Liberation Front (EAM) of which the Greek People's Liberation Army (ELAS) was the military wing. This front was of a leftist nature and dominated by the Communist Party of Greece. The latter, the National Republican Greek League (EDES), was composed of nationalists with a republican background, and the largest of the anti-communist resistance groups. EAM's growth (particularly in the provinces, aided in part by urban communist activists) was rapid and robust, and by 1944, when the German occupation came to an end, EAM/ELAS claimed that its 'support extended to more than one million members'.[16] Despite the Germans' best efforts to suppress the resistance through violence and terror, the resistance not only persisted, in fact, German suppression may have even bolstered the resistance.[17]

The polarisation between Greece's two resistance groups came to a head with the liberation of Greece in 1944 and the ensuing Civil War in the years 1946–1949. Put crudely and very simplistically, the Civil War played out between the Hellenic Army, a coalition of monarchist and republican forces (including both members of EDES and former quislings) supported by the United Kingdom and the United States and in favour of the pre-war status quo, and the Democratic Army of Greece — the military wing of the Communist Party of Greece (KKE) — backed by Yugoslavia and, intermittently, by Albania and Bulgaria. This foreign interference in a Civil War may seem surprising, however, the threat of Greece becoming a Soviet state was a cause for concern for both the United States and Britain owing to its strategic and geographic importance. Greece was considered to be on the 'front line of the struggle between the US and the USSR for world domination'.[18] The Anglo-Americans considered it imperative that the Greek Left be

1939, the British Council's Institute of English Studies made the learning of English available to Greeks who did not attend private schools.

15 Mark Mazower, *Inside Hitler's Greece: the Experience of Occupation, 1941–44* (New Haven, Conn.; London: Yale University Press, 2001), p. xviii.

16 Mazower, *Inside Hitler's Greece*, p. xix.

17 Ibid.

18 Mackridge, 'Introduction', p. 4.

defeated during the Civil War so that Greece did not come to succumb to Soviet expansionism.

Preceding the Civil War, the German occupation of Greece came to an end in the late summer of 1944. Greece was 'taken over by local partisans' — predominately EAM/ELAS who did not accept the provisional government under Georgios Papandreou installed by the British in October 1944.[19] The provisional government was not particularly successful — demands for the partisans to demobilise ultimately resulted in a breakdown of negotiations.[20] This provisional government also desired to reinstate the Greek king.[21]

The British registered the tensions at play in post-liberation Greece with great alarm, reading the popularity and strength of EAM/ELAS as reaching its logical culmination point with Stalin commandeering the Greek state.[22] The British felt that to avoid such a situation, it had to 'neutralize the Greek Communists, whom it could not hope to control'.[23] In fact, as far back as 17 August 1944, Churchill had written a 'Personal and Top Secret' memo to the American president Franklin Roosevelt to say that:

> The War Cabinet and Foreign Secretary are much concerned about what will happen in Athens, and indeed Greece, when the Germans crack or when their divisions try to evacuate the country. If there is a long hiatus after German authorities have gone from the city before organised government can be set up, it seems very likely that EAM and the Communist extremists will attempt to seize the city.[24]

This correspondence between Churchill and Roosevelt is a stark example of how the British were watching the Greek political scene carefully. The British expected their transatlantic neighbour, the United States, to understand that 'extraordinary interventionist

19 Ed Vulliamy and Helena Smith, 'Athens 1944: Britain's dirty secret', *The Guardian*. 30 Nov 2014, https://www.theguardian.com/world/2014/nov/30/athens-1944-britains-dirty-secret

20 Vulliamy, 'Athens 1944: Britain's dirty secret'.

21 Ibid.

22 John O. Iatrides, 'Britain, The United States, and Greece, 1945–9', in *The Greek Civil War, 1943–1950: Studies of Polarization*, ed. by David Close (London: Routledge, 1993) pp. 190–213.

23 Iatrides, 'Britain, The United States, and Greece, 1945–9', p.194.

24 Cited in Vulliamy, 'Athens 1944'. Churchill, 'increasingly prone to intervening directly in Greek affairs and one of the King of Greece's foremost supporters, exhibited an imperious contempt for the resistance: when they were not Bolsheviks, they were — in a celebrated phrase — "miserable banditti"'. Mazower, *Inside Hitler's Greece*, p. 365.

measures were needed if the interests of the entire Western camp were to be safeguarded'.[25] Britain and America's focus on keeping Greece well out of the Soviet grasp meant that their energies were channelled into preventing a Communist victory during the Civil War.[26] The consequence of this was that 'Greece became the object of powerful external forces whose ultimate purpose went far beyond the need to solve Greece's post-war problems'.[27]

With the re-opening of British Council in 1944, the Council's commitment to disseminating and consolidating English gained renewed political impetus in this divisive climate, and with Britain's wider objectives in mind. Yet, it is important to note, that from the time of its 1944 reopening in Greece, the Council itself may not have understood its policies as explicitly political, a point noted by Peter Mackridge in reference to the nature of the British Council: 'there was a stark difference in perception between what British and Greeks considered to be 'apolitical' and 'political'. For the British Council, 'apolitical' simply meant supporting the conservative status quo; with reference to Greece at the time, it therefore entailed supporting the monarchy'.[28] However, British Council documents of the time certainly point to a paternalistic attitude towards Greece in which the Council takes an active interest in engineering Greece's national fate. A British Council memorandum from the mid-1940s, entitled 'British Council Work in Greece', notes that '[w]ith British support and under British protection, an attempt is now being made to find some sort of national government which can gradually attract to itself the more idealistic and progressive elements [i.e., non-Communist elements] in the country, and set them to work on the task of reconstruction'.[29] The same memorandum continues: 'We have, moreover, undertaken in Greece a responsibility such as we have towards no other country in

25 Iatrides, 'Britain, The United States, and Greece, 1945–9', p.192. With the Americans offering financial aid to Greece from 1947, the British were effectively reduced to America's 'junior partner'. Unlike the British, the Americans had 'more resources' and 'fewer compunctions about dictating to the unruly Greeks'. Iatrides, 'Britain, The United States, and Greece, 1945–9', p. 201.

26 Iatrides, 'Britain, The United States, and Greece, 1945–9', p.192.

27 Ibid.

28 Mackridge, 'Introduction', p. 4.

29 Kew, National Archives, box 34, folder 10, Memorandum British Council Work in Greece: 1945/6.

Europe, and Greece therefore has a special claim to our attention'.[30] The British Council hoped specifically to engage the politically ambivalent members of the Greek youth in the hope that they could instil political beliefs of a more 'moderate' nature — 'pulling them away from EAM and other [left-wing] cultural influences'.[31] The Council aimed to achieve this 'in part by accessing the countries' own 'cultural reserves' but also through sustained cultural and educational programmes', as detailed in reports dated 1945–1946.[32] (The educational programmes were primarily the training of teachers for English language provision in Greece, and the establishment of English language.[33]) Koutsopanagou references a 1946 report that suggests two ways that Britain could exert influence — firstly, by countering propaganda against Britain and the West in the immediate present, and secondly, in the long term, through a 'constant flow of books, articles, films and British cultural influences [...] at a steady level'.[34] It is to this long term aim, primarily the translation of English literary works, that we now turn.

30 Memorandum British Council Work in Greece: 1945/6. This 'special claim' is almost certainly a reference to the classical debt that the West owes Greece. This concept is discussed more thoroughly in my journal article 'Perennial Penelope and Lingering Lotus-Eaters: Revaluing Mythological Figures in the Poetry of the Greek Financial Crisis', *Dibur Literary Journal*, 5 (2018), 71–86.

31 According the British Council, EAM could have 'led the way' in national revival and regeneration but upon its seizure by the Greek communist party 'instilled in its members a number of totally un-Greek political conceptions based on general international theory'. Memorandum British Council Work in Greece: 1945/6.

32 Gioula Koutsopanagou, '"To Cast Our Net Very Much Wider": The Re-Opening of the British Council in Athens and Its Cultural Activities in Greece', in *The British Council and Anglo-Greek Literary Interactions*, pp. 39–68 (pp. 54–55).

33 In 1945, the teaching of English became compulsory, alongside French, in state secondary schools, but this was not administered via the Council. A memorandum dated 1945/1946 notes that the 'Greek government are naturally and rightly sensitive to any hint of foreign interference with the schools system in Greece. They are disposed to make a very large place for the English language in the State school curriculum, but they probably would not be disposed to accept a permanent British educational advisor or English language teachers of British nationality for the State schools, even if such teachers were available in the requisite numbers. There is no question, in other words, of the Greek schools inviting or requiring the same sort of assistance as the Egyptian state schools at one time required'. Memorandum British Council Work in Greece: 1945/6.

34 Koutsopanagou, '"To Cast Our Net Very Much Wider"', p. 55.

The British Council's Translation Programme and *Jane Eyre*

The British Council's literary translation programme came into effect in 1949, when a contract was signed for the publication of six translated editions of English classics. A subsidy of £1400 was to be advanced to Ikaros Publishers by the Council during the translation programme's first year, and a further £150 for each publication if the contract was renewed.[35] By March 1950, four plays by Shakespeare (*Macbeth*, *Romeo and Juliet*, *Twelfth Night*, *A Midsummer Night's Dream*), Charles Dickens's *Great Expectations*, and Charlotte Brontë's *Jane Eyre* had been published.[36] A year later, Shakespeare's *The Tempest* and *Much Ado about Nothing*, together with Rudyard Kipling's *Selected Short Stories*, and Jane Austen's *Pride and Prejudice*, had been published.[37] Furthermore, the serialisation of Vasilēs Rōtas's translation of *Troilus and Cressida* — never before translated into Greek — began in the *Anglo-Greek Review*'s January-February 1951 issue. Shakespeare's *Othello*, *King Lear*, and *Troilus and Cressida*, and Lytton Strachey's *Queen Victoria* were published over the course of 1951–1952, whilst Shakespeare's *A Winter's Tale*, *Julius Caesar*, *Hamlet*, and three plays by Oscar Wilde over 1952–1953.[38]

A committee was formed for the selection of titles, translators, etc., although it is unclear who exactly composed this committee and how the translators and titles were decided,[39] or if the publishers were in

35 Ikaros was probably chosen because they had already published influential highbrow poetry and literary criticism by leading Greek writers, including George Seferis who got the Nobel Prize for Literature in 1963. Ikaros published 22 books over the period from 1944 to 1950 — 0.96%. Kasinēs *Bibliography (Volume II) 1901–1950*, p. λθ'.

36 Kew, National Archives, box 34, folder 20, Annual Report 1949/50, Books & Publications Department.

37 Kew, National Archives, box 34, folder 25, Annual Report of Functional Officer (1951). The same report notes that the publication of the other works selected by the Translation Committee was held up by a paper shortage.

38 *Gulliver's Travels* and *Shrew/Merry Wives* (the latter as one volume) were in preparation in 1951–1952. Kew, National Archives, box 34, folder 25, Representative's Annual Report 1951–1952. It is not clear if *Gulliver's Travels* was ever published. It appears that *The Taming of the Shrew* and *The Merry Wives of Windsor* were only finally published after 'innumerable delays' in 1955, together with *The Merchant of Venice*. Kew, National Archives, box 34, folder 30, Representative's Annual Report 1955–1956.

39 Annual Report 1949/50, Books & Publications Department.

any way responsible for the choice of translators.[40] An advance of £50 was made to Ikaros upon the initiation of the programme in 1949 for the translations into Greek.[41] Yet, it is clear that the British Council realised that in some instances no systematic translations of English classics into Greek had ever been attempted and that they hoped that their translations, certainly in the case of Shakespeare, would become the definitive editions. The Council also decided to commission new translations of works that had been previously translated very successfully, as is the case with Dimitrios Vikelas' renderings of *Romeo and Juliet* and *Macbeth*, and Jacob Polylas' *The Tempest*. Owing to the lack of archival evidence, it is difficult to speculate as to why the Council felt it necessary to retranslate existing works, but such a decision could be attributed to any one of the following factors: a desire to offer an updated or more contemporary translation, or to assert or affirm their authority as an institution and preeminent purveyor of British culture.[42] Furthermore, the retranslations could possibly be a product of the personal desire of the translator to interpret a specific work anew.[43] In the very first year of the translation programme,

40 There were two functional officers at the Council: the Books Officer and the Functional Officer (Music, Arts, Theatre). The duties of the Books Officer is described as 'usual routine work' and building connections with important booksellers, but perhaps the role extended into decisions regarding the translation and distribution of books. Kew, National Archives, box 34, folder 20, British Institute Athens Annual Report 1947–48.

41 This advance was also for the publication of Professor Sewell's *The English Mind in the Seventeenth Century*. Annual Report — 1949/50, Books & Publications Department.

42 Lawrence Venuti notes that retranslations can often 'maintain and strengthen the authority of a social institution by reaffirming the institutionalised interpretation of a canonical text'. See: *Translation Changes Everything: Theory and Practice* (London; New York: Routledge, 2013) p. 97.

43 These reasons may have been the motivations behind Vasilis Rotas' translations of Shakespeare. Although pre-WWII, Rotas had been one of the two main Shakespeare translators of the Greek National Theatre, he was unable to return there after the German occupation of Greece and the ensuing Civil War owing to his participation in the Greek resistance as a member of EAM. (Individuals with left-wing sympathies were excluded from public life after the Civil War.) His decision to translate Shakespeare may have been his attempt to reaffirm his expertise as a Shakespearean translator, while also championing his ideological sympathies within the works themselves (e.g., his representation of Shakespeare's female characters is informed by his socialist ideology, unlike Vikelas' readings that reflect his middle-class value system. Dimitra Dalpanagioti, 'The Translation of William Shakespeare's Plays and the Changing Concept of Womanhood in Greece' (1875–1955)' (unpublished doctoral thesis, Aristotle University of Thessaloniki, November 2020),

Shakespeare, Dickens, and Brontë were translated by three different translators. *Jane Eyre* was translated by Ninila Papagiannē.[44]

Maria Papagiannē, informally known as 'Ninila', was born in 1913 in Smyrna in Turkey. Her formative years were spent between Constantinople and Athens, a time when the Ottoman Empire was in a state of flux. Papagiannē's family moved permanently to Greece in 1922 — the year of the compulsory population exchange between Greece and Turkey.[45] After completing her education at the American College of Greece[46] (then known as the Junior College for Girls),[47] Papagiannē went on to become a translator and novelist. Papagiannē's translations, many of which are still available today as reprints, include nineteenth and twentieth century British and American novels. In particular, she translated works by Charlotte Brontë, Jane Austen, Henry James, Stephen A. Larrabee, Herman Melville, Don DeLillo, and Lawrence Durrell.[48]

---

pp. 225–26. Moreover, Rotas chose to translate Shakespeare into demotic Greek (unlike some earlier translations by other translators which were in Katharevousa), which may possibly have made him an appealing choice to the British Council. (Demotic Greek was the contemporary vernacular, unlike Katharevousa that was a cultivated imitation of Ancient Greek that was used for official and literary purposes. The use of these two forms of Modern Greek in different spheres generated a high degree of controversy in the nineteenth and twentieth centuries (known as the 'Language Question'), until 1976 when Demotic was made Greece's official language.)

44 During the period 1901–1950, 2,283 books are translated by 720 individuals (Kasinēs, Bibliography (Volume II) 1901–1950, p. λ'), only 112 of whom are female (Bibliography (Volume II) 1901–1950, p. λε'). During this period, Georgia Deligiannē-Anastasiadē (a famed children's writer responsible for later translations of *Jane Eyre*) translated five books in total, and Ninila Papagiannē three books (Kasinēs, *Bibliography (Volume II) 1901–1950*, p. λε').

45 Georgia Farinou-Malamatari, 'Ninila Papagiannē: A Hidden Presence', in *Modern Greek Literature of the Twentieth-century. A Volume in Honour of Eris Stavropoulou* [*Themata Neoellinikēs Logotechnias tou eikostoy aiōna. Timētikos tomos gia tēn Eri Stavropoulou*], ed. by T. Agathos, L, Iaōkeimidou, and G. Ksourias. (Athens, Gutenberg, 2020), pp. 578–88. (pp.578–79).

46 Farinou-Malamatari, 'Ninila Papagiannē: A Hidden Presence', p. 579.

47 Pierce – American College of Greece, 'Founding and Development', https://www.pierce.gr/en/founding-development/

48 For readers interested in the translation and reception of some of these texts, refer to Elinor Shaffer's book series *The Reception of British and Irish Authors in Europe*. Of particular interest are: Katerina Kitsi-Mitakou and Maria Vara, 'The Reception of Jane Austen in Greece', in *The Reception of Jane Austen in Europe*, ed. by Anthony Mandal and Brian Southam (London: Continuum, 2007), pp. 225–39, and Eleftheria Arapoglou, '"The Art of the Novel": Henry James's Reception in Greece', in *The Reception of Henry James in Europe*, ed. by Annick Duperray (New York: Continuum, 2006), pp. 225–34.

Unfortunately though, there is no archival evidence from either Ikaros or the British Council to explain Papagiannē's connection to the British Council, and why she would have worked with them to produce a translation of *Jane Eyre*. However, we may make some tentative speculations to explain *Jane Eyre*'s inclusion in the translation programme, both thanks to its reputation as a British cultural work, and in relation to Papagiannē's personal life and aesthetic sensibilities. Firstly, *Jane Eyre* was popular from its initial publication, and continued to remain popular well beyond Brontë's death in 1855. Charlotte MacDonald, making further reference to various literary scholars, notes that for late nineteenth or early twentieth century audiences, *Jane Eyre* represented a bygone era, a time of 'province, stage coach, country property', an era that conveyed a 'reassuring and confirming story of England at a moment of early nineteenth-century modernity'.[49] Together with writers like Dickens, *Jane Eyre* fulfilled an 'appetite for stories of Englishness', which would thereby make it a good choice for educational programmes within and outside of Britain that aimed to consolidate or foster a sense of British identity — it has been taught globally, often in former English colonies.[50] In fact, for McDonald, *Jane Eyre*'s 'charisma' as a text fed (and continues to feed) into its appeal to different classes or groups of individuals: for some it is a tale of resistance in which Jane resists power and injustice: she (in own words) may be 'poor, obscure, plain and little' but this governess still stands up to the wealthy and powerful Mr Rochester.[51] She is a symbol of sovereignty, controlling her own destiny and fate. Her 'autonomous self' reflects back to the reader the 'utopian promise that *Jane Eyre* long illuminated in the global imagination'.[52] This sovereignty, of an individual in command of herself, makes Jane a particularly compelling figure for female readers, and perhaps

---

49 Charlotte MacDonald, 'Jane Eyre at Home and Abroad', in *Ten Books That Shaped the British Empire: Creating an Imperial Commons*, ed. by Antoinette Burton and Isabel Hofmeyr (Durham: Duke University Press, 2014), pp. 50–70. (p 57)

50 *Jane Eyre* was on the school matriculation curriculum as a set text, locking into a 'wider colonial legacy in institutions of church and education, in the libraries and literacy associations of paper and print that lived alongside, and often outlasted, formal relations of empire' (MacDonald, "*Jane Eyre* at Home and Abroad", pp. 57–58).

51 MacDonald, '*Jane Eyre* at Home and Abroad', pp. 57–58.

52 MacDonald, '*Jane Eyre* at Home and Abroad', p. 60.

made her appealing to Papagiannē whose novelistic works show a preoccupation with strong or unconventional female protagonists.

Papagiannē's novels, entitled *Πέρασμα Ανέμου* (1968) [*The Wind Passing Through*], and *Μια πόλη μια ζωή* (1969) [*One City, One Life*], were published by Ikaros within a year of each other. In both instances, the novels portray Papagiannē's pronounced interest in history (connecting with her training as a professional tour guide[53]), and are written as 'autobiographies' from the perspective of an unconventional female narrator. The first novel takes place in ancient Greece, and deals with the figure of Mirini: a fife-playing hetaira — a type of ancient Greek prostitute who aside from providing sexual services, was an artist and entertainer. The second novel begins in the pre-World War II period and extends into the 1950s, with particular emphasis on Germany's occupation of Greece. In this book, the novel's protagonist, Maya Constantinou, makes a personal plea to the first mate of the SS to free her childhood friend and neighbour (585).

As Farinou-Malamatari notes, for readers of Greek literature, Papagiannē's second novel, *One City, One Life*, is strongly reminiscent of the novel, *Invalids and Wayfarers* (1964) by Giorgos Theotokas — one of Greece's preeminent novelists and liberal intellectuals.[54] Theotokas' novel, set in Greece, presents a relationship between the female tragedian, Theano Galati, and a SS officer's helper, a director named Ernest Hillenbrand. However, the resonances are far from coincidental: Papagiannē had a personal familial connection to Theotokas: her maternal grandfather was Theotokas' grandmother's brother.[55] In 1962, Papagiannē related to Theotokas in two interviews her personal story of the occupation — the very story that then appeared in *Invalids and Wayfarers*.[56] Theotokas' novel draws the relationship in judgemental terms, borne out of Galati's fear and loneliness, and ultimately as an example of political treason, whereas

53 Farinou-Malamatari, 'Ninila Papagiannē: A Hidden Presence', p. 579.

54 Farinou-Malamatari, 'Ninila Papagiannē: A Hidden Presence', p. 586.

55 Farinou-Malamatari, 'Ninila Papagiannē: A Hidden Presence', p. 578.

56 *The Nations*, published in 2004, offers a literary timeline of *Invalids and Wayfarers*, including important archival materials such as the two interviews. However, Papagiannē's name is not included in the interviews: the editors of *The Nations* limited themselves to the initials, noting 'that it was deemed proper for her name not to be published'. These editors probably were not aware of the fact that Papagiannē herself published the story in fictionalized form in 1968 in her own way. Farinou-Malamatari, 'Ninila Papagiannē', p. 586.

Papagiannē's rendition of the relationship is far more sympathetic, seeing it as a love that transcends political or national boundaries, and in which the SS commander is impressed by Maya's bravery and intelligence.[57] Papagiannē's transgressive behaviour during Greece's savage occupation by Germany points to Papagiannē herself being a strong independent woman, one who functioned outside of societal norms and conventions. It is this subversive ability to push up against convention which may, we speculate, have made *Jane Eyre*, with its spirited and unique female protagonist, an appealing novel for Papagiannē to translate.

Indeed, in lieu of archival evidence of why the British Council chose to include *Jane Eyre* in their translation programme, we could make the following assumptions: that the British Council chose the novel because of its popularity, charisma, and multifactedness, as discussed earlier. Alternatively, Papagiannē herself could have been an advocate for the novel, nominating it to the Council because it embodied some of the features central to her very own novels — a female-centred worldview, and literary universe narrated by a female protagonist who functions outside the traditional female roles of wife or mother. Moreover, she may have advocated for the novel because its emphasis on female agency spoke to some of her own personal values and ideals as a nonconformist and free-thinking woman.[58]

Although Papagiannē's translation of *Jane Eyre* contains omissions of certain paragraphs or sentences (which we discuss later in this chapter), the most famous feminist passages in the novel have been retained, such as Jane's meditation in Chapter 12, where she asserts that 'women feel just as men feel' and laments their unfair treatment in the nineteenth century.[59] Furthermore, one of the novel's most famous instances of female agency in which Jane declares that she chose to marry Rochester — the opening lines of the epilogue: 'Reader, I married him' have been rendered in a manner that maintains Jane's independence and free will. Papagiannē's 'Αναγνώστη, τον παντρεύτηκα' (back translation: 'Reader, I married him') could have been translated variously as 'Reader, we got married' or even as

57 Farinou-Malamatari, 'Ninila Papagiannē: A Hidden Presence', pp. 587–88.

58 There is also the possibility that *Jane Eyre* itself could have influenced Papagiannē's fiction, and offered her an aesthetic model for her own work.

59 *JE*, Ch. 12; Charlotte Brontë, *Jane Eyre* [*Tzeēn Eyr*], trans. by Ninila Papagiannē (Athens: Ikaros, 1949), p. 162.

'Reader, he married me', which is the case with some later Greek translations of the novel.[60]

However, Papagiannē certainly missed some opportunities to assert Jane's agency, as is evidenced in Chapter 23 in Rochester's comment to Jane: 'You — poor and obscure, and small and plain as you are — I entreat to accept me as a husband.' Papagiannē's translation 'Ετσι που είσαι φτωχή και σοβαρή και μικροκαμωμένη σε θέλω για γυναικά μου' can be back translated as 'You who are poor and serious and small, I want as my wife'.[61] In the English source text, Rochester's entreaty requires Jane to agree and allow the marriage: her will is at the very centre of the question. In contrast, Papagiannē's translation highlights Rochester's needs and desires: Rochester is not asking for Jane to accept him as her husband, but rather offers a clear statement of his will in which Jane is an object to be possessed.[62]

Papagiannē's translation, for the most part, is fairly competent. Nonetheless, Papagiannē seems to have struggled with the references to Northern European magical creatures (elves, sprites, goblins). and instead used religious terms to describe the magical creatures with

60 *JE*, Epilogue; Papagiannē, p. 653. In other languages this phrase has been translated in ways that do not emphasise Jane's agency. See: Eleni Philippou, '"Reader, I went through a wedding ceremony with him": Translating *Jane Eyre*', *Creative Multilingualism*. 7 Dec. 2017, https://creativeml.ox.ac.uk/blog/exploring-multilingualism/reader-i-went-through-wedding-ceremony-him-translating-jane-eyre/index.html

61 *JE*, Ch. 23; Papagiannē, p. 366.

62 Jane's comments emphasise her lack of power as a woman in nineteenth century England. She lacks beauty, a high social rank, and wealth: all of which would have offered a limited level of agency as a woman. In fact, throughout the novel the conversational exchanges between Jane and Rochester make clear that there is a power dynamic at play between the two individuals that differ both in age and social station: Jane speaks to Rochester in the third person plural — the formal or polite form of address ordinarily used when speaking to strangers, someone senior or elderly, or a superior — whereas Rochester uses the first person singular to address Jane. In more recent translations, such as that of Dimitris Kikizas, both Jane and Rochester speak to each other in the first person singular. (See: Charlotte Brontë, *Jane Eyre* [*Tzeēn Eyr*], trans. by Dimitris Kikizas (Athens, Smili, 1997).) The shift could be explained by newer translations seeing the interaction between Jane and Rochester as less defined by strict social codes or mores, and less inclined to reinforce the uneven power dynamic between Jane and Rochester. The unpublished doctoral thesis, 'Domestication and Foreignization in *Jane Eyre*' (National and Kapodistrian University of Athens, March 2022), by Sofia-Konstantina Zacharia looks at various retranslations of *Jane Eyre*, focusing in particular on the translations of Polly Moschopoulou (1991), Dimitris Kikizas (1997), and Georgia Deligianni (2019).

which the Greek, predominately Orthodox, readership would have been familiar. Often, the novel's magical creatures were translated simply as demons or devils. For example, when Jane comments that Rochester is no longer affectionate and now treats her with disdain, labelling her a 'provoking puppet', 'malicious elf', 'sprite', 'changeling', Papagiannē translates his comments in the following way 'ενοχλητικό κουταβάκι' 'irritating little puppy', 'ανυπόφορο ζιζάνιο' 'unbearable pest', 'δαίμονα, κουτόπραμα' 'demon, foolish thing'.[63] Although puppet is probably a misreading in which Papagiannē has mistaken the word puppet for puppy, in the instances of elf, sprite, and changeling, it is clear that she is unable to find an appropriate term for these different magical creatures, and therefore condenses the words into one all-encompassing theological term: demon. In the same chapter, where Rochester comments to Jane: 'Is this my pale little elf?', Papagiannē again reverts to familiar biblical imagery translating 'pale little elf' as 'χλομό μου διαβολάκι': 'pale little devil of mine'.[64] (Strangely, the reprints of her translation have not been altered despite accurate terms for these supernatural creatures being in existence.[65]) Papagiannē's translation also tends to miss intertextual references, such as those to Shakespeare.

The Council were unsure of the financial feasibility of their translation initiative, and the covering letter to the 1949/50 Annual Report asserts that no sales figures for the Council's publishing of translations are available yet, but that the writer 'understands from the staff here on leave that the response has not been great. The Shakespeare versions are apparently much more popular than Dickens'.[66] The 1952 sales returns show *Macbeth* as the most popular title followed by *Great Expectations*, with Kipling's stories the least

63 *JE*, Ch. 24; Papagiannē, p. 389.

64 *JE*, Ch. 24; Papagiannē, p. 371.

65 The *Dictionary of Standard Modern Greek* [*Lexiko tēs neas hellēnikēs glōssas*] contains the terms τελώνιο (goblin; hob-goblin), αερικό (pixie/sprite), ξωτικό (elf) for these supernatural creatures. See these entries respectively: https://www.greek-language.gr/greekLang/modern_greek/tools/lexica/triantafyllides/search.html?lq=%CF%84%CE%B5%CE%BB%CF%8E%CE%BD%CE%B9%CE%BF&dq=; https://www.greek-language.gr/greekLang/modern_greek/tools/lexica/triantafyllides/search.html?lq=%CE%B1%CE%B5%CF%81%CE%B9%CE%BA%CF%8C&dq=; https://www.greek-language.gr/greekLang/modern_greek/tools/lexica/triantafyllides/search.html?lq=%CE%BE%CF%89%CF%84%CE%B9%CE%BA%CF%8C&dq=

66 Annual Report 1949/50, Books & Publications Department.

successful.[67] A general comparison between the 1952–1953 records and those of 1950–1951 show sales remain more or less at a steady level, although the report does not specify the number of sales.[68] The sales were presumably low, as the 1953–1954 Annual Report suggests: 'although sales are poor by British standards, demands for Shakespeare is [sic] constant'. The same report states that earlier volumes containing *Macbeth* and *Romeo and Juliet* are now out of print.[69]

Despite the presumably low sales, in the 1949–1950 Annual Report of the Books and Publications department, P. B. de Jongh (the Functional Officer for Books and Publications) unequivocally states that the 'general reception of the public was most favourable and several distinguished Greek literary critics have pointed out in the Press that the initiative taken by the British Council will enable a hitherto very evident gap in Greek libraries to be filled'.[70] The Local Publications section of the same Annual Report states that 'Comment in the Press and outside has been most appreciative [of the translations]. The Ministry of Education has welcomed this project warmly'.[71] Upon closer inspection it appears that the British Council went to some effort to ensure that their translations were promoted and publicised.[72] An Annual Library Report from 1950 (the year that *Jane Eyre* was published) states that the directors of the various British Council's

67 National Archives, Kew, box 34, folder 25, Representative's Annual Report 1952–1953.

68 Representative's Annual Report 1952–1953.

69 Kew, National Archives, box 34, folder 25, Representative's Annual Report 1953–1954.

70 Annual Report 1949/50, Books & Publications Department.

71 Ibid.

72 Although the Council had an interest in promoting books related to their translation programme, they also promoted English books more generally. The Book & Publications Department's Annual Report 1949/50 dated May 1950 shows that 288 press cuttings of reviews of British books were forwarded to Greek publishers. These notices of British books appeared in the Greek press — monthly, weekly, and daily Athenian newspapers. All review copies were obtained through the British Council, and the books mainly comprised of works of literary criticism. A report from the preceding year notes that the Greek literary critics appeared eager to obtain copies of English books for review, and that the reviews feature in a range of publications (across the political spectrum), not simply British Council publications. Reviewers included M. Skouloudes, a translator of Shakespeare and Dostoevsky. Kew, National Archives, box 34, folder 20, Annual Report 1948/49, Books & Publications Department.

Institutes of English Studies that were located around Greece were asked to publicise the Council's translations, promote sales and offer suggestions for new titles to the translations committee.[73] The Report continues that free copies of the translations for press review could be provided by the Council, and that the directors should inform the Books Officer if they want to sell the books in their institutes (however, directors were free to decide their own policy in this respect).[74] There was a level of synergy and support between the British Council's various initiatives for the translations. For example, the introductions to the translated Shakespeare plays were written by Professor Sewell, the Byron Professor at University of Athens. (As mentioned earlier, the Byron Professor position was initiated by the British Council in 1937 for the teaching of English Language and Literature.) In the same year as the publication of *Jane Eyre*, the Institute for English Studies lists in their 'extracurricular activities' a lecture in Greek by Mrs Vafopoulou at the Institute of English Studies on the subject of the Brontës.[75] In the Annual Report of the British Institute of Salonica 1948–49, reference is made to a teaching programme in which Shakespeare is taught with special reference to *Julius Caesar* and *Twelfth Night*, texts that feature as part of the translation programme.[76] Even supposedly innocuous celebrations had the purpose of promoting the translations. The Representative's Annual Report of 1954–1955 notes that the 'actual purpose' of the celebration of the 350th anniversary of performance of *Othello, Lear*, and *Macbeth*, was to 'advertise the Ikaros translations of Shakespeare into Greek, which the Council subsidises'.[77]

Jane Eyre and the Anglo-Greek Review

The magazine *Anglo-Greek Review* (*Anglo-Hellēnikē Epitheōrēsē*) appears to have been extremely useful in airing the translations by the British Council. The first twelve issues of the magazine were published by the Anglo-Greek Information Service (AIS, later AGIS), a

73 Kew, National Archives, box 34, folder 30, Annual Library Report 1950.

74 Annual Library Report 1950.

75 Annual Report 1949/50, Books & Publications Department.

76 Kew, National Archives, box 34, folder 20, Annual Report of the British Institute of Salonica 1948/49.

77 Many of the Shakespeare translations were used for productions at the National Theatre or National Gardens. The Rotas translation of *Twelfth Night* was used by Karolos Koun, one of Greece's foremost directors, for his production at the Arts theatre. Representative's Annual Report 1955–1956.

propaganda organisation that was dissolved at the end of 1945.[78] With AGIS's dissolution, the *Review*'s publication became the responsibility of the British Council.[79] The *Review*, produced in Athens, published reviews and articles about literature rather than literary works, and was edited from around its third issue by George Katsimbalis, the leading Greek literary figure. Katsimbalis gave up his editorial role in 1952, and was succeed by and G. P. Savidis, the literary critic who was later to become the Seferis Professor at Harvard. The *Review* primarily published educational or informative articles, often of a relatively impartial or conservative character: these pieces were not focused on provoking debate or introducing new literary trends, as Dimitris Tziovas also notes.[80] Some of the articles are surveys of developments in English literature or short articles on different aspects of British life, rather than incendiary opinion pieces. Moreover, initially the magazine 'looked to the recent cultural past and tried to canonize it, rather than addressing the present and the future'.[81] Under Savidis's editorial command, contributions from women, younger writers and critics, some of whom were even Left-leaning, became more prominent.[82]

As Peter Mackridge points out, it is difficult to ascertain with complete certainty the objective behind the *Review*'s publication as those responsible for the initiation, development, and running of the *Review* are no longer alive and the *Review* lacks an archive.[83] However, the editorial manifesto in the first *Review* hoped that the readers 'of each country [Britain and Greece] who are learning the language of the other' come to a 'closer understanding'.[84] The magazine asserts itself as a space in which the British reader can gain knowledge of the Greek zeitgeist: about what Greece is 'thinking and feeling today about the

78 AGIS was 'set up by Leeper under the aegis of General Scobie at a time when Greece was under British military occupation' (Mackridge, 'Introduction', p. 11).

79 A late 1940s Annual Report by the British Council's Books and Publications department clearly lists the *Anglo-Greek Review* as a British Council publication together with *British Council Brochures, British Medical Bulletin, English Language Teaching, British Agricultural Bulletin, British Book News, Britain To-day*, and *Prospero* (the literary periodical of the British Council in Corfu). Annual Report 1948/49, Books & Publications Department.

80 Tziovas, 'Between Propaganda and Modernism', p. 133.

81 Tziovas, 'Between Propaganda and Modernism', p. 134.

82 Tziovas, 'Between Propaganda and Modernism', p. 129.

83 Mackridge, 'Introduction', p. 11.

84 Tziovas, 'Between Propaganda and Modernism', p. 127.

problems which confront' her by accessing 'contemporary sources'.[85] Yet the English-Greek bilingual character of the magazine was lost by its fourth issue, and the focus skewed towards an exclusively Greek readership, even though the contents page remained bilingual until 1953.[86] Peter Mackridge even notes that Katsimbalis was particularly keen to publish translated British reviews of Greek works suggesting that he viewed the readership as a Greek audience interested in seeing how Greek literature was faring abroad.[87] The *Review* helped 'familiarise the Greek public with aspects of British life, its arts and institutions.'[88]

The *Review* had a subtle political agenda, advocating the 'values of liberal democracy' by including articles on the 'liberal institutions, democracy and freedom of speech', especially in its early issues.[89] However, the Council itself saw the magazine as a non-partisan space, and prided itself on its reputation as a highbrow publication, appealing to the 'sophisticated taste' of their Greek readership.[90] An Annual Report from 1947–1948 states that the publication is read by 'all intellectuals irrespective of their political sympathies; contributions by writers of the Right and the Left have appeared in the same issue — an almost phenomenal occurrence in post-war Greece'.[91] The same Annual Report notes that the *Review* does much for the Council's 'prestige' and that its 'rigorous abstention from politics is in marked contrast to the vast majority of Greek papers and periodicals'.[92] Yet Tziovas reads this claim for non-partisanship in a rather more nuanced way, suggesting that the *Review* was an 'attempt on the part of the British to support the liberal intelligentsia of Greece and offer them a respectable forum in which to express themselves and promote the country's

85 Ibid.

86 The English character of the magazine probably fell away because of the difficulties of securing English articles, as noted by the Council's Functional Officer in 1951: 'The Problem of English contributions remains acute and every effort should be made during the coming year to find a solution if the review is to survive as an 'Anglo-Greek review'. [underlining in the original] NA, box 34, folder 25, Annual Report of Functional Officer (1951).

87 Mackridge, 'Introduction', p. 11.

88 Tziovas, 'Between Propaganda and Modernism', p. 132.

89 Tziovas, 'Between Propaganda and Modernism', pp. 130, 132.

90 Annual Report 1947–48.

91 Ibid.

92 According to Mackridge, the magazine's prestige is in line with that of *Ta Nea Grammata* (11). *Ta Nea Grammata* was a preeminent magazine that showcased much of the writing of Greece's influential Generation of the '30s.

cultural achievements'.[93] Although the *Review* was no means overtly ideological, nor vulgar propaganda, it definitely locked into a larger system of British Council initiatives within an even broader British strategy of 'promoting liberal democracy and offering a taste of British life and culture'.[94] It largely aimed to create a 'favourable backdrop to the stage upon which politics and diplomacy were conducted.'[95]

It is not clear if the Greek editors had any real say about the magazine's content, or if the British funders of the magazine primarily dictated editorial policy and content. Indeed, Tziovas rightfully asserts that it is unknown 'who chose these pieces [the articles] or where they came from (particularly with earlier issues)'.[96] An Annual Report from 1947–1948 states that '[t]he quality of the material received from the Council in London for publication in the *Review* continued, as during last year, to be of a quality required by the Editor'.[97] This statement suggests that Britain would send articles to the Council, but the Editor was not entirely powerless: it seems as if he may have had some control as to whether the articles were of publishable quality.

Whatever the editorial policy, the overlap between the translation programme and the articles in the magazine suggests that part of the editorial mandate was to support British Council initiatives. The serialisation of *Troilus and Cressida*, *Twelfth Night*, and *The Winter's Tale* (all featured in the translation programme) cannot have been coincidental, and was probably an attempt to increase sales or publicise the texts. The *Review*'s January/February issue of 1949 contains an article by Augustus Muir entitled 'Famous English Women Novelists', that discusses Jane Austen, George Eliot, and the Brontë sisters.[98] The article is probably a translation from English but the source text remains unlocatable, thereby suggesting that the piece may have been specially commissioned for the *Review*. The article coincides with the publication of Charlotte Brontë's *Jane Eyre* (1949), and the prospective publication of Jane Austen's *Pride and Prejudice* (1950), thereby killing two birds with one stone. Muir's reading of *Jane Eyre* is very

93 Tziovas, 'Between Propaganda and Modernism', p. 133. He also suggests that the Greek editors themselves felt that the *Review* had a political agenda (p. 131).

94 Tziovas, 'Between Propaganda and Modernism', p. 133.

95 Ibid.

96 Ibid.

97 Annual Report 1947–48.

98 Muir is a writer who also went by the name of Austin Moore.

progressive, stressing Jane's female agency and independent thought. Muir registers that the novel's publication was controversial and scandalised many readers, noting 'It also shocked some who found in the book a revolutionary attitude against existing societal norms/traditions',[99] but his praise of the book is overt. He squarely comments, '[C]lever and enlightened people, such as the great English novelist [William] Thackeray, recognised its great creative strength'.[100]

An article, 'The English Novel', in the 1951 *Review* by the Greek literary critic, Professor Apostolos Sahinis, directly registers three British Council translations that were published over the course of 1949–1950: *Jane Eyre, Pride and Prejudice*, and *Great Expectations*.[101] Sahinis notes that the collaboration between Ikaros publishers and the British Council has put three English texts into circulation that embody 'the spirit, the climate, the atmosphere and sensitivity of 19th century English literature'.[102] In the article, Sahinis laments the fact that Greek novelists are using Russian and Scandinavian novels as their models for writing prose. According to Sahinis these novels (by Knut Hamsun, for instance) are largely stylistically experimental, or avant garde, and should not be considered worthy of emulation. For Sahinis, Greek novelists should aspire towards the great classic English novels such as *Jane Eyre, Pride and Prejudice*, and *Great Expectations*. Sahinis introduces Charlotte Brontë as the sister of the writer of *Wuthering Heights*, presumably based on the fact that the Greek reader was familiar with Emily Brontë: *Wuthering Heights* had already been translated into Greek in the nineteenth century. Sahinis suggests that *Jane Eyre* and *Wuthering Heights* share an interest in the supernatural and are set in isolated castles in the English countryside where emotions and passions cannot be released or expressed,

99 Augustus Muir, 'Famous English Women Novelists', *Anglo-Greek Review* [*Anglo-Hellēnikē Epitheōrēsē*], 4 (1949), 8–11 (p. 11).

100 Muir, 'Famous English Women Novelists', p. 11.

101 In the July-December 1951 issue of the *Nea Estia* magazine, Lawrence Hanson's *The Four Brontës: the Lives and Works of Charlotte, Branwell, Emily, and Anne Brontë* (1950) published by Oxford University Press was reviewed. The book is regarded by the reviewer (listed as Γ.Ν.Α.) as 'very interesting'. The reviewer notes that the central personality in this book is Charlotte Brontë. The review may have been initiated by the British Council policy of sending out English books for review in Greek publications (see footnote 72), and been part of a general strategy to once again promote authors linked to the translation programme.

102 Apostolos Sahinis, 'The English Novel', *Anglo-Greek Review* [*Anglo-Hellēnikē Epitheōrēsē*], 5 (1951), 157–58 (p. 157).

and as a consequence tyrannize the characters to generate unusual psychological states or situations.[103] Sahinis reduces *Jane Eyre* to a romance, stating that the book is about the life of a poor orphan who becomes a governess and after a series of trials ultimately finds joy in the arms of her beloved Mr Rochester.[104] In a somewhat backhanded compliment, Sahinis notes that what the novel lacks in development and action is compensated by Brontë's sensitivity and pensive, lyrical temperament.[105] He notes that the reader cannot avoid the 'prattling' or 'babbling' characteristic of women's novels, but this is countered by the 'warm feeling of life', the descriptions of the English natural world, and the interesting rendering of the protagonist's emotions.[106] Whereas in Muir's article, *Jane Eyre* is understood as a revolutionary novel that disrupts societal codes through its creative energies, Sahinis sets up *Jane Eyre* as riven of such potential. Sahinis' plainly misogynistic tract aims to be positive, but undoubtedly diminishes the novel by seeing it simply as an expression of emotion.[107]

Sahinis may have read the text in English rather than in translation owing to his knowledge of English from his years as postgraduate student at Kings College London. His derogatory or negative comments about the novel probably do not arise from Papagiannē's translation, but are rather a manifestation of his general literary conservatism. In fact, the Greek translation largely expresses the source text's feminist urgency and vigour when Jane passionately advocates for the rights of women or female independence.[108] In translation, it does not become a sappy sentimental romance. Furthermore, the translation is free of superfluous detail — what Sahinis refers to as 'prattle' — because Papagiannē expunged parts of the text that she found extraneous. (Admittedly, she may have deleted certain sections based on the assumption that the Greek readership would have had difficulty understanding the content, or perhaps because they were too difficult to translate into Greek.) Lastly, the text, at various points, tends to

103 Sahinis, 'The English Novel', p. 158.
104 Ibid.
105 Ibid.
106 Ibid.
107 Katerina Kitsi-Mitakou and Maria Vara discuss Muir's and Sahinis' articles in reference to Jane Austen's reception in Greece. See Katerina Kitsi-Mitakou and Maria Vara, 'The Reception of Jane Austen in Greece', in *The Reception of Jane Austen in Europe*, ed. by Anthony Mandal and Brian Southam (London: Continuum, 2007), pp. 225–39.
108 See, for instance, Papagiannē, pp. 162, 364.

downplay the supernatural elements that Sahinis emphasizes in his review.

For example, one of the instances where Papagiannē has made cuts to the text is the conversation between Rochester and Jane in Chapter 24. Here, the two characters converse: at times playfully and flirtatiously, but then also more seriously. They discuss Rochester's treatment of Blanche Ingram; Jane's aversion to being bedecked in jewels, and their relationship. The source text reads:

> "I never met your likeness. Jane, you please me, and you master me — you seem to submit, and I like the sense of pliancy you impart; and while I am twining the soft, silken skein round my finger, it sends a thrill up my arm to my heart. I am influenced — conquered; and the influence is sweeter than I can express; and the conquest I undergo has a witchery beyond any triumph I can win. Why do you smile, Jane? What does that inexplicable, that uncanny turn of countenance mean?"
>
> "I was thinking, sir (you will excuse the idea; it was involuntary), I was thinking of Hercules and Samson with their charmers —"
>
> "You were, you little elfish —"
>
> "Hush, sir! You don't talk very wisely just now; any more than those gentlemen acted very wisely. However, had they been married, they would no doubt by their severity as husbands have made up for their softness as suitors; and so will you, I fear. I wonder how you will answer me a year hence, should I ask a favour it does not suit your convenience or pleasure to grant."[109]

From this passage, Papagiannē has retained only, 'Ποτέ δεν βρήκα την όμοιά σου, Τζέην. Μ' ευχαριστείς και μ' εξουσιάζεις.', which, when back-translated, reads as, 'I never met your likeness. Jane, you please me, and you master me'. These lines are followed by Jane's words: 'Αναρωτιέμαι, κύριε, (θα μου συγχωρήσετε, πιστεύω, αυτή μου τη σκέψη) αναρωτιέμαι αν θα μείνετε πάντα έτσι, κι αν θα μου κάνατε ποτέ μια χάρη, που δε θα σας ερχότανε και τόσο βολική, κι αυτό για να μ' ευχαριστήσετε μονάχα', which back-translates to 'I wonder, Sir, (and you will forgive, I believe, this thought of mine) wonder if you will always stay like this, and if you would ever do me a favour that would not come to you so conveniently, and that solely to please me'.[110] The deleted sections suggest that Papagiannē may have struggled to translate the supernatural elements (the references to witchery, elfishness; an uncanny turn of countenance, or Hercules and Samson being charmed).

---

109 *JE*, Ch. 24.

110 *JE*, Ch. 24. Papagiannē, p. 375.

Alternatively, and to return to our earlier discussion of the feminist element of the translation, Papagiannē may have consciously chosen not to include the references to Hercules and Samson and 'their charmers', even if a Greek audience may have been familiar with these mythological and biblical stories. She may have been keen not to reinforce misogynistic stereotypes that portray women in a negative light (as manipulative temptresses) or male figures as emasculated or humiliated by women. Both the references to Samson and Hercules present male figures renowned for their strength being denigrated or weakened by a female romantic interest. In the Old Testament, Samson was seduced by Delilah and lost his strength after confessing his secret to her that his strength was a result of his hair never being cut. She not only strips Samson of his strength by cutting his hair in his sleep, but betrays him to the Philistines who then enslave him and blind him. In ancient Greek mythology, Hercules, as punishment for a murder, became the slave of the widow Omphale, Queen of Lydia, with whom he later had three children. In some variations of the myth, as Omphale's slave, he is forced to do women's work, and is thereby emasculated.[111]

The cheeky tone, flirtatiousness, and otherworldly element of the source passage may have been lost in translation, but despite these omissions, the essence of the source passage has been captured. Papagiannē's translation expresses firstly that Rochester has submitted to Jane's mastery (while stripping this mastery of any suggestion of denigration or emasculation), and secondly that Jane feels anxiety at possible changes in Rochester's demeanour in the future.

It is uncertain if Muir's and Sahinis' reviews actually assisted in the sales of the translations, or whether they had any influence on Greek society at all. There is no accurate data on the magazine's dissemination, although we know that the price of the magazine fluctuated and reflected the volatility of the Greek economy during the war, and post-war years. The Council asserts that it had extensive circulation in its early days, but this cannot be substantiated.[112] Nevertheless, these reviews do point to the synergy and energy of the British Council in endorsing and publicising their translations.

111 J.A. Coleman, *Dictionary of Mythology* (London: Arcturus, 2007), p. 781.
112 Tziovas, 'Between Propaganda and Modernism', p. 129.

Conclusion

The translation of *Jane Eyre* was by no means a neutral exercise but rather part and parcel of a wider political and ideological strategy conducted by Britain after the end of the second World War. In the wake of the Cold War — in the struggle for territorial and ideological expansion between the Anglophone West and the Soviet East — Greece was of significant political and geographic importance. As a consequence, Britain's policy of soft power, which was channelled through institutions such as the British Council, aimed to make Greece conducive to British influence. Through lectures, English language classes, the establishment of a University Chair, and a systematic translation programme (among other things), the British Council aimed to promote and disseminate British culture. Although, there is no documentation that discusses why *Jane Eyre* specifically was chosen as part of the British Council's translation programme, its selection speaks to the novel's enduring popularity, its 'Englishness', and ability to appeal to different readers in different ways, as mentioned earlier in this chapter.. Indeed, it is not difficult to speculate that the British thought that the novel would offer a worthy contribution to their literary translation programme, with the tale of this little governess hopefully cultivating Greek sympathies in the ruins of the Second World War and the Greek Civil War.

Works Cited

Arapoglou, Eleftheria, '"The Art of the Novel": Henry James's Reception in Greece', in *The Reception of Henry James in Europe*, ed. by Annick Duperray (New York: Continuum, 2006), pp. 225–34.

Brontë, Charlotte, *Jane Eyre* [Tzeēn Eyr], trans. by Ninila Papagiannē (Athens, Ikaros, 1949).

——, *Jane Eyre* [Tzeēn Eyr], trans. by Dimitris Kikizas (Athens, Smili, 1997).

Coleman, J.A, *Dictionary of Mythology*, (London: Arcturus, 2007).

Dalpanagioti, Dimitra, 'The Translation of William Shakespeare's Plays and the Changing Concept of Womanhood in Greece (1875–1955)', (unpublished doctoral thesis, Aristotle University of Thessaloniki, November 2020).

Denisi, Sophia, *The Translation of Novels and Novellas 1830–1880: An Introductory Study and Record*, [Metafrasis Mithistorimatōn kai Diēgēmatōn 1830–1880: Eisagōgiki Meletē kai Katagrafē] (Athens: Periplus, 1995).

Drinkwater, Derek, 'Leeper, Sir Reginald Wildig Allen [Rex] (1888–1968)', *Oxford Dictionary of National Biography (2011)*, https://doi.org/10.1093/ref:odnb/55366

Farinou-Malamatari, Georgia, 'Ninila Papagiannē: A Hidden Presence' in *Modern Greek Literature of the Twentieth-century. A volume in honour of Eris Stavropoulou [Themata Neoellinikēs Logotechnias tou eikostoy aiōna. Timētikos tomos gia tēn Eri Stavropoulou*], ed. by T. Agathos, L, Iaokeimidou, G. Ksourias. (Athens, Gutenberg, 2020), pp. 578–88.

Iatrides, John O, "Britain, The United States, and Greece, 1945–9" in *The Greek Civil War, 1943–1950: Studies of Polarization*, ed. by David Close (London: Routledge, 1993) pp. 190–213.

Kasinēs, K. G, *Bibliography of Greek Translations of Foreign Literature, 19th–20th Centuries (Volume I)1801–1900*, [Vivliographia Tōn Hellēnikōn Metaphraseōn Tēs Xenēs Logotechnias 19.-20. Ai. Prōtos Tomos] Autoteleis ekdoseis (Athēnai: Syllogos Pros Diadosin Ōphelimōn Vivliōn, 2006).

——, *Bibliography of Greek Translations of Foreign Literature, 19th–20th Centuries (Volume II) 1901–1950*, [Vivliographia Tōn Hellēnikōn Metaphraseōn Tēs Xenēs Logotechnias 19.-20. Ai. Deyphteros Tomos 1901–1950] Autoteleis ekdoseis (Athēnai: Syllogos Pros Diadosin Ōphelimōn Vivliōn, 2013).

Kitsi-Mitakou, Katerina, and Maria Vara, 'The Reception of Jane Austen in Greece', in *The Reception of Jane Austen in Europe*, ed. by Anthony Mandal and Brian Southam (London: Continuum, 2007), pp. 225–39.

Koutsopanagou, Gioula, '"To Cast Our Net Very Much Wider": The Re-Opening of the British Council in Athens and Its Cultural Activities in Greece', in *The British Council and Anglo-Greek Literary Interactions, 1945–1955*, ed. by Peter Mackridge and David Ricks (London and New York: Routledge, 2018) pp. 39–68.

MacDonald, Charlotte, 'Jane Eyre at Home and Abroad', in *Ten Books That Shaped the British Empire: Creating an Imperial Commons*, ed. by Antoinette Burton and Isabel Hofmeyr (Durham: Duke University Press, 2014), pp. 50–70.

Mackridge, Peter, 'Introduction', in *British Council and Anglo-Greek Literary Interactions, 1945–1955*, ed. by Peter Mackridge and David Ricks (London and New York: Routledge, 2018), pp. 1–20.

Mazower, Mark. *Inside Hitler's Greece: The Experience of Occupation, 1941–44*. (New Haven, Conn.; London: Yale University Press, 2001).

Muir, Augustus, 'Famous English Women Novelists', *Anglo-Greek Review* [Anglo-Hellēnikē Epitheōrēsē], 4 (1949), 8–11.

Pierce – *American College of Greece*, 'Founding and Development', https://www.pierce.gr/en/founding-development/

Philippou, Eleni, 'Perennial Penelope and Lingering Lotus-Eaters: Revaluing Mythological Figures in the Poetry of the Greek Financial Crisis', *Dibur Literary Journal*, 5 (2018), 71–86.

——, '"Reader, I went through a wedding ceremony with him": Translating Jane Eyre', *Creative Multilingualism*, 7 Dec. 2017, https://creativeml.ox.ac.uk/blog/exploring-multilingualism/reader-i-went-through-wedding-ceremony-him-translating-jane-eyre/index.html

Sahinis, Apostolos, 'The English Novel', *Anglo-Greek Review* [Anglo-Hellēnikē Epitheōrēsē], 5 (1951), 157–58.

Tziovas, Dimitris. 'Between Propaganda and Modernism: The Anglo-Greek Review and the Discovery of Greece', *The British Council and Anglo-Greek Literary Interactions, 1945–1955*, ed. by Peter Mackridge and David Ricks (London and New York: Routledge, 2018), pp. 123–54.

Venuti, Lawrence. *Translation Changes Everything: Theory and Practice*, (London; New York: Routledge, 2013).

Vulliamy, Ed and Helena Smith, "Athens 1944: Britain's dirty secret", *The Guardian*, 30 Nov 2014, https://www.theguardian.com/world/2014/nov/30/athens-1944-britains-dirty-secret

Zacharia, Sofia-Konstantina. 'Domestication and Foreignization in Jane Eyre', (Unpublished doctoral thesis, National and Kapodistrian University of Athens, March 2022).

Γ.N.A., 'Review of Lawrence Hanson's The Four Brontës (1950)', *Nea Estia*, 50 (1951), 1327.

Archival Materials

Kew, National Archives, box 34, folder 10, Memorandum British Council Work in Greece: 1945/6.

Kew, National Archives, box 34, folder 20, British Institute Athens Annual Report 1947–48.

Kew, National Archives, box 34, folder 20, Annual Report 1948/49, Books & Publications Department.

Kew, National Archives, box 34, folder 20, Annual Report 1949/50, Books & Publications Department.

Kew, National Archives, box 34, folder 25, Annual Report of Functional Officer (1951).

Kew, National Archives, box 34, folder 25, Representative's Annual Report 1951–1952.

Kew, National Archives, box 34, folder 25, Representative's Annual Report 1952–1953.

Kew, National Archives, box 34, folder 30, Representative's Annual Report 1955–1956.

Kew, National Archives, box 34, folder 20, Annual Report of the British Institute of Salonica 1948/49.

Kew, National Archives, box 34, folder 30, Annual Library Report 1950.

Kew, National Archives, box 34, folder 25, Representative's Annual Report 1954–1955.

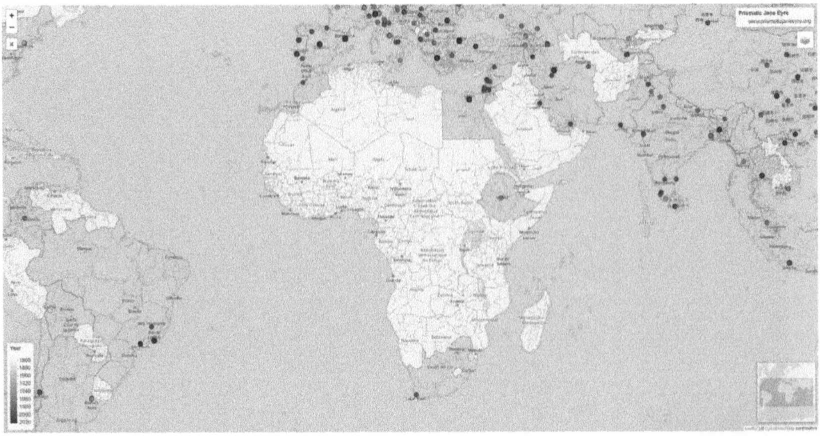

The General Map
https://digitalkoine.github.io/je_prismatic_generalmap/
Created by Giovanni Pietro Vitali; © OpenStreetMap contributors

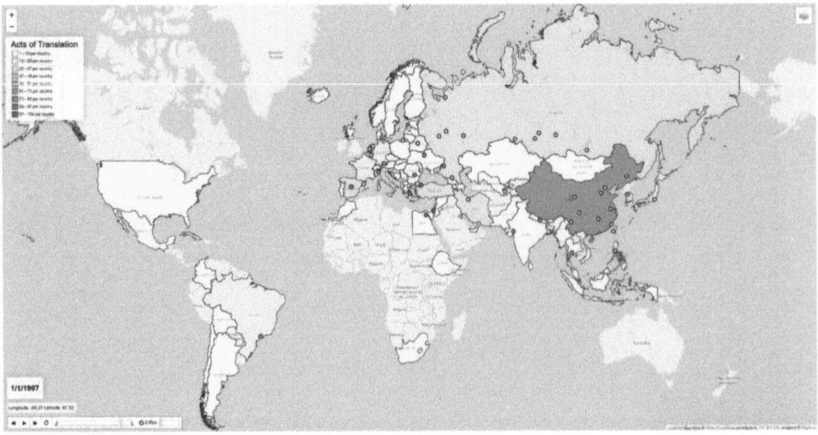

The Time Map
https://digitalkoine.github.io/translations_timemap
Created by Giovanni Pietro Vitali and Simone Landucci; © OpenStreetMap contributors, © Mapbox

7. Searching for Swahili Jane

Annmarie Drury[1]

Although *Jane Eyre* has travelled widely, its sojourn in the languages of sub-Saharan Africa has been limited. Apart from an Amharic translation (1981), there are only learners' 'thesaurus editions' in Afrikaans and Swahili and a drastically abridged Afrikaans translation.[2] My task thus differs somewhat from the work animating other essays here. It is to think about the absence of *Jane Eyre* from one language of sub-Saharan Africa, Swahili, and then to outline a potentiality. Writing about absence is a peculiar task with methodological complications, and in offering this discussion, I do not mean to argue that there *should* be a Swahili *Jane Eyre*. Yet in the context of a 'Prismatic *Jane Eyre*' project, this limitation upon the circulation of the novel — that it has not entered the majority of languages from our second-largest continent — has meaning. If we understand translation as prismatic, then here we find an occlusion, a failure in transmission. Pondering a rich literary sphere that *Jane Eyre* has not entered illuminates aspects of that sphere, I think, and potential meanings of Brontë's novel.

The nineteenth-century British novel has special significance in Swahili literary history because it became a vehicle of colonial language regulation. This happened after the Versailles Treaty gave Tanganyika, formerly part of German East Africa, to Britain as a League of Nations mandate — technically not a colony but indistinguishable from one in most practical terms. Early literary translations from English into

1 I am grateful to Ann Biersteker, Alamin Mazrui, and Clarissa Vierke for discussing ideas with me as I worked on this essay.

2 The Amharic translation is *Žén'éyer* (Addis Ababa: Bolé Mātamiya Bét, 1981). I have found neither the translator's name nor a copy of the book. The 'thesaurus editions' in Afrikaans and Swahili (published by ICON Group International, 2008) propose to assist learners both of English and of the relevant African language, but the Swahili edition appears to have been created by a machine and fails where interpretive nuance is required. The abridged Afrikaans version is translated and ed. by Antoinette Stimie (Kaapstad: Oxford University Press, 2005).

 https://doi.org/10.11647/OBP.0319.11

Swahili, many made in the 1920s, served a policy through which Britain sought to create and promulgate a 'standard' form of Swahili. Based on the southern Swahili dialect of Kiunguja — the Swahili of Zanzibar — though not fully Kiunguja itself, the standard Swahili promoted and enforced by the Inter-Territorial Language Committee (ITLC), a colonial agency created for this purpose, was in its inception a language virtually without a literature. Colonial standardization entailed sidelining much of the Swahili literary canon, which lay in poetry composed in northerly dialects and thus violating 'standard' rules.[3] While translators brought the Bible into Swahili in the nineteenth century — Johann Ludwig Krapf, under the aegis of the Anglican Church Missionary Society, began such work in the 1840s; Edward Steere published his translation of the New Testament in 1879; and William Taylor translated portions including Psalms (1904) — few literary translations from European languages into Swahili existed.[4] An abridged translation of Bunyan's *Pilgrim's Progress* (1888) and two early prose renderings from Shakespeare (1900 and 1867) are notable exceptions.[5] Wanting texts for classroom instruction, colonial

3 I explore this problem in Chapter Five of *Translation as Transformation in Victorian Poetry* (Cambridge: Cambridge University Press, 2015).

4 P. J. L. Frankl, 'Johann Ludwig Krapf and the Birth of Swahili Studies', *Zeitschrift der Deutschen Morgenländischen Gesellschaft*, 142 (1992), 12–20 (p. 13); Robert Marshall Heanley, *A Memoir of Edward Steere: Third Missionary Bishop in Central Africa* (London: George Bell and Sons, 1888, p. 239); and P. J. L. Frankl, 'W. R. Taylor (1856–1927): England's Greatest Swahili Scholar', *AAP*, 60 (1999), 161–74 (p. 168). The earliest date for Steere's translation is 1883 in catalogue records, but Heanley and contemporaneous sources such as the *Dictionary of National Biography* give 1879 as the date of publication in East Africa. These nineteenth-century scriptural translations present different varieties of Swahili. Krapf's work precedes settled orthography for Swahili in the Roman alphabet. Steere's concentration on the dialect of Zanzibar, Kiunguja, pre-dates the British program of standardization based on that dialect; Alamin Mazrui, in *Cultural Politics of Translation: East Africa in a Global Context* (New York: Routledge, 2016, p. 23) deems it 'a pan-Swahili dialect'. Taylor translated into Kimvita, the dialect of Mombasa, and as Frankl explains, the fact that Kimvita was spoken by relatively few Christians contributed to the obscurity of his Swahili psalter.

5 The 1888 version of Bunyan was *Msafiri*, published by the Religious Tract Society for the Universities' Mission. My sources on prose versions of Shakespeare are Mazrui, *Cultural Politics of Translation*, pp. 3–4; and Thomas Geider, 'A Survey of World Literature Translated into Swahili', in *Beyond the Language Issue: The Production, Mediation and Reception of Creative Writing in African Languages*, ed. by Anja Oed and Uta Reuster-Jahn (Köln: Rüdiger Köppe, 2008), pp. 67–84 (p. 69). For more on translations from European languages before the 1920s, see Serena Talento, 'The "Arabic Story" and the

administrators in the 1920s translated fiction, with one man making most of the first generation of translations. This was Frederick Johnson, creator of a dictionary of standard Swahili and the first head of the ITLC, who sometimes translated with the African Edwin (E. W.) Brenn.[6] Johnson was known for translating rapidly at his typewriter,[7] and outside of translation, his work extended to the joint authorship in Swahili of a small book on citizenship, *Uraia*, that, as Emma Hunter shows, delineates a conception of freedom 'as security' rather than 'as political liberty', one consonant with a vision of Tanganyika as part of 'a wider imperial family'.[8] Johnson's translations, favouring Victorian novels, included selections from Rudyard Kipling's *Jungle Book* and *Second Jungle Book*, published in 1929 as *Hadithi za Maugli: Mtoto Aliyelelewa na Mbwa Mwitu* [*Stories of Mowgli: The Child Raised by Wolves*]; an abridged translation with Brenn of Rider Haggard's *King Solomon's Mines*, published as *Mashimo ya Mfalme Sulemani* (1929); a translation with Brenn of Robert Louis Stevenson's *Treasure Island* (1929); an abridged translation of Haggard's *Allan Quatermain*, published in 1934 as *Hadithi ya Allan Quatermain*; and a translation of Swift's *Gulliver's Travels*.[9] This corpus suggests that a type of fiction

Kingwana Hugo: A (Too Short) History of Literary Translation into Swahili', in *Lugha na Fasihi: Essays in Honor and Memory of Elena Bertoncini Zúbková*, ed. by Flavia Aiello and Roberto Gaudioso (Naples: Università degli Studi di Napoli 'L'Orientale', 2019), pp. 59–80 (pp. 63–4); and *Framing Texts — Framing Social Spaces: Conceptualising Literary Translation in three Centuries of Swahili Literature* (Köln: Rüdiger Köppe, 2021), Chapter Five and appendices.

6 Johnson does not clarify the extent of Brenn's work, and it is possible that Brenn contributed to translations beyond those where his 'help' ('msaada') is acknowledged. John Iliffe identifies Brenn as a 'senior clerk in the Education Department' who studied at the Church Missionary Society school in Mombasa, in *A Modern History of Tanganyika* (Cambridge: Cambridge University Press, 1979), p. 266. Mazrui comments on Brenn's translation of *The Arabian Nights* in *Cultural Politics of Translation* (p. 41).

7 Geider, 'A Survey of World Literature Translated into Swahili', p. 73.

8 Emma Hunter, 'Dutiful Subjects, Patriotic Citizens, and the Concept of Good Citizenship in Twentieth-Century Tanzania', *The Historical Journal, 56*, no. 1 (2013), 257–77 (p. 265). Johnson's fellow author was Stanley Rivers-Smith, the first Director of Education in Tanganyika.

9 The Swahili editions are: *Hadithi za Maugli: Mtoto Aliyelelewa na Mbwa Mwitu* (London: Macmillan, 1929); *Mashimo ya Mfalme Sulemani* (London: Longman, 1929; reissued as recently as 1986 by Longmans Kenya in Nairobi); *Kisiwa chenye Hazina* (London: Longmans, 1929); *Hadithi ya Allan Quatermain* (London: Sheldon Press, 1934); *Safari za Gulliver* (London: Sheldon Press, 1932); *Mashujaa: Hadithi Za Kiyunani* (London: Sheldon Press, 1933). My sources for these titles and dates are Marcel van Spaandonck's *Practical and*

favoured by the language-standardizing translators was the boy's adventure story with imperialist resonance. Whether Johnson and his colleagues made their choices for reasons of personal affinity, in that they could most rapidly translate and abridge texts they knew from their youth; out of conscious ideological purpose, as Ousseina Alidou persuasively argues was done by another colonial official with a magazine serialization based on Booker T. Washington's *Up from Slavery* in Zanzibar in the mid-1930s; or because they imagined these fictions would engage school students, primarily boys, one readily perceives how the pattern of selection would have omitted *Jane Eyre*.[10]

Thus the first translations of British novels, often abridged, into Swahili created two registers of problem. First, they turned nineteenth-century British fiction into a literature of linguistic enforcement, through volumes asserting — with the ITLC's literal seal of approval — that the right kind of Swahili was this variety created in translations by British men of books by other British men. Secondly, the very language of the translations signalled alienness from the Swahili literary tradition, for it neglected the art of prose narration as it then existed in Swahili — an art developed in historical chronicles and local storytelling traditions, for example, and influenced by Arabic genres; one feature was the fluidity with which prose accommodated interpolation of poetry.[11] The Kenyan poet Abdilatif Abdalla (b. 1946),

---

Systematical Swahili Bibliography: Linguistics 1850–1963 (Leiden: Brill, 1965), which misspells Brenn's name, and searches in WorldCat and the catalogues of SOAS, University of London and Yale University libraries. Although it is beyond the scope of this essay, Johnson's selections from American literature would reward consideration. As Talento writes, he translated as well *Tales of Uncle Remus* and, with Brenn as collaborator, Longfellow's *Song of Hiawatha*; see Talento, 'The "Arabic Story" and the Kingwana Hugo', pp. 65–6.

10 Ousseina Alidou, 'Booker T. Washington in Africa: Between Education and (Re)Colonization', in *A Thousand Flowers: Social Struggles Against Structural Adjustment in African Universities*, ed. by Silvia Federici, George Caffentzis, and Ousseina Alidou (Trenton, NJ: Africa World Press, 2000), pp. 25–36. Alidou examines G. B. Johnson's Swahili series in *Mazungumzo ya Walimu wa Unguja* in 1935, where the figure of Washington is used to endorse provision of vocational rather than scholarly education for Africans. G. B. Johnson, the Chief Inspector of Schools on Zanzibar, soon published a short biography of Washington in Swahili that included excerpts from *Up from Slavery* in G. B. Johnson's Swahili translation: *Maisha ya Booker T. Washington: Mtu Mweusi Maarufu* (London: Sheldon Press, 1937). G. B. Johnson is not to be confused with Frederick Johnson, first head of the ITLC and the 'Johnson' referred to elsewhere in this essay.

11 Farouk Topan, 'Biography Writing in Swahili', *History in Africa*, 24 (1997), 299–307 (p. 299).

who writes in the Swahili dialect of Kimvita, has remarked on how this early set of translations promulgated a narrative language shaped by English, one in which 'mawako au miundo ya sentensi zile si ya Kiswahili, ya Kiingereza, mpaka maneno pia — maanake kunatumika maneno ya Kiswahili lakini mtungo ule wa sentensi si Kiswahili': 'the construction or forms of the sentences are not Swahili but English, and the words as well — that is, Swahili words are being used but the composition of the sentence is not Swahili.'[12] His comment suggests how these translations, estranged from Swahili literary language, had the potential to alienate readers in the schools of Zanzibar and beyond.

Of course, these translations into (a kind of) Swahili formed but one facet of the identity of British fiction in colonial East Africa. The rich multilingualism of East Africa, in play whenever one considers literary circulation there, invites us to consider as well the experience of English-language readers in colonial schools. Many students who encountered Stevenson's *Treasure Island* or the novels of Haggard in colonial East Africa read the books in English rather than Swahili, and here, too, British literature had strong affiliations with colonial oversight. The Kenyan author Ngũgĩ wa Thiong'o, writing of his years at Alliance High School, the first secondary school in Kenya for Africans, describes his experience learning but never quite gaining satisfaction from British novels he found in the school library. English was the language of instruction at Alliance, and Ngũgĩ, whose first language is Gĩkũyũ, writes of reading in English some of the same fictions I have named as translated into Swahili by colonial translators — including *Treasure Island* and *King Solomon's Mines*. This reading generated a recognition about the pervasiveness of imperial culture, Ngũgĩ explains, an understanding that '[e]ven in fiction I was not going to escape the theme of empire building.' It also created a sense of entrapment: 'I looked in vain for writings that I could identify with fully. The choice, it seemed, was between the imperial narratives that disfigured my body and soul, and the liberal ones that restored my body but still disfigured my soul.' At the same time, Ngũgĩ admired certain authors. He credits Shakespeare with a regeneration of

12 Transcribed (with my translation) from a recording shared by Abdilatif Abdalla of a session at the Swahili Colloquium, University of Bayreuth, Germany, 1 June 2019. Abdalla's interlocutor, the poet Mohammed Khelef Ghassani, produces an example of such an English-inflected Swahili formulation: *mwisho wa siku* (at the end of the day), where Swahili narrative would use the formulation *hatimaye* (finally, at last, in the end).

Swahili drama and recalls how he found in Emily Brontë's *Wuthering Heights* a narrative style that chimed with his experience of stories at home: 'With its many voices, it felt much the way narratives of real life unfolded in my village, an episode by one narrator followed by others that added to it and enriched the same theme.'[13] Stevenson made Ngũgĩ want to write while motivating his 'first major literary dispute', an argument with a friend over whether an aspiring author needed external endorsement, 'license to write'.[14] In illuminating the complicated experience of reading British literature as a colonial East African subject, Ngũgĩ's account suggests associations that might attach to *Jane Eyre* in the multilingual literary sphere a Swahili translation would enter — that might or *might have* attached to it, that is, since generations of East Africans have no experience of colonial education, though they may well have experience of its legacies. The complexity of East African reading publics, in terms of language background and educational profile, emerges vividly as one tries to imagine a Swahili *Jane Eyre*. Ngũgĩ's account brings us, intriguingly, to a sister-novel of *Jane Eyre*, but we have not yet found a Swahili *Jane*.

In the post-independence era, translation of the Anglophone African novel into Swahili had particular importance, with novels by Ngũgĩ, Ayi Kwei Armah, and Chinua Achebe, for example, all appearing in Swahili translation; a translation of Ferdinand Oyono's *Une vie de boi* (1956), made from John Reed's English translation *Houseboy* (1966), appeared in the same series as many of these.[15] Yet translators also revisited the nineteenth-century British novel in a series of new

---

13 Ngũgĩ wa Thiong'o, *In the House of the Interpreter* (New York: Anchor, 2012), pp. 163–4.

14 Ngũgĩ wa Thiong'o, *Dreams in a Time of War* (New York: Anchor, 2010), p. 220.

15 Ngũgĩ wa Thiong'o, *Njia Panda* [translation of *The River Between*], trans. by John Ndeti Somba (Nairobi: East African Publishing House, 1974); and *Usilie Mpenzi Wangu* [translation of *Weep Not, Child*], trans. by John Ndeti Somba (Nairobi: Heinemann Educational, 1975); Ayi Kwei Armah, *Wema Hawajazaliwa*, trans. by Abdilatif Abdalla (Nairobi: Heinemann Educational, 1976); and Chinua Achebe, *Shujaa Okonkwo* [translation of *Things Fall Apart*], trans. by Clement Ndulute (Nairobi: East African Publishing House, 1973); Ferdinand Oyono, *Boi* [translation of *Une vie de boi* via John Reed's translation *Houseboy*], trans. by Mabwana Raphael Kahaso and Nathan Mbwele (Nairobi: Heinemann Educational, 1976). On *Shujaa Okonkwo* see Meg Arenberg, 'Converting Achebe's Africa for the New Tanzanian: *Things Fall Apart* in Swahili Translation', *Eastern African Literary and Cultural Studies*, 2 (2016), 124–35; on *Boi* see Ken Walibora Waliaula, 'The Afterlife of Oyono's *Houseboy* in the Swahili Schools Market: To Be or Not to Be Faithful to the Original', *PMLA*, 128 (2013), 178–84. Sources for bibliographic details are author's

translations published in the years just before independence and reissued in Nairobi in the 1990s, including translations of Charles Dickens's *David Copperfield* and *Oliver Twist*, R. M. Ballantyne's *Coral Island*, and Jules Verne's *Around the World in Eighty Days*, in addition to Mark Twain's *Tom Sawyer*. A chapbook translation of Arthur Conan Doyle's 'The Adventure of the Speckled Band' appeared, sponsored by the Sherlock Holmes Society of Kenya, and a translation of Conan Doyle's *Hound of the Baskervilles* was later published.[16] In this near- and post-independence translating, East African translators (generally with Swahili as a first or second language) play a primary role, more hands are at work, and we see something more of what Donald Frame calls 'free literary translation' — that is, work undertaken at the choice of the translator — even as some similarities to the colonial-era bookshelf emerge.[17] Yet no fiction by a Brontë figures in this phase of translation.

We have thus identified two absences of *Jane* from the body of English-language fiction in Swahili translation, an early and a more recent one, and at this point it is useful to flip the model and ask what place in Swahili literature a Swahili *Jane* might have found, or yet find. What meaning might *Jane Eyre* have in the Swahili literary context? With what Swahili literature might it be in conversation? The poet and scholar Alamin Mazrui encourages us to adopt this kind of approach when he posits that Swahili culture places special emphasis on relations between translated literature and literature written in

copies and searches in WorldCat and the catalogues of SOAS, University of London and Yale University libraries.

16 On the original, pre-independence publication of novels here listed in their 1993 printing, my source is Mazrui (*Cultural Politics of Translation*, p. 5). They are *Visa vya David Copperfield*, trans. by Alfred Kingwe (Nairobi: Macmillan Kenya, 1993); *Visa vya Oliver Twist*, trans. by Amina C. Vuso (Nairobi: Macmillan Kenya, 1993); *Kisiwa cha Matumbawe*, adapted by E. F. Dodd, trans. by Elizabeth Pamba (Nairobi: Macmillan Kenya, 1993); *Kuizunguka Dunia kwa Siku Themanini*, trans. by Yusuf Kingala (Nairobi: Macmillan Kenya, 1993); *Visa vya Tom Sawyer*, trans. by Benedict Syambo (Nairobi: Macmillan Kenya, 1993). The translations of Conan Doyle are *Maajabu ya Utepe Wenye Madoadoa*, trans. by George M. Gatero and Leonard L. Muaka (Nairobi: Battered Silicon Dispatch Box, 1993); and *Mbwa wa Familia ya Baskerville*, trans. by Hassan O. Ali (Shelburne, Ontario: Battered Silicon Dispatch Box, 1999). Sources are searches in WorldCat and the catalogues of SOAS, University of London and Yale University libraries.

17 Donald Frame, 'Pleasures and Problems of Translation', in *The Craft of Translation*, ed. by John Biguenet and Rainer Schulte (Chicago: University of Chicago Press, 1989), pp. 70–92 (p. 70).

Swahili: 'Contrary to the focus of translation studies in the West on the relationship between the translated text and the original text, the most pressing issue in Swahiliphone Africa has been about the relationship of the translated text to the literature of its translating language,' he writes.[18] In imagining such relationships for a Swahili *Jane*, gender emerges as a key consideration.

Most literary translations into Swahili have been created by men, and few novels written by women in any language have been translated into Swahili. Setting aside children's literature, the one novel I know in Swahili translation that was authored by a woman is Mariama Bâ's *Une si longue lettre* (1979), translated by Clement Maganga and published in 2017 in Tanzania.[19] Bâ's epistolary novel, part autobiographical, probes the lives of women in Senegal. In this sense, its entrance into Swahili endorses Mazrui's earlier speculation that for women in Swahiliphone Africa, literary translation has particular value as a vehicle for social change: 'For women, translated texts may function as potential instruments of counterhegemonic discourses against patriarchy.' Mazrui notes that when Khadija Bachoo, 'an East African woman of Swahili-Muslim background', wrote to him in 2004 about her plan to translate Nawal el Saadawi's *God Dies by the Nile*, an interest in social critique inspired the project: '[s]he regarded *God Dies by the Nile* as a way of saying what she as a Swahili woman had wanted to say but was unable to do for reasons of cultural censorship. Because the translated work deals with a "foreign land" and a "foreign culture" out there, she believed it stood a better chance of escaping hostile reception from her patriarchal culture.'[20] Yet the translation never appeared. Here we find a link between feminine figures, real and fictional alike, and social critique. Is this a space where *Jane Eyre* might enter?

Mazrui's thoughts also resonate with the career in Swahili translation of Lewis Carroll's *Alice's Adventures in Wonderland*,

18 Alamin Mazrui, *Swahili Beyond the Boundaries: Literature, Language, and Identity* (Athens, OH: Ohio University Press, 2007), p. 123.

19 Mariama Bâ, *Barua Ndefu Kama Hii*, trans. by Clement Maganga (Dar es Salaam: Mkuki na Nyota, 2017); Mazrui discusses Maganga and the publishing context for his translation in *Cultural Politics of Translation* (pp. 75–76, 152). The children's novel *Under the Hawthorne Tree* by the Irish writer Marita Conlon-McKenna has also been translated into Swahili: Marita Conlon-McKenna, *Chini ya Mti wa Matumaini* (Dar es Salaam: Mkuki na Nyota, 2010); bibliographic records identify no translator.

20 Mazrui, *Swahili Beyond the Boundaries*, p. 144.

which has a few unusual features: to start, it has been translated twice, each time by a woman and with each translation possessing 'counterhegemonic' or quietly countercultural elements; the second, or more recent, translation might be considered richly counterhegemonic, the first in possession of countercultural elements. The first translation of *Alice* into Swahili, *Elisi katika Nchi ya Ajabu* (1940), was created by Ermyntrude Virginia St Lo Conan Davies (E. V. St Lo), who had returned to England after working as an Anglican nun in East Africa. According to Ida Hadjivayanis, Conan Davies felt 'disillusioned' with her order, subsequently studied nursing and midwifery in London, and began translating *Alice* while working as a nurse in Tanganyika, in the mid-1930s.[21] In some ways, *Elisi* aligns with colonial efforts to standardize Swahili; published by Sheldon Press, an arm of the Society for Promoting Christian Knowledge, it received the imprimatur of the Inter-Territorial Language Committee, and its creator was a native speaker of English. Yet *Elisi* also differs from the first generation of translations made by ITLC officials: it was created outside of the colonial bureaucracy *per se*; it was by a woman; and it features a girl protagonist. In her wish to transfigure Alice into a Swahili girl, Conan Davies makes memorable use of John Tenniel's illustrations for Carroll's text. *Elisi* appears as an African child, and the mad hatter wears a fez. The Red Queen is still the same queen, however, as Hadjivayanis, the second translator of *Alice's Adventures*, points out. In her re-translation of the book in 2015, *Alisi Ndani ya Nchi ya Ajabu*, Hadjivayanis scrutinizes the Conan Davies translation — an unusual instance of a re-translation in Swahili elaborating critical commentary on translation choices from the colonial era. Hadjivayanis argues that Alice is and should remain English; that the immutability of the Red Queen in Conan Davies' translation betrays its colonialist agenda; and that the first translation is mistaken in the very naming of its protagonist: the better form of 'Alice' in Swahili is 'Alisi'.[22] In and through the work of Hadjivayanis, we discover the figure of Alice cast and re-cast by women translators to serve a calculated sense of who Alice should *be* to Swahili readers. The career of *Alice's Adventures*

21 Ida Hadjivayanis, 'The Swahili *Elisi*: In Unguja Dialect', in *Alice in a World of Wonderlands: The Translations of Lewis Carroll's Masterpiece*, Vol. 1, ed. by Jon A. Lindseth and Alan Tannenbaum (New Castle, Delaware: Oak Knoll Press, 2015), 567–72 (p. 568).

22 Lewis Carroll, *Alisi Ndani ya Nchi ya Ajabu*, trans. by Ida Hadjivayanis (Port Laois, Ireland: Evertype, 2015), p. viii.

in translation suggests that feminine figures in Swahili literary translation possess potent mutability. There is also a spectre of Jane in Alice. Carroll's novel owes something to *Jane Eyre*, and to *Oliver Twist* behind that: in the successive displacements of its female protagonist and the corresponding encounters with a gallery of interlocutors, in its satire on education and social rituals, and in the threats and violence with which its protagonist contends. Jane is partially translated into Alice, and Alice *is* translated into Swahili.

Intertwined with Mazrui's remarks on women translating, and with the early loneliness of Conan Davies' *Elisi* as a book about a girl for girls first of all, are questions about girls' and women's literacy in East Africa. While there is not opportunity here to explore this subject in depth, we can note that the historian Corrie Decker documents an influential anxiety about women's *writing*, specifically, during the colonial era in Zanzibar — the era of the ITLC's translations of Haggard and Stevenson. Literacy certainly existed in Zanzibar before colonial schools. But a concept of literacy that entailed writing for girls presented special challenges:

> Whereas religious performances and elocution contests were familiar and respectable expressions of a schoolgirl's new literacy skills, writing was suspect. In the Western schools, literacy was understood as the ability to read, speak, *and* write. Many Zanzibaris of the time, though, believed that if a girl learned how to write she would write love letters to boys. This was one of the main reasons parents were initially wary of sending girls to the government schools. Similarly in Kenya, as Lynn Thomas explains, there was a close "association between [girls'] schooling and unrestrained sexuality".[23]

In colonial Zanzibar, Decker documents, schoolgirls on their way to 'modern literacies' negotiated societal fears about their practice of written self-expression.

Brontë, of course, knew about problems faced by women writers, in idea and in fact. Arriving back with her, I would like to ask a question centred in *Jane Eyre* and in the Swahili literary sphere. Is it possible to discern a textual space for a Swahili *Jane Eyre*: to imagine it situated among existing Swahili literature, to see *Jane Eyre* and Swahili literary creations gesturing towards one another? If so, how might that look?

23 Corrie Decker, 'Reading, Writing, and Respectability: How Schoolgirls Developed Modern Literacies in Colonial Zanzibar', *The International Journal of African Historical Studies*, 43 (2010), 89–114 (pp. 101–2).

To explore the question, we can think about passages from *Jane Eyre* and the Swahili canon side by side. When I undertake this experiment, scenes from a contemporary novel and from a classic, mid-nineteenth-century poem surface on the Swahili side and, from *Jane Eyre*, a meditation early in Chapter Twelve on the frustration of women who long for work of more interest than their society allows. Here Jane, having remarked on her own discontent, considers the situation of women generally:

> It is vain to say human beings ought to be satisfied with tranquility: they must have action; and they will make it if they cannot find it. Millions are condemned to a stiller doom than mine, and millions are in silent revolt against their lot. Nobody knows how many rebellions besides political rebellions ferment in the masses of life which people earth. Women are supposed to be very calm generally: but women feel just as men feel; they need exercise for their faculties, and a field for their efforts, as much as their brothers do; they suffer from too rigid a restraint, too absolute a stagnation, precisely as men would suffer; and it is narrow-minded in their more privileged fellow-creatures to say that they ought to confine themselves to making puddings and knitting stockings, to playing on the piano and embroidering bags. It is thoughtless to condemn them, or laugh at them, if they seek to do more or learn more than custom has pronounced necessary for their sex.[24]

Associatively, I connect Jane's musings with a scene from *Rosa Mistika* (1971), the first novel by the Tanzanian author Euphrase Kezilahabi: a fiction in his early, social-realist vein that focuses on inequity and abuse faced by girls in East Africa's educational system, as well as in family life. In this passage, from Chapter Three, Kezilahabi depicts the domestic space where the titular character Rosa and her sisters congregate — the women's compound, *mji wa wanawake* — as a site of profound vulnerability. At this point in the narrative, Rosa is on the threshold of opportunity; she has gained admittance to a girls' secondary school and eagerly awaits her departure. She and her sister Flora are returning from a trip to town to buy Rosa school supplies. At home, they gather companionably with their younger sisters Stella and Honorata and their neighbour Bigeyo, who gives Rosa a haircut while the girls' mother, Regina, washes clothes. Then a hawk comes, revealing the powerlessness of the girls and women:

> Walipofika nyumbani [Rosa na Flora] walimkuta Bigeyo akiwangojea, kwani Rosa alikuwa amemwambia aje amnyoe.

24 *JE*, Ch. 12.

Walikuwa wamekaa kivulini chini ya mchungwa. Regina alikuwa akifua nguo za Rosa. Mkasi ulilia, 'Kacha kacha, kachu' juu ya kichwa cha Rosa. Rosa alikuwa akijitazama ndani ya kioo kila wakati, alimwongoza Bigeyo asijekata sana nywele zake za mbele karibu na uso. Stella aliona kitu fulani kinashuka kasi sana. Alipiga kelele hali akitupa mikono juu.

'Swa! Swa! Swa!'

Wengine pia waliamka na kupiga kelele. Kazi bure. Kifaranga kimoja kilikwenda kinaning'inia kati ya kucha za mwewe. Walibakia kuhesabu vilivyosalia.

'Vilikuwa kumi. Sasa vimebaki vitatu!' Flora alishangaa. Rosa alikaa chini tena kunyolewa. Muda si mrefu mwewe alirudi. Safari hii Honorata ndiye alikuwa wa kwanza kumwona.

'Swa! Swa! Swa!' alitupa mikono juu, 'Swa!' Mwewe alikuwa amekwisha chukua kifaranga kingine. Zamu hii hakuenda mbali. Alitua juu ya mti karibu na mji. Wasichana walianza kumtupia mawe lakini hayakumfikia. Mwewe alikula kifaranga bila kujali. Alipomaliza aliruka kwa raha ya shibe. Vifaranga vilibaki viwili. Ilionekana kama kwamba hata mwewe alifahamu kwamba huu ulikuwa mji wa wanawake.

When they [Rosa and Flora] reached home, they found Bigeyo waiting for them, as Rosa had asked her to come cut her hair.

They were sitting in the shade of an orange tree. Regina was washing Rosa's clothes. The scissors snipped, 'Kacha kacha, kachu', over Rosa's head. Rosa was looking at herself in the mirror constantly, directing Bigeyo not to cut too much around her face. Stella saw something descending at great speed. She shouted, throwing up her arms.

'Swa! Swa! Swa!'

The others, too, started and shouted. But it was useless. One chick went, dangling from the claws of the hawk. The girls were left to count the remaining ones.

'There were ten. Now there are three!' Flora exclaimed. Rosa sat back down for her haircut. Soon the hawk returned. This time Honorata was the first to spot it.

'Swa! Swa! Swa!' she threw up her arms, 'Swa!' The hawk had already snatched another chick. This time it didn't go far. It alighted on a tree near the compound. The girls threw stones at it, but their throws fell short. The hawk ate the chick unconcernedly. When it finished, it leaped about with the delight of a full stomach. Two chicks remained. It seemed even the hawk understood that this was a women's compound.[25]

Rosa and the other schoolgirls in Kezilahabi's pioneering novel, which was banned in schools before becoming a set text there, seek to 'learn more' — to borrow the words of Jane — but in doing so in a

25 Euphrase Kezilahabi, *Rosa Mistika* (Nairobi: Kenya Literature Bureau, 1980 [1971]), p. 22 [my translation].

patriarchal society unprepared to support their aspirations, they meet with failure and tragedy. This early scene in the women's compound foreshadows that loss. As Rosa looks towards secondary school with hopeful apprehension, Kezilahabi signals that her existence is fretted with vulnerabilities. A few pages earlier, as Rosa and Flora journey to town, young men try to stop them on the road, and Kezilahabi describes the girls' flight in imagery that connects to the coming scene in the compound: refusing to look back at the young men whistling at them, the sisters 'kept running, like birds who had barely escaped to safety' ('waliendelea kukimbia kama ndege walionusurika').[26] As much as these girls may desire and deserve educational opportunity, Kezilahabi's imagery suggests, they face incessant risk in pursuing it.

In *Rosa Mistika*, Kezilahabi shares with Brontë a thought: a critical interest in educational structures and modes — in what they should be and in how they fail. His unsparing accounts of the violence Rosa experiences, including sexual violence, and of her sexual and reproductive life no doubt caused the novel's initial banning. Rosa, like Jane (and like Alice in a lighter-hearted rendition), suffers displacements, threats, and violence. Imagery of birds, central to Kezilahabi's representation of Rosa's vulnerability in Chapter Three, circulates in *Jane Eyre*, where Jane reads Thomas Bewick's *History of English Birds* in the novel's opening pages and where Rochester, attempting later to characterize Jane to herself, delivers an assessment in such imagery: 'I see at intervals the glance of a curious sort of bird through the close-set bars of a cage.'[27] While there is not space to elaborate this comparison fully, it is evident that Brontë and Kezilahabi both use imagery of birds to explore questions of power. Bird imagery captures an intertwining of vulnerability and potential liberation that resonates with the circumstances of protagonists who seek only 'a field for their efforts' — or, as Kezilahabi has it in another simile, 'air, water and light' ('maji, hewa na mwanga').[28] Improbably, Kezilahabi entered *Rosa Mistika* for an English-language literary prize, as Roberto

26 Kezilahabi, *Rosa Mistika*, p. 20 [my translation]. Kezilahabi's use of the verb *kunusurika* ('to be saved', 'to just manage to escape') in this image contributes to a sense of ceaseless vulnerability. In the simile, the flight of birds comes not so that they will be saved but because they have (just barely) escaped some danger.

27 *JE*, Ch. 14.

28 Kezilahabi, *Rosa Mistika*, p. 56 [my translation].

Gaudioso reports, 'kwa kuchokoza': to provoke.[29] Possibly the critical stance shared with a writer such as Brontë, in addition to colonial inheritances in the post-colonial educational system, contributed to his choice to do so.

The *Utendi wa Mwana Kupona*, or *Mwana Kupona's Poem*, composed in 1858 by Mwana Kupona binti Msham, centres also in a women's space. It represents a domestic transmission of knowledge from mother to daughter in which the act of writing figures centrally. This is a second scene we might connect with Jane's meditation in Chapter 12. Mwana Kupona, a renowned poet of nineteenth-century Pate, explains to her daughter how to negotiate her world. The provision of ink and paper ('wino na qaratasi') and the daughter's role as her mother's scribe figure in the poem's opening stanzas, here in the translation of J. W. T. Allen:

(1)	
Negema wangu bintu mchachefu wa sanati upulike wasiati asa ukazingatia	Come here, my daughter, and listen to my advice; young though you are, perhaps you will pay attention to it.
(2)	
Maradhi yamenishika hatta yametimu mwaka sikupata kutamka neno lema kukwambia	I have been ill for a whole year and have not had an opportunity to talk properly to you.
(3)	
Ndoo mbee ujilisi na wino na qaratasi moyoni nina hadithi nimependa kukwambia	Come forward and sit down with paper and ink. I have something that I want to say to you.

Among the mother's advice is her admonition that her daughter must win approval from five entities, including God and her husband. The poem then dilates on how the daughter should comport herself to ensure her husband's happiness:

29 Roberto Guadioso, 'To the Eternal Presence of Poetry, to Euphrase Kezilahabi', *Swahili Forum*, 27 (2020), 5–16 (p. 6).

(22)

Mama pulika maneno
kiumbe ni radhi tano
ndipo apate usono
wa akhera na dunia

Listen to me, my dear; a woman requires the approval of five before she has peace in this world and the next.

(23)

Nda Mngu na Mtumewe
baba na mama wayuwe
na ya tano nda mumewe
mno imekaririwa

Of God and His Prophet; of father and mother, as you know; and the fifth of her husband as has been said again and again.

(24)

Naawe radhi mumeo
siku zote mkaao
siku mukhitariwao
awe radhi mekuwea

Please your husband all the days that you live with him and on the day that you receive your call, his approval will be clear.

(25)

Na ufapo wewe mbee
radhi yake izengee
wende uitukuzie
ndipo upatapo ndia

If you die first, seek his blessing and go with it upon you, so you will find the way.

(26)

Siku ufufuliwao
nadhari ni ya mumeo
taulizwa atakao
ndilo takalotendewa

When you rise again the choice is your husband's; he will be asked his will and that will be done.

(27)

Kipenda wende peponi
utakwenda dalhini
kinena wende motoni
huna budi utatiwa

If he wishes you to go to Paradise, at once you will go; if he says to Hell, there must you be sent.

(28)

Keti naye kwa adabu
usimtie ghadhabu
akinena simjibu
itahidi kunyamaa

Live with him orderly, anger him not; if he rebuke you, do not argue; try to be silent.

(29)

Enda naye kwa imani atakalo simkhini we naye sikindaneni ukindani huumia	Give him all your heart, do not refuse what he wants; listen to each other, for obstinacy is hurtful.

(30)

Kitoka agana naye kingia mkongowee kisa umtengezee mahala pa kupumua	If he goes out, see him off; on his return welcome him and then make ready a place for him to rest.[30]

Affiliations between these stanzas and Jane's musings are complex. One might argue that *Utendi wa Mwana Kupona* (titled in one early English translation as a poem 'upon the wifely duty'), in the detailed instruction it sets forth, reveals a world where women live under 'too rigid a restraint'. Or one might agree with an interpretation of the poem — advanced in a reading by Ann Biersteker, in particular — as subverting the social norms it ostensibly embraces.[31] We might also, however else we understand it, highlight the significance of women's writing to the imaginary of this poem, which sets before us a scene of feminine knowledge and agency — the bringing of pen and ink by a daughter, under a mother's instruction; the preparation for writing; the prizing of knowledge-transmission signalled in the phrase 'pulika maneno', 'listen to these words', in the first stanza of line 22 (which Allen's generally sound translation elides to 'listen to me'), a phrase that signals as well the deep intertwining of orality and literacy in Swahili letters — which sets before us all these things, that is, prior to elaborating any explicit instruction for navigating life as a woman on the nineteenth-century Swahili coast. The role of caregiver that Mwana Kupona advises her daughter to assume in relation to her husband bears a resemblance to the role Jane holds in marriage to the blind Rochester in Chapter 38, which intertwines Jane's happiness

30 Mwana Kupona binti Msham, 'Utendi wa Mwana Kupona', in *Tendi: Six Examples of a Classical Verse Form with Translations and Notes*, ed. and trans. by J. W. T. Allen (London: Heinemann, 1971).

31 Ann Biersteker, 'Language, Poetry, and Power: A Reconsideration of "Utendi Wa Mwana Kupona"', in *Faces of Islam in African Literature*, ed. by Kenneth W. Harrow (London: James Currey, 1991), pp. 59–77.

during a decade of marriage with her identity as a writer recording her experience: 'My tale draws to its close [...] I have now been married ten years. I know what it is to live entirely for and with what I love best on earth.' *Utendi wa Mwana Kupona* likewise links writing, and language itself, to 'wifely duty'. As Farouk Topan notes, the poem treats language as the provenance of the wife, while '[t]he husband, on the contrary, is presented as someone who is almost devoid of speech, or someone to be taken as such.'[32] Defining themselves through the act of writing, both Mwana Kupona and Brontë create layers of such self-definition by making the feminine figures at the center of their creations into keepers of language.

But here, having no Swahili *Jane Eyre*, we reach a limit of this line of thought. What words would a Swahiliphone translator choose for the passage on 'a stiller doom' and 'silent revolt'? What would the register of language be? Where might we find lexical resonance with Euphrase Kezilahabi or Mwana Kupona, and what might that suggest to us about the meanings of those writers and their texts in the Swahili sphere? What would Jane's name be, in Swahili? She is unnamed for now, but perhaps not entirely unimagined.

Works Cited

Abdalla, Abdilatif, Personal communication, 2 June 2019.

Achebe, Chinua, *Shujaa Okonkwo*, trans. by Clement Ndulute (Nairobi: East African Publishing House, 1973).

Alidou, Ousseina, 'Booker T. Washington in Africa: Between Education and (Re) Colonization', in *A Thousand Flowers: Social Struggles Against Structural Adjustment in African Universities*, ed. by Silvia Federici, George Caffentzis, and Ousseina Alidou (Trenton, NJ: Africa World Press, 2000), pp. 25–36.

Arenberg, Meg, 'Converting Achebe's Africa for the New Tanzanian: *Things Fall Apart* in Swahili Translation', *Eastern African Literary and Cultural Studies*, 2 (2016), 124–35, https://doi.org/10.1080/23277408.2016.1274357

Armah, Ayi Kwei, *Wema Hawajazaliwa*, trans. by Abdilatif Abdalla (Nairobi: Heinemann Educational, 1976).

Bâ, Mariama, *Barua Ndefu Kama Hii*, trans. by Clement Maganga (Dar es Salaam: Mkuki na Nyota, 2017).

32 Farouk Topan, 'From Mwana Kupona to Mwavita: Representations of Female Status in Swahili Literature', in *Swahili Modernities: Culture, Politics, and Identity on the East Coast of Africa*, ed. by Pat Caplan and Farouk Topan (Trenton, NJ: Africa World Press, 2004), pp. 213–28 (p. 219).

Ballantyne, R. M., *Kisiwa cha Matumbawe*, adapted by E. F. Dodd, trans. by Elizabeth Pamba (Nairobi: Macmillan Kenya, 1993).

Biersteker, Ann, 'Language, Poetry, and Power: A Reconsideration of "Utendi Wa Mwana Kupona"', in *Faces of Islam in African Literature*, ed. by Kenneth W. Harrow (London: James Currey, 1991), pp. 59–77.

Binti Msham, Mwana Kupona, 'Utendi wa Mwana Kupona', in *Tendi: Six Examples of a Classical Verse Form*, ed. and trans. by J. W. T. Allen (London: Heinemann, 1971).

Carroll, Lewis, *Alisi Ndani ya Nchi ya Ajabu*, trans. by Ida Hadjivayanis (Port Laois, Ireland: Evertype, 2015).

Conan Doyle, Arthur, *Maajabu ya Utepe Wenye Madoadoa*, trans. by George M. Gatero and Leonard L. Muaka (Nairobi: Battered Silicon Dispatch Box, 1993).

——, *Mbwa wa Familia ya Baskerville*, trans. by Hassan O. Ali (Shelburne, Ontario: Battered Silicon Dispatch Box, 1999).

Conlon-McKenna, Marita. *Chini ya Mti wa Matumaini* (Dar es Salaam: Mkuki na Nyota, 2010).

Decker, Corrie, 'Reading, Writing, and Respectability: How Schoolgirls Developed Modern Literacies in Colonial Zanzibar', *The International Journal of African Historical Studies*, 43 (2010), 89–114.

Dickens, Charles, *Visa vya David Copperfield*, trans. by Alfred Kingwe (Nairobi: Macmillan Kenya, 1993).

——, *Visa vya Oliver Twist*, trans. by Amina C. Vuso (Nairobi: Macmillan Kenya, 1993).

Drury, Annmarie, *Translation as Transformation in Victorian Poetry* (Cambridge: Cambridge University Press, 2015), https://doi.org/10.1093/res/hgw027

Frame, Donald, 'Pleasures and Problems of Translation', in *The Craft of Translation*, ed. by John Biguenet and Rainer Schulte (Chicago: University of Chicago Press, 1989), pp. 70–92.

Frankl, P. J. L., 'Johann Ludwig Krapf and the Birth of Swahili Studies', *Zeitschrift de Deutschen Morgenländischen Gesellschaft*, 142 (1992), 12–20.

——, 'W. R. Taylor (1856–1927): England's Greatest Swahili Scholar', *Afrikanistische Arbeitspapiere*, 60 (1999), 161–74.

Gaudioso, Roberto, 'To the Eternal Presence of Poetry, to Euphrase Kezilahabi', *Swahili Forum*, 27 (2020), 5–16.

Geider, Thomas, 'A Survey of World Literature Translated into Swahili', in *Beyond the Language Issue: The Production, Mediation and Reception of Creative Writing in African Languages*, ed. by Anja Oed and Uta Reuster-Jahn (Köln: Rüdiger Köppe, 2008), pp. 67–84.

Hadjivayanis, Ida, 'The Swahili *Elisi*: In Unguja Dialect', in *Alice in a World of Wonderlands: The Translations of Lewis Carroll's Masterpiece*, Vol. 1, ed. by

Jon A. Lindseth and Alan Tannenbaum (New Castle, Delaware: Oak Knoll Press, 2015), pp. 567–72.

Haggard, H. Rider, *Mashimo ya Mfalme Sulemani*, trans. by Frederick Johnson and E. W. Brenn (London: Longman, 1929).

——, *Hadithi ya Allan Quartermain*, trans. by Frederick Johnson (London: Sheldon Press, 1934).

Heanley, Robert Marshall, *A Memoir of Edward Steere: Third Missionary Bishop in Central Africa* (London: George Bell and Sons, 1888).

Hunter, Emma, 'Dutiful Subjects, Patriotic Citizens, and the Concept of Good Citizenship in Twentieth-Century Tanzania', *The Historical Journal*, 56, no. 1 (2013), 257–77, https://doi.org/10.1017/S0018246X12000623

Iliffe, John, *A Modern History of Tanganyika* (Cambridge: Cambridge University Press, 1979).

Johnson, G. B., *Maisha ya Booker T. Washington: Mtu Mweusi Maarufu* (London: Sheldon Press, 1937).

Kezilahabi, Euphrase, *Rosa Mistika* (Nairobi: Kenya Literature Bureau, 1980 [1971]).

Kipling, Rudyard, *Hadithi za Maugli: Mtoto Aliyelelewa na Mbwa Mwitu*, trans. by Frederick Johnson (Bombay, Calcutta, Madras, and London: Macmillan, 1929).

Mazrui, Alamin, *Swahili Beyond the Boundaries: Literature, Language, and Identity* (Athens, OH: Ohio University Press, 2007).

——, *Cultural Politics of Translation: East Africa In a Global Context* (New York: Routledge, 2016). https://doi.org/10.4324/9781315625836

Ngũgĩ wa Thiong'o, *Njia Panda*, trans. by John Ndeti Somba (Nairobi: East African Publishing House, 1974).

——, *Usilie Mpenzi Wangu*, trans. by John Ndeti Somba (Nairobi: Heinemann Educational, 1975).

——, *Dreams in a Time of War* (New York: Anchor, 2010).

——, *In the House of the Interpreter* (New York: Anchor, 2012).

Oyono, Ferdinand, *Boi*, trans. by Mabwana Raphael Kahaso and Nathan Mbwele (Nairobi: Heinemann Educational, 1976).

Spaandonck, Marcel van, *Practical and Systematical Swahili Bibliography: Linguistics 1850–1963* (Leiden: Brill, 1965).

Stevenson, Robert Louis, *Kisiwa chenye Hazina*, trans. by Frederick Johnson and E. W. Brenn (London: Longmans, 1929).

Swift, Jonathan, *Safari za Gulliver*, trans. by Frederick Johnson (London: Sheldon Press, 1932).

Talento, Serena, 'The "Arabic Story" and the Kingwana Hugo: A (Too Short) History of Literary Translation into Swahili', in *Lugha na Fasihi: Essays in Honor and Memory of Elena Bertoncini Zúbková*, ed. by Flavia Aiello and

Roberto Gaudioso (Naples: Università degli Studi di Napoli 'L'Orientale', 2019), pp. 59–80.

——, *Framing Texts — Framing Social Spaces: Conceptualising Literary Translation in three Centuries of Swahili Literature* (Köln: Rüdiger Köppe, 2021).

Topan, Farouk, 'Biography Writing in Swahili', *History in Africa*, 24 (1997), 299–307.

——, 'From Mwana Kupona to Mwavita: Representations of Female Status in Swahili Literature', in *Swahili Modernities: Culture, Politics, and Identity on the East Coast of Africa*, ed. by Pat Caplan and Farouk Topan (Trenton, NJ: Africa World Press, 2004), pp. 213–28.

Twain, Mark, *Visa vya Tom Sawyer*, trans. Benedict Syambo (Nairobi: Macmillan Kenya, 1993).

Verne, Jules, *Kuizunguka Dunia kwa Siku Themanini*, trans. by Yusuf Kingala (Nairobi: Macmillan Kenya, 1993).

Waliaula, Ken Walibora, 'The Afterlife of Oyono's *Houseboy* in the Swahili Schools Market: To Be or Not to Be Faithful to the Original', *PMLA*, 128 (2013), 178–84, https://doi.org/10.1632/pmla.2013.128.1.178

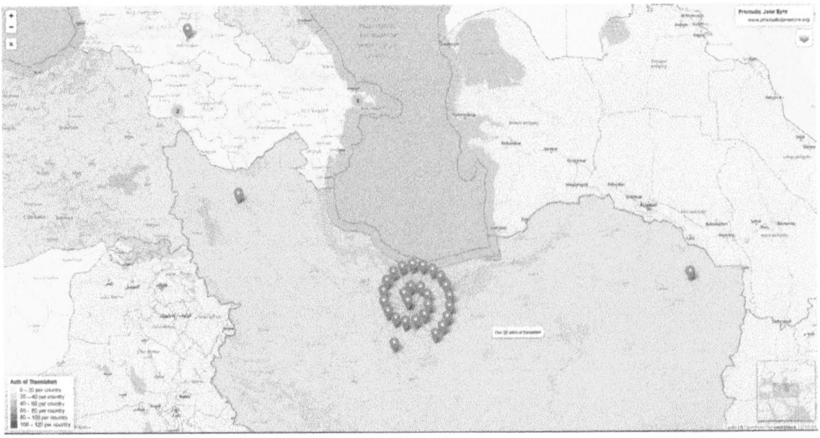

The World Map
https://digitalkoine.github.io/je_prismatic_map
Created by Giovanni Pietro Vitali;
maps © Thunderforest, data © OpenStreetMap contributors

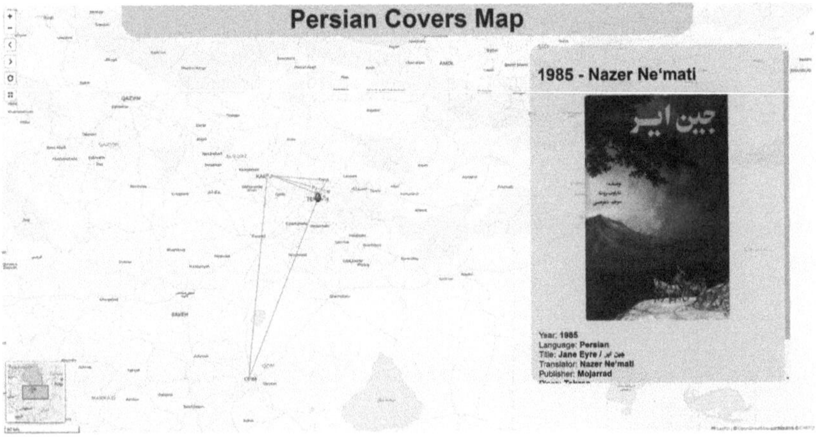

The Persian Covers Map
https://digitalkoine.github.io/persian_storymap/
Researched by Kayvan Tahmasebian; created by Giovanni Pietro Vitali and Simone Landucci

8. The Translatability of Love
The Romance Genre and the Prismatic Reception of *Jane Eyre* in Twentieth-Century Iran

Kayvan Tahmasebian and Rebecca Ruth Gould[1]

> My love has sworn, with sealing kiss,
> With me to live — to die;
> I have at last my nameless bliss.
> As I love — loved am I![2]

In the field of reception studies, Walter Benjamin's description of translation as emerging from the original's survival (*Überleben*) highlights the infinite variety of metamorphoses that literary texts could undergo in their worldly circulation. 'For a translation comes later than the original,' Benjamin asserts, 'and since the most important works never find their chosen translators at the time of their origin, their translation marks a stage in their continuing life [*Fortleben*].'[3] Benjamin remarks that the work's capacity for continuing its life in subsequent translations, its Übersetzbarkeit (translatability),

1 All translations from Persian, French, and German are our own. In addition to being supported by the Prismatic Translation project, this work has been facilitated by the European Union's Horizon 2020 Research and Innovation Programme under the Marie Skłodowska-Curie Grant Agreement No. 842125 and under ERC-2017-STG Grant Agreement No 759346.

2 *JE*, Ch. 24

3 Walter Benjamin, 'Die Aufgabe des Übersetzers', *Gesammelte Schriften*, 7 vols (Frankfurt a.M.: Suhrkamp, 1972), IV/i, p. 11. Our rendering of *Überleben* as 'survival' follows Chantal Wright, who explains in her introduction to Antoine Berman's *The Age of Translation: A Commentary on Walter Benjamin's* 'The Task of the Translator' (London: Routledge, 2018), p. 75, why it is problematic to render this term as 'afterlife'.

 https://doi.org/10.11647/OBP.0319.12

originates in a potential inherent in the work itself. Benjamin's account of translatability as the continued life of a literary text is instructive. Translation can be regarded as a process that brings forth a text's potential life, albeit in different ways every time it is undertaken. If any literary text *can* be translated in innumerable ways then, in theory, translation can be made to encompass any juxtaposition of two or more texts in any relation. The multiplicity of translation's modes of continued life is attested to by the broad spectrum according to which translations vary, ranging from strictly interlinear to free translations. By studying translations in terms of the ways in which they survive following their migration into other languages, we can better apprehend the variety and evolution of readerships that these translations generate across times and places.

The present chapter explores the Persian lives of Charlotte Brontë's novel *Jane Eyre* (1847). As we explore the possibility of comparative reading in a global context and across genres generated through a fundamentally different (premodern and non-European) poetics, we show how the nineteenth-century British novel continues its life in the Persian language and, most particularly, how it was received by Iranian readers according to the well-established tradition of the Persian romance that has given world literature some of its most famous lovers, including Layli and Majnun, Khosrow and Shirin, and Yusof and Zolaykhā. Beyond simply studying the reception of the Persian *Jane Eyre*, we illuminate the romantic potentialities of the narrative that are revealed through its exposure to a discourse of love that developed in a radically different cultural context and according to literary typologies that are without counterpart in the source literature.

Our method of reconstructing the reception of the Persian *Jane Eyre* was developed through extensive work on the numerous translations of the novel into Persian within the framework of the Prismatic *Jane Eyre* project. The prismatic metaphor of translation takes a pluralistic stance towards the relation of the original and the translated. Through the prism of translation, the text is dispersed and redistributed across languages, genres, cultures, and temporalities. In contrast to communicative translation paradigms that evaluate the product in terms of its faithfulness to an original, prismatic translation explores the creative ways in which the translated text deviates from the original. Regarding translation 'as a release of multiple signifying possibilities' instead of 'producing a text in one language that counts as equivalent to a text in another',[4] the prismatic approach is concerned with emancipating dormant interpretive and performative potentialities of the text when they are disjoined from the original language and context.

A prismatic examination of the reception of *Jane Eyre* in Persian will show how this multi-layered novel, with its interwoven strands of realism, romance, gothic, social-comment novel, governess novel, *Bildungsroman*, and spiritual autobiography,[5] undergoes a dispersion through translation whereby the novel's romance dimension is intensified by translational interventions. This approach grew out of our discovery that a considerable share of *Jane Eyre*'s Iranian readership over the past seventy years has been constituted by readers who consider the novel as a work of 'love literature [*adabiyāt-e 'āsheqāna*]' a term that references an established genre of Persian literature. Our survey of around thirty translations into Persian of *Jane Eyre* completed over the course of seventy years draws a trajectory whereby the Persian Jane evolved from the archetypal beloved of a Victorian romance into the independent resolute character favoured by feminist discourses in contemporary Iran, who nevertheless retains the characteristics of the archetypal Persian lover.[6] Over the course of seventy years, Persian translations of the English novel have evolved from early abridged translations that foregrounded the romance constituents of *Jane Eyre*, and which selectively and strategically rewrote the story in Persian, to more realistic refashionings that highlight the protagonist's education and autonomy, represented by elaborate paratextual devices in the most recent Persian versions.

Our reception-oriented reading considers how Jane, Rochester, and St John Rivers are perceived in their interrelations, according to concepts that construct the Persian discourse of love such as the lover's absence or separation (*ferāq*), the lovers' union (*vesāl*), the dialectic of the lover's demanding love and the beloved's demurral or rejection (*nāz va niyāz*), and the beloved's infidelity (*jafā*). Our discussion intersects with the study of gendered aspects of language, comparative

---

4 'Strand 6: Prismatic Translation', Creative Multilingualism, https://www.creativeml.ox.ac.uk/research/prismatic-translation

5 See Zoë Brennan, Brontë's Jane Eyre: *A Reader's Guide* (London and New York: Continuum, 2010), pp. 24–30.

6 Nushin Ebrahimi discusses Iranian feminism in her preface to her translation of *Jane Eyre*, in Charlotte Brontë, *Jeyn 'Eyr*, trans. by Nushin Ebrahimi (Tehran: Ofoq, 2015), pp. 7–14. Hereafter Ebrahimi (2015).

genre studies, the sociology of translation and retranslation, world literature, and popular culture. We explore how the Persian readership of *Jane Eyre* actualises the romantic potentialities of the text by filling its 'gaps' and 'indeterminacies' within an established generic 'horizon of expectation', ably described by Hans Robert Jauss.[7] Concurrently, we investigate the role of translators and publishers in forging an 'interpretive community' that demands particular modes for reading literary texts.[8]

Publishing Contexts for *Jane Eyre* in Iran

Jane Eyre enjoys a special place within the modern Persian literary system. The novel has been extensively read and appreciated by generations of Iranian readers and has occupied a central role in Iranian English language-learning programs, both as supplementary reading material and in Iranian university curricula for English literature. Brontë's novel has existed in Persian ever since 1950, in the translation of Masʿud Barzin. Since then, over thirty translations have been published. This abundance of *Jane Eyre*'s retranslations into Persian contrasts with a striking paucity of critical literature on the novel in Persian. Iranian scholarship on the novel is restricted to merely two scholarly articles: a New Historicist reading of racial ideology in *Jane Eyre* and an analysis of connotations in several translations of the novel into Persian.[9] Joyce Zonana's 1993 feminist reading of *Jane Eyre* has also been translated into Persian.[10]

Much of the online Persian material about *Jane Eyre*, especially on online Iranian booksellers, is directly translated from English sources. Reviews and notes to the novel that are written originally

7 Hans Robert Jauss, 'Literary History as a Challenge to Literary Theory', *New Literary History*, 2 (1970), 7–37.

8 Stanley Fish, *Is There a Text in This Class?: The Authority of Interpretive Communities* (Cambridge, MA: Harvard University Press, 1980).

9 Maʿsumeh Takallu and Behzad Barekat, 'A Study of Charlotte Brontë's *Jane Eyre* through the Prism of New Historicism', *Naqd-e zabān va adabiyāt-e khāreji*, 79 (2019), 79–102; Marjan Dehqani and Ahmad Seddiqi, 'Translating Connotations in Novels from English into Persian: Case Study of Charlotte Brontë's *Jane Eyre*', *Motāleʿāt-e tarjoma*, 36 (2012), 129–43.

10 Joyce Zonana, 'The Sultan and the Slave: Feminist Orientalism and the Structure of Jane Eyre', *Signs: Journal of Women in Culture and Society*, 18 (1993), 592–617, http://tarjomaan.com/article/5949/404.html

in Persian identify it as a 'love story [*dāstān-e ʿāsheqāna*]'.[11] In a note on an abridged Persian translation, a reviewer maintains that the novel narrates a 'love adventure [*mājarā-ye ʿāsheqāna*] full of ups and downs'.[12] Another reviewer classifies the novel as a classical romance novel (*roman-e ʿāsheqāna*) replete with 'suspense, love, absence, union [*vesāl*], failure and patience'.[13] An Iranian website introduces the novel as the third in a list of 'ten love novels everyone should read', a list that also includes Tolstoy's *Anna Karenina*, Proust's *In Search of Lost Time*, Austen's *Pride and Prejudice*, Brontë's *Wuthering Heights*, Flaubert's *Madame Bovary*, F. Scott Fitzgerald's *The Great Gatsby*, Pasternak's *Doctor Zhivago*, Pushkin's *Eugene Onegin*, and Goethe's *The Sorrows of Young Werther*.[14] *Jane Eyre* is routinely included in other similar listings of the greatest love stories in world literature in Iranian media.[15] This coverage attests to the public visibility of the novel, alongside the popularity of its film adaptations.[16]

Jane Eyre's popularity in Iran is also revealed by the large number of its retranslations. The title has been translated, either full or abridged form, by over thirty different translators.[17] Each translation/rewriting has appeared in several prints runs. *Jane Eyre* has also been published by publishers based in Qom, Mashhad, Isfahan, and Tabriz, provincial cities that comprise only a marginal share of the book market in Iran. While the title existed for two decades in only one translation, the first-ever *Jane Eyre* in Persian by Masʿud Barzin (1950),[18] since the 1979 Iranian revolution, around thirty other retranslations have since appeared, including in abridgements, as in Fereidun Kar's translation,[19] or translations of *Jane Eyre* rewritten by other writers, as in Maryam

11 See Moʿin Badpa, 'Dah nokta darbāra-ye romān-e Jeyn Eyr va nevisandash ['Ten remarks about the novel Jane Eyre and its author']', https://www.ettelaat.com/?p=370368

12 See https://taaghche.com/book/98508/جین-ایر

13 See https://www.chetor.com/152574-کتاب-جین-ایر/

14 See http://old.alef.ir/vdceep8w7jh8opi.b9bj.html?296640

15 See https://www.bartarinha.ir/fa/news/244462/10-رمان-عاشقانه-ای-که-هر-کس-باید-بخواند

16 For example, dubbed and subtitled versions of *Jane Eyre*'s 2011 and 1997 film adaptations directed by Cary Fukunaga and Robert Young respectively.

17 The catalog of the National Library of Iran lists 38 translations; however 8 of these were never published.

18 Charlotte Brontë, *Jen 'Er*, trans. by Masʿud Barzin (Tehran: Kanun-e Maʿrefat, 1950). Hereafter Barzin (1950).

19 Charlotte Brontë, *Jeyn 'Eyr*, trans. by Fereidun Kar (Tehran: Javidan, 1990). Hereafter Kar (1990).

Moayyedi's *Jeyn 'Eyr* (2004),[20] which translates Evelyn Attwood's simplified version of the novel.

Plagiaristic translations are also found among the thirty translations. For example, during our work for the *Prismatic Jane Eyre* project, we compared randomly selected excerpts of some translations with the original. Marzieh Khosravi's 2013 translation[21] was revealed to be a complete word-by-word copy of Mohammad-Taqi Bahrami Horran's *Jeyn 'Eyr* (1991).[22] The absence of copyright regulations, the indeterminate legal situation of publications, and the lack of quality checks have contributed to a chaotic market. European classics are frequent targets for such plagiarist acts. Further adding to their suitability for translation in the Islamic Republic of Iran, Victorian novels like *Jane Eyre* do not usually contain material — such as sex, drinking, extra-marital affairs, and obscenities — that often trigger the pre-publication reviews that are part of the government censorship apparatus, determining what can and cannot be published. For this reason, translations of Victorian novels are less likely to attract heavy government oversight. However, even for *Jane Eyre*, censorship has not been entirely avoided. References to 'wine' in the original are altered in Persian translation. In the version by Bahrami Horran, 'an aromatic drink [*nushidani*]' and 'syrup [*sharbat*]' is substituted for 'wine' in the following passage:

> Something of vengeance I had tasted for the first time; as aromatic wine it seemed, on swallowing, warm and racy: its after-flavour, metallic and corroding, gave me a sensation as if I had been poisoned.[23]

20 Charlotte Brontë, *Jeyn 'Eyr*, trans. by Maryam Moayyedi (Tehran: Amir Kabir, 2004). Hereafter Moayyedi (2004).

21 Charlotte Brontë, *Jeyn 'Eyr*, trans. by Marzieh Khosravi (Tehran: Ruzgar, 2013). Hereafter Khosravi (2013).

22 Charlotte Brontë, *Jeyn 'Eyr*, trans. by Mohammad-Taqi Bahrami Horran (Tehran: Jami, 1996 [1991]). Hereafter Bahrami Horran (1991).

23 Brontë, *Jane Eyre*, p. 31. This excerpt is translated in Bahrami Horran (1991), p. 49, as

برای اولین بارمزه انتقام را کمی چشیده بودم. مثل یک نوشیدنی معطر وقتی از گلو پایین میرفت گرم و خوشمزه احساس میشد و به اصطلاح مثل یک شربت اصل بود. مزه دبش و تیز آن به من این احساس را میداد که گفتی مسموم شده‌ام.

A back translation would be as follows: 'For the first time, I had tasted vengeance a little. Like an aromatic drink (*nushidani*), when it went down the throat, it was felt warm and delicious, as it's called, like a genuine syrup (*sharbat*). Its excellent and sharp taste was felt as if I were poisoned.'

In recent years within Iran, the problem of plagiaristic translations has attracted critical and journalistic attention.[24] Alongside full plagiarism, some translations of *Jane Eyre* show traces of having been compiled from a range of past translations. Plagiaristic re-translations of the so-called classical 'masterpieces' benefit both the publisher and the pseudo-translator. They are attractive to those who desire irresponsibly to see their names on the book covers as translators — literary translation is a prestigious occupation in Iran today, though it is not rewarding in terms of payment. Another common reason for fully plagiaristic published translations is that they may enhance the curriculum vitae of those aspiring to university positions. Such inauthentic works are expedient to publishers who must publish a certain quota of books annually in order to retain their permission to publish. Reprinting earlier retranslations of a popular novel, especially those which are no longer in print, is a profitable means of producing a book without paying for translator's rights. It is even common for the pseudo-translator to pay the publisher, requesting that their name appear on the cover as the translator of such and such a masterpiece of world literature.

Jane Eyre in Persian: Three Case Studies

We have excluded plagiaristic translations as well as translations from rewritten or abridged *Jane Eyre*s from our immediate purview. Our examination focuses instead on Barzin (1950), the first ever translation of the novel into Persian, Bahrami Horran (1991), a best-selling translation of the novel reprinted many times, and Reza'i (2010),[25] a recent, accurate, and high-quality translation. Reza'i's translation combines accuracy with detailed paratextual information so that the reader can better understand the historical, biblical, and literary allusions central to *Jane Eyre*, and come to appreciate the narrator as a remarkable educated woman.

Our selection is also informed by the reputation of the three translators, who are among the most prolific and professional of all of the Persian *Jane Eyre* translators. The first, Mas'ud Barzin, was an Iranian journalist, the ex-director general of the former National

24 For the controversy around Khosravi (2013), see http://www.ensafnews.com/47978/یک-روایت-کنایه-آمیز-یک-نقد،-یک-جوابیه/

25 Charlotte Brontë, *Jeyn 'Eyr*, trans. by Reza Reza'i (Tehran: Nashr-e Ney, 2010). Hereafter Reza'i (2010).

Iranian Radio and Television (1979), the first director of the Iranian Trade Union of Writers and Journalists, cultural coordinator in the Iranian embassy in India, and the general director of the public relations office of Farah Diba, the Pahlavi queen prior to the revolution. Barzin also translated *Oliver Twist* (1837–39) and *Gone with the Wind* (1936) and has compiled a glossary of journalistic terms in Persian. Mohammad-Taqi Bahrami Horran has translated around ten works, mostly literary, such as *Alice's Adventures in Wonderland* (1865) and *Le petit prince* (1943). Reza Reza'i, formerly a champion of the Iranian Chess National Team, has published around thirty translations, mostly literary, of Jane Austen, the Brontë sisters, and George Eliot.

The popularity of *Jane Eyre* also resonates with the popularity of Daphne du Maurier's novel, *Rebecca* (1938) in Iran. *Rebecca*'s plot is so similar to that of *Jane Eyre* that it has been understood by some as an adaptation of Brontë's novel.[26] Both du Maurier's novel and its film adaptation by Alfred Hitchcock (1940) were popular classics for Iranian readers and movie-goers. Du Maurier's novel has appeared in at least twenty-five different translations into Persian since the first translation by Shahbaz in 1954. It also appears in the above-mentioned Persian list of the most popular love stories of world literature.

The published Persian translations of *Jane Eyre* foreground romantic aspects, beginning with the cover images selected for Persian versions of the novel. Cover artists for these editions employ familiar melodramatic symbolism pertaining to marriage and love, with motifs of couples, hearts, and roses, as you can see by exploring the Persian Covers Map. One of the covers, of Afshar's 1985 translation,[27] is exemplary in this respect: it depicts a pair of female hands, presumably Jane's, holding to her breast an image of what appears to be Thornfield Hall, with a heart imprisoned behind its columns. Such cover images played a decisive role in shaping Jauss' horizon of expectation for the Iranian reader. They bring into focus the love between Jane and Rochester while barely making reference to other aspects of the protagonist such as her steadfast and independent character.

Translators' prefaces help us see how the novel is introduced to the Iranian reader. Most of the prefaces to translations of *Jane Eyre*

---

26 Heta Pyrhönen, *Bluebird Gothic: Jane Eyre and its Progeny* (Toronto: University of Toronto Press, 2010).

27 Charlotte Brontë, *Jeyn 'Eyr*, trans. by Mahdi Afshar (Tehran: Zarrin, 1982). Hereafter Afshar (1982).

consist primarily of a short biography of the author. Barzin adds a prefatory note in praise of Brontë's genius (*nobugh*).[28] He admits that he has abridged the novel, but insists that 'nothing of the matter [*'asl*] of the story is lost. I have removed only marginal parts [*havāshi*] and passages of merely second-order significance [*daraja-ye dovom*] in this masterpiece which do not please the Iranian reader'.[29] The 'marginal and less significant' removed content, however, includes the allusive texture of the novel (to the Bible, to literary texts, to fairy tales) as well as the protagonist's reflections upon her feelings and her moral progress. With these parts removed, the *Bildungsroman* aspects of the novel are diluted. Bahrami Horran's preface emphasizes the autobiographical nature of the book, not in the sense intended by the 'autobiography' in the original title (*Jane Eyre: An Autobiography*) but by identifying Jane the protagonist with Brontë the author.[30] The identification of Jane and Charlotte is evident also in Barzin's emphasis on Brontë's 'genius' which transformed her from a poor girl into an affluent writer in 'a lifetime battle with poverty and hardship', as indicated in the biography provided for Brontë on the back cover of Barzin's translation. All Persian translations have removed 'an autobiography' from the original title and only a few translations (Ebrahimi, Bahrami Horran, Reza'i) point to the writer's pseudonym, Currer Bell, in their prefaces.

As regards the transliteration of Jane's name in the title, all translators invariably translate it as جین ایر (pronounced *jeyn air*) with the exception of Barzin, who changes the title to *yatim* (orphan), with the *Jane Eyre* as the subtitle spelled unconventionally in Persian, ژن ئر. The spelling looks strange to an Iranian reader, with the 'J' transcribed, in a French fashion, to be pronounced as /*zh*/ and 'Eyre' transcribed in a script that resembles no Persian word and which instead looks like Arabic (without however corresponding to any existing Arabic spelling). Persian and Arabic words do not begin with a joined *hamza*. The change of the protagonist's name resonates with the translator's emphasis on Jane/Charlotte's genius; *zhen* is a homophone to *zheni*, a calque used in modern Persian for French *géni* (genius). Barzin's cover is embellished with a bleak expressionist-like depiction of a female figure which could be ascribed to Jane Eyre's period at Lowood

28 Barzin (1950), pp. 3–4.
29 Barzin (1950), p. 4.
30 Bahrami Horran (1991), pp. 3–4.

School (Figure 13). The artist is unknown. The cover art echoes Fritz Eichenberg's wood engravings for the 1943 Random House edition of the novel, although Eichenberg's depictions differ in many respects.

Fig. 13 Cover image of *Jeyn 'Eyr*, trans. by Mas'ud Barzin (Tehran: Ma'refat, 1950)

In this earliest translation of *Jane Eyre* into Persian, the author/protagonist's genius consists in the moral uprightness of her narrative and her 'interpretation of social problems'.[31] No paratextual aspect of this first translation of *Jane Eyre* foregrounds the romantic

31 Barzin (1950), p. 3.

characteristics of the novel. The protagonist's equilibrium between passion and reason, and between romantic and realist narrative modes, is highlighted instead. Thus, the first image of Jane that presented to the Iranian reader was less concerned with her romantic life than with her gender-specific capacity to transform her life of poverty and weakness into one of joy and strength, which made her a role model for modern Iranian readers.

Barzin's is the only translation of *Jane Eyre* into Persian until the 1979 Iranian revolution, at which point over thirty translations appeared in the period up to 2017. Meanwhile, the novel's pattern of reception has acquired the markers of the love literature (*adabiyāt-e ʿāsheqāna*) genre. Reza'i introduces *Jane Eyre* as a work at the 'summits [*qolla-hā*]' of classical world literature.[32] The translator focuses on the element of balance in the novel by recognising the writer's style in an intermediary state between realism and romanticism. He characterises the heroine as 'an ordinary-looking girl with a sublime spirit, who resists the ties of the world without losing faith in the foundations of her ethics and beliefs [*osul-e akhlāqi va eʿteqādi*]'.[33] At the same time, he describes the novel as a story of 'love, happiness and suffering, duty and morals, patience and victory, separation (*ferāq*) and union (*vesāl*)'.[34] Afshar writes that the most distinguished feature of this 'pleasant romantic story [*dāstān-e romāntik*]' is the chastity of Jane and Master Rochester's love'.[35] Ebrahimi's translation appeared as the first in a book series published by the publishing house Ofoq under the title *ʿAsheqāna-hāye kelāsik*, or 'classical romances'. Other titles in this series include Jane Austin's *Sense and Sensibility* (1811), *Emma* (1815), and *Pride and Prejudice* (1815), Honoré de Balzac's *Eugénie Grandet* (1833), Emily Brontë's *Wuthering Heights* (1847), Louisa May Alcott's *Little Women* (1868), Jean Webster's *Daddy-Long-Legs* (1912), Lucy Maud Montgomery's *The Blue Castle* (1926), and Annemarie Selinko's *Désirée* (1951).

The romantic strand in the popular reception of *Jane Eyre* first captured our attention during our work on *Jane Eyre*'s prismatic Persian translations, as we saw that a considerable number of translations target the typical readers of classical Persian romances, and of other romantic

32 Reza'i (2010).
33 Reza'i (2010), p. 9.
34 Ibid.
35 Afshar (1982), pp. 2–3.

literature. It has been argued that popularization of discourses is better thought of in terms of recontextualization than simplification.[36] The Iranian recontextualization of *Jane Eyre* as a popular romance occurs within a framework in which translations contribute to reclassifying the nineteenth-century British novel within an already established genre of *adabiyāt-e 'āsheqāna*. Many of the simplified or abridged Persian versions of *Jane Eyre* recalibrate the narrative into popular romance frameworks. We will see how the tendency of the modern Persian poetic system to define literary genres by theme contributes to such genre shifts from the original to the translated *Jane Eyre*. In the classical Persian typology, poetic sub-genres are defined in terms of the themes developed in the poem. Examples include the *marsiyya* (elegy), *mofākhara* (boasting poems), *monāzara* (dialogue), *shahrāshub* (complaints against cities), *habsiyya* (prison poem), *monājāt* (prayer), *shekvā* (complaint), *hajv* (satire), and *madiha* (panegyric).

The socio-political implications of introducing world literary masterpieces through distorted translations have been explored by the Iranian writer Reza Baraheni, who contends that such translations, abridged or expanded, intensify the aimlessness and alienation intrinsic to any translation of 'Western' literary and philosophical work into Persian.[37] Baraheni maintains that Iranian readers' alienation has not been resolved by post-revolutionary publishing policies in the so-called campaign against *ebtezāl* (superficiality). He identifies three strands in the Iranian publishing industry that transport readers beyond their objective socio-historical circumstances, two of which are comprised of translations. First, *shāhābādi* (literally, 'land of the shah') translations, a reference to the pre-revolutionary name of the street called after the Islamic Republic (currently Jomhuri Eslami Avenue) in Tehran, once the site of the most concentrated complex of Iranian publishers; second, expansionist translations (explained below); and third, historical romances. Baraheni uses the term *shāhābādi* to refer to the publishing industry that republished masterpieces of world literature in abridged and simplified editions in tens of thousands of copies and with a vast distribution network.

36 Helena Calsamiglia and Teun A. Van Dijk, 'Popularization discourse and knowledge about genome', *Discourse & Society*, 15 (2004), 369–89 (p. 371).

37 Reza Baraheni, *Kimiyā va khāk* [*Elixir and Dust*] (Tehran: Morgh-e Amin, 1985), pp. 96–99.

While the *shāhābādi* type of translations reduce the complexity of the original, expansionist translations rewrite the original by drawing on the translator's imaginative interventions. Instead of condensing the original, expansionist translations add to it by filling the gaps. This 'expansionist [*maktab-e bast*]' type of translation is known to the Persian reader by the name of its most renowned practitioner, Zabihollah Mansuri (1899–1986). Once a legendary Iranian translator of popular literature, Mansuri's translations have been extensively criticised for their infidelity and their imaginary rewritings of the original to the point of devising a new original text. Baraheni's third category is comprised of popular historical novels of Iranian kings and European monarchs such as Napoleon and Russian Tsars that function, according to Baraheni, to satisfy the unconscious thirst of post-revolutionary bourgeois readers for the restoration of the Iranian monarchy. These three strands generate an escapist literature that impedes the establishment and growth of a modern national literary consciousness by bombarding national literature with imprecise and inferior translations.

While the role of so-called expansionist translations of European novels in diminishing the Iranian aesthetic is undeniable, it is equally important to view these texts as gateways to a more serious literature for many Iranian readers. The remainder of this chapter turns to the potential modes of being that these translations, however imperfect and unfaithful they may be, suggest for *Jane Eyre* in its global journey across world literary genres. For this purpose, we first introduce the Persian romance tradition to examine the context within which Brontë's novel was received and categorised by Iranian readers as they integrated the text into their generic horizons of expectation.

Modern Iranian Romances and Serialised Love Stories (*pāvaraqi*)

The sub-genre of *dāstān-e 'āsheqāna* (love story) has always maintained a formidable presence in modern Persian literature. Adventure romances were among the first translated works from European literatures into Persian as early as the late Qajar era, for example, Prince Mohammad Taher Mirza Eskandari's translations of Alexander Dumas's *Le Comte de Monte-Cristo* (1895) and *Les Trois Mousquetaires* (1899). Before that, Iranian picaresque narratives known as *rend-nāma*, after the figure of the profligate (*rind*), which dates back to medieval Sufi literature, delighted Iranian readers. They were published in lithographs for the private use of the literate elite and for public readings for the illiterate in public spaces such as coffee-houses. Folk romances such as *Samak-e ayyār* [*Samak the Knight-errant*], transmitted orally and transcribed during the 12th century, and *Amir Arsalān-e nāmdār* [*The Famous Prince Arsalan*] were read to the Qajar ruler Nasser al-Din Shah and were favoured by ordinary people as well. More sophisticated picaresque prose stories, known in Persian and Arabic as *maqāma*, and marked by elaborate mannerisms, lacked the popularity of these romances. These folk romances are comparable to European chivalric romances in that both are patterned after a quest: the lover must undergo several trials to gain the beloved's favour and union. Early popular romantic legends, such as Mohammad Baqer Mirza Khosravi's *Shams va Toghrā'* (1899) were written in imitation of both Iranian folk legends and the early translated European novels.

Early Iranian popular romances, such as Sheykh Musa Nasri's *'Eshq va saltanat* [*Love and sovereignty*] (1881) or Mirza Hasan Khan Badi''s *Sargozasht-e Shams al-Din va Qamar* [*Tale of Shams al-Din and Qamar*] (1908) were characterised by a double plot of *razm* (battlefield) and *bazm* (feast). The double epic-romantic structure imitates the most popular love stories in Ferdowsi's *Shāhnāma* [*Book of Kings*], including that of Bijan and Manijeh in which an account of the brave deeds and battles of the male prince, Bijan, is given alongside accounts of his love affairs with the female princess, Manijeh. These stories were recited by public oral storytellers (*naqqāl*) or were illustrated in sophisticated manuscripts for the court. 'Abedini has demonstrated how late Qajar romances distracted the masses during the turbulent days of the Iranian Constitutional Revolution (1905–1911) with 'exciting stories of love and war of the princes who had lost their crowns' against the background of Iran's past glory, thus fulfilling the ideological function of generating sympathy with the Qajar dynasty just as it was losing its grips on monarchical power.[38]

With the decline of the Qajar monarchy, these romances embraced more nationalist causes in compliance with the modernist-nationalist cultural policies of Reza Shah (1925–1941). The most remarkable popular romances for this period are rooted in Iran's ancient pasts and focus on Achaemenid, Parthian, or Sassanid kings. Under the

38 Hasan 'Abedini, *Sad sāl dāstān-nevisi-ye Irān* [*One hundred years of fiction writing in Iran*], vol.1 (Tehran: Cheshmeh, 2001), p. 34.

guise of a pseudo-historical account of the wars and loves of Cyrus the Great, Alexander, Ardeshir, and Yazdgerd, the reasons for Iran's power and moral decline are sought. Dreams for a civilizational restoration are elaborated in historical novels (*romān-e tārikhi*), such as ʿAbd al-Hoseyn Sanʿati-zadeh's *Dāmgostarān* [*Mouse-catchers*] (1920–1925), Haydar ʿAli Kamali's *Mazālem-e Tarkān Khātun* [*Lady Tarkan's plea for justice*] (1927), ʿAli Asghar Rahim-zadeh Safavi's *Shahrbānu* and Hoseyn Masrur's *Dah nafar Qezelbāsh* [*Ten Qezelbash soldiers*] (1948). More realist and historicist dimensions are also observed in Mortaza Moshfeq Kazemi's *Tehrān-e makhuf* [*Horrible Tehran*] (1926), the first Iranian social novel.

Since the 1940s, with the spread of newspapers, love stories circulated in serialised forms in weekly magazines known as *pāvaraqi*.[39] These serialised love stories of Hoseynqoli Mostaʿan (with twenty stories) and Javad Fazel (with more than forty stories) attracted a huge number of readers to the extent that, according to ʿAbedini, 'the weekly magazines *Omid, Sabā, Taraqi, Tehrān Mosavvar* and *Ettelāʿat Haftegi* that published them were printed in five to fifteen thousand'.[40] The first translated *pāvaraqi* was published in *Ettelaʿ* magazine in 1936 by Mohammad Hoseyn Forughi under the title, *Jorj-e Engelisi ʿāsheq-e mādmovāzel Mārti-ye Pārisi* [*English George in love with Mademoiselle Marti from Paris*]. These are the best examples of modern Iranian escapist literature with loosely plotted stories and stock expositions, complications, climaxes and resolutions of a love affair between male and female characters who only change names as they appear in different stories. Substantial variation in the plot structures was rare. Authors entertained their readership by adhering to the same conventional protocols between the author and the huge mass of its readers.

The publication of these extraordinarily popular serialised romances coincided with the political oppression that followed after the American and British-led coup in 1953. The previously mentioned 'expansionist' strand of translation, represented by Zabihollah Mansuri's works, grew out of this phenomenal cultural market. His serialised column, *ʿOshāq-e nāmdār* [*Famed Lovers*] delighted Iranian readers of the popular magazine *Sepid va Siyāh* for eight years. His works, transgressing the boundaries of translation and authorship,

39 ʿAbedini, *Sad sāl dāstān- nevisi*, pp. 142–43. See also pp. 279–74.
40 ʿAbedini, *Sad sāl dāstān- nevisi*, p. 142.

are among the most widely read by contemporary Iranian readers. Not only in fiction but also in poetry, Iranian popular magazines of the 1950s and 1960s were haunted by the romance genre. Fereidun Kar, one of the most important poets working within this popular strand, also translated *Jane Eyre* into Persian (1990). With E'temadi's twenty-eight best-selling love novellas, the trajectory of the genre of love story writing (*'Eshqi-nevisi*) had reached its peak.

This trend was abruptly stopped with the 1979 revolution in Iran. The rise in the publication of classics such as *Jane Eyre* in the eighties and nineties should be understood in the context of the anti-superficiality (*zedd-e ebtezāl*) campaigns of the post-1979 revolutionary cultural milieu. In the absence of multitude of love stories, translated classics and their revival as *dāstān-e 'eshqi* offered a way to preserve the huge Iranian romance enthusiast market that had developed prior to the revolution. Although a more conservative form of *'eshqi-nevisi* was revived in the late nineties after the reformist opening in the Iranian political sphere with writers such as the best-selling Fahimeh Rahimi with twenty-three novels, a considerable number of romance readers were drawn to reading translated nineteenth century European novels with romantic overtones.

The Problem of a Comparative Generic Classification

The popular reception of *adabiyāt-e 'āsheqāna* (love literature) is rooted in a lyric sub-genre of classical Persian poetry, named *manzuma-ye 'āsheqāna* (romance verse), which recounts love affairs between an amorous couple in the *masnavi* (couplet) form. The most canonical Persian romances are Nezami Ganjevi's *Layli va Majnun* (1188), *Khosrow va Shirin* (c. 1175–76), and *Seven Beauties* (c. 1197), and Jami's *Yusof va Zolaykhā* (c. 1482). Each of these narratives recounts the affairs of the world-famous literary lover figures.[41] The exact number of these *manzumas* is unknown but around six hundred

41 Nezami's *Laylā va Majnun* has been rendered into English prose by Rudolf Gelpke, with Zia Inayat-Khan and Omid Safi, as *The Story of Layla and Majnun* ([n.p.]: Omega Publications, 1966); his *Seven Beauties* has been translated by Julie Scott Meisami as *Haft Paykar: A Medieval Persian Romance* (New York: Oxford University Press, 1995); Jami's *Yusof va Zolaykhā* has been rendered into prose by David Pendlebury as *Yusuf and Zulaikha: An Allegorical Romance* (London: Octagon, 1980).

extant manuscripts have been identified, mostly in verse.[42] In classical Persian literature, poetic love narratives (*ʿEshq-nāma*) exist either in the lyric form of the *ghazal* (as in Hafez's poetry) or in verse romance narratives considered to have originated in the *ghazal*.[43] The Iranian scholar Hasan Zolfaqari relates the *ghazal* to the *manzuma*, on the grounds that 'in the *ghazal*, the concept of love is expressed implicitly; however in a *manzuma-ye ʿāsheqāna*, the same theme is made explicit and extended in the form of narrative.'[44]

The tradition of Persian romance verse narrative has itself flourished across spatial and temporal boundaries in its global circulation. The first significant contribution to the Persian romance tradition, Fakhr al-Din Asʿad-e Gorgani's *Vis va Rāmin* (c. 1050) is adapted from an earlier Parthian love story.[45] A century later, this work was translated into Georgian prose by Sargis Tmogveli under the title *Visramiani*, and this rendering later helped scholars seeking to reconstruct details of the original Persian.[46] The form reached its maturity with Nezami Ganjevi's *Layli va Majnun* and *Khosrow va Shirin*. These two classics of Persian verse romance received many imitations (*nazira*), adaptations (*eqtebās*) which collectively constitute a rich body of classical Persianate love stories in verse, extending from South Asia to the Balkans.[47] The genre is also popular in other parts of the Persianate world, as seen as in the Kurdish oral legends of *charika*, Azeri *ʿāshiq*'s sung narratives and in the Armenian poems of Sayat Nova in the Caucasus, and countless adaptations of Persian romances into Urdu and other Indian languages in South Asia.

42 For a list of extant Persian *manzumas*, see Hasan Zolfaqari, *Yeksad manzuma-ye ʿāsheqāna-ye fārsi* [*One hundred Persian romance verses*] (Tehran: Charkh, 2013), pp. 37–47.

43 J. C. Bürgel, 'The Romance', in *Persian Literature*, ed. by Ehsan Yarshater (NY: Bibliotheca Persica, 1988), pp. 161–78.

44 Zolfaqari, *Yeksad manzuma-ye ʿāsheqāna-ye fārsi*, p. 19.

45 This work was most recently translated into English by Dick Davis as *Vis and Ramin*, trans. and ed. by Dick Davis (New York: Penguin, 2009).

46 The Georgian text was translated into English by Oliver Wardrop as *Visramiani: The Story of the Loves of Vis and Ramin, a Romance of Ancient Persia* (London: Royal Asiatic Society, 1914).

47 For one such imitation from Persian to Georgian, see Rebecca Ruth Gould, 'Sweetening the Heavy Georgian Tongue: Jāmi in the Georgian-Persianate World', in *Jāmi in Regional Contexts: The Reception of ʿAbd al-Raḥmān Jāmi's Works in the Islamicate World, ca. 9th/15th-14th/20th Century*, ed. by Thibaut d'Hubert and Alexandre Papas (Leiden: Brill, 2018), pp. 802–32.

Persian verse romances pose a challenge to comparative poetics in terms of their literary generic classifications. Attempts have been made by Iranian scholars to categorise these verse narratives according to generic frameworks borrowed from European poetics. Cross-categorization is significant when we consider that famous dramatic works such as Shakespeare's *Romeo and Juliet* and *Anthony and Cleopatra* are at times introduced as *'Eshq-nāma*, following the convention in the modern Persian poetic system of determining the genre membership of a literary work according to its theme. Connecting the term 'lyric [*ghenāyi*]' to European literary theory, the Iranian literary critic Sirus Shamisa categorizes these *manzumas* as 'narrative lyric [*ghenāyi dāstāni*]'.[48] As Shamisa recognises, European lyric poetry deals with an individual's inner desires and emotions, hopes, failures, and ambitions. However, the term *ghenāyi* in the Persian literary system originates in an Arabic literary typology and encompasses a diverse range of themes (*mazāmin*) such as 'panegyric (*madh*), satire (*hajv*), elegy (*marsiyya*), complaint (*shekvā*), separation (*ferāq-nāma*), prison poem (*habsiyya*), pride poem (*mofākhara*), oath (*sowgand-nāma*), praising the wine-bearer (*sāqi-nāma*), prayer (*monājāt-nāma*), happiness (*shādi-nāma*), the Prophet's ascension (*me'rāj-nāma*), praise songs (*moghanni-nāma*), debate poems (*monāzara*), complaints against cities (*shahrāshub*), turning away from the beloved (*vāsukht*), modesty (*voqu'*), and declarations of love (*taghazzol*).'[49] Romance verse (*manzuma-ye 'āsheqāna*) is distinguished because it is inclusive of all other *ghenāyi* themes, that is, some or all of the just-mentioned themes can be included in a *manzuma*.

Debates around the classification of Persian romances arise when a non-Iranian generic classification system, such as the tripartite typology of narrative (epic), lyric, and dramatic, is taken as the comparative measure. With this pre-supposition, it is not easy to classify a *manzuma* either as lyric or as narrative, because it can be both. A *manzuma* is narrative and is also lyric when the term is understood as *ghenāyi* to refer to poetic forms that deal with individual feeling and inner life. The problem arises from the translational identification of European *lyric* and the Arabo-Persian *ghenāyi*. Both words have musical resonances, 'lyric' in its original Greek reference to lyre that accompanied the recitation of poems, and

48 Sirus Shamisa, *Anvā'-e adabi* [*Literary types*] (Tehran: Ferdows, 1999), p. 124.
49 Zolfaqari, *Yeksad manzuma-ye 'āsheqāna-ye fārsi*, p. 19.

ghenāyi from Arabic *ghinā* ('to sing'), a term used for the recitation of poems that were to be performed in musical accompaniment. Shamisa adds the adjective *dāstāni* (narrative) to *ghenāyi* (lyric) in order to bypass the problematic identification of the two terms. Attempts to classify *manzuma* according to a European typology, however, end in ambivalence between the lyric and dramatic in the light of the fact that lyric poetry in European literature is generally non-narrative.

The debate around the generic cross-categorization of Persian romances reveals a significant structural characteristic of the genre in fluctuation between epic and lyric, and between the communal and the individual. This structural duality is reflected in the dual structure of the modern love stories comprising descriptions of *razm* (battles) and *bazm* (love). As regards our study of *Jane Eyre* through the lens of Persian romances, the fact that Persian *manzuma*s can only be called lyric when lyric elements permeate and interrupt the narrative elements resonates with the duality of romance and realism that is essential to Brontë's novel. 'The romantic, concerned with life's more extraordinary moments, including the passionate, is represented by Jane and Rochester's relationship,' argues Zoë Brennan, adding the caveat that 'passion is bridled to morality as Brontë attempts to include it in the realm of everyday. So, the novel can be said to take a realist stance, presenting the domestic and the everyday.'[50]

Having presented a synoptic history of the Persian romance, the next section reads *Jane Eyre* through the lens of Persian romances, with particular attention to their structural characteristics. We will see how the novel has been received by the Persian reader whose 'horizon of expectations' is shaped by romantic forces that eclipse all other generic dimensions of the novel, including the *Bildungsroman*, spiritual autobiography, and gothic.

Jane Eyre as a Persian Romance

Persian love stories progress according to a consistent pattern: A falls in love with B; A and B are initially in a state of separation; A seeks union with B and has to overcome certain obstacles and challenges; the story ends either happily with A and B united, or tragically with A and/or B dead. As regards *Jane Eyre*, the romantic component revolves around a love triangle with Jane and Rochester in mutual love and

50 Brennan, Brontë's *Jane Eyre: A Reader's Guide*, p. 25.

St John Rivers in love with Jane. Lovers in Persian romances can be grouped according to the degree of agency they show with respect to their beloved. While in Nezami's *Khosrow and Shirin*, both Khosrow and Shirin are actively engaged in the game of love — they plot and act to resolve the problems on their way to union — the character of Majnun in his *Layli and Majnun* is the archetypal passive lover of Persian literature, who remains satisfied with a mere image of the beloved until his tragic end in madness on the grave of his beloved Layli, after she has died in despair.

From this point of view, Jane Eyre's conduct and character as a beloved is comparable to Shirin: both have preserved a balance between their passion and their reason. Sattari describes Shirin as 'the symbolic face of a woman in love who refuses to transgress morality, mixing her passion with chastity (*ʿeffat*).'[51] For a substantial proportion of Iranian readers, Jane's refusal of Rochester's proposal to leave England together and live with him in Southern France as his wife would recall Shirin's resistance to Khosrow's seductions for premarital pleasure.

The romantic triangle of Shirin, Khosrow, and Farhad in Nezami's romance also parallels that of Jane, Rochester, and St John in *Jane Eyre*. The double pattern of satisfied and disappointed lovers is present in both texts, under the guise of Khosrow and Farhad in Nezami and Rochester and St John in Brontë, respectively. St John's austere perseverance in his love for Jane and his journey to India is echoed in Farhad, the disappointed lover who dies with the same sense of vocation, as a sculptor cutting the mountains and dreaming of Shirin. Furthermore, Rochester and Khosrow are parallel figures; they both play the role of the capricious aristocratic lover in these love triangles in contrast with the more responsible figures of Farhad and St John. Rochester's mad wife, Bertha, is as much a marital obstacle to Rochester's passion for Jane as is Khosrow's wife, Maryam, the Roman Emperor's daughter. Also, Khosrow's flirtations with Shekar-e Esfahani in order to make Shirin jealous is reminiscent of Rochester's teasing of Jane by showing affection for Blanche. Nezami's romance ends with the death of lovers, with Shirin committing suicide in the arms of her lover, murdered by his son. However, Khosrow's seclusion in a fire temple (*ātashkada*) after yielding all his power to his son is

51 Jalal Sattari, *Sāya-ye Izot va shekar-khand-e Shirin* [*Iseult's shadow and Shirin's sweet smile*] (Tehran: Markaz, 2004), p. 3.

similar to the scene near the end of *Jane Eyre*, with a blind handicapped Rochester in Ferndean after his Thornfield property has been burnt in the fire initiated by Bertha.

These parallels between different roles and positions do not constitute an adequate basis for systematic comparison. However, they point to the horizon of expectations that Iranian readers bring to a novel like *Jane Eyre* when it is introduced to them as a 'classical romance [*'āsheqāna-ye kelāsik*]', as in Ebrahimi's 2009 translation, which formally announces the genre membership of the Persian *Jane Eyre* through the name of the book series to which it belongs. Such converging horizons can also be found on a morphological level. In recent years, several studies have been undertaken by Iranian scholars on the morphology of Persian romances. Most of these studies are inspired by Vladimir Propp's approach to the structural elements of Russian folktale narratives.[52] For example, through an examination of twenty-two Persian romances, Va'ezzadeh introduces the Persian *manzuma* as a distinct narrative genre with an initial situation, twenty-two narrative functions and five main characters.[53] Correspondingly, the narrative of *Jane Eyre* could be reconstructed in a way that reflects its intersection with the classical Persian romance, with Rochester and Jane as 'the lover [*'asheq*]' and 'the beloved [*ma'shuq*]', Rochester's marriage as 'the obstacle', Bertha as 'the villain' and no 'helper' identified. Va'ezzadeh recognises three concluding patterns for Persian romances: union (*vesāl*), death, and the lover's ascension to the throne and beloved's giving birth to the lover's child, which is interesting with respect to Jane and Rochester's marriage in the end and Jane's giving birth to Rochester's son. Rochester's regaining his lost eyesight in the end is also a familiar ending for Persian romance readers, as in Jami's romance where Zolaykha recovers from blindness in the conclusion.

In another morphological approach to Persian romance, again through Propp, Zolfaqari distinguishes twenty narrative functions, many of which are present in the romantic texture of *Jane Eyre*.[54] These can be enumerated as follows: 1) The lover or the beloved's father (the

52 See V. Ia. Propp, *Morphology of the Folktale*, trans. by Louis A. Wagner, 2nd edn (Austin: University of Texas Press, 1968 [1928]).

53 Abbas Va'ezzadeh, 'Rada-bandi-ye dāstān-hā-ye 'āsheqāna-ye fārsi ['Typology of Persian romance narratives']', *Naqd-e adabi*, 33 (2016), 157–89.

54 Hasan Zolfaqari, 'Sākhtār-e dāstani-ye manzuma-hā-ye 'āsheqāna-ye fārsi ['The narrative structure of Persian romance narratives']', *Dorr-e dari (Adabiyāt-e ghenāyi 'erfāni)*, 17 (2016), 73–90.

king) has no child; 2) The father's prayers bring him a child; 3) The lover is born with difficulty and grows up fast. Although these elements are non-existent in *Jane Eyre*, with an orphan protagonist, the pattern nonetheless reverberates throughout the novel. The difficult birth of the protagonist in the Persian romance is a condition of possibility for the story. A Persian love story must start with an improbability. The lover should enter the world with difficulty and in despair, in order for his or her existential value, and therefore the existential value of the story of his or her love, to become evident to the reader. Therefore, as a sign of a continued life (not unlike the image of the translated text with which we opened), the lover's difficult birth at the beginning of the Persian romance suggests the chance to live, and to survive. From this perspective, Jane's survival of the fatal epidemic at Lowood can be regarded as among the essential constituents of the romantic component of *Jane Eyre* despite the fact that the same episode in the original highlights an important stage in the protagonist's spiritual progress towards an ethics of fairness and self-respect that contrasts with the doctrine of angelic humility and self-neglect adopted by Jane's friend Helen Burns.

We have so far identified three elements of the chain of narrative incidents and functions in classical Persian *manzuma* in our attempt to fit *Jane Eyre* into that framework and to map a potentially generative misreading of the novel in Persian. To continue this thread, which interestingly places Jane in the position of the lover and not only the beloved: 4) The lovers meet and fall in love; 5) The lover gets information about the beloved (compare, for example, Chapter 13 where Rochester enquires about Jane); 6) The lovers confess their love to each other and obstacles (religious or class differences, for example) appear on the way to their marriage (compare Chapters 21–22, the declaration of love and Jane's insistence on not being of the same social rank as her master); 7) The lover becomes sick in separation and takes refuge in the wilderness (compare Jane's flight from Thornfield, her wandering and sickness afterward, Chapters 28–29); 8) The lover's relatives cannot do anything to save him or her; 9) The lover's departure for hunting (compare Rochester's leaving Thornfield in Chapter 16); 10) The lover embarks on a dangerous trip, usually a voyage, his ship sinks and he is saved (compare Jane's flight from Thornfield after rejecting Rochester's proposal and being aided by Rivers family); 11) The lover enters an unknown place and is put on trial (compare Jane's residence in Marsh End/Moor House in Chapter 28, and her tedious life in the cottage attached to the school at Morton in Chapters 31–32); 12) The lover is aided miraculously (compare Jane's unexpected inheritance of a large fortune from her dead uncle and gaining a family, that is, her relation to Rivers family); 13) The development of minor love plots in the margin of the main story (compare Blanche Ingram's role in Chapter 18 and Rosamond Oliver in Chapter 32); 14) The lover's rendezvous with the beloved in disguise (compare Rochester's meeting with Jane in a gypsy's disguise in Chapter 19); 15) The lover is tested (compare Rochester's questioning of Jane in Chapters 13–14); 16) The rival impedes the union (compare Bertha's role in the novel); 17) The lover and rival struggle and the lover wins; 18) Letters and messages are exchanged between the lovers; 19) The lover isolates him/herself after having renounced all his power (compare Rochester's isolation in Ferndean after the fire in Thornfield in Chapters 36–37; 20) Finally, the lovers either unite or die (compare to their marriage in the novel's final Chapter).

Beyond revealing a structural truth about the novel, the one-to-one correspondences just noted map a potential misreading of the novel that translates — and which was translated — across languages and accommodated to different generic frameworks. In this regard, it is also relevant to note the translational interventions that confer continued life on the novel's romantic aspects. Persian amorous discourse is founded on particular concepts such as the lover's absence or separation (*ferāq*), the lovers' union (*vesāl*), the lover's demanding and beloved's demurral (*nāz va niyāz*), and the beloved's infidelity (*jafā*) that are fostered through the millennium-old tradition of *adabiyāt-e 'āsheqāna* (romance literature). Iranian translators' use of these terms contributes to the prismatic recontextualization of *Jane Eyre* as a Persian romance.

For example, the concept of *ferāq*, the lovers' state of separation in Persian romances, is a necessary stage in the maturation of carnal desire into a spiritual love. Reza'i translates 'separation' in Rochester's consolation to Jane, 'and you will not dream of separation and sorrow to-night; but of happy love and blissful union' (end of Chapter 26) as *ferāq*.[55] Another instance is the figure of the unfaithful beloved (*mahbub-e jafā-kār*), a ubiquitous object of the lover's complaints in classical Persian poetry. In the following excerpt of Chapter 11, which describes a song

55 Reza'i (2010), p. 729.

sung by little Adèle, Reza'i translates 'perfidy' and 'desertion' as *jafā* and 'the false one' as *mahbub-e jafā-kār*:[56]

> It was the strain of a forsaken lady, who, after bewailing the perfidy of her lover, calls pride to her aid; desires her attendant to deck her in her brightest jewels and richest robes, and resolves to meet the false one that night at a ball, and prove to him, by the gaiety of her demeanour, how little his desertion has affected her.[57]

In addition, different motivations for the protagonist's decisions throughout the narrative are revealed when the novel is read in light of the core concepts of love relations in Persian romances. The Persian semiotics of love regards the lovers' relations as a dialectic of demanding and demurring (*nāz va niyāz*). In classical Persian *manzumas* and *ghazals*, the lover's task is demanding (*niyāz*) and the beloved's response to the lover's demand is to pretend indifference (*nāz*). Dehkhoda defines *nāz* as 'showing independence (*esteghnā*)'.[58] In *Sawānih al-'Ushāq* (Hardships of Lovers), an important 11th century Sufi treatise on love, Ahmad Ghazzali writes that 'the beloved always remains the beloved, hence the beloved's attribute is 'independence [*esteghnā*]', and the lover always remains the lover, hence the lover's attribute is 'lack [*efteqār*]'.[59] The Iranian romance reader's horizon of expectations interprets Jane's rejection of Rochester's proposal to live with him after the failed wedding as a reflection of the beloved's indifference (*nāz*). In this case, the beloved's indifference is only a pretence of 'independence' that is performed in order to blaze the fire of Rochester's love, and to bring about their eventual marriage. It diverges from the classical Persian paradigm, whereby *nāz* signifies the beloved's firm resistance of the temptation to enter into a forbidden and secret relationship.

The Language of Romance

The novel's tendency toward romance in its Persian translations is manifested in the ways the Persian Jane loses her capacity for

---

56 Reza'i (2010), p. 256.

57 *JE*, Ch. 11.

58 'Ali Akbar Dehkhoda, *Loghatnāma*, vol.2, ed. by Mohammad Mo'in and Sayyed Ja'far Shahidi (Tehran: Entesharat va chap-i daneshgah-i Tehran, 1998) p. 2169

59 Ahmad Ghazzali, *Majmu'a āsār-e Fārsi-ye Ahmad Ghazzāli*, ed. by Ahmad Mojahed (Tehran: Entesharat-e Daneshgah-e Tehran, 1979), p. 164.

balancing her passion and her reasoning faculty. The Jane of Victorian England is distinguished by both her emotional intensity and her intellectual judgement. These capacities come to be revised through the heterogeneous resources of the Persian language. This revision derives in part from the limitations and difficulties of the Persian language in clarifying private emotions and feelings. The best example is the lack of clear delineation in Persian for the words 'feelings', 'emotions', and 'sentiments' which have no semantic delineation and are rendered by the same word — *ehsāsāt* — in all Persian versions of the novel.

These limitations also become evident in connection with key words in the novel such as 'passion'. Matthew Reynolds remarks that 'Passion' is one of the terms in Jane's psychomachia, in which context it battles with 'conscience' and 'judgment'.[60] Its meaning approximates to 'love', but can also be distinguished from love as more fleshly and fleeting; and of course there are other passions such as 'rage'. Everyone notices that Jane is 'passionate'. A remarkable part of Jane's intellectual faculties lies in her ability to give detailed descriptions and analyses of what she actually feels and thinks. And exactly these are the parts that are subject to most of the distortions and omissions in Persian translations. These descriptions constitute part of what is usually cut in translations, as in Barzin's. In general, the word 'passion' has been rendered by a wide range of words in Persian meaning 'excitement' (*shur*), 'love' (*'eshq*), 'strong desire' (*tamannā*) and 'anger' (*khashm*). Because of this indeterminacy, Reza'i translates 'passion' into redundant structures by joining two synonymous words by 'and'. For example, in the case of 'I had felt every word as acutely as I had heard it plainly, and a passion of resentment fomented now within me,' Reza'i translates 'passion' as *khashm va 'asabāniyyat* ('anger and rage'),[61] while in the case of 'The passions may rage furiously, like true heathens, as they are', the word is translated as *shur va sowdā* ('excitement and melancholy').[62]

Table 1 shows how different Persian translations of *Jane Eyre* interact with regard to Jane's detailed description of her innermost feelings when she heard Rochester calling out to her in her imagination:

60 See below, Chapter V.
61 *JE*, Ch. 4; Reza'i (2010), p. 84.
62 *JE*, Ch. 19; Reza'i (2010), p. 510.

All the house was still; for I believe all, except St. John and myself, were now retired to rest. The one candle was dying out: the room was full of moonlight. My heart beat fast and thick: I heard its throb. Suddenly it stood still to an inexpressible feeling that thrilled it through, and passed at once to my head and extremities. The feeling was not like an electric shock, but it was quite as sharp, as strange, as startling: it acted on my senses as if their utmost activity hitherto had been but torpor, from which they were now summoned and forced to wake. They rose expectant: eye and ear waited while the flesh quivered on my bones.[63]

1	Najmoddini[64] (1983), p. 174	ناگهان احساس ناشناخته‌ای آنرا از حرکت بازایستاندند. این حس مانند یک شوک الکتریکی نبود. ولی خیلی تند و غریب بود و روی تمام اعصاب من تاثیر گذاشت. در حالی که بدنم می‌لرزید چشم و گوشم منتظر ماندند.
2	Afshar (1982), p. 511	قلبم به شدت می‌تپید، آن چنان که صدای قلب خویش را می‌شنیدم، به ناگاه تپش سریع قلبم، از حرکت بازایستاد و احساسی غریب بر من حاکم شد آن‌چنان که قلبم را دچار لرزشی عظیم کرد. لرزشی که از حوزه قلبم گذشت و اعماق مغزم را به لرزه کشاند، این احساس مانند یک شوک الکتریکی نبود، اما احساسی کاملا غریب بود مانند یک تکان ناگهانی بود و آن‌چنان بر اعصابم اثر گذاشت که با آخرین تاثیر ممکنه اعصابم را به تحرک واداشت با این احساس گوشت بر روی استخوانم لرزید و نگاهم و همه وجودم به حالت انتظار باقی ماند.
3	Kar (1990), p. 269	و قلب من که از چند ساعت پیش دچار هیجان شده بود به تندی می‌طپید، ناگهان اعصابم سست شد و عرق سردی بر بدنم نشست.
4	Bahrami Horran (1991), p. 605	قلبم با سرعت و شدت می‌تپید؛ صدای تپش آن را می‌شنیدم. ناگهان در اثر یک احساس توصیف‌ناپذیر ایستاد. این احساس، که چنین اثری بر آن نهاده بود، یکباره تمام وجودم را در بر گرفت. به رعد و برق شباهتی نداشت اما بسیار شدید، عجیب و تکان‌دهنده بود. تأثیر آن بر حواسم به گونه‌ای بود که گفتی منتهای فعالیت آنها تا این موقع فقط یک حالت خواب مانند بوده، حالا آنها را فراخوانده‌اند و آنها ناگزیر بیدار شده‌اند. وقتی بیدار شدند حالت انتظار داشتند: چشم و گوش در انتظار بودند و گوشت و پوست روی استخوانم می‌لرزیدند.
5	Reza'i (2010), p. 606	قلبم تند و بلند می‌زد. صدای تاپ تاپش را می‌شنیدم. ناگهان احساس وصف‌ناپذیری قلبم را از حرکت انداخت، و این احساس نه تنها قلبم را از حرکت انداخت بلکه به سرم انتقال یافت و بعد هم در کل وجودم منتشر شد. احساسم شبیه برق‌گرفتگی نبود، اما بسیار شدید و عجیب و تکان‌دهنده بود. چنان بر حس‌هایم تاثیر گذاشت که گویی حس‌های من تا آن لحظه فقط در حالتی شبیه به خواب بودند. حالا به این حس‌ها ندا و فرمان می‌رسید که از خواب بیدار شوند. حس‌هایم برخاستند و تیز شدند. چشم و گوشم باز شدند و تمام بدنم به رعشه افتاد.

63 *JE*, Ch. 35.

64 Charlotte Brontë, *Jeyn 'Eyr*, trans. by Parviz Najmoddini (Tehran: Towsan, 1983).

6	Rasuli (2011), p. 426[65]	قلبم به هیجان آمده بود و تند می‌زد. صدایش را می‌شنیدم. ناگهان چیزی آن را از هیجان انداخت و همه وجودم را در بر گرفت. مثل شوک الکتریکی نبود ولی خیلی تکان‌دهنده بود.
7	Ebrahimi (2015), p. 424	ناگهان قلبم ایستاد؛ احساسی وصف‌ناپذیر از قلبم گذشت، به سرم منتقل شد و تمام وجودم را فرا گرفت. احساسم شبیه برق‌گرفتگی نبود، اما شدید، عجیب و تکان‌دهنده بود. به گونه‌ای مر ا برانگیخت که انگار قبلا در رخوت و خمودگی بودم. ذره ذره‌ی وجودم را از خواب بیدار و فعال کرد. هوشیار شدم، چشم و گوشم باز شد و بدنم شروع کرد به لرزیدن.

Table 1: Jane hears Rochester calling out to her in seven Persian translations of *Jane Eyre*:

As the table shows, Iranian translators have had problems especially with the word 'extremities', the material equivalent of Brontë's 'passion'. 'Extremities' has no definite counterpart in Persian. Afshar mistranslates it as 'the field of my heart [*howza-ye qalbam*]'. Najmoddini and Kar omit not only the whole phrase but this entire crucial paragraph. Bahrami Horran condenses the whole phrase as 'all my existence' (*tamām-e vojudam*). Reza'i renders it as 'all my body'.

As regards the verb 'thrill', the translators in Table 1 have either had recourse to explanatory phrases or have omitted the word. In the former case, the translator's imagination plays a significant role in rewriting these descriptions of inner experience, which make the translated text read like a passionate narration of opaque inner experience rather than a precise analysis of emotions. Ebrahimi condenses the entire feeling into the phrase 'an inexpressible feeling'. This conversely generates a sense of indeterminacy and imprecision rather than clarity of mind, thereby depriving Jane of a great part of her intellectual capacity in Persian translation. At the same time, as noted in the twenty narrative functions elucidated earlier, the Persian Jane acquires characteristics of the archetypal Persian beloved that are missing from the original, which renders her more as a lover, who packages her love within the Victorian social structures and behavioural norms that are most likely to ensure its success.

While Persian does not make as precise distinctions in the language of feeling, it does have the grammatical ability to distinguish levels of intimacy. *Jane Eyre*'s Persian translations reveal many different levels of intimacy and power relations that are established by the

65 Charlotte Brontë, *Jeyn 'Eyr*, trans. by Maryam Rasuli (Tehran: Ordibehesht, 2011).

second-person singular form of address. As in French, the singular 'you' takes two forms in the Persian language, *tow* (for simple informal address) and *shomā* (for formal and plural address). In contrast with the neutral 'you' in English dialogues, the Persian translator is able, or even obliged, to impose an intimacy which is non-existent in the English text. In this way, all direct addresses in *Jane Eyre* are naturally divided into formal and informal forms according to the translator's interpretation of the relationship between the interlocutors. This means that the translator of *Jane Eyre* into Persian has tools lacking in the original text to lengthen and shorten the distance between Jane and other characters in the novel in her romantic, domestic, social, and employment relations. For example, in the scene where Jane encounters her bullying cousin, John, we read:

> "What do you want?" I asked, with awkward diffidence.
> "Say, 'What do you want, Master Reed?' was the answer. 'I want you to come here.'"[66]

Bahrami Horran translates these 'you's differently.[67] While John addresses Jane with *tow*, implying his belief in his natural superiority over her as in a master-servant relation, Jane addresses him with formal forms and *shomā*, revealing her intention to maintain a distance between them. However, a few lines later, when Jane bursts into rebellious anger, her address changes to *tow*, breaking the normal superior-inferior relation between them: 'Wicked and cruel boy!' I said. 'You are like a murderer — you are like a slave-driver — you are like the Roman emperors!'[68] Different Iranian translators respond to the challenge of rendering address differently. Jane's addresses to John are rendered in the informal mode throughout Reza'i's translation, reflecting an approach to Jane's character which is uncompromising from the beginning.[69]

Further developing these nuanced uses of *tow* and *shomā*, Jane's relation to her two lovers, Rochester and St John, are represented differently by different translators. In Bahrami Horran's translation, the first encounter between Rochester and Jane is recounted in a mutual formal manner with both Rochester and Jane addressing

66 *JE*, Ch. 1.
67 Bahrami Horran (1991), p. 8.
68 *JE*, Ch. 1.
69 Reza'i (2010), p. 18.

each other with *shomā*.[70] However, while Rochester's address to Jane changes to *tow* when Jane saves him in the fire and in his proposal to Jane afterwards, Jane's address to Rochester remains formal until the end even when they are married. The Iranian reader would interpret this as either a sign of Jane's will to keep her distance, thus actively taking control of the formality involved in her relation to Rochester, or conversely as her passive submission to the master-servant relationship with Rochester even after their intimacy is secured by marriage. These considerations are non-existent in the original *Jane Eyre* and result from filtering the text through the prism of the Persian language, and its meticulous distribution of formal and informal registers.

The relation of Jane with St John is different in regard to forms of address. The first encounters between the two are managed by *shomā* until the scene in which St John informs Jane of her inherited wealth, addressing her with *tow*:[71]

> "And you," I interrupted, "cannot at all imagine the craving I have for fraternal and sisterly love. I never had a home, I never had brothers or sisters; I must and will have them now: you are not reluctant to admit me and own me, are you?"
>
> "Jane, I will be your brother — my sisters will be your sisters — without stipulating for this the sacrifice of your just rights."[72]

The translation of St John's 'you' into *tow* here shows a desire to get closer to Jane after she demands 'fraternal and sisterly love' from him. Meanwhile Jane, using *shomā* throughout, is resolved to keep her distance except for a transitory moment near the end of their dialogue, when the Persian Jane yields to the intimate mode and addresses St John with *tow*: 'And I do not want a stranger — unsympathising, alien, different from me; I want my kindred: those with whom I have full fellow-feeling. Say again you will be my brother: when you uttered the words I was satisfied, happy; repeat them if you can, repeat them sincerely.'[73] In Reza'i's text, this distribution of formality and informality appears somewhat different from Bahrami Horran's. Except for rare moments, St John does not speak to Jane in formal

70 Bahrami Horran (1991), p. 161.
71 Bahrami Horran (1991), p. 558.
72 *JE*, Ch. 33.
73 For translation, see Bahrami Horran (1991), p. 558.

address, while Jane keeps the formality in her relation to St John until the end.

This differentiated intimacy is also revealing with respect to another range of direct addresses in *Jane Eyre*, that is, when the autobiographical narrator directly addresses the reader. Different levels of intimacy between the narrator and the reader are built into Reza'i's and Bahrami Horran's translations. For example, at the end of Chapter 27:

> Gentle reader, may you never feel what I then felt! May your eyes never shed such stormy, scalding, heart-wrung tears as poured from mine. May you never appeal to Heaven in prayers so hopeless and so agonised as in that hour left my lips; for never may you, like me, dread to be the instrument of evil to what you wholly love.[74]

While Reza'i uses the formal address for the reader, Bahrami Horran uses the informal form.[75]

The Education of the Persian Jane

Antoine Berman's 'retranslation hypothesis' posits that translations of a work increase in accuracy with respect to the original the more mediated they are across generations.[76] Our survey of the translations of *Jane Eyre* into Persian over seven decades has confirmed Berman's hypothesis. From Barzin's first abridged translation in 1950, to one Reza'i's more recent 2010 translation, heavily annotated with 116 endnotes explaining the allusive intertexts of the novel to the Persian reader, the Persian Jane develops from being an innocent woman from a lower social class in love with an aristocratic married man into an educated, assertive, and confident young woman who gains in autonomy and integrity as she matures, and who learns to overcome oppressive social and gender hierarchies through her innate intellectual and empathetic capacities.

Most early Persian translations of *Jane Eyre* remove the many allusions in the novel to the Bible, Graeco-Roman mythology, and to writers such as Virgil, Shakespeare, and Walter Scott. This allusive texture is fundamental to the English novel.[77] Reza'i clarifies the novel's

74 *JE*, Ch. 27.

75 Reza'i (2010), p. 822; Bahrami Horran (1991), p. 461.

76 Antoine Berman, 'La retraduction comme espace de traduction', *Palimpsestes*, 13 (1990), 1–7.

77 See Philip C. Rule, 'The Function of Allusion in Jane Eyre', *Modern Language Studies* 15 (1985), 165–71.

allusions in its 116 endnotes, thus attempting to bring the intellectual capacities of the protagonist to light, and making the novel's status as a *Bildungsroman* palpable for the Persian reader. Table 2 shows different translators' renderings of several literary and historical allusions in *Jane Eyre*:

Original reference in *Jane Eyre*	**Reza'i (2010)**	**Bahrami (1991)**	**Kar (1990)**	**Afshar (1982)**
Bewick's *History of British Birds* (Ch. 1, p. 6)	*	TA	×	TR
Pamela and *Henry, Earl of Moreland* (Ch. 1, p. 7)	*	T	T	R
Goldsmith's *History of Rome* (Ch. 1, p. 8)	*	T	×	R
Gulliver's Travels (Ch. 3, p. 17)	*	T	×	R
Guy Fawkes (Ch. 3, p. 21)	*	E	×	R
Ezekiel: 'to take away your heart of stone and give you a heart of flesh' (Ch. 4, p. 27	*	T	×	R
Matthew: 'Love your enemies; bless the that curse you' (Ch. 6, p. 49)	*	T	×	R

Key

TA	translates title and author name
T	translates title only
×	removes reference
*	annotates
E	uses endnote
R	removes reflection evoked by the reference

Table 2: Rendering literary and historical allusions in Persian translations of *Jane Eyre*

When allusions are removed or left untranslated, a considerable part of Jane's intellectual capacity disappears from view. Even when such details are annotated in Persian translations, they are only restored in the paratextual apparatus. They remain external to the normal processes of reading and severed from the unified texture into which they were originally woven. Both in the case of removal and of annotation, they are moved out of the text, to become '*hors-texte*', in Derrida's terms.[78] At the beginning of Chapter 2, Jane is locked (domesticated) in the red-room. Here Jane's knowledge of the French language is disclosed to the reader. Her translational powers become evident while she plays on the French phrase '*hors de moi*', in the sense of being 'beside myself', which is literally translated by the narrator as '*out* of myself':

> I resisted all the way: a new thing for me, and a circumstance which greatly strengthened the bad opinion Bessie and Miss Abbot were disposed to entertain of me. The fact is, I was a trifle beside myself; or rather *out* of myself, as the French would say: I was conscious that a moment's mutiny had already rendered me liable to strange penalties, and like any other rebel slave, I felt resolved, in my desperation, to go all lengths.[79]

Barzin completely removes this reference to Jane's knowledge of the French language, and employs the Persian term '*az khod bikhod shoda*' to refer to both 'beside myself' and 'out of myself'.[80] *Az khod bikhod shodan* means 'to lose one's self', more literally 'to become self-less', which denotes 'losing control'. Reza'i picks up on this meaning but loses the word play completely by translating it as 'I had lost my control' which makes no sense in conjunction with 'as the French would say.'[81] Bahrami Hurran uses two Persian terms: '*az khod bikhod shodan*' and '*be qowl-e farānsavi-hā digar khodam nabudam* [as French would say "I was not myself"]'.[82] 'Not myself' translates 'out of myself' and best epitomises Jane's intellectual and emotional dignity, as manifested in her capacity to get out of herself and to create an autobiographical 'I' that is obliged to see one's self as an other. In Persian literature, 'love' is constituted by estrangement or alienation. 'I was not myself' is a fundamental element of the Persian lover's discourse, and informs the lover's ability to transcend his or her self for the sake of the other.

---

78 See Jacques Derrida, *Of Grammatology*, trans. by Gayatri Chakravorty Spivak (Baltimore, MD: Johns Hopkins University Press, 2013 [1997]), p. 163.

79 *JE*, Ch. 2.

80 Barzin (1950), p. 12.

81 Reza'i (2010), p. 23.

82 Bahrami Horran (1991), p. 11.

By viewing literary texts from outside the system in which they were originally produced, translators, comparatists, and scholars of translation can expand the potentialities of the original text. They can confer on it a continued life (Benjamin's *Fortleben*), ensuring its survival, its Überleben, across space and time. In the case we have examined, of the Iranian *Jane Eyre*, as translation was professionalised, translations became more accurate and adept at capturing the nuances of the original. Clearly, the increase in accuracy was a gain. And yet something of the simplicity of Barzin's inaugural translation may be said to be missing from more recent translations.

Rather than suggesting that one translation methodology is better or more necessary than another, the prismatic approach enables us to insist on the need for both. With inaccurate translations, Iranian readers ran the risk of sentimentalising *Jane Eyre*. Equally, without compelling translations shaped to the contours of the target culture, and specifically to its engagement with the Persian romance tradition, the translation may never have been read at all. The later accurate versions enable Iranian readers to re-read the novel, without displacing the value of the earlier inaccurate versions. New reception paradigms determine new modes of being for works of world literature. The prismatic approach to translation, with its emphasis on the potentiality of literary texts to determine and transform the conditions of their reception, shows how translators give new life to old originals in the act of translation, sometimes changing their original meanings in radical ways. By using prismatic translation to engage with readers' horizons of expectation, we can learn, gradually and imperfectly, to read as we might wish to live: according to the Persian principle of unconditional love for the other.

Works Cited

Translations of *Jane Eyre*

Brontë, Charlotte, *Jeyn 'Eyr*, trans. by Mahdi Afshar (Tehran: Zarrin, 1982).

——*Jeyn 'Eyr*, trans. by Mohammad-Taqi Bahrami Horran (Tehran: Jami, 1996 [1991]).

——*Jen 'Er*, trans. by Mas'ud Barzin (Tehran: Kanun-e Ma'refat, 1950).

——*Jeyn 'Eyr*, trans. by Nushin Ebrahimi (Tehran: Ofoq, 2009).

——*Jeyn 'Eyr*, trans. by Nushin Ebrahimi (Tehran: Ofoq, 2015).

——*Jeyn 'Eyr*, trans. by Fereidun Kar (Tehran: Javidan, 1990).

——*Jeyn 'Eyr*, trans. by Marzieh Khosravi (Tehran: Ruzgar, 2013).

——*Jeyn 'Eyr*, trans. by Maryam Moayyedi (Tehran: Amir Kabir, 2004).

——*Jeyn 'Eyr*, trans. by Parviz Najmoddini (Tehran: Towsan, 1983).

——*Jeyn 'Eyr*, trans. by Maryam Rasuli (Tehran: Ordibehesht, 2011).

——*Jeyn 'Eyr*, trans. by Reza Reza'i (Tehran: Nashr-e Ney, 2010).

Other Sources

'Abedini, Hasan, *Sad sāl dāstān-nevisi-ye Irān* [*One hundred years of fiction writing in Iran*], 3 vols (Tehran: Cheshmeh, 2001).

Badpa, Mo'in, 'Dah nokta darbāra-ye romān-e Jeyn Eyr va nevisandash' [Ten remarks about the novel Jane Eyre and its author], https://www.ettelaat.com/?p=370368

Baraheni, Reza, *Kimiyā va khāk* [Elixir and Dust] (Tehran: Morgh-e Amin, 1985).

Walter Benjamin, 'Die Aufgabe des Übersetzers', *Gesammelte Schriften*, 7 vols (Frankfurt a.M.: Suhrkamp, 1972), IV/i.

Berman, Antoine, 'La retraduction comme espace de traduction', *Palimpsestes*, 13 (1990), 1–7.

——, *The Age of Translation: A Commentary on Walter Benjamin's 'The Task of the Translator*, trans. by Chantal Wright (London: Routledge, 2018).

Brennan, Zoë, *Brontë's Jane Eyre: A Reader's Guide* (London and New York: Continuum, 2010).

Bürgel, J. C., 'The Romance', in *Persian Literature*, ed. by Ehsan Yarshater (New York: Bibliotheca Persica, 1988), pp. 161–78.

Brontë, Charlotte, *Jane Eyre: An Autobiography*, ed. by Richard J. Dunn, 3rd edn (New York: W. W. Norton, 2001).

Calsamiglia, Helena, and Teun A. Van Dijk, 'Popularization discourse and knowledge about genome', *Discourse & Society*, 15 (2004), 369–89.

Dehkhoda, Ali Akbar, *Loghatnāma*, ed. by Mohammad Moin and Sayyed Jafar Shahidi (Tehran: Entesharat va chap-i daneshgah-i Tehran, 1998), II.

Dehqani, Marjan, and Ahmad Saddiqi, 'Translating Connotations in Novels from English into Persian: Case Study of Charlotte Brontë's Jane Eyre', *Motāle'āt-e tarjoma*, 36 (2012), 129–43.

Derrida, Jacques, *Of Grammatology*, trans. by Gayatri Chakravorty Spivak (Baltimore, MD: Johns Hopkins University Press, 2013 [1997]).

Fish, Stanley, *Is There a Text in This Class?: The Authority of Interpretive Communities* (Cambridge, MA: Harvard University Press, 1980).

Ghazzali, Ahmad, *Majmu'a āsār-e Fārsi-ye Ahmad Ghazzāli*, ed. by Ahmad Mojahed (Tehran: Entesharat-e Daneshgah-I Tehran: 1979).

Gould, Rebecca Ruth, 'Sweetening the Heavy Georgian Tongue: Jāmī in the Georgian-Persianate World', in *Jāmī in Regional Contexts: The Reception of 'Abd al-Raḥmān Jāmī's Works in the Islamicate World, ca. 9th/15th-14th/20th Century*, ed. by Thibaut d'Hubertand Alexandre Papas (Leiden: Brill, 2018), pp. 802–32.

Jauss, Hans Robert, 'Literary History as a Challenge to Literary Theory', *New Literary History*, 2 (1970), 7–37.

Pyrhönen, Heta, *Bluebird Gothic: Jane Eyre and its Progeny* (Toronto: University of Toronto Press, 2010).

Propp, V. Ia., *Morphology of the Folktale*, trans. by Louis A. Wagner, 2nd edn (Austin: University of Texas Press, 1968 [1928]).

Reynolds, Matthew, 'Passion', *Prismatic Jane Eyre*, https://prismaticjane eyre.org/passion/

Rule, Philip C., 'The Function of Allusion in Jane Eyre', *Modern Language Studies*, 15 (1985), 165–71.

Sattari, Jalal Sāya-ye, *Izot va shikar-khand-e Shirin* [Iseult's shadow and Shirin's sweet smile] (Tehran: Markaz, 2004).

Shamisa, Sirus, *Anvā'-e adabi* [Literary types] (Tehran: Ferdows, 1999).

Takallu, Masumeh, and Behzad Barekat, 'A Study of Charlotte Brontë's Jane Eyre through the Prism of New Historicism', *Naqd-e zabān va adabiyāt-e khāreji*, 79 (2019), 79–102.

Va'ezzadeh, Abbas, 'Rada-bandi-ye dāstān-hā-ye 'āsheqāna-ye fārsi ['Typology of Persian romance narratives']', *Naqd-e adabi*, 33 (2016), 157–89.

Zonana, Joyce, 'The Sultan and the Slave: Feminist Orientalism and the Structure of Jane Eyre', *Signs: Journal of Women in Culture and Society*, 18 (1993), 592–617.

Zolfaqari, Hasan, *Yeksad manzuma-ye 'āsheqāna-ye fārsi* [One hundred Persian romance verses] (Tehran: Charkh, 2013).

——, 'Sākhtār-e dāstāni-ye manzuma-hā-ye 'āsheqāna-ye fārsi ['The narrative structure of Persian romance narratives']', *Dorr-e dari (adabiyāt-e ghenāyi 'erfāni)*, 17 (2016), 73–79.

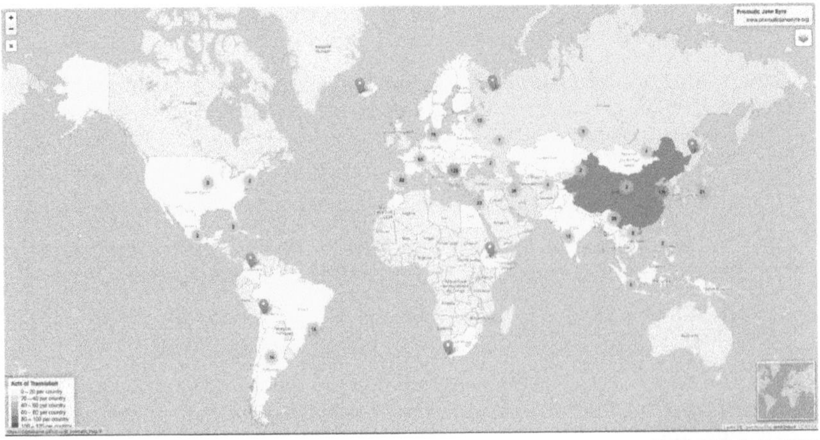

The World Map
https://digitalkoine.github.io/je_prismatic_map
Created by Giovanni Pietro Vitali;
maps © Thunderforest, data © OpenStreetMap contributors

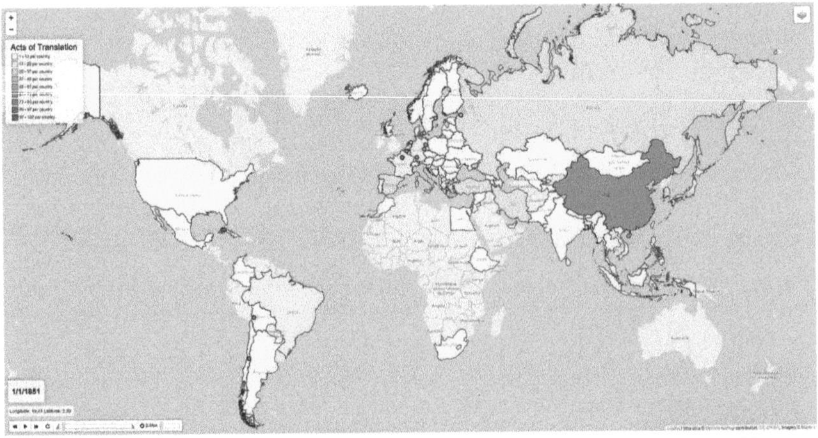

The Time Map
https://digitalkoine.github.io/translations_timemap
Created by Giovanni Pietro Vitali and Simone Landucci;
© OpenStreetMap contributors, © Mapbox

IV Close-Reading the Multiplicitous Text Through Language(s)

Matthew Reynolds

What Sort of Close Reading?

As will be more than clear by now, the phenomenon that we are reading — the world *Jane Eyre* — is vast and varied. It crosses time, geography and language(s). Its internal organization is both complex and fluid, because, as I argued in Chapter I, and as is evident in several of the essays you will have encountered so far, it is not possible to draw a firm distinction between one instance of this world work and another — that is, between one text, in whatever language, and the next. You can never be certain whether something that is made explicit in one text is not implicit in another, nor whether something visibly left out in a later version has not been quietly skipped, forgotten or felt to be superfluous by readers of other versions before. To read several instances of *Jane Eyre* together is, therefore, not a matter of comparing fixed entities but rather of opening up the textuality of each through its intermingling with the others. Hence the ambiguity in the title of this chapter. The text that Brontë wrote is already 'multiplicitous', and it passes 'through language(s)' to generate others (translations, and translations of translations); so, to read them is also to read it. And the whole of the world *Jane Eyre* is an (even more) multiplicitous text, which can be read through the language(s) with which it is composed. This chapter, and the chapters that follow, offer close readings of this plural text, this transtemporal, migratory and multilingual phenomenon, focusing on the transformations of key words.

So this chapter, and Chapters V–VII, bring many threads, from many kinds of languaging, together. In so doing, they provide a centre of gravity, or point of reference, for the many other modes of close reading exhibited in this publication. This volume gathers

 https://doi.org/10.11647/OBP.0319.13

the work of individuals, and both reading and the writing-from-reading that generates 'a reading' are, though taught and shareable, finally individual practices: each participant has their own style. As you will have discovered, what the essays present is not the result of a determinate method applied equally to all the varied texts and locations, translations in India treated in the same way as translations in Greece, and so on. Rather, in the course of the project that has given rise to this volume, shared interests and tactics emerged through conversations in which all the participants joined. The essays were then written from that intellectual context, with each writer pursuing the lines that seemed most interesting to them in dialogue with the wider, collaborative endeavour. This arrangement recognises that Laachir, Marzagora and Orsini's concept of 'significant geography' (which I described in Chapter III) applies not only to the people and texts under discussion but also to the people and texts who are doing the discussing. Each of us enters the phenomenon of the world *Jane Eyre* from a different place, with different points of reference, and can only grasp some areas of it, even while being aware of the other areas explored by our colleagues.[1] Close-reading a world text requires collaboration; and collaboration generates a plurality of readings, from different perspectives and in different modes.

There is some kind of closeness in all the analyses throughout this book. The discussions of contexts of *Jane Eyre* translation in the essays placed earlier in the volume (for instance Essay 1 by Ulrich Timme Kragh and Abhishek Jain on India, Essay 5 by Andrés Claro on Spain and South America, Essay 6 by Eleni Philippou on Greece, or Essay 8 by Kayvan Tahmasebian and Rebecca Gould on Iran), pay close attention to the detail of those contexts, connecting them to features of the translation-texts. In the terms of the early C21st debates about formalist modes of reading in the United States academy, we could say, with Susan J. Wolfson and Marjorie Levinson, that these are instances of 'activist new formalism', that is, of interpretations that recognise the inherence of the literary text in larger textualities of history and ideology.[2] The same recognition runs throughout the volume, even

1 This view builds on the conception of comparative criticism described in Matthew Reynolds, Mohamed-Salah Omri and Ben Morgan, 'Introduction', *Comparative Critical Studies*, special issue on *Comparative Criticism: Histories and Methods*, 12, 2 (2015), 147–59.

2 Marjorie Levinson, 'What is New Formalism?', *PMLA* 122 (2007), 558–69 (p. 559); see Susan Wolfson, 'Reading for Form', *Modern Language Quarterly*

when historical contexts are not explicitly brought into consideration. This is why the essays are not divided into different sections but are rather presented as a sequence, punctuated by orientatory chapters such as this one. The essays introduced by Chapters I and II may have particular relevance to the conceptualisation of translation, and those introduced by Chapter III may give special attention to place, but close reading permeates them all.

The essays and chapters that come next, forming roughly the second half of the book, are, correspondingly, those that focus most tightly on textual and formal aspects of the world *Jane Eyre*, while also being aware of its contexts. In Chapter V, I explore a selection of instances of the word 'passion' in the novel, presenting a synoptic view of how they are transformed in many languages, moments and locations. In Essay 9, Ana Teresa Marques dos Santos and Cláudia Pazos-Alonso study the 'volcanic vehemence' of Jane's self-expression as it comes through in a selection of translations from Portugal and Brazil, paying particular attention to what happens to the word 'mind'. In Essay 10, Ida Klitgård explores, in a similar vein, what becomes of the word 'passion' in Danish. A broader, quantitative approach is then taken by Paola Gaudio in Essay 11: she tracks what happens to all the nouns expressing feeling in the novel, with the aim of gauging how its overall emotional climate may be different in Italian.

Chapter VI then studies instances of the word 'plain' as they are re-made in many languages — a case which, as we will see, is revealingly different from that of 'passion'. This is followed by Essay 12, in which Yunte Huang explores proper nouns and pronouns in Chinese, starting from the coincidence that the name 'Jane Eyre' can be rendered with the characters '简爱' [*jian ai*] which also mean 'simple love': this only-partially-appropriate compound has become the book's dominant title and has strongly affected its reception in China. Mary Frank, in Essay 13, turns to consider an aspect of grammar, the need for German translators to decide whether characters refer to one another with an intimate or formal kind of 'you' — 'du' or 'Sie' — and, in particular, whether Jane and Rochester ever call each other 'du'. Here, attention to the translations opens onto a consideration of the dynamics of intimacy in Brontë's text, including Mr Rochester's use of the diminutive 'Janet'. In Essay 14 Léa Rychen considers the prominence of references to the Bible, and in particular to its 1611

61 (2000), 1–16 (p. 2).

Authorized (or 'King James') Version, asking what becomes of this significant strand of intertextuality in French, where there is no equivalent canonical Bible to quote.

Chapter VII offers a fresh synoptic view, via a consideration of the spiritually inflected terms 'walk' and 'wander', again tracing their shifts of significance and connotation across several tongues; it also presents two 'prismatic scenes', and concludes with a theorisation of 'littoral reading'. In Essay 15, Jernej Habjan focuses on a peculiarity of the style of *Jane Eyre* — its use of free indirect speech in quotation marks, that is, in the way direct speech is more usually presented. He shows German and Slovenian translators working out how to handle this conundrum, and from there develops a new understanding of the representation of speech in the text that Brontë wrote. In the last two essays in the volume, exploration of the source text and of the translations proceeds as a single, dialogic movement. Madli Kütt, in Essay 16, conducts a comparative investigation of first-person presence across the English and Estonian texts, given that 'Estonian has a large variety of means to avoid direct reference to either the speaker or the listener', tending 'to focus instead on the event, possession or experience itself'. Reading this most intensely first-person of novels in Estonian, therefore, means discovering 'new, altered points of view'. Finally, in Essay 17, Eugenia Kelbert asks an apparently simple question: what do the characters look like? From an investigation of six Russian translations, in dialogue with Brontë's text, she proposes that the world *Jane Eyre* creates 'a multiplicity of imagined persons across the globe'. In Chapter VIII, I offer some conclusions to this rich series of readings, and to the volume as a whole.

All these instances of close reading, diverse though they are, have at least one feature in common. They do not conceive of what they are investigating as an object which can be isolated from other textualities. This, then, is not close reading in the tradition of the New Criticism, where what is being read, usually a poem, has to be configured (in the words of Cleanth Brooks) as a 'unity' so as to discover how it organizes 'apparently contradictory and conflicting elements of experience ... into a new pattern'.[3] Rather, the close readings gathered here enter into a textual environment that has no end: they cultivate some patches of it, but maintain an awareness of the unexamined tracts of the world

3 Cleanth Brooks, *The Well Wrought Urn: Studies in the Structure of Poetry* (London: Dobson Books, 1949), p. 195.

Jane Eyre that lie beyond. In this, they owe more to the Roland Barthes of *S/Z*, who insisted that:

> Si l'on veut rester attentif au pluriel d'un texte ... il faut bien renoncer a structurer ce texte par grandes masses, comme le faisaient la rhétorique classsique et l'explicitation scolaire ... tout signifie sans cesse, et plusieurs fois, mais sans délégation à un grand ensemble final, à une structure dernière.
>
> [If we wish to remain attentive to the plural of a text ... we must give up structuring the text into large masses, in the vein of classical rhetoric and scholarly explication ... everything signifies ceaselessly, in several ways, but without having to be referred to a great, final unity, to an ultimate structure].[4]

And they follow the traces of Julia Kristeva, who, in the course of her theorization of intertextuality, saw any given text as a 'productivité' [productivity], born from '*plusieurs pratiques sémiotiques*' [*several semiotic practices*] which are '*translinguistiques*, c'est à dire faites à travers la langue et irréductibles aux categories qui lui sont, de nos jours, assignées' [*translinguistic*, that is to say, they happen across language and are irreducible to the categories imposed on language these days].[5]

Despite her own deeply multilingual repertoire, Kristeva did not pursue her concept of the 'translinguistic' into instances of translation: in this respect, *Prismatic Jane Eyre* is taking a road that was opened but left untravelled by her work. Likewise, Barthes does not offer any explicit discussion of translation. Yet *S/Z* is, just like this volume, an intense close reading of a single piece of prose fiction which, at times, Barthes describes in terms that also fit *Prismatic Jane Eyre*:

> Le texte unique n'est pas accès (inductif) à un Modèle, mais entrée d'un réseau à mille entrées; suivre cette entrée, c'est viser au loin, non une structure légale de normes et d'écarts, une Loi narrative ou poétique, mais une perspective (de bribes, de voix venues d'autres textes, d'autres codes), dont cependant le point de fuite est sans cesse reporté, mystérieusement ouvert.[6]
>
> [The single text does not give (inductive) access to a Model, but is rather the entrance to a network with a thousand entrances; to take this entrance is to set one's sights, in the distance, not on a legal structure of norms and gaps, a narrative or poetic Law, but a perspective (of crumbs,

4 Roland Barthes, *S/Z* (Paris: Seuil, 1970), p. 18.
5 Julia Kristeva, *Semiotiké: Recherches pour une sémanalyse* (Paris: Seuil, 1969).
6 Barthes, *S/Z*, p. 19.

> of voices come from other texts, of other codes) whose vanishing point, however, is ceaselessly pushed back, mysteriously open].

Barthes here is describing how study of a single text can show us something about all literature, making a poststructuralist argument which, when it is confined to the homolingual interpretive environment of Standard French (or indeed Standard English), has to do ceaseless battle against the constraining forces of publishing conventions and interpretive norms. However, when it is applied to the world of literature in translation, Barthes' claim reads more like a straightforward description of incontrovertible cultural and material realities: here, even a notionally single work such as *Jane Eyre* has a thousand entrances (or at least 618), while the voices coming from other texts (including other translations) have a strong and obvious influence, and the other codes are very markedly other, since language-difference can generate real incomprehension, as well as prompt bright insight.

This line of thought gives us an answer to the attack made by Franco Moretti on the role of close reading in world literary contexts:

> The trouble with close reading (in all of its incarnations, from the new criticism to deconstruction) is that it necessarily depends on an extremely small canon. This may have become an unconscious and invisible premiss by now, but it is an iron one nonetheless: you invest so much in individual texts *only* if you think that very few of them really matter. Otherwise, it doesn't make sense. And if you want to look beyond the canon (and of course, world literature will do so: it would be absurd if it didn't!) close reading will not do it. It's not designed to do it, it's designed to do the opposite. At bottom, it's a theological exercise — very solemn treatment of very few texts taken very seriously.[7]

To set this comment against the studies presented in this volume is to see how entirely Moretti overlooks the processes by which texts in fact circulate in world-literary contexts: through language(s), in hundreds of different versions, written by as many different people. This obviously complicates the notion of the canon. To be sure, *Jane Eyre* is a 'canonical' novel. But what that means in world-literary contexts is that it is opened up to all kinds of remaking: irreverent as well as reverent, casual as well as careful — reworkings for kids, for language-learners, for many different purposes in different

7 Franco Moretti, 'Conjectures on World Literature' *New Left Review*, new series 1 (2000), 54–68 (p. 57).

places. And that is just the translations. The film versions, the manga versions, the theatre versions, the erotic versions, the continuations, the blogs, the merchandise — all these are even more carnivalesque. So the textuality that comprises and surrounds only one 'canonical' text in world-literary contexts is not extremely small. It is vast. All this — this individuality, variety, commitment, obstruction, invention, labour — all this is beneath the purview of distant reading. Yet it is through all this, and crucially through language(s), that world literature happens. It is in these trammels that people encounter it, read it, react to it, are changed by it and change it in their turn. And all this can only be seen by close reading, done collaboratively.

Collaboratively, and also selectively. For despite the many people involved in this project, what we have been able to read is still only part of what there is. And that part has not been subjected to a uniform methodology. The discussion of Chinese translations by Yunte Huang in some ways overlaps with the analysis of German translations by Mary Frank; but the two essays also pursue quite different avenues: they are in implicit dialogue, not methodological unison — and the same goes for all the essays. This heterogeneous approach embodies the commitment to collaboration, the openness to alternative epistemologies, and the recognition — indeed, the welcoming — of incompleteness which I announced in the Introduction and have been elaborating in Chapters I, II and III. As we have been seeing, the instances of the world *Jane Eyre* do not obey a uniform global 'system', and neither do they inhabit 'languages' in the sense of standardized structures. They exist in particular repertoires, cultures and temporalities, having been created by individuals in distinct material contexts; and they are encountered by readers who are people. The participants in this project, too, are people. And so, from their varied situations in the significant geography of this project, different aspects of the world *Jane Eyre*, as it is available to them through their own repertoires, strike them as interesting. And what is interesting is what we want to find out. They have selected the translations they wish to analyse on the basis of their judgment, and they have pursued the lines of enquiry that seem most profitable to them, given who they are, their intellectual commitments, and the material they are exploring. In the terms of the social sciences, the readings presented in the essays arise from '*judgment* or *purposive sampling*, or *expert choice*'.[8] This procedure is no use for extracting statistics; but it is the only way of gaining access to a network with a thousand entrances — and that is what reading a world literary text requires us to do.

Almost all the approaches taken in individual essays could be pursued further afield. Widespread study of the handling of pronouns, of the language of appearance, or of indirect speech, for instance, are projects that could obviously be undertaken. That we have not done so is mainly down to practicality — of our capacities but also of yours, as readers, given the dimensions to which this volume has already grown. But it is also the case that these lines of enquiry turn out to be of variable fruitfulness in different locations — though it is impossible to be sure what will be interesting until you have looked. For instance, discussion starting from Léa Rychen's Essay 14 suggested that Biblical intertextuality tended very often to be lost, and there was not much more to be said about it — but this does not mean that in some context and linguistic repertoire not represented in the conversation it might not be very interesting indeed. Likewise, the sort of creative attention to pronouns in German discovered by Mary Frank turned out — in the eyes of Céline Sabiron — not to be matched in French, though as Sowon S. Park pointed out, in languages with very different pronominal conventions, such as Korean, the picture was likely to be complicated in quite different ways. Again, the features described by Madli Kütt seemed to us to be specific to Estonian, with the caveat that there are many languages in which *Jane Eyre* has been translated that we were not able to study in detail. Various other lines of possible comparison across linguistic repertoires were tried out. We looked at rhythm; but it seemed that only Juan G. de Luaces, writing in Spanish in Barcelona in the early 1940s, showed any significant interest in responding to Brontë's rhythms (see Essay 5 above, by Andrés Claro). We looked at patterns of metaphoricity, including pillars, water and fire. Here some points of interesting translinguistic comparison did emerge. For instance, Andrés Claro pointed out that the word 'erect', used by Brontë both for threatening patriarchal figures such as Mr Brocklehurst in Chapter 4 ('the straight, narrow, sable-clad shape standing erect') and for her own self-assertion before Mr Rochester in Chapter 23 ('another effort set me at liberty, and I stood erect before him') could not have

8 Graham Kalton, *Introduction to Survey Sampling* (Beverly Hills, Calif.: Sage Publications, 1983), p. 91.

been matched by Spanish translators with its obvious counterpart 'erecto' because the connotations were 'too immediately phallic'. In Persian on the other hand, as Kayvan Tahmasebian explained, words relating to pillars and erectness tend to connote 'support' and therefore 'dependence', so alternatives have had to be sought. On the whole, however, it seemed that metaphoricity was best attended to in the repertoire-specific essays, as happens with fire in Essay 9 by Ana Teresa Marques dos Santos and Cláudia Pazos-Alonso below. Book-covers provided readier material for translinguistic comparison, as we have seen in Chapter III; and the variations in the titles and subtitles that have been given to the translations are suggestive too, as the following selection shows:

[Jane Eyre, or the Memoirs of a Governess]: *Jane Eyre ou Mémoires d'une gouvernante*, tr. 'Old Nick' (Paul Émile Daurand Forgues), French, 1849; *Jane Eyre, eller en Gouvernantes Memoirer*, translator unknown, Danish, 1850; *Dzhenni Ėĭr, ili zapiski guvernantki* tr. S. I. Koshlakova, Russian, 1857 ... and many more, in many more languages.

[Jane Eyre, or the Orphan of Lowood]: *Jane Eyre oder die Waise von Lowood*, tr. A. Heinrich, German, 1854; *Jane Eyre, of, De wees van Lowood: een verhaal*, translator unknown, 1885; *Dzhenni Ėĭr, Lokvudskaia sirota*, Russian, 1893 ... and many more.

[An Ideal Lady]: *Riso Kaijin*, tr. Futo Mizutani, Japanese, 1896.

[Seeing Light Again]: *Chong guang ji*, tr. Xiaomei Xu, Chinese, 1925.

[The Passion of Jane Eyre]: *A Paixão de Jane Eyre*, tr. 'Mécia' (João Gaspar Simões), Portuguese, 1941.

[Jane Eyre: A Sublime Woman]: *Jane Eyre (A Mulher Sublime)*, tr. Virgínia Silva Lefreve, Portuguese, 1945.

[Orphan: Jane Eyre]: *Yatim*; subtitled ژن ئر, tr. Mas'ud Barzin, Persian, 1950.

[Jane Eyre / Simple Love]: *Jianai*, tr. Fang Li, Chinese, 1954 ... and almost every later Chinese translation.

[The Closed Door: Jane Eyre]: *La porta chiusa (Iane Eyre)*, translator unknown, Italian 1958.

[True Love]: *Kiều giang*, translator unknown, Vietnamese, 1963.

[When Everything Fails: A Novel of Jane Eyre]: *Kapag bigo na ang lahat: hango sa Jane Eyre*, translator unknown, Tagalog, 1985.

[Jane Eyre: Love Story]: *Khwāmrak khǫng: Jane Eyre*, tr. Sotsai Khatiwǫraphong, Thai, 2007.

[Jane Eyre: Happiness Coming After Many Years]: *Jane Eyre: Yıllar Sonra Gelen Mutluluk*, tr. Ceren Taştan, Turkish, 2010.

[The Human Life of the Girl Jane Eyre]: *Bumo Dreng Ar gyi mitse (Bu mo sgreng ar gyi mi tshe)*, tr. Sonam Lhundrub, Tibetan, 2011.[9]

However, our most productive focus, as we looked together across the language(s) of the world *Jane Eyre*, turned out to be on individual words.

Key Words Refracting through Language(s)

In the text that Brontë wrote, networks of meaning grow through the repetition of particular words, words which gather significance as they recur. 'Plain' is a good example: across the span of the novel, Jane tells us that she wears 'plain' clothes (in the sense of 'unelaborate'), looks 'plain' ('unremarkable'), hears 'plainly' ('clearly'), and is 'too plain' in her speech ('blunt'); that her 'Reason' tells her a 'plain, unvarnished tale' ('honest, frank'), and that she herself narrates the 'plain truth' ('unembellished'). This last usage also jumps out of the fictional text into the Preface that Brontë wrote for the second edition, where she describes the novel as 'a plain tale with few pretensions'.[10] We will explore these reappearances of the word fully in Chapter VI below: watching it, as it steps up time and again to put its finger on something and name it, plainly, we may be tempted to feel, as William Empson did in *The Structure of Complex Words*, that:

> a word may become a sort of solid entity, able to direct opinion, thought of as like a person; also it is often said (whether this is the same idea or not) that a word can become a 'compacted doctrine', or even that all words are compacted doctrines inherently.[11]

I would say, slightly differently, that the reiterations of the word signal an argument, one that is implicit also in the unfolding of the plot: plain looks can foster clarity of perception and straightforwardness

9 These titles were researched by Rachel Dryden, Chelsea Haith, Céline Sabiron, Vincent Thierry, Léa Rychen, Ida Klitgård, Eugenia Kelbert, Mary Frank, Jernej Habjan, Ana Teresa Marques dos Santos, Claudia Pazos Alonso, Kayvan Tahmasebian, Yunte Huang, Alessandro Grilli, Yorimitsu Hashimoto, Emrah Serdan, Ulrich Timme Kragh, Livia Demetriou-Erdal.

10 See Chapter VI, '"Plain" through Language(s)' for the references for these quotations, and full discussion.

11 William Empson, *The Structure of Complex Words* (London: The Hogarth Press, 1985 [1951]), p. 39.

of expression, and plainness, in this complex of senses, is a virtue. As the word is repeated, each new use can be tinged by those that have come before, so that its significance grows. We can draw on Empson again to say that, progressively, different senses of the word come to be 'used at once', creating 'an implied assertion that they naturally belong together'.[12]

To take a selection of such key words, and to trace them through the novel, is to sample the endless drift and metamorphosis of vocabulary through time which was well described by Raymond Williams in *Keywords*:

> We find a history and complexity of meanings; conscious changes, or consciously different uses; innovation, obsolescence, specialization, extension, overlap, transfer; or changes which are masked by a nominal continuity so that words which seem to have been there for centuries, with continuous general meanings, have come in fact to express radically different or radically variable, yet sometimes hardly noticed, meanings and implications of meaning.[13]

This is one aspect of the world of language(s), unstoppably burgeoning, subsiding, metamorphosing, and always exceeding the most patient attempts to chronicle it — such as those made by the enormous *Oxford English Dictionary*, a crucial source for both Williams and Empson. As its title announces, that dictionary (like many others) has another limitation: it is concerned only with the area of language(s) that counts as English. Both critics adopt the same focus, a constraint which causes Williams, at least, some frustration. He expresses it in a passage that I shall quote at length, since it is foundational to the volume that you are reading:

> Of one particular limitation I have been very conscious. Many of the most important words that I have worked on either developed key meanings in languages other than English, or went through a complicated and interactive development in a number of major languages. Where I have been able in part to follow this, as in *alienation* or *culture*, its significance is so evident that we are bound to feel the lack of it when such tracing has not been possible. To do such comparative studies adequately would be an extraordinary international collaborative enterprise ... I have had enough experience of trying to discuss two key English Marxist terms — base and superstructure — not only in relation to their German originals, but in discussions with French,

12 Empson, *Structure*, p. 40.

13 Raymond Williams, *Keywords: A Vocabulary of Culture and Society* (London: Harper Collins 1988 [1976; revised edn 1983]), p. 16.

> Italian, Spanish, Russian and Swedish friends, in relation to their forms in these other languages, to know not only that the results are fascinating and difficult, but that such comparative analysis is crucially important, not just as philology, but as a central matter of intellectual clarity. It is greatly to be hoped that ways will be found of encouraging and supporting these comparative inquiries, but meanwhile it should be recorded that while some key developments, now of international importance, occurred first in English, many did not and in the end can only be understood when other languages are brought consistently into comparison.[14]

Prismatic Jane Eyre hopes to provide something of the comparative analysis that Williams wished for, even if it has its own necessary limitation, with its focus on a single world work. Yet this limitation does not mean that the words we have studied develop less complexity of meaning, as they spread across languages, than words like 'base' and 'superstructure' considered as part of transnational political discourse. Words in use can sprout new involutions in all sorts of ways; but a novel like *Jane Eyre* creates an especially charged context for their growth. Close-reading words in a literary text can uncover as much — or more — intricacy than attention to words in broader discourse, because literature is a forcing-house for language.

A quick example: three instances of the word 'mind' in the novel, with their Chinese translations by 宋兆霖 (Zhaolin Song), researched by Yunte Huang, and their Korean translations by 유 종호 (Ju JongHo) researched by Sowon S. Park. Here are the instances:

> Then my sole relief was to walk along the corridor of the third story, backwards and forwards, safe in the silence and solitude of the spot, and allow my mind's eye to dwell on whatever bright visions rose before it (Chapter 12).
>
> Besides, I know what sort of a mind I have placed in communication with my own: I know it is one not liable to take infection: it is a peculiar mind: it is a unique one (Mr Rochester to Jane in Chapter 15).
>
> Your mind is my treasure, and if it were broken, it would be my treasure still (Mr Rochester to Jane in Chapter 27).

In all these cases, Zhaolin Song translates 'mind' into 心灵 [xinling], which would usually be back-translated as 'heart and spirit', and Ju JongHo translates it as 마음 [ma um], which would usually be back-translated as 'heart'. What issues come into play when we consider these

14 Williams, *Keywords*, p. 18.

displacements? We can point to general differences in the distribution of words, and so of their range of meanings, in the language(s) as used in these translations; and we can consider individual interpretive choices made by the translators, together with their cultural moments and the expectations of their audiences. But we can also look again at the text Brontë wrote, and notice the emotiveness and physicality surrounding 'mind' as it appears there. In the first instance, the visions of Jane's mind's eye open onto an imagined tale of 'life, fire, feeling'; while the warmth of Mr Rochester's use of the word is evident in the sentences quoted. In the history of English literary writing, what has more usually been said to be a 'treasure' that can be 'broken' is, not 'mind', but 'chastity'.[15] So, the choices made by the Chinese and Korean translators respond to an energy of imaginative possibility released by Brontë's words. She uses 'mind' in a way that is unusually charged, and so has the potential to be translated into more embodied terms in language(s) that offer that choice.[16]

This instance can help us to articulate the difference between the variants explored by *Prismatic Jane Eyre* and those chronicled in the *Vocabulaire Européen des philosophies: dictionnaire des intraduisibles*, edited by Barbara Cassin, the book which is probably the truest fulfilment to date of Williams's wish for comparative analyses of key words across languages (albeit only European ones in this case). Like Williams, Cassin sees the words as inhabiting a general sphere of usage — for her, the discourse of philosophy. What is discovered in the *Vocabulaire*, then, is:

> la manière dont, d'une langue à l'autre, tant les mots que les réseaux conceptuels ne sont pas superposables — avec mind, entend-on la même chose qu'avec Geist ou qu'avec esprit ... ?[17]
>
> [how, from one language to another, neither words nor conceptual networks map onto one another exactly — by mind does one understand the same thing as by Geist or by esprit...?]

15 For instance, this characteristic C17th instance by James Shirley, *The Wedding* (London: printed for John Groue [etc], 1629), act 2, scene 1, line 75: 'the treasures of her chastity / Rifled'; the idiom survived into the C19th, as in Michael Field, *Brutus Ultor* (Clifton: J. Baker & Son — George Bell & Sons, 1886), p. 26: 'there's no treasure there, / No chastity'. Quoted from *Proquest Literature Online*, https://www.proquest.com/lion.

16 For in-depth discussion of 'mind' in Portuguese, see Essay 9 below, by Ana Teresa Marques dos Santos and Cláudia Pazos-Alonso.

17 Pp. xvii–xviii.

But in *Prismatic Jane Eyre* what comes into focus are not only general differences between what a word might be said to mean in one language and what a roughly equivalent word might mean in another ('mind in English' vs 'Geist in German') — indeed, as we saw in Chapter II, our study puts some pressure on the usefulness of 'a language' as an explanatory category. Rather, we attend to particular instances of usage, with the complexities of meaning, connotation and affect that erupt from them, and see how they are re-made with the always-partly-divergent and always-partly-continuous linguistic resources of translators with different repertoires in disparate moments and locations. Cassin feels able to identify particularly challenging philosophical terms, and label them '*intraduisibles*' ['*untranslatables*'] — a definition which, she says:

> n'implique nullement que les termes en question, ou les expressions, les tours syntaxiques ou grammaticaux, ne soient pas traduits et ne puissent pas l'être — l'intraduisible, c'est plutôt ce qu'on ne cesse pas de (ne pas) traduire. Mais cela signale que leur traduction, dans une langue ou dans une autre, fait problème, au point de susciter parfois un néologisme ou l'imposition d'un nouveau sens sur un vieux mot.
>
> [does not imply for a moment that the terms in question, and the expressions, the syntactic and grammatical constructions, are not translated and cannot be — the untranslatable is rather that which we never stop (not) translating. But this shows that their translation, in one language or another, creates problems, to the extent of sometimes requiring a neologism or the imposition of a new meaning on an old word.]

If unceasing, endlessly regenerative re-translation is the sign of the untranslatable, the index of 'problems', then the whole of *Jane Eyre* is untranslatable in Cassin's sense — not just across Europe, but world-wide.

To see what is really going on here, we need to bring back into the picture all those linguistic fluidities and particularities which I described in Chapters I and II, and which Cassin's conception of language here neglects — the variations in usage and in peoples' repertoires, the continuities across language(s), and the ever-running rills and seepages of change. Any reader comes to *Jane Eyre* from their own location in language(s), and if they write down their reading as a translation it will be different from everyone else's. Translation does not happen into 'one language or another' but always into particular repertoires. In the case of philosophical texts, the repertoires used are typically specialized and comparatively fixed. With these texts it may indeed be the case that a few words stand out as especially problematic and therefore 'untranslatable'. But in the case of *Jane Eyre* — and this seems likely to be true of literature more broadly — anything at all, from a pronoun to a proper noun, can turn out to be, from someone's point of view, and in relation to some linguistic repertoire, a generative crux.

One aspect of this generativity is brilliantly described by the linguist Christian M. I. M. Matthiessen. He adopts the term 'agnate' (which comes to him from H. A. Gleason via the work of Michael Halliday), using it to describe wording that might have been employed by a speaker or writer, but was not:

> At any point in translation it may be one of these agnates rather than the actual expression that serves as the best candidate for translation ... The agnates make up the source text's shadow texts — texts that might have been because they fall within the potential of the language — and these shadow texts are thus also relevant to translation. By the same token, an actual translation exists against the background of shadow translations — possible alternative translations defined by the systemic potential of the target language.[18]

Any instance of a word, then, is haunted by the range of other words that it has been chosen from. The significance of their absent presence is conflicted. On the one hand, they accentuate the fact that the word on the page has been chosen — they prompt us to think that what matters most about it is what distinguishes it from them. On the other hand, they are nevertheless still invisibly there, and they bring with them the emotional and semantic hinterland from which the chosen word has emerged. For Matthiessen, the range of these possible shadow texts is limited by the concept of 'a language'. In his model, there is a text-plus-shadow-texts in one standard language, and another text-plus-shadow-texts in another standard language, and the aim is to make the two sets match as closely as possible. However, once you remember that people do not just inhabit the standard language but have more complex repertoires, which are always varied and often multilingual, then the range of what can be seen as a shadow text expands. A moment from *Jane Eyre* that I discussed above in Chapter II is a good example:

---

18 Christian M. I. M. Matthiessen 'The environments of translation', in *Text, Translation, Computational Processing [TTCP]: Exploring Translation and Multilingual Text Production: Beyond Content*, ed. by Erich Steiner and Colin Yallop (Berlin and New York: Mouton de Gruyter, 2013), pp. 41–126 (p. 83).

> I was a trifle beside myself; or rather *out* of myself, as the French would say.

The shadow text that has come into being in the vicinity of 'beside myself' is from French, 'hors de moi'; and it has then been translated into the sequence of visibly written words, '*out* of myself'. So we need to reconceptualize shadow texts, not as being confined within the system of 'a language', but rather as spreading across space and time through the landscape of language difference — in this case not only 'hors de moi' but (moving to German) 'außer mir', as well as 'I was mad with rage' or 'J'étais folle de rage' or (moving into modern English) 'I had totally lost it', etc, etc, with domino after domino falling in whichever direction you would like to move. Shadow texts are not only what Jane (or Brontë) could have written but did not. They are also (by the same token) what someone else would have said in the same situation. They are, therefore, not only — as Matthiessen thinks them — 'relevant to translation': they are themselves translations into different repertoires. This repertoire may be only slightly divergent — in this case, alternative mid-nineteenth century tendencies in the range of language(s) Brontë knew (Standard English-French-German-Yorkshire). Or it may be located further afield — in modern English or anywhere else in the world landscape of language difference.

So when we watch key words refracting through languages, what we see are shadow text after shadow text appearing, as the world *Jane Eyre* moves into new locations across space and time, and stepping forward to take the place of the words written first by Brontë, just as '*out* of myself' steps in to substitute for 'beside myself'. We have already seen this happening to a small extent with the three instances of the word 'mind' in the Chinese and Korean translations by Zhaolin Song and Ju JongHo. Now let us observe a single instance of the word 'glad', as its shadows form in new repertoires and locations, in a series of translations across French, German, Slovenian, Persian and (again) Chinese, which have been researched, respectively, by Céline Sabiron, Mary Frank, Jernej Habjan, Kayvan Tahmasebian and Yunte Huang. The instance in Brontë's text comes at the start of the second paragraph of the novel, where, having told us about the bad weather and the impossibility of taking a walk, Jane for the first time asserts herself using the first person, and sets herself starkly apart from the mood that has been established: 'I was glad of it: I never liked long walks ...'. Now here are the translations:

> J'en étais contente [I was glad of it] (Lesbazeilles-Souvestre, 1854; also Brodovikoff and Robert, 1946 and Monod, 1966)
>
> Ich war von Herzen froh darüber [I was happy about it from my heart] (von Borch, 1888)
>
> Je n'en étais pas fâchée [I was not angry/upset about it] (Gilbert and Duvivier, 1919)
>
> Je m'en réjouis [I was well pleased about it] (Redon and Dulong, 1946)
>
> Meni je bilo kar všeč [I rather liked it] (Borko and Dolenc, 1955)
>
> J'en étais heureuse [I was happy about it] (Maurat, 1964)
>
> Bilo mi je kar prav [This agreed with me actually] (Legiša-Velikonja, 1970)
>
> Mir war es nur Recht [It was only right to me] (Kossodo, 1979)
>
> خوشحال بودم [I had a good feeling (*khush-hāl*) of it] (Bahrami Horran, 1991; also Reza'i, 2010)
>
> 这倒让我高兴 [It contrarily made me glad, rendering 'glad' as 高兴 (gaoxing), 'high and rising (in spirit or mood)', a Chinese equivalent of feeling 'up'] (Song Zhaolin, 2002)
>
> J'en étais ravie' [I was delighted with it] (Jean, 2008)
>
> Mich freute es [It pleased me] (Walz, 2015)

As always, any of these instances could nourish an interpretation focusing on the contextual factors that have helped it into being (many of the essays in this volume offer such readings). On the other hand, by looking at the quotations together, in a decontextualized array, we can form a vivid sense of the signifying possibilities generated by Brontë's word 'glad' at this point in the text. As it moves into new locations and repertoires, different shadow texts step forward to take its place. We have represented them in English with back translations which are (as ever) not exact equivalents of them, any more than they are exact equivalents of 'glad'. Nevertheless, as shadow texts of shadow texts, the back translations can register in English something of the range that opens up: 'glad' can move in the direction of happy, pleased, delighted, not upset, I liked it, it was right, it agreed with me, I had a good feeling, it made me feel 'up'. Each translator has searched out something that sounds right in their repertoire, a ringing turn of phrase to match the energy of Brontë's. This particular explosion of plurality, then, is an indication of the emotional charge of the moment; and it also directs us back to the particular word that Brontë chose, rather than the alternatives that are thrown up in the back translations. Why 'glad of it', exactly, rather than 'I was pleased' or 'I was happy'?

It turns out that 'glad' is a distinctive word for Jane. She does not use it particularly often (in fact, it appears less frequently in *Jane Eyre* than in comparable novels such as E. C. Gaskell's *North and South* or Dickens's *David Copperfield*). In those books, the word often functions as part of a formula in polite conversation, and this usage does sometimes occur in *Jane Eyre* too: 'Mr. Rochester would be glad if you and your pupil would take tea with him'.[19] But more often (and this is what is distinctive) it is used in the vein we have begun to explore: a powerful expression of individual feeling. Here are some more examples:

> 'I am glad you are no relation of mine: I will never call you aunt again as long as I live.' (The young Jane to Mrs Reed)
>
> How glad I was to behold a prospect of getting something to eat! (at Lowood school)
>
> I felt glad as the road shortened before me: so glad that I stopped once to ask myself what that joy meant: (returning to Thornfield from Mrs Reed's deathbed)
>
> 'Oh, I am glad! — I am glad!' I exclaimed. ... 'I say again, I am glad!' (Jane to St John Rivers on learning that the Rivers family are her relations)
>
> Gladdening words! (At Thornfield after the fire, on learning that Mr Rochester is still alive)
>
> 'God bless you, sir! I am glad to be so near you again.' (To Mr Rochester, near the end of the novel).[20]

As 'glad' recurs in Jane's mouth it becomes a vehement, individual, bodily word, one that voices relief when danger is avoided or suffering escaped, and relish when a joy is gained. In all this, it is differentiated from 'happy' which appears more frequently, and in a wider range of uses, and which often has something conventional about it. These contrasting strands of meaning are signalled right at the start when — as we saw in Chapter II — the novel introduces some key aspects of its language(s) as well as of its spatial and interpersonal dynamics. While Jane is 'glad' at the cancellation of the walk, Mrs Reed is 'perfectly happy' as she reclines 'on a sofa by the fireside with her darlings about her' — a group from which Jane is debarred, as

19 *JE*, Ch. 13.
20 *JE*, Chs 4, 5, 22, 33, 36, 37.

Mrs Reed tells her that 'she really must exclude me from privileges intended only for contented, happy, little children'. So Jane goes to take refuge with 'Bewick's History of British Birds' in the window-seat in the breakfast room, and tells us: 'I was then happy: happy at least in my way.' This sequence puts a question-mark over the value of being 'happy' which lingers throughout the novel, even to the very last appearance of the word in the final chapter: 'my Edward and I, then, are happy: and the more so, because those we most love are happy likewise'. In the sequence of the narrative, the apparent tranquillity of this utterance is disrupted by the turn to St John Rivers, and the jarring, brief description of his work as an 'indefatigable pioneer' in 'India'.[21] This reaffirms what we have already learned from its earlier recurrences: that 'happy' is not a straightforward word. Like other novels in the *Bildungsroman* genre, *Jane Eyre* asks: what happens when the individual joins the couple or the social, when the visceral settles into the conventional. One of the ways it puts the question is by showing 'glad' giving way to 'happy'.

Neither 'glad' nor 'happy' is as complex a word as 'plain' (nor, we will see, as 'passion'). But the relationship between the two terms is part of the network of co-ordinates that organises the signifying material of the novel. Studying the proliferation of shadow texts created by the first appearance of 'glad' has helped us to see this; however, as it turns out, the distinction between 'glad' and 'happy' is not consistently tracked in any of those translations. In all of them, as the novel progresses, words that stand in for 'glad' can also stand in for 'happy', so a significant distinction dissolves into a differently significant continuum. When this happens, one needs to read the translations for the new patterns that they create for themselves, as we will see in the discussions of 'ugly', 'laid(e)' and 'brutto/a', as well as the Persian word 'parsa', in Chapter VII.

Sometimes, a pattern of repetition is preserved almost unchanged through many translations. When this happens, though the look of a word has altered, and probably also its connotations, the structuring influence of its recurrences persists. One striking example is 'conscience', a powerful word in the novel and in Jane's mental life. Its healing strength is urged on the young Jane by Helen Burns at Lowood; and when she discovers the existence of Mr Rochester's wife Bertha

21 See Essay 1, by Ulrich Timme Kragh and Abhishek Jain for discussion of this passage.

it is Conscience (now capitalised) that tells her she must leave him.[22] In translations into French studied by Céline Sabiron, into Spanish studied by Ana Teresa Marques dos Santos, into Danish studied by Ida Klitgård, and into Slovenian studied by Jernej Habjan, the same word recurs wherever 'conscience' recurs ('conscience', 'conciencia', 'samvittighed', 'vest'). And this continues to be true of translations into languages where religious traditions other than Christianity are dominant: of those into Arabic studied by Yousif M. Qasmiyeh (ضمير [*dameer*]), into Persian studied by Kayvan Tahmasebian (وجدان [*vijdān*]), and into Korean studied by Sowon S. Park (양심 [*yang shim*]).

Often, a pattern is partly preserved and partly broken. One instance is 'master', a word which, in Brontë's text, spans the mode of address to a young gentleman ('Master Reed'), the job title of a schoolmaster ('Mr Miles, the master'), and Jane's at once professional and passionate appellation for Mr Rochester ('my master'). In all the translations studied by Mary Frank in German, by Jernej Habjan in Slovenian, by Andrés Claro in Spanish, by Kayvan Tahmasebian in Persian, and by Eugenia Kelbert in Russian, the vocabulary available in those languages splits off the first two kinds of usage from the last. Another, more complex, and more fascinating instance, is 'passion': let us turn to it straight away, in Chapter V.

Works Cited

For the translations of *Jane Eyre* referred to, please see the List of Translations at the end of this book.

Barthes, Roland, *S/Z* (Paris: Seuil, 1970).

Brooks, Cleanth, *The Well Wrought Urn: Studies in the Structure of Poetry* (London: Dobson Books, 1949).

Cayley, John, *Programmatology*, https://programmatology.shadoof.net/index.php

Empson, William, *The Structure of Complex Words* (London: The Hogarth Press, 1985 [1951]).

Kalton, Graham, *Introduction to Survey Sampling* (Beverly Hills, Calif.: Sage Publications, 1983).

Kristeva, Julia, *Semiotiké: Recherches pour une sémanalyse* (Paris: Seuil, 1969).

Levinson, Marjorie, 'What is New Formalism?', *PMLA* 122 (2007), 558–69, https://doi.org/10.1632/pmla.2007.122.2.558

22 *JE*, Chs 8, 27.

Matthiessen, Christian M. I. M., 'The environments of translation', in *Text, Translation, Computational Processing [TTCP]: Exploring Translation and Multilingual Text Production: Beyond Content*, ed. by Erich Steiner and Colin Yallop (Berlin and New York: Mouton de Gruyter, 2013), pp. 41–124, https://doi.org/10.1515/9783110866193.41

Moretti, Franco 'Conjectures on World Literature' *New Left Review*, new series 1 (2000), 54–68.

Reynolds, Matthew, Mohamed-Salah Omri and Ben Morgan, 'Introduction', *Comparative Critical Studies*, special issue on *Comparative Criticism: Histories and Methods*, 12, 2 (2015), 147–59, https://doi.org/10.3366/ccs.2015.0164

Raymond Williams, *Keywords: A Vocabulary of Culture and Society* (London: Harper Collins 1988 [1976; revised edn 1983]).

Wolfson, Susan, 'Reading for Form', *Modern Language Quarterly* 61 (2000), 1–16, https://doi.org/10.1215/00267929-61-1-1

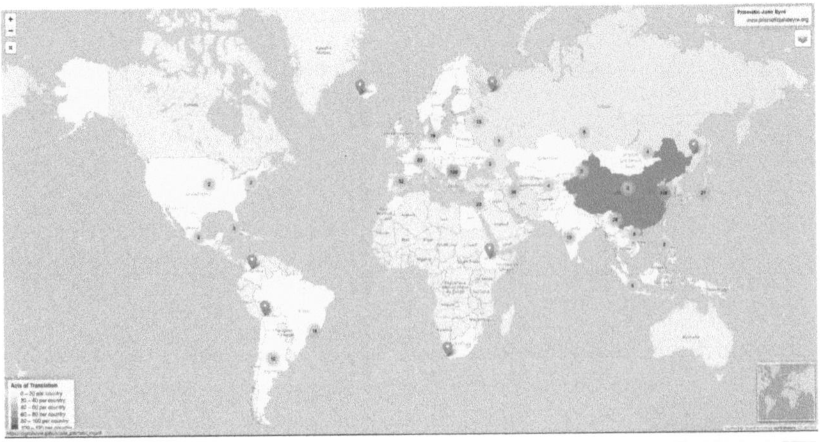

The World Map
https://digitalkoine.github.io/je_prismatic_map
Created by Giovanni Pietro Vitali;
maps © Thunderforest, data © OpenStreetMap contributors

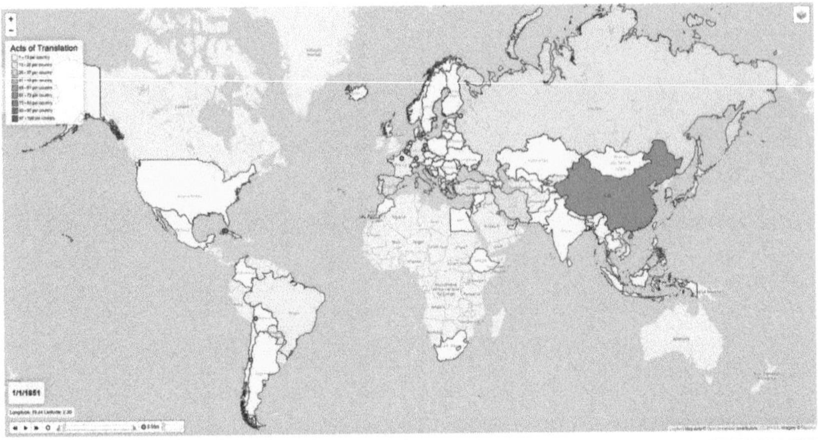

The Time Map
https://digitalkoine.github.io/translations_timemap
Created by Giovanni Pietro Vitali and Simone Landucci;
© OpenStreetMap contributors, © Mapbox

V. ‘Passion’ through Language(s)

Matthew Reynolds

‘You are passionate’, says Mrs Reed to the young Jane early on, and the novel conducts an extended exploration of what that might mean. ‘Passion’ (with ‘passionate’ and ‘impassioned’) appears 43 times, with its varied possible meanings surfacing to different degrees at different moments. Jane is passionate in her resistance to bullying in the Reed family and injustice at Lowood school; she and Mr Rochester are passionate in their relationship with one another; St John Rivers is passionate in his missionary zeal. ‘Passion’ can connote anger, stubbornness, vehemence, suffering, wilfulness, intensity, desire, love, generosity, unhappiness, devotion, and fanaticism. It is a root, perhaps *the* root of selfhood; yet it also needs to be controlled by ‘conscience’ and ‘judgment’.

The word’s reappearances throughout the novel work somewhat like a pattern of rhyme in a poem. They establish connections between the multiple meanings of ‘passion’ and suggest ways of understanding the relationships between them. As with an Empsonian complex word (discussed in Chapter IV), Brontë’s handling of ‘passion’ implies an argument: passion in the sense of love is continuous with passion in the sense of rage; love is a mode of self-assertion and self-fulfilment for women no less than for men. Yet the novel also worries at the word in ways that are too knotted for easy summary: ‘passion’ is exalted, diminished, attacked, and viewed with wonder.

The complexities inherent in the word ‘passion’ were not invented by Brontë, of course, nor are they specific to the English language. Passion is shared with French (*passion*), Italian (*passione*), Spanish (*pasión*), Romanian (*pasiune*), Portuguese (*paixão*), and it derives from the Latin *passio*, itself influenced by translation from the Greek *πάθος* (*pathos*). Tracing ‘passion’ in *Jane Eyre* across these closely related areas of the global landscape of language variation allows us to gauge the distinctiveness of the meaning-making resources of Brontë’s English, and the way she put them to use. Take the French

 https://doi.org/10.11647/OBP.0319.14

'*passion*'. It looks identical to the English version of the word, and can enable moments of perfect word-for-word translation, as in the heart-rending passage in Chapter 27 where, after the failure of the wedding, Jane resolves to leave Thornfield:

> Conscience, turned tyrant, held Passion by the throat
>
> ma conscience devenait tyrannique, tenait ma passion à la gorge (F1854)
>
> ma conscience, muée en tyran, saisit la passion à la gorge (F1964)
>
> et la Conscience, muée en despote, tenait la Passion à la gorge (F1966)
>
> la conscience devenue tyrannique prenait la passion à la gorge (F2008)[1]

But 'passion' in French does not correspond so readily to the angrier reaches of 'passion' in English. In such cases — as Céline Sabiron points out — the French translations 'tend to specify what is meant' using other words, as here in Chapter 2 where Bessie is chiding the young Jane:

> ... if you become passionate and rude, Missis will send you away, I am sure.
>
> si vous devenez brutale et en colère (F1854) [if you become brutal and angry]
>
> si vous devenez violente et grossière (F1946) [violent and rude]
>
> si vous devenez emportée, violente (F1964) [fiery, violent]
>
> si vous devenez coléreuse et brutale (F1966) [quick-tempered and brutal]
>
> vous vous montrez violente et désagréable (F2008) [violent and disagreeable]

The varying translations are interesting for several reasons. They can help us imagine our way into the implications of the English 'passionate' here. They trace a mini-history of shifts in taste and usage in French across different translators and different times. And they show that the French 'passion' and English 'passion' cast different nets

1 As ever, all publication details for the translations quoted can be found in the List of Translations at the end of this volume. The abbreviations used here, and throughout the animations and static arrays that follow, start with an indicator of the language (F = French), followed by the year of first publication, and then — if there is more than one translation into that language for that year — the first letter of the translator's name.

across the material of the novel, joining up experience in different ways.

In other languages, the picture is sometimes quite similar to the French, even though the word that corresponds to 'passion' has a different etymology. In Russian — as Eugenia Kelbert points out — there is 'a direct analogue of "passion" ("страсть [*strast'*]", adj. "страстный [*strastnyĭ*]") but it has strong romantic/sexual connotations, as well as religious significance, since *strasti* refer both to the passions of Christ and to the deadly sins, eight in number in the Russian Orthodox tradition, which include anger as well as lust'. Nevertheless, the angrier instances of 'passion' tend to be rendered by other words. This varies between the translations, though: 'for example, Stanevich's 1950 translation uses "страсть" [*strast'*] twice less frequently than Gurova's in 1999'.

Other tongues draw in a multitude of words to cover the semantic range of Brontë's 'passion'. In Arabic, as Yousif M. Qasmiyeh explains, 'passion has multiple equivalences, depending on the connotation, context and those involved. At times it carries the meaning of a reaction or a response to a state of being: "انفعال [*infiʿāl*]". At other times it connotes anger and frustration: "حنق [*ḥanq*]". When it is associated with love and/or having feelings for other people, the words used are: "حب [*ḥubb*]" (love) which is conventionally modified by an adjective, "عاطفة [*ʿātifa*]", and "هوى [*hawā*]" which is a synonym of "حب [*ḥubb*]" and conveys the act of falling in(to) another state of being.' In Persian too — Kayvan Tahmasebian tells us — '"passion" corresponds to a wide range of diverse words from "شور [*shūr*]" (literally, "excitement"), "عشق [*ʿishq*]" (literally, "love"), "تمنا [*tamannā*]" (literally, "strong desire") and "خشم [*khashm*]" (literally, "anger"). Because of this indeterminacy, "passion" is usually translated into redundant structures where two nearly similar words are joined by "and".'

In what follows, you can explore the various reconfigurations of 'passion' generated by different translations and languages.

A Picture of Passion

We are at the end of Chapter 1, where the young Jane is attacked by her cousin John Reed, and fights back. He 'bellowed out loud' and Mrs Reed arrives with the servants Bessie and Abbott. The fighting children are parted, and Jane hears the words:

> 'Dear! dear! What a fury to fly at Master John!'

'Did ever anybody see such a picture of passion!'

This is the first appearance of 'passion' in the novel, and 'picture' is an interesting word to attach to it. Jane has just been reading the illustrated Bewick's *Book of British Birds*, in which 'each picture told a story'; and later in the novel the pictures she draws will be similarly eloquent. The phrase 'picture of passion' feels as though it might be proverbial; but a database search uncovers only one instance in English-language literature before this moment.[2] In context, it sounds like a colloquial idiom, more likely to be uttered by Abbott or Bessie than by Mrs Reed. And in fact the lady of the house chimes in next, in her commanding tones: '"Take her away to the red-room, and lock her in there."' So a brief social drama unfolds in response to the little Jane's act of resistance: the startled expostulations of the servants creating the conditions in which a member of the gentry lays down the law.

In the translations, as you can see in the animation and static array below, the idea of the picture sometimes remains and sometimes drops away. In French it tends to morph into the slightly less material 'image'; in Dèttore's 1974 Italian translation it becomes more dramatic, a 'scena' or theatrical scene. Almost all the translations continue the idea that what is happening here is something that strikes the sight, that has never been 'seen' before. On the other hand, almost all are required by the habits of their languages to break the link between this moment and Jane's later passion (in the sense of love): they render 'passion' with words that can be back-translated as 'anger', 'stubbornness', 'impertinence', 'mad', 'fury', 'rage', and suchlike. The consequence is that this moment becomes visibly connected to the anger, pain and madness of Bertha Rochester as they are revealed later in the novel. Ana Teresa Marques dos Santos points out that this tendency is especially marked in the Portuguese translations by 'Mécia' (1941) and Ferreira (1951) which use 'monstro' (monster) and 'ferazinha' (little beast'). Adriana X. Jacobs notes that Bar's 1986 Hebrew translation makes a more subtle gesture in the same direction, using a word, 'משולהבת [*meshulhevet*]', which derives from *shalhevet* (flame).

Only Dèttore takes a different tack, making the words express the emotion of whoever it is who speaks them, rather than attributing feeling to Jane: 'Si è mai vista una scena così pietosa?' (Have you ever seen such a pitiful scene?) Paola Gaudio points out that 'pietosa'

2 In James Fenimore Cooper's *Home as Found* (Philadelphia: Lea and Blanchard, 1838), Proquest Literature Online, https://www.proquest.com/lion.

here connotes 'miserable', 'pathetic' and 'embarrassing'. Yet it also perhaps — as Jane is held and then carried off — brings with it a hint of a *Pietà*, the scene of Mary holding Christ's body and mourning him, which follows the passion of Christ on the cross in traditional narratives of the crucifixion. This thread of suggestion cannot be said to be visible in the English alone; but it is latent in the weave of language(s) and culture(s) from which *Jane Eyre* is formed. It becomes more prominent in translation.

These prismatic variants occupy a complex conceptual space. They have come into being successively through time and across geographical distances; but equally they all co-exist simultaneously in the textual reality of the world work *Jane Eyre* as it currently exists. So I present them to you in two ways. First, in an animated form, inspired by the (much more accomplished) digital artworks created by John Cayley;[3] and, second, in a static array, inspired by traditional variorum editions. The two modes of presentation also encourage two modes of reading: the first perhaps more aesthetically receptive, the second perhaps more informational and analytic. As ever, all publication details for the translations quoted can be found in the List of Translations at the end of this volume: the abbreviations in the animations and static arrays start with an indicator of the language, then the year of first publication and then — if there is more than one translation into that language for that year — the first letter of the translator's name. For instance: It2014S means the Italian translation, published in 2014, by the translator whose name begins with S — that is, Stella Sacchini (Milan: Feltrinelli).[4]

Animation 1: a picture of passion

3 John Cayley, *Programmatology*, https://programmatology.shadoof.net/index.php, accessed 6th November, 2021.

4 This animation and array incorporate research by Eugenia Kelbert, Céline Sabiron, Ana Teresa Marques dos Santos, Andrés Claro, Paola Gaudio, Adriana X. Jacobs, Sowon S. Park, Matthew Reynolds, Yousif M. Qasmiyeh, and Jernej Habjan.

https://hdl.handle.net/20.500.12434/60f44705

D2015 **hidsighed** [hot-temperedness]

Por2011 Mas onde é que já se viu uma **fúria** destas?! [Have you ever seen such a fury?]

It2010 Si è mai vista una **collera** simile? [Did you ever see an anger like it?]

F2008 une telle image de la **colère** [such an image of anger]

K2004 꼴 [{***Kkol***} face]

He1986 ראיתם פעם תמונה משולהבת כזאת [{*ra'item pa'am temuna* ***meshulhevet*** *ka-zot*} Did you ever see such an ecstatic picture?]

It1974 Si è mai vista una scena così **pietosa**? [Have you ever seen such a pitiful scene?]

F1964 semblable image de la **passion**! [similar image of passion!]

Sp1941 ¡Con cuánta **rabia**! [With so much rage!]

Por1951 Se já se viu uma coisa destas!... É uma **ferazinha**! [Have you ever seen a thing such as this one?... She's a little beast!]

R1950 Этакая злоба у девочки! [{*Ėtakaia* ***zloba*** *u devochki*} What malice that child has!]

F1946 pareille image de la **colère** [such an image of anger]

Por1941 Onde é que já se viu um **monstro** destes?! [Have you ever seen a monster such as this one?]

F1919 pareille **forcenée** [such a mad person/a fury]

R1901 Видѣлъ-ли кто-нибудь подобное бѣшенное созданіе! [{*Vidiel li kto-nibud' podobnoe* ***bieshennoye*** *sozdaníe*} Has anyone seen such a furious (lit. driven by rabies) creature!]

Did ever anybody see such a picture of **passion**!

R1849 Кто бы могъ вообразить такую страшную картину! Она готова была растерзать и задушить бѣднаго мальчика! [{*Kto by mog voobrazit' takuiu* ***strashnuiu*** *kartinu! Ona gotova byla rasterzat' i zadushit' biednago mal'chika*} Who could have imagined such a terrible sight/picture! She was ready to tear the poor boy apart and strangle him!]

It1904 Avete mai visto una **rabbiosa** come questa? [Have you ever seen a girl as angry as this one?]

Por1926 Já viu alguem tal accesso de **loucura** ! [Has anyone ever seen such a madness fit?]

He1946 הראה אדם מעולם התפרצות כגון זו? [{*hera'e adam me-olam* ***hitpartsut*** *kegon zo*} Has anyone ever seen an outburst like that one?]

Sp1947 ¿Habráse visto nunca semejante **furia**? [Have you ever seen such fury?]

It1951 Non s'è mai vista tanta **prepotenza**! [I've never seen such impertinence]

Sl1955 **jeza** [fury]

Sl1970 **ihta** [stubbornness]

A1985 هل قدر لأي امرئ أن يرى مثل هذا الانفعال من قبل؟ [{*hal quddira li ayy imri' an yarā mithla hadha al* ***infi'āl***} Was anyone ever destined to see such a reaction]

R1999 Просто невообразимо, до чего она разъярилась! [{*Prosto nevoobrazimo, do chego ona* ***raz"arilas'!***} It simply passes imagination how furious she is]

He2007 ראיתם פעם פראות כזאת?! [{*ra'item pa'am pir'ut* ***ka-zot****?*} Did you ever see such wildness?!]

Sp2009 ¡Habrase visto alguna vez **rabia** semejante! [Have you ever seen such rage!]

Pe2010 تا حالا چنین خشم و عصبانیتی از کسی ندیده بودیم [{*tā hālā chunīn* ***khashm va 'asabāniyatī*** *az kasī nadīda būdīm*} We had not seen such a rage and anger]

T2011 སྨྱོན་མ་འདི་འདྲ་སུས་མཐོང་མྱོང་ཡོད་དམ [{***smyon*** *ma 'di 'dra sus mthong myong yod dam*} Has anyone ever seen such a crazy woman?]

D2016 **raseri** [anger, wrath]

A Passion of Resentment

In Chapter 4, the young Jane has been present at the interview between Mrs Reed, her aunt, and Mr Brocklehurst, the forbidding visitor who has come to assess her suitability for Lowood school. She has heard herself described as 'an artful, noxious child' possessing 'a tendency to deceit'. Sitting there, she says, 'I had felt every word as acutely as I had heard it plainly, and a passion of resentment fermented now within me.'

The phrasing, with its emphasis on feeling and hearing, accentuates the sense of 'passion' as the reaction to a stimulus that has come from outside (to which Jane has been *passive*); in response, passion 'ferments' like wine or beer in the making. There is a variant here in the English texts of *Jane Eyre*: the second and third editions print 'fomented' (i.e., warmed, cherished) instead of 'fermented' which is in the manuscript and first edition. Both readings can be found in later editions, and have been used by translators.

In the translations, 'passion of resentment' is rephrased in ways that give rise to different, sometimes more violent back-translations: 'unbearable rage', 'lust for vengeance', 'intense anger'. The hint of liquid in 'fermented' plays out in varied directions: 'passionate thirst for vengeance'; 'indignation started to boil within me'; 'indignation was ready to pour forth torrent-like from my chest'. In the Tibetan translation, which is comprehensively abridged, much of the preceding dialogue and description are cut, but this moment of passion is preserved and intensified.[5]

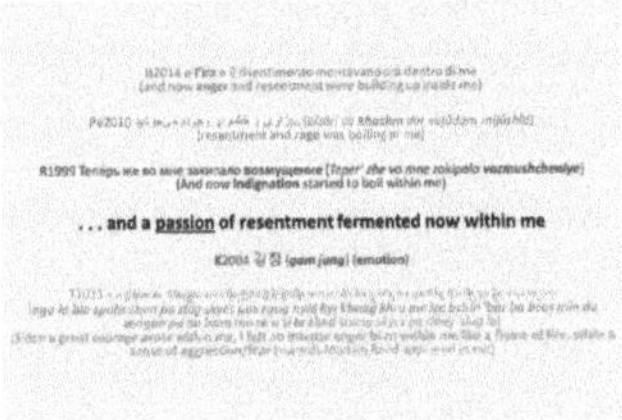

Animation 2: a passion of resentment
https://hdl.handle.net/20.500.12434/3b5761b6

D2016 **lidenskabelig** følelse [passionate feeling]

Pe2010 بیزاری و خشم در وجودم می‌جوشید [{***bīzārī va khashm*** *dar vujūdam mījūshīd*} resentment and rage was boiling in me]

R1999 Теперь же во мне закипало возмущение [{*Teper' zhe vo mne zakipalo* ***vozmushcheniye***} And now indignation started to boil within me]

It1974 un **impeto** di risentimento ribolliva dentro di me [an impetus of resentment was boiling over inside me]

Sl1955 **srd** po maščevanju [lust for vengeance]

R1950 и во мне пробуждалось горячее желание отомстить [{*i vo mne probuzhdalos'* ***goriachee zhelanie*** *otomstit'*} and an ardent wish to avenge myself was awakening within me]

R1901 и безумная жажда мести зародилась и стала рости въ моемъ сердцѣ [{*i* ***bezumnaia zhazhda*** *mesti zarodilas' i stala rosti v"*

5 This animation and array incorporate research by Eugenia Kelbert, Yousif M. Qasmiyeh, Jernej Habjan, Ida Klitgård, Ulrich Timme Kragh, Sowon S. Park, Matthew Reynolds, and Kayvan Tahmasebian.

moem" serdtsie} and an insane thirst for revenge was born and grew in my heart]

I had felt every word as acutely as I had heard it plainly, and a **passion** of resentment fermented now within me.

R1849 и негодованіе готово было излиться бурнымъ потокомъ изъ моей груди [{*i* ***negodovanīe*** *gotovo bylo izlit'sia burnym" potokom" iz" moeĭ grudi*} indignation was ready to pour forth torrent-like from my chest]

It1904 e stavo là, agitata da un **vivo** risentimento [and there I sat, agitated by a vivid resentment]

It1951 un **cupo** risentimento mi agitava tutta [a dark resentment was shaking all of me]

Sl1970 **strastna** maščevalnost [passionate thirst for vengeance]

A1985فاذا بحنق شديد يعتمل في ذات نفسي [{*fa idhā bi* ***ḥanq*** *Shadīd ya'tamil fī dhāt nafsī*} [suddenly/then an unbearable rage began to boil in/at my very core]

K2004 감정[{***gam jung***} emotion]

T2011 ང་ལ་བློ་སྤོབས་ཆེན་པོ་ཞིག་སྐྱེས་པས་རང་ཉིད་ཀྱི་ཁོང་ཁྲོ་མེ་ལྕེ་བཞིན་འབར་བ་བཅོས་མིན་དུ་མངོན་པ་ན་ལྕམ་མོ་རེའུ་ཏི་ལ་ཞེད་སྣང་སྐྱེས་པ་དང་འདུག་ལ། [{*nga la blo spobs chen po zhig skyes pas rang nyid kyi khong khro me lce bzhin 'bar ba bcos min du mngon pa na lcam mo re'u ti la* ***zhed snang*** *skyes pa dang 'dug la*} Since a great courage arose within me, I felt an intense anger burn within me like a flame of fire, while a sense of aggression/fear towards Madam Reed appeared in me]

It2014 e **l'ira** e il risentimento montavano ora dentro di me [and now anger and resentment were building up inside me]

A "Grande Passion"'

In Chapter 15, Mr Rochester explains to Jane how her French pupil Adèle came to be at Thornfield Hall: 'she was the daughter of a French opera dancer, Céline Varens; towards whom he had once cherished what he called a "grande passion." This passion Céline had professed to return with even superior ardour.' Mr Rochester uses a French phrase, though one that is readily comprehensible in English, to veil his affair and distance himself from it, introducing a note of melodrama and exoticism. If you call something a 'grande passion' you may well mean to suggest that it is not so deep-rooted as a 'great passion' would have been ('"une grande passion" is "une grande folie"', as Brontë wrote in a letter to her friend Ellen Nussey.)[6] In the next sentence, Jane, narrating, translates the French 'passion' into English 'passion' as Rochester's passion is reflected by Céline. In this English translation the question of honesty is made explicit: his '"grande passion"' (a French phrase used by an Englishman) may be hot-headed, but her 'passion' (now an English word used of a French woman) is only 'professed'. Translation within the text becomes a means of ethical appraisal.

The translators often recreate the switch from French 'passion' to an equivalent in their language, though nowhere is the spelling identical as it is with the French/English word. Sometimes, a language's liberty with pronouns enables a translator to put the two terms exactly side by side (Hill, Sp2009: '... *passion.* Pasiòn ...'; Pareschi, It2014: '... *passion.* Passione ...'). Sometimes 'passion' is glossed, creating a bridge towards the description of Céline's response (as with Stanevich, R1950); sometimes she is allowed the French word too (Rohde, D2016R); sometimes the connection is made by a switch from verb to noun (Ferreira, Por1951); sometimes the translational jump from Mr Rochester's 'passion' to her equivalent is abandoned, and her professed feeling is described in different terms; and sometimes the same word, in the language of the translation, is used for both Mr Rochester's and Céline's actual or apparent feelings, as in Ben Dov's use of 'תשוקה [*teshuka*]', He1946 (followed by Bar, He1986). As Adriana X. Jacobs comments: 'In Hebrew, "*teshuka*" is related to the root sh.u.k., to run after, often used in the sense of longing and physical desire (in Rabbinic literature, the desire of a wife for her husband)'.

In each case, the translators are re-creating in their own language the sparks (including a spark of irony) that jump between the two kinds — two languages — of passion that Brontë imagined and wrote down. They are answering Brontë's text more intimately than Céline has answered to Mr Rochester.[7]

6 *The Letters of Charlotte Brontë*, 2 vols, ed. Margaret Smith (Oxford, Clarendon Press, 1995–2000), i, p. 233. Online: Intelex Past Masters Full Text Humanities.

7 This animation and array incorporate research by Eugenia Kelbert, Céline Sabiron, Ana Teresa Marques dos Santos, Andrés Claro, Adriana X. Jacobs, Matthew Reynolds, Yousif M. Qasmiyeh, Jernej Habjan, Ida Klitgård, Kayvan Tahmasebian, and Ulrich Timme Kragh.

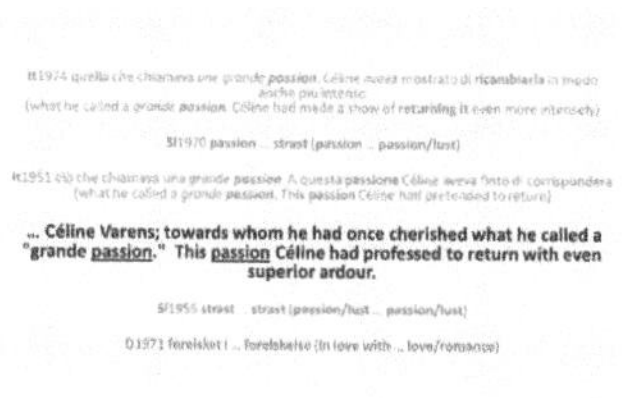

Animation 3: a 'grande passion'
https://hdl.handle.net/20.500.12434/5b33ce52

D2016 grande **passion** … **lidenskab** [passion]

T2011 ཁོ་རང་བུད་མེད་དེ་ལ་ཡིད་སེམས་དབང་མེད་དུ་ཤོར་བས་བུད་མེད་དེས་ཁོ་ལ་དེ་ལས་ལྷག་པའི་བརྩེ་དང་འབྱིན་ངེས་ཡིན་པའི་ཐ་ཚིག་བསྒྲགས་པ་སོགས་གསལ་བོར་བཤད། [{*kho rang bud med de la* ***yid sems*** *dbang med du shor bas bud med des kho la de las lhag pa'i brtse dang 'byin nges yin pa'i tha tshig bsgrags pa sogs gsal bor bshad*} When he felt lost and powerless with attraction {*yid sems*} to this woman, she had given him assurances of an even stronger feeling]

Pe2010

آقای راچستر به او «کششی پرشور» داشت. سلین هم می گفت همین کشش را به آقای راچستر داشته [{*āqāy-i rāchester bi ū* ***kishish-i pur-shūr*** *dāsht. Selīn ham mīguft hamīn* ***kishish*** *rā bi āqāy-i rāchester dāshta*} Mr Rochester had an excited attraction to her. Selin said too she had the same attraction to Mr Rochester]

He2007 … תשוקה גדולה [{***teshuka*** *gedola*} a large/great desire … {no second rendition of 'passion'}]

He1986 תשוקה לוהטת … תשוקה דומה [{***teshuka*** *lohetet*} a fiery/burning desire … {***teshuka*** *doma*} a similar desire]

It1974 quella che chiamava *une grande* ***passion***. Céline aveva mostrato di ricambiarla in modo anche più intenso [what he called a *grande passion*. Céline had made a show of returning it even more intensely]

Sl1970 **passion** … **strast** [passion/lust]

Sp1941 que fue su gran **pasión**. Céline le había asegurado corresponderle con más ardor aún [who was his great passion. Céline had assured him that she responded with even greater ardour]

Por1951 Varens, por quem se **apaixonara** doidamente, **paixão** que, ostensivamente, ela retribuía [Varens, with whom he fell madly in love, a passion that she ostensibly requited]

R1950 une grande **passion** [пылкую страсть (фр.)]. На эту страсть [{*pylkuiu* ***strast'*** (fr.)]. *Na etu* ***strast'***} gloss: ardent passion. To this passion...]

He1946 רחשי תשוקה עזה ... תשוקה [{*rachashei* ***teshuka*** *'aza* ... ***teshuka***} feelings of strong desire ... desire]

R1901 [*cut*]

... Céline Varens; towards whom he had once cherished what he called a 'grande **passion**.' This **passion** Celine had professed to return with even superior ardour.

R1849 une grande **passion**, ... эту страсть [{*etu strast'*} this passion]

It1904 quella che chiamava una gran **passione**. / Celina aveva finto di corrispondervi con un **amore** anche più ardente [what he called a great passion. Celina had pretended to respond to it with a love that was even more ardent]

Sp1947 lo que él llamaba *une grande* ***passion***, a cuya **pasión** parecía ella corresponder aún con más entusiasmo [what he called a *grande passion*, to which passion she seemed to respond with even more enthusiasm]

It1951 ciò che chiamava una *grande* ***passion***. A questa **passione** Céline aveva finto di corrispondere ... [what he called a *grande passion*. This passion Céline had pretended to return]

Sl1955 **strast** ... **strast** [passion/lust]

D1957 **forelsket** i [in love with] ... **forelskelse** [love/romance]

A1985 كان يشعر نحوها في يوم من الأيام بما سماه «حبّا عارما» [{*kāna yash'ur naḥwaha fī yawm min al ayām bimā sammāhu "****ḥubban*** *'ariman"*} he had felt for her, one of those days, what he called "an all-encompassing love"]

R1999 une grande **passion** ... даже еще более пылкой взаимностью [{*dazhe eshche bolee pylkoĭ vzaimnost'iu*} reciprocate even more ardently]

Sp2009 lo que él calificó como una *grande* ***passion***. **Pasión** que, al parecer, devoraba a la citada Céline con más ardor aún si cabe [what he described as a *grande passion*. Passion which, it seemed, devoured the aforementioned Céline with even more ardour, if that were possible]

It2014 quella che definì una *grande* ***passion***. **Passione** che Céline aveva giurato di ricambiare con intensità perfino superiore alla sua

> [what he defined as a *grande passion*. A passion which Cèline had sworn she returned with an intensity even greater than his]
>
> D2015 grande **passion** ... **passion**

Judgment Would Warn Passion

Chapter 15, which begins with Mr Rochester's confession about Céline, and continues with a description of Jane's growing attachment to him, culminates with his bed being set on fire, Jane dousing the flames, and his suggestively tender goodnight to her. After which, she cannot sleep:

> Till morning dawned I was tossed on a buoyant but unquiet sea, where billows of trouble rolled under surges of joy. I thought sometimes I saw beyond its wild waters a shore, sweet as the hills of Beulah; and now and then a freshening gale, wakened by hope, bore my spirit triumphantly towards the bourne: but I could not reach it, even in fancy — a counteracting breeze blew off land, and continually drove me back. Sense would resist delirium: judgment would warn passion. Too feverish to rest, I rose as soon as day dawned.

This was the end of Volume I in the first edition.

How does 'passion' here relate to Mr Rochester's 'passion' for Céline? One clue is that Jane's watery waking dream echoes comments made earlier in the chapter by Mr Rochester, when he said that one day she too would feel love as he did for Céline:

> ... you will come some day to a craggy pass in the channel, where the whole of life's stream will be broken up into whirl and tumult, foam and noise: either you will be dashed to atoms on crag points, or lifted up and borne on by some master-wave into a calmer current — as I am now.

That enigmatic last clause — 'as I am now' — is not remarked on by the narrative. So, at the end of the chapter, Jane is experiencing a mixture of Rochester's 'tumult' and 'calmer current', something that might perhaps be defined as a combination of passion and love. On this reading, 'billows of trouble' would be on the side of 'passion', while the 'freshening gale, wakened by hope' that bears Jane towards a shore 'sweet as the hills of Beulah' would be on the more virtuous side of 'love' (Beulah is associated with matrimony in the Biblical book of Isaiah and Bunyan's *Pilgrim's Progress*).

However, when we try to connect Jane's allegory of her feelings to the explanation she gives of them, the picture becomes more complicated. On the most plausible construal of the grammar, it is the virtuous-seeming gale that strikes her as 'delirium', and as 'passion', while 'sense' and 'judgment' are figured as the 'counteracting breeze' that keeps her from the happy shore. Here we can see the entangled nature of Jane's situation, even before it is revealed that Rochester is married, and the corresponding emotional and ideological complexity of the novel, in which the longing for a happy marriage can figure as a dangerous temptation.

These contradictions play out variously in the translations. Some (e.g., Danish and Korean) use the same word for passion here as for Rochester's 'grande passion'; others use a different one (e.g., al-Baʿalbakī's Arabic, A1985, and Ben Dov's Hebrew, H1946). In Preminger's 2007 Hebrew translation, as Adriana X. Jacobs comments, 'what is interesting is actually the translation for "warn" — "מרסן", "merasen", to bridle, to restrain. This suggests that Preminger reads this primarily as a physical, sexual passion. Also, this language connects to the image of "reason [holding] the reins" in the next example (Chapter 19)'. In other translations too, what judgment does to passion varies as the relationship between the two terms is re-imagined by different minds in different languages: in the animation and array that follow, you will see verbs that can be back-translated as 'cool', 'stand up to', 'push back' and 'resist'.

For the anonymous 1904 Italian translator, on the other hand, the significance of the contrasting winds switches round: here, it is delirium that conquers judgment, and passion that conquers wisdom, both of them pushing Jane back from the sweet, safe shore. It is possible that this translator felt the pressure of a famous Petrarch sonnet about a storm of desire, 'Passa la nave mia colma d'oblio', in which both 'arte' (skill) and ragione ('reason') die beneath the waves.[8] As Charlotte Brontë may well have known the almost equally famous English version of the Petrarch by Thomas Wyatt ('My galy charged with forgetfulnes'),[9] perhaps what we are seeing here are a writer and a translator responding differently to a shared Anglo-Italian cultural inheritance.[10]

8 *Le Rime di Francesco Petrarca*, ed. Giuseppe Salvo Cozzo (Florence: G. C. Sansoni, 1904), p. 189.

9 *Collected Poems of Thomas Wyatt*, eds Kenneth Muir and Patricia Thomson (Liverpool: Liverpool University Press, 1969), pp. 21–22.

10 This animation and array incorporate research by Eugenia Kelbert, Adriana X. Jacobs, Yousif M. Qasmiyeh, Jernej Habjan, Ida Klitgård, Ulrich Timme Kragh, Sowon S. Park, Matthew Reynolds, and Kayvan Tahmasebian.

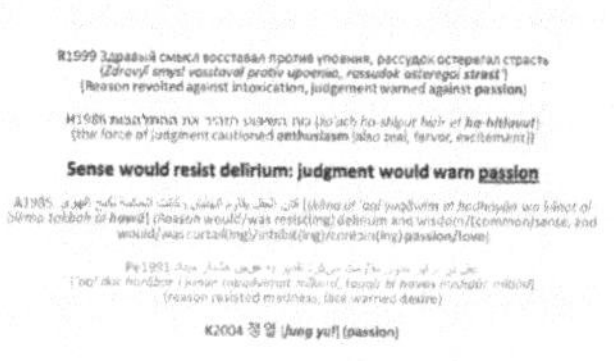

Animation 4: judgment would warn passion
https://hdl.handle.net/20.500.12434/266540ab

It2014 La ragione si opponeva al delirio, e il senno ammoniva la **passione** [Reason stood in the way of delirium, and good sense admonished passion]

H2007 תשוקה [{**teshuka**} desire]

Pe1991 عقل در برابر جنون مقاومت می‌کرد تقدیر به هوس هشدار میداد [*ʿaql dar barābar-i junūn muqāvimat mīkard, taqdīr bi* ***havas*** *hushdār mīdād* reason resisted madness; fate warned desire]

H1986 כוח השיפוט הזהיר את ההתלהבות [{*ko'ach ha-shiput hizir et* ***ha-hitlavut***} the force of judgment cautioned enthusiasm (also zeal, fervor, excitement)]

It1974 il giudizio respingeva la **passione** [judgement pushed passion back]

Sl1970 **strast** [passion]

It1951 Il buon senso voleva resistere al delirio, la saggezza opporsi alla **passione** [good sense tried to resist delirium, wisdom to stand up to passion]

H1946 שיפוט השכל — מתרה בגיאות הרגש [{*shiput ha-sekhel — matre be-ge'a'ot* ***ha-regesh***} good judgement warns the tides of emotion]

R1901 [*cut*]

Sense would resist delirium: judgment would warn **passion**

R1849 passage abridged to: Усталая и вполнѣ измученная этими лихорадочными грёзами [{*Ustalaya i vpolne izmuchennaia ėtimi likhoradochnymi grëzami*} Tired and quite exhausted by these delirious dreams]

It1904 Invano il buon senso voleva resistere al delirio; la saggezza alla **passione**! [In vain good sense tried to resist delirium, and wisdom to resist passion]

R1950 Здравый смысл противостоял бреду, рассудок охлаждал страстные порывы [{*Zdravyĭ smysl protivostoial bredu, rassudok okhlazhdal* ***strastnye poryvy***} Reason opposed delirium, judgement cooled passionate urges]

Sl1955 **strasti** [passions]

D1957 **lidenskaben** [passion] — Also in **D**2016R (lidenskab) and **D**2016P

A1985 كان العقل يقاوم الهذيان وكانت الحكمة تكبح الهوى. [{*kāna al ʿaql yuqāwim al hadhayān wa kānat al ḥikma takbaḥ al* ***hawā***} Reason would/was resist(ing) delirium and wisdom/(common)sense, and would/was curtail(ing)/inhibit(ing)/contain(ing) passion/love]

R1999 Здравый смысл восставал против упоения, рассудок остерегал страсть [{*Zdravyĭ smysl vosstaval protiv upoeniia, rassudok osteregal* ***strast'***} Reason revolted against intoxication, judgement warned against passion]

K2004 정열[{***jung yul***} passion]

T2011 passage abridged to: ང་སླར་རང་ཉིད་ཀྱི་མལ་ཁྲིའི་སྟེང་ཉལ་མོད་ཡེ་ནས་མ་ཁུགས་པར་དགའ་སྤྲོས་དང་སེམས་ཁྲལ་གཉིས་ཀྱི་འགལ་དུའི་ཁྲོད་ནམ་གསལ་རག་བར་དུ་གཡོ་འཁྱོམ་བྱས་སོང་། [{*nga slar rang nyid kyi mal khri'i steng nyal mod ye nas ma khugs par dga' spros dang sems khral gnyis kyi 'gal du'i khrod nam gsal rag bar tu g.yo 'khyom byas song/*} I laid down again in my own bed, but I never fell asleep. I was swayed strongly back and forth between opposite extremes of excitement and worry]

The Passions May Rage Furiously

This passage comes near the end of the strange scene, in Chapter 19, where Rochester is disguised as a gypsy and pretends to tell Jane's fortune. He has probed her feelings for him, and betrayed something of his feelings for her; now he ventriloquizes the traits that he sees in her face:

> The forehead declares, "Reason sits firm and holds the reins, and she will not let the feelings burst away and hurry her to wild chasms. The passions may rage furiously, like true heathens, as they are; and the desires may imagine all sorts of vain things: but judgment shall still have the last word in every argument, and the casting vote in every decision."

Rochester must feel these words as a challenge to his own behaviour and intentions, for a few moments after uttering them he cannot keep up the gipsy disguise, and throws it off.

Here we see 'passions' in the plural rather than the singular 'passion' that we have been exploring hitherto. These 'passions' seem to have a narrower range than the singular word, and the way they appear in Rochester's discourse defines them quite precisely: they are a subset of 'feelings', and are distinguished from 'desires'. We can infer that feelings such as rage and resentment would be 'passions', while love and attraction would be 'desires'. 'Heathens' — to whom Rochester likens the passions — have appeared once before in the novel, near the start of the chapters at Lowood school, in a scene that echoes here. The angry young Jane protested to the saintly Helen Burns: 'I must dislike those who, whatever I do to please them, persist in disliking me; I must resist those who punish me unjustly'; and Helen replied: 'Heathens and savage tribes hold that doctrine, but Christians and civilised nations disown it'. No doubt Helen would approve of the discipline of the psyche that Rochester ascribes to Jane's forehead, but the whole course of the novel (together with the range of uses of 'passion') suggests a more complex definition of virtue, one more open to resistance and rage.

In the translations, 'passions' is occasionally translated with a different word from the earlier appearances of 'passion', for instance al-Baʿalbakī's 1985 Arabic translation: 'الأهواء [whims {*al ahwaa*}]'. But much more often the same word is used — for instance, Italian 'passioni', Russian 'страсти' or Slovenian 'strasti'. In Emilia Dobrzańska's 1880 Polish translation, a gendered dynamic emerges, as Kasia Szymanska explains: 'rozum' [reason] — here singular — is masculine, while 'namiętność' [passion] is feminine, and the word for 'heathen', 'poganka' is also given in the feminine form. Rochester 'is personifying passion by comparing it to a female heathen (individual)', in contrast to 'the masculine reason'. Reason and passion continue, of course, to be gendered in the later Polish translations, though the contrast becomes less stark when passions and heathens are pluralised.

Here, as in our previous example from Chapter 15, the prismatic potential of the scene can sometimes emerge more from the words connected to 'passion' than from 'passion' itself. In Portuguese, as Ana Teresa dos Santos points out, there is fascinating variation in the translation of the word 'heathens': by 'Mècia' (Por1941) as 'bacantes' (Bacchantes), suggesting wild revelry; by Cabral do Nascimento (Por1975) as 'bárbaros' (barbarians), suggesting rejection by society; by Goettems (Por2010) as 'selvagens' (wild things/animals); and by Rocha (Por2011) as 'idolaters', connecting Jane's love for Rochester to idolatry.

This sequence of words, with its emotional extremity, also leaves its mark on the translations in another way: by being cut, from several of them — as you will see in the animation and array below. The anonymous Russian translation of 1901, the 1921 Polish translation by Zofia Sawicka and the 1957 Danish translation by Aslaug Mikkelsen were all abridged (and the first two were aimed squarely at younger readers), so they omit other parts of the novel as well. But it is striking that this passage is one that they all think needs to be excluded.[11]

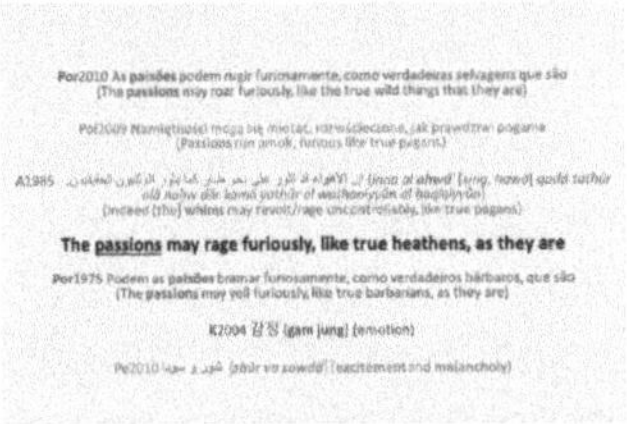

Animation 5: The passions may rage furiously
https://hdl.handle.net/20.500.12434/65df9373

It2014 Le **passioni** possono scatenarsi con la furia barbarica che è loro propria [the passions can run wild, with the barbaric fury that is proper to them]

Por2010 As **paixões** podem rugir furiosamente, como verdadeiras selvagens que são [the passions may roar furiously, like the true wild things that they are]

Pol2009 **Namiętności** mogą się miotać, rozwścieczone, jak prawdziwi poganie [passions run amok, furious like true pagans]

A1985 ان الأهواء قد تثور على نحو ضار كما يثور الوثنيون الحقيقيون. [{*inna al* ***ahwā̓*** *(sing.* ***hawā****) qadd tathūr ʿalā naḥw ḍār kamā yathūr al wathaniyyūn al ḥaqīqiyyūn*} Indeed [the] whims may revolt/rage uncontrollably, like true pagans]

It1974 Le **passioni** possono infuriare con la violenza pagana loro propria [the passions may flare up with their proper (own) pagan violence]

Sl1955 **strasti** [passions]

R1950 & 1999 страсти [{***strasti***} passions]

11 This animation and array incorporate research by Eugenia Kelbert, Ana Teresa Marques dos Santos, Sowon S. Park, Kasia Szymanska, Matthew Reynolds, Yousif M. Qasmiyeh, Jernej Habjan, Kayvan Tahmasebian, and Ida Klitgård.

Pol1930 Niech sobie **namiętności**, pogańskie plemię szaleją wściekle [passions, a pagan tribe, rage furiously]

It1904 La **passione** potrà urlare furiosamente, da vera pagana com'è [passion may howl furiously, like the true pagan that she is]

Pol1880 **namiętność**, jako prawdziwa poganka [passion, like a true heathen]

The **passions** may rage furiously, like true heathens, as they are

R1849 Пусть бушуютъ страсти [{*Pust' bushuuut" strasti*} let passions rage]

R1901 [*cut*]

Pol1921 [*cut*]

Por1941 As **paixões** podem desencadear-se, furiosas como bacantes [the passions may thrive, furious like bacchantes] — using Roman mythology to associate "passion" and revelry, frenzy, lack of control, and rage

It1951 La **passione** potrà scatenarsi furiosamente, da vera pagana com'è [passion may run wild furiously, like the true pagan that she is]

D1957 [*cut*]

Por1975 Podem as **paixões** bramar furiosamente, como verdadeiros bárbaros, que são [the passions may yell furiously, like true barbarians, as they are]

K2004 감정[{**gam jung**} emotion]

Pe2010 شور و سودا [{***shūr va sowdā***} Excitement and melancholy]

Por2011: As **paixões** bem podem grassar desvairadamente, como os autênticos idólatras que de facto são [the passions may disseminate in a wild manner, like the true idolaters that they are]

D2015&16 **lidenskaberne** [passions]

A Solemn Passion Is Conceived in my Heart

Now we are in the complex, emotionally harrowing Chapter 27, which follows the collapse of the wedding and the revelation of Bertha. Mr Rochester narrates the story of his marriage and reaffirms his love for Jane:

> After a youth and manhood, passed half in unutterable misery and half in dreary solitude, I have for the first time found what I can truly love — I have found *you*. You are my sympathy — my better self — my

> good angel — I am bound to you with a strong attachment. I think you good, gifted, lovely: a fervent, a solemn passion is conceived in my heart; it leans to you, draws you to my centre and spring of life, wraps my existence about you, and, kindling in pure, powerful flame, fuses you and me in one.

Jane accepts that this is true love ('not a human being that ever lived could wish to be loved better than I was loved'), and forgives Rochester for his deception of her; and yet she is clear that she cannot stay with him, and leaves Thornfield in agony of heart.

This is the consummation of all the uses of 'passion' hitherto: here, 'passion' appears in its most positive light, as a power leading to good, yet it is also connected to the darker senses (suffering, anger, stubbornness) that have appeared in our earlier examples. Rochester's phrasing ('a fervent, a solemn ... conceived in my heart') pushes those other connotations away (this is the *good* kind of passion, he wants to assert); and yet, in doing so, he cannot but acknowledge that they exist.

In the translations into European languages, similar phrasing is used to similar effect: as you can see below, the Italian and Russian translations reveal the 'shadow texts', the cluster of related words, that hover around Rochester's adjectives 'fervent' and 'solemn' and feed into their signification even though they are not visibly written in the English. The Arabic and Persian translations, in contrast, both reach for different nouns than those that have been used for our earlier instances of 'passion', continuing their work of rendering Brontë's word into a varied vocabulary. As Kayvan Tahmasebian comments, the Persian word '*hāl*', used by Reza Reza'i (Pe2010), 'has a wide range of meanings. Primarily, it denotes the present time. It is also used in reference to one's own state, how one feels. Its other meanings are "adventure", "great pleasure", "*jouissance*".' Those kinds of intensity all feel appropriate here.[12]

12 This animation and array incorporate research by Eugenia Kelbert, Kayvan Tahmasebian, Ida Klitgård, Ulrich Timme Kragh, Sowon S. Park, Matthew Reynolds, Yousif M. Qasmiyeh, Jernej Habjan.

Animation 6: a solemn passion is conceived in my heart
https://hdl.handle.net/20.500.12434/e70765ab

D2015&16 **lidenskab** [passion]

T2011 [*cut*]

K2004 정열 [{***jung yul***} passion]

A1985 إن فؤادي ليضمر لك عاطفة مهيبة متقدة. [{*inna fuādī la yuḍmira laka* ***'ātifa*** *mahība muttaqida*} Indeed it is my heart that holds/keeps/preserves burning, majestic passion for you]

Sl1955 & 1970 **strast** [passion]

R1950 живет благоговейная и глубокая страсть [{*zhivet blagogoveĭnaia i glubokaia* ***strast'***} lives passion characterised by awe and depth]

R1901 [*cut*]

a fervent, a solemn **passion** is conceived in my heart

R1849 Пылкая и торжественная страсть [{*Pylkaia i torzhestvennaia* ***strast'***} Fervent and solemn passion]

It1904 ho concepito nel cuore una **passione** solenne e fervente [I have conceived a solemn, fervent passion in my heart]

It1951 il mio cuore ha concepito una **passione** grave e fervida [my heart has conceived a solemn, vivid passion]

It1974 c'è nel mio cuore una **passione** fervida e viva [in my heart there is a fervent, lively passion]

R1999 Жаркая благороднейшая любовь [{*Zharkaia blagorodneĭshaia* ***liubov'***} Ardent, most noble love]

Pe2010 شور و حال [{***shūr va hāl***} excitement and ecstasy]

It2014 nel mio cuore c'è una **passione** grande e fervida [in my heart there is a great and fervent passion]

Works Cited

For the translations of *Jane Eyre* referred to, please see the List of Translations at the end of this book.

Cozzo, Giuseppe Salvo, ed., *Le Rime di Francesco Petrarca* (Florence: G. C. Sansoni, 1904).

Muir, Kenneth and Patricia Thomson, eds., *Collected Poems of Thomas Wyatt* (Liverpool: Liverpool University Press, 1969).

Proquest Literature Online, https://www.proquest.com/lion

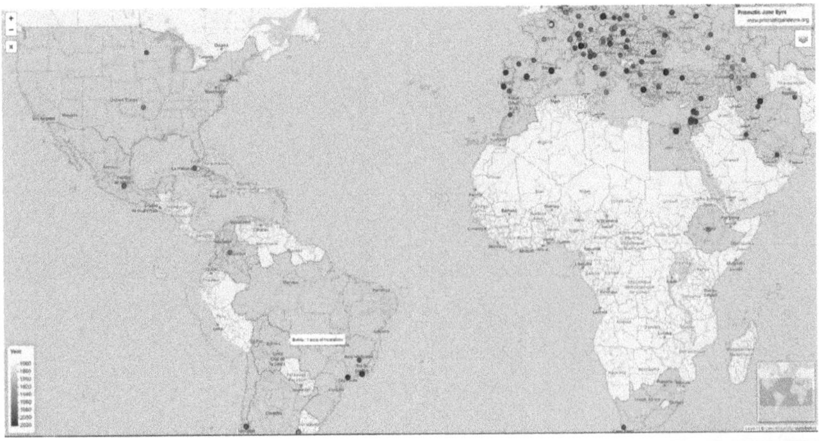

The General Map
https://digitalkoine.github.io/je_prismatic_generalmap/
Created by Giovanni Pietro Vitali; © OpenStreetMap contributors

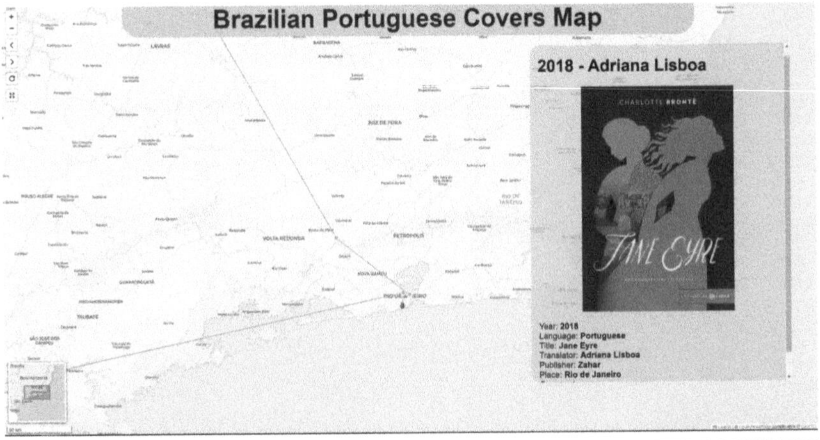

The Brazilian Portuguese Covers Map
https://digitalkoine.github.io/brazilian_portuguese_storymap/
Researched by Ana Teresa Marques dos Santos; created by Giovanni Pietro Vitali and Simone Landucci

9. A Mind of her Own
Translating the 'volcanic vehemence' of *Jane Eyre* into Portuguese

Ana Teresa Marques dos Santos and Cláudia Pazos-Alonso

The first image of Jane offered to the reader is that of a young girl trapped indoors. After she picks a book to read, she hides behind the window-seat curtains, paradoxically opting for a form of self-confinement, in order to break mentally free. This *incipit* hints at the centrality of the prison-escape leitmotif within the novel. In this essay we explore several Portuguese language renditions of *Jane Eyre*, ranging from the earliest known translation, published in instalments in the nineteenth-century periodical *O Zoophilo* [Zoophile], through to two twenty-first-century versions, in a selection that spans both Brazil and Portugal. In the process of so doing, we note how, at key moments in the twentieth century, the yearning for freedom that characterizes Brontë's heroine may acquire further resonances in political contexts informed by dictatorship and censorship (1932–1974 in Portugal and 1964–1985 in Brazil) and, indeed, in their immediate aftermath.

Seven translations were considered: in book-form, three from Brazil and three from Portugal, ranging from 1926 to 2011, with an equal number of male and female translators.[1] In addition, we examined

1 Joanna Eyre, unsigned translation, in *O Zoophilo* [Zoophile] (Lisbon, 1877–82); Joanna Eyre, trans. by anonymous (Petropolis: Typographia das 'Vozes de Petropolis', 1926). This is presumably a male translator according to the masculine form 'o traductor' used to sign the 'translator's preface'; *O Grande Amor de Jane Eyre*, trans. by Leyguarda Ferreira (Lisbon: Edição Romano Torres, 1951); *Jane Eyre*, trans. by João Cabral do Nascimento (Porto: Editorial Inova, 1975); *Jane Eyre*, trans. by Marcos Santarrita (Rio de Janeiro: Francisco Alves, 1983); *Jane Eyre*, trans. by Doris Goettems (São Paulo: Landmark, 2010); *Jane Eyre*, trans. by Alice Rocha (Barcarena: Editorial Presença, 2011). The

 https://doi.org/10.11647/OBP.0319.15

the (incomplete) first known translation into European Portuguese, published in *O Zoophilo* between 1877 and 1882, by an anonymous (but demonstrably female) translator. An eighth version, *A Paixão de Jane Eyre*, the first European Portuguese translation in book-form (1941), signed by Mécia and João Gaspar Simões, formed part of the project, until it became apparent that the two excerpts chosen were entirely absent from this bowdlerised version.[2]

The Portuguese language renditions of the imprisonment versus resistance motif in *Jane Eyre* are explored here through the analysis of two pivotal moments: first, shortly before Jane meets Rochester and, second, as she comes to realize that she cannot possibly marry St John Rivers (Chapters 12 and 34 respectively). Through a close textual analysis of the expressions that surround the prismatic keyword 'mind', we discuss not only the explosive captivity-freedom tension, but also, crucially, the decisive expression of Jane's own subjectivity, tellingly described as 'volcanic vehemence' earlier in Chapter 34.[3]

It is noteworthy that both passages chosen culminate in one long sentence each, thus arguably using style to transmit 'volcanic vehemence'. As we shall see, in two out of three instances, it is within these meandering sentences that the keyword 'mind' appears. Additionally, both passages include references to Jane's 'nature' in close proximity with the semantic field of 'fire' (another two prismatic keywords) and, last but not least, her body. This suggests that for Brontë the expression of female subjectivity (the word 'inward(ly)' tellingly features in both extracts) is in fact closely linked with *both* the mind and the body.

Physical and Mental Evasion

The opening of Chapter 12 recounts Jane's state of mind whenever she 'took a walk by [herself] in the grounds; [...] or when [...] [she] climbed the three staircases, raised the trap-door of the attic, and having reached the leads, looked out afar over sequestered field and hill, and

translations will henceforth be referred to as *Zoophilo*, 1926 anon., Ferreira, Nascimento, Santarrita, Goettems, and Rocha, respectively.

2 *A Paixão de Jane Eyre*, trans. by Mécia and João Gaspar Simões (Lisbon: Editorial Inquérito, 1941). Cuts are extensive, sometimes corresponding to whole pages.

3 It is not possible to consider the 1877–82 translation of 'mind' in Chapter 34 because the last instalment of *Joanna Eyre*, published in *O Zoophilo* on 28 September 1882, corresponds to Chapter 27.

along dim sky-line'. Significantly, the reader is reminded that Jane is a woman who resists imprisonment, just before she meets Rochester for the first time.

After stating that in these moments she 'longed for a power of vision that might overpass that limit', the narrator addresses her readers directly:

> Who blames me? Many, no doubt; and I shall be called discontented. I could not help it: the restlessness was in my nature; it agitated me to pain sometimes. Then my sole relief was to walk along the corridor of the third storey, backwards and forwards, safe in the silence and solitude of the spot, and allow my mind's eye to dwell on whatever bright visions rose before it — and, certainly, they were many and glowing; to let my heart be heaved by the exultant movement, which, while it swelled it in trouble, expanded it with life; and, best of all, to open my inward ear to a tale that was never ended — a tale my imagination created, and narrated continuously; quickened with all of incident, life, fire, feeling, that I desired and had not in my actual existence.[4]

Together with 'to walk', 'mind' indicates the process through which Jane attempts to break free. The narrator blurs the distinction between physical and mental dimensions by placing them on a similar level. 'To walk' is implicitly associated with 'feet', yet here 'mind' is not an abstract entity, but appears linked to the body ('mind's eye') — implying that it is through her mind that Jane obtains 'that power of vision that might overpass that limit'. Thus, Jane's interiority is paradoxically signalled through a corporeality that becomes strengthened with two further anatomical references — the heart (an internal organ) and the ear, qualified as an 'inward ear'. The direction of the movement evoked is not simply, then, from the inside to the outside: in fact, it is external social limitations that lead Jane to her expansive inner world.

The translations by Santarrita and Goettems successfully hint at Jane's interiority by resorting to similar associations: 'mind's eye' is 'olhos da mente' (Goettems) [the mind's eyes], and 'visão mental' (Santarrita) [mental vision]. In contrast to their Brazilian counterparts, the European Portuguese versions unanimously evoke the opposition between material and spiritual world by translating 'mind' as 'espírito' [spirit]:

4 *JE*, Ch. 12. See Chapter VI below for further discussion of this passage.

Brontë	Zoophilo (1877–82)	Ferreira (1951)	Nascimento (1975)	Rocha (2011)
'allow my mind's eye to dwell on whatever bright visions rose before it'	'dar redea ás fulgurantes visões do meu espirito'[5] (give free rein to my spirit's dazzling visions)	'deixava o meu espírito abandonar-se às visões brilhantes luminosas'[6] (let my spirit abandon itself to the brilliant visions full of light)	'deixar a imaginação expandir-se; quantas visões se me ofereciam ao espírito'[7] (let my imagination expand; how many visions offered themselves to my spirit)	'dar licença aos olhos do meu espírito para se deleitarem com quaisquer visões auspiciosas que se lhe deparassem'[8] (allow my spirit's eyes to take delight in whichever auspicious visions came before them)

Rocha's text maintains Brontë's association of 'mind' and 'body' because it keeps the reference to 'olhos' ('os olhos do meu espírito' [the eyes of my spirit]). The other texts, however, resorted to 'visões' [visions] in order to avoid the oddness of that pairing in Portuguese, with Nascimento adding a reference to imagination for clarity. Their preference shifts the focus from the observer to the observed, and thus reduces some of Jane's 'power of vision'. In Nascimento's and Ferreira's cases, this is complemented by the failure to acknowledge Jane's own agency, as her 'spirit' abandons itself to, or is offered, visions.

As for 'inward ear', it becomes 'audição interior' (Rocha) or 'ouvido interior' (Santarrita and Goettems) [inner hearing, or inner ear, respectively] — or, more figuratively still, 'ouvidos da alma' [the ears of the soul], the choice of Cabral do Nascimento.

By Chapter 12, thus, and unlike the opening scene of the novel, the escape from the multiple constraints afflicting Jane is carried out

5 *Zoophilo*, 13 December 1877, p. 2.
6 Ferreira, p. 128.
7 Nascimento, p. 118.
8 Rocha, p. 148.

through her own body as well as the tale she imagines. The sequence of seven possessives that punctuates the excerpt ('my nature', 'my sole relief', 'my mind's eye', 'my heart', 'my inward ear', 'my imagination', 'my actual existence') corresponds to a robust assertion of both the power of Jane's self, and her own awareness of that power to circumvent the limits imposed upon her.

Besides being a translator of English, American, and French literature, Cabral do Nascimento (1897–1978) was a poet himself, linked to the early twentieth-century literary Portuguese saudosismo and modernist movement. This may explain why he seems to have stylistic reasons to reject the reiterated use of the possessive adjective 'my' (which he only used for the first instance, 'minha natureza' [my nature]) — a reluctance also in evidence when it comes to Chapter 34. In fact, despite the important role of the possessive 'my' in foregrounding Jane's selfhood and connecting it with her body, only *Zoophilo*'s, Santarrita's, and Goettems's versions included nearly as many such markers as Brontë had. On the other hand, while Ferreira's and Rocha's renditions of Jane's acknowledgement of an indomitable force within her ('I could not help it: the restlessness was in my nature') left the possessive out, through their choice of the idiomatic expression 'estava-me no sangue' [it was in my blood] for 'was in my nature', they creatively established an opportune link between the idea of inward activity and the bodily references that the next long and meandering sentence will explore.

Brontë also emphasizes interiority and its ability to provide evasion through the use of the alliteration that immediately precedes 'my mind's eye': 'safe in the silence and solitude of the spot'. The literal Portuguese correspondents 'silêncio' [silence] and 'solidão' [solitude] conveniently facilitated the maintenance of a similar alliteration in all translations except for Leyguarda Ferreira's. In some cases, a third sibilant sound was added by either the translation of 'safe' or the inclusion of a different term:

Brontë	*Zoophilo* (1877–82)	1926 anon. and Santarrita (1983)	Nascimento (1975)	Rocha (2011)
'safe in the silence and solitude of the spot'	'do seu silêncio e solidão'[9] [of its silence and solitude]	'segura no silêncio e na solidão'[10] [safe in the silence and solitude]	'na solidão e no silêncio desse lugar'[11] [in the solitude and silence of that place]	'no silêncio e na solidão, e dar licença aos'[12] [in the silence and solitude, and give permission to]

A later alliteration that describes the 'tale my imagination created' ('quickened with all of incident, life, fire, feeling'), however, was ignored by all the translations considered, except that published in *O Zoophilo*: 'animada por grande variedade de peripecias, pelo fogo, pelo sentimento' [animated by a great variety of incident, by fire, by feeling]. Santarrita and Rocha did nonetheless reproduce Brontë's style by copying her asyndetic construction for that phrase. The 1926 Brazilian translator and Nascimento preferred alternative strategies, namely a metaphor ('todos os incidentes, a vida e paixão abrasada' [all incidents, life and a fiery passion]) and an antithesis ('possuidora do que nunca tivera e sempre desejara' [in possession of that which I had never had and had always wished for]), respectively.

Santarrita, Rocha, and the two early anonymous translators paid further close attention to Brontë's stylistic mastery by maintaining the strikingly long sentence at the core of this passage (from '[t]hen my sole relief was[...]' to 'in my actual existence'). Although very long sentences are frequently found in Portuguese, several translators broke Brontë's sentence into smaller ones, whereas this quartet did not modify Brontë's punctuation. The length of the sentence contributes to the overall effect of conveying the complexity of this multi-faceted evasion experience for Jane, in which her entire self is involved and

9 *Zoophilo*, 13 December 1877, p. 2.
10 1926, p. 172 and Santarrita p. 101.
11 Nascimento, p. 118.
12 Rocha, p. 148.

immersed, evoking both her exterior and, especially, her interior dimensions.

Jane's personal experience leads to the claim that Brontë makes about women in general in the paragraph that follows ('[w]omen are supposed to be very calm generally: but women feel just as men feel; they need exercise for their faculties, and a field for their efforts, as much as their brothers do'), an often-cited searing critique of society's limited expectations of women. While the feminist perspective embraced in *O Zoophilo* by the 1877 translator in their rendition of this famous indictment of double standards falls outside our brief here, it is worth mentioning that this translator's creative version of the verb 'to walk' as 'evadir-me' [to evade] spotlights, even more explicitly than the English text does, that Jane's experience is about escaping. Tellingly, this contrasts with all later translations, which opted for literal synonyms of the English verb 'to walk'. The choice is not altogether surprising since this anonymous early version of *Jane Eyre* can be attributed to Francisca Wood (1802–1900), the Editor of the first overtly feminist periodical in Portugal.[13] Wood published feminist versions of the Grimm brothers' short stories in this periodical, *A Voz Feminina* (The Female Voice).[14] Furthermore, her first-hand knowledge of Britain, where she lived at the time of the publication of *Jane Eyre*, meant she was ideally placed to subsequently translate a novel that would come to occupy a privileged position in the feminist canon. Her invisible authorship of the serialized translation therefore provides a fitting explanation for the underscoring, through lexical choice in the sentence considered above, of the idea of transcending oppressive patriarchal constraints.

Jane's rebellious struggle and visceral desire for agency are also successfully reinforced in this nineteenth-century version through the translation of 'a tale my imagination created' as 'uma historia **filha** da minha imaginação' (a story daughter of my imagination),

13 See Cláudia Pazos-Alonso, *Francisca Wood and Nineteenth-Century Periodical Culture: Pressing for Change* (Oxford: Legenda, 2020), pp. 178–80, and Ana Teresa Marques dos Santos, 'A primeira Jane Eyre portuguesa, ou como o Órgão da Sociedade Protetora dos Animais trouxe Charlotte Brontë para Portugal (1877–1882)', *Revista de Estudos Anglo-Portugueses* (forthcoming) for the multiple contextual and stylistic arguments that support such an attribution.

14 Maria Teresa Cortez, *Os Contos de Grimm em Portugal. A recepção dos Kinder- und Hausmärchen entre 1837 e 1910* (Coimbra: Minerva and Universidade de Aveiro, 2001), pp. 89–103.

thereby throwing into relief the materiality of (gendered) creativity. Interestingly, a couple of additions allow the *Zoophilo* text to hint more explicitly than the English original at the connection between Jane and Bertha Mason. Although the reader is not yet aware of the gothic motif of the double, since at this juncture Bertha is merely a mysterious figure still identified with Grace Poole, the *Zoophilo*'s translation connects the two characters by expanding 'the corridor of the third storey' into 'aquelle medonho corredor do terceiro andar de que já falei' [that terrifying corridor on the third storey which I have already mentioned].

Nearly one century later, faith in the eradication of women's metaphorical imprisonment was heightened after the fall of the forty year-long Portuguese New State regime, when the translation by Nascimento was published at the end of 1975, more than one year after the peaceful revolution that brought back democracy to the country. The newly-gained sense of freedom that pervaded life in Portugal, in addition to the publisher's commitment to 'contribute to freedom from fascist obscurantism', enabled him to be particularly attuned to Jane's expressions of freedom.[15] Having preferred the verb 'errar' [to wander] as a translation of 'to walk', Nascimento seizes a different opportunity to convey the idea of 'evasion', and renders 'safe' as 'livre' [free]: 'livre na solidão e no silêncio desse lugar' [free in the silence and solitude of the spot]. Similarly, the Brazilian translator of 1926 transfers a closely related notion to yet another sentence by adding the term 'liberdade' [freedom] to the translation of 'to let my heart be heaved by the exultant movement': '*onde eu tinha liberdade* de deixar arfar com pulsações exultantes o coração' [*where I had the freedom to* let my heart heave with exultant throbs] (our emphasis). As their lexical choices are contrasted with the ones made by the other translators (e.g., 'isolava-me' [isolated myself] and 'refugiando-me' [sheltering], Ferreira and Rocha's versions respectively), *Zoophilo*, 1926 anon, and Nascimento emerge as taking Brontë's implied criticism one step further, since their versions enhance Jane's free-spirited escape.

15 *1968–1978. Editorial Inova/Porto: Uma Certa Maneira de Dignificar o Livro* (n.p.: Inova, 1978), p. 85.

'Mind'

'Mind' is a word that occurs 136 times in the course of *Jane Eyre*. As we saw in the first of the two excerpts under analysis, it is a core term that conveys the prison-escape dichotomy while foregrounding the protagonist's subjectivity. Nowhere is this clearer than in the second extract, from Chapter 34, where the word 'mind' is repeated twice in the space of three sentences, precisely as Jane, through internal monologue in this instance, comes to the realization that the prospect of being shackled and stifled by a marriage to her cousin is intolerable:

> I looked at his features, beautiful in their harmony, but strangely formidable in their still severity; at his brow, commanding but not open; at his eyes, bright and deep and searching, but never soft; at his tall imposing figure; and fancied myself in idea *his wife*. Oh! it would never do! As his curate, his comrade, all would be right: I would cross oceans with him in that capacity; toil under Eastern suns, in Asian deserts with him in that office; admire and emulate his courage and devotion and vigour; accommodate quietly to his masterhood; smile undisturbed at his ineradicable ambition; discriminate the Christian from the man: profoundly esteem the one, and freely forgive the other. I should suffer often, no doubt, attached to him only in this capacity: **my body would be under rather a stringent yoke, but my heart and *mind* would be free. I should still have my unblighted self to turn to: my natural unenslaved feelings with which to communicate in moments of loneliness. There would be recesses in my *mind* which would be only mine**, to which he never came, and sentiments growing there fresh and sheltered which his austerity could never blight, nor his measured warrior-march trample down: but as his wife — at his side always, and always restrained, and always checked — forced to keep the fire of my nature continually low, to compel it to burn inwardly and never utter a cry, though the imprisoned flame consumed vital after vital — *this* would be unendurable.

The keyword 'mind' is translated in several different ways, and a distinction can be drawn between the choices in European and in Brazilian Portuguese. For the latter, in both passages, 'mind' is generally 'mente' or connected to 'mente', which in English corresponds to the most intellectual sense of the word, as in 'mental' processes. The exception to this, among the Brazilian translations, is the anonymous 1926 version which omits both references to 'mind' in Chapter 34 — having also avoided the earlier 'mind's eye', in Chapter 12, through the introduction of the idea of 'imagination': 'vista imaginativa' [imaginative vision]. The expression 'my heart and mind would be free' is conflated with 'my natural unenslaved feelings', and results in a combination that spared the translator the trouble of finding a way to convey 'unenslaved' in Portuguese: 'ficando assim livres meu coração e meus sentimentos naturaes' [my heart and natural feelings would thus be free].

In fact, in this translation the whole excerpt is heavily cut, condensed, and reduced to around six lines of text. The translator removes the references to St John Rivers's physique and, hence, to his cold harshness, possibly in order to avoid criticism of a clergyman (whilst keeping his positive aspects, 'his courage and devotion and vigour' as 'sua coragem, sua devoção, seu vigor'). The translator summarised the passage, conveying only its gist (Jane looks at St John, states the extent to which she could accompany him, briefly refers to what type of freedom she would retain, and how constrained she would be, and expresses the intensity of her sacrifice through similar fire imagery). The richly vivid details provided by the English text for each one of these ideas are missing. The justification for this, and, moreover, the acknowledgement of the poetic worth of what was left out, can be found in the preface signed by the anonymous translator:

> Na segunda metade [do livro] [...] tomei a liberdade de cortar desapiedadamente tudo quanto pudesse impedir a carreira dos eventos para o desenlace final. Mais de uma nuance de sentimentos, aliás subtilissima, mais de uma flôr poetica, aliás fragantissima, ficaram esmagadas pela marcha inexoravel que os factos peremptoriamente exigiam.[16]
>
> [In the second half of the book, I took the liberty to cut ruthlessly everything that could prevent the flow of events towards the final denouement. More than one nuance of feelings, however subtle, more than one poetic flower, however fragrant, was crushed by the relentless march categorically demanded by the facts.]

In the European Portuguese versions of Chapter 34, alternative terms for 'mind' appear. A chronological overview of the lexical choices reveals a slow move towards a twenty-first-century interpretation of 'mind' that foregrounds Jane's intellect:

16 'Prefácio do Tradutor' [Translator's Preface], 1926 anon, p. 8.

Brontë	Ferreira (1951)	Nascimento (1975)	Rocha (2011)
'my heart and my **mind** would be free'	'o meu coração e o meu **espírito** conservar-se-iam livres'	'o coração e a **alma** continuariam livres'	'o meu coração e a minha **mente** seriam livres'
'There would be recesses in my **mind** which would be only mine'	'no meu **espírito** existiriam recantos que me pertenceriam unicamente'[17]	'haveria recessos na minha **mente** que seriam só meus'[18]	'haveria recessos na minha **mente** que seriam só meus'[19]

While Ferreira opted for a term connected to spirituality for both instances of 'mind', Nascimento chose the association with 'intellect' in one instance, and finally Rocha settled for 'intellect' in both cases (our emphasis in bold). Looking at the 1975 and 2011 versions, the option of 'alma' in the 1975 text arguably suggests a lexical choice still predominantly informed by the religious context promoted by the dictatorship up to 1974, whereas the 2011 translation moves away from 'espírito' and 'alma' [spirit, and soul] and prefers the more cerebral 'mente'. Implied here is also a different understanding of what Jane was attempting to express and, consequently, of her subjectivity: her intellectual freedom was important to her and not to be sacrificed in a marriage to St John Rivers. In short, by 2011, Jane's faculty of reasoning has gained more prominence.

The different weight of 'mente', as opposed to 'espírito' or 'alma', is all the more evident in Nascimento's text, where having interpreted the second instance of 'mind' as 'mente', he is led to correct Brontë's seemingly contradictory subsequent allusion to 'sentiments':

> Brontë: There would be recesses in my **mind** which would be only mine, to which he never came, and **sentiments** growing there fresh and sheltered [...]
>
> Nascimento: Haveria recessos na minha **mente** que seriam só meus, e **ideias** que ali se desenvolveriam, frescas e abrigadas [...][20]
>
> [There would be recesses in my mind which would be only mine, and ideas which would develop there, fresh and sheltered]

17 Ferreira, p. 371.
18 Nascimento, p. 420.
19 Rocha, p. 533.
20 Nascimento, p. 420.

While Rocha chooses the same word to translate 'mind' in both cases, Nascimento's preference for 'mente' instead of 'alma' [soul] in the second instance may be explained by the wish to allow the Portuguese Jane to use the alliteration, besides the double possessive, to vigorously reiterate her selfhood, as in English: 'minha mente ... meus' [my mind ... mine].

Master and Slave

In Chapter 12, imprisonment arises from limits imposed mainly by Jane's physical, social, and gender circumstances. In Chapter 34, however, it becomes directly bound up with systemic constraints generated by unequal male-female relations. A number of devices in Brontë's text combine to create a feeling of entrapment, ultimately in order to justify Jane's rejection of the possibility of a marriage that, by the standards of Victorian society, would have been considered advantageous. Several terms used to characterise her putative union to St John conjure up unambiguous images of curtailment of freedom: 'masterhood', 'imprisoned', 'yoke', 'restrained', and 'checked'. This contrasts with Jane's yearning to remain 'unenslaved'.

Leyguarda Ferreira's 1951 version of the excerpt does not shy away from portraying the relationship in terms of male dominance. As shown below, the Portuguese text resorts to the repetition of different forms of the verb 'to dominate' (our emphasis in bold):

Brontë	Ferreira (1951)
'at his tall imposing figure; and fancied myself in idea *his wife*'	'para o seu vulto imponente que parecia **dominar-nos** e supus-me *sua mulher*'
'but as his wife — at his side always, and always restrained, and always checked — forced to keep the fire of my nature continually low'	'Mas como sua mulher — constantemente **dominada**, obrigada a **dominar-me**'[21]

On the one hand, the notion of 'dominance' is foregrounded, but on the other hand, following the reference to physical dominance, the second allusion, 'constantemente dominada', is ambiguously vague

21 Ferreira, p. 371.

in comparison to the original poly-syndetic tricolon describing the marital relationship (i.e., 'at his side always, and always restrained, and always checked'). The same could be said of 'obrigada a dominar-me' [forced to control myself] as a laconic translation of 'forced to keep the fire of my nature continually low'. The possible sexual connotation does not seem to explain the smoothing over of Brontë's metaphor, considering that the translation keeps the fire imagery of the next sentence ('forced [...] to compel it to burn inwardly and never utter a cry') graphically conveying it as 'obrigada [...] a consumir-me nas próprias chamas sem soltar um grito' [forced to consume myself in my own flames without uttering a cry]. Rather, Ferreira's habitual shortening practice, which has been criticized as resulting in 'free adaptations' rather than complete translations, seems to be a more plausible reason.[22]

Even when imagining herself working alongside St John as his comrade rather than his wife, the everyday subjugation that Jane would be forced into, as a result of her gender, is highlighted: she would be 'controlled' by him ('constantemente dominada') as well as by herself ('obrigada a dominar-me'). While the reference to self-control expands the scope in order to signal that systemic expectations of feminine modesty entail self-disciplining, Ferreira strengthens the idea of female pliability to male dominance through additional lexical choices:

Brontë	Ferreira (1951)
'[...] I would [...] accommodate quietly to his masterhood'	'[...] estava disposta [...] a sujeitar-me à sua autoridade'[23]
	(I was willing to subject myself to his authority)

22 See Afonso Reis Cabral, 'Leyguarda Ferreira', http://romanotorres.fcsh.unl.pt/?page_id=59#F, and Daniel Melo, *História e Património da Edição em Portugal — A Romano Torres* (Famalicão: Edições Húmus, 2015), p. 80. Maria Leonor Machado de Sousa considers this '<<simplifying>> habit' a regular practice by the publisher. Maria Leonor Machado de Sousa, 'Dickens in Portugal', in *The Reception of Charles Dickens in Europe*, ed. by Michael Hollington (London: Bloomsbury, 2013), pp. 197–211 (p. 198, p. 206).

23 Ferreira, p. 371.

Through the rendition of 'to accommodate quietly' as 'sujeitar-me' [to subject myself] and 'masterhood' as 'autoridade' [authority], Ferreira reinforces the image of female subjection to unequivocal male domination. Such rendition chimed with the prevailing Portuguese conservative patriarchal ideology of the 1950s, according to which men were indeed the figures of authority (and explicitly so within marriage: for example 'the 1933 Constitution stated that the husband was head of the family and that it was he who wielded authority').[24] On the other hand, by highlighting Jane's forced subordination, Brontë's phrasing may strike the modern reader as subtly bolstering her character's justification for ultimately rejecting St John Rivers' supremacy.

A chronological perspective of the translational choices for 'masterhood' in the corpus can again be useful in highlighting shifting interpretations of the relationship between Jane and her suitor. As the choices become less charged, they hint at the way the distribution of power in the male/female relationship becomes increasingly perceived as more balanced over time:

Brontë	Ferreira (1951)	Nascimento (1975)	Rocha (2011)
'masterhood'	'autoridade'[25]	'primado'[26]	'orientação'[27]
	['authority', with connotations of power and control, entailing subjection]	['primacy', implying a hierarchy of sorts, but with a subtler connection with the idea of power]	['directions, guidance', with connotations of help, and no explicit mention of power dynamics]

Likewise, in the Brazilian versions, the 2010 option for 'direção' [guidance] is very similar to the choice of 'orientação' by the

24 See Anne Cova and António Costa Pinto, 'Women under Salazar's Dictatorship', *Portuguese Journal of Social Science* 1(2), (2002), 129–46 (129). An analysis of a different translation by Ferreira reached a similar conclusion regarding another aspect of the dictatorship values: patriotism. See Jorge Bastos da Silva, 'A Lusitanian Dish: Swift to Portuguese Taste', in *The Reception of Jonathan Swift in Europe*, ed. by Hermann J. Real (London: Continuum, 2005), pp. 79–92.

25 Ferreira, p. 371.

26 Nascimento, p. 420.

27 Rocha, p. 533.

Portuguese Rocha in 2011, whereas the 1983 translation by Santarrita still preferred 'domínio' [dominance].

Jane's consideration of the dire consequences of her imprisonment through marriage is also aptly captured by the use of adjectives with prefixes of negation. These represented an interesting challenge for the translators, though in most cases they were able to use similarly prefixed adjectives available in Portuguese, and thus keep the negativity underlying the English expression: for instance, the final 'unendurable' was translated within the range of the ideas of 'intolerable' or 'unbearable', as 'intolerável' (Nascimento and anon. 1926) and 'insuportável' (Rocha and Santarrita), with Goettems instead choosing 'inaceitável' [unacceptable], perhaps doubly referring to the marriage offer itself.

In this excerpt, one sentence stands out not only because it contains two adjectives prefixed by 'un', but also because it is located between the two sentences featuring the word 'mind': 'I should still have my unblighted self to turn to: my natural unenslaved feelings with which to communicate in moments of loneliness'. Both 'unblighted' and 'unenslaved' have a positive resonance. For 'unenslaved feelings' Santarrita and Rocha kept the suggestion of a master-slave relationship, using the expression 'sentimentos não escravizados' [non enslaved], whereas others lost that allusion by preferring the positive but more abstract 'freed' ('sentimentos libertos', Nascimento). Goettems's translation, 'pensamentos livres' [free thoughts], accentuates the cerebral by commuting 'feelings' into 'thoughts'.

Moreover, this sentence is pivotal in communicating Jane's inner resistance and self-preservation, since it is one of the only two times in the course of the entire novel where the expression 'my [...] self' features. Conveying 'my unblighted self' as 'o meu eu intato' [my intact self] (Santarrita) or 'a minha identidade intacta' [my intact identity] (Rocha) is matched by a choice for 'unenslaved' which necessarily implies a skewed relationship with someone else: 'não escravizados' [non-enslaved] (Santarrita and Rocha). By contrast, a less personalized rendition of 'my unblighted self' as 'o meu mundo indestrutível' [my indestructible world] corresponds to a more abstract paraphrase of the adjective 'unenslaved' as 'livres' [free] (Goettems).

Striving for Selfhood: The Possessives 'my' Versus 'his'

One of the most effective devices employed by Brontë to underscore Jane's subjectivity is the repeated use of the possessive 'my'. Significantly, in this passage, it only makes an appearance in the second part of the paragraph, when the focus shifts to the mainly inner consequences that her marriage, considered in the first, would have upon her. She is at pains to describe not merely the suffering arising from the envisaged curtailment of freedom, but, crucially, its pervasive extent. She does so with such efficiency that, in the words of Jean Wyatt, '[n]ot even Virginia Woolf's Mrs Dalloway could conjure up a more frightening vision of patriarchal domination invading every room of the soul'.[28]

No doubt for stylistic reasons, both Nascimento and Santarrita, both male, preferred to ignore the mark of possession on two occasions, and have 'my body' simply as 'o corpo' [the body] and 'my heart and mind' as 'o coração e a alma' (Nascimento) and 'o coração e a mente' (Santarrita) [the body and the soul, and the body and the mind, respectively]. This is entirely permissible in Portuguese, and indeed a stylistically superior choice under most circumstances. As we have seen, the 1926 Brazilian translation and Leyguarda Ferreira's version were abridged, which accounts for a lower number of occurrences of 'my' in those texts.

The 2010 and 2011 translations, on the other hand, have each added two more possessive forms to the seven that can be found in the English source text:

---

28 Jean Wyatt, 'A Patriarch of One's Own: Jane Eyre and Romantic Love', *Tulsa Studies in Women's Literature*, 4 (1985), 199–216 (208).

Brontë	Goettems (2010)	Rocha (2011)
‘**my** body’	‘**Meu** corpo’	‘o **meu** corpo’
‘**my** heart and mind’	‘**meu** coração e **minha** mente’	‘o **meu** coração e **minha** mente’
‘**my** unblighted self	‘o **meu** mundo’	‘a **minha** identidade’
‘**my** natural unenslaved feelings’	‘**meus** pensamentos...’	‘os **meus** sentimentos...’
‘**my** mind’	‘na **minha** mente’	‘na **minha** mente’
‘only **mine**’	‘só **meus**’	‘só **meus**’
‘the fire of **my** nature’	‘da **minha** natureza’	‘da **minha** natureza’
‘consumed vital after vital’	‘consumisse **minhas** entranhas’[29]	
‘burn inwardly’		‘arder no **meu** íntimo’[30]

Even though it could be argued that in this instance the later translations once again emerge as being more receptive to the reinforcement of female subjectivity, the added possessives are intimately bound to the translational options in lexical terms: ‘coração’ (heart) and ‘mente’ (mind) are masculine and feminine nouns respectively and, although not compulsory, each can be preceded by its respective gendered possessive adjective. It is therefore impossible to pinpoint whether the use of the possessive was the consequence or the cause of the lexical choice. Choosing to translate ‘vital after vital’ as ‘entranhas’ [entrails] may also lead to the addition of the possessive (although Santarrita managed to use ‘entranha(s)’ without a possessive), as does conveying ‘inwardly’ as ‘no meu íntimo’ [in my inner core].

Consistency in terms of attention devoted to Brontë’s use of the possessive can, nonetheless, help to support the claim that more recent translators were particularly mindful of the effect this marker has. Goettems’s version paid a similar degree of attention to Brontë’s use of ‘my’ in the Chapter 12 passage (where it occurs seven times in English and six times in Portuguese), and here to the prevalence of the contrasting ‘his’. The latter is initially present in Jane’s physical description of St John through a series of parallel constructions that include both favourable and critical comments. Whereas other

29 Goettems, p. 358.
30 Rocha, p. 533.

translations seem to ignore or downplay the repeated occurrences of this marker, Goettems's text offers a solution which helps to avoid the redundant tone that the repetition of 'his' at the beginning of the passage could easily entail in Portuguese — it uses Brontë's pauses to break the sentence into smaller units (our emphasis in bold):

> I looked at **his** features, beautiful in their harmony, but strangely formidable in their still severity; at **his** brow, commanding but not open; at **his** eyes, bright and deep and searching, but never soft; at **his** tall imposing figure; and fancied myself in idea ***his*** *wife*.

> Olhei para os **seus** traços, belos em **sua** harmonia, mas estranhamente temíveis na **sua** severidade. Para **sua** fronte autoritária, mas não aberta. Para os **seus** olhos, brilhantes e profundos e inquisidores, mas ainda assim nunca ternos. Para **sua** figura alta e imponente; e me imaginei como ***sua*** *esposa*...[31]

Breaking up this description into a series of short nominal sentences creates a lingering, slow motion effect. It arguably lengthens perception (both Jane's and the reader's) underscoring a self-conscious thought-process. Moreover, Goettems's translation of her suitor's 'strangely formidable' features as 'estranhamente temíveis' [strangely fearsome] emphasises Jane's own awareness (and concomitant rejection) of gender-based domination, also present both in Rocha's identical rendering of this phrase and in Nascimento's choice of a similar qualifier ('estranhamente assustadoras' [strangely frightening]).

Last but not least, there is a compelling argument in favour of the hypothesis that recent translations seek to self-consciously spotlight Jane's assertive subjectivity: both Goettems and Rocha, unlike their predecessors, opt to convey the start of the sentence 'I should still have my unblighted self to turn to' as 'Eu ainda teria' [I would still have] and 'Eu continuaria a ter' [I would keep on having] respectively. Bearing in mind that in Portuguese the use of the first-person pronoun is unnecessary here and therefore redundant, its presence speaks volumes.

Conclusion

In Chapter 35, when Jane declines to become his wife, St John remonstrates with her as follows: 'Your words are such as ought not to be used: violent, unfeminine, and untrue. They betray an unfortunate

31 Goettems, p. 358.

state of mind'. This is the only time that Jane is explicitly qualified as 'unfeminine' in the course of the novel. According to prevailing social codes of mid-nineteenth-century England which undoubtedly extended well into the long twentieth century, her rebellious state of mind may indeed be labelled 'unfeminine' and even 'violent', but surely the real purpose of *Jane Eyre* is to challenge these codes and stifling expectations: in the first passage Jane escapes by bursting from the straitjacket of convention through the power of her imagination; in the second, even more radically, she does so by asserting vehemently to herself and the reader her right to an authentic self, outside marriage. Yet 'volcanic vehemence', situated as she put it between 'absolute submission' and 'determined revolt', does not belong exclusively to Jane: ultimately it is a rhetorical means for Brontë to explore the prison-escape leitmotif that underpins the novel. Through the volcanic self-expression of her fictional character, then, Brontë exposes gender politics by insistently interrogating the right to refuse limitative patriarchal expectations of women.

The communicative immediacy of a transgressive first-person voice hinges on Brontë's subtle deployment of a host of stylistic features including, as was observed here, sentence length, alliteration, adjectives with negating prefixes as well as a proliferation of possessives. These present multiple challenges for translators. To what extent did successive translations into Portuguese over the last century-and-a-half manage to communicate the fire and restlessness that inhabit the mind of both the author and her creation, in order to transmit Jane's visceral need to be true to her 'self'?

As might be expected, the last four versions considered here, published from 1975 onwards, reveal a growing willingness on the part of translators to showcase Jane's spirited 'nature' and intellect. It seems that the two twenty-first-century female translators were, on the whole, more closely attuned to the textual devices in the English original that articulated subjectivity and, as such, they accentuated it, for instance through the liberal use of possessives. Rocha's rendition of life-affirming vehemence is especially striking in her version of the first passage, while Goettems's translation generates an arguably more cerebral Jane, especially in the second passage.

At their best, translators resort to devices such as metaphor and antithesis, in addition or as alternatives to Brontë's rhetorical strategies. Their creativity enables them to forge opportunities unavailable in the English text to reinforce Brontë's revolutionary criticism of a woman's role and place in society. In that light, it is highly significant that the earliest known translation into European Portuguese, the nineteenth-century incomplete rendition published in *O Zoophilo*, proved to be comfortable with the unfettered expression of subjectivity and inner revolt as a means of female self-actualization. Interestingly, it threw into relief the gendering of creativity by describing the tale that Jane wove inwardly as 'uma historia filha da minha imaginação' [a story daughter of my imagination].

While, more broadly speaking, this pioneer version is underscored by the belief in women's intellectual freedom, conversely some early- and mid-twentieth-century translators reacted to volcanic vehemence with ambivalence or even silence. As we saw, the 1926 Brazilian version suppresses later sections of the text. More significantly, in the 1951 Portuguese version, Ferreira's condensing practice allows her to elide significant bits and avoid ideological difficulties, as she seems to re-interpret both female yearnings and male-female relationships in line with the conservative gendered logic of the dictatorship. The most extreme case of muteness in a cultural landscape informed by censorship, however, is to be found in the earliest European Portuguese translation in book-form (1941) where Mécia and João Gaspar Simões handled the complexity of the material underpinning the source text through conspicuous avoidance altogether, in other words, through the glaring omission of both passages chosen for analysis here. Perhaps nowhere is the seismic power of Jane's mind more strikingly evident than when the transmission of core moments, where 'natural unenslaved feelings' are vocally articulated, is considered so perilously transgressive that it can only be met with absolute suppression and deafening silence.

Works Cited

Translations of *Jane Eyre*

Brontë, Charlotte, 'Joanna Eyre', *O Zoophilo* (14 January 1877, p. 4 to 28 September 1882, pp. 1–2).

——, *Joanna Eyre* (Petropolis: Typographia das 'Vozes de Petropolis', 1926).

——, *A Paixão de Jane Eyre*, trans. by Mécia and João Gaspar Simões (Lisbon: Editorial Inquérito, 1941).

——, *O Grande Amor de Jane Eyre*, trans. by Leyguarda Ferreira (Lisbon: Edição Romano Torres, 1951).

——, *Jane Eyre*, trans. by João Cabral do Nascimento (Porto: Editorial Inova, 1975).

——, *Jane Eyre*, trans. by Marcos Santarrita (Rio de Janeiro: Francisco Alves, 1983).

——, *Jane Eyre*, trans. by Doris Goettems (São Paulo: Landmark, 2010).

——, *Jane Eyre*, trans. by Alice Rocha (Barcarena: Editorial Presença, 2011).

Other Sources

1968–1978. Editorial Inova/Porto: Uma Certa Maneira de Dignificar o Livro (n.p.: Inova, 1978).

Cabral, Afonso Reis, 'Leyguarda Ferreira', http://romanotorres.fcsh.unl.pt/?page_id=59#F

Cortez, Maria Teresa, *Os contos de Grimm em Portugal. A recepção dos Kinder-und Hausmärchen entre 1837 e 1910* (Coimbra: Minerva (Centro Interuniversitário de Estudos Germanísticos) and Universidade de Aveiro, 2001).

Cova, Anne and António Costa Pinto, 'Women under Salazar's Dictatorship', 1.2 (2002), 129–46.

Marques dos Santos, Ana Teresa, 'La capacidad de visibilidad de la traductora invisible: mujeres y traducción en el caso de la *Jane Eyre* portuguesa del siglo XIX', in *Traducción literaria y género: estrategias y práticas de visibilización*, ed. by Patricia Álvarez Sánchez (Granada: Editorial Comares, 2022), 51–62.

——, 'A primeira *Jane Eyre* portuguesa, ou como o Órgão da Sociedade Protetora dos Animais trouxe Charlotte Brontë para Portugal (1877–1882)', *Revista de Estudos Anglo-Portugueses* (forthcoming).

Melo, Daniel, *História e Património da Edição em Portugal—A Romano Torres* (Famalicão: Edições Húmus, 2015).

Pazos-Alonso, Cláudia, *Francisca Wood and Nineteenth-Century Periodical Culture: Pressing for Change* (Oxford: Legenda, 2020), https://doi.org/10.2307/j.ctv16kkzkt

Silva, Jorge Bastos da, 'A Lusitanian Dish: Swift to Portuguese Taste', in *The Reception of Jonathan Swift in Europe*, ed. by Hermann J. Real (London: Continuum, 2005), pp. 79–92.

Sousa, Maria Leonor Machado de, 'Dickens in Portugal', in *The Reception of Charles Dickens in Europe*, ed. by Michael Hollington (London: Bloomsbury, 2013), pp. 197–211.

Wyatt, Jean, 'A Patriarch of One's Own: Jane Eyre and Romantic Love', *Tulsa Studies in Women's Literature*, 4 (1985), 199–216.

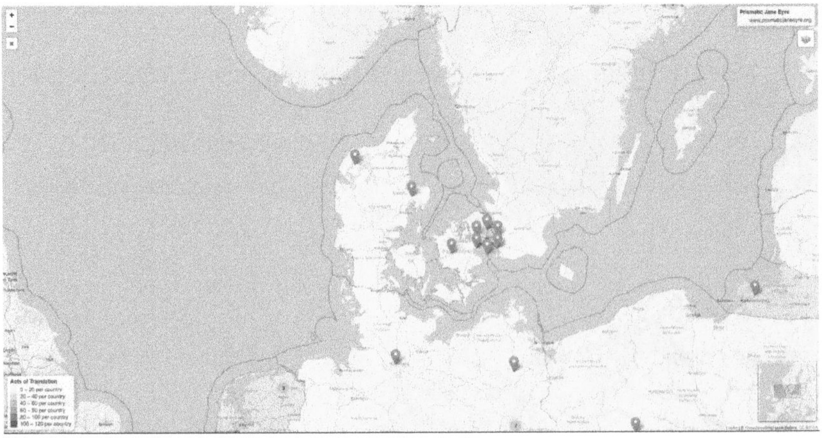

The World Map
https://digitalkoine.github.io/je_prismatic_map
Created by Giovanni Pietro Vitali;
maps © Thunderforest, data © OpenStreetMap contributors

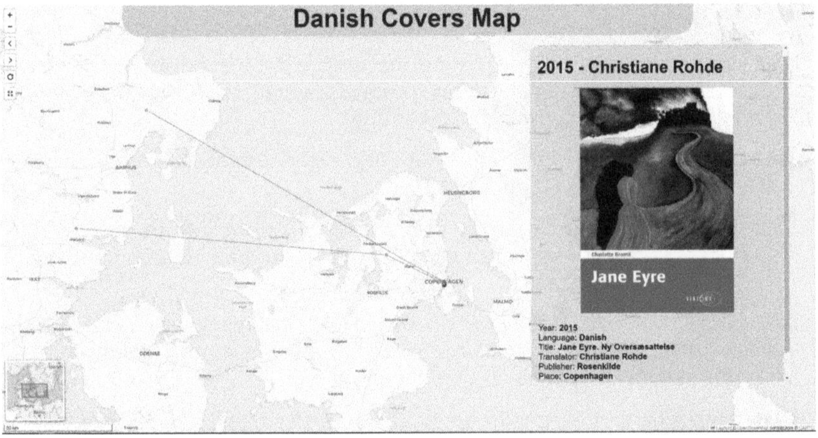

The Danish Covers Map
https://digitalkoine.github.io/danish_storymap/
Researched by Ida Klitgård; created by Giovanni Pietro Vitali and Simone Landucci

10. The Movements of Passion in the Danish *Jane Eyre*

Ida Klitgård

Introduction

This essay sets out to study the movements of the word 'passion' in the novel, both as a movement of feeling and as a movement of meanings. Here movement is to be understood as a pun on the changing semantic nature of the word 'passion' and a key passionate feature of Jane Eyre's nature: she is both moved and moves her reader. But as the translation of a word does not happen in a vacuum, the translation stands and falls with the translations of the contextual words. These contexts may make the word in focus slip and slide in mysterious ways, revealing the translators' specific understanding of the text. My analysis of both the word and its contexts reveals that even though the word contains many complex meanings in English, the Danish translations seem to release a limited variety which portray Jane in a certain way.

There are several Danish translations of *Jane Eyre*, especially old ones (see the Translations List at the end of this volume). The first translation is from 1850 by an unknown translator. Then follow two further translations in 1894 and 1895 by Vilhelm Møller and Sofie Horten. Horten's translation was reprinted several times before a new translation by Emma Sunde was published in 1917. I have, however, decided to focus on the three most recent translations as they are readily available to current readers of *Jane Eyre*. The first was translated in 1944 by the Danish translator and writer of books on Victorianism, Aslaug Mikkelsen (1846–1964). This translation has been reprinted several times, including the edition used here, from 1971. The most recent reprint is from 2011. The two more recent translations were made by Christiane Rohde (1944-) in 2015 and by the translator Luise Hemmer Pihl (1940-) in 2016. The first translation

 https://doi.org/10.11647/OBP.0319.16

is typical of the period as it proves to be an abridged version. In those years it was not uncommon to turn major foreign novels into briefer works, aimed at entertainment only. The same is the case with Peter Freuchen's translation of Herman Melville's *Moby Dick* into a so-called 'man's novel', as it says on the back of the cover.[1] The two recent translations depart from such abridgement and translate the novel in full. Together, the three translators release specific readings which emphasise that there is no real one and only translation, even if reviewers often forget this fact, as Matthew Reynolds has noted:

> Reviewers of translations rarely keep this fact in mind. Typically, a translation is either ticked off or praised (but usually ticked off) for catching or failing to catch the 'tone' or 'spirit' of 'the original'. But the original has no tone or spirit in itself: it takes the readers to imagine those qualities into being. In fact, there is fundamentally no such thing as 'an original': there is only the source text that gives rise to interpretations in collaboration with the readers. So what is really happening when a reviewer feels that a translation 'fails to catch the tone of the original' is that the printed translation is doing something different from the implicit translation that is in the reviewer's mind.[2]

Aslaug Mikkelsen is a particularly clear example of this. The novel has indeed been abridged, but not just because the times cried for light entertainment, for Mikkelsen had mixed feelings about Charlotte Brontë's achievements as a writer. In her book, *Foregangskvinder i engelsk litteratur* [Pioneering women in English literature] (1942) Mikkelsen criticises what she terms Brontë's unbalanced and unequal development of plot, and she deplores the pretentious melodrama of interludes which, she says, break all laws of realism.[3] She also has no admiration for 'de lange, stærkt konstruerede, til Tider fuldkommen umulige samtaler mellem personerne' [the long, strongly constructed, at times completely impossible conversations between the characters] which may be due to Brontë's unfamiliarity with how real people actually express themselves. Brontë has no sense of humour, Mikkelsen argues, and her language is often too hysterically bombastic.[4] It

1 See Ida Klitgård, 'Translation, Adaptation or Amputation? Arctic Explorer-Writer-Anthropologist Peter Freuchen's Little-Known Danish Translation of Moby Dick', *Across Languages and Cultures*, 16 (2015), 119–41.

2 Matthew Reynolds, *Translation: A Very Short Introduction* (Oxford: Oxford University Press, 2016), p. 59.

3 Aslaug Mikkelsen, *Foregangskvinder I engelsk litteratur* (Copenhagen: P. Haase & Søns Forlag, 1942), p. 138.

4 Mikkelsen, *Foregangskvinder*, pp. 139–40.

is exactly such passages that Mikkelsen has abridged or deleted altogether. On the other hand, Mikkelsen admits, Brontë is also blessed with the talent of capturing her reader in the way she conveys her perceptions through vivid observations: she has the gift of 'den dybe, lidenskabelige Følelse' [the deep, passionate feeling]. In fact, the word passion [lidenskab] is identified by Mikkelsen as the key quality in the novel, and that is why I have chosen to focus on it.[5]

Even though we have no such translational reflections from the two most recent translators, they are also interesting figures. Christiane Rohde is in fact an actress, not someone educated in languages, and Luise Hemmer Pihl has a degree in English and Italian, and her translation is printed by her own small publishing house. She has also translated a number of La Fontaine's fables as well as Emily Brontë's *Wuthering Heights* and Jane Austen's *Northanger Abbey*. So, unlike Aslaug Mikkelsen, who also translated George Eliot, Jack London, Upton Sinclair, Harriet Beecher Stowe and Rudyard Kipling, we are thus not dealing with any of the prolific, established translators of British fiction in Denmark, but with passionate readers and translators who, for the first time in decades, have introduced the complete text to a Danish audience.

Therefore, my analysis will not follow any pre-existing methodology of translation criticism but will move in a philological way through various reflections generated by the three translations. I adopt the methodology of attention to 'key words' introduced in Chapter IV, adding my particular emphasis on contextual words: even when a key word is translated in the same way, the words around it can introduce significant differences. To emphasise my point, it is impossible to analyse the implications of the translations of a single word without involving the contextual words by which it is surrounded.

The Word 'Passion' in English and Danish

As noted in Chapter III above, the noun 'passion' has several meanings according to *The Oxford English Dictionary* (*OED*). Here are the main definitions of the word's meanings in English, which I give in full from the online *OED*, as this is a philological study:

1. Senses relating to physical suffering and pain (such as Christ's)
2. The sufferings of a martyr

5 Mikkelsen, *Foregangskvinder*, p. 140.

3. A suffering or affliction of any kind
    a. A painful disorder, ailment or affliction of the body or a part of the body
    b. A fit or seizure; a faint
4. In oaths and asseverations, with reference to 1.
5. Senses relating to emotional or mental states
    a. Any strong, controlling, or overpowering emotion, as desire, hate, fear, etc.; an intense feeling or impulse
    b. A fit, outburst, or state marked by or of strong excitement, agitation, or other intense emotion
6. Intense anger; rage; temper
    a. A fit of temper; an outburst of anger or rage
7. Strong affection; love
    a. Sexual desire or impulses
    b. An object of love or sexual desire
8. An intense desire or enthusiasm of something; the zealous pursuit of an aim

If we look at the vertical, and thus chronological, development of this list, it is interesting to observe how the meanings move from Christian connotations of Christ's pain and suffering to the pain and suffering of humankind, both physically, mentally and emotionally. Such states are characterised by fits or outbursts and may cover both spectrums of emotions from hate to love, as long as they are intense. Later on, such states of passion turn into metaphors of sexual desire. We have come a long way from the old pious context. The list ends with a blander meaning of the word, covering a want or need for something.[6]

When we turn to a modern thesaurus, it offers the following links that encapsulate the continuing complexity of the word in contemporary usage:

> resentment; sentiment; spirit; temper; warmth; zeal; agony; animation; distress; dolor; eagerness; ecstasy; fire; fit; flare-up; frenzy; heat; hurrah;

6 The online etymological dictionary, too, testifies to the fact that sexual desire and fondness are late meanings. See https://www.etymonline.com/word/passion#etymonline_v_7291

> indignation; ire; misery; outbreak; outburst; paroxysm; rapture; storm; suffering; transport; vehemence; wrath; zest; affectivity.[7]

Thus, the word refers to intense and often explosive feelings, whether they be lovable or disagreeable.

In Cassin's *Dictionary of Untranslatables*, the philosophical untranslatability of the word is divided into three categories: 1. Passion and suffering: the passions of the soul that affect, as Descartes said, 'the union of the soul and the body', which constitute the 'irrational substance of life'; 2. Passion as both love and suffering, related to pain and pleasure, action, and passivity; 3. Passion as opposite to wisdom as wisdom constitutes an ability to resist, a constancy or courage of the soul.[8] Thus, human existence seems to be a tug-of-war between diametrically opposite emotions in which passion paradoxically forms both one of the sides, and constitutes a tug-of-war in itself as it forms a divided state of being. As we will see in *Jane Eyre*, it is precisely this double split between passion as both love and pain, faced with the restraints of Cassin's 'wisdom', or 'reason' as it is called in the novel, which haunts Jane throughout. This dilemma is supported by Giulia Sissa in her philosophical discussion of the split between the active and the passive represented in the word 'pathos', which is related to passion:

> Psychic life is movement. The mind moves. Psychic life is passion. The mind is, in fact, moved. The vocabulary of feeling in European languages is organized around these two poles: on one hand, the idea of turbulence, a becoming, an instability — something starts moving and transforms itself, there is a psychic activity; on the other hand, such an activity is the effect of an external cause to which the mind finds itself exposed, which it undergoes, passively. Something happens to it and transforms it. Agitation is the form that passivity takes.[9]

So let us now look at one of those European languages: Danish. At first sight the translation of 'passion' into Danish does not offer major obstacles as we have the same word 'passion' alternating with the more habitually used 'lidenskab' (equivalent to and derived from the German *Leidenschaft*). In the great *Dictionary of the Danish Language*

---

7 http://www.thesaurus.com/browse/passion

8 *Dictionary of Untranslatables: A Philosophical Lexicon*, ed. by Barbara Cassin (Princeton: Princeton University Press, 2014), p. 745.

9 Giulia Sissa, 'Pathos/perturbatio', in *Dictionary of Untranslatables: A Philosophical Lexicon*, ed. by Barbara Cassin (Princeton: Princeton University Press, 2014), pp. 745–49 (p. 745).

(*Ordbog over det danske sprog*) which covers the language from 1700 to 1950, 'passion' is defined not only as the suffering of Christ, but also as a strong mental movement, such as desire, especially erotic desire. The dictionary also refers to the expression 'have en passion for' [have a passion for] meaning having a preference for something, to like something.[10] Thus, the Danish word seems to follow the development from the religious to the worldly meanings as detected in the *OED*.

In the modern *Danish Dictionary* (*Danske Ordbog*) the word firstly covers a strong feeling based on urges, inclinations or instincts. Secondly, it refers to having an interest in or love for something. Lastly, it refers to a piece of classical music, such as an oratorium.[11] In this way, the modern definitions lean more towards the last, bland definition in the *OED*.

When turning to a major English-Danish dictionary, *Engelsk-dansk Ordbog*, 'passion' is defined as 1) equal to 'lidenskab'; 2) an emotional outburst or affect; or 3) the passion of Christ.[12]

To sum up, the Danish definitions cover the same variations as the English definitions, except for the ones referring to compassion, indignation, hate or wrath, which are nowhere mentioned. Also, the split between love and pain or passion and reason is never indicated in either of the two works. So the general impression to the modern reader is that 'passion' is a more pleasing and less inherently complex experience in Danish than in English. Thus, modern translators may invest something more one-sided in the word than was the case in the England of the 1840s.

What about the other Danish word 'lidenskab'? According to *Dictionary of the Danish Language*, it arrived from Germany in the mid-eighteenth century as a 'foreign' substitute for 'passion'. It derives from 'leiden', to suffer, in German. It was received with a certain amount of skepticism, as a sarcastic source from 1759 says:

> '"Lidenskaber! hvad vil det siige? Er det en liden Skabere?" — "Nej. Lidenskaberne ere de Affecter, som sætter Sindet i Bevægelse, saasom Vrede, Had, Kiærlighed, Misundelse." — "Naa, nu begriber jeg det, det er Sinds Lidelser".'

10 See 'Passion', in *Ordbog over det danske sprog*, https://ordnet.dk/ods/ordbog?query=passion.

11 See 'Passion', in *Danske Ordbog*, https://ordnet.dk/ddo/ordbog?query=passion.

12 'Passion', in Helge L. Schwarz, Marianne Holmen, Freddy Volmer Hansen, Egon Foldberg, and Ida Klitgård, *Engelsk-dansk ordbog* (Copenhagen: Munksgaard, 1996), p. 1087.

> ('"Passions! What does that mean? Is it a small [the Danish word 'liden' is archaic for 'small'] creator?" — "No. The passions are the affects which put the mind in motion, such as anger, hatred, love, envy." — "Ah, now I understand, it is mental illnesses"' [the Danish word 'lidelser' may both mean sufferings and 'illnesses'].)

Another old source suggests that the word should not be incorporated in any dictionary as:

> 'Affect og Passion ere [...] meget forstaaeligere end vort nye Lidenskab, som er hverken tydsk eller jydsk, og kunde af en Ulærd antages for Lidenhed, sat imod Storhed'
>
> ('Affect and passion are [...] much more intelligible than our new "Lidenskab", which is neither German, nor Jutlandish, and could be reckoned as smallness compared with greatness by an unskilled person [here there is a pun on the word 'Lidenhed' which means smallness and connotes sufferings at the same time] put against grandeur').[13]

Thus, the new word 'lidenskab' in Danish is at first perceived as less important than 'passion'. However, the development of its meaning is very similar to the development of the meanings of 'passion'. In the modern Danish dictionary, the meanings span from 1) a violent feeling which is difficult to control and which may lead to unfavourable behaviour, such as an obsession; 2) a strong interest for or love of something; to 3) irresistible erotic love.[14] So interestingly, in opposition to 'passion', which has more pleasing connotations in Danish, 'lidenskab' may indeed be used in cases of anger and hate, and situations where the movement has negative consequences. This is a plausible guess because the word was received with hostility in the Danish language.

Translation Analysis

The analysis will reveal which word, 'passion' or 'lidenskab', the translators select to emphasise the contextual situation of negative vs. positive feelings. This development becomes clear when traversing the following selection of examples in the novel.[15]

13 See 'lidenskab', in *Ordbog over det danske sprog*, https://ordnet.dk/ods/ordbog?query=lidenskab&tab=for

14 See 'lidenskab', in Danske Ordbog, https://ordnet.dk/ddo/ordbog?query=lidenskab&tab=for

15 The translations discussed are Charlotte Brontë, *Jane Eyre*, trans. by Aslaug Mikkelsen (Aarhus: Det Danske Forlag, 1971); Charlotte Brontë, *Jane Eyre*, trans. by Christiane Rohde (Copenhagen: Lindhardt og Ringhof, 2015); and Charlotte Brontë, *Jane Eyre*, trans. by Luise Hemmer Pihl (Mørke: Grevas Forlag, 2016).

Passion and Wrath

1.

Brontë	Mikkelsen	Rohde	Pihl
“*Dear! dear!* What a *fury* to *fly at* Master John!” “Did ever anybody see such a picture of **passion**!” (Ch. 1)	“*Vorherre bevares*! Sikken en lille furie — at *fare sådan løs på* hr. John” [the second line has been left out] (p. 14).	“*Gud bevare os*! Sikken en *heks* og *lige i struben på* Master John!” “Jeg har aldrig set magen til **hidsighed**!” (p. 12).	“*Du milde*! Sikken en *furie*, som hun *farer løs på* Master John!” “Har man nogen sinde set mage til sådan et **raseri**?” (p. 10).

Here the young Jane is attacked by her cousin John Reed, but she fights back. The children are then separated, and Jane is scolded. The expression ‘picture of passion’ brings associations of a painting of a passionate scene as if what is going on is prototypical behaviour when angry. The three translations here all neglect the idiom of the ‘picture’ and reformulate it. As for ‘passion’, Mikkelsen avoids translating the whole sentence altogether. Rohde, in turn, translates ‘passion’ into ‘hidsighed’ [hot-temperedness] which is more on a par with the source text. Pihl translates it into ‘raseri’ meaning anger or wrath. The picture allusion has been rephrased into ‘jeg har aldrig set magen til...’ [I have never seen anything like such hot-temperedness] or ‘Har man nogen sinde set mage til...’ [has anybody ever seen anything like such anger].

When it comes to the surrounding context, the translations undergo a development from Jane as a Fury and her attack described as ‘fare’ [get at]. In Mikkelsen’s translation the sentence can be back-translated into ‘For goodness’/God’s sake! What a little Fury — to attack Mr. John like that!’ Rohde translates it into ‘For God’s sake! What a witch — and directly at Master John’s throat!’ In this way the contextual picture of Jane transforms in a more violent fashion from a hot-tempered child to a wicked witch almost about to strangle Master John. Pihl opts for a calmer solution by translating ‘Dear, dear’ into ‘Du milde!’, i.e., ‘Oh my!’ The rest is close to Mikkelsen’s translation. This example is in alignment with the Danish use of the word ‘passion’ as a positive state. If it had been used here, the reader would have been in doubt as to whether Jane's fit was being perceived as a good thing, contrary to the source text's rendering of it as the work of a Fury.

2.

Brontë	Mikkelsen	Rohde	Pihl
[Bessie] "if you become **passionate** and rude, Missis will *send you away, I am sure.*" (Ch. 2)	[this sentence and others have been left out] (p. 15)	"hvis De er **hidsig** og *uartig, sender fruen Dem bort,* og det er *så sikkert som amen i kirken.*" (p. 14)	"hvis De bliver **vred** og *uforskammet*, er jeg *sikker på*, at fruen vil *sende Dem bort*" (p. 12).

In this passage, 'passionate' is either translated into 'hidsig' [hot-tempered] or 'vred' [angry]. Again, we see two diverging interpretations of Jane's passion. It is as if Jane becomes more and more cross over time, and thus the Danish adjective 'passioneret' would be impossible here, as it would give connotations of a positive trait. In Rohde, Jane is hot-tempered and 'uartig', that is, 'naughty', and in Pihl she is angry and 'uforskammet', or 'rude'. So in Rohde, Jane comes across in a childish manner, whereas in Pihl she appears stubbornly exasperated in a more adult way.

The threat of expulsion, 'send you away', is translated into the Danish equivalents of being sent away. The same is, however, not true of Bessie's expression of certainty 'I am sure'. Pihl translates this into a phrase with the same form and content, whereas Rohde adds an emphatic 'så sikkert som amen i kirken': this is roughly equivalent to 'which is as certain as the amen [being said] in church' which is again equivalent to the English expressions 'as sure as fate' or 'as sure as eggs is eggs'.

It is noteworthy that both translators decide to translate 'you' into 'De' and 'Dem' which are the formal addresses equivalent to the French 'vous' or the German 'Sie', even though Jane is a child. It might have been expected that the recent translations would abandon this, at this address is very formal in modern Danish. On the other hand, they signal that there is a master-servant relationship involving distance and reverence at stake here.

3.

Brontë	Mikkelsen	Rohde	Pihl
'I had felt every word as acutely as I had heard it plainly, and a **passion** of resentment *fomented* now within me.' (Ch. 4)	'[the first part has been left out] og jeg ligefrem *kogte* af harme' (p. 32)	*'Jeg havde følt hvert ord som et stik i hjertet*. Hele mit sind *kogte* af harme' (p. 40)	*'Jeg havde hørt hvert eneste ord lige så skarpt som tydeligt*, og nu *gærede* en **lidenskabelig følelse** af nag i mig' (p. 39)

It must be noted that in this passage there is a textual variant. Brontë's manuscript and the first edition read 'fermented' (to undergo a chemical process involving yeast; to excite), whereas the second and third editions, both published during Brontë's lifetime, give 'fomented' (to soak with heated liquid, to stimulate), as here. Both variants have been perpetuated in later editions. In our case, it seems likely that Mikkelsen and Rohde were working from source texts with 'fomented', since they both give 'kogte' ['boiled'], while Pihl was faced with 'fermented', since she translates 'gærede' ['fermented']. However, given the similarity between the two words it is impossible to be sure.

In this example, Jane feels a passion of resentment. The most recent translation by Pihl is the only one to include a translation of this: 'en lidenskabelig følelse' ['a passionate feeling'] whereas the others leave it out and only speak of the fermenting/fomenting issue. Here the German derivative 'lidenskabelig' has been selected to denote a negative psychic movement inside Jane where 'passioneret' would have given the reader a different impression.

The phrase 'I had felt every word as acutely as I had heard it plainly' also receives different treatments by the translators. Mikkelsen leaves it out, and the two others focus on Jane hearing the words, and thus they struggle to render Jane's emotional experience of what is being said. Rohde says that Jane had felt every word as a stab in the heart, which correctly merges listening and feeling, but Pihl settles with a more limited explanation of Jane hearing every single word acutely and plainly. Her emotions are instead carried into 'en lidenskabelig følelse af nag' ['a passionate feeling of resentment'].

So far we have learned that when passion and being passionate is a sentiment of pain, suffering and rage, either the sentences are completely reformulated, or the Danish 'lidenskab' or 'lidenskabelig' is preferred, which give us the impression of situations in which Jane is a victim of damaging feelings she is unable to control. The next examples tell us about the translators' choices when 'passion' refers to love.

Passion and Love

4.

Brontë	Mikkelsen	Rohde	Pihl
'Celine Varens, towards whom he had once cherished what he called a "grande **passion**." This **passion** Celine had professed to return with even superior *ardour*' (Ch. 15)	'Celine Varens, som han sagde at han en gang havde været **forelsket i**, og denne **forelskelse** havde Celine tilsyneladende besvaret med en endnu større *lidenskab*' (p. 110)	'Céline Varens, mod hvem han engang nærede, hvad han kaldte en "grande **passion**". Denne **passion** havde Céline foregivet at gengælde med endnu større *lidenskab*' (p. 163)	'Céline Varens, som han en gang havde næret, hvad han kaldte en "grande **passion**", for. Denne **lidenskab** havde Céline foregivet at gengælde med endnu stærkere *glød*' (p. 166)

In this passage, all the translators except Mikkelsen have maintained the melodramatic French expression and thus maintained a foreignising effect. Mikkelsen, however, seems to have domesticated everything into 'being in love' as this is what 'forelsket' [being in love with (verb)] and 'forelskelse' [being in love (noun)] refer to. In this way, the ambiguities of the great passion have been reduced to plainly being in love, which has a simple, romantic air to it.

When it comes to the English mention of 'passion', Rohde keeps the Danish direct equivalent, which has positive connotations, whereas Pihl translates it into 'lidenskab', which has mixed connotations of powerful emotions out of one's reach. This word is, paradoxically, also used for 'ardour' by Mikkelsen and Rohde. Ardour refers to fervour, intense devotion or burning heat, so it could certainly be another way to describe passion, and thus 'lidenskab'. But Pihl is the only one who incorporates the 'burning heat' motif as she chooses 'glød' ['glow'].

5.

Brontë	Mikkelsen	Rohde	Pihl
'Real *affection*, it seemed, he could not have for me; it had been only *fitful* **passion**: that was *balked*; he would want me no more.' (Ch. 26)	'Virkelig *kærlighed* til mig syntes det ikke, at han kunne have næret; det havde kun været en *opblussende* **lidenskab**, som var blevet *skuffet*; han ville ikke have mere brug for mig' (p. 207)	'Han kunne ikke føle ægte *hengivenhed* for mig, det havde kun været en *krampagtig blind* **lidenskab.** Den *var forbi*, og jeg var uønsket' (p. 344)	'Det forekom mig, at han ikke kunne nære sand *hengivenhed* for mig; det havde kun været en *ustadig* **lidenskab**; den *havde stødt på en hindring*, han ville ikke vide af mig mere' (p. 351)

Jane's constant worries about Rochester's feelings for her are represented in various ways. Rochester's 'affection' is either translated into 'kærlighed' ['love'] or 'hengivenhed' ['devotion'], thus representing it as something strong or something more tempered.

The 'fitful passion' (i.e., a sporadic spell of passion) is translated into either 'opblussende lidenskab' ['blazing/rising passion'], 'krampagtig blind lidenskab' ['convulsively/forcibly blind passion'] or 'ustadig lidenskab' ['changeable/fickle passion']. Even though these interpretations all agree on the negative aspects of 'lidenskab', they leave us with different impressions of Rochester and may have a bearing on our analysis of how Jane sees their relationship. Mikkelsen and Rohde have taken the liberty to forecast the thematic spheres of fire and blindness, but it may not be appropriate to explicate these at this moment in the novel.

The fitful passion is 'balked', meaning stopped and prevented from going on by her resistance. Mikkelsen translates this as 'skuffet' ['disappointed'], Rohde 'den var forbi' ['it was over'], and Pihl 'havde stødt på en hindring' ['had met with an obstacle']. All these examples are very different and do not quite describe Rochester's stubbornness as Jane imagines it.

In the following examples, we leave behind passion as simply anger, hate or fickle love and turn to the complexity of passion as both pleasure and pain in the face of wisdom, reason and sense, which is so characteristic of the adult Jane and the entire scope of the novel.

Passion and Wisdom

6.

Brontë	Mikkelsen	Rohde	Pihl
'[in Jane's mind] *Sense* would resist *delirium*: *judgment* would warn **passion**.' (Ch. 15)	'*Fornuft* kæmpede mod *fantasier*; *den kolde dømmekraft* advarede **lidenskaben**' (p. 118)	'*Fornuften* kunne ikke modstå *den vidunderlige drøm*, min *dømmekraft* kunne ikke hamle op med min **lidenskab**' (p. 175)	'*Fornuften* blev ved med at modstå *vildelsen*: *dømmekraften* blev ved at advare **lidenskaben**' (p. 180)

Jane's inner self is in turmoil after having both heard about Rochester's passion for Céline and having heard sweet words from his lips towards her. She has received mixed messages and does not know what to think, so there is a raving tug-of-war between being sensible and feeling a strong love for Rochester. The three translations all translate 'passion' into 'lidenskab' rather than 'passion', which would truly refer to passions of the heart in a more elevated way. As for the noun 'delirium', it refers metaphorically to a temporary disorder of the mental faculties, as in fevers, disturbances of consciousness, characterised by restlessness, excitement, delusions, hallucinations, etc. Mikkelsen has decided on 'fantasier' in the plural ['fantasies'], and Pihl translates it as 'vildelsen' ['the delirium']. Here Rohde's translation is the odd one out as her translation reads 'den vidunderlige drøm' equivalent to 'the wonderful dream'. This lifts the torturous inner frenzy into a much narrower range as the translator passes her judgment on the meaning of 'delirium' as constituting merely girlish fancies. In fact, both Mikkelsen and Rohde give the impression of Jane's state as being mere reveries of the imagination.

Such biased interpretation can also be found in Mikkelsen's translation of 'judgment' into 'den kolde dømmekraft' ['cold judgment’]. Here the others just have the most obvious equivalent, ‘min dømmekraft’ [‘my sense of judgment’] or ‘dømmekraften’ [‘judgment’].

7.

Brontë	Mikkelsen	Rohde	Pihl
‘[Rochester as gipsy reading Jane’s face] The forehead declares, “Reason sits firm and holds the reins, and she will not *let the feelings burst away and hurry her to wild chasms.* The **passions** may rage furiously, like true heathens, as they are; and the desires may imagine all sorts of vain things: but judgment shall still have the last word in every argument, and the casting vote in every decision. *Strong wind, earthquake-shock, and fire may pass by*: but I shall follow the guiding of that still small voice which *interprets the dictates of conscience*.”’ (Ch. 19)	‘Det er som om, panden siger: Jeg kan leve alene, hvis min selvagtelse og forholdene tvinger mig til at gøre det. Jeg behøver ikke sælge min sjæl for at købe salighed. Jeg har en skat i mig selv, som kan holde mig i live, hvis alle ydre glæder bliver mig nægtet eller bliver mig budt til en pris, som jeg ikke har råd til at betale. [This passage combines the first sentence with the forehead with the preceding passage in the source text. Thus the remaining passage with the raging passion etc. has been left out]’ (p. 146)	‘Panden erklærer: “Fornuften sidder fast i sadlen og holder tømmerne, og fornuften vil ikke *slippe følelserne løs og kaste sig ud på det dybe vand.* **Lidenskaberne** kan rase heftigt, som de hedninger de er, og attråen kan forestille sig alle mulige forfængelige fornøjelser, men dømmekraften får stadig det sidste ord i enhver argumentation, og alle beslutninger bliver vejet for og imod. *Orkaner, jordskælv og vulkanudbrud kan vel overfalde mig*, men jeg følger den rolige lille stemme, som *tolker og dikterer samvittigheden*”’ (p. 231)	‘Panden erklærer: “Fornuften står fast og holder tømmerne, og hun vil ikke *lade følelserne bryde ud og drive hende til vildsomme afgrunde.* Nok kan **lidenskaberne** rase vildt som de sande hedninger, de er, og begæret kan forestille sig alle mulige forfængelige ting; men dømmekraften vil alligevel have det sidste ord i enhver diskussion og den afgørende stemme i enhver beslutning. *Kraftig blæst, jordskælv og flammer kan komme forbi*, men jeg vil følge vejledningen fra den lille stille stemme, der *fortolker det, som samvittigheden dikterer*”’ (p. 238)

Rochester imagines that the cast of Jane's forehead expresses that she will stay in control of things, no matter what primitive 'heathen' passions may rage inside her mind on a par with a wild, uncontrollable weather — she will obey the voice of conscience diligently. It is a key passage, but it has been severely abbreviated and adapted by Mikkelsen. This means that the word 'passions', this time in the plural, is only translated by Rohde and Pihl. And they both opt for 'lidenskaberne', which by now in the translations has proven to be their favourite option.

Interesting challenges are presented by, for instance, the personification of Jane's reason as sitting on a horse, which is imagined as an animal of wild feelings: 'she will not let the feelings burst away and hurry her to wild chasms'. The expression 'burst away' refers to a sudden and forcible break away or issuing forth, e.g., from confinement, or a sudden, violent letting-go of emotions. The path to 'wild chasms' refers to a deep cleft or gorge in the surface of the earth. Pihl translates the wild chasms into equivalent Danish words, but Rohde translates it into 'deep water'. I believe the chasms are important as stock props in tales of the Romantic sublime. When they are deleted in favour of the drowning metaphor, we are left with a less typical literary landscape of the period.

Other natural elements of the sublime, such as 'Strong wind, earthquake-shock, and fire may pass by' have also been translated differently. They are absent in Mikkelsen, but Rohde heightens the drama of natural disasters by representing them as 'Orkaner, jordskælv og vulkanudbrud kan vel overfalde mig' [hurricanes, earthquakes and volcano eruptions may overtake me]. As volcanos are oddly out of place in the Yorkshire scenery, they appear more cataclysmic than the intended fire in the source text. This effect is heightened because they also seem to seize her, not just to pass by, which, as in many of the examples above, turns Jane into a helpless victim. One guess is that Rohde has interpreted 'earthquake-shock and fire' as one event: a volcano eruption where fire is spurted out. Pihl, on the other hand, translates it more loyally as 'Kraftig blæst, jordskælv og flammer kan komme forbi' ['strong wind, earthquake, and flames may pass by'], and thus she preserves an instance of the fire leitmotif in the novel.

As for the still small inner voice of wisdom that interprets the dictates of conscience — which is in opposition to the passions raging within Jane — the two most recent translators have interpreted this differently. Pihl translates it more or less directly, but Rohde misses the point by saying that the small voice both interprets and dictates conscience. This gives us the impression that Jane's inner voice rules over her conscience, but it is in fact the other way round.

8.

Brontë	Mikkelsen	Rohde	Pihl
'I wrestled with my own resolution: I wanted to be weak that I might avoid *the awful passage of further suffering I saw laid out for me*; and Conscience, *turned tyrant*, held **Passion** by the throat, told her *tauntingly*, she had yet but dipped her dainty foot in the slough, and swore that with that arm of iron *he would thrust her down to unsounded depths of agony*.' (Ch. 27)	'Jeg rejste mig i pludselig rædsel over den kamp mellem samvittighed og **lidenskab**, som jeg følte, jeg ikke kunne komme udenom [this has been adapted, and the rest has been left out]' (p. 208)	'Jeg kæmpede med min egen beslutning. Jeg ønskede at være svag, så jeg kunne undgå *yderligere kvaler*. Samvittigheden *blev rasende* og greb **Lidenskaben** i struben og fortalte hende *vredt*, at med sin jernarm ville han *kaste hende i endnu kvalfuldere dybder*' (p. 346)	'Jeg kæmpede med min egen beslutning, jeg ønskede at være svag, så jeg kunne undgå den *yderligere lidelses rædselsfulde vej, som jeg så ligge udstrakt foran mig*; og Samvittigheden *blev en tyran* og holdt **Lidenskaben** i kvælertag, fortalte hende *spottende*, at hun hidtil kun havde dyppet foden i sumpen, og svor at han med sin jernarm *ville kaste hende ned i uanede dybder af kval*' (p. 353)

In the personification of a tyrant, the (male) iron fist of conscience now forcefully dictates Jane to hold her horses, as it were, and not let herself get swayed by her (female) passion for Rochester. If she crosses the line, she will go to hell. Jane longs to let herself be swayed to avoid the constant tug-of war between painful and pleasurable passion and wisdom, but the struggle must go on as she tries to be a good woman.

Once again the word 'passion' does not offer major obstacles in the Danish translations. It is translated into 'lidenskaben' as so many times before. It is the context that alters the various renditions. When it comes to 'the awful passage of further suffering I saw laid out for me', Rohde and Pihl are the only translators who dare translate this phrase. Rohde, however, is quickly done with the description of Jane's visualisation of a passage of suffering. And here 'passage' may refer to a route, a transit or a voyage, or an opening into suffering. Rohde translates it into 'yderligere kvaler' ['further woe'] which completely rids the description of its metaphorical understanding of Jane's possible transformation as a journey. Pihl translates it more directly into 'yderligere lidelses rædselsfulde vej, som jeg så ligge udstrakt foran mig' ['further suffering's terrible road, which I saw lying stretched out in front of me'].

Jane feels that her conscience is like a tyrant. Again, Rohde does not adhere directly to the source text but represents her conscience becoming furious ('blev rasende'). This is not exactly the same as feeling that conscience has become one's ruler as it dictates in a powerful manner what Jane has to do. Pihl, instead, renders the translation faithfully, describing her conscience as a tyrant. The tyrant's taunting voice is translated into 'vredt' ['angrily'] by Rohde, which echoes the furious conscience. Pihl translates it into 'spottende' which is a more direct translation. The depths of agony where Jane may be hurled by the iron arm of conscience are 'unsounded', i.e., deep, unfathomed. Rohde translates this into 'endnu kraftfuldere dybder' ['even more powerful depths'], and Pihl translates it into 'uanede dybder af kval' ['unknown depths of agony']. Thus again Pihl seems more faithful to the exact wording of the novel — and in this case also more lyrical — than Rohde, who translates more freely.

Passion and Warmth

In Chapter 27 we reach a key passage where Rochester confesses his true love for Jane. Here, the word 'passion' takes on the complex meanings of movement as suggested by Cassin and Sissa previously.

9.

Brontë	Mikkelsen	Rohde	Pihl
'[Rochester] I think you good, gifted, lovely: *a fervent, a solemn* **passion** is conceived in my heart; it leans to you, draws you to my centre and spring of life, *wraps my existence about you, and, kindling in pure, powerful flame, fuses you and me in one.'* (Ch. 27)	'Jeg anså dig for god, højt begavet og en elskelig karakter [the rest has been left out and this sentence merges with the next paragraph]' (p. 218)	'Jeg synes, du er vidunderlig, begavet og yndig. Mit hjerte er fyldt af *en brændende oprigtig* **lidenskab**. Mit hjerte søger dit, drager dig til mig og *omslynger dig med mit liv, og en ren blussende kraftig flamme smelter dig og mig til ét'* (p. 366)	'Jeg anser dig for at være god, begavet, yndig; *en brændende, en højtidelig* **lidenskab** er undfanget i min [*sic*] hjerte; den hælder mod dig, trækker mig til mit livs centrum og kildevæld, *smyger min væren omkring dig; og antændt i en ren, stærk flamme smelter den dig og mig til ét'* (p. 374)

Rochester describes his feelings for Jane: 'a fervent, a solemn passion' breeds in his heart. Once again, the Danish authors all translate this new elevated 'passion' into 'lidenskab'. It is simply impossible to find a word that brings with it the new connotations of warmth and gentleness. So we must look for the contextual choices made in translation. The 'fervent' and 'solemn' nature of this passion takes on different forms. The adjective 'fervent' refers to a great sense of warmth or intensity, and 'solemn' means that it is grave, sober, earnest. Rohde interprets the passion as 'brændende, oprigtig' ['burning, sincere'] and Pihl as 'brændende, højtidelig' ['burning, solemn']. Even though they differ, they both agree on representing the fire motif in this situation.

The burning nature of Rochester's passion is repeated in the subsequent poetic expression of his love: it 'wraps my existence about you, and, kindling in pure, powerful flame, fuses you and me in one'. His fire reaches out for Jane and pulls her close to him so that they may burn and blend as one single flame, encapsulating both pain and pleasure, passion and wisdom. This merging of the two souls is described as both pure and powerful, thus fusing the purity and the passion of the Victorian and Romantic spirit of the time — or the beautiful and the sublime. Only the recent translators retain this passage. Rohde's version can be back-translated into the following: 'embraces you with my life, and a pure burning powerful flame melts you and me into one'. Pihl writes: 'clings my being around you, and lit in a pure, strong flame it melts you and me into one'. In this way, they both preserve the novel's crucial duality of passivity and action, immaculacy and potency.

Conclusion

My philological analysis — i.e., asking what does this word mean? — has attempted to capture the Danish understandings of the word 'passion' in *Jane Eyre*. Aslaug Mikkelsen noted how this particular word and trait in Jane's complex character was a key concern in the scope of the novel. And since the Danish direct equivalent may not be used about negative movements of the soul, in contrast to English, a Danish translator may have to use the Danish synonym 'lidenskab' or else entirely rephrase matters. Correspondingly, it turns out from these selected, but representative, examples that when passion is linked to wrath, either the Danish word 'lidenskab' is chosen, or the passages are explicated by way of paraphrase. When passion is linked to love in its multiple forms, more strategies may be used. Either it can be rendered as 'passion' or 'lidenskab', or it may be translated by way of the translator's interpretation of the word as something romantic rather than emotionally dramatic and forceful. When passion is presented in opposition to wisdom, the word 'lidenskab' tends to be used. The same is the case with the ultimate link to warmth and gentleness. So, 'lidenskab' is clearly the preferred word overall, even though it had a late and unwelcome inclusion in the Danish language. It has simply grown more versatile than 'passion'. The word 'passion' is only used in the one instance of 'grande passion ... passion'. One possibility is that translators have chosen to use 'lidenskab' consistently, roughly as Brontë uses 'passion', to cover a similar range. Another might be that they have wanted to avoid using 'passion' precisely because it looks the same as the English word, so it would not feel like enough of a translation.

This small spectrum of solutions decided upon by the translators has far-reaching implications — not only for the word itself, but for the contextual meanings of the selected cases in point. In the majority of the examples, the Danish Jane is represented as a victim of strong, often negative, emotions that are out of her control. As Sissa said, in European languages the vocabulary of feelings is organized around, on the one hand, turbulence and transformation; in short, activity; and on the other hand, exposure and agitation; in short, passivity. In this respect, the Danish Jane Eyre comes across as more passive than active. And thus, paradoxically, the movements of passion in the Danish translations may seem more under control than the raging passions in the source text. In this way, the translators sit firm and hold the reins. They do not let the Danish versions burst away and hurry them to wild chasms. Their judgment has the last word.

Works Cited

Translations of *Jane Eyre*

Brontë, Charlotte, *Jane Eyre*, trans. by Aslaug Mikkelsen (Aarhus: Det Danske Forlag, 1971).

——, *Jane Eyre*, trans. by Christiane Rohde (Copenhagen: Lindhardt og Ringhof, 2015).

——, *Jane Eyre*, trans. by Luise Hemmer Pihl (Mørke: Grevas Forlag, 2016).

Other Sources

Cassin, Barbara (ed.). *Dictionary of Untranslatables: A Philosophical Lexicon* (Princeton: Princeton University Press, 2014).

Klitgård, Ida, 'Translation, Adaptation or Amputation? Arctic Explorer-Writer-Anthropologist Peter Freuchen's Little-Known Danish Translation of Moby Dick', *Across Languages and Cultures*, 16 (2015), 119–41, https://doi.org/10.1556/084.2015.16.1.6

Mikkelsen, Aslaug, *Foregangskvinder I engelsk litteratur* (Copenhagen: P. Haase & Søns Forlag, 1942).

Reynolds, Matthew, *Translation: A Very Short Introduction* (Oxford: Oxford University Press, 2016).

Schwarz, Helge L., Marianne Holmen, Freddy Volmer Hansen, Egon Foldberg, and Ida Klitgård, *Engelsk-dansk ordbog* (Copenhagen: Munksgaard, 1996).

Sissa, Giulia, 'Pathos/perturbatio', in *Dictionary of Untranslatables: A Philosophical Lexicon*, ed. by Barbara Cassin (Princeton: Princeton University Press, 2014), pp. 745-49.

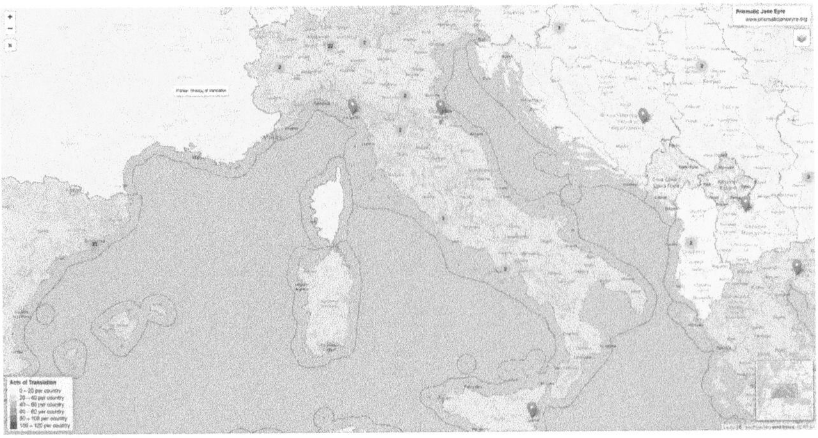

The World Map
https://digitalkoine.github.io/je_prismatic_map
Created by Giovanni Pietro Vitali;
maps © Thunderforest, data © OpenStreetMap contributors

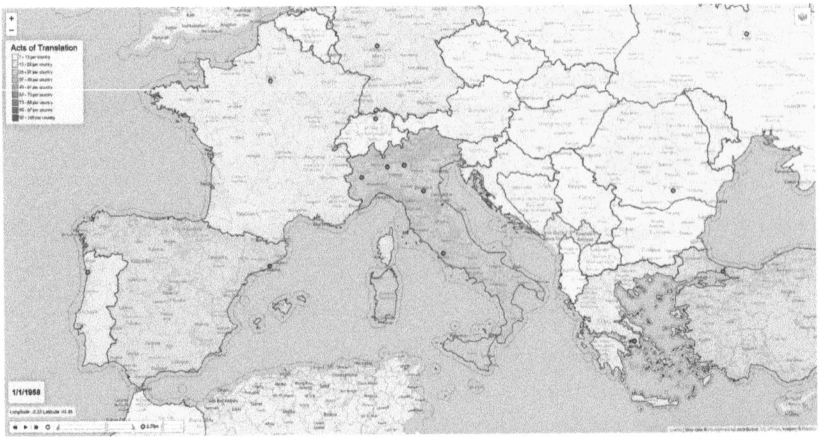

The Time Map
https://digitalkoine.github.io/translations_timemap
Created by Giovanni Pietro Vitali and Simone Landucci;
© OpenStreetMap contributors, © Mapbox

11. Emotional Fingerprints
Nouns Expressing Emotions in *Jane Eyre* and its Italian Translations

Paola Gaudio

Introduction

Good writers are able to make every novel a unique representation of emotional dynamics, a cognitive roller-coaster of emotional ups and downs, as their empathic readers let the narrator take their hand and lead them across the universe of narrative fiction, which is fraught with emotions of all kinds. If this is possible, it is because writers have a finely-tuned knack for triggering vicarious emotions by using mere words, and they can differentiate very subtly among the vast array of emotions made available by their language.

Charlotte Brontë had a natural talent for story-telling, and her passionate nature ensured that her novels should be imbued with a wide range of emotions.[1] It has been almost two centuries now since her novel was first published, and the main reason it is still such an engaging story today is because of the stirring emotions that capture

1 That Charlotte Brontë was passionate is testified by her numerous biographers, and it is no coincidence that one of them, Lyndall Gordon, entitled her work *Charlotte Brontë: A Passionate Life* (London: Vintage, 1994). Charlotte Brontë's passionate nature can also be appreciated in her early writings, with the intricate adventures of the heroes and heroines of the Glass Town Saga and the Kingdom of Angria — the latter presumably named after the pirate Angria (Christine Alexander, *The Early Writings of Charlotte Brontë*, Oxford: Basil Blackwell, 1983, p. 113), and homophonic of the adjective *angrier*. The reception of *Jane Eyre* itself, which 'impressed its original readers as nothing less than revolutionary' (Patsy Stoneman, *Charlotte Brontë Transformations: The Cultural Dissemination of* Jane Eyre *and* Wuthering Heights, London: Prentice Hall/Harvester Wheatsheaf, 1996, p. 7) bears testimony to the passionate nature of its author as it inevitably reflects onto her narratives.

https://doi.org/10.11647/OBP.0319.17

its readers.[2] Even though times change and cultures develop in different directions, it seems that we share an inner core of empathy that responds emotionally to the (mis)adventures of others' lives, even though these go back two hundred (or even two thousand for that matter) years and never really existed beyond the written page. Sometimes emotions can be stirred without even labelling them as such in the narrative, and a love scene can be such even if the word *love* is not mentioned at all. It is, however, revealing to observe the type and frequency of those that are actually present in a canonical novel such as *Jane Eyre* and see how these relate to the characters and the plot. High frequency of use is certainly a key indication of the relevance of a certain emotion in the novel. Sometimes, however, what is missing can be equally revealing in terms of themes and narrative style, hence it deserves some attention. The first part of this essay addresses the issue of frequency of emotion-nouns in *Jane Eyre* and, on the basis of all the data collected, insights are then gained and discussed with regard to the themes of the novel and the depiction of its characters.

As one of the classics of nineteenth-century British literature, *Jane Eyre* is not published in English only, but in a variety of languages, including Italian. The second part of this study is an attempt to understand whether and to what degree the quantitative pattern of emotion-nouns in the original English text is duplicated in Italian. In order to do this, the consistency in the frequency of Italian emotion-nouns is first analysed across the translations, then compared with the findings from the English original. Lexical correspondences between English and Italian emotion-nouns are thus identified and quantified.

The results of the quantitative analysis of emotion-nouns in individual translations are finally presented in the form of what are

2 This is how Vinaya, a reviewer on Goodreads.com, aptly puts it: 'I have read *Jane Eyre* a million times, but I never tire of the story. Every time I reach the scene where she professes her love to Mr Rochester, I come out in goosebumps. Every single time. [...] There is a reason why millions of people the world over remember and revere a book written a hundred and fifty-odd years ago while the bestsellers of our times slip quickly and quietly from our memories. *Jane Eyre* is more than just a beautiful book about a love story that transcends all boundaries; it is a testament to the power of pure emotion, that can be felt through the ages and across all barriers of time and culture'; from 'Five Reasons Why *Jane Eyre* Would Never Be a Bestseller in Our Times' (December 2010), https://www.goodreads.com/review/show/135963844?book_show_action=true&from_review_page=1

called *emotional fingerprints*, i.e., a visual representation, by means of word clouds, of the emotions characterizing each version of the book.

The following methodological section accounts for the selection method of emotion-nouns in the English original as well as in the translations; it sheds light on the issues deriving from the syntactic asymmetries between English and Italian in relation to this specific research; and it outlines some basic statistical principles applied to process the data and gain insight on the whys and hows of the results obtained.

Methodology

The approach to the study of emotions in both *Jane Eyre* and its translations is definitely inductive, meaning that the intent of this research is not to implement any specific theory on quantitative or comparative analysis of data, on inter- or intra-linguistic translation, or on the definition of emotions, but rather to observe the specificities of the texts at stake and, from that, apply any type of analysis, statistical or otherwise, that appears to be able to point to patterns and anomalies. Such an approach applies to all sections of this essay, from the discussion of emotions in the source text, to the analysis of the corpora, to the statistical data, and to the creation of emotional fingerprints in the form of word clouds as a means to visually represent the idiosyncrasies of the translations. What I am offering is neither a close reading nor a distant one: it is rather a transversal reading through the eyepiece of emotional lexis across the source text and its translations.

Given the general framework, a few words on how the data was gathered, and on the constraints, limitations, and exceptions that were necessary to lend rigour and coherence to the results, are certainly required. The English source text is the 2006 Penguin edition of *Jane Eyre* in .txt format. The Italian texts are .txt files of eleven translations, ranging from the anonymous one published back in 1904 to the more recent 2014 translations by Stella Sacchini and by Monica Pareschi.

The focus being emotions, namely an over-reaching, all-encompassing category, the object of study is narrowed down to the lexical items expressing emotions and belonging in the syntactic category of nouns, whether singular or plural. As a consequence, it should be noted that, because of this, the figures underestimate emotions expressed by other parts of speech (adjectives, adverbs, and verbs). Thus, in the case of *love*, only the noun is considered, but not any of its derivatives *loved, loving, lovingly, loveless, unloving, lovely*, etc. The same applies to other words such as *fear, hope* or *wish*, and their derivative forms (*fearful, fearless, fearlessly*, etc.). Even though there is a quantitative underestimation of emotions as expressed by other parts of speech, the peculiarity of nouns is that, whilst verbs describe what someone does,[3] adverbs indicate how something is done, and adjectives are descriptive by nature, nouns are either subjects or objects of any statement, they either originate the predicate or complete it: in other words, they constitute the fulcrum of any utterance by naming what topic is being discussed, evoked, analysed, commented upon, or dealt with — either by the characters themselves or by the fictional narrator — and this is precisely why a noun-focused analysis cannot be overlooked. There is another reason for narrowing down the field of research to nouns only, and it has to do with the comparability — or lack thereof — of syntactic roles between languages. Even excluding all derivatives, in English the word *love* can still be a noun or a verb; not so in Italian, where there are two different words: the noun *amore*, and the verb *amare*. *Sorpresa*, in contrast, can be both a verb and a noun, just like its English equivalent *surprise*. Yet, there is no correspondence between the syntactic roles of these verb-forms in the two languages: *surprise* is either present indicative, imperative, or exhortative in English; but in Italian, the verb-form *sorpresa* is a female singular past participle, also used as adjective. Similarly, *sorprese* and *surprises*, in addition to being plural nouns, can also be verbs in the third person singular: in Italian, *sorprese* is a past tense (*lei mi sorprese*, 'she surprised me'), in English it is a present ('she surprises me'). Like the singular *sorpresa*, its plural *sorprese* can be past participle and adjective too — not so in English.

Syntactic ambiguity applies to words which can be nouns, verbs, or adjectives:[4] *love* and *loves*, *doubt* and *doubts*, *regret* and *regrets*, etc. these can all be either nouns or verbs — which is actually a common phenomenon. Therefore disambiguation is necessary. More in detail, plural nouns can be homonymous with a past participle or a

---

3 Not all verbs are dynamic, there are stative verbs too, but even these are predicative in nature.

4 Syntactic ambiguity also occurs between nouns and adverbs, as in 'today is a beautiful day', where *today* is a noun, and 'today it is going to rain', where *today* is an adverb. However, there is no such ambiguity in the nouns selected for this study.

second person singular of the verb in Italian; in English, they can be homonymous with a third person singular of the present indicative. Sometimes — not always — the ambiguity is symmetric and occurs in both languages: *desideri* and *desires*, *tormenti* and *torments* can all be either plural nouns or verbs (respectively, second person singular of the verbs *desiderare* and *tormentare* in Italian; third person singular of the verbs *to desire* and *to torment* in English).

For the corpora to be genuinely comparable, syntactic roles must not be mixed up. Following these adjustments, and since the scope of this study comprises exclusively nouns, each token should — ideally — have its equivalent in the translations. This latter claim however, is not at all a given since — as will be extensively shown — there are substantial variations in the translations, with certain emotion-nouns popping up a lot more often than in the original or disappearing altogether.

As to what constitutes an emotion and what not, the plethora of taxonomies of emotions varies greatly in the scientific world, depending on the aim of the classification and the perspective from which they are considered (psychological, cognitive, neurological, anthropological, etc.).[5] Things are complicated even further by the relationship between emotion and reading, which implies a different way of experiencing emotion, and which is based on empathy.[6] The aim of this essay is not, however, to recreate any taxonomy of emotions, neither it is to describe the dynamics at play between text and emotional reactions on the part of the readers. Since the approach is inductive, emotion theories such as Paul E. Griffiths's[7]

5 In his *Emotion. The Science of Sentiment* (Oxford University Press: Oxford, 2001), Dylan Evans provides a concise account of the main issues and traditional approaches to emotion.

6 See Maria Chiara Levorato, *Le emozioni della lettura* (Bologna: il Mulino, 2000), and Ed S. Tan, 'Emotion, Art and the Humanities', in *Handbook of Emotions*, 2nd edn, ed. by Michael Lewis and Jannete M. Haviland-Jones (New York and London: Guilford Press, 2000), pp. 116–34. Particularly interesting are the insights that have developed from affect studies on the relationship between emotions and literature: see *The Palgrave Handbook of Affect Studies and Textual Criticism*, ed. by Donald R. Wehrs and Thomas Blake (Cham: Palgrave Macmillan, 2017); whereas Patrick Colm Hogan's 'Affect Studies', in *Oxford Research Encyclopedia—Literature* (USA: Oxford University Press, 2016) provides an insightful description of the differences between affective science and affect theory, and of their relevance to literature.

7 Paul E. Griffiths, *What Emotions Really Are. The Problem of Psychological Categories* (Chicago and London: University of Chicago Press, 1997).

and Antonio Damasio's[8] have only worked as general guidelines in the initial approach to the source text. The inductive process that led to identifying the spectrum of emotion-nouns used by Charlotte Brontë in *Jane Eyre* took place by analysing the word-frequency list of the novel in English. The nouns that were thus recognized as expressing emotions in English have then paved the way to the identification of emotion-nouns in the Italian translations, whose word lists were also individually examined.

Etymologically, an emotion stirs something inside and, for the purposes of this study, it can be defined as whatever arises instinctively or spontaneously in the perceiver's consciousness following a stimulus. Such stimulus can range from an actual event to a mere mental image. An emotion is not the same as a physical sensation (feebleness, coldness, etc.), even though the two are closely related as emotions always involve some physical response like increased heart-beat or dilated pupils; and it is not a behaviour either (kindness, rudeness, etc.) even though behaviours are often either causes or consequences of an emotional response. Within this general framework, any noun which could arguably be considered some type of emotion was included in the selection. The word *emotion* itself has also been included in the research for obvious reasons of self-reference, along with its near-synonyms *passion*, *sentiment*, *sensation*, and *feeling*. It goes without saying that these words do not express any specific emotion themselves. However, their relevance stems from the purpose they serve of indicating that the semantic field of the portion of text in which they occur revolves indeed around emotions.

A broad parameter for the quantitative selection of the emotional lexis for the contrastive analysis is that, for a noun to be taken into consideration, it needs to have a frequency equal to or higher than ten occurrences, either in the source text or in one of the translations. There is one exception to this rule and it concerns the word *misery*, which was included because of its peculiarity, and which will be analysed in the section 'English–Italian equivalents and outliers'. Such inclusion does not skew the analysis, because the emphasis of the contrastive analysis is not so much on the quantitative identification of emotional-nouns in the novel — which is dealt with in the next section — but on the differences and similarities between source text

8 Antonio Damasio, *Descartes' Error: Emotion, Reason and the Human Brain* (London: Picador, 1994).

and target texts: thus, the addition of one more case simply makes the enquiry a little more extensive.

Once the data were gathered, statistics provided the tools necessary to gain insights on the results. At the basis of the statistical analysis there is the fundamental notion of the normal curve, which is a bell-shaped, symmetric curve representing a great part of natural and societal phenomena. The assumption is that, in the infinite world of possibilities offered by translation, the different translations of a word are normally distributed (i.e., their distribution follows the normal curve). The word *hate*, for example, is likely to be translated as *odio* by the vast majority of Italian translators and on most occasions. Some, however, will now and then translate it with *disprezzo* (contempt), *repulsione* (repulsion) or maybe omit it altogether, with frequencies which decrease as the target word becomes more and more unusual. In this research, the standard deviation (SD) measures the variability of the translations for each emotion-noun: if the standard deviation is low, there is greater consistency in how a word is translated, if it is high, there is little consistency in its translations. Z-scores represent the frequency of a certain value (in this case, the number of occurrences of an emotion-noun) expressed into standard deviations. The more a z-score is closer to zero, the more it approaches the mean, i.e., the more similar its frequency is to the average frequency of that same noun across the translations. Most values fall within the interval ±1 SD (i.e., their z-score is between –1 and +1). Values that fall outside this interval are considered outliers, if the values lie outside the interval ±2 SD, they are extreme outliers.

One more statistic that will be used is the standard error (SE), which is another measure of dispersion. In fact, in the analysis that follows, the standard error is a measure of dispersion of the distribution of standard deviations. In other words, the standard error tells us whether the variability observed per each emotion-noun in the eleven translations is normal or not. Since the standard error is basically just a type of standard deviation, the same rules apply, therefore values that fall outside the interval ±1 SE will be considered outliers; and those that fall outside the interval ±2 SE will be considered extreme outliers.

Hence, the present research shows which emotion-nouns are used with similar frequencies across the translations and which are not. The mean frequency of every Italian emotion-noun is then compared to the frequency of its usual equivalent in the English source text. This allows us to determine whether and to what extent there actually exists a correspondence between English and Italian emotion-nouns in *Jane Eyre*. Lastly, since z-scores measure how typical or unusual the frequency of an emotion-noun is, they will be the reference values used to recreate the emotional fingerprints of each translation in the final section.

Emotions in *Jane Eyre*

The list of nouns expressing emotions in the original English version of *Jane Eyre* is provided in Table 1. As can be seen at a glance, *love* ranks first (81 occurrences), *pleasure* second (78), *hope* third (57), *doubt* (52) fourth, and *fear* fifth (47). Overall, there are at least 78 types of emotions and an average of 30.3 tokens per chapter. The list, however, is not exhaustive, since it contains only the most frequent emotions (>10) and a selection of the lesser used ones, and does not account for those which occur only once, like *apprehension, disdain, envy, foreboding, tedium, trepidation,* etc. The number of nouns expressing emotions in *Jane Eyre* is therefore noteworthy, especially with regard to the sheer linguistic variety of the emotions Charlotte Brontë mentions in her narrative.

Emotion-noun	**Freq.**	**Emotion-noun**	**Freq.**
love	81	anguish	10
pleasure	78	disgust	10
hope	57	melancholy	10
doubt	52	jealousy	9
fear	47	anxiety	8
wish	35	impatience	8
pain	33	misery	8
affection	30	anger	7
passion	30	hate	7
delight	27	regret	7
solitude	25	woe	7
pride	24	concern	6
happiness	23	ire	6
pity	23	loneliness	6
courage	22	sadness	6
suffering	22	satisfaction	6
sympathy	22	scorn	6

Emotion-noun	Freq.	Emotion-noun	Freq.
joy	21	tenderness	6
excitement	18	repentance	4
emotion	17	wrath	4
grief	17	aversion	5
surprise	17	contempt	5
terror	17	distress	5
despair	16	indignation	5
shame	16	desperation	4
sorrow	16	hesitation	4
desire	14	agitation	3
fury	14	compassion	3
enjoyment	13	humiliation	3
horror	13	longing	3
curiosity	12	rage	3
disappointment	12	restlessness	3
dread	12	yearning	3
agony	11	bewilderment	2
gratitude	11	bitterness	2
mercy	11	fun	2
relief	11	torment	2
remorse	11	wretchedness	2
wonder	11		
admiration	10		

TOT Types:	78
TOT Tokens:	1,152
Mean:	14.8
SD:	15.4
Mean per chapter:	30.3
Word Count:[9]	58,598
Emotion-nouns %:	1.96

Table 1: Emotion-nouns in Jane Eyre

9 Does not include function words.

As to the ranking of individual emotions, *love* trumps them all — as any respectable Victorian female *Bildungsroman* is expected to do.

Pleasure is a bit more problematic. The first instinct would be to disregard it altogether because of its recurrent use in today's everyday language, which often has little to do with actual emotions and refers rather to fixed expressions like 'it's a pleasure to meet you' — which are commonly uttered even when the underlying emotion is closer to indifference or nuisance rather than true pleasure. However, on reading the various instances of *pleasure* in the novel, and given the extremely high frequency of the word itself, it cannot be altogether dismissed — at least not without first wondering whether or not it plays some significant role in *Jane Eyre*.

It does. Many instances of the word occur in relation to Rochester and refer either to his dissolute lifestyle prior to proposing to Jane, or to the pleasure both Rochester and Jane find in sharing each other's company. In all such cases it is evident that the word carries with it sensual rather than spiritual overtones. Still, the novel does not point to purely hedonistic quests, and those Jane Eyre narrates have also to do with small, everyday pleasures that derive, for example, from her enjoying Miss Temple's company in an otherwise hostile environment, from experiencing genuine sisterhood for the first time, or from running in the wind:

> [Miss Temple] kissed me, and still keeping me at her side [...] where I was well contented to stand, for I derived a child's pleasure from the contemplation of her face.[10]

> There was a reviving pleasure in this intercourse, of a kind now tasted by me for the first time — the pleasure arising from perfect congeniality of tastes, sentiments, and principles.[11]

> It was not without a certain wild pleasure I ran before the wind, delivering my trouble of mind to the measureless air-torrent thundering through space.[12]

Even when sensual in nature, the pleasures Jane craves are very much delimited by her sense of modesty, her rationality, and her greater intent to be an independent, self-respecting woman. She is in fact well aware of the dangers posed by the unrestrained pleasures Rochester himself succumbed to, that 'heartless, sensual pleasure — such as

10 *JE*, Ch. 8.
11 *JE*, Ch. 30.
12 *JE*, Ch. 25.

dulls intellect and blights feeling'.[13] And when he claims that, 'since happiness is irrevocably denied me, I have a right to get pleasure out of life: and I will get it, cost what it may', Jane's reply is: 'then you will degenerate still more, sir'.[14]

However, within the limits imposed extra-diegetically by Victorian values, and intra-diegetically by Jane's very nature, she herself gleefully and unhesitatingly appreciates the pleasures life can give, the 'so many pure and sweet sources of pleasure'[15] she is granted daily at Moor House, for example, or the short-lived pleasure of the conqueror's solitude she enjoyed when she stood up to Mrs Reed in chapter 2. Along the same lines, when St John proposes, she refuses to succumb to a life devoid of pleasures and filled with miseries only, because 'God did not give her [her life] to throw away'.[16]

Jane Eyre is thus a hedonistic quest to the extent that pleasure and love are the ultimate goals of any human being — unless it is St John, of course. His endgame is misery, to the point that not only does he willingly endure it — not unlike Helen Burns — but he actively pursues it. Yet even to him, in his eyes, suffering — and its siblings: endurance, perseverance, and restraint — become indeed pleasures, for it is them that allow him to actually enjoy life, giving it the meaning he craves and, ultimately, to be reunited with his beloved Jesus Christ.

Hence, considering the occurrence of individual emotions, it is *love* and *pleasure* that stand out the most, followed by *hope, doubt, fear*, and *wish.*

Things change a little if we pool together synonyms or near-synonyms (e.g., *pain* and *suffering, despair* and *desperation*), as well as lexical labels that refer to some common underlying emotion, even though there may be different nuances involved (e.g., *terror* is *fear* felt to the utmost degree; *affection* is a bland type of *love*, etc.). The more complex an emotion is, the more it shares traits with other emotions: *jealousy*, for example, which in the array stands for an independent category — like *courage, curiosity*, and *pride* — might easily be perceived as inherent in love and desire. This is why other similar groupings could certainly be created on the basis of perceived contiguity between emotions. The groupings suggested here are

13 *JE*, Ch. 20.
14 *JE*, Ch. 14.
15 *JE*, Ch. 30.
16 *JE*, Ch. 35.

represented in Figure 14, and they are labelled by the most frequent emotion within the sub-set:

- pleasure, happiness, joy, excitement, enjoyment, delight, relief, satisfaction, fun;
- love, affection, tenderness, gratitude, admiration;
- pain, suffering, grief, sorrow, agony, anguish, woe, misery, distress, torment;
- hope, wish, desire, longing, yearning;
- fear, terror, horror, dread, anxiety, concern, aversion, disgust;
- fury, anger, rage, ire, wrath, hate, scorn, contempt, indignation, bitterness;
- pity, mercy, sympathy, compassion;
- passion, emotion;
- shame, remorse, regret, repentance, humiliation;
- solitude, loneliness;
- melancholy, sadness, wretchedness, disappointment;
- surprise, wonder;
- doubt, hesitation, bewilderment;
- despair, desperation;
- impatience, restlessness, agitation.

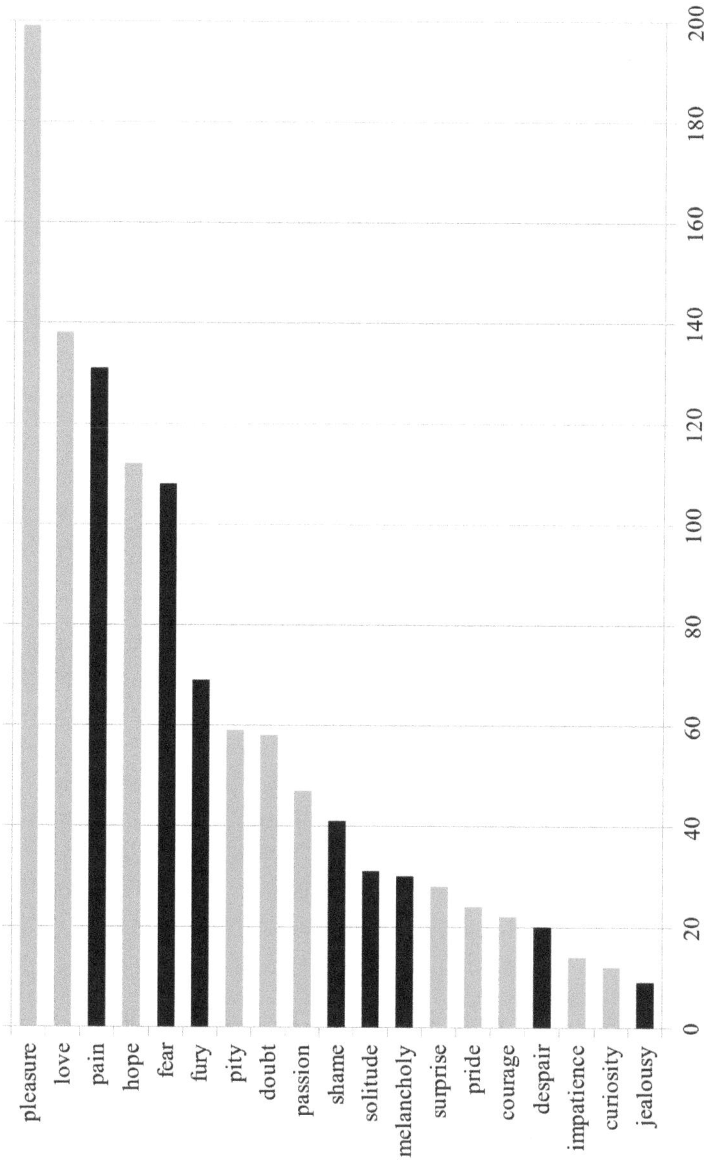

Fig. 14 Grouped emotions

A further differentiation is suggested by colour: positive emotions are represented in pink, negative emotions in black, mixed emotions in green. Like in any fairy tale, in *Jane Eyre* too, good triumphs over evil, as positive emotions grouped under the label *pleasure* are by far the most frequent ones, followed by *love* and competing closely with a long tail of negative and mixed emotions, making the battle even more engaging. If we pool all positive emotions (in pink, 449 occurrences) and all negative ones (in black, 439 occurrences), their frequency is roughly the same, with positive emotions exceeding the negative by only 10 points. It is even more interesting to notice that negative emotions are scattered among a greater variety of nouns (40 nouns in 8 groupings), whereas the range of nouns expressing positive emotions is much more limited (19 in 3 groupings). Even so, both *pleasure* and *love* still trump all other groupings — with an inversion if compared to the individual frequencies of Table 1.

Love ranks second then, and it is in good company, because its existential synonym — *pain* — ranks third by just a few occurrences. In Italian, *love* (*amore*) actually rhymes with *pain* (*dolore*), and they do tend to go hand in hand, as the latter swiftly replaces the former if its object is made unavailable for whatever reason. If *love* and *pain* belong in the realm of reality — albeit fictional — *hope* and *fear* are their parallels in the realm of possibility. *Hope* that difficulties will be surmounted eventually and that love, in whatever form, will conquer all; and *fear* that the positive emotions might be taken away and replaced by everlasting negative ones.

The words *hope*, *wish*, *desire*, *longing*, and *yearning* have been pooled together because they all indicate a void to be filled: from Jane's perspective it may be sexual desire for Rochester, but also a melancholic longing for the affection of a loving family, the material wish for food and shelter when she had neither, an intense desire for liberty or, were this not to be granted, at least for a new servitude:

> I desired liberty; for liberty I gasped; for liberty I uttered a prayer; it seemed scattered on the wind then faintly blowing. I abandoned it and framed a humbler supplication. For change, stimulus. That petition, too, seemed swept off into vague space. 'Then,' I cried, half desperate, 'grant me at least a new servitude!'.[17]

This desire to fill some existential void is naturally not peculiar to Jane, since it characterizes any existential quest — in fiction no less than in real

17 *JE*, Ch. 10.

life — and clearly affects other characters as well, from Helen's desire to forgive and accept, to John Reed's unquenchable thirst for vice, Eliza's wish for quiet and order, St John's visionary mission, and Rochester's predicament since before he met Jane (i.e., the difficulty he repeatedly experienced in his quest to find a soulmate able to fill his need for companionship in order to avert his deep-seated solitude). Even Bessie and Miss Temple are ultimately defined by their desire to have a family of their own, and finally embrace the love this entails.

Jane Eyre is therefore primarily a novel about pleasure, love, pain, hope, and fear, but it also concerns doubt, solitude, fury, pride, courage, and an amazing plurality of further emotions, whether considered individually or grouped as in Figure 14. These kinds of emotion are not at all dissimilar from those usually experienced, to varying degrees, in any ordinary life: their peculiarity in *Jane Eyre* lies in the unique entanglement provided by the plot and by the narrative skills of its author.

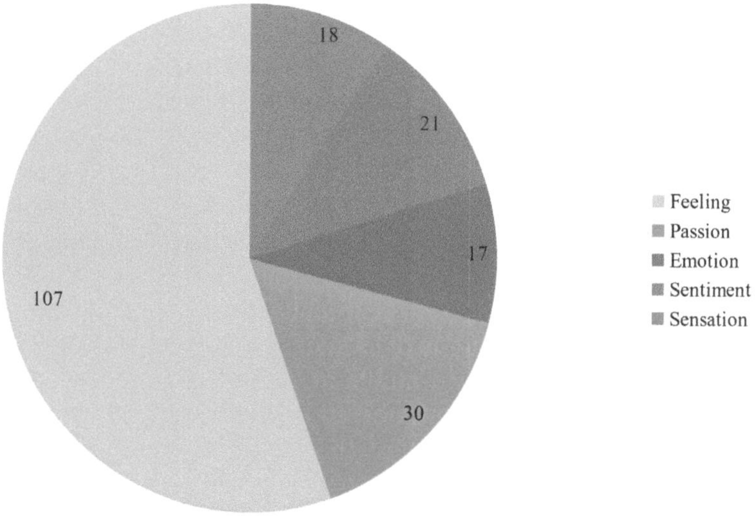

Fig. 15 Frequency of 'emotion' and its near-synonyms

As for the word *emotion* itself and its near-synonyms *feeling*, *sensation*, *passion*, and *sentiment*, they occur 193 times altogether (Figure 15) i.e., an average of 5 times per chapter and, together with the tokens in Table 1, they amount to 2.2 % of the total word-count (function words excluded).

That the noun *feeling* should be the one used the most is not surprising given its overarching meaning. A different matter is the word *passion*.

Hidden in its high frequency lurks a potentially disruptive challenge affecting the Victorian values of modesty and restraint. Even though not an emotion itself, passion works as an intensifier of emotions. If felt with passion — which etymologically derives from the Latin *patior*, to suffer, and thus indicates that the intensity of what is felt is such that it actually becomes painful — any emotion becomes excessive, uncompromising, difficult if not impossible to control — much less to suppress — and thus poses a genuine threat to the established order.

Emotion-Nouns in the Italian Translations

In an ideal — slightly boring — universe, each word would have its equivalent in any other language: the occurrences of, say, *love* would repeat themselves with the same frequency in all translations, in all languages — and the same would be true of any other noun, verb, adjective, etc. In an infinite number of translations, the distribution of occurrences of the equivalents of *love* would be normal, its variability extremely low (i.e., small standard deviation) and due to the occasional random error. The real world is of course a little more complicated. So it happens that such hypothetical equivalence tends to go awry. Not always, though. In the prismatic variability of translation, constants can still be identified.

These occur when the measure of variability of translation-equivalents is below average. From a statistical point of view, every distribution of values (in this case, the occurrence of emotion-nouns in Italian) varies to a certain degree from its mean. One of the possible measures of such variability is the standard deviation and its related z-score statistic. The observed minimum and maximum range of the standard deviation in the data gathered here is 0.8 and 20. The higher the standard deviation, the more the distribution varies (i.e., the frequency of the same emotion-noun varies across the translations); the lower the standard deviation, the less variable the distribution (i.e., there is more consistency in the frequency of the same emotion-noun in the translations). As to z-scores, these measure how far the variability of a certain value is from the average. In the following tables, z-scores refer to the standard error (SE), i.e., they indicate whether the standard deviation of a particular emotion-noun is higher (z-score >0) or lower (z-score<0) than the average standard deviation (z-score=0). High SE z-scores indicate that there is little or no consistency in the frequency with which an emotion-noun occurs across all translations; low SE z-scores indicate consistency, and SE z-scores equal to or close to zero indicate that the variability of that emotion-noun is around average.

The nouns in the table below therefore represent, in decreasing order, emotions whose frequency is most consistent across the translations,[18] with *rimorso* (remorse) ranking first. It will be noticed that the mean frequency of some of them is rather low: hence, by virtue of the scarcity of occurrences, their consistency is only partially significant. Of greater interest are those words whose mean frequency is relatively high, such as *felicità* (happiness, 37 occurrences on average), *disperazione* (despair/desperation, 23.2 occurrences on average) and *orgoglio* (pride, 20.4 occurrences on average), which appear with close to the same frequency in all translations: the frequency of — for example — *felicità* is exactly the same in Pozzo Galeazzi, Reali, D'Ezio and Sacchini (40), with the other translators using it slightly less, like Gallenzi (39), Déttore (36), etc., down to Pareschi, with her 32 occurrences, who therefore lowers the mean value a bit more. That SE z-scores should point to a lower-than-normal dispersion rate in the frequencies of *disperazione* (–0.60), *felicità* (–0.55), and *orgoglio* (–0.52), across the translations is significant precisely because of their relatively high frequencies.

The list of emotion-nouns that are consistently reproduced in all the translations are therefore listed in Table 2 below. Nouns with the highest mean frequencies are highlighted in grey:

	Emotion-noun	**Usual English equivalent**	**Mean**	**SD**	**SE z-score**
1	rimorso	remorse	11.8	0.8	–1.21
2	gelosia	jealousy	8.6	1.1	–1.13
3	commozione	stirring emotion	1.1	1.2	–1.10
4	agonia	agony	1.5	1.4	–1.03
5	rimpianto	regret	7.6	1.6	–0.99
6	delusione	disappointment	10.6	1.7	–0.95
7	ammirazione	admiration	13.5	1.8	–0.93
8	disprezzo	contempt	11.9	1.9	–0.91
9	infelicità	misery	2.8	1.9	–0.89
10	curiosità	curiosity	14.7	2.1	–0.85

18 Since the 1904 anonymous translation is semi-abridged, it was not included in these calculations so as to avoid that the distributions should be skewed.

	Emotion-noun	Usual English equivalent	Mean	SD	SE z-score
11	divertimento	fun	4.9	2.5	–0.72
12	impazienza	impatience	12.0	2.6	–0.70
13	disgusto	disgust	8.6	2.8	–0.65
14	odio	hate	12.9	2.8	–0.64
15	amarezza	bitterness	9.9	2.8	–0.64
16	malinconia	melancholy	7.7	2.9	–0.62
17	godimento	enjoyment	6.3	2.9	–0.61
18	delizia	delight	3.1	2.9	–0.60
19	disperazione	despair/desperation	23.2	2.9	–0.60
20	felicità	happiness	37.0	3.1	–0.55
21	sconforto	discouragement	2.4	3.1	–0.54
22	eccitamento/ eccitazione	excitement/ excitation	7.1	3.1	–0.54
23	preoccupazione	concern	7.7	3.2	–0.54
24	gratitudine	gratitude	12.5	3.2	–0.53
25	orgoglio	pride	20.4	3.2	–0.52
26	meraviglia	wonder	6.2	3.3	–0.50

Table 2: High consistency

At the other end of the spectrum, there are those emotions that do not have much consistency in the frequency with which they appear in each translation, and whose SE z-score is >0.5 (here it is nouns with the lowest mean frequencies that are highlighted in grey):

	Emotion-noun	Usual English equivalent	Mean	SD	SE z-score
1	ansia	anxiety	10.7	7.2	0.61
2	timore	dread	19.4	7.4	0.66
3	pietà	mercy	25.3	7.7	0.76
4	collera	choler/wrath	10.8	8.2	0.89
5	piacere	pleasure	86.8	8.3	0.92
6	simpatia	sympathy	15.5	8.6	1.00
7	amore	love	88.0	8.7	1.04
8	sofferenza	suffering	27.1	8.8	1.07

9	pena	pity	29.3	10.8	1.64
10	dubbio	doubt	48.7	13.0	2.25
11	gioia	joy	57.6	13.0	2.26
12	dolore	pain	39.8	13.6	2.43
13	paura	fear	81.2	20.0	4.26

Table 3: Low consistency

Unsurprisingly, their mean frequency is relatively high. Indeed, the correlation coefficient between frequencies and z-scores happens to be strongly positive (+0.7): in other words, emotion-nouns whose frequency is higher tend to have greater variability, and *vice versa*. That such correlation should only be strong and not perfect explains why even lower frequency words like *ansia* (anxiety, 10.7 occurrences on average) and *collera* (choler, 10.8 occurrences on average) make it among the least consistent ones (SE z-score >0.5), whereas the z-score of *amore* (love, 1.04 SE z-score), which has the highest mean frequency in the selection (88), is virtually identical with that of *simpatia* (sympathy, 1 SE z-score), whose frequency is much lower (15.5).[19]

One last case that is worth commenting on is the least consistent of all, *paura* (fear): its frequency in each translation varies so much that it is impossible to identify anomalies since there is no 'normal' value — even more so considering that its usual equivalent in the source text is used 47 times only, against a mean of 81 occurrences in the translations. As a matter of fact, the frequency of *paura* ranges

19 It needs to be pointed out that *simpatia* is not exactly the same as its English correspondent *sympathy*. They both share the same Greek etymology (*σὺν*, meaning 'with' and *πάθος*, 'passion'), but the Italian term — while still partially retaining the original meaning of 'compassion' — is used in everyday language to express congeniality. Clearly this explains the inconsistency in numbers. Of the 22 occurrences of *sympathy* in the source text, the Italian translations range from the 28 occurrences in Pozzo, to the mere 3 in D'Ezio. Further, there seems to be a temporal decrease in the use of *simpatia* on the part of the translators, as the highest frequencies can be observed in the oldest translations, those from the nineteen-fifties and seventies: Pozzo Galeazzi (28 occurrences), Spaventa Filippi (25), and Dettore (24). With Reali in 1996 (16 occurrences) and, even more, with Gallenzi in 1997 (8 occurrences), the use of the term decreases dramatically, probably due to a parallel and gradual diversion of the word from its etymological meaning. Lamberti's is the only twenty-first-century translation where *simpatia* occurs over 20 times, but this exception is due to the strong influence Spaventa Filippi's translation exerted on Lamberti's (see Essay 2 above, 'Who Cares What Shape the Red Room is?').

from the 55 occurrences in Pareschi to more than twice as many in D'Ezio (119). The impact this has on the texts is clearly remarkable as Pareschi's turns out to be a *fear*less translation, whereas D'Ezio's is a *fear*ful one.

English-Italian Equivalents and Outliers

The preceding section focuses on the consistency of nouns expressing emotions throughout the translations. This section relates such data to equivalent emotion-nouns in the original anglophone version of *Jane Eyre*.

If it is true that there is no exact correspondence between lexical systems of different languages, it is also true that, especially when languages have common origins — as is the case with English and Italian — overlapping areas do exist and can be quite broad, with occasional equivalence. *Terror*, for example, finds its unquestionable counterpart in the Italian *terrore*, there is no tangible difference between *solitude* and *solitudine*, *remorse* and *rimorso*: their substantially similar semantic core is proven not simply by common etymologies — as etymologically equivalent words can gain completely different meanings across languages and develop, for example, into false friends like *actually* and *attualmente* (currently), *eventually* and *eventualmente* (possibly) — but by semantic and pragmatic similarities. Indeed, even when etymologically different, there is no doubt that the overwhelmingly most common equivalent of *love* in Italian is *amore*, *hate* corresponds to *odio*, *bitterness* to *amarezza*, and so on and so forth. Appendix 1, at the end of this paper, provides the English-Italian equivalents for each emotion-noun as found in *Jane Eyre*. For the most part, the parameters applied for identifying such correspondences are: etymology, semantics, and pragmatics. Sometimes, however, the equivalence is not straightforward: in those cases, equivalence was determined on the basis of similarity in frequency and, in exceptional cases, similar words had to be grouped[20] — so it happens that *rage* was pooled with *anger*, *excitement* with *excitation*, *solitude* with *loneliness*, etc.[21]

20 All details are in Appendix 1, along with the measure of the correspondence expressed in z-scores.

21 Since English was influenced by both Latin and Germanic languages, the co-existence of synonyms or near-synonyms deriving one from Latin, the other from Germanic (as in *solitude* and *loneliness*) is not unusual.

In spite of these adjustments, which are due to the inevitable differences in languages, there is a hefty equivalence in the frequency of most emotion-nouns between the anglophone version of *Jane Eyre* and the Italian ones. In light of the many factors that can and do affect the outcome of translations, which never turn out to be identical, such consistencies are indeed noteworthy. Here is a selection of the most similar emotion-nouns in terms of frequency:

English	**Italian**	**Eng. Freq.**	**Mean It. Freq.**
contempt/scorn	disprezzo	11	11.9
despair/desperation	disperazione	20	23.2
emotion	emozione	17	17.8
fury	furia	14	13.6
hope	speranza	57	60.1
jealousy	gelosia	9	8.6
love	amore	81	88
passion	passione	30	27.6
regret	rimpianto	7	7.6
relief	sollievo	11	10.2
remorse	rimorso	11	11.8
shame	vergogna	16	16.1
solitude/loneliness	solitudine	31	31.3
terror	terrore	17	17.3

Table 4: Similar frequencies of emotion-nouns

It could certainly be argued that there might be discrepancies between source text and target texts as to where these words occur, because each occurrence of every Italian emotion-noun is not necessarily a systematic translation of always the same corresponding English word. The most representative such case is possibly *gioia*, which can translate a whole range of emotions besides *joy*, including *delight*, *enjoyment* and *bliss* (see infra). This, however, does not invalidate the evidence that the impact these emotion-nouns have on the English novel as a whole is nearly identical to the one they have on the Italian translations, because what matters is the sheer amount of emotion-nouns rather than their displacement. Besides, the evidence pointing to substantial consistency is impressive.

There are exceptions, though, and they can be even more revealing than the consistencies. It could be assumed that the lack of correspondence in the frequency of emotion-nouns would concern special cases with little or no semantic overlap between English and Italian words. That is not the case. Surprisingly, common emotions such as *agony, courage, excitement, happiness, joy,* and the above-mentioned *bitterness* and *hate* — which all find ready-to-use equivalents in Italian — are substantially inconsistent. In Table 5, the inconsistency between English and Italian emotion-nouns is expressed in z-scores: when z-score is >+2, the emotion is under-represented in the translations, when it is <–2, it is over-represented. These reference values indicate that the frequency with which they occur in *Jane Eyre* is higher or lower than 95% of all other values in the normal distribution — which makes them truly exceptional. Table 5 also shows the mean difference between the mean frequency of the emotion in the Italian translations and its English equivalent in the original text:

English	Italian	JE Z-score	Mean difference
delight	delizia	8.2	–23.5
excitement/excitation	eccitamento/eccitazione	3.8	–12.2
agony	agonia	6.6	–9.0
enjoyment	godimento	2.3	–6.4
misery	infelicità	2.7	–5.5
hate	odio	–2.1	5.7
bitterness	amarezza	–2.8	7.4
affection	affetto	–2.1	8.7
sadness	tristezza	–2.3	11.5
courage	coraggio	–2.4	14.1
happiness	felicità	–4.5	14.1
joy	gioia	–2.8	36.6

Table 5: Emotion-nouns whose frequency in Italian is not consistent with the source text

Figure 16 further elaborates the data by representing English occurrences as reference point (zero on the Y axis) and the bars indicating the difference between the frequency of emotion-nouns in the translations and the frequency of corresponding emotion-nouns in the source text (which is given in parentheses).

Thus, *delight* and *excitement* appear much less in Italian (as *delizia* and *eccitamento*) than in the original (on average –23.5 and –12.2 times respectively). Likewise, *agony*, *enjoyment*, and *misery* do not occur in Italian as often as in English. In Stella Sacchini's and Bérénice Capatti's translations, for example, *agony* is never used, whereas in the original there are 11 such occurrences. A close reading of the text reveals that, for example, Sacchini tends to systematically translate *agony* with *angoscia* or also *miserie* (miseries), but never with its closer equivalent *agonia*. Bars above zero indicate that the opposite is true: *hate*, *bitterness*, *affection*, *sadness*, *courage*, *happiness*, and *joy* are to be found much more in the translations than in the original text. Among these, the frequency of *joy* is outstanding. Its frequency in Italian (*gioia*) is higher by up to 61 occurrences (in Luisa Reali). This means that Italian readers' general impression of the novel will be a lot more *joy*ful than it is for readers of the English text.

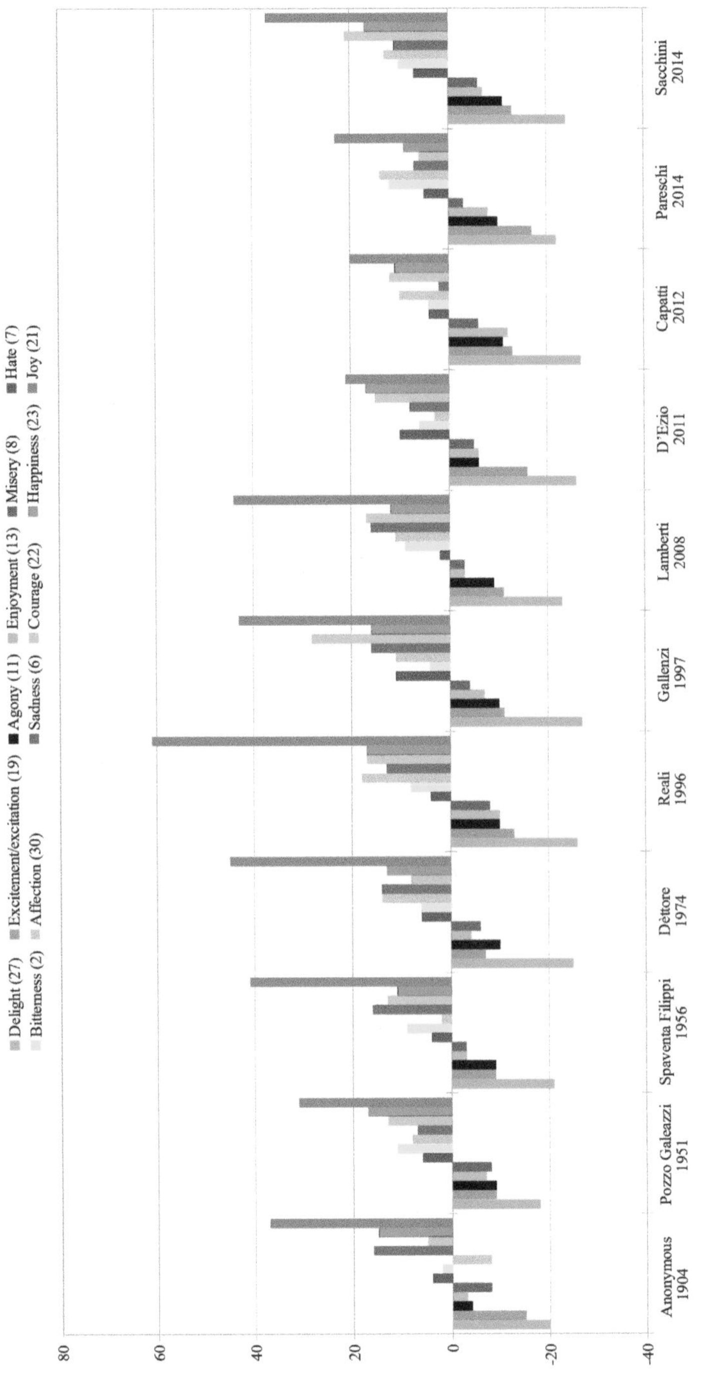

Fig. 16 Difference in frequency of emotion-nouns in English and Italian

At this point it remains to be seen what happens to those emotions that tend to disappear from the translations or pop up where there is no trace of them in the original. Let us consider *joy*, which is the most extreme case of asymmetry, and see the reasons why there are so many instances of *gioia* in the Italian translations.

Reali uses the word *gioia* 82 times, whereas in English there are only 21 occurrences of *joy* — four times as many as in the original. On a closer reading of the occurrences within the text, it transpires that *gioia* works as a *passe-partout* word to be used here and there every time the translator finds it suitable: in particular, it appears that Reali systematically uses *gioia* to translate *delight* (as a matter of fact, Reali never uses its corresponding *delizia* at all):

> it is my *delight* to be entreated[22]

> È una *gioia* per me sentirmi pregare[23]

> I permitted myself the *delight* of being kind to you[24]

> Mi concessi la *gioia* di essere gentile con te[25]

This thus explains, on the one hand, the remarkably high frequency of *gioia* in Reali, as the 27 occurrences of the word *delight* add to the frequency of *joy* (21) in the source text; and, on the other hand, why the word *delight* is under-represented in Italian.

The following examples are from Dèttore's translation instead. As in Reali, here too *joy* is nowhere to be found in the original:

> I seemed to distinguish the *tones* of Adèle, when the door closed.[26]

> mi parve distinguere le grida di *gioia* di Adèle, quando la porta venne chiusa.[27]

> Oh, it is *rich* to see and hear her![28]

> Oh, non è una *gioia* vederla e udirla?[29]

---

22 *JE*, Ch. 24.
23 Charlotte Brontë, *Jane Eyre*, trans. by Luisa Reali, with an Introduction by Franco Buffoni (Milano: Mondadori, 1996), p. 309. Hereafter 'Reali'.
24 *JE*, Ch. 27.
25 Reali, p. 371.
26 *JE*, Ch. 12.
27 Charlotte Brontë, *Jane Eyre*, trans. by Ugo Dèttore, with an Introduction by Paolo Ruffilli (Milano: Garzanti, 1974, 1995), p. 140. Hereafter 'Dèttore'.
28 *JE*, Ch. 24.
29 Dèttore, p. 317.

> I have at last my nameless *bliss*: As I love — loved am I![30]
>
> Raggiunto ho infine la mia *gioia* infinita: Amare... essere amato.[31]
>
> and my eyes seemed as if they had beheld the fount of *fruition*.[32]
>
> e gli occhi sembravano aver contemplato la fonte della *gioia*.[33]

The one systematic tendency that can be appreciated in Dèttore lies in the translation of *enjoyment* with *gioia* (even the example above, concerning *fruition*, is a reflection of such tendency, as the obsolete Middle English meaning of *fruition* is indeed *enjoyment*):[34]

> Much *enjoyment* I do not expect in the life opening before me.[35]
>
> Non mi aspetto molta *gioia* dalla vita che mi si apre dinanzi.[36]
>
> It is not like such words as Liberty, Excitement, *Enjoyment*.[37]
>
> [...] non è davvero come Libertà, Esultanza e *Gioia*.[38]

To the outliers in Figure 16 must be added the noun *infelicità*, which deserves some attention. It is the only case included in the selection of emotion-nouns to be used less than 10 times, either in the translations or in the source text. As a matter of fact, its usual English equivalent, *unhappiness*, is never used by Charlotte Brontë in *Jane Eyre*. Yet, it pops up here and there across the translations, with up to 5 occurrences (in Lia Spaventa Filippi, Luca Lamberti, and Monica Pareschi — while Giuliana Pozzo Galeazzi and Luisa Reali remain faithful to the original and never mention it). *Infelicità* is the opposite of *felicità*, just as *unhappiness* is the opposite of *happiness*, but Charlotte Brontë prefers using *misery*, never *unhappiness*. *Misery* occurs 8 times in English and it can surely be translated as *miseria* (there are actually several such

30 *JE*, Ch. 24.

31 Dèttore, p. 322.

32 *JE*, Ch. 24.

33 Dèttore, p. 303.

34 See 'fruition, *n.*', *OED*, https://www.oed.com/view/Entry/75089

35 *JE*, Ch. 31.

36 Dèttore, p. 423. Reali too translates this occurrence of *enjoyment* with *gioia* ('Non mi aspetto molte *gioie* dalla vita che mi si apre davanti'; see Reali, p. 422).

37 *JE*, Ch. 10. Even though there are several instances in both Déttore and Reali of *enjoyment* being translated with *gioia*, it is not always the case. This very line is translated by Reali as 'non come le parole Libertà, Vitalità, *Godimento*'(Reali, p. 98) — with *godimento* as a more straightforward correspondent for *enjoyment*.

38 Dèttore, p. 103.

occurrences in the translations), but the Italian word — not unlike the English one, only to a much greater extent — tends to be associated with a condition of destitution or poverty (therefore not an emotion), and this is why it happens that some Italian translators express the emotion of feeling miserable with *infelicità*, thus reserving the use of *miseria* to refer to the condition of poverty. Besides, as is well known, unhappiness is not necessarily associated with destitution — albeit just moral — and may befall anyone, even the rich and wealthy, or the otherwise non-destitute.

That *unhappiness* is nowhere to be found in the source text may be surprising, but it is not uncommon, since the word itself is sparsely used in other nineteenth-century novels as well: it appears only twice in Jane Austen's *Pride and Prejudice*, in William Thackeray's *Vanity Fair*, and in Charles Dickens's *Oliver Twist*; it is also never mentioned by Charlotte Brontë's sisters Anne in *The Tenant of Wildfell Hall*, and Emily in *Wuthering Heights*.

Emotional Fingerprints

The lexical idiosyncrasies of the translations in relation to the number and frequency of outliers is visually represented by means of word clouds constituting the emotional fingerprint of each translation. The aim of the previous sections was to identify those emotion-nouns that are consistently reproduced in the target texts, those that are not, and what emotions differ quantitatively the most in relation to the source text. This section revolves instead around the identification of outliers in each translation, so as to characterize them on the basis of their idiosyncrasies. Such idiosyncrasies are the actual emotional fingerprints of the translations, making them unique and distinguishable from all the others, and affecting the emotional impact of the novel on its readers. All translations have some emotional fingerprint: this is revealed by identifying and visualizing[39] the extent to which the emotion-nouns that are used by a specific translator differs from the source text and from all other translations. The translation's emotional fingerprint is therefore not a mere representation of the most frequent emotion-nouns, because it reveals what emotions set

39 An online word cloud generator, WordClouds.com, was used for the creation of the emotional fingerprints, which were subsequently fine tuned in Adobe Photoshop. https://wordclouds.com/

that particular translation apart from the others, hence making it one of a kind.

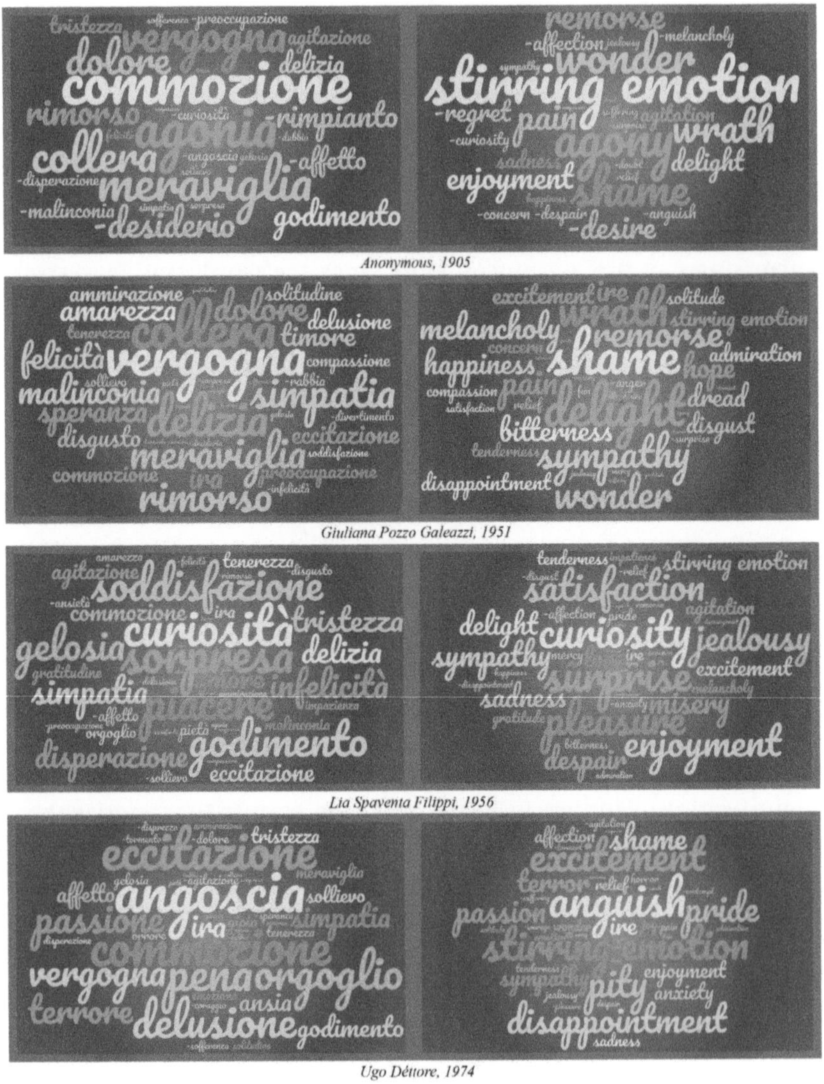

Fig. 17 Emotional fingerprints (i)

Luisa Reali, 1996

Alessandro Gallenzi, 1997

Luca Lamberti, 2008

Marianna D'Ezio, 2011

Fig. 18 Emotional fingerprints (ii)

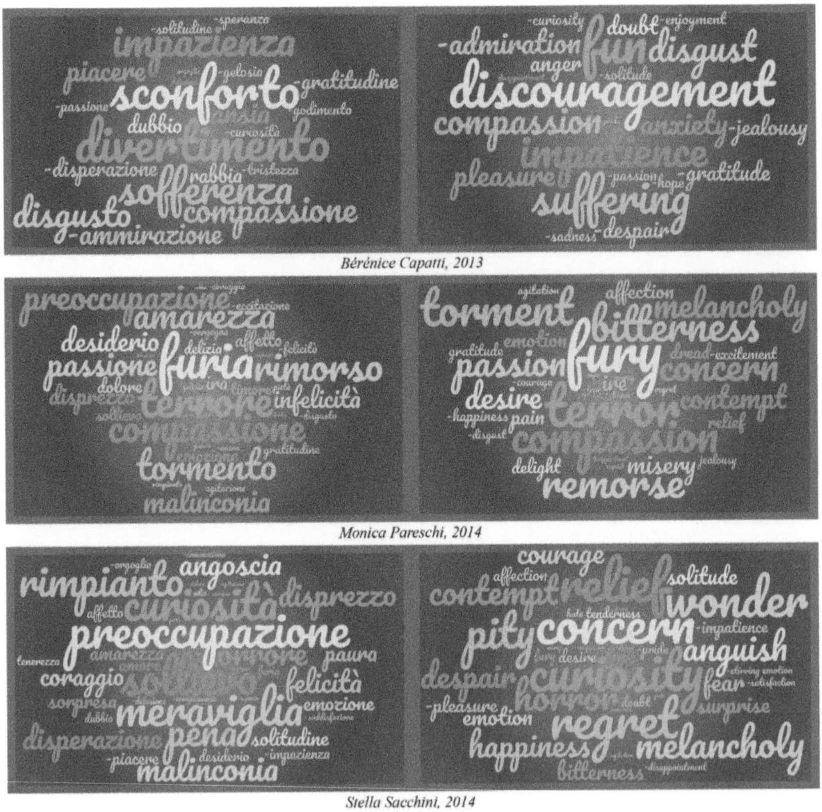

Fig. 19 Emotional fingerprints (iii)

The statistics used as a basis for creating emotional fingerprints are emotion-nouns' z-scores, calculated with reference to the mean and standard deviation of the distribution of each emotion-noun in the source text as well as in the translations. For an emotional fingerprint to be significant, it is not necessary that there should be outliers: even where all emotions are within the norm (their variability from the mean is non-remarkable), it is revealing to appreciate the idiosyncrasies of the translations, as the values fed to the cloud generator are based on the individual emotions' z-scores in each translation. They include all z-scores >+0.1 (which indicate that the noun is used more than average). Yet, since a translation's emotional fingerprint can also be characterized by low frequencies of certain emotions, these are likewise comprised in the cloud, with the ten lowest z-scores (i.e., the words that are used the least) coloured in grey and preceded by a minus sign. As in the previous sections, emotion-nouns lying outside the range mean ±2 standard deviations — i.e., whose z-score is either >+2 or <–2 — are considered extreme outliers.

Whenever the use of a certain item is particularly recurrent, it sticks out more. In the emotional fingerprints, the bigger the word, the more unusual it is — with the most unusually frequent words popping out with greater visibility and flashy colours, as opposed to the colour of the unusually infrequent ones, which is always grey.[40]

Translator	**Extreme outliers**	
	In excess	**In dearth**
Anonymous	*agonia* (agony), *collera* (wrath), *commozione* (stirring emotion), *dolore* (pain), *meraviglia* (wonder), *vergogna* (shame)	*affetto* (affection), *amarezza* (bitterness), *angoscia* (anguish), *curiosità* (curiosity), *desiderio* (desire), *disperazione* (despair), *dubbio* (doubt), *malinconia* (melancholy), *preoccupazione* (concern), *rimpianto* (regret), *sorpresa* (surprise)
Pozzo Galeazzi	*delizia* (delight), *vergogna* (shame)	*rabbia* (rage)
Spaventa Filippi	—	—
Dèttore	—	—
Reali	*dubbio* (doubt), *orrore* (horror)	—
Gallenzi	*agitazione* (agitation), *coraggio* (courage)	
Lamberti	—	—
D'Ezio	*agonia* (agony)	—

40 Besides grey, the palette comprises 8 colours: yellow is assigned to the most unusually frequent words, followed — in descending order — by magenta, fuchsia, green, light blue, orange, purple, and pink. The sequence of colours then repeats itself down to the least unusually frequent word. Words with similar frequencies are sorted alphabetically in English, and coloured accordingly. The Italian fingerprints follow the same colouring sequence as in English.

Translator	**Extreme outliers**	
	In excess	**In dearth**
Capatti	*divertimento* (fun), *sconforto* (discouragement)	*ammirazione* (admiration), *disperazione* (despair), *gelosia* (jealousy), *gratitudine* (gratitude), *solitudine* (solitude).
Pareschi	*furia* (fury), *terrore* (terror)	—
Sacchini	—	—

Table 6: Extreme outliers (for complete data see Appendix 2)

The 1904 anonymous translation is a semi-abridged one, therefore it is unavoidable that some nouns should be fewer than average.[41] In this case, then, outliers by dearth are not really significant as their lower frequency may be due to the text being abridged. For the very same reason, the anonymous translator's outliers in excess are particularly remarkable. Those which are used with unusual frequency are: *agonia* (agony), *vergogna* (shame), *meraviglia* (wonder), *collera* (wrath), *dolore* (pain), and, above all, *commozione* (stirring emotion) — whose z-score is a good +9.27. *Stirring emotion* is a label used here for a word that does not have a ready equivalent in English, and which the anonymous translator uses 12 times, i.e., once every three chapters on average. *Commozione* means being stirred or touched, often to tears, sometimes out of joy, sometimes out of grief — hence, *stirring emotion* seems to be its closest equivalent. The anonymous translator is not the only one to use *commozione*, as Pozzo Galeazzi (2), Spaventa Filippi (2), Dèttore (3), and Reali (2) use it too, albeit with a much lower frequency. From the gathered data, it can be evinced that there is a temporal decrease in its use, as it disappears altogether from Gallenzi's 1997 translation onward.[42] In the translations that did use it, the words *commozione* and *emozione* are equivalents of the same word *emotion*, even though their meaning — in current Italian — is

41 See Chapter 1 above for discussion of this translation, including its debt to the 1854 French translation by Noëmi Lesbazeilles-Souvestre.

42 As with *sympathy* (see note 19), the one exception is Lamberti's 2008 translation, with its 2 occurrences of *commozione*, but it bears little relevance because Lamberti was remarkably affected by Spaventa Filippi's translation and it is therefore no coincidence that, in his translation, *commozione* is used twice.

not at all interchangeable, as *commozione* is a hyponym of *emozione*. That the 1904 translation should be one of a kind is consistent with its publication date — which certainly sets its language apart from the more recent translations — and is also compatible with the tendency this translator shows to omit whole sentences, which again is in line with the higher occurrence of negative outliers. With such a tendency to abridge, the higher frequency of positive outliers really stands out — as can be appreciated by observing its emotional fingerprint (see Figure 17).

Moving on to the second most emotionally peculiar translation, Capatti's, there are here seven outliers: two in excess (*divertimento, sconforto*) and five in dearth (*ammirazione, disperazione, gelosia, gratitudine, solitudine*). Among these, the most remarkable is the frequent use of *sconforto* (discouragement), a word which is barely used by all other translators (Pozzo, Reali, Lamberti, and D'Ezio use it just once, Déttore, Pareschi, and Sacchini twice, Gallenzi three times), or never at all (anonymous, Spaventa Filippi), but which Capatti repeats 11 times. The higher frequency of such word is to be explained in several ways. A couple of occurrences, for example, are the result of the nominalization of adjectives:

> All I see has made me thankful, not *despondent*.[43]
>
> Tutto ciò che vedo mi ha fatto provare gratitudine e non *sconforto*.[44]
>
> the most troubled and *dreary* look.[45]
>
> uno sguardo pieno di ansia e *sconforto*.[46]

In this latter case, two pre-modifiers (the past-participle 'troubled', and the adjective 'dreary') are replaced by post-modifying nouns (*ansia e sconforto*). Capatti uses *sconforto* also when translating 'dejection' (3 occurrences), usually in the expression 'to sink into dejection' or simply 'to sink' (1), where *sconforto* clearly constitutes an over-interpreting addition:

> my heart again sank[47]

43 *JE*, Ch. 31.
44 Charlotte Brontë, *Jane Eyre*, trans. by Bérénice Capatti (Milano: Rizzoli, 2013), p. 510. Hereafter 'Capatti'.
45 *JE*, Ch. 19.
46 Capatti, p. 286.
47 *JE*, Ch. 3.

il mio cuore sprofondò nuovamente nello *sconforto*.[48]

[I] sank into inevitable *dejection*[49]

sprofondavo nello *sconforto*[50]

sank with *dejection*[51]

sprofondato nello *sconforto*.[52]

The remaining occurrences of *sconforto* variously translate *distress* (2), *depression* (1), and *damp* (2).

After the anonymous translator's and Capatti's, third in order of peculiarity is Pozzo's translation, with three extreme outliers, two of which are in excess (*vergogna* and *delizia*) and one in dearth (*rabbia*). The rest of the translations have only a couple of extreme outliers each, or none at all — which points to a substantial uniformity in the use of emotion-nouns across the Italian translations. Among the extreme outliers, Reali's repetitive use of the word *dubbio* (doubt, 77 occurrences) is particularly striking as it concerns a highly variable word (the anonymous translation and hers are in fact the only translations to have extreme outliers in highly variable distributions). Also, the increase in frequency of such a word in the other translations, which can be observed after hers was published, might be due to an influence she might have exerted on them by virtue not only of her skills as translator but also of her renowned publisher Mondadori (Gallenzi's 1997 translation came out just a few months after Reali's and was probably not affected at all): be that as it may, the frequency of the word *dubbio* in all subsequent translations is >40, whereas before 1996 it was always <40.

As a conclusion to this section, the emotional fingerprint of Charlotte Brontë's *Jane Eyre* (Figure 20) is a suggestive way to summarize what it feels like to read her novel in its original form rather than in translation.

48 Capatti, p. 25.
49 *JE*, Ch. 22.
50 Capatti, p. 348. The adjective *inevitable* is omitted in the translation.
51 *JE*, Ch. 32.
52 Capatti, p. 519.

Fig. 20 Emotional fingerprint of Charlotte Brontë's *Jane Eyre*

Conclusion

Analysing emotions in fiction is a mammoth task. Novels play with emotions by definition — or else they would be non-fictional pieces of writing. Simply differentiating between what expresses an emotion and what does not is in itself problematic. Comparing patterns of emotional lexis in the original as well as in eleven translations is even harder.

The first challenge of this study was to define a methodology aimed at isolating a significant portion of emotionally relevant items in the source and target texts. This portion was defined as lexical labels expressing emotions, and falling into the category of singular and plural nouns.

The second challenge was to rank the relevance of such lexis in *Jane Eyre* as originally written by Charlotte Brontë, in English. In order to do that, it was not only the mere frequency of individual words that was considered, but — wherever possible — similar emotions were pooled together so as to account for the reading experience, regardless of subtle differentiations in the use of synonyms or near-synonyms (e.g., *despair, desperation*). It goes without saying that a close reading of all 78+ emotions would comprise an analysis of nearly every single sentence of the novel — which is why the focus was limited to pointing out a few outstanding cases: *love, pain, pleasure, hope, fear, wish,* and *passion.*

The third challenge was to compare the emotional lexis in the original with that of the translations. The first step in the comparison procedure was to analyse the frequency of emotion-nouns in the translations so as to assess their consistency — or lack thereof. The findings show a general homogeneity in the frequency of most emotion-nouns, with *rimorso* (remorse) ranking first for consistency and *disperazione* (despair), *felicità* (happiness), and *orgoglio* (pride) sticking out for greater relevance given their relatively high frequency. At the other end of the consistency spectrum, there are *gioia* (joy), *dolore* (pain), and *paura* (fear), the latter showing a most impressive level of variability among the translations. The focus was then shifted to the similarity in frequency between the Italian emotion-nouns and their corresponding English ones, revealing them to be substantially similar in most cases, with virtually identical frequency in emotion-nouns such as *contempt* and *disprezzo, emotion* and *emozione, fury* and *furia, jealousy* and *gelosia,* along with several more pairs. Exceptions to the many and substantial English-Italian equivalents are a handful of emotion-nouns whose differences are illustrated in Figure 16, with *delight* (*delizia*) and *joy* (*gioia*) being, respectively, the most under-represented and the most over-represented emotion-noun in the translations.

Finally, the emotional fingerprint of each translation was the ultimate challenge, as its goal is to summarize in one image the peculiarities of something as complex as the emotional dimension of different translations of the same text. To this purpose, the use of word clouds has proven to be effective.

There are still questions that remain to be answered. Among these, there is one which is not explicitly addressed by this transversal reading of the novel, but which the emotional fingerprints silently point to: besides the usual factors influencing translatorial outputs — such as time period, intended readership, ideology, or gender — what specifically accounts for the degrees of variability and idiosyncrasies in the representation of emotions? Surely it must be a reflection of the translators' psyche, of their subjectivity as individuals, of their poetics as writers.

Works Cited

Edition and Translations of *Jane Eyre*

Brontë, Charlotte, *Jane Eyre*, ed. with an Introduction and Notes by Stevie Davies (London: Penguin 2006).

——, *Jane Eyre o le memorie di un'istitutrice*, 2 vols., trans. by anonymous (Milano: Fratelli Treves, 1904).

——, *Jane Eyre*, trans. by Giuliana Pozzo Galeazzi, with an Introduction by Oriana Palusci (Milano: Rizzoli, 1951, 1997).

——, trans. by Lia Spaventa Filippi, with an Introduction by Giuseppe Lombardo (Roma: Newton & Compton, 1956, 2002).

——, trans. by Ugo Dèttore, with an Introduction by Paolo Ruffilli (Milano: Garzanti, 1974, 1995).

——, trans. by Luisa Reali, with an Introduction by Franco Buffoni (Milano: Mondadori, 1996).

——, trans. by Alessandro Gallenzi (Milano: Frassinelli, 1997).

——, trans. by Luca Lamberti, with an Introduction by Carlo Pagetti (Torino: Einaudi, 2008).

——, trans. by Marianna D'Ezio (Firenze: Giunti Editore, 2011).

——, trans. by Bérénice Capatti (Milano: Rizzoli, 2013).

——, trans. by Monica Pareschi (Milano: Neri Pozza, 2014).

——, trans. by Stella Sacchini, with an Afterword by Remo Ceserani (Milano: Feltrinelli, 2014).

Other Sources

Alexander, Christine, *The Early Writings of Charlotte Brontë* (Oxford: Basil Blackwell, 1983).

Damasio, Antonio, *Descartes' Error: Emotion, Reason and the Human Brain* (London: Picador, 1994).

Evans, Dylan, *Emotion: The Science of Sentiment* (Oxford: Oxford University Press: 2001).

Gordon, Lyndall, *Charlotte Brontë: A Passionate Life* (London: Vintage, 1994).

Griffiths, Paul E., *What Emotions Really Are: The Problem of Psychological Categories* (Chicago and London: University of Chicago Press, 1997).

Hogan, Patrick C., 'Affect Studies', in *Oxford Research Encyclopedia of Literature* (USA: Oxford University Press, 2016), http://doi.org/10.1093/acrefore/9780190201098.013.105

Levorato, Maria Chiara, *Le emozioni della lettura* (Bologna: il Mulino, 2000).

Stoneman, Patsy, *Brontë Transformations: The Cultural Dissemination of Jane Eyre and Wuthering Heights* (London: Prentice Hall/Harvester Wheatsheaf, 1996).

Tan, Ed S., 'Emotion, Art and the Humanities', in *Handbook of Emotions*, 2nd edn, ed. by Michael Lewis and Jeannette M. Haviland-Jones (New York and London: Guilford Press, 2000), pp. 116–34.

Vinaya, 'Five Reasons Why Jane Eyre Would Never Be A Bestseller in Our Times' (December 2010), https://www.goodreads.com/review/show/135963844?book_show_action=true&from-review_page=1

WordClouds.com (Vianen: Zygomatic, 2003–2020), https://www.wordclouds.com/

Wehrs, Donald R. and Thomas Blake (eds.), *The Palgrave Handbook of Affect Studies and Textual Criticism* (Cham: Palgrave Macmillan, 2017), http://doi.org/10.1007/978-3-319-63303-9

Appendices

(1) English-Italian emotion-nouns.

(2) Italian emotion-noun frequency and z-scores.

Appendix 1: English-Italian Emotion Nouns[53]

English	Italian	Eng. freq.	It. mean freq.	It. SD	Eng. z-score
affection	affetto	30	40.4	5.0	–2.092
agitation	agitazione	3	7.4	3.7	–1.193
agony	agonia	11	1.5	1.4	6.626
bitterness	amarezza	2	9.9	2.8	–2.815
admiration	ammirazione	10	13.5	1.8	–1.967
love	amore	81	88.0	8.7	–0.805
anguish/distress	angoscia	15	20.1	5.6	–0.910
anxiety	ansia	8	10.7	7.2	–0.377
wrath/choler	collera	5	10.8	8.2	–0.709
stirring emotion	commozione	0	1.1	1.2	–0.919
compassion	compassione	3	10.4	4.1	–1.798
courage	coraggio	22	37.0	6.3	–2.372
curiosity	curiosità	12	14.7	2.1	–1.312
delight	delizia	27	3.1	2.9	8.176

53 In this table, z-scores range from –4.477 ('happiness') to +8.176 ('delight'). Z-scores equal to zero indicate perfect correspondence between the frequency of a word in the original English text and in its Italian translations (e.g.: 'ire' and '*ira*'). Values between –1 and +1 (e.g., 'anxiety' and '*ansia*', z-score –0.377) indicate a substantial — yet not perfect — correspondence in their frequency, with normal variability (i.e., the frequency of the English word lies within ±1SD from the mean of the frequency of its correspondent word in Italian). Z-scores lower than –1 indicate that the frequency of the English word (e.g., 'impatience') is remarkably lower than in Italian, therefore the translations over-represent that emotion-noun as compared to the source text. Conversely, z-scores higher than +1 indicate that the word (e.g., 'misery') is used a lot more frequently in the source text than in the translations, which therefore under-represent it.

English	Italian	Eng. freq.	It. mean freq.	It. SD	Eng. z-score
disappointment	delusione	12	10.6	1.7	0.817
desire/wish[54]	desiderio/voglia	60	61.7	5.1	–0.335
disgust	disgusto	10	8.6	2.8	0.508
despair/ desperation	disperazione	20	23.2	2.9	–1.090
contempt/scorn	disprezzo	11	11.9	1.9	–0.486
fun	divertimento	2	4.9	2.5	–1.153
pain/grief	dolore	50	39.8	13.6	0.752
doubt	dubbio	52	48.7	13.0	0.255
excitement/ excitation	eccitamento/ eccitazione	19	7.1	3.1	3.786
emotion	emozione	17	17.8	5.7	–0.142
happiness	felicità	23	37.0	3.1	–4.477
fury	furia	14	13.6	5.4	0.074
jealousy	gelosia	9	8.6	1.1	0.372
joy	gioia	21	57.6	13.0	–2.820
enjoyment	godimento	13	6.3	2.9	2.304
gratitude	gratitudine	11	12.5	3.2	–0.473
impatience	impazienza	8	12.0	2.6	–1.549
misery	infelicità	8	2.8	1.9	2.691
ire	ira	6	6.0	3.6	0.000
melancholy	malinconia	10	7.7	2.9	0.802
wonder	meraviglia	11	6.2	3.3	1.458
hate	odio	7	12.9	2.8	–2.102
pride	orgoglio	24	20.4	3.2	1.124
horror	orrore	13	11.5	3.7	0.400
passion	passione	30	27.6	5.5	0.433

54 Also includes *craving* (5), *longing* (3) and *yearning* (3).

English	Italian	Eng. freq.	It. mean freq.	It. SD	Eng. z-score
fear	paura	47	81.2	20.0	–1.711
pity	pena	23	29.3	10.8	–0.584
pleasure	piacere	78	86.8	8.3	–1.066
mercy	pietà	11	25.3	7.7	–1.853
concern	preoccupazione	6	7.7	3.2	–0.537
anger/rage	rabbia	10	11.9	5.4	–0.353
remorse	rimorso	11	11.8	0.8	–1.014
regret	rimpianto	7	7.6	1.6	–0.380
discouragement	sconforto	0	2.4	3.1	–0.766
sympathy	simpatia	22	15.5	8.6	0.760
satisfaction	soddisfazione	6	12.6	3.8	–1.747
suffering/sorrow	sofferenza	38	27.1	8.8	1.237
solitude/ loneliness	solitudine	31	31.3	5.5	–0.055
relief	sollievo	11	10.2	4.3	0.185
surprise	sorpresa	17	12.1	4.3	1.152
hope	speranza	57	60.1	4.6	–0.670
tenderness	tenerezza	6	13.4	4.5	–1.635
terror	terrore	17	17.3	6.1	–0.049
dread	timore	12	19.4	7.4	–1.005
torment	tormento	2	10.0	5.3	–1.512
sadness	tristezza	6	17.0	4.8	–2.277
shame	vergogna	16	16.1	3.3	–0.030

Appendix 2: Italian Emotion-Noun Frequency and Z-Scores[55]

	Anonymous		Pozzo		Spaventa		Dèttore		Reali		Gallenzi		Lamberti		D'Ezio		Capatti		Pareschi		Sacchini	
	z-score	freq.	z-score	freq.	z-score	freq.	z-score	freq.	z-score	freq.	z-score	freq.	z-score	freq.	z-score	freq.	z-score	freq.	z-score	freq.	z-score	freq.
affetto	-3.701	22	-0.483	38	-1.690	32	0.724	44	1.529	48	0.121	41	0.121	41	-1.489	33	-0.080	40	0.724	44	0.523	43
agitazione	0.976	11	-0.108	7	0.705	10	-1.464	2	-0.922	4	2.061	15	0.434	9	0.163	8	-0.651	5	0.434	9	-0.651	5
agonia	3.836	7	0.349	2	0.349	2	-0.349	1	-0.349	1	-0.349	1	0.349	2	2.441	5	-1.046	0	-0.349	1	-1.046	0
amarezza	-2.102	4	1.104	13	0.392	11	-0.677	8	0.036	10	-1.390	6	0.392	11	-0.677	8	-1.390	6	1.461	14	0.748	12
ammirazione	-0.281	13	0.843	15	0.281	14	0.281	14	-0.281	13	0.843	15	0.281	14	0.843	15	-2.529	9	-0.281	13	-0.281	13
amore	-0.690	82	-0.230	86	1.035	97	-0.345	85	1.035	97	-1.496	75	1.265	99	0.345	91	-1.150	78	-1.035	79	0.575	93
angoscia	-2.515	6	-0.731	16	0.161	21	1.944	31	-0.375	18	0.339	22	-0.018	20	-1.088	14	-1.445	12	0.161	21	1.052	26
ansia	-1.075	3	-0.377	8	-1.214	2	0.879	17	1.996	25	0.042	11	-1.075	3	-0.656	6	0.879	17	0.042	11	-0.516	7
collera	2.838	34	1.981	27	0.147	12	0.269	13	1.248	21	-1.076	2	0.147	12	-0.587	6	-1.199	1	-0.587	6	-0.342	8
commozione	9.104	12	0.752	2	0.752	2	1.587	3	0.752	2	-0.919	0	0.752	2	-0.919	0	-0.919	0	-0.919	0	-0.919	0
compassione	0.146	11	0.632	13	-0.826	7	-0.583	8	-1.069	6	-0.826	7	0.146	11	0.875	14	1.118	15	1.604	17	-1.069	6
coraggio	-1.581	27	-0.316	35	-0.316	35	-1.107	30	0.316	39	2.055	50	0.316	39	0.000	37	-0.474	34	-1.423	28	0.949	43
curiosità	-2.284	10	0.146	15	1.604	18	-0.340	14	0.146	15	-0.340	14	-0.340	14	-0.340	14	-1.798	11	-0.340	14	1.604	18
delizia	1.334	7	2.018	9	0.992	6	-0.376	2	-0.718	1	-1.061	0	0.308	4	-0.718	1	-1.061	0	0.650	5	-0.034	3
delusione	-0.934	9	0.817	12	-0.934	9	1.401	13	1.401	13	-0.350	10	-1.518	8	-0.350	10	0.234	11	0.234	11	-0.934	9
desiderio/voglia	-4.273	40	-1.319	55	0.059	62	-0.138	61	0.847	66	-1.319	55	-0.926	57	1.437	69	-0.335	60	1.241	68	0.453	64
disgusto	-1.306	5	0.871	11	-1.306	5	-0.218	8	0.871	11	0.871	11	-1.306	5	0.145	9	1.233	12	-1.306	5	0.145	9
disperazione	-2.452	16	-0.068	23	0.954	26	0.272	24	-0.068	23	-0.068	23	0.954	26	-0.068	23	-2.452	16	-0.409	22	0.954	26
disprezzo	-0.486	11	-1.025	10	0.054	12	-1.025	10	-0.486	11	-1.025	10	1.673	15	0.054	12	-0.486	11	1.133	14	1.133	14

55 Extreme outliers in excess (>+2 SD) are highlighted in green, in dearth (<–2 SD) are highlighted in pink.

	Anonymous		Pozzo		Spaventa		Dèttore		Reali		Gallenzi		Lamberti		D'Ezio		Capatti		Pareschi		Sacchini	
divertimento	-1.551	1	-1.551	1	-0.358	4	0.040	5	0.437	6	0.040	5	0.040	5	-0.358	4	2.426	11	-0.358	4	-0.358	4
dolore	2.741	77	1.267	57	-0.648	31	-1.312	22	-0.354	35	0.309	44	-0.427	34	1.857	65	-0.722	30	0.678	49	-0.648	31
dubbio	-2.138	21	-0.749	39	-0.749	39	-0.903	37	2.185	77	-0.980	36	-0.594	41	0.255	52	0.795	59	0.332	53	0.409	54
eccitamento/ eccitazione	-0.986	4	0.923	10	0.923	10	1.559	12	-0.350	6	0.286	8	0.286	8	-1.305	3	-0.350	6	-1.623	2	-0.350	6
emozione	-0.318	16	-1.026	12	-0.318	16	0.389	20	1.627	27	-1.911	7	0.035	18	0.212	19	-0.495	15	0.743	22	0.743	22
felicità	0.320	38	0.959	40	-0.959	34	-0.320	36	0.959	40	0.640	39	-0.640	35	0.959	40	-0.959	34	-1.599	32	0.959	40
furia	-1.218	7	-0.295	12	-0.295	12	-0.111	13	-0.480	11	-0.664	10	-0.295	12	0.812	18	-1.402	6	2.288	26	0.443	16
gelosia	0.372	9	0.372	9	1.302	10	0.372	9	0.372	9	-0.558	8	0.372	9	0.372	9	-2.419	6	0.372	9	-0.558	8
gioia	0.031	58	-0.431	52	0.339	62	0.647	66	1.880	82	0.493	64	0.570	65	-1.202	42	-1.279	41	-1.048	44	0.031	58
godimento	1.272	10	-0.103	6	1.272	10	0.929	9	-1.135	3	-0.103	6	1.272	10	0.241	7	-1.823	1	-0.447	5	-0.103	6
gratitudine	-0.473	11	0.158	13	0.473	14	-0.158	12	1.419	17	-0.473	11	0.473	14	0.473	14	-2.365	5	0.473	14	-0.473	11
impazienza	-0.775	10	0.000	12	0.387	13	0.000	12	-1.162	9	0.000	12	0.387	13	0.775	14	1.936	17	-0.775	10	-1.549	8
infelicità	-1.449	0	-1.449	0	1.139	5	-0.414	2	-1.449	0	0.621	4	1.139	5	0.104	3	-0.414	2	1.139	5	-0.414	2
ira	-1.405	1	1.124	10	0.562	8	1.124	10	-1.686	0	-0.843	3	0.000	6	-1.124	2	0.000	6	1.124	10	-0.281	5
malinconia	-2.684	0	1.150	11	0.453	9	0.105	8	-0.244	7	-1.638	3	-0.244	7	-0.592	6	-1.289	4	1.150	11	1.150	11
meraviglia	2.976	16	1.458	11	-0.061	6	0.547	8	-0.972	3	-1.579	1	-0.668	4	0.547	8	-0.364	5	-0.364	5	1.458	11
odio	-0.677	11	0.036	13	-0.677	11	0.036	13	-0.677	11	1.817	18	-1.390	9	1.461	17	-0.677	11	-0.321	12	0.392	14
orgoglio	-0.125	20	-1.061	17	0.499	22	1.436	25	1.748	26	-0.437	19	-0.125	20	-0.437	19	0.187	21	-0.437	19	-1.373	16
orrore	-0.934	8	-0.400	10	-0.400	10	0.400	13	2.000	19	-0.400	10	-1.200	7	-1.200	7	-0.133	11	0.133	12	1.200	16
passione	-0.469	25	-0.289	26	-0.108	27	1.155	34	0.433	30	0.794	32	0.072	28	-1.371	20	-1.732	18	1.335	35	-0.289	26
paura	-1.460	52	-0.760	66	-0.310	75	-0.210	77	-0.310	75	1.290	107	-0.410	73	1.891	119	-0.660	68	-1.310	55	0.790	97
pena	-0.120	28	-0.491	24	0.250	32	1.548	46	0.343	33	-0.120	28	0.436	34	-1.603	12	-0.676	22	-1.047	18	1.362	44
piacere	-0.218	85	-0.097	86	1.356	98	-0.945	79	-0.097	86	-0.218	85	0.630	92	1.114	96	0.751	93	-0.581	82	-1.914	71
pietà	-1.723	12	-1.205	16	0.479	29	0.350	28	0.091	26	0.739	31	-0.168	24	1.905	40	-1.335	15	-1.075	17	0.220	27
preoccupazione	-2.434	0	0.727	10	-0.853	5	-0.221	7	0.411	9	-1.169	4	-0.853	5	-0.221	7	-0.853	5	1.359	12	1.675	13

	Anonymous		Pozzo		Spaventa		Dèttore		Reali		Gallenzi		Lamberti		D'Ezio		Capatti		Pareschi		Sacchini	
rabbia	-1.096	6	-2.024	1	-0.353	10	-0.910	7	0.019	12	1.504	20	0.204	13	0.947	17	0.761	16	0.204	13	-0.353	10
rimorso	1.521	13	1.521	13	-1.014	11	0.254	12	-1.014	11	0.254	12	-1.014	11	0.254	12	-1.014	11	1.521	13	0.254	12
rimpianto	-4.184	1	-1.014	6	-0.380	7	-0.380	7	1.521	10	0.254	8	-0.380	7	0.254	8	-1.648	5	0.254	8	1.521	10
sconforto	-0.766	0	-0.447	1	-0.766	0	-0.128	2	-0.447	1	0.191	3	-0.447	1	-0.447	1	2.744	11	-0.128	2	-0.128	2
simpatia	0.292	18	1.461	28	1.111	25	0.994	24	0.058	16	-0.877	8	0.643	21	-1.461	3	-0.877	8	-0.526	11	-0.526	11
soddisfazione	-1.483	7	0.371	14	1.430	18	-0.159	12	0.371	14	-1.483	7	1.694	19	-0.688	10	-0.159	12	-0.424	11	-0.953	9
sofferenza	0.556	32	0.329	30	-0.125	26	-1.033	18	1.577	41	-1.033	18	-0.125	26	-0.011	27	1.804	43	-0.806	20	-0.579	22
solitudine	-1.691	22	0.673	35	-0.055	31	0.309	33	1.219	38	0.127	32	0.127	32	0.127	32	-2.419	18	-0.782	27	0.673	35
sollievo	0.649	13	0.649	13	-1.205	5	0.649	13	-0.973	6	-0.742	7	-1.205	5	0.881	14	-0.278	9	0.649	13	1.576	17
sorpresa	-2.374	2	-1.199	7	1.622	19	0.212	13	-1.199	7	-0.024	12	1.387	18	-0.729	9	-0.024	12	-0.729	9	0.682	15
speranza	-0.886	56	1.058	65	-0.238	59	-0.886	56	1.058	65	0.410	62	-0.454	58	1.490	67	-1.750	52	-0.454	58	-0.238	59
tenerezza	-0.309	12	0.574	16	0.574	16	0.353	15	1.458	20	-0.972	9	0.574	16	-1.635	6	-1.414	7	0.133	14	0.353	15
terrore	-0.708	13	-1.037	11	0.280	19	1.103	24	0.280	19	-0.708	13	-0.379	15	-0.872	12	-0.872	12	2.091	30	0.115	18
timore	0.081	20	1.032	27	-0.054	19	-0.733	14	0.624	24	1.167	28	0.353	22	-1.955	5	-1.140	11	0.624	24	0.081	20
tormento	-1.323	3	-1.134	4	-0.189	9	-1.134	4	-0.378	8	1.890	20	0.000	10	0.189	11	-0.567	7	1.512	18	-0.189	9
tristezza	1.035	22	-0.828	13	1.035	22	0.621	20	0.414	19	1.035	22	1.035	22	-0.621	14	-1.863	8	-0.828	13	0.000	17
vergogna	2.957	26	2.061	23	-0.030	16	1.165	20	-0.030	16	-0.329	15	-0.329	15	-0.329	15	-1.225	12	-1.225	12	0.269	17

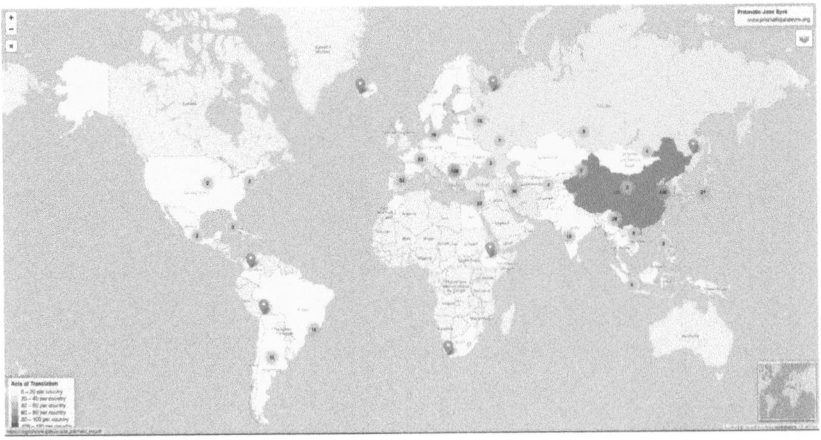

The World Map
https://digitalkoine.github.io/je_prismatic_map
Created by Giovanni Pietro Vitali;
maps © Thunderforest, data © OpenStreetMap contributors

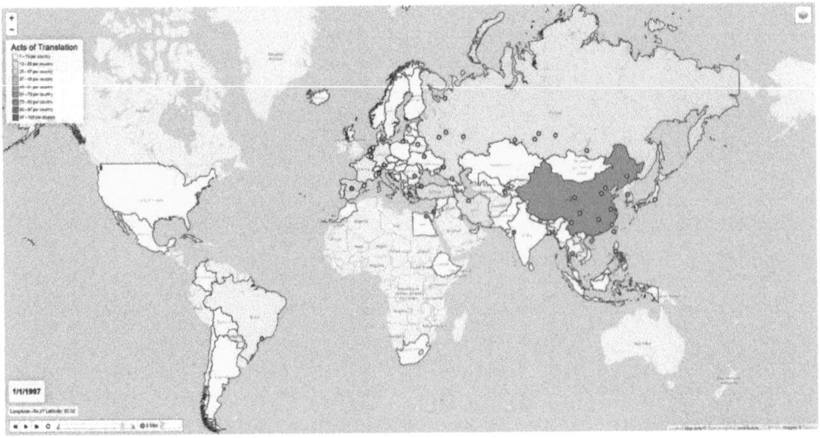

The Time Map
https://digitalkoine.github.io/translations_timemap
Created by Giovanni Pietro Vitali and Simone Landucci;
© OpenStreetMap contributors, © Mapbox

VI. 'Plain' through Language(s)

Matthew Reynolds

The word 'plain', with its derivatives 'plainly' and 'plainness', appears in the novel 48 times. As we saw in Chapter IV, it covers a wide semantic range: in this, it is like 'passion' (which we explored in Chapter V), only the spread of meanings and suggestions is even more expansive. 'Plain' can refer to physical looks — Jane is frequently called 'plain', by herself and others — and to dress, hairstyle and food: plain uniforms and 'plain fare' form part of the grim regime at Lowood School. But it is also, crucially, used of perception and speech, and especially so as they are performed by Jane: she sees and hears things plainly, and speaks 'the plain truth'. Her behaviour in the book shares these traits with the narrative that she is imagined as having written: when the second edition of *Jane Eyre* came out in 1848, Brontë described it in the 'Preface' as 'a plain tale'.

Again, as with 'passion', the reiterations of 'plain' in the English text imply an argument about values. To put it briefly: it does not matter if a woman looks plain; what is important is that she perceives things plainly (i.e., gets at the truth) and utters them plainly, whether she is speaking to Mr Rochester or writing for the public. As we will see in more detail below, no one word in any translation covers the same range as Brontë's 'plain' (though the Slovenian 'preprosto' comes close). Indeed, research by Caterina Cappelli has shown that, in thirteen Italian translations of *Jane Eyre*, 'plain' is translated by a total of 68 separate terms (see figures 21 and 22 for details), and there are also about 60 occasions on which no equivalent is provided for the word. So, when it comes to lexical patterning, none of the translations makes exactly the same connections as the source text.

 https://doi.org/10.11647/OBP.0319.18

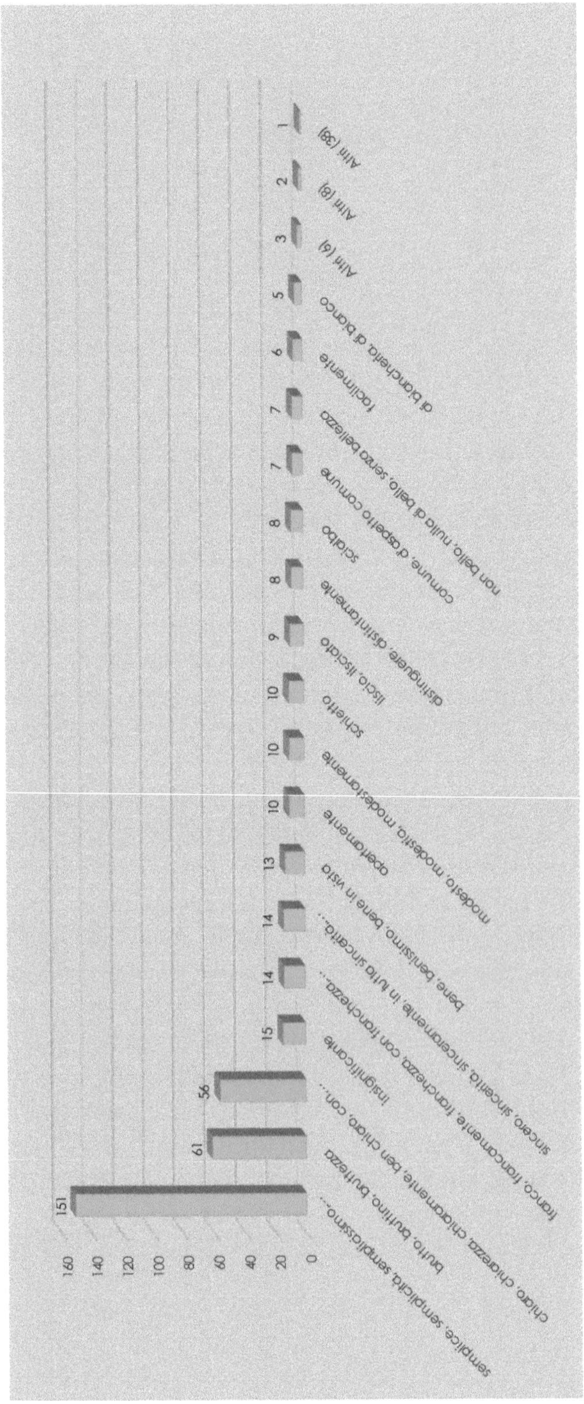

Fig. 21 Translations of 'plain' and its derivatives in 13 Italian translations, researched and created by Caterina Cappelli

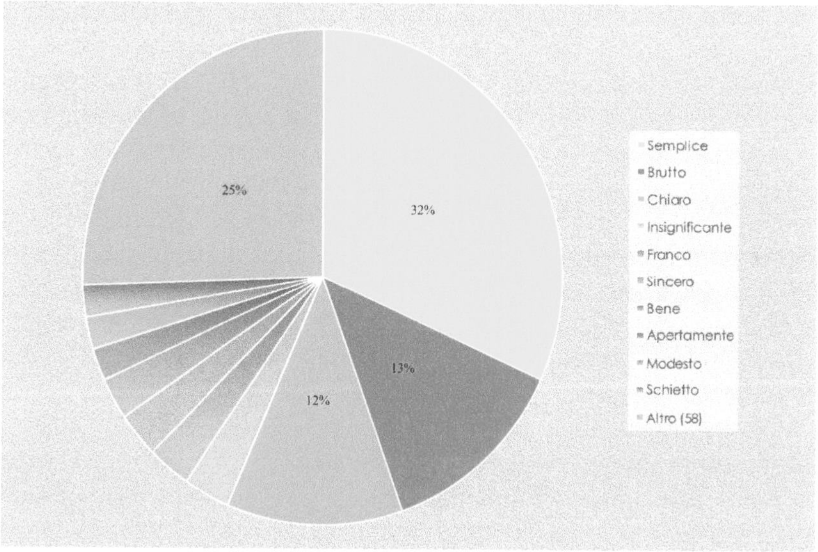

Fig. 22 A prismatic visualization of the data presented in Figure 21, researched and created by Caterina Cappelli

But the argument about plainness is not made only through particular vocabulary. It is also made through the plot, the sequence of events in which the novel's valuations are acted out by its protagonists. In this dramatic unfolding of meaning, Jane's looks and language are still, broadly speaking, 'plain', whatever words are used to describe them. So when we study the source text and the translations together we can see, in the English, the particular lexical texture that helped Brontë develop her powerful understanding of the significance of plainness; and then, in the translations, an explosion of re-wordings, through which the nuances of that understanding shift as it is re-formed with different linguistic materials. What in English is the plain truth may be described with words that can be back-translated as 'naked', 'simple' or 'unadorned' (and many more), while plain speech might be seen as 'hasty', 'blunt' or 'open'. These re-wordings then establish new connections across the texts and contexts in which they appear. For instance — as we will see — where Brontë's English maintains a distinction between 'plain' and 'ugly', several French and Italian translations use just one word ('laid' or 'brutto') to span both English terms.

In Brontë's text, 'plain' establishes various fleeting and perhaps accidental relationships with other words to which it is connected by phonetics and/or etymology. It rhymes with 'pain' and has a kinship to 'explain'. It overlaps with its homonyms 'to plain' — that is, to lament, as when, in Chapter 28, Jane's heart 'plained of its gaping wounds' — and 'a plain' in the sense of a flat stretch of landscape, as when, in Chapter 24, Mr Rochester plans to take Jane to 'Italian plains' after the wedding. And of course it rhymes with the protagonist's own name. The phrase 'plain Jane' never exactly appears in the novel (a database search suggests that it first appeared in print in a play by M. Rophino Lacy, *Doing for the Best,* which premièred in 1861, and which has some thematic similarities to *Jane Eyre,* though no explicit indebtedness).[1] Nevertheless, 'plain' is at the heart of Jane's being, and her book charges the word with new energies.

In the translations, the linguistic phosphorescence of rhyme of course plays out differently, across other words. But the feminist thrust of Jane's association with plainness — in all its meanings — does not therefore lose its force, as essays by Andrés Claro, Maria Claudia Pazos Alonso and Ana Teresa Marques dos Santos and others in this volume have already shown. Jane may no longer rhyme with 'plain', but — in the eyes of many translators — her tale still speaks plain truths.

The Plain Truth

Our first prismatic expansion of the word 'plain' is from Chapter 12, not long after Jane's arrival at Thornfield Hall. She has already got used to her new situation, and is even a little bored of it: often, she climbs to the roof and longs to see beyond the horizon to the 'busy world', or walks back and forth along the corridor of the 'third story', in which storied realm she opens her 'inward ear to a tale that was never ended — a tale my imagination created, and narrated continuously; quickened with all of incident, life, fire, feeling, that I desired and had not in my actual existence'.[2] Here too she makes the feminist declaration that would inspire many readers of the novel and its translations: 'women are supposed to be very calm generally: but women feel just as men feel; they need exercise for their faculties, and a field for their efforts as much as their brothers do; they suffer from too rigid a restraint, too absolute a stagnation, precisely as men would suffer ....'

1 *Proquest Literature Online,* https://www.proquest.com/lion

2 See Essay 9 above, by Ana Teresa Marques dos Santos and Cláudia Pazos-Alonso.

The sentence that is our focus joins this play of tensions between lived stagnation and the freedom that is imagined and desired. For, while she is alone and occupied with such thoughts, Jane 'not unfrequently' hears the laugh that she thinks to be Grace Poole's: 'the same peal, the same low, slow ha! ha! which, when first heard, had thrilled me: I heard too her eccentric murmurs, stranger than her laugh'. These fascinating sounds contrast with what Jane sees of Grace, and it is this that calls out the word 'plain':

> she would come out of her room with a basin, or a plate, or a tray in her hand, go down to the kitchen and shortly return, generally (oh, romantic reader, forgive me for telling the plain truth!) bearing a pot of porter. Her appearance always acted as a damper to the curiosity raised by her oral oddities: hard-featured and staid, she had no point to which interest could attach.

The wishes of the imagined romantic reader align with Jane's: both hope for more excitement than Thornfield currently provides. The word 'plain' seems to describe the way things are — not eventful enough to satisfy Jane's desires (earlier in the chapter the same has been said of Adèle and Mrs Fairfax). Yet there is also a counter-current in the word, for as the novel proceeds it will turn out that the plain truth about Grace Poole's liking for porter (a black beer) is not the whole truth about the thrilling laugh. There is a hint of this in the address to the reader, which has a knowingness about it, given that what is being read is a novel in which some elements of romance are likely to appear. If readers forgive the narrator for telling the plain truth here, it may be because they are pretty sure that Jane's wish will come true, and greater excitements soon appear.

As you can see in the animation and array below, three of the earliest translations skip the whole address to the reader: the feeling seems to be that Jane's chatty, almost flirtatious relationship with her imagined reader is superfluous, perhaps disconcerting, and can happily be left out. In Elvira Rosa's 1925 Italian version, on the other hand, the phrase 'romantic reader' is itself romanticised, to become 'anime romantiche' ('romantic souls'): this is in line with the generally sentimental tendency of her translation.

Some translators find in their languages words that approximate quite closely to 'plain': 'escueta' (María Fernanda Peredá, Sp1947); 'schietta' (G. Pozzo Galeazzi, It1951); 'preprosto' (Borko and Dolenc, Sl1955); or 'schlichte' (Melanie Walz, Ge2015). Other translations turn the quality of the 'truth' in different directions, such as 'vsakdanjo' ('everyday', Božena Legiša-Velikonja, Sl1970) or 'пошлую' ('vulgar', Irina Gurova, R1999); 'desnuda' or 'nøgne' ('naked', Juan G. de Luaces, Sp1943; Luise Hemmer Pihl, D2016); or 'sin adornos' or 'usmyikkede' ('unadorned', Toni Hill, Sp2009; Christian Rohde, D2015). When the plain truth is turned into a 'détail' or 'particolare' (Gilbert and Duvivier, Fr1919; Elvira Rosa, It1925) it takes on a scientific, almost forensic feel; but it can also — in contrast — assume a legal, or even religious tonality, as with 'la vérité entière' ('the whole truth', Noémie Lesbazeilles-Souvestre, F1954) or 'la semplice verità' ('the simple truth', Ugo Dèttore, It1974). All these variants have something in common, in that they can all be set in opposition to the genre of romance; but each one angles the binary slightly differently. What is at stake between the 'romantic' and the 'plain' can become a matter of adornment vs nakedness, complication vs simplicity, gentility vs vulgarity, or vagueness vs detail.[3]

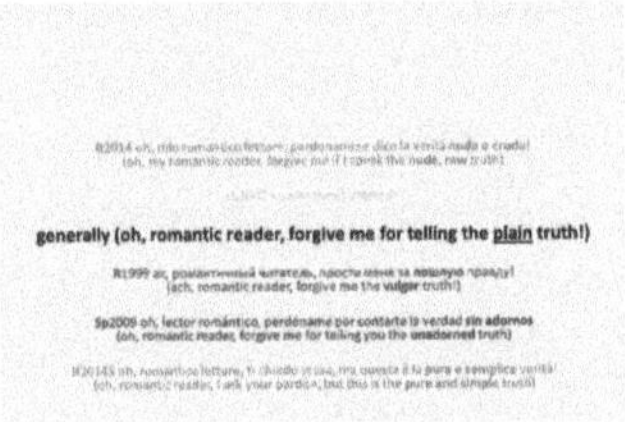

Animation 7: the plain truth
https://hdl.handle.net/20.500.12434/3360ced7

D2016 **nøgne** sandhed [naked truth]

Ge2015 der romantisch Leser vergebe mir, dass ich die **schlichte** Wahrheit sage [forgive me, romantic reader, for telling the plain truth]

It2014 oh, mio romantico lettore, perdonami se dico la verità **nuda e cruda**! [oh, my romantic reader, forgive me if I speak the nude, raw truth]

Hi2002 <parenthesis deleted>

Ge1979 romantischer Leser, verzeih mir, wenn ich **die Wahrheit** sage [romantic reader, forgive me, if I tell the truth]

Sl1970 povem tako **vsakdanjo** stvar [talk of such everyday things]

3 This animation and array incorporate research by Caterina Cappelli, Andrés Claro, Mary Frank, Jernej Habjan, Abhishek Jain, Eugenia Kelbert, Madli Kütt, and Céline Sabiron.

E1959 oo, romantiline lugeja, andesta, et **karmi** tõtt kõnelen [oh, romantic reader, forgive me for telling the harsh truth]

It1951 tu, romantico lettore, perdonami se dico la **schietta** verità [you, romantic reader, forgive me if I speak the plain truth]

Sp1947 perdona, lector romántico, que te diga la verdad **escueta** [forgive me, romantic reader, that I tell you the plain truth]

Sp1943 perdona, lector romántico, que te diga la verdad **desnuda** [forgive me, romantic reader, that I tell you the naked truth]

F1919 ce **détail** [this detail]

R1901 <parenthesis deleted>

F1854 la vérité **entière** [the whole truth]

generally (oh, romantic reader, forgive me for telling the **plain** truth!) bearing a pot of porter

R1849 <parenthesis deleted>

Ge1888 oh, verzeihe mir, romantische Leserin, wenn ich **die Wahrheit** sage [oh, forgive me, romantic woman reader, if I tell the truth]

It1904 <parenthesis deleted>

It1925 perdonatemi questo **particolare**, anime romantiche [forgive me this particular, romantic souls]

F1946, 1946B, 2008 la **simple** vérité [the simple truth]

R1950 прости мне эту **грубую** правду, романтический читатель [forgive me this rough truth, romantic reader]

Sl1955 razodenem **preprosto** resnico [reveal the plain truth]

F1966 la vérité **toute nue** [the wholly naked truth]

It1974 oh! romantico lettore, perdonami se dico la **semplice** verità! [oh! romantic reader, forgive me if I speak the simple truth]

R1999 ах, романтичный читатель, прости меня за **пошлую** правду! [ach, romantic reader, forgive me the vulgar truth!]

Sp2009 oh, lector romántico, perdóname por contarte la verdad **sin adornos** [oh, romantic reader, forgive me for telling you the unadorned truth]

It2014S oh, romantico lettore, ti chiedo scusa, ma questa è la **pura e semplice** verità! [oh, romantic reader, I ask your pardon, but this is the pure and simple truth]

D2015 **usmyikkede** sandhed [unadorned truth]

Hear Plainly

Our next instance comes from later in the same chapter. Jane has taken the opportunity to get out of the house and carry a letter to the nearby village of Hay. Halfway there, she pauses on a stile and looks at the landscape around:

> On the hill-top above me sat the rising moon; pale yet as a cloud, but brightening momently: she looked over Hay, which, half lost in trees, sent up a blue smoke from its few chimneys; it was yet a mile distant, but in the absolute hush I could hear plainly its thin murmurs of life.

This passage joins the interplay of sight and sound which we have observed earlier in the chapter, though with an opposite emphasis. There, 'eccentric murmurs' could not be explained by the 'plain truth' which presented itself to Jane's eyes; but here 'thin murmurs' can be heard 'plainly', though their origin is distant and not wholly visible. And if, earlier, the 'plain truth' was in a flirtatious relationship with the desires of the 'romantic reader', appearing to deny excitements which nonetheless remained a possibility, here again a plain appearance seems connected to the energies of romance. For just as Jane's ear is completing its audit of little, everyday sounds, something quite different breaks in: a 'rude noise' which — like the 'third story' and the thrilling laugh at Thornfield — sparks her imagination, this time summoning fairy tales and the folkloric figure of the Gytrash, and heralding the encounter with Mr Rochester.

The translations gathered here show how distinctive a feature of Brontë's English it was that the same term could be used in both this and the earlier quotation, for the translators all have to reach for different words, generally shifting the quality of Jane's hearing towards distinctness or clarity, though sometimes leaving it with no adverb at all. Several of them also reveal, by turning away from it, the insistence Brontë gives to Jane's first-person, always liking her to be the subject of verbs, as she is here. Madli Kütt points out that Elvi Kippasto's 1959 Estonian translation opts for an impersonal construction (part of a trend which she explores at length below in Essay 16); and the same move is made by several other translators.[4]

4 This animation and array incorporate research by Caterina Cappelli, Mary Frank, Jernej Habjan, Abhishek Jain, Eugenia Kelbert, Ida Klitgård, Madli Kütt, and Céline Sabiron.

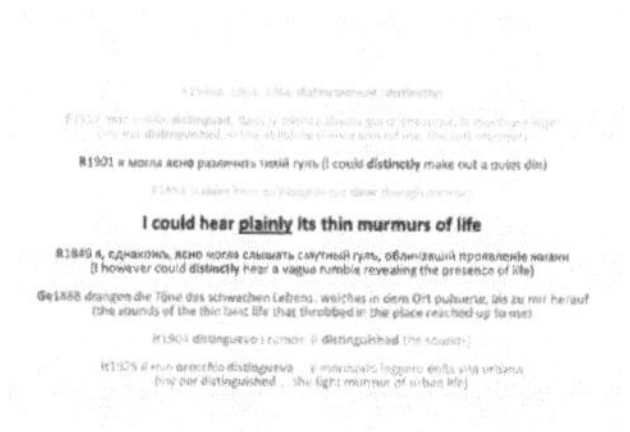

Animation 8: hear plainly
https://hdl.handle.net/20.500.12434/613b7725

Ge2015 konnte ich die leisen Lebensregungen des Dorfes vernehmen [I could hear the soft movements of life in the village]

It2014 sentivo **chiaramente** il brusio di vita che di là si levava [I heard clearly the murmur of life that arose from there]

Hi2002 मैं उसके जीवन की मन्द ध्वनि स्पष्ट सुन रही थी [{*maĩ uske jīvan kī mand dhvani* ***spaṣṭa*** *sun rahī thī* } I was clearly hearing its low/soft sound]

Ge1979 konnte ich … das dünne Gemurmel seines Lebens vernehmen [I could hear … the thin murmur of its life]

Sl1970 **razločno** slišala [distinctly hear]

D1957, 2015, 2106 **tydeligt** [clearly]

It1951 ne distinguevo **nitidamente** i rumori [I clearly distinguished its sounds]

F1946B, 1964, 1966 **distinctement** [distinctly]

F1919 mon oreille **distinguait**, dans le silence absolu qui m'entourait, le murmure léger [my ear distinguished, in the absolute silence around me, the soft murmur]

R1901 я могла **ясно** различить тихій гулъ [I could distinctly make out a quiet din]

F1854 si **clairs** bien qu'éloignés [so clear though remote]

I could hear **plainly** its thin murmurs of life

R1849 я, однакожъ, **ясно** могла слышать смутный гулъ, обличавшій проявленіе жизни [I however could distinctly hear a vague rumble revealing the presence of life]

Ge1888 drangen die Töne des schwachen Lebens, welches in dem Ort pulsierte, bis zu mir herauf [the sounds of the thin faint life that throbbed in the place reached up to me]

It1904 **distinguevo** i rumori [I distinguished the sounds]

It1925 il mio **orecchio distingueva** … il mormorio leggero della vita urbana [my ear distinguished … the light murmur of urban life]

R1950 уже доносились ко мне несложные звуки ее жизни [unsophisticated/simple sounds of its life could already reach me]

Sl1955 **natančno** zaznati [clearly register]

E1959 kuid täielikus vaikuses oli kaugeid külaeluhääli **selgesti** kuulda [the faraway sounds of village life could be clearly heard]

It1974 potevo udire **distintamente** i lievi sussurri della sua vita [I could hear distinctly the soft whispers of its life]

R1999 до меня уже доносились легкие отголоски тамошней жизни [light echoes of life of over there already reached me]

Fr2008 **nettement** [clearly]

It2014S potevo percepire **chiaramente** i suoi tenui mormorii di vita [I could perceive clearly its faint murmurs of life]

Plain ... Too Plain

In Chapter 14 there are successive appearances of 'plain'; and as they are more tightly linked than those in Chapter 12 we will consider them together. First, Mr Rochester summons Adèle and Jane to join him after dinner:

> I brushed Adèle's hair and made her neat, and having ascertained that I was myself in my usual Quaker trim, where there was nothing to retouch — all being too close and plain, braided locks included, to admit of disarrangement — we descended.

Then, down in the dining room, after Mr Rochester has asked if Jane thinks him handsome and she has replied 'no, sir', Jane's Quaker look, together with the idea of disarrangement, recurs in his speech to her. He says she has 'the air of a little nonnette' (a word, meaning 'little nun', that appears in French dictionaries and not in English ones — though, since Jane and Mr Rochester both mix French and English in their language use, it is not marked as foreign in the text); and he elaborates with words that echo the 'qu' of 'Quaker': 'quaint, quiet, ...'. But this reserved exterior conceals disruptive energies: 'when one asks you a question ... you rap out a round rejoinder, which, if not blunt, is at least brusque. What do you mean by it?' In her reply, Jane reaches for the word 'plain':

> 'Sir, I was too plain: I beg your pardon. I ought to have replied that it was not easy to give an impromptu answer to a question about appearances; that tastes differ; that beauty is of little consequence, or something of that sort.'

Rochester feels there to be a contrast between the modest look and assertive speech; but Jane conceives of both as manifesting the same quality: plainness, which eschews both ornament and circumlocution.

Just as with Chapter 12, none of the translators find it possible to use the same word for both these occurrences of 'plain'. In some cases, their choices make Jane seem to share Rochester's view, as when Aslaug Mikkelsen (D1957) presents Jane's dress as 'ordentlig' ('decent'), in contrast to her speaking 'så ligeud' ('so bluntly'). In others, the English Jane's idea comes through more fully: both Elvira Rosa (It1925) and Ugo Dèttore (It1974) see Jane's dress as 'simple' ('semplice', possessing 'semplicità'), while her speech is 'sincere' ('sincera'). Though obviously not the same as exact repetition, this pairing does suggest a continuity of values.

Overall, these two new instances of 'plain' give yet more evidence of the enormous semantic productivity of Brontë's repeated use of the word. Just occasionally you can find an equivalent that has appeared before: for instance, Dèttore (It1974) chooses 'semplice' both for Jane's clothing here and for 'the plain truth' in Chapter 12, while Monica Pareschi (It2014) and Stella Sacchini (It2014S) both employ 'schietta' for Jane's speech, a word that had also been used for 'the plain truth' by G. Pozzo Galeazzi in 1951. It is all the more striking that Pareschi and Sacchini both sought other terms for 'the plain truth', while Pozzo Galeazzi chooses a different word ('franca', 'frank') for Jane's plain speech here.[5]

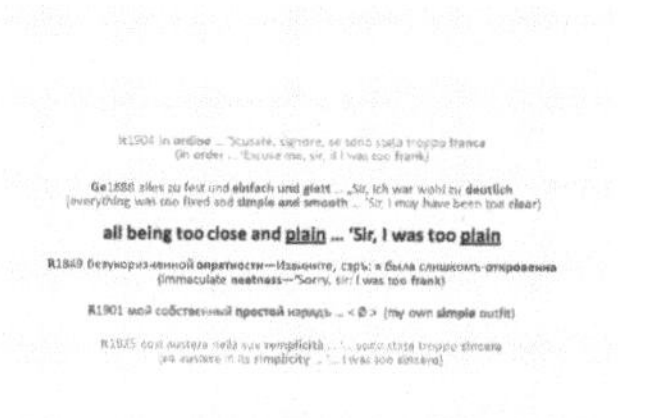

Animation 9: plain ... too plain
https://hdl.handle.net/20.500.12434/d4aae74d

D2016 **enkelt** ... talte for **ligefremt** [simple/plain ... put it too bluntly]

D2015 < Ø > ... var for **hurtig** [was too quick]

5 This animation and array incorporate research by Caterina Cappelli, Mary Frank, Jernej Habjan, Abhishek Jain, Eugenia Kelbert, Ida Klitgård, and Madli Kütt.

It2014 era troppo essenziale e **austero** ... 'Signore, sono stata troppo **schietta** [it was too basic and austere ... 'Sir, I was too plain]

R1999 такой **скромной простоте ...** — Сэр, я была слишком **прямолинейна** [such modest simplicity ... 'Sir, I was too direct]

It1974 tutto infatti era troppo **semplice** e raccolto ... 'Signore, sono stata troppo **sincera** [all indeed was too simple and gathered ... 'Sir, I was too sincere]

D1957 **ordentlig** ... '... sagde min mening så **ligeud** [decent ... '... spoke my opinion so bluntly]

R1950 < Ø > ... — Сэр, я слишком **поторопилась** ['Sir, I was too hasty]

It1904 **in ordine** ... 'Scusate, signore, se sono stata troppo **franca** [in order ... 'Excuse me, sir, if I was too frank]

Ge1888 alles zu fest und **einfach und glatt** ... „Sir, ich war wohl zu **deutlich** [everything was too fixed and simple and smooth ... 'Sir, I may have been too clear]

all being too close and **plain** ... 'Sir, I was too **plain**

R1849 безукоризненной **опрятности** — Извините, сэръ: я была слишкомъ-**откровенна** [immaculate neatness ... 'Sorry, sir: I was too frank]

R1901 мой собственный **простой** нарядъ ... < Ø > [my own simple outfit]

It1925 così austera nella sua **semplicità** ... '... sono stata troppo **sincera** [so austere in its simplicity ... '... I was too sincere]

It1951 la mia **semplice** veste e la **liscia** acconciatura ... 'Scusi, signore, sono stata troppo **franca** [my simple dress and smooth hairstyle ... 'Excuse me, sir, I was too frank]

E1959 kõik oli **ülimalt lihtne** ja range ... 'Palun vabandust, sir, ma olin liiga **avameelne** [everything was extremely simple and strict ... 'I beg your pardon, sir, I was too frank]

Ge1979 **ordentlich** aussah ... »Ich war zu **offen** [looked tidy ... 'I was too open]

Hi2002 किसी परिवर्तन की या पुनः पूसाधन की आवश्यकता नहीं है [{*kisī parivartan kī yā punaḥ prasādhan kī āvaśyaktā nahī̃ hai*} no necessity for change or again dressing / toilet] ... महाशय, मैं बेढब बोल गई। [{*mahāśay, maĩ* ***beḍhab*** *bol gaī*} Sir, I spoke ugly]

It2014S era tutto troppo composto e **semplice** ... 'Signore, sono stata troppo **schietta** [it was all too composed and simple ... 'Sir, I was too plain]

Ge2015 mein **schlichtes**, enganliegendes Kleid ... »Sir, ich war zu **offen**
[my simple, close-fitting dress ... 'Sir, I was too open]

Plain, Unvarnished ... Poor, and Plain

After the nocturnal fire in Mr Rochester's bed, which Jane puts out with a water jug, the pair share a tender moment holding hands. Jane is left 'feverish' with emotional confusion and passes a sleepless night. The next day is described in Chapter 16, which, in the first edition, was the start of the second volume. Jane longs to see Mr Rochester, but it turns out that he has gone to stay at another house, miles away, where a party of gentlefolk is assembled. Mrs Fairfax tells Jane of the beautiful young ladies who will be there, especially the much-admired Blanche Ingram, with whom Mr Rochester once sang a beautiful duet.

Later, alone, Jane takes a stern view of the 'hopes, wishes, sentiments' about Mr Rochester that had been budding inside her, and the word 'plain' pops up to express it:

> Reason having come forward and told, in her own quiet way, a plain, unvarnished tale, showing how I had rejected the real and rabidly devoured the ideal; — I pronounced judgment to this effect: —
>
> That a greater fool than Jane Eyre had never breathed the breath of life ...

The judgment continues, getting fiercer and fiercer: 'your folly sickens me ... Poor stupid dupe! ... Blind puppy!' — and it culminates in punishment where 'plain' appears again:

> 'Listen, then, Jane Eyre, to your sentence: to-morrow, place the glass before you, and draw in chalk your own picture, faithfully; without softening one defect: omit no harsh line, smooth away no displeasing irregularity; write under it, "Portrait of a Governess. Disconnected, poor, and plain."'

(According to the *Oxford English Dictionary*, 'disconnected' means 'without family connections of good social standing; not well connected'. You will see that other possible nuances emerge in the translations.) Jane is also to paint, as a contrast, a beautiful fantasy portrait on a piece of ivory, to represent Blanche Ingram.

Here we have the first use of the word to describe Jane's physical appearance (in Chapter 14, as we have just seen, it is used of her clothes and hairstyle, but not her face). So here, at this moment of emotional distress, she stamps the word on her body: someone who looks like this, she tells herself, is never going to be loved by Mr Rochester. It is a despairing, decisive act of self-definition.

Yet this is not all that is happening. Because of its previous appearances with different meanings, 'plain' has become charged with other energies, and their traces are latent here. Plain is not only about how you look: it is also about speaking plainly, about hearing clearly, about maintaining dignity, about seeing things as they are. As she tells the plain truth about her own, plain looks, Jane makes it possible for her readers to understand that there is more to plainness than meets the eye.

Physical plainness is not only an addition to the other kinds: it also helps them to come into being. Jane's unremarkable physical appearance makes it easier for her to see and say things as they are. Beautiful, rich creatures like Blanche are caught up in a world that is in many ways not 'real': privileged, idealised, puffed with compliments and romantic possibilities. Condemned to — or blessed with — plainness, Jane must stand outside those gossamer realms, and therefore can see through them, as when, later in the novel, she understands that Mr Rochester does not really love Blanche, however much he might be acting as though he does.

In the animation and array, you will see that only one of the translations — Božena Legiša-Velikonja's Slovenian version of 1970 — uses the same term for these two instances of 'plain'. Some of the other translations connect the first instance to 'the plain truth' in chapter 12: Marie von Borch (Ge1888), Elvi Kippasto (E1959), and Ugo Dèttore (It1974) all use words approximating to 'simple' in both cases. The two Italian translations published in 2014 perform a switcharound: Monica Pareschi chooses 'semplice' ('simple') here and 'nuda e cruda' ('nude and raw') back in chapter 12, while Stella Sacchini does exactly the reverse.

Overall, though, it is again the semantic plurality bursting out in the translations that is most striking. Beyond 'simple', the 'plain' of 'plain, unvarnished tale' is rendered by words approximating to 'sobriety', 'unadorned', 'as they really stood', 'without spices', and more; while the 'plain' of 'poor, and plain' morphs into words that roughly correspond to 'ugly', 'simple', 'dull', 'insignificant', 'ordinary' and 'unimpressive'. One especially surprising and suggestive shift is created by Irinarkh Vvedenskii's Russian translation of 1849. It renders the second 'plain' as безпріютной, 'shelterless', thereby bringing in the sense of 'plain' when used as a noun: a flat expanse of landscape. It is as though Jane is anticipating her later wanderings on the moors around Whitcross: disconnected, poor, an outcast on the plain.[6]

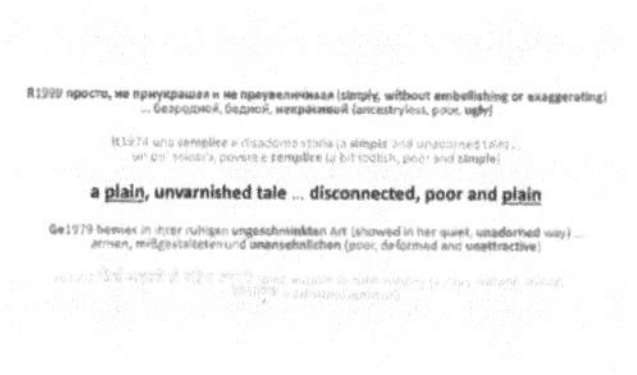

Animation 10: plain, unvarnished ... poor, and plain
https://hdl.handle.net/20.500.12434/7fac4507

D2016 **usmykket** [unadorned] ... **uanselig** [unimpressive]

D2015 **ligefrem** [straightforward] ... **grim** [ugly]

It2014 una storia **semplice** e senza fronzoli [a simple tale without frills] ... povera, **scialba** e sola al mondo [poor, dull and alone in the world]

R1999 **просто, не приукрашая и не преувеличивая** [simply, without embellishing or exaggerating] ... безродной, бедной, **некрасивой** [ancestryless, poor, ugly]

It1974 una **semplice** e disadorna storia [a simple and unadorned tale] ... un po' sciocca, povera e **semplice** [a bit foolish, poor and simple]

E1959 talle omase **lihtsa** ning ilustamata seletuse [a simple, unvarnished tale] ... Üksiku, vaese ja **inetu** [lonely, poor and ugly]

It1951 le cose **così come realmente stavano** [things as they really stood] ... **brutta**, povera, e senza parentela [ugly, poor, and without kin]

It1925 un **semplicissimo** racconto [a very simple tale] ... povera, **brutta** e senza famiglia [poor, ugly, and without family]

Ge1888 eine **einfache**, ungeschmückte Erzählung [a simple, unadorned tale] ... armen, alleinstehenden, **hässlichen** [poor, single, ugly]

a **plain**, unvarnished tale ... disconnected, poor and **plain**

6 This animation and array incorporate research by Caterina Cappelli, Mary Frank, Jernej Habjan, Abhishek Jain, Eugenia Kelbert, Ida Klitgård, and Madli Kütt.

Ru1849 и выслушавъ рядъ взведенныхъ **обвиненій** [having heard a series of accusations brought (against me)] ... безродной, бѣдной, **безпріютной** [ancestryless, poor, shelterless]

It1904 le cose **così com'erano** [things as they were] ... **brutta**, povera e senza attinenze di famiglia [ugly, poor, and without family connections]

R1950 со свойственной ему **трезвостью** [with his characteristic sobriety] ... одинокой, неимущей **дурнушки** [solitary, poor, unattractive]

Sl1955 **jasno** [clearly] ... **preproste** [plain]

Sl1970 **preprosto** [plainly] ... **preproste** [plain]

Ge1979 bewies in ihrer ruhigen **ungeschminkten** Art [showed in her quiet, unadorned way] ... armen, mißgestalteten und **unansehnlichen** [poor, deformed and unattractive]

Hi2002 मिर्च-मसाले से रहित कहानी [{**mirc-masāle se rahit** kahānī} a story without spices] ... साधारण [{sādhāraṇ} general]

It2014S una storia, **nuda** e cruda [a nude, raw tale] ... senza famiglia, povera e **insignificante** [without family, poor and insignificant]

Ge2015 einen **unverblümten**, ungeschminkten Bericht [a blunt, unadorned report] ... ohne Verbindungen, arm und **gewöhnlich** [without ties, poor and ordinary]

Plain, and Little

We are in Chapter 23 and a lot has happened since our last point of focus. There has been the house party at Thornfield, during which Mr Rochester seemed to woo Blanche Ingram; there has been his appearance in disguise as a gypsy fortune teller; there has been the arrival and mysterious wounding of Mr Mason, from Jamaica; and then Jane has gone away for a month to attend the death-bed of Aunt Reed at Gateshead Hall. Since her return to Thornfield there has been 'a fortnight of dubious calm'.

Now, Jane has encountered Mr Rochester in the garden, and he — with what must seem extraordinary cruelty — has been goading her with the news that he will soon marry Miss Ingram, and she will have to go away. In response, her love for what she would have to leave behind bursts out of her:

> 'I love Thornfield ... I have talked, face to face, with what I reverence; with what I delight in, — with an original, a vigorous, an expanded

> mind. I have known you, Mr. Rochester; and it strikes me with terror and anguish to feel I absolutely must be torn from you forever.'

Startlingly, he then changes tack and tells her that she won't have to leave after all. Distraught, she reacts again:

> 'Do you think I can stay to become nothing to you? Do you think I am an automaton? ... Do you think, because I am poor, obscure, plain, and little, I am soulless and heartless? — You think wrong! — I have as much soul as you, — and full as much heart! ... I am not talking to you now through the medium of custom, conventionalities, nor even of mortal flesh: — it is my spirit that addresses your spirit; just as if both had passed through the grave, and we stood at God's feet, equal, — as we are!'

The word 'plain' appears here with the same pained meaning of physical unattractiveness that we saw in Chapter 16. Yet Jane's utterance also embodies the other, more positive senses of 'plain': seeing things clearly, and speaking out in defiance of convention.

Her speech strikes home. Rochester declares that he loves Jane, not Blanche Ingram. He proposes in words that echo hers:

> 'You — you strange — you almost unearthly thing! — I love as my own flesh. You — poor and obscure, and small and plain as you are — I entreat to accept me as a husband.'

In the animation and array, you will see the prismatic diffractions of the first appearance of 'plain' in this chapter: 'I am poor, obscure, plain, and little'. One thing to bear in mind is that the translators are — as always — faced, not with the word by itself, but as part of a phrase or sentence. In this case, the sequence 'poor, obscure, plain, and little' has a marked, emotive rhythm: 'tum, ti tum, tum, ti tum ti'. When Juan G. de Luaces leaves out 'plain, and little' from his Spanish translation in 1943 it is probably not because he dislikes those words, and not from carelessness, but because he wants to keep a strong rhythm pulsing through the sentence that he writes, helped by a pattern of alliteration ('P—p—p—sc—c—c'): '¿Piensa que porque soy pobre y oscura carezco de alma y de corazón?' ('Do you think that because I am poor and obscure I am lacking in soul and heart'). For Lesbazeilles-Souvestre in 1854, on the other hand, the closeness of French to English enabled her to match word with word while keeping almost the same rhythm: 'je suis pauvre, obscure, laide et petite'.

'Laide' is an obvious term for a French translator to adopt: it means roughly the same as 'plain' in this context, is a monosyllable, and even has three letters in common with the English word. Yet

Lesbazeilles-Souvestre's choice makes a decisive change in the novel's web of words, for 'laide', or 'laid' in the masculine, is also used to translate 'ugly'.

This shift will be explored more fully in the next section. Here, in our prismatic expansion of 'I am poor, obscure, plain and little', we can see a similar choice being made by translators who opt for 'hässlich' in German, 'brutta' in Italian or 'grim' in Danish. Others take a different path, avoiding the conflation of 'plain' with 'ugly', and further opening up its semantic complexity as they do so.

Animation 11: plain, and little[7]
https://hdl.handle.net/20.500.12434/cb0d066a

D2015 **grim** [ugly]

It 2014S sono povera, sconosciuta, **insignificante** e piccola [I am poor, unknown, insignificant and small]

Sp2009 soy pobre, silenciosa, **discreta** y menuda [I am poor, silent, modest and small]

Hi2002 निर्धन, परिवारविहीन, सामान्य शक्ल-सूरत की और छोटी हूँ [{*nirdhan parivārvihīn,* ***sāmānya*** *śakla-sūrat kī aur choṭī hūṁ*} poor, without family, ordinary looking, and small]

Ge1979 ich arm, unbedeutend, **häßlich** und klein bin [I am poor, insignificant, ugly and small]

F1966 je suis pauvre, insignifiante, **laide** et menue [I am poor, insignificant, ugly and slight]

E1959 ma olen vaene ja tähtsusetu, **ilutu** ja väike [poor and unimportant, unlovely and little]

Sl1955, 1970 **preprosta** [plain]

7 This animation and array incorporate research by Caterina Cappelli, Andrés Claro, Mary Frank, Abhishek Jain, Eugenia Kelbert, Ida Klitgård, Madli Kütt, and Céline Sabiron.

R1950 если я небогата и незнатна, если я мала ростом и **некрасива** [if I am not rich and not noble, if I am of small stature and plain]

Sp1943 soy pobre y oscura [I am poor and obscure]

It1904 son povera, oscura, **brutta**, piccina [I am poor, obscure, ugly, little]

F1854 je suis pauvre, obscure, **laide** et petite [I am poor, obscure, ugly and little]

I am poor, obscure, **plain**, and little

R1849 я бѣдна и не принадлежу къ вашему блистательному кругу [I am poor and do not belong to your brilliant circle]

Ge1888 weil ich arm und klein und **hässlich** und einsam bin [I am poor and small and ugly and alone]

It1925 son povera, umile, piccola e **senza bellezza** [I am poor, humble, small and without beauty]

Sp1947 soy pobre, insignificante y **vulgar** [I am poor, insignificant and vulgar]

It1951 sono povera, oscura, **brutta** e piccola [I am poor, obscure, ugly and small]

D1957 **ubetydelig** [insignificant]

F1964 je suis pauvre, humble, **sans agrément**, petite [I am poor, humble, without pleasant features, little]

It1974 sono povera, oscura, **semplice** e piccola [I am poor, obscure, simple and small]

R1999 я бедна, безродна, **некрасива** и мала ростом [I am poor, ancestry-less, plain and of small stature]

F2008 je suis pauvre, obscure, **quelconque** et menue [I am poor, obscure, ordinary and slight]

It2014 sono povera, oscura, **brutta** e piccola [I am poor, obscure, ugly and small]

Ge2015 ich arm bin, unbedeutend, **unansehnlich** und klein [I am poor, insignificant, unattractive and small]

D2016 **uanselig** [unimpressive]

Ugly and Laid(e)

As we saw in the last section, Noémi Lesbazeilles-Souvestre's French version of 1854 translates 'plain' in Chapter 23, with a word, 'laid(e)', which she also uses to translate 'ugly'. This matters because Brontë maintains a firm distinction between those two terms. 'Plain' is associated with Jane and has the range of meanings that we have been exploring. 'Ugly' is associated with Mr Rochester: it is used mainly of his physical appearance, but it can also apply to his behaviour ('bigamy is an ugly word!' — as he exclaims in Chapter 26.) A good three-word summary of *Jane Eyre* in English might be 'plain meets ugly', with all that this entails: feminine meets masculine, directness meets deceit, clarity meets obfuscation, poverty meets wealth, innocence meets exploitation. But in the French of Lesbazeilles-Souvestre the verbal dynamic is altered. The differences between Jane and Rochester are reduced and the likeness is made more visible. In her translation, 'laide' meets 'laid'.

This shift is in tune with the idiom of French nineteenth-century fiction. Women characters in novels by Balzac, Sand, Hugo, Sue and others frequently declare 'je suis laide' ('I am ugly'), as a search of the *ARTFL-FRANTEXT* database reveals, whereas the equivalent English database, *LION*, yields only one instance of a woman saying 'I am ugly' in a nineteenth-century novel (Priscilla, in George Eliot's *Silas Marner*).[8] So, as a translation choice in this instance, 'laide' is entirely justifiable. Neverthelesss, as similar decisions are made throughout the novel, and the word 'laid(e)' proliferates, a decisive change is effected in the web of words describing people's looks. In Lesbazeilles-Souvestre's translation, 'laid(e)' (or, in one case, 'laideurs') appears in all the following instances, where it is used to translate the English words that I have put in bold in the animation and array.

8 *ARTFL-FRANTEXT*, https://artfl-project.uchicago.edu/content/artfl-frantext; *Proquest Literature Online*, https://www.proquest.com/lion

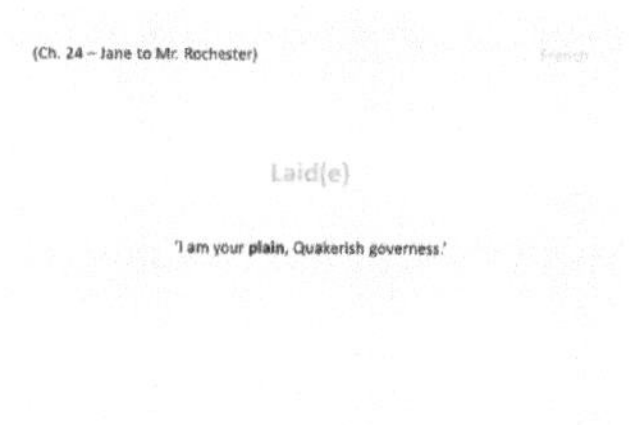

Animation 12: ugly and laid(e)
https://hdl.handle.net/20.500.12434/628b4f4d

Ch. 3 (Mr. Lloyd)
he had a **hard-featured** yet good-natured looking face

Ch. 11 (Grace Poole)
a set, square-made figure, red-haired, and with a hard **plain** face

Ch. 14 (Mr. Rochester)
I am sure most people would have thought him an **ugly** man; yet there was so much unconscious pride in his port; so much ease in his demeanour

Ch. 15 (Mr. Rochester and Céline)
He thought himself her idol, **ugly** as he was

Céline; who even waxed rather brilliant on my personal defects — **deformities** she termed them

(the possibility that Adèle is his daughter)
and perhaps she may be; though I see no proofs of such **grim** paternity written in her countenance

And was Mr. Rochester now **ugly** in my eyes?

Ch. 16 (Jane worries Mr. Rochester may have had a liaison with Grace Poole)
But, having reached this point of conjecture, Mrs. Poole's square, flat figure, and **uncomely**, dry, even coarse face, recurred so distinctly to my mind's eye, that I thought 'No; impossible! my supposition cannot be correct.'

'Portrait of a Governess, disconnected, poor, and **plain**.'

Ch. 17 (of Mr. Rochester)
Most true is it that 'beauty is in the eye of the gazer.' [The French back-translates as 'what some find **ugly** can seem beautiful to others')

(Blanche Ingram exclaims)
I grant an **ugly** *woman* is a blot on the fair face of creation ['*woman*' is italicised in Brontë's text]

Ch. 18 (the Gypsy — Mr. Rochester in disguise)
'A shockingly **ugly** old creature, Miss; almost as black as a crock.'

Ch. 21 (Jane describes Mr Rochester to Bessie, on her visit to Gateshead)
I told her he was rather an **ugly** man, but quite a gentleman

(Georgiana sees Jane's sketch of Mr. Rochester)
but she called that 'an **ugly** man.'

Ch. 23 (Jane to Mr. Rochester in the garden — the instance we explored in the last section)
'because I am poor, obscure, **plain** and little'

(Mr. Rochester to Jane)
'You — poor and obscure, and small and **plain** as you are — I entreat to accept me as a husband.'

Ch. 24 (Jane)
I looked at my face in the glass, and felt it was no longer **plain**

(Jane to Mr. Rochester)
'I am your **plain**, Quakerish governess.'

Ch. 35 (Jane to Diana about the idea of marrying St John Rivers)
'And I am so **plain**, you see, Die. We should never suit.'
'**Plain**! You?'

Ch. 37 (Mr. Rochester asks)
'Am I **hideous**, Jane?'

(And jealously he asks about St John Rivers)
'Is he a person of low stature, phlegmatic, and **plain**?'

As you can see, in Brontë's English these instances are divided between 'plain' and 'ugly' — and occasionally other terms. In the French of Lesbazeilles-Souvestre they are all brought together into the embrace of a single word.

Ugly and Brutto/a

The anonymous translator of the first Italian *Jane Eyre*, published in 1904, had Lesbazeilles-Souvestre's French version open in front of them as they worked, alongside Brontë's English. And they followed Lesbazeilles-Souvestre in abolishing the English distinction between 'plain' and 'ugly'. Where she wrote 'laid(e)', they put the nearest Italian equivalent — 'brutto' and its derivatives — in almost every instance. There is just one case where the Italian translator deviates from Lesbazeilles-Souvestre's example: right at the end of the novel, in Chapter 37, where Rochester asks Jane if he is 'hideous', the Italian gives, not 'brutto', but 'orribile' (horrible).

Yet 'brutto' does not have exactly the same range as 'laid'. It can be used more casually, for instance to talk about bad weather: 'brutto tempo'. The 1904 Italian translator exploits this flexibility in the word: 'brutto' and its derivatives appear 29 times in their translation where 'laid' etc had appeared only 22 times in Lesbazeilles-Souvestre — this despite the fact that the 1904 Italian version shrinks the text to about 145,000 words in length, by contrast with Brontë's c. 189,000 and Lesbazeilles-Souvestre's c. 193,000. To the list of instances translated by Lesbazeilles-Souvestre with 'laid', the 1904 Italian translator adds one 'ugly' used of James Reed in Chapter 1 (Lesbazeilles-Souvestre had rendered this with 'repoussante', 'repulsive'):

> I knew he would soon strike, and while dreading the blow, I mused on the disgusting and *ugly* appearance of him who would presently deal it.

Thereafter, 'brutto' and its derivatives draw all the following extra moments into their net (again, bold indicates the word(s) translated with 'brutto' or a derivative):

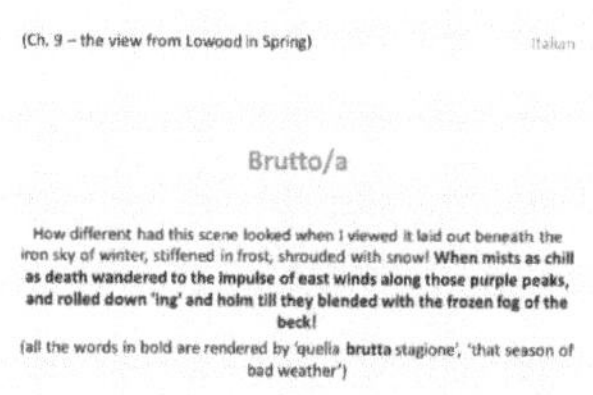

Animation 13: ugly and brutto/a
https://hdl.handle.net/20.500.12434/f7205298

Ch. 4
'Deceit is, indeed, a **sad** fault in a child,' said Mr. Brocklehurst

Ch. 5 (at Lowood School)
Above twenty of those clad in this costume were full-grown girls; or rather young women: it suited them **ill**, and gave an **air of oddity** even to the prettiest

Ch. 9 (the view from Lowood in Spring)
How different had this scene looked when I viewed it laid out beneath the iron sky of winter, stiffened in frost, shrouded with snow! **When mists as chill as death wandered to the impulse of east winds along those purple peaks, and rolled down 'ing' and holm till they blended with the frozen fog of the beck!** [all the words in bold are rendered by 'quella brutta stagione', 'that season of bad weather']

Ch. 11 (the first morning at Thornfield)
I looked at some pictures on the walls (one I remember represented a

> **grim** man in a cuirass, and one a lady with powdered hair and a pearl necklace)
>
> Ch. 16 (Reason attacks Jane's dream of closeness to Rochester)
> 'is it likely he would waste a serious thought on this indigent and **insignificant** plebeian?'
>
> Ch. 29 (Jane gets up for the first time at Marsh-End / Moor-House)
> My clothes hung loose on me; for I was much wasted: but I covered **deficiencies** with a shawl

These additional instances soften the linguistic focus of the text. They help us to see, by contrast, how it matters that Brontë's English gave particular attention to 'plain', together with its relation to 'ugly'; and indeed how it matters — in a different way — that the French of Lesbazeilles-Souvestre merged the two terms of that articulation, so as to give distinctive prominence to the 'laid(e)'.

Works Cited

For the translations of *Jane Eyre* referred to, please see the List of Translations at the end of this book.

Artfl-Frantext, https://artfl-project.uchicago.edu/content/artfl-frantext

Proquest Literature Online, https://www.proquest.com/lion

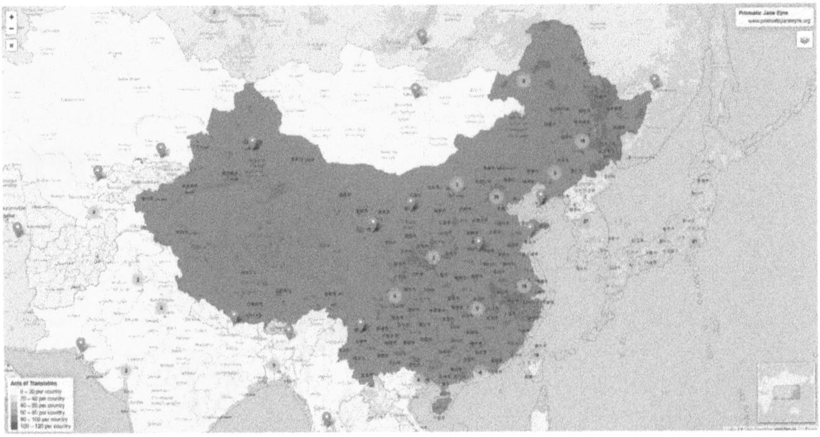

The World Map
https://digitalkoine.github.io/je_prismatic_map
Created by Giovanni Pietro Vitali;
maps © Thunderforest, data © OpenStreetMap contributors

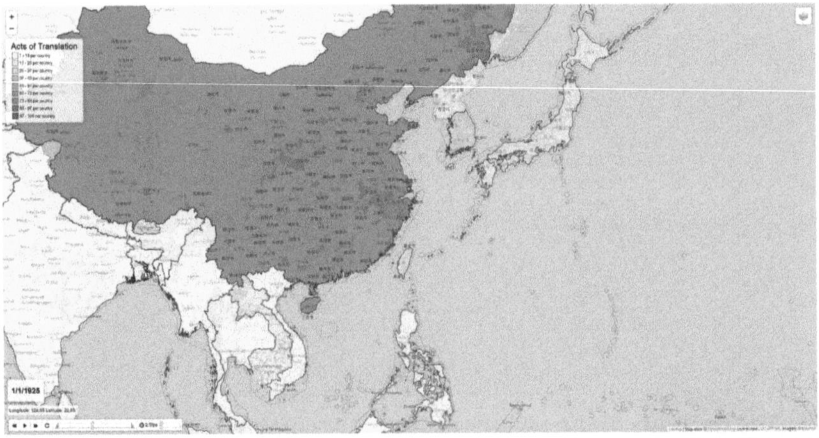

The Time Map
https://digitalkoine.github.io/translations_timemap
Created by Giovanni Pietro Vitali and Simone Landucci;
© OpenStreetMap contributors, © Mapbox

12. Proper Nouns and Not So Proper Nouns
The Poetic Destiny of *Jane Eyre* in Chinese

Yunte Huang

To grasp what I would like to call the poetic destiny of Charlotte Brontë's *Jane Eyre* in Chinese, and to explore the reasons for the book's tremendous success in Chinese-language translations, let us start with some facts and figures.

In 1925, the first Chinese translation of *Jane Eyre* appeared under the title, '重光记' (Seeing the Light Again). In this condensed rendition, the translator Zhou Shoujuan (周瘦鹃), more on whom later, reduced the original novel of about 190,000 English words to less than 9,000 characters in Chinese. Ten years later, in 1935, a lengthier abridged translation, by Wu Guangjian (伍光建), was published under the title '孤女飘零记' (Record of a Wandering Orphan Girl). In August of the same year, a complete translation, by Li Jiye (李霁野), began serialization in a magazine, leading to the publication of the book in September, 1936. Li's version bears the title '简爱自传' (An Autobiography of Jane Eyre).

In this period, when China experienced the impact of the New Culture Movement, which called for abolishing old ideologies and embracing new ideas and cultural practices, *Jane Eyre* was warmly received by Chinese readers for its perceived expression of free love and for its ostensible portrayal of a 'new woman'. Like the protagonist Nora in Henrik Ibsen's play *A Doll's House*, which was the talk of the town in China at the time, Jane Eyre was celebrated as an icon of feminism.

However, after the founding of the People's Republic of China in 1949, there was no more new translation of *Jane Eyre* in the Mainland because the novel was virtually banned. It was regarded as an expression of petty bourgeois sentimentality, which did not jibe well with the revolutionary spirit promoted by the Communist government.

 https://doi.org/10.11647/OBP.0319.19

As seen in the following poem 'Inscription on a Photograph of Militia Women' composed by Mao Zedong in 1961, the kind of 'new woman' idolized in this era was not a lady wearing 'silk or satin', but a militia fighter in a proletarian revolution, an almost androgynous figure who prefers her 'battle attire':

> **为女民兵题照**
> 飒爽英姿五尺枪，
> 曙光初照演兵场。
> 中华儿女多奇志，
> 不爱红装爱武装。

> **Inscription on a Photograph of Militia Women**
> Bright and brave figures bear rifles five-foot long,
> On the parade ground lit up by the first rays of dawn.
> So high these China's daughters aspire,
> Loving not silk or satin, but battle attire.[1]

Indeed, Jane may hate it when Rochester buys her silk dresses, preferring instead to stay as his 'plain, Quakerish governess', but she doesn't go so far as to put on battle attire.[2] By contrast, in Taiwan, under the rule of the Nationalist Party, new Chinese translations of *Jane Eyre* continued to appear from the 1950s to 1970s.[3]

When the tumultuous decade of the Cultural Revolution ended in 1976, Jane Eyre's fortune changed again in the Mainland. With the death of Mao and the subsequent loosening of ideological control by the Communist Party, China saw a renewed interest in *Jane Eyre*. Especially during the Culture Fever, a period in the 1980s when translations of Western literature, philosophy, religion and other subjects flooded the Chinese market, multiple Chinese editions of the novel appeared to appease the growing hunger of Chinese readers. In fact, the first complete translation of *Jane Eyre* after the Cultural Revolution, an edition by Zhu Qingying (祝庆英) published in 1988, allegedly boasted a print run of over three million copies. Since 1976, there have been well over one hundred Chinese versions, including complete translations, abridged editions, edited editions, annotated

---

1 Mao Zedong [毛泽东], *Maozhuxi shici sanshiqi shou* [毛主席诗词三十七首] (Thirty-seven Poems by Chairman Mao) (Beijing: Wenwu Press, 1964), p. 17 (translation mine).

2 *JE*, Ch. 24.

3 See the Time Map and the List of Translations at the end of this volume.

editions, and bilingual editions.[4] Symptomatically, in October 2015, in his speech during a state visit to Great Britain, President Xi Jinping spoke fondly of *Jane Eyre*, along with Shakespeare's plays and Dickens' *Oliver Twist*, as examples of British things that had exerted positive and lasting influences in the Middle Kingdom.[5]

Proper Nouns

> A noun is a name of anything, why after a thing is named write about it. A name is adequate or it is not. If it is adequate then why go on calling it, if it is not then calling it by its names does no good.
>
> — Gertrude Stein, 'Poetry and Grammar'[6]

Looking back at the vicissitudes of *Jane Eyre* in Chinese translation, I would like to venture a thesis: *Jane Eyre*'s popularity is augmented by the creative rendering of proper nouns by Chinese translators.

Contrary to Gertrude Stein's skepticism, as seen in the epigraph, about names or proper nouns, there is a very different approach to the issue. Ezra Pound, for instance, likes to refer to a dialogue in *The Confucian Analects*: When his disciple Tze-Lu asked Confucius, 'The Lord of Wei is waiting for you to form a government, what are you going to do first', the master replied, 'Settle the names (determine a precise terminology)'. The Chinese concept in question here, '正名' (*zheng ming*), is variously translated as 'correct naming', 'precise definition', or 'reification of name'. It constitutes a pillar of the Confucian thought that 'if words (terminology) are not (is not) precise, they cannot be followed, or completed in action according to specifications'. As Confucius went on to say in the *Analects*, 'Therefore the proper man must have terms that can be spoken, and when uttered be carried into effect; the proper man's words must cohere to things, correspond to them (exactly)'.[7]

---

4 Shouhua Qi, 'No Simple Love: The Literary Fortunes of the Brontë Sisters in Post-Mao, Market-Driven China', in *The Brontë Sisters in Other Worlds*, ed. by Shouhua Qi and Jacqueline Padgett (New York: Palgrave Macmillan, 2014), pp. 19–49.

5 Xi Jinping, 'Work Together to Promote Openness, Inclusiveness and Peaceful Development', https://www.fmprc.gov.cn/eng/topics_665678/2015zt/xjpdygjxgsfw/201510/t20151022_705452.html

6 Gertrude Stein, *Lectures in America* (New York: Random House, 1935), p. 209.

7 Ezra Pound, *Poems and Translations*, ed. by Richard Sieburth (New York: The Library of America, 2003), pp. 711–12.

Keeping in mind this notion of 'correct naming', let us look at the way certain names or proper nouns have been handled in Chinese translations of *Jane Eyre.* In fact, ever since the first complete translation by Li Jiye in 1936, the Chinese title of the book has been, with rare exceptions, '简爱'. The character '简' (*jian*), which is the homophonic rendering of 'Jane', means 'simple'. The character '爱' (*ai*), the acoustic equivalent of 'Eyre', means 'love'. Therefore, the Chinese title, while a close approximation in sound of the English original, semantically suggests 'simple love'. In most Chinese versions of the novel, Jane Eyre is simply addressed as '爱小姐', or Miss Love. Such a poetically rendered title, as well as the choice of an almost aphrodisiac sobriquet of the protagonist, surely adds much to the appeal of the novel to Chinese readers looking for a romantic love story.

Perhaps the only exception to the brand name of 'simple love' as popularized by Li Jiye was a failed translation attempt, and its failure speaks volumes of the power of proper nouns. In 2017, the Shanghai Library discovered a manuscript of a partial translation of *Jane Eyre* by Mao Dun, circa 1935, right around the time Li Jiye had completed his translation and was looking for a publisher. In this green-covered notebook, there are sixteen pages of Mao Dun's translation of the first three chapters of *Jane Eyre*. Most noteworthy for our interest is that Mao Dun (茅盾), one of the greatest modern Chinese writers, renders the title as '珍雅儿'. Granted that it is not so bad a translation of 'Jane Eyre', for it captures the English acoustics as well as enriching the semantics of the name with elegant, cute words like '珍' (*zhen*, 'precious'), '雅' (*ya*, 'elegant'), '儿' (*er*, 'little'), it is still no competition for the marvellous, almost magical, choice of '简爱'. In fact, the brand of '简爱' has become so popular and predominant in the literary marketplace that Mao Dun's manuscript, donated by his son to the Shanghai Library in 1996, went unnoticed for over twenty years, mostly because Mao Dun's working title does not command, pardon my pun, any name recognition.[8]

I am not trying to suggest that the poetic rendition of 'Jane Eyre' as '简爱' has ensured the novel's success in China. Even a pornographic novel with a most salacious title and a most alluring personal name (say,

8 Li Ting [李婷], 'Maodun ceng liangci fanyi Jianai [茅盾曾两次翻译《简爱》] (Maodun Twice Tried to Translate *Jane Eyre*)', *Wenhui* [文汇报] (Literary Newspaper) (7 September 2018), http://m.xinhuanet.com/book/2018-09/07/c_129948806.htm

Stormy Daniels) cannot secure its success without the usual features that make a book a good read or a good sell. However, we should not underestimate the power of branding, or rather, re-branding when a product, literary or otherwise, crosses linguistic boundaries, creating opportunities as well as traps for re-naming.

In addition to the intellectual weight of the aforementioned Confucian concept of 'correct naming', I do not think I need to go to great lengths to explain the importance of branding to the success of a product, or the poetic allure in commercial brand names like Coca-Cola, Kodak, PowerBook, and Blackberry. Saturated in sound symbolism, defined as the way sounds convey meaning independent of what a word actually signifies, these brand names are intangible assets that often make or break the companies' fortunes, especially upon the launch of new products. For example, in 1957, when the Ford Motor Company was looking for a name for its newly engineered and designed mid-priced car, they asked the poet Marianne Moore for help. In response to the company's request for a name that would 'convey, through association or other conjuration, some visceral feeling of elegance, fleetness, advanced features and design', Moore provided a list that includes Intelligent Bullet, Utopian Turtletop, Bullet Cloisone, Pastelogram, Mongoose Civique, and Andante con Moto. Unable to reach an agreement, Ford executives eventually named the car after Henry Ford's son Edsel. 'Launched with an unprecedented, fifty-million-dollar advertising and marketing campaign', the Edsel was a spectacular business flop. While clearheaded materialists would attribute Edsel's misfortune to changes in the car market, it is no denying that 'the name has become synonymous with failure'.[9]

By contrast, clever branding could change the fate of a product, literary or otherwise. Just imagine what would have happened to the novel *The Great Gatsby* if it had become known to us by F. Scott Fitzgerald's preferred title, 'Trimalchio in West Egg'? Or, how would *Pride and Prejudice* have fared under Jane Austen's original title, 'First Impressions'? In a similar fashion, the Patagonian toothfish, after being renamed as the Chilean sea bass, became popular among diners, as did the slimehead, reborn as the orange roughy, and rapeseed oil as canola.[10]

9 John Colapinto, 'Famous Names: Does It Matter What a Product Is Called?', *The New Yorker* (3 October 2011), p. 39.

10 Colapinto, 'Famous Names', p. 41.

Our concern, however, is not just with how words make things saleable, but with how words in translation make things marketable. The rule of thumb in the age of globalization is that ideal names must work across languages. As John Colapinto tells us in his article 'Famous Names', 'the industry [of naming] abounds in tales of cross-linguistic gaffes, like Creap coffee creamer from Japan, Bum potato chips from Spain, and the Chevy Nova — in Spanish, the "no go"'.[11] And the industry is also full of examples of successful cross-linguistic rebranding, many of which may be construed as happy accidents of meaning and sound, instances such as the Chinese translation of Coca-Cola as '可口可乐', Starbucks as '星巴克', or even Dr Sun Yat-sen's appropriation and condensation of Abraham Lincoln's famous phrase 'of the people, by the people, for the people' as '三民主义' (*sanmin zhuyi*, Three People Principle).[12]

In the case of literary products, for example, the original title of Pearl Buck's novel *The Good Earth* was 'Wang Lung', named after the protagonist. Her publisher and future husband, Richard Walsh, very wisely convinced her that no English reader would be interested in a book with a title that sounds like 'one lung'.[13] Also, it is reasonable to speculate that 'Wang Lung' is most likely '王龙' (*wang long*, 'king dragon'), indeed an august and auspicious name in Chinese, and its semantic value would have been severely undercut by the acoustic suggestion of 'one lung'.

The revised title, *The Good Earth*, certainly went a long way to foreground the central narrative, a Chinese peasant's rise and fall by the fortune of the land. Published in 1931, a novel with such a title was quite appealing to the nation of the United States in the throes of the Great Depression and the Dust Bowl. In addition, the title word 'earth' resonates with the name of the novel's female protagonist, O-Lan (O Land), which is also a not-so-distant echo of another land-based popular novel, Willa Cather's *O Pioneers!* At the very least, the title *Good Earth* avoided a potentially disastrous interlingual mishearing as in the case of 'Wang Lung'.

---

11 Colapinto, 'Famous Names', p. 39.

12 For those who don't know Chinese, let's take the translation of coca-cola as an example. The Chinese rendition of coca-cola is 可口可乐, pronounced as kekou kele. 可口 means appetizing, and 可乐 means entertaining or pleasing.

13 Peter J. Cohn, *Pearl S. Buck: A Cultural Biography* (New York: Cambridge University Press, 1996), 165.

'简爱' (simple love) for Jane Eyre, or '爱' (love) for Eyre, is equally a case of interlingual mishearing, albeit in this case it achieves the intended effect. Likewise, as we will see in the next section, the first Chinese translation of *Jane Eyre*, by Zhou Shoujuan, contains plenty of examples of the translator mining the rich potentials for mishearing, double hearing, reverberations, and acoustic puns in proper nouns.

Not So Proper Nouns: Mandarin Duck and Butterfly

Zhou Shoujuan (1895–1968) was a leader of the School of Mandarin Duck and Butterfly (MDB), a genre of popular fiction that features romantic love, knights-errant, scandals, and detective mysteries. In the Chinese tradition, both mandarin ducks and butterflies are symbols for love and lasting companionship. A prolific writer, Zhou translated Charlotte Brontë, Daniel Defoe, Charles Dickens, Mark Twain, Washington Irving, Harriet Beecher Stowe, and many others.

Zhou's translation of *Jane Eyre* was published in *Heartstrings* (心弦), a collection of his translations from foreign fiction with a common theme of love and romance, including Samuel Richardson's *Clarissa*, Nathaniel Hawthorne's *Scarlet Letter*, Prosper Merimee's *Carmen*, Charles Reade's *Love Me Little, Love Me Long*, and others. In his rendering of *Jane Eyre*, Zhou shrank the original text down to less than 9,000 words and turned it into a novella on love akin to an MDB story. With the title referring to Mr Rochester's regaining of vision at the end of the narrative, *Seeing the Light Again* is divided into four chapters: '怪笑声' (Strange Laughter), '情脉脉' (Bubbling Emotions), '疯妇人' (The Mad Woman), and '爱之果' (Fruits of Love).[14]

This is no place to discuss Zhou's translation in great detail, but I do want to draw attention to his treatment of proper nouns, which was a key part of his strategy of rebranding *Jane Eyre* as a sui generis MDB love story. First, Zhou translated the author's name Charlotte Brontë as '嘉绿白朗蝶', which roughly means 'fair green white open butterfly'. Secondly, his rendering of the name of Jane Eyre was particularly noteworthy: '嫣痕伊尔'. In this Chinese version, the name for Jane, '嫣痕', literally means 'pretty traces', with '痕' (*hen*, 'traces') being one of the favourite choice of words for MDB writers as well

14 Zhou Shoujuan [周瘦鹃], *Chongguang ji* [重光记] (Seeing the Light Again), in *Xinxian* [心弦] (Heartstrings) (Shanghai: Dadong shuju, 1925), pp. 1–24.

as in classical Chinese novels and poetry. Often paired with such words as 'tears' or 'love', '痕' is also a homophone of '恨' (*hen*, 'hate, lament, regret'). Together with the condensation of the content, such re-branding of proper nouns framed the reading of *Jane Eyre* upon the novel's debut in Chinese. As one Chinese scholar puts it, 'Zhou Shoujuan intentionally put a "love" label on *Jane Eyre*' (周瘦鹃是有意为《简爱》贴上'言情'标签).[15] But such a label — call it a birthmark, if you will — also doomed the novel in the later, revolutionary period when the ruling ideology turned against literary schools such as the MDB. Persecuted and publicly humiliated during the Cultural Revolution, Zhou committed suicide in 1968.

Pronouns

> Pronouns are not as bad as nouns because in the first place practically they cannot have adjectives go with them. That already makes them better than nouns...they of course are not really the name of anything. They represent some one but they are not its or his name. In not being his or its or her name they already have a greater possibility of being something than if they were as a noun is the name of anything...there is at least the element of choice even the element of change.
>
> — Gertrude Stein, 'Poetry and Grammar'[16]

Given Gertrude Stein's fondness for pronouns for their flexibility, she might have hated what happened to personal pronouns in early twentieth-century China. Rather than providing choice and change and hence allowing for escape from fixed labels (identity, gender, sexuality, ethnicity, etc.) — Stein's sensitivity towards pronouns derived from the fact that she was living as a lesbian Jew in wartime Europe — new personal pronouns were invented in China to specify gender and other categories. For thousands of years, in classical Chinese, there was no differentiation between genders in the use of third person pronoun. '他' was the catch-all word for third person pronoun, regardless of gender or personhood. It referred to a man, woman, or nonhuman being.

15 Li Jin [李今], 'Zhou Shoujuan dui jianai de yanqinghua gaixie jiqi yanqingguan [周瘦鹃对《简爱》的言情化改写及其言情观] (Zhou Shoujuan's Sentimentalizing Revision of *Jane Eyre* and His Sentimentalism), *Wenxue pinglun* [文学评论] (Literary Review), 1 (2013), 70.

16 Stein, p. 212.

The encounter with western languages in the nineteenth and early twentieth centuries made Chinese literati rethink their millennial-old language habit. The first two experiments took place in grammar books. In 1823, in the first English grammar book written in Chinese, 英国文语凡例传, the famous Anglo-Scottish Protestant missionary, Rev. Robert Morrison (马礼逊), translated 'he' as '他男', 'she' as '他女', and 'it' as '他物'. He likewise translated 'his', 'her', and 'its' respectively as '他男的', '他女的', and '他物的'. Then in 1878, in his Chinese translation of an English grammar book, 文法初阶, Guo Zansheng (郭赞生) appropriated a classical word '伊' and adopted it as the Chinese equivalent of the English pronoun 'she'.

The person eventually responsible for the neologisms we are now familiar with was the writer and linguist, Liu Bannong (刘半农, 1891–1934), who in 1917 came up with the idea of using the traditional '他' for a man and a new word '她' to refer to a woman. Publicized by Zhou Zuoren (周作人), Liu's proposal was later modified by others, who added variations such as '它' and '牠' for nonhuman beings, and '祂' for nonhuman but sacred beings. Supposedly, it was in the following poem by Liu Bannong that he first used, in 1920, the feminine pronoun '她' (she, or her):

教我如何不想她
天上飘着些微云,
地上吹着些微风,
啊……
微风吹动了我的头发,
教我如何不想她?

How Can I Not Miss Her
Light clouds drift in the sky
Gentle breezes blow on earth
Alas!
Gentle breezes brushing my hair
How can I not miss her?[17]

Liu's neologism triggered a firestorm, with many leading intellectuals jumping into the fray, debating the pros and cons of adopting gender-specific pronouns. While the supporters advocated the usefulness of the newly minted pronouns, especially in the context of translating

17 *The Big Red Book of Modern Chinese Literature: Writings from the Mainland in the Long Twentieth Century*, ed. by Yunte Huang (New York: W. W. Norton, 2016), p. 35.

from foreign languages, the detractors of various ideological camps raised objections for very different reasons. The cultural conservatives wanted to preserve the language habit of China, characterizing the neologism as a case of 'cutting one's foot to fit the new shoe'. The women's rights group, surprisingly, also vocalized their objection. As their rationale goes, if the central issue of women's rights is gender equality and gender desegregation, enabling women to function and compete in cultural arenas previously reserved for men, then adopting gender-specific pronouns would only defeat the purpose of the cause. An editorial in a women's magazine took issue with the word '她', arguing that since the former catch-all pronoun '他' contains the radical '人' (person), using '她' for women only is to deprive them of their personhood or humanity. Another commentator opined that since many Chinese words with negative connotations contain the radical '女' (woman), such as '奸' (rape), '嫉' (envy), '妒' (jealousy), and '奴' (slave), adding one more word of the kind to the list would make matters worse for women.[18]

Despite the objections, the convenience of the new pronouns became too apparent. Especially after the founding of the People's Republic, the government sponsored a few rounds of language reforms, codifying all aspects of Chinese ranging from spelling to grammar. Three different third person pronouns became the standard: '他' for 'he', '她' for 'she', and '它' for 'it'. The proverbial cow was out of the barn.

Given that somewhat complicated, entangled history of these pronouns in China, I would now like to examine the use of third person pronouns, particularly'她' (she) and '它' (it), in half a dozen representative Chinese translations of a section of *Jane Eyre*. As most readers of the novel know, the following dialogue between Jane and Mr Rochester, in which she recalls an eerie encounter with Bertha Mason, encapsulates a dynamic motif in the narrative, that is, in the words of Sandra M. Gilbert and Susan Gubar, the 'parallels between Jane and Bertha':[19]

> 'Shall I tell you of what it reminded me?'

---

18 Lang Bo [朗博], 'Weile yige hanzi [为了一个汉字] (For the Sake of a Chinese Word)', *Shijie Huaren Zhoukan* [世界华人周刊] (World Chinese Weekly) (23 October 2018), https://www.sohu.com/a/272476071_176673

19 Sandra M. Gilbert and Susan Gubar, *The Madwoman in the Attic: The Woman Writer and the Nineteenth-Century Literary Imagination* (New Haven: Yale University Press, 1979), p. 360.

> 'You may.'
> 'Of the foul German spectre — the Vampyre.'
> 'Ah? — What did it do?'
> 'Sir, it removed my veil from its gaunt head, rent it in two parts, and flinging both on the floor, trampled on them.'
> 'Afterwards?'
> 'It drew aside the window-curtain and looked out: perhaps it saw dawn approaching, for, taking the candle, it retreated to the door. Just at my bedside the figure stopped: the fiery eye glared upon me — she thrust up her candle close to my face, and extinguished it under my eyes. I was aware her lurid visage flamed over mine, and I lost consciousness: for the second time in my life — only the second time — I became insensible from terror.'[20]

In what has now become a classic interpretation of the novel, Gilbert and Gubar associate the 'madwoman in the attic' with the female protagonist, calling Bertha 'Jane's truest and darkest double'. The feminist critics deem the gothic scene as 'the book's central confrontation', an encounter between Jane and 'her own imprisoned "hunger, rebellion, and rage," a secret dialogue of self and soul on whose outcome [...] the novel's plot, Rochester's fate, and Jane's coming-of-age all depend'.[21]

Given the high stakes of the psychodrama here, it is important to pay attention to the shifting pronouns that Jane uses to describe the 'spectre', the 'Vampyre', which is, to quote Gilbert and Gubar again, 'her own secret self'.[22] As seen in the passage quoted above, Jane begins by using the pronoun 'it' to describe the figure that entered her bedroom: 'of what it reminded me', 'it removed my veil', 'It drew aside the window-curtain', and so on. Then she switches to the female third person pronouns of 'she' and 'her': 'she thrust up her candle', and 'her lurid visage' (or 'her wild visage' in the first edition). The switch, or rather, ambiguity, between the menacing figure as an animal and as a person, highlights the doubling of Jane/Bertha; rather than simply a demonic other, Jane recognizes the figure as part of her rebellious, angry, almost beastly self.

In translation, sensitivity, or the lack thereof, to the subtle and meaningful variations of the pronouns in the English original would also help us assess the degree to which the translator understands the

---

20 *JE*, Ch. 25. See Chapter VII below for further discussion, together with a verbal animation of this prismatic scene.
21 Gilbert and Gubar, *The Madwoman in the Attic*, pp. 360, 339.
22 Gilbert and Gubar, *The Madwoman in the Attic*, p. 348.

psychodrama at play in the novel. Interestingly, without the coinage of new pronouns as we discussed above, a Chinese translator would have had much difficulty rendering those pronoun changes in the English passage. But even with the new pronouns at their disposal, some Chinese translators, as we shall see, still fail to produce a version that does justice to the original.

To make comparison easier, I outline the chain of pronouns used in the English original as follows:

> It—it—it—she—her—her

Now let's look at some of the Chinese translations.

It is worth noting that in Zhou Shoujuan's abridged translation in 1925, the first ever in Chinese, the famous MDB writer rejected the new pronouns and consistently used the classical Chinese '伊' for third person female pronoun. A heavily condensed version, Zhou's text does not contain the passage in question.

In comparison, in the 1935 translation by Wu Guangjian, the translator did adopt the new pronoun '她', but did not use the other pronoun '它' to create a sense of differentiation:

> 她拉开窗帘往外看：　也许她看见天破晓了，拿了蜡烛，向房门走。走过我的床边，站住脚，她两只冒火的眼瞪住看我——把蜡烛凑近我的脸，就在我眼前，把烛吹灭了。我觉得她的冒火眼照住我的眼，我就不省人事。

Disregarding the pronoun variations in the original, Wu used the third person female pronoun '她' throughout the passage: '她—她—她—她的', or to back-translate, 'she—she—her—her'. To add another wrinkle here, the word 'figure' in the original passage contains ambivalence over beast/human. In fact, the sentence 'Just at my bedside the figure stopped' is where the narrator transitions from the use of 'it' to that of 'she'. Since he ignored the pronoun shift, Wu omitted translating the word 'figure' by restructuring the sentence to the equivalent of 'Passing by my bedside and stopping, she stared at me with two fiery eyes'.[23]

In contrast, Li Jiye in his first complete Chinese translation of *Jane Eyre* in 1936, managed to make use of the newly minted pronouns '她' and '它', thus retaining the word play in the original on pronouns as well as the word 'figure':

---

23 Charlotte Brontë, *Gunu piaoling ji* [孤女飘零记] (Record of a Wandering Orphan Girl), trans. by Wu Guangjian [伍光建] (Shanghai: Commercial Press, 1935), p. 424.

它把窗帘拉到一旁，向外看：或许它看到黎明快到了，因为，它拿着蜡烛，退到门那里。正在我床边，这形体站住了。火般眼睛闪视着我——她把蜡烛伸到我脸跟前，给我看着吹熄了。我觉得她的青白的脸面在我的脸上发着光，于是我晕过去了。

The chain of pronouns Li used: '它—它—它—她—她的', or to back-translate, 'it—it—it—she—her'. And he translates 'figure' as '形体', literally 'body form', as ambivalent and noncommittal as the original English word.[24]

Fast forward a few decades, to after the Cultural Revolution, when we saw a sudden surge in the number of Chinese renditions of *Jane Eyre*, and we find that translators differed in their treatments of the key pronouns in the passage. In his version published in 1990, Wu Junxie (吴钧燮) followed the path paved by the earlier translator Li and retained the play on pronouns:

它拉开窗帘，望望外面，也许它发现天快黎明了，因为它拿起蜡烛，朝门口走去。正走到我床边，这个人影停住了。火一样的目光瞪着我，——她猛地把蜡烛一直伸到我的脸跟前，就在我的眼皮底下把它吹灭了。我感觉到她那张可怕的鬼脸在我的脸上面闪闪发光，我昏了过去。

The chain of pronouns Wu used: '它—它—它—她—她', or to back translate, 'it—it—it—she—her'. One difference between Wu and Li, however, lies in that Wu rendered 'figure' as '人影', literally 'human shadow', thus losing the ambiguity.[25]

Another version from that period, by Huang Yuanshen (黄源深), published in 1993, the translator also retained the wordplay on pronouns but killed off the ambiguity by going in the opposite direction in his rendition of 'figure':

它拉开窗帘，往外张望。也许它看到已近拂晓，便拿着蜡烛朝房门退去。正好路过我床边时，鬼影停了下来。火一般的目光向我射来，她把蜡烛举起来靠我的脸，在我眼皮底下把它吹灭了。我感到她白煞煞的脸朝我闪着光，我昏了过去。

As we see, the chain of pronouns Huang used: '它—它—她—她'. And he renders 'figure' as '鬼影', literally 'shadow of a ghost'. Just like Wu's 'human shadow', Huang's choice also eliminated the room for ambivalence between human/nonhuman.[26]

---

24 Charlotte Brontë, *Jianai* [简爱] (Jane Eyre), trans. by Li Jiye [李霁野] (1936; reprint, Xian: Shaanxi People's Press, 1982), p. 348.

25 Charlotte Brontë, *Jianai* [简爱] (Jane Eyre), trans. by Wu Junxie [吴钧燮] (Beijing: People's Literature Press, 1990), p. 381.

26 Charlotte Brontë, *Jianai* [简爱] (Jane Eyre), trans. by Huang Yuanshen [黄源深] (first published in 1993; reprint, Nanjing: Yilin Press, 2016), p. 284.

The most extreme would be the 2005 version by Song Zhaolin (宋兆霖), who used the nonhuman '它' throughout the passage:

> 它拉开窗帘，朝外面看了看，也许是它看到天快要亮了，因为它拿起蜡烛，朝门口退去。正走到我床边，那身影停了下来，一双火红的眼睛恶狠狠直朝我瞪着。它猛地把蜡烛举到我面前，在我的眼皮底下把它吹灭了。我感到它那张可怕的脸在我的脸上方闪出微光，我失去了知觉。

The chain of pronouns Song used: '它—它—它—它—它—它', or to back translate, 'it—it—it—it—it—it'. Like Wu Guangjian in his 1935 version, Song completely eliminated the play on pronouns, although he did so by consistently using the nonhuman '它' whereas Wu had chosen the human '她'. And just like Wu, Song might also claim a redeeming factor, that is, he rendered 'figure' as '身影', literally 'body shadow'.[27]

All things considered, it was the translation by Zhu Qingying, the 1988 edition that enjoyed a phenomenal print run of three million copies, that gave us the most even-handed treatment of pronouns and related issues. Zhu's version reads:

> 它拉开窗帘，朝外边看看；也许它看到了黎明来临，因为它拿起蜡烛退到门口去。这个身影就在我床边停了下来；火一样的眼睛瞪着我——她把蜡烛猛地伸到我前面，让我看着她把它吹熄。我感觉到她那灰黄的脸在我的脸上方闪出微光，我失去了知觉。

The chain of pronouns Zhu used: '它—它—它—她—她—她', or to back translate, 'it—it—it—she—her—her'. And she translated the word 'figure', as Song would do later, as '身影', ('body shadow').[28]

Half a century after Li's first complete translation, through the undulations of the Chinese experience as dramatic as the Cultural Revolution, or as seemingly trivial as the minting of new pronouns, we finally find in Zhu a translation that does poetic justice to the sentimental pilgrimage of Jane Eyre, or '简爱', Simple Love. But as we know, the book is no simple love story, and neither is the translational journey of this beloved novel in the Chinese language.

27 Charlotte Brontë, *Jianai* [简爱] (Jane Eyre), trans. by Song Zhaolin [宋兆霖] (first published in 2005; reprint, Shanghai: Shanghai Art and Literature Press, 2007), p. 305.

28 Charlotte Brontë, *Jianai* [简爱] (Jane Eyre), trans. by Zhu Qingying [祝庆英] (Shanghai: Shanghai Yiwen Press, 1988), p. 372.

Works Cited

Translations of *Jane Eyre*

Brontë, Charlotte, *Chongguang ji* [重光记] (Seeing the Light Again), trans. by Zhou Shoujuan [周瘦鹃], in *Xinxian* [心弦] (Heartstrings) (Shanghai: Dadong shuju, 1925), pp. 1–24.

——, *Gunu piaoling ji* [孤女飘零记] (Record of a Wandering Orphan Girl), trans. by Wu Guangjian [伍光建] (Shanghai: Commercial Press, 1935).

——, *Jianai* [简爱] (*Jane Eyre*), trans. by Li Jiye [李霁野] (1936; reprint, Xian: Shaanxi People's Press, 1982).

——, *Jianai* [简爱] (*Jane Eyre*), trans. by Zhu Qingying [祝庆英] (Shanghai: Shanghai Yiwen Press, 1988).

——, *Jianai* [简爱] (*Jane Eyre*), trans. by Wu Junxie [吴钧燮] (Beijing: People's Literature Press, 1990).

——, *Jianai* [简爱] (*Jane Eyre*), trans. by Song Zhaolin [宋兆霖] (2005; reprint, Shanghai: Shanghai Art and Literature Press, 2007).

——, *Jianai* [简爱] (*Jane Eyre*), trans. by Huang Yuanshen [黄源深] (1993; reprint, Nanjing: Yilin Press, 2016).

Other Sources

Cohn, Peter J., *Pearl S. Buck: A Cultural Biography* (New York: Cambridge University Press, 1996).

Colapinto, John, 'Famous Names: Does It Matter What a Product Is Called?', *The New Yorker* (3 October 2011).

Gilbert, Sandra M., and Susan Gubar, *The Madwoman in the Attic: The Woman Writer and the Nineteenth-Century Literary Imagination* (New Haven: Yale University Press, 1979).

Huang, Yunte (ed.), *The Big Red Book of Modern Chinese Literature: Writings from the Mainland in the Long Twentieth Century* (New York: W. W. Norton, 2016).

Lang, Bo [朗博], 'Weile yige hanzi [为了一个汉字] (For the Sake of a Chinese Word)', *Shijie Huaren Zhoukan* [世界华人周刊] (World Chinese Weekly) (23 October 2018), https://www.sohu.com/a/272476071_176673

Li, Jin [李今], 'Zhou Shoujuan dui jianai de yanqinghua gaixie jiqi yanqingguan [周瘦鹃对《简爱》的言情化改写及其言情观] (Zhou Shoujuan's Sentimentalizing Revision of *Jane Eyre* and His Sentimentalism)', *Wenxue pinglun* [文学评论] (Literary Review), 1 (2013), 70.

Li, Ting [李婷], 'Maodun ceng liangci fanyi Jianai [茅盾曾两次翻译《简爱》] (Maodun Twice Tried to Translate *Jane Eyre*)', *Wenhui* [文汇报] (Literary Newspaper) (7 September 2018), http://m.xinhuanet.com/book/2018-09/07/c_129948806.htm

Mao, Zedong [毛泽东], *Maozhuxi shici sanshiqi shou* [毛主席诗词三十七首] (Thirty-seven Poems by Chairman Mao) (Beijing: Wenwu Press, 1964).

Pound, Ezra, *Poems and Translations*, ed. by Richard Sieburth (New York: The Library of America, 2003).

Qi, Shouhua, 'No Simple Love: The Literary Fortunes of the Brontë Sisters in Post-Mao, Market-Driven China', in *The Brontë Sisters in Other Worlds*, ed. By Shouhua Qi and Jacqueline Padgett (New York: Palgrave Macmillan, 2014), pp. 19–49.

Stein, Gertrude, *Lectures in America* (New York: Random House, 1935).

Xi, Jinping, 'Work Together to Promote Openness, Inclusiveness and Peaceful Development', https://www.fmprc.gov.cn/eng/topics_665678/2015zt/xjpdygjxgsfw/201510/t20151022_705452.html

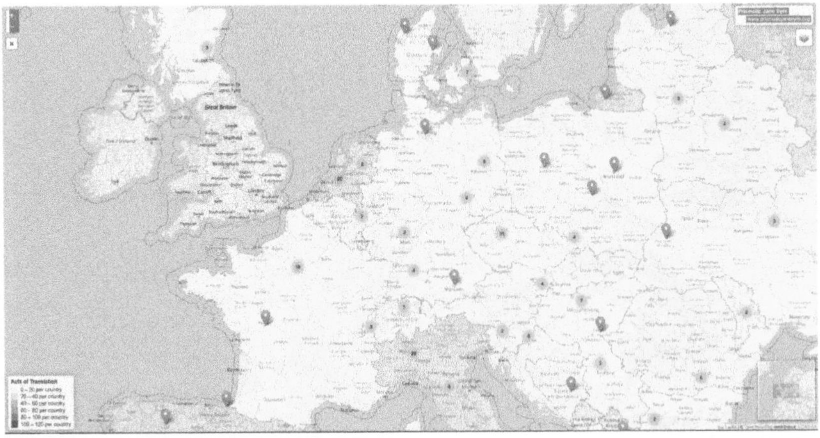

The World Map
https://digitalkoine.github.io/je_prismatic_map
Created by Giovanni Pietro Vitali;
maps © Thunderforest, data © OpenStreetMap contributors

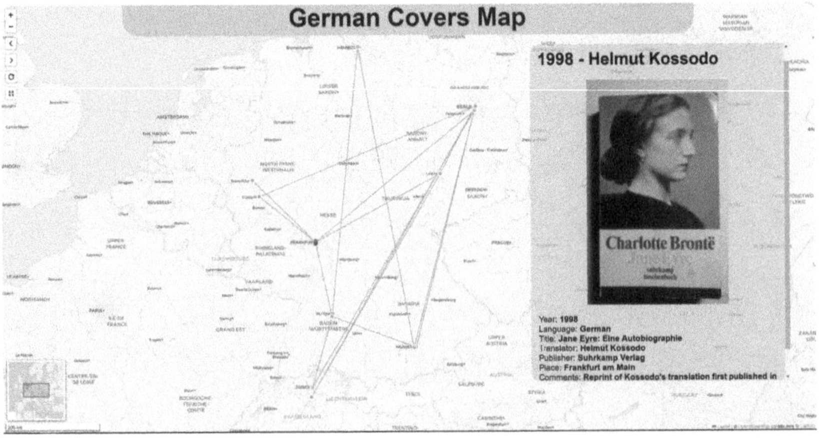

The German Covers Map
https://digitalkoine.github.io/german_storymap/
Researched by Mary Frank and Tom Cheesman; created by
Giovanni Pietro Vitali and Simone Landucci

13. Formality of Address and its Representation of Relationships in Three German Translations of *Jane Eyre*

Mary Frank

German is among the many languages that use both a formal second-person personal pronoun (*Sie*, accompanied by the second-person plural verb form) and an informal one (*du*, accompanied by the second-person singular verb form). The requirement for the translator from English into German to choose either *Sie* or *du* where English has only the undifferentiated *you* will inevitably influence the target-text reader's perception of the degree of formality of a particular relationship. This essay traces the decisions made by three translators of *Jane Eyre* into German about the use of *Sie* and *du*. It does so through the lens of Jane's interactions with three characters: Mrs Reed, Edward Rochester and St John Rivers. In the case of the relationship between Jane and Rochester, it further relates these decisions to the translators' handling of a marker of formality vs. informality already present in the original text: Rochester's addressing of Jane with the diminutive 'Janet'. It asks what effects arise from three translators' decisions about the use of *Sie* or *du*, compared with the original text, and whether these effects can be considered a gain or a loss in translation.

The translations used for this investigation are: Marie von Borch's, first published in 1887–90 — this was the first translation into German that did not omit large parts of the source text; Helmut Kossodo's, first published in 1979 — this was the first largely complete twentieth-century translation and is also the translation that has been most

 https://doi.org/10.11647/OBP.0319.20

reprinted;[1] Melanie Walz's, first published in 2015 — at the time of writing, this is the most recent translation.

It has not been possible to obtain any biographical information about von Borch, but it is clear that she was a quite prominent translator into German of her time, notably of works by pioneering Scandinavian writers such as Jens Peter Jabobsen, Knut Hamsun, and Henrik Ibsen. Kossodo (1915–1994) set up his own publishing house in 1945 that gained a reputation in the 1960s for promoting unorthodox and provocative authors. When this venture failed in the mid-1970s, he turned to translation, from both English and French, to make his living.[2] Walz (born 1953) is a literary translator from English and French whose many translations range from Charles Dickens and Jane Austen, to Salman Rushdie and A. S. Byatt.

Knowing something of the translators' backgrounds and their other works makes it possible to consider, as a secondary question, whether any connections may exist between a translator's handling of *Sie* and *du* in this instance and his or her broader life and career. Further, the translations to be discussed here together span almost 150 years, and this will also allow consideration of the extent to which each translation reflects its historical moment.

Sie/*du* in Jane's Relationship with Mrs Reed

All three translators have Jane address her aunt Mrs Reed formally as *Sie*. Given the coldness between the two, it would be unthinkable for Jane to use *du*. Furthermore, even in close aunt-niece relationships, it would have been expected in the nineteenth century that a niece would address her aunt as *Sie*.[3] It is significant, then, that von Borch has Jane switch temporarily to the informal *du* form in Chapter 2 when pleading with her aunt to be released from the terror of the red room (here shown by singular verb forms, in bold):

1 A detailed history of translations of *Jane Eyre* into German until the 1990s can be found in Stefanie Hohn, *Charlotte Brontës* Jane Eyre *in deutscher Übersetzung: Geschichte eines kulturellen Transfers* (Tübingen: Gunter Narr Verlag, 1998), pp. 211–12.

2 'Zeitmosaik', 28 October 1984, https://www.zeit.de/1994/44/zeitmosaik

3 Until the early nineteenth century, middle- and upper-class children even addressed their parents as *Sie*. See Werner Besch, *Duzen, Siezen, Titulieren: Zur Anrede im Deutschen heute und gestern* (Göttingen: Vandenhoeck & Ruprecht, 1996), p. 105.

> „Oh, Tante, **hab** Erbarmen! **Vergib** mir doch! Ich kann, ich kann es nicht ertragen. — **Bestrafe** mich doch auf andere Weise!“[4]
>
> (‘O aunt, have pity! Forgive me! I cannot endure it — let me be punished some other way!’)

In Chapter 4 of von Borch, Jane again switches temporarily to addressing her aunt informally when, in another moment of emotional turmoil, she objects to having been portrayed to Mr Brocklehurst as a liar (shown here by *du* in the accusative and dative cases, in bold):

> „Ich bin nicht falsch, nicht lügnerisch, wäre ich es, so würde ich sagen, dass ich **dich** liebe, aber ich erkläre **dir**, dass ich **dich** nicht liebe, ich hasse **dich** ...“[5]
>
> (‘I am not deceitful: if I were, I should say I loved you; but I declare I do not love you: I dislike you ...’)[6]

Immediately following this exchange, and perhaps somewhat unconvincingly given that Jane is still ‘thrilled with ungovernable excitement’, von Borch has her regain control and revert to addressing her aunt as *Sie*. This does, however, produce a marked contrast when Jane subsequently quotes the words with which, in *du* form, she had earlier pleaded with her aunt to be released from the red room (in this quotation the *Sie* form is marked in italics and the *du* form in bold):

> „Ich werde niemals vergessen, wie *Sie* mich heftig und rau in das rote Zimmer *zurückstießen* und mich dann *einschlossen* — bis zu meiner Sterbestunde werde ich es nicht vergessen. Obgleich die Todesangst mich verzehrte, obgleich ich vor Jammer und Entsetzen fast erstickend aus allen Kräften schrie und flehte: „**Hab** Erbarmen, Tante Reed! **Hab** Erbarmen“ Und diese Strafe *ließen Sie* mich erdulden ...“[7]
>
> (‘I shall remember how you thrust me back — roughly and violently thrust me back — into the red-room, and locked me up there, to my dying day; though I was in agony; though I cried out, while suffocating with distress, “Have mercy! Have mercy, Aunt Reed!” And that punishment you made me suffer...’)[8]

---

4 Von Borch, p. 8. Page numbers refer to the edition (very lightly) revised by Christian Reichenberg as it is the most easily available printing: all quotations have been checked against the 1887–90 Ph. Reclam text as presented in TextGrid Repository (2012). Brontë, Charlotte. Jane Eyre. Digitale Bibliothek. https://hdl.handle.net/11858/00-1734-0000-0002-454B-6

5 von Borch, p. 18.

6 *JE*, Ch. 4.

7 von Borch, p. 19.

8 *JE*, Ch. 4.

These juxtapositions of *Sie* and *du* in von Borch create two potential effects on the reader. The first is to give a signal of Jane's emotional turmoil that is not present in the original text. In this rendering into German, Jane's very grammar displays her fear and despair, so great that she forgets herself and addresses her aunt informally. The second is to suggest traits in Jane's character that are also not apparent in the original text, since — it might appear — she can switch between the *Sie* and *du* forms at will. In the first instance she does so deliberately to manipulate her aunt, seeking with her informality to establish a closeness between them that will move the latter to compassion. In the second instance, she does so to offend her aunt.

Whether these effects should be considered positive or negative, a gain or a loss in translation, depends on one's view of what translation can and should do. Should a translation offer additional or alternative readings of the source text? Given that the translator into German has no choice but to opt for either *Sie* or *du*, the effect will inevitably be one of destabilisation: a single personal pronoun in English must become one of two in German, with the corresponding effects that this choice brings. One might regard the fact that the juxtaposition of *du* and *Sie* heightens the sense of emotional turmoil as a positive effect of translation, building on what is already present in the text. On the other hand, for this juxtaposition to also suggest new character traits might be considered rather problematic.

Neither Kossodo nor Walz have Jane switch, even *in extremis*, to addressing her aunt informally. As outlined above, this may, or may not, be considered a lost opportunity in terms of the potential effects of switching to *du*. What *is* clear is that any switch between *Sie* and *du* needs careful handling by the translator. In Kossodo, Jane uses the *Sie* form when pleading for release from the red room:

> »Ach, Tante! Haben *Sie* Mitleid! Verzeihen *Sie* mir doch! Ich kann es nicht ertragen! Strafen *Sie* mich anderswie!«[9]

However, when in Kossodo Jane later reminds her aunt of this episode, she quotes words that are in the *du* form (*Sie* form marked in italics and *du* form in bold):

> »Bis zu meiner letzten Stunde werde ich es *Ihnen* nie vergessen, wie *Sie* mich hart und grausam *zurückstießen*, wie *Sie* mich in das Rote Zimmer gestoßen *haben* und trotz meiner Todesangst und Verzeiflung dort

9 Kossodo, p. 24.

eingeschlossen, trotz meiner flehentlichen Bitten, ›**hab** Erbarmen! **hab** Erbamen, Tante Reed!‹ Und diese Strafe *haben Sie* mir auferlegt ...«[10]

It is possible that, like von Borch, Kossodo felt that the emotional intensity of Jane's rebellion against her aunt merited a switch to the *du* form. If this is the case, then he overlooked the fact that, in the original exchange in Chapter 2, he had remained with the *Sie* form. Alternatively, Kossodo may simply have been drawing on an earlier translation and failed to remember that he had altered the words in Chapter 2. In either case, the effect is incongruous: Jane's sudden and fleeting use of the *du* form simply leaves the reader puzzled.

Sie/*du* in Jane's Relationship with Edward Rochester

In all three translations, Jane's relationship with Edward Rochester begins on a formal footing, each using the *Sie* form as would befit the master-servant hierarchy. As their relationship turns to love, each translation introduces informality, but with significant contrasts, both between translations and between how Jane and Rochester each use *du*. These contrasts will be explored below, but should be prefaced by setting the wider social context. In the nineteenth century, German-speaking middle-class women generally addressed their husband formally as *Ihr* (later replaced by *Sie*), while they were addressed by their husband informally as *du*.[11]

It is possibly with this context in mind that none of the three translators ever have Jane cross the barrier into using *du* with Rochester when addressing him face-to-face. On his first proposal, Rochester invites Jane to 'give me my name'.[12] Despite this, even in Chapter 38 (when they have been married for ten years) she refers to him more often as 'Mr Rochester' than 'Edward', and it seems all three translators felt that this persistent formality in his presence indicated against the switch to *du* that would normally accompany using a person's first name. It is only when Jane speaks to him in his absence or in her mind that the translators consider switching to *du*. This is first seen at the end of Chapter 24, during their month of courtship.

10 Kossodo, p. 50.
11 Besch, *Duzen, Siezen, Titulieren*, p. 105.
12 *JE*, Ch. 23.

Here, von Borch and Walz both have Jane use the *du* form when she speaks to Rochester in her mind:

> „Jetzt vermag ich **dich** durch vernünftige Behandlung im Schach halten," dachte ich bei mir … (von Borch)[13]
>
> ('I can keep you in reasonable check now,' I reflected …)
>
> »Ich weiß jetzt, wie ich mit **dir** umspringen muss«, dachte ich … (Walz)[14]

Jane's continued use of *Sie* when addressing Rochester directly shows appropriate respect from a nineteenth-century wife for her husband, especially a husband who is a former employer. However, these two translators' decision to shift to *du* when she speaks to him indirectly mirrors the overall plot context in which these words are spoken and arguably enhances their effect. At this point, Jane is determined to show that she cannot be won over too easily by Rochester. Her use of *du* in von Borch and Walz places the couple on equal terms, indeed even highlights the way in which Jane subtly manipulates Rochester while outwardly appearing compliant and meek (reflecting her words, 'I thus thwarted and afflicted him').

In Chapter 35, all three translators have Jane call out to Rochester in the *du* form in response to hearing his voice. In contrast with the use of *du* casting Jane as consciously manipulative in the example above, here it seems an involuntary response to deep emotion:

> „Ich **komme**!" rief ich. „**Warte** auf mich! Oh, ich will kommen!" Ich flog an die Tür und sah in den Korridor hinaus, er war dunkel. Ich lief in den Garten; er war leer. „Wo **bist du**?" rief ich aus. (von Borch)[15]
>
> ('I am coming!' I cried. 'Wait for me! Oh, I will come!' I flew to the door, and looked into the passage: it was dark. I ran out into the garden: it was void. 'Where are you?' I exclaimed.)
>
> »Ich **komme**!« rief ich. »**Warte**, ich komme!« Ich lief zur Tür und schaute in den Gang. Es war dunkel. Ich lief in den Garten. Er war leer.
>
> »Wo **bist du**?« rief ich laut. (Kossodo)[16]
>
> »Ich **komme**!« rief ich. »**Warte** auf mich! Oh, ich komme bald!« Ich eilte zur Tür und sah in den Flur: Dunkelheit. Ich lief in den Garten hinaus. Niemand war dort. »Wo **bist du**?«, rief ich. (Walz)[17]

---

13 von Borch, p. 157.
14 Walz, p. 362.
15 von Borch, p. 241.
16 Kossodo, p. 549.
17 Walz, p. 554.

In all three translations, Rochester switches to addressing Jane informally as *du* at the point of his first proposal in Chapter 23. On the one hand, the translator can treat this event, like Jane's pleading to be released from the red room, as a point of particularly heightened emotion that can be highlighted in translation with an apparent involuntary shift to informal address. On the other, it can be treated as an 'official' milestone in their relationship which 'entitles' Rochester to now address Jane as *du*. In von Borch and Walz, the shift from *Sie* to *du* is highlighted through its occurring in the course of a single sentence (*Sie* form marked in italics and *du* form in bold):

> „*Kommen Sie* zu mir — *kommen Sie* für Zeit und Ewigkeit zu mir," [...] „**Mach du** mein Glück." (von Borch)[18]
>
> ('Come to me — come to me entirely now,' [...] 'Make my happiness...')
>
> »*Kommen Sie* zu mir — *kommen Sie* und *seien Sie* die Meine«, [...] »**Mach** mich glücklich.« (Walz)[19]

It is in the latter sense that von Borch and Kossodo pursue Rochester's switch to addressing Jane informally: after this point, they do not have him revert to using *Sie* to her. In contrast, Walz seems to pursue the former sense, treating the proposal as a passing moment of heightened emotion that can be spotlighted by, but only merits, a temporary switch to *du*. This appears to be confirmed by the fact that, in Chapter 37, Walz again has Rochester 'lapse' into the *du* form at a point of heightened emotion, when he is recalling the moment at which he called out to her:

> »Wie verlangte es mich nach **dir**, Janet! Oh, wie verlangte es mich nach **dir** seelisch und körperlich!«[20]
>
> ('I longed for thee, Janet! Oh, I longed for thee both with soul and flesh!')

It is interesting to note that this one of only two points in the novel where Brontë uses the old-fashioned *thee* instead of *you*. It is possible to speculate that, alongside this being a moment of emotional intensity, Walz's choice of the *du* form at this point was influenced by the fact that *thee* is a cognate of the Low German *di*. If this was the case, then it did not influence Walz's decision-making at the other point (in Chapter 23) where Brontë uses *thee*. Here, having had Rochester temporarily

18 von Borch, p. 145.
19 Walz, p. 337.
20 Walz, p. 589.

switch to *du* when proposing to Jane a short time before, Walz has swiftly had him firmly revert to *Sie* (*Sie* form marked in italics):

> »Ich hätte bis zum Morgen so mit *Ihnen* sitzen können, Jane.«
>
> ('I could have sat with thee till morning, Jane')[21]

Sie/*du* in Jane's Relationship with St John Rivers

It has been noted that the translator may regard a proposal scene as a turning point at which it becomes appropriate to have characters switch from using *Sie* to using *du*, both because it is a moment of emotional intensity and because it represents a 'formal' milestone. This was seen to pertain in all three translations in the case of Rochester's first proposal to Jane, albeit only temporarily in Walz. In contrast, however, von Borch is the only translation in which the same rationale is applied when Jane's cousin St John proposes to her in Chapter 34. In this translation, St John switches from *Sie* to *du* in the space of an intervening sentence (*Sie* form marked in italics and *du* form in bold):

> „Und was sagt *Ihr* Herz *Ihnen*?" fragte St. John.
>
> „Mein Herz ist stumm — mein Herz ist stumm," entgegnete ich bebend und schaudernd.
>
> „Dann muss ich für dasselbe sprechen," [...] „Jane, **komm** mit mir nach Indien! **Komm** mit mir als meine Helferin, meine Mitarbeiterin."[22]
>
> ('And what does *your* heart say?' demanded St. John.
>
> 'My heart is mute, — my heart is mute,' I answered, struck and thrilled.
>
> 'Then I must speak for it,' continued the deep, relentless voice. 'Jane, come with me to India: come as my helpmeet and fellow-labourer.')

The absence of a switch from formal to informal address can say as much as its presence. One can interpret the fact that Kossodo and Walz do not have St John switch to addressing Jane as *du* at this point of emotional intensity as reflecting their response to Brontë's portrayal of St John as a man who puts religious duty before love. While he may have feelings for Jane, St John's religious calling is his highest priority and he perceives her first and foremost as somebody who can help him fulfil this calling, rather than as a wife to be loved in her own right. The decision of these translators thus reveals a value

21 Walz, p. 338.
22 von Borch, p. 231.

judgment: in their view, he is not sufficiently capable of true love to call Jane *du*. Given that the translators must choose between *Sie* or *du*, a value judgment is inevitable, but it is one that steers the target-text reader towards forming an additional impression of St John that is not present in the source text.

In the light of St John's privileging of duty over love, it is somewhat surprising that, in von Borch, his switch to addressing Jane informally is permanent. By analogy with the cases discussed above, where the switch from *Sie* to *du* takes place at moments of emotional intensity when the person concerned is temporarily swept away by their feelings, one might expect that von Borch would have St John swiftly return to his usual rational self and revert to *Sie*. The fact that this is not the case suggests to the reader, whether deliberately or not on von Borch's part, that St John should perhaps not be regarded as entirely devoid of human feeling.

For her part, Jane does not deviate in any of the three translations from addressing St John as *Sie*. This would have been normal between male and female cousins at the time (in contrast, Jane and St John's sisters Mary and Diana address each other as *du* in von Borch and Walz even before they know they are cousins, and in Kossodo thereafter), and is thus not marked in Kossodo and Walz. In von Borch, the fact that St John switches to using *du* towards Jane means that her continued use of *Sie* towards him becomes marked. It is a lexical sign of what is contained in the original text but does not sit directly on the surface in the way that the contrast between *du* and *Sie* in this translation does: while St John wants to bind Jane to him in pursuing his calling, her continued love for Rochester means that she cannot forge an emotional connection with St John, a state made clear in the target text through her failure to switch from using *Sie*.

The Contrast Between 'Jane' and 'Janet' as a Marker of Formality

Brontë uses 'Janet', a diminutive of Jane, to signal the increasing closeness of the relationship between Rochester and Jane. Rochester first uses this term of endearment in Chapter 22, at the point when Jane returns from having spent a month at her aunt Reed's deathbed (one could speculate that this is intended to suggest that her absence has increased his affection towards her, and their relationship is now entering a new phase of intimacy). In total, he addresses Jane as Janet four times before his first proposal in the following chapter, and fifteen times thereafter. One can trace some interesting connections between the use of the informal and formal personal pronouns between Rochester and Jane and his addressing of her as Janet.

None of the three translators replicate Rochester's pre-proposal use of Janet, except, on just one occasion, Walz. If one sets this single use in Walz aside as statistically insignificant, then it is possible to construct an understanding of the use of a diminutive in the translators' eyes as being necessarily connected with, indeed triggered by, the switch from *Sie* to *du* by Rochester at the point of his proposal. Kossodo and Walz show a very similar pattern, the former using Janet the first time that the name is used by Brontë after the proposal, and on eleven of the fifteen occasions thereafter, and the latter using Janet twelve times after the proposal. It is as if, in these translators' minds, a term of endearment cannot be used unless, at the same time, the person to whom it is directed can also be addressed as *du*. In the case of Walz, this use of *du* does not need to be permanent. Recall that, in this translation, Rochester reverts to addressing Jane as *Sie*. It is apparent that, for Walz, there is no contradiction between using a term of endearment together with the formal mode of address, as long as that term has been introduced hand-in-hand with informal address.

In contrast, von Borch delays replicating Rochester's use of Janet until Chapter 37. Stefanie Hohn argues that many of the decisions present in this translation (lexical choices, additions and omissions) suggest that, motivated by her religious beliefs, 'Von Borch ist ganz offenbar bemüht, das leidenschaftliche Temperament der weiblichen Hauptfigur in respektablen Grenzen zu halten' ('Von Borch is very clearly concerned to keep the passionate temperament of the female main character within respectable boundaries').[23] Hohn does not mention von Borch's significant delay in introducing Rochester's use of Janet compared with the original text in this regard, but it can be seen to correspond with the pattern that she identifies. In addressing Jane familiarly as Janet, Rochester suggests a (possibly physical) closeness with her that von Borch, seeking to portray Jane as innocent and pure, does not wish to allow to enter the narrative until Jane is a mature, independent woman and Rochester is at last free to marry her, thus making their closeness respectable.

23 Hohn, *Charlotte Brontës* Jane Eyre, p. 103 (my translation).

One could regard Brontë's placing of the term Janet in Rochester's mouth as to some degree an 'equivalent' device to the ability of the translators into German to have him switch from *Sie* to *du* in addressing Jane, in that both devices allow the signalling of a growing intimacy in their relationship. In this case, one can detect both similarities and differences in usage between the English and German devices. Compared with the use of Janet, all three translators have Rochester switch to using *du* later. On the other hand, Kossodo then replicates Brontë's placing of Janet in his mouth by having Rochester consistently use *du* thereafter. Walz both follows and deviates from Brontë's usage: to some degree, the effect of using Janet to signal growing intimacy is negated by Walz's decision to have Rochester revert to addressing Jane as *Sie*. Finally, von Borch delays the replication of the term of endearment the longest. While this appears to be a deliberate measure designed to cast Jane as innocent and pure, the loss of a sense of intimacy that would have arisen from its usage is to some degree mitigated by the permanent switch to Rochester addressing Jane as *du* at the point of the first proposal.

It should be noted, finally, that the effect of Rochester's use of Janet on the German-speaking reader is of course dependent on that reader understanding that this is a term of endearment. None of the translators exploit any of the measures that would have been at their disposal to explicate the term. Such measures might have included a footnote, a neologism constructed on German diminutive patterns, such as Janelein, or a gloss on first usage, along the lines of 'Meine liebe, kleine Jane, meine Janet' ['My dear little Jane, my Janet']. Kossodo and Walz, however, exploit the power of the contrast between *Sie* and *du* to provide guidance for their readers as to the significance of Janet. By delaying the term's introduction until after Rochester has proposed (and addressed Jane as *du*), they signal that his use of Janet should be read as similarly indicating that the couple's relationship has entered a new phase. In von Borch, the time that elapses between the proposal and Rochester's use of Janet may well be too long for the reader to make this connection. Instead, the term's sudden appearance in Chapter 37 seems rather unmotivated.

Discussion

Any translator from English into German, and indeed from English into many other languages, cannot avoid having to choose between the formal and the informal second-person personal pronouns. In her introduction to the notes that accompany her translation, Walz draws attention to the difficulty this can pose the translator:

> ... es bleibt [...] der Phantasie des Lesers und des Übersetzers anheimgestellt, an welchen Stellen die Personen des Romans sich duzen können oder sollen. Dass die kleine Jane von ihrer Tante geduzt wird und sie siezt, ist naheliegend; schwieriger wird es, wenn Rochester Jane umwirbt und ihr Liebesworte ins Ohr flüstert, denn auch wenn er noch so vertraulich zu ihr spricht, bleibt sie in ihren Kommentaren an die Adresse der Leserschaft immer bei der distanzierten Bezeichnung *my master*, und sie nennt Rochester nie beim Vornamen, nur das eine Mal, als er sie darum bittet.[24]
>
> (... it is a matter for the imagination of the reader and the translator to decide where in the novel the characters can or should call each other du. It is obvious that young Jane is addressed as du by her aunt and that she calls her aunt Sie; it becomes harder when Rochester courts Jane and whispers words of love in her ear, because even though he speaks to her very intimately, she continues to refer to him in her comments to her readers with the formal term *my master*, and she never uses Rochester's first name apart from on the one occasion when he asks her to do so.)

Walz's assessment of this issue can be expanded. It is the translator who must first make decisions about whether to use *Sie* or *du*. As Walz indicates, these decisions are sometimes uncomfortable. Inevitably, too, they will influence the readers' perceptions of the relationships between characters. But as Walz also indicates, readers are not passive 'consumers' of a translator's decision-making. The fact that the translator has chosen either *Sie* or *du*, or indeed has deliberately contrasted the two, then invites — even forces — the reader to ask in turn whether, in his or her view, the use of *Sie* or *du* sits well with a particular character at a particular moment of the plot. Readers must make their own decisions and engage with the text in a way that the neutral *you* of the original text does not require them to.

If the need to choose between *Sie* and *du* prompts the reader to engage with the text, it is regrettable that the tone of Walz's statement

24 Walz, p. 631 (My translation).

also verges on the apologetic, suggesting that this choice could damage the original text. One can also pursue a line of argument that challenges the idea that the existence of two possible levels of formality prompts reader engagement with the text. According to this view, it inhibits it. The choice made by opting for either *Sie* or *du*, with their clear implications of (in)formality which do not exist in the neutral *you*, brings a layer of explicature to the target text that does not exist in the original. The original reader gradually assesses for him- or herself the various characters' closeness, or distance, on the basis of Brontë's lexical clues (as Walz further points out in her note, Jane's use of *my master* indicates the hierarchy of their relationship, for example), whereas in the case of the target text that assessment has been made already by the translator and sits on the surface in its very grammar, already set out for the reader rather than awaiting discovery. Something of the 'mystery' of the original has thus been lost.

To take this argument further, it has been seen that a translator's decision-making with regard to shifts between *Sie* and *du* can have the effect of suggesting a value judgment on a character or of suggesting character traits not present in the original text. By either having St John continue to address Jane as *Sie* after proposing to her (Kossodo and Walz), or by having him switch to *du* (von Borch), the translators implicitly judge him as somebody who is either relentlessly cold or, alternatively, capable of loving. In the case of von Borch's decision-making regarding shifts between *Sie* and *du* in the relationship between Jane and her aunt, the introduction of a shift from *Sie* to *du* can be interpreted by the reader not as a character's involuntary response at a time of heightened emotion, but as a signal of a deliberate violation of the conventions of formal and informal address, in order to manipulate or cause offence. This, then, suggests a character trait that is not present in the original. For the translator's decision-making to have the effect of shaping the reader's view of a character can again be seen as undermining the reader's own journey of discovery and interpretative abilities.

One can, on the other hand, regard the contrast between *Sie* and *du* as introducing a welcome and enriching nuancing into *Jane Eyre* in German. The availability of two second-person personal pronouns in German can be seen as filling a gap left by the neutrality of the English term *you*. The target-text readers' experience is enhanced by the existence of an additional means of tracing the shifts in the various relationships. One cannot help wondering whether, if an equivalent device had been available to Brontë, she would have gladly used it (indeed, her use of the diminutive Janet to signal the growing closeness between Jane and Rochester could be interpreted as her seeking precisely such a device). In particular, the way in which the contrast between *Sie* and *du* is used in translation to signal and add emphasis to a moment of emotional intensity can hardly be seen as a translation 'loss'. Rather, the way the translators allow grammar to work hand in hand with lexis and plot to create such moments should be seen as an example of how a text, necessarily disquietened as it moves from one language to another, can gain in translation. This effect is particularly successful in the von Borch and Walz translations of Rochester's first proposal, where the shift from *Sie* to *du* takes place within a single sentence and is thus especially marked. No language can ever be complete in itself. In this case, German can give *Jane Eyre* something that English lacks. The necessity of choosing between *Sie* and *du* becomes a virtue.

The foregoing discussion has highlighted trends in the usage of *Sie* and *du* in these three translations that can now be considered in the light of the individual translators' backgrounds and of the wider socio-cultural contexts in which the translations were undertaken.

One might expect that von Borch, the translation made only a few decades after *Jane Eyre* was published, would demonstrate the most formality in address. In fact, the opposite is the case. As has been seen, it is in this translation that the possibility of switching from *Sie* to *du* at moments of emotional intensity is most exploited (it is the only translation to use this technique in relation to Jane's relationship with her aunt). It is possible to read into this — for the time — progressive stance on formality a connection between von Borch and the modern Scandinavian authors she was also translating and, more generally, a connection with the arrival of this literature in Germany. On the other hand, however, this translation can be regarded as the most conservative in its treatment of the use of the term Janet, which is very delayed compared with Kossodo and Walz. It stands, then, on a cusp between the traditional moral context of the early and mid-nineteenth century and the emerging literary world of the late nineteenth century. It seems that, at this point, von Borch judged that to also use Janet, Brontë's own device for indicating familiarity, would have taken informality too far.

In line with a general trend for *du* to be used increasingly readily nowadays, one might expect that the most recent translation, Walz, would show a tendency in this direction. Again, the opposite is the case. This is the only translation in which Rochester switches only temporarily to addressing Jane as *du* at the moment when he proposes to her. One might understand Walz's opting for greater formality between Jane and Rochester as a conscious effort to return *Jane Eyre* to its nineteenth-century context. The fact that this translation was made to mark the 200th anniversary of Brontë's birth may well have strongly influenced Walz to adopt this strategy. In the same vein, this translation is subtitled 'Eine Autobiographie' (*An Autobiography*), as was the novel when first published. It should be noted, too, that Walz's other translations include a considerable number of literary classics.

A return to greater formality in *Jane Eyre* in translation may also be an indication of a changing tide in translational interpretation of the novel. Hohn observes how Kossodo, in the notes to his translation, highlights Jane's desire to be a strong, independent woman.[25] Kossodo's observation firmly aligns with the context of production, the Women's Liberation Movement being very active in the years running up to 1979, the year of first publication of this translation. It is somewhat surprising, then, that Kossodo does not tend towards greater equality between Jane and Rochester in terms of the formality of their address. As in von Borch, dating from nearly one hundred years earlier, in Kossodo Rochester addresses Jane as *du* after his proposal, but she continues to address him as *Sie*. There is, however, a very notable non-grammatical marker of greater informality in Kossodo compared with the original text and with the other two translations. Here, many of Jane's uses of the words *sir* and *master* are omitted, or greater equality between the two is introduced through these words being rendered with the less loaded *Mr Rochester* or *er* (he). Here, then, it is possible to discern some connection with Kossodo's desire, during his career as a publisher that preceded his work as a translator, to promote progressive views.

25 Hohn, *Charlotte Brontës* Jane Eyre, p. 92.

Conclusion

Studying the contrasting formality and informality of address in three translations of *Jane Eyre* into German has highlighted the fact that translation cannot be a neutral process. Every time the translator chooses between the personal pronouns *Sie* and *du*, there is potential for this choice to shape readers' perceptions of the relationships between characters. Juxtaposing *Sie* and *du* can both heighten emotional intensity and, in the case of Jane's interaction with her aunt, suggest character traits that are not apparent in the original text. Switching from *Sie* to *du* indicates a dimension of meaning in the progression of relationships, especially that of Rochester and Jane, that is not contained in the neutral English personal pronoun *you*. Even the fact of the absence of a switch, in the case of Jane's addressing of St John, indicates more than is present in the original text. To some observers, the explicitation that accompanies the use of either *Sie* or *du* is a loss in translation, a transformation that robs the original text of some of its mystery. A sensitive translator, however, can turn the inevitability of having to switch between *Sie* and *du* into a virtue. Through creative decisions that will challenge readers, the translator's handling of formality of address has the potential to invite deeper engagement with the text.

Works Cited

Translations of *Jane Eyre*

Brontë, Charlotte, *Jane Eyre, die Waise von Lowood, eine Autobiographie*, trans. by Maria von Borch, revised by Christian Reichenbach (Belle Époque, n.d.).

——, *Jane Eyre, Eine Autobiographie*, trans. by Helmut Kossodo (Frankfurt aM/ Leipzig: Insel Verlag, 2008 [1979]).

——, *Jane Eyre: Eine Autobiographie*, trans. by Melanie Walz (Berlin: Insel Verlag, 2015).

Other Sources

Besch, Werner, *Duzen, Siezen, Titulieren: Zur Anrede im Deutschen heute und gestern* (Göttingen: Vandenhoeck & Ruprecht, 1996).

Hohn, Stefanie, *Charlotte Brontës Jane Eyre in deutscher Übersetzung: Geschichte eines kulturellen Transfers* (Tübingen: Gunter Narr Verlag, 1998).

'Zeitmosaik', 28 October 1984, https://www.zeit.de/1994/44/zeitmosaik

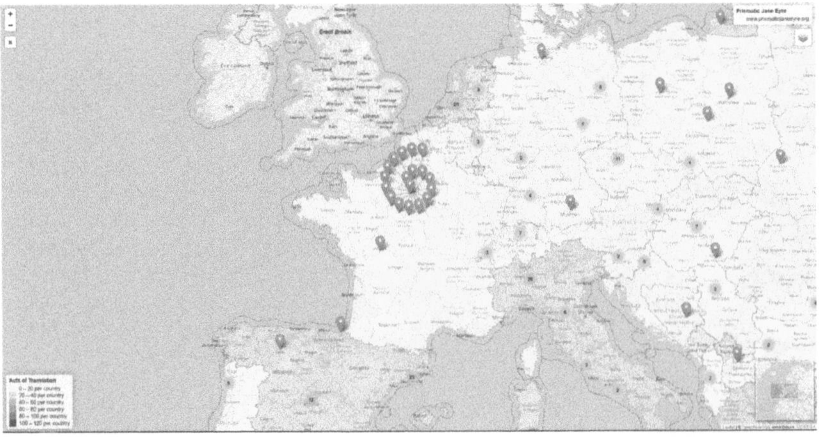

The World Map
https://digitalkoine.github.io/je_prismatic_map
Created by Giovanni Pietro Vitali;

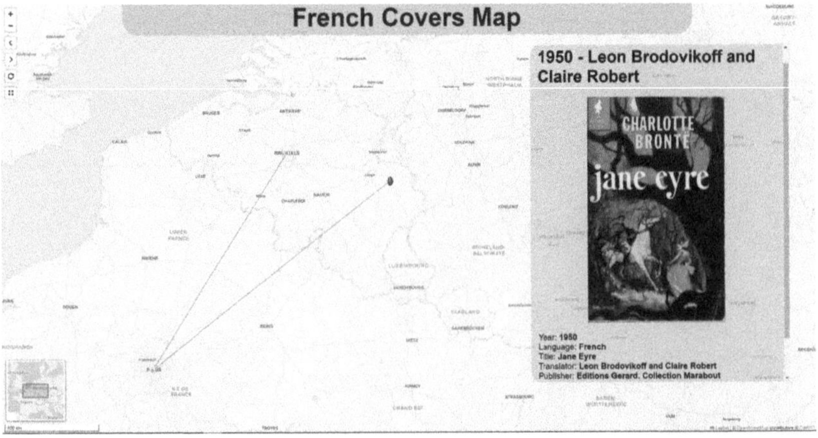

The French Covers Map
https://digitalkoine.github.io/french_storymap/
Researched by Céline Sabiron, Léa Rychen and Vincent Thierry;
created by Giovanni Pietro Vitali and Simone Landucci

14. Biblical Intertextuality in the French *Jane Eyre*

Léa Rychen

Introduction: The Bible of Jane Eyre in *Jane Eyre*

In the mid-nineteenth century, English novelists tended to expect from their readership an extended knowledge of the Biblical texts, and Charlotte Brontë certainly did not depart from this principle. She was born in a parsonage as the daughter of a clergyman, and her upbringing in an Evangelical Anglican household profoundly influenced her own reading and writing.[1] The centrality of Christianity in Brontë's works is evidenced in her 1853 novel *Villette* and its virulent criticism of Roman Catholicism, but *Jane Eyre* also echoes the Christian faith. Time and again, the novel published in 1847 quotes the Bible, especially the iconic language of the King James version.[2] This translation produced by the Church of England, commissioned by James VI and I in 1604 and published in 1611, is even considered by some 'the most important book in English religion and culture'.[3] Biblical intertextuality is paramount to the understanding of *Jane Eyre*. Along her journey, the protagonist encounters characters such as Brocklehurst, Helen and St John, whose immersion in religion radically defines their choices of actions and words. As will be studied later, Jane's interactions with them often present her own radical interpretation of the Christian

1 See Phyllis Kelson Jones, 'Religious Beliefs of Charlotte Brontë, as Reflected in her Novels and Letters' (unpublished doctoral thesis, The Open University, 1997).

2 This rings true for countless English literary works, from Shakespeare to Shelley, via Bacon, Bunyan, and Blake. See Richard E. Crook, 'The Influence of the Bible on English Literature', *The Irish Church Quarterly*, 4 (1911), 283–95.

3 David Norton, cited by Arnold Hunt, '400 years of the King James Bible', *The Times Literary Supplement*, (February 9 2011).

https://doi.org/10.11647/OBP.0319.21

sacred text, which serves as a foundation for her reflections on life, love, meaning and purpose.

In the twenty-one different translations of *Jane Eyre* in French, the web of intertextual references to the Christian Bible has suffered many changes. *Traduttore, traditore*, as the famous saying goes: is the Biblical intertextuality of *Jane Eyre* betrayed in the French translations? Many factors account for such a loss, from the translators' own styles, the cuts in the original texts, and the various translation choices, to the very history of the culture the translations are produced for. Indeed, as the history of Christianity in France dramatically differs from that in England, so too does the place of the Biblical texts and language in the literary culture. There is no French equivalent of the 1611 English Authorized Version, no canonical Bible to attach one's religious imagery to. And as the process of secularization accelerated in the French-speaking world, that same religious imagery drastically faded for Charlotte Brontë's future readership. *Jane Eyre* is written not only in English but also in the language of the Bible, with connections to its characters and stories. A comparison of seven different translations written between 1854 and 2008 shows that the French translators very often alter the significance of the Biblical allusions.[4]

A revelation on Revelation

> 'Do you read your Bible?'
>
> 'Sometimes.'
>
> 'With pleasure? Are you fond of it?'
>
> 'I like Revelations, and the book of Daniel, and Genesis and Samuel, and a little bit of Exodus, and some parts of Kings and Chronicles, and Job and Jonah.'
>
> 'And the Psalms? I hope you like them?'
>
> 'No, sir.'[5]

Early in the novel, ten-year-old Jane meets the sinister Brocklehurst who confronts her about her knowledge of the Bible. The young girl shows her singularity by citing difficult, prophetic books as her favourite ones: among them is the last book of the New Testament canon. A translation of the first word in Koine Greek, *apokalypsis*

---

4 The seven French translations under study are those of Noëmi Lesbazeilles-Souvestre (1854), Marion Gilbert and Madeleine Duvivier (1919), Léon Brodovikoff and Claire Robert ([1946] 1950), R. Redon and J. Dulong (1946), Charlotte Maurat (1964), Sylvère Monod (1966), and Dominique Jean (2008).

5 *JE*, Ch. 4.

(which means 'unveiling' or 'revelation'), the English title ranges from *The Book of Revelation*, *Revelation to John*, and *Apocalypse of John*, to simply *The Revelation* or *Revelation*. In French, according to tradition the title *L'Apocalypse* is used, after the Latin Vulgate translation *apocalypsis*, but the book is sometimes referred to as *Livre de la Révélation* or *Révélation de Jésus-Christ*. It is interesting to note that Charlotte Brontë writes 'Revelations' in the plural, an unusual form of the title which might be thought a misquotation. In the mouth of ten-year-old Jane Eyre, however, it could mean both the apocalyptic book and the apocalyptic genre, to which Daniel and Job might also pertain.

Some French translators closely follow the original and translate quite literally 'les Révélations' (Lesbazeilles-Souvestre, 1854;[6] Brodovikoff and Robert, 1946;[7] Maurat, 1964;[8] and Jean, 2008),[9] while the others choose 'l'Apocalypse'.[10] For the French readership, the first choice tends to obscure the direct relation to the Bible. Is the aim to draw the reader away from the clear mention of the controversial Biblical book? Is it to stick to the script of the original novel, with the equivocal word in the plural form? A comparison with another mention in the novel can help understand these translation choices.

The second instance when the book of Revelation is mentioned is in Chapter 35, when St John Rivers gives the evening reading. The shift is apparent: 'la Révélation' appears in one translation (Brodovikoff and Robert, 1946);[11] 'l'Apocalypse' in all the others. The standard title is reinstated; the possibility of a play on words with all Biblical revelations disappears. However, the term 'la Révélation' also alludes to the Revelation of God through Jesus Christ — that is, the Christian message in its entirety — and thus gives a broader perspective on what is revealed. In the 1897 Service and Paton edition of Brontë's text — the one reproduced electronically in Project Gutenberg — there is an evolution between the two passages, and 'Revelations' becomes 'Revelation'.[12] Although the original text has the plural form in both cases, the shift is significant. In between, Jane has endured all kinds of revelations as she has grown up and walked on her faith journey

6 Lesbazeilles-Souvestre, The Project Gutenberg electronic text.
7 Brodovikoff and Robert, p. 39.
8 Maurat, p. 47. 'Révélations' is italicised.
9 Jean, p. 75.
10 See for example Redon and Dulong, p. 32.
11 Brodovikoff and Robert, p. 497.
12 See Essay 2 above for a discussion of this edition.

(the book is indeed often viewed as a female *Bildungsroman*). The revelations and emotions she wrestles with pave the way for a much more linear, consistent, solid truth. Jane's vision of God, her understanding of the Bible and of herself, her own character and vision for the future have become clearer. In the novel, other instances of the term 'revelation' (in singular or plural form, but with a lower-case 'r') include the encounter with the gypsy woman (Chapter 18), Jane's Christic vision over the bed of the wounded Mason (Chapter 20), and Jane's critical conversations about love and duty with Rochester and St John (Chapters 20, 27, and 34). Jane's path is fraught with revelations that lead to her own search for (Biblical) truth.

In French, translators Léon Brodovikoff and Claire Robert keep this same tension with the evolution from 'les Révélations' to 'la Révélation': this suggests that they used the Service and Paton text, or another edition that included the same variant, and that they kept very close to the English, allowing for double meanings while making the reference to the Bible less obvious. On the contrary, Marion Gilbert and Madeleine Duvivier, R. Redon and J. Dulong, and Sylvère Monod have kept 'l'Apocalypse' all the way through, asserting the allegiance to the Biblical book and placing Jane Eyre in a Biblical frame, while losing the possible correspondences with the character's personal revelations. Noëmi Lesbazeilles-Souvestre, Charlotte Maurat and Dominique Jean give 'les Révélations' (in italics for Maurat) in the first instance, keeping ten-year-old Jane's own words when describing the Bible, and re-establishing the official title of the Biblical book ('l'Apocalypse') when it is actually read through and quoted.

Jane as Felix: A Multi-Dimensional Characterisation

> Still I felt that Helen Burns considered things by a light invisible to my eyes. I suspected she might be right and I wrong; but I would not ponder the matter deeply; like Felix, I put it off to a more convenient season.[13]

The Biblical intertextuality also lies in historical references. The allusion to Felix, the Roman procurator of Judea between 52 and 58 CE, has its roots in the Biblical passage of Acts 24, when the apostle Paul stood trial before Felix in Caesarea: 'And after certain days, when Felix came with his wife Drusilla, which was a Jewess, he sent for Paul,

13 *JE*, Ch. 6.

and heard him concerning the faith in Christ. And as he reasoned of righteousness, temperance, and judgment to come, Felix trembled, and answered, Go thy way for this time; when I have a convenient season, I will call for thee'.[14] In Charlotte Brontë's text, Helen is equated to Paul preaching patience, acceptance and duty to a Felix-like Jane who feels compelled to embrace these truths, but postpones the commitment that such a decision entails.

The treatment of the reference in the French translations is varied: it is either cut (in Lesbazeilles-Souvestre, and Redon and Dulong), simply translated 'comme Félix' (in Gilbert and Duvivier,[15] and Brodovikoff and Robert)[16] or similarly translated with the addition of an explanatory footnote (in Monod,[17] and Maurat)[18] or endnote (in Jean).[19] As for Redon and Dulong, they repeatedly cut Biblical references. Their translation seems to demonstrate the frailty of the Biblical presence in French literature. Still, the disappearance of this specific comparison can be viewed as an attempt to erase its masculinity, rather than its Biblical nature. Indeed, scholar Rachel Williams suggests that Lesbazeilles-Souvestre consistently negates the 'masculine' elements in the novel with the aim of producing a female-oriented translation.[20]

While the Biblical intertextuality cannot survive radical cuts, a simple reference requires the reader's active participation and knowledge. On the other hand, accompanying notes (see following table) influence the reader's perception of the reference, as they may emphasise several aspects of it.

---

14 Acts 24.24–25, in the King James Version.
15 Gilbert and Duvivier, p. 77.
16 Brodovikoff and Robert, p. 68.
17 Monod, p. 98.
18 Maurat, p. 72.
19 Jean, p. 111.
20 Noëmi Lesbazeilles-Souvestre 'actively attempted to construct *Jane Eyre* as a text that is proper both for a female writer to have produced and for female readers to consume by consistently negating the so-called "masculine" elements she found in the novel. The character of Jane Eyre is significantly altered in the translation in ways that bring her more in line with conventional feminine values.' Rachel Williams, 'The reconstruction of feminine values in Mme Lesbazeille-Souvestre's 1854 translation of *Jane Eyre*' [Abstract], *Translation and Interpreting Studies*, 7 (2012), 19–33 (p. 19).

Translator	Date	Note
Maurat	1964	'Félix, proconsul, gouverneur de la Judée pour les Romains, avait épousé Drusille, princesse juive, fille du vieux roi Agrippa Ier. C'est devant Félix que comparut saint Paul à Césarée; il retint l'apôtre en prison pour plaire aux Juifs.'[21]
Monod	1966	'Gouverneur de Judée (cf Actes, 24, 25).'[22]
Jean	2008	'Allusion aux Actes des apôtres, XXIV, 25: « Mais, comme Paul discourait sur la justice, sur la tempérance, et sur le jugement à venir, Félix, effrayé, dit: Pour le moment retire-toi; quand j'en trouverai l'occasion, je te rappellerai. »'[23]

Monod's note provides the reader with information as to the referent and the origin of the comparison. It gives historical as well as Biblical background, though it emphasises the position of the man rather than his personality or actions. Maurat's note focuses on explaining who Felix actually was. The choice of words and names denotes a wish for historical accuracy. It seems to insist on the man's prejudicial sense of justice — using imprisonment as a springboard for his own popularity: 'pour plaire aux Juifs' ('to please the Jews'). Jean's note differs in the sense that it does not specifically explain, but instead gives the Biblical verse that the passage alludes to. Felix is only presented in his refusal to listen to and accept Paul's teaching.

The Biblical intertextuality here resides in the syntagm 'comme Félix' but also in the additional comments, which shed a different light on this comparison to Jane. Felix's portrayal — as a governor, as a man of power, as a manipulative politician, as a sceptic, as a possible truth-seeker — necessarily affects Jane Eyre's characterisation. With one single translation, the texts then colour the protagonist in different ways.

21 Maurat, p. 72.
22 Monod, p. 98.
23 Jean, p. 805.

A Proverbial Shaping of Culture

> Well has Solomon said — 'Better is a dinner of herbs where love is, than a stalled ox and hatred therewith.'[24]

Charlotte Brontë here quotes Proverbs 15.17 from the King James Bible. Comparison of both Catholic and Protestant Biblical verses with the French translations of *Jane Eyre* suggests that most of them follow the English wording rather than an official Biblical French version. Phrases like 'un dîner d'herbe' (chosen by Lesbazeilles-Souvestre and Maurat)[25] or 'dîner d'herbes' (chosen by Monod,[26] and Brodovikoff and Robert)[27] are direct literal translations from the English text. This shows that the centrality of the Bible (especially the 1611 King James version) in nineteenth-century English literature has no parallel in the French literary spectrum. Indeed, whereas the Reformation in England led to a rejection of the Catholic Church and preservation of the Bible, in France it did quite the opposite. The Catholic Church kept its political and religious influence, but the Bible was set aside. As a result, the Bible did not shape the French language and culture, as was the case in England or Germany. Prominent writers and philosophers such as Blaise Pascal read the Bible in Latin. The Vulgate subsequently infused their works, and not a French version. There is no benchmark translation of the Bible in French, but rather many individual translations produced either by Catholics or Protestants, which differ in their choice of Hebrew and Greek or Latin as the language of the translation. It is then up to the readers to choose which translations to read.

In this passage, some translators indicate the reference of the verse, but that does not mean they quoted it from an actual French Bible. Monod mistakes Chapter 15 for 25,[28] thus altering the reference. Although Maurat adds it in a note,[29] she does not follow the same translation pattern as with other Biblical verses in her work (she states in a footnote that 'toutes les références bibliques de cette traduction

24 *JE*, Ch. 8.
25 Maurat, p. 94.
26 Monod, p. 130.
27 Brodovikoff and Robert, p. 91.
28 'Proverbe de Salomon issu de la Bible (références 25,17)', Monod, p. 130, note 3.
29 Maurat, p. 94, note 2.

sont tirées de la Bible de Crampon[30]')[31] and provides her own version of the proverb. In fact, only Jean directly quotes from a French Bible, the Louis Segond version,[32] which he says he uses for all Biblical quotations in his translation.[33]

Both Gilbert and Duvivier's, and Redon and Dulong's translations cut the whole reference altogether. It is of note that both translations are published in a post-World-War France (1919 and 1946 respectively), at a time when religious faith was strongly decreasing. Furthermore, the beginning of the twentieth century in France was marked by a series of laws undermining the Catholic Church and denying its legitimacy in the educational field. The 1904 law denied religious congregations the right to teach; the following year saw the official separation of the Church and the State. The concept of *laïcité* was being given a legal basis. This was a time of growing tensions, both between France and the Vatican, and within the country. The traumatic Vichy regime reinstated the funding of Catholic private schools and authorized religious congregations to teach. To counteract this, the 1946 Constitution gave *laïcité* a constitutional weight. The text clearly marked a separation between religion and education — considered as a 'temporal power' belonging only to the State. In such an atmosphere, it is understandable that some editors would be reluctant to associate forms of teaching (Jane giving a proverb) with Christianity, simply erasing the Biblical quote.

Rochester Between Job, Hobbes and Moby Dick

> 'I wish to be a better man than I have been, than I am; as Job's leviathan broke the spear, the dart, and the habergeon, hindrances which others count as iron and brass, I will esteem but straw and rotten wood.'[34]

Jane's encounters with Rochester are occasions of much mystery and Jane slowly uncovers the veil of his enigmatic, poignant character. At the beginning of Chapter 15, as he opens up about his past with Céline Varens, his personality is also portrayed through a reference to the book of Job: 'The sword of him that layeth at him cannot hold: the

30 *La Sainte Bible de Crampon* (1923), a Catholic Bible translated from the Hebrew, Aramaic, and Greek manuscripts.
31 Maurat, p. 47, note 1.
32 *La Bible Segond* ([1880] 1910), a Protestant Bible translated from the Hebrew, Aramean, and Greek manuscripts.
33 Jean, p. 141; p. 807.
34 *JE*, Ch. 15.

spear, the dart, nor the habergeon. He esteemeth iron as straw, [and] brass as rotten wood.'[35] In this passage of the Bible, God is talking to Job and his three accusing friends to manifest his almighty powers and his control over creation. The parallel between Rochester's words and the Biblical text makes him a fate-stricken, agonising man in the image of Job, as well as a control-seizing, powerful defender in the image of a God-created monster. It surrounds Rochester with an atmosphere of mystique that complexifies the character.

The reference is absent in Gilbert and Duvivier,[36] and in Redon and Dulong,[37] who performed major cuts to Rochester's discourse. As we have seen, the choice to cut the Biblical reference can be viewed as an appropriation of the text in a cultural context (two post-World War periods, respectively 1919 and 1946) when secularism was intensifying and personal allegiance to Christianity was questioned. In the other translations (like Proverbs 15.17 in Chapter 8), the Biblical intertextuality does not seem to call for any correspondence with existing Biblical translations in French. The translators rather freely adapted the text in its rhythms and choice of words.

Interestingly, Lesbazeilles-Souvestre, and Brodovikoff and Robert translate 'Leviathan' with 'baleine',[38] thus creating an overlap between the books of Job and Jonah. Indeed, the French term 'baleine' appears in some Biblical versions (e.g., 1744 Martin) to translate the Hebrew *hattannûn*, sea monster or *gā·ḏō·wl dāḡ*, great fish. It is specifically the term *gā·ḏō·wl dāḡ* that appears in the book of Jonah when it is said, 'Now the LORD had prepared a great fish to swallow up Jonah. And Jonah was in the belly of the fish three days and three nights'.[39] When exegetes pondered over the kind of great fish Jonah could have been swallowed up by, the possibility of a whale appeared because of its great size. But in this Chapter of Job, the Hebrew word is *liw·yā·ṯān* (serpent, sea monster, or dragon) which quite literally gave the English 'Leviathan' and the French 'Léviathan', sometimes translated by 'crocodile'.

However, the French translators are not alone in the cross-over between 'Leviathan' and 'whale'. Nowadays, *liw·yā·ṯān* means 'whale'

35 Job 41.26–27 in the King James Version. The precise reference depends on the Biblical versions.
36 See passage in Gilbert and Duvivier, pp. 154–55.
37 See passage in Redon and Dulong, pp. 133–35.
38 'la baleine de Job', Brodovikoff and Robert, p. 177.
39 Jonah 1.17, King James Version.

in Modern Hebrew. This is also to be found in literature: the rabbinic literature traditionally associates Job and Jonah, and the Talmud suggests that the whale is doomed to be killed by the Leviathan. In his 1851 *Moby-Dick*, Herman Melville also describes the Leviathan as being 'Job's whale' — and thus it was translated as 'la baleine de Job' in *Moby Dick*'s French translations, the first being in 1928.[40] Such a phrase has the effect of drawing attention away from God (the one in the book of Job who mentions the Leviathan as an instrument of his almighty power) to Job, a mere man, and thus humanizes the reference. But by turning the Leviathan into a whale, it creates a new kind of image: the possible allusion to Hobbes disappears, and so does the fear that such a monstrous creature provokes. The whale is a much more accessible animal that one can visualize, and even hunt and dominate. With Lesbazeilles-Souvestre's, and Brodovikoff and Robert's translations, the intertextuality goes beyond the relationship between *Jane Eyre* and the Bible: it also creates a dialogue between languages (Hebrew, English and French), and several texts.

Les liaisons dangereuses, or the Aftermath of Iconic Couples

> 'Now, King Ahasuerus! What do I want with half your estate? Do you think I am a Jew-usurer, seeking good investment in land? I would much rather have all your confidence. You will not exclude me from your confidence if you admit me to your heart?'
>
> 'You are welcome to all my confidence that is worth having, Jane; but for God's sake, don't desire a useless burden! Don't long for poison — don't turn out a downright Eve on my hands!'[41]

Several Biblical references are intertwined in the dialogue between Jane and Rochester. The proposition of giving out half the estate out of love or admiration recalls King Ahasuerus and Esther in the Old Testament (as well as Herod and Salome in the New Testament), when the king makes the extravagant promise of answering any of his lady's wishes. The mention of Eve may refer to the woman's temptation of her husband leading both of them to sin — or to the desire for knowledge that the fruit represents. This exchange between Jane and Rochester is

40 For example, see Herman Melville, *Moby Dick*, trans. H. Guex-Rolle (Paris: Garnier-Flammarion, 1989), p. 220.

41 *JE*, Ch. 24.

therefore coloured by the echo of major ethical themes and complex couples taken from the Bible.

Again, the French translations make varying use of these references, leaving the Biblical intertextuality challenged. The whole passage is cut in Gilbert and Duvivier,[42] while Lesbazeilles-Souvestre cuts the comparison with Eve. The remaining translations (including, unusually, Redon and Dulong) preserve both references. What is striking though is the use of notes, which lead to different interpretations. Both Jean and Monod felt the need to give their readership explanations about 'roi Assuérus', but the two explanations are radically different. Jean (as with the example from Chapter 6) quotes the whole verse from the Bible[43] whereas Monod provides historical background and moves away from the strictly Biblical framework.[44] He focuses on the marriage between King Ahasuerus and Esther — who hid her Jewishness from her husband following the advice of her uncle Mordecai — hence insisting on the lack of honesty within the couple. This once again proves how a single reference can foster multiple interpretations.

Jane Eyre's Song of Lament

> 'Be not far from me, for trouble is near: there is none to help.'
>
> It was near: and as I had lifted no petition to Heaven to avert it — as I had neither joined my hands, nor bent my knees, nor moved my lips — it came: in full heavy swing the torrent poured over me. The whole consciousness of my life lorn, my love lost, my hope quenched, my faith death-struck, swayed full and mighty above me in one sullen mass. That bitter hour cannot be described: in truth, 'the waters came into my soul; I sank in deep mire: I felt no standing; I came into deep waters; the floods overflowed me.'[45]

As our protagonist evolves throughout her coming-of-age journey, her own language goes through a process of refinement, being whetted against the cultural language with which she has grown up. In her despair regarding the situation with Bertha, the Psalms of David are

42 See Gilbert and Duvivier, pp. 274–75.

43 'Allusion à Esther, V, 6: « Et pendant qu'on buvait le vin, le roi dit à Esther: Quelle est ta demande? Elle te sera accordée. Que désires-tu? Quand ce sera la moitié du royaume, tu l'obtiendras. »' Jean, p. 818, note 2.

44 'Le roi Assuérus (485 à 465 avant l'ère courante), petit-fils de Cyrus, après avoir répudié son épouse Vashti, choisit pour nouvelle reine la belle Esther. Mais Esther n'avait pas révélé au roi qu'elle était juive, sur les conseils de son oncle Mordékhaï.' Monod, p. 441, note 1.

45 *JE*, Ch. 26.

intertwined with her own lament. Two references to Psalms follow closely in the passage quoted above, both announced by quotation marks. Here, the Biblical intertextuality wraps Brontë's text and protagonist with a certain degree of sacredness. The first reference is to Psalm 22: 'Be not far from me; for trouble is near; for there is none to help.'[46] The second reference is an adaptation of the beginning of Psalm 69: 'Save me, O God; for the waters are come in unto my soul. I sink in deep mire, where there is no standing: I am come into deep waters, where the floods overflow me.'[47] While the introductory words 'in truth' reinforce the Biblical authority, the rewording of the psalm somewhat questions its legitimacy. Whose voice is true? This is a question this text seems to ask, as often with the Biblical references in *Jane Eyre*.

The Biblical intertextuality in French is kept more or less visible through devices such as punctuation, notes, and direct mentions of God and Scripture. Just as in the original, the psalmist's and Jane's words overlap. In this respect, it is interesting to note that most translations of Psalm 69 are gender neutral; but Gilbert and Duvivier's translation denotes a male speaker ('je suis entré', 'les flots m'ont submergé');[48] while Redon and Dulong's translation denotes a female speaker ('je suis tombée', 'je me suis enfoncée').[49] Whose voice is this then? It is either David's in the Bible, Jane's in the novel, or both undifferentiated. These grammatical additions, due to the gender-marked agreements in French, question the notion of the appropriation and interpretation of the Biblical text.

In this passage, most translators make a didactic use of notes, suggesting how little the French readership might know of the Bible. Lesbazeilles-Souvestre's (1854) and Brodovikoff and Robert's (1946) are the only translations without accompanying notes; they are also the only ones that insert 'Mon Dieu !'[50] or 'par Dieu !'[51] at the beginning of the Biblical quotation, turning it into a direct address to God and placing the passage in a more vehemently spiritual (though not explicitly *Biblical*) light.

46 Psalms 22.11, King James Version.
47 Psalms 69.2, King James Version.
48 Gilbert and Duvivier, p. 305.
49 Redon and Dulong, p. 289.
50 Lesbazeilles-Souvestre, The Project Gutenberg electronic text.
51 Brodovikoff and Robert, p. 345.

A Theological Debate at the Heart of the Novel: St John and Calvinism

> The heart was thrilled, the mind astonished, by the power of the preacher: neither were softened. Throughout there was a strange bitterness; an absence of consolatory gentleness; stern allusions to Calvinistic doctrines — election, predestination, reprobation — were frequent; and each reference to these points sounded like a sentence pronounced for doom. When he had done, instead of feeling better, calmer, more enlightened by his discourse, I experienced an inexpressible sadness; for it seemed to me — I know not whether equally so to others — that the eloquence to which I had been listening had sprung from a depth where lay turbid dregs of disappointment — where moved troubling impulses of insatiate yearnings and disquieting aspirations. I was sure St. John Rivers — pure-lived, conscientious, zealous as he was — had not yet found that peace of God which passeth all understanding: he had no more found it, I thought, than had I with my concealed and racking regrets for my broken idol and lost elysium — regrets to which I have latterly avoided referring, but which possessed me and tyrannised over me ruthlessly.[52]

When she is around St John, Jane is in contact with not only the poetic language but also the systematic doctrines of the Bible. Later systematized by the sixteenth-century reformer John Calvin and his successors, the three doctrines mentioned in this passage (election, predestination and reprobation) find their roots in the writings of one of the first theologians, the apostle Paul. A few verses in his epistle to the Romans are often cited as justification for these doctrines: 'Even so then at this present time also there is a remnant according to the election of grace'[53] (i.e., election); 'For whom he did foreknow, he also did predestinate to be conformed to the image of his Son, that he might be the firstborn among many brethren'[54] (i.e., predestination); 'Israel hath not obtained that which he seeketh for; but the election hath obtained it, and the rest were blinded'[55] (i.e., reprobation, the opposite of the election). The term 'reprobation' itself does not appear in the Bible: it comes from Latin *probare* (prove, test) and *reprobates* (reproved, condemned) and describes the fate of 'the rest', that is, those God has not elected and predestined.

---

52 *JE*, Ch. 30.
53 Romans 11.5, King James Version.
54 Romans 8.29, King James Version.
55 Romans 11.7, King James Version

In this passage, Jane criticizes St John's sermons for being sternly Calvinistic. Now, in order to understand the subtle criticism, it is important to recognize in this description a striking contrast with Charlotte Brontë's own religious beliefs. Indeed, her letters and writings show that her Evangelical faith leans towards Arminianism: a theology regarding the atonement of sins as the consequence of God's desire to see all redeemed.[56] According to this view, humans' free will and their own decision whether or not to reject God determines whether or not they will be redeemed and brought into a relationship with God. Calvinism, on the other hand, insists on man's total depravity and inability to choose God. God's gift of faith is only directed to those he eternally elected, and eternal punishment awaits those his grace did not touch.

Brontë grew up during 'the heyday of Evangelical controversies', with prominent Evangelical preachers such as Whitfield and Wesley gaining in popularity against the status quo of the Church of England.[57] This led to profound divisions 'among and between Wesleyan Methodists, Primitive Methodists, Calvinists, Arminians, and various "high" and "low" Tractarian and Evangelical Anglicans'.[58] In this context, Brontë might have witnessed the fierce dispute between Calvinists and Arminianists on questions of salvation even in her own family and parsonage.[59] This definitely left a mark on her novel and tainted her protagonist's spiritual struggles when facing the differing theologies of Brocklehurst, Helen Burns and St John.

In French, there are different translations for the 'stern allusions to Calvinistic doctrines — election, predestination, reprobation'. As we will see in the following table, the choice of words and punctuation is highly significant as it changes the meaning of the words and turns a doctrinal, heavily theological passage into a more philosophical reflection.

56 See Elisabeth Jay, 'Jane Eyre and Biblical Interpretation', in *Jane Eyre, de Charlotte Brontë à Franco Zeffirelli*, ed. by Frédéric Regard and Augustin Trapenard (Paris: Sedes, 2008), pp. 65–76.

57 Franklin J. Jeffrey, 'The Merging of Spiritualities: Jane Eyre as Missionary of Love', *Nineteenth-Century Literature*, 49 (1995), 456–82 (p. 459).

58 Jeffrey, 'The Merging of Spiritualities', p. 459.

59 Jones, 'Religious Beliefs of Charlotte Brontë', p. 8.

Translator	Date	Translation
Lesbazeilles-Souvestre	1854	'sombres allusions aux doctrines calvinistes, aux élections, aux prédestinations, aux réprobations'[60]
Gilbert and Duvivier	1919	passage cut
Brodovikoff and Robert	1946	'allusions sévères à des doctrines calvinistes, aux choix, aux prédestinations, aux réprobations'[61]
Redon and Dulong	1946	'allusions sévères aux doctrines de Calvin [...] le choix, la méditation, la réprobation'[62]
Maurat	1964	'allusions aux sévères doctrines calvinistes sur le libre arbitre, la prédestination, la réprobation'[63]
Monod	1966	'allusions sévères aux doctrines calvinistes (élection, prédestination, réprobation)'[64]
Jean	2008	'austères allusions aux doctrines calvinistes — élection, prédestination, réprobation'[65] + endnote: 'réprobation s'entend ici au sens religieux de jugement par lequel Dieu réprouve le pécheur ou refuse de le compter au nombre des élus.'[66]

The whole passage is cut by Gilbert and Duvivier, in line with the recurrent excision of explicit Christian references in their 1919 translation, which perhaps responds to the political context of growing secularism, as we have seen. Lesbazeilles-Souvestre, and Brodovikoff and Robert use the plural form ('aux élections, aux prédestinations, aux réprobations'; 'aux choix, aux prédestinations, aux réprobations'). This suggests an enumeration of separate facts or experiences, which the simple commas emphasise: it is not clear from the syntax whether they are conceived of as examples of Calvinist doctrines, or other themes alluded to by St John. Redon and Dulong, by stating 'doctrines de Calvin', put an emphasis on the reformer, presenting the man rather than the theological branch: this gives a historical more than a religious perspective. Also, the term 'choix' carries fewer Biblical

60 Lesbazeilles-Souvestre, The Project Gutenberg electronic text.
61 Brodovikoff and Robert, p. 419.
62 Redon and Dulong, p. 342.
63 Maurat, p. 406.
64 Monod, p. 593.
65 Jean, p. 576.
66 Jean, p. 824.

connotations than 'election' and does not specifically refer to the Pauline verses (the same comment can be made about Brodovikoff and Robert's translation). Therefore, both 1946 translations seem to reduce the Biblical intertextuality. This is even more obvious with Redon and Dulong translating 'predestination' with 'méditation', which is radically different. Meditation is not a doctrine, but rather a spiritual or even philosophical practice. One cannot but think of Descartes' *Méditations sur la philosophie première* (1641) — a cornerstone in French history of thought. In the same vein, it is interesting that Maurat translates 'election' (God choosing those who will believe in him) by 'le libre arbitre' (man's own choice to believe in God) and thus completely shifts the focus from God to man. It sheds light on Calvin as a philosopher more than a theologian, and it draws a less religious portrait of St John. Again, it seems that the spiritual is preferred over the Biblical, and the philosophical over the religious. Yet, this shift of discipline from a God-centred theology to a more humanistic philosophy comes in a passage of clear theological reflection. Indeed, Jane overtly comments on St John's positions as 'stern' and invokes a Pauline expression ('that peace of God which passeth all understanding')[67] to counterbalance his theology with her own. In the philosophical turn brought about by the French translators, one might wonder where St John might find that kind of peace. Could it come from the works of our modern philosophers?

Jane Eyre, a Marian Figure

> Reader, it was on Monday night — near midnight — that I too had received the mysterious summons: those were the very words by which I replied to it. I listened to Mr. Rochester's narrative, but made no disclosure in return. The coincidence struck me as too awful and inexplicable to be communicated or discussed. If I told anything, my tale would be such as must necessarily make a profound impression on the mind of my hearer: and that mind, yet from its sufferings too prone to gloom, needed not the deeper shade of the supernatural. I kept these things then, and pondered them in my heart.[68]

As we have seen, Biblical intertextuality allows for a superimposition of several voices: that of the Biblical author, that of the people in the Biblical account, that of Jane Eyre, and behind all of them that of Charlotte Brontë. This passage parallels the account of the birth of Jesus in Luke's Gospel. When the shepherds visit Joseph and Mary and the newborn Jesus, they

67 Philippians 4.7.
68 *JE*, Ch. 37.

praise the baby as being the promised Saviour and Christ. They repeat in amazement what the angels told them. They go and spread the news all around. Luke goes on to say that 'Mary kept these things then, and pondered them in her heart' (Luke 2.19). It is a moment when reality (the pain of giving birth, the simplicity of the manger, the smell of the cattle) and the supernatural meet. Revelations have been made and wait to be implemented. Under the pen of Charlotte Brontë, Jane Eyre before Rochester becomes Mary the mother of God — the bearer of amazing truths and great responsibilities, the witness and author of pure love. This Biblical reference affects not only the characterisation of Jane, but also that of Rochester and their tumultuous, profound relationship.

In the original, the wording exactly parallels the Biblical verse, with the only change occurring in the grammatical pronouns. However, it appears in the French translations that there is very little correspondence with official Biblical versions, either Catholic or Protestant:

Translator	**Date**	**Translation**
Lesbazeilles-Souvestre	1854	'Je gardai ces choses ensevelies dans mon cœur et je les méditai.'[69]
Gilbert and Duvivier	1919	'Je gardai donc ces choses et les repassai dans mon cœur.'[70]
Brodovikoff and Robert	1946	'Je gardai donc ces choses-là dans mon cœur et les méditai.'[71]
Redon and Dulong	1946	'Je gardai pour moi mes réflexions sur cet incident.'[72]
Maurat	1964	'Je gardai donc toutes ces choses pour moi, et les méditai dans mon cœur.'[73]
Monod	1966	'Aussi je ne dis mot de ce mystère et le méditai dans mon cœur.'[74]
Jean	2008	'Aussi conservai-je en moi-même toutes ces choses que je repassai dans mon cœur.'[75] + endnote 'Citation de l'Évangile selon Luc, II, 19'[76]

69 Lesbazeilles-Souvestre, The Project Gutenberg electronic text.
70 Gilbert and Duvivier, p. 460.
71 Brodovikoff and Robert, p. 536.
72 Redon and Dulong, p. 435.
73 Maurat, p. 515.
74 Monod, p. 753.
75 Jean, p. 726.
76 Jean, p. 829.

Gilbert and Duvivier are probably the most faithful to the Bible, as their translation follows the verse in the Louis Segond Bible: 'Marie gardait toutes ces choses, et les repassait dans son cœur'. The only adaptation is the substitution of 'donc' by 'toutes'.

The other translations look similar but show some differences in the syntax and choice of words, which makes it harder to recognize Luke's verse in them: Lesbazeilles-Souvestre adds the adjective 'ensevelies' ('buried'), Maurat adds 'pour moi' ('to myself'), Jean 'en moi-même' ('for myself') and Brodovikoff and Robert write 'ces choses-là' ('those things'). Redon and Dulong's and Monod's translations are the most inventive with further lexical changes: 'réflexions sur cet incident' ('reflexions on this incident'), 'ce mystère' ('this mystery'). On the whole, the translators seem to be willing to provide their own version of the verse. Even Jean, who gives the Biblical reference in a note, rewrites it in his own way.

The superimposition of voices is then enriched by that of the translator. At first sight, the Biblical intertextuality could appear to be jeopardized. But the rewriting is also a way to give a new breath to the Biblical text, to play with the literary words and let the magic of intertextuality operate.

An Apocalyptic End: Jane, St John(s), and the Translators' Voices

> His own words are a pledge of this —
>
> 'My Master,' he says, 'has forewarned me. Daily He announces more distinctly, — "Surely I come quickly!" and hourly I more eagerly respond, — "Amen; even so come, Lord Jesus!"'[77]

The novel ends with a final Biblical reference, which is the penultimate verse of the Bible: 'He which testifieth these things saith, Surely I come quickly. Amen. Even so, come, Lord Jesus.'[78] In the intricate game of the interaction of texts and superimposition of voices, Jane tells of St John, who writes to her by quoting from the Bible. The novel ends thus suspended, almost unfinished, with the promise of a change to come. It announces a death, more than the Second Coming, but the intertextuality allows for an array of interpretations. What is clear is that, by concluding her novel with the Bible (and its own conclusion for

77 *JE*, Ch. 38.
78 Revelation 22.20, King James Version.

that matter) she adds a final touch of sacredness to her text. However, it can be argued that this sacredness does not systematically appear in the French translations:

Translator	**Date**	**Translation**
Lesbazeilles-Souvestre	1854	'« Mon maître, dit-il, m'a averti; chaque jour il m'annonce plus clairement ma délivrance. J'avance rapidement, et à chaque heure qui s'écoule, je réponds avec plus d'ardeur: « Amen; Venez, Seigneur Jésus! »'[79]
Gilbert and Duvivier	1919	' — Mon Maître, dit-il, m'a averti. Chaque jour il me le fait savoir plus nettement: « Je viens bientôt ! » et, d'heure en heure, je réponds avec plus d'ardeur: « Amen; viens, Seigneur Jésus! »'[80]
Brodovikoff and Robert	1946	'« Mon Maître », dit-il, « m'a prévenu. Journellement Il m'annonce plus distinctement: sans aucun doute. Je viens rapidement » et d'heure en heure je Lui réponds plus passionnément: « Amen, même ainsi, venez, Mon Seigneur! »'[81]
Redon and Dulong	1946	'« Mon Maître, dit-il, m'a donné l'avertissement; chaque jour il me l'annonce avec plus de netteté: je viens sûrement et rapidement, et à chaque heure je réponds avec plus de ferveur: Amen, venez, Seigneur Jésus. »'[82]
Maurat	1964	'« Mon maître m'a averti. De jour en jour son message se fait plus net: "J'arrive bientôt, sache-le." Et, d'heure en heure, je réponds avec plus de ferveur: "Amen; viens donc, Seigneur Jésus." »'[83]
Monod	1966	'« Mon Maître, écrit-il, m'a averti d'avance. Chaque jour il m'annonce plus distinctement: Sois-en sûr, je viens promptement ! Et d'heure en heure, je réponds avec plus d'empressement: Amen, qu'il en soit ainsi; viens, Seigneur Jésus! »'[84]
Jean	2008	'« Mon Maître m'a averti. Chaque jour il annonce plus distinctement: "Oui, je viens bientôt !" et, chaque heure, je réponds: "Amen, viens Seigneur Jésus!". »'[85]

79 Lesbazeilles-Souvestre, The Project Gutenberg electronic text.
80 Gilbert and Duvivier, p. 466.
81 Brodovikoff and Robert, p. 542.
82 Redon and Dulong, p. 440.
83 Maurat, p. 520.
84 Monod, p. 761.
85 Jean, p. 733.

Only Gilbert and Duvivier and Jean keep the Biblical reference with quotation marks and the most common French translation of that verse: 'Je viens bientôt'.[86] The other translators take away the quotation marks (apart from Maurat) and provide their own translation of the phrase, thus distancing themselves from any Biblical version. The subsequent variations both in the verb ('venir' ('come'), 'avancer' ('advance'), 'arrive' ('arrive')) and the adverb ('rapidement' ('rapidly'), 'sûrement' ('certainly'), 'promptement' ('promptly')) highlight the paradox that St John's 'own words' are, in reality, those of another St John — the Biblical writer. This confusion of voices might have encouraged the translators to find their own voices, too.

Conclusion: Emerging New Voices

From the interactions with Brocklehurst and Helen Burns, to the tumultuous and conflicting relationships with Rochester and St John; in the evolution from the passionate, rebellious child to the tempered, collected woman; in all stages of her life from the pupil to the teacher, the character of Jane Eyre is made to reflect on the teaching of the Christian Bible and its incarnation in her own life. She talks to God and quotes from the King James Version. Charlotte Brontë and her protagonist, along with thousands of young English people, learnt how to read and speak with the Bible: they were influenced by its tone, its powerful imagery, its morals, and its poetry. Although we could argue that Biblical reception in Britain had been undermined by eighteenth-century rationalists and nineteenth-century scientific theories, Brontë's readership was still used to seeing the sacred text as a reference, both in life and through literature. All in all, we can see the several faces of the Bible in *Jane Eyre*: a hypotext sustaining the novel, a closely read text studied and understood differently by the characters, and a reservoir of words and images that the author and her protagonist (and possibly her readership) were plunged into and shaped by.

The first French translation of *Jane Eyre* was published in 1854, at a time when France had long undergone a profound dechristianization which was to become officially institutionalized at the beginning of the following century. The place of the Bible as sacred scripture had

86 This Biblical translation is to be found in the following versions: Ostervald, Crampon, Darby, Martin, Segond, Traduction Oecuménique de la Bible, Semeur.

gradually moved to the margins due to the hegemony of a ritualized and politicized Catholic Church, the violence of the Reformation, and the ever-growing influence of liberals and atheists among the French elite. This historical context necessarily had an impact on the number of Biblical references in the novel. Indeed, in all the French translations, the Biblical references suffer changes, metamorphoses, distortions, cuts, transformations of all sorts. Biblical verses disappear, mentions of Biblical characters or stories are cut, Brontë's words are translated directly from the English without reference to a French Bible. The translations then appear to be a French version of the King James Bible. In their choice of words, the French translators tend to prefer the spiritual over the Biblical and the philosophical over the religious.

Biblical intertextuality thus undergoes important changes in the French translations of *Jane Eyre*. There seems to be a tendency to hide or disguise the Biblical verses behind the garment of the translator's own style. Or else the translators decided to follow Jesus' parable when he said: 'No one tears a piece out of a new garment to patch an old one. Otherwise, they will have torn the new garment, and the patch from the new will not match the old'.[87] They preferred to sew on another piece with new voices altogether, even if that meant losing the subtlety of Brontë's intertextual fabric.

87 Luke 5.36, New International Version.

Works Cited

Translations of *Jane Eyre*

Brontë, Charlotte, *Jane Eyre ou les mémoires d'une institutrice*, trans. by Noémie Lesbazeilles-Souvestre (Paris: D. Giraud, 1854). The version used here is the electronic version provided by The Project Gutenberg.

——, *Jane Eyre*, trans. by R. Redon and J. Dulong (Paris: Éditions du Dauphin, 1946).

——, *Jane Eyre*, trans. by Marion Gilbert and Madeleine Duvivier (Paris: GF Flammarion, 1990 [1919]).

——, *Jane Eyre*, trans. by Dominique Jean (Paris: Gallimard, 2012 [2008]).

——, *Jane Eyre*, trans. by Léon Brodovikoff and Claire Robert (Verviers, Belgique: Gérard and Co., 1950 [1946]).

——, *Jane Eyre*, trans. by Sylvère Monod (Paris: Pocket, 2011 [1966]).

——, *Jane Eyre*, trans. by Charlotte Maurat (Paris: Le Livre de Poche, 1992 [1964]).

Other Sources

La Bible Segond, trans. by Louis Segond (Oxford, Paris, Lausanne, Neuchatel, Geneva: United Bible Societies, [1880] 1910).

La Sainte Bible, trans. by Augustin Crampon (Paris, Tournai, Roma: Desclée et Cie, 1923).

Les Saints Livres connus sous le nom de Nouveau Testament, trans. by John Nelson Darby (Vevey: Ch. F. Recordon, 1859).

Le Nouveau Testament, trans. by David Martin (New York: American Bible Society, 1861).

La Sainte Bible, trans. by Jean-Frédéric Ostervald (Neuchatel: A. Boyve et Cie, 1744).

La Bible du Semeur, trans. by Alfred Kuen, Jacques Buchhold, André Lovérini and Sylvain Romerowski, (Charols: Excelsis, 1992).

La Traduction œcuménique de la Bible (Villiers-le-Bel: United Bible Society, Paris: Éditions du Cerf, 1975).

Brontë, Charlotte, *Villette*, in The Project Gutenberg, produced by Delphine Lettau, Charles Franks and Distributed Proofreaders.

Crook, Richard E., 'The Influence of the Bible on English Literature', *The Irish Church Quarterly*, 4 (1911), 283–95, https://doi.org/10.2307/30067106.

Hunt, Arnold, '400 years of the King James Bible', *The Times Literary Supplement*, 9 February 2011.

Jay, Elisabeth, 'Jane Eyre and Biblical Interpretation', in *Jane Eyre, de Charlotte Brontë à Franco Zeffirelli*, ed. by Frédéric Regard and Augustin Trapenard (Paris: Sedes, 2008), pp. 65–76.

Jeffrey, Franklin J., 'The Merging of Spiritualities: Jane Eyre as Missionary of Love', *Nineteenth-Century Literature*, 49 (1995), 456–82, https://doi.org/10.2307/2933729.

Jones, Phyllis Kelson, 'Religious Beliefs of Charlotte Brontë, as Reflected in her Novels and Letters' (unpublished doctoral thesis, The Open University, 1997).

Melville, Herman, *Moby Dick*, trans. H. Guex-Rolle (Paris: Garnier-Flammarion, 1989).

Williams, Rachel, 'The reconstruction of feminine values in Mme Lesbazeille-Souvestre's 1854 translation of *Jane Eyre*', *Translation and Interpreting Studies: The Journal of the American Translation and Interpreting Studies Association*, 7 (2012), 19–23, https://doi.org/10.1075/tis.7.1.02wil

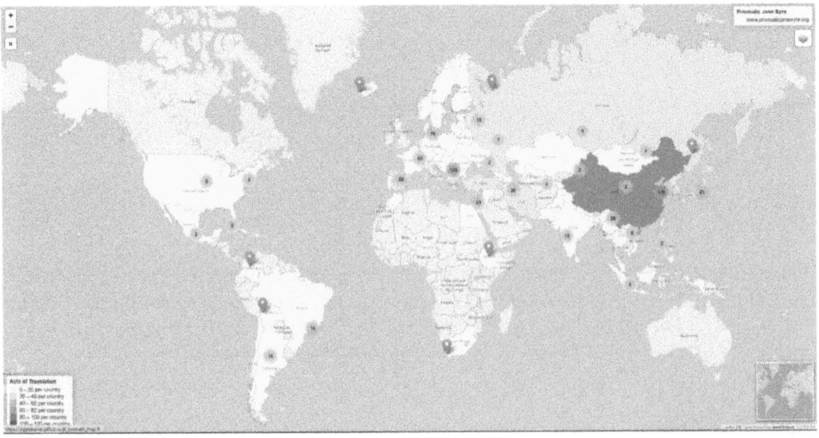

The World Map
https://digitalkoine.github.io/je_prismatic_map
Created by Giovanni Pietro Vitali;
maps © Thunderforest, data © OpenStreetMap contributors

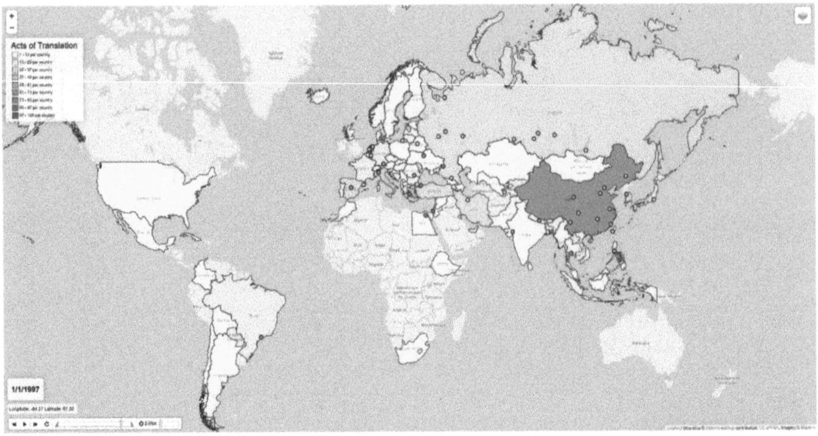

The Time Map
https://digitalkoine.github.io/translations_timemap
Created by Giovanni Pietro Vitali and Simone Landucci;
© OpenStreetMap contributors, © Mapbox

VII. 'Walk' and 'Wander' through Language(s);
Prismatic Scenes; and Littoral Reading

Matthew Reynolds

Like 'plain' and 'ugly' (discussed in Chapter V), 'walk' and 'wander' form a significant contrast, one that is threaded throughout the text. A walk appears in the novel's very first sentence, and wandering appears in its second:

> There was no possibility of taking a walk that day. We had been wandering, indeed, in the leafless shrubbery an hour in the morning ...

Headlined in this way, the words gesture towards a long history of literary works made from walks and wanderings. John Bunyan's *The Pilgrim's Progress* — a strong influence on *Jane Eyre* — begins:

> As I walk'd through the wilderness of this world[1]

Dante's *Commedia* starts, not only *in medias res* (as Horace recommended epics should), but also in the middle of a walk:

> Nel mezzo del cammin di nostra vita
>
> (In the middle of the walk of our life)[2]

There is a Christian tonality to these echoes which is in tune with the Biblical references discussed by Léa Rychen in Essay 14; but the roots of wandering and walking also spread wider. Homer's *Odyssey*, in its opening lines, describes Odysseus as a man 'wandering from

1 John Bunyan, *The Pilgrim's Progress*, ed. W. R. Owens (OUP, new edn, 2003), p. 10.

2 Dante Alighieri, *Inferno*, ed. Anna Maria Chiavacci Leonardi (Milan: Mondadori, 2016), p. 57.

 https://doi.org/10.11647/OBP.0319.22

clime to clime'[3] — at least, that is Alexander Pope's translation, the one the Brontës were most likely to have known. Nearer to Charlotte Brontë's own time, Wordsworth had made much poetry from country walks, and Book 1 of his 1814 volume *The Excursion* was called 'The Wanderer'. Dickens's *Oliver Twist, or the Parish Boy's Progress* (1838) was a bestseller in the years of *Jane Eyre*'s gestation, and a decisive early turn in the plot happens when, as the title of Chapter 8 announces, 'Oliver Walks to London'.

So with its opening sentence, 'There was no possibility of taking a walk that day', *Jane Eyre* both marks its difference from these precedents and taps their energy to create a potential: when *will* the walk be possible? It signals the likelihood that the obstruction or achievement of journeys may play a substantial part in the novel; and so it turns out to be, with Jane's variously troubled displacements from one defining location to another: Gateshead to Lowood; Lowood to Thornfield; Thornfield to Whitcross, Marsh End and Morton; back to Thornfield, and finally on to Ferndean. None of these journeys is merely physical; each represents some kind of step, whether happy or not, in the personal development that the *Bildungsroman* genre (to which *Jane Eyre* is affiliated) encourages readers to expect.

The distinction between 'walk' and the alternative provided by the second sentence, 'wandering', gives readers a miniature, two-word thesaurus with which to begin to make sense of the novel's physical and mental journeys. 'Walk' is more decisive, and implies a direction. Charlotte Brontë herself relished a long, brisk walk: though walking was her everyday mode of transport — to church, shops, friends — her letters are still full of the enjoyment of striding across the moors. Jane, however, announces her opposite view in the second paragraph of the book, and she uses the inaugural appearance of her assertive first-person pronoun to do so: 'I was glad of it; I never liked long walks'. At that moment, we can sense the young character being separated from her heartier adult author; but as Jane grows up, she too comes to like the independence of walking alone, as when, on her return from Mrs Reed's deathbed in Chapter 22, she chooses to walk from Millcote to Thornfield, a distance that (as we know from Chapter 11) is 'a matter of six miles'. Walking is not always done so vigorously, yet even when

3 Alexander Pope, *The Odyssey of Homer: Books I–XII* (*The Poems of Alexander Pope*, vol. 9), ed. Maynard Mack (London: Methuen & Co, and New Haven: Yale University Press, 1967), p. 25.

there is no physical destination, there is always an emotional purpose. This is especially so in the charged moments when a man is walking with a woman. When Rochester walks with Jane in Chapter 15 he tells her of his past with Céline Varens; and when they walk together in Chapter 23 he proposes marriage, as St John Rivers in his turn will do during a walk in Chapter 34.

'Wandering', on the other hand, has no evident physical or emotional direction. It can be carefree, as when the young Jane 'wandered far' with Mary Ann at Lowood, or desperate, as when the older Jane, having fled from Thornfield to Whitcross, 'wandered about like a lost and starving dog'.[4] Wandering also lends itself — much more than 'walk' — to metaphor: there can be wandering from the straight and narrow, as with Rochester's past life in Chapter 20; and thoughts and words can wander in the mind, whether in a daydream during dull lessons at Lowood school (Chapter 6) or in the agony of Jane's despair after the failed wedding (Chapter 26).

'Wander' in Hebrew and Estonian

If you trace recurrences of 'walk' and 'wander' through the novel, you see the words gathering significance; and all the more so if you have the never-exactly-parallel texts of some translations alongside. In Hebrew, as Adriana X. Jacobs notes, there are many overlapping terms for 'wander' and, since wandering features crucially in the Hebrew Bible, the choice of words can carry a particular charge. In Chapter 3, after the incident in the red room, Jane seeks consolation in *Gulliver's Travels*, a book she usually loves. Only now it has lost its former charm:

> ... all was eerie and dreary; ... Gulliver a most desolate wanderer in most dread and dangerous regions.

Jacobs points out that Sharon Preminger, in 2007, translates 'wanderer' as 'נווד' [navad], a Modern Hebrew word 'closely associated with wandering as migration, as exile. In Genesis 4, Cain flees to the city of "Nod", which is etymologically related to "navad".' And the suggestion of exile continues: just a few lines later, when Bessie starts singing a song, 'in the days when we went gypsying', Preminger draws on the same verbal field: 'בימי נדודינו' ([*be-yamei nedudeinu*] in the days of our

4 *JE*, Ch. 28.

wanderings).[5] Six decades earlier, another Hebrew translator, Hana Ben Dov, gave similarly focused imaginative attention to wandering, translating the description of Gulliver as 'נודד בודד בארץ אויבת' ([*noded boded be-erets oyevet*] a solitary wanderer in an enemy land).[6] Jacobs comments that the phrase '"erets oyevet" is striking, and one wonders whether Ben Dov's language is shaped by her historical context, namely, the Second World War and the conditions of Jewish life in the final years of the British Mandate'. In these translations, we can see the influence of a Biblical understanding of wandering, which Brontë would have partly shared, passing through the text of *Jane Eyre* and emerging with distinctive force in new historical moments and imaginative communities.

In Elvi Kippasto's 1959 Estonian translation, studied by Madli Kütt, we can discover the range of significance that Brontë spans with the word 'wander'. In this selection of instances, Kippasto reaches for a different Estonian word each time.

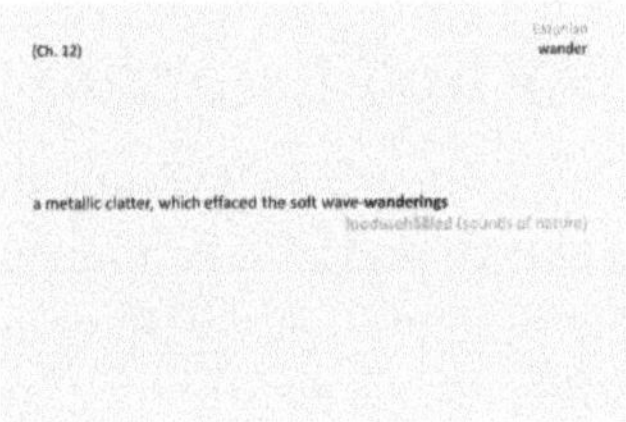

Animation 14: 'wander' in Estonian
https://hdl.handle.net/20.500.12434/06db0996

Ch. 1 We had been **wandering**, indeed, in the leafless shrubbery
uitasime (wandering)

Ch. 3 Gulliver a most desolate **wanderer**
kes eksleb (who is wandering, with a connotation of getting lost)

Ch. 6 your thoughts never seemed to **wander**
püsivad (always stay)

Ch. 9 when mists as chill as death **wandered**
liikusid (were moving)

Ch. 12 a metallic clatter, which effaced the soft wave-**wanderings**
loodusehääled (sounds of nature)

---

5 Preminger (2007), p. 29.
6 Ben Dov (1946), p. 18.

Ch. 17 vague suggestions kept **wandering** across my brain
vilksatas (skimmed)

Ch. 20 Is the **wandering** and sinful, but now rest-seeking and repentant, man justified
ränduril (wanderer)

Ch. 28 I drew near houses; I left them, and came back again, and again I **wandered** away
minna (went)

Ch. 37 I arrested his **wandering** hand, and prisoned it in both mine.
otsiva (searching)

As Kütt points out, more is going on in each of these examples than the isolated choice of a word. The instance from Chapter 9, where the mists simply 'liikusid' ('were moving') rather than 'wandered', is part of a general lightening of the metaphorical weight of that passage: in Kippasto's Estonian, the mists are also just mists, no longer 'chill as death'. In Chapter 17, the suggestions that Jane might leave Thornfield seem to be just starting, rather than continuing ('*kept* wandering'). In Chapter 6, where Helen's thoughts never seem to wander, Kippasto keeps the verb for 'wander' that she used at the start of the novel, 'uitama', for Jane's own thoughts, which, a bit further on in the English sentence, 'continually rove away'. So 'wander' wanders in this translation: we can observe, not only the variety of meanings that become explicit in Kippasto's Estonian, but also, by contrast, the insistence with which Brontë re-uses the English word in different, variously literal and metaphorical contexts, charging it with meaning.

'Parsa' in Persian

In Hebrew and Estonian we have seen translators opening out the significances of the word 'wander' by choosing varied possible equivalences at different moments of the text and under the pressure of distinct historical circumstances. But this splitting and diffraction of meaning is not the only way that translation can go to work upon the verbal material of the source. It can also do the opposite, linking what had been occurrences of different words in the source, and binding them together into new key terms.

Kayvan Tahmasebian has traced this happening in Persian. Two recent translators, Bahrami Horran (1996) and Reza'i (2010), have both translated the novel's first 'wander', 'we had been wandering, indeed, in the leafless shrubbery', with 'پرسه زده بودیم' {*parsa zadan*}. Tahmasebian notes that the word ‘parsa’ which is used for “wandering” contains the same connotations of aimlessness as indicated in the context of the original novel. However, etymologically, it is a contracted form of the Persian word ‘pārsa’ which means “to beg” as well as “a beggar”. It originally denotes the movement of beggar, here and there, in order to ask for (*porsidan*) something. It was part of the customs in some Sufi sects in which a disciple was asked to wander around the town, like a beggar, and recite poems, in order to suppress pride and vanity in him (*Dehkhoda Dictionary*).

Tahmasebian has traced the word ‘parsa’ throughout Reza’i’s translation, and has found that it renders a variety of English words, establishing a new network of association between the moments when they appear. The words are ‘walk’, ‘stroll’, ‘fly’, ‘stray’, ramble’ and — interestingly — ‘haunt’. Here are their occurrences (every word in bold is translated using ‘parsa’).

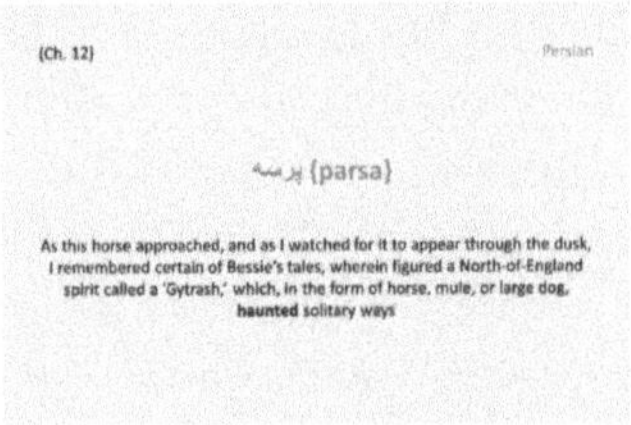

Animation 15: ‘parsa’
https://hdl.handle.net/20.500.12434/3121b8ca

Ch. 4 (Jane alone in the nursery)
I then sat with my doll on my knee till the fire got low, glancing round occasionally to make sure that nothing worse than myself **haunted** the shadowy room

Ch. 5 (Jane waits in an inn on her way to Lowood school)
Here I **walked** about for a long time, feeling very strange, and mortally apprehensive of someone coming in and kidnapping me

Ch. 12 (Jane awaits the appearance of the figure who turns out to be Mr. Rochester)
As this horse approached, and as I watched for it to appear through the dusk, I remembered certain of Bessie’s tales, wherein figured a North-of-England spirit called a ‘Gytrash’, which, in the form of horse, mule, or large dog, **haunted** solitary ways

Ch. 15 (Mr. Rochester, before he sees Céline with the vicomte)
and I was tired with **strolling** through Paris

Ch. 23 (Jane in the orchard, before Mr. Rochester proposes)
Here one could **wander** unseen. While such honey-dew fell, such silence reigned, such gloaming gathered, I felt as if I could **haunt** such shade forever

Ch. 24 (Mr. Rochester)
Ten years since, I **flew** through Europe half mad

Ch. 25 (Jane waits for Mr. Rochester to return on the evening before their planned wedding)
Here and there I **strayed** through the orchard

Ch. 25 (Jane narrates one of her dreams from the night before)
I **wandered**, on a moonlight night, through the grass-grown enclosure within

Ch. 26 (on the way to the church to be wed)
and I have not forgotten, either, two figures of strangers **straying** amongst the low hillocks and reading the mementoes graven on the few mossy head-stones

Ch. 28 (Jane penniless near Whitcross)
I **rambled** round the hamlet, going sometimes to a little distance and returning again, for an hour or more

Ch. 28 (Jane reluctant to approach houses, again near Whitcross)
I left them, and came back again, and again I **wandered** away

Ch 36 (The innkeeper describes Mr. Rochester's behaviour after Jane's departure)
He would not cross the door-stones of the house, except at night, when he **walked** just like a ghost about the grounds and in the orchard as if he had lost his senses

Tahmasebian comments:

> the network thus established between English words (mediated by the Persian word "parsa") has expected and unexpected knots. While the word "wander" can be easily associated with "walk", "stroll", "stray" and "ramble", the association with "haunt" seems a bit far-fetched. In Persian, this association is made possible through the collocation "ruh-e sargardān" which means "wandering spirit" or "wandering ghost". These words have been used in the context of popular horror stories that depict ghosts wandering at night. The stories are not rooted in Iranian folk tales but have been imported into modern Iranian culture from European origins. Thus, they have an "originally" translational existence within Iranian culture.

So this new conjunction of moments of 'parsa' in the Iranian *Jane Eyre* opens a new web of associations, centred in Jane's beggarly wandering around Whitcross, and spreading connotations of dislocation, dispossession and ghostliness into other moments of the novel.

'Walk' in Greek

As we have seen, the word 'walk' does not have such a wide range of meanings as 'wander'; but Brontë still recurs to the word insistently. One striking example is in Chapter 27 when, in the wake of the failed wedding, Jane insists that she and Rochester must part:

> He turned away; he threw himself on his face on the sofa. 'Oh, Jane! my hope — my love — my life!' broke in anguish from his lips. Then came a deep, strong sob.
>
> I had already gained the door: but, reader, I walked back — walked back as determinedly as I had retreated. I knelt down by him; I turned his face from the cushion to me; I kissed his cheek; I smoothed his hair with my hand.

In Greek, the usual word for walk (περπατάω) would sound odd in this context; so the three Greek translations studied by Eleni Philippou have each found different ways of phrasing 'I walked back — walked back':

> Όμως γυρνούσα πίσω, αναγνώστη, γυρνούσα πίσω (But I was coming back, reader, I was coming back) tr. Ninila Papagiannē, 1949.
>
> Αλλά ξαναγύρισα, ξαναγύρισα (But I returned again, I returned again) tr. Dimitris Kikizas, 1997.
>
> Όμως, καλέ μου αναγνώστη, γύρισα πίσω — γύρισα πίσω (But, my good reader, I turned back — I turned back) tr. Maria Exarchou, 2011.

These alternatives show us something about the Greek language and the choices of the three translators; but they also alert us to similar English alternatives — shadow texts — which Brontë did not use. Not 'I turned back'; not 'I returned'; but 'I walked back', a choice of words that connects this action, this merely momentary change of direction, to the other decisive walks throughout the novel.

'Walk' and 'Wander' in Italian and Chinese

Now let us observe a selection of walks, then a selection of wanderings, and finally the two sequences braided together, all given in English, in the recent Chinese translation by Song Zhaolin (Beijing, 2002), and in the anonymous first Italian translation (Milan, 1904). These are obviously very different languages and contexts, yet we can discern similar dynamics at work in both translations as, on the one hand, new connotations and connections appear while, on the other, key contours in Brontë's handling of both words are followed, and indeed thrown into relief.

The Chinese text, studied by Yunte Huang, translates the opening contrast between 'walk' and 'wandering' with 散步 ({*sanbu*} random or scattered footsteps) and 漫步 ({*manbu*}, wandering footsteps). Both expressions, Huang explains, contain the character 步, which 'is an ideograph of two feet: the upper half 止 is an image of a foot with toes sticking out, and the lower half is the reverse image.' As you look down the columns of 'walk' and 'wander' you can watch this character recurring. As with the instances we have explored above, Song finds varied ways of translating Brontë's repeated words; but he also establishes patterns of reiteration — most notably when the 'walk' 散步 (*sanbu*) that could not be taken at the novel's beginning makes a marked reappearance as the 'walk' 散步 (*sanbu*) that Jane and Rochester will for evermore be able to take together after they are reunited at its end.

In Italian, there is a similar mixture of prismatic diffraction of Brontë's words, and partially matching repetition. Italian has two obvious verbs for walk: 'passeggiare', which is more in the sense of going for a walk or stroll, and 'camminare', which is more in the sense of being able to walk, or just walking. The anonymous translator makes her or his own patterns with these words. You will see in the animation and array that 'camminare' figures on one occasion in the 'wander' column (Ch. 23), and it can also appear elsewhere in the novel where Brontë does not write of either walking or wandering. There are likewise two obvious Italian words for 'wander': 'errare', which includes the sense of error, and 'vagare' which is more carefree, a bit like the English 'drift'. In the animations and array below, you can trace the recurrences of 'passeggiare' (including 'passeggerò') and 'errare' (including 'errato', 'errante' and 'erravo'). Just like Song Zhaolin a century later, the anonymous Italian translator reaches for the same verb, 'passeggiare', for both the first 'walk', which cannot be taken, and the last, which Jane and Mr Rochester will take together. It makes another, similar arc with the verb 'errare' which appears both at the novel's beginning and (used of Rochester's hand) near its end.

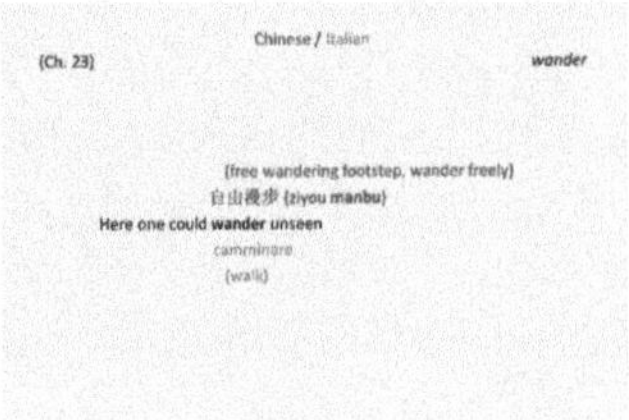

Animation 16: 'walk'
https://hdl.handle.net/20.500.12434/d9f915c9

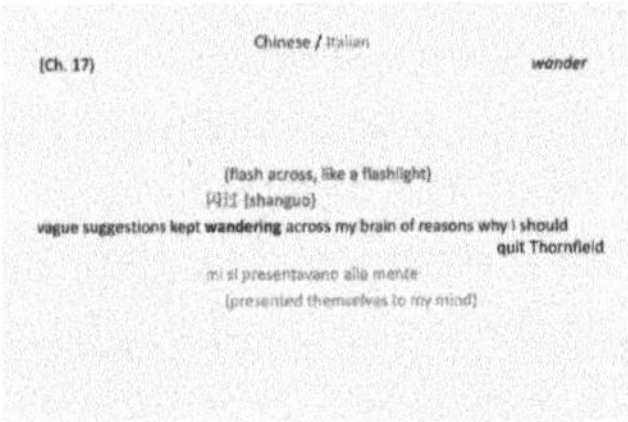

Animation 17: 'wander'
https://hdl.handle.net/20.500.12434/4c9ac8ca

Walk	Wander
Ch. 1 the first sentence **散步 (*sanbu***, random or scattered footsteps) There was no possibility of taking a **walk** that day. **passeggiare** (to walk)	
	Ch. 1 the second sentence **漫步 (*manbu***, wandering footsteps) We had been **wandering**, indeed, in the leafless shrubbery an hour in the morning; **errato** (wandered)
	Ch. 3 Jane fails to find consolation in *Gulliver's Travels* after the episode in the red room 流浪汉 (*liulang han*, homeless fellow, bum) Gulliver a most desolate **wanderer** in most dread and dangerous regions viaggiatore disperato **errante** (desperate traveller wandering)
Ch. 3 the apothecary Mr Lloyd queries why Jane has fallen 走路 (*zoulu*, walk the road) Can't she manage to **walk** at her age? camminare (to walk)	
	Ch. 6 at Lowood, Jane admires Helen Burns 走神 (*zoushen*, walking mind, absent-minded) your thoughts never seemed to **wander** while Miss Miller explained the lesson vagasse (wandered)

Walk	Wander
Ch. 12 at Thornfield 踱步 (*duobu*, back and forth footsteps) Then my sole relief was to **walk** along the corridor of the third story, backwards and forwards, **passeggiare** (to walk)	
	Ch. 12 just before her first meeting with Rochester, the clatter of hooves is heard above the murmur of streams 荡漾 (*dangyang*, up and down {of waves}) a metallic clatter, which effaced the soft wave-**wanderings** [–]
Ch. 15 **散步 (*sanbu*,** random or scattered footsteps) Mr Rochester ... asked me to **walk** up and down a long beech avenue seguirlo (follow him)	
	Ch. 17 Rochester has left Thornfield to spend time with Blanche and others at the Leas 闪过 (*shanguo*, flash across, like a flashlight) vague suggestions kept **wandering** across my brain of reasons why I should quit Thornfield mi si presentavano alla mente (presented themselves to my mind)
Ch. 20 an instruction after the wounding of Mason 走进 (*zoujin*, walk enter, walk into) go down into my bedroom, and **walk** straight forward into my dressing-room; [–]	

Walk	**Wander**
	Ch. 20 Rochester's description of himself, after the incident with Mr. Mason 流浪 (liulang, to be homeless) the **wandering** and sinful, but now rest-seeking and repentant, man [–]
Ch. 22 Jane's return to Thornfield after Aunt Reed's death 步行 (*buxing*, footsteps walk) … Millcote. I proposed to **walk** the distance quietly by myself; fare la via a piedi (to do the journey on foot)	
	Ch. 23 Jane tries to avoid Rochester in the winding walk bordered with laurels 自由**漫步** (*ziyou* ***manbu***, free wandering footstep, wander freely) Here one could **wander** unseen camminare (to walk)
Ch. 23 the walk on which Rochester toys with Jane's feelings before proposing **散步** (***sanbu***, random or scattered footsteps) I did not like to **walk** at this hour alone with Mr Rochester in the shadowy orchard **passeggiare** (to walk)	

Walk	**Wander**
Ch. 25 while waiting for Rochester to return the night before the wedding 小径 (*xiaojing*, little path) Descending the laurel **walk**, I faced the wreck of the chestnut-tree; viale (avenue)	
Ch. 27 she returns to kiss him before (as she thinks) leaving him for ever 走 (*zou*, walk) I had already gained the door; but, reader, I **walked** back tornai addietro (I returned back)	
	Ch. 28a after she has fled Thornfield, Jane wanders hungry and homeless around Whitcross 慢慢走开 (*manman zoukai*, slowly walk away) and again I **wandered** away mi accostavo di nuovo (I approached again)
	Ch. 28b still wandering around Whitcross 到处乱转 (*daochu luanzhuan*, everywhere chaotically turn) while I thus **wandered** about like a lost and starving dog **erravo** (I wandered)
Ch. 34 St John is about to propose **散散步 (*san san bu*)** Unlike 散步, adding one more 散 makes it sound more invitational, casual, or friendly [St John] 'Now, Jane, you shall take a **walk**; and with me.' **passeggiare** (to walk)	

Walk	**Wander**
Ch. 37a Jane sees the blinded Rochester at Ferndean 走动走动 (*zoudong zoudong*, walk move walk move) Mr Rochester now tried to **walk** about: vainly — all was too uncertain camminare (to walk)	
	Ch. 37 reunited with Rochester 胡乱摸着 (*huluan mozhe*, disorderly touch or feel about) I arrested his **wandering** hand, and prisoned it in both mine. **errante** (wandering)
Ch. 37b they are re-united **散步 (*sanbu*)** I will be your companion — to read to you, to **walk** with you, **passeggerò** (I will walk)	

Prismatic Scenes (i): The 'Red-Room'

A step on from the multilingual readings of words that I have offered so far is to attempt something like them for whole episodes of the novel. We have done this for two prismatic scenes: the 'red-room', from Chapter 2, and the 'shape' in Jane's bedroom, from Chapter 25. We present the material in the form of animations, created in JavaScript by Paola Gaudio: they ask for your participation as follows. The English text appears in blocks, so you have time to read it. Click on the revolving globe in the bottom right-hand corner to start the translations appearing. You will see that colour is used in two ways: the colour of the text is keyed to the language of the translation, while the colour of the frame around each translation shows you which English words it corresponds to. When all the translations have appeared around a given block of text, click on the revolving globe again to move forward, and click once more to launch the next set of translations. You can also navigate using the numbers in the left-hand margin or the triangles in the bottom left-hand corner. The background is dark so that the colours show up effectively: you may find you want to zoom in on your browser to make the text more legible.

First, the 'red-room' — the iconic episode in Chapter 2, where the young Jane, having stood up to John Reed's bullying, is confined as a punishment. We pick up the scene after the look of the room has been sketched in: the bed with its massive pillars and red damask curtains, the red carpet, the chairs, the glaring white piled-up pillows and mattresses, the windows and the 'visionary hollow' of the mirror; after we have learned that Jane's kind uncle Mr Reed had died there; and after Jane has lamented the injustice of her situation.[7]

The 'Red-Room': JavaScript animation by Paola Gaudio
https://hdl.handle.net/20.500.12434/b84f8bc9

The scene in the 'red-room' is generative: elements of it recur throughout the novel, from the red and white colour scheme of the drawing room at Thornfield Hall to Jane's repeated fretting at her life's restrictions; from the confinement imposed on Bertha Rochester to the possibility of supernatural intervention which, so feared in the red-room itself, is so welcomed near the end of the novel, when it takes the form of Rochester's voice echoing magically across the moors (Jane's heart beats 'thick' on both occasions).[8]

In the many plays, films and free re-writings that *Jane Eyre* has prompted, the scene has continued its recurrent metamorphoses.

7 The animation presents Danish translations by Aslaug Mikkelsen (1957), Christina Rohde (2015) and Luise Hemmer Pihl (2016), selected and back-translated by Ida Klitgård; French translations by Marion Gilbert & Madeleine Duvivier (1919), R. Redon & J. Dulong (1946), Léon Brodovikoff & Claire Robert (1946), Charlotte Maurat (1964), Sylvère Monod (1966) and Dominique Jean (2008), selected and back-translated by Céline Sabiron (with a few additions by Matthew Reynolds); and Russian translations by Irinarkh Vvedenskii (1849), Anon (1849), Anon (1901), Vera Stanevich (1950) and Irina Gurova (1999), selected and back-translated by Eugenia Kelbert. As ever, full publication details are in the List of Translations at the end of this volume.

8 *JE*, Ch. 35.

In Charlotte Birch-Pfeiffer's stage version (1853) it shrinks to an encounter with a portrait of Mr Reed; in Robert Stevenson's film of 1943 it morphs into a cluttered cupboard; while in Daphne du Maurier's *Rebecca* (1938) it blends with the windowless room occupied by Bertha Rochester and expands into the eerie west wing of Manderley, the domain of the dead first Mrs de Winter.[9]

In the translations shown in the animation there are, of course, no such free re-makings. Instead, we can watch the translators responding to the challenges of Brontë's language. The first of these is a particular vocabulary of mental struggle which has its roots in nonconformist writers of Christian spirituality such as John Bunyan and William Blake, but which Brontë moulds to her own emotional purpose in phrases like 'consternation of soul', 'heart in insurrection', 'mental battle'. In the animation, you can see some translators matching that phraseology while others reach for alternative terms. Further on, the renderings of words like 'vassalage' and 'heterogeneous' show translators responding in different ways to the markedly elaborate, adult vocabulary with which Jane, as narrator, recounts the trauma suffered by her younger self. A few changes here and there — like the introduction of a chiming clock, or the upgrading of the hall to a castle — add touches that register and perhaps amplify the gothic tension. And at moments of inward feeling or imagination ('I was a discord', 'a haloed face') translators find their own ways of expressing Jane's pain, and her hope which then fades and darkens into terror.

Some of these changes derive from the translators' individual styles: Eugenia Kelbert points out that the anonymous 1901 Russian translator has a general 'tendency to translate one word by two close synonyms'. Other choices bear the imprint of their historical and cultural moment — for instance Vera Stanevich's phrase 'phosphoric

---

9 Charlotte Birch-Pfeiffer, 'Die Waise aus Lowood. Schauspiel in zwei Abtheilungen und vier Acten. Mit freier Benutzung des Romans von Currer Bell', in *Gesammelte dramatische Werke*, vol. 14 (Leipzig: Reclam, 1876), 33–147; *Jane Eyre*, dir. By Robert Stevenson (20th Century Fox, 1943); Daphne du Maurier, *Rebecca* (London: V. Gollancz, 1938).

('фосфорическим') brilliance' in her translation from 1950, and her substitution of 'mother ('матерью') for 'parent'. In our second prismatic scene we will see such circumstances exerting a more transformative pressure.

Prismatic Scenes (ii): The 'Shape' in Jane's Bedroom

Our second prismatic scene is from near the end of Chapter 25: Jane's narration to Mr Rochester, on the eve of their planned wedding, of a strange and threatening incursion into her bedroom the night before, by a figure whom she does not yet know to be his current wife, Bertha.

The passage has always been one of the most provocative in the book. It was omitted from the 1849 French version by 'Old Nick' (Paul Émile Daurand Forgues), which — as we saw in Chapter I — served as the basis for several later translations into Spanish, German, Swedish and Russian. It nourished some of the novel's most influential interpretations: Sandra Gilbert and Susan Gubar's, which reads Bertha as Jane's double, and Gayatri Chakravorti Spivak's, which critiques the racism by which her portrayal is afflicted.[10]

And, as we will see, translators — those who have not gone so far as to cut the passage — have tended to veil it in various ways, perhaps not wanting (or not managing) to match the breathless vividness of Brontë's style here, while also demurring at the means by which Bertha is dehumanized. When we look at these translations closely, we get a detailed, fresh impression, both of the challenge of this passage, and of how it has been received by readers in different places, languages and times.[11]

10 See Chapter I above for references and discussion.

11 The animation presents translations into Spanish, by Juan G. de Luaces (1943), María Fernanda Pereda (1947), Jesús Sánchez Diaz (1974) and Toni Hill (2009), selected and back-translated by Andrés Claro; into Estonian, by Elvi Kippasto (1959), selected and back-translated by Madli Kütt; into Slovenian, by France Borko and Ivan Dolenc (1955) and Božena Legiša-Velikonja (1970), selected and back-translated by Jernej Habjan; into Arabic by Munīr' al-Ba'albakī (1985), selected and back-translated by Yousif M. Qasmiyeh; into Polish by Emilia Dobrzańska (1880), Teresa Świderska (1930), selected and back-translated by Kasia Szymanska; and into Greek by Polly Moschopoulou (1991) and Maria Exarchou (2011), selected and back-translated by Eleni Philippou. As ever, full publication details are in the List of Translations at the end of this volume.

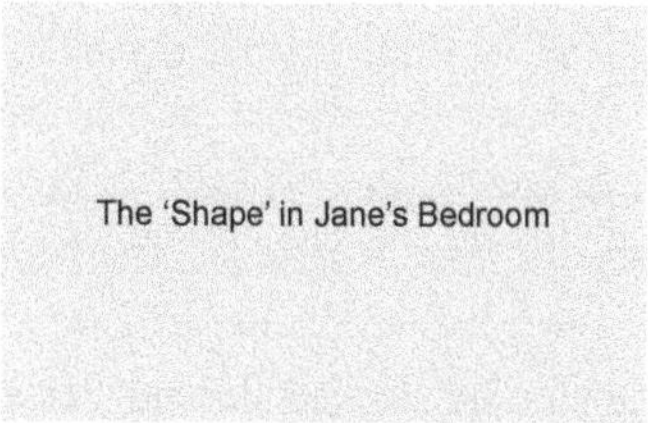

The 'Shape' in Jane's Bedroom: JavaScript animation by Paola Gaudio
https://hdl.handle.net/20.500.12434/f6c70608

'The second time in my life' — in the last sentence of this passage — points to the first time Jane had lost consciousness from terror: almost a decade, and twenty-three chapters, earlier, in the 'red-room'. There are some similarities between the scenes: enclosure in a bedroom, and a vividly imagined threat. But the style of the two passages is quite different. In the first, the mature Jane employs all the sophisticated resources of her written language to render the impressions of the child, with complex sentences and (as we have seen) words like 'consternation', 'vassalage' and 'cordiality', which few ten-year-olds would know. In the second, Jane as a young woman is shown speaking in her own urgent, colloquial tongue, with short, simple sentences and everyday words: 'I thought — oh, it is daylight!' One way in which translators tame her energy here is by constructing the syntax in more formal ways — as Madli Kütt has remarked of the Estonian translation of this phrase by Kippasto (1959), which can be back-translated, not as 'I thought — oh', but 'I thought that...' (similar things happen in this and other translations throughout the passage).

Jane has been very frightened, and she reaches for varied means to express her terror. One is the language of racial othering: the 'savage face', the 'red eyes', the 'blackened inflation of the lineaments'. Another is the imaginary figure of 'the Vampyre'. In the prismatic animation we can see translators emphasising this second aspect of the description (al-Baʿalbakī, for instance, adds explanatory words that can be back-translated as 'the sucker of people's blood'), while downplaying the first. Andrés Claro points out that both the 1940s Spanish translators, Luaces and Pereda, avoid the word 'savage' — and in Essay 5, above, he traces the reasons in their historical moments and political commitments. In such cases, the translators' muzzling of an aspect of their source can become a form of ethical critique.

Another feature of the text that Brontë wrote to represent Jane's speech is its wavering as to whether what Jane has encountered is human, or not; a 'she' or an 'it'. What first emerges from the closet was not a person but 'a form ... it was not Leah, it was not Mrs Fairfax'; then 'it seemed ... a woman' and becomes a 'she'; but then again, via the description of the face ('it was a discoloured face'), the figure becomes an 'it' again: 'it removed my veil'; only finally to veer back into humanity and gender: 'her lurid visage flamed over mine'. Translators vary in their handling of this variation, depending on their choices and also on how pronouns work in the languages they are using: Yunte Huang, in Essay 12, above, has explored several Chinese translations in this regard, while Madli Kütt, in Essay 16, below, provides a detailed discussion of the differently distinctive affordances of Estonian. Reading the translations together, we find a vivid record of the haunting, goading quality of this scene.

It already has that quality in the novel Brontë wrote. Right at the start of Chapter 25, Jane tells us that something strange has happened, and also that she will not explain what it was until later. We are also given an oddly charged description of the 'closet' in her bedroom, and the 'wraith-like apparel' it contains (i.e., the wedding dress), together with the weighted comment that Mrs Rochester is 'not I ... but a person whom as yet I know not'. None of this makes full sense until the scene of the invasion of the bedroom has been narrated several pages later; and yet, by the time that narration happens, these puzzling details may well have been forgotten — and indeed the scene itself is not fully explained until later again. Where then does this scene belong? In Brontë's text it floats, eery and ungraspable; and it continues to haunt the translations that encounter it.

Littoral Reading

The prismatic words and scenes that we have explored, throughout Chapters IV, V, VI and VII, have given us a way into the heterolingual complexity of the world *Jane Eyre*. Reading them, we can see how verbal patterns shape the signifying material of the text that Brontë wrote, and how those shapes morph in translation. To a large extent, the transformations are compelled by the medium the translator is working with and in: their language, repertoire, publishing context and cultural moment; but they are also motivated by individual taste and choice. Studying these never-quite-parallel texts together, we discover the creativity of linguistic, cultural and historical difference, as well as of individual translational imaginations. We also gain a better sense of what was there to be transformed — of the potential that is revealed in the source text through its being translated.

Not all words and scenes yielded the rich variety of those to which I have given full treatment here. Of the words that we researched, some, like 'mind', 'glad', 'conscience', 'master' produced a narrower range of interest, as we have seen. Others, like 'duty', 'elf' or 'strange' did not — so far as the research group could ascertain — reveal more than fleeting energies in the translations. This must show us something about the variable imaginative charge that words and their shadows carry, not only within what is defined as being 'their language' but across broader landscapes of language variety. But it may also be a sign of our comparatively restricted sample from the vast and variegated word hoard that is the world *Jane Eyre*. Perhaps, in other translations, and other languages and moments, those other words and their shadows turn out to be deeply interesting.

The approach described in these chapters does not exhaust itself in the discoveries that we have made about the particular words and scenes that we have studied. It also offers itself as a mode of reading suited to world works — that is to say, works that it is impossible to read in all their plural, multilingual vastness. If you can, sample a work in more than one language version. If you cannot do that, you can still read with an awareness that the words and scenes in front of you are translational: they have a disposition to be re-made differently, because they are haunted by shadow texts that can become actual in other repertoires, times and places. This is as true of texts that have not yet been translated as it is of those that are already translations. Read, not literally, but littorally, knowing that the words before you have been cast up onto the white page from the boundlessly transformative seas of language, and will inevitably float off again towards new strands. Reading a world text means being open to the traces of these horizons of meaning, even if the vast majority of them are beyond our ken.

I invite you to keep this wide perspective open, in counterpoint with the tighter focus of the essays that follow, as the volume begins to draw towards its close.

Works Cited

For the translations of *Jane Eyre* referred to, please see the List of Translations at the end of this book.

Birch-Pfeiffer, Charlotte, 'Die Waise aus Lowood. Schauspiel in zwei Abtheilungen und vier Acten. Mit freier Benutzung des Romans von Currer Bell', in *Gesammelte dramatische Werke* (Leipzig: Reclam, 1876), XIV, pp. 33–147.

Bunyan, John, *The Pilgrim's Progress*, ed. W. R. Owens, new edition (Oxford: Oxford University Press, 2003).

Dante Alighieri, *Inferno*, ed. Anna Maria Chiavacci Leonardi (Milan: Mondadori, 2016).

du Maurier, Daphne, *Rebecca* (London: V. Gollancz, 1938).

Pope, Alexander, *The Odyssey of Homer: Books I–XII* (*The Poems of Alexander Pope*, vol. 9), ed. Maynard Mack (London: Methuen & Co, and New Haven: Yale University Press, 1967).

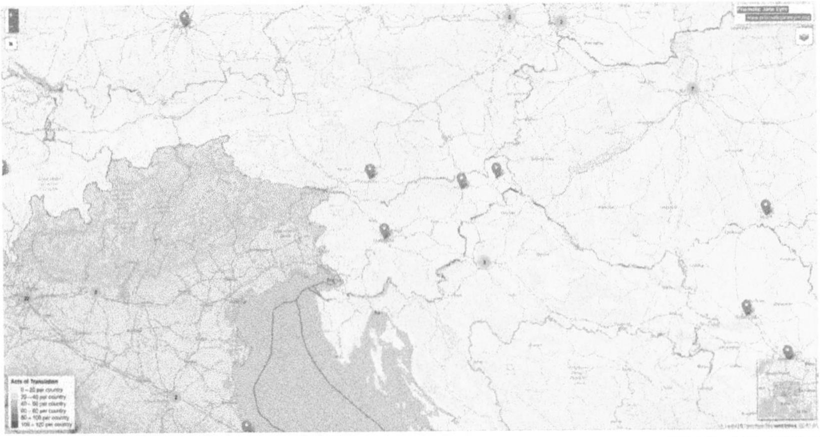

The World Map
https://digitalkoine.github.io/je_prismatic_map
Created by Giovanni Pietro Vitali;
maps © Thunderforest, data © OpenStreetMap contributors

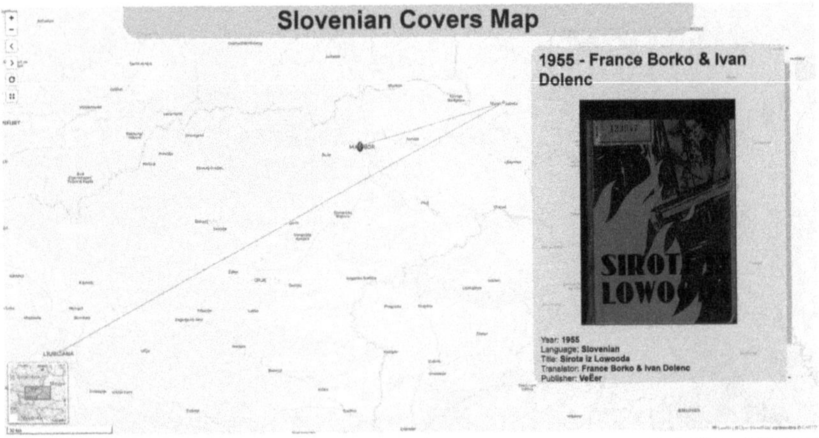

The Slovenian Covers Map
https://digitalkoine.github.io/slovenian_storymap/
Researched by Jernej Habjan; created by Giovanni Pietro Vitali and Simone Landucci

15. Free Indirect *Jane Eyre*

Brontë's Peculiar Use of Free Indirect Speech, and German and Slovenian Attempts to Resolve It

Jernej Habjan

Pursuing a close reading of a global novel across languages, it makes sense to start with an element of analysis which is found in as many languages as possible without being limited to the abstract linguistic material common to those languages; an element which is in common without being simply common.[1] One such element may arguably be free indirect speech: 'an interlinguistic process'[2] — as Marguerite Lips calls it in her book-length study — that uses linguistic units found globally to reach the realm of *metalinguistics* — to use Mikhail Bakhtin's term for the study of polyphonic literary devices such as free indirect speech.[3] Gertraud Lerch, a major influence on the Bakhtin Circle in matters of free indirect speech,[4] delineates this stylistic device as follows:

> In direct as well as indirect speech, the author starts by using a speech verb, a thought verb, etc. (*Il dit: 'Mon père te hait!'* or *Il dit que son père la haïssait*) to pin the responsibility of what was said to his characters,

1 This book chapter was written at the Research Centre of the Slovenian Academy of Sciences and Arts in the framework of the research programme 'Studies in Literary History, Literary Theory and Methodology' (P6-0024 [B]), which was funded by the Slovenian Research Agency.

2 Marguerite Lips, *Le style indirect libre* (Paris: Payot, 1926), p. 216. Translation mine.

3 See Mikhail Bakhtin, *Problems of Dostoevsky's Poetics*, trans. by Caryl Emerson (Minneapolis: University of Minnesota Press, 1984), pp. 181–85, 202.

4 See Valentin N. Vološinov, *Marxism and the Philosophy of Language*, trans. by Ladislav Matejka and I. R. Titunik (New York and London: Seminar Press, 1973), pp. 141–59.

 https://doi.org/10.11647/OBP.0319.23

> from whom he distances himself precisely by using this verb. In free indirect speech, however, he supresses the verb and arranges the expressions of his characters as if he took them seriously, as if these were facts and not mere utterances or thoughts (*Il protesta: Son père la haïssait!*). This is possible only due to the poet's empathy with the creations of his fantasy, due to his identification with them[.][5]

As a unit of analysis, free indirect speech is firmly based in linguistic features whose spread is almost as global as language itself, namely direct and indirect speech.[6] It mixes these features in cognitively interesting and historically dynamic ways, using what is common to modern languages to yield results that are often anything but common. Indeed, as we will see, there is a form of free indirect speech used in *Jane Eyre* that is so uncommon that many translations of the novel resolve it in favour of either direct or indirect speech. In fact, the more recent the translation, the more likely it will relay this peculiar and uncommon form of free indirect speech as either common direct speech or common indirect speech.

Defined as merger of direct speech's tone and indirect speech's tenses and personal pronouns, there is hardly any free indirect speech in *Jane Eyre*; defined in this standard way, one would have to look for it in what some have recently presented as the other camp, that of Jane Austen. Indeed, John Mullan even credits Austen for inventing free indirect speech in his *Intelligence Squared* defence of Austen against Emily Brontë.[7] Moreover, introducing his evolutionary tree of free indirect speech as the final figure of his *Graphs, Maps, Trees*, Franco Moretti writes that free indirect speech by leaving the individual voice

---

5 Gertraud Lerch, 'Die uneigentliche direkte Rede', in *Idealistische Neuphilologie: Festschrift für Karl Vossler*, ed. by Victor Klemperer and Eugen Lerch (Heidelberg: C. Winter, 1922), pp. 107–19 (p. 108). Translation mine. The examples in French translate as 'He said: "My father hates you!"', 'He said that his father hated her', and 'He protested: his father hated her!' respectively; the combination of the reporter's tenses and pronouns and the reportee's exclamation point (or, in negative terms, the absence of both quotation marks and the conjunction *that*) makes the final example a mix of the other two.

6 Language typologist Tom Güldemann even claims that one of these two features, direct speech, may be 'universal'; following such a strong category, his formulation that the other feature is 'missing' from or 'restricted' in 'a number of languages' does nothing to suggest that it is not global. See Tom Güldemann, *Quotative Indexes in African Languages: A Synchronic and Diachronic Survey* (Berlin: Mouton de Gruyter, 2008), p. 9.

7 See Erica Wagner et al., 'Jane Austen vs. Emily Brontë: The Queens of English Literature Debate' (*Intelligence²*, 2014), https://intelligencesquared.com/events/jane-austen-vs-emily-bronte/

a certain amount of freedom, while permeating it with the impersonal stance of the narrator', brought about 'an unprecedented "third" voice, intermediate and almost neutral in tone between character and narrator: the composed, slightly resigned voice of the *well-socialized individual*, of which Austen's heroines — these young women who speak of themselves *in the third person*, as if from the outside — are such stunning examples'.[8]

Hence, when it comes to what we today perceive as standard free indirect style, Brontë, any Brontë, is indeed in a different camp than Austen. There is, however, quite a lot of talk in *Jane Eyre* that only makes sense as free indirect speech in quotation marks: speech that merges with the tenses and personal pronouns of indirect speech not only the tone of direct speech but also its quotation marks.[9] Once this kind of talk in *Jane Eyre* is understood in this way, even the quotation marks themselves seem to start making sense: as they are invariably used in those cases of free indirect speech that the narrator finds harmful, they seem to be bracketing out that speech. And vice versa, the standard type of free indirect speech, the one without quotation marks, as rare as it is in *Jane Eyre*, seems to be opening itself up to the speech it is relaying, as this speech tends to be dear to the narrator. As a result, even standard indirect speech is anything but standard in *Jane Eyre*. In subsequent realist and modernist prose, free indirect speech will go on to become the main device for achieving, neither an opening up to the relayed speech nor a bracketing out of it, but Moretti's '"third" voice', a position that is neither the relaying narrator's nor the relayed character's; in *Jane Eyre*, however, it seems to achieve both, but by means of two distinct linguistic forms: free indirect speech without quotation marks (the standard), and free indirect speech

---

8 Franco Moretti, *Graphs, Maps, Trees: Abstract Models for Literary History* (London and New York: Verso, 2005), p. 82.

9 The habit of novelists to add quotation marks to indirect and free indirect speech has been noted by scholars, as has been the fading of this convention around the time Charlotte Brontë became a novelist. That the change in the convention might imply a change in free indirect speech itself has not been considered, however, even though free indirect speech has been rightly approached as precisely a set of conventions. See Norman Page, *Speech in the English Novel: Second Edition* (Houndmills and London: Macmillan, 1988), p. 31; Monika Fludernik, *The Fictions of Language and the Languages of Fiction* (London and New York: Routledge, 1993), pp. 226, 150; Anne Toner, *Jane Austen's Style: Narrative Economy and the Novel's Growth* (Cambridge: Cambridge University Press, 2020), p. 173.

within them. As a result, neither the standard nor its opposite seem to produce Moretti's '*well-socialized individual*' of an Austen heroine; in *Jane Eyre*, the '"third" voice' is not the voice of Austen's third-person narrator, but the voice of Jane herself: Jane the narrator bracketing out those who hurt Jane the heroine and embracing those who do not. If the Brontë camp is really different from the Austen camp, it is because it has more nuance in its free indirect speech, not less.

Free Indirect Speech within Quotation Marks

The kind of free indirect speech that uses elements of both direct and indirect speech, including the former's quotation marks, is certainly non-standard. There is a passage in *Jane Eyre* where the text itself is, as it were, aware of this, as it resolves its own free indirect speech in quotation marks by taking the direction of direct speech, making the pronouns and the sequence of tenses conform to the presence of quotation marks. And since the type of free indirect speech used in this passage renders, as already mentioned, even the standard type quite non-standard, let us open with it.

> I entered the shop: a woman was there. Seeing a respectably-dressed person, a lady as she supposed, she came forward with civility. How could she serve me? I was seized with shame: my tongue would not utter the request I had prepared. I dared not offer her the half-worn gloves, the creased handkerchief: besides, I felt it would be absurd. I only begged permission to sit down a moment, as I was tired. Disappointed in the expectation of a customer, she coolly acceded to my request. She pointed to a seat; I sank into it. I felt sorely urged to weep; but conscious how unseasonable such a manifestation would be, I restrained it. Soon I asked her '**if there were** any dressmaker or plain-workwoman in the village?'
>
> 'Yes; two or three. Quite as many as there **was** employment for.'
>
> I reflected. I was driven to the point now. I was brought face to face with Necessity. I stood in the position of one without a resource, without a friend, without a coin. I must do something. What? I must apply somewhere. Where?
>
> 'Did **she** know of any place in the neighbourhood where a servant **was** wanted?'
>
> 'Nay; **she** couldn't say.'
>
> 'What **was** the chief trade in this place? What **did** most of the people do?'
>
> 'Some **were** farm labourers; a good deal **worked** at Mr. Oliver's needle-factory, and at the foundry.'
>
> '**Did** Mr. Oliver employ women?'
>
> 'Nay; it **was** men's work.'

> 'And what do the women do?'
> 'I knawn't,' was the answer.[10]

Even though it contains indirect speech's tenses and pronouns, the exchange in quotation marks might seem a mere linguistic alternative to the usual version of direct speech in Brontë's time; in fact, we can trace this alternative back to the first chapter of her first novel, *The Professor*, in which the first-person narrator reproduces a letter in which he had written the following: 'When I had declined my uncles' offers they asked me "what **I intended** to do."'[11] However, in the last two utterances, the above exchange does use the usual version of direct speech ('And what do the women do?' 'I knawn't'), as if to imply that the preceding utterances were indeed a mix of direct and indirect speech, a mix that places them beyond any linguistic alternative and in the realm of Bakhtinian metalinguistics, the study of free indirect speech as precisely a mix of direct and indirect speech. Despite the quotation marks, the utterances only make sense as instances of free indirect speech; they can only be read in a non-contradictory manner if they are read as reported, indirect speech which is quoted, that is, as quoting while reporting.

This tension is all the more obvious if we look at translations, as they tend to resolve it in the direction of either quoting or reporting. To this end, it is sufficient to look at a couple of languages. Here, selected translations of *Jane Eyre* in German and Slovenian will be consulted: a Germanic language like English, and a Slavic one; a language that has produced not only numerous translations of *Jane Eyre* but also a scholarly monograph on them,[12] and a language that has rendered *Jane Eyre* but twice and that has received the novel through a dramatisation written and staged precisely in the other language;[13] and, finally,

---

10 *JE*, Ch. 28. Here and in subsequent quotations I bold those quotation marks, tenses, and pronouns which together create what I call non-standard free indirect speech.

11 Currer Bell, *The Professor* (London: Smith, Elder & Co., 1857), p. 4.

12 See Stefanie Hohn, *Charlotte Brontës* Jane Eyre *in deutscher Übersetzung. Geschichte eines kulturellen Transfers* (Tübingen: Narr, 1998); for an English-language chapter-length study based on this book, see Lynne Tatlock, 'Canons of International Reading: *Jane Eyre* in German around 1900', in *Die Präsentation Kanonischer Werke um 1900. Semantiken, Praktiken, Materialität*, ed. by Philip Ajouri (Berlin: de Gruyter, 2017), pp. 121–46.

13 See Charlotte Birch-Pfeiffer, 'Die Waise aus Lowood. Schauspiel in zwei Abtheilungen und vier Acten. Mit freier Benutzung des Romans von Currer Bell', in *Gesammelte dramatische Werke*, vol. 14 (Leipzig: Reclam, 1876),

a language of the imperial metropole and a language of a province that had only started its struggle for sovereignty at the time when *Jane Eyre* was written. But all these differences curiously make the selection equally easy in both languages: the German translations are so large in number that one can simply take the first nearly complete translation and trace its fate in a very recent revision of that same translation; and the Slovenian ones are so scarce that one can just take each in one hand and consult them both at once.

None of these translations retains the original combination of quotation marks and tenses and pronouns. The strange tension between quotation marks and past tenses from the beginning of the exchange ('Soon I asked her "**if there were** any dressmaker or plain-workwoman in the village?"') is resolved by Marie von Borch in the first nearly complete German translation by simply dropping the quotation marks: 'Gleich darauf fragte ich sie, ob im Dorfe eine Schneiderin oder eine einfache Handarbeiterin sei.'[14] This solution is retained also in Martin Engelmann's 2008 revision of the translation: 'Ich fragte sie, ob es im Dorf wohl eine Schneiderin oder eine einfache Handarbeiterin geben würde?'[15] The same holds for the two most recent German translations,[16] as well as for both Slovenian translations, which respectively read 'Čez nekoliko časa sem jo vprašala, ali imajo v vasi kakšno šiviljo ali krojačnico.' and 'Čez nekaj časa sem jo vprašala, ali je v vasi kakšna krojačica ali šivilja.'[17]

---

pp. 33–147; for the Slovenian translation, see Charlotte Birch-Pfeiffer, *Lowoodska sirota: igrokaz v dveh oddelih in 4 dejanjih / po Currer Bellovem romanu nemški spisala Charlotte Birch-Pfeifer*, trans. by Dav.[orin] Hostnik (Ljubljana: Dramatično društvo, 1877). For the dual-language German-English edition, see Charlotte Birch-Pfeiffer, *Jane Eyre or The Orphan of Lowood: A Drama in Two Parts and Four Acts* [trans. by Clifton W. Tayleure] (New York: Fourteenth Street Theatre, 1870).

14 Currer Bell, *Jane Eyre, die Waise von Lowood. Eine Autobiographie*, trans. by M.[arie] von Borch (Leipzig: Philipp Reclam jun.[, 1888]), p. 522.

15 Charlotte Brontë, *Jane Eyre, die Waise von Lowood. Eine Autobiographie*, trans. by Martin Engelmann (Berlin: Aufbau-Taschenbuch, 2008), p. 503.

16 See Charlotte Brontë, *Jane Eyre. Eine Autobiographie*, trans. by Melanie Walz (Berlin: Insel, 2015), p. 432; and Charlotte Brontë, *Jane Eyre. Roman*, trans. by Andrea Ott (Zürich: Manesse, 2016), p. 403.

17 Charlotte Brontë, *Sirota iz Lowooda*, trans. by France Borko and Ivan Dolenc (Maribor: Večer, 1955), p. 448; and Charlotte Brontë, *Jane Eyre*, vol. II, trans. by Božena Legiša-Velikonja (Ljubljana: Založništvo slovenske knjige, 1991), p. 316.

Yet as soon as Jane asks her second question, von Borch's early German translation follows this strange type of free indirect speech to the quotation mark, as it were. As a result,

> 'Did **she** know of any place in the neighbourhood where a servant **was** wanted?'
> 'Nay; **she** couldn't say.'

is rendered as:

> '**Ob sie** von irgend einer Stelle in der Nachbarschaft **wisse**, wo eine Dienerin gebraucht **werde**?'
> 'Nein, **sie wisse** von keiner.'[18]

Moreover, the translation follows this paradoxical pattern even after it has been resolved by the original itself. There, as we have seen, the exchange ends with a pair of lines of this non-standard free indirect speech followed by a pair of lines of plain direct speech:

> '**Did** Mr. Oliver employ women?'
> 'Nay; it **was** men's work.'
> 'And what do the women do?'
> 'I knawn't,' was the answer.

Von Borch, however, turns the penultimate line's direct speech back into that peculiar type of free indirect speech:

> '**Ob** Mr. Oliver auch Frauen **beschäftige**?'
> 'Nein, es **sei** Männerarbeit.'
> 'Und womit **beschäftigten** sich die Frauen?'
> 'Weiß nicht,' lautete die Antwort.[19]

It seems, then, that von Borch's 1887–90 translation is more Catholic than the Pope; for where the original uses the final two lines of the exchange to resolve this tension in the direction of direct speech ("'And what do the women do?'"), the translation reintroduces the tension ("'Und womit **beschäftigten** sich die Frauen?'" instead of "'beschäftigen"') after it has already resolved it in the direction of indirect speech ('Gleich darauf fragte ich sie, ob im Dorfe eine Schneiderin [...] sei.' instead of 'fragte ich sie, **"ob** im Dorfe eine Schneiderin [...] **sei"**.').

This is resolved in 2008, when Engelmann's revision of von Borch's 1887–90 translation applies the initial solution in the direction of

18 Bell, *Jane Eyre*, trans. by von Borch, p. 522.
19 Bell, *Jane Eyre*, trans. by von Borch, p. 522.

indirect speech throughout the exchange, omitting the quotation marks also in the penultimate line:

> Und womit beschäftigten sich die Frauen?
> 'Keine Ahnung,' lautete die Antwort.[20]

This is also the direction in which the tension reintroduced by the early translation ("'Und womit **beschäftigten** sich die Frauen?'") is solved in one of the two most recent German translations, by Melanie Walz:

> Und was taten die Frauen?
> 'Weiß nicht', lautete die Antwort.[21]

However, the most recent German translation chooses the opposite direction: following the original itself, Andrea Ott renders the last two utterances of the exchange as direct speech:

> 'Und was tun die Frauen?'
> 'Weiß nicht', kam die Antwort[.][22]

The same holds also for the two Slovenian translations. Here is the one by France Borko and Ivan Dolenc:

> 'In s čim se ukvarjajo pri vas ženske?'
> 'Ne bi mogla povedati,' je bil odgovor.[23]

And here is the one by Božena Legiša-Velikonja:

> 'Kaj delajo pa ženske?'
> 'Ne vem,' je bil odgovor.[24]

Hence, insofar as von Borch's 1887–90 translation is updated by Engelmann in 2008 in the same way the original exchange itself is altered by its final pair of lines, one could say that the dynamics of this passage in English are refracted in the history of its German translations. In turn, this translation history mirrors the history of English prose itself: much like Engelmann and other contemporary translators of *Jane Eyre* (Walz or Ott in German, Borko and Dolenc or Legiša-Velikonja in Slovenian), the English novel after the Brontës, too, seems increasingly uncomfortable with the tension of quoted reporting, or, reported quoting.

---

20 Brontë, *Jane Eyre*, trans. by Engelmann, p. 503.
21 Brontë, *Jane Eyre*, trans. by Walz, p. 433.
22 Brontë, *Jane Eyre*, trans. by Ott, p. 404.
23 Brontë, *Sirota iz Lowooda*, trans. by Borko and Dolenc, p. 449.
24 Brontë, *Jane Eyre*, vol. 2, trans. by Legiša-Velikonja, p. 317.

But let us return to Whitcross. Jane looking for work is not the only example of this tension between direct and reported speech. In the very next substantial exchange, quotation marks are again merged with third-person pronouns and past tenses:

> An old woman opened: I asked was this the parsonage?
> 'Yes.'
> '**Was** the clergyman in?'
> 'No.'
> '**Would** he be in soon?'
> 'No, he **was** gone from home.'
> 'To a distance?'
> 'Not so far — happen three mile. He **had been** called away by the sudden death of his father: he **was** at Marsh End now, and **would** very likely stay there a fortnight longer.'
> '**Was** there any lady of the house?'
> 'Nay, there **was** naught but **her**, and **she was** housekeeper;' and of her, reader, I could not bear to ask the relief for want of which I was sinking; I could not yet beg; and again I crawled away.[25]

In German, this tension is retained in von Borch's 1887–90 translation, but not in Engelmann's 2008 revision, where sentences like '"**Ob** er bald nach Hause kommen **würde**."'[26] are relieved of their quotation marks and thus resolved as simple indirect speech,[27] a solution chosen also by the two most recent translations.[28] Conversely, the two Slovenian translations keep the original quotation marks and instead turn conditional verbs like the one in '"**Would** he be in soon?"' into future verbs to get plain direct speech, as in '"Se bo kmalu vrnil?"',[29] which could be back-translated as '"Will he be in soon?"'

Similarly, as the exchange ends with Jane trying to sell her gloves and the housekeeper retorting '"No! what **could she** do with them?"',[30] this mix is retained in German in 1887–90[31] but resolved as indirect speech by Engelmann in 2008, Walz in 2015, and Ott in 2016;[32] indirect

---

25 *JE*, Ch. 28.
26 Bell, *Jane Eyre*, trans. by von Borch, p. 525.
27 See Brontë, *Jane Eyre*, trans. by Engelmann, p. 506.
28 See Brontë, *Jane Eyre*, trans. by Walz, p. 434; and Brontë, *Jane Eyre*, trans. by Ott, p. 406.
29 Brontë, *Sirota iz Lowooda*, trans. by Borko and Dolenc, p. 451; and Brontë, *Jane Eyre*, vol. 2, trans. by Legiša-Velikonja, p. 318.
30 *JE*, Ch. 28.
31 See Bell, *Jane Eyre*, trans. by von Borch, p. 525.
32 See Brontë, *Jane Eyre*, trans. by Engelmann, p. 506; Brontë, *Jane Eyre*, trans. by Walz, p. 435; and Brontë, *Jane Eyre*, trans. by Ott, p. 406.

speech is also the solution chosen by the first Slovenian translation, while the second one chooses direct speech.[33]

The opposite solution, indirect speech, is chosen early on by von Borch's translation,[34] as well as by all the other translations,[35] as they confront this mixture:

> She had taken an amiable caprice to me. She said I was like Mr. Rivers, only, certainly, she allowed, 'not one-tenth so handsome, though **I was** a nice neat little soul enough, but he **was** an angel.' I was, however, good, clever, composed, and firm, like him. I was a *lusus naturæ*, she affirmed, as a village schoolmistress: she was sure my previous history, if known, would make a delightful romance.
>
> [...] She was first transfixed with surprise, and then electrified with delight.
>
> '**Had I** done these pictures? **Did I** know French and German? What a love — what a miracle **I was**! **I drew** better than **her** master in the first school in S—. **Would I** sketch a portrait of **her**, to show to papa?'[36]

The first Slovenian translation is the only partial exception here in that it renders the final paragraph as direct rather than indirect speech. It does join the other translations, though, when it comes to rendering as plain indirect speech the following direct-indirect mix:

> St. John arrived first. [...] Approaching the hearth, he asked, '**If I was** at last satisfied with housemaid's work?'[37]

In this case, the second Slovenian translation is the exception, only not for turning free indirect speech into direct speech like the first Slovenian translation of the previous case, but, much more surprisingly, for retaining the original tension:

> Najprej se je pokazal St. John. [...] Ko je stopil k štedilniku, me je vprašal, '**ali se nisem** končno že naveličala prostaškega dela služkinje?'[38]

But the very first example of what can only be understood as non-standard free indirect speech is to be found as early as the book's

33 See Brontë, *Sirota iz Lowooda*, trans. by Borko and Dolenc, p. 452; and Brontë, *Jane Eyre*, vol. 2, trans. by Legiša-Velikonja, p. 318.

34 See Bell, *Jane Eyre*, trans. by von Borch, pp. 589–90.

35 See Brontë, *Jane Eyre*, trans. by Engelmann, pp. 568–69; Brontë, *Jane Eyre*, trans. by Walz, p. 487; Brontë, *Jane Eyre*, trans. by Ott, pp. 457–58; Brontë, *Sirota iz Lowooda*, trans. by Borko and Dolenc, pp. 507–8; and Brontë, *Jane Eyre*, vol. 2, trans. by Legiša-Velikonja, pp. 356–57.

36 *JE*, Ch. 32.

37 *JE*, Ch. 34.

38 Brontë, *Jane Eyre*, vol. 2, trans. by Legiša-Velikonja, pp. 378–79.

third paragraph. Even before Mrs Reed starts to address Jane Eyre in the third person instead of the second to signal hierarchy, Jane the narrator returns the favour with interest and quotes Mrs Reed in the third person instead of the first. The result is free indirect speech that is even more polyphonic than that of Mrs Reed:

> Me, she had dispensed from joining the group; saying, '**She regretted** to be under the necessity of keeping **me** at a distance; but that until **she heard** from Bessie, and **could** discover by **her** own observation, that **I was** endeavouring in good earnest to acquire a more sociable and childlike disposition, a more attractive and sprightly manner — something lighter, franker, more natural, as it were — **she** really must exclude **me** from privileges intended only for contented, happy, little children.'[39]

When, much later in the novel, Mrs Reed is reintroduced together with her third-person address, Jane the narrator does the same to Mrs Reed's daughters, Eliza and Georgiana, quoting them in the third person instead of the first:

> I asked if Georgiana would accompany her.
>
> 'Of course not. Georgiana and **she had** nothing in common: **they** never **had** had. **She would** not be burdened with her society for any consideration. Georgiana should take her own course; and **she**, Eliza, **would** take **hers**.'
>
> 'It would be so much better,' she said, 'if **she** could only get out of the way for a month or two, till all was over.'[40]

In Eliza's case, this tension between quotation marks and the sequence of tenses is resolved in favour of the latter starting from 1887–90;[41] the first Slovenian translation is the only one that does the opposite and drops, not the quotation marks, but the sequence of tenses to turn the original mix into direct speech.[42] In Georgiana's case, this latter solution is chosen also by the other Slovenian translation,[43] as well as by von Borch's early German edition[44] and its recent revision by Engelmann, where '"It would be so much better," she said, "if **she** could

39 *JE*, Ch. 1.
40 *JE*, Ch. 21.
41 See Bell, *Jane Eyre*, trans. by von Borch, pp. 372–73; Brontë, *Jane Eyre*, trans. by Engelmann, pp. 358–59; Brontë, *Jane Eyre*, trans. by Walz, p. 310; Brontë, *Jane Eyre*, trans. by Ott, p. 286; and Brontë, *Jane Eyre*, vol. 1, trans. by Legiša-Velikonja, p. 223.
42 See Brontë, *Sirota iz Lowooda*, trans. by Borko and Dolenc, p. 319.
43 See Brontë, *Jane Eyre*, vol. 1, trans. by Legiša-Velikonja, p. 224.
44 See Bell, *Jane Eyre*, trans. by von Borch, p. 373.

only get out of the way for a month or two [...]"' reads '"Es wäre so viel besser," pflegte sie zu sagen, "wenn ich auf ein oder zwei Monate fort könnte [...]"'.[45]

As for the book's third paragraph, Mrs Reed is everywhere translated in the same way as Eliza, that is, as ordinary indirect speech without quotation marks.[46]

The early translation is less averse to mixing direct and indirect speech when it comes to sentences such as '"**Did I** like **his** voice?" he asked' in Chapter 24: in 1887–90, von Borch translated this into German as '"**Ob seine** Stimme **mir** denn eigentlich so sehr **gefiele**?" fragte er.'[47] Engelmann's 2008 revision, however, omits the quotation marks to turn the sentence into indirect speech: 'Ob seine Stimme mir denn eigentlich gefiele?, fragte er.'[48] This is also the direction taken by the most recent German translations,[49] while the Slovenian translations take the opposite, direct path, turning past tense into present tense and the first and third person into the second and first: '"Ali ti ugaja moj glas?" je vprašal.'[50] and '"Ti je všeč moj glas?" je vprašal.'[51] — which could both be back-translated as '"Do you like my voice?" he asked.'

As soon as this singing voice leads to serious questions, von Borch's 1887–90 translation sobers up, as it were, and turns the free indirect style of the question into plain direct speech rather than leaving that task to Engelmann's 2008 revision. In 1887–90 as well as 2008, the section

> as he reached me, I asked with asperity, 'whom **he was** going to marry now?'
>
> 'That **was** a strange question to be put by **his** darling Jane.'[52]

45 Brontë, *Jane Eyre*, trans. by Engelmann, p. 359.

46 See Bell, *Jane Eyre*, trans. by von Borch, pp. 3–4; Brontë, *Jane Eyre*, trans. by Engelmann, p. 5; Brontë, *Jane Eyre*, trans. by Walz, p. 13; Brontë, *Jane Eyre*, trans. by Ott, p. 5; Brontë, *Sirota iz Lowooda*, trans. by Borko and Dolenc, p. 5; and Brontë, *Jane Eyre*, vol. 1, trans. by Legiša-Velikonja, p. 5.

47 Bell, *Jane Eyre*, trans. by von Borch, p. 432.

48 Brontë, *Jane Eyre*, trans. by Engelmann, p. 414.

49 See Brontë, *Jane Eyre*, trans. by Walz, p. 358; and Brontë, *Jane Eyre*, trans. by Ott, p. 331.

50 Brontë, *Sirota iz Lowooda*, trans. by Borko and Dolenc, p. 371.

51 Brontë, *Jane Eyre*, vol. 2, trans. by Legiša-Velikonja, p. 264.

52 *JE*, Ch. 24. In *Charlotte Brontë: Style in the Novel* (Madison: University of Wisconsin Press, 1973), p. 36, Margot Peters characterises this passage as 'direct indirect discourse', a term that tries to say as much as my 'free indirect speech within quotation marks', but whose elegance comes at the price of entirely losing the connection with the concept of free indirect speech.

is translated as

> Als er neben mir stand, fragte ich streng: 'Nun, wen werden Sie denn jetzt heiraten?'
>
> 'Das ist eine seltsame Frage von den Lippen meines Lieblings, Jane!'[53]

This holds also for the following paragraph:

> 'Indeed! I considered it a very natural and necessary one: **he** had talked of **his** future wife dying with **him**. What did **he** mean by such a pagan idea? *I* had no intention of dying with **him** — **he** might depend on that.'[54]

Both in 1887–90 and 2008, the ending '"he might depend on that."' is translated as '"darauf können Sie sich verlassen."'[55] instead of '"darauf **könnte er** sich verlassen."'

Accordingly, the beginning of the section

> '**Would I** be quiet and talk rationally?'
>
> '**I would** be quiet if **he liked**, and as to talking rationally, I **flattered** myself I **was** doing that now.'[56]

is translated in 1887–90 as well as 2008 as '"Willst du jetzt still sein oder vernünftig mit mir reden?"'[57] instead of '"**Ob sie** jetzt still sein oder vernünftig mit **ihm** reden **wolle**?"'

Incidentally, the second and latest Slovenian translation is the most surprising again, as it keeps the original tension of the last three examples,[58] rather than resolving it in the direction of either direct or indirect speech.

To conclude this list, here is an utterance that keeps both of the two elements that are omitted in the standard type of free indirect speech, that is, not only direct speech's quotation marks but also indirect speech's third-person speech verbs (in this case, '"he had [...] remarked"' and '"he feared"'):

Perhaps this is the reason why Peters applies the term only to this example of what I describe as free indirect speech within quotation marks.

53 Bell, *Jane Eyre*, trans. by von Borch, pp. 433–34; Brontë, *Jane Eyre*, trans. by Engelmann, p. 417.

54 *JE*, Ch. 24.

55 Bell, *Jane Eyre*, trans. by von Borch, p. 434; Brontë, *Jane Eyre*, trans. by Engelmann, p. 417.

56 *JE*, Ch. 24.

57 Bell, *Jane Eyre*, trans. by von Borch, p. 434; Brontë, *Jane Eyre*, trans. by Engelmann, p. 418.

58 See Brontë, *Jane Eyre*, vol. 2, trans. by Legiša-Velikonja, pp. 265–66.

> This silence damped me. I thought perhaps the alterations had disturbed some old associations he valued. I inquired whether this was the case: no doubt in a somewhat crest-fallen tone.
>
> 'Not at all; **he had**, on the contrary, **remarked that I had** scrupulously respected every association: **he feared**, indeed, **I** must have bestowed more thought on the matter than it was worth. How many minutes, for instance, **had I** devoted to studying the arrangement of this very room? — By-the-bye, could **I** tell **him** where such a book **was**?'[59]

The first Slovenian translation turns this into direct speech, rendering '"Not at all; **he had**, on the contrary, **remarked that I had** [...]"' as '"Nikakor ne," je dejal. '"Nasprotno! Opazil sem, da ste [...]"'.[60] The other translations simply omit the original quotation marks to create plain indirect speech.[61] But this bifurcation, where the first Slovenian edition resolves non-standard free indirect speech in the opposite direction than the second one or the recent German translations, is to be expected by now; what is also to be expected is that, in the early German translation, the tension of the final paragraph is not simply turned into direct rather than indirect speech, as in the early Slovenian translation, but, much more interestingly, retained:

> Sein Schweigen dämpfte meine Freude. Ich glaubte, daß die Veränderungen vielleicht einige alte Erinnerungen gestört hätten, welche ihm wert und lieb gewesen. Ich fragte, ob dies der Fall sei. Vielleicht in sehr niedergeschlagenem Ton.
>
> 'Durchaus nicht. **Er bemerke** im Gegenteil, daß **ich** mit der größten Gewissenhaftigkeit alles, was **ihm** wert **sei**, geschont **habe**; **er fürchte** in der That, daß **ich** der Sache mehr Wichtigkeit **beigelegt**, als sie wert **sei**. Wieviel Minuten **hätte ich** zum Beispiel damit zugebracht, über das Arrangement dieses Zimmers nachzudenken? — Übrigens, **könne ich ihm** denn nicht sagen, wo dies und jenes Buch **sei**?'[62]

Finally, if we return to the beginning of Jane's exchange with the Whitcross shop-keeper, we can also return to the standard type of free indirect speech, where quotation marks are omitted rather than kept. For the sentence 'How could she serve me' can now be read as free indirect speech as well:

---

59 *JE*, Ch. 34.

60 See Brontë, *Sirota iz Lowooda*, trans. by Borko and Dolenc, p. 541.

61 See Brontë, *Jane Eyre*, trans. by Engelmann, p. 606; Brontë, *Jane Eyre*, trans. by Walz, p. 518; Brontë, *Jane Eyre*, trans. by Ott, p. 488; and Brontë, *Jane Eyre*, vol. 2, trans. by Legiša-Velikonja, p. 379.

62 Bell, *Jane Eyre*, trans. by von Borch, p. 627.

> I entered the shop: a woman was there. Seeing a respectably-dressed person, a lady as she supposed, she came forward with civility. **How could she serve me?** I was seized with shame: my tongue would not utter the request I had prepared.[63]

Indeed, all the German translations we have been consulting read 'How could she serve me' as free indirect speech, namely 'Womit sie mir dienen könne?'.[64] Similarly, the latest Slovenian translation has 'S čim mi lahko postreže?', and only the other Slovenian edition merges the sentence with the previous one to come up with a sentence characteristic of indirect speech: 'je prodajalka vljudno prišla k meni in me vprašala, s čim mi lahko postreže.', or, in back-translation, 'she came forward with civility and asked me how she could serve me.'

Free Indirect Speech without Quotation Marks

If this example of standard free indirect speech seems banal, let us conclude with two examples that are far from being banal and that, moreover, are the clearest examples of this type of free indirect speech in *Jane Eyre*. As early as Chapter 2, Jane relays her own past speech without using either quotation marks or third-person speech verbs:

> What a consternation of soul was mine that dreary afternoon! How all my brain was in tumult, and all my heart in insurrection! Yet in what darkness, what dense ignorance, was the mental battle fought! I could not answer the ceaseless inward question — ***why*** I thus **suffered**; **now, at the distance of — I will not say how many years, I see it clearly**.

Here, Jane's past exclamations merge with her present report — that is, past exclamation points merge with the present use of the past tense — so that even her final comment on the difference between her past and her present cannot fully revoke the merger (which all the consulted translations seem to understand as they retain even the italics of '*why*').[65]

But we also find free indirect speech at the opposite end of the book, in Chapter 37, where the respective positions of Jane and Rochester

63 *JE*, Ch. 28.

64 Bell, *Jane Eyre*, trans. by von Borch, p. 521; Brontë, *Jane Eyre*, trans. by Engelmann, p. 502; Brontë, *Jane Eyre*, trans. by Walz, p. 432; and Brontë, *Jane Eyre*, trans. by Ott, p. 403.

65 See Bell, *Jane Eyre*, trans. by von Borch, p. 17; Brontë, *Jane Eyre*, trans. by Engelmann, p. 18; Brontë, *Jane Eyre*, trans. by Walz, p. 24; Brontë, *Jane Eyre*, trans. by Ott, p. 16; Brontë, *Sirota iz Lowooda*, trans. by Borko and Dolenc, p. 17; and Brontë, *Jane Eyre*, vol. 1, trans. by Legiša-Velikonja, p. 13.

finally merge. The paragraph starts as indirect speech but then loses the latter's features without gaining those of direct speech. So, at first, speech is relayed not by direct quotation but by a speech verb conjugated for a third-person pronoun, in this case 'he said'; in time, however, this, too, is abandoned. And as the introductory 'he said' is gradually omitted, 'his' (that is, Rochester's) speech merges with the narrator's (that is, Jane's):

> I should not have left him thus, **he said**, without any means of making my way: I should have told him my intention. I should have confided in him: he would never have forced me to be his mistress. Violent as he had seemed in his despair, he, in truth, loved me far too well and too tenderly to constitute himself my tyrant: he would have given me half his fortune, without demanding so much as a kiss in return, rather than I should have flung myself friendless on the wide world. I had endured, **he was certain**, more than I had confessed to him.

Both here and in the translations,[66] the result is an account irreducible to either of the two subject positions involved; not even the return of 'he said' in the form of 'he was certain' can revoke the merger of the two positions — especially since, as the reader already knows by this point, she indeed deliberately confessed a mere portion of what she had endured.

Whereas the quotation marks in the non-standard examples seemed to be bracketing out free indirect speech, here, in these two standard examples, the narrator relays speech as if to embrace it: as if Jane were trying to embrace first her own past speech and then Rochester's present speech; first her past as an orphan of Lowood and then her future as Mrs Rochester; first her past self and then her future other; first her virtue and then her reward. And as an item, the two standard examples of free indirect speech, the one from the second chapter and the one from the second last chapter, seem to embrace *Jane Eyre* itself.

Finally, as the type of free indirect speech represented by these two examples has been made standard simply by the subsequent development of prose narrative, be it original or translated, one could say that this type, where Jane Eyre and hence *Jane Eyre* are embraced, is in turn embraced by translators and rewriters, to the point that it is

66 See Bell, *Jane Eyre*, trans. by von Borch, p. 705; Brontë, *Jane Eyre*, trans. by Engelmann, pp. 681–82; Brontë, *Jane Eyre*, trans. by Walz, p. 581; Brontë, *Jane Eyre*, trans. by Ott, pp. 549–50; Brontë, *Sirota iz Lowooda*, trans. by Borko and Dolenc, p. 610; and Brontë, *Jane Eyre*, vol. 2, trans. by Legiša-Velikonja, p. 424.

now standard. Conversely, the other kind of example, where speech harmful to Jane is bracketed out, is itself increasingly avoided and thus made non-standard by those who translate and write in the wake of *Jane Eyre*. *Jane Eyre* itself belongs to the historical moment when novelists were still allowed to rely on quotation marks to produce the effect of free indirect style while already having the possibility of dispensing with quotation marks and practising free indirect style as it is known today. As a whole, *Jane Eyre* is a kind of merger of these two ways of merging direct and indirect speech, one of which has since become the standard and one of which this essay has tried to valorise by looking at how it has fared in translation.

Works Cited

Translations of *Jane Eyre*

Brontë, Charlotte, *Jane Eyre*, trans. by Božena Legiša-Velikonja (Ljubljana: Založništvo slovenske knjige, 1991).

——, *Jane Eyre, die Waise von Lowood. Eine Autobiographie*, trans. by Martin Engelmann (Berlin: Aufbau-Taschenbuch, 2008).

——, *Jane Eyre. Eine Autobiographie*, trans. by Melanie Walz (Berlin: Insel, 2015).

——, *Jane Eyre. Roman*, trans. by Andrea Ott (Zürich: Manesse, 2016).

——, *Sirota iz Lowooda*, trans. by France Borko and Ivan Dolenc (Maribor: Večer, 1955).

Other Sources

Bakhtin, Mikhail, *Problems of Dostoevsky's Poetics*, trans. by Caryl Emerson (Minneapolis: University of Minnesota Press, 1984).

Bell, Currer, *Jane Eyre, die Waise von Lowood. Eine Autobiographie*, trans. by M.[arie] von Borch (Leipzig: Philipp Reclam jun., [1887–90]).

Birch-Pfeiffer, Charlotte, 'Die Waise aus Lowood. Schauspiel in zwei Abtheilungen und vier Acten. Mit freier Benutzung des Romans von Currer Bell', in *Gesammelte dramatische Werke* (Leipzig: Reclam, 1876), XIV, pp. 33–147.

——, *Jane Eyre or The Orphan of Lowood: A Drama in Two Parts and Four Acts*, trans. by Clifton W. Tayleure (New York: Fourteenth Street Theatre, 1870).

——, *Lowoodska sirota: igrokaz v dveh oddelih in 4 dejanjih / po Currer Bellovem romanu nemški spisala Charlotte Birch-Pfeifer*, trans. by Dav.[orin] Hostnik (Ljubljana: Dramatično društvo, 1877).

Brontë, Charlotte, *The Professor* (London: Smith, Elder & Co., 1857).

Fludernik, Monika, *The Fictions of Language and the Languages of Fiction* (London and New York: Routledge, 1993).

Güldemann, Tom, *Quotative Indexes in African Languages: A Synchronic and Diachronic Survey* (Berlin: Mouton de Gruyter, 2008), https://doi.org/10.1515/9783110211450

Hohn, Stefanie, *Charlotte Brontës* Jane Eyre *in deutscher Übersetzung. Geschichte eines kulturellen Transfers* (Tübingen: Narr, 1998).

Lerch, Gertraud, 'Die uneigentliche direkte Rede', in *Idealistische Neuphilologie: Festschrift für Karl Vossler*, ed. by Victor Klemperer and Eugen Lerch (Heidelberg: C. Winter, 1922), pp. 107–19.

Lips, Marguerite, *Le style indirect libre* (Paris: Payot, 1926).

Moretti, Franco, *Graphs, Maps, Trees: Abstract Models for Literary History* (London and New York: Verso, 2005).

Page, Norman, *Speech in the English Novel: Second Edition* (Houndmills and London: Macmillan, 1988).

Tatlock, Lynne, 'Canons of International Reading: *Jane Eyre* in German around 1900', in *Die Präsentation Kanonischer Werke um 1900. Semantiken, Praktiken, Materialität*, ed. by Philip Ajouri (Berlin: de Gruyter, 2017), pp. 121–46, https://doi.org/10.1515/9783110549102-008

Toner, Anne, *Jane Austen's Style: Narrative Economy and the Novel's Growth* (Cambridge: Cambridge University Press, 2020), https://doi.org/10.1017/9781108539838

Vološinov, Valentin N., *Marxism and the Philosophy of Language*, trans. by Ladislav Matejka and I. R. Titunik (New York and London: Seminar Press, 1973).

Wagner, Erica, et al., 'Jane Austen vs. Emily Brontë: The Queens of English Literature Debate' (*Intelligence²*, 2014), https://intelligencesquared.com/events/jane-austen-vs-emily-bronte/

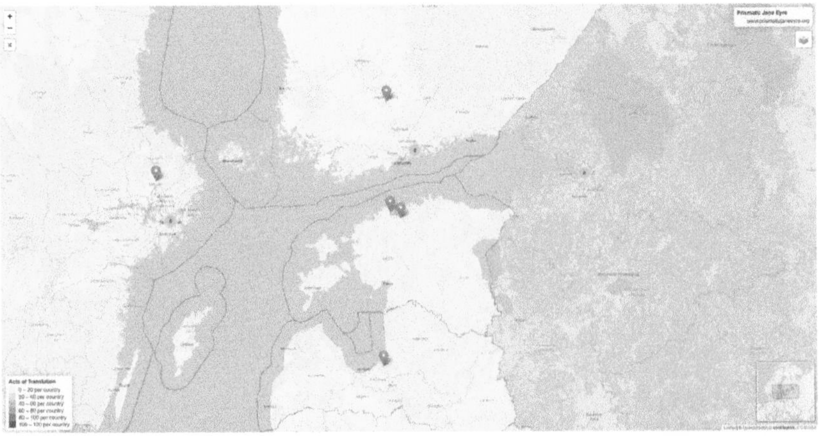

The World Map
https://digitalkoine.github.io/je_prismatic_map
Created by Giovanni Pietro Vitali;
maps © Thunderforest, data © OpenStreetMap contributors

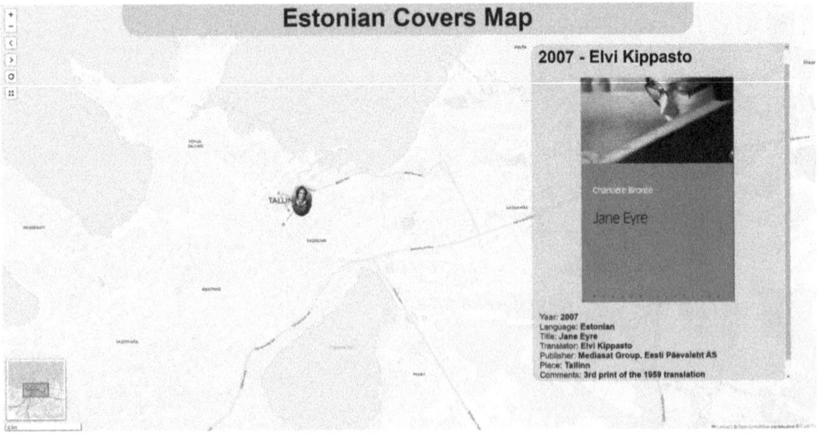

The Estonian Covers Map
https://digitalkoine.github.io/estonian_storymap/
Researched by Madli Kütt; created by Giovanni Pietro Vitali and Simone Landucci

16. 'Beside myself; or rather *out* of myself'

First Person Presence in the Estonian Translation of *Jane Eyre*

Madli Kütt

Jane Eyre is undoubtedly a narrator who is very present in her storytelling, on many levels. This presence is both intense and polyvalent, but for the most part it inheres in a first-person narrator who is at the centre of her own story. Jane presents herself as someone who acts, perceives, thinks and remembers, and gives a great deal of attention to her own thoughts and feelings. She explicitly separates her two narrative selves into the character in the scene and the retrospective writer. As a character, she controls her inner point of view by referring often to herself as she is experiencing something ('I heard', 'I saw'): I will call this her 'experiencer' role. In her 'narrator' role, she keeps her knowledge mostly in line with the chronological progress of the story, and whenever she seems to have more information than she should, she takes good care to explain to her reader how and when she got it, thereby asserting the truthfulness of her story. This does not mean that her narration is without inconsistencies: in fact, there have been fruitful and passionate studies by Charlotte Fiehn, Kevin Stevens and Lisa Sternleib, asserting Jane's dubious or even unreliable position as a narrator.[1] Yet the fact that, after a century-and-a-half of criticism, these scholars still feel the need to announce such disparities only goes to emphasise Jane's strong personal presence in the novel.

1 Charlotte Fiehn, 'The Two Janes: *Jane Eyre* and the Narrative Problem in Chapter 23', *Brontë Studies*, 41 (2016), 312–21; Lisa Sternlieb, '*Jane Eyre*: "Hasarding Confidences"', *Nineteenth-Century Literature*, 53 (1999), 452–79; Kevin Stevens, '"Eccentric Murmurs": Noise, Voice, and Unreliable Narration in *Jane Eyre*', *Narrative*, 26 (2018), 201–20.

https://doi.org/10.11647/OBP.0319.24

In this essay, I would like to discuss the ways that Jane's intense presence is changed in Estonian translations, putting forward the hypothesis that these changes significantly affect the image and the functioning of the first person in the novel. I have two reasons for this hypothesis. The first comes from one of the remarkable differences between English and Estonian: their ways of expressing the subject in a clause. Estonian, together with other Finno-Ugric languages, is considered as a 'passive' language: there is a natural tendency to prefer passive constructions, which may lead to concealing the subject, especially in its functions as possessor and experiencer, in both oral and written forms. Estonian also has a large variety of means to avoid direct reference to either the speaker or the listener, and to focus instead on the event, possession or experience itself.[2] This tendency has somewhat weakened in the last thirty years (mainly due to contacts with Indo-European languages like German or Russian, and more recently, and contrastingly, English), but it is still present and recognisable today,[3] and was even more so during the time when *Jane Eyre* first appeared in Estonian in 1959. It is fair to expect that such a tendency might also have left its prints on the translation of a first-person narrative from English into Estonian.

The second reason is the possibility of what I will call an 'immersion effect' during the translation process. A fictional immersion effect, as explained by Jean-Marie Schaeffer in *Pourquoi la fiction*?, is a way for the author and the reader (or viewer, or player) to engage with the fictional world, an affective investment that, as Schaeffer insists, 'operates not only at the reception of works but also at their creation'.[4] The translator as both a reader and a co-creator is indeed right at the heart of these dynamics, and their effects would be even stronger in case of a first-person narration. In other words, when a translator is rewriting in her own language a novel in which someone keeps using the first-person perspective, it is possible that, at least in some respects,

2 Liina Lindström, 'Kõnelejale ja kuulajale viitamise vältimise strateegiaid eesti keeles [Strategies of avoidance of reference to the speaker and hearer in Estonian]', *Emakeele Seltsi aastaraamat* [*Yearbook of the Estonian Mother Tongue Society*], 55 (2010), 88–118.

3 Mati Erelt and Helle Metslang, 'Kogeja vormistamine eesti keeles: nihkeid *SAE* perifeerias' [Expression of the experiencer in Estonian: Shifts in the periphery of the SAE]', *Emakeele Seltsi aastaraamat* [*Yearbook of the Estonian Mother Tongue Society*], 53 (2007), 9–22.

4 Jean-Marie Schaeffer, *Why Fiction*? trans. by Dorrit Kohn (Lincoln and London: University of Nebraska Press, 2010), pp. 153–54.

the translator might start to see herself in that 'I' as well. Clearly, the identification with the first person is not entirely straightforward, not even in translation. The translator's 'I' is obviously not the same as the author's 'I'. This understanding has led translation theorists to recognise that translation brings along a multiplication of voices which may be present in the text to different degrees. Theo Hermans is the first to call this phenomenon by the term 'Translator's voice', by which he argues for a discursive presence of the translator in any translated text, including first-person narratives.[5] In *The Conference of the Tongues* (2014), Hermans demonstrates that translator's voice can become especially visible in translating strongly ideological first-person writings, such as Adolf Hitler's *Mein Kampf*, where the translator may be openly intervening in a text to mark disapproval or reservation towards the anterior speaker's values. He recognises, however, that translators can struggle with the first-person perspective in the text, not only when translating a work with which their personal views do not agree but 'even when they are in sympathy with what they translate'.[6] When translating a work of fiction, these processes are bound to be even more complex because of different voices and modalities involved in the 'I'. In translation, these various instances of subjectivity can converge through the translator's immersion and affect the first-person appearance in both her experiencer and her narrator roles.

An Estonian translator of *Jane Eyre* is thus torn between these tendencies of language, translation and fiction, which can cause various movements and momentums to manifest themselves in the text. However, more than the causes of these movements, I will focus on their effects on the performance of the first person. For this purpose, I have chosen to address the translator's immersive experience by comparing some narrative aspects of the translations and the source text, such as the enhancement or masking of the first-person expression in the text, the presentation of a different point of view, or a change in the spatial perspective. These aspects will allow us to understand how the translator's immersive experience may alter the first-person narrative in the course of translation. Which moments tend to increase or decrease the presence of the 'I' in the text? How do changing degrees of closeness to or distance from the first person alter

5 Theo Hermans, 'The Translator's Voice in Translated Narrative', *Target*, 8:1 (1996), 23–48.

6 Theo Hermans, *The Conference of the Tongues* (London: Routledge, 2014), p. 57.

the point of view and other narrative functions? How does Jane come across through her narration in the Estonian version?

The Presence of *Jane Eyre* in Estonian

Before looking more closely at the changes that Jane goes through when translated into Estonian, a few points in the Estonian history of translating *Jane Eyre* need clarification. The novel entered into this small Finno-Ugric language, of about a million native speakers, in 1959 in Elvi Kippasto's translation (published first under her married name Raidaru), with verses translated by Edla Valdna. In 1981, a second edition was issued with some proofreading corrections and under the translator's maiden name Kippasto. The 1981 text was reprinted in 2007 with no alterations, and the edition of 2013 brought some additional minimal changes.[7] All of these editions also include Valdna's translation of the verses but only the edition of 1981 gives her the credit; the two more recent editions only refer to Elvi Kippasto as translator and relate themselves to the 1981, not the 1959 edition.

In 2000, another version of Jane Eyre was published, and this time it bore a different name for the translator, Ira Inga Vilberg. This is an interesting case of publishing that falls between making a new translation and editing an existing one, where the two activities merge in practice. Although Brigitta publishing house issued the text as a new translation, comparative reading of Kippasto's and Vilberg's versions indicates a great similarity between them, which points to the fact that Vilberg has worked with Kippasto's text as a source. Such cases are not unfamiliar to translation history, as Kaisa Koskinen and Outi Paloposki demonstrate in their study of retranslations in Finland; they note that reasons for such incidents are complex and case specific, and they can sometimes happen without a consent of the translators or editors themselves.[8] In addition to these reasons, Ira Inga Vilberg's case seems to be related to its publishing period. The publication of this version

7 Charlotte Brontë, *Jane Eyre* (Tallinn: Mediasat Group, Eesti Päevaleht AS, 2007); Charlotte Brontë, *Jane Eyre* (Tallinn: Tänapäev, 2013). The changes in the 2013 print include spelling '*söör*' [sir] phonetically instead of using the loan word 'sir' like the earlier editions, and occasionally adjusting the syntax by one word.

8 Kaisa Koskinen, and Outi Paloposki, *Sata kirjaa, tuhat suomennosta. Kaunokirjallisuuden uudelleenkääntäminen* [A Hundred Books, A Thousand Translations: Retranslating Fiction] (Helsinki: Suomalaisen kirjallisuuden seura [Finnish Literature Society], 2015).

falls into a time of cultural adjustments in Estonian history. In 2000, with Estonia's recently regained independence nine years earlier, publishing norms were undergoing a phase of significant changes and had not yet properly set in. Many small publishing companies worked for financial purposes and were not immediately concerned by copyright laws.[9] The publishing house Brigitta from Tallinn seems to fit the profile: it was active from 1994–2000, and Vilberg's *Jane Eyre* is their last publication in a series of youth-oriented classical literature, historical and crime novels. Attempts to find out about the translator-editor Vilberg as a person have turned out unsuccessful as of yet, which points to a likelihood that a pseudonym was used. The fact that Valdna's verse translations have been completely removed (possibly due to copyright issues), as well as the presence of many proofreading mistakes in the text (letters and words left out or misspelt) also indicate a low-budget publishing situation. This however does not discredit Vilberg's effort on working with the text in this particular situation in which she found herself. The changes that Vilberg has made are mostly motivated by the intent of modernising the language (adjustments in syntax, grammar, and vocabulary). Occasionally, the changes have also increased accuracy towards the English source text, though this goal has not been followed consistently. In the context of this essay, I have chosen to use Kippasto's edition of 1981 as the main source since this is the most well-known and republished version, and differences in Vilberg's version are discussed where they concern the first-person presence in the text. Comparing the two versions will provide valuable insight into the alternative ways in which the first-person presence can be affected. However, due to a great number and frequency of similarities between the two versions, the comparison is not followed systematically but is undertaken only when Vilberg's version provides additional understanding of the topic.

'Moving where all else was still': Feeling with the Protagonist

I would like to begin my discussion by looking into some ways by which the translation increases the presence of the first person and

9 Aile Möldre, *Kirjastustegevus ja raamatulevi Eestis aastail 1940–2000* [Publishing and Book Distribution in Estonia in 1940–2000] (Tallinn: TLÜ kirjastus [Tallinn University Press], 2005), pp. 232–34.

moves closer to the character-level of the narration. Indeed, despite the linguistic tendency of Estonian to conceal the subject, there are some moments where Kippasto's translation seems to intensify this presence. The very first scene of the novel offers an example of this movement. It is the moment of Jane's solitary reading behind the curtains, on the window sill, which she expects to be interrupted 'too soon'.

> *JE*, Ch. 1: I feared nothing but interruption, and that came **too** soon.[10]
>
> EK 9: Ma ei kartnud midagi rohkem, kui et **mind** segatakse. **Ja minu kurvastuseks** juhtuski see õige peatselt.
>
> BT: I feared nothing more than that **I** would be interrupted. **And to my regret**, this happened shortly.
>
> IIV 7: Ma ei kartnud midagi muud, kui et **mind** segatakse. **Kuid kahjuks** juhtuski see kohe.
>
> BT: I feared nothing more than that **I** would be interrupted. **But unfortunately**, this happened shortly.

Kippasto's translation adds two more mentions of the first person in that short sentence. This has also caused some changes in the syntax, so that there are now two separate sentences, both of which focus on the first person. In the first sentence, the translation changes a shorter, nominal form — 'interruption' — into a full sub-clause 'that I would be interrupted' [*et mind segatakse*]. In the second, a temporary adverb 'too' becomes a first-person experiencer-phrase which makes explicit Jane's feelings of 'regret' [*kurvastuseks*] towards the upcoming event. In Vilberg's version, one of these additions of 'I' has been removed but the other one remains.

The translation can move closer to the first person also through other characters' speech. Such is the case with Miss Abbot's comment at the beginning of the red-room passage, directed in English only to Bessie. Abbot refers to Jane in the third person throughout this reply, excluding her completely from the conversation. Jane is left to herself, and in God's care.

10 The examples in this essay are taken from Charlotte Brontë, *Jane Eyre*, trans. by Elvi Kippasto (Tallinn: Kirjastus Eesti Raamat, 1981), abbreviated to 'EK'; and Charlotte Brontë, *Jane Eyre*, trans. by Ira Inga Vilberg (Tallinn: Brigitta, 2000), abbreviated to 'IIV'. All emphases in the examples as well as the back-translations ('BT') are by the author of this essay.

JE, Ch. 2: 'Besides,' said Miss Abbot, 'God will punish **her**: he might strike **her** dead in the midst of **her** tantrums, and then where would **she** go? Come, Bessie, we will **leave her**: (...)'

EK 13: "Pealegi võib Jumal ise **teid** karistada," ütles miss Abbot. "Ta võib **teid** keset niisugust vihahoogu surmaga rabada, ja mis siis...? Tulge, Bessie, **lähme** ära. (...)"

BT: 'Besides, God himself may punish **you**,' said miss Abbot. 'He may strike **you** dead in the midst of such a fit of anger, and what then...? Come, Bessie, let us **go**. (...)'

IIV 12: "Peale selle," ütles miss Abbot, "jumal ise võib **teda** karistada. Ta võib **teda** keset sellist purset surmaga tabada, ja kuhu ta hind [sic!] siis läheb...? Tulge, Bessie, lähme ära. (...)"

BT: "Besides, God himself may punish **her**,' said miss Abbot. 'He may strike **her** dead in the midst of such a burst, and where would her soul go then...? Come, Bessie, let us go. (...)'

In Kippasto's translation, this comment addresses Jane by using a formal second person 'you' [*teid*], making this a three-way conversation. As is characteristic in Estonian, there are also fewer personal addresses — two of the 'her's have been left out. Abbot's words are still strict and threatening, and it could be argued that her threats have now a more personal direction and thus more power to take their effect. On the other hand, by including Jane as a participant in this conversation, and by using the formal address, the translation also allows more respect and sympathy towards the child. Vilberg's version corrects this dialogue significantly, by switching the personal pronouns back to the third person, and thus removing Jane from the conversation again. Still, Vilberg's corrections do not touch the way Abbot invites Bessie to go with her, rather than leave Jane behind as she does in the English version. Thus, by leaving out the final 'her', Jane in this version is even more intensely pushed away.

However, Kippasto's movement against the linguistic distance of Estonian happens only rarely. More often, the effect of increased closeness becomes apparent through less direct devices. For example, translation can interfere with the dramatic setting of the scene, as we can see in the red-room passage. Jane has been locked up in the red-room which has a certain effect of magic on her. Although inwardly full of movements of thought and emotion, Jane is physically rather immobile in the room, being imprisoned ('Alas! yes: no jail was ever more secure') and 'left riveted' by Bessie and Abbott on 'a low ottoman near the marble chimney-piece'. She moves around once, to confirm that the door is indeed locked, and returns right to her stool. On her way back, she takes an 'involuntary' look into the mirror which opens a view into a magical world, a 'visionary hollow'. She also notices her own reflection there, 'a strange little figure' in contrast with the surroundings: 'a white face and arms specking the gloom'.[11] She sees the little figure's eyes moving, in contrast with 'all else' that is 'still'.

> *JE*, Ch. 2: with [...] glittering eyes of fear **moving** where **all else** was **still**
>
> EK 14: hirmust läikivate silmadega, kus **ainsana elu** näis **tuksuvat toas**, mis oli otsekui **surnud**
>
> BT: with glittering eyes of fear, which [were] **the only place** where **life** seemed to be **throbbing** in a **room** that was like **dead**

Translation makes this scene more dynamic, as it adds a description of the movement in the eyes, a 'throbbing' [*tuksuvat*]. It also pushes the contrast between the figure and its surrounding to an extreme by interpreting movement as 'life' [*elu*], and stillness as 'dead' [*surnud*]. More importantly, translation takes this otherworldly vision back into the reality: the mirror starts to work as a mirror again, bringing Jane's gaze back into the 'room' [*toas*] where she was, and her being there becomes even more real as it is now a question of life and death.

These dynamics continue into the next example from the red-room scene, where Jane is still sitting on her stool, looking at the room around her. Her field of vision is again described as rather static, and consists of only two still frames: the bed and the walls form one single frame, and the mirror forms another.

> *JE*, Ch. 2: and **now, as I sat** looking **at** the white bed **and** overshadowed walls — occasionally also turning a fascinated eye towards the dimly gleaming mirror —
>
> EK 16: Mu **rahutu pilk eksles** valgelt voodi**lt** hämarusse uppuvaile seinte**le** ja **sealt uuesti** tuhmilt läikivale peeglile, ning...
>
> BT: My **restless glance was wandering from** the white bed **to** the overshadowed walls drowned into the darkness and **from there again** to the dimly gleaming mirror, and...

Translation has let go of Jane's sitting body altogether, and instead follows her 'glance' [*pilk*] which has gained some emotion and momentum. It has become 'restless' [*rahutu*], and it is 'wandering' [*eksles*] around more, switching between different frames, going from

11 *JE*, Ch. 2.

the bed to the walls (the spatial movement in Estonian is indicated by declinations *-lt*, and *-le*), and 'from there again' [*sealt uuesti*] to the mirror.

The above examples convey a certain degree of increase in the first person presence in Kippasto's translation. Vilberg's version seems to have been sensitive to these increases of the subject's presence and has sometimes guided the translation back towards a greater distance. Interestingly, Vilberg's changes mostly concern the times where subjects are directly mentioned but do not interfere with the dynamics of the scenes. The stronger presence of the first person indicates the immersion effect in Kippasto's version, which has two major effects on Jane's experiencer role: at these moments, the character-Jane becomes more active than in the English version; and other characters have more ability to interact with her directly. It is perhaps not without interest that most of these moments where the translation seems to be approaching the first person perspective come from the first few chapters of the book, where Jane is still a child. This seems to indicate that Kippasto as the translator has more sympathy for young Jane and thus moves closer to her also in her expression. However, as the following analysis will demonstrate, this closeness is not prevalent in the rest of Kippasto's translation.

Dimming the First-Person Presence

The dominant tendency in the Estonian *Jane Eyre* is to omit the first-person experiencer or alter and dim her position in other ways. This has consequences on both the narrator and the character levels.

On the narrator level, losing the first person as the focal point shifts the point of view towards a more diffused, general perspective. In descriptive passages, the first person can easily be left out. In the following example, Jane has taken a rest on her way to Hay, just before meeting Mr Rochester for the first time. She is again describing what she could see from where she was sitting.

> *JE*, Ch. 12: From **my** seat **I could look down** on Thornfield: the gray and battlemented hall was the principal object in the vale **below me**;
>
> EK 108: **Siit oli** kogu **Thornfield** selgesti näha: oru põhjas **kõrgus** sakmelise katusevalliga maja helehall **massiiv**,
>
> BT: **Thornfield was** easily visible from **here**: in the vale, the monolithic, light gray and battlemented **hall was towering**

IIV 133: **Minu** kohalt oli kogu Thornfield hästi näha: oru põhjas kõrgus sakilise katusega maja hall massiiv,

BT: From **my** seat, Thornfield was easily visible: in the vale, the monolithic, gray and battlemented hall was towering

In the first phrase, Kippasto's translation maintains the deictic reference with 'from here' [*siit*] so that the point of view is still relatable to the first person, but any mention of the experiencer herself, as well as the spatial indicator 'below me' in the second phrase, have been omitted. The role of the subject has been given to Thornfield Hall instead. Vilberg makes the first person presence only slightly more explicit, by reintroducing the possessive 'from my seat' [*minu kohalt*] instead of Kippasto's more generic deixis, but still leaving out the subject 'I' who 'could look down' in the English text.

Some omissions of the experiencer may bring more crucial changes to the narrative point of view. When, in Chapter 1, Jane and John Reed have had their fight, others come and separate them. Jane recalls: 'I heard the words', and quotes what she heard. The dialogical form indicates that there is more than one speaker.

JE, Ch. 1: We were parted: **I heard the words** —
'Dear! dear! What a fury to fly at Master John!'
'Did ever anybody see such a picture of passion!'

EK 11–12: Meid lahutati.
"Helde taevas! Küll on metsaline! Tormab noorhärra Johnile kallale!"
"Kes niisugust raevuhoogu enne on näinud!" **kostsid hüüded läbisegi**.

BT: We were parted. / "Good Heavens! What a savage! Storming at Master John!" / "Who has seen such a fit of fury before!" **the voices sounded, mixed**.

In translation, the first-person phrase has been lost and, instead, the plurality of voices is given focus. There are indeed many speakers present in the scene, but in addition to the dialogical form, we learn about this from a separate phrase. The first person does not form a focal point any longer, and thus the voices are given the freedom to 'sound' [*kostsid*] of their own accord, and are allowed to disperse and to get 'mixed' [*läbisegi*] with one another.

Similarly, the first person may disappear in a cognitive function, as with the red-room scene's vision in the mirror where Jane compares herself to 'a strange figure':

> *JE*, Ch 2: **I thought it** like one of the tiny phantoms, half fairy, half imp,
>
> EK 14: **See oli** midagi tillukese haldja ja väikese kuradikese taolist,
>
> BT: **It was** something like a tiny fairy and a little devil,

The translation does not preserve the act of intellection expressed in the first-person phrase. The Estonian sentence is simply stating the nature of the figure, without any personal input into the image, which presents the view as a general description rather than someone's imagination.

These cases demonstrate the loss of a focal point but more importantly they indicate the gain of another, more open one. The descriptions are no longer a strict account of what Jane could see or hear or what she was thinking, but of what was visible and audible from that place, which operate as an implicit invitation to the reader to experience it as well.

In addition to the effect of giving up the experiencer's remarks in favour of a more generalised point of view, Kippasto's translation also often disregards the re-phrasings and correctional additions which show the narrator hesitating, rethinking, re-remembering, or otherwise revising her expression. This may be a more deliberate choice by the translator who perhaps sees these reiterations as author's 'mistakes' and tries to edit them out by writing the 'correct' version right away. These corrections have also survived in Vilberg's version where they have been considered relevant enough to keep.

Such a correction of corrections happens already in the red-room scene where the narrator is describing the room as one 'very seldom slept in', and then specifying: 'I might say never, indeed', making the room seem even more drastically solitary.

> *JE*, Ch. 2: The red-room was a spare chamber, very seldom slept in; **I might say never, indeed; unless** when a chance influx of visitors at Gateshead-hall rendered it necessary to turn to account all the accommodation it contained:
>
> EK 13: Punane tuba oli seisnud kasutamata. Seal magati noil äärmiselt harvadel juhtudel, kui Gateshead-halli nii rohkesti külalisi kokku voolas, et kõik majas olevad toad ära tuli kasutada.
>
> BT: The red-room had remained unused. It was only slept in on those rare occasions when there was such an influx of visitors at Gateshead-hall that it became necessary to turn to use all the rooms in the house.

The Estonian version does not provide any equivalent for the first-person specification in the English text, and changes the comment into a conclusive passive tense sentence: 'It was only slept in on those rare occasions when' [*Seal magati noil äärmiselt harvadel juhtudel, kui*]. This omission does not change the information given about the room; however, it does cancel out the first-person narrator's input. What remains is a straightforward, general informative description of how the room was used, without any personal comment or opinion about it.

Omission of the narrator's corrective comment occurs more drastically in Chapter 15, where Jane hears Bertha's laughter behind her door, just before she discovers the fire that Bertha has set on Mr Rochester's bed. In this scene, however, Jane does not yet have the knowledge of the real source of that 'demoniac laugh'. Instead, the laughter itself is personified as a 'laugher': it 'stood at my bedside' as a human would, but then, changing her mind, the narrator corrects herself. She is shifting the position of the laugher into 'crouched by my pillow', as if crouching would seem more like something a goblin would do.

> *JE*, Ch. 15: and I thought at first, the goblin-laugher **stood** at my bedside — **or rather, crouched** by my pillow:
>
> EK 145: ja algul tundus mulle, nagu **kostaks** õel naer otse mu kõrval padja juures.
>
> BT: and at first it seemed to me, as if the **evil laughter was coming** from right beside me, near the pillow

In the Estonian translation, there is no personification, which makes the laughter just a sound that also behaves like a sound. It comes from a certain place 'right beside me, near the pillow', but there is no information given about the position of the one who laughs, whether standing or crouching, so no correction is needed. In addition, the laughter is characterised not as 'goblin' but as 'evil' [õel], so all the references to a possibly non-human source of the laughing sound have also disappeared. Again, the Estonian sentence has a conclusory effect: it contains both the bedside and the pillow, the visual references in the room, but not the narrator's correction which binds them in the English version.

These corrections or hesitations also reach into the speech of other characters in the novel, as with this comment made by Mrs Fairfax on Mr Rochester's character, where she repeatedly points out that the opinion expressed is her own.

> *JE*, Ch. 11: 'Oh! his character is unimpeachable, **I suppose**. He is rather peculiar, **perhaps**: he has travelled a great deal, and seen a great deal of

> the world, **I should think**. **I dare say** he is clever: but I never had much conversation with him.'
>
> EK 102: "Oo, iseloom on tal laitmatu. **Tõsi küll**, ta on veidi omapärane. Ta on palju reisinud ja palju maailma näinud. **Küllap** ta on tarkki, aga ma pole temaga palju vestelnud."
>
> BT: 'Oh, his character is unimpeachable. **However**, he is rather peculiar. He has travelled a great deal and seen a great deal of the world. He is **probably** clever as well, but I haven't had much conversation with him.'

All of the remarks in the first person have disappeared in the translation. Some indication of the presence of Mrs Fairfax's opinion in these words is still conveyed, but only with the use of impersonal adverbs 'however' [*tõsi küll*] and 'probably' [*küllap*]. This does not change the point of view — Mrs Fairfax is still the source of information — but it focuses on learning about Rochester and pays less attention to how Mrs Fairfax comes across, herself. Considering Jane's opinion about the lady which she offers a few lines further on ('There are people who seem to have no notion of sketching a character ...'),[12] this is not an entirely insignificant change in the narrator's point of view as well.

The process of editing out the narrator's comments sometimes extends to moments where the narrator does not introduce a qualification or correction, but adds a specification. In this example, where Jane has had the rather mystical experience of hearing a voice through the air, the narrator explains that she only heard her name three times — and nothing more.

> *JE*, Ch. 35: I heard a voice somewhere cry —
> "Jane! Jane! Jane!" **Nothing more**.
>
> EK 411: kusagilt kaugusest kuulsin ma hüüdu:
> "Jane! Jane! Jane!"
>
> BT: from somewhere far away I heard a cry: / "Jane, Jane, Jane!"

The Estonian text drops that comment, as if to point out that when there is 'nothing more' to be said, it does not really need saying.

The changes in translation can also add more distance towards the diegetic level of the acting character in the scene. These are often changes that happen in the rhythm of the text. They may be brought about through various means, such as changing the syntax or tense of the verbs, or adding logical connectors to the text. The rhythm thus

12 *JE*, Ch. 11.

becomes less dramatically charged and the scene is narrated in a more neutral tone. This happens for example at the beginning of Chapter 28 where, for two paragraphs, Jane gives her story in a present-tense narration, describing her arrival at Whitcross:

> *JE*, Ch. 28: Two days **are** passed. It **is** a summer evening;
>
> EK 313: **Möödusid** kaks päeva. **Oli** suveõhtu.
>
> BT: Two days **passed**. It **was** a summer evening.

This dramatic effect does not come across in Kippasto's translation where all of the present tense use has been disregarded and the story continues in its usual retrospective manner. Vilberg brings the narration slightly closer to the scene by switching back to the present tense, although for her the scene begins a couple of sentences later:

> *JE*, Ch. 28: The coach **is** a mile off **by this time**; **I am** alone.
>
> EK 313: **Nüüd oli** postitõld **juba** miili võrra edasi **sõitnud ja** mina **seisin ristteel** üksinda.
>
> BT: **Now** the coach **had driven** for a mile **already** and I **stood** on the **crossroad**, alone.
>
> IIV 392: Nüüd **on** postitõld juba miili võrra edasi sõitnud ja mina **seisan** üksinda ristteel.
>
> BT: Now the coach **has** driven for a mile already and I **stand** alone on the crossroad.

However, Vilberg keeps Kippasto's translation in other discursive points like the altered syntax and a more descriptive approach which manifests in adding the verbs 'has/had driven' [*oli/on sõitnud*] and 'stood/stand' [*seisin/seisan*] as well as in placing the subject 'on the crossroad' [*ristteel*]. Thus it becomes clear that despite the temporal differences, both Estonian versions opt for a more descriptive account of the situation and stay with the narrator-Jane rather than permitting the character-Jane to actively experience the scene.

The increased distance may be created also in the form of a more external point of view. In this case, the translator distances herself both from the character-Jane and the narrator-Jane. This may be observed in a scene in Chapter 8 where Jane and Helen are invited by Miss Temple to have tea and toast, and Jane describes a change in Helen's appearance and behaviour. She first attributes the change to the warm atmosphere and friendship, but then suggests that 'perhaps, more than all these', there is something 'within her', Helen's intrinsic powers that generate the change. Jane observes these powers becoming active: 'they woke, they kindled', 'they glowed' and 'they shone'. Still, Jane does not give up her own point of view either, but alludes to her presence through what she sees from the outside, on Helen's cheek, and through memory when she reminds herself that she 'had never seen [her cheek] but pale and bloodless'. Jane is present here both as narrator and as character, and thus she sees Helen at once from the inside and from the outside.

> *JE*, Ch. 8: The refreshing meal, the brilliant fire, the presence and kindness of her beloved instructress, or **perhaps more than all these**, something in her own unique mind, had roused her powers within her. **They woke, they kindled**: first, **they glowed** in the bright tint of her cheek, **which till this hour I had never seen but** pale **and bloodless**; **then they shone** in the liquid lustre of her eyes, which had suddenly acquired a beauty more singular than that of Miss Temple's.
>
> EK 70: **Võib-olla et** kosutav toit, hele kaminatuli, armastatud kasvataja leebus ja ligidus või ka tema enda ainulaadses vaimus peituv miski olid temas uusi jõude äratanud ja süütitanud. Heleni kahvatud **põsed kattusid õhetava punaga**, silmadesse **tekkis niiske sära**, **andes neile** ebatavalise ilu, mis oli veelgi haruldasem kui miss Temple'i silmade oma.
>
> BT: **Perhaps** the refreshing meal, the brilliant fire, the kindness and presence of the beloved instrcutress, or something hidden in her own unique mind **had roused and kindled** new powers in her. Helen's pale **cheeks became covered** with a bright tint, a **liquid lustre appeared** in her eyes, **giving them** an unusual beauty, more singular than that of Miss Temple's.

Such a double vision is not preserved in translation. Interestingly, we notice a loss on both sides. The Estonian text does not give any voice to Helen's inner powers — they are no longer the subject of the verbs, but are instead observed through visible effects: 'Helen's pale cheeks became covered with a bright tint' [*Heleni kahvatud põsed kattusid õhetava punaga*], 'a liquid lustre appeared in her eyes' [*silmadesse tekkis niiske sära*]. The Estonian narrator no longer sees what is happening inside Helen, and at the same time we have also lost most of the first person's presence. Firstly, the narrator's suggestion 'perhaps' [*võib-olla et*], even if still present, has become shorter and moved to the beginning of the sentence, which makes it valid for all possible effects on Helen's new appearance, not just the inner powers. Secondly, Jane's memory of seeing Helen's cheek before as 'pale and bloodless' has changed into a mere impersonal description of 'Helen's pale cheeks' [*Heleni kahvatud põsed*].

Just a few moments later, at the farewell to Miss Temple, Jane's perspective undergoes another translational change. In English, this perspective manifests in a rather particular view of Helen and Miss Temple's relationship which becomes apparent in a rhythm of short clauses with a repetitive emphasis on Helen, and in a comparison between Helen and Jane herself. This perspective is very personal and even gives a hint of jealousy. We can almost hear Jane's regretful voice behind the text continuing 'it was her, and not me' who got Miss Temple's attention. Truthfully, it is unclear whether this is a sign of a sisterly competitiveness belonging to the teenager Jane in the scene or the narrator-Jane of the later years expressing her own regret, knowing Helen's fate; but this distinction is not necessary to conclude that it is a moment where Jane's person (and personality) is strongly present in the text.

> *JE*, Ch. 8: Helen she held a little longer **than me**: she let **her** go **more** reluctantly; **it was** Helen her eye followed to the door; **it was for her** she **a second time** breathed a sad sigh; **for her** she wiped a tear from her cheek.
>
> EK 71: Helenit hoidis ta oma süleluses veidi kauem, **nagu** oleks tal kahju olnud teda ära lasta. Saatnud teda pilguga ukseni, ohkas miss Temple kurvalt, ja ta põsel **hiilgas pisar**.
>
> BT: Helen she held in her arms a little longer, **as if** she had regretted letting her go. Having followed her to the door with her glance, Miss Temple sighed sadly, and **a tear shone** on her cheek.

The translation bears practically no signs of this emotion. The emphasis has moved away from Helen except for the beginning of the first sentence. The syntax in the Estonian paragraph shows no distinctive repetitions. It also has a less rhythmical structure: the five clauses of the English text have been connected into two longer sentences, with a hypothesis as a connection in one case ('as if she had regretted' [*nagu oleks tal kahju olnud*]), and a temporal succession in the other ('having followed her' [*saatnud teda*]). In the last subordinate clause, the subject of the verb has switched from Miss Temple to the 'tear' [*pisar*] that 'shone' [*hiilgas*] on her cheek. The hypothesis and the changing of the subject again suggest a more external point of view, one from which the narrator can guess but does not know of Miss Temple's feelings, and sees the instructress, her cheek and a tear on it, from the outside.

Thus we can conclude that the narrator in the Estonian translation, although less present in the text in the first-person form, comes across as more confident and better prepared for telling the story. The narration in the Estonian *Jane Eyre* is focusing on the story to be told and hiding the storyteller character in ways that are provided for the translator by her language and her translating practices. Comparing Kippasto's translation with Vilberg's edits confirms this conclusion in most aspects. Despite slight differences, Vilberg's version has a very similar effect on the narrator. Her alterations are more linguistically oriented and almost never interfere with the settings or the dynamics of the scenes which often remain the same as Kippasto's, word for word. This suggests that the appearance of the first person in its grammatical forms is more sensitive to an editor's alterations (and perhaps more generally, to the changes in language) than other literary devices which create the immersion effect. However, as the prevailing distance of the narrator's point of view indicates, the immersion effect which comes through from the Estonian versions has indeed been greatly influenced by the Finno-Ugric tendency to conceal the subject, in both discursive and narrative aspects.

The Vampyre with a Wedding Veil

Having observed several processes emphasising or dimming the presence of the first person in translation and altering the point of view, I would now like to read more closely one particular scene which helps us to understand the function of the narrator's new position in the Estonian text. This is what we might call the 'Vampyre' scene, a tale within the tale where, the night before their wedding, Jane tells Rochester about a mysterious 'shape' that had intruded into her bedroom and ripped her wedding veil. In order to address the narrator's position in the scene, there are two main questions to be discussed: who or what is the form that emerges from the closet and vents her frustration on the wedding garments? And to whom do these garments really belong?

Throughout Jane's tale, the being whom she sees and hears in her room that night is named as a questionable, possibly non-human thing: 'a shape', 'a form', 'a ghost', 'a figure'. It remains unrecognised: 'this was not Sophie, it was not Leah, it was not Mrs Fairfax: it was not — no, I was sure of it, and am still — it was not even that strange woman, Grace Poole'.[13] It is referred to with neuter pronouns 'it' and 'its', most of the time. Though it seems like a woman by appearance

13 *JE*, Ch. 25.

and on a few occasions Jane does use the pronoun 'she', it is not recognised by Jane as a living person (this feature of the narration is also discussed by Yunte Huang in Essay 13, above, in connection with the Chinese translations). Instead, it reminds her '[o]f the foul German spectre — the Vampyre'.[14]

The Estonian translator deals with this uncertainty in two ways. On three occasions, all in the first part of the tale where the intruder has not yet been seen by Jane, the subject of the verb is replaced with something less personal.

> *JE*, Ch. 25: **I heard** a rustling there.
>
> EK 274: Sealtpoolt **kostis** mingit **sahinat**.
>
> BT: a **rustling sounded** from there.

Here the experiencer phrase 'I heard' is replaced by 'a rustling' [*sahinat*] 'sounded' [*kostis*], which points to the sound itself, not a person hearing or making it.

> *JE*, Ch. 25: **No one** answered:
>
> EK 274: **Vastust** ei tulnud
>
> BT: The **answer** did not come,

In this example, 'the answer' [*vastus*] becomes the subject of the negative verb 'did not come' [*ei tulnud*].

> *JE*, Ch. 25: "Sophie! Sophie!" I again cried: and still **it** was silent.
>
> EK 274: "Sophie! Sophie!" hõikasin ma uuesti, aga **kõik** jäi vaikseks.
>
> BT: "Sophie! Sophie!" I cried again, but **everything** remained silent.

Next, the pronoun 'it' referring to the intruder is replaced by a broad and impersonal pronoun 'everything' [*kõik*].

On the other hand, when the figure becomes visible, the Estonian text identifies the intruder immediately as a living human being.

> *JE*, Ch. 25: but **a form emerged from** the closet: **it** took the light
>
> EK 274: kuid **keegi ligines** kapi **poolt**, võttis küünla
>
> BT: but **someone approached** from **the direction of** the closet, took the candle

The noun that Jane uses here, 'a form', is translated with the personal pronoun 'someone' [*keegi*], and the verb 'emerged' — an action

14 *JE*, Ch. 25.

proper to spirits and ghosts — is changed into 'approached' [*ligines*], an action more appropriate to humans. The pronoun 'it' is not translated separately, so the subject of the verb 'took' [*võttis*] is still the 'someone' from the previous clause. There is also a change in the spatial movement. In the English version, the form 'emerged from the closet', which is consistent with the idea of a ghost. The Estonian translation sees the someone coming from that 'direction' [*kapi poolt*], but not necessarily originating from the closet: this is more suited to the idea of a human being.

On the second occasion on which the intruder is named with a noun, 'the shape' decidedly becomes a 'person' [*inimene*], and a relative personal pronoun 'who' [*kes*] is added:

> *JE*, Ch. 25: The **shape** standing before me
>
> EK 274: See **inimene, kes** mu ees seisis,
>
> BT: The **person who** was standing before me

Throughout the scene, the neuter pronoun 'it' by which Jane refers to the creature is translated, where present, by a personal pronoun 'he/ she' [*ta*]. '*Ta*' does not have a gender in Estonian and may sometimes refer to inanimate things, especially in spoken form. Still, given the context of nouns and pronouns the translator uses in this passage, '*ta*' is perceived clearly as a personal pronoun:

> *JE*, Ch. 25: Shall I tell you of **what it** reminded me?'
>
> EK 275: "Kas ütelda teile, **keda ta** mulle meenutas?"
>
> BT: Shall I tell you of **whom she** reminded me?

Here, for instance, both pronouns 'what' and 'it' are translated as personal 'whom' [*keda*] and 'he/she' [*ta*].

The comparison to the vampire itself does not undergo any significant changes in translation, neither in the discourse nor in the point of view.

> *JE*, Ch. 25: 'Of the foul German spectre — the Vampyre.'
>
> EK 275: "Jälki viirastust — vampiiri!"
>
> BT: 'Of [a] foul spectre — [a] vampire!'

The German reference is missing, however, so that the vampire becomes a less specific reference. As the creature is leaving Jane's room, it is once more named by a noun, 'the figure'.

> *JE*, Ch. 25: Just at my bedside, **the figure** stopped:

EK 275: Otse minu voodi kõrval **ta** seisatas.

BT: Just at my bedside **she** stopped.

The translation replaces it by a pronoun, which makes 'the figure' again into a personal 'he/she' [*ta*].

I leave it to every reader of the English text to decide how believable is Jane's claim to have really met a vampire that night, but it is clear that the Estonian translator has not taken this claim very seriously. To Kippasto, this creature is definitely a human being, and if yet unknown to the character-Jane, then seemingly already known to the translator who is likely to be familiar with the continuation of the novel.

As for our second question, 'who do the wedding garments really belong to?', we also get a slightly different answer from the Estonian text. At the first mention, they clearly belong to the first person of the tale, Jane, in both languages.

JE, Ch. 25: and the **door** of the closet, where, **before going to bed,** I had hung **my** wedding-dress and veil, stood open:

EK 274: ja kapp, kuhu ma **oma** laulatuskleidi ja loori olin riputanud, oli lahti.

BT: and the closet, where I had hung **my** wedding-dress and veil, stood open.

In this sentence, the translation drops a couple of spatio-temporal indicators. The 'door' is not mentioned but left to the reader's implicit deduction. Secondly, the temporal indicator for Jane's action of hanging her garments 'before going to bed' is also left out. The attention of the translator is here centred on anticipation of the event that is about to happen, and is not concerned with past circumstances.

The spatial reference becomes crucial in the following example, as the next time the garments are mentioned, the English narrator identifies them by that spatial attribute. They are the garments that are 'pendent from the portmanteau', but their belonging is left somewhat open: they belong in that space and are now potentially accessible to anyone who can reach the portmanteau.

JE, Ch. 25: and surveyed the garments **pendant from the portmanteau**.

EK 274: silmitses **mu** laulatusrõivaid.

BT: surveyed **my** wedding garments.

However, the translator does not go along with this move. She leaves out the spatial indicator and replaces it with a possessive pronoun. The garments in translation still belong to 'me', wherever they may be.

When, in the next example, the intruder takes the veil, the Jane of the English text needs to try to reclaim it by affirming that the veil is still hers, even though it has been taken 'from its place'.

> *JE*, Ch. 25: But presently she took **my** veil **from its place**; she held it up
>
> EK 275: aga siis võttis ta loori **enda kätte**,
>
> BT : but then she took the veil to **her hands**,

That claim is lost in translation, but so is the indication of the spatial belonging. The veil no longer has its own place, and is now in the 'hands' [*kätte*] of the intruder. What happens next is interesting for two reasons. First, Jane says that the intruder throws the veil 'over her own head', stressing Jane's comment that the veil is now on the wrong head, the intruder's, not Jane's. The second is the intruder's movement when she turns to the mirror. This allows Jane to see the reflection of her 'visage and features'.

> *JE*, Ch. 25: and then she threw it over **her own** head, and **turned** to the mirror.
>
> EK 275: ja heitis **endale** pea ümber ning **vaatas** peeglisse.
>
> BT: and threw over **her** head and **looked** into the mirror.

In translation, that opposition is not stressed. The woman throws the veil on her head, but there is no objection to that by the storyteller. The second point of interest brings us back to the woman's identity, as her movement towards the mirror changes in translation into 'looking' [*vaatas*]. This makes her act more explicitly dialogical, because Bertha is no longer just an object of Jane's gaze or imagination but is given the ability to look back. She is recognised as a partner, not just a shape or a creature.

A bit later, Jane tries once more to reclaim her veil by calling it hers. Bertha has become again an 'it' with 'its gaunt head':

> *JE*, Ch. 25: 'Sir, **it** removed **my** veil from **its gaunt head**,
>
> EK 275: "**Oh**, sir, **ta** kiskus loori peast,
>
> BT: '**Oh** sir, **she** tore the veil from [the] head,

The translation is rather emotional here, calling out an 'Oh' and describing the action with a more dynamic verb 'tore' [*kiskus*]. But the veil is no longer Jane's, it is just a veil; and Bertha is a person, a 'he/she' [*ta*], whose head is just a head, no stranger or gaunter than any other human being's.

This passage also reveals the visual aspect of the immersion effect, where visuality is increased in translation. Just as we saw above, with Bertha being given the ability to look into the mirror instead of just turning towards it, we can notice more visual activity in Jane's character too. In addition to allowing more visual contact between the characters, there are also indications of a desire to see better.

The scene begins with Jane hearing some noise and noticing a light in the room, but it takes a while before she can actually see the intruder. When she does, however, she leaves her listener, Rochester, and her reader in a momentary suspense, describing her own movement and feelings rather than saying directly what was in front of her.

> *JE*, Ch. 25: I had risen up in bed, I bent forward: first, surprise, then bewilderment, came over me; and then my blood crept cold through my veins.
>
> EK 274: Tõusin voodis istukile, kummardusin ettepoole, **et teda näha**: algul üllatusin, sattusin segadusse, ent siis tardus mul veri soontes.
>
> BT: I rose up in bed, I bent forward **to see her**: at first I was surprised, became bewildered, but then the blood froze in my veins.

This does not seem to be enough for the translator who adds an explanatory purpose for Jane's movement: Jane bends forward in order 'to see her' [*et teda näha*]. The translator's impulse to enter the fictional scene becomes almost tangible here — it is as if the translator had stretched up together with Jane to reach out for a better position in order to see what Jane has seen. Something similar happens a little while later when Jane describes the dress that the intruder was wearing.

> *JE*, Ch. 25: I know not what dress she had on: **it** was white and straight;
>
> EK 274: Ma ei tea, missugune ta kleit oli, **nägin ainult, et tal oli seljas** midagi valget ja laia.
>
> BT: I know not what her dress was like, **I only saw that she was wearing** something white and loose.

Here too the translation takes a more descriptive approach and fills the rhythmical hiatus with an explanation in a first-person form, spelling out that the narrator had indeed had visual proof of her information about the dress. Through these additions, which seem somewhat contradictory to Kippasto's usual way of avoiding the first-person subject where possible, the translation makes the experience of seeing more visible in the text. Seeing becomes an additional confirmation to Jane's story: she now has even more concrete proof of the reality of her intruder.

Through these questions of identity and belonging, and the increased aspect of visuality, the Estonian translation gives more credibility to Bertha, both as a person and as a truthful (or at least lawful) owner of the wedding veil. By doing so, the translation also puts the narrator in a more neutral position, allowing the two female rivals to be recognised as equals rather than showing the duel from the jealous Jane's point of view. This equality is something that Kevin Stevens, among others, has shown to be missing from Jane's narration in its English version.[15] Through his analysis of auditory thematics in the novel, Stevens demonstrates how Jane deliberately deprives Bertha of the ability to speak and to appear human: Jane claims Bertha's murmurs to be unintelligible noise while she also 'frames Bertha's sounds to evoke horror and disgust'.[16] Stevens also observes that Jane builds her narrative strategically to conceal and misdirect Bertha's identity for many chapters, although she offers freely her retrospective knowledge on other issues. These findings lead him to conclude that 'Jane crucially privileges aesthetics over ethics: withholding Bertha's existence also withholds her very humanity, as she is alive in the narrative only through noises — demonic laughter and seemingly non-linguistic murmurs'.[17] To Stevens, Jane Eyre is an unreliable and manipulative narrator who is trying to mislead her reader and present the story with her own personal agenda.

The image of the first person that comes across from the translation is rather different from her English counterpart, at least as seen by Stevens, Fiehn, or Sternlieb, but she acquires her own entirely coherent and functional existence. To answer Stevens's concern: Jane translated into Estonian does seem to become more 'trustworthy' as a narrator, in the sense that she now presents a more external point of view. We meet with a Jane who is less of a character in her story and more of the detached, autobiographical storyteller that she claims to be. She does not get so absorbed in her story, does not go along so easily with

15 Stevens, '"Eccentric Murmurs"', pp. 201–20.
16 Stevens, '"Eccentric Murmurs"', p. 214.
17 Stevens, '"Eccentric Murmurs"', p. 209.

its movements and emotions, but rather gives a more neutral account of the events and experiences retrospectively. Her storytelling also becomes more confident and ethical. She does not have to correct herself so often: it is as if she has had a chance to think through and edit her words before (re-)writing them. And she has more consideration both towards her main adversary, Bertha, and towards her own younger self.

Furthermore, the translational changes in the first-person presence reveal some pervasive tendencies in the translator's attitudes towards Jane. For the most part, Kippasto seems not to absorb Jane's 'I' fully, but rather to remain a bystander, literally "beside myself", so as to represent new, altered points of view. Among these additional points of view, we can perhaps recognise that of someone who feels empathy for the poor child and moves closer to her, as well as that of a more neutral storyteller who is taking her distance, and also the point of view of an editor who corrects the hesitations and shifts the attitudes. However, this is not something to be regretted or disapproved in the work of the translator, although that has been many a translator's fate. Instead of interpreting these changes as losses of the novel's versatile aspects, translation offers a new opportunity for interpretation. Thomas Pavel has noted that readers or viewers immersed in the world of a work of art 'have no actual power to modify what happens in the fictional world, but [they] still project [their] desires, exercise [their] will, even though, in fact, [they] do it only homeopathically and with little effect on the world of the work of art'.[18] Yet, translating is a work that consists precisely in this power to modify a text, to interact with its world more actively and effectively. It is the translator's job to, figuratively speaking, move around in the spaces of the fictional world, have a relationship with its characters, tell the story and record the experience of immersion. Clive Scott has described this experience through the notion of fieldwork and he points out that translation is in fact more of a live recording, 'an encounter-in-action' of the experience than an account after the fact: it is 'the interlocution between *an* I and *a* you, not a treatment of *the* it'.[19] This experience has revealed itself in the Estonian *Jane Eyre* as a certain shift in the points of view which is brought about by adding

18 Thomas Pavel, 'Immersion and distance in fictional worlds', *Itinéraires*, 1 (2010), 99–109 (p. 103).

19 Clive Scott, *The Work of Literary Translation* (Cambridge: Cambridge University Press, 2018), p. 6.

a new linguistic, cultural and historical situation, and simply another set of eyes. We have seen how the translator has been immersed into the fictional world but has done so not quite as the narrator, nor as the character, and not quite as her own self either. So, just as much as this is an encounter between an author and a translator (and eventual editors), it is also an encounter with Jane's roles and attitudes. Like a prism, it brings forth different aspects of her character as a narrator.

Works cited

Translations of *Jane Eyre*

Brontë, Charlotte, *Jane Eyre*, trans. by Elvi Kippasto (Tallinn: Kirjastus Eesti Raamat, 1981).

——, *Jane Eyre*, trans. by Ira Inga Vilberg (Tallinn: Brigitta, 2000).

——, *Jane Eyre*, trans. by Elvi Kippasto (Tallinn: Mediasat Group, Eesti Päevaleht AS, 2007).

——, *Jane Eyre*, trans. by Elvi Kippasto (Tallinn: Tänapäev, 2013).

Other Sources

Erelt, Mati, and Metslang, Helle, 'Kogeja vormistamine eesti keeles: nihkeid SAE perifeerias [Expression of the experiencer in Estonian: Shifts in the periphery of the SAE]', *Emakeele Seltsi aastaraamat* [*Yearbook of the Estonian Mother Tongue Society*], 53 (2007), 9–22.

Fiehn, Charlotte, 'The Two Janes: *Jane Eyre* and the Narrative Problem in Chapter 23', *Brontë Studies*, 41 (2016), 312–21, https://doi.org/10.1080/14748932.2016.1222698

Hermans, Theo, 'The Translator's Voice in Translated Narrative', *Target*, 8:1 (1996), 23–48.

Hermans, Theo, *The Conference of the Tongues* (London: Routledge, 2014), https://doi.org/10.4324/9781315759784

Lindström, Liina, 'Kõnelejale ja kuulajale viitamise vältimise strateegiaid eesti keeles [Strategies of avoidance of reference to the speaker and hearer in Estonian]', *Emakeele Seltsi aastaraamat* [*Yearbook of the Estonian Mother Tongue Society*], 55 (2010), 88–118.

Koskinen, Kaisa and Paloposki, Outi, *Sata kirjaa, tuhat suomennosta. Kaunokirjallisuuden uudelleenkääntäminen* [A Hundred Books, A Thousand Translations: Retranslating Fiction] (Helsinki: Suomalaisen kirjallisuuden seura [Finnish Literature Society], 2015).

Metslang, Helle, 'Estonian grammar between Finnic and SAE: some comparisons', *Language Typology and Universals*, 62 (2009), 49–71, https://doi.org/10.1524/stuf.2009.0004

Möldre, Aile, *Kirjastustegevus ja raamatulevi Eestis aastail 1940–2000* [Publishing and Book Distribution in Estonia in 1940–2000], (Tallinn: TLÜ kirjastus [Tallinn University Press], 2005).

Pavel, Thomas, 'Immersion and distance in fictional worlds', *Itinéraires*, 1 (2010), 99–109, https://doi.org/10.4000/itineraires.2183

Schaeffer, Jean-Marie, *Why Fiction*? trans. by Dorrit Kohn (Lincoln and London: University of Nebraska Press, 2010).

Scott, Clive, *The Work of Literary Translation* (Cambridge: Cambridge University Press, 2018).

Sternlieb, Lisa, '*Jane Eyre*: "Hasarding Confidences"', *Nineteenth-Century Literature*, 53 (1999), 452–79, https://doi.org/10.2307/2903027

Stevens, Kevin, '"Eccentric Murmurs": Noise, Voice, and Unreliable Narration in *Jane Eyre*', *Narrative*, 26 (2018), 201–20, https://doi.org/10.1353/nar.2018.0010

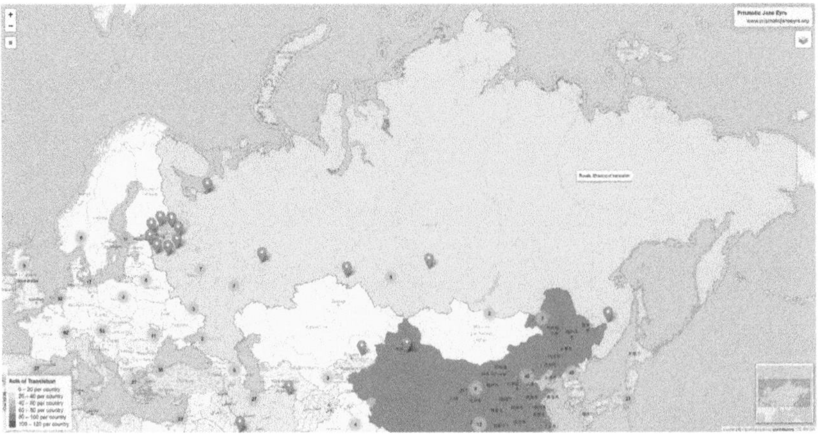

The World Map
https://digitalkoine.github.io/je_prismatic_map
Created by Giovanni Pietro Vitali;
maps © Thunderforest, data © OpenStreetMap contributors

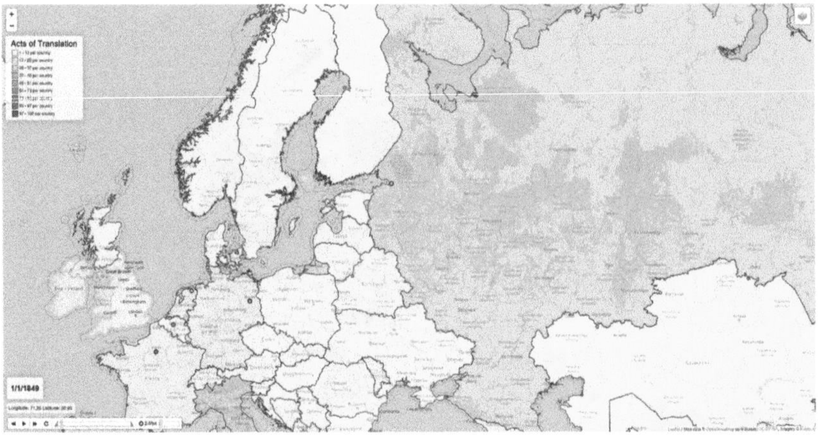

The Time Map
https://digitalkoine.github.io/translations_timemap
Created by Giovanni Pietro Vitali and Simone Landucci;
© OpenStreetMap contributors, © Mapbox

17. Appearing Jane, in Russian

Eugenia Kelbert

Introduction[1]

Few aspects of the novelistic genre reveal the prismatic character of translation variation in a way that is more visible than character description, or more visual. Unlike most aspects of translation, descriptions of appearance rely on a disproportionately small number of well-chosen words destined to form the top of a cognitive iceberg in the reader's mind. Whenever particular characters are on stage, and often when they are spoken of or otherwise relevant to our interpretation of the story, we cannot but imagine their expressions and gestures, their physical presence. The resulting mental image thus remains an aspect of the reading experience even when the initial literary portrait is very scarce. In other words, appearances, once established, are a silent factor we literally must bear in mind as readers as well as critics, throughout the novel.

Yet how aware are we of how the characters we identify and empathise with, or perhaps detest, would look if we met them in the street? We may not give it much thought, but few readers could, given sufficient artistic skill, draw even the most beloved, intimately known character from a favourite novel off the top of their head. This may explain why many readers watch screen adaptations, a form of semiotic 'matching' between distinct systems of signifiers that many

1 For a detailed analysis of the Russian translations of appearance in *Jane Eyre* that complements this article, see 'Appearances: Character Description as a Network of Signification in Russian Translations of *Jane Eyre*', *Target: International Journal of Translation Studies*, 34.2 (2021), 219–50. This research was supported by a Leverhulme Early Career Fellowship. I would also like to acknowledge the contribution of Aruna Nair and three research assistants: Karolina Gurevich, Alesya Volkova, and Olga Nechaeva.

 https://doi.org/10.11647/OBP.0319.25

critics consider a near-impossibility.[2] For an avid reader, the book, as a rule, comes first, and the best adaptation is secondary. Yet most readers will flock to the cinema to welcome — or criticise — a new Emma Woodhouse, Anna Karenina, or Jane Eyre. 'Emma was nothing like Emma,' they will say afterwards, 'though she is the right type.' Such analysis, paradoxically, informs the reader of their own vision of the character. If it happens to coincide with that offered by the film, the adaptation acts as a visual aid that helps reaffirm that vision. And what if it does not? Then the jarring sensation becomes, in itself, a way to flesh out 'the reader's own personal idea'.[3]

There are good reasons for the combination of precision and vagueness in how we imagine a literary character. As Heier points out, gaps in key information about character appearance form a major step in the evolution of the literary portrait: as the genre developed, the detailed descriptions we find in Balzac or Dickens were increasingly replaced by 'mere signals and meagre suggestions by which the portrait is to take shape'.[4] Once the traditional at-length portrait goes, 'the reader depends on his own aesthetic sensitivities; he is left with his own imagination to complete the full portrait. Although this manner may initiate a highly sophisticated aesthetic process in the reader's mind, one no longer is dealing with the portrait created by the author'.[5] As the modern literary portrait becomes a literary sketch, the author's job is no longer to supply an image to the reader, but rather to direct the reader's imagination with well-chosen strokes. The actual process that leads the director to a casting decision, and the reader to the impression that 'they got it completely wrong,' is a matter of cognitive poetics and part and parcel of the reader's mental model of a given character.[6] Brontë, whose work is contemporary with Dickens's greatest novels even if he claimed to have never read it,[7] seems to have

2 Dudley Andrew, 'The Well-Worn Muse: Adaptation in Film History and Theory', in *Narrative Strategies: Original Essays in Film and Prose Fiction*, ed. by Syndy M. Conger and Janet R. Welsh (Macomb: Western Illinois University Press, 1980), pp. 9–19 (pp. 12–13).

3 E. Heier, '"The Literary Portrait" as a Device of Characterization', *Neophilologus*, 60 (1976), 321–33 (p. 323).

4 Heier, '"The Literary Portrait"', p. 323.

5 Heier, '"The Literary Portrait"', p. 323.

6 See Lisa Zunshine, *Why We Read Fiction: Theory of Mind and the Novel* (Columbus, OH: Ohio State University Press, 2006).

7 Lisa Jadwin, '"Caricatured, Not Faithfully Rendered": *Bleak House* as a Revision of *Jane Eyre*', *Modern Language Studies*, 26 (1996), 111–33 (p. 112).

anticipated this trend. Indeed, her work may have contributed, as this analysis helps to demonstrate, to the way it came to develop.

When it comes to *Jane Eyre*, the pieces of this visual puzzle are handed out very sparingly indeed.[8] Edward Fairfax Rochester, for example, is of medium height, has a broad chest, and is supposedly unattractive. But does he have facial hair? In fact, Rochester has 'black whiskers', but we only glean that bit of information when Jane sketches his portrait when visiting Mrs Reed, half-way through their courtship.[9] How was the reader to imagine his face until then? What happens to that mental representation once this information is revealed? What is more, Russian translators of *Jane Eyre* interpret this gem of insight very differently: two abridged or rewritten versions skip it altogether, and these Rochesters may as easily be clean-shaven as wear a beard, three more adorn him with sideburns, and only one — but the one that reached by far the widest readership — gives him a moustache. The looks produced as a result of the omission or different interpretations of the word 'whiskers' by the given translator can therefore differ widely. This also affects screen adaptations: a Rochester with sideburns is inevitably less relatable than one that wears a kind of facial hair we associate with our own times.

When it comes to Jane, the effects of such translation nuances can become especially complex. She is, on the one hand, a romantic heroine and the object of the disenchanted protagonist's passion, and as such, her looks are of primary importance to the narrative. Like Rochester, she is not attractive, but while a physically unattractive hero carries something of a demonic halo, an unattractive heroine narrator has a different effect entirely. Insofar as the reader (often a female reader) identifies with Jane, her supposed plainness, and the nature of that plainness, not only subverts pre-existing conventions of the genre, but makes her relatable in a new and radical way. Jane

---

8 This makes for a particularly revealing case study of the literary portrait as a network of signification in translation, as argued in Kelbert, 'Appearances'. (See also Antoine Berman, 'La Traduction comme épreuve de l'étranger', *Texte*, 4 (1985), 67–81; and 'Translation and the Trials of the Foreign', trans. by Lawrence Venuti, in *The Translation Studies Reader*, ed. by Lawrence Venuti (London: Routledge, 2000), pp. 240–53). Cf. Yiying Fan and Jia Miao, 'Shifts of Appraisal Meaning and Character Depiction Effect in Translation: A Case Study of the English Translation of Mai Jia's *In the Dark*', *Studies in Literature and Language*, 20 (2020), 55–61 for further examples of character description variation in translation.

9 *JE*, Ch. 21.

has no fairy godmother and never turns into a beautiful princess; instead, she remains herself and wins tangible happiness through sheer personality and self-respect. Unlike the stories of conventional romantic heroines, hers becomes one any reader can aspire to, regardless of their origins or looks. In this respect, the story of Jane and Rochester's romance as told by the servants (which Jane herself is treated to when she returns incognito) foreshadows the novel's trace in the popular consciousness: 'nobody but him thought her so very handsome. She was a little small thing, they say, almost like a child'.[10]

Jane is, however, not only the protagonist but also the first-person narrator and, for all her introspection, poorly placed to supply a badly needed verbal portrait of herself in the style of an omniscient narrator. While she is a keen observer of others, what we know of her own appearance must come from observers of her as she quotes them, and the resulting image is inevitably sketchy, an elusive Picasso-like sketch made from a dozen different perspectives. It relates as much, and often more, information about these perspectives as about the heroine. In this, the reader is only offered two crutches to lean on: the consensus multiple characters seem to share of what beauty or the lack of beauty seems to be, and the equally shared notions of phrenology and physiognomy the novel's characters refer to, again, as a shared truth.[11]

---

10 *JE*, Ch. 36.

11 See Kelbert, 'Appearances', for a more detailed discussion of physiognomy in *Jane Eyre*. To quote Sally Shuttleworth, '[i]n many places, where the study of human character from the face became an epidemic, the people went masked through the streets' (Sally Shuttleworth, *Charlotte Brontë and Victorian Psychology* (Cambridge: Cambridge University Press, 1996), p. 56). See Alexander Walker, *Physiognomy founded on Physiology* (London: Smith, Elder and Co., 1834), and Samuel R. Wells, *New Physiognomy; or, Signs of Character* (London: L. N. Fowler & Co., 1866) for contemporary accounts. For further background on the uses of physiognomy in Victorian literature, see Rhonda Boshears and Harry Whitaker, 'Phrenology and Physiognomy in Victorian Literature', in *Literature, Neurology, and Neuroscience: Historical and Literary Connections*, ed. by Anne Stiles, Stanley Finger, and François Boller (Amsterdam: Elsevier, 2013), pp. 87–112; Lucy Hartley, *Physiognomy and the Meaning of Expression in Nineteenth-Century Culture* (Cambridge: Cambridge University Press, 2005); Michael Hollington, 'Physiognomy in *Hard Times*', *Dickens Quarterly*, 9 (1992), 58–66; Ian Jack, 'Physiognomy, phrenology and characterisation in the novels of Charlotte Brontë', *Brontë Society Transactions*, 15 (1970), 377–91; John Graham, 'Character Description and Meaning in the Romantic Novel', *Studies in Romanticism*, 5 (1966), 208–18; and Sharrona Pearl, *About Faces: Physiognomy in Nineteenth-Century Britain* (Cambridge, MA: Harvard University Press, 2010).

Ultimately, neither source of objectivity proves very reliable. Rochester calls Jane a 'changeling — fairy-born and human-bred', and while her personality makes her seem like a pillar of stability to his temperamental and whimsical self, the unseizable quality at the protagonist's core extends to the more technical ways her character is crafted.[12] The fact that she is the teller of her own story, the observer as well as the focus of attention, makes the novelist's — and the translator's — task all the more delicate.

This essay, then, focuses on character description as an exploration of the way prismatic processes permeate even the most fundamental aspects of a novel in translation. It traces the way Jane's appearance refracts in the novel's transition from English to Russian, from the first Russian translation, completed only two years after the novel's publication, to its last, and sixth Russian version, published as recently as 1999. While I explore character description in *Jane Eyre* more generally as a case study in Bermanian networks of signification elsewhere,[13] Jane's appearance is a special case that deserves closer scrutiny. This case study highlights the nuances of translating both narrative voice and characterisation in a setting where the stakes of individual word choices in translation are particularly high, not only for what is but also for what is not put in words.

Of the six Russian incarnations of *Jane Eyre*, three were published in the nineteenth century and three more in the twentieth. The first four are pre-revolutionary and use the old spelling system, later reformed by the Bolshevik government; two of these are full versions of the novel and two more are rewritten or abridged. The first is by Irinarkh Vvedenskii, a brilliant translator and early translation theorist, who gave Russian readers vivid and highly readable (though sometimes embellished by his own — often very tasteful — improvements) versions of Dickens and Thackeray, as well as Brontë.[14] His reaction to Brontë's novel was immediate: the first Russian translation came out as early as 1849. Curiously, Vvedenskii later claimed that, in contrast to his heartfelt respect and love for Dickens and Thackeray, he had, for reasons he would keep to himself, neither love nor respect ('вовсе

12 *JE*, Ch. 37.

13 Kelbert, 'Appearances'.

14 See Anna Syskina, 'Perevody XIX veka romana "Dzhen Eĭr" Sharlotty Brontë: peredacha kharaktera i vzgliadov geroini v perevode 1849 goda Irinarkha Vvedenskogo', *Vestnik Tomskogo gosudarstvennogo politekhnicheskogo universiteta*, 3 (2012), 177–82.

не люблю и не уважаю'[15]) for the 'English governess' who wrote the novel and therefore had no qualms in improving the text to suit his own taste: 'The novel "Jane Eyre" was indeed not translated but rather refashioned by me' ('Романъ "Дженни Эйръ" дѣйствительно не переведенъ, а передѣланъ мною').[16]

The second translation, by Sofia Koshlakova (1857), is done from the French adaptation of *Jane Eyre* by Paul-Émile Daurand Forgues, published under the pseudonym of Old Nick (1849).[17] This version stands out in that the novel is not only abridged considerably, but also recast as an epistolary novel where Jane is telling her story to a female friend called Elizabeth. The choice to work from this early adaptation may or may not have something to do with the fact that the book was marketed as part of a 'Library for summer retreats, steamboats and railways': in 1855, Old Nick's French text had similarly been re-published by Hachette in its 'Bibliothèque des Chemins de Fer'

---

15 Vvedenskii, Irinarkh, 'O perevodah romana Tekkereia "Vanity Fair" v "Otechestvennykh" Zapiskakh" I "Sovremennike"' *Otechestvennye zapiski*, 1851, Vol. 78, № 9/8, 61–81 (p. 75). For more about the context of this polemic and on Vvedenskii's method, see also Levin, Yu. D., *Russkie perevodchiki XIX veka i razvitie khudozhestvennogo perevoda* (Leningrad: Nauka, 1985), 124–36.

16 I thank Ekaterina Samorodnitskaya for pointing me to Vvedenskii's remarks. Charlotte Brontë's identity became known in 1848, but it does not seem that the information had reached Russia by 1849 when Vvedenskii's translation came out in five instalments of *Otechestvennye zapiski* throughout the year. Notably, the summary of the novel published in the same year in another journal Vvedenskii contributed to regularly, *Biblioteka dlia chteniia*, still speculates on whether the author is male or female. Vvedenskii's bitter words published in 1851, then, come across as an afterthought rather than an actual description of his motivation for the extensive changes he made. While he may have been less keen to go to great pains to convey the spirit (his alleged goal as a translator) of some 'English governess', his treatment of *Jane Eyre* is not that different from that of Thackeray or Dickens. In fact, in the same essay, Vvedenskii argues about Thackeray that the translator will '*inevitably* and *certainly* destroy the particular colour of this writer if he translates him <...> too closely to the original, sentence by sentence.' ('*неизбѣжно* и *непремѣнно* уничтожитъ колоритъ этого писателя, если станетъ переводить его <...> слишкомъ-близко къ оригиналу, изъ предложенія въ предложеніе' italics in the original, ibid, p. 69). Vvedenskii's wording leaves it ambiguous if his alleged disrespect was to do with the qualities of *Jane Eyre* or merely with the author's identity; his jabs both at Brontë and at his fellow translators who, he points out, treat the 'English governess' author just as poorly suggest, however, that his stepping forward to take credit as the Russian novel's co-creator was related to the discovery of the person behind the pseudonym.

17 See Chapters I & II above for a discussion of this version and its translation into other languages.

('Railway Library').[18] In addition, the Russian public was exposed to early digests or excerpts from the novel.[19] The end of the century saw a full retranslation by V. Vladimirov in 1893 (which largely followed Vvedenskii's), and the twentieth century started off in 1901 with an anonymous abridged version for a youth audience.

Two more translations enter the scene after the Revolution and remain the only ones currently in print. One, by Vera Stanevich, came out in 1950 and became a classic; this was essentially the only version available, in enormous runs sponsored by the State's considerable publishing and distribution mechanism, until the USSR became a thing of the past.[20] Unfortunately, several passages, especially concerning religion, were removed by the Soviet censor,[21] and another translator, Irina Gurova, republished this version with the missing parts restored in 1990. Gurova also published her own translation, which differs considerably from Stanevich's.[22] It goes without saying that many things have changed for the Russian Jane over a century and a half of retranslations. Notably, three of the six translators considered changing or adapting the novel to be part of their job description, and all but one version were censored to a lesser or greater degree. From the content of the novel to spelling, the translator's priorities and the very literary language of the time, we are dealing here with six different books. Focusing specifically on appearance offers a visual and compelling window into these differences.

---

18 See Chapter I above.

19 Anna Syskina, 'Russian Translations of the Novels of Charlotte Brontë in the Nineteenth Century', *Brontë Studies*, 37 (2012), 44–48 (p. 45).

20 Stanevich may have gained the Soviet establishment's official seal of approval, but she was, as a translator, anything but a product of the Soviet system. A symbolist poet and founder of a literary salon, she was an active member of pre-revolutionary literary circles, and her language expertise and stylistic intuition were formed within a world that disappeared in 1917.

21 Vvedenskii's and Vladimirov's translations, like Stanevich's, cut out the novel's final passage about St John's letter, betraying a curious agreement between the Soviet censor's anti-religious feeling and, presumably, the aesthetic sense of the nineteenth-century translators.

22 Iuliia Iamalova (3) claims that Gurova's translation was published the same year, i.e., in 1990 (see 'Istoriia perevodov romana Sharlotty Brontë "Dzheĭn Eĭr" v Rossii', *Vestnik Tomskovo gosudarstvennogo universiteta*, 363 (2012), 38–41, p. 40). It seems, however, that the first edition of Gurova's translation came out in 1999, under the same cover as a novel by Barbara Ford. I thank Alexey Kopeikin for his advice that helped locate this edition.

No Beauty, or Translating Imperfection

Jeanne Fahnestock argues that character description in British letters evolved drastically between the early nineteenth century and the 1860s. In the beginning of this period, the appearance of characters, and especially heroines, was referred to in a cursory fashion, so that a novelist may have noted, for instance, feminine features, beautiful in every respect. Towards, the end, what Fahnestock calls the 'heroine of irregular features' takes centre stage, largely under the influence of physiognomy. As the heroines' features grow less regular and harmonious, the heroines themselves gain license to imperfection and, as a result, also personal growth. This had hitherto been, with few exceptions, the privilege of the hero. In fact, a new 'aesthetic of the imperfect' became so much part of the *air du temps* that by 1868 a popular article declared women with perfectly regular features to be dull.[23]

Jane Eyre falls squarely in the middle of this period and exemplifies this change: 'the minutely described heroine has a much harder time being perfectly beautiful; she is often a heroine of irregular features instead'.[24] Jane is, indeed, a heroine of irregular features if ever there was one. This makes sense in physiognomic terms: insofar as character is expressed in salient features, asymmetrical by definition, striking personality must be accompanied by irregularity in appearance (with St John the exception that proves the rule). Indeed, Brontë's motivation behind the novel, as reported by Gaskell, plays out this very drama in her argument with her more conventionally minded sisters, who claimed that only a beautiful heroine could be interesting. 'Her answer was, "I will prove to you that you are wrong; I will show you a heroine as plain and as small as myself, who shall be as interesting as any of yours."'[25]

Jane herself, in her capacity as the story's narrator, also assumes that appearance and personality are related; for example, living up to St John's expectations is to her 'as impossible as to mould my irregular features to his correct and classic pattern, to give to my

23 Jeanne Fahnestock, 'The Heroine of Irregular Features: Physiognomy and Conventions of Heroine Description', *Victorian Studies*, 24 (1981), 325–50 (p. 333).

24 Fahnestock, 'The Heroine of Irregular Features', p. 329.

25 Elizabeth Gaskell, *The Life of Charlotte Brontë* (London: Smith, Elder, and Co., 1906), n.p. https://www.gutenberg.org/files/1827/1827-h/1827-h.htm

changeable green eyes the sea-blue tint and solemn lustre of his own'.[26] The irregularity of her appearance, however, does not make her a 'minutely described' heroine; on the contrary. In fact, we never find out what about Jane's features is 'so irregular and so marked': A prominent nose? A large mouth? Or do her ears stick out? We know Jane is of small stature and has a slight figure, which makes Rochester think of an elf or a fairy when looking at her, but there is little else, particularly when it comes to facial features.[27] With her protagonist, Brontë manages to combine early-century vagueness with an aesthetic of the imperfect.

Each translator must then pick a side in terms of where to place Jane on the novel's elusive scale of physical attractiveness. Jane is not a beauty, granted, and repeatedly contrasted with regular-featured belles such as Georgiana in her childhood and Blanche in her youth. Yet, the opposite of beauty is ugliness, and is Jane actually ugly? Abbott calls her 'a little toad' at age ten, St John declares hers an 'unusual physiognomy' that 'would always be plain', as the 'grace and harmony of beauty are quite wanting in those features', Jane's female cousins are of the opinion that, when in good health, 'her physiognomy would be agreeable', and Rochester at one point pronounces her to be 'truly pretty this morning'.[28] Even though she looks unusually happy when this last pronouncement is made and he is a man in love, the image goes badly with extreme bad looks and suggests rather a lack of particular beauty, now made up for by happy emotion.[29]

Given this fragile balance of points of view in the original, the translator's seemingly minor decisions lead to significant variation. In some translations, carefully wrought negatives such as 'you are not beautiful either' become in Russian *nekrasiva* — literally, the word means 'not-beautiful' but in Russian it is actually much closer to a description of extreme plainness than to a lack of the quality we

---

26 *JE*, Ch. 34.
27 *JE*, Ch. 11.
28 *JE*, Chs 3, 29, and 24.
29 A Russian 1850 resumé of the novel adds another, much earlier compliment, translating Rochester's 'you are no more pretty than I am handsome, yet a puzzled air becomes you' as 'You are far from being a beauty, just as I am not a handsome man; but at this moment you are rather pretty' ('Вы далеко не красавица, также какъ и я не красивый мужчина; но въ эту минуту вы довольно-миловидны'). 'Dzhen Eĭr, roman Korrer Bellia', *Sovremennik*. St Petersburg, 1850. Vol. 21/6, Seg. 4, pp. 31–38 (p. 32).

call beauty.[30] If the first translation, by Vvedenskii, keeps to vague expressions such as 'you are not a beautiful woman either / вѣдь и ты — не красавица',[31] the second by Koshlakova exaggerates the effect consistently. In fact, Koshlakova goes so far as to mention, speaking of the child Jane, her plainness that 'apparently repelled my relatives / свою некрасивость, по-видимому, отталкивающую близких моих';[32] elsewhere, again, she consistently makes Jane's looks actively unpleasant. For example, where Rochester tells Jane she is 'not pretty any more than [he is] handsome', Koshlakova adds an extra edge to it with 'nature has been just as unmerciful to your appearance as to mine[33] / хоть природа была такъ же немилостива къ вашей наружности, какъ къ моей'.[34] The last nineteenth-century translation, by Vladimirov, strikes a somewhat shaky balance between Betsy declaring Jane 'недурна'[35] (not bad-looking, one can even imagine it used to describe someone as being attractive) and 'некрасива', that is to say bad-looking. Vladimirov goes further still, for example, in translating 'features so irregular and so marked' as 'черты моего блѣднаго лица неправильны и невыразительны' ('that the features of my pale face [were] irregular/incorrect and inexpressive').[36] Suddenly, Jane's features are the opposite of marked in Russian — they are bland instead, completely skewing our idea of the heroine. Of the three nineteenth-century versions, then, the first makes Jane other-than-beautiful (rather like the original in this respect), the second somewhat repellent-looking, and the third uninteresting as well as unattractive.

In the twentieth century, the anonymous 1901 translation, abridged for a youth audience, omits most of the rare references to Jane's looks altogether. She is small, slight, and pale and was no beauty as a child but that is about it. Finally, the two modern translations (Stanevich in 1950, and Gurova in 1999) bring their own nuances to the table. Gurova's translation is scattered with colloquial and somewhat disparaging epithets such as *замухрышка*[37] (for 'no beauty'; this term, evocative

30 *JE*, Ch. 16.
31 Vvedenskii, p. 132.
32 Koshlakova, p. 21.
33 33 *JE*, Ch. 14.
34 Koshlakova, p. 128.
35 Vladimirov, p. 567.
36 *JE*, Ch. 11.
37 Gurova, p. 51.

of Cinderella, could be translated loosely as mousy-looking or drab) and *худышка*[38] ('scrawny', for Rochester's 'assez mince').[39] This adds a nuance to our perception of Jane: she seems easier to overlook or look down at. Her marked features are here 'unusual / необычные'; Jane lacks not only even 'a shade of beauty' ('и тени красоты') but even any prettiness ('лишена миловидности').[40] Stanevich is kinder to Jane: rather than having nothing to recommend her, she merely regrets that she is 'not beautiful enough / недостаточно красива'.[41] On the whole, her word choices are more restrained and consistent, with a Jane who looks serious, focused, and by no means a beauty — but that may well be her virtue. Overall, the six translations imply six different Janes, the effect of whose appearance on others varies from unpleasant to other than dazzling.

Jane, with Russian Eyes

Perhaps the closest to a literary portrait of the heroine we get in the novel is a scene where, the morning after the proposal scene, Rochester praises Jane's 'dimpled cheek and rosy lips', 'satin-smooth hazel' hair and 'radiant hazel eyes'.[42] This is the first reference we get to Jane's eye and hair colour (though we know she brushes her hair smooth from before). With a highly characteristic ambiguity, however, Brontë undermines that description: the whole point of this welcome sketch is that on that particular morning Jane does not look like her usual self. How much of this liberally bestowed information can then be applied to her normal appearance on days when she is not blissfully happy and observed by an ardent lover? Not much, we learn at once as Jane adds, in an aside: '(I had green eyes, reader; but you must excuse the mistake: for him they were new-dyed, I suppose.)' How much can any description in the novel be trusted if the eye of the keenest of observers — a man in love, supposedly looking straight at Jane's face at the moment of speaking — is so easily deceived?

Smooth brown hair and green eyes, then. And this is as much as we gather of Jane's appearance. Elsewhere, any reference to it is either vague and general, or comes from clearly unreliable observers, or both.

38 Ibid. p. 66.
39 *JE*, Ch. 13.
40 Gurova, p. 55.
41 Stanevich, p. 104.
42 *JE*, Ch. 24.

The only exception is Jane's height, the one point that is corroborated by several reliable sources. Lloyd, the apothecary, judges her to be eight or nine years of age when she is actually ten and Brocklehurst's first impression is that 'her size is small'; in the red room mirror she also sees herself as 'a strange little figure'.[43] As an adult, Bessie estimates that she is a head and shoulders shorter than Eliza and about twice slighter than Georgiana Reed; Rochester, as reported by Adèle, describes her to the little girl as 'une petite personne, assez mince et un peu pâle', and Adèle also thinks this a fitting description of her mademoiselle.[44] Jane's paleness is also corroborated by herself,[45] so we can safely add it to the slim list of the four or five things we will have gathered about her looks by the end of the novel: small stature, slight figure, a pale face, smooth brown hair, and what she later refers to, once more, as 'changeable green eyes'.[46]

The Russian translators vary in how they treat these grains of information we glean to imagine a face and figure to which we could attribute the novel's 183,858 words. For instance, Rochester's description quoted above is omitted entirely in the 1901 version. As for the available translations of his description of Jane, only Gurova's 1990 translation renders each element faithfully (and even she makes Jane's hair silky 'шелковистые' rather than satin-smooth, referring to their texture rather than implying also a hairstyle). Gurova is also the only one to make an attempt at translating 'sunny-faced' or mention the dimple on Jane's cheek, with Stanevich going for 'rosy / румяные'[47] cheeks and the other translators omitting the reference and focusing on the more conventional rosy lips. The notions of Jane as a 'pale, little elf' and a 'sunny-faced girl' in the same scene baffles the translators as well. Stanevich and Gurova differ in their choice for 'girl', which is ambiguous in Russian. Stanevich goes for 'девушка'[48] (young woman) while Gurova chooses 'девочка'[49] (usually, a little girl, making Jane, who is already 'almost like a child' in stature, at once a lot more childlike). Their nineteenth-century predecessors forego the elf (Vvedenskii goes for a 'little friend, pale and doleful / маленькій

43 *JE*, Chs 4 and 2.
44 *JE*, Ch. 13.
45 *JE*, Ch. 11.
46 *JE*, Ch. 34.
47 Stanevich, p. 104.
48 Ibid. p. 249.
49 Gurova, p. 145.

другъ, блѣдный и печальный'[50]) but make up for it by then reaching for another mythical creature and translating 'sunny-faced girl' as an 'aerial nymph / воздушная нимфа' as a way to cover both problematic phrases.

Perhaps most strikingly, any reference to Jane's eyes is omitted from the exchange in the novel's first translation (though Vvedenskii does mention their green colour towards the end of the novel). In Koshlakova's epistolary version, the matter of green eyes is particularly interesting: rather than simply say that are green, Jane reports to her correspondent that Rochester showered her with compliments on her *beauty* and the radiance of her pretty *dark* eyes, italicises both 'beauty' and 'dark' as clearly ludicrous suppositions and refers to her friend's common sense about her eyes which are 'as you well know, entirely green' ('Осыпав комплиментами и мой веселый вид, и *красоту*, и блеск моих хорошеньких *темныхъ* глаз...которые, как вам извѣстно, другъ мой, у меня совершенно зеленые'[51]).[52] In this version alone, then, the green colour of Jane's eyes becomes a trait both implicitly corroborated by another and evident to an objective observer, which only Rochester is blinded to, by the same emotion that blinds him to her lack of beauty. Unsurprisingly, Jane's description of the scene also exaggerates the original's gentle irony at Rochester's expense.

'Satin-smooth hazel' hair is another element worth dwelling on, as a paradigmatic example where the idiomatic arsenal of the Russian language changes the protagonist's appearance ever so gently. Namely, hazel is simply not used to describe either hair or eyes in Russian, the most idiomatic first choice for hair being 'chestnut' (каштановый) and for eyes 'brown' (карий, which encompasses a range of hues from hazel to dark brown), and these are the words the Russian translators reach for. While culturally and idiomatically equivalent, both chestnut and brown evoke a slightly different (and darker) hue than the original. It goes without saying that Rochester's touching notion that Jane's hair colour matches her eyes goes out of the window together with the word 'hazel' in all the translations.

---

50 Vvedenskii p. 66.

51 Koshlakova, p. 74.

52 In this, Koshlakova translates accurately from 'Old Nick''s French: 'Lorsqu'il m'eut félicitée sur ma bonne mine, sur ma *beauté* même, et sur l'éclat de mes jolis yeux *bruns*, — ils sont verts, comme vous le savez, ma chere [sic] amie...' (*Jane Eyre*, tr. Old Nick, 1855, p. 86)

The repercussions of these seemingly slight changes, however, go deeper than we may anticipate. As translation variation goes, they adjust the little we know of Jane's appearance. In terms of the relationship between appearance and interpretation, however, they also do away with a nuance Brontë was probably aware of from observation (or else why would she have planted the word 'changeable' in the second reference to Jane's eyes, or come up with Rochester's striking blunder in the first place): namely, that in reality, it is easy to mistake hazel eyes for green, while the opposite is impossible. Hazel eyes have some green in them, as well as brown; the two eye colours share the same pigment, pheomelanin, dominant in the green eye colour and supplemented with another dominant pigment, brownish-black eumelanin, in hazel irises. In other words, rather than going with Jane's unlikely interpretation that Rochester's love made her eyes 'new-dyed' for him that morning, it is safe to assume that Jane's 'changeable green' eyes are in fact hazel, i.e., light brown with a green tinge to them. In other words, Rochester, not Jane, identifies her eye colour most accurately, although Jane is unaware of the fact and, as we know, is quick to reject the suggestion. The fact that Russian does not distinguish between these colours for eyes makes this ambiguity near-impossible to preserve in translation.

Choosing how to translate 'hazel', most people imagine this eye colour as a kind of light brown, and when an exact equivalent is lacking, would lean in that direction as the closest equivalent available, just as the Russian translators did. Yet brown eyes are common, while both hazel and especially green are a rarity. The fact that Jane clearly identifies as being green-eyed is, in other words, a matter not of objective truth, as she — and Koshlakova's version — make it appear, but of Jane's self-perception (quite in harmony with the little green men Rochester, too, associates her with independently from her eye colour). In other words, this seemingly minor detail reveals Jane to us as a less than objective narrator. These are the eyes through which we perceive the novel's entire world, which later become Rochester's eyes as well: how reliably do they perceive themselves?

As well as making us wonder about the reliability of the many other 'objective' pronouncements Jane makes in the novel, Rochester's alleged mistake provides a unique insight into Jane's sense of identity. The forgivable and very human bias of identifying entirely with one aspect of her eye colour may be aesthetic, as she is an artist, or reflect her sense of being different, or both. Can it be that, reconciled with what she, and most people around her, perceive as her lack of beauty, she takes comfort in her unusual and striking eyes that she would never acknowledge even to herself? If so, Brontë's game in terms of the character's psychologisation may be even subtler and even more modern here (coming from an author writing half a century before Freud) than most critics, including Shuttleworth's meticulous study of Brontë and Victorian psychology, give her credit for. Unsurprisingly, Charlotte Brontë's eyes may have been hazel as well, which would explain the inside joke and imply a note of self-irony in Jane's portrayal (the novel was, after all, billed as an autobiography).[53]

Invisibly Centre Stage: A Prismatic Approach

Jane Eyre is, in general, notoriously attentive to the processes of both observing and interpreting from observation. We can recall Jane scrutinising Grace Poole or comparing St John's looks to Rosamond's to estimate the likelihood of their union. Characters are constantly aware — or, indeed, unaware — of being observed (we recall Jane's discomfort under Mr Brocklehurst's 'two inquisitive-looking grey eyes which twinkled under a pair of bushy brows'[54]), or learn of having been observed in the past (e.g., when Rochester tells Jane the story of their first encounters from his perspective, or Mrs Reed explains many

53 Brontë was, like Jane, of very short stature and had notoriously irregular features; Ann Thackeray Ritchie notes 'a general impression of chin about her face,' (*Letters of Anne Thackeray Ritchie*, ed. by Hester Ritchie (London: John Murray, 1924), pp. 269–70), and Elizabeth Gaskell a 'crooked mouth' and a 'large nose'. The latter describes her eyes as follows: 'They were large, and well shaped; their colour a reddish brown; but if the iris was closely examined, it appeared to be composed of a great variety of tints' (Gaskell, *The Life of Charlotte Brontë*, Ch. 6, n.p.). Elsewhere, Gaskell makes the same apparent mistake as Rochester: having mentioned her 'soft brown hair', she then describes Brontë's eyes as '(very good and expressive, looking straight and open at you) of the same colour as her hair' (*The Life of Charlotte Brontë*, Ch. 7). Even though others, notably Matthew Arnold and Gaskell's daughter, refer to Brontë's eyes as grey, the very confusion in Gaskell's description seems to suggest eyes that were, like Jane's, multi-coloured with a predominance of brown, supplemented with green, grey, or a variety of tints: in other words, hazel. Indeed, another visitor once referred to them as 'chameleon-like, a blending of various brown and olive tints' (*The Brontës: Interviews and Recollections*, ed. by H. Orel (London: Palgrave Macmillan, 1997), p. 166). Brontë's drawing entitled 'Study of eyes' provides an eloquent, if black-and-white, testimonial of her fascination with eyes and their structure (reprinted in Shuttleworth, *Charlotte Brontë*, n.p.).

54 *JE*, Ch. 4.

years later how she perceived the rebellious child in the red room). From physiognomic reading of personality to interpreting emotions, making decisions based on a deliberate reading of appearance is a large aspect of both of the novel's courtships, perhaps best expressed in a scene where St John, Jane tells us, 'seemed leisurely to read my face, as if its features and lines were characters on a page'.[55] In a sense, this mirrors not only the fake gypsy's intense focus on Jane's features (which, again, does nothing to help us imagine them visually) but also Rochester's proposal, when Jane asks to read his countenance, an ordeal Rochester finds it hard to endure, despite his prediction that she would 'find it scarcely more legible than a crumpled, scratched page' (217).[56] The peculiar 'art of surveillance' that characterises the novel is part and parcel of what Shuttleworth calls 'Brontë's challenge to realism', and compensates for her tendency to narrators 'devoted as much to concealing as to revealing the self'.[57]

The way in which characters consistently find an interpretative resource in physical appearance, visible to them but concealed from the reader, keeps us aware that appearances contain the key to interpretation, and that we have no access to it as readers. There is a good reason for that. Very much a precursor to the modernists where sparse character description is concerned, Brontë is also an author preoccupied with the power of the imagination: it suffices to recall Jane's intense inner life, as reflected in her drawings. While regularly emphasising the importance of what we cannot see, she leaves much to the reader's imagination. A few key features are scattered carefully throughout the text, and the rest is up to us. Lessing points out that, due to the nature of literature, where a portrait has to unfold in time, phrase by phrase, and no unified impression is possible as it is in painting, the only way to approximate such instantaneous impact is to focus on one salient trait and let the reader's mind do the rest.[58] Brontë's way of handling the inherent differences between literature and reality is to refuse to compensate for the reader's inability to see the whole picture. Instead, she embraces this limitation by providing a portrait that, far from standing for a visual image, may be as complete,

55 *JE*, Ch. 30.
56 *JE*, Ch. 23.
57 Shuttleworth, *Charlotte Brontë*, p. 17.
58 Cited in Heier, '"The Literary Portrait"', p. 327.

or as approximate, as reliable, or as inaccurate, as suits the author's design.

In Jane's case, this principle is elevated to the level of what Yuri Lotman calls a 'minus-device', i.e., a marked lack or omission that becomes a literary device in itself.[59] A salient example is the well-known episode where Jane sets herself the unforgiving task of drawing her own image and that of her rival (ironically, the latter is at that point based on a verbal description alone). The novelist tantalises the reader with Jane's drawing of her 'real head in chalk' that, unlike her sketch of Rochester, reveals nothing to us: 'Listen, then, Jane Eyre, to your sentence: to-morrow, place the glass before you, and draw in chalk your own picture, faithfully; without softening one defect: omit no harsh line, smooth away no displeasing irregularity; write under it, "Portrait of a Governess, disconnected, poor, and plain"'.[60] We already cannot reach Jane through a literary portrait; similarly, her actual portrait is marked by the defiant absence of any description.

Apart from a few basic facts and a few subjective references, descriptions to Jane's looks are not only sparse but deliberately apophatic. A chorus of detailed — indeed, minute — epithets lists, from the very first page of the novel, all the things Jane is *not*. As a child, she is *not* attractive or sprightly, light, frank, natural, physically strong, sanguine, brilliant, careless, exacting, handsome, romping, nice, or pretty. Betty thinks she was 'no beauty' as a child.[61] When Jane grows up, she regrets she is 'not handsomer' and cannot boast 'rosy cheeks, a straight nose, and small cherry mouth', or being 'tall, stately, and finely developed in figure'; her features are, as we have discussed, *not* regular and she looks like she is not from *this* world.[62] The only predicates ever applied to Jane that are not apophatic in themselves describe her as difficult to describe or place: she has 'cover', appears to be of an unclear age, and so on.[63] In the rare instances a positive description does occur, the epithets used, though they imply something about appearance, tend to really refer to personality instead, such as the bounty of four whole adjectives that actually tell us nothing about

59 Yuri, Lotman, *The Structure of the Artistic Text*, trans. by Gail Lenhoff and Ronald Vroon (Ann Arbor: Dept. of Slavic Languages and Literature, University of Michigan, 1977), p. 51.
60 *JE*, Ch. 16.
61 *JE*, Ch. 10.
62 *JE*, Chs 11 and 13.
63 *JE*, Chs 2 and 13.

how Jane looks ('quaint, quiet, grave, and simple'), or descriptions such as 'queer, frightened, shy, little thing', or 'gentle, gracious, genial stranger'.[64]

How does a 'minus-device' fare in translation? Not too well, as it turns out. On the one hand, seemingly minor choices gain in significance as a result, leading to larger shifts in emphasis. On the other, different translators' strategies tend to be consistent despite variation in the translation choices, which suggests that the translators' reading of the text is affected by Brontë's apophatic portrayal of her heroine. One such strategy is to make anything resembling appearance more salient; for instance, where Jane imagines that she may have been a 'sanguine, brilliant, careless, exacting, handsome, romping child', good looks are only mentioned in passing; yet they are emphasised in every single Russian translation of this description.[65] Another is to avoid any suggestion of appearance altogether. The four Russian translations that feature the quotation involving the 'gentle, gracious, genial stranger', for example, choose adjectives that refer clearly to Jane's personal qualities rather than (as the English 'gentle' and 'gracious' suggest) at least tangentially to the outward impression she may make. In Russian, Jane becomes, in the earliest translation, noble and magnanimous / 'великодушную и благородную особу',[66] then turns into a 'sweet, nice, loving creature / милое, симпатичное, любящее существо'[67] in the 1893 version, and finally a 'meek, elevated and merciful soul / кроткой, возвышенной, милосердной души'[68] in 1990.[69]

In the context of a minus-device, connotations also gain in importance. The translator cannot avoid interpretation, and often already suggestive adjectives lead us to divergent impressions in Russian. Rochester's comparison of Jane to a 'nonnette' is one case in point.[70] Vvedenskii's (1849) very free translation goes with 'институтка'[71] (an institute girl). This is an interesting choice in itself:

64 *JE*, Chs 14, 4, and 20.
65 *JE*, Ch. 2.
66 Vvedenskii, p. 220.
67 Vladimirov, p. 266.
68 Gurova, p. 123.
69 A similar transformation occurs with the list of adjectives describing the qualities Jane lacked as a child. Russian translations make them more about Jane's kindness: evil, bad, cunning, not kind, not tender etc. Yet, Brontë's carefully selected adjectives tend to imply appearance.
70 *JE*, Ch. 14.
71 Vvedenskii, p. 98.

though Lowood is an 'institution' rather than an 'institute', the word may seem like a potentially felicitous solution given Jane's background. Yet the Russian analogue conjures up a very different image: that of a young graduate of the Smolny Institute for aristocratic young ladies. The cultural connotations this evokes are hardly nun-like or Quakerish, and would suggest, in 1849, a well-bred and sheltered young lady from an excellent family. Interestingly, just a year before Vvedenskii's translation came out, Smolny Institute had opened a two-year class to train female teachers, which may or may not have influenced this translator's choice.

Unsurprisingly, once the notion of a Smolny girl is introduced, Vvedenskii then cannot convincingly translate the other adjectives in the passage ('quaint, quiet, grave, and simple') and makes them refer to Jane's 'composed, serious and somewhat naive pose / спокойной, серьёзной и нѣсколько наивной позѣ'.[72] Koshlakova (1857), who translated from Old Nick's adaptation, follows the French to turn Jane into more of a nun: 'priggish, composed, serious, simple, with constantly folded hands / напыщенную, спокойную, серьезную, простую, съ вѣчно сложенными руками'[73] (in English, Jane only looks like a nun in that moment, with folded arms, not constantly). Stanevich, a century later, makes her 'quiet, grave, calm / тихая, строгая, спокойная',[74] and Gurova, in 1990, 'old-fashioned, quiet, grave, naive/unsophisticated / старомодная, тихая, серьезная, бесхитростная.'[75] The range of the images projected is telling: from Vvedenskii's sophisticated young lady via the rather Eliza-like imposing figure of a nun, and finally to Gurova's old-fashioned simpleton.

In certain paradigmatic cases, prismatic variation in emphasis is amplified by linguistic variation. Consider the moment where Rochester admits to his inability to guess Jane's age, a precious clue as to her looks: Jane's 'features and countenance are so much at variance', he explains.[76] But what does this mean? Quite apart from the cryptic nature of the remark itself, Russian is hard put to trace the distinction between features and countenance. While technical analogues may be found, they are inexact and, when not juxtaposed, the two words are likely to be translated in the same way. So, while a couple of the

72 Ibid. p. 105.
73 Koshlakova, p. 124.
74 Stanevich, p. 134.
75 Gurova, p. 74.
76 *JE*, Ch. 13.

translations go down the cryptic route (e.g., 'features' vs 'expression'), two attempt interpretation: the very first translation of the novel into Russian, by Vvedenskii, juxtaposes Jane's figure (her body silhouette) with her 'physiognomy / физiономiею',[77] while the canonical Stanevich translation decodes the enigma in its own way: 'childlike appearance and seriousness / детский облик и серьезность'.[78] Thus, dealing with the ambiguity of Jane's looks in the novel leads, in one case, to a reference to Jane's body, exceptional in the novel, and in the other — to her making a childlike impression.

Prismatic variation in translation is already striking when it comes to a key trope as dependent on a handful of carefully chosen words as character description. The effect is further amplified in Jane's case, given how little of her appearance we can pin down. The Russian translations of Rochester's remark 'you have rather the look of another world. I marvelled where you had got that sort of face'[79] are another example of the extent to which cross-lingual difference can direct the translator's hand in such an ambivalent setting. Russian has two words for 'world', one ('*мир*') homonymous with the word for peace and the other ('*свет*') with that for light. The latter has strong connotations of the afterlife, and that is the word used by both Vladimirov and the anonymous 1901 translator. Accordingly, all the pre-1950 translations lean towards the look not so much of 'another' as 'the other' world, making Jane not so much a fairy as something of a revenant. The modern two translations diverge: Stanevich goes for 'you look like a creature from another world / вы похожи на существо из другого мира'[80] (a stronger image than merely having the look of another world) and Gurova for 'there is something about you that is not from this world / в вас сквозит что-то не от этого мира.'[81] Here, the overall effect of the minus-device pushes the translators to make Jane even more of an otherworldly being than she already is in English, and a good deal more sinister.

To conclude, it seems clear that variation in translation goes beyond descriptive nuances and affects the novel's deepest structures, such as the visual representation of a character and, by extension, that character's relationships and motivations. For instance, the same

77 Vvedenskii, p. 123.
78 Stanevich, p. 127.
79 *JE*, Ch. 13.
80 Stanevich, p. 126.
81 Gurova, p. 68.

story reads differently with a repellent-looking Jane as opposed to one that is perhaps underappreciated but rather pretty. In certain cases, as with 'hazel' for Jane's eye colour, the translation affects not only her appearance but also, potentially, the way we think of her looks (standard or exotic) and how Jane comes across as a narrator (objective or biased). There is only so much we can do to trace the exact image that each version of a text produces for each reader. Yet an analysis of the prompts that such an image is based on lifts the veil on prismatic variation that goes beyond a given translation or language: as well as a multiplicity of books, *Jane Eyre*'s many translations create a multiplicity of imagined persons across the globe.

Paradoxically, with an underdescribed character such as Jane, the effect can be even stronger, as evident from one compelling testimony. A Russian summary of the novel, published in 1850, muses on Jane's appearance as follows: 'Jane Eyre was no beauty, not even pretty. But her characteristic facial features cannot be imagined in any way other than as the imprint of great resources of the soul: a firm, unshakeable will and a readiness for an anything but lustreless fight with destitution and grief.'[82] The author of this review bases their summary on Vvedenskii's translation, which they cite extensively word for word, and has evidently derived from it a clear notion of Jane's features and of the importance of that strong mental image for characterisation. The character's actions successfully fill in the gaps in Jane's portrait, resulting in a convincing image — an image based on mere crumbs of description Brontë scatters for her readers and now refracted through the prism of another language — which the contemporary Russian critic confidently declares the only one imaginable. The image itself, however, is transient, and succeeded, with new translations, by mental representations where Jane comes across as now plain, now priggish, now pretty, or otherworldly: forever a changeling, fairy-born and human-bred.

82 'Дженъ Эйръ не была красавицей, не была даже хорошенькой. Но характерныя черты лица ея нельзя вообразить иначе, какъ съ отпечаткомъ великихъ силъ душевныхъ: воли твердой, непреклонной, и готовности на небезславную борьбу съ нуждой и горемъ.' (*Sovremennik*, p. 32).

Works Cited

Russian Translations of *Jane Eyre* (in chronological order)

List researched and compiled by Eugenia Kelbert and Karolina Gurevich

April 1849, summary with translated excerpts:

"Literaturnye Novosti v Anglii: Dzhenni Ir: Avtobiografiia," *Biblioteka dlia chteniia*, 1849, Vol. 94/2, Seg. 7, pp 151–72.[83]

May 1849, first translation by Irinarkh Vvedenskii (divided in 5 parts):

Irinarkh Vvedenskii, "Dzhenni Ir. Roman," *Otechestvennye zapiski*, 1849, Vol. 64/6, Seg. 1, pp 175–250; Vol. 65/7, Seg. 1, pp. 67–158; Vol. 65/8, pp 179–262; Vol. 66/9, Seg. 1, pp 65–132, Vol. 66/10, Seg. 1, pp 193–330. Extracts from this translation were included in "Dzhen Eĭr, roman Korrer Bellia." *Sovremennik*. St Petersburg, 1850. Vol. 21/6, Seg. 4, pp 31–38.

1857, translation by S. I. Koshlakova, abridged and recast as an epistolary novel (three parts). Translated from the French adaptation *Jane Eyre. Mémoires d'une gouvernante, Imité par Old Nick* (Paris: Hachette, 1855):

Bronte Sh. *Dzhenni Eĭr, ili Zapiski guvernantki*, trans. S. I. K...voĭ, Biblioteka dlia dach, parokhodov i zheleznykh dorog, St. Petersburg: Tipografiia imperatorskoĭ akademii nauk, 1857.

Translation of the German play adaptation by Charlotte Birch-Pfeiffer, *Die Waise aus Lowood* (1853):

Charlotte Birch-Pfeiffer, *Lovudskaya sirota: Zhan Eyre*, trans. by D. A. Mansfeld, Moscow: Litographia Moscowskoy teatralnoy biblioteki E. N. Rassohinoy, 1889.

1893, translation by V.D. Vladimirov:[84]

Bronte Sh. *Dzhenni Eĭr (Lokvudskaia Sirota). Roman-avtobiografiia v 2kh chastiakh*. Trans. V. D. Vladimirov, St Petersburg: M.M. Lederle & Ko, 1893.

1901, anonymous translation, abridged for a youth audience:

"Dzheni Eĭr, istoriia moeĭ zhizni," Sharloty Bronte. Sokraschennyĭ perevod s angliĭskogo. *IUnyĭ chitatel', zhurnal dlia deteĭ starshego vozrasta*, Vol. 3, 5, St Petersburg, 1901

83 Other published summaries included, notably, *Sovremennik* (1850, Vol. 21/6, Seg. 4, pp 31–38), a second summary in *Biblioteka dlia chteniia* (1852, 116: 23–54) and a brief summary in *Mir Bozhii* (1893, 9: 162–65).

84 Vladimirov's real name was Vladimir Dmitrievich Vol'fson.

1950, canonical Soviet translation by Vera Oskarovna Stanevich:

Bronte, Sharlotta. *Dzhen Eĭr*, Trans. V. Stanevich, Moscow: Goslitizdat (Leningrad: 2ia fabrika det. Knigi Detgiza), 1950

1990, Vera Stanevich's translation with censored passages restored by Irina Gurova:

Bronte, Sharlotta. *Dzhen Eĭr*, Trans. V. Stanevich (omissions in the texts reconstructed by I. Gurova), Moscow: Khudozhestvennaia literatura, 1990

1999, translation by Irina Gurova:

Bronte, Sharlotta. *Dzheĭn Ėĭr*, trans. I. Gurova and *Rozhdestvo v Indii* by Barbara Ford, trans. V. Semenov. Moscow: AST, 1999

The Gurova and Stanevich translations have both been much reprinted: Figure 23 shows their relative popularity.

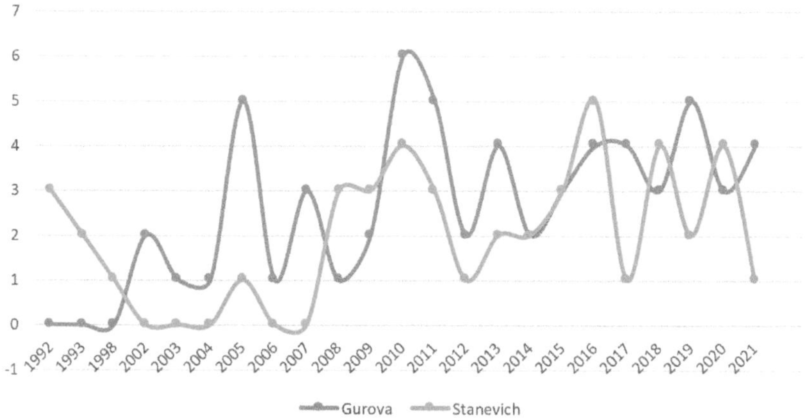

Fig. 23 Reprints and re-editions of the Gurova and Stanevich translations, researched and created by Karolina Gurevich

Other Sources

Andrew, Dudley, 'The Well-Worn Muse: Adaptation in Film History and Theory', in *Narrative Strategies: Original Essays in Film and Prose Fiction*, ed. by Syndy M. Conger and Janet R. Welsh (Macomb: Western Illinois UP, 1980), pp. 9–19.

Berman, Antoine, 'La Traduction comme épreuve de l'étranger', *Texte*, 4 (1985), 67–81.

——, 'Translation and the Trials of the Foreign', trans. Lawrence Venuti, in *The Translation Studies Reader*, ed. by Lawrence Venuti (London: Routledge, 2000), pp. 240–53.

Boshears, Rhonda and Harry Whitaker, 'Phrenology and Physiognomy in Victorian Literature', in *Literature, Neurology, and Neuroscience: Historical and Literary Connections*, ed. by Anne Stiles, Stanley Finger, and François Boller (Amsterdam: Elsevier, 2013), https://doi.org/10.1016/B978-0-444-63273-9.00006-X

Brontë, Charlotte, *Jane Eyre: An Authoritative Text, Contexts, Criticism*, 3rd edn, ed. by Richard J. Dunn (New York: W.W. Norton & Company, 2001).

Demidova, O. R., 'The Reception of Charlotte Brontë's Work in Nineteenth-Century Russia', *The Modern Language Review*, 89 (1994), 689–96.

Fahnestock, Jeanne, 'The Heroine of Irregular Features: Physiognomy and Conventions of Heroine Description', *Victorian Studies*, 24 (1981), 325–50.

Fan, Yiying and Jia Miao, 'Shifts of Appraisal Meaning and Character Depiction Effect in Translation: A Case Study of the English Translation of Mai Jia's *In the Dark*', *Studies in Literature and Language*, 20 (2020), 55–61, http://dx.doi.org/10.3968/11484

Gaskell, Elizabeth, *The Life of Charlotte Brontë* (Smith, Elder, and Co., 1906), https://www.gutenberg.org/files/1827/1827-h/1827-h.htm

Graham, John, 'Character Description and Meaning in the Romantic Novel', *Studies in Romanticism*, 5 (1966), 208–18.

Hartley, Lucy, *Physiognomy and the Meaning of Expression in Nineteenth-Century Culture* (Cambridge: Cambridge University Press, 2005).

Heier, E., '"The Literary Portrait" as a Device of Characterization', *Neophilologus*, 60 (1976), 321–33.

Hollington, Michael, 'Physiognomy in *Hard Times*, *Dickens Quarterly*, 9 (1992), 58–66.

Iamalova, Iuliia, 'Istoriia perevodov romana Sharlotty Brontë "Dzheĭn Eĭr" v Rossii', *Vestnik Tomskovo gosudarstvennogo universiteta*, 363 (2012), 38–41.

Jadwin, Lisa, '"Caricatured, Not Faithfully Rendered": *Bleak House* as a Revision of *Jane Eyre*', *Modern Language Studies*, 26 (1996), 111–33.

Jack, Ian 'Physiognomy, phrenology and characterisation in the novels of Charlotte Brontë', *Brontë Society Transactions*, 15 (1970), 377–91.

Kelbert, Eugenia, 'Appearances: Character Description as a Network of Signification in Russian Translations of Jane Eyre', *Target: International Journal of Translation Studies*, 34.2 (2021), 219–50, https://doi.org/10.1075/target.20079.kel

Klinger, Suzanne 'Translating the Narrator', in *Literary Translation*, ed. by J. Boase-Beier, A. Fawcett, and P. Wilson (London: Palgrave Macmillan, 2014), pp. 168–81.

Levin, Yu. D., *Russkie perevodchiki XIX veka i razvitie khudozhestvennogo perevoda* (Leningrad: Nauka, 1985).

Lotman, Yuri, *The Structure of the Artistic Text*, trans. by Gail Lenhoff and Ronald Vroon (Ann Arbor: Dept. of Slavic Languages and Literature, University of Michigan, 1977).

Macdonald, Frederika, *The Secret of Charlotte Brontë* (London: T. C. & E. C. Jack, 1914), https://www.gutenberg.org/files/41105/41105-h/41105-h.htm.

Orel, H. [John Stores Smith], 'Personal Reminiscences: A Day with Charlotte Brontë', in *The Brontës. Interviews and Recollections*, ed. by H. Orel (London: Palgrave Macmillan, 1997).

Pearl, Sharrona, *About Faces: Physiognomy in Nineteenth-Century Britain* (Cambridge, MA: Harvard University Press, 2010).

Reynolds, Matthew, ed., *Prismatic Translation* (Cambridge: Legenda, 2020).

Sarana, Natal'a V., 'Traditsiia angliĭskogo romana vospitaniia v russkoĭ proze 1840–1870h godov' (unpublished doctoral thesis, National Research University Higher School of Economics, 2018).

Shuttleworth, Sally, *Charlotte Brontë and Victorian Psychology* (Cambridge: Cambridge University Press, 1996).

Syskina, Anna, 'Perevody XIX veka romana "Dzhen Eĭr" Sharlotty Brontë: peredacha kharaktera i vzgliadov geroini v perevode 1849 goda Irinarkha Vvedenskogo', *Vestnik Tomskogo gosudarstvennogo pedagogicheskogo universiteta*, 3 (2012), 177–82.

——, 'Russian Translations of the Novels of Charlotte Brontë in the Nineteenth Century', *Brontë Studies*, 37 (2012), 44–48.

Syskina, Anna A. and Vitaly S. Kiselev, 'The Problem of Rendering Psychological Content in V. Vladimirov's Translation of *Jane Eyre* (1893)', *Brontë Studies*, 40 (2015), 181–86.

Thackeray Ritchie, Anne. *Letters of Anne Thackeray Ritchie, with Forty-two Additional Letters from her Father William Makepeace Thackeray*, ed. by Hester Ritchie (London: John Murray, 1924).

Vvedenskii, Irinarkh, 'O perevodakh romana Tekkereia "Vanity Fair" v "Otechestvennykh" Zapiskakh" i "Sovremennike"' *Otechestvennye zapiski*, 1851, Vol. 78, № 9/8, pp. 61–81 (p. 75).

Walker, Alexander. *Physiognomy founded on Physiology* (London: Smith, Elder, and Co., 1834), https://archive.org/details/physiognomyfound00walk/page/14

Wells, Samuel R., *New Physiognomy; or, Signs of Character, as manifested through Temperament and External Forms, and especially in "The Human Face Divine"* (London: L. N. Fowler & Co., 1866).

Zunshine, Lisa, *Why We Read Fiction: Theory of Mind and the Novel* (Columbus, OH: Ohio State University Press, 2006.

VIII. Conclusions

Matthew Reynolds

We invite each reader to draw their own conclusions from this volume, and hopefully to re-draw them in the course of an ongoing conversation with it. Here are some of the conclusions that I have drawn, as prompts to that activity.

Reading in world-literary contexts means reading heterolingually.

Reading heterolingually entails reading collaboratively. This can be a matter of actual interpersonal collaboration (I think there should be more translingual shared reading projects like this one) but it can also be a disposition of mind.

Understanding in world-literary contexts is necessarily incomplete, and this incompleteness should be welcomed.

Abridgement is fundamental to *Jane Eyre*'s existence in the world, and probably to that of all world novels.

The distinction between translations and other kinds of re-writing, such as versions and adaptations, is pragmatic; but it still has value because a translation makes a claim on the identity of the work.

A world work consists of the originary text and all its translations together.

Translation moves through language difference, not between languages; it participates in the organisation and regulation of language difference.

Texts are written with repertoires, not in languages.

Jane Eyre's multilingual repertoire takes on salience in a world-literary context. No one translation known to me is as heterolingual as the text that Brontë wrote; but together the translations constitute a massive realisation of the heterolingual potential of the source.

https://doi.org/10.11647/OBP.0319.26

Re-publication of an existing translation in a new place can play an important role in the diffusion of the work: it is an 'act of translation'.

Jane Eyre translation has sometimes been promoted as part of a programme of English soft power (as in Greece after World War II).

But more often the choice to translate is an active one on the part of writers and publishers in the ingurgitative culture.

In these cases, translation can be a vehicle for imaginative and ideological freedom (as in Spain under Franco, or Iran after the 1979 revolution).

Translations in India and South America have reconfigured the racist portrayal of Bertha Rochester, diffusing and defusing it. This matters to the politics of the work.

Jane Eyre has had a powerful feminist impact in many contexts, such as late C19th Portugal and 1940s South America.

Abridgement can reveal what readers feel to be the core of the work; equally, censorship can indicate its moments of sharpest ideological challenge, by erasing them.

Thinking about the absence of translations from a language or culture (as of *Jane Eyre* from Swahili) is also a revealing literary historical exercise.

Aspects of the novel can grow when it is moved into a medium that has specific sensitivities and affordances, as with the vocabulary of touching in Arabic, proper nouns in Chinese, and *Sie* and *du* in German.

On the other hand, Brontë's text can hold out challenges which translators have not yet found a way to meet — as with the Biblical and other intertextualities, and French translations of the French in the novel.

Perhaps the most complex mode of reading afforded by the linguistic plurality of a world work is when translations are found to pursue interesting departures from their sources, and in so doing give new visibility to what they are departing from — as in the handling of free indirect speech across German and Slovenian, the imagining of appearance in Russian, and the presentation of narratorial selfhood in Estonian. The prismatic texts (including the source) can be read in themselves, and in their differences from one another, together.

This case study reveals something that is true of all translation, and that entails collaborative and open-ended practices of research and writing.

All translation invites a littoral reading.

All translation is prismatic translation.

Lives of Some Translators

Many translators have been mentioned, and their work discussed, throughout the volume: please use the index to encounter them. Here, we provide information on only a few of them: those whose translations feature in the book and for whom we were able to gather enough information to exhibit in the form of short biographies. This appendix therefore represents only a tiny proportion of the hundreds of *Jane Eyre* translators that there have been. The aim is to give some sense of the individuals who have dedicated themselves to translating the novel, of their variety, and also of the patchiness of what can be known about them.

Amal Omar Baseem al-Rifayii

Yousif M. Qasmiyeh

Language: Arabic; *Jane Eyre* translation: 2014

Amal Omar Baseem al-Rifayii is the only female Arabic translator of *Jane Eyre* identified throughout the course of the research. Al-Rifayii is Syrian and previously studied Law and Business Administration in Syria and France respectively. She worked for UNESCO and conducted research on various subjects, including on the extent to which the work environment and employees' psychological readiness affect administrative changes at work. In addition to assembling the dictionaries of Diplomatic and Legal Idioms, Administrative and Economic Idioms (both in Arabic-English and English-Arabic), Idioms of Business Administration, and Samples of Commercial Correspondences (English-Arabic), al-Rifayii has translated selected poems by the Brontë sisters, *The Snows of Kilimanjaro* by Hemingway, *A Child in the Grave* by Andersen, *The Unforgotten One* by Montgomery, *God Sees the Truth, But Waits* by Tolstoy, and *The McWilliamses and the Burglar Alarm* by Twain.

Yousif Ata Al-Tarifi

Yousif M. Qasmiyeh

Language: Arabic; *Jane Eyre* translation: 2017

Yousif Ata Al-Tarifi is a prolific author who has written extensively on classical as well as contemporary topics ranging from classical Arabic literature and grammar to modernist Arab literary figures, including the lives and writings of Jibran Khalil Jibran (Lebanon), Ibrahim Touqan (Palestine), Abu Al-Qasim Al-Shaabi (Egypt/Tunisia), Ahmad Shawqi (Egypt), Badr Shakir Al-Sayaab (Iraq), and Nazik Al-Malaa'eka (Iraq). There is limited information about his education (although it seems likely he completed Arabic studies). Some of Al-Tarifi's translations beyond *Jane* Eyre include *Christ Recrucified* by Nikos Kazantzakis (2017), *Metamorphosis, and The Trial* and *Letter to His Father* by Kafka. I am of the opinion that Al-Tarifi has only translated texts from English, including the works of Kazantzakis and Kafka.

Munīr' al-Baʿalbakī (1918–1999)

Yousif M. Qasmiyeh

Language: Arabic; *Jane Eyre* translation: 1985

Munīr' al-Baʿalbakī is easily considered a giant of the field and is nicknamed the 'sheikh of translators in the modern era' by fellow translators, literary critics and philologists alike. From the translations of *Jane Eyre* that I have reviewed (circa 10), the vast majority of these translations relied extensively on al-Baʿalbakī 1988 translation. It is as if Baalbaki's translation had become 'the original of the original' by virtue of constituting itself as a new canon within translation studies in Arabic. Baalbaki read Arabic literature and Islamic studies at the American University of Beirut (AUB) and pursued further postgraduate studies in Baghdad where he also taught and further acquainted himself with Pan-Arabism. He founded, with his friend Baheej Othman, the publishing house Dar El Ilm Lilmalayin (House of Education for the Millions) which has continued to publish his English-Arabic dictionary *Al-Mawrid* (now in different formats; complete, concise, pocket, bilingual, middle-sized, etc) which has exceeded its 40th edition. He translated more than a hundred books from English, including *The Story of My Experiments with Truth* by M. Ghandi, *A Tale of Two Cities* by Dickens, *A Farewell to Arms, The Old Man and the Sea* and *The Snows of Kilimanjaro* by Hemingway, *A History of Socialist Thought* by G.D. Cole, *The Iron Heel* by Jack London, and *History of the Arabs* by P. Hitti.

Amīr Masʿūd Barzīn (1920–2010)

Kayvan Tahmasebian

Language: Persian; *Jane Eyre* translation: 1950

Masʿūd Barzīn was an Iranian journalist who became director-general of the former National Iranian Radio and Television, the first director of The Iranian Trade Union of Writers and Journalists, the cultural coordinator in the Indian Embassy in Tehran, the general director of the Iranian Queen's Public Relations Office. He also translated Charles Dickens's *Oliver Twist* and Margaret Mitchell's *Gone with the Wind*, several books about Indian culture, Gandhi and his non-cooperation movement. He edited a glossary of journalism in Persian.

Masʿūd Barzīn's 1950 translation is interesting as a prototype to the numerous retranslations of *Jane Eyre* into Persian. It is also interesting in that, although abridged, it remained the only translation available to the Persian readership for around three decades. In his brief introductory note, the translator explains that 'he has abridged and then translated the work for several reasons. It should be noted that nothing of the matter of the story is lost; I only omitted secondary and tertiary subjects in this masterpiece which are not interesting to the Persian reader'.[1]

Marie von Borch (1853–1895)

Mary Frank

Language: German; *Jane Eyre* translation: 1887

An experienced translator of Scandinavian literature, including Hamsun's *Sult* (1890), Von Borch seems to have translated mainly from Norwegian, and *Jane Eyre* seems to be her only translation from English. Her translation from Norwegian to German of Alexander L. Kielland's *Siesta* was translated into English by Charles Flint McClumpha and published in *Modern Ghosts* (1890).

Georgia Deligiannē-Anastasiadēs (1904–1998)

Eleni Philippou

Language: Greek; *Jane Eyre* translation: 1963

Deligiannē-Anastasiadēs was a poet and translator born in Smyrna, Asia Minor, in 1904. After completing her secondary schooling in Smyrna, she moved to Athens. As a journalist she worked with many magazines of the time under the aliases 'Zoe' and 'Louise'. Her poem 'Lament' was set to music by the Greek composer Mikis Theodorakis and included in

1 *Jane Eyre: Yatim* [Orphan] (Tehran: Maʿrefat, 1950), p. 4.

the album 'Songs of the Match'. She translated more than forty literary works, including books by Cervantes, Victor Hugo, Karl Marx, and Honore de Balzac. She died in Athens in 1998.[2]

Emilia Dobrzańska, née Karczewska (1852–1925)

Kasia Szymanska

Language: Polish; *Jane Eyre* translation: 1880

Dobrzańska was a Polish noblewoman, translator from French and English, and educational activist. Educated in a school for girls in Piotrków Trybunalski, then part of Congress Poland within the Russian Partition, Dobrzańska stayed on as a teacher of botany and French after her graduation. After the Russian authorities closed down the school, she opened her own one and continued to fight for independent education in Poland. Besides translating French writers such as Henry Gréville, Réné de Pont-Jest, and André Valdés, she also translated English works, most notably, Shakespeare's *Venus and Adonis*. Her translation of *Jane Eyre*, probably based on the French rendering by Noëmi Lesbazeilles Souvestre from 1854, was published in instalments (1880–1881) in the weekly *Tydzień* edited by her husband Mirosław Dobrzański.[3]

Maria Faleńska, neé Trębicka (Trembicka) (1821–1896)

Kasia Szymanska

Language: Polish; *Jane Eyre* translation: 1865

A Polish novelist active in the literary circles of nineteenth-century Warsaw, translator from English, Italian and French, and author (under various pseudonyms) of features and columns for Warsaw and Cracow-based newspapers. Besides the first Polish rendering of *Jane Eyre*, her translations include Charles Dickens' *Dombey and Son*, Lady Georgiana Fullerton's *Lady-bird* and Giovanni Verga's *Eros*. Daughter of Stanisław Trębicki, one of the Polish generals leading the 1830–1831 November Uprising against the Russian Empire; a long-time correspondent and friend of Polish Romantic poet Cyprian Kamil Norwid; married to

2 Hellenic Authors' Society, *Georgia Deligiannē-Anastasiadēs*, https://www.authors.gr/deligianni_anastasiadi_gewrgia-article-574.html?category_id=15

3 Dagmara Hadyna, 'A Relayed Translation. Looking for the Source Text of the First Polish Translation of Charlotte Brontë's *Jane Eyre*', *Studia Litteraria Universitatis Iagellonicae Cracoviensis* 11.2 (2016), 73–81; Monika Roszkowska, 'The Evolution of Translation Standards as Illustrated by the History of Polish Translations of *Jane Eyre* by Charlotte Brontë,' *Crossroads. A Journal of English Studies* 2 (2013), 43–57.

Felicjan Medard Faleński, a representative of Polish Parnassianism, poet, playwright and translator.

Carmen Martín Gaite (1925–2000)

Andrés Claro

Language: Spanish; *Jane Eyre* translation: 1999

Carmen Martín Gaite was a well-known, award-winning Spanish novelist who also wrote criticism and translated prose from the French, English, Italian, and Portuguese languages. She was educated privately, with strong influence from her father, a liberal notary who did not want her to be educated by religious institutions. After the Civil War, she would be educated at the Women's Institute of Salamanca and go on to study Literature and Philology at the University of Salamanca. Giving up her academic career, she travelled widely in several European countries and devoted herself to writing fiction (novels and short stories). In 1978 she was the first woman to obtain the National Prize for Literature with her book *The Back Room*. She wrote literary criticism and scripts for Spanish television series (*Santa Teresa de Jesús; Celia*). In addition to her translation of *Jane Eyre*, for which she posthumously received the Ángel Crespo annual award for best translation in Catalonia (2000), she translated *Mme. Bovary*, by G. Flaubert; *Tales of Perrault*, by C. Perrault; *To the Lighthouse*, by V. Woolf; *Victorian Fairy Tales*, by J. Ruskin; *Senescence*, by I. Svevo; *The Sailor*, by F. Pessoa; *A Grief Observed*, by C. S. Lewis; *The Periodic System*, by P. Levi; and *French Letters to Merline*, by R. M. Rilke.

Marion Gilbert (1876–1951) and Madeleine Duvivier (dates unknown)

Céline Sabiron, Léa Rychen and Vincent Thiery

Language: French; *Jane Eyre* translation: 1919

These names are both pseudonyms. Marion Gilbert was in fact called Odette Bussard, born Maurel, and Madeleine Duvivier was Madeleine Noémi Tournier, born Maurel. They were sisters, daughters of a Protestant pastor and a British mother, who died when Odette was three years old. They were both actively involved in feminist movements (as early as the 1910s), but there is no archive on Madeleine Duvivier.

Marion Gilbert founded with George Sand's granddaughter, Aurore Sand, 'the George Sand Club', a charitable organization for women of letters. She became a member of the first women's gourmet club called 'Les Belles Perdrix' and one of the first contributors to the collection of recipes of the same name, published in 1930. In the same year, she participated in the exhibition of writers and painters, along with Lucie Delarue-Mardrus and Anna de Noailles. She was part of the jury of the Viking Prize and the literary circle named 'La Française'. In the 1930s she took part in the Women's Academy of Letters founded by Marie de Wailly. Interested in writing from a young age, she first worked for local newspapers before writing novels from 1913 (*Le Sang sur la falaise*) onwards. Most of her literary production was published as a serial in *La Petite Illustration*, e.g., *Celle qui s'en va* (1921). She received a couple of prizes, including in 1926 the 'Bookman' prize for her novel entitled *Le Joug* (a prize won the year before by François Mauriac for *Le Désert de l'Amour*). *La Maison du doute* (1929), then considered as one of the best novels written by a female writer, was shortlisted for the Femina Prize, finally awarded to Georges Bernanos. In 1902 she had married Léon Bussard, an agricultural engineer with whom she had three children: the death of one of her sons inspired her collection of poems entitled *Son tombeau* (1936). On top of writing original works, she acted as a translator of English texts, such as *Just Crime* by British journalist and writer of popular fiction Headon Hill (1910) or *Jane Eyre*, published in French in 1919. She is also credited with several translations of Pelham Grenville Wodehouse's and Nicholas Wiseman's works, as well as a translation of Dickens's *David Copperfield* (1924) and *The Adventures of Mr. Pickwick* (1929). Most of her translations were done in collaboration with her sister.[4]

Irina Gavrilovna Gurova, née Gordon (1924–2010)

Eugenia Kelbert

Language: Russian; *Jane Eyre* translation: 1999

Gurova's father was born to an educated family, and knew Latin, Greek, French and German. He was a tutor in the famous art collector Schukin's house. He was later twice arrested by the Soviets as a 'spy', and at Solovki prison camp shared a cell with the renowned Russian linguist Dmitrii Likhachev. He translated Maupassant, and worked at the publishing house Academia. Gurova's mother came from a merchant/clergy family. She worked as a housekeeper at a special needs' home for children, and later as a watchwoman. Gurova's aunt, an actress, had access to the library for actors, which was not overly censored. At this library, Gurova first read English literature in translation, e.g., Poe.

4 https://fr.wikipedia.org/wiki/Marion_Gilbert

Gurova graduated from the Moscow State University in French and German in 1947, and taught English at a high school until 1956. Her first translation, a story by Jack London, was published in 1954. She translated Faulkner, Austen, Steinbeck, Wodehouse, Poe, King, other classics, as well as several writers of sci-fi and fantasy, and edited numerous translations.

Toni Hill (1966-)

Andrés Claro

Language: Spanish; *Jane Eyre* translation: 2009

Toni Hill, a graduate in psychology, is a Spanish writer and translator published by the transnational group Penguin Random House. He is the author of three detective novels starring Inspector Hector Salgado of the Troopers, the autonomous Catalonian police force, in Barcelona: *El verano de los juguetes muertos*, *Los buenos suicidas*, and *Los amantes de Hiroshima*; also of the gothic mystery novel *Los ángeles de hielo* and of the modern thriller *Tigres de cristal*. In addition to *Jane Eyre*, he has translated authors such as David Sedaris, Jonathan Safran Foer, Glenway Wescott, Rosie Alison, Peter May, Rabbih Alameddine, and A. L. Kennedy.[5]

Sofie Horten (1857–1928)

Ida Klitgård

Language: Danish; *Jane Eyre* translation: 1911

Sofie Horten was one of Denmark's first women journalists. She made her debut as a freelance journalist in 1888 and was later appointed editor of the magazine *Husmoderen* [*The House Wife*] which was to be renamed *Hus og hjem* [*House and Home*]. Sofie Horten was also an active translator of German, Swedish and English books and participant in the movement for women's right to vote.[6]

5 https://es.wikipedia.org/wiki/Toni_Hill
6 http://www.kvinfo.dk/side/597/bio/378/origin/170/

Gabriela Jaworska, now: Iwasyk (b. 1978)

Kasia Szymanska

Language: Polish; *Jane Eyre* translation: 2007

A Kraków-based English teacher, literary translator, blogger, and poet. She graduated from Jagiellonian University in Film studies and Literary Translation. Besides rendering *Jane Eyre*, Jaworska translated Jane Austen's *Mansfield Park*, detective fiction (Sue Grafton), and children's literature (Jenny Nimmo, Wendy Orr).[7]

Helmut Kossodo (1915–1994)

Mary Frank

Language: German; *Jane Eyre* translation: 1979

Kossodo was a Jew who fled from Germany to Switzerland in 1933. He studied music with the aim of becoming a conductor but was interned on the outbreak of war and undertook forced labour. He used inherited money to set up his own publishing business in 1945, specialising in little-known authors. The business went bankrupt in the mid-1970s and he then turned to translating (from French and English) and reviewing.[8]

Noémi Lesbazeilles, née Souvestre (1834–1887)

Céline Sabiron, Léa Rychen & Vincent Thiery

Language: French; *Jane Eyre* translation: 1854

On top of being a good musician, Noëmi Souvestre learnt how to speak both English and German, like most women of her background (middle class) at the time. In 1852 she married Eugène Lesbazeilles, her father's secretary. Lesbazeilles was of reformed religion, and so were many of their friends. According to a friend of the family, Pierre-Paul Guieysse (a French Socialist politician of a Protestant family), Noëmi converted to Protestantism at the end of her life, but he said the same thing for M. Souvestre, while this information has never been confirmed by his other friends.[9] A year and a half after the marriage, on 22 January 1854, the couple had a girl, Suzanne, (who died in 1876) and then on 14 August 1857 a boy, Paul, who mobilised his parents all his life owing to his poor health and life-long depression — this did not prevent him from

---

7 Monika Roszkowska, 'The Evolution of Translation Standards as Illustrated by the History of Polish Translations of *Jane Eyre* by Charlotte Brontë,' *Crossroads. A Journal of English Studies* 2 (2013), 43–57.

8 https://de.wikipedia.org/wiki/Helmut_Kossodo

9 https://ouestfigureshistoriques.wordpress.com/famille-souvestre/noemi-souvestre/

studying brilliantly, and in 1881 he passed the agrégation competitive examination in philosophy ahead of two young men who became famous: Henri Bergson and Jean Jaurès. In 1862 Eugène and Noëmi had another son, Albert, who did not live very long and on 13 January 1865 a girl, Madeleine. In 1864 the Lesbazeilles had moved to Versailles because Noëmi's husband had found a job as a library assistant, and his mother followed them and moved in opposite their house. It seeems that Noëmi's freedom was very limited. At the time Versailles was a rather dull city in which few Parisians wanted to live. Yet, with the arrival of the Charton family in April 1863 a friendly group of people was formed and the families often met. During the 1870 war the Lesbazeilles fled to Roscoff in Britanny where they learnt that their house had been plundered. Her son Paul's health problems and the premature death of her daughter Suzanne affected her health. It is believed Noëmi died of cancer at her home in Versailles on 12 January 1902, followed by her husband two years later (1904).

Very little is known about Noëmi Lesbazeilles-Souvestre's literary life: she is mostly remembered for her translation of *Jane Eyre* published in 1854. It has been praised for its excellent quality and therefore republished many times since its first publication. Contrary to Lesbazeilles-Souvestre's protestations of complete fidelity in the preface to the translation, critic Rachel Williams argued that 'In the translation itself, however, and in contradiction to her stated goal, she actively attempted to construct *Jane Eyre* as a text that is proper both for a female writer to have produced and for female readers to consume by consistently negating the so-called 'masculine' elements she found in the novel. The character of *Jane Eyre* is significantly altered in the translation in ways that bring her more in line with conventional feminine values'.[10] After a very long pause of almost twenty-five years, Noëmi's name reappeared in 1875 with popular scientific texts on wild animals : *Les oiseaux de nuit* (Night Birds), *Le gorille* (The Gorilla), *Le gypaète* (The Bearded Vulture) and *Le tigre* (The Tiger), which appeared in the *Journal de la jeunesse*. Her husband wrote texts of similar content in the same issue. Perhaps some of the texts authored by her husband had been co-written by Noëmi but there is no evidence of this. For example, Hachette et Cie published *Les forêts* (The Forests) by Eugène Lesbazeilles in 1884. Thanks to Colette Cosnier

10 Rachel Williams, 'The Reconstruction of Feminine Values in Mme Lesbazeille-Souvestre's 1854 Translation of *Jane Eyre*', *Translation and Interpreting Studies* 7 (2012), 19–33 (p. 19).

in her book *Le silence des filles: De l'aiguille à la plume* (Fayard, 2001), it is now known that Noëmi translated at least one German author, Friedrich Adolf Krummacher, a writer and theologian who died in 1845 and who wrote books for children and is best known for his *Parables*.

Juan González-Blanco de Luaces (1906–1963)

Andrés Claro

Language: Spanish; *Jane Eyre* translation: 1943

Juan G. de Luaces, a poet and novelist in his own right as well as a literary critic before the Civil War, became one of the most prolific post-war Spanish translators. Raised in a family of intellectuals who had maintained close contacts with prominent representatives of Spanish culture (Ortega y Gasset, the Machados, Unamuno) and a Republican militant in his youth, he published an early book of poems (*Saetas de oro*, 1925), historical novels and biographies (*Los amores de Cleopatra* (1928), *La dramática vida de Miguel Bakunin* (1930)), followed in the post-war years by *La guerra de los sapos* (1947), *La ciudad vertical* (1948), *La nave de los cien condenados* (1949), *La huella de la noche* (1949), and *Un hombre de mucha suerte* (1950). Other of his original post-war literary works, however, did not succeed in evading censorship or were rejected by uneasy editors. It was in this context of 'internal exile' imposed by the changed political situation that, to feed his family and continue writing, Luaces began to translate for several publishing houses, producing more than a hundred literary translations in the 1940s (including a dozen in 1943 alone, the year of his compressed *Jane Eyre*), mainly from English (Chaucer, the Brontës, Dickens, Somerset, Maugham, Conrad, Cooper, Lehmann, Churchill, and others), but also from French, German, Italian, Portuguese, and Russian (Dostoevsky and Turgenev).[11] Luaces, then, must be counted among those writers whose literary careers were curtailed by Franco's dictatorship: he was censored, spent time in prison, and tried to escape to Latin America during the War.

11 Marta Ortega Sáez, 'Juan González-Blanco de Luaces: el traductor desconocido de la posguerra española'. *Arbor*, 740 (2009), 1339–1352; see also Ortega Sáez's PhD thesis, *Traducciones del franquismo en el mercado literario español contemporáneo: el caso de Jane Eyre de Juan G. De Luaces*, Universitat de Barcelona (2013), http://hdl.handle.net/2445/46345

Charlotte Maurat

Céline Sabiron, Léa Rychen & Vincent Thiery

Language: French; *Jane Eyre* translation: 1964

Little is known about Charlotte Maurat and she does not feature in the literary world. She is a contemporary figure, a Brontë fan who has clearly worked a lot on the writer's biography and her world. In the preface to her translation, she warned the reader of her boundless admiration for Charlotte Brontë, using hyperbolic adjectives to describe her style ('splendidly', 'quite exceptional', 'happily treated', 'magnificent', 'incomparable storyteller').[12] Apart from translating *Jane Eyre* in 1964, three years later she wrote a book entitled *The Secret of Brontë: or Charlotte Brontë according to Juvenilia: her letters and those who knew her* (Paris: Buchet-Chastel, 1967). She is not known for any other translations and she does not seem to have worked on any other authors.

Aslaug Møller (Mikkelsen) (1876–1964)

Ida Klitgård

Language: Danish; *Jane Eyre* translation: 1944

Aslaug Møller was a writer and translator. As the first academic in her family, she received a degree in English language and literature from University of Copenhagen in 1903 where she was a student of the internationally acclaimed linguist Otto Jespersen. As a translator of mostly British and American literature, such as George Elliot, Jack London, Upton Sinclair, Harriet Beecher Stowe and Rudyard Kipling, she often wrote under the pseudonym of Aslaug Mikkelsen which was her maiden name. She is also the author of four books on Victorian women, such as *Victoria* (1938), *Tre søstre* [*Three sisters*] (1953) about the Brontë sisters, *Florence Nightingale* (1956) and *Kvindernes Vej gennem Victorias England* [*Women's Way through Victoria's England*] (1959). Throughout her career she was an ardent member of the women's movement in Denmark and worked especially to improve the housing and living conditions for women academics and women students. In 1926 she became chair of the Danish branch of the international Federation of University Women.[13]

---

12 Charlotte Brontë, *Jane Eyre*, trans. by Charlotte Maurat (Paris: Le Livre de Poche, 1944), pp. i–iii.

13 https://kvindebiografiskleksikon.lex.dk/Aslaug_M%C3%B8ller
https://biografiskleksikon.lex.dk/Aslaug_M%C3%B8ller
https://da.wikipedia.org/wiki/Aslaug_Mikkelsen
https://www.litteraturpriser.dk/aut/MAslaugMoeller.htm

Sylvère Monod (1921–2006)

Céline Sabiron, Léa Rychen & Vincent Thiery

Language: French; *Jane Eyre* translation: 1966

As a laureate (aged only 21) of the Agrégation competitive examination for entry into the teaching profession in France and a specialist of Charles Dickens (on whom he focused his PhD thesis, also writing a seminal book on *Dickens the Novelist*, published in France by Hachette in 1953, and in the USA by Oklahoma University Press in 1968), he taught in secondary schools, then lectured at Université de Caen (1949–1964) where he greatly contributed to the rebirth of Université de Basse-Normandie, which had been destroyed by the war. He was then appointed full professor at Université Sorbonne (Paris III) from 1964 to 1982, i.e. until his retirement, and after a brief period at Université Paris VIII, of which he was one of the founders. As an academic he dedicated his time to the writers of the nineteenth century, and then of the twentieth, as his *History of English Literature from Victoria to Elizabeth II* (1970) shows. He had two passions for two different writers, both of major importance in the English literary heritage: Dickens and Conrad. In order to make them better known and loved by French-speaking readers, he made translations of them for the Bibliothèque de la Pléiade. He also worked on texts by Emily and Charlotte Brontë, Walter Scott and Shakespeare. His translations were usually accompanied by a comprehensive preface and extensive notes. He also translated more contemporary authors such as Peter Ackroyd among others.

A former president of the foreign literatures committee of the National Book Center (Centre National du Livre, CNL), a member of the association promoting literary translation (Assises de la Traduction Littéraire en ArleS, ATLAS), founded in 1984 under the aegis of the Association of the Literary Translators of France—of which he was president from 1989 to 1992—, Sylvère Monod was awarded the 'Grand Prix national de la traduction' for his commitment to translation. He wrote a novel, *Madame Homais*, published by Belfond in 1988.[14]

---

14 https://fr.wikipedia.org/wiki/Sylv%C3%A8re_Monod https://www.cairn.info/revue-etudes-anglaises-2006-3-page-383.htm

Luise Hemmer Pihl (1940–)

Ida Klitgård

Language: Danish; *Jane Eyre* translation: 2016

She has a degree in English and Italian from Aarhus University and is a translator. She has translated from Italian, French and English, such as Charlotte Brontë's *The Professor* and Jane Austen's *Northanger Abbey*. She is the owner of the small publishing house Grevas Forlag.[15]

Christiane Rohde (1944–)

Ida Klitgård

Language: Danish; *Jane Eyre* translation: 2015

Christiane Rohde is a Danish actor. She made her breakthrough as the particularly stupid kitchen maid Miss Hollenberg in the famous Danish TV series *Matador* (1978–81). In 1969 she married the Danish artist Per Arnoldi. Besides *Jane Eyre*, she has also translated works by H. Rider Haggard, Anne Tyler, Margaret Mitchell, E.M. Forster, Lewis Carroll and Wilkie Collins.[16]

Jesús Sánchez Díaz (1901–1981)

Andrés Claro

Language: Spanish; *Jane Eyre* translation: 1974

Jesús Sánchez Díaz (Caudete, 1901–1981) was born into a family of day labourers to illiterate parents. He was educated from an early age in religious institutions (Carmelite friars) at his mother's insistence, and in 1912 entered a Salesian school, where he would be a student and teacher for the next decade, ultimately declining to enter the priesthood. In 1926 he returned to Caudete, where he established a private school as well as undertaking other work in notaries and unions. He was editor of the weekly publication *El Ideal Caudetano* and was elected as a council member. Between 1930 and 1934 he worked as a teacher on Gran Canaria and in various Spanish towns, returning after the Civil War once again to Caudete, where he continued to be employed as a schoolteacher. It was then that, out of financial necessity, he began to produce translations from French and Italian commissioned by Ediciones Paulinas, including several ascetic and apostolic books (he also wrote biographies of Blanca de Castilla and Pope John XXIII commissioned by the same Catholic publisher). In addition to his condensed paraphrase of *Jane Eyre*, which relied heavily

15 http://danskforfatterleksikon.dk/1850/PLuisePihl.htm
16 https://da.wikipedia.org/wiki/Christiane_Rohde
https://danskefilm.dk/skuespiller.php?id=190

on Antonini's earlier compressed version first published in Buenos Aires (1941), his abridged versions of English works include titles such as *Uncle Tom's Cabin* and *Robinson Crusoe*. He was a regular contributor to the magazine *Moros y Cristianos* and wrote a *History of Caudete*.

Zofia Sawicka, a.k.a. Zofja Sawicka

Kasia Szymanska

Language: Polish; *Jane Eyre* translation: 1921

Polish novelist, translator, compiler and editor of children's literature active during the Interwar period. She was affiliated with the literary circles in Lviv, then part of Poland, as well as the publishing press Kultura i sztuka (Culture and Art) run by Hermana Stachel.

She translated multiple books by Karl May, Jacob Grimm's fairy tales and Rudolf Raspe's tall tales about Baron Münchhausen. She also compiled and edited several books with fantastical tales, most notably *Świat czarów* (*The World of Wonders*) featuring Hans Christian Andresen, Charles Dickens, and Rudyard Kipling. Her novels focused on individual experiences of Polish women, e.g., *Paniątko* (*Little Miss)*, Sielanka aktorka (*The Idyll of an Actress*), Czwarte krzesło (*The Fourth Chair*), *Idealistka* (*The Idealist Woman*). Her version of *Jane Eyre* for a juvenile audience with illustrations was entitled *Sierota z Lowood* (*An Orphan from Lowood*) and first published in Lviv in 1921, but then also printed by Warsaw and Chrzanów presses.[17]

Vera Oskarovna Stanevich (1890–1967)

Eugenia Kelbert

Language: Russian; *Jane Eyre* translation: 1950

Vera Oskarovna Stanevich was a poet and one of the foremost 20th century translators of Western European and American literature into Russian. She was educated at the Moscow Higher Courses for Women (Philosophy). Before her long career as a literary translator, she had her first literary life as a Silver Age symbolist poet, and published a number of short stories in 1917. (Five of her poems appeared in an almanac alongside those of Pasternak and others in 1913.) Stanevich was the wife of another minor symbolist, Anisimov, who himself translated Langston

17 Irena Gruchała, 'Herman Stachel – lwowski wydawca piśmiennictwa popularnego', *Folia Toruniensia* 18 (2018), 35–56; Bogumiła Krassowska, Alina Grefkowicz, *Bibliografia literatury dla dzieci i młodzieży, 1918–1939: literatura polska i przekłady* (Warsaw: Biblioteka Publiczna m. st. Warszawy/The Public Library of Warsaw City, 1995), pp. 9, 304, 331, 424–25.

Hughes and Rilke's *Das Stunden-Buch* (with Stanevich and under Pasternak's guidance). Their apartment became a salon frequented by the likes of Bely, Pasternak, Esenin, Mayakovsky and others. With her husband, Stanevich founded the literary group Serdara, which included Pasternak among its members. She was also known, then, as an extravagant woman who tended to defy gender norms (by wearing trousers sometimes etc.) and was hopelessly in love with Andrei Bely.[18] She was an active member of the literary circles of the time, which must have been a formative part of her training as a literary professional and ultimately translator. She worked at the Rumyantsev museum in 1919–20.

She was also, for several years, a prominent anthroposophist and a student of Steiner, whom she also started to translate towards the end of her life[19] (her anthroposophy group was on the hook of the OGPU). A fellow anthroposophist recalls her generous nature full of idiosyncrasies and contradictions. She was the adopted daughter of the head of the Penza hospital and, it seems, encouraged rumours that she had been abandoned by gypsies (the same friend attributes a prophetic ability to Stanevich, which she allegedly mistrusted and repressed). Her son, Boris, died in 1934 of scarlet fever; her husband, Anisimov, in 1940.

Under her maiden name, Stanevich published translations of Goethe (*Egmont*), Heine, Brontë, Thomas Mann's *The Magic Mountain*, Balzac, Feuchtwanger, Remarque, Kafka etc., and was a member of the Soviet literary establishment (Union of Translators). Stanevich wrote two theoretical articles about translation.[20]

Teresa Świderska

Kasia Szymanska

Language: Polish; *Jane Eyre* translation: 1930

A Polish translator from English and author of children's literature. Her other translations include Walter Scott's *Waverley*, *Rob Roy*, and *The Bride of Lammermoor*, Charles Dickens's *David Copperfield* and *A Tale of Two Cities*, as well as Woodrow Wilson's memoirs. She wrote a children's book entitled *Pamiętniki Neptuna: Opowiadania dla dzieci, które lubią psy* (Neptune's Memoirs: Short Stories for Children Who Like Dogs).[21]

18 http://mpgu.su/graduates/stanevich-vera-oskarovna/
19 http://www.rmuseum.ru/data/authors/a/anisimovavo.php
20 http://feb-web.ru/feb/kle/kle-abc/ke7/ke7-1412.htm
21 Monika Roszkowska, 'The Evolution of Translation Standards as Illustrated by the History of Polish Translations of *Jane Eyre* by Charlotte Brontë,' *Crossroads. A Journal of English Studies* 2 (2013), 43–57.

Pipina Tsimikalē (1903–1987)

Eleni Philippou

Language: Greek; *Jane Eyre* translation: 1969

An important Greek writer born in Gytheio in the Peloponnese. She is primarily known as a children's writer and poet, but she has written works for adults too. She published many volumes of fairy tales with Astir and Ankyra publishing houses. Her translations include Harriet Beecher-Stowe, Alexandre Dumas, and Charlotte Brontë. She died in 1987, after receiving multiple honours, such as awards from Children's Book Circle (Κύκλο Παιδικού Βιβλίου) and Women's Literary Society (Γυναικεία Λογοτεχνική Συντροφιά).[22]

Irinarkh Vvedenskiĭ (1813–1855)

Eugenia Kelbert

Language: Russian; *Jane Eyre* translation: 1849

Vvedenskiĭ himself experienced much that must have made him empathetic to topics and opinions expressed in *Jane Eyre*. He was a skilled teacher who was responsible for the literary education of military cadets. He had first-hand experience of poverty and also of an institution not dissimilar to Lowood. At age eight, he was sent to a seminary, where he was taught Russian grammar, Latin, Ancient Greek, arithmetic, theology, church history and singing. However, the teaching methodology was mostly limited to learning lessons by heart and to the rod, as Vvedenskiĭ himself testified. Mostly, Vvedenskiĭ owed his education to his abilities as an autodidact.

He continued his education at the Saratov seminary, where literature, philosophy and theology were taught in Latin. He was among the first in his class and especially enjoyed writing dissertations. In 1834, aged 21, he was qualified to become a priest but chose to enrol as a university student in Moscow. However, he was unable to pursue his university studies due to poverty, and therefore went to a theological academy instead and audited university classes on the side. He was expelled four years later owing to a story that involved his courting a policeman's daughter (a topic Brontë explored!). Poverty-stricken, he was aided by a university professor who enrolled him as a student and hired him as a teacher. The professor also used him as a translator for his publications.

The famous nineteeth century poet Afanasii Fet wrote of him that he spoke Latin as fluently as Russian and also mastered written German,

22 https://el.wikipedia.org/wiki/Πιπίνα Τσιμικάλη

French, English and Italian, despite an abhorrent accent in these languages. Upon leaving for St Petersburg, Vvedenskiĭ was finally able to get a university degree and was charged with the instruction and the development of the course of literary study for military institutions. At the same time, Osip Senkovskiĭ engaged him as translator and critic for his *Biblioteka dlia chteniia* periodical.

Vvedenskiĭ 's interest in English literature was originally due to his conviction that it had influenced Russian literature. He and a friend initially learned the language by themselves (like Mary and Diana, without any other master than the dictionary), and then got a native-speaker teacher. Vvedenskiĭ translated Thackeray and several of Charles Dickens' novels, among other things, alongside his teaching job and occasional critical writings. He is also credited with being among the first translation theorists in Russia.

In 1853, Vvedenskiĭ took a voyage across Europe and spent 3 months in Germany, France and England. He hated Paris and loved London, although his planned meeting with Dickens did not take place as both he and Thackeray were away that month.

His translations of English authors are lively and accurate (except when they are not, as Vvedenskiĭ considered it his job to change and improve the original, as he claimed, in its own spirit). His translations use characteristic language, which his contemporaries criticised as too colloquial.

Vvedenskiĭ described his own productivity as non-stop working for ten hours a day. By 1851, he estimated having translated 5248 pages alongside teaching for 23 hours a week. No wonder that soon after his return from Europe, his strained sight gave way and he went blind, his health weakened and eventually, he died. He was only 42.

Melanie Walz (1953–)

Mary Frank

Language: German; *Jane Eyre* translation: 2015

Walz has been translating prolifically from French and English since the 1980s. She won the Zuger translation prize in 1999 for her translation of John Cowper Powys' *Weymouth Sands*, the Heinrich Maria Ledig-Rowohlt prize in 2001 (in particular for her translations of works by A.S. Byatt), and a literary grant in 2005 from the City of Munich for her translation of texts by Marcel Proust. She received the City of Munich translation prize the same year. Mainly translates living authors, but has translated Virginia Woolf, Jane Austen and Dickens.[23]

Yu JongHo 유 종호 (1935–)

Sowon S. Park

Language: Korean; *Jane Eyre* translations: 1970, 2004

One of Korea's major 'new' literary critics. Former Chair of Korean Literature at Yonsei University, Professor of English at Ewha University and the 36th President of the Korean National Academy of Arts. He debuted with *Valley of Language* (언어의 유곡(幽谷)) in 1957 in *Verbal Art* (문학예술). He is author and translator of over 100 books including *What is Literature?* and *The Pessimism of Korea*. His most influential critical essays were republished in a five-volume collection in 1995 (*The Collected Critical Essays of Yu JongHo* vol 1–5). He was awarded, among others, the *Order of Silver Cultural Merit* in 2001, the *Inchon* Prize for Literature in 2002 and the *Manhae* Prize in 2007.[24] Yu's Korean translation of *Jane Eyre* (Seoul: Dongwha Press, 1970; 2nd edition, 1973) was awarded the Best Translation of British Classics prize by the *Translation Evaluation Committee* of the *Research Society of British and American Literatures* (1995-) in 2004. Funded by the Korean National Research Foundation (대한학술 진흥재단, 韓國學術進興財團), a 44 member committee drew up a short list of 36 best translations between independence (1945) and 2003. Prizes were awarded to 14 works in American literature and 22 in British Literature. *Jane Eyre* was among the 22 titles and 25 translations of *Jane Eyre* were closely read and evaluated. Judges pointed to the precision and accuracy of his words, the text's fidelity to the original and praised his concerted effort to recreate as much nuance as possible as well as the preservation of the overall flow in the longer sentences. After Yu won this award, he revised the 1973 version, in which he used ornate and literary Chinese vocabulary, producing a more up-to-date modern Korean translation (Minum Press: Seoul).

---

23 https://de.wikipedia.org/wiki/Melanie_Walz

24 http://www.naa.go.kr/site/eng/naa/member/view?memId=273

List of Translations

This list is drawn from many sources: WorldCat, https://www.worldcat.org/; UNESCO's Index Translationum, and all the national library catalogues associated with the languages in the list. Translations have also been found in other sources: when this has happened it is recorded in the notes. The German section is indebted to Stefanie Hohn, *Charlotte Brontës Jane Eyre in deutscher Übersetzung. Geschichte eines kulturellen Transfers* (Tübingen: Narr, 1998) and Lynne Tatlock, *Jane Eyre in German Lands: The Import of Romance, 1848–1918* (New York: Bloomsbury Academic, 2022); the Spanish section is indebted to Marta Ortega Sáez, *Traducciones del franquismo en el mercado literario español contemporáneo: el caso de Jane Eyre de Juan G. De Luaces* (PhD thesis, Universitat de Barcelona, 2013). All the co-authors of this volume, together with the other participants in the project recorded in the Acknowledgements, have provided data for this list. Particular contributions have been made by Hongtao Wang and his students who researched the vast number of recent Chinese translations, Karolina Gurevich, who unravelled the complicated history of re-editions in Russian, and Jay Dillon who shared his unique knowledge of the earliest translations in several languages.

The work of compiling and correcting the list was done by Rachel Dryden, Eleni Philippou, Chelsea Haith, Joseph Hankinson and Matthew Reynolds.

The rules of thumb that we have used to distinguish translations from adaptations, versions and other kinds of re-working are explained in Chapter I (where the fuzziness of this distinction is also explained). Under 'known reprints' we make no distinction between 'reprints' and 'new editions': that distinction can be complex, and in most cases we do not have exact enough information to make it. There will undoubtedly be translations that we have missed, especially in languages that are not a focus of this volume. The list does not claim to be perfect and complete; rather, it represents the corpus on which we have based our research.

Afrikaans

2005 *Jane Eyre*. Cape Town, Oxford University Press Southern Africa
Translator: Antoinette Stimie

Known reprint: 2013

Notes: Abridged; juvenile edition

Albanian

2003 *Xhein Airi/Jane Eyre*. Tirana, Unknown
Translator: Dritan Koka

2014 *Xhein Airi/Jane Eyre* Tirana, Pegi
Translator: Alina Karaulli

Amharic

1981 *Žén'éyer/Jane Eyre*. Addis Ababa, Bolé Mātamiya Bét
Translator: Unknown

Arabic

1956 جين اير/*Jane Eyre*. Cairo, Kitābī Series
Translator: Ismāʿīl Kāmil

1965 جين اير/*Jane Eyre*. Cairo, Egyptian Radio Station
Translator: Nūr al-Dimirdāsh

1984 جين اير/*Jane Eyre, or a Tale of an Orphan*. Beirut, Al-Mʿārif Press
Translator: Unnamed group of translators

Known reprint: 2008

1985 جين ايير/*Jane Eyre*. Beirut, Dār Al-ʿIlm Lil-Malāyīn
Translator: Munīr al-Baʿalbakī

Known Reprint: 2006

Notes: 2006 edition published simultaneously in Casablanca, by Al-Markaz al-Thaqāfī Al-ʿArabī, and Beirut, by Dār Al-ʿIlm Lil-Malāyīn, in memory of Munīr al-Baʿalbakī (1919–1999); n.d. print on demand edition, جَين إير/*Jane Eyre*, Morroco, Maktabat al-Yusr (this is an online bookshop offering print on demand).

1993 جين اير/*Jane Eyre*. Cairo, Dār al-Hilāl
Translator: Nabīl Rāghib

Known reprints: 1996, 2007

Notes: Bilingual edition; later editions are with Al-Gharīb Publishing House

1999 جين اير/*Jane Eyre*. Damascus, Dār al-Biḥār/Cairo, Dār Wa Maktabat Al-Hilāl
Translator: Unnamed

Notes: Abridged; bilingual edition, joint publication

2004 جين اير/*Jane Eyre*. Cairo, Al Usra Press
Translator: Ṣabrī al-Faḍl

Notes: Juvenile edition

2005 جين اير/*Jane Eyre*. Amman, Al-Ahliyya Press
Translator: Samīr Izzat Naṣṣār

2010 جين اير/*Jane Eyre*. Beirut, Dār Al-Ḥarf al-ʿArabī
Translator: Riḥāb ʿAkāwī

2012 جين اير/*Jane Eyre*. Cairo, Modern Arab Foundation
Translator: Ḥilmī Murād

2014 قصة جين اير/*Story of Jane Eyre*. Kuwait City, Dār Nāshirī Lil Nashr al-Ilikitrūni
Translator: Amal al-Rifāʿī

Notes: Electronic version

2016 جين اير/*Jane Eyre*. Dubai, Dār Al Hudhud Publishing and Distribution
Translator: Unknown

Notes: Translation of a simplified original (English) version of a graphic novel; Author listed as Jill Tavens

2016 جين اير/*Jane Eyre*. Giza, Bayt al-Lughāt al-Duwaliyya
Translator: Unknown

Notes: Bilingual edition, used to teach English

2017 جين اير/*Jane Eyre*. Aleppo, Dār al-Nahj/Dār al-Firdaws
Translator: Aḥmad Nabīl al-Anṣārī

Notes: Abridged

2017 جين اير/*Jane Eyre*. Amman, Al-Ahliya Press
Translator: Yūsif ʿAṭā al-Ṭarīfī

2017 جين اير/*Jane Eyre*. Cairo, Dār al-Alif Publishing House for Printing and Distribution
Translator: Unknown

Armenian

1908 *Chēyn Ēyr*. Erevan, Tpagrutʻiwn H. Mattʻēosean
Translator: Marinos H Stampōlluean

1959 *Jeyn Ēyr*. Erevan, Haypethrat
Translator: Aram Budaghyan

Known reprints: 1988, 2018.

Notes: Source for the 1959 edition: Jay Dillon Rare Books + Manuscripts

Assamese

1999 জেন আয়ার/*Jane Eyre*. Kamrup Metropolitan, Pūrbāñcal Prakāś
Translator: Subhadra Baruwa

Notes: Possibly abridged

Azeri

2013 *Ceyn Eyr*. Baku, Qanun, 'Äli vä Nino'
Translator: Nadir Bədəlov

Notes: Translated from Russian (probably one of the Stanevich, Stanevich-Gurova or Gurova translations). Source: Jay Dillon Rare Books + Manuscripts

Basque

1998 *Jane Eyre*. Guipúzcoa, Elkarlanean
Translator: Iñaki Mendiguren

Known reprint: 2011

Notes: Possibly abridged

Bengali

1977 জেন আয়ার/*Jane Eyre*. Dhaka, Muktadhārā Press
Translator: Suraiya Akhtar Begum

Notes: Abridged

1990 জেন আয়ার/*Jane Eyre*. Dhaka, Muktadhārā Press
Translator: Kabir Chaudhuri

Notes: Abridged

1991 জেন আয়ার/*Jane Eyre*. Kolkata, Dēv Sāhitya Kuṭār
Translator: Sudhīndranāth Rāhā

Notes: Abridged

2006 কিশোর ক্লাসিক জেন আয়ার লিটল উইমেন ভ্যানিটি ফেয়ার/*Teenager Classics: Jane Eyre, Little Women, Vanity Fair*. Dhaka, Sebā Prakāśanī
Translator: Qazi Shahnoor Husain

Notes: Abridged

2010 শালর্ট ব্রন্টি জেন আয়ার/*Charlotte Brontë: Jane Eyre*. Dhaka, Pāñjērī Pāblikēśans
Translator: Dhrub Nīl

Notes: Abridged and illustrated: 'Teenage Classics Series'

2011 শালর্ট ব্রন্টি জেন আয়ার/*Charlotte Brontë: Jane Eyre*. Dhaka, Phrēṇḍs Buk Karṇār
Translator: Khurram Hosahim

2018 শালর্ট ব্রন্টি পাঠকনন্দিতা ও শিল্পোত্তীর্ণা উপন্যাস জেন আয়ার/*Charlotte Brontë's Delightful and Artistic Novel: Jane Eyre*. Dhaka, Biśbasāhitya Bhaban
Translation: Muhaq Zakir
Notes: Abridged, edition for teenagers

2019 শালর্ট ব্রন্টি জেন আয়ার/*Charlotte Brontë: Jane Eyre*. Dhaka, Uttaraṇ
Translator: Sālēhā Chowdhury
Notes: Abridged

Bulgarian

1959 *Джейн Еър/Jane Eyre*. Sofia, Nar. kultura
Translator: Hristo K'nev
Known reprint: 1979

2013 *Джейн Еър: автобиография/Jane Eyre: An Autobiography*. Sofia, Šambala
Translator: Natalya Georgieva, Dimit'r Tonin & Silvia Serafimova Velikova

Burmese

1953 *Gyain-è-yà/Jane Eyre*. Rangoon, Burma Translation Society
Translator: Unknown

Catalan

1992 *Jane Eyre*. Barcelona, Proa
Translator: Maria Dolors Ventós
Known reprints: 1996, 2010
Note: 2010 edition is with Labutxaca

2001 *Jane Eyre*. Barcelona, Columna
Translator: Jordi Arbonès i Montull

2010 *Jane Eyre*. Barcelona, Teide
Translator: Anna Llisterri

Chinese

1925 重光记/*Chong guang ji/Seeing Light Again*. Shanghai, Dadong Press
Translator: Shoujuan Zhou (周瘦鹃)

1935 孤女飘零记/*Gunv piaolingji/Record of a Wandering Orphan*. Shanghai, Commercial Press
Translator: Guangjian Wu (伍光建)
Known reprints: 1977, 2013
Notes: 2013 reprinted as 简爱/*Jianai/Jane Eyre* with Jilin, Shidai Wenyi Press

1936 简爱自传/*Jianai zizhuan*/*Jane Eyre: An Autobiography*. Shanghai, Shenghuo Shudian
Translator: Jiye Li (李霁野)

Known reprints: 1952, 1982

Notes: 1952 reprinted as 简爱/*Jianai zizhuan*/*Jane Eyre* with Wenhua Shenghuo Press; 182 reprint is with Shanxi Renmin Press in Beijing

1954 简爱/*Jianai*/*Jane Eyre*. Taipei, Taipei Xinxing Press
Translator: Fang Li (李方)

1961 简爱/*Jianai*/*Jane Eyre*. Taipei, Taipei Dazhongguo Press
Translator: Wen Li (李文)

1963 简爱/*Jianai*/*Jane Eyre*. Taipei, Taipei Wenhua Press
Translator: Weitang Lin (林维堂)

1971 简爱/*Jianai*/*Jane Eyre*. Kaohsiung, Gaoxiong Dazhong Press
Translator: Zhicheng Zhang (张志成)

1972 简爱/*Jianai*/*Jane Eyre*. Tainan, Tainan Xinshiji Press
Translator: Xiaomei Xu (许小美)

1973 简爱/*Jianai*/*Jane Eyre*. Tainan, Tainan Wangjia Press
Translator: Ninglan Lin (林宁兰)

1975 简爱/*Jianai*/*Jane Eyre*. Tainan, Tainan Biaozhun Press
Translator: Mengdai Zhao (赵梦黛)

1975 简爱/*Jianai*/*Jane Eyre*. Taipei, Taipei Wuzhou Press
Translator: Yundai Liu (刘云迨)

Known reprint: 1984

1975 简爱/*Jianai*/*Jane Eyre*. Taipei, Taipei Qingliu Press
Translator: Zhong Wen (文仲)

1980 简爱/*Jianai*/*Jane Eyre*. Shanghai, Shanghai Yiwen press
Translator: Qingying Zhu (祝庆英)

1983 简爱/*Jianai*/*Jane Eyre*. Shenyang, Liaoning Meishu Press
Translator: Zunyi Li (李遵义)

Notes: Comic book; adapted

1988 简爱/*Jianai*/*Jane Eyre*. Taipei, Taipei Zhiwen Press
Translator: Xuting Liang (梁绪婷)

1990 简爱/*Jianai*/*Jane Eyre*. Beijing, Renmin Wenxue Press
Translator: Junxie Wu (吴钧燮)

Known reprints: 2019

Notes: 2019 reprinted with Taipei, Xinchaoshe Wenhua Shiye

1991 简爱/*Jianai*/*Jane Eyre*. Hangzhou, Zhejiang Wenyi Press
Translator: Wen Ling (凌雯)

1993 简爱/*Jianai*/*Jane Eyre*. Fuzhou, Haixia Wenyi Press
Translator: Derong Li (李德荣)

1994 简爱/*Jianai*/*Jane Eyre*. Nanjing, Yilin press
Translator: Yuanshen Huang (黄源深)

1995 简爱/*Jianai*/*Jane Eyre*. Jilin, Shidai Wenyi Press
Translator: Hong Liang (梁虹)

1995 简爱/*Jianai*/*Jane Eyre*. Chengdu, Sichuan Renmin Press
Translator: Naixiu Sun (孙乃修)
Notes: Abridged

1995 简爱/*Jianai*/*Jane Eyre*. Xining, Qinghai Renmin Press
Translator: Qi Zhao (赵琪)

1995 简爱/*Jianai*/*Jane Eyre*. Changsha, Hunan Wenyi Press
Translator: Shuren Huang (黄淑仁)

1996 简爱/*Jianai*/*Jane Eyre*. Shijazhuang, Hebei University Press
Translator: Ming Lu (卢铭)
Notes: Abridged

1996 简爱/*Jianai*/*Jane Eyre*. Beijing, Beijing Broadcast College Press
Translator: Peng'en Li (李彭恩)
Notes: Abridged

1996 简爱/*Jianai*/*Jane Eyre*. Beijing, Qinghua University Press
Translator and Chief Editor: Shensheng Yang (杨慎生)

1996 简爱/*Jianai*/*Jane Eyre*. Shijiazhuang, Huashan Wenyi Press
Translator: Xiao Li (小莉)

1997 简爱/*Jianai*/*Jane Eyre*. Lijiang, Lijiang press
Translator: Jianhua Hu (胡建华)

1997 简爱/*Jianai*/*Jane Eyre*. Tainan, Tainan Hanfeng Press
Translator: Shuping Xu (徐淑萍)

1997 简爱/*Jianai*/*Jane Eyre*. Beijing, Jiuzhou Tushu Press
Translator: Xiaohong Yang (杨晓红)

1998 简爱/*Jianai*/*Jane Eyre*. Nanjing, Jiangsu Jiaoyu Press
Translator: Ailing Wu (吴艾玲) (译注)

1999 简爱/*Jianai*/*Jane Eyre*. Yanbian, Yanbian Renmin Press
Translator: He Wu (武合)

1999 简爱/*Jianai*/*Jane Eyre*. Beijing, China Xiju Press
Translator: Shibi Yang (杨诗碧)

1999 简爱/*Jianai*/*Jane Eyre*. Chengdu, Sichuan Renmin Press
Translator: Suxian Wei (魏素先)

1999 简爱/*Jianai*/*Jane Eyre*. Taipei, Taipei Yuanzun Wenhua Press

Translator: Wenqi Li (李文绮)

Known reprints: 2010

Notes: 2010 edition is in Hefei, with Anhui Jiaoyu Press

1999 简爱/*Jianai*/*Jane Eyre*. Beijing, Dazhong Wenyi Press
Translator: Xiaowei Wang (王晓卫)

1999 简爱/*Jianai*/*Jane Eyre*. Taipei, Taipei Xidai Press
Translator: Youling Huang (黄友玲)

1999 简爱/*Jianai*/*Jane Eyre*. Beijing, China Xiju Press
Translator: Zijian Han (韩子剑)

2000 简爱/*Jianai*/*Jane Eyre*. Harbin, Harbin Publishing House
Translator: Lin Zi (林子)

2000 简爱/*Jianai*/*Jane Eyre*. Tainan, Tainan Daxia Press
Translator: Xinci Zhang (张心慈)

2000 简爱/*Jianai*/*Jane Eyre*. Yanbian, Yanbian Renmin Press
Translator: Yu Sun (孙宇)

2001 简·爱 (缩写本)/*Jianai (suoxieben)*/*Jane Eyre, Abridged Version*. Chengdu, Sichuan Wenyi Chubanshe (四川文艺出版社)
Translator: Daming Li (李大明) and Jing Li (李晶)

Known reprint: 2011

Notes: Chinese abridged version. This abridged version was the basis for the 2011 translation into Tibetan printed together with the Chinese text

2001 简爱/*Jianai*/*Jane Eyre*. Hong Komg, Wenhua Yishu Press
Translator: Fei Gao

2001 简爱/*Jianai*/*Jane Eyre*. Beijing, Beijing yanshan press
Translator: Jianghao Wu (吴江皓) and Fanhai Zeng (曾凡海)

2001 简爱/*Jianai*/*Jane Eyre* (英汉对照). Jilin, Shidai Wenyi Press
Translator: Xiaofeng Shen (沈小凤)

2001 简爱/*Jianai*/*Jane Eyre*. Hulun Buir, Neimenggu Wenhua Press
Translator: Xiaojuan Dong (董晓娟)

2001 简爱/*Jianai*/*Jane Eyre*. Hulun Buir, Neimenggu Wenhua Press
Translator: Xiaojuan Wang (王晓娟)

2001 简爱/*Jianai*/*Jane Eyre*. Shanghai, Shanghai Shijie Tushu Corporation
Translator and editor: Yixin Fan (樊一昕)

2002 简爱/*Jianai*/*Jane Eyre*. Hong Kong, Wenhua Yishu Press
Translator: Xijiang Fan

2002 简爱/*Jianai*/*Jane Eyre*. Beijing, China Wenlian Press
Translator: Zhaolin Song (宋兆霖)

Known reprints: 2005, 2007

Notes: 2005 and 2007 with Taipei, Taipei Shangzhou Press

2003 简爱/*Jianai*/*Jane Eyre*. Hangzhou, Zhejiang Wenyi Press
Translator: Jinghai Shi (史津海), Huiliang Liu (刘微亮) and Wenwen Wang (王雯雯)

2003 简爱/*Jianai*/*Jane Eyre*. Hefei, Anhui Wenyi Press
Translator: Shen Guo (郭深) and Zhen Liu (刘珍)

2003 简爱/*Jianai*/*Jane Eyre*. Hefei, Anhui Renmin Press
Translator: Na Li (李娜) and Xia Li (李霞)

2003 简爱/*Jianai*/*Jane Eyre*. Beijing, Huaxia Press.
Translator: Li Ling (凌力)

Notes: Abridged

2004 简爱/*Jianai*/*Jane Eyre*. Jilin, Shidai Wenyi Press
Translator: Ping Zhou (周萍)

2004 简爱/*Jianai*/*Jane Eyre*. Beijing, Hangkong Gongye Press
Translator: Chunfang Yue (岳春芳)

Notes: Adaptation

2005 简爱/*Jianai*/*Jane Eyre*. Taipei, Taipei Shangzhou Press
Translator: Zhaolin Song (宋兆霖)

Known reprints: 2007

2005 简爱/*Jianai*/*Jane Eyre*. Beijing, Zhongyang Bianyi Press
Translator: Chengwu Zhang (张成武)

2005 简爱/*Jianai*/*Jane Eyre*. Beijing, Zhongyang Bianyi Press
Translator: Hui Chen (陈辉)

2005 简爱/*Jianai*/*Jane Eyre*. Beijing, Renmin Ribao Press
Translator and editor: Jialin Zhang (张家林)

2005 简爱/*Jianai*/*Jane Eyre*. Beijing, China Shuji Press
Translator: Guangjia Fu (傅光甲)

Known reprints: 2012

Notes: 2005 is Chinese-English bilingual edition; 2012 with China Zhigong Press

2006 简爱/*Jianai*/*Jane Eyre*. Guangzhou, Guangzhou Press
Translator: Xiongfei Li (李雄飞)

2006 简爱/*Jianai*/*Jane Eyre*. Hohhot, Neimenggu Renmin Press
Translator: Yuanshang Jin (金元尚)

Known reprint: 2007

2006 简爱/*Jianai*/*Jane Eyre*. Beijing, Guangming Daily Press
Notes: Subtitle "Notes from Renowned Teachers" (名师伴读版)

Translator: Yongtao Zhao (赵永涛)

2007 简爱/*Jianai*/*Jane Eyre*. Tianjin, Tianjin Keji Fanyi Press Co.
Translator: Baoying Tian (田宝英)

2007 简爱/*Jianai*/*Jane Eyre*. Hohhot, Neimenggu Renmin Press
Translator and editor: Jiyong Li (李继勇)

2007 简爱/*Jianai*/*Jane Eyre*. Harbin, Harbin Publishing House
Translator: Linxiu Chen (陈林秀)

2007 简爱/*Jianai*/*Jane Eyre*. Wuhan, Changjiang wenyi press
Translator: Min Xia (夏旻), Zijia Dian (奠自佳) and Chunhai Fan (范纯海)

2007 简爱/*Jianai*/*Jane Eyre*. Kaifeng, Henan Wenyi Press
Translator: Yao Xiao (肖遥)

2008 简爱/*Jianai*/*Jane Eyre*. Beijing, Nongcun Duwu Press
Translator: Yue Fu (付悦)

2008 简爱/*Jianai*/*Jane Eyre*. Chongqing, Chongqing Press
Translator: Houkai Wu (伍厚恺)

2008 简爱/*Jianai*/*Jane Eyre*. Dalia, Dalian University of Technology Press
Translator: Jing Zhang (张静)
Notes: Annotated by translator

2008 简爱/*Jianai*/*Jane Eyre*. Shenyang, Liaoning Jiaoyu press
Translator: Kan Dai (戴侃)

2008 简爱/*Jianai*/*Jane Eyre*. Xi'an, Shaanxi Renmin Jiaoyu Press
Translator and editor: Qingong Du (杜勤功)

2009 简爱/*Jianai*/*Jane Eyre*. Beijing, China International Radio Press
Translator: Jing Zhang (张兢) and Su Liu (刘素)

2009 简爱/*Jianai*/*Jane Eyre*. Beijing, Huayi Press
Translator: Shengyao Zhan (詹圣耀)

2009 简爱/*Jianai*/*Jane Eyre*. Changchun, Beifang Funv Ertong Press
Translator: Dongmei Shi (史东梅)

2010 简爱/*Jianai*/*Jane Eyre*. Jilin, Shidai Wenyi Press
Translator: Jiachun Zhou (周家春)

2010 简爱/*Jianai*/*Jane Eyre*. Beijing, Zhongyang Bianyi Press
Translator: Jianhua Shi (施建华)

2010 简爱/*Jianai*/*Jane Eyre*. Chengdu, Tiandi Press
Translator and editor: Li Ren (立人)

2010 简爱/*Jianai*/*Jane Eyre*. Changchun, Jilin Wenshi Press
Translator: Min Zhang (张敏)

2011 简爱/*Jianai*/*Jane Eyre*. Hohhot, Yuanfang Press

Translator and editor: Yongqian Wu (吴永谦)

2011 简爱/*Jianai*/*Jane Eyre*. Jilin, Jilin Publishing Group
Translator: Yi Tang (唐译)

2011 简爱/*Jianai*/*Jane Eyre*. Wuhu, Anhui Normal University Press
Translator: Xingye Zhao (赵星冶)

2012 简爱/*Jianai*/*Jane Eyre*. Changsha, Changsha Wenyi Press
Translator: Xiaoyan Feng (冯小晏)

2012 简爱/*Jianai*/*Jane Eyre*. Harbin, Beifang Wenyi Publishing House
Translator: Chengbin Zhang (张承滨)

2012 简爱/*Jianai*/*Jane Eyre*. Hong Kong, Haodoo Press
Translator: Peifang Liu (刘珮芳) and Xiaowan Chen (陈筱宛)

2012 简爱/*Jianai*/*Jane Eyre*. Nanjing, Yilin press
Translator: Yajing Ma (马亚静)

2012 简爱/*Jianai*/*Jane Eyre*. Taipei, Licun Wenhua
Translator: Zhiyun Si (斯志云)

2012 简爱/*Jianai*/*Jane Eyre* (彩绘版). Beijing, China Shuji Press
Translator and editor: Zhangxia Pu (蒲章霞)

2013 简爱/*Jianai*/*Jane Eyre*. Beijing, Foreign Language Teaching and Research Press
Translator: Jianren Huang (黄健人)

2013 简爱/*Jianai*/*Jane Eyre*. Beijing, China Kexue Puji Press
Translators and editors: Xiufang Ye (叶秀芳), Ying Zeng (曾颖), and Baohong Zhu (朱葆红)

2013 简爱/*Jianai*/*Jane Eyre*. Shanghai, Shanghai Wenyi Press
Translator: Mengmei Wang (王梦梅)
Notes: Adaptation

2014 简爱/*Jianai*/*Jane Eyre*. Shantou, Shantou University Press
Translator: Xun Gong (龚勋)

2014 简爱/*Jianai*/*Jane Eyre*. Beijing, Beijing University of Technology Press
Translator: Wenjie Liu (刘文杰)

2015 简爱/*Jianai*/*Jane Eyre*. Harbin, Harbin Publishing House
Translator: Guokui Zhang （张国奎）

2015 简爱/*Jianai*/*Jane Eyre*. Nanning, Jieli Press
Translator: Wei Yang (杨伟) and Xiaoli Li (李晓丽）

2015 简爱/*Jianai*/*Jane Eyre*. Qingdao, Qingdao Press
Translator: Biqing Xie (谢碧卿)
Notes: Adapted by translator, illustrated by Li Huang (黄丽)

2015 简爱/*Jianai*/*Jane Eyre*. Urumqi, Xinjiang Meishu Sheying Press

Translator and editor: Jiayuan Fang (方家元)

2016 简爱/*Jianai*/*Jane Eyre*. Beijing, China Zhigong Press
Translator: Qing Run (青闰)

2016 简爱/*Jianai*/*Jane Eyre*. Chengdu, Sichuan Shaonian Ertong Publishing House
Translator: Jinghao Zhang (张经浩)

2016 简爱/*Jianai*/*Jane Eyre*. Harbin, Heilongjiang Meishu Publishing House
Translator: Zhonglei Cui (崔钟雷)

2016 简爱/*Jianai*/*Jane Eyre*. Nanchang, Jiangxi Meishu Publishing House
Translator: Yihong Liu (刘益宏)

2016 简爱/*Jianai*/*Jane Eyre*. Nanning, Jiangsu Renmin Publishing
Translator: Hongliang Tao (陶红亮)

2016 简爱/*Jianai*/*Jane Eyre*. Taipei, Taiwan Shangwu Press
Translator: Xuanzhu Zhang (张玄竹)

2016 简爱/*Jianai*/*Jane Eyre*. Wuhan, Changjiang Press
Translator and editor: Yi Zheng (郑毅)

2016 简爱/*Jianai*/*Jane Eyre*. Xi'an, Sanqin Press
Translator: Feng Yu (枫雨)

2017 简爱/*Jianai*/*Jane Eyre*. Beijing, Foreign Languages Press
Translator: Hongchang Cai (蔡红昌)

2017 简爱/*Jianai*/*Jane Eyre*. Chengdu, Tiandi Press
Translator: Di Fan (范蒂)

2017 简爱/*Jianai*/*Jane Eyre*. Harbin, Heilongjiang Meishu Publishing House
Translator and chief editor: Qian Lei (雷倩)

2017 简爱/*Jianai*/*Jane Eyre*. Harbin, Heilongjiang Meishu Publishing House
Translator and editor: Qingfeng Jiao (焦庆峰)

2017 简爱/*Jianai*/*Jane Eyre*. Hong Kong, Chenxing Press
Translator: Xiangmei Wu (吴湘湄)

2017 简爱/*Jianai*/*Jane Eyre*. Nanjing, Jiangsu Wenyi Publishing House
Translator: Rongyue Liu (刘荣跃)

2017 简爱/*Jianai*/*Jane Eyre*. Nanning, Guangxi Normal University Press
Translator: Tianfei Cao (曹天飞)

2017 简爱/*Jianai*/*Jane Eyre*. Yinchuan, Ningxia Renmin Jiaoyu Press
Translator: Shuqin Zhao (赵书琴)

2017 简爱/*Jianai*/*Jane Eyre*. Beijing, Beijing University of Technology Press

Translator: Yanbo Liu (刘彦波)

2017 简爱/*Jianai*/*Jane Eyre*. Beijing, China International Radio Press
Translator: Fubo Tan (谭付波)
Notes: Subtitle: "Analysis and Quick Read" (精解速读)

2017 简爱/*Jianai*/*Jane Eyre*. Changchun, Jilin Wenshi Press
Translator: Donghai Xie (谢东海)
Notes: Subtitle: "Analysis and Quick Read" (精解速读)

2017 简爱/*Jianai*/*Jane Eyre*. Beijing, Beijing University of Technology Press.
Translator and chief editor: Tian Sang (桑田)
Notes: 'Full interpretation' (足本解读)

2018 简·爱/*Jianai*/*Jane Eyre*. Beijing, Unity Press
Translator: Yu Li (李语)

2018 简·爱/*Jianai*/*Jane Eyre*. Chengdu, Sichuan Minzu Press
Translator: Shizhong Zhao (赵世忠）and Nan Wu (吴楠)

2018 简爱/*Jianai*/*Jane Eyre*. Nanjing, Jiangsu Fenghuang Wenyi Publishing
Translator: Hongyan Lv (吕红艳)

2018 简爱/*Jianai*/*Jane Eyre*. Nanjing, Nanjing University Press
Translator: Shuyang Zou (邹抒阳)
Note: Adaptation

2018 简爱/*Jianai*/*Jane Eyre*. Beijing, Beijing Ribao Press
Translator: Committee of Translators (名家编译委员会)
Notes: Subtitle: "Analysis and Quick Read" (精解速读).

2019 简爱/*Jianai*/*Jane Eyre*. Taipei, Xinchaoshe Wenhua Shiye Co., Ltd.
Translator: Junxie Wu (吴钧燮)

2019 简爱/*Jianai*/*Jane Eyre*. Suzhou, Suzhou University Press
Translator and editor: Lei Wu (吴磊)

2019 简爱/*Jianai*/*Jane Eyre*. Tianjin, Tianjin Renmin Press
Translator: Hongji Li (李继宏)

Cornish

2020 *Jane Eyre*. Dundee, Evertype
Translator: Nicholas Williams
Notes: With illustrations by Edmund H. Garrett and E. M. Wimperis

Croatian

1974 *Jane Eyre*. Zagreb, Nakladni zavod MH
Translator: Giga Gračan & Andrijana Hjuit

Known reprints: 1975, 1976

1974 *Jane Eyre*. Zagreb, Naprijed
Translator: Karlo Budor

2008 *Jane Eyre*. Zagreb, Naklada Ljevak
Translator: Giga Gračan

Known reprint: 2012

Note: modernized version of the 1974 translation, introducing post-independence linguistic forms

Czech

1875 *Jane Eyre, sirotek Lowoodský/Jane Eyre, The Lowood Orphan*. Prague, Libuše
Translator: P. M. Chorušická

1895 *Johana Eyre-ová; aneb, Sirotek lowoodský/Johana Eyre; or, the Lowood Orphan*. Prague, Alois Hynek
Translator: Unknown

Known reprints: 1897?, c. 1910, 1929

Notes: Published 1895–96 in twenty-one parts; then in three volumes. Source: Jay Dillon Rare Books + Manuscripts

1907 *Sirotek lovoodský (Johanna Eyrová)/Orphan of Lowood (Joanna Eyre)*. Prague, B. Kočí
Translator: Karel Funk

Notes: Probably abridged

1932 *Sirotek lowoodský/Orphan of Lowood*. Prague, Vojtěch Šeba
Translator: Tereza Turnerová

Notes: Pro dívky' ('for girls'); illustrated by A.L. Salač

1938 *Sirotek lowoodský (Johanna Eyre)/Orphan of Lowood (Joanna Eyre)*. Prague, K. Hlouška
Translator: Ročák, Josef

Notes: Abridged

1954 *Sirotek lowoodský/The Lowood Orphan*. Prague, Mladá fronta
Translator: Jarmila Fastrová

Known reprints: 1957, 1991, 1994, 1998, 2007

Notes: 1991 edition is with Albatross; 1994 with Český spisovatel; 1998 with X-Egem; 2007 in Frýdek-Místek with Alpress

2012 *Jane Eyreová*. Prague, Československý spisovatel
Translator: Pavla a Matouš Iblovi

2013 *Jana Eyrová*. Prague, Dobrovský
Translator: Petr Polák

2018 *Jana Eyrová*. Říčany, Sun
Translator: Hana Jovanovičová
Known reprint: 2020

2018 *Jana Eyrová*. Voznice, LEDA
Translator: Miroslav Kaftan

2019 *Jana Eyrová*: Prague, CooBoo
Translator: Petra Diestlerová

2020 *Jane Eyre*. Dunicko, INFOA
Translator: Karolina Doláková

Danish

1850 *Jane Eyre, eller en Gouvernantes Memoirer/Jane Eyre, or the Memoirs of a Governess*. Copenhagen, Jordans Forlag
Translator: Unknown
Known reprints: 1856–7, 1884
Notes: 3rd edition published with Jacob Erslev

1894 *Jane Eyre*. Slagelse, Sorø Amtstidende
Translator: Vilhelm Møller

1897 *Et Vajsenhusbarn eller Jane Eyre. En Gouvernantes Memoirer/An Orphan or Jane Eyre. The Memoirs of a Governess*. Copenhagen, R. Stjernholm (Roman-Bazar)
Translator: Sofie Horten
Known reprints: 1905, 1909, 1911, 1913, 1914, 1944
Notes: 1905 edition is with Vort Lands Feuilletori; 1909 is with Østjydsk Forlagsforretning and is titled Et Vaisenhusbarn: (Jane Eyre); 1911 is with Frederiksbergs Biblioteks Forlag and may be abridged; 1913 is with Romanforlaget; 1914 is with Danmark; 1944 is with Det Danske forlag

1909 *Jane Eyre*. Copenhagen, Chr. Flor
Translator: Unknown

1913 *Et Vajsenhusbarn/An Orphan*. Copenhagen, Forlaget Danmark
Translator: Emma Sunde

1944 *Jane Eyre*. Copenhagen, Unknown
Translator: Aslaug Mikkelsen
Known reprints: 1957, 1963, 1965, 1971(i), 1971(ii), 1978, 1984, 1987, 2011

Notes: 1963 edition with Spectator; 1965 and 1978 with Det Danske Forlag; 1971 with Edito (Verdenslitteraturens Perler); a second 1971 edition with Danske Forlag, Nyt Dansk; 1984 and 1987 with Nyt Dansk Litteraturselskab Litteraturselskab; 2011(i) with Lindhardt og Ringhof; 2011(ii) and 2012 with Bechs Forlag; 2015 with Rosenkilde

2015 *Jane Eyre*. Copenhagen, Rosenkilde
Translator: Christiane Rohde

Notes: 2016 edition with Lindhardt og Ringhof

2016 *Jane Eyre*. Syddjurs, Grevas
Translator: Luise Hemmer Pihl

Dutch

1849 *Jane Eyre, of het leven eener gouvernante/Jane Eyre or the Life of a Governess*. Groningen, C.M. Van Bolhuis Hoitsema
Translator: Unknown

Notes: Two volumes; second volume published in 1850

1874 *Jane Eyre, de wees van Lowood, of Het leven eener gouvernante/Jane Eyre, the orphan of Lowood, or The life of a governess*. Deventer, Ter Gunne
Translator: Unknown

1885 *Jane Eyre, of, de wees van Lowood: een verhaal/Jane Eyre, or, The orphan of Lowood: a story*. Gouda, G.B. van Goor Zonen
Translator: Unknown

1914 *Jane Eyre (de wees van Lowood)/Jane Eyre (the orphan of Lowood)*. Amsterdam, Amsterdam Mij voor Goede en Goedkoope Lectuur
Translator: J Kuylman; Leo Simons

1935 *Jane Eyre of het leven eener gouvernante/Jane Eyre or the life of a governess*. Amsterdam, Hollandsch Uitgeversfonds
Translator: Unknown

Notes: Date is approximate

1948 *Jane Eyre*. Amsterdam, Contact
Translator: Elisabeth de Roos

Known reprints: 1950, 1951, 1959, 1967, 1978

Notes: 1978 with Veen

1965 *Jane Eyre*. Amsterdam, L.J. Veen's Uitgeversmij N.V.
Translator: M. Foeken-Visser

Known reprints: 1971, 1974, 1985, 1991, 1995, 2001, 2003, 2004, 2005, 2006, 2007

Notes: 1971 with L.J. Veen's Uitgeversmij N.V (Wageningen); 1985 with Veen (Utrecht); 1995, 2001, 2003, 2005 published with Pandora; 2006 with Just Publishers; 1991, 2004, 2007 with Veen (Amsterdam)

1970 *Jane Eyre*. Haarlem, Spaarnestad
Translator: Clara Eggink

Known reprint: 1978; 2008

Notes: 1970 date is approximate. 1978 with Amsterdam Boek; 2008 with Just Publishers.

1980 *Jane Eyre: een autobiografie*. Antwerpen, Spectrum
Translator: Heleen Kost

Known reprint: 1994

1981 *Bronte Omnibus*. Dronten, Casterman
Translator: F. Mitchell

1984 *Jane Eyre*. Antwerpen, Deltas
Translator: Martha van Bergen

1994 *Jane Eyre*. Amsterdam, Reader's Digest
Translator: Unknown

Notes: probably a reprint of one of the existing translations

1995 *Charlotte Bronte: Jane Eyre*. Paterswolde, Dalcomtext
Translator: Sam de Bruijn; C Bosker

1995 *Jane Eyre*. Liège, Hemma
Translator: A Spitzers; Philippe Henriot

1998 *Jane Eyre*. Groningen, BoekWerk
Translator: Akkie de Jong

Known reprint: 2006; 2012; 2016; 2017

Notes: 2006 with Muntinga Pockets; 2012 with BoekWerk; 2016 and 2017 with Uitgeverij Rainbow bv

2008 *Jane Eyre: een autobiografie*. Houten, Spectrum
Translator: Unknown

2011 *Jane Eyre*. Amsterdam, L.J. Veen
Translator: Unknown

2013 *Jane Eyre*. Amsterdam, Reader's Digest
Translator: Unknown

2013 *Jane Eyre*. Arnhem, Bontekoe
Translator: Bies van Ede

Notes: Gill Tavner's adaption

2014 *Jane Eyre*. Amsterdam, Athenaeum-Polak & Van Gennep
Translator: Babet Mossel; Marja Pruis

Esperanto

1931 *Jane Eyre*. Zutphen, W.J. Thieme
Translator: Hendrik Jan Bulthuis

2001 *Jane Eyre*. Tyresö, Inko
Translator: Unknown

Estonian

1959 *Jane Eyre*. Tallinn, Eesti Riiklik Kirjastus
Translator: Elvi Raidaru (Kippasto), verses translated by Edla Valdna
Known reprints: 1981, 2007, 2013
Notes: 1981 with Eesti Raamat, a corrected text with the translator's surname changed to Kippasto, her married name; 2007 with Mediasat Group, an exact reprint of 1981; 2013 with Tänapäev incorporating some minor changes

2000 *Jane Eyre*. Tallinn, Brigitta
Translator: Ira Inga Vilberg
Notes: Closely based on Kippasto's translation, though Valdna's verses are omitted. Nothing is known of Ira Inga Vilberg, so the name may be a pseudonym

Finnish

1915 *Kotiopettajattaren romaani/The Novel of a Governess*. Porvoo, WSOY
Translator: Tyyni Haapanen (Tyyni Tuulio)
Known reprints: 1919, 1939, 1945, 1947, 1950, 1954, 1963, 1965, 1968, 1972, 1980, 1986, 1991, 2016

1973 *Kotiopettajattaren romaani/The Novel of a Governess*. Hämeenlinna, Kristo
Translator: Kaarina Ruohtula
Known reprints: 1974, 1985, 1987, 1988, 2000, 2001 (tape), 2008

French

1849 *Jane Eyre ou Mémoires d'une gouvernante/Jane Eyre or Memoirs of a Governess*. Paris, *Le National*; Brussels, *La Revue de Paris* and *L'Indépendance belge*
Translator: 'Old Nick' (Paul Émile Daurand Forgues)
Known reprints: 1855

Notes: 'Old Nick' was the pseudonym of Paul Émile Daurand Forgues. The translation was serialised virtually simultaneously in *Le National* (15 April – 11 June), *La Revue de Paris* (April – June), and *L'Indépendance belge* 29 April – 28 June 1849; the same text was issued in two volumes by Lebègue (Brussels, 1849) and republished by Hachette (Paris, 1855) in its Bibliothèque des Chemins de Fer (Railway Library). See Jay Dillon, '"Reader, I found it": The First *Jane Eyre* in French', *The Book Collector*, 72 (2023), 11–19.

1854 *Jeanne Eyre ou les mémoires d'une institutrice (1854).* Paris, D. Giraud

Translator: Noëmi Lesbazeilles-Souvestre

Known reprints: 1862, 1883, 1897, 1900, 1903, 1908, 1912, 1920, 1947, 1949, 1965, 1970, 2008, 2010, 2011, 2013, 2014

Notes: From 1862, titled Jane Eyre ou les mémoires d'une institutrice

1919 *Jane Eyre.* Paris, Ernest Flammarion

Translator: Marion Gilbert & Madeleine Duvivier

Known reprints: 1954, 1990

Notes: Still in print in Flammarion, 1990

1946 *Jane Eyre.* Lausanne, J. Marguerat

Translator: Jan-Ewan Jaermann-Landry

Known reprint: 1960

Notes: Nouvelle adaptation

1946 *Jane Eyre.* Lausanne, J. Marguerat, and Éditions du Dauphin

Translator: R. Redon & J. Dulong

Known reprint: 1953

1946 *Jane Eyre.* Paris, Éditions La Boétie, and then Verviers, Gérard et Cie (from 1950)

Translator: Léon Brodovikoff & Claire Robert

Known reprints: 1950, 1967

Notes: English abridgement for French market, title: The Girlhood of Jane Eyre

1946 *La Vie passionnée de Jane Eyre/The Passionate Life of Jane Eyre. Paris, S. I. E. P.*

Translator: Max Roth

Notes: Roman adapté de l'anglais'

1947 *Jane Eyre.* Paris, Stock, Delamain et Boutellau, then Le Club français du livre and Éditions C.R.J

Translator: Jules Castier

Known reprints: 1952, 1956 (2), 1957, 1982

Notes: Preface by Rene Lalou

1947 *Jane Eyre*. Paris, Grund
Translator: Renée Masson
Notes: Illustrations by Patrick de Manceau

1948 *Jane Eyre*. Poitiers, Fonteneau
Translator: Jacques Marcireau
Known reprints: 1948, 1950, 1954,
Notes: Adapté de l'anglais'

1948 *Jane Eyre: Une autobiographie*. Paris, Fernand Nathan
Translator: Robert & André Prophétie
Notes: Adaptation

1949 *Jane Eyre*. Paris, Hatier
Translator: Marguerite Faguer
Known reprint: 1953

1950 *Jane Eyre*. Paris, Gedalge
Translator: J.C. Gourdon
Known reprint: 1952

1950 *Jane Eyre*. Paris, Les Compagnons du livre, 2 vol.
Translator: Marcelle Sibon
Known reprint: 1956

1953 *Jane Eyre*. Paris, Editions du Panthéon
Translator: Geneviève Nanteuil

1957 *Jane Eyre*. Paris, Editions G.P.
Translator: Geneviève Méker
Known reprints: 1960, 1971

1964 *Jane Eyre*. Paris, Le Livre de Poche, Collection «Classiques»
Translator: Charlotte Maurat
Known reprints: 1972, 1992, 2016

1965 *Jane Eyre*. Paris, Delagrave et Éditions Lito
Translator: Frédérique Sauvage
Known reprints: 1965, 1977

1966 *Jane Eyre*. Paris, Garnier-Frères, and Presses Pocket, and Le Grand Livre du Mois
Translator: Sylvère Monod
Known reprints: 1981, 1984, 1988, 1990, 1998, 1999, 2011, 2012

1967 *Jane Eyre*. Lausanne, Editions Rencontres, and Edito-service, and Rombaldi

Translator: Henriette Guex-Rolle

Known reprints: 1973, 1995

Notes: Traduit de & Roman d'amour.

2008 *Jane Eyre*. Paris, Gallimard (Folio Classique), and Gallimard Jeunesse

Translator: Dominique Jean

Known reprints: 2012, 2016

Georgian

1964 ჯეინ ეარი/*Jane Eyre*. Tbilisi, Literatura da Xelovneba

Translators: T'. Maġraże and Z. Xaxanašvili

Known reprints: 1976, 2004, 2011, 2012, 2015

Notes: Introduction by Elguja Maġraże. Source: Jay Dillon Rare Books + Manuscripts

German

1848 *Johanna Eyre*. Berlin, Duncker & Humblot

Translator: Ernst Susemihl

1850 *Jane Eyre: Memoiren einer Gouvernante/Jane Eyre: Memoirs of a Governess*. Leipzig, Grimma, Verlags-Comptoir

Translator: Ludwig Fort

Notes: Translated from 'Old Nick''s 1849 French version—see entry above.

1850 *Jane Eyre*. Stuttgart, Franckh

Translator: Christoph Friedrich Grieb1854

Jane Eyre oder die Waise aus Lowood/Jane Eyre or the Orphan of Lowood. Pest, Vienna and Leipzig, Hartleben

Translator: A. Heinrich

Notes: Jay Dillon points out that this was the first translation to adopt the title of Charlotte Birch-Pfeiffer's popular 1853 stage adaptation (on which, see Chapter I).

1854 *Jane Eyre, die Waise von Lowood/Jane Eyre the Orphan of Lowood*. Altona, Hamburg: Heilbutt

Translator: Unknown. Tatlock describes this text as being adapted from Ludwig Fort's 1850 translation.

1882 *Jane Eyre, die Waise von Lowood, oder Gott führt die Seinen wunderbar. Für's Volkerzählt/Jane Eyre, the Orphan of Lowood, or God wonderfully guides his own*. Told for the people. Reutlingen, Enßlin & Laiblin

Translator: Otto Berger

Notes: Source: Tatlock

1887 *Jane Eyre, die Waise von Lowood, eine Autobiographie/Jane Eyre, the Orphan of Lowood, an Autobiography. Leipzig, Ph.* Reclam
Translator: Marie von Borch

Known reprints: Jay Dillon advises that there were ten printings from 1888 to 1917, 34,000 copies in all; recent reprints include 2008, 2011, 2013

Notes: Dates 1887–90. The 2008 edition, with later reprints, was revised by Martin Engelmann.

1890 *Jane Eyre, die Waise von Lowood von Currer Bell. Aus dem Englischen für die reifere weibliche Jugend bearbeitet/Jane Eyre, the Orphan of Lowood by Currer Bell.* Adapted from the English for Older Girls. 5th edition. Berlin, Leo

Notes: The date of this edition is approximate and that of the first edition is unknown. Source: Tatlock.

1892 *Johanna Eyre, die Waise von Lowood/Jane Eyre, the Orphan of Lowood.* Teschendorf, Prochaska
Translator: Unknown

Known reprints: 1902

Notes: Tatlock describes this text as a revised and abridged version of Susemihl's 1848 translation.

1894 *Jane Eyre oder die Waise aus Lowood/Jane Eyre or the Orphan of Lowood. Wien, A.* Hartleben
Translator: Unknown

Notes: Tatlock describes this text as a revised and abridged version of Heinrich's 1854 translation.

1904 *Jane Eyre, Die Waise von Lowood/Jane Eyre, the Orphan of Lowood.* Stuttgart, Franckhsche Verlh
Translator: G.A. Volchert

Known reprints: 1912 (described as 6th edition)

Notes: Hohn gives the date of first publication of this edition as 1904; Tatlock, who has examined the 1912 edition, describes the text as being a re-worked version of the 1850 Grieb translation — see entry above.

1904 *Jane Eyre, die Waise von Lowood/Jane Eyre, the Orphan of Lowood. Halle, O.* Hendel

Translator: Eduard von Bauernfeld. Tatlock describes this text as being based on the 1854 adaptation of Fort's 1850 translation — see entries above.

1905 *Die Waise von Lowood/The Orphan of Lowood.* Berlin, Jugendhort
Translator: Gertrude Reichard

1906 *Jane Eyre, die Waise von Lowood/Jane Eyre, the Orphan of Lowood.* Berlin: Globus

Translator: Rudolf Reichhardt

Known reprints: 1917, 1927, 1935

Notes: Tatlock describes this text as relying heavily on Borch's translation, and as being aimed at younger readers.

1911 *Die Waise von Lowood/The Orphan of Lowood.* Berlin, Weichert
Translator: Ilka von Hartung

Notes: Aimed at younger readers.

1927 *Jane Eyre.* Leipzig, Hesse und Becker Verlag
Translator: Bertha Tucholsky

1945 *Jane Eyre.* Zürich, Manesse
Translator: Paola Meister-Calvino

Known reprints: 1963, 1994, 1996, 1997

1947 *Jane Eyre.* Zürich, Büchergilde Gutenberg
Translator: Ursula Markun

1948 *Die Waise von Lowood/The Orphan of Lowood.* Wien, Verkauf
Translator: Carl Haus

Notes: Published simultaneously in Zurich; republished in Cologne in 1950 by Kiepenheue

1950 *Jane Eyre.* Zürich, Buchclub Ex Libris
Translator: Carl Bach

1958 *Jane Eyre, eine Autobiographie.* Zürich, Diogenes
Translator: Bernhard Schindler

Known reprints: 1959, 1961, 1978, 1988

1958 *Jane Eyre: Roman.* Frankfurt, Ullstein
Translator: Elisabeth von Arx

Known reprints: 1981, 1986, 1988, 1989, 1990, 1992, 1993, 1996

1961 *Jane Eyre, die Waise von Lowood/Jane Eyre, the Orphan of Lowood.* Klagenfurt, Eduard Kaiser Verlag
Translator: Hertha Lorenz

1963 *Die Waise von Lowood/The Orphan of Lowood.* Berlin, Kinderbuchverlag
Translators: Bernhard Schindler and Renate Jessel

1979 *Jane Eyre, Eine Autobiographie.* Frankfurt, Insel
Translator: Helmut Kossodo

Known reprints: 1986, 1987, 1989, 1990, 1992, 1993, 1994, 1997, 1998, 2004, 2008, 2015

1990 *Jane Eyre, Eine Autobiographie.* Stuttgart, Philipp Reclam
Translator: Ingrid Rein

Known reprints: 1996, 1998, 2011

1997　*Jane Eyre: Roman.* München, Deutscher Taschenbuch Verlag
Translator: Gottfried Röckelein
Known reprints: 1998, 1999, 2000, 2008, 2014, 2018

2004　*Jane Eyre: Roman.* Zürich, Manesse
Translator: Andrea Ott
Known reprint: 2016

2015　*Jane Eyre Eine Autobiographie.* Berlin, Suhrkamp/Insel
Translator: Melanie Walz

Greek

1949　*Τζέην Έϋρ: Μυθιστόρημα/Jane Eyre: A Novel.* Athens, Ikaros
Translator: Ninila Papagiannē
Known reprint: 1954/1955 (vol 1/vol 2); 1993
Notes: 1993 with Zacharopoulos S.I.

1950　*Τζέην Έυρ by Charlotte Bronde [sic]/Jane Eyre.* Athens, D. Darema
Translator: Polyvios Vovolinēs
Notes: Dates are approximate: 1950–1955

1954　*Τζέην Έϋρ/Jane Eyre.* Athens, Parthenōn
Translator: Sotiris Patatzē

1955　*Τζέην Έϋρ: Ο Πύργος του πονου/Jane Eyre: The Tower of Pain.* Athens, Romantso
Translator: George Tarsatopoulou

1963　*Τζέην Έυρ: μυθιστόρημα/Jane Eyre: A Novel.* Athens, Minōas
Translator: Georgia Deligiannē-Anastasiadē
Known reprints: 1992, 2002
Notes: Juvenile edition

1968　*Τζέην Έυρ/Jane Eyre.* Athens, Aylos
Translator: Eletherias Siola

1969　*Τζέην Έυρ/Jane Eyre.* Athens, Ankyra
Translator: Pipina Tsimikalē
Known reprint: 2016
Notes: Juvenile edition

1979　*Τζέην Έυρ/Jane Eyre.* Thessaloniki, Rekos
Translator: Thanasis Georgiadēs
Notes: Date is approximate

1981　*Τζέην Έυρ/Jane Eyre.* Athens, ASTĒR-Papadēmētriou
Translator: Dora Kominē-Dialetē

Known reprints: 1986, 1990

Notes: Juvenile edition

1990 *Τζέην Έηρ/Jane Eyre*. Athens, Damianos
Translator: Vasilis Liaskas

1990 *Τζέιν Έυρ/Jane Eyre*. Athens, Pella
Translator: George Tarsatopoulou

1991 *Τζέιν Έιρ/Jane Eyre*. Athens, Kaktos
Translator: Polly Moschopoulou

1997 *Τζέην 'Έυρ/Jane Eyre*. Athens, Smilē
Translator: Dimitris Kikizas

Known reprint: 2015

1998 *Τζέιν Έυρ/Jane Eyre*. Athens, Patakē
Translator: Marilena Alevizou

1999 *Τζέιν Έιρ/Jane Eyre*. Athens, Modern Times
Translator: Sophia Tsiledakē

Notes: Adaption

2001 *Τζέιν Έιρ/Jane Eyre*. Athens, Aposperitis
Translator: Yiannis Karouzos

2002 *Τζέην Έϋρ/Jane Eyre*. Athens, DeAgostini Hellas
Translator: Georgia Deligiannē-Anastasiadē

Known reprint: 2004

2008 *Τζέιν Έιρ/Jane Eyre*. Athens, Harlenik Bell
Translator: Klairē Laina

2011 *Τζέιν Έιρ/Jane Eyre*. Athens, Savvalas
Translator: Beatrice Kantzola-Zambatakou

Notes: Juvenile edition

2011 *Τζέιν Έιρ/Jane Eyre*. Athens, Tessera Pi
Translator: Maria Exarchou

2017 *Τζέιν Έιρ/Jane Eyre*. Athens, Susaeta
Translator: Theodora Darvirē

Notes: Juvenile edition

2018 *Τζέην Εϋρ/Jane Eyre*. Athens, Fourfouri
Translator: Stella Feikou

Notes: Juvenile edition

Gujarati

1993 શાર્લોટ બ્રોન્ટે કૃત જેન એયર/*Charlotte Brontë's Creation Jane Eyre.* Ahmedabad, Navbharat Sāhitya Mandir
Translator: Hansā C. Patel
Notes: Abridged. Source: researcher's copy (Abhishek Jain)

2009 વેઈકફીલ્ડનો ભલો પાદરી, બિચારી અનાથ છોકરી/*The Vicar of Wakefield, The Poor Orphan Girl.* Ahmedabad, Bālavinōd Prakāśan;
Translator: Manasukh Kākaḍiyā
Notes: Abridged, and printed alongside a translation of Oliver Goldsmith's The Vicar of Wakefield. Source: researcher's copy (Abhishek Jain)

Hebrew

1946 ג'יין אייר/*Jane Eyre. Jerusalem, M.* Newman Press
Translator: Hana Ben Dov

1968 ג'יין אייר/*Jane Eyre.* Ramat Gan, Massada Press
Translator: Yitzhak Levanon
Notes: Abridged

1986 ג'יין אייר/*Jane Eyre.* Tel Aviv, Or 'Am
Translator: Tala Bar

1987 ג'יין אייר/*Jane Eyre.* Tel Aviv, Zmora Bitan
Translator: Liora Herzig

1996 ג'יין אייר/*Jane Eyre.* HaDarom, Korim
Translator: Asi Weinstein
Notes: Abridged; juvenile edition

2002 ג'יין אייר בתמונות/*Jane Eyre.* HaMerkaz, Ofarim
Translator: Smadar Kugo
Notes: Abridged with illustrations by Richard Lauter (English adaptation part of Treasury of Illustrated Classics, likely source of this Hebrew adaptation)

2007 ג'יין אייר/*Jane Eyre.* Tel Aviv, Yediot Sfarim
Translator: Sharon Preminger

Hindi

2002 जेन आयर/*Jane Eyre.* New Delhi, Rajkamal Prakashan
Translator: Vidyā Sinhā

Hungarian

1873 *Jane Eyre: önéletírás/Jane Eyre: Autobiography*. Budapest, Légrády
Translator: Huszár Imre

1918 *A lowoodi árva/The Orphan of Lowood*. Budapest, Kultúra Kvk
Translator: Karinthy Frigyes

1942 *A lowoodi árva: [regény]/The Orphan of Lowood: [novel]*. Budapest, Bibliotheca
Translator: Fónagy Iván

1963 *Jane Eyre 1–3. köt.: regény/Jane Eyre Vol. 1–3: Novel*. Budapest, Szépirodalmi Kiadó
Translator: Mária Ruzitska

Known reprints: 1964, 1967, 1968, 1969, 1972, 1976, 1977, 1986, 1991, 1999

Notes: 1968, 86 and 91 are with Európa; 1999 with Móra; the other re-editions are in Bratislava with Krásnej lit.

1984 *Jane Eyre. Regény/Jane Eyre. Novel*. Budapest, Európa
Translator: Gábor Görgey; Mária Ruzitska

Known reprint: 2005

Notes: Abridged; with running English-Hungarian thesaurus; 2005 with Palatinus

2005 *A lowoodi árva: Jane Eyre/The Orphan of Lowood: Jane Eyre*. Szeged, Könyvmolyképző
Translator: Mária Ruzitska and Imre Szász

Known reprint: 2007

2014 *Jane Eyre*. Budapest, Ulpius-ház
Translator: Kiss Zsuzsa

Icelandic

1948 *Jane Eyre*. Reykjavík, Ísafoldarprentsmiðja hf
Translator: Sigurður Björgólfsson

Known reprints: 1975, 1982

Notes: reprints are with Sogysafn Heimilanna. Source: Jay Dillon Rare Books + Manuscripts

Indonesian

1977 *Jane Eyre*. Jakarta, P. T. Gramedia
Translator: Unknown

Notes: Abridged

1977 *Jane Eyre*. Jakarta, Pancar Kumala
Translator: Yurida Kasmara

1984 *Jane Eyre*. Jakarta, Pustaka Jaya
Translator: Unknown
Notes: Abridged. Source: Jay Dillon Rare Books + Manuscripts

2010 *Jane Eyre*. Jakarta, Gramedia Pustaka Utama
Translator: Lulu Wijaya

Italian

1904 *Jane Eyre, o Le memorie d'un' istitutrice/Jane Eyre or the Memoirs of a Governess*. Milan, Fratelli Treves
Translator: Unknown

1925 *Jane Eyre: romanzo*. Milan, Sonzogno
Translator: Elvira Rosa
Known reprint: 1941

1935 *Jane Eyre: il romanzo di un' istitutrice/Jane Eyre: the novel of a governess. Milan, A.* Barion Casa per edizioni popolari
Translator: C. Marazio
Known reprint: 1946

1946 *Gianna Eyre*. Rome, Perrella
Translator: Lucilla Kànizsa Jacchia
Known reprint: 1947

1950 *Jane Eyre: romanzo*. Milan, Cavallotti
Translator: Berto Minozzi
Known reprints: 1951, 1956, 1957

1951 *Jane Eyre*. Milan, Rizzoli
Translator: G. Pozzo Galeazzi
Known reprints: 1991, 1993, 1994, 1995, 1996, 1997, 1998, 1999, 2003, 2004, 2006, 2009, 2012, 2013
Notes: 1991, 1995, 1996, 2004 with Fabbri imprint (Fabbri taken over by Rizzoli in 1990). 1993 introduced by Oriana Palusci; 2006 with Rizzoli introduced by Virginia Woolf essay; 2013 with *Corriere della Sera*.

1954 *Jane Eyre*. Turin, SAS
Translator: Virginia Galante Garrone
Known reprints: 1956, 1957, 1966, 1980, 1998
Notes: Abridged ('riduzione'). 1966 with Edizioni Paoline, Catania, known to have been reprinted there in 1980, 1983

1956 *Jane Eyre: romanzo*. Milan, Boschi
Translator: D. L. C. Tenconi
Known reprints: 1958, 1964

Notes: Illustrated by Guido Bertello; collection 'Romanzi celebri'

1956 *Tre romanzi*. Rome, R. Casini
Translator: Lia Spaventa Filippi

Known reprints: 1965, 1973, 1976, 1987, 1995, 1998, 2002, 2004, 2006, 2008, 2009, 2010, 2015

Notes: *Tre romanzi* by Brontë sisters, includes *Agnes Grey*, *Cime tempestuose*, *Jane Eyre*, and edited by Lia Spaventa Filippi with introduction by Maria Luisa Astaldi; collection 'I grandi maestri'. 1973 with Geneva, Edito-Service is *Jane Eyre* only. 1995 with Biblioteca Economica Newton (series of Newton & Compton) is *Jane Eyre* only, with introduction by Giuseppe Lombardo; repr. 1998, 2002; c. 1997 is the 3 Brontë novels; 2004, 2010, 2015 with Newton & Compton, and introduction by Lombardo; same again published by Societa Europea de Edizioni 2006; 2008 is the 3 novels with Rizzoli; 2009 is *Jane Eyre* with *Il giornale*.

1957 *Jane Eyre: romanzo*. Milan, Lucchi
Translator: Curzio Siniscalchi

Known reprints: 1962, 1964, 1968, 1970

Notes: Illustrated by Edgardo dell'Acqua

1958 *Jane Eyre*. Bologna, Capitol
Translator: Dante Virgili

Known reprints: 1959, 1968

Notes: SBN says Virgili is editor; Gaudio says translator, referencing BNCF Marucelliana

1958 *La porta chiusa (Iane Eyre)/The Closed Door (Jane Eyre)*. Brescia, La Scuola
Translator: Unknown

Notes: Abridged

1961 *Jane Eyre*. Milan, Fabbri
Translator: E. Giroldo Inglese

Known reprints: 1968, 1972,

Notes: Collection 'libri deliziosi'

1962 *Jane Eyre*. Brescia, La Scuola
Translator: V. Trabeschi De Toni

1962 *Jane Eyre*. Florence, Sansoni
Translator: C. G. Cecioni

Known reprint: 1967

Notes: Edizioni scolastiche Sansoni. Collana di classici inglesi

1963 *Jane Eyre: romanzo*. Milan, C. Del Duca
Translator: Unknown

1966 *Jane Eyre*. Rome, G. Casini
Translator: C. Egidi Mattei

1967 *Jane Eyre*. Milan, Bietti
Translator: Liliana Battistelli
Known reprints: 1974, 1978
Notes: Abridged

1967 *Jane Eyre*. Milan, AMZ
Translator: Unknown
Known reprints: 1970, 1974
Notes: Probably abridged; cover by B. Bodini; illustrated by C. Colombi; another SBN entry says cover by Ivan Gongalow

1967 *Jane Eyre: romanzo*. Milan, Boschi
Translator: Emma De Mattia
Notes: Illustrated by Musati

1974 *Jane Eyre*. Milan, Garzanti
Translator: U. Dèttore
Known reprints: 1976, 1978, 1980, 1982, 1984, 1986, 1987, 1989, 1990, 1991, 1992, 1995, 1996, 1997, 2004, 2007, 2009, 2012, 2014, 2017
Notes: 1987 with introduction by Franco Cordelli; 1995 introduction by Paolo Ruffilli; 2017 with Centauria

1983 *Jane Eyre*. Bologna, Malipiero
Translator: R. Cenni
Notes: Abridged; collection 'Bestseller per I ragazzi'; illustrated by Serenella De Vita

1986 *Jane Eyre*. Milan, A Peruzzo
Translator: Caterina Niceta
Known reprints: 1987, 1995

1987 *Jane Eyre: versione integrale*. La Spezia, Melita
Translator: Unknown
Notes: Collection 'i classici'

1995 *Jane Eyre*. Milan, La Spiga
Translator: M. De Maria, A. Tenconi Fasoli
Known reprint: 1999

1996 *Jane Eyre*. Milan, Mondadori
Translator: Luisa Reali
Known reprints: 1999, 2004, 2008, 2011, 2012, 2016
Notes: Introduction by Franco Buffoni

1996 *Jane Eyre*. Milan, Editoriale Zeus
Translator: Unknown
Notes: Introduction by Maria Luisa Astaldi

1997 *Jane Eyre*. Milan, Frassinelli
Translator: Alessandro Gallenzi

2004 *Jane Eyre*. Rimini, Rusconi
Translator: Unknown
Notes: Collection 'I grandi classici'

2007 *Jane Eyre*. Naples, La nuova scuola
Translator: Caterina Lerro, Luisa Marro
Notes: Very abridged. Collection 'Flowers of Literature: Classics by Steps'

2008 *Jane Eyre*. Turin, Einaudi
Translator: L. Lamberti
Known reprint: 2017

2011 *Jane Eyre*. Florence, Giunti
Translator: Marianna D'Ezio
Notes: Introduction by Joyce Carol Oates

2011 *Jane Eyre*. Milan, Dalai
Translator: Fosca Belli

2013 *Jane Eyre*. Milan, Rizzoli
Translator: Berenice Capatti
Known reprints: 2016, 2018
Notes: La biblioteca delle ragazze

2014 *Jane Eyre*. Milan, Feltrinelli
Translator: Stella Sacchini
Notes: Postface by Remo Ceserani

2014 *Jane Eyre*. Salerno, Editrice Gaia
Translator: Francesco Torraca
Notes: Possibly 2nd edn, introduction by Erica D'Antuono

2014 *Jane Eyre*. Vicenza, Neri Pozza
Translator: Monica Pareschi
Notes: Intro Tracy Chevalier

2017 *Jane Eyre*. Milan, Einaudi
Translator: Carlo Pagetti

Japanese

1896 理想佳人/*Riso Kajin*/*An Ideal Lady*. Tokyo, Hakubunkan
Translator: Futo Mizutani
Notes: Abridged, incomplete, abandoned after 14 chapters

1930 ヂエイン・エア/*Jane Eyre*. Tokyo, Kaizosha
Translator: Hisako Endo
Known reprints: 1957, 2003

1931 ジエイン・エア/*Jane Eyre*. Tokyo, Shinchosha
Translator: Gisaburo Jyuichiya
Known reprint: 1952

1949 ジエーン・エア/*Jane Eyre*. Tokyo, Okakura Shobo
Translator: Yasuo Okubo
Known reprints: 1951, 1954, 2012

1954 嵐の孤児: ジェーン・エア/*Arashi no Koji*/*Orphan of the Storm–Jane Eyre*. Tokyo, Kaiseisha
Translator: Yoichi Nakagawa
Notes: Adaptation

1955 ジェイン・エア/*Jane Eyre*. Tokyo, Kodansha
Translator: Tomoji Abe

1957 ジェーン・エア/*Jane Eyre*. Tokyo, Kadokawa Shoten
Translator: Ryuji Tanabe
Known reprints: 1967, 1996

1963 みなし子ジェーン/*Minashigo Jein*/*Jane the Orphan*. Tokyo, Iwasaki Shoten
Translator: Suzue Okanoue
Known reprints: 1967, 1969, 1976, 1989

1964 ジェイン・エア/*Jane Eyre*. Tokyo, Syueisha
Translator: Seijiro Tanaka

1967 ジェーン・エア/*Jane Eyre*. Tokyo, Iwasaki Shoten
Translator: Hanako Muraoka

1967 ジェーン・エア/*Jane Eyre*. Tokyo, Obunsha
Translator: Taeko Kamiyama

1968 ジェイン・エア/*Jane Eyre*. Tokyo, Chuo Koronsha
Translator: Ichiro Kono
Known reprint: 1994

1968 ジェイン・エア/*Jane Eyre*. Tokyo, Syueisha
Translator: Kenichi Yoshida

Known reprint: 1979

1971 ジェーン・エア/*Jane Eyre*. Tokyo, Kaiseisha
Translator: Eiji Shinba

1974 ジェイン・エア/*Jane Eyre*. Tokyo, Kodansha
Translator: Koji Oi

1974 ジェーン・エア/*Jane Eyre*. Tokyo, Syueisha
Translator: Yoshiharu Suzuki

1995 ジェイン・エア/*Jane Eyre*. Tokyo, Misuzu Shobo
Translator: Shigeru Koike

2002 ジェーン・エア/*Jane Eyre*. Kyoto, Kyoto Syugakusha
Translator: Yasuo Tanaka

2006 ジェイン・エア/*Jane Eyre*. Tokyo, Kobunsha
Translator: Fusa Obi

2007 ジェイン・エア/*Jane Eyre*. Tokyo, HQ Fast Fiction
Translator: Akiko Minami
Notes: Abridged

2013 ジェイン・エア/*Jane Eyre*. Tokyo, Iwanami Shoten
Translator: Hiromi Kawashima

Kannada

2014 ಜೇನ್ ಐರ್/*Jane Eyre*. Bengaluru, Tēju Pablikēṣans
Translator: Śyāmalā Mādhava

Korean

1957 제인 에어/*Jane Eyre*. Seoul, Ewha Women's University/홍문사 이화여대출판사
Translator: Ewha University English Novel Class
Known reprint: 1958

1963 제인 에어/*Jane Eyre*. Seoul, 을류문화사 중앙문화사 신영출판사 중앙미디어 중앙출판사
Translator: Lee, Kunsam
Known reprints: 1982, 1988, 1987, 1994, 1996

1969 제인 에어/*Jane Eyre*. Seoul, 창도사 동서문화사
Translator: Won, UngSeo
Known reprints: 1969, 1976

1970 제인 에어/*Jane Eyre*. Seoul, Donghwa Publishing Corporation Ltd/ 동화출판공사 동화출판사
Translator: Yu, JongHo
Known reprint: 1973

Notes: See 2004 entry.

1971 제인 에어/*Jane Eyre*. Seoul, 정음사
Translator: Chung, Bongwha
Known reprint: 1984

1971 제인 에어/*Jane Eyre*. Seoul, Daeyang Co/주부생활 4월호 부록/대양출판사
Translator: Yun, JongHyuk
Known reprint: 1975

1972 제인 에어/*Jane Eyre*. Seoul, 제문출판사/영흥문화사/흥신문화사/오성출판사/삼금출판사
Translator: Jung, SungKuk
Known reprints: 1976, 1977, 1979, 1981

1974 제인 에어/*Jane Eyre*. Seoul, 휘문출판사
Translator: Yu, Ryung

1975 제인 에어/*Jane Eyre*. Seoul, Minumsa Publisher 삼중당
Translator: Lee, Jaehun

1976 제인 에어/*Jane Eyre*. Seoul, Samsung Publishing Co/삼성출판사
Translator: Lee, KunChul
Known reprint: 1986

1980 제인 에어/*Jane Eyre*. Seoul, Whimoon Publishing Company/범우사/휘문출판사/신원문화사
Translator: Bae, YoungWon
Known reprints: 1983, 1984, 1996, 2002

1981 제인 에어/*Jane Eyre*. Seoul, 지성출판사/시대문화사/천호출판사
Translator: Ku, JungSeo
Known reprints: 1983, 1985

1982 제인 에어*Jane Eyre*. Seoul, 풍년
Translator: Kim, SunHo

1982 제인 에어/*Jane Eyre*. Seoul, Gakwon Publishing Corporation 문공사/삼성당/학원출판공사
Translator: Park, SunNyeo
Known reprints: 1982, 1992, 2016

1986 제인 에어/*Jane Eyre*. Seoul, 청화
Translator: Kim, YongGil

1988 제인 에어/*Jane Eyre*. Seoul, 계몽사
Translator: Jang, MunPyong
Known reprint: 1993

1988 제인 에어/*Jane Eyre*. Seoul, Education Library/교육서관/하서
Translator: Kim, MunYoung

Known reprint: 2002

1988 제인 에어/*Jane Eyre*. Seoul, Ilshin/일신서적공사
Translator: Kim, SuYeon
Known reprints: 1988, 1994

1990 제인 에어/*Jane Eyre*. Seoul, 세명문화사
Translator: Lee, JungKee
Known reprint: 1994

1992 제인 에어/*Jane Eyre*. Seoul, Hongshin Culture History/홍신문화사
Translator: Park, JongHak
Known reprint: 2001

1994 제인 에어/*Jane Eyre*. Seoul, Samsung Publisher/삼성기획/육문사
Translator: Kim, JungWhan
Known reprints: 1995, 2000

1994 제인 에어/*Jane Eyre*. Seoul, Sodam Publishing Company/소담출판사
Translator: Yu, HaeKyung

1999 제인 에어/*Jane Eyre*. Seoul, 청목사
Translator: Kim, SungKu

2004 제인 에어/*Jane Eyre*. Seoul, 민음사
Translator: Yu, JongHo
Known reprints: 2008, 2017
Notes: Inspired by the award of a prize to his 1970 translation, the translator produced a new translation in more colloquial and modern language.

2005 제인 에어/*Jane Eyre*. Seoul, 신아사
Translator: Jo, AeRi
Notes: Bilingual Korean-English edition

2014 제인 에어/*Jane Eyre*. Seoul, The Classic/더클래식
Translator: Na, SunSook
Known reprint: 2017

2016 제인 에어/*Jane Eyre*. Seoul, Brown Hill/브라운힐
Translator: Park, JungSook

Latvian

1976 *Džeina Eira: romāns/Jane Eyre: Novel*. Riga, Izdevniecība "Liesma"
Translator: Helga Gintere
Known reprint: 2008

Lithuanian

1957 *Džeinė Eir*. Vilnius, Valstybinė grožinės literatūros leidykla
Translator: Unknown
Notes: Source: Jay Dillon Rare Books + Manuscripts

1983 *Džeinė Eir*. Kaunas, FD
Translator: Vytautas Karsevičius
Notes: Abridged; with running English-Lithuanian thesaurus

1985 *Džeinė Eir*. Vilnius, Vaga
Translator: Marija Kazlauskaitė and Juozas Subatavičius
Known reprint: 2006
Note: reprint is with Alma littera

Macedonian

1984 *Džejn Ejr*. Skopje, Naša kniga
Translator: Ilinka Smilevska

Malay

1979 *Jane Eyre*. Kuala Lumpur, Dewan Bahasa dan Pustaka
Translator: Sharifah Hasnah Abdullah

Malayalam

1983 ഷാർലറ്റ ബ്രോൺടി ജെയ്ൻ എയർ/*Charlotte Brontë: Jane Eyre*. Kottayam, D. C. Books
Translator: N. Govindan Nair
Notes: Abridged

2020 ജെയ്ൻ എയർ/*Jane Eyre*. Kothamangalam, Saikatam Buks
Translator: Sāṟa Dīpa Ceṟiyān

Moldavan

1988 *Džejn Ejr*. Chişinău, Literatura artistike
Translator: Iskimži, Nina; Kurekeru-Vatamanu, E.

2004 *Jane Eyre*. Chişinău, Arc
Translator: Paul B. Marian and D. Mazilu
Notes: In two volumes. First published in Bucharest in 1956, when it counted as being in Romanian.

Mongolian

2014 *Delhiyn songodog zohioluud/Selected World Classics*. Ulan Bator, Bolor Sudar Publishing
Translator: D. Altanchimeg

Notes: Title of collection can also be roughly translated to mean The "best" Works of Literature. Within the collection, only parts of Jane Eyre translated. Within collection: Жейн Эйр: Шарлотте Бронтегийн бүтээлээс хэсэгчлэн авав/*Jyeyn Eyr: Sharlotte Brontyegiyn büteelees hesegchlen avav/Jyeyn Eyr: An Excerpt Taken from Charlotte Brontë's Work/works.*

Nepali

1993 जेन एयर/*Jane Eyre*, Kathmandu, Abhivyākti Chāpākhānā (Expression Press, Chabahil), for PEN Nepal

Translator: Mrs Sarayu Rāī

Notes: Mrs Sarayu Rai was a retired schoolteacher at Kurseong, near Darjeeling. Source: Jay Dillon Rare Books + Manuscripts.

North-East Scots

2018 *Jean Eyre*. Dundee, Evertype

Translator: Sheena Blackhall and Sheila Templeton

Norwegian

1902 *Jane Eyre*. Oslo, *Norsk Familie-Journal*

Translator: Unknown

Notes: published as a free supplement to *Norsk Familie-Journal*. Source: Jay Dillon Rare Books + Manuscripts

1911 *Jane Eyre eller en Gouvernantes Memoirer*. Efter det Engelske. 1.-3. Del. Roman/*Jane Eyre, or, a Governess's Memoir. Translated from English, parts 1–3, novel.* Oslo, Kristiania

Translator: Unknown

1948 *Jane Eyre*. Oslo, Nasjonalforlaget

Translator: Unknown

1986 *Jane Eyre*. Oslo, Mortensen

Translator: Othar Bertelsen

1989 *Jane Eyre*. Bærum, Den norske bokklubben

Translator: Elise Horn

1999 *Jane Eyre*. Oslo, Pax

Translator: Ragnfrid Stokke

Persian

1950 یتیم: Subtitled ژن ئر/*Yatim/Orphan*. Tehran, Ma'refat

Translator: Mas'ud Barzin

Notes: Abridged

1982 جین ایر/*Jane Eyre*. Tehran, Zarrin

Translator: Mahdi Afshar

Known reprints: 1987, 1991, 2005, 2009

1983 جین ایر/*Jane Eyre*. Tehran, Towsan
Translator: Parviz Najmoddini
Notes: Translation of E. M. Attwood's simplified version

1985 جین ایر/*Jane Eyre*. Tehran, Mojarrad
Translator: Nazer Ne'mati
Notes: Abridged

1990 جین ایر/*Jane Eyre*. Tehran, Javidan
Translator: Fereidun Kar
Notes: Abridged

1991 جین ایر/*Jane Eyre*. Tehran, Mohammad-Taqi Bahrami Horran
Translator: Mohammad-Taqi Bahrami Horran
Known reprints: 1996, 2001, 2010, 2014
Notes: Self-published; 1996 with Jami

1991 جین ایر/*Jane Eyre*. Tehran, Abnus
Translator: Nastaran Jame'i
Known reprints: 1996, 2014
Notes: Abridged

1991 جین ایر/*Jane Eyre*. Tehran, Ketab-e Afarin
Translator: Parvin Qa'emi
Known reprint: 1995
Notes: Abridged

1997 جین ایر/*Jane Eyre*. Tehran, Hezar Aftab
Translator: Shahla Naqash, Fatemeh Naqash
Notes: Abridged

1998 جین ایر/*Jane Eyre*. Tehran, Jaddeh-ye Abrisham
Translator: Hojjatollah Soleymani
Notes: Persian Rewriting

2004 جین ایر/*Jane Eyre*. Tehran, Amir Kabir
Translator: Maryam Moayyedi
Known reprint: 2015
Notes: Translation of Evelyn Attwood's simplified version

2004 جین ایر/*Jane Eyre*. Tehran, Sarvestan
Translator: Zohreh Bakubi
Known reprint: 2008
Notes: Abridged

2006 جین ایر/*Jane Eyre*. Mashad, Nush

Translator: Ayat Tabasiyan

Notes: Abridged

2009 جین ایر/*Jane Eyre*. Tehran, Ofoq
Translator: Nushin Ebrahimi

Known reprint: 2013

Notes: Translation of Anna Claybourne's rewriting

2010 جین ایر/*Jane Eyre*. Tehran, Nashr-e Ney
Translator: Reza Reza'i

Notes: Complete

2011 جین ایر/*Jane Eyre*. Tehran, Ordibehesht
Translator: Maryam Rasuli

2011 جین ایر/*Jane Eyre*. Tehran, Marefat, Zaban-amuz
Translator: Sho'leh Moradi

Notes: Abridged

2012 جین ایر/*Jane Eyre*. Tehran, Zaban-e mehr
Translator: Maryam Dastum

Notes: Translation of the Oxford Bookworms Series

2013 جین ایر/*Jane Eyre*. Tehran, Fararuy
Translator: Hanieh Chupani

2013 جین ایر/*Jane Eyre*. Tehran, Ruzgar
Translator: Marzieh Khosravi

2013 جین ایر/*Jane Eyre*. Tehran, Qasidak Saba & Hegmatan
Translator: Mirinda Moqimi

2014 جین ایر/*Jane Eyre*. Tehran, Bongah-e tarjomeh va nashr-e ketab-e parseh
Translator: Armin Hedayati

Notes: Abridged illustrated version

2014 جین ایر/*Jane Eyre*. Tehran, Atefeh Moradmand
Translator: 'Atefeh Moradmand

Notes: Abridged

2015 جین ایر/*Jane Eyre*. Qom, Navid Zohur
Translator: Majid Qolami Shahedi

2015 جین ایر/*Jane Eyre*. Tehran, Mahya
Translator: Leyla Jahani

Notes: Abridged

2015 جین ایر/*Jane Eyre*. Tehran, Panjareh
Translator: Mahshid Mojtahedzadeh

2015 جین ایر/*Jane Eyre*. Tehran, Ofoq
Translator: Nushin Ebrahimi

2016 جین ایر/*Jane Eyre*. Tabriz, Yaran & Azarbaijan
Translator: Batul Ja'farzadeh

Notes: Abridged

2016 جین ایر/*Jane Eyre*. Tehran, Shahr-i qesseh
Translator: Mahta Labafi

Notes: Translation of Maggie Pearson's illustrated version

2016 جین ایر/*Jane Eyre*. Tehran, Mo'asseseh-ye negaresh-e elektronik-e ketab
Translator: Sepideh Habibi

Notes: Abridged illustrated version

2017 جین ایر/*Jane Eyre*. Qom, Atashkadeh; Jakan; Piramid
Translator: Maliheh Vafa'i

2017 جین ایر/*Jane Eyre*. Tehran, Matn-e digar/Badban
Translator: Morvarid Qasempur

2018 جین ایر/*Jane Eyre*. Tehran, Atisa
Translator: Leila Sane'i Movaffagh

2018 جین ایر/*Jane Eyre*. Tehran, Vajeh
Translator: Mahdi Ashraf al-Kottabi & Hossein Ashraf al-Kottabi

2018 جین ایر/*Jane Eyre*. Tehran, Parmis
Translator: Parisa Moqimi

2019 جین ایر/*Jane Eyre*. Qom, Ava-ye biseda
Translator: Akram Afshar

2019 جین ایر/*Jane Eyre*. Tehran, Ghadiani
Translator: Saba Karami

2019 جین ایر/*Jane Eyre*. Tehran, Nikfarjam
Translator: Zahra Yaqubian

Polish

1865 *Joanna Eyre. Powieść*/*Joanna Eyre. A Novel*. Warsaw,
Translator: Maria Faleńska

Notes: Published in *Tygodnik Mód* (*Fashion Weekly*), Issues 9–27. Magazine published the novel in instalments. Source: Jay Dillon Rare Books + Manuscripts

1880 *Janina. Powieść z angielskiego*/*Jane. English Novel*. Piotrków Trybunalski, Tydzień
Translator: Emilia Dobrzańska

Known reprint: 2006

Notes: Abridged; published in instalments 1880–1881

1921 *Sierota z Lowood. Powieść z angielskiego z kolorowanemi obrazkami/The Orphan of Lowood. An English Novel with colour pictures.* Chrzanów, Ksiegarnia i Drukarnia Związkowa w Chrzanowie

Translator: Zofia Sawicka

Known reprint: 1922

Notes: Abridged; juvenile edition with illustrations. Date is approximate. Jay Dillon advises that there seem to have been two related editions at the same time: Lviv: Kultura i Sztuka (Herman Stachel), no date, no copy known, and Berlin: Drukarnia Nakładowa Chrzanów (Chrzanów), for Eugen Bartels, no date, 'Copyright 1921 by E. Bartels', two copies at Łódź, as well as 'a similar version in German, Berlin: Bartels, no date, which was probably the source of the Polish translation'.

1930 *Dziwne losy Jane Eyre/The Strange Fate of Jane Eyre.* Poznań, Księgarnia św. Wojciecha

Translator: Teresa Świderska

Known reprints: 1959, 1971, 1974, 1976, 1991, 1993, 1996, 1997, 1998, 2008, 2009

2007 *Jane Eyre.* Kraków, Zielona Sowa

Translator: Gabriela Jaworska

Known reprint: 2009

Portuguese

1877 *Joanna Eyre.* Lisbon, *Zoophilo*

Translator: Unknown

Notes: Serialised between 1877 and 1882 in *Zoophilo*, a periodical. Incomplete. Authorship has been attributed to Francisca Wood (1802–1900) (see Cláudia Pazos Alonso, *Francisca Wood and Nineteenth-Century Periodical Culture. Pressing for Change*, Cambridge: Legenda, 2020; and Ana Teresa Marques dos Santos, 'A primeira *Jane Eyre* portuguesa, ou como o Órgão da Sociedade Protetora dos Animais trouxe Charlotte Brontë para Portugal (1877–1882)', *Revista de Estudos Anglo-Portugueses* (forthcoming)

1916 *Joanna Eyre.* Petrópolis, Vozes de Petrópolis

Translator: Unknown

Known reprints: 1926, 1953

Notes: first date is approximate.

1941 *A Paixão de Jane Eyre/The Passion of Jane Eyre.* Lisbon, Editorial Inquérito

Translators: Mécia and João Gaspar Simões

Known reprints: 1951, 1964, 1971, 1983, 2003, 2004, 2011

Notes: Bowdlerised version, but later editions claim to have been revised. Different editions don't mention dates, only the number of the edition. 1983 and 2004 are with Difel. 2003 is in Beja with Europa-América; 2011 with Relogio d'Agua

1942 *Jane Eyre*. Rio de Janeiro, Irmãos Pongetti
Translator: Sodré Viana

Known reprints: 1943, 1944, 1946, 1954, 1956, 1958, 1960, 1964, 1965, c.1970 , 2018
Notes: c. 1970 with Ediouro; 2018 with Editora Nova Fronteira

1945 *Jane Eyre (A Mulher Sublime)/Jane Eyre (A Sublime Woman)*. São Paulo, Edições e Publicações Brasil S.A.
Translator: Virgínia Silva Lefreve (sic)

1951 *O Grande Amor de Jane Eyre/The Great Love of Jane Eyre*. Lisbon, Romano Torres
Translator: Leyguarda Ferreira

Known reprints: 1955, 1957, 1965, 1976

Notes: Slightly abridged version.

1953 *Jane Eyre*. Rio de Janeiro, Ebal
Translator: Unknown

Known reprint: 1956

Notes: Graphic novel; published in two different periodicals: Maravilhosa (June 1953, nr. 69) and Pequenina (June 1956, nr. 27)

1958 *Jane Eyre*. Porto, Civilização
Translator: Maria Fernanda Cidrais

Known reprints: 1977, 2012

1970 *Jane Eyre*. Rio de Janeiro, Editora Vecchi
Translator: Unknown

1971 *Jane Eyre*. Rio de Janeiro, Ediouro
Translator: Miécio Táti

Known reprints: 198?, 1996

Notes: Juvenile Edition

1974 *Jane Eyre*. Lisbon, Verbo
Translator: Maria das Mercês de Mendonça Soares

Known reprint: 1988

Notes: Juvenile edition, with illustrations. Abridged.

1974 *Jane Eyre*. Lisbon, Emissora Nacional Portuguesa
Translator: Unknown

Notes: Radio version; never published.

1975 *Jane Eyre*. Porto, Inova
Translator: João Cabral do Nascimento

1978 *A Paixão de Jane Eyre/The Passion of Jane Eyre*. Lisbon, Círculo de Leitores
Translator: Maria Auta Monteiro Costa
Known reprints: 1987, 2007

1983 *Jane Eyre*. Rio de Janeiro, Francisco Alves
Translator: Marcos Santarrita

1988 *Jane Eyre*. Porto, Edinter
Translator: Isabel Patrícia and Martins da Rocha
Notes: Juvenile edition, with illustrations. Very abridged.

1994 *Jane Eyre*. Madrid, Ediclube, S.A.P.E.
Translator: Translation Agency P.A.R.
Known reprints: 1997, 2002

1996 *Jane Eyre*. São Paulo, Paz & Terra
Translator: Lenita Maria Remoli Esteves and Almiro Piseta

2007 *Jane Eyre*. Amadora, Ediclube
Translator: Unknown

2008 *Jane Eyre*. Belo Horizonte, Editora Itatiaia
Translator: Waldemar Rodrigues de Oliveira
Known reprint: 2009

2009 *Jane Eyre*. Porto, Modo de Ler
Translator: Unknown

2010 *Jane Eyre*. São Paulo, Landmark
Translator: Doris Goettems
Known reprint: 2016
Notes: Bilingual and Illustrated

2011 *Jane Eyre*. Lisbon, Presença
Translator: Alice Rocha

2011 *Jane Eyre*. Matosinhos, Book.it
Translator: Mafalda Dias
Known reprint: 2012

2011 *Jane Eyre*. Rio de Janeiro, Edições Bestbolso
Translator: Heloísa Seixas
Known reprints: 2013, 2014, 2016, 2018?

2014 *Jane Eyre*. São Paulo, Martin Claret
Translator: Carlos Duarte and Anna Duarte

2018 *Jane Eyre*. Rio de Janeiro, Zahar
Translator: Adriana Lisboa
Notes: With comments and illustrations

2018 *Jane Eyre*. São Paulo, Folha São Paulo
Translator: Unknown

2021 *Jane Eyre*. São Paulo, Penguin-Companhia
Translator: Fernanda Abreu

Punjabi

1981 ਸਰਵੇਤਮ ਵਿਸ਼ਵ ਮਾਰਿਤ ਜੇਨ ਆਇਰ/*The World-Renowned Jane Eyre*. Patiala, Bhāṣā Vibhāg
Translator: Kesar Singh Uberoi
Notes: Likely abridged

Romanian

1930 *Singură pe lume: Jane Eyre: roman/The Only One in the World*. Bucharest, Editura ziarului "Universul"
Translator: Unknown

1956 *Jane Eyre*. Bucharest, Editura de Stat pentru Literatură şi Artă
Translator: Paul B. Marian; Dumitru Mazilu
Known reprints: 1966, 1970, 1972, 1991, 2004
Notes: 2004 edition is in Chișinău, Moldova (2004)

1982 *Jane Eyre*. New York, Washington Square Press
Translator: Unknown

1993 *Jane Eyre*. Bucharest, Prietenii Cărţii
Translator: Unknown

2005 *Jane Eyre*. Bucharest, Leda
Translator: Mirella Acsente
Known reprints: 2013, 2015
Notes: Preface by Cornel Mihai Ionescu; 2015 edition is with Editura Corint

2009 *Jane Eyre*. Bucharest, Adevărul Holding : Leda
Translator: Radu Lazăr

2017 *Jane Eyre*. Bucharest, Editura Rao
Translator: Graal Soft
Notes: Translation attributed to Graal Soft, a company that offers interpreting and translation services, including literary translation

Romansch

1971 *Giuanna Eyre: Roman/Jane Eyre: Novel.* Mustér , Switzerland, Calender Romontsch

Translator: Ida Columberg-Nay

Notes: In Calendar Romontsch, Vol. 112, pp. [49]–171. Published by Stamparia de Pl. Condrau. Source: Jay Dillon Rare Books + Manuscripts

Russian

1849 *'Literaturnyia novosti v Anglii: Dzhenni Ir": Avtobiografiia' (Литературныя новости Англіи: Дженни Иръ: Автобіографія)/England's Literary News: Jane Eyre: Autobiography.* St Petersburg, Biblioteka dlia chteniia, vol. 94/2, 151–172

Translator: Unknown

Notes: Summary with translated excerpts

1849 *Dzhenni Ir" (Дженни Иръ)/Jane Eyre.* St Petersburg, Otechestvennye zapiski, vol. 64/6, 175–250; vol. 65/7, 67–158; vol. 65/8, 179–262; vol. 66/9, 65–132; vol. 66/10, 193–330

Translator: Irinarkh Vvedenskiĭ

Note: Extracts from this translation were included in a very short summary of the novel, printed as *Dzhen Ėĭr (Дженъ Эйръ)/Jane Eyre.* St Petersburg, Sovremennik, vol. 21/6 (1850), 31–38.

1857 *Dzhenni Ėĭr" ili zapiski guvernantki (Дженни Эйръ или записки гувернантки)/Jane Eyre, or The memoirs of a Governess.* St Petersburg, Biblioteka dlia dach, parokhodov i zheleznykh dorog

Translator: S. I. Koshlakova

Notes: Translated from 'Old Nick''s French version, *Jane Eyre. Mémoires d'une gouvernante* (Paris and Brussels 1849; reprinted Paris 1855). See French section above.

1893 *Dzhenni Eĭr": Lovudskaia sirota. Roman»-avtobiografiia v dvukh" chastiakh" (Дженни Эйръ: Ловудская сирота. Романъ-автобиография в двухъ частяхъ)/Jane Eyre, the orphan of Lowood. Novel-Autobiography in two parts.* St Petersburg, Lederle i Ko

Translator: V. D. Vladimirov

Notes: Name alias of Vladimir Dmitrievich Vol'fson. A short summary of this translation was published in Mir Bozhiy (God's peace), 9 (1893).

1901 *Dzheni Ėĭr". Istoriia moeĭ zhizni (Джени Эйръ. Исторія моей жизни)/Jane Eyre: The Story of My Life. St Petersburg, IUnyĭ chitatel': zhurnal" dlia dieteĭ starshago vozrasta, Vol.* 3, 5

Translator: Anonymous

Notes: Abridged for a juvenile audience

1950 *Dzhen Eĭr (Джен Эйр)/Jane Eyre.* Leningrad (now St Petersburg), Goslitizdat: 2ja fabrika detskoj knigi Detgiza

Translator: V. O. Stanevich

Reprints: 1952, 1955, 1956, 1956, 1957, 1958, 1959, 1960, 1983, 1983, 1985, 1986, 1987, 1988, 1988, 1988, 1989, 1989, 1989, 1989, 1990, 1990, 1991, 1992, 1992, 1992, 1992, 1992, 1992, 1992, 1992, 1992, 1992, 1992, 1992, 1993, 1993, 1993, 1993, 1994, 1994, 1996, 1997, 1998, 1998, 2003, 2004, 2005, 2005, 2007, 2008, 2008, 2008, 2009, 2009, 2009, 2010, 2010, 2010, 2010, 2011, 2011, 2011, 2012, 2013, 2013, 2014, 2014, 2015, 2015, 2015, 2016, 2016, 2016, 2016, 2016, 2017, 2018, 2018, 2018, 2018, 2019, 2019, 2020, 2020, 2020, 2020, 2021

Notes: Simultaneously published in Moscow. 1952 edition with Goslitizdat, Moscow; 1955 with Lenizdat, Leningrad; 1956 (i) with Kazgoslitizdat, Alma Ata; 1956 (ii) with Rad. pys'mennyk, Kiev; 1957 with Gosizdat BSSR, Minsk; 1958 with Altaiskoe kn. Izdatel'stvo and Gor'kovskoe knizhnoe izd-vo, Barnaul; 1959 with Goslitizdat USSR, Tashkent; 1960 with Gor'kovskoe knizhnoe izd-vo, Gorkii (now Nizhnii Novgorod); 1983 (i), 1988 (i), and 1989 (i) with Pravda, Moscow; 1983 (ii) with Vyshcha shkola, Kiev; 1985 with Krasnodarskoe knizhnoe izdatel'stvo, Krasnodar; 1986 with Khudozhestvennaia literature, Makhachkala; 1987 with Dnipro, Kiev; 1988 (ii) with Vysheĭsh. Shk., Minsk; 1988 (iii) and 1989 (ii) with Mordovskoe kn. Izdatel'stvo, Saransk; 1989 (iii), 1990 (ii), and 1994 (i) with Khudozh, Moscow; 1989 (iv) with Yazychi, Baku; 1990 (i) with Tsentral'no-Chernozemskoe kn. Izdatel'stvo, Voronezh; 1991 with Detskaja literatura, Moscow; 1992 (i) with Yuzh. zvezda, Krasnodar; 1992 (ii) with Sovetskii pisatel', Moscow; 1992 (iii) and 1998 (i) with OLMA-PRESS, Moscow; 1992 (iv) with Dom, Moscow; 1992 (v) with Grotesk, Krasnoyarsk; 1992 (vi) with Germes, Rostov-on-Don; 1992 (vi) with Ural-BISI, Izhevsk; 1992 (viii) with Znamenitaya kniga, Moscow; 1992 (ix) with Belarus', Minsk; Aktsiia, Khimki; 1992 (x) with Orakul, Minsk; 1992 (xi), 1992 (xii), 1993 (i) with Korum, Moscow; 1993 (ii) with IPF Zeus, Moscow; 1993 (iii) with Izd-vo Tomskogo universiteta, Tomsk; 1993 (iv) with Tatarskoe kn. Izdatel'stvo, Kazan; 1994 with Buryatskoe kn. Izdatel'stvo, Ulan-Ude; 1996 with Izvestia, Moscow; 1997 with El'-fa, Nalchik; 1998 (ii), 2004, 2005 (i), 2005 (ii), 2007, 2008 (i), 2008 (ii), 2008 (iii), 2009 (i), 2009 (ii), 2010 (i), 2010 (ii), 2011 (i), 2011 (ii), 2013 (i), 2014 (i), 2014 (ii), 2015 (i), 2015 (ii), 2016 (i), 2016 (ii), 2016 (iii), 2016 (iv), 2016 (v), 2018 (i), 2018 (ii), 2018 (iii), 2018 (iv), 2019 (i), 2020 (i), 2020 (ii), 2020 (iii), and 2020 (iv) with Eksmo, Moscow; 2009 (iii) with Leningradskoe izdatel'stvo, St Petersburg; 2010 (iii), 2011 (iii), 2013 (ii), 2015 (iii) with RIPOL klassik, Moscow; 2010 (iv) with Profizdat, Moscow; 2012 with Martin, Moscow; 2017 with Pesochnye chasy, Moscow; 2019 (ii) with Izdatel'skij dom Mescherjakova; 2021 with Kacheli, St Petersburg.

The following editions published in Moscow with unknown translators are likely to reprint the Stanevich text: 1952, Khud. lit.; 1957, Vysheĭsh. Shk.; 1960, Izd-vo Pravda; 1983 and 1985, Yuzhnaia Zvezda; 1989, Khudozhestvennaia literature; 1990, Detskaja literature. The following editions with unknown translators, printed in different cities, probably reproduce the Stanevich translation.

1990 *Dzhen Eĭr (Джен Эйр)/Jane Eyre*. Moscow, Khudozhestvennaia literatura

Translator: V. O. Stanevich, with omissions reconstructed by I. Gurova

Notes: The following editions with unknown translators may reproduce either the original Stanevich translation or the text as augmented by Gurova: 1990, Privolzhskoe kn. Izdatel'stvo: SO NPO "Insolar", Saratov; 1990, I͡Azychy, Baku; 1991, Vneshiberika, Moscow and St Petersburg; 1992, Severo-zapadnoe kn. Izdatel'stvo/ *VPPO*, Arcangelo; 1992, *ADIB*, Dushanbe; 1992, Kn. Izdatel'stvo, Novosibirsk; 1993, Tovarischestvo "Vol'noe slovo", Ivanovo; 1993, Sovremennai͡a lit-ra, Minsk (bound together with Rozhdestvo v Indii by Barbara Ford); 1994, Literatura, Minsk (re-edition of the 1993 Minsk publication); 1994, Vysheĭshaia Shkola, Minsk; 1994, Kudozhestvennai͡a Literatura, Moscow

1999 *Dzheĭn Ėĭr (Джейн Эйр)/Jane Eyre, with Rozhdestvo v Indii (Рождество в Индии)/Christmas in India by Barbara Ford, trans. by V. Semenov*. Moscow: AST, 1999

Translator: I. G. Gurova

—Moscow reprints: 2003, 2004, 2005, 2005, 2005, 2005, 2005, 2007, 2007, 2007, 2009, 2010, 2010, 2010, 2010, 2010, 2011, 2011, 2011, 2011, 2013, 2015, 2016, 2016, 2016, 2017, 2017, 2017, 2018, 2018, 2018, 2019, 2019, 2019, 2019, 2019, 2020, 2020, 2021, 2021, 2021, 2021

Notes: 2003, 2004, 2005 (i), 2005 (ii), 2005 (iii), 2009, 2010 (i), 2010 (ii), 2010 (iii), 2010 (iv), 2010 (v), 2011 (i), 2011 (ii), 2011 (iii), 2013, 2016 (i), 2017 (i), 2018 (i), 2019 (i), 2019 (ii), 2019 (iii), 2019 (iv), 2020 (i), 2021 (i), and 2021 (ii) with AST; 2005 (iv) with Literatura: mir knigi; 2005 (v) with Geleos; 2005 (iii) and 2007 (ii) with Profizdat; 2007 (i) and 2015 with TERRA--Knizhnyi Klub Knigovez; 2007 (iii) with Komsomol'skaya pravda; 2011 (iv) and 2018 (ii) with Inostranka; 2016 (ii) and 2016 (iii) with Martin; 2017 (ii) and 2021 (iii) with Veche; 2017 (iii) with Vremja; 2018 (iii) with Al'fa-kniga; 2019 (v) with Rech'; 2020 (ii) with NEB Svet; 2021 (iv) with ROSMEN

—St Petersburg reprints: 2006, 2008, 2009, 2010, 2011, 2012, 2012, 2013, 2013, 2013, 2014, 2014, 2015, 2015, 2016, 2017, 2019, 2020

Notes: all with Azbuka-klassika except 2012 (ii) which is with Leninzdat and 2019 which is with Rech'

—Minsk reprints: 2011

Notes: with Harvest

The following editions with unknown translators are likely to use one of the Stanevich, the Stanevich-Gurova or the Gurova translations: 2006, Minnetonka, Russian publisher unknown (distributed by East View Information Services in the US); 2009, 20010, 2011, Minsk, Kharvest (including Barbara Ford, *Rozhdestvo v Indii*); 2011, Charkiv, Izdatel'stvo Klub Semeĭnogo Dosuga

Serbian

1952 *Џејн Ејр/Jane Eyre*. Belgrade, Novo pokolenje
Translator: Radmila Todorović

Known reprints: 1953, 1964, 1965, 1966, 1967, 1971, 1973, 1976, 1978, 1980, 1986, 1990, 1994, 2011, 2012, 2014, 2016, 2017
Notes: 2012 is in Novi Sad with Kuća dobre knjige

1990 *Džejn Ejr, buntovnica/Jane Eyre, the Rebel*. Sarajevo, Oslobođenje
Translator: Budislava Šćekić

Notes: Abridged by Eugenio Sotillos

Sinhalese

1955 ජේන් අයර්/*Jane Eyre. Colombo, M. D.* Gunasena and Company
Translator: R. N. H. Perera

Known reprints: 1956, 1977, 1985, 1991, 1995, 2000, 2015

Notes: Source: Jay Dillon Rare Books + Manuscripts

1999 ජේන් අයර්/*Jane Eyre. Colombo, S.* Godage
Translator: H. M. Moratuwagama,

Notes: Abridged for children. Source: Jay Dillon rare Books + Manuscripts

2015 *Jane Eyre*. Colombo, Sarasavi Publishing
Translator: Pramitha Rohini Wanigaratne

Slovak

1954 *Jana Eyrová*. Bratislava, Mladé letá
Translator: Štefan Kýška

Known reprints: 1964, 1985

Slovenian

1955 *Sirota iz Lowooda/Orphan of Lowood*. Maribor, Večer
Translator: France Borko & Ivan Dolenc

1970 *Sirota iz Lowooda/Orphan of Lowood*. Murska Sobota, Pomurska založba

Translator: Božena Legiša-Velikonja

Known reprint: 1980

1991 *Jane Eyre*. Ljubljana, Založništvo slovenske knjige
Translator: Božena Legiša-Velikonja

Notes: Reprint of 1970 translation under a new title

Spanish

1849 *Juana Eyre: Memorias de un aya/Jane Eyre: Memoirs of a Governess.* Paris, Administración del Correo de Ultramar (Xavier de Lassalle)
Translator: Unknown

Notes: Translated from 'Old Nick''s French version published in Paris and Brussels in 1849: here 'Oldt-Nick' (sic) is given as author, with no mention of Brontë. Source: Jay Dillon Rare Books + Manuscripts

1850 *Juana Eyre. Memorias de un aya.* Santiago de Chile, Imprenta del Progreso
Translator: Unknown

Notes: Serialisation in the newspaper *El Progreso*, 7th February – 4th April. Author is given as 'Oldt-Nick', with no mention of Brontë, as in the Paris 1849 translation which this edition reprints

1850–1 *Juana Eyre: memorias de un aya.* Havana, *Diario de la Marina*
Translator: Unknown

Known Reprint: 1851

Notes: Author is given as 'Old Nick'. Serialisation in the newspaper *Diario de la Marina* during 1850–1851; also printed as a volume by Imprenta del Diario de la Marina, 1851.
Reprints the 1849 Paris translation

1851 *Juana Eyre: Memorias de un aya.* La Paz, Imprenta Paceña
Translator: Unknown

Notes: Serialised in *La época* newspaper. Probably reprints the 1849 Paris translation. Also printed as a volume of 105 pages. Source: J. R. Guttérez, *Datos para la Bibliografía Boliviana* (La Paz, Imprenta de la Libertad de Ezéquiel Arzadum (1875)

1851 *Juana Eyre: Memorias de un aya.* Matanzas, Imprenta de gobierno por S.M
Translator: Unknown

Notes: This translation is probably a reprint of Havana 1850–51, and is probably incomplete. Source: Jay Dillon Rare Books + Manuscripts

1882 *Juana Eyre; ó, Memorias de una institutriz.* Madrid, *El globo*

Translator: Unknown

Notes: Serialised in *El globo* newspaper, 9 September 1882 – 7 February 1883, in 134 instalments. An anonymous relay translation from Noëmi Lesbazeilles-Souvestre's 1854 French translation, discovered by Sara Medina in 2016. Source: Jay Dillon Rare Books + Manuscripts

1889 *Juana Eyre*. New York, D. Appleton y Compañía
Translator: Leopoldo Terrero

Known reprints: 1898, 1903

Notes: 1889, (Siglo XIX), 1898 (Siglo XIX), 1903 (Siglo XX: 1900–1936). Source: M. Ortega Sáez

1928 *Juana Eyre*. Barcelona, Juventud
Translator: José Fernández Z.

Known reprints: 1945, 1958, 1976, 1996, 1998, 2003

Notes: José Fernández Z. is José Zendrera Flecha (1894–1969), owner and founder of the publishers Juventud. It is likely that José Zendrera Flecha was not the translator himself, and that he was simply registering the books under his name. Source: M. Ortega Sáez

1928 *Juana Eyre*. Barcelona, Mentora
Translator: Unknown

1941 *Jane Eyre*. Buenos Aires, Acme Agency (Amadeo Bois)
Translator: M. E. Antonini

Known reprints: 1944, 1948, 1957

1941 *Juana Eyre*. Buenos Aires, Editorial Juventud Argentina
Translator: Unknown

1943 *Jane Eyre*. Barcelona, Iberia, Joaquin Gil
Translator: Juan G. de Luaces

Known reprints: 1948, 1954, 1955, 1958, 1961, 1961 (ii), 1966, 1967, 1972, 1973, 1974, 1979, 1984, 1985, 1987, 1989, 1995, 1996, 1997, 1998, 2000, 2003, 2004, 2005, 2007, 2011, 2011, 2015

Notes: 1961(i) edition is with Vergara (Obras de Carlota, Emilia y Ana Bronte); 1967, 1973, 1974, 1984, 1987, 1995, 1997, 1998, 2000, 2003, 2005, 2007, 2011 with Madrid, Espasa Calpe; 1974 with Círculo de Amigos de la Historia; 1984, 1987, 1996, 1998, 2000, 2003, 2004 with Planeta; 1985 with Bogota, Oveja Negra; 2005 with Altaya; 1954, 1955, 1972, 2011, 2015 with Buenos Aires, Espasa-Calpe Argentina; 1966, 1979, 1996 with Barcelona, Círculo de Lectores

1944 *Jane Eyre*. Buenos Aires, Sopena
Translator: Rafael Jiménez Orderiz

Known reprints: 1946, 1983, 2004

Notes: 1946 with Buenos Aires, Sopena Argentina; 1983 and 2004 with Mexico City, Porrúa

1944 *Jane Eyre*. Santiago de Chile, Zig-zag
Translator: Unknown

1945 *Jane Eyre*. Barcelona, Renguera
Translator: Javier de Zengotita

1945 *Jane Eyre*. Barcelona, Bruguera
Translator: Juan Ruiz de Larios

Known reprints: 1954, 1968, 1971, 1972, 1973, 1974, 1976

1945 *Juana Eyre: novela completa*. Madrid, Revista Literaria « Novelas y Cuentos »
Translator: Unknown

1946 *Jane Eyre*. Barcelona, Molino
Translator: Rosa S. de Naveira

1946 *Jane Eyre*. Buenos Aires, W. M. Jackson
Translator: Fernando M. Ungría

Known reprints: 1952, 1961, 1968

Notes: 1952 and 1961 with Barcelona, Éxito; 1968 with Mexico City, Cumbre

1947 *Jane Eyre*. Madrid, Aguilar
Translator: María Fernanda Pereda

Known reprints: 1949, 1953, 1959, 1962, 1972, 1974, 1977, 1990, 1994, 1997, 2009, 2012, 2016

Notes: 1972 and 1977 with Barcelona, Plaza & Janés; 1990, 1994, 1997, 2009, 2012, 2016 with Madrid, Orbis

1956 *Jane Eyre*. Barcelona, Fama
Translator: Elena García Ortiz

Notes: Source: M. Ortega Sáez

1962 *Jane Eyre*. Barcelona, Toray
Translator: José Villalva Pinyana

Notes: Source: M. Ortega Sáez

1966 *Jane Eyre*. Barcelona, Círculo de Lectores
Translator: E. Vergara

Known reprints: 1979, 1996

1970 *Jane Eyre*. Barcelona, Rodegar
Translator: E. Reguera

Known reprint: 1972, 1977

1972 *Jane Eyre*. Madrid, Salvat + Alianza Editorial
Translator: Camila Batlles

Known reprints: 1986, 1987, 1995

Notes: 1986, 1987, 1995 with Barcelona, Salvat. Source: M. Ortega Sáez

1973 *Jane Eyre*. Barcelona, Petronio
Translator: J. Ribera

1974 *Jane Eyre*. Santiago de Chile, Paulinas
Translator: Jesus Sánchez Díaz

Notes: abridged for younger readers

1976 *Jane Eyre*. Madrid, Alonso
Translator: Juan Alarcón Benito

1982 *Jane Eyre*. Barcelona, Toray
Translator: Eugenio Sotillos

Notes: Juvenile edition

1989 *Jane Eyre*. Santiago de Chile, Zig Zag
Translator: S. Robles

Notes: abridged for younger readers

1991 *Jane Eyre*. Madrid, Gaviota
Translator: José Enrique Cubedo Fernández-Trapiella

Known reprint: 2013

Notes: 2013 with León, Everest. Source: M. Ortega Sáez

1996 *Jane Eyre*. Madrid, Cátedra
Translator: Elizabeth Power

Known reprints: 2006, 2008 (i), 2008 (ii), 2009, 2012, 2016

Notes: 2006 and 2008 (ii) with Alianza Editorial

1999 *Jane Eyre*. Barcelona, Alba
Translator: Carmen Martín Gaite

Known reprints: 2003(i), 2003(ii), 2004, 2007, 2009, 2012, 2016

Notes: 2003(ii) and 2007 are with Debolsillo; 2004 is with RBA

Source: M. Ortega Sáez

1999 *Jane Eyre*. La Habana, Instituto Cubano del Libro
Translator: Unknown

Notes: Possibly a reprint of the 1999 translation by Gaite.

2000 *Jane Eyre*. Santiago de Chile, Zig-Zag
Translator: Unknown

Notes: possibly a reprint of the 1989 translation by Robles.

2001 *Jane Eyre*. Madrid, Edaf
Translator: Alejandro Pareja Rodríguez

Known reprint: 2016

Notes: reprint is in Barcelona with Austral

2007 *Jane Eyre*. Madrid, Rueda
Translator: Unknown

Notes: En 2 v.

2009 *Jane Eyre*. Barcelona, Mondadori
Translator: Toni Hill

Known reprints: 2010, 2011, 2015

Notes: 2011 with Debolsillos; 2015 with Penguin Clásicos

2014 *Jane Eyre*. Barcelona, Plutón
Translator: Benjamin Briggent

Known reprint: 2016

2014 *Jane Eyre*. Madrid, Susaeta
Translator: Sara Torrico

2016 *Jane Eyre*. Barcelona, Ediciones B
Translator: Nuria González Esteban

Notes: Source: M. Ortega Sáez

Swedish

1850 *Jane Eyre: en sjelf-biographie/Jane Eyre: An autobiography*. Stockholm, Albert Bonniers förlag
Translator: Unknown

1855 *Jane Eyre: En sjelfbiografi/Jane Eyre : An autobiography*. Uppsala,
Translator: Carl Johan Backman

Known reprints: 1873

Notes: the 1873 edition is substantially revised (information from Jay Dillon Rare Books + Manuscripts

1943 *Jane Eyre*. Helsinki, Söderströms Förlags Ab
Translator: Ingegärd von Tell

Known reprints: 1957, 1984, 1989, 1992, 1994, 1996, 2014

Notes: 1984, 94, 96 are in Stockholm with Natur och kultur; 2014 withModernista

1999 *Jane Eyre*. Stockholm, Bonnierförlagen
Translator: Gun-Britt Sundström

Known reprints: 2000, 2005, 2007, 2009, 2011, 2013

Notes: 2000 printing is with Månpocket; 2005 with Bonnier

2005 *Jane Eyre*. Stockholm, LL-förlaget
Translator: Unknown

Tagalog

1985 *Kapag bigo na ang lahat: hango sa Jane Eyre ni Charlotte Bronte/ When Everything Fails: a Novel of Jane Eyre by Charlotte Brontë.* Mandaluyong, Cacho Hermanos

Translator: Unknown

1992 *Kapag bigo na ang lahat/When Everything Fails. Manila, Solar Pub. Corp.*

Translator: Unknown

Tajik

2010 *Jen Ėĭr: roman.* Dushanbe, TJB "Istijbol

Translator: Unknown

Notes: In Cyrillic script

Tamil

1953 ஜேன் அயர்: உலகப் புகழ் பெற்ற நாவல்/*Jēṉ Ayar: Ulakap pukal̲ per̲r̲a nāval/Jane Eyre: A World Renowned Novel.* Tirunelvēli, Tirunelvēlit Teṉṉintiya Cavacittānta Nūr̲patippuk Kal̲akam

Translator: K. Appātturai

2003 ஜேன் அயர்: உலகப் புகழ் பெற்ற நாவல்/*Jēṉ Ayar: Ulakap pukal̲ per̲r̲a nāval/Jane Eyre: A World Renowned Novel.* Chennai, Cāratā Māṇikkam Patippakam

Translator: K. Appātturai

Notes: Enlarged edition of 1953

Thai

1993 *Rak dīeo khọ̄ng Čhēn Čhirā/My Only Love.* Bangkok, Mư̄kčhīn

Translator: Unknown

2007 ความรักของเจน แอร์/*Khwām rak khọ̄ng yēn 'œ/Jane Eyre: Love Story.* Bangkok, Phrǣo

Translator: Sotsai Khatiwō̜raphong

2009 เจน แอร์-- รักแท้ชั่วนิรันดร์/*Ghane 'œ-- rak thǣ chūaniran/Jane Eyre: Love Forever.* Bangkok, Sī'etyūkhēchan

Translator: 'Anchasā Phatthawansō̜n; Clare West

2013 ความรักของเยน แอร์/*Khwām rak khọ̄ng yēn 'œ/A Love Story.* Bangkok, Sǣngdāo

Translator: Chanit Sāipradit

Tibetan

2011 *Bumo Dreng Ar gyi mitse (Bu mo sgreng ar gyi mi tshe)/The human life of the girl Jane Eyre*. Chengdu, Sichuan Publishing House (Si khron dpe skrun tshogs pa)
Translator: Sonam Lhundrub
Notes: Abridged. The Tibetan translation was made on the basis of the abridged Chinese translation by Daming Li and Jing Li (2001). The book begins with the Tibetan text, followed by the Chinese text.

Turkish

1945 *Jane Eyre*. Istanbul, Türkiye Yayınevi
Translator: Saffet Orgun
Known reprints: 1946, 1955, 1962

1946 *Jane Eyre*. Istanbul, Pulhan Matbaası
Translator: Fahrünnisa Seden
Notes: Abridged for children by A. Sweaney

1954 *Jane Eyre*. Istanbul, Varlık Yayınevi
Translator: Tahsin Yücel
Known reprints: 1957, 1961, 1966, 1972, 1995

1962 *Jane Eyre*. Istanbul, Altın Kitaplar
Translator: Eser Tutel

1968 *Jane Eyre*. Istanbul, Hayat Yayınları
Translator: Nihal Yeğinobalı
Known reprints: 1969, 1971, 1975, 1985, 1990, 2007, 2008

1970 *Jane Eyre*. Istanbul, İnkılâp ve Aka Yayınevi
Translator: Ömer M. Karacık

1973 *Jane Eyre*. Istanbul, İnkılâp ve Aka Yayınevi
Translator: Leyla Moralı
Known reprint: 1974

1974 *Jane Eyre*. Istanbul, İnkılâp ve Aka Yayınevi
Translator: Filiz Borak
Known reprint: 1981
Notes: Revised juvenile edition

1976 *Jane Eyre*. Istanbul, Oymaktaş Yayınları
Translator: Emel Ulutaş

1981 *Jane Eyre*. Istanbul, Çağdaş Yayıncılık
Translator: Deniz Oral

1986 *Jane Eyre*. Istanbul, Ülkü Yayınevi

Translator: Suna Güler Asımgil

1994 *Jane Eyre*. Istanbul, Nurdan Yayınları
Translator: Zafer Yurt
Notes: Abridged, under "Children's Classics" series

1995 *Jane Eyre*. Istanbul, Morpa Kültür Yayınları
Translator: Bekir Balcı
Notes: Misprinted, by "Carlotte Bronte" [sic]

1997 *Jane Eyre*. Istanbul, Remzi Kitabevi
Translator: Hüseyin Yumrukçal
Known reprints: 1999, 2001, 2011
Notes: Abridged, under "Children's Classics" series

2002 *Jane Eyre*. Istanbul, Oda Yayınları
Translator: Nurten Tunç
Known reprints: 2011, 2016

2002 *Jane Eyre*. Izmir, Gonca Yayınları
Translator: Tahsin Yıldırım

2003 *Jane Eyre*. Istanbul, Gizem Çocuk Yayınları
Translator: Celâl Oğuz
Notes: Abridged, under "Children's Classics" series

2003 *Jane Eyre*. Istanbul, Morpa Kültür Yayınları
Translator: Cevat Ulkut

2003 *Jane Eyre*. Istanbul, Timaş Yayınları
Translator: Çiğdem Özmen
Known reprints: 2008, 2009, 2011, 2013

2003 *Jane Eyre*. Istanbul, İnkılap Yayınları
Translator: Öner Kemal
Known reprints: 2004, 2010
Notes: Juvenile edition

2004 *Jane Eyre*. Istanbul, Bordo Siyah Yayınevi
Translator: Ayşe Düzkan
Known reprints: 2007, 2013
Notes: Subtitled 'Aristokrasiye Yenilmeyen Aşk' (The love that survived against the aristocracy)

2004 *Jane Eyre*. Istanbul, İlya Yayınevi
Translator: Didem Koçak
Notes: Published in two slim volumes

2005 *Jane Eyre*. Ankara, Ankara Yıldırım Dağıtım

Translator: Esra Özkan

Notes: Abridged

2006 *Jane Eyre*. Istanbul, Buhan Yayıncılık
Translator: Gülhan Küçükturgay

Notes: Abridged and illustrated

2007 *Jane Eyre*. Istanbul, Sīmge Yayıncılık
Translator: Cemal Telci

Known reprint: 2009

Notes: Rewritten by the translator

2008 *Jane Eyre*. Ankara, Kılavuz Yayıncılık
Translator: Sevgi Alişarlı

Notes: Abridged

2010 *Jane Eyre*. Istanbul, Bahar Yayınevi
Translator: Edibe Atar

Notes: Marketed as a "comprehensive summary".

2010 *Jane Eyre: Yıllar Sonra Gelen Mutluluk*/*Jane Eyre: Happiness Coming After Many Years*. Istanbul, Martı Yayıncılık
Translator: Ceren Taştan

Known reprint: 2011

2011 *Jane Eyre*. Istanbul, Bahar Yayınevi
Translator: Mesut Yıldırım

Notes: Abridged

2013 *Jane Eyre*. Istanbul, Gendaş Yayınevi
Translator: F. Deniz Abamor

Notes: Unavailable; presumably abridged

2014 *Jane Eyre*. Istanbul, Gugukkuşu Yayınları
Translator: M. Ali Ayyıldız

Notes: Abridged and illustrated

2015 *Jane Eyre*. Ankara, Yason Yayınları
Translator: Göksu Birol

2016 *Jane Eyre*. Istanbul, Epsilon Yayınevi
Translator: Nilgün Erzik

Notes: Abridged

2016 *Jane Eyre*. İstanbul, Büyülü Fener Yayıncılık
Translator: Sibel Alaş

Notes: "Retold" Children's Classics

2017 *Jane Eyre*. Istanbul, Yabancı Yayınları

Translator: Arzu Altınanıt

2017 *Jane Eyre*. Istanbul, Gece Kitaplığı
Translator: Mustafa Baştürk
Notes: Subtitled 'Gözlerimi yaklaşan sonuma dikip huzur içinde yaşıyorum' (I look at my impending doom and live peacefully)

Ukrainian

1939 *Ìdealìstka: povìst' u 2 tomah/The Idealist: A novel in two parts*. L'viv, Dilo
Translator: Ol'ga Slìpa

1983 *Džen Ejr*. Kiev, Višča škola
Translator: Petro Sokolovs'kyĭ
Known reprints: 1984, 1987, 1999, 2004
Notes: 1987 with Kiev, Dnipro; 1999 with Kiev, Osnovy'; 2004 with Kharkiv, Folio. 1999 and 2004 transliterated as Dz͡heĭn Eĭr.

1995 *Dz͡heĭn Eĭr*. Kiev, BMP 'Borisfen'
Translator: Unknown

Urdu

1975 جین آئر/*Jane Eyre*. Lahore, Maktabah-e-Shakar
Translator: Saifuddīn Hassām
Known reprint: 2021
Notes: 2021 is published in Jhelum by Book Corner (Amar Shahid); Jay Dillon notes that it is a a new edition, edited by Salman Khalid. Source for the 1975 edition: Jay Dillon Rare Books + Manuscripts

2020 جین آئر/*Jane Eyre*. Karachi, City Book Point (Muhammad Asad)
Translator: Aurang Zeb Qasmi
Notes: Source: Jay Dillon Rare Books + Manuscripts

Vietnamese

1963 *Kiều giang; tiểu thuyết phóng tác nguyễn bản của Charlotte Bronti/ True Love: Charlotte Brontë's original version.* Chợlơn, Khải minh
Translator: Unknown

1971 *Kieu giang/Jane Eyre.* Saigon, Chieu Duong
Translator: Unknown

1979 *Kiều Giang: nguyên bản, Jane Eyre/Jiane Eyre, original, Jane Eyre.* Fort Smith, Sống Mới
Translator: Hải Thủy Hoàng

2006 *Jane Eyre: tiểu thuyết/Jane Eyre: a novel.* Hà Nội, Văn hóa thông tin
Translator: Liên Thảo Bùi; Thị Hợp Nguyễn; Thu Hà Vũ

2010 *Jên Erơ.* Hà Nội, Văn Học
Translator: Anh Kim Trần; Đức Nam Nguyễn

2016 *Jane Eyre.* Hà Nội, Nhà Xuất Bản Văn Học
Translator: Y Thư Trịnh

West Frisian

2020 *Jane Eyre.* Dundee, Evertype
Translator: Jant Van Der Weg-Laverman
Notes: With Illustrations by Edmund H. Garrett and E. M. Wimperis

Data and Code

The code for the Time Map was written by Giovanni Pietro Vitali and Simone Landucci. The code for all the other maps was written by Giovanni Pietro Vitali alone.

The data for the Time Map, General Map and World Map was gathered by the whole Prismatic *Jane Eyre* team, and compiled by Rachel Dryden, Eleni Philippou, Chelsea Haith, Joseph Hankinson and Matthew Reynolds: see the Acknowledgements at the start of this volume and the headnote to the List of Translations for details. The data for the Covers Maps was provided by the researchers named on each map's first page.

The code for the two Prismatic Scenes was written by Paola Gaudio; the data was provided by the researchers listed in the introductory page for each scene.

All this material is preserved both in GitHub (https:/github.com/Prismatic-Jane-Eyre) and on Oxford University's Sustainable Digital Scholarship platform (https:/www.sds.ox.ac.uk/home). It is freely available to use according to the licenses provided on GitHub and at Oxford SDS.

The locations are as follows:

General Map

https:/github.com/Prismatic-Jane-Eyre/je_prismatic_generalmap

https:/portal.sds.ox.ac.uk/articles/educational_resource/General_Map/22133510

https:/doi.org/10.25446/oxford.22133510.v1

World Map

https:/github.com/Prismatic-Jane-Eyre/je_prismatic_map

https:/portal.sds.ox.ac.uk/articles/educational_resource/World_Map/22134059

https:/doi.org/10.25446/oxford.22134059

Time Map

https:/github.com/Prismatic-Jane-Eyre/translations_timemap

https:/portal.sds.ox.ac.uk/articles/educational_resource/Time_Map/22134077

https:/doi.org/10.25446/oxford.22134077.v1

Arabic Covers Map

https:/github.com/Prismatic-Jane-Eyre/arabic_storymap

https:/portal.sds.ox.ac.uk/articles/educational_resource/Covers_Map_Arabic/22134173

https:/doi.org/10.25446/oxford.22134173.v1

Brazilian Portuguese Covers Map

https:/github.com/Prismatic-Jane-Eyre/brazilian_portuguese_storymap

https:/portal.sds.ox.ac.uk/articles/educational_resource/Covers_Map_Brazilian_Portuguese/22134401

https:/doi.org/10.25446/oxford.22134401.v1

Danish Covers Map

https:/github.com/Prismatic-Jane-Eyre/danish_storymap

https:/portal.sds.ox.ac.uk/articles/educational_resource/Covers_Map_Danish/22134206

https:/doi.org/10.25446/oxford.22134206.v1

Dutch Covers Map

https:/github.com/Prismatic-Jane-Eyre/dutch_storymap

https:/portal.sds.ox.ac.uk/articles/educational_resource/Covers_Map_Dutch/22134212

https:/doi.org/10.25446/oxford.22134212.v1

Estonian Covers Map

https:/github.com/Prismatic-Jane-Eyre/estonian_storymap

https:/portal.sds.ox.ac.uk/articles/educational_resource/Covers_Map_Estonia/22134218

https:/doi.org/10.25446/oxford.22134218.v1

Finnish Covers Map

https:/github.com/Prismatic-Jane-Eyre/finnish_storymap

https:/portal.sds.ox.ac.uk/articles/educational_resource/Covers_Map_Finnish/22134233

https:/doi.org/10.25446/oxford.22134233.v1

French Covers Map

https:/github.com/Prismatic-Jane-Eyre/french_storymap

https:/portal.sds.ox.ac.uk/articles/educational_resource/Covers_Map_French/22134245

https:/doi.org/10.25446/oxford.22134245.v1

German Covers Map

https:/github.com/Prismatic-Jane-Eyre/german_storymap

https:/portal.sds.ox.ac.uk/articles/educational_resource/Covers_Map_German/22134260

https:/doi.org/10.25446/oxford.22134260

Greek Covers Map

https:/github.com/Prismatic-Jane-Eyre/greek_storymap

https:/portal.sds.ox.ac.uk/articles/educational_resource/Covers_Map_Greek/22134281

https:/doi.org/10.25446/oxford.22134281.v1

Hebrew Covers Map

https:/github.com/Prismatic-Jane-Eyre/hebrew_storymap

https:/portal.sds.ox.ac.uk/articles/educational_resource/Covers_Map_Hebrew/22134311

https:/doi.org/10.25446/oxford.22134311

Hungarian Covers Map

https:/github.com/Prismatic-Jane-Eyre/hungarian_storymap

https:/portal.sds.ox.ac.uk/articles/educational_resource/Covers_Map_Hungarian/22134326

https:/doi.org/10.25446/oxford.22134326.v1

Japanese Covers Map

https:/github.com/Prismatic-Jane-Eyre/japanese_storymap

https:/portal.sds.ox.ac.uk/articles/educational_resource/Covers_Map_Japanese/22134359

https:/doi.org/10.25446/oxford.22134359.v1

Persian Covers Map

https:/github.com/Prismatic-Jane-Eyre/persian_storymap

https:/portal.sds.ox.ac.uk/articles/educational_resource/Covers_Map_Persian/22134368

https:/doi.org/10.25446/oxford.22134368.v1

Polish Covers Map

https:/github.com/Prismatic-Jane-Eyre/polish_storymap

https:/portal.sds.ox.ac.uk/articles/educational_resource/Covers_Map_Polish/22134380

https:/doi.org/10.25446/oxford.22134380.v1

Romanian Covers Map

https:/github.com/Prismatic-Jane-Eyre/romanian_storymap

https:/portal.sds.ox.ac.uk/articles/educational_resource/Covers_Map_Romanian/22134407

https:/doi.org/10.25446/oxford.22134407.v1

Slovenian Covers Map

https:/github.com/Prismatic-Jane-Eyre/slovenian_storymap

https:/portal.sds.ox.ac.uk/articles/educational_resource/Covers_Map_Slovenian/22134455

https:/doi.org/10.25446/oxford.22134455.v1

Spanish Covers Map

https:/github.com/Prismatic-Jane-Eyre/spanish_storymap

https:/portal.sds.ox.ac.uk/articles/educational_resource/Covers_Map_Spanish/22134479

https:/doi.org/10.25446/oxford.22134479.v1

Swedish Covers Map

https:/github.com/Prismatic-Jane-Eyre/swedish_storymap

https:/portal.sds.ox.ac.uk/articles/educational_resource/Covers_Map_Swedish/22134500

https:/doi.org/10.25446/oxford.22134500.v1

Turkish Covers Map

https:/github.com/Prismatic-Jane-Eyre/turkish_storymap

https:/portal.sds.ox.ac.uk/articles/educational_resource/Covers_Map_Turkish/22134512

https:/doi.org/10.25446/oxford.22134512.v1

Prismatic Scene: The ‘Shape’ in Jane’s Bedroom

https:/github.com/Prismatic-Jane-Eyre/the_shape

https:/portal.sds.ox.ac.uk/articles/educational_resource/Prismatic_Scene_The_Shape_in_Jane_s_Bedroom/22140506

https:/doi.org/10.25446/oxford.22140506.v2

Prismatic Scene: The ‘Red-Room’

https:/github.com/Prismatic-Jane-Eyre/the_red_room

https:/portal.sds.ox.ac.uk/articles/educational_resource/Prismatic_Scenes_The_Red-Room/22140488

https:/doi.org/10.25446/oxford.22140488.v3

The animations of Prismatic Words, created by Matthew Reynolds, have also been archived on the Oxford Sustainable Digital Scholarship platform, with the following DOIs. The researchers who provided the data are named in the introductory page for each animation.

Prismatic Words: ‘Passionate’
https:/doi.org/10.25446/oxford.22134575.v1

Prismatic Words: ‘Picture of Passion’
https:/doi.org/10.25446/oxford.22134584.v4

‘Passion of Resentment’
https:/doi.org/10.25446/oxford.22134626.v2

Prismatic Words: ‘Grande Passion’
https:/doi.org/10.25446/oxford.22134629.v1

Prismatic Words: ‘Judgment and Passion’
https:/doi.org/10.25446/oxford.22134653.v2

Prismatic Words: ‘Passions Rage Furiously’
https:/doi.org/10.25446/oxford.22134662.v2

Prismatic Words: ‘A Solemn Passion’
https:/doi.org/10.25446/oxford.22134689.v1

Prismatic Words: ‘Hear Plainly’
https:/doi.org/10.25446/oxford.22134701.v1

Prismatic Words: ‘Plain Truth’

https:/doi.org/10.25446/oxford.22134695.v1

Prismatic Words: 'Plain, Too Plain'
https:/doi.org/10.25446/oxford.22134704.v2

Prismatic Words: 'Plain, Unvarnished, Poor and Plain'
https:/doi.org/10.25446/oxford.22134713.v2

Prismatic Words: 'Plain, and Little'
https:/doi.org/10.25446/oxford.22134719.v2

Prismatic Words: 'Ugly and Laid(e)'
https:/doi.org/10.25446/oxford.22134722.v2

Prismatic Words: 'Ugly and brutto/a'
https:/doi.org/10.25446/oxford.22134734.v1

Prismatic Words: '"Wander" in Estonian'
https:/doi.org/10.25446/oxford.22134737.v2

Prismatic Words: '"Parsa" in Persian'
https:/doi.org/10.25446/oxford.22134740.v2

Prismatic Words: '"Walk" in Chinese and Italian'
https:/doi.org/10.25446/oxford.22134749.v2

Prismatic Words: '"Wander" in Chinese and Italian'
https:/doi.org/10.25446/oxford.22134758.v1

Prismatic Words: 'The Interplay of "Walk" and "Wander" in Chinese and Italian'
https:/doi.org/10.25446/oxford.22134764.v1

M.R.

Notes on the Co-Authors

Andrés Claro (Santiago, Chile) is a philosopher, essayist and university professor. He undertook his postgraduate studies in philosophy and Literature at the École des Hautes Études en Sciences Sociales (Paris) and at Oxford University. His work has interrogated extensively the ways in which poetic conceptions and figurations shape characteristic worlds, spatial-temporal configurations, with particular attention to translation processes. To a series of essays on poetics, theory of language and culture — most recently, the trilogy of books *La Creación* (2014), *Imágenes de mundo* (2016), and *Tiempos sin fin* (2018) — he adds two major books: *La Inquisición y la Cábala, un capítulo de la diferencia entre ontología y exilio* (1996; 2nd. ed., 2009) and *Las Vasijas Quebradas, cuatro variaciones sobre la 'tarea del traductor'* (2012). He has published collections of poems and literary translations from various languages. He teaches in the Doctorate in Philosophy (Aesthetics) at the Universidad de Chile and has been visiting professor in universities in Latin America, Europe and the United States.

Annmarie Drury is the author of *Translation as Transformation in Victorian Poetry* (2015), the translator and editor of *Stray Truths: Selected Poems of Euphrase Kezilahabi* (2015), and the editor of The Imaginative Vision of Abdilatif Abdalla's Voice of Agony, which is forthcoming. She studies poetry and cultures of translation in the British nineteenth century and in Swahiliphone East Africa, and she writes and translates poetry. She is writing a book about tropes and politics of listening in Victorian poetry. She is Associate Professor of English at Queens College, City University of New York.

Mary Frank is a freelance translator from French and German to English. She also researches translation and teaches translation theory and practice. Her research interests are the interplay/opposition of translation theory and practice and the development of approaches to translating in the presence of significant cultural gaps between the source and target cultures. She made the first translations into English of satirical short stories by popular East German author

Ottokar Domma. She has served on the editorial board of *The Linguist* magazine and on the committee of Women in German Studies.

Paola Gaudio is Aggregate Professor of English Language and Translation at the University of Bari Aldo Moro (Italy), where she teaches undergraduate and postgraduate courses in English for Statistics. Her research interests range from nineteenth and twentieth century anglophone literature to translation theory and specialized languages. More recently, she has worked as Literary Translation expert for the European Commission, and as Quality Assurance expert for the Italian National Agency for the Evaluation of Universities and Research Institutes. She enjoys approaching literary studies from a Digital Humanities perspective — which has led to the creation of visual representations of her findings, such as the emotional fingerprints of source and target texts, and 2D animations of prismatic scenes ('Red-Room' and 'Shape' in Jane's bedroom passages).

Rebecca Ruth Gould is the author of *Writers and Rebels: The Literature of Insurgency in the Caucasus* (2016), which won the University of Southern California Book Prize in Literary and Cultural Studies and the best book of the year award from the Association for Women in Slavic Studies, *The Persian Prison Poem: Sovereignty and the Political Imagination* (2021), and, most recently, *Erasing Palestine: Free Speech and Palestinian Freedom*, forthcoming in 2023. She is Professor of Islamic World and Comparative Literature, at the University of Birmingham, where she directs the ERC-funded Global Literary Theory Project.

Jernej Habjan is a fellow at the Research Centre of the Slovenian Academy of Sciences and Arts. Recently, he was a postdoctoral fellow in the research group 'Globalization and Literature' at the University of Munich and a Fung Global Fellow at the Princeton Institute for International and Regional Studies, Princeton University. He sits on the ICLA Research Committee on Literary Theory and is the author of *Ordinary Literature Philosophy: Lacanian Literary Performatives between Austin and Rancière* (2020). His essays in literary theory have appeared in *Interventions*, the *Journal of Global History*, *Neohelicon*, and *South Atlantic Quarterly*.

Yunte Huang is a professor of English at the University of California, Santa Barbara. A Guggenheim Fellow, he is the author of *Transpacific Imaginations* (2008) and *Charlie Chan* (2010), which won the Edgar Award and was a National Book Critics Circle Award finalist. His most recent book *Inseparable* (2018), also a finalist for the NBCC award, was named

Best Book of the Year by the *New York Times*, *NPR*, and *Newsweek*. He has published articles in the *New York Times*, *Wall Street Journal*, *Chicago Tribune*, *PMLA*, and others, and has been featured on NPR, CBS, C-SPAN, and others. His new book, *Chinese Whispers*, is forthcoming in 2022.

Abhishek Jain is Bhagwan Mallinath Visiting Assistant Professor of Jain Studies and Comparative Theology at Loyola Marymount University in Los Angeles. He was previously a research fellow of classical and medieval Indian studies at the International Institute for Asian Studies at Leiden University in the Netherlands. Having completed an education in Sanskrit and Indian philosophy in India, he became a doctoral student in the project 'Narrative Modes of Historical Discourse in Asia' funded by the European Research Council. He obtained the PhD degree from Adam Mickiewicz University in 2021 with the dissertation 'Emplotment and Historicity: Narrative Modes of Historical Discourse in the Prabandhakośa'. His research is focused on Indian philosophy, the religion of Jainism, and theories of narrative and history.

Eugenia Kelbert is a Leverhulme Early Career Fellow at the University of East Anglia and Co-Director of UEA's East Centre for the study of East-Central Europe and the former Soviet space. She specialises in comparative literature, translation studies, literary bilingualism, modernism, poetry, stylistics and digital humanities (especially stylometry). Her dissertation on translingual literature (Yale University, 2015) won the ACLA's Charles Bernheimer Prize; she is completing a monograph on translingualism and researching a second book project on translation and cross-lingual stylistics. Other projects include recent and forthcoming publications, notably, in *Target: International Journal of Translation Studies*, *Meta: Translators' Journal*, *and Modernism/Modernity*.

Ida Klitgård is an Associate Professor at the Department of Communication and Arts, Roskilde University, Denmark. She holds a Danish cand.mag. degree in English and Translation Studies and an MPhil degree in Modernist Studies from Glasgow University. In 2007 she was awarded a Dr.Phil (Habilitation doctoral degree) with the monograph *Fictions of Hybridity: Translating Style in James Joyce's Ulysses* (2007). Klitgård has published widely on Virginia Woolf, James Joyce and translation studies. Recent studies include covert interlingual translation in Danish university students' academic writing and studies in satire, disinformation and health communication.

Léa Rychen is Chief Editor of imagoDei, a French-speaking multimedia platform reflecting on the interactions between culture, the arts, and beliefs. While completing a Master's degree in English, Spanish, and Translation at the Université de Lorraine in Nancy, France, she worked as a translator for various publishing houses and companies. She then studied Theology and Apologetics at Oxford, where she completed the Certificate in Theological Studies at Wycliffe Hall and the program of OCCA the Oxford Centre for Christian Apologetics. She now lives in Geneva and develops the imagoDei media for the French-speaking world.

Ulrich Timme Kragh is a scholar of Asian Languages and Cultures, currently researching as a Visiting Fellow at the Apabhramsha Sahitya Academy in Jaipur, India. He has previously taught at Florida State University and the University of Sydney. He has also served as a researcher at Harvard University, Geumgang University, Leiden University, the Australian National University, the University of Copenhagen, and Adam Mickiewicz University. He was the principal investigator of the project 'Narrative Modes of Historical Discourse in Asia' funded by the European Research Council. His publications concern medieval Indian philosophy and religion, yogic traditions in Tibet and Pakistan, and theories of history and literature in East Asia, India, and Tibet.

Madli Kütt is an Estonian translator and lecturer in French language at the Estonian Military Academy. She is currently working on her dissertation 'The Fictional Subject and Imaginative Views in Marcel Proust's 'A la recherche du temps perdu' and its translation into Estonian', and has published articles on the topic. Her research interests are centred on literary translation, particularly concentrating on theories of fictionality, mental imagery in the processes of writing and translation, and 'small literatures'.

Ana Teresa Marques dos Santos holds a Ph.D. in Translation Studies (University of Warwick), and is a Lector at the University of Aveiro in Portugal. Her key research interests are in translation history, including flows and reception. She has published on radio broadcast translations, the translation and censorship of William Faulkner and Oscar Wilde, and the dissemination of Brazilian translations and Spanish literature during the Portuguese New State regime. She is a member of the 'Intercultural Literature in Portugal 1930-2000' research project, based at three universities in Lisbon. She is currently researching literary women translators in Portugal.

Cláudia Pazos-Alonso is Professor of Portuguese and Gender Studies, University of Oxford. Her research interests range across nineteenth and twentieth-century Lusophone literature. Book publications include *Francisca Wood and Nineteenth-Century Periodical Culture: Pressing for Change* (2020); *Antigone Daughters? Gender, Genealogy, and the Politics of Authorship in 20th-Century Portuguese Women's Writing* (2011, with Hilary Owen), *Imagens do Eu na Poesia de Florbela Espanca* (1997). She has also co-edited the volumes *Reading Literature in Portuguese* (2013), *A Companion to Portuguese Literature* (2009), and *Closer to the Wild Heart: Essays on Clarice Lispector* (2002) and guest-edited journal issues on major contemporary authors such as Lidia Jorge and Mia Couto.

Eleni Philippou is a Postdoctoral Research Fellow at the Oxford Comparative Criticism and Translation Research Centre at the University of Oxford. She is also the Principal Investigator of the AHRC-funded Prismatic Jane Eyre Schools project, which follows on from her postdoctoral work on the OWRI-funded Creative Multilingualism project. Her monograph, *Speaking Politically: Adorno and Postcolonial Fiction* (2021), explores the implications of Adorno's philosophy for literary studies, particularly in relation to texts that emerge from situations of political extremity. Her key research interests are postcolonial and world literature, contemporary poetry, critical theory, comparative literature, and translation studies. Furthermore, she is an award-winning poet, with a number of poems published in both British and international anthologies and journals.

Yousif M. Qasmiyeh is a poet and translator whose DPhil research at the University of Oxford's English Faculty explores containment and time in 'refugee writing' in English and Arabic. His collection, *Writing the Camp* (2021), was the Poetry Book Society's recommendation for spring 2021; was highly commended by the 2021 Forward Prizes for Poetry; and was shortlisted for the 2022 Royal Society of Literature Ondaatje Prize. His second collection, *Eating the Archive*, was published in 2023. His work has appeared in journals and magazines including *Modern Poetry in Translation, Stand, Critical Quarterly, GeoHumanities, Cambridge Literary Review, New England Review, Poetry London* and *PN Review*. He is Creative Encounters Editor of the Migration and Society journal, Writer-in-Residence of the Refugee Hosts research project, and Joint Lead of the Imagining Futures Baddawi Camp Lab.

Matthew Reynolds is Professor of English and Comparative Criticism at the University of Oxford, where he chairs the Oxford Comparative Criticism and Translation Research Centre (OCCT) and leads the Prismatic Translation and Prismatic Jane Eyre projects. Among his books are *Prismatic Translation* (2019), *Translation: A Very Short Introduction* (2016), *The Poetry of Translation: From Chaucer & Petrarch to Homer & Logue* (2011), *Likenesses* (2013), *The Realms of Verse: English Poetry in a Time of Nation-Building* (2001), and the novels *Designs for a Happy Home* (2009) and *The World Was All Before Them* (2013).

Céline Sabiron is Senior Lecturer in British literature at Université de Lorraine (Nancy, France). Her research deals with the concept of literary transfers through her main focus which is translation, both in the sense of a change of languages, and of a transaction between two cultures, and in particular Britain (Scotland) and France in the eighteenth and nineteenth centuries. Her recent publications include *Romanticism and Time* (2021) co-edited with S. Laniel-Musitelli, *Textuality and Translation* (2020) with C. Chauvin, and a special EJES issue *Decentering Commemorations* (2021), with J. Tranmer. She is one of the three organisers of the ARIEL project (ariel.univ-lorraine.fr).

Kayvan Tahmasebian is a research fellow at the Global Literary Theory project (University of Birmingham) and a Bahari Visiting Fellow in the Persian Arts of the Book, at the Bodleian Libraries, Oxford. With Rebecca Ruth Gould he translated *House Arrest: Poems of Hasan Alizadeh* (2022) and *High Tide of the Eyes: Poems by Bijan Elahi* (2019).

Giovanni Pietro Vitali is Associate Professor in Digital Humanities at the University of Versailles Saint Quentin en Yvelines–Paris-Saclay University. Previously, he was lecturer in Italian studies at the University of Lorraine and University of Poitiers, and a Marie S. Curie Research Fellow working on *Last Letters from the World Wars: Forming Italian Language, Identity and Memory in Texts of Conflict*. He is the author of *Voices of Dissent Interdisciplinary Approaches to New Italian Popular and Political Music* (2020). He is widely active in the field of Digital Humanities, specializing in NPL, Textometry, Stilometry, Mapping and Data Visualization, and participating in initiatives at the Universities of Lepizig, Lorraine, Poitiers, Neuchâtel and Verona, and the École Normale Supérieure in Paris, as well as in Prismatic Jane Eyre. His code can be found at https://github.com/digitalkoine.

Index

About the Team

Alessandra Tosi was the managing editor for this book.

Lucy Barnes performed the proofreading and indexing.

Katy Saunders designed the cover. The cover was produced in InDesign using the Fontin font.

Jeremy Bowman typeset the book in InDesign. The text and heading font is Noto Serif.

Cameron Craig produced the paperback and hardback editions.

Cameron produced the EPUB, PDF, XML and HTML editions. The conversion is performed with open source software such as pandoc (https://pandoc.org/) created by John MacFarlane and other tools freely available on our GitHub page (https://github.com/OpenBookPublishers).

This book need not end here...

Share

All our books — including the one you have just read — are free to access online so that students, researchers and members of the public who can't afford a printed edition will have access to the same ideas. This title will be accessed online by hundreds of readers each month across the globe: why not share the link so that someone you know is one of them?

This book and additional content is available at:

https://doi.org/10.11647/OBP.0319

Donate

Open Book Publishers is an award-winning, scholar-led, not-for-profit press making knowledge freely available one book at a time. We don't charge authors to publish with us: instead, our work is supported by our library members and by donations from people who believe that research shouldn't be locked behind paywalls.

Why not join them in freeing knowledge by supporting us: https://www.openbookpublishers.com/support-us

You may also be interested in:

Creative Multilingualism
A Manifesto
Katrin Kohl, Rajinder Dudrah, Andrew Gosler, Suzanne Graham, Martin Maiden, Wen-chin Ouyang (editors)

https://doi.org/10.11647/OBP.0206

Romanticism and Time
Literary Temporalities
Sophie Laniel-Musitelli (editor)

https://doi.org/10.11647/OBP.0232

Middlemarch
Epigraphs and Mirrors
Adam Roberts

https://doi.org/10.11647/OBP.0249

Jane Austen
Reflections of a Reader
Nora Bartlett (author), Jane Stabler (editor)

https://doi.org/10.11647/OBP.0216

Milton Keynes UK
Ingram Content Group UK Ltd.
UKHW020324031123
431792UK00001B/1

9 781800 648